T0189570

Lecture Notes in Artificial Intelligence 13753

Subseries of Lecture Notes in Computer Science

More information about this subseries at https://link.springer.com/bookseries/1244

Reyhan Aydoğan · Natalia Criado · Jérôme Lang ·
Victor Sanchez-Anguix · Marc Serramia (Eds.)

PRIMA 2022:
Principles and Practice
of Multi-Agent Systems

24th International Conference
Valencia, Spain, November 16–18, 2022
Proceedings

Springer

Editors
Reyhan Aydoğan ⓘD
Özyeğin University
Istanbul, Turkey

Natalia Criado ⓘD
Universitat Politècnica de València
Valencia, Spain

Jérôme Lang
Université Paris-Dauphine
Paris, France

Victor Sanchez-Anguix ⓘD
Universitat Politècnica de València
Valencia, Spain

Marc Serramia ⓘD
King's College London
London, UK

ISSN 0302-9743   ISSN 1611-3349 (electronic)
Lecture Notes in Artificial Intelligence
ISBN 978-3-031-21202-4   ISBN 978-3-031-21203-1 (eBook)
https://doi.org/10.1007/978-3-031-21203-1

LNCS Sublibrary: SL7 – Artificial Intelligence

This Springer imprint is published by the registered company Springer Nature Switzerland AG
The registered company address is: Gewerbestrasse 11, 6330 Cham, Switzerland

Preface

Welcome to the proceedings of the 24th International Conference on Principles and Practice of Multi-Agent Systems (PRIMA 2022), held in Valencia and online during November 16–18, 2022. Originally started as a regional (Asia-Pacific) workshop in 1998, PRIMA has become one of the leading and most influential scientific conferences for research on multi-agent systems. Since 2009, PRIMA has brought together active researchers, developers, and practitioners from both academia and industry to showcase, share, and promote research in several domains, ranging from foundations of agent theory and engineering aspects of agent systems to emerging interdisciplinary areas of agent-based research. PRIMA's previous editions were held in Nagoya, Japan (2009), Kolkata, India (2010), Wollongong, Australia (2011), Kuching, Malaysia (2012), Dunedin, New Zealand (2013), Gold Coast, Australia (2014), Bertinoro, Italy (2015), Phuket, Thailand (2016), Nice, France (2017), Tokyo, Japan (2018), Torino, Italy (2019), and online (2020).

This year we received 100 full paper submissions from 33 countries. Each submission was carefully reviewed by at least three members of the Program Committee (PC), composed of 116 prominent world-class researchers, in a double blind process. In addition, 28 sub-reviewers were called upon to review submissions. The review period was followed by PC discussions. At the end of the reviewing process, authors received the technical reviews. PRIMA 2022 accepted 31 full papers (an acceptance rate of 31%), while 15 submissions were selected to appear as short papers and one as a demo paper. In addition to the paper presentations, the conference included three tutorials. Finally, the conference included two invited talks sponsored by EurAI, one by Carles Sierra on the engineering of social values, and the other by Serena Villata on AI at the service of society to analyse human arguments.

We would like to thank all the individuals and institutions that supported PRIMA 2022. Mainly we thank the authors for submitting high-quality research papers, confirming PRIMA's reputation as a leading international conference in multi-agent systems. We are indebted to our PC members and additional reviewers for spending their valuable time to provide careful reviews and recommendations on the submissions, and for taking part in follow-up discussions. Finally, we thank our sponsors EurAI and the Artificial Intelligence Journal.

November 2022

Reyhan Aydoğan
Natalia Criado
Jérôme Lang
Victor Sanchez-Anguix
Marc Serramia

Organisation

Conference Chairs

Reyhan Aydoğan   Özyeğin University, Turkey
Victor Sanchez-Anguix   Universitat Politècnica de València, Spain

Program Chairs

Natalia Criado   Universitat Politècnica de València, Spain
Jérôme Lang   CNRS, France

Web Chairs

Joan Ciprià Moreno Teodoro   Universitat Politècnica de València, Spain
Victor Sanchez-Anguix   Universitat Politècnica de València, Spain

Publications Chair

Marc Serramia   King's College London, UK

Local Organisation

Juan Miguel Alberola Oltra   Universitat Politècnica de València, Spain
  (Financial Chair)
Carlos Carrascosa   Universitat Politècnica de València, Spain
Joan Ciprià Moreno Teodoro   Universitat Politècnica de València, Spain
Stella Heras   Universitat Politècnica de València, Spain
Jaume Jordan   Universitat Politècnica de València, Spain
Vicente Julian   Universitat Politècnica de València, Spain

PRIMA Steering Committee

Guido Governatori (Chair)   NICTA, Australia
Takayuki Ito (Deputy Chair)   Kyoto University, Japan
Aditya Ghose (Immediate Past   University of Wollongong, Australia
  Chair)
Abdul Sattar (Treasurer)   Griffith University, Australia
Makoto Yokoo (Chair Emeritus)   Kyushu University, Japan
Bo An   Nanyang Technological University, Singapore

Program Committee

Rem Collier	University College Dublin, Ireland
Silvano Colombo Tosatto	CSIRO, Italy
Juan Corchado	University of Salamanca, Spain
Massimo Cossentino	National Research Council of Italy, Italy
Ângelo Costa	University of Minho, Portugal
Stefania Costantini	University dell'Aquila, Italy
Célia da Costa Pereira	Université Côte d'Azur, France
Mehdi Dastani	Utrecht University, Netherlands
Dave de Jonge	IIIA-CSIC, Spain
Fernando De La Prieta	University of Salamanca, Spain
Marina De Vos	University of Bath, UK
Ronald de Haan	University of Amsterdam, Netherlands
Yves Demazeau	CNRS - LIG, France
Yali Du	King's College London, UK
Barbara Dunin-Keplicz	University of Warsaw, Poland
Animesh Dutta	NIT Durgapur, India
Alberto Fernandez	University Rey Juan Carlos, Spain
Angelo Ferrando	University of Genova, Italy
Zack Fitzsimmons	College of the Holy Cross, USA
Nicoletta Fornara	Università della Svizzera Italiana, Italy
Katsuhide Fujita	Tokyo University of Agriculture and Technology, Japan
Naoki Fukuta	Shizuoka University, Japan
Rustam Galimullin	University of Bergen, Norway
Enrico Gerding	University of Southampton, UK
Guido Governatori	NICTA, Australia
Önder Gürcan	Université Paris-Saclay, CEA, LIST, France
Rafik Hadfi	Kyoto University, Japan
Adrian Haret	The ILLC, University of Amsterdam, Netherlands
Hiromitsu Hattori	Ritsumeikan University, Japan
Stella Heras	Universitat Politècnica de València, Spain
Michael Ignaz Schumacher	U. of Applied Sciences Western Switzerland, Switzerland
Jaume Jordán	Universitat Politècnica de València, Spain
Vicente Julian	Universitat Politècnica de València, Spain
Franziska Klügl	Örebro University, Sweden
Nadin Kokciyan	University of Edinburgh, UK
Dominique Longin	CNRS, IRIT, France
Henrique Lopes Cardoso	University of Porto, Portugal
Emiliano Lorini	IRIT, France
Michael Luck	King's College London, UK
Marin Lujak	University Rey Juan Carlos, Spain

Xudong Luo   Guangxi Normal University, China
Jan Maly   Vienna University of Technology, Austria
Elisa Marengo   Free University of Bozen-Bolzano, Italy
Iván Marsa Maestre   University of Alcala, Spain
Pasqual Marti   Universitat Politècnica de València, Spain
Viviana Mascardi   University of Genova, Italy
Shigeo Matsubara   Osaka University, Japan
David Mercier   Université d'Artois, France
Roberto Micalizio   Universita' di Torino, Italy
Yasser Mohammad   Assiut University, Egypt
Stefania Monica   Università degli Studi di Modena e Reggio
                                  Emilia, Italy
Jörg P. Müller   TU Clausthal, Germany
Aniello Murano   University of Naples Federico II, Italy
Yí Nicholas Wáng   Sun Yat-sen University, China
Pablo Noriega   IIIA-CSIC, Spain
Paulo Novais   University of Minho, Portugal
Arianna Novaro   Université Paris 1 Panthéon-Sorbonne, France
Francesco Olivieri   Griffith University, Australia
Andrea Omicini   Alma Mater Studiorum–Università di Bologna,
                                  Italy
Hirotaka Ono   Nagoya University, Japan
Nir Oren   University of Aberdeen, UK
Julian Padget   University of Bath, UK
Simon Parsons   University of Lincoln, UK
Juan Pavón   Universidad Complutense de Madrid, Spain
Tiago Pinto   Universidade de Trás-os-Montes e Alto
                                  Douro/INESC-TEC, Portugal
Agostino Poggi   University of Parma, Italy
R. Ramanujam   Institute of Mathematical Sciences, Chennai,
                                  India
Alessandro Ricci   University of Bologna, Italy
Juan Antonio Rodriguez Aguilar   IIIA-CSIC, Spain
Luca Sabatucci   ICAR-CNR, Italy
Francesco Santini   Università di Perugia, Italy
Alberto Sardinha   Universidade de Lisboa, Portugal
Giuseppe M.L. Sarnè   University of Milan Bicocca, Italy
Isabel Sassoon   Brunel University London, UK
Ken Satoh   National Institute of Informatics and Sokendai,
                                  Japan
Francois Schwarzentruber   École normale supérieure de Rennes, France
Valeria Seidita   Università degli Studi di Palermo, Italy

Marc Serramia	King's College London, UK
Emilio Serrano	Universidad Politécnica de Madrid, Spain
Sujoy Sikdar	Binghamton University, UK
Marija Slavkovik	University of Bergen, Norway
Zoi Terzopoulou	ILLC, Netherlands
Ingo J. Timm	German Research Center for Artificial Intelligence, Germany
Alice Toniolo	University of St Andrews, UK
Behnam Torabi	The University of Texas at Dallas, USA
Jan Treur	Vrije Universiteit Amsterdam, Netherlands
Paolo Turrini	University of Warwick, UK
Leon van der Torre	University of Luxembourg, Luxembourg
Laurent Vercouter	LITIS lab, INSA de Rouen, France
Serena Villata	CNRS - I3S, France
Giuseppe Vizzari	University of Milano-Bicocca, Italy
Anaëlle Wilczynski	Université Paris-Saclay, France
Neil Yorke-Smith	Delft University of Technology, Netherlands
Dongmo Zhang	Western Sydney University, Australia
Dengji Zhao	ShanghaiTech University, China

Additional Reviewers

Mubashara Akhtar	King's College London, UK
Gabriel Amaral	King's College London, UK
Annemarie Borg	Utrecht University, Netherlands
Jan Buermann	University of Southampton, UK
Furkan Canturk	Ozyegin University, Turkey
Theodor Cimpeanu	Teesside University, UK
Victor Hugo Contreras Ordoñez	Hes-so, Switzerland
Francesco Faloci	University of study of Perugia, Italy
Maksim Gladyshev	Utrecht University, Netherlands
Zixin Gu	ShanghaiTech University, China
Miao Li	ShanghaiTech University, China
Xiaolong Liang	Department of Philosophy (Zhuhai), Sun Yat-sen University, China
Xingzhou Lou	Institute of Automation, Chinese Academy of Sciences, China
Enrico Marchesini	Northeastern University, Italy
Ivan Mercanti	IMT Institute for Advanced Studies, Italy
Daphne Odekerken	Utrecht University, Netherlands
Gideon Ogunniye	University College London, UK
Jianglin Qiao	Western Sydney University, Australia

Manel Rodríguez-Soto	Spanish National Research Council (IIIA-CSIC), Spain
Inga Rüb	Warsaw University, Poland
Katsuhiko Sano	Faculty of Humanities and Human Sciences, Hokkaido University, Japan
Emre Sefer	Ozyegin University, Turkey
Andrzej Szalas	University of Warsaw, Poland
Carlo Taticchi	Università degli Studi di Perugia, Italy
Giovanni Varricchione	Utrecht University, Netherlands
Francis Rhys Ward	Imperial College London, UK
Junyu Zhang	ShanghaiTech University, China

Invited talks

On the Engineering of Social Values

Carles Sierra

Artificial Intelligence Research Institute (IIIA-CSIC)

Abstract. Ethics in Artificial Intelligence is a wide-ranging field which encompasses many open questions regarding the moral, legal and technical issues that arise with the use and design of ethically-compliant autonomous agents. Under this umbrella, the computational ethics area is concerned with the formulation and codification of ethical principles into software components. In this talk, I will take a look at a particular problem in computational ethics: the embedding of moral values into autonomous agents. I will argue that the right ethical perspective comes from the consideration of the agreements on functionality by groups of humans whose interactions are mediated by technology. The mapping of values into operational norms enables the use of game theoretical tools to quantify the alignment between group behaviour and group value semantics [2, 3]. Furthermore, the representation of interactions in the form of extensive form games allows using simulation techniques to analyse the alignment between norms and values [1]. Also, autonomous agent technologies can further support group interactions by suggesting norms to adopt that might steer group behaviour towards the goals associated with a set of desired social values.

References

1. Montes, N., Osman, N., Sierra, C.: A computational model of ostrom's institutional analysis and development framework. Artif. Intell. **311**, 103756 (2022)
2. Montes, N., Sierra, C.: Value-guided synthesis of parametric normative systems. In: Proceedings of the 20th AAMAS, pp. 907–915 (2021)
3. Montes, N., Sierra, C.: Synthesis and properties of optimally value-aligned normative systems. J. Artif. Int. Res. **74** (2022)

Artificial Intelligence at the Service of Society to Analyse Human Arguments

Serena Villata

I3S Laboratory, Université Côte d'Azur,
CNRS, Inria, France

Abstract. Artificial Intelligence (AI) aims to understand the principles that govern intelligent behaviour and to encode these principles into machines. Argumentation pervades human intelligent behavior, and it is a mandatory element to conceive artificial machines that can exploit argumentation models and tools in the cognitive tasks they are required to carry out. To do so, artificial argumentation combines formal argumentation, based on critical reasoning, with human natural argumentation extracted through argument mining methods. Intelligent machines enriched with computational argumentation models can extract, analyse, summarise and generate natural language argumentative structures from different contexts, such as clinical trials and political debates. Argument(ation) mining (AM) is the dimension of artificial argumentation aiming at automatically processing natural language arguments and reason upon them. More precisely, argument mining is the research area aiming at extracting natural language arguments and their relations from text, with the final goal of providing machine-processable structured data for computational models of argument. In this invited talk, I will first introduce this recent research area, addressing the challenge of identifying argumentative structures from texts (e.g., clinical trial articles, social media content). Then, I will discuss how these methods can be used to identify fallacious arguments in political debates. Fallacies play a prominent role in argumentation since antiquity due to their contribution to argumentation in critical thinking education. Their role is even more crucial nowadays as contemporary argumentation technologies face challenging tasks as misleading and manipulative information detection in news articles and political discourse, and counter-narrative generation. Finally, I will conclude with some thoughts on the challenge of automatic generation of counter-arguments to fight online disinformation and hate speech.

Keywords: Argument mining · Natural language processing · Argumentation theory

Contents

Short Papers

Demo Papers

Full Papers

Robustness of Congestion Pricing in Traffic Networks with Link-Specific Noise

Naohiro Yoshida$^{(\boxtimes)}$ and Katsuhide Fujita

Tokyo University of Agriculture and Technology, Koganei, Tokyo, Japan
yoshida@katfuji.lab.tuat.ac.jp, katfuji@cc.tuat.ac.jp

Abstract. Road pricing has been attracting attention as a method to alleviate road congestion. In recent years, applying tolls dynamically has become technically feasible owing to information communication technology and the advancement of connected and autonomous vehicles. Marginal cost tolls (MCT) are a well-known method guaranteed to achieve optimal system performance. However, it is difficult to accurately calculate MCT, and it is unclear how MCT affects the system performance in noisy environments.

In this study, we show the theoretical noise conditions that do not decrease the system performance when using MCT with link-specific noise expressed as a constant factor. First, this study defines the *Price of Anarchy Safety Zone* (PoASZ) as the set of theoretical conditions of noise that guarantees that the system performance of applying inaccurate MCT will not lead to worse traffic than the scenario without tolls. We further demonstrate the simulation experiments under various traffic networks and discuss the effect of tolls on the system performance. Simulation results verify the theoretical conditions of this study using the simulation-based Price of Anarchy Safety Zone (PoASZ) in some traffic networks.

Keywords: Road pricing · Marginal cost pricing · Congestion games

1 Introduction

Traffic congestion is widespread across the world. In the United States in 2019, road congestion increased by 8.7 billion hours of travel time and 3.5 billion gallons of additional consumed fuel, whose costs reached 190 billion dollars [12]. One of the methods to alleviate road congestion is to implement road pricing by applying tolls. In the recent years, owing to the advancement of connected and automated vehicles and information communication technology such as mobile phones, the widespread application of more flexible tolls is becoming technically feasible. The discordance between the *user equilibrium* (UE) and *system optimum* (SO) is an important problem to solve road congestions in traffic engineering and game theory. In other words, in congested traffic networks, a result of the users' selfish

© The Author(s), under exclusive license to Springer Nature Switzerland AG 2023
R. Aydoğan et al. (Eds.): PRIMA 2022, LNAI 13753, pp. 3–19, 2023.
https://doi.org/10.1007/978-3-031-21203-1_1

routing to minimize each cost does not match the state where the total system travel time is at its minimum.

Marginal cost tolls (MCT), which represents a tolling method, is theoretically guaranteed to lead a user equilibrium to the system optimum [1]. Therefore, MCT is the optimal toll to alleviate road congestion, and thus minimize the total travel time. However, an accurate calculation of MCT is difficult, because a differentiable delay function is unknown. Recent research presented Δ-tolling [16,17], which approximates MCT, but does not guarantee its accurate calculation. Another study [15] assumed MCT with network-specific noise expressed as a constant factor and analyzed the influence of such tolls on the system performance, but did not reveal the influence of MCT with link-specific noise (i.e., MCT multiplied by a link-specific constant factor). This uncertainty to link-specific noise is an important aspect for road administrators and the government to be able to consider MCT as a solution to traffic congestion.

In this study, we show the theoretical noise conditions that do not decrease the system performance when using MCT with link-specific noise expressed as a constant factor from the scenario without tolls. We also provide experimental results obtained by simulation under various traffic networks and discuss the effects of this tolls on system performance. First, this study defines the *Price of Anarchy Safety Zone* (PoASZ) as the set of theoretical conditions of noise that guarantees that the system performance of applying inaccurate MCT will not lead to worse traffic than the scenario without tolls. We assume that the link-specific constant coefficient multiplied by MCT is the inaccurate MCT. Next, we show PoASZ by solving the upper bound the system performance when MCT with noise is applied. Finally, we perform simulation experiments and discuss a robustness to link-specific noises of MCT by demonstrating that the theoretically proved PoASZ holds the results of simulations under various traffic networks[1].

The main contributions of this study are summarized as follows:

- theoretical conditions of noise that do not decrease the system performance when applying MCT with link-specific noise compared to that without applying tolls;
- simulation results support the theoretical findings and elucidate the influence of inaccurate MCT on the system performance.

The rest of this paper is organized as follows. Section 2 introduces preliminary information including definitions, theorems, and assumptions related to the traffic network analysis used in this paper. Section 3 introduces related works on road pricing. Section 4 defines PoASZ and demonstrates PoASZ using the upper bounds of system performance. Section 5 presents simulation experiments verifying the theoretical aspects in this study and discusses the influence of inaccurate MCT on system performance. Section 6 concludes the paper and proposes future research directions.

---

[1] Note that this paper does not focus on technical or political issues in applying tolls.

2   Preliminaries

This section describes definitions, theorems, and assumptions related to the traffic network analysis used in this paper [15,18].

2.1   Traffic Network Model

A directed graph $G(V, E)$ represents a traffic network where V is vertex set, and E is link set. Each link $e \in E$ is affiliated with a latency function $l_e = l_e(f_e)$, where f_e is the flow of the link. The following assumptions on the latency function are often used in transportation literature: it is non-negative, convex, and $dl_e/df_e > 0$ for each link.

A demand $R(s,t) \geq 0$ represents the flow between $(s,t) \in V^2$. $\mathcal{P}_{st}$ is a simple path set, where a simple path does not include a cycle, and p is its element.

The following assumes a feasible flow defined as following: $f_p \geq 0$ $(\forall(s,t) \in V^2, \forall p \in \mathcal{P}_{st})$, $f_e = \sum_{p \in \mathcal{P}_e} f_p$ $(\forall e \in E)$, $\sum_{p \in \mathcal{P}_{st}} f_p = R(s,t)$ $(\forall(s,t) \in V^2$, and $\forall p \in \mathcal{P}_{st})$, where $\mathcal{P}_e$ is the set of paths including link e.

2.2   User Equilibrium

User equilibrium (UE) is known as the possible condition resulting from the users' routing behavior and road congestion. In UE, it is assumed that all users in the traffic network are rational; that is, they always choose a path that has the minimum cost, and they have complete information about available routes.

In UE, among all paths that exist between $(s,t) \in V^2$, the cost of the used paths is equal. The cost is less than or equal to that of the unused paths. In this study, the cost is taken as the sum of the travel time and the time conversion of the toll. In this section, we first consider only the travel time.

UE is thus formulated as follows:

$$f_p(c_p - c_{st}) = 0, \quad c_p - c_{st} \geq 0 \quad (\forall p \in \mathcal{P}_{st}, \forall(s,t) \in V^2) \tag{1}$$

where f_p and c_p is the flow and cost of path $p \in \mathcal{P}_{st}$ between (s,t), and c_{st} is the minimum cost of paths between (s,t).

UE assignment denotes flows in the UE. To obtain the UE assignment, the simultaneous equations shown in Eq. (1) must be solved under the feasible flow constraint (see Sect. 2.1). However, this can be solved only when the network structure is simple (including a few links).

Then, we consider transforming Eq. (1) into an optimization problem.

Theorem 1. (optimization problem equivalent to UE) *The UE is equivalent to the following optimization problem:*

$$minimize \quad \sum_{e \in E} \int_0^{f_e} l_e(\omega) \, d\omega$$

$$subject\ to \quad R(s,t) = \sum_{p \in \mathcal{P}_{st}} f_p, \ f_p \geq 0, \ f_e \geq 0 (\forall(s,t) \in V^2, \forall p \in \mathcal{P}_{st}, \forall e \in E).$$

The UE is also equivalent to the following variational inequality problem.

Theorem 2. (variational inequality problem equivalent to UE) *The UE is equivalent to the following variational inequality problem:*

$$\text{Find } \bar{\boldsymbol{f}} \text{ such that } \sum_{e \in E} l_e(\bar{f}_e)\left(f_e - \bar{f}_e\right) \geq 0 (\forall \boldsymbol{f}). \tag{2}$$

2.3 Applying Tolls

UE Under the Application of Tolls. We assume that the value of time (VOT) for all users is homogeneous. When tolls are applied, users on the traffic network perceive the travel time and tolls as their own costs; hence, the cost c_e of a link e is $c_e(f_e) = l_e(f_e) + \tau_e(f_e)$, where l_e and τ_e denotes the travel time and the toll of the link. The formulation of UE in applying tolls is the cost c_p of a path $p \in \mathcal{P}_{st}$ in Eq. (1), which is replaced by $c_p = l_p + \tau_p$ where $\tau_p = \sum_{e \in E} \delta_{e,p} \tau_e$.
System Optimum and Marginal Cost Tolls (MCT). The total system travel time is defined by $T(\boldsymbol{f}) = \sum_{e \in E} l_e(f_e) f_e$. A *system optimum* (SO) is the condition in which $T(\boldsymbol{f})$ is minimized.

In general, the UE flow does not match the SO flow. However, to alleviate road congestion, it is desirable that the UE flow matches the SO flow. Therefore, we try to match them by applying the optimal toll. In other words, we attempt to determine MCT, which is a tolling scheme in which UE matches SO.

Definition 1. (marginal cost toll) *The marginal cost toll (MCT) of each link $e \in E$ is defined as*

$$\tau_e^*(f_e) = f_e \frac{dl_e}{df_e}. \tag{3}$$

In Eq. (3), dl_e/df_e denotes the increase rate of travel time caused by increase in flow. Thus, MCT τ_e^* of the link e, which is dl_e/df_e multiplied by the flow f_e, indicates the influence of increased traffic flow to all users in the link e.

2.4 System Performance

Let $\boldsymbol{f}^*$ be an SO flow. We define the price of anarchy (PoA) [9] in a UE flow $\bar{\boldsymbol{f}}$ as $\rho(\bar{\boldsymbol{f}}) = T(\bar{\boldsymbol{f}})/T(\boldsymbol{f}^*) \geq 1$. In this study, the system performance of a traffic network is measured by PoA. When the delay function of each link is expressed by the β-th order equation, the upper bound of the PoA when tolls are not applied is $[1 - \beta(1 + \beta)^{-(1+\beta)/\beta}]^{-1}$ [11].

3 Related Work

Road pricing to alleviate road congestion has been studied for a long time. The survey and practical aspects of road pricing are detailed in [3]. Recent studies on alleviating road congestion by using artificial intelligence are summarized in

[13]. There are two main types of its approaches in the research of alleviating road congestion by road pricing: one is based on game theory, while the other is based on reinforcement learning.

Sharon et al. [16,17] proposed Δ-tolling, a model-free tolling scheme based on game theory. In particular, if the delay function follows the BPR (Bureau of Public Roads) function described below, tolls calculated by Δ-tolling are equal to MCT. Even in the contrary case, experimental results show that applying the tolls can reduce the total system travel time by up to 32 %. Other existing studies examine the problems in applying the MCT-based tolling scheme to the real world based on game theory. Sharon et al. [15] also focused on the case of applying tolls expressed by MCT with a fixed error factor r. Theoretical proofs and simulation experiments show that the total system travel time expressed by a function of r is monotonically non-increasing if $0 \leq r \leq 1$ and monotonically non-decreasing if $r \geq 1$. Yang et al. [19] theoretically demonstrated the upper bounds of the system performance upon application of MCT-like tolls. Sharon et al. [14] and Hanna et al. [6] focused on MCT considering the influences of partial compliance.

Mirzaei et al. [8] proposed Enhanced Δ-tolling, which is a method that generalizes the network-wide constant parameters β and R used in Δ-tolling to take different values for each link and tunes them by using policy gradient reinforcement learning. The simulation results show that this method reduces the total system travel time by up to 38 % compared to Δ-tolling. This suggests that the best performance is achieved with link-specific R and keeping β global. Chen et al. [2] also considered reinforcement learning to propose a more realistic tolling policy than Δ-tolling by including the changes in demand and using a multi-agent reinforcement learning. This study defines the reward function as the difference in the total travel time at each time step, and the tolling policy is learned to maximize the expected total reward. They demonstrate that Δ-tolling applies the policy gradient that can reduce the total system travel time by up to 15 %.

This study considers more general cases of applying MCT with link-specific noise than the existing study by Sharon et al. [15]. Meanwhile, we assume that each link has individual r_e and analyze the influence of the tolls on the system performance through both theory and simulation experiments. Furthermore, we show the concrete conditions of noise that guarantees that the system performance of applying inaccurate MCT will not lead to worse traffic than the scenario without tolls by considering Yang et al. [19].

4 Price of Anarchy Safety Zone (PoASZ)

4.1 Inaccurate MCT

Assumption of Noise. We consider a scenario where the tolls that apply to all links in a traffic network deviate from the exact MCT due to noise expressed by a link-specific fixed factor. Let this toll be called the inaccurate MCT.

Definition 2. (inaccurate MCT) *Define the inaccurate MCT of each link* $e \in E$ *as* $\tilde{\tau}_e^*(f_e) = r_e \tau_e^*(f_e)$ *where* $r_e \geq 0$ *is the noise factor specific to the link* e.

The noise of MCT is caused by that delay function. l_e is unknown in real traffic. Hence, when applying MCT as the tolls in real traffic, it is necessary to use an approximation method such as Δ-tolling [16,17]. However, approximation methods are not guaranteed to calculate MCT accurately, and thus noise can occur.

In this study, we consider the delay function as the BPR function: $l_e(f_e) = l_{e0}[1 + \alpha (f_e/c_e)^\beta]$ where $l_{e0} \geq 0$ is the free-flow travel time of the link $e \in E$, $c_e > 0$ is the road capacity, and $\alpha, \beta > 0$ are constant parameters in the entire network. When the BPR function is used as the delay function, the inaccurate MCT is expressed by $\tilde{\tau}_e^*(f_e) = \beta r_e \alpha_e f_e^\beta$ $(\alpha_e = l_{e0}\alpha/c_e^\beta)$. With regard to the inaccurate MCT, we only consider the case of (a): $0 \leq r_e \leq 1$, $\forall e \in E$ (i.e., tolls are lower than the MCT on all links) and (b): $r_e \geq 1$, $\forall e \in E$ (i.e., tolls are higher than the MCT on all links) for simplicity.

Let r be the noise factor vector of all links, and $\bar{f}(r)$ be the UE flow under the inaccurate MCT by r. The total system travel time $T(\bar{f}(r))$ and PoA $\rho(\bar{f}(r))$ in this case are abbreviated as $T(r)$ and $\rho(r)$, respectively. Let $\mathbf{0}$ and $\mathbf{1}$ be the vector r when $r_e = 0$, $\forall e \in E$ (i.e., when no tolls are assigned on all links) and when $r_e = 1$, $\forall e \in E$ (i.e., when exact MCT are assigned on all links).

4.2   Formulation of UE Under Inaccurate MCT and Uniqueness of Solution

We show the optimization problem equivalent to the UE under inaccurate MCT, which is formulated based on [15].

Lemma 1. (UE under inaccurate MCT) *The UE under application of inaccurate MCT is equal to the following optimization problem:*

$$minimize \quad \sum_{e \in E} r_e l_e(f_e) f_e + \sum_{e \in E} (1 - r_e) \int_0^{f_e} l_e(\omega)\, d\omega \qquad (4)$$

$$subject\ to \quad R(s,t) = \sum_{p \in \mathcal{P}_{st}} f_p, \ f_p \geq 0, \ f_e \geq 0 \quad (\forall(s,t) \in V^2, \forall p \in \mathcal{P}_{st}, \forall e \in E).$$

Proof. The Lagrangian function is

$$L(\boldsymbol{f}, \boldsymbol{\lambda}) = \sum_{e \in E} r_e l_e(f_e) f_e + \sum_{e \in E} (1 - r_e) \int_0^{f_e} l_e(\omega)\, d\omega - \sum_{(s,t) \in V^2} \left[\lambda_{st} \left(\sum_{p \in \mathcal{P}_{st}} f_p - R(s,t) \right) \right].$$

This results in the following KKT optimality conditions:

$$f_p \geq 0, \quad \frac{\partial L}{\partial f_p} \geq 0 \quad \Longleftrightarrow \quad (l_p + r_e f_p l_p') - \lambda_{st} \geq 0 \qquad (\forall (s,t) \in V^2, \ \forall p \in \mathcal{P}_{st}),$$

$$f_p \frac{\partial L}{\partial f_p} = 0 \quad \Longleftrightarrow \quad f_p[(l_p + r_e f_p l_p') - \lambda_{st}] \geq 0 \qquad (\forall (s,t) \in V^2, \ \forall p \in \mathcal{P}_{st}),$$

$$\frac{\partial L}{\partial \lambda_{st}} = 0 \quad \Longleftrightarrow \quad R(s,t) = \sum_{p \in \mathcal{P}_{st}} f_p \qquad (\forall (s,t) \in V^2)$$

where $l_p = \sum_{e \in E} \delta_{e,p} l_e(f_e)$ and $r_p f_p l_p' = \sum_{e \in E} \delta_{e,p} r_p f_e \, dl_e/df_e$. Let the cost of the path $p \in \mathcal{P}_{st}$ be $c_p = l_p + r_p f_p l_p'$ and λ_{st} be regarded as the minimum cost c_{st} between (s,t). Thus, the optimization problem in Lemma 1 is equivalent to the UE (Eq. (1)) with travel time $l_e(f_e)$ and tolls $\tilde{\tau}_e^* = r_e f_e \, dl_e/df_e$ perceived by users as the cost.

Next, we demonstrate the uniqueness of the UE flow in applying the inaccurate MCT. To do so, it is sufficient to show that the objective function (4) is strictly convex. Let the objective function (4) be Z. The Hessian matrix of Z is $H = \mathrm{diag}(d^2 Z/df_e^2) = \mathrm{diag}((1 + r_e) \, dl_e/df_e + r_e f_e \, d^2 l_e/df_e^2) \in \mathbb{R}^{|E| \times |E|}$. Because $r_e \geq 0$ by Definition 2, $dl_e/df_e > 0$ and $d^2 l_e/df_e^2 \geq 0$ by the assumptions of the delay function, and $f_e \geq 0$ by the feasible flow constraint, H is a diagonal matrix with positive diagonal components. In other words, because H is positive definite, Z is strictly convex. Note that this proof shows the uniqueness of the solution for link flows and does not guarantee that for path flows.

4.3   Upper Bound of System Performance and PoASZ

In the following, we assume that the PoA in applying no tolls $\rho(\mathbf{0}) = T(\mathbf{0})/T(\mathbf{1}) \in [1, [1 - \beta(1 + \beta)^{-(1+\beta)/\beta}]^{-1}]$ is determined by measurement in real traffic or simulation. First, *Price of Anarchy Safety Zone* (PoASZ) is defined as follows.

Definition 3. (Price of Anarchy Safety Zone) *The Price of Anarchy Safety Zone (PoASZ) is defined as the noise condition such that the system performance $\rho(\mathbf{r})$ under applying inaccurate MCT cannot decrease below that under applying no tolls.*

The theoretical determination of PoASZ is useful for adjusting the parameters employed in an MCT estimation method and developing and evaluating the method.

Next, based on [19], we derive the PoASZ theoretically using the upper bound of PoA as a function of the noise. For the UE flow under inaccurate MCT $\bar{\mathbf{f}}(\mathbf{r})$, the variational inequality problem equivalent to UE

$$\sum_{e \in E} \left(l_e(\bar{f}_e) + \tilde{\tau}_e^*(\bar{f}_e) \right) (f_e - \bar{f}_e) \geq 0 \quad (\forall \mathbf{f}),$$

i.e.,

$$T(\bar{f}) = \sum_{e \in E} l_e(f_e)f_e + \sum_{e \in E} \left[\left(l_e(\bar{f}_e) - l_e(f_e) \right) f_e + (f_e - \bar{f}_e)\tau_e \right] \quad (\forall f) \quad (5)$$

holds from the variational inequality problem equivalent to UE.

(a) In the case of $0 \le r_e \le 1$ ($\forall e \in E$) For the noise r, such that $0 \le r_e \le 1$ ($\forall e \in E$), let $\gamma_{1,e}$ be

$$\gamma_{1,e} = \max_{f_e \ge 0} \frac{\left(l_e(\bar{f}_e) - l_e(f_e) \right) f_e + (f_e - \bar{f}_e)\tilde{\tau}_e^*(\bar{f}_e)}{l_e(\bar{f}_e)\bar{f}_e} \quad (6)$$

$$= \max_{f_e \ge 0} \frac{\alpha_e(\bar{f}_e^{\beta} - f_e^{\beta})f_e + (f_e - \bar{f}_e)\beta r_e \alpha_e \bar{f}_e^{\beta}}{(l_{e0} + \alpha_e \bar{f}_e^{\beta})\bar{f}_e}.$$

As $l_{e0} \ge 0$,

$$\gamma_{1,e} \le \max_{f_e \ge 0} \frac{(\bar{f}_e^{\beta} - f_e^{\beta})f_e + (f_e - \bar{f}_e)\beta r_e \bar{f}_e^{\beta}}{\bar{f}_e^{1+\beta}}. \quad (7)$$

Because the denominator of the right side of Eq. (7) is constant, it is sufficient to consider the maximization of the numerator $F_{1,1}(f_e) = (\bar{f}_e^{\beta} - f_e^{\beta})f_e + (f_e - \bar{f}_e)\beta r_e \bar{f}_e^{\beta}$. $dF_{1,1}/df_e = 0$ leads to f_e that maximizes $F_{1,1}(f_e)$: $f_e = [(1+\beta r_e)/(1+\beta)]^{1/\beta}\bar{f}_e$. Therefore, Eq. (7) is

$$\gamma_{1,e} \le \beta \left[\left(\frac{1 + \beta r_e}{1 + \beta} \right)^{\frac{1+\beta}{\beta}} - r_e \right] =: F_{1,2}(r_e). \quad (8)$$

Regarding $F_{1,2}(r_e)$ ($0 \le r_e \le 1$) at the right side of Eq. (8), $F_{1,2}(r_e)$ decreases monotonically with $0 \le r_e \le 1$ since $dF_{1,2}/dr_e \le 0$. Thus,

$$\gamma_{1,e} \le F_{1,2}(r_e) \le \beta \left[\left(\frac{1 + \beta r_{\min}}{1 + \beta} \right)^{\frac{1+\beta}{\beta}} - r_{\min} \right] \quad (\forall e \in E) \quad (9)$$

where $r_{\min} = \min_{e \in E} r_e$ and $0 \le F_{1,2}(r_e) < 1$ as $F_{1,2}(0) < 1$ and $F_{1,2}(1) = 0$.

Because $\left[\left(l_e(\bar{f}_e) - l_e(f_e) \right) f_e + (f_e - \bar{f}_e)\tilde{\tau}_e^*(\bar{f}_e) \right] / (l_e(\bar{f}_e)\bar{f}_e) \le \gamma_{1,e}$ ($\forall e \in E$) by Eq. (6), Eq. (5) is

$$T(\bar{f}) \le \sum_{e \in E} l_e(f_e)f_e + \sum_{e \in E} \gamma_{1,e}l_e(\bar{f}_e)\bar{f}_e$$

$$\le T(f) + \beta \left[\left(\frac{1 + \beta r_{\min}}{1 + \beta} \right)^{\frac{1+\beta}{\beta}} - r_{\min} \right] T(\bar{f}) \quad (\forall f)$$

using Eq. (9). Replacing f by the system optimum flow f^* yields

$$T(\bar{f}) \le T(f^*) + \beta \left[\left(\frac{1 + \beta r_{\min}}{1 + \beta} \right)^{\frac{1+\beta}{\beta}} - r_{\min} \right] T(\bar{f}).$$

Note that $\beta\{[(1+\beta r_{\min})/(1+\beta)]^{(1+\beta)/\beta} - r_{\min}\} \in [0,1)$. Hence, we obtain the upper bound of the PoA $\rho(\boldsymbol{r})$ as the function of $r_{\min}$:

$$\rho(\boldsymbol{r}) = \frac{T(\bar{\boldsymbol{f}})}{T(\boldsymbol{f}^*)} \leq \frac{1}{1 - \beta\left[\left(\frac{1+\beta r_{\min}}{1+\beta}\right)^{\frac{1+\beta}{\beta}} - r_{\min}\right]} \qquad (0 \leq r_{\min} \leq 1). \qquad (10)$$

Because the right hand of Eq. (10) decreases monotonically with $r_{\min} \in [0,1]$, the PoASZ in the case of $0 \leq r_e \leq 1$ ($\forall e \in E$) is

$$\dot{\rho}(\boldsymbol{0}) \geq \frac{1}{1 - \beta\left[\left(\frac{1+\beta r_{\min}}{1+\beta}\right)^{\frac{1+\beta}{\beta}} - r_{\min}\right]} \qquad (0 \leq r_{\min} \leq 1). \qquad (11)$$

However, when the noise is constant throughout the network (i.e., $r_e = r, \forall e \in E$, r: const.), PoASZ is $0 < r \leq 1$ regardless of Eq. (11). This is because the total system travel time that is expressed as a function of r decreases monotonically for $0 \leq r \leq 1$ [15].

(b) In the case of $r_e \geq 1$ ($\forall e \in E$) For the noise $\boldsymbol{r}$, such that $r_e \geq 1$ ($\forall e \in E$), let $\gamma_{2,e}$ be

$$\gamma_{2,e} = \max_{f_e \geq 0} \frac{\left(l_e(\bar{f}_e) - l_e(f_e)\right) f_e + (f_e - \bar{f}_e)\tilde{\tau}_e^*(\bar{f}_e)}{l_e(f_e)f_e} \qquad (12)$$

$$= \max_{f_e \geq 0} \frac{\alpha_e(\bar{f}_e^\beta - f_e^\beta)f_e + (f_e - \bar{f}_e)\beta r_e \alpha_e \bar{f}_e^\beta}{(l_{e0} + \alpha_e f_e^\beta)f_e}.$$

Because $l_{e0} \geq 0$,

$$\gamma_{2,e} \leq \max_{f_e \geq 0}\left[-1 + \frac{\bar{f}_e^\beta f_e + (f_e - \bar{f}_e)\beta r_e \bar{f}_e^\beta}{f_e^{1+\beta}}\right]. \qquad (13)$$

We define $F_{2,1}(f_e) = -1 + \frac{\bar{f}_e^\beta f_e + (f_e - \bar{f}_e)\beta r_e \bar{f}_e^\beta}{f_e^{1+\beta}}$. Solving $dF_{2,1}/df_e = 0$ leads to f_e that maximizes $F_{2,1}(f_e)$: $f_e = \frac{1+\beta}{\beta}\frac{\beta r_e}{1+\beta r_e}\bar{f}_e$. Therefore, Eq. (13) is

$$\gamma_{2,e} \leq -1 + \left(\frac{1+\beta r_e}{1+\beta}\right)^{1+\beta}\left(\frac{1}{r_e}\right)^\beta =: F_{2,2}(r_e). \qquad (14)$$

Regarding $F_{2,2}(r_e)$ ($r_e \geq 1$) in the right hand of Eq. (14), $F_{2,2}(r_e)$ increases monotonically with $r_e \geq 1$ since $dF_{2,2}/dr_e \geq 0$. Thus,

$$\gamma_{2,e} \leq F_{2,2}(r_e) \leq -1 + \left(\frac{1+\beta r_{\max}}{1+\beta}\right)^{1+\beta}\left(\frac{1}{r_{\max}}\right)^\beta \qquad (15)$$

where $r_{\max} = \max_{e \in E} r_e$.

As $[(l_e(\bar{f}_e) - l_e(f_e)) f_e + (f_e - \bar{f}_e)\tilde{\tau}_e^*(\bar{f}_e)]/(l_e(f_e)f_e) \le \gamma_{2,e}$ $(\forall e \in E)$ by Eq. (12), Eq. (5) is

$$T(\bar{f}) \le \sum_{e \in E} l_e(f_e)f_e + \sum_{e \in E} \gamma_{2,e}l_e(f_e)f_e$$

$$\le T(f) + \left[-1 + \left(\frac{1 + \beta r_{\max}}{1 + \beta}\right)^{1+\beta} \left(\frac{1}{r_{\max}}\right)^{\beta}\right] T(f) \qquad (\forall f) \qquad (16)$$

using Eq. (15). By replacing f by the system optimum flow f^*, we obtain the upper bound of the PoA $\rho(r)$ as the function of $r_{\max}$:

$$\rho(r) = \frac{T(\bar{f})}{T(f^*)} \le \left(\frac{1 + \beta r_{\max}}{1 + \beta}\right)^{1+\beta} \left(\frac{1}{r_{\max}}\right)^{\beta} \qquad (r_{\max} \ge 1). \qquad (17)$$

Because the right hand of Eq. (17) increases monotonically with $r_{\max} \in [1, \infty)$, PoASZ in the case of $r_e \ge 1$ $(\forall e \in E)$ is

$$\rho(0) \ge \left(\frac{1 + \beta r_{\max}}{1 + \beta}\right)^{1+\beta} \left(\frac{1}{r_{\max}}\right)^{\beta} \qquad (r_{\max} \ge 1). \qquad (18)$$

Notably, the PoASZ when the noise is constant throughout the network (i.e., $r_e = r$, $\forall e \in E$, r: const.) is given by replacing $r_{\max}$ in Eq. (18) in r.

Summarizing the above discussion for both cases, we obtain the following theorem for the PoASZ.

Theorem 3. (PoASZ) *For each link $e \in E$ in the traffic network $G(V, E)$, $l_e(f_e) = l_{e0} + \alpha_e f_e^\beta$ ($l_{e0}, \alpha_e \ge 0$, $\beta > 0$) and the inaccurate MCT $\tilde{\tau}_e^* = \beta r_e \alpha_e f_e^\beta$ are set as the delay function and the toll. The PoASZ is*

$$\rho(0) \ge \begin{cases} \dfrac{1}{1 - \beta\left[\left(\frac{1+\beta r_{\min}}{1+\beta}\right)^{\frac{1+\beta}{\beta}} - r_{\min}\right]} & (0 \le r_e \le 1, \forall e \in E) \\[4ex] \left(\dfrac{1 + \beta r_{\max}}{1 + \beta}\right)^{1+\beta} \left(\dfrac{1}{r_{\max}}\right)^{\beta} & (r_e \ge 1, \forall e \in E) \end{cases} \qquad (19)$$

where $\rho(0)$ is the PoA in applying no tolls and $r_{\min} = \min_{e \in E} r_e$, $r_{\max} = \max_{e \in E} r_e$.

For example, if $\beta = 4$, the upper bound of the PoA is

$$\rho(r) \le \begin{cases} \dfrac{1}{1 - 4\left[\left(\frac{1+4r_{\min}}{5}\right)^{5/4} - r_{\min}\right]} & (0 \le r_e \le 1, \forall e \in E) \\[4ex] [(1 + 4r_{\max})/5]^5 \, r_{\max}^{-4} & (r_e \ge 1, \forall e \in E) \end{cases} \qquad (20)$$

from Eq. (10) and (17). These graphs are shown as blue lines in Fig. 1. When the PoA in applying no tolls is determined to $\rho(0) = 1.4$ by measurement in real traffic or simulation, the PoASZ calculated by Eq. (20) is $0.23404 \le r_{\min} \le 1$ for $0 \le r_e \le 1$ $(\forall e \in E)$ and $1 \le r_{\max} \le 2.77612$ for $r_e \ge 1$ $(\forall e \in E)$ from Eq. (19).

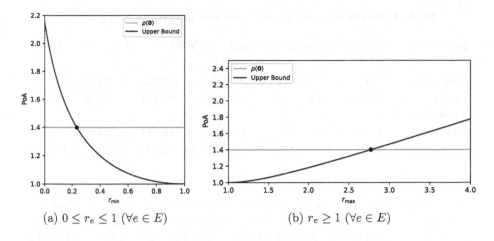

(a) $0 \le r_e \le 1 \ (\forall e \in E)$ (b) $r_e \ge 1 \ (\forall e \in E)$

Fig. 1. Upper bound of PoA (the blue line) and $\rho(0) = 1.4$ (the red line) at $\beta = 4$. (Color figure online)

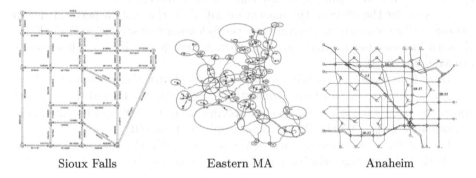

Sioux Falls   Eastern MA   Anaheim

Fig. 2. Traffic networks used in the simulation experiments [10].

5   Simulation Experiments

To confirm the theoretically derived PoASZ and consider the effect of the inaccurate MCT on the PoA, we simulate four traffic scenarios.

5.1   Experiment Condition

Each traffic scenario is determined by the traffic network $G(V, E)$ and the demand $R(s, t) \ (\forall (s, t) \in V^2)$. The traffic network specifies the set of vertices V and links E. Each is partitioned into traffic analysis zones, and each zone has a vertex called a centroid. All traffic demand is assumed to occur between centroids. The demand $R(s, t)$ between non-centroid vertices (s, t) is set to 0.

The BPR function is used for the delay function l_e of each link $e \in E$ with the commonly used parameters $\alpha = 0.15$ and $\beta = 4$. The toll τ_e on each link

Table 1. Specification of the traffic scenario used in the experiment.

Network	Vertices	Links	Zones	Total demand	$T(\mathbf{0})$	$T(\mathbf{1})$	$\rho(\mathbf{0})$
Sioux falls	24	76	24	360,600	7,480,225	7,194,256	1.0397
Eastern massachusetts	74	258	74	65,576	28,181	27,324	1.0313
Anaheim	416	914	38	104,694	1,419,914	1,395,015	1.0178
Chicago sketch	933	2,950	387	1,260,907	18,377,326	17,953,268	1.0236

e is set to the inaccurate MCT $\tilde{\tau}_e^*$ shown in Definition 2. The noise factor r_e of each link e is set randomly according to a uniform distribution. The interval $I = [a, b]$ ($a \le b$) of the uniform distribution is (a) $I \subset [0.00, 1.00]$ with the step width of the end points of 0.01 for an experiment for $0 \le r_e \le 1$ ($\forall e \in E$) or (b) $I \subset [1.0, 10.0]$ with the step width of 0.1 for an experiment for the case of $r_e \ge 1$ ($\forall e \in E$). We simulate twenty runs for each interval.

To consider the effect of the inaccurate MCT on the system performance in various traffic scenarios, we demonstrate the following four scenarios: Sioux Falls, Eastern Massachusetts, Anaheim, and Chicago Sketch (see Fig. 2). All scenarios are available at [10].

Table 1 presents the following scenario specifications: the number of vertices $|V|$, links $|E|$, zones, and total demand $\sum_{(s,t)\in V^2} R(s,t)$. In addition, Table 1 shows the total system travel time in applying no tolls $T(\mathbf{0})$ and in the system performance $T(\mathbf{1})$, and the PoA without applying tolls $\rho(\mathbf{0})$.

The UE flows are computed using Algorithm B [4][2]. The convergence condition is that the average relative gap of each bush is less than 1×10^{-8}.

5.2   Results

Table 2 presents the PoA without tolls, where the PoASZ calculated by Eq. (19), and the maximum PoA toward the noise satisfying PoSAZ. The maximum PoA satisfying the theoretically derived PoASZ is lower than the PoA without tolls. These results support our theoretical claims regarding the PoASZ.

For case (b), the blue points in Fig. 3 present the noise conditions (minimum and maximum of the uniform distribution that determines the noise r_e) PoA is no more than $\rho(\mathbf{0})$. The red points also present the condition that PoA is higher than $\rho(\mathbf{0})$. Notably, in case (a), all PoA under all conditions do not exceed $\rho(\mathbf{0})$, which is also relevant for Eastern Massachusetts in case (b), such that these figures are omitted. From these results, the noise condition for PoA stating that the system performance must not be lower than that without tolls is not as strict as the PoASZ. The reasons of it are as follows.

---

[2] The source code of Algorithm B in language C (https://sboyles.github.io/teaching/ce392c/tap.zip) is modified for the purpose of this experiment.

Table 2. $\rho(0)$, PoASZ and $\max_{r \in S} \rho(r)$ in four traffic scenarios. $\rho(0)$ is PoA without tolls. $\max_{r \in S} \rho(r)$ is the maximum PoA toward noise satisfying PoASZ, obtained by simulation experiments (S is the noise set satisfying PoASZ).

Network	$\rho(0)$	(a) $0 \leq r_e \leq 1$ ($\forall e \in E$)		(b) $r_e \geq 1$ ($\forall e \in E$)	
		PoASZ	$\max_{r \in S} \rho(r)$	PoASZ	$\max_{r \in S} \rho(r)$
Sioux falls	1.0397	$0.70073 \leq r_{\min} \leq 1$	$1.0012 < \rho(0)$	$1 \leq r_{\max} \leq 1.3807$	$1.0007 < \rho(0)$
Eastern massachusetts	1.0313	$0.73203 \leq r_{\min} \leq 1$	$1.0009 < \rho(0)$	$1 \leq r_{\max} \leq 1.0957$	$1.0005 < \rho(0)$
Anaheim	1.0178	$0.79510 \leq r_{\min} \leq 1$	$1.0002 < \rho(0)$	$1 \leq r_{\max} \leq 1.2397$	$1.0002 < \rho(0)$
Chicago sketch	1.0236	$0.76573 \leq r_{\min} \leq 1$	$1.0003 < \rho(0)$	$1 \leq r_{\max} \leq 1.2811$	$1.0001 < \rho(0)$

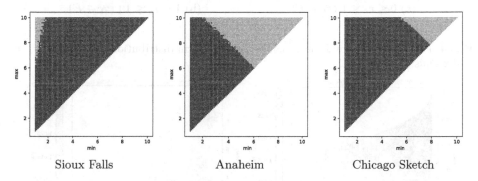

| Sioux Falls | Anaheim | Chicago Sketch |

Fig. 3. Noise conditions (minimum and maximum of uniform distribution) indicating that PoA is lower than $\rho(0)$ (blue points) and higher than $\rho(0)$ (red points). All figures fall. within case (b): $r_e \geq 1$ ($\forall e \in E$). Notably, in case (a), the PoA under all conditions does not exceed $\rho(0)$, which is also valid for Eastern Massachusetts in case (b), such that these figures are omitted. (Color figure online)

- The deterioration of the system performance due to the increase in noise is unremarkable.
- the PoA without tolls $\rho(0)$ is lower than its theoretical upper bound. $[1 - \beta(1+\beta)^{-(1+\beta)/\beta}]^{-1}$ is known as the upper bound of $\rho(0)$ [11]. Because $\beta = 4$ in these experiments, the upper bound of $\rho(0)$ is 2.1505. However, as noted by [5], the PoA without tolls in the traffic scenarios is significantly lower than the theoretical upper bound. Hence, in Fig. 1, the intersection of the curve representing the upper bound of the PoA and the line representing $\rho(0)$ is located more to the right in case (a) or more to the left in case (b); in other words, the PoASZ is obtained as a strict condition in both cases.

Figure 4, 5 and 6 present the relation between the mean and variance of the uniform distribution that determines the noise and the average of twenty PoAs obtained in the simulation. Because the Anaheim result is almost the same as the one of Eastern Massachusetts, the former is not shown. Regarding the relation between the variance and PoA in the four traffic scenarios, a smaller variance indicates better system performance. The strength of this tendency is most remarkable for Sioux Falls in both cases (a) and (b). These results provide

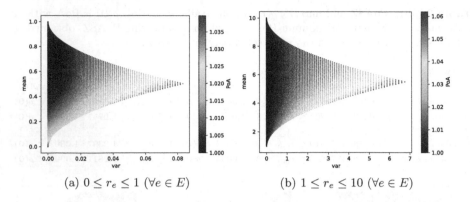

(a) $0 \leq r_e \leq 1 \ (\forall e \in E)$ (b) $1 \leq r_e \leq 10 \ (\forall e \in E)$

Fig. 4. PoA, the mean, and the variance of the uniform distribution determining r_e in Sioux Falls.

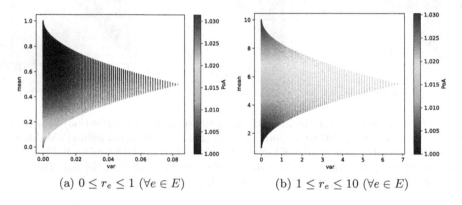

(a) $0 \leq r_e \leq 1 \ (\forall e \in E)$ (b) $1 \leq r_e \leq 10 \ (\forall e \in E)$

Fig. 5. PoA, the mean, and the variance of the uniform distribution determining r_e in Eastern Massachusetts.

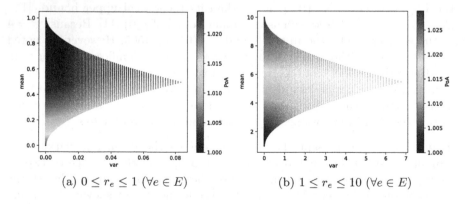

(a) $0 \leq r_e \leq 1 \ (\forall e \in E)$ (b) $1 \leq r_e \leq 10 \ (\forall e \in E)$

Fig. 6. PoA, the mean, and the variance of the uniform distribution determining r_e in Chicago Sketch.

a basis for setting parameter β used in Δ-tolling [16,17] to be constant across the entire network. This tendency that a smaller variance indicates better system performance is also observed in case (a) of the other three networks, although it is not as remarkable as Sioux Falls. The similar tendency is observed for Chicago Sketch in case (b). Nevertheless, the variance has little relation to the system performance for the other two traffic scenarios. The possible reasons behind this tendency is the concentration of traffic on links with lower tolls, which increases the total system travel time.

The result regarding the variance of link-specific noise r_e and the system performance provides an expectation that a smaller variance in the VOT of each user would lead to a better the system performance when the VOT is heterogeneous for each user, and the toll is equal to the accurately calculated MCT (i.e., $\tau_e = \tau_e^*$, $\forall e \in E$).

The relation between the mean of the uniform distribution and the PoA differs between Sioux Falls and the other networks. As the mean is larger in case (a) and smaller in case (b), the system performance tends to be better the three networks except for Sioux Falls. This result is predicted when MCT with a constant noise coefficient r for the whole network is applied as a toll (i.e., $\tau_e = r\tau_e^*$, $\forall e \in E$) [15]. In contrast, the overall system performance tends to be higher for Sioux Falls, in both cases (a) and (b), as the mean is larger. While this tendency is predictable from [15] for case (a), but different from [15] for case (b)[3]. However, if the variance is small, there is little relation between the mean and the system performance, even for (b). Regarding the relation between the PoA, variance, and mean, no clear correlation is found with each specification of the traffic scenarios (shown in Table 1).

The following is a summary of the simulation results.

- Smaller variance in the noise of the inaccurate MCT leads to better system performance.
- The mean of the noise of the inaccurate MCT close to 1 with small variance leads to better system performance.

6   Conclusion

This study focuses on MCT under the traffic network with link-specific noise. We defined the PoASZ as a noise condition. By PoASZ, the system performance of the cases with tolls could not be lower than the ones with no tolls. We considered two cases: 1) the tolls that are lower than MCT and 2) the tolls that are higher than MCT. PoASZ was theoretically derived as a function of the minimum noise in the former case and the maximum noise in the latter case. The simulation results demonstrate that the theoretical PoASZ was confirmed by the simulation results of PoASZ in some traffic networks. Furthermore, we showed that the

---

[3] Even in case (b), when the variance is equal to 0, i.e., when the noise is constant across the network ($\tau_e = r\tau_e^*$, $\forall e \in E$, r: const.), the result supports the conclusion of [15] that the system performance increases monotonically for $r \geq 1$.

system performance is better when the variance of the noise of the inaccurate MCT is smaller, and when the variance of the noise of the inaccurate MCT is smaller at a mean close to 1.

A possible future task would be to consider more realistic traffic environments. This study assumes the most basic user equilibrium, including the deterministic users' route choice behaviors, static traffic models, and transportation service levels. By considering stochastic user equilibrium, the deterministic users' route choice can be assumed. While such static traffic assignment is an effective tool for long-term traffic plans, it cannot represent the dynamic traffic congestion phenomenon. To consider the progress of time, dynamic user equilibrium (DUE) can be used as a model [7]. In the case of a dynamic model, the marginal cost tolls can also be estimated using an approximating calculation method, such as Δ-tolling [16,17].

References

1. Beckmann, M.J., McGuire, C.B., Winsten, C.B.: Studies in the Economics of Transportation. Yale University Press (1956)
2. Chen, H., et al.: DyETC: dynamic electronic toll collection for traffic congestion alleviation. In: Proceedings of AAAI-18, vol. 32 (2018)
3. de Palma, A., Lindsey, R.: Traffic congestion pricing methodologies and technologies. Transp. Res. Part C: Emerg. Technol. **19**(6), 1377–1399 (2011). https://doi.org/10.1016/j.trc.2011.02.010
4. Dial, R.B.: A path-based user-equilibrium traffic assignment algorithm that obviates path storage and enumeration. Transp. Res. Part B: Methodol. **40**(10), 917–936 (2006). https://doi.org/10.1016/j.trb.2006.02.008
5. Grange, L.d., Melo-Riquelme, C., Burgos, C., González, F., Raveau, S.: Numerical bounds on the price of anarchy. J. Adv. Transp. **2017**, 9 (2017)
6. Hanna, J.P., Sharon, G., Boyles, S.D., Stone, P.: Selecting compliant agents for opt-in micro-tolling. In: Proceedings of AAAI-19 (2019). https://doi.org/10.1609/aaai.v33i01.3301565
7. Mahmassani, H., Herman, R.: Dynamic user equilibrium departure time and route choice on idealized traffic arterials. Transp. Sci. **18**(4), 362–384 (1984). https://doi.org/10.1287/trsc.18.4.362
8. Mirzaei, H., Sharon, G., Boyles, S., Givargis, T., Stone, P.: Enhanced delta-tolling: traffic optimization via policy gradient reinforcement learning. In: Proceedings of ITSC 2018, pp. 47–52 (2018). https://doi.org/10.1109/ITSC.2018.8569737
9. Papadimitriou, C.: Algorithms, games, and the internet. In: Proceedings of STOC 2001. pp. 749–753 (2001). https://doi.org/10.1145/380752.380883
10. For Research Core Team, T.N.: Transportation networks for research https://github.com/bstabler/TransportationNetworks
11. Roughgarden, T.: The price of anarchy is independent of the network topology. J. Comput. Syst. Sci. **67**(2), 341–364 (2003). https://doi.org/10.1016/S0022-0000(03)00044-8
12. Schrank, D., Albert, L., Eisele, B., Lomax, T.: 2021 urban mobility report (2021)
13. Sharon, G.: Alleviating road traffic congestion with artificial intelligence. In: Proceedings of IJCAI-21, pp. 4965–4969 (2021). https://doi.org/10.24963/ijcai.2021/704

14. Sharon, G., Albert, M., Rambha, T., Boyles, S., Stone, P.: Traffic optimization for a mixture of self-interested and compliant agents. In: Proceedings of AAAI-18 (2018). https://doi.org/10.1609/aaai.v32i1.11444
15. Sharon, G., Boyles, S.D., Alkoby, S., Stone, P.: Marginal cost pricing with a fixed error factor in traffic networks. In: Proceedings of AAMAS 2019, pp. 1539–1546 (2019)
16. Sharon, G., et al.: Real-time adaptive tolling scheme for optimized social welfare in traffic networks. In: Proceedings of AAMAS 2017, pp. 828–836 (2017)
17. Sharon, G., Michael, W.L., Hanna, J.P., Rambha, T., Boyles, S.D., Stone, P.: Network-wide adaptive tolling for connected and automated vehicles. Transp. Res. Part C: Emerg. Technol. **84**, 142–157 (2017). https://doi.org/10.1016/j.trc.2017.08.019
18. Sheffi, Y.: Urban Transportation Networks. Prentice-Hall, Hoboken (1985)
19. Yang, H., Xu, W., Heydecker, B.: Bounding the efficiency of road pricing. Transp. Res. Part E: Logist. Transp. Rev. **46**(1), 90–108 (2010). https://doi.org/10.1016/j.tre.2009.05.007

Explanation-Based Negotiation Protocol for Nutrition Virtual Coaching

Berk Buzcu[1]([✉]), Vanitha Varadhajaran[2], Igor Tchappi[2],
Amro Najjar[3], Davide Calvaresi[4], and Reyhan Aydoğan[1,5]

[1] Computer Science, Özyeğin University, Istanbul, Turkey
berk.buzcu@ozu.edu.tr , reyhan.aydogan@ozyegin.edu.tr
[2] University of Luxembourg, Esch-sur-Alzette, Luxembourg
igor.tchappi@uni.lu
[3] Luxembourg Institute of Science and Technology, Esch-sur-Alzette, Luxemburg
amro.najjar@list.lu
[4] University of Applied Sciences and Arts Western Switzerland, Delémont,
Switzerland
davide.calvaresi@hevs.ch
[5] Interactive Intelligence, Delft University of Technology, Delft, The Netherlands
https://expectation.ehealth.hevs.ch/

Abstract. People's awareness about the importance of healthy lifestyles
is rising. This opens new possibilities for personalized intelligent health
and coaching applications. In particular, there is a need for more than
simple recommendations and mechanistic interactions. Recent studies
have identified nutrition virtual coaching systems (NVC) as a technological solution, possibly bridging technologies such as recommender,
informative, persuasive, and argumentation systems. Enabling NVC to
explain recommendations and discuss (argument) dietary solutions and
alternative items or behaviors is crucial to improve the transparency
of these applications and enhance user acceptability and retain their
engagement. This study primarily focuses on virtual agents personaliz-
ing the generation of food recipes recommendation according to users'
allergies, eating habits, lifestyles, nutritional values, etc. Although the
agent would nudge the user to consume healthier food, users may tend
to object in favor of tastier food. To resolve this divergence, we propose
a user-agent negotiation interacting over the revision of the recommendation (via feedback and explanations) or convincing (via explainable
arguments) the user of its benefits and importance. Finally, the paper
presents our initial findings on the acceptability and usability of such a
system obtained via tests with real users. Our preliminary experimental
results show that the majority of the participants appreciate the ability
to express their feedback as well as receive explanations of the recommendations, while there is still room for improvement in the persuasiveness
of the explanations.

Supported by CHIST-ERA (grant CHIST-ERA-19-XAI-005).

1   Introduction

According to the World Health Organization (WHO), non-communicable diseases (e.g., cardiovascular diseases, chronic respiratory diseases, and diabetes) are responsible for 63% of all deaths worldwide[1]. Moreover, WHO outlines that these diseases are preventable by effectively tackling shared risk factors such as unhealthy diets. Personal preferences and constraints (e.g., cultural, religious, and sustainable diets [7]) and unhealthy derivatives possibly hidden (or overlooked) in a large variety of food items highlight the need for guidance. To this end, food recommender systems are increasingly proposed to guide people in selecting suitable recipes [30]. Indeed, food recommenders have dramatically grown, primarily fueled by globalization (more availability and broader variety) and the rise of ultra-processed food that has skyrocketed metabolic and overweight issues [12].

One may argue that they can find countless recipes over the internet. However, picking the "best" one for a given individual in a specific situation is highly complex. Objectively handling such a vast collection of possibilities and crossing variables such as allergens, nutrition values, personal needs, calories already intake, historical values, and the *preference* of the moment is challenging. Therefore, a personalized support system is needed. Nutrition virtual coaches (NVC) are intended to recommend the most fitting recipes to the user according to a broad set of variables. NVC can, indeed, consider users' health [29] as well as their needs, requests, and historical consistency over time. NVC can support a wide range of goals, ranging from gaining muscles, to weight loss, even for individuals with nutrition-related diseases (i.e., obesity[2]). Such support is envisioned to be educative. Instructing the user would allow reducing the dependency on the NVCs progressively.

Existing solutions both from research [5] and industry [25] tried to cope with such goals. However, they lack clarity and transparency, generating a lack of trust and efficacy. Explainable AI (XAI) techniques have been adopted in several tangential applications domains, such as transportation [20], fleet management [16], neurosciences [9] etc. to bring such transparency. Moreover, some studies have approached explainable food recommendations by proposing a semantic model [21] and incorporating negotiation to gently navigate the user towards a certain quality of life goal [18]. While these works have been considered recommender systems, to the best of our knowledge, no existing system qualifies as a whole Nutrition Virtual Coach allowing the agents to explain the recommendations to the user, and contend interactively over it for the sake of achieving the desired behavior change.

This work presents an interactive and explainable protocol enabling an NVC to promote healthy(-ier) food. To do so, we have developed a simple health score calculation module, a module with a multi-criteria additive utility function to

---

[1] https://www.who.int/news-room/fact-sheets/detail/noncommunicable-diseases.

[2] https://www.cdc.gov/chronicdisease/resources/publications/factsheets/nutrition.html.

rank the recipes logically, and an OWL ontology to classify/relate users and ingredients (best fitting). Moreover, we tested and assessed the protocol with individuals characterized by various backgrounds.

The rest of this paper is organized as follows. Section 2 presents the related work. Section 3 presents the explainable argumentation negotiation module for NVC. Section 4 evaluates and discusses the obtained results. Finally, Sect. 5 concludes the paper and outlines future works.

2   Related Works

This section briefly overviews the literature on recommender systems in the context of food recommender systems (Sect. 2.1) and evolving towards explainable and interactive recommendations (Sect. 2.2).

2.1   Conventional Food Recommendation

One of the first concepts of a food recommender system, CHEF, dates back to 1986 [14]. It tests case-based planning, defining a few success/failure conditions and attempting to replace/improve food items within recipes. The cased-based planning model used in CHEF requires an extensive initial knowledge base, remarkable pre-processing, and the creation of plans and backup plans for each recipe. Freyne and Berkovsky implement the general intuition of recommender algorithms such as collaborative filtering (CF), and content-based (CB) approaches to recommend recipes [10]. Their strategy to determine ingredient weights and use them with the CF and CB performs better when making predictions than directly using the recipes. Ge, Ricci and Massimo introduce concepts of personalization of the recommendations subordinating taste to health [11]. Chi, Chen and Tasi focus on recommending food for chronic individuals (i.e., kidney diseases) [6]. The authors architected a specific Ontology Web Language (OWL) ontology embedding health-relevant aspects rather than specific calculations. A more generalized healthy recommendation framework is proposed by Chen et al. [5]. It focuses on modifying unhealthy recipes from a dataset of unhealthy food. They propose a new deep learning-based method (IP-embedding) to match recipes with desired ingredients. The IP-Embedding is used to build a pseudo recipe (a set of ingredients forming the desired outcome) from the requirements, which is then matched to healthy ingredients, and finally matched with a real recipe via the MSE metric. Similarly, Teng, Lin and Adamic seeks to build a pointwise comparison metric to understand how to realize recipes from ingredients and swap them with healthier alternatives [27]. Ingredients/food substitution has also been tackled by Elsweiler, Trattner and Harvey [8]. They metricize the nutritional values for fat, sodium, etc., for a predetermined healthy range. Then, images of the recipes push users to prefer healthier food rather than unhealthy options.

2.2 Early Interactive Recommendation System

Explainable AI (XAI) is pervading humans' daily lives. AI predictors and classifiers are no longer allowed to be opaque. To be trusted and make a real impact on humans, they need to be more transparent, understandable, and inspectable [2]. Indeed, recommender systems are expected to equip their outcomes with explanations [13]. Such explanations should allow for justification, control, and discovery of new aspects of the proposed outcome [1]. Padhiar *et al.* propose a food recommender system drafting explanations from knowledge-based ontology [21]. Samih, Adadi and Berrada push the concept further, proposing a knowledge-based explainable recommender system where they generate explanations using the probabilistic soft-logic framework [24]. Finally, to increase the interaction between the user and the virtual assistants, Lawo *et al.* define a cluster of consumers with ethical and social priorities and include them in the recommendation process negotiation as central concerns — recording positive feedback w.r.t. concerning the alternatives proposed [18].

Overall, recommendation systems are not new in the nutrition domain. Pursuing healthy, sustainable, and taste-based combinations are the most targeted goals. Recent studies tried to embed explanations in the recommendations to foster transparency — henceforth trust and acceptability. Aligned with this trend, the following section presents an interactive communication/negotiation protocol enabling explainable mechanisms to dive into specific topics and to learn from the user's feedback promptly.

3 Ontology-Based Negotiation for NVC

The well-known tendency to prefer unhealthy food is worsened by the plethora of internet-sourced popular recipes which foster unhealthy habits [26]. Accordingly, the NVCs aim to improve dietary choices and reduce health risks through personalized recommendations. To do so, there is a need to resolve the conflict between user preferences regarding the food's taste and the recipes' healthiness. Furthermore, the system should explain well-grounded reasons why the given recipe is recommended to the user so that the NVC can persuade its users to improve their eating habits.

This section proposes an NVC leveraging ontology-based reasoning to interact with the user in a turn-based fashion. The goal is to understand their needs and interests, and make healthy recommendations, while still considering their preferences. The interaction between the user and the NVC is governed by the explanation-based negotiation protocol presented in this work. Section 3.1 describes the food ontology required for ontological reasoning. Section 3.2 describes the explanation-based negotiation protocol, Sect. 3.3 explains our basic recommendation algorithm and finally, Sect. 3.4 elaborates on the explanation generation algorithm.

3.1   Food Ontology and Recipe Repository

An OWL-based ontology database is utilized in Protege to represent the relationship between the users and their eating habits and to capture the structural similarities among the ingredients of the recipes. The ontology consists of two main concepts: *User* and *Food*. The *User* concept captures the users eating habits, such as religious or lifestyle restrictions. We define object properties such as *doesNotEat* to determine what kind of food ingredients the user would not consume. Figure 1 shows a small part of the ontology indicating user eating habits. Here, the restrictions (e.g., Muslims do not eat pork) are encoded by connecting the object properties (shown in diamonds) to both the *User* and *Food* ends.

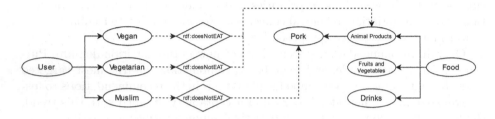

Fig. 1. A sample of the general structure of the OWL based ontology

The *Food* concept involves a hierarchy of food recipe ingredients (e.g., *Beef* is a sub-concept of *Animal Products*, a *Cucumber* is a sub-concept of *Vegetables* etc.). Figure 2 shows the Protege view of some food classifications and some of their ingredients or instances. The agent can query the OWL ontology and decide whether the user can consume the given recipe based on their eating habits.

We realized a repository by incorporating two different datasets: *foodRecSys*[3] and *FoodBase Corpus* [22]. *foodRecSys* contains around 46K recipes with comprehensive nutritional values. It also contains each recipe's name, photo, ingredients, and cooking steps. However, the dataset lacks the structural information our system needs to construct our ingredient concept hierarchy on the ontology. Therefore, we use *FoodBase Corpus* [22], which contains a structured annotation of recipe ingredients from the same source. Using this annotation, we automatically construct the ontology structure. Then, we manually adapted it to fit our recipe repository.

Since the content of the recipes involves more complex structures (e.g., *slice of a tomato* instead of *tomato*), we need to pre-process the ingredients to match our ontological instances. In this process, we apply the Levenshtein Distance[4]

---

[3] https://www.kaggle.com/datasets/elisaxxygao/foodrecsysv1?resource=download&select=core-data_recipe.csv.

[4] https://blog.paperspace.com/measuring-text-similarity-using-levenshtein-distance/.

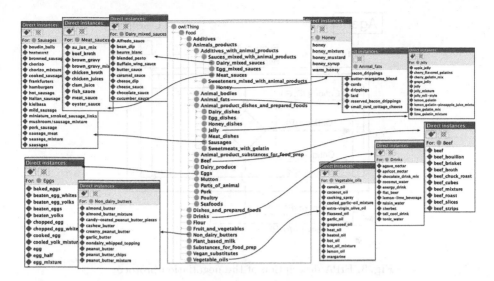

Fig. 2. Protege view of the Food class and some of their ingredients using OWL

to detect the best match. This match is mapped onto our repository, enabling the reasoner to use the food ontology. Furthermore, the recipe repository does not include cuisine information. Thus, we used an additional cuisine dataset[5] to incorporate the cuisine information into the recipe repository. Finally, we filtered the recipes that we could not find the corresponding cuisine information. Ultimately, the remaining number of recipes is 15K.

3.2   Explanation-Based Negotiation Protocol

The bilateral negotiation protocol enables the user to specify their constraints w.r.t. preferences and proactively give feedback while allowing the NVC agent to generate personalized recommendations along with explanations. Note that the explanation is about why the agent chooses a given recommendation. Similar to the Alternating Offer Protocol [3, 23], the interaction follows turn-taking fashion (see Fig. 3).

According to the proposed protocol, the user initiates the interaction by sending their constraints (C), which may consist of the ingredients the user may be allergic (e.g., milk, peanuts) to; the (dis)liked ingredients (e.g., specific meat/vegetables); and the desired type of cuisine (e.g., Middle Eastern, Italian, French). After receiving the user's constraints, the agent recommends a recipe (R) along with its explanation (ϵ). Then the user can: Accept R, leave without an agreement, criticize R, ϵ, or both. When the user makes a critique, the agent can revise its recommendation/explanation, regenerating (R'), (ϵ'), or both. This interaction continues in a turn-taking fashion until reaching a termination condition (i.e., Accept or Leave w/o Recommendation) or the time deadline is reached.

---

[5] https://cosylab.iiitd.edu.in/culinarydb/.

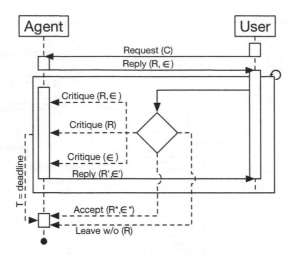

Fig. 3. FIPA description of the negotiation protocol

In our current implementation, a user can criticize the given recommendation by referring to pre-structured critiques as follows, where Y denotes one of the ingredients chosen by the user. (i) I ate Y recently, (ii) I'm allergic to Y, (iii) I don't like Y, and (iv) I want to give custom feedback.

Similarly, the user can criticize the explanations communicated alongside the recommendations with the pre-defined statements such as (i) The explanation is not convincing, (ii) The explanation does not fit my case, (iii) The explanation is incomplete, (iv) The explanation is not clear enough, and (v) I disagree with the explanation.

It is worth mentioning that the protocol is flexible enough to allow any kind of explanation and critique. For simplicity, this work only covers some basic structured phrases as mentioned above.

3.3 The Baseline Recommendation Strategy

Filtering and Scoring Recipes. To analyze the applicability of the designed protocol, we have developed a basic recommendation strategy relying on filtering and scoring the recipes with respect to the user's constraints and healthiness, as seen in Algorithm 1. The agent first filters the recipes according to the user's eating habits/constraints via ontology reasoning on what kind of ingredients the user would not consume (Lines 1–3). Assuming that the user is vegan, then the agent first filters the recipes containing animal-related products. Then, if the same user specifies that they do not like "zucchini", the agent removes the recipes containing zucchini from the remaining candidate list, R_u. In turn, the utilities of the remaining candidate are calculated by considering both healthiness and their alignment with the user preferences. Then, the recipes are ordered according to the calculated utilities (Lines 4–5)[6]. The recipe with the highest utility is taken

---

[6] The details of the utility calculation are explained below.

as a candidate recipe, and the system retroactively generates an explanation in line with the recipe's properties (Lines 6–7). This candidate recipe and its corresponding explanation are given to the user.

When the agent receives feedback from the user regarding the recipe, F_r, it filters the candidate recipes according to the updated constraints given by the feedback and selects the highest-ranked recipe similarly (Lines 10–15). When the agent receives feedback from the user regarding the explanation, F_ϵ, it simply generates a new explanation with the underlying recipe (Lines 16–18).

Algorithm 1: AgentDecisionFunction

Data: R: Recipes, U: User;

$R_u \subset R$: Recipe dataset tailored for the user;

H_u: Eating habits of the user, P_u: User Constraints/Preferences;

r_c: Candidate recipe, ϵ: Explanation for candidate recipe;

F_r: Feedback to the recipes, F_ϵ: Feedback to the explanation;

1 **if** *firstRecommendation* **then**
2     $R_u \leftarrow$ filterRecipesByCondition(R, H_u);
3     $R_u \leftarrow$ filterRecipesByCondition(R_u, P_u);
4     $U_{R_u} \leftarrow$ calculateUtilities(R_u);
5     $R_u \leftarrow$ rankRecipes(R_u, U_{R_u});
6     $r_c \leftarrow$ getHighestRankRecipe(R_u);
7     $\epsilon \leftarrow$ generateExplanation(r_c);
8 **end**
9 **else**
10   **if** F_r *exists* **then**
11        $R_u \leftarrow$ filterRecipesByCondition(R_u, F_r);
12        $U_{R_u} \leftarrow$ calculateUtilities(R_u);
13        $R_u \leftarrow$ rankRecipes(R_u, U_{R_u});
14        $R_c \leftarrow$ getHighestRankRecipe(R_u);
15   **end**
16   **if** F_ϵ *exists* **then**
17        $\epsilon \leftarrow$ generateExplanation(r_c);
18   **end**
19 **end**
20 **return** (r_c, ϵ);

Utility Estimation. To select the suitable recipe, this paper relies on a multi-criteria decision-making [17]. Multi-criteria decision analysis allows decisions among multiple alternatives evaluated by several conflicting criteria [31]. In this paper, the multi-criteria decision analysis is done by ranking recipes through a multi-criteria function. The multi-criteria function gives each recipe a score in the dataset. One of the main advantages of using a mathematical function is the transparency of the function and its outcomes. This feature is well suited for our proposed NVC due to the explainability of the generated behavior.

Now let us explain how our agent calculates the overall utility of the recipes. Based on the multi-criteria, the agent considers three criteria: Active Metabolic

Rate (AMR) score, nutrition value score, and users' Satisfaction score. The final score of the recipes is the weighted sum of the score provided by each module as presented by Eq. 1 where w_a, w_n, w_u denote the weights of each AMR score, nutrition value score, and users' satisfaction score, respectively. Note that each score is normalized to ensure that the overall score is ranged within $[0, 1]$.

$$recipeScore = w_n * nutrientsScore + w_a * amrScore + w_u * UsersScore \quad (1)$$

The nutrient-based score is calculated according to the nutritional information of the recipes, such as proteins, lipids, carbohydrates, cholesterol, sodium, and saturated fats. These nutrients have respective recommended amounts for a healthy life [28]. In this work, we take into account the nutrition intake limits specified by the WHO organization[7]. Accordingly, the nutrition-based score is calculated as seen in Eq. 2 where each individual nutrition score is calculated according to Eq. 3. We assume that consuming less than each nutrient's minimum amount (min_n) is better than its maximum amount (max_n). By following this heuristic, the individual score of each nutrient is calculated.

$$nutrientScore(recipe) = score(pro) + score(lip) + score(cb) + \\ score(ch) + score(sod) + score(sat) \quad (2)$$

$$score(n) = \begin{cases} 5 & \text{if } n \in [min_n, max_n] \\ 3 & \text{if } n < min_n \\ 1 & \text{else} \end{cases} \quad (3)$$

AMR is the number of calories that a person must consume daily depending on his height, sex, age, weight, and activity level. Such preliminary information is taken during the registration of the users. The value of AMR is based on the value of Basal Metabolic Rate (BMR), the number of calories required to keep a body functioning at rest, the activity level of the person, and the desire of the person to maintain or reduce his current weight. Table 1 presents the values to keep the current weight. To compute the AMR score based on the minimum and maximum amount of calories required for a given user available in literature [28], we rely on the same assumption of Eq. 3 that is consuming fewer calories than required ($score = 3$) is better than consuming more calories than required ($score = 1$). In addition, when the amount of calories computed is between the minimum and maximum amount of calories, the score is set to 5. Historically, the most used formula to compute BMR is the [15] equation with Eqs. 4 and 5, for men and women respectively. The authors estimated the constants of Eqs. 4 and 5 by several statistical experiments [15].

$$BMR = 10 * weight + 6.25 * height - 5 * age + 5 \quad (4)$$

$$BMR = 10 * weight + 6.25 * height - 5 * age + 161 \quad (5)$$

---

[7] https://www.who.int/news-room/fact-sheets/detail/healthy-diet, http://www.myd ailyintake.net/daily-intake-levels/.

Table 1. Daily recommended kilocalories (kcal) intake to maintain weight [28]

Activity level	Daily calories
Too little exercise	$calories = BMR * 1.2$
Light exercise	$calories = BMR * 1.375$
Moderate exercise	$calories = BMR * 1.55$
Strong exercise	$calories = BMR * 1.725$
Very strong exercise	$calories = BMR * 1.9$

User Satisfaction Score. Lastly, the user satisfaction score is calculated by considering the popularity of the recipe among all users and the current user's preferences equally. For the popularity of the recipe, we use the ratings given by the other users between [1, 5]. These values are normalized to [0, 1]. Meanwhile, regarding the user's preferences, we check how many ingredients are considered to be liked by the user. Here, to determine whether an ingredient is liked or not, we can use the explicit feedback from the user as well as rely on user profiling to predict whether the given ingredient is likely to be preferred to be consumed. Here, we use Jaccard Similarity [4] to estimate the individual user satisfaction (the rate of the number of the preferred ingredients over the number of all the ingredients of a given recipe).

Let us assume the user-submitted his preference for ingredients (i_1, i_2, i_3) and we have a recipe such that $R_1 = i_1, i_2, i_5, i_6$. Each ingredient that exists with the liked constraint is considered to be 1 and 0 otherwise. The mean of this operation is 0.5, which is effectively the score of R_1 for this user. For all the recipes, the scores are then max-normalized to place the values between [0, 1], resulting in a relative level of importance for the given recipe. For instance, let's assume that the system knows that the user likes the ingredients i_1, i_2, and i_3 and calculate the score of a recipe consisting of the following ingredients:i_1, i_2, i_5, i_6. The individual user satisfaction would be 2/4 according to Jaccard similarity. If the overall user rating of that recipe is equal to 4 out of 5, then the overall score would be equal to 0.65 ((0.5+0.8)/2).

3.4 Explanation for Recommendation

We present a straightforward explanation generation approach to demonstrate how the NVC agent interacts with its users. Two types of explanations are considered: health-related and preference-related. Six promising health-related explanations are generated from our dataset by taking the nutritional values into consideration, such as protein, vitamin coverage, and cholesterol counts. If the recommended recipe satisfies the given health conditions, we need to identify the main ingredient contributing to this condition, as seen in Table 2, where X is the amount of the nutrition. Note that more sophisticated explanations could be produced by consulting some nutritionists and enhancing ontology reasoning.

Three different explanations are presented regarding the user preferences: chosen cuisine, chosen ingredient, and overall popularity of the recipe (i.e., community score S) as seen in Table 2. To generate such explanations, we match the ingredients of the recipe (i.e., Y, Z) with the corresponding explanation. Finally, the agent generates its complete explanations by combining a fixed starting statement and randomly chosen health and preference-related explanations.

Table 2. Explanation variables and examples

Criteria	Example
Health related explanations	
Protein amount covers user needs for a meal	This recipe contains X grams of protein, which is about X% of your daily requirement. Your body needs proteins from your organs to your muscles and consuming the necessary amount of it is important!
Calorie count is above 30% of BMR	You should eat this food because it covers a good portion of your necessary daily calorie intake by X. You should eat X for a balanced diet and maintain a healthy weight!
Vitamin B amount covers the user needs for a meal	B vitamins have a direct impact on your energy levels, brain function, and cell metabolism, and you should consume X gram for a healthy vitamin B level in a meal!
Vitamin C amount covers the user needs for a meal	Vitamin C is needed for the growth and repair of tissues in all parts of your body. This recipe contains: X% of it and eating it will make you feel more energetic!
The amount of iron must be enough for a meal	Lack of Iron in your system could be critical, causing a disease that is known as iron deficiency anemia. This recipe supplies you with X of it.
The cholesterol must be below a threshold	This recipe has a very low cholesterol count. Cholesterol is linked with a higher risk of cardiovascular disease, and this food is great for low amounts of it.
Preference related explanations	
Users' chosen cuisine matches the recipe cuisine	This recipe is also a part of the cuisine you like: Z
Users' chosen ingredient matches the recipe	This recipe contains the ingredient you wanted: Y_1 and Y_2.
The recipes community score is above a threshold	This recipe was rated S stars by the community, and you might like it too!

4   Evaluation

The acceptability and appreciation of the proposed framework are evaluated via a user study involving 53 participants. This section presents the experimental setup and participants, and discusses the results of the user experiments.

4.1   Experimental Setup

To investigate the effect of interactive explanations and critiques introduced by the proposed protocol, we leverage a Web-based platform allowing the users to experience both the explanation-based negotiation protocol (i.e., the interactive recommender) and its replica without the explanations and critiques component (i.e., a regular recommender) — see Fig. 4.

Prior to the experiments, each user is asked to fill out a pre-survey and registration form to specify their gender, age, height, weight, sports activity level, eating habits, and allergies[8]. This information is used to estimate the healthiness score of recipes recommended to the user (see Sect. 3.3). Seeking to instill different experiences, the two environments (i.e., regular and interactive e-coach/food recommenders) are proposed randomly to each user with a 5-minute break between the two sessions. At the end of the test, the users are asked to fill a questionnaire consisting of mostly 5-point Likert scale questions regarding their experience in both sessions, employing a within-subject design [19].

4.2   Participants

We have recruited 53 users (i.e., 33 men and 20 women with various back-grounds). The mean age is 25.9 with a max of 51 and the min is 19 years old. The participants were asked to rank the importance of five criteria: "Nutritional factors", "Past experience with taste", "How it looks", "Price of the ingredients", and "Cooking style" while making their decisions on a food recommendation. Figure 5 shows the histogram analysis of this ranking. Twenty-eight users seem to prefer the recipes they knew already. Ten users have chosen nutritional factors among those that they prefer or consider healthier.

---

[8] We would like to state that the experiment protocol adopted in this study was approved by the Ethics Committee of Özyeğin university, and informed consent was obtained from all participants.

(a) Regular Recommender Session   (b) Interactive Recommender Session

Fig. 4. Regular and interactive recommendation sessions

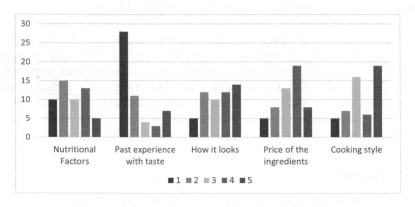

Fig. 5. Pre-survey questionnaire ranking question histogram

4.3 Experimental Results

This section analyzes the findings of the tests and the users' responses to the post-test survey. Since the experiment is composed of two sessions (i.e., Interactive and Regular) and the comparative questions are the same for both, we performed a within-analysis statistical tests. The data is not normally distributed which is one of the main assumptions made by the pairwise T-test. Thus, we apply its corresponding non-parametric test called the Wilcoxon sign rank test [19]. For all tests, the Confidence Interval (CI) is set to 0.95, $\alpha = 1 - CI = 0.05$.

Figure 6 shows the box plot (including the mean) and the p-values of the first set of questions in the experiments between the regular and interactive sessions respectively. The yellow lines represent the median, the triangles in green the means, and the small blue circles the outliers. The results show that for Q1 (p = 0.001) and Q2 (p = 0.011) the interactive session is significantly better than the regular session. Indeed, these two questions aim at the sociability of the system, and the difference may stem from the engagement provided by the interactive session. Q3 (p = 0.002) is about the completeness of the system. The users answered that the interactive session provided a better set of information than the regular session to make an informed decision. Q4 (p = 0.931), Q5 (p − 0.431), and Q6 (p = 0.506) qualify the usability of the system. Assessing them, we can convene that adding an interactive dimension to the system can still be effective and efficient. Nevertheless, only a minor part of the users (12 out of 53 users or 23% of them) still prefer the regular one over the interactive system.

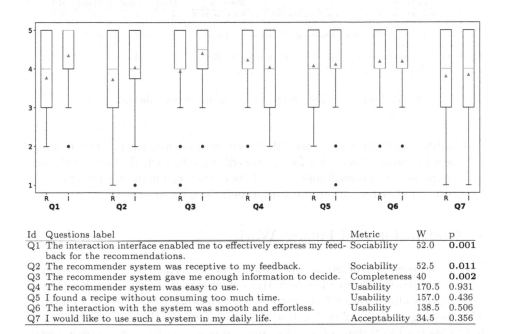

Id	Questions label	Metric	W	p
Q1	The interaction interface enabled me to effectively express my feed-back for the recommendations.	Sociability	52.0	**0.001**
Q2	The recommender system was receptive to my feedback.	Sociability	52.5	**0.011**
Q3	The recommender system gave me enough information to decide.	Completeness	40	**0.002**
Q4	The recommender system was easy to use.	Usability	170.5	0.931
Q5	I found a recipe without consuming too much time.	Usability	157.0	0.436
Q6	The interaction with the system was smooth and effortless.	Usability	138.5	0.506
Q7	I would like to use such a system in my daily life.	Acceptability	34.5	0.356

Fig. 6. Box plot and p-values of the first set of questions

Furthermore, we questioned the users regarding their experiences with the explanations, as illustrated in Fig. 7. Concerning Q8, mean, median, and mode are greater or equal to 4 ("Agree"). Moreover, three quartiles of Q8 are equal or greater than 4 ("Agree") which means most of the users (about 75%) were satisfied with the explanations. Regarding question Q9 related to the usefulness of the explanations, two quartiles are greater or equal to 4 ("Agree") and two quartiles are between 2 ("Disagree") and 3 ("Neutral"). That means at least half of the participants agree with the usefulness of the explanation while others either disagree or are neutral. Finally, concerning Q10, three quartiles are equal or greater than 4 ("Agree"), which means most of the users appreciate receiving explanations in addition to recommendations. Moreover, since the mode is 5, users who strongly agree are greater than those who agree to receive explanations.

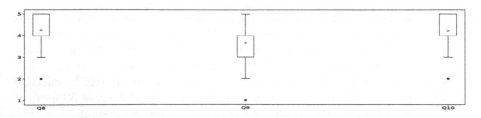

Id	Questions label	Metrics	Mode	Median	Mean	std
Q8	The explanations exchanged during the interaction were satisfactory.	Satisfaction	4	4	4.26	0.79
Q9	The explanations for recommendations have impacted my choice.	Usefulness	4	4	3.67	1.02
Q10	Rate your appreciation of the idea of receiving explanation in addition to recommendations.	Usefulness	5	4	4.23	0.80

Fig. 7. Average ratings of the explanation related questionnaire

Finally, the experiment revealed that while users scored the looks of an image to be less important than other factors contributing to their decision, at the end of the experiment, a considerable 55% of them gave the highest score (Strongly Agree) to whether the images influenced their decision or not.

5 Conclusion and Future Work

This study developed an interaction protocol for the XAI-based NVCs to improve the system's transparency via interactive explanations. To this end, it proposes a specialized alternating offers protocol, an OWL-based ontology for ontological reasoning, and a utility function that considers nutritional information to determine the healthiness of a recipe and the user's preferences. Such a contribution has been tested with 53 individuals who, in the final questionnaire, have remarked the concrete contribution conveyed by the interactive explanation-base interaction w.r.t. conventional recommender systems. In future work, we plan to design a more sophisticated explanation mechanism and recommendation strategy to be framed in a reconciling and scalable agent-based framework.

Acknowledgments. This work has been par ally supported by the CHIST-ERA grant CHIST-ERA-19-XAI-005, and by *(i)* the Swiss National Science Foundation (G.A. 20CH21_195530), *(ii)* the Italian Ministry for Universities and Research, *(iii)* the Luxembourg National Research Fund (G.A. INTER/CHIST/19/14589586), *(iv)* the Scientific and Research Council of Turkey (TÜBİTAK, G.A. 120N680).

References

1. Alexandra, V.A., Badica, C.: Recommender systems: an explainable AI perspective. In: 2021 International Conference on INnovations in Intelligent SysTems and Applications (INISTA), pp. 1–6. IEEE (08 2021)

2. Anjomshoae, S., Najjar, A., Calvaresi, D., Främling, K.: Explainable agents and robots: results from a systematic literature review. In: AAMAS, Montreal, Canada, May 13–17, pp. 1078–1088 (2019)
3. Aydoğan, R., Festen, D., Hindriks, K.V., Jonker, C.M.: Alternating offers protocols for multilateral negotiation. In: Fujita, K., et al. (eds.) Modern Approaches to Agent-based Complex Automated Negotiation. SCI, vol. 674, pp. 153–167. Springer, Cham (2017). https://doi.org/10.1007/978-3-319-51563-2_10
4. Ayub, R., Ghazanfar, M.A., Maqsood, M., Saleem, A.: A jaccard base similarity measure to improve performance of CF based recommender systems, pp. 1–6 (01 2018). https://doi.org/10.1109/ICOIN.2018.8343073
5. Chen, M., Jia, X., Gorbonos, E., Hoang, C.T., Yu, X., Liu, Y.: Eating healthier: exploring nutrition information for healthier recipe recommendation. Inf. Process. Manage. **57**(6), 102051 (2020)
6. Chi, Y.L., Chen, T.Y., Tsai, W.T.: A chronic disease dietary consultation system using owl-based ontologies and semantic rules. J. Biomed. Inform. **53**, 208–219 (2015)
7. Corrado, S., Luzzani, G., Trevisan, M., Lamastra, L.: Contribution of different life cycle stages to the greenhouse gas emissions associated with three balanced dietary patterns. Sci. Tot. Environ. **660**, 622–630 (2019)
8. Elsweiler, D., Trattner, C., Harvey, M.: Exploiting food choice biases for healthier recipe recommendation. In: Proceedings of the 40th International ACM SIGIR Conference, pp. 575–584. Association for Computing Machinery (2017)
9. Fanda, L., Cid, Y.D., Matusz, P.J., Calvaresi, D.: To pay or not to pay attention: classifying and interpreting visual selective attention frequency features. In: Calvaresi, D., Najjar, A., Winikoff, M., Främling, K. (eds.) EXTRAAMAS 2021. LNCS (LNAI), vol. 12688, pp. 3–17. Springer, Cham (2021). https://doi.org/10.1007/978-3-030-82017-6_1
10. Freyne, J., Berkovsky, S.: Recommending food: reasoning on recipes and ingredients. In: De Bra, P., Kobsa, A., Chin, D. (eds.) UMAP 2010. LNCS, vol. 6075, pp. 381–386. Springer, Heidelberg (2010). https://doi.org/10.1007/978-3-642-13470-8_36
11. Ge, M., Ricci, F., Massimo, D.: Health-aware food recommender system. In: Proceedings of the 9th ACM Conference on Recommender Systems, pp. 333–334. RecSys '15, Association for Computing Machinery, New York, NY, USA (2015)
12. Gibney, M.J., Forde, C.G., Mullally, D., Gibney, E.R.: Ultra-processed foods in human health: a critical appraisal. Am. J. Clin. Nutr. **106**(3), 717–724 (2017)
13. Gunning, D., Aha, D.: Darpa's explainable artificial intelligence (xai) program. AI Mag. **40**(2), 44–58 (2019). Jun
14. Hammond, K.J.: Chef: a model of case-based planning. In: AAAI (1986)
15. Harris, J.A., Benedict, F.G.: A biometric study of human basal metabolism. Proc. Natl. Acad. Sci. **4**(12), 370–373 (1918)
16. Igor, T., Jean, E., Ndamlabin, M., Amro, N., Yazan, M., Stéphane, G.: A decentralized multilevel agent based explainable model for fleet management of remote drones. Procedia Comput. Sci. **203**, 181–188 (2022)
17. Ishizaka, A., Siraj, S.: Are multi-criteria decision-making tools useful? an experimental comparative study of three methods. Eur. J. Oper. Res. **264**(2), 462–471 (2018)
18. Lawo, D., Neifer, T., Esau, M., Stevens, G.: Buying the 'right' thing: designing food recommender systems with critical consumers. In: Proceedings of the 2021 CHI Conference on Human Factors in Computing Systems. CHI 2021, Association for Computing Machinery, New York, NY, USA (2021)

19. Lazar, J., Feng, L.H., Hochheiser, H.: Research Methods in Human-Computer Interaction. Willey (2010)
20. Mualla, Y., et al.: The quest of parsimonious XAI: a human-agent architecture for explanation formulation. Artif. Intell. **302**, 103573 (2022)
21. Padhiar, I., Seneviratne, O., Chari, S., Gruen, D., McGuinness, D.L.: Semantic modeling for food recommendation explanations. In: ICDEW, pp. 13–19. IEEE (2021)
22. Popovski, G., Seljak, B., Eftimov, T.: Foodbase corpus: a new resource of annotated food entities. Database J. Biolog. Databases Curation **11**, baz121 (2019)
23. Rubinstein, A.: Perfect equilibrium in a bargaining model. Econometrica: J. Econ. Soc. **50**(1), 97–109 (1982)
24. Samih, A., Adadi, A., Berrada, M.: Towards a knowledge based explainable recommender systems. In: Proceedings of the 4th International Conference on Big Data and Internet of Things. BDIoT2019, Association for Computing Machinery, New York, NY, USA (2019)
25. Soutjis, B.: The new digital face of the consumerist mediator: the case of the 'Yuka' mobile app. J. Cultural Econ. **13**(1), 114–131 (2020)
26. Starke, A., Trattner, C., Bakken, H., Johannessen, M., Solberg, V.: The cholesterol factor: balancing accuracy and health in recipe recommendation through a nutrient-specific metric. In: CEUR Workshop Proceedings, vol. 2959 (2021)
27. Teng, C.Y., Lin, Y.R., Adamic, L.A.: Recipe recommendation using ingredient networks. In: Proceedings of the 4th Annual ACM Web Science Conference, pp. 298–307. WebSci 2012 (2012)
28. Toledo, R.Y., Alzahrani, A.A., Martinez, L.: A food recommender system considering nutritional information and user preferences. IEEE Access **7**, 96695–96711 (2019)
29. Trang Tran, T.N., Atas, M., Felfernig, A., Stettinger, M.: An overview of recommender systems in the healthy food domain. J. Intell. Inf. Syst. **50**(3), 501–526 (2017). https://doi.org/10.1007/s10844-017-0469-0
30. Tran, T.N.T., Felfernig, A., Trattner, C., Holzinger, A.: Recommender systems in the healthcare domain: state-of-the-art and research issues. J. Intell. Inf. Syst. **57**(1), 171–201 (2021)
31. Wang, L., et al.: A dynamic multi-attribute group emergency decision making method considering experts' hesitation. Int. J. Comput. Intell. Syst. **11**(1), 163–182 (2018)

Cooperative Driving at Intersections Through Agent-Based Argumentation

Stefano Mariani$^{(\boxtimes)}$ ⓘ, Dario Ferrari, and Franco Zambonelli ⓘ

Department of Sciences and Methods of Engineering, University of Modena
and Reggio Emilia, Reggio Emilia, Italy
{stefano.mariani,dario.ferrari,franco.zambonelli}@unimore.it

Abstract. In a future of self-driving and connected vehicles, cooperative driving will be the key to guarantee that not only isolated vehicles can hit the road safely on their own, but that the collective of vehicles displays efficient and safe behaviours. Intersection crossing is arguably the most challenging problem for cooperative driving, as vehicles need to coordinate their relative movements while avoiding collisions and optimising intersection throughput. In this paper, we propose a multi-agent based approach exploiting computational argumentation to coordinate vehicles at intersections: vehicles approaching an intersection, represented by agents, argue about their right of way, while an arbitration process resolves conflicting arguments (i.e., leading to vehicle collisions) by applying a configurable conflicts resolution policy and suggesting alternative routes to vehicles. Extensive simulation results show that – in most situations – the argumentation-based approach enables increasing the overall throughput at intersections while decreasing vehicles' delay.

Keywords: Cooperative driving · Intersection crossing · Multi-agent system · Argumentation · Coordination

1 Introduction

Connected self-driving vehicles (aka "autonomous" vehicles) will eventually populate our streets [4,8,18] to relieve us from the duty of driving and possibly paying attention, thus making it possible to exploit travel time in other activities. Also, such vehicles will reduce crashes, now mostly due to bad human behaviors and errors [1], reduce traffic (hence pollution) thanks to route optimization [23], and pave the way for a number of innovative mobility services [31].

Most of the current applied research in the area concerns the methods and tools to enable *individual* vehicles to hit the road safely. However, it is getting increasingly recognized that, to take full advantage of autonomous vehicles, *coordinating* the relative activities and movements of vehicles [21] is required by

This work has been partially supported by the MIUR PRIN 2017 Project N. 2017KRC7KT "Fluidware".

many urban situations. This trend is witnessed by initiatives such as the Grand Cooperative Driving Challenge, focussing on *cooperative automated driving* [7]. One notable case of such situations requiring proper coordination is crossing intersections: there, vehicles need to either cooperatively agree on a crossing order to avoid collisions, or a third party has to be delegated the duty to regulate the competitive access to the intersection—while still guaranteeing absence of collisions. The literature about intersection crossing for autonomous vehicles has plenty of approaches to deal with such problem [21], many of which model vehicles as autonomous agents, and borrow coordination techniques from the multi-agent systems literature [5].

In this paper, we propose a yet unexplored approach to coordinate vehicles at intersections, based on *computational argumentation* [33]. The key idea of the approach is to modell vehicles as autonomous agents engaging in argumentative dialogues: when vehicles approach an intersection they start interacting with each other by exchanging arguments about, e.g., final destination, own traveling parameters, their partial knowledge about the traffic situation, with the goal to solve conflicts and find an agreement on the crossing order—thanks to a distributed arbitration process. Accordingly, in this paper, we:

- detail the argumentation-based approach proposed for conflicts resolution in intersection crossing problems;
- evaluate its performances by comparing different conflict resolution policies, and show that – in most situations – such an approach enables increasing the overall throughput at intersections while decreasing vehicles' delay.

The remainder of this paper is structured as follows: Sect. 2 provides an overview of the problem domain and of existing solutions; Sect. 3 describes the argumentation-based coordination framework we propose for realising cooperative driving at intersections; Sect. 4 reports the experimental results assessing the positive impact of our approach. Finally, Sect. 5 concludes the paper with closing remarks and an outlook to future works.

2   Problem Formulation and Related Works

Intersection crossing is the problem of *coordinating* vehicles while concurrently crossing intersections [30]. As such, it is a *competitive* and *resource-oriented* problem [21], since vehicles are self-interested agents only caring about getting their right-of-way across the intersection as soon as possible.

Today, intersection management is realized either by a central controller, usually the traffic light, or by imposing to vehicles pre-defined coordination rules, as in the presence of stop signs and precedence rules. This puts the responsibility for safety fully in charge of humans, and does not promote efficiency. For instance, the traffic lights impose unnecessary stops whenever the intersection is under-exploited. Future autonomous vehicles scenarios will make it possible to conceive safer and more efficient solutions, eventually making traffic lights and stop signs obsolete. In particular, three main classes of coordination approaches have been explored so far in the related literature [21]. Here we briefly recall them.

Centralised Approaches. They somewhat represent the natural evolution of traffic lights for autonomous vehicles. One coordinator (also called *intersection manager*), is associated with each intersection with the goal to: *(1)* receive information from approaching vehicles such as origin, destination, distance, speed; *(2)* elaborate a set of collision free trajectories enabling vehicles to safely cross the intersection, which may require some vehicles to slow down or change lane; and *(3)* instruct the vehicles about what to do (e.g. slow down or speed up), or informing them about what constraints they must abide to while crossing (e.g. start crossing in T seconds at speed S). The most representative centralized approach is the so called *reservation-based* one [5], where vehicles incoming to the intersection contact the intersection manager to communicate their expected trajectory, and the intersection manager "reserves" the required segments of the intersection to vehicles, if not reserved by others, or post-pones requests otherwise. However, many different alternative schemes have been proposed [11,13–15,35,36].

Centralized approaches are easy to design because they assume full knowledge of the situation. Most importantly, simulations show that such approaches reduce the waiting time of vehicles with respect to traditional approaches based on stop signs or traffic lights [5]. However, a problem of centralized approaches is that they require an infrastructural element, the intersection manager, that represents a single point of failure and a potential bottleneck for system performance.

Negotiation-Based Approaches. Here, vehicles are required to actively participate in a multi-agent protocol aimed at establishing in which order they will gain access to the intersection. Such protocol, given the competitive nature of the problem, can take the form of an *auction* [2,3,29,32]. The intersection manager, now acting only as broker and not as a central authority, collects "bids" placed by vehicles approaching the interaction, each representing an offer to "buy" the portion of the intersection required for crossing. The value of the bid may express the urgency of the vehicle in crossing, it is autonomously set by each individual vehicle according to its own strategy, and can correspond to some real-world currency or some sort of "road credits" assigned to vehicles. The intersection manager collects the bids, gives the right-of-way to the set of vehicles that are in a collision free trajectory and, among those that are in collision, to the ones having placed the highest bid(s)—depending on the winner selection mechanism.

Negotiation-based strategies can exhibit performances comparable to centralised approaches, but highly depend on the specific assumptions (e.g. the type of "money" involved) and mechanisms (e.g. the type of auction adopted) underpinning the approach. A problem intrinsic of any auction mechanism concerns liveness, i.e., starvation of vehicles, in that the strategy of vehicles in bidding can sometimes prevent others to win auctions, with the risk for them to experience indefinitely long waiting times.

Self-organizing Approaches. The way human-driven vehicles cross unsignalled intersections in many over-congested African and Asian cities is based on drivers trying to guess each other's actions while making subtle movements strategically aimed at affecting others', and leading to an overall spontaneous collective self-organization of behaviours [10].

There have been proposals to apply similar emergent, self-organizing approaches to autonomous vehicles. In [20], for instance, the authors interpret the intersection crossing problem using *game theory*, that is, modeling each car as the player of a game involving other approaching cars, each playing its own game, thus each having different payoffs and utility models. Another family of emergent self-organizing approaches adopt some nature-inspired metaphor to harness natural ecosystems self-organisation capabilities, such as in the case of *pheromone-based coordination* [25,34]. There, each vehicle is modelled as an agent-ant that deposits virtual pheromones along its way, to signal its presence and other traffic-related information. Such pheromones are aggregated by an intelligent road infrastructure, making it available to other vehicles to ease routing and enable intersection crossing.

Self-organizing approaches are potentially very effective. However, they may be difficult to deploy in the real-world, as delivering guarantees about safety and liveness may be prohibitively difficult or impractical, given that this kind of approaches often exploit stochastic decision making, partial, local information only, and no explicit communication.

3   Argumentation for Intersection Crossing

In the attempt to pick the best of two worlds, argumentation-based coordination lies halfway between negotiation and emergent self-organizing approaches: on the one hand, it can be implemented in a decentralised way, by assuming that vehicles agree on the argumentation framework but carry out the reasoning independently; on the other hand, without imposing a predefined coordination protocol vehicles are free to change their strategy depending on the dynamic situation of each intersection and their inner goals.

The investigation of argumentation, as the discipline of studying how humans debate and reason [33], in computer science led to the development of the field of *computational argumentation* and, in the field of multi-agent systems, to argumentation-based coordination protocols [22]. Argumentation-based approaches have been already exploited successfully for solving several coordination problems in multi-agent systems, such as for cooperative planning [26], and as a general purpose underpinning of negotiation protocols [28]. As far as cooperative driving is concerned, argumentation-based approaches are advocated by other conceptual proposals as a way to solve conflicts and increase trustworthiness and safety of decisions [9], but limited to an individual vehicle, or never fully developed [16,17].

We envision that agents representing vehicles engage in open dialogues while approaching the intersection, discussing their beliefs about the best way to cross

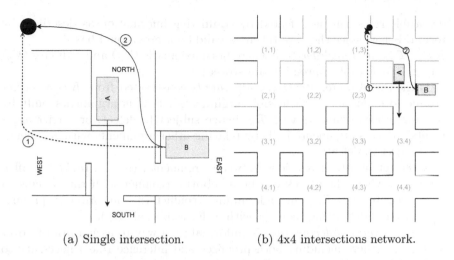

(a) Single intersection.   (b) 4x4 intersections network.

Fig. 1. Example of argumentation-based coordination. Vehicles A and B would be in conflict if B followed path (1). A argues that B should turn right, following path (2), to avoid conflict while reaching destination anyways.

it, and in case of conflicting needs, arguing with each other about possible ways to resolve that conflict. For instance, as depicted in Fig. 1a, a vehicle A approaching the intersection in the north-to-south direction can express arguments about its urgency to cross, and argue that vehicle B in the east-to-west direction – thus conflicting with A – could/should decide to cross right, as B would reach in any case destination, while avoiding conflict with A. Persuaded by A's argument, B could eventually decide to turn right.

In this paper, we develop this conceptual proposal and implement it in a concrete algorithm evaluated via simulation.

3.1 Computational Argumentation Framework

We chose to adopt the *ASPIC+* (Argumentation Service Platform with Integrated Components) structured argumentation framework [24], where arguments are based on strict and defeasible rules (explained below), and a notion of defeat is defined based on the notion of *preference ordering*. Intuitively, an argument is any claim accepted to be true on a provisional basis, that is, until it becomes disproven by a counter-argument. Such a disproof is expressed by the defeat relation. In *ASPIC+*, a *structured argumentation framework* (SAF) is formally defined as $SAF = \langle \mathcal{A}, \mathcal{C}, \preceq \rangle$ by an *argumentation theory* $AT = \langle AS, KB \rangle$, where

- $AS = \langle \mathcal{L}, \mathcal{R}, n \rangle$ is the *argumentation system* expressing formulas in logic language $\mathcal{L}$ (e.g. first-order logic), having strict ($\mathcal{R}_s$) and defeasible ($\mathcal{R}_d$) inference rules, and a (partial) naming function for such rules $n : \mathcal{R}_d \to \mathcal{L}$— to conveniently refer to rules. Strict inference rules, by definition, cannot be defeated, as the convey reasoning grounded in classical logic, whereas

defeasible rules can be defeated by conflicting information as described by
term $\mathcal{C}$ below, since they are taken as valid on a provisional basis;
- $KB \subseteq \mathcal{L}$ is the *knowledge base* where both axiomatic ($\mathcal{K}_n$) and ordinary ($\mathcal{K}_p$)
  – that is, defeasible – premises are stored;
- $\mathcal{A}$ is the set of finite, *structured arguments* constructed from KB as either
  atomic formulas in $\mathcal{L}$, "defeasible arguments", that is arguments built by
  relating other arguments with $\mathcal{R}_d$, hence subject to defeat, or "strict arguments", that is arguments built by relating other arguments with $\mathcal{R}_s$, hence
  not subject to defeat;
- $\mathcal{C}$ is the set of attack relations between arguments, that is, $(a, b) \in \mathcal{C}$ iff a
  attacks b, where the attack can be a rebuttal (conflict with the conclusion
  of a defeasible rule $\mathcal{R}_d$), an undermining (conflict with an ordinary premise
  $\mathcal{K}_p$), or an undercutting (conflict with a defeasible rule $\mathcal{R}_d$).
- $\preceq$ is a *preference ordering*, that is (informally), a way to assign priority over
  arguments (there including both premises and inference rules) necessary to
  define defeats—that is, successful attacks.

We refer the interested reader to [24] for a complete description of *ASPIC+*.

Exemplification. Consider the situation depicted in Fig. 1a. We can represent
conflicting arguments as per Fig. 2. There, the defeasible argument D_1 rebuts
the defeasible argument D_2, and vice versa, and the strict argument S_1 rebuts
D_2, too. In this case, the argumentation semantics establishes that argument
D_1 "wins" the dispute, as its validity, although compromised by D_2 itself, is
"restored" by S_1. This means that vehicle v_A gets the right of way while v_B
doesn't. Such a semantics is usually defined in terms of *acceptability* of arguments [6], that by contrasting an argument in a set with the others establishes
whether the argument is either undefeated, or defeated by arguments that are
themselves defeated (thus *restoring*, or defending, the original argument).

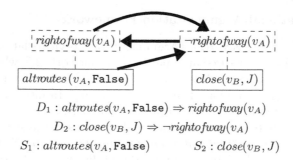

$$D_1 : altroutes(v_A, \texttt{False}) \Rightarrow rightofway(v_A)$$
$$D_2 : close(v_B, J) \Rightarrow \neg rightofway(v_A)$$
$$S_1 : altroutes(v_A, \texttt{False}) \qquad S_2 : close(v_B, J)$$

Fig. 2. Example of rebutting attacks between 2 defeasible arguments (D_1, D_2) and 1
strict argument (S_1).

3.2   Dynamic Preference Ordering for Conflicts Resolution

However, it may be the case that no argument in a set satisfies such accept-ability notion, hence *ASPIC+* introduces the notion of *preference ordering* to further resolve conflicting arguments when no undisputed restoring is available. Figure 3 shows what happens if we add another rebuttal from S_2 to D_1 to Fig. 2. Now, only through definition of a preference ordering over arguments the argu-mentation framework can allow for detection of a winning one (e.g., D_2 in this case). Nonetheless, this is one feature of *ASPIC+* we chose to by-pass with a custom solution. The reason being that such ordering is *statically* defined in *ASPIC+*, without the possibility to account for *contextual* information drawn from the argumentation graph itself during reasoning. As we want to *(a)* have a more flexible argumentation process, capable of defining a sort of *dynamic pref-erence ordering* where contextual information available in the argumentation graph itself determines such ordering, and *(b)* give to users of our framework the freedom to define their own preference orderings in a more familiar way than through *ASPIC+* theories – that is, through Java programming – we intro-duce the notion of a *custom conflict resolution policy*. Such a policy is seen as a "black-box" by the *ASPIC+* argumentation theory, called by the argumenta-tion process itself when no argument defeats all others without being defeated itself in turn. This way, we don't rely on *ASPIC+* built-in preference ordering implementation, but exploit our own more flexible one.

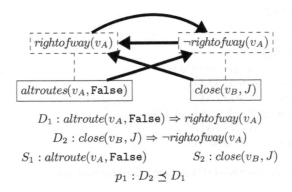

$$D_1 : altroute(v_A, \textbf{False}) \Rightarrow rightofway(v_A)$$
$$D_2 : close(v_B, J) \Rightarrow \neg rightofway(v_A)$$
$$S_1 : altroute(v_A, \textbf{False}) \qquad S_2 : close(v_B, J)$$
$$p_1 : D_2 \preceq D_1$$

Fig. 3. Example of preference ordering: only thanks to preference p_1 argument D_2 wins the debate, as its defeasible rule is preferred over D_1.

Algorithm 1 describes the argumentation process in pseudocode while abstracting away technical details due to the specific software library used, that is, the *ASPIC+* implementation provided by the TweetyProject[1]. Whenever due, e.g. at each simulation step, a car needs to be checked for its right to cross the intersection (function ASSIGNRIGHTOFWAY). It is thus checked for conflicts

---

[1] https://tweetyproject.org.

against every other car (pairwise, without loss of generality), and: if conflict is not detected, gets its right of way, otherwise argues against the conflicting car (function ARGUE). Arguing amounts to checking attacks in the argumentation graph dynamically created (and similar to the one exemplified in Figs. 2, 3): if any argument is successfully restored, the corresponding car gets its right of way (whereas the other one is bound to wait for the next argumentation round), if all arguments are defeated successfully (i.e. conflicts cannot be resolved under the exploited grounded semantics), the pluggable black-box conflicts resolution policy is delegated to find the winner argument.

Algorithm 1. Argumentation process organised in modular functions, called by the simulation routine. Dot notation denotes access to data fields or method invocations (aka function calls) as borrowed from object-oriented languages.

Require: $junction, junctionArbiter, car$

> **function** ASSIGNRIGHTOFWAY(car)   ▷ argumentation process
>   **for all** $c \in cars \setminus \{car\}$ **do**
>   **if** $\neg junctionArbiter.conflict(c, car)$ **then**
> $car.state \leftarrow CROSSING$
>   **else**
>   ARGUE($junctionArbiter.graph$)   ▷ conflict to resolve
>   **end if**
>   **end for**
>   **return** $leaving$
> **end function**
>
> **function** ARGUE($graph$)
>   **if** $graph.car1 \Rightarrow graph.car2$ **then**   ▷ attacking arguments
> $car1.state \leftarrow CROSSING$
> $car2.state \leftarrow WAITING$
>   **else if** $graph.car2 \Rightarrow graph.car1$ **then**
> $car1.state \leftarrow WAITING$
> $car2.state \leftarrow CROSSING$
>   **else**   ▷ neither car defeats the other
> $junction.policy.rightOfWay(graph.car1, graph.car2)$
>   **end if**
> **end function**

---

4 Experimental Results

To measure the impact of argumentation-based coordination on intersection crossing, we performed simulations and tracked 3 fundamental metrics:

– the number of times vehicles *change route* by selecting an alternative one from their pool (aka "# alternative routes used"). This is useful to assess to what extent argumentation is effective in solving conflicts.

- the throughput across the whole network of intersections, measured as the number of vehicles managing to cross an intersection (aka "# crossings").
- the delay (aka "# waitings") introduced by the conflict resolution policy, as the number of slowdowns (or complete stops) vehicles need to do to avoid collisions while respecting the right of way.

Both "# crossings" and "# waitings" are useful to assess the extent to which the argumentation-based approach can improve the traffic situation. The resolution policy we want to evaluate in our simulations, called `AltRoutesPolicy`, scans the alternative routes of the conflicting vehicles looking for a *conflict-free combination*: if it finds one, the conflict is resolved and vehicles can cross the intersection simultaneously; otherwise the conflict is not solved and either vehicle has to give way (according to some application-specific symmetry-breaking strategy, such as "give way to the vehicle closer to the intersection").

4.1   Simulation Setup

There exist many simulation softwares dedicated to micro-simulation (i.e. simulating individual vehicles behaviour) of traffic flow, such as SUMO [19] and MATsim [12], However, they do not explicitly support engineering of complex coordination protocols amongst vehicles, and do not offer an adequate level of abstraction to multi-agent systems researchers, as they force developers to deal with low-level aspects such as micro-management of vehicles' lateral and longitudinal control. For this, and because our proposed argumentation-based approach abstracts away many technical details of vehicles behaviour, which are instead the focus of such simulators, we developed our own software for the validation. The software developed is available on Github, together with the Python scripts used for results analysis and plotting: https://github.com/DarioFerrari-git/AutoA.

Each simulation automatically spawns new vehicles in the junctions network according to a vehicles generation strategy implemented by users. A few builtin strategies are already provided; in particular, `Random` creates vehicles with fully random properties (e.g. speed, urgency, routes, etc.), whereas `ControlledAlt` creates vehicles with a desired number of alternative routes available to reach a random destination requiring to cross a desired number of junctions. These parameters are described in Table 1. To ensure reproducibility of simulations, every random number generator exploited can be configured with a seed. Besides spawning vehicles, each simulation step *(i)* removes already served vehicles from the simulation, *(ii)* populates the argumentation graph by translating the current junction and (remaining) vehicles situation into arguments, *(iii)* triggers the argumentation process to assign the right of way to remaining vehicles, and *(iv)* relocates vehicles in the next junction of the network (if existing, depending on the car position and route in the network) and updates it travelling parameters (e.g. state, position, route).

We simulated 3 different grid-like intersections networks, having the topology exemplified in Fig. 1b, with an increasing number of junctions: from 16 to 256,

Table 1. Some of the parameters available for configuring simulations, and the values used to perform the experiments of Sect. 4.

Param name	Param value per grid size		
	4×4	8×8	16×16
Routes length (L)	2, 4	8	16
# of available routes (A)	2, 3, 4	4, 6, 8	8, 12, 16
Policy	AltRoutes / Urgency / Precedence		
Gen. strategy	ControlledAlt		

that is, from a 4×4 grid, to a 16×16 one. Several simulations have been run with different *route lenghts* (the number of intersections a vehicle has to cross to reach destination) and different number of *available routes* vehicles have to reach their destination, as better explained for each plot we show in the following.

4.2   Effectiveness in Solving Conflicts

Figure 4 plots the number of alternative routes adopted (y axis) against the simulations steps (x axis), in the case of the 3 different intersections networks and the alternative routes parameter ("A") denoted in the legend. The conflict resolution policy is kept fixed as AltRoutesPolicy, and routes length ("L") is fixed, too, as equal to the junctions network diameter (i.e. 4, 8, and 16 according

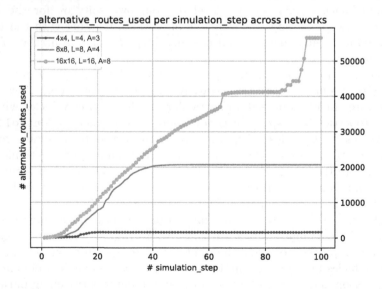

Fig. 4. Number of alternative routes used (y axis) against the simulations steps (x axis) for different intersections networks and alternative routes available (parameter "A" in legend). Routes length ("L") equals the junctions network diameter.

to network size). As intuitively expected, the larger the network, hence the more vehicles are in the simulation, *(i)* the more conflicts are likely to happen during the coordination process, *(ii)* hence the more the opportunity to take alternative routes becomes appealing to resolve such conflicts (provided that vehicles' routes are reasonably long and enough alternatives are available).

4.3   Impact on Traffic Situation

Figure 5 plots the throughput (in terms of the number of intersections crossed, on the y axis) of the intersections network against the simulation steps (x axis) in the case of the 8×8 and 16×16 networks, but with an increasing number of alternative routes available—the 4×4 network is too small to show meaningful results. The "precedence" baseline is also added for comparison with traditional approaches, where vehicles get their right of way based on usual precedence rules. The main takeaways of this graph are two: *(i)* the argumentation-based approach is always better than the precedence baseline, and *(ii)* the more the alternative routes available to vehicles during argumentation (the "A" parameter as per legend), the better the throughput of the network. It is worth noting that, in the 16×16 network, increasing the number of alternative routes available to

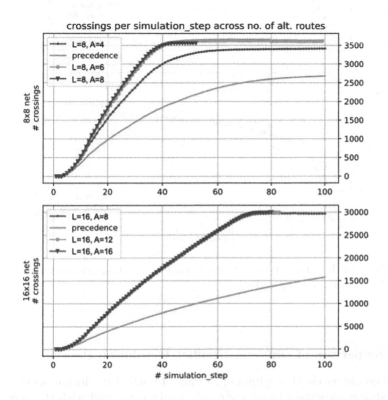

Fig. 5. Throughput of the network in terms of intersections crossed.

vehicles beyond a certain number (half the network diameter in this case) does not further improve performance.

Figure 6 is complementary to Fig. 5, and shows the delay introduced by the approach (in terms of the number of times vehicles are forced to wait, hence slowdown or stop, to give way to others) in the same network and routes conditions of Fig. 5. Considering that the y axis is on a `log` scale, here *(i)* the increase of performance with respect to the precedence baseline, and *(ii)* the performance difference across the number of alternative routes, within the same network size, are both much more evident. However, here increasing the number of alternative routes seems to continue improving performance even for larger networks, differently from the case of throughput commented in Fig. 5.

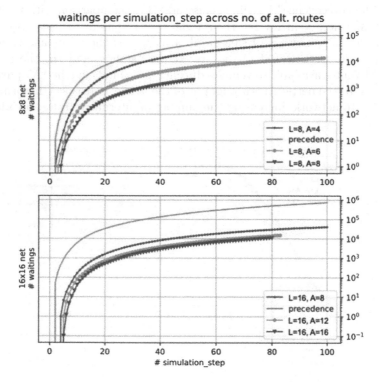

Fig. 6. Delay of the intersections network in terms of waitings/slowdowns experienced by vehicles. y axis is on `log` scale.

4.4   Comparison of Different Conflict Resolution Policies

Figure 7 compares the throughput of 2 different conflict resolution policies for our proposed argumentation-based approach, again compared with the precedence baseline and for different network sizes. In particular, we compare the already

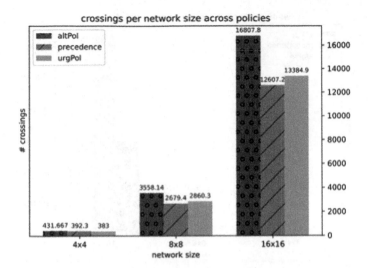

Fig. 7. Comparison of throughput for different conflict resolution policies, across network sizes. `AltRoutesPolicy` gives the best performance.

described `AltRoutesPolicy` with the so called `UrgencyPolicy`, that gives the right of way to the vehicle with the highest urgency value (generated randomly from 0 to 1). The `AltRoutesPolicy` is the best one across network sizes, with a stronger difference from the 2nd best when the intersections network is larger. This demonstrates that looking for conflict-free alternative routes can improve the overall network throughput. Figure 8 does the same but comparing the delay introduced by the policies. The difference between the `AltRoutesPolicy` and the others is much greater than for throughput, confirming the positive impact of alternative routes adoption on overall network performance.

4.5   Discussion

In this subsection we take the chance to discuss assumptions, limitations, and threats to validity of our proposed approach and simulation experiments.

First of all our approach assumes presence of a "smart" transportation infrastructure: sensors and actuators must be available on the road infrastructure (as well as on vehicles, such as to ensure collision avoidance) and connected in a network, to guarantee that the necessary data is available and can be communicated to entities participating in the argumentation-based coordination process. Such an infrastructure is not currently widespread to most cities, but recent initiatives such as the Grand Cooperative Driving Challenges of 2011 and 2016 [7, 27] demonstrate that it may become reality soon.

One notable assumption we made in our simulations is that there is no cost for vehicles associated to changing route. This is simplistic as one should consider factors such as the slowing down due to turning, and the speed of other vehicles. In this paper we abstracted away from these issues as we wanted to emphasise

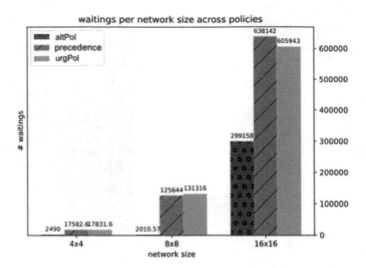

Fig. 8. Comparison of delay introduced by different conflict resolution policies, across networks. `AltRoutesPolicy` gives the best performance.

the overall feasibility, fairness, and benefits to global traffic congestion of the approach. Future works will be devoted to improving this aspect.

One threat to validity of our approach is that we only consider a road network where every road has two directions with one lane each, although most of the related literature considers two directions with three lanes each (turn right, go straight, turn left). However, expanding to such a setting would only impact the self-driving controller for changing lane before the junction, which is something we abstract away in our formulation.

Finally, one threat to validity of our evaluations is that we do not compare to existing approaches to intersection management. We emphasise that our approach is mostly complementary to those, not a competitor, as provides a way to either inject any conflict resolution policy in any coordination approaches, provided that it is expressed within an argumentation framework, or to work side by side with those approaches providing for alternative paths.

5   Conclusion and Outlook

Besides the improvement to raw performance just discussed, argumentation-based cooperative driving paves the way to a number of improvements in traffic flow management, especially regarding intersections crossing:

– it can seamlessly complement existing strategies, such as reservation-based ones [5], by intervening on the coordination process only when conflicts cannot be resolved by the specific approach (for instance, by arguing in favour of an alternative route instead of making vehicles stop)

- the argumentation process is orthogonal to the policy for resolving conflicts; this means, such a policy can be changed at will, depending on any criteria, and possibly during operation
- argumentation is naturally suitable for any scenario mixing humans and machines, as it is one of the most natural way of thinking for humans, and lends itself to providing human-comprehensible explanations.

In the future, we will explore such aspects in due detail, for instance translating reservation-based strategies into our framework and then adding the alternative routes policy to investigate whether improvements can be measured. We plan to integrate our framework into a state-of-the-art micro-scale traffic simulator, such as MATsim [12], to further confirm our analysis on more realistic road networks and with fully realistic vehicles dynamics.

References

1. Bimbraw, K.: Autonomous cars: past, present and future a review of the developments in the last century, the present scenario and the expected future of autonomous vehicle technology. In: Informatics in Control. Automation and Robotics (ICINCO), 2015 12th International Conference on, vol. 1, pp. 191–198. IEEE, IEEE (2015)
2. Cabri, G., Gherardini, L., Montangero, M.: Auction-based crossings management. In: Proceedings of the 5th EAI International Conference on Smart Objects and Technologies for Social Good, pp. 183–188. GoodTechs 2019, ACM, New York, NY, USA (2019). https://doi.org/10.1145/3342428.3342689
3. Carlino, D., Boyles, S.D., Stone, P.: Auction-based autonomous intersection management. In: 16th International IEEE Conference on Intelligent Transportation Systems (ITSC 2013), pp. 529–534. IEEE (2013)
4. Coppola, R., Morisio, M.: Connected car: technologies, issues, future trends. ACM Comput. Surv. (CSUR) **49**(3), 46 (2016)
5. Dresner, K., Stone, P.: A multiagent approach to autonomous intersection management. J. Artif. Intell. Res. **31**, 591–656 (2008)
6. Dung, P.M.: On the acceptability of arguments and its fundamental role in non-monotonic reasoning, logic programming and n-person games. Artif. Intell. **77**(2), 321–357 (1995). https://doi.org/10.1016/0004-3702(94)00041-X
7. Englund, C., et al.: The grand cooperative driving challenge 2016: boosting the introduction of cooperative automated vehicles. IEEE Wirel. Commun. **23**(4), 146–152 (2016). https://doi.org/10.1109/MWC.2016.7553038
8. Fagnant, D.J., Kockelman, K.: Preparing a nation for autonomous vehicles: opportunities, barriers and policy recommendations. Trans. Res. Part A: Policy Pract. **77**, 167–181 (2015)
9. Fridman, L., Ding, L., Jenik, B., Reimer, B.: Arguing machines: human supervision of black box AI systems that make life-critical decisions (2017)
10. Gonzalez, C.L., Zapotecatl, J.L., Alberola, J.M., Julian, V., Gershenson, C.: Distributed management of traffic intersections. In: Novais, P., et al. (eds.) ISAmI2018 2018. AISC, vol. 806, pp. 56–64. Springer, Cham (2019). https://doi.org/10.1007/978-3-030-01746-0_7

11. Hamouda, A.H., Mahfouz, D.M., Elias, C.M., Shehata, O.M.: Multi-layer control architecture for unsignalized intersection management via nonlinear MPC and deep reinforcement learning. In: 24th IEEE International Intelligent Transportation Systems Conference, ITSC 2021, Indianapolis, IN, USA, 19–22 September 2021, pp. 1990–1996. IEEE (2021). https://doi.org/10.1109/ITSC48978.2021.9565126

12. Horni, A., Nagel, K., Axhausen, K. (eds.): Multi-Agent Transport Simulation MATSim. Ubiquity Press, London (2016). https://doi.org/10.5334/baw

13. Kowshik, H., Caveney, D., Kumar, P.: Provable systemwide safety in intelligent intersections. IEEE Trans. Veh. Technol. **60**(3), 804–818 (2011). https://doi.org/10.1109/TVT.2011.2107584

14. Lee, J., Park, B.: Development and evaluation of a cooperative vehicle intersection control algorithm under the connected vehicles environment. IEEE Trans. Intell. Transp. Syst. **13**(1), 81–90 (2012). https://doi.org/10.1109/TITS.2011.2178836

15. Li, B., Zhang, Y., Jia, N., Peng, X.: Autonomous intersection management over continuous space: A microscopic and precise solution via computational optimal control. **53**, 17071–17076 (2020). https://doi.org/10.1016/j.ifacol.2020.12.1611

16. Lippi, M., Mamei, M., Mariani, S., Zambonelli, F.: An argumentation-based perspective over the social iot. IEEE Internet Things J. **5**(4), 2537–2547 (2018). https://doi.org/10.1109/JIOT.2017.2775047

17. Lippi, M., Mamei, M., Mariani, S., Zambonelli, F.: Coordinating distributed speaking objects. In: Lee, K., Liu, L. (eds.) 37th IEEE International Conference on Distributed Computing Systems, ICDCS 2017, Atlanta, GA, USA, 5–8 June 2017, pp. 1949–1960. IEEE Computer Society (2017). https://doi.org/10.1109/ICDCS.2017.282

18. Litman, T.: Autonomous vehicle implementation predictions. Victoria Transport Policy Institute Victoria, Canada (2017)

19. Lopez, P.A., et al.: Microscopic traffic simulation using sumo. In: The 21st IEEE International Conference on Intelligent Transportation Systems. IEEE (2018). https://elib.dlr.de/124092/

20. Mandiau, R., Champion, A., Auberlet, J.M., Espié, S., Kolski, C.: Behaviour based on decision matrices for a coordination between agents in a urban traffic simulation. Appl. Intell. **28**(2), 121–138 (2008). https://doi.org/10.1007/s10489-007-0045-3

21. Mariani, S., Cabri, G., Zambonelli, F.: Coordination of autonomous vehicles: Taxonomy and survey. ACM Comput. Surv. **54**(1), 1–33 (2021). https://doi.org/10.1145/3431231

22. Maudet, N., Parsons, S., Rahwan, I.: Argumentation in multi-agent systems: context and recent developments. In: Maudet, N., Parsons, S., Rahwan, I. (eds.) ArgMAS 2006. LNCS (LNAI), vol. 4766, pp. 1–16. Springer, Heidelberg (2007). https://doi.org/10.1007/978-3-540-75526-5_1

23. Menon, N., Barbour, N., Zhang, Y., Pinjari, A.R., Mannering, F.: Shared autonomous vehicles and their potential impacts on household vehicle ownership: An exploratory empirical assessment. Int. J. Sustain. Transp. **13**(2), 111–122 (2018)

24. Modgil, S., Prakken, H.: The ASPIC$^+$ framework for structured argumentation: a tutorial. Argument Comput. **5**(1), 31–62 (2014). https://doi.org/10.1080/19462166.2013.869766

25. Nguyen, T., Jung, J.J.: Ant colony optimization-based traffic routing with intersection negotiation for connected vehicles. Appl. Soft Comput. **112**, 107828 (2021). https://doi.org/10.1016/j.asoc.2021.107828

26. Pardo, P., Pajares, S., Onaindia, E., Godo, L., Dellunde, P.: Multiagent argumentation for cooperative planning in DeLP-POP, vol. 2, pp. 913–920. International Foundation for Autonomous Agents and Multiagent Systems (IFAAMAS) (2011)

27. Ploeg, J., Shladover, S., Nijmeijer, H., van de Wouw, N.: Introduction to the special issue on the 2011 grand cooperative driving challenge. IEEE Trans. Intell. Transp. Syst. **13**(3), 989–993 (2012). https://doi.org/10.1109/TITS.2012.2210636
28. Rahwan, I., Ramchurn, S.D., Jennings, N.R., Mcburney, P., Parsons, S., Sonenberg, L.: Argumentation-based negotiation. Knowl. Eng. Rev. **18**(4), 343–375 (2003)
29. Rey, D., Levin, M.W., Dixit, V.V.: Online incentive-compatible mechanisms for traffic intersection auctions. Eur. J. Oper. Res. **293**(1), 229–247 (2021). https://doi.org/10.1016/j.ejor.2020.12.030
30. Rios-Torres, J., Malikopoulos, A.: A survey on the coordination of connected and automated vehicles at intersections and merging at highway on-ramps. IEEE Trans. Intell. Transp. Syst. **18**(5), 1066–1077 (2017). https://doi.org/10.1109/TITS.2016.2600504
31. Röth, T., Pielen, M., Wolff, K., Lüdiger, T.: Urban vehicle concepts for the shared mobility. ATZ worldwide **120**(1), 18–23 (2018). https://doi.org/10.1007/s38311-017-0163-4
32. Vasirani, M., Ossowski, S.: A market-inspired approach for intersection management in urban road traffic networks. J. Artif. Int. Res. **43**(1), 621–659 (2012)
33. Walton, D.: Argumentation theory: a very short introduction. In: Simari, G., Rahwan, I. (eds.) Argumentation in Artificial Intelligence. Springer (2009). https://doi.org/10.1007/978-0-387-98197-0_1
34. Wu, J., Abbas-Turki, A., Moudni, A.E.: Cooperative driving: an ant colony system for autonomous intersection management. Appl. Intell. **37**(2), 207–222 (2012). https://doi.org/10.1007/s10489-011-0322-z
35. Wu, W., Zhang, J., Luo, A., Cao, J.: Distributed mutual exclusion algorithms for intersection traffic control. IEEE Trans. Parallel Distrib. Syst. **26**(1), 65–74 (2015). https://doi.org/10.1109/TPDS.2013.2297097
36. Zohdy, I.H., Kamalanathsharma, R.K., Rakha, H.: Intersection management for autonomous vehicles using iCACC. In: 2012 15th International IEEE Conference on Intelligent Transportation Systems, pp. 1109–1114. IEEE (2012). https://doi.org/10.1109/ITSC.2012.6338827

Dyadic Obligations: Proofs
and Countermodels via Hypersequents

Agata Ciabattoni[1]([✉]) [iD], Nicola Olivetti[2]([✉]) [iD], and Xavier Parent[1]([✉]) [iD]

[1] TU Wien, Vienna, Austria
{agata,xavier}@logic.at
[2] Aix-Marseille Univ, Université de Toulon, CNRS, LIS, Marseille, France
nicola.olivetti@univ-amu.fr

Abstract. The basic system **E** of dyadic deontic logic proposed by
Åqvist offers a simple solution to contrary-to-duty paradoxes and allows
to represent norms with exceptions. We investigate **E** from a proof-
theoretical viewpoint. We propose a hypersequent calculus with good
properties, the most important of which is cut-elimination, and the consequent subformula property. The calculus is refined to obtain a decision
procedure for **E** and an effective countermodel computation in case of
failure of proof search. By means of the refined calculus, we prove that
validity in **E** is Co-NP and countermodels have polynomial size.

1 Introduction

Deontic logic deals with obligation and other normative concepts, which are
important in a variety of fields—from law and ethics to artificial intelligence.

Obligations are contextual in nature, and take the form of conditional statements ("if-then"). Their formal analysis rely on dyadic deontic systems. The
family of those systems that come with a "preference-based" semantics is the
best known one. It was originally developed by [6,11], and adapted to a modal
logic setting by Åqvist [2] and Lewis [16]. The framework has roots in the so-
called classical theory of rational choice, sharing the assumption that a normative
judgment is based on a maximization process of normative preferences. In that
framework, $\bigcirc(B/A)$ (reading: "B is obligatory, given A") is true when the best
A-worlds are all B-worlds. The framework was early recognized as a landmark,
due to its ability to handle at once two different kinds of deontic conditionals, whose treatment within a usual Kripke semantics had proved elusive: (a)
Contrary-to-duty (CTD) conditionals, and (b) Defeasible deontic conditionals.
The former are obligations that come into force when some other obligation is
violated. As is well-known (e.g. [7]), deontic logicians have struggled with the
problem of giving a formal treatment to CTD obligations. According to Hansson [11], van Fraassen [29], Lewis [16] and others, the problems raised by CTDs

© The Author(s), under exclusive license to Springer Nature Switzerland AG 2023
R. Aydoğan et al. (Eds.): PRIMA 2022, LNAI 13753, pp. 54–71, 2023.
https://doi.org/10.1007/978-3-031-21203-1_4

call for an ordering on possible worlds in terms of preference (or relative good-ness, or betterness), and Kripke-style models fail in as much as they do not allow for grades of ideality. The use of a preference relation has also been advocated for the analysis of defeasible conditional obligations. In particular, Alchourrón [1] argues that preferential models provide a better treatment of this notion than the usual Kripke-style models. Indeed, a defeasible conditional obligation leaves room for exceptions. Under a preference-based approach, we no longer have the deontic analogue of two laws, the failure of which constitutes the main formal feature expected from defeasible conditionals; these are "deontic" modus-ponens (or Factual Detachment): $\bigcirc(B/A)$ and A imply $\bigcirc B$, and Strengthening of the Antecedent: $\bigcirc(B/A)$ entails $\bigcirc(B/A \wedge C)$. (There is an extensive literature on the treatment of contrary-to-duties, e.g. [16,17,23,26,29], and defeasible condi-tional obligations, e.g. [3,13,18,28], in a preference-based framework.)

The meta-theory of the framework has been the focus of much research in recent years (for an overview, see [22]). Like in traditional modal logic, different properties of the relation in the models yield different Hilbert systems. Early axiomatisation results [16,25,29] were tailored to the case where the betterness relation comes with many properties. These have been criticized as being too demanding in some contexts. Therefore subsequent research investigated how to extend these results to models equipped with a betterness relation meeting less conditions, if any at all [10,21]. Åqvist's system **E**, corresponds to the most general case, involving no commitment to any structural property of the relation. Stronger systems–like **F** and **G**–are obtained by adding extra constraints on the betterness relation. (A roadmap of existing systems is, e.g., in [10,22].) In this paper we focus on **E**, the weakest known preference-based dyadic deontic logic.

So far for preference-based deontic logics there has been an almost exclusive focus on the connection between semantic properties and Hilbert systems. Very little research has been done on Gentzen-style calculi. To our knowledge only **G**, due to its equivalence with Lewis's VTA and van Fraassen's CD, has an analytic Gentzen calculus [9]. As is well known such calculi have significant practical and theoretical advantages compared to Hilbert systems. In analytic calculi proof search proceeds indeed by step-wise decomposition of the formulas to be proven. For this reason they can be employed to establish important meta-logical properties for the formalized logics (e.g., decidability, complexity and interpolation), and facilitate the development of automated reasoning methods. In general, analytic calculi serve to find derivations and hence provide forms of constructive *explanations* for normative systems; e.g. showing which hypotheses have been used in deriving certain obligations given specific facts. They also facilitate counter-model construction from non-derivable statements, and hence provide explanations of why "something should not be done".

The present paper aims at filling in this gap, focusing on Åqvist's system **E**. We introduce an analytic Gentzen-style calculus **HE** for **E**, and use (a reformu-lation of) it to provide an alternative decidability proof for **E** and a complexity result. The calculus is also employed to generate formal explanations for a well-known CTD paradox [7] from the deontic logic literature.

HE admits the elimination of the key rule of cut—which simulates Modus Ponens in Hilbert systems—and the consequent (relaxed version of the) subformula property; moreover its completeness proof is independent from the logic's semantics. An "optimized" version **HE+** of **HE** is also given, that supports automated proof search and counterexample constructions.[1] **HE+** is used to prove that the validity problem of **E** is co-NP and countermodels have polynomial size.

We highlight two salient features of our approach.

- Since **E** is tightly connected with the modal logic S5 ($S5$ is actually a sublogic of **E**), our calculi are defined using the hypersequent framework [4]—a simple extension of Gentzen's sequent framework—needed to provide a cut-free calculus for $S5$ [4,14,19], i.e. a calculus in which the cut rule is redundant.
- Similarly to previous work on modal interpretation of conditionals, e.g., [8,27], we encode maximality by a unary modal operator. Intuitively the fact that x is among the best worlds that force a formula A may be understood as saying that all the worlds accessible from x via the betterness relation (or "above" x according to the ranking) force not-A. This is encoded as $\mathcal{B}et\neg A$, where $\mathcal{B}et$ is a K-type modal operator. The conditional obligation $\bigcirc(B/A)$ can be indirectly defined as $\square(A \wedge \mathcal{B}et\neg A \rightarrow B)$, where $\square$ obeys the laws of S5. Here "indirectly" indicates that the reduction schema is not explicitly introduced. $\mathcal{B}et$ is not part of the language of **E**, but is used at the meta-level in the Gentzen-style system to define suitable rules for the conditional.

We remark that although our calculus in some sense "translates" **E** into the bi-modal logic $S5+K$, its complexity turns out to be the same as for classical logic: co-NP; this contrasts with the P-SPACE complexity of $S5+K$.

2   System E

In this section we present the logic **E** both syntactically and semantically.

Definition 1. The language $\mathcal{L}$ is defined by the following BNF:

$$A ::= p \in \text{PropVar} \mid \neg A \mid A \rightarrow A \mid \square A \mid \bigcirc(A/A)$$

$\square A$ is read as "A is settled as true", and $\bigcirc(B/A)$ as "B is obligatory, given A". The Boolean connectives other than $\neg$ and $\rightarrow$ are defined as usual.

Definition 2. The axiomatization of **E** consists of any Hilbert system for classical propositional logic, the Modus Ponens rule (MP): If $\vdash A$ and $\vdash A \rightarrow B$ then $\vdash B$, the rule (Nec): If $\vdash A$ then $\vdash \square A$ and the following axioms:

---

[1] See [5] for an alternative method for generating countermodels.

$$\text{S5 axioms for } \Box \tag{S5}$$
$$\bigcirc (B \to C/A) \to (\bigcirc(B/A) \to \bigcirc(C/A)) \tag{COK}$$
$$\bigcirc (A/A) \tag{Id}$$
$$\bigcirc (C/A \wedge B) \to \bigcirc(B \to C/A) \tag{Sh}$$
$$\Box(A \leftrightarrow B) \to (\bigcirc(C/A) \leftrightarrow \bigcirc(C/B)) \tag{Ext}$$
$$\bigcirc (B/A) \to \Box \bigcirc (B/A) \tag{Abs}$$
$$\Box A \to \bigcirc(A/B) \tag{O-Nec}$$

The notions of derivation and theoremhood are as usual.

An intuitive reading of the axioms is as follows. A basic design choice of the logic $\mathbf{E}$ is that necessity is interpreted as in the modal logic S5. (COK) is the conditional analogue of the familiar distribution axiom K. (Abs) is the absoluteness axiom of [16], and reflects the fact that the ranking is not world-relative. (O-Nec) is the deontic counterpart of the necessitation rule. (Ext) permits the replacement of necessarily equivalent sentences in the antecedent of deontic conditionals. (Id) is the deontic analogue of the identity principle. Named after Shoham [24, p. 77] who seems to have been the first to discuss it, (Sh) can be seen as expressing a "half" of deduction theorem or a "half" residuation property. The question of whether (Id) is a reasonable law for deontic conditionals has been much debated (see [23] for a defense).

The semantics of $\mathbf{E}$ can be defined in terms of *preference models*. They are possible-world models equipped with a comparative goodness relation $\succ$ on worlds so that $x \succ y$ can be read as "world x is *better* than world y". Conditional obligation is defined by considering "best" worlds: intuitively, $\bigcirc(B/A)$ holds in a model, if all the best worlds in which A is true also make B true.

Definition 3. A preference model is a structure $M = (W, \succ, V)$ $(W \neq \emptyset)$ whose members are called possible worlds, $\succ \subseteq W \times W$, $V : W \to \mathcal{P}(PropVar)$. The following evaluation rules are used, for all $x \in W$:

- $M, x \vDash p$ iff $p \in V(x)$
- $M, x \vDash \neg A$ iff $M, x \nvDash A$
- $M, x \vDash A \to B$ iff if $M, x \vDash A$ then $M, x \vDash B$
- $M, x \vDash \Box A$ iff $\forall y \in W \; M, y \vDash A$
- $M, x \vDash \bigcirc(B/A)$ iff $\forall y \in best(A) \; M, y \vDash B$

where $best(A) = \{y \in W \mid M, y \vDash A \text{ and there is no } z \succ y \text{ such that } M, z \vDash A\}$. A formula A is valid in a model M if for all worlds x in M, $M, x \vDash A$. A formula A is *valid* iff it is valid in every preference model.

Observe that we do not assume any specific property of $\succ$.

To the purpose of the calculi developed in the following, we introduce the modality $\mathcal{B}et$, which will allow us to represent the "Best" worlds: $M, x \vDash \mathcal{B}et A$ iff $\forall y \succ x \; M, y \vDash A$. By this definition, we get $x \in best(A)$ iff $M, x \vDash A$ and $M, x \vDash \mathcal{B}et \neg A$. However, the modality $\mathcal{B}et$ is not part of $\mathcal{L}$. As a notational convention, when no confusion arise, we write $x \vDash A$ for $M, x \vDash A$. The following result from [21] is needed for subsequent developments:

Theorem 1. E *is sound and complete w.r.t. the class of all preference models.*

The completeness proof in [21] uses another notion of maximality, call it best′, where $y \in$ best′(A) iff $y \models A$ and $y \succ z$ for all z s. t. $z \models A$ and $z \succ y$. Although best and best′ are not equivalent, our result follows almost at once. Indeed, starting with a model $M = (W, \succ, V)$ in which obligations are evaluated using best′, one can derive an equivalent model $M' = (W, \succ', V)$ (with W and V the same) in which obligations are evaluated using best.[2]

We end this section with two remarks. The first one concerns reductions of conditional logics to modal logics. In the literature various such reductions have been introduced; perhaps the best-known is the embedding of conditional logic into S4 put forth by Lamarre and Boutilier (see the discussion in [18] and the references therein). There are similarities with their approach, but also important differences. They define indeed an embedding of a conditional logic, different from **E**, into S4. In contrast, we do *not* embed **E** into any (bi)modal logic. **E** contains an $S5$ modality as a primitive notion, whose meaning is independent from the dyadic modality $\bigcirc(B/A)$.

The second remark concerns the suitability of **E** to handle exceptions. Readers familiar with [13,23] may question this suitability. We think that **E** does provide a minimal account of exceptions. However, we agree with [28] that a more adequate treatment of exceptions within a preference-based framework calls for the combined use of a normality relation and a betterness relation.

3 A Cut-Free Hypersequent Calculus for E

We introduce the hypersequent calculus **HE** for the logic **E**. **HE** is defined in a modular way by adding to the calculus for the modal logic $S5$ suitable rules for the dyadic obligation, and the $\mathcal{B}et$ operator. Introduced in [19] to define a cut-free calculus for $S5$, hypersequents consist of sequents working in parallel.

Definition 4. A *hypersequent* is a multiset $\Gamma_1 \Rightarrow \Pi_1 \mid \ldots \mid \Gamma_n \Rightarrow \Pi_n$ where, for all $i = 1, \ldots, n$, $\Gamma_i \Rightarrow \Pi_i$ is an ordinary sequent, called *component*.

The hypersequent calculus **HE** is presented in Definition 5. It consists of initial hypersequents (i.e., axioms), logical/modal/deontic and structural rules. The latter are divided into *internal* and *external rules*. **HE** incorporates the sequent calculus for the modal logic S4 as a sub-calculus and adds an additional layer of information by considering a single sequent to live in the context of hypersequents. Hence all the axioms and rules of **HE** (but the external structural rules) are obtained by adding to each sequent a context G (or H), representing a possibly empty hypersequent. For instance, the (hypersequent version of the)

---

[2] Put $x \succ' y$ iff $x \succ y$ and $y \not\succ x$. We can easily verify that an arbitrarily chosen world satisfies exactly the same formulas in both models, viz. for all worlds x, $M, x \models A$ iff $M', x \models A$. (The sole purpose of this construction is to extend the result in [21] to the current setting.).

axioms are $\Gamma, p \Rightarrow \Delta, p \mid G$. The external structural rules include ext. weakening (ew) and ext. contraction (ec) (see Fig. 1). These behave like weakening and contraction over whole hypersequent components. The hypersequent structure opens the possibility to define new such rules that allow the "exchange of information" between different sequents. It is this type of rules which increases the expressive power of hypersequent calculi compared to sequent calculi, allowing the definition of cut-free calculi for logics that seem to escape a cut-free sequent formulation (e.g., $S5$). An example of external structural rule is the ($s5$) rule in [14] (reformulated as ($s5'$) in Fig. 1 to account for the presence of $\bigcirc$), that allows the peculiar axiom of $S5$ to be derived as follows:

$$
\dfrac{
\dfrac{
\dfrac{
\dfrac{
\dfrac{\Box A \Rightarrow \Box\neg\Box A, \Box A}{\Box A \Rightarrow \mid \Rightarrow \Box\neg\Box A, \Box A}\;(s5')
}{\Rightarrow \neg\Box A \mid \Rightarrow \Box\neg\Box A, \Box A}\;(\neg\mathrm{R})
}{\Rightarrow \Box\neg\Box A, \Box A \mid \Rightarrow \Box\neg\Box A, \Box A}\;(\Box\mathrm{R})
}{\Rightarrow \Box\neg\Box A, \Box A}\;(\mathrm{ec})
}{\Rightarrow \neg\Box A \to \Box\neg\Box A}\;(\to\mathrm{R})+(\neg\mathrm{L})
$$

$$
\dfrac{G}{G \mid \Gamma \Rightarrow \Pi}\;(ew)
\qquad
\dfrac{G \mid \Gamma \Rightarrow \Pi \mid \Gamma \Rightarrow \Pi}{G \mid \Gamma \Rightarrow \Pi}\;(ec)
\qquad
\dfrac{G \mid \Gamma^{\Box}, \Gamma^{O}, \Gamma' \Rightarrow \Pi'}{G \mid \Gamma \Rightarrow \mid \Gamma' \Rightarrow \Pi'}\;(s5')
$$

Fig. 1. External structural rules

$$
\dfrac{\Gamma^{\Box}, \Gamma^{O}, A, \mathcal{B}et\,\neg A \Rightarrow B \mid G}{\Gamma \Rightarrow \bigcirc(B/A), \Delta \mid G}\;(\bigcirc\mathrm{R})
\qquad
\dfrac{\Gamma^{\Box}, \Gamma^{O}, \Gamma^{b\downarrow} \Rightarrow A \mid G}{\Gamma \Rightarrow \Delta, \mathcal{B}et\,A \mid G}\;(\mathcal{B}et)
$$

$$
\dfrac{\Gamma^{\Box}, \Gamma^{O} \Rightarrow A \mid G}{\Gamma \Rightarrow \Delta, \Box A \mid G}\;(\Box\mathrm{R})
\qquad
\dfrac{\Gamma, \Box A, A \Rightarrow \Delta \mid G}{\Gamma, \Box A \Rightarrow \Delta \mid G}\;(\Box\mathrm{L})
$$

$$
\dfrac{\Gamma, \bigcirc(B/A) \Rightarrow \Delta, A \mid G \quad \Gamma, \bigcirc(B/A) \Rightarrow \Delta, \mathcal{B}et\,\neg A \mid G \quad \Gamma, \bigcirc(B/A), B \Rightarrow \Delta \mid G}{\Gamma, \bigcirc(B/A) \Rightarrow \Delta \mid G}\;(\bigcirc\mathrm{L})
$$

Fig. 2. Deontic and modal rules

The rules in Fig. 1 and 2 make use of the following notation:
$$\Sigma^{b\downarrow} = \{G : \mathcal{B}et\,G \in \Sigma\} \qquad \Sigma^{\Box} = \{\Box G : \Box G \in \Sigma\}$$
$$\Sigma^{O} = \{\bigcirc(C/D) : \bigcirc(C/D) \in \Sigma\}$$

Definition 5. The hypersequent calculus **HE** consists of the hypersequent version of Gentzen LK sequent calculus for classical propositional logic, the external structural rules in Fig. 1 and the modal and deontic rules in Fig. 2.

A *derivation* in **HE** is a tree obtained by applying the rules bottom up. A *proof* $\mathcal{D}$ is a derivation whose leafs are axioms. This distinction will be used in Sect. 4.

The soundness of **HE** is proved with respect to preference models. Although we can interpret directly an hypersequent H into the semantics, it is easier (and more readable) to interpret it as a formula $I(H)$ of the extended language $\mathcal{L}+\mathcal{B}et$ and show the validity of this formula whenever H is provable.

Theorem 2. *If there is a proof in* **HE** *of* $H := \Gamma_1 \Rightarrow \Pi_1 \mid \ldots \mid \Gamma_n \Rightarrow \Pi_n$, *then* $I(H) := \Box(\bigwedge \Gamma_1 \to \bigvee \Pi_1) \vee \ldots \vee \Box(\bigwedge \Gamma_n \to \bigvee \Pi_n)$ *is valid.*

Proof. By induction on the proof of H. We show $(\bigcirc R)$, $(\mathcal{B}et)$ and *(s5')*.

$(\bigcirc R)$ Suppose the premise is valid but not the conclusion. Thus for some model M and world x, $x \not\models \Box(\bigwedge \Gamma \to \bigvee \Delta \vee \bigcirc(B/A)) \vee \Box G$. Thus (1) $x \not\models \Box(\bigwedge \Gamma \to \bigvee \Delta \vee \bigcirc(B/A))$ and $x \not\models \Box G$. Since the premise is valid: $x \models \Box(\bigwedge \Gamma^\Box \wedge \bigwedge \Gamma^O \wedge A \wedge \mathcal{B}et \neg A \to B) \vee \Box G$ so that (2) $x \models \Box(\bigwedge \Gamma^\Box \wedge \bigwedge \Gamma^O \wedge A \wedge \mathcal{B}et \neg A \to B)$. From (1) there is y s.t. (3) $y \models \bigwedge \Gamma$, $y \not\models \bigvee \Delta$ and $y \not\models \bigcirc(B/A)$; from the latter there is some z such that $z \in best(A)$ and $z \not\models B$ [evaluation rule for $\bigcirc$]. So $z \models A$ and $z \models \mathcal{B}et \neg A$ [def of $\mathcal{B}et$]. From (3), $y \models \bigwedge \Gamma^\Box \wedge \bigwedge \Gamma^O$, whence also for z, as $\Gamma^\Box$ and Γ^O express global assumptions, holding in all worlds in the model. Thus $z \models \bigwedge \Gamma^\Box \wedge \bigwedge \Gamma^O \wedge A \wedge \mathcal{B}et \neg A$. By (2) $z \models B$, a contradiction.

$(\mathcal{B}et)$ Suppose that the premise is valid but not the conclusion. Thus for a model M and world x (ignoring the context G) $x \not\models \Box(\bigwedge \Gamma \to \bigvee \Delta \vee \mathcal{B}etA)$, but $(*)$ $x \models \Box(\bigwedge \Gamma^\Box \wedge \bigwedge \Gamma^O \wedge \bigwedge \Gamma^{b\downarrow} \to A)$ thus for some world y: (1) $y \models \bigwedge \Gamma$ (2) $y \not\models \mathcal{B}etA$. Observe that (3) $y \models \bigwedge \Gamma^\Box \wedge \bigwedge \Gamma^O$ and that (4) $y \models \mathcal{B}et C$ for all $\mathcal{B}et C \in \Gamma$. By (2) there is z with $z \succ y$ s.t. $z \not\models A$. Hence $z \models \bigwedge \Gamma^\Box \wedge \bigwedge \Gamma^O$. But by (4) we also get $z \models \Gamma^{b\downarrow}$. Therefore by $(*)$ we get $z \models A$, a contradiction.

(s5') Suppose that the premise is valid but not the conclusion. Thus for some M and x, $x \not\models \Box \neg \bigwedge \Gamma \vee \Box(\bigwedge \Gamma' \to \bigvee \Pi')$, so that $x \not\models \Box \neg \bigwedge \Gamma$ and $x \not\models \Box(\bigwedge \Gamma' \to \bigvee \Pi')$. Therefore there are $y, z \in W$, such that $y \not\models \neg \bigwedge \Gamma$, meaning (1) $y \models \bigwedge \Gamma$ and $z \not\models \bigwedge \Gamma' \to \bigvee \Pi'$, which entails (2) $z \models \bigwedge \Gamma'$ and (3) $z \not\models \bigvee \Pi'$. By validity of the premise, $z \models \bigwedge \Gamma^\Box \wedge \bigwedge \Gamma^O \wedge \bigwedge \Gamma' \to \bigvee \Pi'$, so that by (3), (4) $z \not\models \bigwedge \Gamma^\Box \wedge \bigwedge \Gamma^O \wedge \bigwedge \Gamma'$. But by (1), $z \models \bigwedge \Gamma^\Box \wedge \bigwedge \Gamma^O$ so that by (2) and (4) we have a contradiction.

Theorem 3. (Completeness with cut) *Each theorem of* **E** *has a proof in* **HE** *with the addition of the cut rule:*

$$\frac{G \mid \Gamma, A \Rightarrow \Delta \qquad H \mid \Sigma \Rightarrow \Pi, A}{G \mid H \mid \Gamma, \Sigma \Rightarrow \Delta, \Pi} \ (cut)$$

Proof. As Modus Ponens corresponds to the provability of $A, A \to B \Rightarrow B$ and two applications of cut, it suffices to show that (Nec) and all the axioms of **E** are provable in **HE**. As an example, we show a proof of (COK):

$$\cfrac{B \to C, B \Rightarrow C \quad \cfrac{A \Rightarrow A}{\mathcal{B}et \, \neg A \Rightarrow \mathcal{B}et \, \neg A}(\mathcal{B}et)^\star \quad A \Rightarrow A}{\cfrac{\cfrac{B \to C, \bigcirc(B/A), A, \mathcal{B}et \, \neg A \Rightarrow C}{}(\bigcirc L)_\star \quad \cfrac{\cfrac{A \Rightarrow A}{\mathcal{B}et \neg A \Rightarrow \mathcal{B}et \, \neg A}(\mathcal{B}et)^\star \quad A \Rightarrow A}{}(\bigcirc L)_\star}{\cfrac{\bigcirc(B \to C/A), \bigcirc(B/A), A, \mathcal{B}et \, \neg A \Rightarrow C}{\cfrac{\bigcirc(B \to C/A), \bigcirc(B/A) \Rightarrow \bigcirc(C/A)}{\Rightarrow \bigcirc(B \to C/A) \to (\bigcirc(B/A) \to \bigcirc(C/A))}(\to R)\times 2}(\bigcirc R)}}$$

($\star$ in the above proof stands for additional applications of internal weakening, and $(\mathcal{B}et)^\star$ stands for $(\mathcal{B}et) + (\neg L) + (\neg R)$)

Cut-Elimination

Theorem 3 heavily relies on the presence of the cut rule. In this section we give a constructive proof that cut can in fact be *eliminated* from **HE** proofs. This result (cut elimination) implies (a relaxed form of) the *subformula property*: all formulas occurring in a cut-free **HE** proof are subformulas (possibly negated and under the scope of $\mathcal{B}et$) of the formulas to be proved.

Proof idea: To reduce the complexity of a cut on a formula of the form $\neg A$ or $A \to B$ we can exploit the rule invertibilities (Lemma 1). Some care is needed to deal with cut-formulas of the form $\Box A$, $\mathcal{B}et \, A$ and $\bigcirc(B/A)$. There we cannot use the invertibility argument and cuts have to be shifted upward till the cut-formula is introduced. Notice however that the $(\Box R)$, $(\bigcirc R)$ and $(\mathcal{B}et)$ rules do not allow to shift *every* cut upwards: only those involving sequents of a certain "good" shape. The proof hence proceeds by shifting uppermost cuts upwards in a specific order: first over the premise in which the cut formula appears on the right (Lemma 4) and then, when a rule introducing the cut formula is reached (and in this case the sequent has a "good" shape), shifting the cut upwards over the other premise (Lemma 3) till the left cut formula is introduced and the cut can be replaced by smaller cuts. The hypersequent structure does not require major changes; as the $(s5')$ rule allows cuts with "good" shaped sequents to be shifted upwards, to handle (ec) we consider the hypersequent version of the multicut: cutting one component (i.e. sequent) against possibly many components.

The *length* $|\mathcal{D}|$ of an **HE** proof $\mathcal{D}$ is (the maximal number of applications of inference rules) $+1$ occurring on any branch of d. The *complexity* $\ulcorner A \urcorner$ of a formula A is defined as: $\ulcorner A \urcorner = 0$ if A is atomic, $\ulcorner \neg A \urcorner = \ulcorner A \urcorner + 1$, $\ulcorner A \to B \urcorner = \ulcorner A \urcorner + \ulcorner B \urcorner + 1$, $\ulcorner \mathcal{B}et \, A \urcorner = \ulcorner A \urcorner + 1$, $\ulcorner \Box A \urcorner = \ulcorner A \urcorner + 1$, and $\ulcorner \bigcirc(A/B) \urcorner = \ulcorner A \urcorner + \ulcorner B \urcorner + 3$. The *cut rank* $\rho(\mathcal{D})$ of $\mathcal{D}$ is the maximal complexity $+1$ of cut formulas in $\mathcal{D}$, noting that $\rho(\mathcal{D}) = 0$ if $\mathcal{D}$ is cut-free. We use A^n to indicate n occurrences of A.

It is easy to see that the rules of the classical propositional connectives remain invertible, as stated in the lemma below.

Lemma 1. *Given an* **HE** *proof* $\mathcal{D}$ *of a hypersequent containing a compound formula* $\neg A$ *(resp.* $A \to B$*), we can find a proof* $\mathcal{D}'$ *of the same hypersequent ending in an introduction rule for* $\neg A$ *(resp.* $A \to B$*) and with* $\rho(\mathcal{D}') \le \rho(\mathcal{D})$.

In **HE** any cut whose cut formula is immediately introduced in left and right premise can be replaced by smaller cuts. More formally,

Lemma 2. *Let A be a compound formula and $\mathcal{D}_l$ and $\mathcal{D}_r$ be* **HE** *proofs such that $\rho(\mathcal{D}_l) \leq \ulcorner A \urcorner$ and $\rho(\mathcal{D}_r) \leq \ulcorner A \urcorner$, and*

1. *$\mathcal{D}_l$ is a proof of $G \mid \Gamma, A \Rightarrow \Delta$ ending in a rule introducing A*
2. *$\mathcal{D}_r$ is a proof of $H \mid \Sigma \Rightarrow A, \Pi$ ending in a rule introducing A*

We can find an **HE** *proof of $G \mid H \mid \Gamma, \Sigma \Rightarrow \Delta, \Pi$ with $\rho(\mathcal{D}) \leq \ulcorner A \urcorner$.*

Proof. We show the only non-trivial case: $A = \mathcal{B}et\, B$, where a cut

$$\dfrac{\dfrac{H \mid \Sigma^{\square}, \Sigma^{O}, \Sigma^{b\downarrow}, B \Rightarrow C}{G \mid \Sigma, \mathcal{B}et\, B \Rightarrow \mathcal{B}et\, C, \Pi}\,{\scriptstyle(\mathcal{B}et)} \quad \dfrac{H \mid \Gamma^{\square}, \Gamma^{O}, \Gamma^{b\downarrow} \Rightarrow B}{H \mid \Gamma \Rightarrow \mathcal{B}et\, B, \Delta}\,{\scriptstyle(\mathcal{B}et)}}{G \mid H \mid \Gamma, \Sigma \Rightarrow \mathcal{B}et\, C, \Delta, \Pi}\,{\scriptstyle(cut)}$$

is replaced by

$$\dfrac{\dfrac{H \mid \Sigma^{\square}, \Sigma^{O}, \Sigma^{b\downarrow}, B \Rightarrow C \quad G \mid \Gamma^{\square}, \Gamma^{O}, \Gamma^{b\downarrow} \Rightarrow B}{G \mid H \mid \Sigma^{\square}, \Sigma^{O}, \Sigma^{b\downarrow}\Gamma^{\square}, \Gamma^{O}, \Gamma^{b\downarrow} \Rightarrow C}\,{\scriptstyle(cut)}}{G \mid H \mid \Gamma, \Sigma \Rightarrow \mathcal{B}et\, C, \Delta, \Pi}\,{\scriptstyle(\mathcal{B}et)}$$

Lemma 3. *Let $\mathcal{D}_l$ and $\mathcal{D}_r$ be* **HE** *proofs such that:*

1. *$\mathcal{D}_l$ is a proof of $G \mid \Gamma_1, A^{\lambda_1} \Rightarrow \Delta_1 \mid \ldots \mid \Gamma_n, A^{\lambda_n} \Rightarrow \Delta_n$;*
2. *A is a compound formula and $\mathcal{D}_r := H \mid \Sigma \Rightarrow A, \Pi$ ends with a right logical rule introducing an indicated occurrence of A*
3. *$\rho(\mathcal{D}_l) \leq \ulcorner A \urcorner$ and $\rho(\mathcal{D}_r) \leq \ulcorner A \urcorner$;*

Then we can construct an **HE** *proof $\mathcal{D}$ of $G \mid H \mid \Gamma_1, \Sigma^{\lambda_1} \Rightarrow \Delta_1, \Pi^{\lambda_1} \mid \ldots \mid \Gamma_n, \Sigma^{\lambda_n} \Rightarrow \Delta_n, \Pi^{\lambda_n}$ with $\rho(\mathcal{D}) \leq \ulcorner A \urcorner$.*

Proof. We distinguish cases according to the shape of A. If A is of the form $\neg B$ or $B \to C$, the claim follows by Lemmas 1 and 2. If A is $\square B$, $\bigcirc(B/C)$ or $\mathcal{B}et\, B$ the proof proceeds by induction on $|\mathcal{D}_l|$. If $\mathcal{D}_l$ ends in an initial sequent, then we are done. If $\mathcal{D}_l$ ends in a left rule introducing one of the indicated cut formulas, the claim follows by (i.h. and) Lemma 2. Otherwise, let (r) be the last inference rule applied in $\mathcal{D}_l$. The claim follows by the i.h., an application of (r) and/or weakening. Some care is needed to handle the cases in which r is $(s5')$, $(\square R)$, $(\bigcirc R)$ or $(\mathcal{B}et)$ and A is not in the hypersequent context G. Notice that when $A = \square B$ (resp. $A = \bigcirc(B/C)$) the conclusion of $\mathcal{D}_r$ is $\Sigma \Rightarrow \square B, \Pi$ (resp. $\Sigma \Rightarrow \bigcirc(B/C), \Delta$), but we can safely use the "good"-shaped sequent $\Sigma^{\square}, \Sigma^{O} \Rightarrow \square B$ (resp. $\Sigma^{\square}, \Sigma^{O} \Rightarrow \bigcirc(B/C)$), that allows cuts to be shifted upwards over all **HE** rules, and we apply weakening afterwards. When $A = \mathcal{B}et\, B$, notice that the cut formula does not appear in the premises of these rules. For example let $(r) = (s5')$, $A = \square B$, and $\mathcal{D}_l$ ends as follows

$$\begin{array}{c} \vdots\, d'_l \\ \dfrac{G \mid \Gamma^{\square}, \square B, \Gamma^{O}, \Gamma' \Rightarrow \Pi' \mid \ldots \mid \Omega, \square B \Rightarrow \Delta}{G \mid \Gamma, \square B \Rightarrow \mid \Gamma' \Rightarrow \Pi' \mid \ldots \mid \Omega, \square B \Rightarrow \Delta}\,{\scriptstyle(s5')} \end{array}$$

The claim follows by i.h. applied to the conclusion $G \mid \Gamma^\square, \square B, \Gamma^O, \Gamma' \Rightarrow \Pi' \mid$ $\dots \mid \Omega, \square B \Rightarrow \Delta$ of d'_l (and $\Sigma^O, \Sigma^\square \Rightarrow \square B$), followed by an application of $(s5')$ and weakening. The case $A = \bigcirc(B/C)$ is the same. The cases involving $(\square R)$, $(\bigcirc R)$ and $(\mathcal{B}et)$ are handled in a similar way.

Lemma 4. *Let $\mathcal{D}_l$ and $\mathcal{D}_r$ be* **HE** *proofs such that:*

1. $\mathcal{D}_l$ *is a proof of* $G \mid \Gamma, A \Rightarrow \Delta$;
2. $\mathcal{D}_r$ *is a proof of* $H \mid \Sigma_1 \Rightarrow A^{\lambda_1}, \Pi'_1 \mid \dots \mid \Sigma_n \Rightarrow A^{\lambda_n}, \Pi'_n$;
3. $\rho(\mathcal{D}_l) \leq \ulcorner A \urcorner$ *and* $\rho(\mathcal{D}_r) \leq \ulcorner A \urcorner$.

Then a proof $\mathcal{D}$ can be constructed in **HE** *of $G \mid H \mid \Sigma_1, \Gamma^{\lambda_1} \Rightarrow \Pi'_1, \Delta^{\lambda_1} \mid \dots \mid \Sigma_n, \Gamma^{\lambda_n} \Rightarrow \Pi'_n, \Delta^{\lambda_n}$ with $\rho(\mathcal{D}) \leq \ulcorner A \urcorner$.*

Proof. Let (r) be the last inference rule applied in $\mathcal{D}_r$. If (r) is an axiom, then the claim holds trivially. Otherwise, we proceed by induction on $|\mathcal{D}_r|$, using Lemma 3 when (one of) the indicated occurrence(s) of A is principal. Assume A is not principal. If (r) acts only on H or is a rule other than $(s5')$, $(\square R)$, $(\bigcirc R)$ and $(\mathcal{B}et)$ the claim follows by the i.h. and an application of (r). For the remaining rules notice that A is not in the rule premise (in case of $(s5')$ the "critical" component in the conclusion has empty right-hand side), hence the claim follows by applying (the i.h. to the other components, and) the respective rule followed by weakening.

Theorem 4. (Cut Elimination) *Cut elimination holds for* **HE**.

Proof. Let $\mathcal{D}$ be an **HE** proof with $\rho(\mathcal{D}) > 0$. We proceed by a double induction on $\langle \rho(\mathcal{D}), n\rho(\mathcal{D}) \rangle$, where $n\rho(\mathcal{D})$ is the number of applications of cut in $\mathcal{D}$ with cut rank $\rho(\mathcal{D})$. Consider an uppermost application of (cut) in $\mathcal{D}$ with cut rank $\rho(\mathcal{D})$. By applying Lemma 4 to its premises either $\rho(\mathcal{D})$ or $n\rho(\mathcal{D})$ decreases.

Corollary 1. (Completeness) *Each theorem of* **E** *has a proof in* **HE**.

4   A Proof Search Oriented Calculus for E

The properties of the calculus **HE** include modularity, cut-elimination and a completeness proof which is independent from the semantics of **E**. However **HE** supports neither automated proof search nor counterexample constructions.

Here we introduce the calculus **HE**$^+$ having terminating proof search, thereby providing a decision procedure for **E**, and in case of termination with failure a countermodel of the starting formula can be extracted checking a *single* failed derivation. Similarly to the calculus for S5 in [15], **HE**$^+$ is obtained by making in **HE** all rules invertible, and all structural rules (including the external ones) admissible. Looking at the rules bottom up, this is achieved by copying the introduced formulas and the component containing it in the rule premises; the "simulation" of $(s5')$ is obtained by introducing additional left rules for $\square$ and $\bigcirc(A/B)$ which add subformulas to different components of the hypersequent.

Using **HE**$^+$ we will show that the validity problem of **E** is co-NP.

Definition 6. The $\mathbf{HE^+}$ calculus consists of: the initial hypersequents $\Gamma, p \Rightarrow \Delta, p \,|\, G$, together with the following rules:

– Rules for the propositional connectives that repeat the formulas introduced in the premises, for example

$$\frac{\Gamma, A \to B \Rightarrow \Delta, A \,|\, G \quad \Gamma, A \to B, B \Rightarrow \Delta \,|\, G}{\Gamma, A \to B \Rightarrow \Delta \,|\, G} \ (\to L) \qquad \frac{\Gamma, A \Rightarrow \Delta, A \to B, B, \,|\, G}{\Gamma \Rightarrow \Delta, A \to B \,|\, G} \ (\to R)$$

– Rules for $\bigcirc$

$$\frac{\Gamma \Rightarrow \bigcirc(B/A), \Delta \,|\, A, \mathcal{B}et \ \neg A \Rightarrow B \,|\, G}{\Gamma \Rightarrow \bigcirc(B/A), \Delta \,|\, G} \ (\bigcirc R+)$$

$$\frac{\Gamma, \bigcirc(B/A) \Rightarrow \Delta, A \,|\, G \quad \Gamma, \bigcirc(B/A) \Rightarrow \Delta, \mathcal{B}et \ \neg A \,|\, G \quad \Gamma, \bigcirc(B/A), B \Rightarrow \Delta \,|\, G}{\Gamma, \bigcirc(B/A) \Rightarrow \Delta \,|\, G} \ (\bigcirc L+)$$

$$\frac{\Gamma, \bigcirc(B/A) \Rightarrow \Delta \,|\, \Sigma \Rightarrow \Pi, A \,|\, G \quad \Gamma, \bigcirc(B/A) \Rightarrow \Delta \,|\, \Sigma \Rightarrow \Pi, \mathcal{B}et \ \neg A \,|\, G \quad \Gamma, \bigcirc(B/A) \Rightarrow \Delta \,|\, \Sigma, B \Rightarrow \Pi \,|\, G}{\Gamma, \bigcirc(B/A) \Rightarrow \Delta \,|\, \Sigma \Rightarrow \Pi \,|\, G} \ (\bigcirc L2)$$

– Rule for $\mathcal{B}et$

$$\frac{\Gamma \Rightarrow \Delta, \mathcal{B}et \ A \,|\, \Gamma^{b\downarrow} \Rightarrow A \,|\, G}{\Gamma \Rightarrow \Delta, \mathcal{B}et \ A \,|\, G} \ (\mathcal{B}et+)$$

– Rules for $\square$

$$\frac{\Gamma \Rightarrow \Delta, \square A \,| \Rightarrow A \,|\, G}{\Gamma \Rightarrow \Delta, \square A \,|\, G} \ (\square R+) \qquad \frac{\Gamma, \square A, A \Rightarrow \Delta \,|\, G}{\Gamma, \square A \Rightarrow \Delta \,|\, G} \ (\square L+) \qquad \frac{\Gamma, \square A \Rightarrow \Delta \,|\, \Sigma, A \Rightarrow \Pi \,|\, G}{\Gamma, \square A \Rightarrow \Delta \,|\, \Sigma \Rightarrow \Pi \,|\, G} \ (\square L2)$$

The notion of proof and derivation is as for $\mathbf{HE}$. The following lemma collects standard structural properties of $\mathbf{HE^+}$.

Lemma 5. *(i) All rules of* $\mathbf{HE^+}$ *are height-preserving invertible. (ii) Rules applications permute over each other (with the usual exceptions). (iii) Internal and external weakening and contraction are admissible in* $\mathbf{HE^+}$.

Proof. (i) Follows by the fact that the premises already contain the conclusion. (ii) and (iii) are standard (and hence omitted).

As a consequence of this lemma the order of application of the rules is irrelevant.

Theorem 5. *If there is a proof of H in* $\mathbf{HE^+}$ *then $I(H)$ is valid.*

Proof. We first show that the rules of $\mathbf{HE^+}$ can be simulated in $\mathbf{HE}$. This holds for all the $\mathbf{HE^+}$ rules but $(\bigcirc L2)$ and $(\square L2)$ by simply applying weakening, internal and external contraction. For $(\square L2)$ we have

$$
\cfrac{
\cfrac{
\cfrac{
\cfrac{G \mid \Gamma, \square A \Rightarrow \Delta \mid \Sigma, A \Rightarrow \Pi}{G \mid \Gamma, \square A \Rightarrow \Delta \mid \Sigma, \square A \Rightarrow \Pi} \text{\scriptsize($\square$L)}
}{G \mid \Gamma, \square A \Rightarrow \Delta \mid \square A \Rightarrow \mid \Sigma \Rightarrow \Pi} \text{\scriptsize(s5$'$)}
}{G \mid \Gamma, \square A \Rightarrow \Delta \mid \Gamma, \square A \Rightarrow \Delta \mid \Sigma \Rightarrow \Pi} \text{\scriptsize(w)}
}{G \mid \Gamma, \square A \Rightarrow \Delta \mid \Sigma \Rightarrow \Pi} \text{\scriptsize(ec)}
$$

The argument for $(\bigcirc L2)$ is analogous. The claim follows by Theorem 2.

We have adopted a "kleene'd" formulation of the calculus to make easier countermodel construction and termination of proof-search. They are both based on the notion of *saturation* that we define next. Given a hypersequent H, we write $\Gamma \Rightarrow \Delta \in H$ to indicate that $\Gamma \Rightarrow \Delta$ is a compontent of H.

Definition 7. (Saturation) A hypersequent H is *saturated* if it is not an axiom and satisfies the following conditions associated to each rule application

$(\to L)_S$ if $\Gamma, A \to B \Rightarrow \Delta \in H$ then either $A \in \Delta$ or $B \in \Gamma$

$(\to R)_S$ if $\Gamma \Rightarrow \Delta, A \to B \in H$ then $A \in \Gamma$ and $B \in \Delta$

$(\neg L)_S$ if $\Gamma, \neg A \Rightarrow \Delta \in H$ then $A \in \Delta$

$(\neg R)_S$ if $\Gamma \Rightarrow \Delta, \neg A \in H$ then $A \in \Gamma$

$(\bigcirc L+)_S$ if $\Gamma, \bigcirc(B/A) \Rightarrow \Delta \in H$ then either $A \in \Delta$ or $\mathcal{B}et\neg A \in \Delta$ or $B \in \Gamma$

$(\bigcirc L2)_S$ if $\Gamma, \bigcirc(B/A) \Rightarrow \Delta \in H$ and $\Sigma \Rightarrow \Pi \in H$ then either $A \in \Pi$ or $\mathcal{B}et\neg A \in \Pi$ or $B \in \Sigma$

$(\bigcirc R+)_S$ if $\Gamma \Rightarrow \bigcirc(B/A), \Delta \in H$ then there is $\Sigma \Rightarrow \Pi \in H$ such that $A \in \Sigma$, $\mathcal{B}et\neg A \in \Sigma$, and $B \in \Pi$

$(\mathcal{B}et+)_S$ if $\Gamma \Rightarrow \Delta, \mathcal{B}etA \in H$ then there is $\Sigma \Rightarrow \Pi \in H$ such that $\Gamma^{b\downarrow} \subseteq \Sigma$ and $A \in \Pi$

$(\square R+)_S$ if $\Gamma \Rightarrow \Delta, \square A \in H$ then there is $\Sigma \Rightarrow \Pi \in H$ such that $A \in \Pi$

$(\square L+)_S$ if $\Gamma, \square A \Rightarrow \Delta \in H$ then $A \in \Gamma$

$(\square L2)_S$ if $\Gamma, \square A \Rightarrow \Delta \in H$ and $\Sigma \Rightarrow \Pi \in H$ then $A \in \Sigma$

The key to obtain termination is to avoid the application of a rule to hypersequents which in a sense already contains the premise of that rule.

Definition 8. (Redundant application) A backward application of a rule (R) to an hypersequent H is *redundant* if H satisfies the saturation condition $(R)_S$ associated to that application of (R).

We call a derivation/proof *irredundant* if (i) no rule is applied to an axiom, and (ii) it does not contain any redundant application of rule. It is easy to see that by the admissibility of internal weakening and external contraction (Lemma 5) redundant applications of the rules can be safely removed.

Lemma 6. *Every hypersequent provable in* $\mathbf{HE}^+$ *has an irredundant proof.*

Proof. By induction on the height of a uppermost redundant application. To illustrate the argument consider a redundant application of the $(\mathcal{B}et+)$ rule

$$\frac{\Gamma \Rightarrow \Delta, \mathcal{B}et \; A \mid \Gamma^{b\downarrow} \Rightarrow A \mid \Gamma^{b\downarrow}, \Sigma' \Rightarrow \Pi', A \mid G}{\Gamma \Rightarrow \Delta, \mathcal{B}et \; A \mid \Gamma^{b\downarrow}, \Sigma' \Rightarrow \Pi', A \mid G} \; (\mathcal{B}et+)$$

this is transformed as follows:

$$\frac{\dfrac{\Gamma \Rightarrow \Delta, \mathcal{B}et \; A \mid \Gamma^{b\downarrow} \Rightarrow A \mid \Gamma^{b\downarrow}, \Sigma' \Rightarrow \Pi', A \mid G}{\Gamma \Rightarrow \Delta, \mathcal{B}et \; A \mid \Gamma^{b\downarrow}, \Sigma' \Rightarrow \Pi', A \mid \Gamma^{b\downarrow}, \Sigma' \Rightarrow \Pi', A \mid G} \; (Wk)}{\Gamma \Rightarrow \Delta, \mathcal{B}et \; A \mid \Gamma^{b\downarrow}, \Sigma' \Rightarrow \Pi', A \mid G} \; (ec)$$

The above property justifies the restriction to irredundant proofs from a syntactical point of view, although this justification is not really needed for completeness (Theorem 7 below).

We now use the calculus $\mathbf{HE}^+$ to give a decision procedure for the logic $\mathbf{E}$; the key issue here is to restrict proof-search to irredundant derivations.

We denote by $|A|$ the size of a formula A considered as a string of symbols.

Theorem 6. *Every* $\mathbf{HE}^+$ *derivation of a formula A of $\mathbf{E}$ is finite and it is either a proof or it contains a saturated hypersequent.*

Proof. Let $\mathcal{D}$ be any derivation built from $\Rightarrow A$ by backwards application of the rules. We first prove that all hypersequents in $\mathcal{D}$ are finite and provide an upper bound on their size. To this purpose let $|A| = n$ and consider $SUB^+(A) = \{B \mid B$ is a subformula of $A \} \cup \{\mathcal{B}et \neg C \mid \bigcirc(D/C)$ occurs in A, for some $C\}$. Clearly the cardinality of $SUB^+(A)$ is $O(n)$ and so it is the size of each formula in it.

Let $H := \Gamma_1 \Rightarrow \Delta_1 \mid \ldots \mid \Gamma_k \Rightarrow \Delta_k$ be any hypersequent occurring in $\mathcal{D}$. The size of each component is bounded by $O(n^2)$: it contains $O(n)$ formulas each one of size $O(n)$. To estimate the size of H, we estimate the number of its components (i.e. k). Observe that the rules which "create" new components are $(\Box R+)$, $(\bigcirc R+)$, and $(\mathcal{B}et+)$. Consider first $(\Box R+)$: by the irredundancy restriction this rule is applied *exactly once* to each formula, say $\Box C$, occurring in the consequent of a component and creates only *one* new component, no matter if $\Box C$ appears in the consequent of many components. To illustrate the situation, consider, e.g.,

$$\frac{\ldots \Gamma_i \Rightarrow \Delta_i, \Box C \mid \; \Rightarrow C \mid \ldots \mid \Gamma_j \Rightarrow \Delta_j, \Box C \mid \ldots \mid \Gamma_k \Rightarrow \Delta_k}{\ldots \Gamma_i \Rightarrow \Delta_i, \Box C \mid \ldots \mid \Gamma_j \Rightarrow \Delta_j, \Box C \mid \ldots \mid \Gamma_k \Rightarrow \Delta_k}$$

the irredundancy restriction ensures that if $(\Box R+)$ is applied to $\Gamma_i \Rightarrow \Delta_i$, it cannot be applied to the component $\Gamma_j \Rightarrow \Delta_j, \Box C$. This means that the number of components created by $(\Box R+)$ is bounded by $\Box$-ed subformulas of A, whence it is $O(n)$. The situation for $(\bigcirc R+)$ is similar.

For the rule $(\mathcal{B}et+)$, first observe the following fact:
Given any derivation $\mathcal{D}$ having at its root a formula of $\mathbf{E}$ (that is a hypersequent $\Rightarrow A$) at most one $\mathcal{B}et$ formula can occur in the antecedent Γ_i of any component of any hypersequent in $\mathcal{D}$, that is $\Gamma_i^{b\downarrow}$ contains at most one formula.

By this fact the rule $(\mathcal{B}et+)$ may be applied when $\Gamma_i^{b\downarrow}$ contains a formula and when $\Gamma_i^{b\downarrow} = \emptyset$, in both cases the applications are not duplicated, for instance in the former case, we may have:

$$\frac{\ldots \Gamma_i, \mathcal{B}et \ \neg E \Rightarrow \mathcal{B}et \ \neg F \mid \neg E \Rightarrow \neg F \mid \ldots \mid \Gamma_j, \mathcal{B}et \ \neg E \Rightarrow \mathcal{B}et \ \neg F \mid \ldots}{\ldots \Gamma_i, \mathcal{B}et \ \neg E \Rightarrow \mathcal{B}et \ \neg F \mid \ldots \mid \Gamma_j, \mathcal{B}et \ \neg E \Rightarrow \mathcal{B}et \ \neg F \mid \ldots}$$

Thus there is at most one application of the $(\mathcal{B}et+)$ rule for any pair of $\mathcal{B}et$ formulas (case $\Gamma_i^{b\downarrow} \neq \emptyset$) plus possibly an application for any $\mathcal{B}et$ formula (case $\Gamma_i^{b\downarrow} = \emptyset$). Since $\mathcal{B}et$ formulas come from the decomposition of O-subformulas and there are $O(n)$ of them, the number of components created by the $(\mathcal{B}et+)$ rule is $O(n^2 + n) = O(n^2)$. We can conclude that the number of components of any hypersequent in $\mathcal{D}$ is $O(n^2)$, whence the size of each hypersequent is $O(n^4)$.

We get also an upper bound on proof branches: since any backward application of a rule is irredundant, it must add some formula/component. Therefore the length of each proof branch is also bounded by $O(n^4)$ and the derivation is finite. Finally each leaf must be an axiom or a saturated hypersequent otherwise a rule would have been applied to it.

The next theorem shows the completeness of $\mathbf{HE}^+$.

Theorem 7. *Every valid formula A of $\mathbf{E}$ has a proof in $\mathbf{HE}^+$.*

Proof. We prove the contrapositive: if A is not provable in $\mathbf{HE}^+$ then there is a model in which A is not valid. Suppose that A is not provable in $\mathbf{HE}^+$, by the previous theorem any derivation of $\Rightarrow A$ as root contains at least one branch ending with a saturated hypersequent. Fix a derivation and let the intended saturated sequent be $H = \Gamma_1 \Rightarrow \Delta_1 \mid \ldots \mid \Gamma_n \Rightarrow \Delta_n$ be the intended saturated hypersequent. We build a countermodel of A based on H. First we enumerate the components of H, calling H' the corresponding structure:

$$H' = 1 : \Gamma_1 \Rightarrow \Delta_1 \mid 2 : \Gamma_2 \Rightarrow \Delta_2 \ldots \mid n : \Gamma_n \Rightarrow \Delta_n$$

We then define a model $M = (W, \succ, V)$ by stipulating:

$W = \{1, \ldots, n\}, \quad V(i) = \{P \mid P \in \Gamma_i\}$ with $i : \Gamma_i \Rightarrow \Delta_i \in H'$
$j \succ i$ where $i : \Gamma_i \Rightarrow \Delta_i \in H', j : \Gamma_j \Rightarrow \Delta_j \in H'$, if we have $\Gamma_i^{b\downarrow} \subseteq \Gamma_j$ and there is a formula $\mathcal{B}et \ C \in \Delta_i$ such that $C \in \Delta_j$.

Notice that in the definition of the preference relation it may be $i = j$. We now prove the fundamental claim (truth lemma); to this purpose we do not need to consider formulas with $\mathcal{B}et$, thus for $B \in \mathcal{L}$:

(a) for any $i \in W$, if $B \in \Gamma_i$ then $M, i \models B$

(b) for any $i \in W$, if $B \in \Delta_i$ then $M, i \not\models B$

Both claims (a) and (b) are proved by structural induction on B.

- Let B be an atom P, then (a) holds by definition of $V(i)$. Concerning (b), let $P \in \Delta_i$, since H is saturated, $P \notin \Gamma_i$, otherwise H would be an axiom; thus $P \notin V(i)$ whence $M, i \not\models P$.
- the propositional cases use saturation conditions and induction hypothesis.
- Let $B = \bigcirc(D/C)$. (a) suppose $\bigcirc(D/C) \in \Gamma_i$. We have to show that for every $j \in W$ the following holds: (case 1) $M, j \not\models C$, or (case 2) there is $k \in W$ with $k \succ j$ such that $M, k \models C$, or (case 3) $M, j \models D$. By saturation conditions $(\bigcirc L+)_S$ or $(\bigcirc L2)_S$ according to $i = j$ or $i \neq j$, we have that either $C \in \Delta_j$ or $\mathcal{B}et\neg C \in \Delta_j$ or $D \in \Gamma_j$, in the first case by i.h. we get $M, j \not\models C$ (case 1), in the third case, by i.h. we get $M, j \models D$ (case 3). Thus we are left with the case $\mathcal{B}et\neg C \in \Delta_j$. By saturation condition $(\mathcal{B}et)_S$, there is $k : \Gamma_k \Rightarrow \Delta_k \in H'$ such that $\Gamma_j^{b\downarrow} \subseteq \Gamma_k$ and $\neg C \in \Delta_k$. Observe that by construction it holds $k \succ j$. Moreover, by saturation condition $(\neg R)_S$, $C \in \Gamma_k$, whence by inductive hypothesis $M, k \models C$.
  (b) Suppose $\bigcirc(D/C) \in \Delta_i$. We have to show that there is $j \in W$ such that: $M, j \models C$; for all $k \in W$ with $k \succ j$ $M, k \not\models C$; and $M, j \not\models D$. By $(OR)_S$ there is $j : \Gamma_j \Rightarrow \Delta_j \in H'$ such that $C \in \Gamma_j$, $\mathcal{B}et\neg C \in \Gamma_j$, and $D \in \Delta_j$; by i.h. we get $M, j \models C$ and $M, j \not\models D$. We have still to prove that for all $k \in W$ with $k \succ j$ $M, k \not\models C$. To this aim, suppose $k \succ j$, by construction we have that there is $j : \Gamma_k \Rightarrow \Delta_k \in H'$ such that $\Gamma_j^{b\downarrow} \subseteq \Gamma_k$ and for some formula $\mathcal{B}et E \in \Delta_j$ it holds $E \in \Delta_k$. Since $\mathcal{B}et\neg C \in \Gamma_j$, $\neg C \in \Gamma_j^{b\downarrow} \subseteq \Gamma_k$, whence by $(\neg L)_S$ $C \in \Delta_k$; by i.h. we conclude $M, k \not\models C$ and we are done.
- $B = \Box C$. (a) suppose $\Box C \in \Gamma_i$. We have to show that for every $j \in W$, $M, j \models C$. Let $j \in W$ this means that $j : \Gamma_k \Rightarrow \Delta_k \in H'$ (it might be $j = i$), by saturation condition $(\Box L+)_S$ or $(\Box L2)_S$, according to $i = j$ or $i \neq j$ we have $C \in \Gamma_j$, whence by i.h. $M, j \models C$.
  (b) Suppose $\Box C \in \Delta_i$. By saturation condition $(\Box R+)_S$ there is $j : \Gamma_j \Rightarrow \Delta_j \in H'$ such that $C \in \Delta_j$, thus by i.h. $M, j \not\models C$.

Being $\Rightarrow A$ the root of the derivation, for some $i : \Gamma_i \Rightarrow \Delta_i \in H'$, we have $A \in \Delta_i$, and by claim (b) $M, i \not\models A$, showing that A is not valid in M.

This allows us to obtain a complexity bound for validity in **E**.

Theorem 8. *Validity of formula of* **E** *can be decided in Co-NP time.*

Proof. Given A, to decide whether A is valid, we consider a non-deterministic algorithm which takes as input $\Rightarrow A$ and guesses a saturated hypersequent H: if it finds it, the algorithm answers "non-valid", otherwise, it answers "valid". As shown in the proof of the Theorem 6, the size of the candidate saturated hypersequent H is polynomially bounded by the size of A ($= O(|A|^4)$), moreover checking whether H is saturated can also be done in polynomial time in the size of A (namely $O(|A|^8)$). More concretely, the algorithm can try to build H

by applying the rules backwards in an arbirary but fixed order, applying the first applicable (i.e. non-redundant) rule and then choosing non-deterministically one of its premises if there are more than one. The number of steps is polynomially bounded by $O(|A|^4)$ and checking whether a rule is applicable to a given hypersequent is linear in the size of the hypersequent. Thus the whole non-deterministic computation is polynomial in the size of the input formula.

By the previous results **E** turns out to have the polysize model property.

Corollary 2. *If a formula A of* **E** *is satisfiable (that is $\neg A$ is not valid), then it has a model of polynomial size in the length of A.*

We end the section with an example of explanation, obtained by countermodel construction, of a well-known CTD paradox.

"Gentle Murder" [7]. Consider the following norms and fact: (i) You ought not kill (ii) If you kill, you ought to kill gently (iii) Killing gently is killing (iv) You kill. In many deontic logics, these sentences are inconsistent and in particular (ii)-(iv) allow to derive the obligation to kill, contradicting (i)–hence the "paradox". We formally show that this does not happen in the logic **E**. To this purpose let the above sentences be encoded by: $\bigcirc(\neg k/\top), \bigcirc(g/k), \Box(g \to k), k$ with the obvious meaning of propositional atoms. We first verify that the above formulas are consistent, thus we begin a derivation with root hypersequent

$$\bigcirc(\neg k/\top), \bigcirc(g/k), \Box(g \to k), k \Rightarrow \bot$$

One of the saturated hypersequents we find by applying the rules backwards is

$$\bigcirc(\neg k/\top), \bigcirc(g/k), \Box(g \to k), k, g \to k, g \Rightarrow \bot, \mathcal{B}et\neg\top \mid g \to k, \neg k \Rightarrow \neg\top, g$$

Following the construction of Theorem 7, we enumerate the components (respectively) by 1,2 and get the model $M = (W, \succ, V)$ where $W = \{1, 2\}$, the preference relation is $2 \succ 1$ and $V(1) = \{k, g\}, V(2) = \emptyset$. It is easy to see that $i \models g \to k$, for $i = 1, 2$, both $\bigcirc(\neg k/\top), \bigcirc(g/k)$ are valid in the model and $1 \models k$. Notice in particular that 1 is the "best" world where "kill" holds and in that world also "killing gently" holds.

We can also verify that the sentences (ii)-(iv) do not derive the obligation to kill. Notice that this claim in **E** is not entailed by what we have just proved. To this purpose we initialise the derivation by $\bigcirc(g/k), \Box(g \to k), k \Rightarrow \bigcirc(k/\top)$ and we get (among others) the following saturated hypersequent:

$$\bigcirc(g/k), \Box(g \to k), k, g \to k, g \Rightarrow \bigcirc(k/\top) \mid \top, \mathcal{B}et\neg\top, g \to k \Rightarrow k, g$$

We get the model $M = (W, \succ, V)$, where W and V are as before (1 and 2 are now constructed using the new hypersequent), but $\succ$ is empty meaning that all worlds are best. Now 2 is a "best" world in an absolute sense (i.e., for $\top$) and k does not hold there. By the evaluation rule (cf. Definition 3), $\bigcirc(k/\top)$ fails both in 1 and 2. Hence killing is not best overall, and you are not obliged to kill.

Acknowledgements. Work funded by the projects FWF M-3240-N and WWTF MA16-028. We thank the anonymous reviewers for their valuable comments.

References

1. Alchourrón, C.: Philosophical foundations of deontic logic and the logic of defeasible conditionals. In: Meyer, J.-J., Wieringa, R. (eds.) Deontic Logic in Computer Science, pp. 43–84. John Wiley & Sons Inc, New York (1993)
2. Åqvist, L.: Deontic logic. In: Gabbay, D., Guenthner, F. (eds.) Handbook of Philosophical Logic, vol. II, pp. 605–714. Springer, Dordrecht (1984). https://doi.org/10.1007/978-94-007-6730-0_1002-1
3. Asher, N., Bonevac, D.: Common sense obligation. In: Nute [20], pp. 159–203
4. Avron, A.: The method of hypersequents in the proof theory of propositional non-classical logics. In Logic: from Foundations to Applications, pp. 1–32. OUP, New York (1996)
5. Benzmüller, C., Farjami, A., Parent, X.: Åqvist's dyadic deontic logic E in HOL. IfCoLog 6, 715–732 (2019)
6. Danielsson, S.: Preference and Obligation. Filosofiska Färeningen, Uppsala (1968)
7. Forrester, J.: Gentle murder, or the adverbial samaritan. J. Phil. 81, 193–197 (1984)
8. Giordano, L., Gliozzi, V., Olivetti, N., Pozzato, G.L.: Analytic tableaux calculi for KLM logics of nonmonotonic reasoning. ACM Trans. Comput. Log. 10(3), 1–47 (2009)
9. Girlando, M., Lellmann, B., Olivetti, N., Pozzato, G.L.: Standard sequent calculi for Lewis' logics of counterfactuals. In Proceedings JELIA, pp. 272–287 (2016)
10. Goble, L.: Axioms for Hansson's dyadic deontic logics. Filosofiska Notiser 6(1), 13–61 (2019)
11. Hansson, B.: An analysis of some deontic logics. Noûs, 3(4), 373–398 (1969)
12. Hilpinen, R. (ed.): Deontic Logic. Reidel, Dordrecht (1971). https://doi.org/10.1007/978-94-010-3146-2
13. Horty, J.: Deontic modals: why abandon the classical semantics? Pac. Philos. Q. 95(4), 424–460 (2014)
14. Kurokawa, H.: Hypersequent calculi for modal logics extending S4. In: Nakano, Y., Satoh, K., Bekki, D. (eds.) JSAI-isAI 2013. LNCS (LNAI), vol. 8417, pp. 51–68. Springer, Cham (2014). https://doi.org/10.1007/978-3-319-10061-6_4
15. Kuznets, R., Lellmann, B.: Grafting hypersequents onto nested sequents. Log. J. IGPL 24(3), 375–423 (2016)
16. Lewis, D.: Counterfactuals. Blackwell, Oxford (1973)
17. Loewer, B., Belzer, M.: Dyadic deontic detachment. Synthese 54, 295–318 (1983)
18. Makinson, D.: Five faces of minimality. Stud. Logica. 52(3), 339–379 (1993)
19. Minc, G.: Some calculi of modal logic. Trudy Mat. Inst. Steklov 98, 88–111 (1968)
20. Nute, D. (ed.): Defeasible Deontic Logic. Kluwer, Dordrecht (1997)
21. Parent, X.: Completeness of Åqvist's systems E and F. Rev. Symb. Log. 8(1), 164–177 (2015)
22. Parent, X.: Preference semantics for Hansson-type dyadic deontic logic: a survey of results. In: Handbook of Deontic Logic and Normative Systems. vol. 2, pp. 7–70. College Publications, London (2021)
23. Prakken, H., Sergot, M.: Dyadic deontic logic and contrary-to-duty obligations. In Nute [20], pp. 223–262
24. Shoham, Y.: Reasoning About Change. MIT Press, Cambridge, MA, USA (1988)
25. Spohn, W.: An analysis of Hansson's dyadic deontic logic. J. Phil. Logic 4(2), 237–252 (1975)

26. J. Tomberlin. Contrary-to-duty imperatives and conditional obligation. Noûs, pp. 357–375 (1981)
27. van Benthem, J., Girard, P., Roy, O.: Everything else being equal: a modal logic for ceteris paribus preferences. J. Phil. Logic **38**(1), 83–125 (2009)
28. van der Torre, L., Tan, Y.-H.: The many faces of defeasibility in defeasible deontic logic. In: Nute [20], pp. 79–121
29. van Fraassen, B.: The logic of conditional obligation. J. Phil. Logic **1**(3/4), 417–438 (1972)

On Normative Reinforcement Learning via Safe Reinforcement Learning

Emery A. Neufeld$^{(\boxtimes)}$, Ezio Bartocci, and Agata Ciabattoni

TU Wien, Vienna, Austria
{emeric.neufeld,ezio.bartocci,agata.ciabattoni}@tuwien.ac.at

Abstract. Reinforcement learning (RL) has proven a successful technique for teaching autonomous agents goal-directed behaviour. As RL agents further integrate with our society, they must learn to comply with ethical, social, or legal norms. Defeasible deontic logics are natural formal frameworks to specify and reason about such norms in a transparent way. However, their effective and efficient integration in RL agents remains an open problem. On the other hand, linear temporal logic (LTL) has been successfully employed to synthesize RL policies satisfying, e.g., safety requirements. In this paper, we investigate the extent to which the established machinery for safe reinforcement learning can be leveraged for directing normative behaviour for RL agents. We analyze some of the difficulties that arise from attempting to represent norms with LTL, provide an algorithm for synthesizing LTL specifications from certain normative systems, and analyze its power and limits with a case study.

1 Introduction

As artificial intelligence (AI) continues to pervade human society, more and more societal roles are prescribed to autonomous agents, and the demand for efficient, adaptable, and safe technology grows. Reinforcement learning (RL) – a machine learning technique that teaches agents optimal policies by assigning rewards and punishments to specific behaviours – has been successfully employed in the training of autonomous agents that exhibit these characteristics. Simultaneously, interest in agents that conform to legal, ethical, and social norms has increased as well, and RL has also been employed for these purposes (see, e.g., [22,26,32]). However, existing approaches to learning compliant behaviour rely on directly punishing individual illegal or unethical behaviours or rewarding praiseworthy ones. This approach is not scalable; in large environments and complex normative systems, specifying non-compliant behaviours individually might not be feasible. Without a way to identify rules and patterns governing compliant behaviour,

This work was supported by the DC-RES run by the TU Wien's Faculty of Informatics and the FH-Technikum Wien and by the project WWTF MA16–028.

R. Aydoğan et al. (Eds.): PRIMA 2022, LNAI 13753, pp. 72–89, 2023.
https://doi.org/10.1007/978-3-031-21203-1_5

the comprehensive numerical assignment of rewards and punishments to specific events can be extremely tedious (if possible at all), not to mention lacking in understandability and therefore transparency.

Normative systems are best represented by deontic logics, which capture the essential logical features of obligations and related concepts. Many such logics have been introduced; among them, Defeasible Deontic Logic (DDL) provides a computationally feasible yet expressive framework to specify and reason about norms in a modular and transparent way [14,15].

In [20,21] the authors use DDL (and its theorem prover SPINdle [19]) in combination with RL; they develop a normative supervisor that prevents a RL agent from selecting actions that would lead to an immediate violation of certain norms. Norms and the current state of the agent's environment are encoded as DDL rules, and a theorem prover is used to derive a set of compliant actions (or, if none exists, a set of 'lesser evil' actions). However, the use of a theorem prover introduces computational overhead during the enactment of the agent's policy while the complete decoupling of the policy from the normative reasoning prevents the agent from thinking ahead and taking steps to avoid undesirable situations. A better integration of RL and DDL (and deontic logics in general) seems out of the reach, with current tools.

Meanwhile, in the last decade there has been significant progress with the use of linear temporal logic (LTL) for synthesizing RL policies under safety constraints, e.g. [2,16,18,27,31]. For instance, an emerging approach in safe RL is the use of *shielding* [2,18], which involves synthesizing from a requirement expressed in the *safety fragment* of LTL a reactive system called a *shield* that lets the agent act freely, provided safety specifications are not violated.

The main question we investigate in this paper is whether the established machinery for safe reinforcement learning can be used for directing normative behaviour for RL agents, which amounts to understanding which normative systems can be represented in LTL and how. This has been a debated topic in the literature, where diverging opinions can be found (e.g. [1,10,12,23]). Our answer is affirmative, albeit with qualifications. We first clarify what we mean by "representing norms with LTL" and discuss two different approaches: (i) *explicit*/syntactic representation (constructing an LTL operator that directly represents an obligation in the way deontic logic does) that matches the approach in [10], and (ii) *implicit*/semantic representation (describing non-violating patterns of behaviour with LTL formulae) which matches the approach in [1]. We prove the impossibility of the former, and elucidate the limitations on the latter.

We propose an algorithm to synthesize in the safety fragment of LTL implicit representations of normative systems from the rule-based representations of these systems in a defeasible deontic logic. The algorithm works in the presence of defeasible mechanisms (e.g. prioritized norms) and constitutive norms [4], but encounters problems due to imperfect accounting for actions, and obligations which come into force when another obligation is violated (contrary-to-duty obligations). Our findings are tested on the Merchant – an RL agent playing a resource-collecting game we created. The game is enriched with two normative systems (simulating "ethical" rules) that we synthesize in LTL; the behaviour complying with these specifications is compared with the behaviour elicited by the normative supervisor of [20,21], which can handle contrary-to-duty norms.

2 Preliminaries

2.1 Safe Reinforcement Learning with LTL

Linear Temporal Logic (LTL) [24] extends classical propositional logic with the temporal operators $X\phi$ ("ϕ next") and $\phi\,U\psi$ ("ϕ until ψ"); using them we can define $F\phi$ ("eventually ϕ") as $F\phi \equiv \top U\phi$, and $G\phi$ ("always ϕ") as $G\phi \equiv \neg F\neg\phi$.

LTL formulas are specified over a set of atomic propositions AP, and the semantics are defined with respect to a set of states S and a labelling function $L : S \rightarrow 2^{AP}$. In particular, the satisfiability of an LTL formula is defined over paths, or infinite sequences of states $\sigma = s_0, s_1, s_2, \dots$.

For the semantics, we introduce the notation $\sigma[i] = s_i$ and $\sigma[i..] = s_i, s_{i+1}, \dots$. The semantics for the propositional part is defined as usual: $\sigma \vDash p$ iff $p \in L(\sigma[0])$; $\sigma \vDash \neg\phi$ iff $\sigma \nvDash \phi$; and $\sigma \vDash \phi \wedge \psi$ iff $\sigma \vDash \phi$ and $\sigma \vDash \psi$. For the primitive temporal operators: $\sigma \vDash X\phi$ iff $\sigma[1..] \vDash \phi$, and $\sigma \vDash \phi\,U\psi$ iff $\exists j \geq 0$ such that $\sigma[j..] \vDash \psi$ and for all $0 \leq i < j$, $\sigma[i..] \vDash \phi$.

LTL is a popular tool for system specification, and has been used extensively for specifying safety-related properties. The fragment of LTL used for this purpose is the U-free subset of LTL formulas (that is, formulas using only the operators X, G, and F), known as *the safety fragment*.

Techniques for generating control policies for reinforcement learning (RL) agents which maximize the probability of satisfying a given LTL formula have been extensively studied, and used, e.g., to synthesize policies which operate with certain safety properties [2,16,18,27,31]. This is done within the context of a labelled Markov Decision Process (MDP):

Definition 1 (Labelled MDP). A labelled MDP is a tuple $\langle S, A, P, R, L\rangle$, where S is a set of states, A is a set of actions, $P : S \times A \times S \rightarrow [0,1]$ is a probability function that gives the probability $P(s, a, s')$ of transitioning from state s to state s' after performing action a, $R : S \times A \rightarrow \mathbb{R}$ is a reward function over states and actions, and $L : S \rightarrow 2^{AP}$ is a labelling function.

The goal of RL is to find a policy $\pi : S \rightarrow A$ which designates optimal behaviour for the agent. When learning within a labelled MDP to satisfy an LTL specification ϕ, this involves learning a policy π^* that generates a path $\sigma^{\pi^*} = s_0, s_1, s_2, \dots$ such that $\sigma^{\pi^*} \vDash \phi$ with maximal probability.

As [9] notes, the standard approach to learning policies satisfying an LTL formula ϕ is to translate it into a deterministic or semi-deterministic automaton (many different algorithms for this exist, e.g. [7,29]) that takes the label $L(s_i) \subseteq$

AP of each state s_i the agent enters as its input alphabet. The next step is to relate the automaton to a given MDP (usually as a product MDP with the state space $S^{\times} = S \times Q$, where Q is the set of automaton states), and then synthesize a policy that maximizes the probability of hitting the set of accepting end states corresponding to the automaton's acceptance conditions. Another approach is *shielding* [2,18]. From a simplified MDP abstracted from the states of the environment and the behaviour of "adversaries" within the environment, action valuations can be computed for each state, giving the probability that the agent will violate the specification from that state [18]. A shield can then be computed that will prevent the agent from taking actions with high probability of leading to a violation. The shield can intervene before (*pre-shielding*) or after (*post-shielding*) the RL agent chooses an action. In the former case, the shield provides the agent only with the safe actions, while in the latter case the shield monitors the actions chosen by the agent and corrects them only when their actuation would cause a safety violation.

2.2 Norms and Normative Reasoning

A normative system is a set of norms. We consider two kinds of norms, which both present as conditional rules: *regulative* and *constitutive norms*. The former describe obligations, prohibitions and permissions that apply in certain contexts. The latter take the form "X counts as Y in context C", or $\mathbf{C}(X, Y | C)$, for some concepts X,Y [4]; they are used to define what Searle [28] calls *institutional facts* from brute (or other institutional) facts.

Deontic logic is a popular tool for formalizing normative reasoning; most deontic logics extend classical logic with deontic operators. The primitive operator is typically taken to be obligation; we will work with dyadic obligations of the form $\mathbf{O}(p|q)$, which means "when q is true, p is obligatory". Generally, when we have $q \wedge \mathbf{O}(p|q)$, we can infer the unary obligation $\mathbf{O}(p)$, or "p is obligatory" (this is called factual detachment). Prohibitions can be defined as obligations of a negative statement (that is $\mathbf{F}(p|q) := \mathbf{O}(\neg p|q)$) and weak permission as the dual operator to obligation (that is, $\mathbf{P}_w(p|q) := \neg \mathbf{O}(\neg p|q)$). As the term *weak permission* suggests, many deontic logics also possess a notion of *strong permission* $\mathbf{P}_s$, which acts as an exception to an obligation or prohibition.

For the sake of simplicity, instead of entire normative systems, we discuss only *single* regulative norms, for now. Notice there is no inherent temporal dimension to the obligation operator; we will take all obligations to be what are called *maintenance obligations* in [13]. The violation condition for a maintenance obligation $\mathbf{O}(p|q)$ is that there is a point in time in which $\mathbf{O}(p) \wedge \neg p$ is true. If a path contains no such points in time we call that path compliant. We formalize below properties of obligations and compliance to them in the context of LTL semantics, with respect to a set of paths Σ.

Definition 2 (Violation and Compliance). A state s_i ($i \in \mathbb{N}$) violates $\mathbf{O}(p|q)$ if q is true at s_i but p is not. A path $\sigma \in \Sigma$ violates $\mathbf{O}(p|q)$ ($\sigma \nvDash_{compl} \mathbf{O}(p|q)$) if it contains a violating state; σ complies with $\mathbf{O}(p|q)$ ($\sigma \vDash_{compl} \mathbf{O}(p|q)$) otherwise.

Note that the negation of an obligation – "p is not obligatory" or "$\neg p$ is permitted" – cannot be violated; in other words, permissions are not violable.

Defeasible Deontic Logic (DDL). Introduced in [15], DDL allows reasoning with literals (propositional atoms p and their negations $\neg p$), modal literals (literals with a modality, e.g. $\mathbf{O}(p)$), and rules defined over them. Rules can be strict ($\rightarrow$), defeasible ($\Rightarrow$), or defeaters ($\rightsquigarrow$). For strict rules, the consequent always follows from the antecedent, while the consequents of defeasible rules follow from the antecedent, unless there is evidence to the contrary. This evidence can come in the form of conflicting rules or defeaters, which prevent a conclusion from being reached by a defeasible rule. Rules, representing norms, can be constitutive or regulative. For example, if we have a dyadic obligation $\mathbf{O}(p|q)$ that we want to hold defeasibly, we would write $q \Rightarrow_O p$.

A *defeasible theory* [11] is a collection of facts F, together with a normative system defined in the language above (consisting of sets of constitutive and regulative rules) and a superiority relation over conflicting rules.

The theorem prover for DDL, SPINdle [19], takes a defeasible theory as input and outputs a set of literals tagged to indicate whether they are provable or not. The derived conclusions can be *negative* or *positive*, *definite* or *defeasible*, *factual* or *deontic*. We only reference defeasible conclusions in this paper: the tag $+\partial_*$ indicates a defeasibly provable conclusion, which is not refuted by any facts or conflicting rules, and is implied by some undefeated rule; meanwhile, $-\partial_*$ indicates defeasibly refutable conclusions which are conclusions for which their complemented literal is defeasibly provable, or an exhaustive search for a constructive proof for the literal fails. For factual conclusions, $* := C$; for deontic conclusions, $* := O$. For example, if we can conclude defeasibly that $\mathbf{O}(p)$, we would get $+\partial_O p$. We say that a violation has been committed when we can prove $+\partial_O p, -\partial_C p$ (that is, we can prove $\mathbf{O}(p)$ but cannot prove p).

3 Representing Norms in LTL

Whether or not norms can be represented with LTL has been a matter of controversy. The precise meaning of "representing norms" has an impact on the nature of the question. There are two distinct approaches that we consider here, which we refer to as explicit representation and implicit representation of norms. By *explicit representation*, we mean the construction of an LTL operator that behaves as an obligation; [10,12] conjecture that this cannot be done. With *implicit representation* we refer to the formal specification of non-violating paths; this is the idea put forth, e.g., in [1], arguing against the conjecture of [10].

Below, we will discuss why the former approach is impossible and introduce a synthesis algorithm for the latter, while pointing out its intrinsic limits.

3.1 Explicit Representation

The case study in [10] shows why translating the statement "it is obligatory that p" as $G(p) := $ "p is always true" is problematic – in part because the dual operator of obligation, weak permission, is semantically incompatible with the dual operator of G (i.e., F, or "eventually") – but we will show that any such translation will prove so. When we talk about explicit representation of norms, we are referring to the following claim:

Conjecture 1. (1) we can construct an LTL operator $O(p, q)$ that directly represents the proposition $\mathbf{O}(p|q)$ (that is, "p is obligatory when q"), such that (2) for any path $\sigma \in \Sigma$, $\sigma \vDash_{compl} \mathbf{O}(p|q)$ if and only if $\sigma \vDash O(p, q)$.

As it turns out, this conjecture is quite unreasonable, specifically if we make the sensible assumption that within the environment we are working in, there exists some obligation with which we can comply. More formally (by $\mathcal{O}_{AP}$ we denote the set of all obligations defined over the atomic propositions in AP):

Property 1. For a set AP associated with a labelled MDP, there exists an obligation $\mathbf{O}(p|q) \in \mathcal{O}_{AP}$ such that there exists a $\sigma \in \Sigma$ such that $\sigma \vDash_{compl} \mathbf{O}(p|q)$.

Theorem 1. *If Property 1 holds, Conjecture 1 must be false.*

Proof. Suppose both Property 1 and Conjecture 1 hold. By Property 1 there is an obligation $\mathbf{O}(p|q)$ for which there is a $\sigma \in \Sigma$ such that $\sigma \vDash_{compl} \mathbf{O}(p|q)$. Then by Conjecture 1(1), there is an LTL operator O such that $\sigma \vDash O(p, q)$. Since we are directly representing "p is obligatory when q" with $O(p, q)$, its negation $\neg O(p, q)$ should represent "p is not obligatory when q". However $\sigma \vDash_{compl} \neg\mathbf{O}(p|q)$, as this formula (which is a permission) cannot be violated. Thus, $\sigma \vDash \neg O(p, q)$ must hold. Hence $\sigma \vDash O(p, q) \wedge \neg O(p, q)$, and so $\sigma \vDash \bot$, a contradiction. $\qquad \square$

Remark 1. In the case of compliance (which differs from truth), $\sigma \vDash_{compl} \phi$ does not imply $\sigma \nvDash_{compl} \neg\phi$. It cannot be true simultaneously that $\mathbf{O}(p|q)$ and $\mathbf{P}_w(\neg p|q)$, but we *can* find a path that complies with both norms posed individually, because the latter cannot, in fact, be violated.

Since point (2) of Conjecture 1 is crucial to this exercise, we can conclude that it is point (1) that should be abandoned. We discuss this in the next section.

3.2 Implicit Representation

We now turn to what we call the implicit representation of norms in LTL. To do so, we consider the notion of a *compliance specification*:

Definition 3 (Compliance Specification). A *compliance specification* is an LTL formula $\phi_{\mathbf{O}p|q}$ such that for a path $\sigma \in \Sigma$, $\sigma \vDash_{compl} \mathbf{O}(p|q)$ iff $\sigma \vDash \phi_{\mathbf{O}p|q}$. A compliance specification ϕ_{NS} for a normative system NS is an LTL formula such that $\sigma \vDash \phi_{NS}$ iff no norm in NS is violated.

With this definition in mind, our revised claim (extended to entire normative systems) is this:

Conjecture 2. (1) There is a compliance specification for any obligation, and (2) there is a compliance specification for any normative system NS.

Remark 2. The second part of the claim is relative to the limitations in the expressive power of LTL, which cannot specify *every* path (see, e.g., [17]).

There are some immediate problems with this approach. Perhaps the most obvious is the question of how we get ϕ_{NS} from a normative system. In the easy case of a single obligation $\mathbf{O}(p|q)$, the appropriate translation is $\phi_{Op|q} := G(q \to p)$, or "always p if q". Note that this is different from the translation of the norm $\mathbf{O}(p)$ to $G(p)$, as discussed in [10]; $G(q \to p)$ is not meant to stand in for "p is obligatory when q"; rather, it characterizes all paths that comply with the obligation. This is essentially the approach taken in [1].

Another issue is the inherent defeasibility of normative systems, which might appear while, e.g., dealing with (and resolving) conflict between norms, and in the presence of strong permissions. The latter are often characterized as conditional exceptions to obligations. For the former, various mechanisms for prioritizing some obligations over others (e.g., the superiority relation in [14] and the hierarchy of norms from [3]) are common and similar to the case with strong permission, the lower priority norm will be suspended temporarily while the other norm is in force.

LTL does not allow for defeasibility in the specifications expressed; however, we can encode exceptions into the conditions under which the norms are in force, as was done in the second formalization considered in [10]. For example, instead of an obligation $\mathbf{O}(p|\top)$ with a strong permission $\mathbf{P}_s(\neg p|q)$, we could use a single obligation $\mathbf{O}(p|\neg q)$. This approach involves taking into account all exceptions to a norm when specifying it, which might be tedious, but not impossible. The task of specifying ϕ_{NS}, however, becomes more difficult as the normative system of interest becomes more complex. Below, we provide a framework for accomplishing this automatically.

Synthesis of Specifications. Given an environment modelled as a labelled MDP and a normative system formalized with deontic logic, we introduce a brute force algorithm for synthesizing compliance specifications expressed as LTL formulas within the safety fragment. The specifications could then be used to synthesize compliant policies with a safe RL technique such as shielding [2, 18]. As it bases its output on Defeasible Deontic Logic (DDL) conclusions, the algorithm has a defeasibility mechanism built in, along with the capability to take constitutive norms into account while reasoning. The algorithm takes a normative system NS expressed in DDL[1] and set of atomic propositions AP associated with the labelling function of a labelled MDP. NS, Γ represents the defeasible theory created when we use $\Gamma \subseteq AP$ as the set of facts F and the norms from NS as rules.

The algorithm checks whether a state violates NS, which happens when we can prove $\mathbf{O}(p)$ (i.e., $+\partial_O p$ in DDL notation) and cannot prove p (i.e. $-\partial_C p$);

---

[1] Any defeasible deontic logic equipped with a theorem prover could in theory be used.

```
input  : AP, NS
output : badStates
begin
    badStates ← ∅;
    for Γ ∈ 2^AP do
        Compute obliged = {p|NS, Γ ⊢ +∂_O p};
        if ∃p ∈ obliged s.t. NS, Γ ⊢ −∂_C p then
            badStates.add(Γ);
        end
    end
    return badStates
end
```

Algorithm 1: FindBadStates

if it does, the state is added to *badStates*. From the output set *badStates*, we can create an LTL compliance specification insisting that the agent stays out of states characterized by these sets of labels:

$$\Phi := \bigwedge_{\Gamma \in badStates} G(\neg \bigwedge_{p \in \Gamma} p) \tag{1}$$

Theorem 2. *For any labelled MDP with a set of states S associated with a labelling function $L : S \to 2^{AP}$, Φ is a compliance specification for NS (provided NS references only atoms from AP or defined from them via constitutive norms).*

Proof. Suppose that a path $\sigma = s_0, s_1, ...$ is not compliant with all norms in NS; i.e., there is an s_i such that it is the case that $\mathbf{O}(p) \wedge \neg p$ for a $\mathbf{O}(p)$; in this case, we will have $NS, L(s_i) \vdash +\partial_O p, -\partial_C p$. So $p \in obliged$ in Algorithm 1, and since $NS, L(s_i) \vdash -\partial_C p$, $L(s_i) \in badStates$. Then Φ is a conjunct that includes $G(\neg \bigwedge_{q \in L(s_i)} q)$. Then, since at s_i it is the case that $\bigwedge_{q \in L(s_i)} q$, σ does not satisfy Φ. Suppose then that Φ is not satisfied by $\sigma = s_0, s_1, ...$ Then there is some s_i such that $L(s_i) \in badStates$, which means that for some p, $NS, L(s_i) \vdash +\partial_O p$, but $NS, L(s_i) \vdash -\partial_C p$. So there is a violation in σ. □

The above algorithm however does not account for norms over actions. Normative systems regularly reference actions or events that cannot be captured by state labels – which is all we have access to in the context of a labelled MDP. As a result, there could be states in *badStates* that can actually be compliant provided the correct action is taken, and states not in *badStates* that could result in a violation if the wrong action is taken. E.g., if we had a state where *red_light* was true (indicating that we are at a red light) and we had an obligation $\mathbf{O}(stop|red\_light)$, this would have ended up in *badStates* after Algorithm 1 because we could not have proven *stop* even though we can prove $\mathbf{O}(stop)$; alternatively, if we are in a state where *driving* is true, and we have a prohibition $\mathbf{F}(drink|driving)$, this would not have ended up in *badStates*; however, if we perform action *drink* while in this state, we are violating the prohibition.

To remedy this, we introduce Algorithm 2. We reference something new there: *transitions*, which are ordered triples $tr := (tr_{act}, tr_{init}, tr_{next})$, where tr_{act} is an action label, tr_{init} an "initial signature" (an expression containing only atoms in AP that describes the initial conditions under which the action can be completed), and tr_{next} a "next signature" (an expression containing only atoms in AP that describes the conditions resulting from performing the action). The algorithm will output a modified set of *badStates*, as well as two new sets: *mandatoryActs* and *prohibitedActs* whose elements are pairs of $\Gamma \in 2^{AP}$ and some tr from *transitions*.

---

input : *AP, transitions, NS, badStates*
output: *badStates, mandatoryActs, prohibitedActs*
begin
    $mandatoryActs \leftarrow \langle \, , \, \rangle$;
    $prohibitedActs \leftarrow \langle \, , \, \rangle$;
    for $\Gamma \in 2^{AP}$ **do**
        for $tr \in transitions$ **do**
            Compute $obliged = \{p|NS, \Gamma \cup \{tr_{act}\} \vdash +\partial_O p\}$;
            if $\forall p \in obliged$ s.t. $NS, \Gamma \cup \{tr_{act}\} \vdash +\partial_C p$ & $\Gamma \in badStates$ **then**
                $badStates.remove(\Gamma)$;
                $mandatoryActs.add(\langle \Gamma, \, tr \rangle)$;
            end
            else
                if $\exists p \in obliged$ s.t. $\Gamma \cup \{tr_{act}\} \vdash -\partial_C p$ & $\Gamma \notin badStates$ **then**
                    $prohibitedActs.add(\langle \Gamma, \, tr \rangle)$;
                end
            end
        end
    end
    return *badStates, mandatoryActs, prohibitedActs*
end

Algorithm 2: ClassifyActions

This algorithm does two things. It constructs a set *mandatoryActs* which contains actions that, if performed, actually constitute compliance despite the fact that the state the action is performed in was in *badStates*. Algorithm 2 removes this state from *badStates* and adds it to *mandatoryActs*. We create the following specification for *mandatoryActs*:

$$\bigwedge_{\langle \Gamma, tr \rangle \in mandatoryActs} G(\bigwedge \Gamma \to (tr_{init} \wedge X(tr_{next}))) \tag{2}$$

The second thing the algorithm does is construct *prohibitedActs*. These are actions that, if performed in an otherwise compliant state, will result in non-compliance. For these we construct the following specification:

$$\bigwedge_{\langle \Gamma, tr \rangle \in prohibitedActs} G(\bigwedge \Gamma \to \neg(tr_{init} \wedge X(tr_{next}))) \tag{3}$$

Though we have presented Algorithms 1 and 2 separately for didactic purposes, they can be compiled into a single process (and we implemented them this way, see footnote 2).

Remark 3. Since DDL conclusions can be computed in time linear with respect to the size of the theory [14] (which does not change), Algorithms 1 and 2 have both an exponential time complexity. However, despite their high complexity, these algorithms need only be executed once, before training.

Potential Issues. We discuss below two limitations of our algorithms, which will be demonstrated in Sect. 4.

(a) **Imperfect translation from actions to state transitions.** We cannot get the same guarantees from Algorithm 2 that we got for Algorithm 1; though we will be able to account for all non-compliant states and courses of action, whether or not we can effectively represent those actions will depend on the setting. Indeed, we might not be able to describe all state transitions associated with an action as a single formula, and even if we manage to, we might end up describing other actions that cause the same transition. This can happen when different actions can lead to the same state. We demonstrate this issue in the case study we present in Sect. 4.1 (the extension).

Setting aside this potential issue with actions, the above algorithms synthesize compliance specifications for most normative systems containing conflicting norms, strong permission, and constitutive norms; however, another problem remains: (b) **Handling Contrary-to-duty Obligations (CTD).** These are obligations which come into force when another obligation is violated. One of the classic CTD scenarios from the deontic logic literature is the "gentle murder" [8]; the scenario consists of two obligations: "you ought not kill" and "if you kill, you ought to kill gently". That is: ideally, we never kill, but if we must, we should do it gently. With this scenario in mind, we revisit the concept of compliance and give the following definitions inspired by the discussion in [10] and its addressal in [1], and extend Definition 2 to entire normative systems.

Definition 4. A path σ is fully compliant with a normative system NS if for every obligation $O \in NS$, $\sigma \vDash_{compl} O$. σ is weakly compliant with NS if for every obligation $O_1 := \mathbf{O}(p|q) \in NS$ such that $\sigma \nvDash_{compl} O_1$, there exists another obligation $O_2 := \mathbf{O}(r|s)$ such that $s \leftrightarrow \neg p \wedge q$ and $\sigma \vDash_{compl} O_2$.

In the above definition, O_1 is a primary obligation that is violated, and O_2 is the associated CTD obligation. Note also that if a path is fully compliant, it is weakly compliant as well. So we have two choices for specifying compliance – full or weak. However, both fail to capture the subtleties of CTD reasoning. The below propositions apply to normative systems with CTDs (and without obligations conflicting with the primary and contrary-to-duty obligations):

Proposition 1. *Given a normative system NS with primary obligation $O_1 := \mathbf{O}(p|q) \in NS$ and CTD obligation $O_2 := \mathbf{O}(r|s)$ (where $s \leftrightarrow \neg p \wedge q$), the full compliance specification ϕ_{NS} for NS is semantically equivalent to the full compliance specification $\phi_{NS'}$ for $NS' = NS \setminus \{O_2\}$.*

Proof. Suppose $\sigma \vDash \phi_{NS}$; then since O_2 is not triggered at any point in σ, its removal cannot trigger any extant norms in NS'. So since for all $O_i \in NS'$, $\sigma \vDash_{compl} O_i$, $\sigma \vDash \phi_{NS'}$. For the converse direction assume $\sigma \vDash \phi_{NS'}$; for every $O_i \in NS'$, $\sigma \vDash_{compl} O_i$. Since $\sigma \vDash_{compl} O_1$ it is never the case that $q \wedge \neg p$. Then since $s \leftrightarrow \neg p \wedge q$, it is never the case that s, and O_2 is never triggered, so it cannot be violated. So σ complies with every obligation in NS and $\sigma \vDash \phi_{NS}$. $\square$

Proposition 1 makes intuitive sense; if we want full compliance with the "gentle murder" scenario, for instance, we will simply not murder at all, making the obligation to murder gently superfluous. In other words, there is no point in specifying O_2. We run into a similar case when we look at weak compliance.

Proposition 2. *Take NS, O_1 and O_2 as in Proposition 1 and assume in addition that there are no norms in NS that are triggered by $\boldsymbol{O}(p)$, and O_2 is not itself the primary obligation of a CTD. Then the weak compliance specification ϕ_{NS} for NS is semantically equivalent to the weak compliance specification $\phi_{NS'}$ for $NS' = NS \setminus \{O_1\}$.*

Proof. Suppose $\sigma \vDash \phi_{NS}$; since O_1 is not a strong permission, its removal does not trigger any extant obligations in NS'. So $\sigma \vDash \phi_{NS'}$. Then assume $\sigma \vDash \phi_{NS'}$. As there are no obligations in NS (or NS') that depend on the triggering of $\boldsymbol{O}(p)$, the only obligations that may be violated in NS have associated CTD obligations that are complied with; this includes O_1, as O_2 (which is in NS') was not violated. So $\sigma \vDash \phi_{NS}$. $\square$

In other words, with the exception of the specific case where some obligation is only triggered when the primary obligation is, the primary obligation has no effect when we are discussing weak compliance.

If a normative system *does* have CTD obligations, our algorithms will simply return LTL formulas that specify adherence to the primary obligation (i.e. it only considers *full compliance*). Alternatively, as implied by Property 2 we in some cases can remove the primary obligation to model weak compliance. The use of weak compliance works in the legal compensation-based scenario discussed in [10] (for which full and weak compliance are both represented in LTL in [1]), but not in the case of the moral imperative in [8]. The statement "if you kill, you ought to kill gently" should not give us license to murder, so long as we do so gently.

4   Case Study: The Merchant

We present a case study that illustrates the use of the synthesis algorithms and their discussed limitations, which stem from the use of LTL to implicitly represent norms and their deployment in conjunction with RL agents.

The case study is a simple game[2] we have created, where the agent, a merchant, must travel through a forest (divided into cells, where each cell can contain

---

[2] An implementation of Algorithms 1 and 2 can be found here: https://github.com/lexeree/normative-player-characters.

rocks, ore, trees, or wood) and extract and collect *resources* (wood extracted from trees, or ore from rocks). The goal is to make it to the market on the other side of the map with items to sell. There are dangerous areas where the agent will be attacked by bandits, and the agent has three options: it can fight (which ends the attack), negotiate (which entails giving the bandits the agent's inventory, and also ends the attack), or try to escape (which has a high risk of failing; in the case of failure, the agent receives damage, and the attack continues). The agent has a total of seven actions available to it: moving north, south, east, or west, fighting, extracting resources (*extract*), picking up resources (*pickup*), and unloading its inventory (*unload*). The agent is not allowed to backtrack; if it leaves a cell, it is not allowed to return to it in the next move.

We employ a fully deterministic version of this environment (the probability of escape failing is 1) with the layout depicted in Fig. 1(a). The merchant is rewarded whenever it extracts or picks up resources, and then once more at the end when it delivers them to the market – we train the RL agent based on these rewards. The optimal behaviour this results in is pictured in Fig. 1(b).

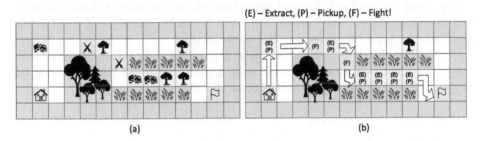

Fig. 1. (a) shows the 'Merchant' environment. Dangerous areas are red, and areas with resources are green. (b) shows the optimal path through the environment. (Color figure online)

In our merchant environment MDP, states are labelled with where the agent is, its immediate surroundings, and what it has in its inventory. In other words, a state can be given the following labels in AP: "attacked", "has_{wood, ore}", "{at, north, south, east, west}_{tree, wood, rock, ore, danger}", and "at_collected", which refers to cells from which the agent has extracted and picked up resources; this label is only true after the agent has picked up a resource, and before it moves on to the next cell. States where, e.g., *at_tree* holds are states where the agent is in the same cell as a tree; if the action *extract* is performed when *at_tree* holds, then *at_wood* holds in the next state. Similarly, when *pickup* is performed while *at_wood*, *at_collected* holds in the next state and the agent *has_wood*. Only one tree/wood or rock/ore can be in each cell.

Utilizing these labels and the available actions, we construct below two normative systems, simulating "ethical" norms. Algorithms 1 and 2 are used to generate LTL specifications for these systems. Our environment can be modelled as a labelled MDP, so we are able to do regular model-free RL (in particular, Q-learning [30]), or use techniques for learning policies constrained by LTL specifications, such as shielding [2,18] or LCRL [16]. We compare[3] the specified compliant behaviours with the behaviour elicited by an existing framework (the normative supervisor in [20], which uses a mechanism similar to pre-shielding that filters out undesirable actions from the agent's arsenal).

4.1   The Environmentally Friendly Merchant

This normative system includes constitutive norms and strong permissions. It forces the merchant to follow the "ethical" behaviour of being environmentally-friendly, that is, not doing something explicitly harmful to the environment ($\Rightarrow_C env$, in DDL), which translates into the norm $\mathbf{O}(env|\top)$ ($\Rightarrow_O env$ in DDL); Deforestation is an activity considered *not* environmentally friendly, leading to the constitutive norm $\mathbf{C}(deforest, \neg env|\top)$ ($deforest \rightarrow_C \neg env$). For now we will look at an initial normative system that asserts that collecting wood counts as deforestation, i.e. $\mathbf{C}(pickup, deforest|at\_wood)$ ($at\_wood, pickup \rightarrow_C deforest$). However, an exception is made; the agent is allowed to pick up wood if it does not already have any wood in its inventory, $\mathbf{P}_s(pickup|\neg has\_wood)$ ($\neg has\_wood \Rightarrow_P pickup$). We will know that the agent obeyed these norms as well as engaged in optimal behaviour if there is exactly one piece of wood in the agent's inventory when it reaches the marketplace.

We will need to translate the action *pickup* into a state transition in order to synthesize a compliance specification with Algorithms 1 and 2; we use at_wood as the initial condition and $at\_collected$ as the next condition and get

$$G(at\_wood \ \land \ has\_wood \ \rightarrow \ \neg(at\_wood \ \land \ X(at\_collected)) \quad (4)$$

This compliance specification is made over actions in $prohibitedActs$, specifying that the agent is only allowed to perform *pickup* with wood when it does not already have wood in its possession. Though we do not mention *pickup* in the specification, it is clear that it is the action *pickup* that is being prevented; if the agent is in a cell with a piece of wood, the only way it can transition into a state where $at\_collected$ is true is to pick up that wood.

The optimal behaviour compliant with this specification matches the behaviour induced by limiting the agent with the normative supervisor (see Fig. 2(a)) under these same norms.

Notice that the agent still extracts the wood, even though it cannot pick it up; that is because during training, the agent still gets a small reward, even for just extracting the wood.

A More Complex Variant. We assert now that even if the wood is not being removed from the forest, cutting down trees still counts as deforestation; i.e., we add a new constitutive norm, $\mathbf{C}(extract, deforest|at\_tree)$ ($at\_tree, extract \rightarrow_C$

---

[3]   The LTL specifications have not been implemented as shields, since the shielding tool TEMPEST [25] is still under development. We instead manually chose optimal paths from among those paths obeying the compliance specifications.

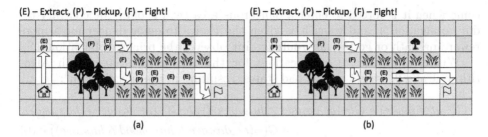

Fig. 2. Compliant journeys for both implementations of the environmentally friendly merchant.

deforest). Additionally, we account for including *extract* in the action *deforest* by adding a new strong permission; if the agent is permitted to pick up wood, it is also permitted to extract wood: $\mathbf{P}_s(pickup) \rightarrow \mathbf{P}_s(extract)$, extending the earlier strong permission to *pickup* over this new form of deforestation.

This normative system further complicates the constitutive norms, and presents the same challenge of a permission being implied by another permission that is seen in [10]. When we synthesize it, we need to translate the action *extract* as well. We take *at_tree* as the initial condition, and *at_wood* as the next condition. When we use Algorithms 1 and 2 to synthesize a specification, we get:

$$G(at\_tree \wedge has\_wood \rightarrow \neg(at\_tree \wedge X(at\_wood))$$
$$\wedge\, G(at\_wood \wedge has\_wood \rightarrow \neg(at\_wood \wedge X(at\_collected))) \quad (5)$$

These are again specifications made over actions in *prohibitedActs*, and serve to prevent the agent from extracting wood from a tree and picking that wood up when the agent has wood in its inventory. We can see how they direct the agent to extract and pick up from only one tree in Fig. 2(b), again matching the behaviour induced by the normative supervisor.

However, this normative system falls prey to the lack of behavioural guarantees discussed in Sect. 3.2; the translation of the action *extract* with wood as *at_tree* $\wedge X(at\_wood)$ creates a compliance specification that is too broad. If we consider the possibility that there could be a cell with wood already present somewhere in the forest, this specification would prevent us from entering that cell if it is adjacent to a cell with a tree. In other words, this specification could result in us prohibiting an action beyond extracting wood from a tree.

4.2   The Pacifist Merchant

This time we require the merchant to be "pacifist": the agent should avoid dangerous areas, $\mathbf{F}(at\_danger|\top)$, but if it *is* in danger, its response should be to *negotiate*, $\mathbf{O}(negotiate|at\_danger)$. Bribing the bandits during an attack counts as negotiating, $\mathbf{C}(unload, negotiate|at\_danger)$.

This normative system contains a contrary-to-duty obligation, and a simple structure of constitutive norms. The biggest test of the agent's behaviour will come when it is forced to enter a dangerous area (will it obey the contrary-to-duty obligation?), and when it is given the choice to enter danger for a more rewarding path or go the safe route (will it observe the primary obligation?).

When we synthesize specifications for this normative system with Algorithms 1 and 2, we get several bad states, resulting in the specification[4]:

$$G(\neg at\_danger) \wedge G(\neg(at\_danger \wedge has\_wood)) \wedge G(\neg(at\_danger \wedge has\_ore))$$
$$\wedge G(\neg(at\_danger \wedge has\_wood \wedge has\_ore)) \quad (6)$$

It is clear that this will result in the merchant being unable to leave its home area because to do so it ends up in a situation where it has no choice but to enter a dangerous area; clearly, these specifications are too restrictive?).

We now turn to weak compliance instead. We remove the primary obligation (cfr. Property 2) and run the synthesis algorithms to get the following specification[5]:

$$G(at\_danger \rightarrow (\neg empty \wedge X(empty)))$$
$$\wedge G(at\_danger \wedge has\_wood \rightarrow (\neg empty \wedge X(empty)))$$
$$\wedge G(at\_danger \wedge has\_ore \rightarrow (\neg empty \wedge X(empty)))$$
$$\wedge G(at\_danger \wedge has\_wood \wedge has\_ore \rightarrow (\neg empty \wedge X(empty))) \quad (7)$$

where $\neg empty := has\_wood \vee has\_ore$, so the initial and next conditions for *unload* are $\neg empty$ and $empty$ respectively. We can see that this specification derived from *mandatoryActs* does not prevent us from entering the dangerous areas at all, so the optimal path under these conditions will lead through both dangerous areas (see Fig. 3(a)).

We implemented this normative system with the normative supervisor, which instead achieves the desired behaviour (Fig. 3(b)).

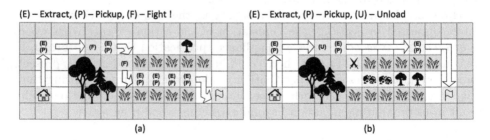

Fig. 3. (a) the optimal path the agent can take while adhering to Spec. 7. (b) The path taken by the agent while under the influence of the normative supervisor.

---

[4] Note that Spec. (6) is semantically equivalent to $G(\neg at\_danger)$.

[5] Note that Spec. (7) is semantically equivalent to $G(at\_danger \rightarrow (\neg empty \wedge X(empty)))$.

5   Conclusion

We investigated the problem of imposing normative constraints on autonomous agents that use RL. Since the current state-of-the-art tools limit the practical integration of normative reasoning into RL, we examined the question of whether we could achieve this goal by leveraging the well-established machinery for safe reinforcement learning that uses the safety fragment of LTL. While discussing the different ways norms could be represented in LTL and their feasibility, we concluded that compliance specifications in LTL constitute a viable option, gave algorithms for synthesizing them from normative systems expressed in defeasible deontic logic, and explored their limitations.

We demonstrated the ability of our approach to synthesise compliance specifications from normative systems in a case study involving an RL agent playing a resource-collecting game. A normative system referring to actions with ambiguous state transitions and another containing a contrary-to-duty obligation serve to clearly showcase our method's limitations, supporting our conclusion that while existing safe RL frameworks based on LTL specifications are capable of implementing a variety of normative systems, some remain out of reach.

In the future, we hope to mitigate the limitations we have outlined in this paper using multi-objective RL; by integrating multiple objectives into a single policy we could use these techniques to synthesize policies that pursue full compliance whenever possible, but resort to imposing weak compliance in cases where the former is unlikely. There exist more expressive logics that may be better suited for the subtleties of normative constraints; one example (an extension of LTL over finite traces) is Linear Dynamic Logic over finite traces (LDL_f) [5], which has been shown to be capable of naturally expressing weak compliance. It has already been used in conjunction with RL (e.g. in [6]), and we intend to further explore how such logics can be used for normative RL. Finally, we plan also to investigate proper mechanisms to incorporate constraints over actions into the reinforcement learning process.

References

1. Alechina, N., Dastani, M., Logan, B.: Norm specification and verification in multi-agent systems. J. Appl. Logics **5**(2), 457 (2018)
2. Alshiekh, M., Bloem, R., Ehlers, R., Könighofer, B., Niekum, S., Topcu, U.: Safe reinforcement learning via shielding. In: Proceedigs of AAAI, pp. 2669–2678 (2018)
3. Boella, G., van der Torre, L.: Permissions and obligations in hierarchical normative systems. In: Proceedings of ICAIL, pp. 81–82 (2003)
4. Boella, G., van der Torre, L.: Regulative and constitutive norms in normative multiagent systems. In: Proceedings of KR 2004, pp. 255–266. AAAI Press (2004)
5. De Giacomo, G., De Masellis, R., Grasso, M., Maggi, F.M., Montali, M.: Monitoring business metaconstraints based on LTL and LDL for finite traces. In: Sadiq, S., Soffer, P., Völzer, H. (eds.) Business Process Management, pp. 1–17 (2014)
6. De Giacomo, G., Iocchi, L., Favorito, M., Patrizi, F.: Foundations for restraining bolts: reinforcement learning with LTLf/LDLf restraining specifications. In: Proceedings of ICAPS, vol. 29, pp. 128–136 (2019)

7. Esparza, J., Křetínský, J.: From LTL to deterministic automata: a safraless compositional approach. In: Biere, A., Bloem, R. (eds.) CAV 2014. LNCS, vol. 8559, pp. 192–208. Springer, Cham (2014). https://doi.org/10.1007/978-3-319-08867-9_13

8. Forrester, J.W.: Gentle murder, or the adverbial samaritan. J. Philos. **81**(4), 193–197 (1984)

9. Fu, J., Topcu, U.: Probably approximately correct MDP learning and control with temporal logic constraints. In: Proceedings of RSS (2014)

10. Governatori, G.: Thou shalt is not you will. In: Proceedings of ICAIL, pp. 63–68 (2015)

11. Governatori, G.: Practical normative reasoning with defeasible deontic logic. In: d'Amato, C., Theobald, M. (eds.) Reasoning Web 2018. LNCS, vol. 11078, pp. 1–25. Springer, Cham (2018). https://doi.org/10.1007/978-3-030-00338-8_1

12. Governatori, G., Hashmi, M.: No time for compliance. In: Proceedings of EDOC, pp. 9–18. IEEE (2015)

13. Governatori, G., Hulstijn, J., Riveret, R., Rotolo, A.: Characterising deadlines in temporal modal defeasible logic. In: Orgun, M.A., Thornton, J. (eds.) AI 2007. LNCS (LNAI), vol. 4830, pp. 486–496. Springer, Heidelberg (2007). https://doi.org/10.1007/978-3-540-76928-6_50

14. Governatori, G., Olivieri, F., Rotolo, A., Scannapieco, S.: Computing strong and weak permissions in defeasible logic. J. Philos. Logic **42**(6), 799–829 (2013)

15. Governatori, G., Rotolo, A.: BIO logical agents: norms, beliefs, intentions in defeasible logic. J. Auton. Agents Multi Agent Syst. **17**(1), 36–69 (2008)

16. Hasanbeig, M., Abate, A., Kroening, D.: Cautious reinforcement learning with logical constraints. In: Proceedings of AAMAS, pp. 483–491 (2020)

17. Hodkinson, I., Reynolds, M.: Temporal logic. In: Blackburn, P., Van Benthem, J., Wolter, F. (eds.) Handbook of Modal Logic, vol. 3, pp. 655–720. Elsevier (2007)

18. Jansen, N., Könighofer, B., Junges, S., Serban, A., Bloem, R.: Safe Reinforcement Learning Using Probabilistic Shields. In: Proceedings of CONCUR. LIPIcs, vol. 171, pp. 1–16 (2020)

19. Lam, H.P., Governatori, G.: The making of SPINdle. In: Proc. of RuleML. LNCS, vol. 5858, pp. 315–322 (2009)

20. Neufeld, E., Bartocci, E., Ciabattoni, A., Governatori, G.: A normative supervisor for reinforcement learning agents. In: Proceedings of CADE, pp. 565–576 (2021)

21. Neufeld, E.A., Bartocci, E., Ciabattoni, A., Governatori, G.: Enforcing ethical goals over reinforcement-learning policies. J. Ethics Inf. Technol. **24**, 43 (2022). https://doi.org/10.1007/s10676-022-09665-8

22. Noothigattu, R., et al.: Teaching AI agents ethical values using reinforcement learning and policy orchestration. In: Proceedings of IJCAI, LNCS, vol. 12158, pp. 217–234 (2019)

23. Panagiotidi, S., Alvarez-Napagao, S., Vázquez-Salceda, J.: Towards the norm-aware agent: bridging the gap between deontic specifications and practical mechanisms for norm monitoring and norm-aware planning. In: Balke, T., Dignum, F., van Riemsdijk, M.B., Chopra, A.K. (eds.) COIN 2013. LNCS (LNAI), vol. 8386, pp. 346–363. Springer, Cham (2014). https://doi.org/10.1007/978-3-319-07314-9_19

24. Pnueli, A.: The temporal logic of programs. In: Proceedings of FOCS, pp. 46–57 (1977)

25. Pranger, S., Könighofer, B., Posch, L., Bloem, R.: TEMPEST - synthesis tool for reactive systems and shields in probabilistic environments. In: Hou, Z., Ganesh, V. (eds.) ATVA 2021. LNCS, vol. 12971, pp. 222–228. Springer, Cham (2021). https://doi.org/10.1007/978-3-030-88885-5_15

26. Rodriguez-Soto, M., Lopez-Sanchez, M., Rodriguez Aguilar, J.A.: Multi-objective reinforcement learning for designing ethical environments. In: Proceedings of IJCAI, pp. 545–551 (2021)
27. Sadigh, D., Kim, E.S., Coogan, S., Sastry, S.S., Seshia, S.A.: A learning based approach to control synthesis of markov decision processes for linear temporal logic specifications. In: Proceedings of CDC, pp. 1091–1096 (2014)
28. Searle, J.R.: Speech acts: an essay in the philosophy of language. Cambridge University Press, Cambridge, England (1969)
29. Sickert, S., Esparza, J., Jaax, S., Křetínský, J.: Limit-deterministic büchi automata for linear temporal logic. In: Proceedings of CAV, LNCS, vol. 9780, pp. 312–332 (2016)
30. Watkins, C.J.C.H.: Learning from Delayed Rewards. Ph.D. thesis, King's College, Cambridge, UK (1989). https://www.cs.rhul.ac.uk/~chrisw/thesis.pdf
31. Wen, M., Ehlers, R., Topcu, U.: Correct-by-synthesis reinforcement learning with temporal logic constraints. In: Procedings of IROS, pp. 4983–4990. IEEE (2015)
32. Wu, Y.H., Lin, S.D.: A low-cost ethics shaping approach for designing reinforcement learning agents. In: Proceedings of AAAI, pp. 1687–1694 (2018)

Analysis of Carbon Neutrality Scenarios of Industrial Consumers Using Electric Power Market Simulations

Masanori Hirano[✉][ID], Ryo Wakasugi, and Kiyoshi Izumi[ID]

The University of Tokyo, Tokyo, Japan
research@mhirano.jp, b2019rwakasugi@socsim.org, izumi@sys.t.u-tokyo.ac.jp

Abstract. This study analyzed various electricity procurement scenarios for a factory in terms of carbon neutrality, using multi-agent simulations. We performed a multi-agent simulation with power-consuming and power-generating agents to simulate the electric power market. Additionally, we developed a factory model reflecting the actual electricity consumption patterns and implemented multiple electricity procurement methods for the factory: market procurements, photovoltaic power generation (PV), fuel cells (FC), and batteries. Using this simulation model, we analyzed the total CO_2 emissions and total cost of carbon neutrality by changing the factory's capacity for PV, FC, batteries, and the generation cost of FC. As a result, we found that batteries can enhance the effects of PV. Furthermore, unfortunately, when the capacity of the batteries is larger, the generation cost of FC for FC activation will be required to become lower, which leads to a discussion of the future price target of FC. Our study successfully demonstrated that realistic multi-agent simulations enable complex phenomenon analyses.

Keywords: Electricity power market · Multi-agent simulation · Carbon neutrality · Factory

1 Introduction

Climate risk is a significant problem worldwide, and, with the expansion of environmental, social, and governance (ESG) investments, many companies have taken steps to mitigate global warming. Individual companies are increasingly expected to reduce and neutralize CO_2 emissions, which may also enhance their value creation. At present, various means should be combined to achieve carbon neutrality, such as energy conservation, the introduction of renewable energy, and the purchase of renewable energy certificates (REC), guarantees of origin (GO), or international renewable energy certificates (I-REC). Thus, the electricity procurement strategy, such as how much renewable energy is introduced or how many certificates are necessary, is vital for each consumer to achieve carbon neutrality.

R. Aydoğan et al. (Eds.): PRIMA 2022, LNAI 13753, pp. 90–105, 2023.
https://doi.org/10.1007/978-3-031-21203-1_6

In particular, factory-owning companies have vast choices to achieve carbon neutrality because factories have enough space to operate numerous devices, and factories can diversify electricity procurement methods due to a high volume of energy consumption. For example, photovoltaic power generation (PV) is widespread, and factories can facilitate many solar panels using plenty of places, such as rooftops. Moreover, equipping batteries for electricity charging at night is also a possible choice for factories because base-load power sources, such as hydroelectric power generation, frequently emit lower CO_2 emissions than peak-load power sources.

Fuel cells (FC) are considered a more challenging way for factories to achieve carbon neutrality. The advantage of hydrogen fuel cells is that energy can be stored in the form of hydrogen. Although hydrogen itself can also be generated using fossil fuels, in the future, it is assumed that it will be entirely generated by renewable energy sources such as PV. It is usually difficult to transform energy into a form that can be stored, except by using fossil fuels. Currently, hydrogen is a realistic medium for this purpose.

However, these methods have difficulties; thus, it is currently difficult to achieve carbon neutrality without combining them. For example, PV is unstable, dependent on the weather, and requires a large operating area. In the case of batteries, the power conservation efficiency per volume is low, and it is far from possible to cover all the power needs of factories. Meanwhile, FC technologies are still being developed; thus, FC-based electricity costs several times more than conventional ones, and it will take a long time before the price drops.

In the electricity market, there has recently been significant pricing uncertainty. Because of the seasonality of electricity demand and the difficulty of electricity storage, the price under deregulated markets frequently has high fluctuations. In Japan, on January 15, 2021, the price increased to 251 yen/kWh, which is approximately 25 times the usual price because of substantial electricity demands. In addition to these fluctuations, markets have complex interactions whereby prices are decided based on the supply-demand balance, which includes compiling all participants' orders in the market. In summary, the ordering actions of each individual affect the market. Especially when the bidding volume is massive, such as in the case of factories, the effect could be very significant, which is well-known as "market impacts."

Therefore, this study newly analyzed the electricity procurement strategy to achieve carbon neutrality in a factory using a multi-agent simulation. We focused on one factory pertaining to a major Japanese company in the electricity industry and simulated carbon neutrality scenarios by changing the capacity of PV, batteries, FC, and the price of FC in the Japan Electric Power Exchange Market (JEPX). Based on the results obtained, we will discuss the strategy of combining PV, batteries, and FC, as well as the impact of FC prices on CO_2 emissions. By utilizing multi-agent simulations, we successfully analyzed realistic scenarios.

2 Related Work

To analyze the electric power market, it is crucial to consider the complex interactions because the prices are decided by the supply-demand balance, which includes the compilation of all participants in the market. Therefore, a multi-agent simulation is a promising approach [4,7]. We used multi-agent simulation to simulate the interaction of all participants in the market and investigate the micro-macroscopic results of their interactions. Multi-agent simulations have been applied to the electric power market [13].

Sensfuss [10] proposed a multi-agent simulation-based platform for Germany called PowerACE, which included a power supply, power demand, renewable energy generation, power market, and the use of batteries. Further, Sensfuss *et al.* [11] used PowerACE to analyze the impact of the emergence of renewable energy on the German electric power market. Weiss *et al.* [14] discussed the investment incentives for power generation plants under an electric power grid, in which all power sources are renewable, using a multi-agent model. Ken *et al.* [6] analyzed the effect and design of feed-in premiums in Japan by using an electric power market simulation.

Similarly, Chuang *et al.* [1] applied the Cournot model to a competitive electric power market to analyze the expansion of power generation and showed the advantages of a competitive market in comparison to a centralized market. Day *et al.* [2] used the supply function equilibrium model, in which all players submit prices and the corresponding volumes, analyzed the impact of the policy introduced in England and Wales to improve market efficiency, and argued the need for continuous strict price monitoring and control. Jiang *et al.* [5] proposed a game-theoretic pricing model for peer-to-peer (P2P) electricity trading in a blockchain for energy, showing that P2P electricity trading could be beneficial and contribute to the development of electric power markets. Ghaffari *et al.* [3] discussed models for tradeable green certificates based on game theory and concluded that the Stackelberg game model was the most appropriate. However, because these game theory-based analyses typically employ strong assumptions, it is difficult to include the complex real-world situations of an electric power market [10].

Hence, Kok *et al.* [8] proposed Power Matcher, a framework with multi-agents, and showed that the flexibility of generation and consumption is essential when demand response (DR) is widely used. In this framework, agents control electricity consumption, generate devices, and strategically publish their orders in the market. Oh *et al.* [9] utilized a multi-agent simulation to investigate the best bidding strategy and showed that DR could contribute to market efficiency. In addition, Zhou *et al.* [15] conducted simulation experiments on the DR of commercial buildings using a multi-agent model and investigated its effect.

3 Simulation Model

We employed the spot market (previous day trading; main market) in JEPX as the basis of our simulation model. In the simulation, there were 48 markets for every 30 mins of power usage with a blinded single-price batch auction mechanism, which is the same as the spot market. Some agents join these markets and submit orders based on their power usage plans. This type of simulation is generally called "multi-agent simulation." We regarded one step as one day, and all experiments completed these 365 steps.

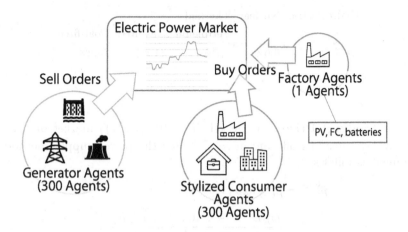

Fig. 1. Simulation model outline

An outline of our simulation is shown in Fig. 1. As explained in more detail in the continuation, one type of generator agent and two types of consumer agents constituted the simulation. Each type of agent had a plan for power usage or generation and a strategy for power procurement or provision. The simulation was similar to the actual power market through the aggregation of their actions.

3.1   Generator Agent

We employed 300 generator agents to supply electric power to the grid. Each agent had a hydroelectric power plant, nuclear power plant, petroleum thermal plant, gas-fired thermal plant, and coal-fired thermal plant. Next, agents decided on their limit sell order based on their unit cost of electricity by source, as explained below.

Power Supply Configuration and Unit Cost. First, we set the total supply configuration of the 300 agents based on the actual Japanese power supply configuration[1]. The configuration is listed in Table 1. Based on the total supply configuration, volumes of each generation type are randomly distributed to 300 agents (by scaling 300 random variables generated from a uniform distribution). Thus, each power supply configuration for the 300 agents was set. Based on

---

[1] https://www.enecho.meti.go.jp/statistics/total_energy/results.html.

each power supply configuration, an agent's unit cost of power generation was determined using each type of generation's configuration and unit costs. We also referred to the Japanese unit costs of each generation type based on actual data[2].

Table 1. Power supply configuration in the entire power market

Hydroelectric	Nuclear	Thermal		
		Petroleum	Gas-fired	Coal-fired
8.8%	6.6%	7.7%	41.8%	35.2%

Offering (Selling) Price. At the kth ($k \in \{0, \cdots, 47\}$) market on day t ($\in \{0, \cdots, 364\}$), agent i's offering price $\hat{p}_t^{k,i,s}$ for the power supply method s is determined as follows:

$$\hat{p}_t^{k,i,s} = p_{t-1}^k \exp\left(\hat{r}_t^{k,i,s}\right), \tag{1}$$

$$\hat{r}_t^{k,i,s} = \frac{w_B^i B_t^{k,i,s} + w_C^i C_t^{k,i,s} + w_N^i N_t^{k,i,s}}{w_B^i + w_C^i + w_N^i}, \tag{2}$$

where p_{t-1}^k is the previous day's market price in the kth market, and w_B^i, w_C^i, and w_N^i are the random weights for the base term $B_t^{k,i,s}$, technical (chart) term $C_t^{k,i,s}$, and noise term $N_t^{k,i,s}$, respectively. w_B^i, w_C^i, and w_N^i are generated from the uniform distributions $[0, W_B^g], [0, W_C^g]$, and $[0, W_N^g]$, respectively. W_B^g is set to 1.0, and W_C^g, W_N^g are set via a parameter grid search to obtain realistic results (see Sect. 4). Each term was calculated as follows:

$$B_t^{k,i,s} = \frac{g_t^s}{\epsilon^{i,s}}(1 + r^{i,s}), \tag{3}$$

$$C_t^{k,i,s} = \frac{1}{\tau} \sum_{l=1}^{\tau} \ln \frac{p_{t-l}^k}{p_{t-l-1}^k}, \tag{4}$$

$$N_t^{k,i,s} \sim \mathcal{N}(0,1), \tag{5}$$

where g_t^s is the previously mentioned unit cost for power generation method s on day t, $\epsilon^{i,s}$ is the power generation efficiency variable from a uniform distribution $[0.8, 1.2]$, $r^{i,s}$ is agent i's additional profit ratio for the generation method s from the uniform distribution $[0.0, 0.2]$, τ is a technical analysis window set to 7 in this study, and $\mathcal{N}(0,1)$ represents a standard normal distribution. This was referred to [12]. Through these calculations that imitate actual decision-making scenarios, agents display heterogeneity and make the market more realistic with merit orders (the lower order of the marginal cost of each power generation).

---

[2] https://www.enecho.meti.go.jp/committee/council/basic_policy_subcommittee/index.html.

Offering (Selling) Volume. Agent i's electric power offering volume for the power generation method s in the kth market on day t is calculated as follows:

$$q_t^{k,i,s} = \overline{q}_t^{k,i,s} + \Delta q_t^{k,i,s}, \tag{6}$$

where $\overline{q}_t^{k,i,s}$ is the reference power generation volume and $\Delta q_t^{k,i,s}$ is the controlled power generation volume. Because base-load power plants cannot control their power output instantaneously, hydroelectric and nuclear power plants were set to their $\Delta q_t^{k,i,s}$ to 0. By contrast, thermal plants can easily control their supply. Thus, we assumed that thermal plants control their power generation volume according to the predicted demand based on the previous week's demand, as given below.

$$\Delta q_t^{k,i,s} = \eta_i \frac{(D_{t-7}^k - S_{t-7}^k)q_{t-7}^{k,i}}{S_{t-7}^k} \lambda_t^{k,i,s}, \tag{7}$$

where D_{t-7}^k and S_{t-7}^k represent the total demand and supply in kth market on the same day in the previous week, respectively. $q_{t-7}^{k,i}$ is agent i's total supply in the market, η_i is agent i's responsiveness to the supply-demand imbalance obtained from a uniform distribution $[0.5, 2.0]$, and $\lambda_t^{k,i,s}$ represents the share of the power generation method s in the total controllable power generation volume of agent i.

3.2   Stylized Consumer Agent

The stylized consumer agent is the only type of consumer agent except for one factory agent. We employed 300 stylized consumer agents. This type of agent was introduced to represent actual consumers. The demands of this type of agent are predefined, and they only change their bidding prices.

Agent j's bidding price in the kth market on day t is calculated as follows:

$$\hat{p}_t^{k,j} = p_{t-1}^k \exp{(\hat{r}_t^{k,j})}, \tag{8}$$

$$\hat{r}_t^{k,j} = \frac{w_F^j F_t^{k,j} + w_C^j C_t^{k,j} + w_N^j N_t^{k,j}}{w_F^j + w_C^j + w_N^j}, \tag{9}$$

where w_F^j, w_C^j, and w_N^j are the random weights for the fundamental term $F_t^{k,j}$, technical (chart) term $C_t^{k,j}$, and noise term $N_t^{k,j}$, respectively. w_F^j, w_C^j, and w_N^j are generated from the uniform distributions $[0, W_F^d], [0, W_C^d]$, and $[0, W_N^d]$, respectively. W_F^d was set to 1.0, and W_C^d and W_N^d were set via a parameter grid search to obtain realistic results (see Sect. 4). Each term was calculated as follows:

$$F_t^{k,j} = \ln{\frac{p_F^*}{p_{t-1}^k}}, \tag{10}$$

$$C_t^{k,j} = \frac{1}{\tau} \sum_{l=1}^{\tau} \ln{\frac{p_{t-l}^k}{p_{t-l-1}^k}}, \tag{11}$$

$$N_t^{k,j} \sim \mathcal{N}(0,1), \tag{12}$$

where p_F^* is the theoretical fundamental price and is set to 10 in this study; the other notations are the same as those of the generator agents. These were based on [12].

The bidding volume was set externally based on actual Japanese demand data[3]. We distributed the actual consumption volume among the 300 agents in the market for each period.

3.3   Factory Agent

This agent was introduced to analyze the factory's electricity procurement scenarios for carbon neutrality. Thus, its behavior was modeled to imitate the actual factory demand pattern. The big differences from stylized traders are the demand modeling and various ways of electricity procurements such as PV, FC, and batteries. We modeled the demand based on the data's principal component analysis (PCA) to realize the actual demand pattern. Then, after determining the combination of various electricity procurement methods, such as PV, FC, and batteries, to satisfy its electricity demands by an algorithm, the factory published the necessary orders to the market. The details of this process are provided below.

PCA and Demand Modeling. We found two major components for actual factory power usage according to our PCA analysis:

- First principal component: This component contributed 68.7% and was significant only in the daytime on a weekday. Thus, we regarded it as a base demand for production activities.
- Second principal component: This component had a contribution of 9.1% and was more significant in summer and winter than in spring and autumn. Thus, we regarded it as a seasonal factor, including air conditioners (AC).
- Other components: We regarded the remaining 22.2%, which could not be explained, by the first and second components, as noise factors.

Based on these components, we modeled the demand for this factory as follows:

$$d_t^{k,\star} = w_B^\star B_t^{k,\star} + w_A^\star A_t^{k,\star} + w_N^\star N_t^{k,\star}, \tag{13}$$

where $B_t^{k,\star}$, $A_t^{k,\star}$, and $N_t^{k,\star}$ are the base, AC, and noise factors, respectively, which are modeled based on the aforementioned components, and $w_B^\star, w_A^\star$, and $w_N^\star$ are their respective weights. $w_B^\star$ and $w_A^\star$ are determined according to the actual demand and $w_N^\star$ is set to 10% of the total demand. (This is because the contribution of each component of PCA does not imply the scale of each component.) Moreover, the factory's total demand share in the market is set to 2.26×10^{-6} based on the actual share.

---

[3] https://www.tepco.co.jp/forecast/html/area_data-j.html;
https://powergrid.chuden.co.jp/denkiyoho/;
https://www.kansai-td.co.jp/denkiyoho/area-performance.html.

Power Procurement Methods

Procurement from Market: For market procurement, this agent submitted orders whose prices were assumed to be sufficiently high for execution. This is because a factory requires a predetermined amount of power. Thus, according to the volume determined by the algorithm, explained later, this agent submitted orders.

PV: In this study, we assumed that all the PV electricity generated by the factory was used or stored on its premises. Moreover, the generated volume was not controlled by the agent.

The actual PV-generated volume at the kth market on day t is given as

$$q_t^{k,\star,\mathrm{pv}} = \min\left\{\overline{q_t}^{k,\star,\mathrm{pv}} C_{\mathrm{pv}} o_{\mathrm{pv}} \exp\left(N_t^{k,\star,\mathrm{pv}}\right), C_{\mathrm{pv}}\right\} \tag{14}$$

$$N_t^{k,\star,\mathrm{pv}} \sim \mathcal{N}(\mu_{\mathrm{pv}}, \sigma_{\mathrm{pv}}), \tag{15}$$

where $\overline{q_t}^{k,\star,\mathrm{pv}}$ is the reference power generation volume per capacity at each time period calculated from the actual data[4], C_{pv} is the capacity volume of PV of the factory, o_{pv} is the average utilization rate, $N_t^{k,\star,\mathrm{pv}}$ is the disturbance term for randomness in the simulation, μ_{pv} is the mean of the disturbance term, and σ_{pv} is the standard deviation of the disturbance term. In short, $\overline{q_t}^{k,\star,\mathrm{pv}} \times o_{\mathrm{pv}}$ is the actual mean generated volume per capacity at each time calculated from the actual data, and $\overline{q_t}^{k,\star,\mathrm{pv}}$ reflects the effect of the actual weather and time of day (at night, this is 0). In our simulation, we employed $o_{\mathrm{pv}} = 0.15$, $\mu_{\mathrm{pv}} = 0.0$, and $\sigma_{\mathrm{pv}} = 0.1$[5].

The PV generation cost, p_{pv}, is set to 0 for simplification because PV usually requires minimal running cost.

FC: The factory can always use FC. The condition that must be satisfied is

$$0 \le q_t^{k,\star,\mathrm{fc}} \le e_{\mathrm{fc}} C_{\mathrm{fc}}, \tag{16}$$

where $q_t^{k,\star,\mathrm{fc}}$ is the electricity volume generated by FC at the kth market on day t, e_{fc} is the efficiency of FC, and C_{fc} is the capacity of FC of the factory. $q_t^{k,\star,\mathrm{fc}}$ is fully controllable by the agent under the condition. In this study, we employed $e_{\mathrm{fc}} = 0.5$ based on the actual data[6].

The generation cost of FC, p_{fc}, is set in the experiments to be changed. Moreover, all the FC used in the factory are assumed to be generated by carbon-neutral generation methods, and the usage of FC is assumed not to emit CO_2.

---

[4] https://www.kansai-td.co.jp/denkiyoho/download/index.html, and the effect of the utilization ratio o_{pv} is excluded.

[5] According to https://www.nedo.go.jp/content/100926249.pdf.

[6] https://www.meti.go.jp/committee/kenkyukai/energy/suiso_nenryodenchi/pdf/001_04_00.pdf.

Batteries: The factory can also use batteries. The batteries had a capacity of C_b. Thus, if the factory charged $\Delta q_t^{k,\star,\mathrm{bt}}$ at the kth market on day t (if $\Delta q_t^{k,\star,\mathrm{bt}}$ is negative, it means discharging), the following equation must be satisfied:

$$0 \leq q_t^{k,\star,\mathrm{bt}} + \Delta q_t^{k,\star,\mathrm{bt}} \leq C_b. \tag{17}$$

This means that batteries could not be charged over their capacity and discharged when they were empty.

Algorithm for Matching Demand and Procurement Methods. We built an algorithm to assume the actual decision flow and determine the combination of various electricity procurement methods, such as PV, FC, and batteries, that would satisfy the factory's electricity demands. Figure 2 shows the daily flow of procurements. Because JEPX's spot market closed its orders at 10:00 AM on the previous day, there could have been a gap between procurements and actual usage. Although Japanese electricity grids allow the gap called "in-balance," usually consumers minimize the gap because in-balance is charged with additional costs.

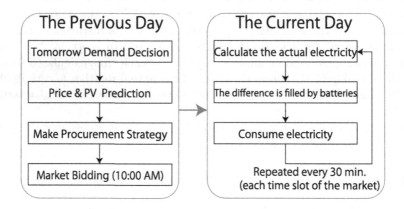

Fig. 2. Daily flow of the procurements.

In the flow illustrated by Fig. 2, the agents devise a procurement strategy based on the next day's demand, estimated electricity price at the market, and PV generation prediction. For simplification, we estimated that the agent could predict exactly tomorrow's demand for the factory, which means that the actual and predicted demand is the same as in the calculation from Eq. 13.

In terms of price and PV prediction, we employed historical data. They are defined as:

$$\hat{p}_t^{k,\star} = p_{t-7}^k, \tag{18}$$

$$\hat{q}_t^{k,\star,\mathrm{pv}} = q_{t-1}^{k,\star,\mathrm{pv}}, \tag{19}$$

where $\hat{p}_t^{k,\star}$ is the predicted market price of the factory agent, p_{t-7}^k is the actual market price of the same market on the same day of the previous week, $\hat{q}_t^{k,\star,\mathrm{pv}}$ is the predicted PV generation of the factory, and $q_{t-1}^{k,\star,\mathrm{pv}}$ is the actual PV generation of the factory at the same timeslot of the previous day. They show that the market price has a weekly cycle, and the PV does not.

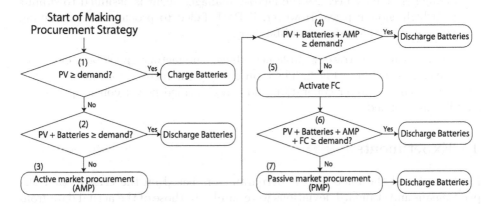

Fig. 3. Procurement strategy (Sub-routine of making procurement strategy in Fig. 2)

Based on these predictions, the factory agent formulates a procurement strategy, namely, a mix of several procurement methods, the details of which are illustrated in Fig. 3. The following explains step-by-step the details of the strategy:

(1) Check if the predicted PV generation volume can exceed the demand. If it can, no procurement except for PV is necessary, and surplus electricity is charged to the batteries.
(2) Check if the sum of the predicted PV generation volume and the usable capacity of batteries can exceed the demand. Because PV is unstable and dependent on the weather, we set the batteries' minimum reserved capacity to 10% of the total daily demand of the factory, and the reserved capacity was granted as the unusable capacity. When the current charged electricity was below the reserved capacity, the usable capacity of batteries was set to 0.
(3) When the second step cannot cover the total demand, "active market procurement (APM)" is carried out. APM sources electricity only when $p_t^k \leq p_{\mathrm{fc}}$ because the only remaining procurement method is FC. Here, the battery's rechargeable (discharged) capacity was used to obtain the lowest procurement price under the condition that the procurements are enough before the demand. It means that the total net electricity cannot be negative at any time. The optimized APM strategy is calculated by dynamic programming according to the condition.
(4) If the APM cannot procure enough electricity because of the restriction of $p_t^k \leq p_{\mathrm{fc}}$, go to the next step.

(5) FC can supplement the insufficient procurement as much as possible under the condition of Eq. 16.
(6) If FC cannot complete the insufficient volume, go to the next step.
(7) Finally, "passive market procurement (PMP)" was carried out. PMP procures insufficient electricity from the market in addition to AMP without any consideration about prices. It is possible for PMP to consistently procure enough electricity because the factory manager agent is assumed to submit at a high enough price. However, if PMP failed to procure, the remaining volume of the batteries would be used.

According to the strategy explained above, the factory agent bids orders to the market, as shown in Fig. 2. Then, on the day the factory consumes electricity, the actual PV power generation and other decided power consumption and supplies are applied.

4   Experiments

First, we tuned the undecided hyperparameters based on the criteria that the price means and standard deviations were similar to those of the actual data from JEPX. Consequently, we obtained $W_C^g = 10.0, W_N^g = 12.5, W_C^d = 1.0, W_N^d = 12.5$. We confirmed that the intraday electricity price changes in the simulations using these parameters and successfully captured the characteristics of actual price changes.

In our experiments, we changed the following parameters.

- The capacity of PV [kWh]: $C_{pv} = 0, 1000, 3000, 5000$
- The capacity of FC [kWh]: $C_{fc} = 0, 500, 1000, 2000$
- The capacity of batteries [kWh]: $C_b = 1000, 3000, 5000, 10000$
- The price of FC generation cost [yen/kWh]: $p_{fc} = 0, 1, 2, \cdots, 20, 8.7$

Notably, $C_{pv} = 3000$ or $C_{fc} = 1000$ can cover the average electricity demand of the factory and $C_{fc} = 2000$ can cover its instantaneous maximum electricity demand[7]. Moreover, $p_{fc} = 8.7$ corresponds to the converted price of LNG of \$10/MMBtu (CIF price) in the calorific equivalent conversion.

In addition to these parameter sets, we tested the case of $C_{pv} = C_b = 0$. Under our assumption, the factory batteries were necessary to cover the uncertainty of PV. Thus, we were able to test the situation where $C_b = 0$ only when $C_{pv} = 0$.

For each parameter set, we ran ten attempts and calculated the mean and standard deviation. The first 61 days (2 months) were used for simulation stabilization, and the remaining 304 days (10 months) were used for evaluation.

As evaluation metrics, we employed the total CO_2 emissions and total carbon-neutral costs. The CO_2 emission coefficient per kWh of the market procurements was calculated according to the simulated power supply configuration at each time slot (usually high in high-demand times and low in others; see Sect. 3.1).

---

[7] This calculation is considered under the generation efficiency assumed in this study.

Moreover, procurement from the market is not carbon neutralized. Thus, to calculate the total carbon-neutral costs, the additional cost of buying certificates to offset the CO_2 emissions from market procurements was considered. In our simulation, we set the price of the certificate to 0.3 yen/kWh based on a survey conducted in Japan[8].

5   Results

Figures 4, 5, 6, 7, and 8 show all the results.

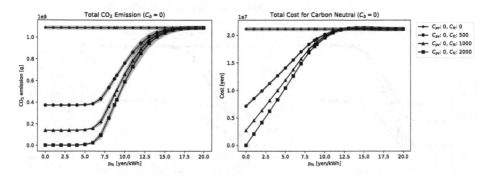

Fig. 4. Results of $C_b = 0$. The filled area is 95% confidential interval (CI).

From Fig. 4, we can observe the pure effects of FC. The figure on the left shows the results of the total CO_2 emissions for each FC generation price (p_{fc}; the horizontal axis). The figure on the right shows the results of the total cost of carbon neutrality. According to these, CO_2 emissions show dynamic changes in the FC price within the range of 5.0–15.0. However, the total cost of carbon neutrality is gradually reduced when the FC price is below 10.0.

Figure 5 shows all results for $C_b = 1000$. According to these, although the effect of PV is significant, it is significantly reduced over $C_{pv} = 3000$. In contrast, the effect of FC is similar, independent of C_{pv}, and shrunk in a homothetic manner.

Figure 6 shows all results for $C_b = 3000$. Although the results are similar to those in Fig. 5, the effect of PV seems more significant than in Fig. 5 because of the greater capacity of the batteries. In contrast to the case of $C_b = 1000$, the combination of $C_b = 3000$ and $C_{pv} = 5000$ can reduce CO_2 emission significantly and help achieve carbon neutrality at a significantly low cost.

Figures 7 and 8 show the results for $C_b = 5000, 10000$, respectively. These results were almost the same because the effect of PV was already saturated. In the case of $C_b = 10000$ (Fig. 8), even $C_{pv} = 3000$, carbon neutrality can be achieved even only by PV.

[8] https://www.meti.go.jp/shingikai/enecho/denryoku_gas/denryoku_gas/
seido_kento/pdf/057_03_01.pdf.

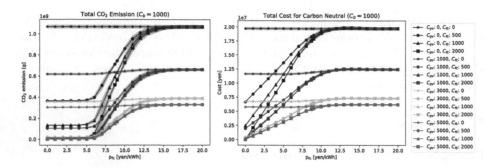

Fig. 5. Results of $C_b = 1000$. The filled area is 95% CI.

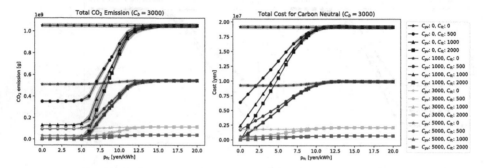

Fig. 6. Results of $C_b = 3000$. The filled area is 95% CI.

6   Discussion

First, we found that the batteries enhanced the effect of PV. According to the results, although the CO_2 emission is still high even if $C_{pv} = 5000$ under $C_b = 1000$, it becomes almost zero only if a larger battery capacity ($C_b \geq 3000$) is employed. This is because PV is significantly unstable depending on the weather. Thus, batteries are essential when the factory employs PV.

In terms of FC, its effect was significant when FC prices were low. Because we assumed that the CO_2 emission of FC is zero, the effect of FC is significant once FC is activated. However, in the factory procurement algorithm, we set the FC to be activated only when the FC price is lower than the marginal market price. This means that FC also faces price competition in the factory procurement strategy. Thus, when p_{fc} is over 15 yen/kWh, the FC is not activated, and FC produces no effects. However, if p_{fc} becomes somewhat low, FC is activated, and this effect emerges. Based on the results, the threshold of partial FC activation is almost 12.5 to 15 yen/kWh, depending on the capacity of the batteries. This is because a larger capacity of the batteries can store a larger volume of electricity, which is procured when the market price is low. Thus, the larger capacity of the batteries affects the FC activation threshold via average market procurement prices. If p_{fc} became sufficiently low (under approximately 5 yen/kWh), the effect of FC on

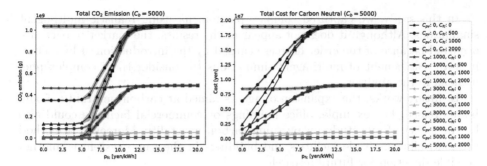

Fig. 7. Results of $C_b = 5000$. The filled area is 95% CI.

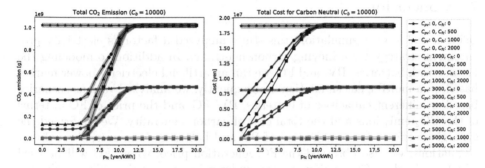

Fig. 8. Results of $C_b = 10000$

the CO_2 emission was saturated. This is because it is improbable for the market price to fall below p_{fc}, except when the market price goes almost 0 on a sunny day. (On a sunny day, the market price sometimes goes 0.01 yen/kWh due to the high supply from PV on the same electricity grid.)

Next, we discuss the FC price target by comparing the results with current FC price targets. Although the future FC price targets depend on surveys and vary across countries, in this study, we refer to the Japanese roadmap[9]. The price target is 8.7 to 17 yen/kWh (depending on the time horizon). According to our results, 17 yen/kWh seems ineffective, but 8.7 yen/kWh is somehow effective in terms of CO_2 emission reduction even when market competition also applies to FC. This CO_2 emission reduction via price competition can be achieved even by subvention or incentives for companies, such as the indirect effect of ESG investment.

The batteries are important throughout the discussion. As explained above, due to their larger capacity, the effects of PV were enhanced, and the threshold of FC activation was affected. However, interestingly, the capacity of batteries is not significantly important when it is sufficiently large.

---

[9] https://www.meti.go.jp/shingikai/energy_environment/suiso_nenryo/ roadmap_hyoka_wg/pdf/002_01_00.pdf.

In this study, we captured complex phenomena using realistic multi-agent simulations. Although it does not appear in the results, the market impact also occurred because of the order decrease caused by the introduction of FC. Thus, it is a great benefit of multi-agent simulations to consider these complex phenomena in the analysis.

In future works, the expansion of agents aimed at carbon neutrality should be addressed. For example, office buildings or commercial facilities could also be the target of our study on pursuing carbon neutrality. Moreover, a method for controlling multiple facilities and buildings in the same system is another possible direction for future research.

7   Conclusion

Using a multi-agent simulation, this study analyzed a factory's electricity procurement strategy for achieving carbon neutrality. In addition to modeling the factory with batteries, PV, and FC, we ran an artificial electricity power market based on a multi-agent simulation. Subsequently, we analyzed various scenarios based on different capacities of batteries, PV, FC, and the price of FC in terms of the CO_2 emissions and the total cost of carbon neutrality. We confirmed the synergistic effect of a combination of PV and batteries. Moreover, through our simulations, we also observed the FC generation price, where FC will be used widely and reduce CO_2 emissions even under price competition. This study successfully performed the analysis by realizing complex phenomena using realistic simulations based on a multi-agent simulation. Finally, expanding the scope of application beyond factories should be addressed in future research.

Acknowledgements. This work was supported by Panasonic Holdings Corporation.

References

1. Chuang, A.S., Wu, F., Varaiya, P.: A game-theoretic model for generation expansion planning: problem formulation and numerical comparisons. IEEE Trans. Power Syst. **16**(4), 885–891 (2001)
2. Day, C.J., Bunn, D.W.: Divestiture of generation assets in the electricity pool of england and wales: a computational approach to analyzing market power. J. Regulat. Econ. **19**(2), 123–141 (2001)
3. Ghaffari, M., Hafezalkotob, A., Makui, A.: Analysis of implementation of Tradable Green Certificates system in a competitive electricity market: a game theory approach. J. Ind. Eng. Int. **12**(2), 185–197 (2016)
4. Helleboogh, A., Vizzari, G., Uhrmacher, A., Michel, F.: Modeling dynamic environments in multi-agent simulation. Auton. Agents Multi-Agent Syst. **14**(1), 87–116 (2007)
5. Jiang, Y., Zhou, K., Lu, X., Yang, S.: Electricity trading pricing among prosumers with game theory-based model in energy blockchain environment. Appl. Energy **271**, 115239 (2020)

6. Kan, S., Shibata, Y.: Study on FIP policy design by using multi-agent based electric power market simulation model (2020). https://eneken.ieej.or.jp/en/report_detail.php?article_info_id=8918
7. Kitano, H., Tadokoro, S.: RoboCup rescue: a grand challenge for multiagent and intelligent systems. AI Maga. **22**(1), 39–39 (2001)
8. Kok, J.K., Warmer, C.J., Kamphuis, I.G.: PowerMatcher: multiagent control in the electricity infrastructure. In: Proceedings of the Fourth International Joint Conference on Autonomous Agents and Multiagent Systems, pp. 75–86. Association for Computing Machinery (ACM) (2005)
9. Oh, H.S., Thomas, R.J.: Demand-side bidding agents: modeling and simulation. IEEE Trans. Power Syst. **23**(3), 1050–1056 (2008)
10. Sensfuß, F.: Assessment of the impact of renewable electricity generation on the German electricity sector: an agent-based simulation approach (2007). https://doi.org/10.5445/IR/1000007777
11. Sensfuß, F., Ragwitz, M., Genoese, M.: The merit-order effect: a detailed analysis of the price effect of renewable electricity generation on spot market prices in Germany. Energy Policy **36**(8), 3086–3094 (2008)
12. Torii, T., Izumi, K., Yamada, K.: Shock transfer by arbitrage trading: analysis using multi-asset artificial market. Evol. Inst. Econ. Rev. **12**(2), 395–412 (2015)
13. Trigo, P., Marques, P.: The electricity market as a multi-agent system. In: 5th International Conference on the European Electricity Market, pp. 1–6. IEEE (2008)
14. Weiss, O., Bogdanov, D., Salovaara, K., Honkapuro, S.: Market designs for a 100% renewable energy system: case isolated power system of Israel. Energy **119**, 266–277 (2017)
15. Zhou, Z., Zhao, F., Wang, J.: Agent-based electricity market simulation with demand response from commercial buildings. IEEE Trans. Smart Grid **2**(4), 580–588 (2011)

Task Allocation on Networks with Execution Uncertainty

Xiuzhen Zhang, Yao Zhang, and Dengji Zhao[(✉)]

Shanghai Engineering Research Center of Intelligent Vision and Imaging,
ShanghaiTech University, Shanghai, China
{zhangxzh1,zhangyao1,zhaodj}@shanghaitech.edu.cn

Abstract. We study a single task allocation problem where each worker connects to some other workers to form a network and the task requester only connects to some of the workers. The goal is to design an allocation mechanism such that each worker is incentivized to invite her neighbours to join the allocation, although they are competing for the task. Moreover, the performance of each worker is uncertain, which is modelled as the quality level of her task execution. The literature has proposed solutions to tackle the uncertainty problem by paying them after verifying their execution. Here, we extend the problem to the network setting. The challenge is that the requester relies on the workers to invite each other to find the best worker, and the performance of each worker is also unknown to the task requester. In this paper, we propose a new mechanism to solve the two challenges at the same time. The mechanism guarantees that inviting more workers and reporting/performing according to her true ability is a dominant strategy for each worker. We believe that the new solution can be widely applied in the digital economy powered by social connections such as crowdsourcing and contests.

Keywords: Task allocation · Social networks · Mechanism design

1 Introduction

Task allocation is an important part of real-world applications such as crowdsourcing [4,16] and market supply [3]. A common goal of task allocation is to find suitable workers to achieve a good performance at a low cost. Previous studies have made great progress in finding the best allocations under cases with a fixed number of workers. For example, the task requester seeks suitable workers in third-party platforms (e.g., Amazon Mechanical Turk) or holds a contest with attractive rewards [1]. Yet, such cases are less scalable due to the relatively fixed number of participants. Generally, we hope to involve more workers so that the task requester is capable of finding more suitable workers. Also, nowadays, people are connected with others via social networks. Therefore, a straightforward

R. Aydoğan et al. (Eds.): PRIMA 2022, LNAI 13753, pp. 106–121, 2023.
https://doi.org/10.1007/978-3-031-21203-1_7

approach is to make full use of their connections such that we can involve more workers. The challenge remains such as workers are competitors for the task and they are unwilling to provide their connections.

More precisely, we consider a single-task allocation problem where the task is allocated to a single agent and the task performance of an agent is measured by the finished quality. Each agent has a cost to perform the task. Before conducting the tasks, agents are uncertain about their actual performance and only know their *probability distributions over the quality levels*, which is also known as the execution uncertainty. Then, another challenge arises to the task requester for the robustness of the task allocation to the execution uncertainty.

We propose the *PEV-based Diffusion Mechanism* to handle the challenges one by one. Firstly, to solve the issue of agents unwilling to invite others, the proposed mechanism tries to reward them such that each agent will invite all her neighbours to maximize her utility. Then, the task requester is able to reach as many agents as possible. Secondly, to allow for the execution uncertainty, the proposed mechanism gives agents payoffs based on their actual performance, which guarantees that agents will not misreport their abilities and the task requester will not have a deficit in expectation. More importantly, previous studies focused on the uncertain successful performance, introducing the probability of success (PoS) to describe the probability of an agent successfully completing the task [11,12], e.g., 70 % to fail and 30 % to finish the task. Yet such a metric is weak to accurately describe agents' abilities. In our setting, we define the probability of quality (PoQ), which represents the probability distribution on completion qualities, e.g., 30 % to finish with a good quality, 20 % to finish with a low quality, and 50 % to totally fail.

To sum up, the goal of this paper is to design a mechanism to incentivize agents to invite all their neighbours, report their PoQs and costs to perform the task. The mechanism should also guarantee that the task requester will not suffer a loss compared to the case where the participating agents are all the task requester's neighbours. We first consider the case where the task requester has no requirements for agents' abilities such that each agent can perform the task in the same quality with a probability of one. We show that the Information Diffusion Mechanism [7,8] can be applied in such a case. However, when the task requester is sensitive to agents' completion qualities and uncertain about agents' performance, the Information Diffusion Mechanism fails in incentive compatibility. To solve this issue, we then propose the PEV-based Diffusion Mechanism to meet these requirements.

1.1 Related Work

The social network is an effective medium to get access to more potential agents. Mechanism design in social networks has been widely utilized in auctions [6,7], answer querying [14], social advertising [9] and influence maximization [13]. An overview and prospect of all these topics that focus on diffusion mechanism design can be seen in [17]. In this paper, we are inspired by the idea of the Information Diffusion Mechanism [6–8], which is proposed to increase the seller' revenue in auctions via social networks. The Information Diffusion Mechanism designs the payoffs based on their contributions to find the buyer with the highest bid. Though there has also been work studying task allocation problems on social networks [5,15], diffusion incentives and strategic actions to hide connections were not taken into their consideration, while these are the main concerns in our setting.

In traditional task allocation problems, the performance and cost that each agent achieves are private information. To achieve truthfully reporting, the task scheduling mechanisms with verification were first proposed to take both agents' declarations and their actual performance into consideration [2,10]. Later, since there exist cases where agents may fail to reach the same performance as they declared in real-world applications, the execution uncertainty is considered in mechanism design problems. To describe the execution uncertainty, probability of success (PoS) is introduced to describe the probability of an agent successfully completing the tasks [11,12,19].

The remainder of this paper is organized as follows. Section 2 describes the model of the single-task allocation problem in social networks and introduces desirable properties. Section 3 presents the Information Diffusion Mechanism in the setting without the execution uncertainty and shows the failure of its application in the general setting. Following that, we propose our PEV-based Diffusion Mechanism and prove its remarkable performance. We conclude in Sect. 4.

2   The Model

Consider a social network represented by a graph $G = (V, E)$, where $V = \{s\} \cup N$ is the node set and E is the edge set. The task requester s has a single task to be performed and $N = \{1, 2, \cdots, n\}$ is the set of all other agents in the network. Each edge $\{i, j\} \in E$ indicates that agent i can directly communicate with agent j. For $i \in V$, let $r_i = \{j \in V \mid \{i, j\} \in E\}$ be the neighbour set of i. Given the task to be performed, let $Q \subset \mathbb{R}^+ \cup \{0\}$ be the set of all possible completion qualities. Let the discrete random variable Q_i be the completion quality of agent i and $q_i \in Q$ denote a realization of Q_i. Let f_i be the probability density function of Q_i, i.e., $P(Q_i = q_i) = f_i(q_i)$. The probability distribution f_i is called agent i's probability of quality (PoQ). There is also a fixed cost $c_i \geq 0$ for i to perform the task. Define $\theta_i = (f_i, c_i, r_i)$ as agent i's type, which is only known to her. Let Θ_i be the type space of agent i and $\theta = (\theta_1, \cdots, \theta_n)$ be the type profile of all agents.

Under the above setting, the goal of the task requester is to assign the task to an agent who can perform it with a high quality and a low cost. Initially, only the task requester's neighbours r_s know the task and they may not be the best worker for the task. Hence, the task requester needs a mechanism to attract more participants, which is done by incentivizing agents to diffuse the task information to all their neighbours. Thus, each agent's action consists of reporting her PoQ, her cost to perform the task and inviting her neighbours, i.e., reporting her type. For agent $i \in N$, let $\theta'_i = (f'_i, c'_i, r'_i)$ be her report, where f'_i is a probability distribution over Q, $r'_i \subseteq r_i$ and $c'_i \geq 0$. Let $\theta' = (\theta'_1, \theta'_2, \cdots, \theta'_n)$ be a report profile of all agents in N. Denote the graph constructed from θ' by $G(\theta') = (V, E(\theta'))$, where $E(\theta') = r_s \cup \{\{i, j\} \mid i \in N, j \in r'_i\}$. Let $I(\theta')$ be the set of all participants under θ', and $i \in I(\theta')$ holds if and only if there exists a path from s to i in the graph $G(\theta')$. Let Θ be the space of all possible type profiles.

Generally speaking, the mechanism consists of two steps. The task requester first announces a contract including a task allocation policy and a payoff policy and then assigns the task to an agent according to their declarations (in our setting, we only consider the case where the task is assigned to at most one agent). After the task requester verifies the completion quality, she will give payoffs to agents according to the announced contract. We call such a mechanism the verified contract mechanism and provide the formal definition below.

Definition 1 (Verified Contract Mechanism). *A **verified contract mechanism** is defined by $\mathcal{M} = (\pi, p)$, where $\pi : \Theta \rightarrow \{0, 1\}^N$ and $p : \Theta \times Q \rightarrow \mathbb{R}^N$ are the allocation and payoff policies respectively. Given a set of agents N and all agents' report profile $\theta' \in \Theta$, set $\pi_i(\theta') = 0$ and $p_i(\theta', q) = 0$ for all $i \notin I(\theta')$, q is the quality that the task requester receives.*

Given a verified contract mechanism and a report profile θ', let $\pi(\theta')$ be the allocation of the verified contract mechanism. $\pi_i(\theta') = 1$ means that the task is allocated to agent i, otherwise she will not perform the task. Since the task can only be assigned to at most one agent, we have $\sum_{i \in N} \pi_i(\theta') \leq 1$. The actual completion quality under the allocation π is drawn from the true PoQ of the selected agent, denoted by q_π. Then $p_i(\theta', q_\pi)$ is the payoff to agent i given from the task requester s. We assume that the utilities of the task requester and the agents are quasi-linear, i.e., $u_s(\theta', q_\pi) = q_\pi - \sum_{i \in N} p_i(\theta', q_\pi)$ and $u_i(\pi(\theta'), p(\theta', q_\pi)) = p_i(\theta', q_\pi) - \pi_i(\theta')c_i$ for all $i \in N$ (In reality, we can map the evaluation of the quality into the same measure of payoffs and costs). In the following, we define several properties concerned in our model. The first one is the efficiency of the mechanism in terms of the expected social welfare.

Definition 2 (Efficiency). *A verified contract mechanism is **efficient** if for all $\theta' \in \Theta$,*

$$\pi(\theta') \in \arg\max_{\pi' \in \Pi} \mathbb{E}_{f'_{\pi'}} \left[q_{\pi'} - \sum_{i \in N} \pi'_i c'_i \right]$$

where Π is the space of all feasible allocations, $f'_{\pi'}$ is the PoQ reported by the selected agent under π' (may not be her true PoQ) and $\mathbb{E}_f[X]$ is the expected value of X taken over f.

In other words, the social welfare equals the completion quality minus the performing cost. An efficient mechanism maximizes the expected social welfare of all agents in the network. Another property is called incentive compatibility, which requires that for each agent i participating in the mechanism, reporting her type θ_i truthfully is a dominant strategy.

Definition 3 (Incentive Compatibility). *A verified contract mechanism is* ***incentive compatible*** *(IC) if for all $i \in N$ and $\theta_i \in \Theta_i$, for all $\theta'_{-i} \in \Theta_{-i}$,*

$$\theta_i \in \arg\max_{\theta'_i \in \Theta_i} \mathbb{E}_{f_i}\left[u_i(\pi((\theta'_i, \theta'_{-i})), p((\theta'_i, \theta'_{-i}), q_{\pi((\theta'_i, \theta'_{-i})))})\right],$$

where θ'_{-i} is the report profile of all agents without i, Θ_{-i} is the space of all possible θ'_{-i}.

Intuitively, incentive compatibility ensures that agents are incentivized to truthfully reveal their abilities and costs to finish the task, and propagate the task information to all their neighbours. The next property ensures that the expected utility of an agent is non-negative when she truthfully reports.

Definition 4 (Individual Rationality). *A verified contract mechanism is* ***individually rational*** *(IR) if for all $i \in N$ and $\theta_i \in \Theta_i$, for all $\theta'_{-i} \in \Theta_{-i}$,*

$$\mathbb{E}_{f_i}\left[u_i(\pi((\theta_i, \theta'_{-i})), p((\theta_i, \theta'_{-i}), q_{\pi((\theta_i, \theta'_{-i})))})\right] \geq 0.$$

The property of individual rationality ensures that agents will not lose to participate in the mechanism. The last desirable property is that the task requester should not suffer a deficit in the task allocation. More precisely, the task requester should consistently achieve a non-negative expected utility, which guarantees the applicability of the mechanism.

Definition 5 (Weakly Budget Balance). *A verified contract mechanism is* ***weakly budget balanced*** *(WBB) if for all $\theta' \in \Theta$,*

$$\mathbb{E}_{f_{\pi(\theta')}}\left[u_s(\theta', q_{\pi(\theta')})\right] \geq 0,$$

where $f_{\pi(\theta')}$ is the true PoQ of the selected agent under θ'.

3   The Mechanism

In this section, we first consider a setting without the execution uncertainty. When no special skills are required to finish the task, all agents perform the given task with the same quality though their costs can differ. We show that the Information Diffusion Mechanism is effective in this setting. However, when the task requires special skills, agents may perform the task with different qualities. We find that the Information Diffusion Mechanism fails in incentive compatibility in this setting. Accordingly, we propose our mechanism, called the PEV-based Diffusion Mechanism, to adapt to both settings. In the PEV-based Diffusion Mechanism, agents are incentivized to diffuse the task information and truthfully report their abilities and costs. The details are illustrated below.

3.1   Without Execution Uncertainty

We first consider the setting where the task performance doesn't require special skills. The task requester gets the same quality no matter which agent the task is assigned to. Then, it is without loss of generality to assume that $Q = \{q\}$ and $f_i(q) = 1$ for all $i \in N$. However, agents may need different costs to perform the given task (e.g., time). Thus, to maximize both the task requester's utility and the social welfare, a mechanism should allocate the task to an agent who can perform the task with the least cost.

Without considering the social network diffusion, all participants are the task requester's direct neighbours. The VCG (Vickrey-Clarke-Groves) mechanism is proposed to incentivize truthfully reporting in auctions. It can be applied here if the goal is changed to select an agent who can perform the task with the least cost rather than selecting the agent with the highest bid. Applying the VCG mechanism, the task requester selects the agent who performs with the least cost among her neighbours, and the agent's payoff equals the decrease in others' utilities due to her participation. Yet the agent may not be the best worker in the social network. For example, let's consider a network in Fig. 1. Without diffusion, the task requester will choose agent 2 while agent 4 can perform the task with the least cost among 7 possible workers. To maximize social welfare, the goal here is to design a mechanism where all agents are incentivized to truthfully report their costs and invite all their neighbours.

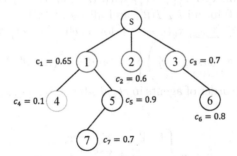

Fig. 1. Given a task, agents' costs to perform the task are shown in the figure. Each agent i can perform the task with $f_i(q) = 1$ and $q = 1$. Without diffusion, the task requester s can only know agent 1, 2 and 3, and agent 2 is chosen. If agents invite all their neighbours, s can know the whole network and then chooses the agent 4.

When considering network diffusion, the VCG mechanism cannot be applied since it will cause deficits for the task requester. An intuitive example is shown in Example 1.

Example 1. Consider the social network shown in Fig. 1, agent 4 is chosen as the agent to perform the task. Let w be the social welfare under this allocation and w_i be the maximal social welfare without i's participation. Then we have

$w_1 = q - c_2 = 0.4$, $w_4 = q - c_2 = 0.4$ and $w = q - c_4 = 0.9$. Therefore, the payoff to agent 1 is $p_1 = q - c_4 - w_1 = 0.5$, the payoff to agent 4 is $p_4 = q - w_4 = 0.6$ and the payoffs to all other agents are 0. Then, the utility of the task requester is $u_s = q - p_1 - p_4 = -0.1$.

To tackle this issue in this setting, we can apply the Information Diffusion Mechanism [8]. The Information Diffusion Mechanism is proposed to incentivize the auction information diffusion to sell a single item in a social network. Similarly, the goal is also changed to select the agent with the least cost. Before giving the mechanism, we first define *critical agents* as follows.

Definition 6. *Given a report profile θ', for agent $i, j \in I(\theta')$, j is one of i's **critical agent** if j exists in all simple paths from the task requester s to agent i in the graph $G(\theta')$. The set of i's all critical agents is denoted by $ct_i(\theta')$ and the sequence order of agents in $ct_i(\theta')$ is denoted by $(s, j_1, \cdots, j_m)$, where $j_m = i$ and $k < k'$ if and only if $j_k \in ct_{j_{k'}}$.*

Then, with the definition above, we apply the Information Diffusion Mechanism in our setting as the following.

Information Diffusion Mechanism

INPUT: a report profile θ'.

---

1. Choose $j \in \arg\max_{i \in I(\theta')} \{q - c_i'\}$ with random tie breaking.
2. Set $\pi_i = 0, p_i = 0$ for all $i \notin I(\theta')$ and all $i \notin ct_j(\theta')$.
3. Compute $w_i = \sum_{k \neq i} \pi_k'(q - c_k')$ for each $i \in ct_j(\theta')$, where $\pi' = \left\{ \pi_i'(\hat{\theta}) = \mathbb{I}\left(i \in \arg\max_{k \in I(\hat{\theta})} q - c_k' \right) \right\}_{i \in N}$ and $\hat{\theta} = (nil, \theta_{-i}')$.
4. Let the sequence order of agents in $ct_j(\theta')$ be $(s, i_1, \cdots, i_m)$, where $i_m = j$. For $k = 1 : m - 1$,

$$\pi_{i_k} = \begin{cases} 1 & \text{if } q - c_{i_k}' = w_{i_{k+1}} \\ & \text{and } \sum_{l=1}^{k-1} \pi_{i_l} = 0 \\ 0 & \text{otherwise} \end{cases}$$

and $\pi_j = 1$ if $\sum_{k=1}^{m-1} \pi_{i_k} = 0$.
5. Suppose i_t be the chosen agent, i.e., $\pi_{i_t} = 1, 1 \leq t \leq m$. Then, the payoff of each agent $i_k \in ct_j(\theta')$ will be

$$p_{i_k} = \begin{cases} w_{i_{k+1}} - w_{i_k} & k < t \\ q - w_{i_t} & k = t \\ 0 & k > t. \end{cases}$$

OUTPUT: the allocation π and the payoff p.

Intuitively, the Information Diffusion Mechanism allocates the task to one agent in the sequence of j's critical agents. More precisely, the mechanism will choose the first agent with the least cost when the next agent in the sequence did not participate[1]. The payoff of the chosen agent equals the least cost reported by other agents who can still participate without her invitation. The payoff of each agent before the chosen agent in the sequence is determined by the difference between the maximum social welfare without her next agent's participation and that without her participation.

Theorem 1 (Li et al. [8]). *The Information Diffusion Mechanism is individually rational, incentive compatible and weakly budget balanced.*

Failure in the Quality-Aware Setting. We then consider another setting without execution uncertainty. In this setting, the task needs special skills to be performed, and then agents may perform the task with different qualities, i.e., $f_i(q_i) = 1$ for $q_i \in Q$ and $i \in N$. Each agent reports her PoQ as f_i', where $f_i'(q_i') = 1$ with $q_i' \in Q$. Then, the task requester also focuses on the qualities that agents will perform the given task with, and we call this setting a quality-aware setting. In this setting, the Information Diffusion Mechanism will try to choose an agent with high-quality performance and a low cost, which then leads to the application failure. The failure lies in no guarantee for incentive compatibility since the payoff to the selected agent is always related to her reported ability. The mechanism will also cause a deficit to the task requester since she may get low-quality performance and give a high payoff to some agent misreporting her ability. Similarly, the Information Diffusion Mechanism cannot be applied when considering the execution uncertainty.

3.2 With Execution Uncertainty

Consider a more general case with execution uncertainty, each agent herself probably performs the task with different qualities. To incentivize the task information diffusion, we apply the idea of the Information Diffusion Mechanism, i.e., agents are rewarded for their contributions in finding the chosen task performer. However, the Information Diffusion Mechanism fails in incentive compatibility in this setting. To mitigate this issue, we propose the **Post Execution Verification-based Diffusion Mechanism** (PEV-based Diffusion Mechanism). The PEV-based Diffusion Mechanism chooses the agent to perform the task based on agents' reports. After the task requester verifies the chosen agent's actual performance, the task requester assigns a payoff to the chosen agent based on her actual performance. Given a report profile $\theta' \in \Theta$, define an allocation that maximizes expected social welfare as

$$\pi^*(\theta') = \left\{ \pi_i^*(\theta') = \mathbb{I}\left(i \in \arg\max_{k \in I(\theta')} \{\mathbb{E}_{f_k'}[Q_k] - c_k'\} \right) \right\}_{i \in N}.$$

---

[1] Assume that there exists at least one agent whose cost to perform the task is less than q, otherwise we can add a dummy agent d with $c_d = q$, and the payoff to the dummy agent is always 0 to ensure the social welfare will be non-negative.

The PEV-based Diffusion Mechanism is defined as follows.

PEV-based Diffusion Mechanism

INPUT: a report profile θ'.

---

1. Choose $j \in \arg\max_{i \in N}\{\mathbb{E}_{f_i'}[Q_i] - c_i'\}$ with random tie breaking.
2. Set $\pi_i = 0, p_i = 0$ for all $i \notin I(\theta')$ and all $i \notin ct_j(\theta')$.
3. For each agent $i \in ct_j(\theta')$, compute $w_i = \sum_{k \neq i} \pi_k' \left(\mathbb{E}_{f_k'}[Q_k] - c_k'\right)$ where $\pi' = \pi^*((nil, \theta'_{-i}))$.
4. Let the sequence order of agents in $ct_j(\theta')$ be $(s, i_1, i_2, \ldots, i_m)$, where $i_m = j$. For $k = 1 : m - 1$,

$$
\pi_{i_k} = \begin{cases} 1 & \text{if } \mathbb{E}_{f_{i_k}'}[Q_{i_k}] - c_{i_k}' = w_{i_{k+1}} \\ & \text{and } \sum_{l=1}^{k-1} \pi_{i_l} = 0 \\ 0 & \text{otherwise} \end{cases}
$$

and $\pi_j = 1$ if $\sum_{k=1}^{m-1} \pi_{i_k} = 0$.
5. Suppose $\pi_{i_t} = 1$ $(1 \leq t \leq m)$. After agent i_t finishes the task, the task requester receives q_π.
6. The payoff of each agent $i_k \in ct_j(\theta')$ is defined as

$$
p_{i_k} = \begin{cases} w_{i_{k+1}} - w_{i_k} & k < t \\ q_\pi - w_{i_t} & k = t \\ 0 & k > t \end{cases}
$$

OUTPUT: the allocation π and the payoff p.

Intuitively, the PEV-based Diffusion Mechanism allocates the task to one agent in the sequence of critical agents. The chosen agent achieves the highest expected welfare when the next agent in the sequence did not participate. The payoff of the chosen agent is determined by her actual execution quality. In the sequence, each critical agent before the chosen agent gets a payoff based on her contribution. Each critical agent's contribution is measured by the increase of the expected social welfare from her participation when the next critical agent did not participate. We give an example to show how the PEV-based Diffusion Mechanism works.

Example 2. Consider the network in Fig. 2, suppose that $Q = \{1, 2, \cdots, 10\}$, all agents' quality distributions f and costs c in their types are listed in the Table 1. Thus, agent 9 is the one maximizing expected social welfare and the sequence order of her critical agents is $(s, 2, 6, 9)$. We can compute that $w_2 = \mathbb{E}_{f_3}[Q_3] - c_3 = 4$, $w_6 = \mathbb{E}_{f_3}[Q_3] - c_3 = 4$ and $w_9 = \mathbb{E}_{f_{10}}[Q_{10}] - c_{10} = 4.5$.

Applying the PEV-based Diffusion Mechanism, we choose agent 9 to perform the task.

Suppose that the actual execution quality of agent 9 is $q_\pi = 8$. Then, the payoffs given to agents 2, 6 and 9 are $p_2 = w_6 - w_2 = 0$, $p_6 = w_9 - w_6 = 0.5$ and $p_9 = q_\pi - w_9 = 3.5$, so their utilities will be $u_2 = p_2 = 0$, $u_6 = p_6 = 0.5$ and $u_9 = p_9 - c_9 = 2.5$. Finally, the utility of the task requester is $u_s = q_\pi - (p_2 + p_6 + p_9) = 4$.

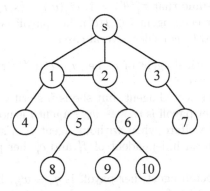

Fig. 2. An example for the PEV-based diffusion mechanism

Table 1. Types of the agents in Fig. 2.

i	f_i	c_i	Expected welfare
1	$f_1(2) = .5, f_1(3) = .5$	$c_1 = 0.5$	2
2	$f_2(1) = 1$	$c_2 = 0.2$	.8
3	$f_3(5) = 1$	$c_3 = 1$	4
4	$f_4(3) = 1$	$c_4 = 1$	2
5	$f_5(4) = .4, f_5(6) = .6$	$c_5 = 1.6$	3.6
6	$f_6(3) = .3, f_6(4) = .6, f_6(7) = .1$	$c_6 = 0.9$	3.1
7	$f_7(6) = .5, f_7(8) = .5$	$c_7 = 4.2$	2.8
8	$f_8(1) = .2, f_8(3) = .8$	$c_8 = 0$	2.6
9	$f_9(8) = .8, f_9(10) = .2$	$c_9 = 1$	7.4
10	$f_{10}(4) = .5, f_{10}(5) = .3, f_{10}(6) = .2$	$c_{10} = 0.2$	4.5

In the following, we will prove the properties of the PEV-based Diffusion Mechanism by first giving two lemmas.

Lemma 1. *Given a report profile $\theta' \in \Theta$, for each agent j, the set of her critical agents $ct_j(\theta')$ and the sequence order of critical agents $(s, i_1, i_2, \ldots, i_m)$ with $i_m = j$, we have $w_{i_k} \leq w_{i_{k'}}$, for all $k < k'$.*

Proof. With the above setting, $i_k \in ct_{i_{k'}}(\theta')$ holds for all $k < k'$. w_{i_k} and $w_{i_{k'}}$ are the maximum expected social welfare for agents in $I((nil, \theta'_{-i_k}))$ and $I((nil, \theta'_{-i_{k'}}))$ respectively. Since agent i_k is before agent i'_k in the sequence, we have that $I((nil, \theta'_{-i_k})) \subset I((nil, \theta'_{-i_{k'}}))$. Then, $w_{i_k} \le w_{i_{k'}}$ holds for all $k < k'$.

Lemma 2. *In the PEV-based Diffusion Mechanism, agent i's payoff p_i is independent of f'_i and c'_i for all $i \in N$ and $\theta' \in \Theta$.*

Proof. Given a report profile θ', let π be the allocation in the PEV-based Diffusion Mechanism. Assume that $\pi_j^*(\theta') = 1$, $ct_j(\theta') = (s, i_1, i_2, \ldots, i_m)$ and i_t is the selected agent. For each agent $i \notin I(\theta')$, her payoff is zero. For each other agent $i \in I(\theta')$, we need to consider several cases.

- If agent i is not a critical agent of i_t, i.e., $i \notin ct_j(\theta')$ or $i = i_k \in ct_j(\theta')$ with $k > t$, her payoff is zero.
- If agent i is not the selected agent, but she is i_t's critical agent, i.e., $i = i_k \in ct_j(\theta')$ with $k < t$, her payoff is $w_{i_{k+1}} - w_{i_k}$. Agent i is not the one maximizing the expected social welfare when without agent i_{k+1}'s participation. Thus, $w_{i_{k+1}}$ and w_{i_k} are both independent of f'_i and c'_i, her payoff is independent of f'_i and c'_i.
- If agent i is the selected agent, her payoff is $q_\pi - w_{i_t}$. Her execution quality q_π is only determined by f_i in her type and w_{i_t} is independent of f'_i and c'_i.

Hence, for all agent $i \in N$, i's payoff is independent of f'_i and c'_i in the PEV-based Diffusion Mechanism.

With these two lemmas, we show that our mechanism satisfies incentive compatibility, individual rationality and weakly budget balance in the following theorem.

Theorem 2. *The PEV-based Diffusion Mechanism is individually rational, incentive compatible and weakly budget balanced.*

Proof. **Individual Rationality.** For each agent $i \in N$, her type θ_i, for all other agents' report profile $\theta'_{-i} \in \Theta_{-i}$, assume that $\pi_j^*((\theta_i, \theta'_{-i})) = 1$. Let $ct_j((\theta_i, \theta'_{-i}))$ be the set of agent j's critical agents, and $(s, i_1, i_2, \ldots, i_m)$ be the sequence order of agents in $ct_j((\theta_i, \theta'_{-i}))$. Applying the PEV-based Diffusion Mechanism, let π be the allocation and i_t be the selected agent, $1 \le t \le m$. For all agents who are not in $I((\theta_i, \theta'_{-i}))$, their payoffs and costs are zero, which means that their utilities are all zero. For each agent $i \in I(\theta')$, her payoff depends on the relationship between her and agent i_t.

(i) If agent i is not agent i_t's critical agent, i.e., $i \notin ct_j$ or $i = i_k \in ct_j$ with $k > t$, her payoff and actual cost are zero.

(ii) If $i \ne i_t$, but i is i_t's critical agent, i.e., $i = i_k \in ct_j$ with $k < t$, her utility is $u_{i_k} = p_{i_k} = w_{i_{k+1}} - w_{i_k}$. According to Lemma 1, her expected utility is always non-negative.

(iii) If agent i is the chosen agent i_t, her expected utility is $\mathbb{E}_{f_i}[q_\pi - w_{i_t} - c_{i_t}] = \mathbb{E}_{f_i}[q_\pi - c_{i_t}] - \mathbb{E}_{f'_{\pi'}}[q_{\pi'} - \sum_{k \ne i} \pi'_k c'_k] \ge 0$, where $\pi' = $

$\pi^*((nil, \theta'_{-i}))$. The inequality holds since agent i must be the one maximizing the expected social welfare for agents in $I((nil, \theta'_{-i})) \cup \{i\}$, otherwise she won't be selected.

Hence, each agent's expected utility is non-negative when truthfully reporting, and our mechanism is **IR**.

Incentive Compatibility. Given agent i's type θ_i, let θ'_{-i} be all other agents' report profile. Assume agent j is the agent maximizing the expected social welfare when i truthfully reports, i.e., $\pi^*_j((\theta_i, \theta'_{-i})) = 1$. Let $(s, i_1, i_2, \ldots, i_m)$ be the sequence order of agents in $ct_j((\theta_i, \theta'_{-i}))$. Applying the PEV-based Diffusion Mechanism, let i_t be the selected agent under (θ_i, θ'_{-i}), $1 \leq t \leq m$. Note that for all $i \notin I((\theta_i, \theta'_{-i}))$, agent i's expected utility is zero for all her possible reports. Thus, we only consider the cases where agent i is in $I((\theta_i, \theta'_{-i}))$.

(i) If $i \notin ct_j((\theta_i, \theta'_{-i}))$, i cannot change the allocation by only misreporting r'_i, and then i's expected utility is zero. Her expected utility changes only when she misreports f'_i or c'_i to be selected. Now her expected utility is $\mathbb{E}_{f_i}[q - w_i - c_i]$, where q is her actual completion quality and $w_i = \mathbb{E}_{f'_{\pi'}}[q_{\pi'}] - \sum_{k \neq i} \pi'_k c'_k$ and $\pi' = \pi^*((nil, \theta'_{-i}))$. $\mathbb{E}_{f_i}[Q_i - c_i] \leq \mathbb{E}_{f'_j}[Q_j - c_j]$ holds for $\pi^*_j((\theta_i, \theta'_{-i})) = 1$. Since $j \in I((nil, \theta'_{-i}))$, we have $\pi'_j = 1$ and $w_i = \mathbb{E}_{f'_j}[Q_j - c'_j]$. Then, her utility is $\mathbb{E}_{f_i}[q - w_i - c_i] = \mathbb{E}_{f_i}[Q_i - c_i] - \mathbb{E}_{f'_j}[Q_j - c'_j] \leq 0$. Then, agent i's utility will not increase if she misreports.

(ii) If $i = i_k \in ct_j((\theta_i, \theta'_{-i}))$ with $k > t$, agent i_t is still selected for all possible θ'_i and agent i's expected utility is always zero.

(iii) If $i = i_k \in ct_j((\theta_i, \theta'_{-i}))$ with $k < t$, agent i's expected utility is $\mathbb{E}_{f_i}[w_{i_{k+1}} - w_{i_k}] = w_{i_{k+1}} - w_{i_k}$, where w_l is the maximum expected social welfare for all agents in $I((nil, \hat{\theta}_{-l}))$ with $\hat{\theta} = (\theta_i, \theta'_{-i})$. If i misreports her type as θ'_i, denote all agents' report profile by $\hat{\theta}' = (\theta'_i, \theta'_{-i})$. Applying the PEV-based Diffusion Mechanism, let j' be the selected agent under $\hat{\theta}'$, and $(s, i'_1, i'_2, \ldots, i'_{m'})$ be the sequence order of agents in $ct_{j'}(\hat{\theta}')$.

1. If $i \notin ct_{j'}(\hat{\theta}')$, her expected utility decreases to zero.
2. If agent i is a critical agent of agent j', agent j' is also a critical agent of j, i.e., $j' = i_{k'} \in ct_j(\hat{\theta})$ with $k' > k$, agent i's expected utility is unchanged.
3. If agent i is a critical agent of j' and j' is not critical agent of agent j, i.e., $i = i'_{k'} \in ct_{j'}(\hat{\theta}')$ and $j' \notin ct_j(\hat{\theta})$, agent i's expected utility is $\mathbb{E}_{f_i}[w'_{i'_{k'+1}} - w'_{i'_{k'}}] = w'_{i'_{k'+1}} - w'_{i'_{k'}}$, where w'_l is the maximum expected social welfare for agents in $I((nil, \hat{\theta}'_{-l}))$. $w'_{i'_{k'}} = w_{i_k}$ holds since $I((nil, \hat{\theta}'_{-i})) = I((nil, \hat{\theta}_{-i}))$. Since $j' \notin ct_j(\hat{\theta}')$, agent i_{k+1} cannot be informed of the task information. Thus, $I((nil, \hat{\theta}'_{-i'_{k'+1}})) \subset I((nil, \hat{\theta}_{-i_{k+1}}))$ and $w'_{i'_{k'+1}} \leq w_{i_{k+1}}$. Accordingly, we have $w'_{i'_{k'+1}} - w'_{i'_{k'}} \leq w_{i_{k+1}} - w_{i_k}$, which means i's expected utility decreases.
4. If $i = j'$, let q be i's completion quality. Her expected utility is $\mathbb{E}_{f_i}[q - w_{i_k} - c_i] = \mathbb{E}_{f_i}[q - c_i] - w_{i_k}$. Since $i \in I((nil, \hat{\theta}_{-i_{k+1}}))$, and agent

i is not the one maximizing the expected social welfare when without agent i_{k+1}'s participation under $\hat{\theta}$, we have that $\mathbb{E}_{f_i}[q - c_i] - w_{i_k} - (w_{i_{k+1}} - w_{i_k}) = \mathbb{E}_{f_i}[q - c_i] - w_{i_{k+1}} = \mathbb{E}_{f_i}[Q_i - c_i] - w_{i_{k+1}} \leq 0$, which means that agent i's expected utility decreases when misreporting.

(iv) If $i = i_t$, her expected utility is $\mathbb{E}_{f_i}[q_\pi - c_i - w_{i_t}]$. If agent i misreports her type as θ_i', denote all agents' report profile by $\hat{\theta}' = (\theta_i', \theta_{-i}')$ and the original one by $\hat{\theta} = (\theta_i, \theta_{-i}')$. Applying the PEV-based Diffusion Mechanism, let j' be the selected agent under $\hat{\theta}'$ and $ct_{j'}(\hat{\theta}') = (s, i_1', i_2', \ldots, i_{m'}')$.

1. If $i = j'$, her expected utility is unchanged, which can be referred from the Lemma 2.
2. If $i \notin ct_{j'}(\hat{\theta}')$, her expected utility decreases to zero.
3. If $i \neq j'$, but agent i is one critical agent of agent j', i.e., $i = i_{k'}' \in ct_{j'}(\hat{\theta}')$ and $k' < m'$, her expected utility is $\mathbb{E}_{f_i}[w_{i_{k+1}'}' - w_{i_k'}'] = w_{i_{k+1}'}' - w_{i_k'}'$, where w_l' is the maximum expected social welfare under $(nil, \hat{\theta}_{-l}')$. Then, $w_{i_k'}' = w_{i_t}$ holds for $I((nil, \hat{\theta}_{-i}')) = I((nil, \hat{\theta}_{-i}))$.

   Since $\pi_i(\hat{\theta}) = 1$, then we have $i = j$ or $w_{i_{t+1}} = \mathbb{E}_{f_i}[Q_i - c_i]$ if $t < m$. In the first case, $\mathbb{E}_{f_i}[q_\pi - c_i] \geq w_{i_{k+1}'}'$ always holds. In the second case, if $j' \in ct_j(\hat{\theta})$, we have $i_{k+1}' = i_{t+1}$, which means that $w_{i_{k+1}'}' \leq w_{i_{t+1}} = \mathbb{E}_{f_i}[Q_i - c_i]$. If $j' \notin ct_j(\hat{\theta})$, agent i_{t+1} must not be informed of the task information. Then, we have $I((nil, \hat{\theta}_{i_{k+1}'}')) \subset I((nil, \hat{\theta}_{i_{t+1}}))$ and $w_{i_{k+1}'}' \leq w_{i_{t+1}} = \mathbb{E}_{f_i}[Q_i - c_i]$. Thus, the relationship between her current utility and her original one is $w_{i_{k+1}'}' - w_{i_k'}' - (\mathbb{E}_{f_i}[q_\pi - c_i] - w_{i_t}) = w_{i_{k+1}'}' - \mathbb{E}_{f_i}[q_\pi - c_i] = w_{i_{k+1}'}' - \mathbb{E}_{f_i}[Q_i - c_i] \leq 0$.

In summary, for each $i \in N$, agent i's expected utility is maximized when she is truthful. Hence, the PEV-based Diffusion Mechanism is **IC**.

Weakly Budget Balance. Given a report profile $\theta' \in \Theta$, let π be the allocation π under θ', the expected utility of s is

$$\mathbb{E}_{f_\pi'}\left[q_\pi - \sum_{i \in N} p_i(\theta', q_\pi)\right]$$
$$= \mathbb{E}_{f_\pi'}\left[q_\pi - (q_\pi - w_{i_t}) - \sum_{k=1}^{t-1}(w_{i_{k+1}} - w_{i_k})\right]$$
$$= \mathbb{E}_{f_\pi'}[w_{i_1}] = w_{i_1} \geq 0$$

Hence, the PEV-based Diffusion Mechanism is **WBB**.

Notice that the expected utility of the task requester equals w_{i_1}, i.e., the maximum expected social welfare when the first agent in the critical agent sequence did not participate. It also means that the expected utility of the task requester will be no less than that when only the neighbours of the task requester participate. Notice that our mechanism cannot always guarantee efficiency since the task may not be allocated to the best worker. Below, we give a proposition to show that no mechanism simultaneously satisfies IR, IC, WBB and efficiency.

Proposition 1. *There is no verified contract mechanism satisfying individual rationality, incentive compatibility, weak budget balance and efficiency in the social networks.*

Proof. We can prove this statement by showing that no individually rational, incentive compatible and efficient verified contract mechanism can satisfy weakly budget balance in the social networks.

Fig. 3. A counterexample: the task requester s is connected to agent 1, and agent 1 has two neighbours: s and agent 2.

Let $\mathcal{M}$ be an IR, IC and efficient verified contract mechanism. Consider a graph shown in Fig. 3, there are only three agents. Given the task to be performed, and suppose that the performance level set is Q. Assume that $f_1(q_1) = 1$, $f_2(q_2) = 1$, $q_1 = q_2$ and $\mathbb{E}_{f_2}[Q_2 - c_2] > \mathbb{E}_{f_1}[Q_1 - c_1] > 0$.

- When agent 1 does not invite agent 2, the mechanism $\mathcal{M}$ will allocate the task to agent 1 and agent 1 must get a payoff of q_1. Otherwise, agent 1 can misreport her cost c_1'.
- When agent 1 invites agent 2, agent 2's payoff should be at least c_2'. However, to guarantee IC, agent 1 should get a payoff of at least $q_1 - c_1'$. Then, agent 1 must get at least $q_1 - c_2$ otherwise agent 1 can misreport her cost to get higher payoff. Similarly, agent 2's payoff must be at least c_1. Then, the utility of the sponsor will be at most $q_2 - p_1 - p_2 \le q_2 - (q_1 - c_2) - c_1 = c_2 - c_1 < 0$. Then, the mechanism $\mathcal{M}$ is not WBB.

4 Conclusion

In this paper, we focus on the single-task allocation problem in the social network. We propose the PEV-based Diffusion Mechanism to incentivize agents to propagate the task information, thus involving more participants and finding a better worker. Then, the PEV-based Diffusion Mechanism can increase the expected utility of the task requester. There also exist open problems worth further investigations. For example, applicable mechanisms are still missing in multiple-task allocation settings where tasks have combinatorial qualities or there exist dependencies between tasks. More importantly, we do expect our work can inspire the research community in the future, especially under decentralized systems such as blockchain [18].

Acknowledgement. This work is supported by Science and Technology Commission of Shanghai Municipality (No. 22ZR1442200).

References

1. Chawla, S., Hartline, J.D., Sivan, B.: Optimal crowdsourcing contests. Games Econ. Behav. **113**, 80–96 (2019)
2. Conitzer, V., Vidali, A.: Mechanism design for scheduling with uncertain execution time. In: Proceedings of the Twenty-Eighth AAAI Conference on Artificial Intelligence, AAAI 2014, pp. 623–629. AAAI Press (2014)
3. Dash, R.K., Vytelingum, P., Rogers, A., David, E., Jennings, N.R.: Market-based task allocation mechanisms for limited-capacity suppliers. IEEE Trans. Syst. Man Cybern.-Part A: Syst. Hum. **37**(3), 391–405 (2007)
4. Goel, G., Nikzad, A., Singla, A.: Allocating tasks to workers with matching constraints: truthful mechanisms for crowdsourcing markets. In: Proceedings of the 23rd International Conference on World Wide Web, pp. 279–280 (2014)
5. Jiang, Y., Zhou, Y., Wang, W.: Task allocation for undependable multiagent systems in social networks. IEEE Trans. Parallel Distrib. Syst. **24**(8), 1671–1681 (2012)
6. Li, B., Hao, D., Gao, H., Zhao, D.: Diffusion auction design. Artif. Intell. **303**, 103631 (2022)
7. Li, B., Hao, D., Zhao, D.: Incentive-compatible diffusion auctions. In: Proceedings of the Twenty-Ninth International Joint Conference on Artificial Intelligence, IJCAI 2020, pp. 231–237. ijcai.org (2020)
8. Li, B., Hao, D., Zhao, D., Zhou, T.: Mechanism design in social networks. In: Proceedings of the Thirty-First AAAI Conference on Artificial Intelligence, pp. 586–592. AAAI Press (2017)
9. Li, Y.M., Shiu, Y.L.: A diffusion mechanism for social advertising over microblogs. Decis. Supp. Syst. **54**(1), 9–22 (2012)
10. Nisan, N., Ronen, A.: Algorithmic mechanism design. Games Econ. Behav. **35**(1–2), 166–196 (2001)
11. Porter, R., Ronen, A., Shoham, Y., Tennenholtz, M.: Fault tolerant mechanism design. Artif. Intell. **172**(15), 1783–1799 (2008)
12. Ramchurn, S.D., Mezzetti, C., Giovannucci, A., Rodriguez-Aguilar, J.A., Dash, R.K., Jennings, N.R.: Trust-based mechanisms for robust and efficient task allocation in the presence of execution uncertainty. J. Artif. Intell. Res. **35**, 119–159 (2009)
13. Shi, H., Zhang, Y., Si, Z., Wang, L., Zhao, D.: Maximal information propagation with budgets. In: ECAI 2020–24th European Conference on Artificial Intelligence, vol. 325, pp. 211–218. IOS Press (2020)
14. Tang, J.C., Cebrian, M., Giacobe, N.A., Kim, H.W., Kim, T., Wickert, D.B.: Reflecting on the darpa red balloon challenge. Commun. ACM **54**(4), 78–85 (2011)
15. de Weerdt, M.M., Zhang, Y., Klos, T.: Multiagent task allocation in social networks. Auton. Agents Multi-Agent Syst. **25**(1), 46–86 (2012)
16. Wu, X., Huang, D., Sun, Y.-E., Bu, X., Xin, Yu., Huang, H.: An efficient allocation mechanism for crowdsourcing tasks with minimum execution time. In: Huang, D.-S., Hussain, A., Han, K., Gromiha, M.M. (eds.) ICIC 2017. LNCS (LNAI), vol. 10363, pp. 156–167. Springer, Cham (2017). https://doi.org/10.1007/978-3-319-63315-2_14
17. Zhao, D.: Mechanism design powered by social interactions. In: Proceedings of the 20th International Conference on Autonomous Agents and Multi-Agent Systems, pp. 63–67 (2021)

18. Zhao, D.: Mechanism design powered by social interactions: a call to arms. In: Raedt, L.D. (ed.) Proceedings of the Thirty-First International Joint Conference on Artificial Intelligence, IJCAI-22, pp. 5831–5835. International Joint Conferences on Artificial Intelligence Organization (2022), early Career
19. Zhao, D., Ramchurn, S.D., Jennings, N.R.: Fault tolerant mechanism design for general task allocation. In: Proceedings of the 2016 International Conference on Autonomous Agents & Multiagent Systems, pp. 323–331. ACM (2016)

Incorporating AI Methods
in Micro-dynamic Analysis to Support
Group-Specific Policy-Making

Shuang Chang[(✉)], Tatsuya Asai, Yusuke Koyanagi, Kento Uemura,
Koji Maruhashi, and Kotaro Ohori

Fujitsu Research, 4-1-1 Kamikodanaka, Nakahara-ku, Kawasaki 211-8588, Japan
{chang.shuang,asai.tatsuya,koyanagi.yusuke,uemura.kento,
maruhashi.koji,ohori.kotaro}@fujitsu.com

Abstract. An agent-based modelling approach is a powerful means of understanding social phenomena by modelling individual behaviours and interactions. However, the advancements in modelling pose challenges in the model analysis process for understanding the complex effects of input factors, especially when it comes to offering concrete policies for improving system outcomes. In this work, we propose a revised micro-dynamic analysis method that adopts advanced artificial intelligence methods to enhance the model interpretation and to facilitate group-specific policy-making. It strengthens the explanation power of the conventional micro-dynamic analysis by eliminating ambiguity in the result interpretation and enabling a causal interpretation of a target phenomenon across subgroups. We applied our method to understand an agent-based model that evaluates the effects of a long-term care scheme on access to care. Our findings showed that the method can suggest policies for improving the equity of access more efficiently than the conventional scenario analysis.

Keywords: Analysis method · Agent-based model · Long-term care services

1 Introduction

Agent-based modelling (ABM) is a powerful means of modelling socio-economic systems by capturing the core characteristics of system complexities from a bottom-up perspective [10]. It complements conventional social science approaches by providing the ability to model individuals' interactive behaviours against a socially constructed environment for investigating complex social systems. By articulating this intricate link between micro-level interactions and the emergent macro-level phenomenon, it becomes a promising tool for evaluating policy effects on social systems, offering evidence-based recommendations and facilitating communication among relevant stakeholders [2,5].

© The Author(s), under exclusive license to Springer Nature Switzerland AG 2023
R. Aydoğan et al. (Eds.): PRIMA 2022, LNAI 13753, pp. 122–138, 2023.
https://doi.org/10.1007/978-3-031-21203-1_8

However, this advancement in modelling poses challenges in the model analysis process, particularly when analysing the non-linear relation between input parameters and the model output. First, agent-based simulation normally generates a large volume of multidimensional simulation logs comprising details on agents' attributes, their interactive and adaptive behaviours, and environmental parameters, which complicates the analysis when it comes to understanding their combined effects [20]. Second, an agent-based model is generally simulated with random sequences in order to provide statistically robust results, which renders the explanation of these results sensitive to the varied experimental settings [16]. Third, an agent-based model not only looks at the aggregate-level outcome but also at the individual-level description. Simulating and exploring all of the possible behaviours and scenarios will thus be extremely time consuming [4]. At present, a thorough yet efficient analysis process on simulation logs is vital to understand the model behaviour, to identify important and relevant patterns, and to deliver insightful knowledge for guiding the design of policies [16,20], which forms the motivation of this work.

1.1 Relevant Works

To enable transparent and reliable analysis of model behaviours quantitatively, modellers have been developing and deploying various techniques to analyse the simulation outputs. For example, statistical methods have been applied to determine the minimum number of simulation runs for generating a sufficient number of samples [12]; optimization methods such as genetic algorithms and sensitivity analysis have been applied to explore the parameter space for identifying the link between parameters and specific model outputs [29]; artificial intelligence methods, such as random forests, have been applied to train metamodels for understanding the model dynamics [8], and a variety of visualization techniques incorporating other methods, such as classification and clustering, have been developed to represent simulation outcomes for facilitating the communication between modellers and other relevant stakeholders [17]. A survey of ABM analysis methods along with a discussion of their challenges and suggested solutions can be found in [16].

On the other hand, the use of quantitative methods solely is not sufficient for explaining the simulation outcome, especially in the case of modelling complex social systems [3]. To enable a qualitative explanation of the model behaviour, Ohori et al. proposed a micro-dynamics analysis method that explains emergent phenomena from the perspective of agents' behaviours and facilitates the communication among stakeholders [19]. Yamane et al. later proposed a systematic micro-dynamics analysis method that relies less on modellers' skills and domain knowledge for analysis [28]. This method automatically identifies the most important causes of a target phenomenon in light of which policies can be offered for improving the phenomenon. Yamada et al. subsequently improved the method by efficiently eliminating causes that are neither useful nor sufficient, termed "small causes" and "simple causes", for suggesting ways to improve the phenomenon [27].

Limitations. While the micro-dynamic analysis methods have proven effective and efficient in suggesting policies to improve system outcomes, there are still a few problems to be tackled. First, there is some ambiguity in the interpretation of identified causes, which requires extra effort for explaining the model behaviours and results. Second, it is not possible to determine causes for different subgroups regarding the phenomenon. This is particularly important for the application of ABM in the realm of social policy analysis, which aims to reduce inequalities across different social groups in terms of access to various kinds of services, such as health and social care [15].

Contribution. On the basis of the discussion above, we aim to propose a revised micro-dynamic analysis method for eliminating the ambiguity in results interpretation and offering policies that target particular subgroups to improve system outcomes. By leveraging advanced artificial intelligence methods, our method can identify subgroups with unique patterns regarding a target phenomenon and discover the causal relations between input factors and the target phenomenon across various subgroups.

We provide a brief review of the conventional micro-dynamic analysis method and introduce our new method in Sect. 2. In Sect. 3, we apply our method to the simulation outcomes of an agent-based model on evaluating a long-term care (LTC) insurance system for clarifying its underlying mechanisms. We demonstrate how this method can strengthen the explanation of the model and efficiently suggest informed policies toward improving the equity of access to LTC services for the most-in-need subgroups, compared with the conventional scenario analysis method. We conclude in Sect. 4 with a brief summary and mention of future work.

2   Method

We first briefly review the conventional micro-dynamics analysis method [27,28] and discuss its limitations. We then propose and explain the procedures of our improved method, as illustrated in Fig. 1.

2.1   Conventional Micro-dynamic Analysis Method

The conventional method consists of four steps: define target phenomenon, label agents leading to the phenomenon, cluster agents, and identify candidates of causes.

S1 Define Target Phenomenon. An operational definition of a phenomenon observed from the macro-level is provided such that the causes leading to it can be analysed. For example, in the case of pedestrian flow simulation, congestion is defined as the target phenomenon and can be distinguished from non-congestion situations by spatial and temporal factors.

S2 Label Agents Leading to the Phenomenon of Interest. Agents relevant to the phenomenon of interest are labelled as target agents. The characteristics

(or features) of the target agents are considered as potential causes of the phenomenon. For example, in the case of pedestrian flow simulation, agents who are
waiting at a particular facility during a particular time slot will be labelled.

S3 Cluster Agents' Features. Agent features are clustered on the basis of
corresponding data type. Features can be static (e.g., personal traits) or dynamic
(e.g., behaviour trajectories). A k-means clustering algorithm is applied, where
k is selected as maximizing the similarity between feature clusters and target
agents. In the case of pedestrian flow simulation, for instance, the passengers'
routes as they visit various airport facilities will be clustered, where each cluster
represents the percentage of agents having visited each facility.

S4 Identify Candidates of Causes. Candidates of causes are extracted and
sorted from the intersections of all combinations of clusters from S3. The similarity between a candidate and the target agents is measured by the F-score,
and a higher value indicates a high probability of being the cause of the target phenomenon. In the case of pedestrian flow simulation, gaining most of the
information from a particular sign could be one of the identified causes.

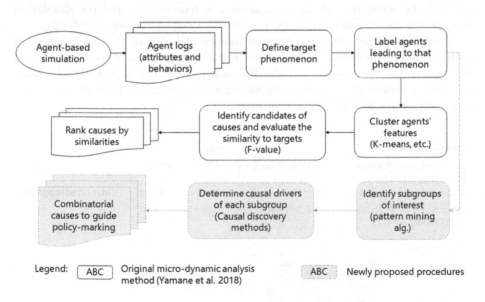

Legend: [ABC] Original micro-dynamic analysis method (Yamane et al. 2018)   [ABC] Newly proposed procedures

Fig. 1. A revised micro-dynamic analysis method.

Limitations of Current Method. The automated clustering method in step
3 (S3) generates clusters similar to each other [27], which makes the interpretation of causes ambiguous. For example, in its application to the pedestrian
flow simulation for evaluating an airport signage system with the congestion situation as the target phenomenon, S3 will cluster all passengers' routes as they
visit various airport facilities. This leads to the generation of similar clusters,

and extra effort is thus required for differentiating and explaining which route leads to the congestion situation. In addition, the suggested policies for relieving the congestion situation are targeted at all passengers, thus extra analyses are required to come up with strategies targeted at particular groups.

2.2 Proposed Method

We incorporate an efficient knowledge discovery technology and a set of causal discovery methods to tackle the above problems as replacing S3 and S4. Instead of clustering agents and evaluating the similarity between target agents and various combinations of agent clusters, we propose two new steps: (S3) identify subgroups that are highly associative with the target phenomenon and (S4) explore causal links between subgroup characteristics and the target phenomenon for each subgroup of interest.

S3 Identify Subgroups of Interest. We aim to identify subgroups having the same value of particular features that are highly related to the target phenomenon. The target phenomenon is denoted by a binary variable indicating whether the occurrence of the phenomenon is true or not, and the simulation logs are separated into two classes, positive and negative, correspondingly.

We deploy a knowledge discovery technology utilizing an efficient constrained pattern-mining algorithm [13] to identify relevant subgroups. This algorithm can also be utilized for learning and classification models and is proved to be more accurate in binary classification experiments than other learning methods such as logistic regression and random forests.

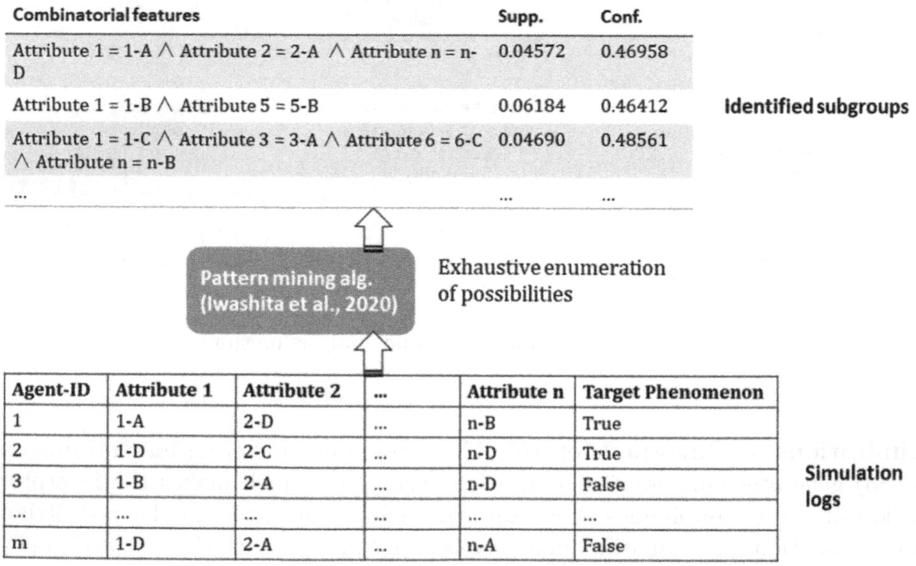

Combinatorial features	Supp.	Conf.	
Attribute 1 = 1-A ∧ Attribute 2 = 2-A ∧ Attribute n = n-D	0.04572	0.46958	
Attribute 1 = 1-B ∧ Attribute 5 = 5-B	0.06184	0.46412	**Identified subgroups**
Attribute 1 = 1-C ∧ Attribute 3 = 3-A ∧ Attribute 6 = 6-C ∧ Attribute n = n-B	0.04690	0.48561	
...	...	...	

Pattern mining alg. (Iwashita et al., 2020)

Exhaustive enumeration of possibilities

Agent-ID	Attribute 1	Attribute 2	...	Attribute n	Target Phenomenon	
1	1-A	2-D	...	n-B	True	
2	1-D	2-C	...	n-D	True	
3	1-B	2-A	...	n-D	False	**Simulation logs**
...	...	...	...	...	...	
m	1-D	2-A	...	n-A	False	

Fig. 2. Format of input features and output patterns.

The format of the input features and output patterns is illustrated in Fig. 2. With tabular data composed of agent attributes and the target phenomenon as input, the method identifies emerging patterns that can discriminate binary classes by searching over and evaluating all combinations of agent features. The combinatorial features, as emerging patterns or subgroups, are measured and ranked by the ratio of agents in positive class of this subgroup to all agents of this subgroup [7], denoted as "Conf.", and the ratio of agents in positive class of this subgroup to all agents, denoted as "Supp.". For example, a subgroup having 100 agents in the positive class and 20 agents in the negative class will be ranked higher than a subgroup having 100 agents in the positive class and 50 agents in the negative class. In this work, we utilize this algorithm to efficiently search over all combinations of input features and discover the conjunctions of features with higher ranks as subgroups that are highly related to the phenomenon. Subgroups can be further filtered according to customized rules with regard to different applications.

Since this method thoroughly and explicitly evaluates the combined effects of all input features and ranks the most influential ones, it eliminates any ambiguity in interpretation, which is a problem arising due to the similarity among agent clusters in the conventional micro-dynamic analysis method.

S4 Determine Causal Drivers for Each Subgroup. For each subgroup, we aim to formulate qualitative explanations of the target phenomenon or collective behaviours invoked by discovering individual causal relations. We apply a set of causal discovery methods to learn the causal relations among agent features from simulation logs, and to represent the relations by directed acyclic graphs. The derived causal relations can be further utilized to guide concrete policies or interventions for improving the target phenomenon.

In contrast to the co-variate analysis, a causal discovery task is focused more on the causal effects among variables rather than mere associative relations. Causal discovery methods have been applied in various fields and have proven useful in discovering causal relations that approximate well-established and known evidence [23]. Such methods can be roughly categorized as constraint-based methods, score-based methods, and methods based on functional causal models [11]. Constraint-based methods statistically estimate the conditional independence among variables to describe the causal structure, while score-based methods select the causal structure among a number of generated ones on the basis of the corresponding score associated with each of them. Functional causal models impose additional assumptions on the data distribution and represent each variable as a deterministic function of its causes and unmeasurable noises [11,23].

Since these methods pose different assumptions on the input datasets, handle confounders differently, and are hard to verify, it is challenging to use them in practical applications. To provide more informative results, we apply multiple causal discovery methods and select those causal relations commonly identified by more than one method [14]. We choose the classic or the most widely applied methods from these types, namely, Greedy Fast Causal Inference (GFCI) [18],

PC [25], and DirectLiNGAM [24], and compare them in Table 1 in terms of the type of variables they can handle, whether the presence of latent confounders is assumed, and whether they can output exact causal structures. GFCI is a combination of the constraint-based method Fast Causal Inference (FCI) [26] and the score-based method Fast Greedy Equivalence Search (FGES) [22], and has been proved to perform better than FCI in some applications [11]. DirectLiNGAM can be used to indicate the sign of causal effects, either positive or negative.

Table 1. A comparison of causal discovery methods

Method	Data type	Confounder	Output
GFCI [18]	Mixed	Yes	Markov equivalence class
PC [25]	Mixed	No	Markov equivalence class
DirectLiNGAM [24]	Continuous	No	Exact structure

3 Application

We apply the above method to understand an agent-based model [6] that evaluates the effects of a long-term care (LTC) nursing insurance scheme launched in a Chinese city, Qingdao, on access to care by simulating individuals' care-seeking behaviours under this particular LTC scheme. The case description and agents' characteristics and behaviours are reviewed first, followed by the analysis provided by the proposed method.

3.1 Qingdao's LTC Scheme

This pilot LTC scheme provides various types of assistance to the elderly individuals who may have difficulty in conducting daily activities via three types of facilities: 1) hospital care providing intensive care for elderly persons with critical LTC needs, 2) nursing home care providing continuous care for elderly persons having substantial difficulties in daily activities, and 3) home-based care providing regular home-visiting care on a weekly basis by doctors and nurses. Key LTC features include eligibility rules and service costs are defined as follows.

Eligibility. Participants who have LTC needs determined by an Activity Daily Living questionnaire, and are enrolled in either Urban Employee Insurance (UEI), which covers urban residents with formal employment, or Urban Resident Insurance (URI), which covers urban residents without formal employment.

Service Costs. Reimbursement rates are different for participants in different insurance schemes, ranging from 90% for UEI participants to 80% for URI participants.

3.2   Agent-Based Model

Two types of agent are defined and modelled: individuals and service providers.

Characteristics of Agents. Individuals are defined by their age, gender, ADL limitations, insurance type, household income, type of caregiver, and district. The structure of age pyramid approximates that of four districts in Qingdao, China. Values of individual characteristics are calibrated using datasets drawn from the China Health and Retirement Longitudinal Study (CHARLS) (http://charls.ccer.edu.cn/en), a nationally representative cross-sectional dataset, as well as local statistics on population. The descriptive statistics of the population in comparison with the national representative sample and local population statistics of Qingdao are provided in Tables 2 and 3 (Tables 1 and 2 in [6]).

Service providers are defined by type, number of LTC beds, service quality, service costs, and district. Values of providers' monthly costs and number of beds are determined from local statistics on health facilities [21], whilst values of service quality are set against qualitative evidence [9]. Nursing home providers are further classified into four types based on differences in monthly cost and quality [9]. We assume a sufficient number of LTC beds is allocated to each district.

Table 2. Descriptive statistics of baseline population

Percentage*	District 1	District 2	District 3	District 4
Age: 0–19	14.7% (14.1%)	16.1% (15.4%)	20.0% (18.2%)	18.3% (17.8%)
Age: 20–29	20.7% (19.7%)	21.00% (19.4%)	23.9% (23.0%)	24.9% (27.0%)
Age: 30–39	16.2% (17.0%)	15.5% (15.9%)	19.1% (19.0%)	19.1% (15.1%)
Age: 40–49	16.9% (16.6%)	15.0% (17.1%)	13.9% (14.9%)	14.1% (16.3%)
Age: 50–59	15.0% (16.7%)	14.2% (15.6%)	11.0% (12.8%)	10.9% (12.5%)
Age: 60–69	9.2% (7.8%)	9.3% (8.5%)	5.8% (6.4%)	6.2% (6.3%)
Age: 70–	7.3% (8.1%)	8.9% (8.2%)	6.3% (5.7%)	6.4% (5.0%)

*Value in our model (from Qingdao population statistics)

Care-Seeking Behaviour. A two-stage care-seeking behaviour is defined for individuals who have LTC needs, i.e., $adl >= 2$, by considering the characteristics of service providers and LTC policies [1]. Following the eligibility rules laid out in the LTC policies, individuals first select an eligible type of service on the basis of their age, income, type of caregiver, insurance status, and number of ADL limitations as $exp(V_{st})/\sum_{st} exp(V_{st})$, where V_{st} is defined in Eq. 1. $st \in \{0, 1, 2\}$ denotes hospital care, nursing home care, and home-based care, respectively. $Inx(x)$ is defined as $1 - e^{-x}$, and β_i represents the weight.

Second, individuals select a particular service provider by evaluating each in terms of service quality, costs, and number of available beds by Eqs. 2 and

Table 3. Descriptive statistics of baseline population aged above 45

	District 1	District 2	District 3	District 4	CHARLS*
Gender (*gender*)					
Male (1)	50.58%	50.63%	50.26%	50.1%	51.36%
Female (0)	49.42%	49.37%	49.74%	49.9%	48.64%
Insurance (*insurance*)					
UEI (1)	35.98%	33.13%	30.36%	31.44%	43.48%
URI (2)	16.91%	18.42%	16.71%	18.9%	19.11%
Number of ADL (*adl*)					
1–2	3.16%	3.98%	3.43%	4.73%	3.73%
3–4	0.82%	0.7%	0.46%	0.56%	0.71%
5–6	0.79%	0.93%	0.69%	0.38%	0.88%
Carer type (*carer*)					
Spouse or paid (1)	50.12%	48.34%	59.87%	69.02%	51.23%
Children (2)	18.28%	22.16%	23.41%	10.59%	20.58%
Relatives (3)	23.9%	19.9%	10.03%	15.69%	17.87%
No one (4)	7.66%	9.6%	6.69%	4.7%	9.96%
Household Income (RMB) (*income*)					
Mean	12956	14511	19282	17637	17976
S.D	28964	27739	31458	32014	42797

*Distribution of urban samples only

3, where c represents the discrepancy between household income and service costs, sq represents the service quality, t represents the period of stay at the provider, and w_i represents the preference of each factor. Characteristics of service providers, i.e., vacancy and service quality, will be changed dynamically along with individuals' selections.

$$V_{st} = \begin{cases} \beta_1 * Inx(insurance_i) + \beta_2 * Inx(age_i) + \beta_3 * Inx(income_i) & \text{for } st = 0 \\ \beta_1' * Inx(carer_i) + \beta_2' * Inx(age_i) + \beta_3' * Inx(income_i) & \text{for } st \in \{1, 2\} \end{cases} \quad (1)$$

$$Util(t) = U(w_1, c) + U(w_2, sq) + U(w_3, t) \quad (2)$$

$$U(x, y) = x * (1 - e^{-y}) \quad (3)$$

3.3   Micro-dynamic Analysis Results

The ABM model is calibrated using empirical datasets at the micro-level and reproduced the pattern of care use across different types of care, as validated against macro-level evidence. By using the proposed method, we aim to improve the equity in access to such services by identifying subgroups that are most likely to use a particular type of LTC service, forming a causal explanation of their care choices, and based on which offering policy suggestions targeted at particular subgroups.

We run the model for 20 times and the changes of all agents' attributes and their choice of care over 20 iterations are logged. Each record contains the individual's age, gender, insurance, number of ADL limitations, type of caregiver, income, and the type of care they have chosen. We randomly select simulation logs from the final iteration and apply the proposed analysis method on them.

S1 Define Target Phenomenon. We define the use of LTC services across different types of services (i.e., hospital care, nursing home care, and home-based care) as the target phenomenon. Our focus here is the equity of access to different types of services under the current LTC scheme. To this end, we seek to discover subgroups closely related to the selection of each type of care, as well as the main causes of such selection within each subgroup.

S2 Label Agents Causing the Phenomenon of Interest. We retain the simulation records of individuals who have LTC needs, which we define as those having more than 2 ADL limitations and who are eligible to use LTC services under the current LTC policy. This leaves us with the records of a total of 50147 individuals who have made their care choice among hospital care, nursing home care, and home-based care on the basis of their characteristics and eligibility rules.

Table 4. Characterized subgroups for choosing nursing home care and home-based care

Subgroups	Supp.	Conf.	Num.
Nursing home care			
Income $\geq$ 2211.83 $\wedge$ gender = 1 $\wedge$ carer < 4	0.113021	0.275898	3813
Income $\geq$ 2211.83 $\wedge$ adl < 3 $\wedge$ carer < 4	0.107005	0.339237	2936
Insurance = 2 $\wedge$ income $\geq$ 2211.83 $\wedge$ gender = 2	0.079072	0.273708	2689
Insurance = 2 $\wedge$ income $\geq$ 2211.83 $\wedge$ adl < 3	0.061667	0.327439	1753
–	–	–	–
Income $\geq$ 1369.17 $\wedge$ gender = 2 $\wedge$ carer $\geq$ 4	0.041255	0.287856	1334
Home-based care			
Income $\geq$ 2211.83 $\wedge$ carer < 4	0.406981	0.453840	10431
Income $\geq$ 2211.83 $\wedge$ adl $\geq$ 3 $\wedge$ carer < 4	0.321355	0.498732	7495
Carer < 4 $\wedge$ income $\geq$ 2211.83 $\wedge$ gender = 2	0.276994	0.486854	6618
Insurance = 1 $\wedge$ income $\geq$ 2211.83 $\wedge$ gender = 2	0.237878	0.577059	4795
–	–	–	–
Income $\geq$ 2211.83 $\wedge$ adl $\geq$ 5.0 $\wedge$ carer < 4	0.221974	0.578146	4455

S3 Identify Subgroups. We apply the pattern mining algorithm with default parameter settings on the individual records to extract the most influential combinations of individual characteristics, i.e., subgroups of individuals, for each type of care. Python is used for implementation.

We limit our analysis to the selection of nursing home care and home-based care. We present the most influential subgroups sorted by "Supp.", the ratio of support in all agents, for choosing nursing home care and home-based care separately in Table 4, where "Conf." is the ratio of support in agents of this subgroup, and "Num" indicates the number of agents in this subgroup. We are interested in subgroups identified by the same influential attributes but of different values across different care choices. For example, women (*gender* = 2) with a household income (*income* $\geq RMB1369$) above the poverty line in China may prefer nursing home care when there is no caregiver (*carer* ≥ 4), and in contrast, they may prefer home-based care when a caregiver is available regardless of the caregiver type (*carer* < 4). This suggests that when income is not a major concern, the availability of a caregiver becomes important. Another interesting group is women (*gender* = 2) above the poverty line (*income* $\geq RMB1369$), who may prefer different types of services if they are enrolled in different insurance schemes.

S4 Determine Causal Drivers for Each Subgroup. We plot the causal structures discovered by the causal discovery methods on all agents and only on subgroups of interest from the previous step in Fig. 3 and Fig. 4 respectively. Legends are the same for both figures. Python and TETRAD, a software package that implements a set of causal discovery tools (http://www.ccd.pitt.edu), are used to perform the causal search with graphical representations of causal relations.

We incorporate some prior knowledge to prohibit causal relations on demographic features (e.g., age and gender) to improve the accuracy of the results [23]. We also do not allow any individual characteristic caused by the care choice, denoted by "*label_nurse*" and "*label_home*" in the figures for the preference of nursing home care and home-based care respectively. We conduct bootstrap sampling 20, 50, 100, 200, and 300 times until we obtain a stable result.

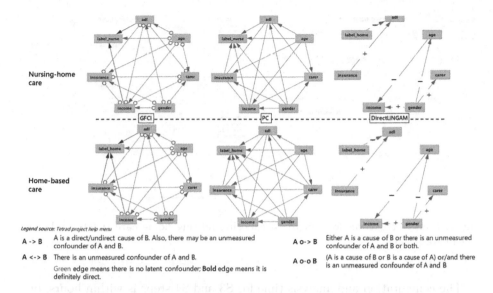

Fig. 3. Causal structures generated by GFCI, PC and DirectLiNGAM respectively.

For the whole population (Fig. 3), the GFCI and PC algorithms managed to find common causal relations that are nearly consistent with the rules encoded in the simulation in the sense that age, income, and number of ADL limitations have a causal effect on the choice of nursing home care and home-based care. The performance of DirectLiNGAM is not satisfactory, probably due to the existence of latent confounders (as reported by GFCI), but is improved for subgroups with a reduced number of variables, probably due to having the confounding variables constant.

For subgroups of interest (Fig. 4), since the GFCI and PC algorithms generate similar results, we only plot the causal structures generated by GFCI and DirectLiNGAM. We can observe that for women with an income above the poverty line, income, number of ADL limitations, and insurance status are direct causes for choosing nursing-home care when they have no caregiver at home, while for women who are enrolled in URI and are above the poverty line, the availability of a caregiver becomes one of the main causes and income may not have a direct effect. For home-based care, income and number of ADL limitations have a direct effect on the preference of home-based care for women with a caregiver regardless of the type, while no direct cause without the existence of confounders is reported for women enrolled in UEI.

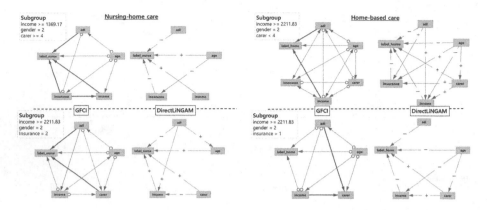

Fig. 4. Causal structures for subgroups choosing nursing home care (left) and home-based care (right).

The computation and analysis time for S3 and S4 steps is within hours, but may increase when the number of samples and variables increases. In addition, when the number of variables increases, extra analysis efforts are required to identify the subgroups of interest, since step S3 will generate a relatively larger number of combinations of agent attributes that are highly related to the target phenomenon.

3.4 Proposed Policy Evaluation

LTC policies can be viewed as changing the characteristics of the target population directly, e.g., providing benefit packages, or indirectly through care delivery, e.g., relocating care facilities. Informed by the above-discovered causal relations, we propose policies targeting particular subgroups for improving the equity of access and compared the effects with conventional scenario analysis.

For nursing home care, we focus on the subgroup identified above—namely, women without a caregiver and with an income above the poverty line—and suggest a policy that provides a monthly subsidy and a discount for using government-funded nursing home care to this subgroup (Scenario 2). We re-simulate the model under this policy and compare the results with a baseline scenario without any policy and with Scenario 1, which provides the same policy to another subgroup (namely, lower-income elderly without a caregiver, known as "three-nos" in China), as suggested in [6].

We evaluate the equity by plotting a Lorenz curve that represents the use of nursing home care (y-axis) against cumulative household income (x-axis). The average results from 20 runs are plotted in Fig. 5. We can observe that both scenarios improved the usage rate across different income groups, but since the number of target individuals in Scenario 2 (278) is much smaller than that in Scenario 1 (1,258), the equity is improved with less subsidy given in our proposed

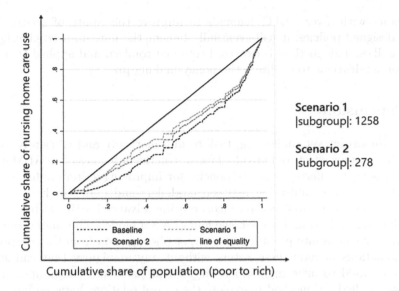

Fig. 5. Use of nursing home care in different scenarios.

policy. In other words, we have identified the subgroup most in need of nursing home care and proposed a well-informed policy to improve their care use.

Similarly, we can propose policies to reduce the disparities in use of the home-based care. For example, the number of ADL limitations has a direct causal effect on choosing home-based care. Therefore, when allocating home-based care to different districts, allocation in accordance with the number of individuals who need more support for daily living activities would be more effective than random allocation or allocation with respect to population size, as proposed and discussed in [6].

3.5   Discussion

The original analysis of this agent-based model [6] revealed that considerable discrepancies exist in the access to care among individuals, but the factors leading to this inequity across various subgroups remain unclear.

Conventional scenario analysis methods typically propose policies targeting at subgroups characterized by social-economic status or depending on domain knowledge, and evaluate them against some macro-level metrics of interest by re-simulation. In contrast, our method enables us to more accurately and efficiently characterise subgroups that are closely related to the access to a particular type of care. Further, it provides a causal explanation of the care choices across subgroups with diverse LTC needs. To this end, it not only strengthens the explanation power of the analysis, but also effectively informs policies as changing the influential population characteristics.

It has demonstrated that our method can support systematic group-specific LTC policy-making by identifying vulnerable subgroups and refining policies in accordance with diverse LTC demands to improve the equity of access. With better designed policies, it will eventually benefit the most-in-need elderly and their families. This method is expected to be customized and applied to a wide range of applications to facilitate the policy-making process.

4   Conclusion

It is an important yet challenging task to automatically and efficiently understand the complex effects of individual factors on the outcomes of an ABM model when it comes to offering concrete policies for improving system outcomes and facilitating the communication between modellers and policy makers. To this end, we proposed a novel method incorporating advanced artificial intelligence algorithms for understanding the behaviour of ABM models. Our method enables a qualitative causal interpretation of a target phenomenon from the perspective of combinations of individual factors without any ambiguity that can subsequently be used to offer suggestions targeted at particular subgroups. In this work, we applied our method to explore the causal relations between individual characteristics and LTC care choices of an LTC system reproduced in silicon by an ABM model. Our findings show that it can efficiently offer group-specific policies compared with conventional scenario analysis for improving the equity of access. It not only saves computational power by decreasing the number of necessary experiments but also provides an explanation that does not rely heavily on expert knowledge.

The ABM model tested in this work has a relatively smaller number of variables and generated a large number of samples, which to certain extent guarantees reliable results by causal discovery methods. Future works may include generalizing this method to be applicable to ABM models with a larger number of variables. Also, a more rigorous evaluation metric should be defined for interpreting the causal structures and automatically determining the main causes to form a basis for guiding the policy-making process.

Acknowledgements. This work was partially supported by JSPS KAKENHI Grant Number 20K18958.

References

1. Andersen, R.M.: Revisiting the behavioral model and access to medical care: Does it matter? J. Health Soc. Behav. **36**(1), 1–10 (1995). http://www.jstor.org/stable/2137284
2. Atun, R.: Health systems, systems thinking and innovation. Health Policy Plan. **27**(SUPPL. 4), 4–8 (2012)
3. Auchincloss, A.H., Garcia, L.M.: Brief introductory guide to agent-based modeling and an illustration from urban health research. Cad. Saude Publica **31**(1), 65–78 (2015). https://doi.org/10.1590/0102-311X00051615

4. Bonabeau, E.: Agent-based modeling: Methods and techniques for simulating human systems. Proc. Natl. Acad. Sci. **99**(suppl 3), 7280–7287 (2002). https://doi.org/10.1073/pnas.082080899
5. Braithwaite, J.: Growing inequality: bridging complex systems, population health and health disparities. Int. J. Epidemiol. 351–353 (2018). https://doi.org/10.1093/ije/dyy001, http://academic.oup.com/ije/advance-article/doi/10.1093/ije/dyy001/4819238
6. Chang, S., Yang, W., Deguchi, H.: Care providers, access to care, and the long-term care nursing insurance in china: An agent-based simulation. Soc. Sci. Medicine **244**, 112667 (2020). https://doi.org/10.1016/j.socscimed.2019.112667
7. Dong, G., Li, J.: Efficient mining of emerging patterns: Discovering trends and differences. In: Proceedings of the Fifth ACM SIGKDD International Conference on Knowledge Discovery and Data Mining, KDD 1999, pp. 43–52. Association for Computing Machinery, New York (1999). https://doi.org/10.1145/312129.312191
8. Edali, M., Yücel, G.: Exploring the behavior space of agent-based simulation models using random forest metamodels and sequential sampling. Simulation Model. Practice Theory **92**, 62–81 (2019). https://doi.org/10.1016/j.simpat.2018.12.006, https://www.sciencedirect.com/science/article/pii/S1569190X18301941
9. Feng, Z., Liu, C., Guan, X., Mor, V.: China's rapidly aging population creates policy challenges in shaping a viable long-term care system. Health Affairs **31**, 2764–73 (2012). https://doi.org/10.1377/hlthaff.2012.0535
10. Gilbert, G.N.: Agent-based models. Quantitative applications in the social sciences. Sage (2008)
11. Glymour, C., Zhang, K., Spirtes, P.: Review of causal discovery methods based on graphical models. Front. Genet. **10**, 524 (2019). https://doi.org/10.3389/fgene.2019.00524
12. Hamill, L.: Agent-based modelling: The next 15 years. J. Artif. Societies Soc. Simul. **13**(4), 7 (2010). https://doi.org/10.18564/jasss.1640, https://www.jasss.org/13/4/7.html
13. Iwashita, H., Takagi, T., Suzuki, H., Goto, K., Ohori, K., Arimura, H.: Efficient constrained pattern mining using dynamic item ordering for explainable classification. CoRR abs/ arXiv: 2004.08015 (2020)
14. Kotoku, J., et al.: Causal relations of health indices inferred statistically using the DirectLiNGAM algorithm from big data of Osaka prefecture health checkups. PLoS ONE **15**(12), e0243229 (2020). https://doi.org/10.1371/journal.pone.0243229
15. Langellier, B.A.: An agent-based simulation of persistent inequalities in health behavior: Understanding the interdependent roles of segregation, clustering, and social influence. SSM - Popul. Health **2**, 757–769 (2016). https://doi.org/10.1016/j.ssmph.2016.10.006, https://www.sciencedirect.com/science/article/pii/S2352827316301112
16. Lee, J.S., et al.: The complexities of agent-based modeling output analysis. J. Artifi. Societies Soc. Simul. **18**(4), 4 (2015). https://doi.org/10.18564/jasss.2897, http://jasss.soc.surrey.ac.uk/18/4/4.html
17. Malleson, N., Heppenstall, A., See, L., Evans, A.: Using an agent-based crime simulation to predict the effects of urban regeneration on individual household burglary risk. Environ. Planning B: Planning and Design **40**(3), 405–426 (2013). https://doi.org/10.1068/b38057

18. Ogarrio, J.M., Spirtes, P., Ramsey, J.: A hybrid causal search algorithm for latent variable models. In: Antonucci, A., Corani, G., Campos, C.P. (eds.) Proceedings of the Eighth International Conference on Probabilistic Graphical Models. Proceedings of Machine Learning Research, vol. 52, pp. 368–379. PMLR, Lugano, Switzerland (2016)

19. Ohori, K., Takahashi, S.: Market design for standardization problems with agent-based social simulation. J. Evol. Econ. **22**(1), 49–77 (2012). https://doi.org/10.1007/s00191-010-0196-y

20. Pereda, M., Santos, J.I., Galán, J.M.: A brief introduction to the use of machine learning techniques in the analysis of agent-based models. In: Hernández, C. (ed.) Advances in Management Engineering. LNMIE, pp. 179–186. Springer, Cham (2017). https://doi.org/10.1007/978-3-319-55889-9_11

21. Qingdao Municipal Bureau of Human Resource and Social Secure: A list of LTC service providers of qingdao six districts (2016). http://www.qdhrss.gov.cn/pages/hdjl/fwdh/59947.html/

22. Ramsey, J., Glymour, M., sanchez romero, R., Glymour, C.: A million variables and more: the fast greedy equivalence search algorithm for learning high-dimensional graphical causal models, with an application to functional magnetic resonance images. Int. J. Data Sci. Anal. **3**, 121–129 (2017). https://doi.org/10.1007/s41060-016-0032-z

23. Shen, X., Ma, S., Vemuri, P., Simon, G.: Alzheimer's Disease Neuroimaging Initiative: Challenges and opportunities with causal discovery algorithms: Application to alzheimer's pathophysiology. Sci. Rep. **10**(1), 2975 (2020). https://doi.org/10.1038/s41598-020-59669-x

24. Shimizu, S., et al.: Directlingam: A direct method for learning a linear non-gaussian structural equation model. J. Mach. Learn. Res. **12**(null), 1225–1248 (2011)

25. Spirtes, P., Glymour, C., Scheines, R. (eds.): Causation, Prediction, and Search. LNS, vol. 81. Springer, New York (1993). https://doi.org/10.1007/978-1-4612-2748-9

26. Spirtes, P., Glymour, C., Scheines, R., Kauffman, S., Aimale, V., Wimberly, F.: Constructing bayesian network models of gene expression networks from microarray data. In: Proceedings of the Atlantic Symposium on Computational Biology (2000). https://doi.org/10.1184/R1/6491291.v1

27. Yamada, H., Yamane, S., Ohori, K., Kato, T., Takahashi, S.: A method for microdynamics analysis based on causal structure of agent-based simulation. In: Bae, K.H., Feng, B., Kim, S., Lazarova-Molnar, S., Zheng, Z., Roeder, T., Thiesing, R. (eds.) 2020 Winter Simulation Conference (WSC), pp. 313–324. IEEE Press, Piscataway, New Jersey (2020)

28. Yamane, S., et al.: Systematic analysis of micro dynamics in agent based simulation. In: Rabe, M., Juan, A., Mustafee, N., Skoogh, A., Jain, S., Johansson, B. (eds.) 2018 Winter Simulation Conference (WSC), pp. 4214–4215. IEEE Press, Piscataway, New Jersey (2018)

29. Yang, C., Kurahashi, S., Kurahashi, K., Ono, I., Terano, T.: Agent-based simulation on women's role in a family line on civil service examination in chinese history. J. Artif. Societies Soc. Simul. **12**(2), 5 (2009). https://www.jasss.org/12/2/5.html

False-Name-Proof Facility Location on Wheel Graphs

Koji Osoegawa, Taiki Todo$^{(\boxtimes)}$, and Makoto Yokoo

Graduate School of Information Science and Electrical Engineering (ISEE),
Kyushu University, Fukuoka 819-0395, Japan
osoegawa@agent.inf.kyushu-u.ac.jp, {todo,yokoo}@inf.kyushu-u.ac.jp

Abstract. In this paper, we consider the study of two classes of mechanism design problems for locating a facility on a wheel graph with $k \geq 4$ vertices, where a vertex is located at the center, which is surrounded by a cycle graph with $k - 1$ vertices and connected to each vertex in the cycle. Two domains of agents' preferences are considered; the single-peaked domain and the single-dipped domain. We are interested in the existence of anonymous social choice functions that are false-name-proof and Pareto efficient. For both domains of preferences, we provide the necessary and sufficient condition on the graph parameter k to guarantee the existence of such social choice functions. Namely, for the single-peaked preference domain, such social choice functions exist if and only if $k \leq 5$. On the other hand, for the single-dipped preference domain, such social choice functions exist if and only if $k \leq 7$.

Keywords: Mechanism design · Facility location games · False-name-proofness · Wheel graphs

1 Introduction

Mechanism design is a well-known research direction in the literature of microeconomics. It has been widely studied over the last decades at the intersection of computer science and economics, and has recently expanded to cover other various application fields such as politics, transportation science, and electricity markets. The main goal of mechanism design is to develop *mechanisms* (also known as *social choice functions* when monetary compensation is not allowed), which are defined as a mapping from agents' preferences to a social outcome, so that some incentive properties, such as strategy-proofness and false-name-proofness, are fulfilled. Strategy-proofness requires that for each agent, reporting her true preference is a dominant strategy, i.e., a best action against every possible profile of the actions of the others. False-name-proofness refines strategy-proofness for the anonymous environments such as the Internet, which requires that just using a single identity and reporting her true preference is a dominant strategy for every agent, even though arbitrarily adding many fake identities is possible.

R. Aydoğan et al. (Eds.): PRIMA 2022, LNAI 13753, pp. 139–155, 2023.
https://doi.org/10.1007/978-3-031-21203-1_9

The application domain of mechanism design covers various problems in economics, from combinatorial auction to matching, exchange, and *facility location*.

Facility location, sometimes also known as facility location games, is one of the most popular mechanism design problems. In a facility location problem, given a space of outcomes, a social choice function builds a public good (or a public bad) on a point in the space of outcomes, based on the profile of the agents' preferences. A space of outcomes is typically represented as a certain mathematical structure such as a line, a Euclidean space, or a discrete graph. When the facility is a public good (or a public bad, respectively), agents' preferences are often assumed to be *single-peaked* (or single-dipped, resp.); each agent has a best outcome in the space of all the outcomes, where having a public good closer to it is better for her (or having a public bad farther away from it is better for her, resp.). We focus on locating a facility in a *Pareto efficient* manner, which is a well-motivated requirement in the literature of economics. Given a profile of agents' preferences and a location returned by a Pareto efficient social choice function, there is no other outcome that is weakly better for all the agents and is strictly better for at least one agent. See Sect. 3 for the formal definitions of these preferences and Pareto efficiency.

In the literature of strategy-proof/false-name-proof facility location, investigating the existence of desirable social choice functions on specific outcome spaces is one of the research trends. For continuous outcome spaces, where any point in the space is available for locating a facility, Moulin [17] pointed out the existence of strategy-proof and Pareto efficient social choice functions for a real line, Schummer and Vohra [25] described the existence of anonymous, Pareto efficient, and strategy-proof social choice functions for acyclic networks, and Todo et al. [30] showed the existence of anonymous, Pareto efficient, and false-name-proof social choice functions for acyclic networks. For discrete outcome spaces, where the facility can be located only on vertices, Dokow et al. [8] studied the existence of strategy-proof social choice functions for cycle graphs, Todo et al. [31] studied the existence of false-name-proof social choice functions for both grid and cycle graphs, and Nehama et al. [18] considered a more general class of graph structures for false-name-proof social choice functions.

In this paper, we first consider false-name-proof facility location on a special class of discrete graphs, called *wheel graphs* [21], which have not been investigated in previous works. A wheel graph W_k with k vertices has a cycle graph with $k-1$ vertices, and there is an additional vertex inside the cycle, which is connected to all the vertices in the cycle. From the perspective of facility location in practice, the class of wheel graphs can naturally approximate the structure of various cities in the world, such as Moscow (the city at its center, which is surrounded by a loop train called "Moscow Central Circle"), Paris (the 1st Arrondissement at its center, which is surrounded by the 2nd to the 9th Arrondissements), Rome (the city at its center, which is surrounded by the ring road called the "Grande Raccordo Anulare"), and Tokyo (the Imperial Palace at its center, which is surrounded by a loop train called the "Yamanote Line"). A number of streets go through the surrounding cycle from the center of the city, in a radial manner, which corresponds to the edges from the vertex inside[1]. Several amusement parks such as Disneyland in Los Angeles also have quite a similar wheel-like structure, e.g., the Fantasyland at its center, surrounded by other zones.

Our main question in this paper focuses on the existence of anonymous social choice functions for wheel graphs that simultaneously satisfy false-name-proofness and Pareto efficiency , i.e., to what extent of wheel graphs we can find such social choice functions. We provide the necessary and sufficient condition on the parameter k of wheel graphs to guarantee the existence of such social choice functions for these graphs, which completely answers the question. For single-peaked preferences, we show that such social choice functions exist only if $k \leq 5$, while its if-side was already recently proven by Nehama et al. [18]. On the other hand, for single-dipped preferences, we show that such social choice functions exist if and only if $k \leq 7$. For both preference domains, it is intuitive and unsurprising that having more preferences/outcomes, i.e., increasing the value of the parameter k, makes the mechanism design problem more difficult to solve. However, providing the exact threshold value is still important for deepening our understanding concerning the extent to which such social choice functions can be designed.

This paper is organized as follows. Section 2 describes previous works on mechanism design for facility location games and false-name-proof mechanism design without money. Section 3 defines the necessary notations and technical terms. In Sect. 4, we provide both the possibility and impossibility results for the domain of single-peaked preferences. Then, in Sect. 5, we provide both possibility and impossibility results for the domain of single-dipped preferences. Section 6 discusses how and to what extent the obtained results can be generalized. Finally, Sect. 7 summarizes the paper and overviews possible directions for future works.

2   Literature Review

The traditional facility location problem has been studied on a continuous line, rather than discrete structures, in the pure economics literature. Moulin [17] investigated strategy-proof and Pareto efficient social choice functions on a continuous line and proposed a class of such social choice functions, so-called generalized median voter schemes. Indeed, it is the only class of deterministic, strategy-proof, Pareto efficient, and anonymous social choice functions. Procaccia and Tennenholtz [23] initiated the research on approximate mechanism design, for which a facility location problem was chosen as a case study. They evaluated the worst case performance of strategy-proof social choice functions on a line from the perspective of competitive ratio. Recently, some new models of facility locations have been investigated, including dynamic facility locations [12,32] and locating multiple heterogeneous facilities [4,11,26]. Some other research also considered the strategy-proof facility location on discrete structures, such as

---

[1] In the field of urban planning, such a city structure is usually called a "radial city" or "radial concentric city.".

grids [9,28] and cycles [2,3,8], while no prior work has considered wheel graphs as an outcome space of facility location.

Locating a public bad, or almost equivalently, social choice with single-dipped preferences, has also been widely studied, from economics to computer science. Manjunath [16] gave a characterization of strategy-proof social choice functions on an interval; for the case of single-dipped preferences, handling unbounded outcome space is technically not straightforward. Lahiri et al. [13] studied a model for locating two public bads on an interval. Both Alcalde-Unzu and Vorsatz [1] and Feigenbaum et al. [10] considered situations where single-peaked and single-dipped preferences coexist. Roy and Storken [24] investigated the preference domain of voting for which strategy-proof, unanimous, and non-dictatorial social choice functions exist. Nevertheless, all of these works just focused on strategy-proof social choice functions.

Over the last two decades, false-name-proof social choice functions have also been scrutinized in various problems [5,22,29,33–35], as an alternative incentive property for such open and anonymous environments as the Internet. For literature on voting and facility location, Bu [6] clarified a connection between false-name-proofness and population monotonicity in general social choice. Conitzer [7] provided a characterization of false-name-proof randomized social choice functions. Todo et al. [30] provided a complete characterization of false-name-proof and Pareto efficient mechanisms for the facility location problem with single-peaked preferences on a continuous line. Lesca et al. [15] also addressed false-name-proof mechanisms that are associated with monetary compensation. Sonoda et al. [27] considered the case of locating two homogeneous facilities. Ono et al. [20] studied discrete structures, although they focused on randomized mechanisms. Nehama et al. [18] clarified a specific class of graph structures under which false-name-proof and Pareto efficient mechanisms exist for single-peaked preferences.

3   Model

In this section, we describe our model of the facility location problem. For any integer $k \geq 4$, let $W_k = (V, E)$ be the *wheel graph* [21] with k vertices, defined by a set V of vertices and a set E of edges as follows:

$$V := \{v_0, v_1, v_2, \ldots, v_{k-1}\}$$

$$E := \{(v_0, v_s)_{1 \leq s \leq k-1}, (v_t, v_{t+1})_{1 \leq t \leq k-2}, (v_{k-1}, v_1)\}$$

In words, vertex v_0 is located at the center, which is surrounded by a cycle graph with $k - 1$ vertices and connected to each vertex in the cycle. Center vertex v_0 is sometimes called a *hub*. Figure 1 shows three examples of wheel graphs, namely W_4, W_5, and W_6. We assume that the edges are undirected. Agents' preferences are determined based on a distance function $D : V^2 \to \mathbb{N}_{\geq 0}$, such that for any $v, w \in V$, $D(v, w) := \#\{e \in s(v, w)\}$, where $s(v, w)$ is the shortest path between v and w. Unlike in cycle graphs, the distance between any two distinct vertices

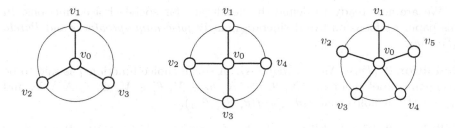

Fig. 1. Wheel graphs W_4, W_5, and W_6

is either 1 or 2 in wheel graph W_k for any $k \geq 4$, due to the existence of the hub vertex.

To handle false-name manipulations in the framework of social choice, we need to define both *potential* agents/identities and *participating* agents. Let $\mathcal{N}$ be a set of potential agents, and let $N \subseteq \mathcal{N}$ be a set of participating agents. Each agent $i \in N$ has a *type* $\theta_i \in V$. When agent i has type θ_i, agent i is said to be *located on* vertex θ_i. Let $\theta := (\theta_i)_{i \in N} \in V^{|N|}$ denote a profile of the agents' types, and let $\theta_{-i} := (\theta_{i'})_{i' \neq i}$ denote a profile without i's. Given θ, let $I(\theta) \subseteq V$ be a set of vertices on which at least one agent is located, i.e., $I(\theta) := \bigcup_{i \in N} \theta_i$. Given θ and $v \in I(\theta)$, let θ_{-v} be a profile obtained by removing all the agents at vertex v from θ. By definition, $I(\theta_{-v}) = I(\theta) \setminus \{v\}$.

Given W_k and $v \in V$, let $\succsim_v$ be the preference of the agent located on vertex v over set V of the outcomes, where $\succ_v$ and $\sim_v$ indicate the strict and indifferent parts of $\succsim_v$, respectively. Preference $\succsim_v$ is *single-peaked* (resp. *single-dipped*) under W_k if, for any $w, x \in V$, $w \succ_v x$ if and only if $D(v, w) < D(v, x)$ (resp. $D(v, w) > D(v, x)$), and $w \sim_v x$ if and only if $D(v, w) = D(v, x)$. That is, an agent located on v strictly prefers outcome w, which is strictly closer to (resp. farther from) v than other outcome x, and is indifferent between these outcomes when they are the same distance from v.

A (deterministic) social choice function is a mapping from the set of possible profiles to the set of vertices. Since each agent might pretend to be multiple agents in our model, a social choice function must be defined for different-sized profiles. To describe this feature, we define a social choice function $f = (f_N)_{N \subseteq \mathcal{N}}$ as a family of functions, where each f_N is a mapping from $V^{|N|}$ to V. When set N of agents participates, social choice function f uses function f_N to determine the outcome. Function f_N takes profile θ of types jointly reported by N as an input, and returns $f_N(\theta)$ as an outcome. We denote f_N as f if it is clear from the context. We further assume that social choice function f is anonymous, i.e., for any input θ and its permutation θ', $f(\theta') = f(\theta)$ holds.

Definition 1 *(Social Choice Function).* An (anonymous and deterministic) *social choice function* (SCF) f is defined as a family of mappings $(f_n)_{n \in \mathbb{N}}$, where each f_n indicates the function that takes n reported preferences as input and returns an outcome for the cases when n agents participate.

We are now ready to define the desiderata for social choice functions. In this paper we focus on two desiderata namely *false-name-proofness* and *Pareto efficiency*.

Definition 2 *(False-Name-Proofness).* A social choice function f is said to be false-name-proof if for any N, θ, $i \in N$, $\theta_i \in V$, $\theta_i' \in V$, $\Phi_i \subseteq \mathcal{N} \setminus N$, and $\theta_{\Phi_i} \in V^{|\Phi_i|}$, it holds that $f(\theta) \succsim_{\theta_i} f(\theta_i', \theta_{\Phi_i}, \theta_{-i})$.

Definition 3 *(Pareto Efficiency).* An outcome $v \in V$ is said to *Pareto dominate* $w \in V$ under θ if $v \succsim_{\theta_i} w$ for all $i \in N$ and $v \succ_{\theta_j} w$ for some $j \in N$. A social choice function f is said to be *Pareto efficient* (PE) if for any N and θ, no outcome $v \in V$ Pareto dominates $f(\theta)$.

Given θ, $PE(\theta)$ denotes the set of vertices that are not Pareto dominated by any other vertex under θ.

The following property, called *ignoring duplicate ballots (IDB)*, helps us to compactly describe the behavior of the false-name-proof and Pareto efficient social choice functions.

Definition 4 *(Ignoring Duplicate Ballots (IDB)).* A social choice function f is said to be *ignoring duplicate ballots* (or satisfies IDB) if for any pair θ, θ', $I(\theta) = I(\theta')$ implies $f(\theta) = f(\theta')$.

Theorem 1 (Okada et al. *[19]*)*. Assume there exists a social choice function f that satisfies both false-name-proofness and Pareto efficiency but does not satisfy IDB. Then, there also exists another social chocie function f' that satisfies false-name-proofness, Pareto efficiency, and IDB simultaneously, and $\forall \theta$ and $\forall i \in N$, $f(\theta) \sim_{\theta_i} f'(\theta)$ holds, regardless whether agents' preferences are single-peaked or single-dipped.*

The intuitive description of IDB is that a social choice function which satisfies it only considers whether, for each vertex, agents are present or not. By focusing on social choice functions satisfying IDB, we can describe the behavior of them concisely; infinitely many possible inputs for general social choice functions with variable populations vs. $2^n - 1$ possible profiles for those satisfying IDB. Due to Theorem 1, which shows that such a restriction is without loss of generality, we can focus our attention to social choice functions that satisfy IDB, as long as the mechanism designers are indifferent among all the possible outcomes and are only interested in the social welfare among agents.

4   Single-Peaked Preferences

In this section we focus on single-peaked preferences on wheel graph W_k and show the necessary and sufficient condition on k to guarantee the existence of false-name-proof and Pareto efficient social choice functions. We first show that $k \leq 5$ is a sufficient condition by referring to the existing results by Nehama et al. [18].

Theorem 2. *Assume that the agents' preferences are single-peaked over wheel graph W_k. Then, there exists a social choice function that simultaneously satisfies false-name-proofness and Pareto efficiency for $k \leq 5$.*

Proof. For W_4 and W_5, Nehama et al. [18] presented false-name-proof and Pareto efficient social choice functions[2]. □

Both social choice functions proposed by Nehama et al. [18] for W_4 and W_5 are priority-based social choice functions; for a given priority over all the vertices, they check, for an input profile, whether the first prioritized vertex is Pareto efficient. If so, they locate the facility at the vertex. Otherwise, they check the second prioritized vertex, and so on. Since W_4 is a complete graph, the priority does not matter; any priority order can define a false-name-proof and Pareto efficient social choice function. On the other hand, for W_5, they provided a specific ordering $v_1 \to v_0 \to v_3 \to v_2 \to v_4$, which defines a false-name-proof and Pareto efficient social choice function.

We then show that the sufficiency condition, $k \leq 5$, is indeed necessary. The following lemma intuitively shows that if the current outcome, $f(\theta)$, is still Pareto efficient after deleting all the agents on some specific vertex v, the same outcome must still be chosen. The following theorem also says that, for any $k \geq 6$, there is no social choice function that simultaneously satisfies both of the properties for W_k.

Lemma 1 (Todo et al. *[31]*). *Let Γ be an arbitrary graph. Assume that agents' preferences are single-peaked under a graph Γ. Then, for any false-name-proof social choice function f, any θ and any $v \in I(\theta)$, $[f(\theta) \in I(\theta) \wedge f(\theta) \in I(\theta_{-v})] \Rightarrow [f(\theta_{-v}) = f(\theta)]$.*

Theorem 3. *Assume that the agents' preferences are single-peaked over wheel graph W_k. Then, there is no social choice function that simultaneously satisfies false-name-proofness and Pareto efficiency for $k \geq 6$.*

Proof. For the sake of contradiction, assume that there is a social choice function f that is false-name-proof and Pareto efficient for single-peaked preferences over $W_k = (V, E)$. Also, let θ be an arbitrary profile such that $I(\theta) = V$, and θ' be an arbitrary profile such that $I(\theta) = V \setminus \{v_0, v_1\}$. The profiles used in the proof are summarized in Fig. 2.

We first show that $f(\theta) \neq v_0$. Assume for contradiction that $f(\theta) = v_0$. Also assume, without loss of generality, that $f(\{v_1, v_2\}) = v_1$ because the geometric symmetry of the two vertices, v_1 and v_2, relative to vertex v_0 allows us to apply the same argument for the case of $f(\{v_1, v_2\}) = v_2$. Then, consider the profile $\{v_1, v_2, v_3\}$. If $f(\{v_1, v_2, v_3\}) = v_2$, then the agent at v_2 will add v_3 when the true profile is $\{v_1, v_2\}$, which violate false-name-proofness. If $f(\{v_1, v_2, v_3\}) = v_1$, then the agent at v_3 will add $\{v_0, v_4, \ldots, v_{k-1}\}$ to move the facility to v_0, which

---

[2] In their paper the subscript indicates the number of vertices in the cycle surrounding the hub, i.e., W_4 in this paper is referred to as W_3 in their paper, and W_5 is referred to as W_4.

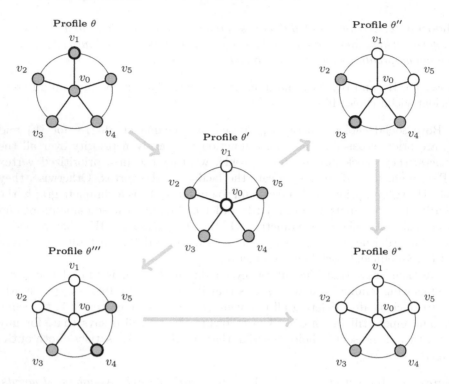

Fig. 2. Five profiles used in the proof of Theorem 3, for the case of $k = 6$. There is at least one agent on each gray vertex. Facility is located at the vertex with the thick border. For the bottom right profile θ^*, there is no vertex on which we can locate the facility.

also violates false-name-proofness. The same argument holds for the case of $f(\{v_1, v_2, v_3\}) = v_3$ for v_1.

We therefore assume, without loss of generality, that $f(\theta) = v_1$. Note that $PE(\theta') = V \setminus \{v_1\}$. Then, from false-name-proofness, it must be the case that $f(\theta') = v_0$. If $f(\theta') \in PE(\theta') \setminus \{v_0, v_{k-2}, v_{k-1}\} = \{v_2, ..., v_{k-3}\}$, then the agent at vertex v_{k-1} has an incentive to add two votes at both v_0 and v_1, which moves the facility to v_1 and reduces her cost, violating false-name-proofness. Similarly, if $f(\theta') \in \{v_{k-2}, v_{k-1}\}$, then the agent at vertex v_2 has an incentive to move the facility to v_1. Therefore, $f(\theta') = v_0$ holds. See the central profile in Fig. 2 for the case of $k = 6$.

Table 1. Behavior of false-name-proof and Pareto efficient social choice function f for single-dipped preferences on W_6, which is defined by ordering $v_1 \to v_2 \to v_5 \to v_3 \to v_4$ over vertices. Note that vertex v_0 is ignored without loss of generality , as explained in the first paragraph of the proof of Theorem 4.

$I(\theta)$	$f(\theta)$	$I(\theta)$	$f(\theta)$	$I(\theta)$	$f(\theta)$	$I(\theta)$	$f(\theta)$
$\{v_1\}$	v_3	$\{v_2\}$	v_5	$\{v_3\}$	v_1	$\{v_4\}$	v_1
$\{v_5\}$	v_2	$\{v_1, v_2\}$	v_4	$\{v_1, v_3\}$	v_5	$\{v_1, v_4\}$	v_2
$\{v_1, v_5\}$	v_3	$\{v_2, v_3\}$	v_5	$\{v_2, v_4\}$	v_1	$\{v_2, v_5\}$	v_3
$\{v_3, v_4\}$	v_1	$\{v_3, v_5\}$	v_1	$\{v_4, v_5\}$	v_2	$\{v_1, v_2, v_3\}$	v_5
$\{v_1, v_2, v_4\}$	v_1	$\{v_1, v_2, v_5\}$	v_3	$\{v_1, v_3, v_4\}$	v_1	$\{v_1, v_3, v_5\}$	v_1
$\{v_1, v_4, v_5\}$	v_2	$\{v_2, v_3, v_4\}$	v_1	$\{v_2, v_3, v_5\}$	v_1	$\{v_2, v_4, v_5\}$	v_1
$\{v_3, v_4, v_5\}$	v_1	$\{v_1, v_2, v_3, v_4\}$	v_1	$\{v_1, v_2, v_3, v_5\}$	v_1	$\{v_1, v_2, v_4, v_5\}$	v_1
$\{v_1, v_3, v_4, v_5\}$	v_1	$\{v_2, v_3, v_4, v_5\}$	v_1	$\{v_1, v_2, v_3, v_4, v_5\}$	v_1	-	-

Here, we show that for any integer j such that $3 \leq j \leq k - 2$, it must be the case that $f(\{v_{j-1}, v_j, v_{j+1}\}) = v_j$. That is, for any profile consisting of three adjacent vertices around the wheel (but not including v_1), the median one must be chosen. If $f(\{v_{j-1}, v_j, v_{j+1}\}) \neq v_j$, i.e., $f(\{v_{j-1}, v_j, v_{j+1}\}) \in \{v_{j-1}, v_{j+1}\}$, then there is at least one agent among them who has a distance of two to the facility. Such an agent then has an incentive to add votes to make the profile identical to θ', under which the facility would be located at v_0, violating false-name-proofness.

Now we can easily obtain a contradiction. From the above argument, for two arbitrary profiles θ'' such that $I(\theta'') = \{v_2, v_3, v_4\}$ and θ''' such that $I(\theta''') = \{v_3, v_4, v_5\}$, both $f(\theta'') = v_3$ and $f(\theta''') = v_4$ hold. See the top-right and bottom-left profiles of Fig. 2 for the case of $k = 6$. Lemma 1 of Todo et al. [31] then implies that for arbitrary profile θ^* such that $I(\theta^*) = \{v_3, v_4\}$ both $f(\theta^*) = v_3$ and $f(\theta^*) = v_4$ hold, which yields a contradiction. □

5 Single-Dipped Preferences

Now we turn to consider single-dipped preferences over wheel graphs W_k. We first show that $k \leq 7$ is a sufficient condition to guarantee the existence of desirable social choice functions. Due to space limitations, we only present a social choice function for W_6 in the proof and show that it satisfies both Pareto efficiency and false-name-proofness. For W_4, W_5, and W_7, the same proof strategy works.

Theorem 4. *Assume that the agents' preferences are single-dipped over wheel graph W_k. Then, there exists a social choice function that simultaneously satisfies false-name-proofness and Pareto efficiency for $k \leq 7$.*

Proof. (For W_6). Let us consider a priority-based social choice function f with priority order $v_1 \to v_2 \to v_5 \to v_3 \to v_4$, which is defined as follows.

$$
f(\theta) = \begin{cases}
v_1 & \text{if } v_1 \in PE(\theta) \\
v_2 & \text{else if } v_2 \in PE(\theta) \\
v_5 & \text{else if } v_5 \in PE(\theta) \\
v_3 & \text{else if } v_3 \in PE(\theta) \\
v_4 & \text{else if } v_4 \in PE(\theta)
\end{cases}
$$

When considering the combination of vertices, we can ignore vertex v_0 without loss of generality. This is because, for any θ and for any $v_i \in V \setminus \{v_0\}$, if $v_i \in PE(I(\theta) \setminus \{v_0\})$, $v_i \in PE(\theta)$ holds, and if $v_i \notin PE(I(\theta) \setminus \{v_0\})$, $v_i \notin PE(\theta)$ holds. In other words, the existence of agents at vertex v_0 never affects the behavior of f. Furthermore, under f, the cost of agents at v_0, if any, does not change at all by any possible false-name manipulation since, for those agents at v_0, all the vertices except v_0 are the best options. According to these facts, the behavior of f is compactly summarized by excluding the existence of v_0, as in Table 1.

By definition, social choice function f clearly satisfies Pareto efficiency because it checks the Pareto efficiency of a vertex before it locates the facility there. To complete the proof, it is then sufficient to show that f satisfies false-name-proofness. Note that, from the structure of wheel graphs, for any θ, any $i \in N$, any $\theta_i \in V$, and any $v \in V$, $D(\theta_i, v) \le 2$ holds[3]. Thus, in what follows we focus on false-name manipulations by agent i whose current distance to the facility is either 0 or 1, i.e., those who are at the same vertex with the facility, or those who are at an adjacent vertex from the facility.

Here, we can summarize the agent's manipulations on some profile against f as Table 2. Note that we omit profiles that include only agents who have no incentive to manipulate, such as $I(\theta) = \{v_1, v_2\}$, which lets agents manipulate because $f(\theta) = v_4$ is optimal for them. To clarify this proof, we explain the first row and the seventh row (whose profile has two types of a manipulator) of the Table 2.

- Consider any profile θ s.t. $I(\theta) = \{v_1, v_3\}$, and $f(\theta) = v_5$. Among the vertices in which at least one agent exists, the vertex with a distance of 0 or 1 from v_5 is v_1, which means that the agents at v_1 want to be far from the facility under profile θ. Since agent i at v_1 can make any profile θ' s.t. $I(\theta') \supseteq \{v_3\}$ and $f(\theta') = v_1$ or v_5, i cannot make a profit.
- Consider any profile θ s.t. $I(\theta) = \{v_1, v_2, v_4\}$, and $f(\theta) = v_1$. Among the vertices in which at least one agent exists, the vertices with a distance of 0 or 1 from v_1 are v_1 and v_2.
  - Since agent i at v_1 can make any profile θ' s.t. $I(\theta') \supseteq \{v_2, v_4\}$ and $f(\theta') = v_1$, i cannot make a profit.
  - Since agent i at v_2 can make any profile θ' s.t. $I(\theta') \supseteq \{v_1, v_4\}$ and $f(\theta') = v_1$ or v_2, i cannot make a profit.

Therefore no agent has an incentive to add fake votes, guaranteeing false-name-proofness.   □

---

[3] This is true for any wheel graph, i.e., for any $k \ge 4$.

Since W_4 is a complete graph, any priority order produces a false-name-proof and Pareto efficient social choice function. For W_5, we found that a priority-based social choice function with priority order $v_1 \rightarrow v_3 \rightarrow v_2 \rightarrow v_4$ also satisfies false-name-proofness and Pareto efficiency. Finally, for W_7, we found that a priority-based social choice function with priority order $v_1 \rightarrow v_2 \rightarrow v_6 \rightarrow v_3 \rightarrow v_5 \rightarrow v_4$ is false-name-proof and Pareto efficient.

Table 2. Summary of possible profiles and possible false-name manipulations under proposed social choice function f for W_6. Each cell of a row, from left to right, indicates all vertices $I(\theta)$ in true profile θ, outcome $f(\theta)$ under the profile, manipulator i, possible manipulated profile θ', and manipulated outcome $f(\theta')$. Observe that, for each row, the manipulator never benefits by moving the facility from $f(\theta)$ to any vertex in $f(\theta')$.

$I(\theta)$	$f(\theta)$	i	θ'	$f(\theta')$
$\{v_1, v_3\}$	v_5	at v_1	$I(\theta') \supseteq \{v_3\}$	v_1 or v_5
$\{v_1, v_4\}$	v_2	at v_1	$I(\theta') \supseteq \{v_4\}$	v_1 or v_2
$\{v_2, v_4\}$	v_1	at v_2	$I(\theta') \supseteq \{v_4\}$	v_1 or v_2
$\{v_2, v_5\}$	v_3	at v_2	$I(\theta') \supseteq \{v_5\}$	v_1, v_2, or v_3
$\{v_3, v_5\}$	v_1	at v_5	$I(\theta') \supseteq \{v_3\}$	v_1 or v_5
$\{v_1, v_2, v_3\}$	v_5	at v_1	$I(\theta') \supseteq \{v_2, v_3\}$	v_1 or v_5
$\{v_1, v_2, v_4\}$	v_1	at v_1	$I(\theta') \supseteq \{v_2, v_4\}$	v_1
		at v_2	$I(\theta') \supseteq \{v_1, v_4\}$	v_1 or v_2
$\{v_1, v_2, v_5\}$	v_3	at v_2	$I(\theta') \supseteq \{v_1, v_5\}$	v_1, v_2, or v_3
$\{v_1, v_3, v_4\}$	v_1	at v_1	$I(\theta') \supseteq \{v_3, v_4\}$	v_1
$\{v_1, v_3, v_5\}$	v_1	at v_1	$I(\theta') \supseteq \{v_3, v_5\}$	v_1
		at v_5	$I(\theta') \supseteq \{v_1, v_3\}$	v_1 or v_5
$\{v_1, v_4, v_5\}$	v_2	at v_1	$I(\theta') \supseteq \{v_4, v_5\}$	v_1
$\{v_2, v_3, v_4\}$	v_1	at v_2	$I(\theta') \supseteq \{v_3, v_4\}$	v_1
$\{v_2, v_3, v_5\}$	v_1	at v_2	$I(\theta') \supseteq \{v_3, v_5\}$	v_1
		at v_5	$I(\theta') \supseteq \{v_2, v_3\}$	v_1 or v_5
$\{v_2, v_4, v_5\}$	v_1	at v_2	$I(\theta') \supseteq \{v_4, v_5\}$	v_1
		at v_5	$I(\theta') \supseteq \{v_2, v_4\}$	v_1
$\{v_3, v_4, v_5\}$	v_1	at v_5	$I(\theta') \supseteq \{v_3, v_4\}$	v_1
$\{v_1, v_2, v_3, v_4\}$	v_1	at v_1	$I(\theta') \supseteq \{v_2, v_3, v_4\}$	v_1
		at v_2	$I(\theta') \supseteq \{v_1, v_3, v_4\}$	v_1
$\{v_1, v_2, v_3, v_5\}$	v_1	at v_1	$I(\theta') \supseteq \{v_2, v_3, v_5\}$	v_1
		at v_2	$I(\theta') \supseteq \{v_1, v_3, v_5\}$	v_1
		at v_5	$I(\theta') \supseteq \{v_1, v_2, v_3\}$	v_1 or v_5
$\{v_1, v_2, v_4, v_5\}$	v_1	at v_1	$I(\theta') \supseteq \{v_2, v_4, v_5\}$	v_1
		at v_2	$I(\theta') \supseteq \{v_1, v_4, v_5\}$	v_1 or v_2
		at v_5	$I(\theta') \supseteq \{v_1, v_2, v_4\}$	v_1
$\{v_1, v_3, v_4, v_5\}$	v_1	at v_1	$I(\theta') \supseteq \{v_3, v_4, v_5\}$	v_1
		at v_5	$I(\theta') \supseteq \{v_1, v_3, v_4\}$	v_1
$\{v_2, v_3, v_4, v_5\}$	v_1	at v_2	$I(\theta') \supseteq \{v_3, v_4, v_5\}$	v_1
		at v_5	$I(\theta') \supseteq \{v_2, v_3, v_4\}$	v_1
$\{v_1, v_2, v_3, v_4, v_5\}$	v_1	at v_1, v_2, or v_5	$4 \leq |I(\theta')| \leq 5$	v_1

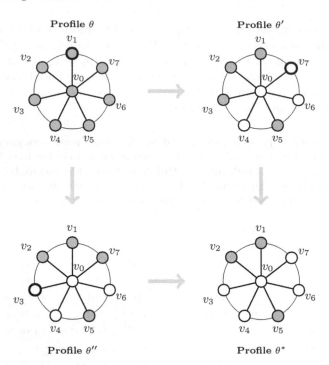

Fig. 3. Four profiles used in the proof of Theorem 5, for the case of $k = 8$. Agents exist at gray vertices, and facility should be located at the vertex with thick border. For the bottom right profile θ^*, there is no vertex on which we can locate a facility.

Next, we show that condition $k \leq 7$ is actually necessary. For any W_k with $k \geq 8$, there is no social choice function that simultaneously satisfies false-name-proofness and Pareto efficiency for single-dipped preferences.

Lemma 2. *Assume that the agents' preferences are single-dipped over wheel graph W_k with $k \geq 8$. If there is a false-name-proof and Pareto efficient social choice function for W_k, then it holds that $f(\theta) \neq v_0$ for any θ such that $I(\theta) = V$.*

Proof. For the sake of contradiction, let us assume that there exists social choice function f that is false-name-proof and Pareto efficient, and returns $f(\theta) = v_0$ for θ such that $I(\theta) = V$.

For any integer $j \in \{1, \ldots, k-1\}$, let us consider an arbitrary profile θ_{-0j} such that $I(\theta_{-0j}) = V \setminus \{v_0, v_j\}$. Note that $PE(\theta_{-0j}) = V \setminus \{v_0\}$. Therefore, if $f(\theta_{-0j}) \neq v_j$, then $f(\theta_{-0j}) \in PE(\theta_{-0j}) \setminus \{v_j\} = V \setminus \{v_0, v_j\} = I(\theta_{-0j})$ holds, indicating that there is at least one agent whose location is chosen as the outcome. Such an agent has an incentive to add two additional votes at vertices v_0 and v_j, which moves the facility to v_0 and reduces her cost. Thus, it must hold that $f(\theta_{-0j}) = v_j$.

Now let us consider an arbitrary profile θ' such that $I(\theta') = V \setminus \{v_0, v_1, v_2\}$. Note that $PE(\theta') = \{v_1, v_2, v_5, \ldots, v_{k-3}\} = V \setminus \{v_3, v_4, v_{k-2}, v_{k-1}\}$. If $f(\theta') = v_1$, then the agent at vertex v_{k-1}, which is directly connected to vertex v_1, has an incentive to add a vote at v_1, which changes the profile to θ_{-02} and thus moves the facility to v_2. This violates the false-name-proofness of f. From the symmetry, $f(\theta') = v_2$ also violates the false-name-proofness of f. If $f(\theta') \in \{v_5, \ldots, v_{k-3}\}$, it holds that $f(\theta') \in I(\theta') \setminus \{v_3, v_4, v_{k-2}, v_{k-1}\}$, indicating that there is at least one agent whose location is chosen as the outcome. Such an agent has an incentive to add three additional votes at vertices v_0, v_1, and v_2, which moves the facility to v_0 and reduces her cost, which violates the false-name-proofness of f. Therefore, it holds that $f(\theta) \neq v_0$.   □

Theorem 5. *Assume that the agents' preferences are single-dipped over wheel graph W_k. Then, there is no social choice function that simultaneously satisfies false-name-proofness and Pareto efficiency for $k \geq 8$.*

Proof. For the sake of contradiction, let us assume that there exists a social choice function f that is false-name-proof and Pareto efficient for single-dipped preferences over W_k with $k \geq 8$. From Lemma 2, $f(\theta) \neq v_0$ for arbitrary profile θ such that $I(\theta) = V$. From the symmetry of wheel graph W_k, we can assume without loss of generality that $f(\theta) = v_1$. The top-left figure in Fig. 3 represents this situation for the case of $k = 8$.

Now let us consider arbitrary profile θ' such that $I(\theta') = V \setminus \{v_0, v_4, v_{k-2}, v_{k-1}\} = \{v_1, v_2, v_3, v_5, \ldots, v_{k-3}\}$. Note that, for any $k \geq 8$, it holds that $PE(\theta') = \{v_3, \ldots, v_{k-5}, v_{k-2}, v_{k-1}\}$. Obviously, $f(\theta') \notin I(\theta') \cap PE(\theta') = \{v_3, v_5, \ldots, v_{k-5}\}$, since in each of these vertices there is at least one agent, who has then an incentive to add fake votes to make the profile identical to the above θ such that $I(\theta) = V$, which returns v_1. Furthermore, if either $f(\theta') = v_4$ or $f(\theta') = v_{k-2}$, at least one agent exists in adjacent vertex v_3 or v_{k-3}, respectively, who then has an incentive to move the facility to v_1. Therefore, it must hold that $f(\theta') = v_{k-1}$. The top-right figure in Fig. 3 represents this situation.

Here, let us consider arbitrary profile θ^* such that $I(\theta^*) = I(\theta') \setminus \{v_3\} = \{v_1, v_2, v_5, \ldots, v_{k-3}\}$. Note that, for any $8 \leq k \leq 11$, $PE(\theta^*) = \{v_3, v_4, v_{k-2}, v_{k-1}\}$ holds, and for any $k \geq 12$, $PE(\theta^*) = \{v_3, v_4, v_7, \ldots, v_{k-5}, v_{k-2}, v_{k-1}\}$ holds. The following intuition explains why $PE(\theta^*)$ changes at $k = 11$. All vertices with agents on the bottom half of the cycle are Pareto dominated by either v_4 or v_{k-1} up to $k = 11$. On the other hand, for $k = 12$, there are some vertices that are not Pareto dominated by any other vertices. For either case, if $f(\theta^*) \neq v_{k-1}$, then there exists at least one agent who has an incentive to add a fake vote on v_3 to move the facility to v_{k-1}. Therefore, it must be the case that $f(\theta^*) = v_{k-1}$.

On the other hand, let us consider another profile θ'' such that $I(\theta'') = I(\theta') \cup \{v_{k-1}\} \setminus \{v_3\}$. See the bottom-left figure in Fig. 3. Note that $PE(\theta'') = \{v_3, v_4, v_7, \ldots, v_{k-1}\}$ holds for any $k \geq 8$. From a similar argument for the case of θ', it must hold that $f(\theta'') = v_3$. Furthermore, since $I(\theta'') \setminus \{v_{k-1}\} = I(\theta^*)$ holds, it must be the case that $f(\theta^*) = v_3$, which contradicts the argument in the previous paragraph. In Fig. 3, no vertex can be chosen as an outcome on the bottom-right figure.   □

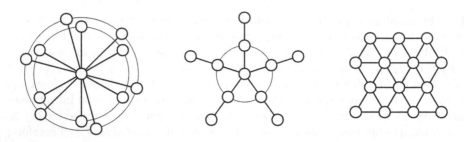

Fig. 4. Double wheel graph, Helm graph, and Triangular grid

6 Discussions

As Todo et al. [31] showed, when a discrete graph G, in which no desirable Pareto efficient social choice function exists for single-peaked preferences, is included in another graph G' as a distance-preserving induced subgraph, then G also never admits the existence of such a social choice function. Therefore, for single-peaked preferences, false-name-proof and Pareto efficient social choice functions do not exist for, e.g., double wheel graphs [14], helm graphs, or triangular grids (see Fig. 4 for examples of these graphs). On the other hand, for single-dipped preferences, no such applications of impossibilities from smaller graphs to larger ones have been proved.

Note that all the proofs provided in this paper strictly rely on the assumption that preferences are distance-based; each agent is indifferent among multiple vertices that are in the same distance from her location. In the literature of economic theory, however, more rich single-peaked/single-dipped preferences on acyclic graphs metric have been studied; agent i located at v_i prefers a vertex x to another vertex y if $x \in s(v_i, y)$. We are not sure whether the threshold parameter would become strictly smaller for such general single-peaked/single-dipped preferences.

In cycle graphs, which have been studied in e.g., Dokow et al. [8] and Todo et al. [31], when the number of vertices increases, the outcome space converges to a circle metric studied by Schummer and Vohra [25], for which it is shown that the dictatorship mechanism is the only strategy-proof and Pareto efficient social choice function. On the other hand, it is not straightforward to extend the results for discrete wheels to infinite space; when the number of vertices increases, then the surrounding cycle becomes similar to a cycle metric, but there is still a vertex in the center, and the distance between two adjacent vertices in the cycle must be equal to the radius of the cycle, from the definition of wheel graphs.

7 Concluding Remarks

In this paper we provided a complete answer for the existence of false-name-proof and Pareto efficient social choice functions for wheel graphs W_k under single-peaked/single-dipped preferences. For single-peaked preferences, $k \leq 5$ is the necessary and sufficient condition for the existence of such social choice functions. On the other hand, for single-dipped preferences, $k \leq 7$ is the necessary and sufficient condition. Future works include a further clarification of the key structure of outcome spaces that allow the existence of false-name-proof and Pareto efficient social choice functions. Although Nehama et al. [18] provided a sufficient condition, it did not even cover most of the wheel graphs. Another important direction is to investigate strategy-proofness on wheel graphs.

Acknowledgements. This work is partially supported by JSPS KAKENHI Grant Numbers JP20H00587, JP20H00609, and JP21H04979.

References

1. Alcalde-Unzu, J., Vorsatz, M.: Strategy-proof location of public facilities. Games Econom. Behav. **112**, 21–48 (2018). https://doi.org/10.1016/j.geb.2018.06.010
2. Alon, N., Feldman, M., Procaccia, A.D., Tennenholtz, M.: Strategyproof approximation of the minimax on networks. Math. Oper. Res. **35**(3), 513–526 (2010). https://doi.org/10.1287/moor.1100.0457
3. Alon, N., Feldman, M., Procaccia, A.D., Tennenholtz, M.: Walking in circles. Discret. Math. **310**(23), 3432–3435 (2010). https://doi.org/10.1016/j.disc.2010.08.007
4. Anastasiadis, E., Deligkas, A.: Heterogeneous facility location games. In: Proceedings of the 17th International Conference on Autonomous Agents and Multiagent Systems (AAMAS 2018), pp. 623–631 (2018)
5. Aziz, H., Paterson, M.: False name manipulations in weighted voting games: splitting, merging and annexation. In: Proceedings of the Eighth International Joint Conference on Autonomous Agents and Multiagent Systems (AAMAS 2009), pp. 409–416 (2009)
6. Bu, N.: Unfolding the mystery of false-name-proofness. Econ. Lett. **120**(3), 559–561 (2013). https://doi.org/10.1016/j.econlet.2013.06.011
7. Conitzer, V.: Anonymity-proof voting rules. In: Proceedings of the Fourth International Workshop on Internet and Network Economics (WINE 2008), pp. 295–306 (2008). https://doi.org/10.1007/978-3-540-92185-1_36
8. Dokow, E., Feldman, M., Meir, R., Nehama, I.: Mechanism design on discrete lines and cycles. In: Proceedings of the 13th ACM Conference on Electronic Commerce (EC 2012), pp. 423–440 (2012). https://doi.org/10.1145/2229012.2229045
9. Escoffier, B., Gourvès, L., Kim Thang, N., Pascual, F., Spanjaard, O.: Strategy-proof mechanisms for facility location games with many facilities. In: Proceedings of the 2nd International Conference on Algorithmic Decision Theory (ADT 2011), pp. 67–81 (2011). https://doi.org/10.1007/978-3-642-24873-3_6
10. Feigenbaum, I., Li, M., Sethuraman, J., Wang, F., Zou, S.: Strategic facility location problems with linear single-dipped and single-peaked preferences. Auton. Agent. Multi-Agent Syst. **34**(2), 49 (2020). https://doi.org/10.1007/s10458-020-09472-9
11. Fong, C.K.K., Li, M., Lu, P., Todo, T., Yokoo, M.: Facility location game with fractional preferences. In: Proceedings of the 32nd AAAI Conference on Artificial Intelligence (AAAI 2018), pp. 1039–1046 (2018). https://doi.org/10.1609/aaai.v32i1.11458

12. de Keijzer, B., Wojtczak, D.: Facility reallocation on the line. In: Proceedings of the 27th International Joint Conference on Artificial Intelligence (IJCAI 2018), pp. 188–194 (2018). https://doi.org/10.24963/ijcai.2018/26
13. Lahiri, A., Peters, H., Storcken, T.: Strategy-proof location of public bads in a two-country model. Math. Soc. Sci. **90**, 150–159 (2017). https://doi.org/10.1016/j.mathsocsci.2016.07.001
14. Le Bras, R., Gomes, C.P., Selman, B.: Double-wheel graphs are graceful. In: Proceedings of the Twenty-Third International Joint Conference on Artificial Intelligence (IJCAI 2013), pp. 587–593 (2013)
15. Lesca, J., Todo, T., Yokoo, M.: Coexistence of utilitarian efficiency and false-name-proofness in social choice. In: Proceedings of the 13th International Joint Conference on Autonomous Agents and Multiagent Systems (AAMAS 2014), pp. 1201–1208 (2014)
16. Manjunath, V.: Efficient and strategy-proof social choice when preferences are single-dipped. Internat. J. Game Theory **43**(3), 579–597 (2014). https://doi.org/10.1007/s00182-013-0396-4
17. Moulin, H.: On strategy-proofness and single peakedness. Public Choice **35**(4), 437–455 (1980). https://doi.org/10.1007/BF00128122
18. Nehama, I., Todo, T., Yokoo, M.: Manipulation-resistant false-name-proof facility location mechanisms for complex graphs. Auton. Agent. Multi-Agent Syst. **36**(1), 12 (2022). https://doi.org/10.1007/s10458-021-09535-5
19. Okada, N., Todo, T., Yokoo, M.: Sat-based automated mechanism design for false-name-proof facility location. In: Proceedings of the 22nd International Conference on Principles and Practice of Multi-Agent Systems (PRIMA 2019), pp. 321–337 (2019). https://doi.org/10.1007/978-3-030-33792-6_20
20. Ono, T., Todo, T., Yokoo, M.: Rename and false-name manipulations in discrete facility location with optional preferences. In: Proceedings of the 20th International Conference on Principles and Practice of Multi-Agent Systems (PRIMA 2017), pp. 163–179 (2017). https://doi.org/10.1007/978-3-319-69131-2_10
21. Pemmaraju, S., Skiena, S.: Computational Discrete Mathematics: Combinatorics and Graph Theory with Mathematica. Cambridge University Press (2003). https://doi.org/10.1017/CBO9781139164849
22. Penna, P., Schoppmann, F., Silvestri, R., Widmayer, P.: Pseudonyms in Cost-Sharing Games. In: Leonardi, S. (ed.) WINE 2009. LNCS, vol. 5929, pp. 256–267. Springer, Heidelberg (2009). https://doi.org/10.1007/978-3-642-10841-9_24
23. Procaccia, A.D., Tennenholtz, M.: Approximate mechanism design without money. ACM Trans. Econ. Comput. **1**(4), 18 (2013). https://doi.org/10.1145/2542174.2542175
24. Roy, S., Storcken, T.: A characterization of possibility domains in strategic voting. J. Math. Econ. **84**, 46–55 (2019). https://doi.org/10.1016/j.jmateco.2019.06.001
25. Schummer, J., Vohra, R.V.: Strategy-proof location on a network. J. Econ. Theory **104**(2), 405–428 (2002). https://doi.org/10.1006/jeth.2001.2807
26. Serafino, P., Ventre, C.: Heterogeneous facility location without money on the line. In: Proceedings of the 21st European Conference on Artificial Intelligence (ECAI 2014), pp. 807–812 (2014). https://doi.org/10.3233/978-1-61499-419-0-807
27. Sonoda, A., Todo, T., Yokoo, M.: False-name-proof locations of two facilities: Economic and algorithmic approachess. In: Proceedings of the 30th AAAI Conference on Artificial Intelligence (AAAI 2016), pp. 615–621 (2016)
28. Sui, X., Boutilier, C., Sandholm, T.: Analysis and optimization of multidimensional percentile mechanisms. In: Proceedings of the 23rd International Joint Conference on Artificial Intelligence (IJCAI 2013), pp. 367–374 (2013)

29. Todo, T., Conitzer, V.: False-name-proof matching. In: Proceedings of the 12th International Conference on Autonomous Agents and Multiagent Systems (AAMAS 2013), pp. 311–318 (2013)
30. Todo, T., Iwasaki, A., Yokoo, M.: False-name-proof mechanism design without money. In: Proceedings of the 10th International Conference on Autonomous Agents and Multiagent Systems (AAMAS 2011), pp. 651–658 (2011)
31. Todo, T., Okada, N., Yokoo, M.: False-name-proof facility location on discrete structures. In: Proceedings of the 24th European Conference on Artificial Intelligence (ECAI 2020), pp. 227–234 (2020). https://doi.org/10.3233/FAIA200097
32. Wada, Y., Ono, T., Todo, T., Yokoo, M.: Facility location with variable and dynamic populations. In: Proceedings of the 17th International Conference on Autonomous Agents and Multiagent Systems (AAMAS 2018), pp. 336–344 (2018)
33. Wang, Q., Ye, B., Tang, B., Guo, S., Lu, S.: ebay in the clouds: False-name-proof auctions for cloud resource allocation. In: Proceedings of the 2015 IEEE 35th International Conference on Distributed Computing Systems (ICDCS 2015), pp. 153–162 (2015). https://doi.org/10.1109/ICDCS.2015.24
34. Yokoo, M., Sakurai, Y., Matsubara, S.: The effect of false-name bids in combinatorial auctions: new fraud in internet auctions. Games Econom. Behav. **46**(1), 174–188 (2004). https://doi.org/10.1016/S0899-8256(03)00045-9
35. Zhang, L., Chen, H., Wu, J., Wang, C.J., Xie, J.: False-name-proof mechanisms for path auctions in social networks. In: Proceedings of the 22nd European Conference on Artificial Intelligence (ECAI 2016), pp. 1485–1492 (2016). https://doi.org/10.3233/978-1-61499-672-9-1485

Improving Problem Decomposition and Regulation in Distributed Multi-Agent Path Finder (DMAPF)

Poom Pianpak[✉] and Tran Cao Son

New Mexico State University, Las Cruces, NM, USA
{ppianpak,tson}@cs.nmsu.edu

Abstract. *Distributed Multi-Agent Path Finder* (DMAPF) is a novel distributed algorithm to solve the *Multi-Agent Path Finding* (MAPF) problem, where the objective is to find a sequence of movements for agents to reach their assigned locations without colliding with obstacles, which include other agents. The idea of *DMAPF* is to decompose a given MAPF problem into smaller sub-problems, then solve them in parallel. It has been shown that *DMAPF* can achieve higher scalability compared to centralized methods. This paper addresses two problems in the previous works. First, the previous works only divide problem maps in a simple, rectangular manner. This can create sub-problems with unbalanced numbers of locations in their maps when the shape of the original map is not rectangular or when the obstacles are not uniformly distributed. Having sub-problems that vary in sizes diminishes the effectiveness of parallelism. Second, the idea of *DMAPF* is to have agents move across sub-problems until they reach the sub-problems that contain their goals, but the previous works do not have a mechanism to regulate the number of agents residing in the sub-problems, thus it may fail to find the solution when a sub-problem is overcrowded. To mitigate the problems, we introduce (*i*) a method to decompose MAPF problems with balanced numbers of vertices; and (*ii*) a mechanism to regulate the number of agents in sub-problems. We also improve the performance of the *Answer Set Programming* (ASP) encoding, that was used in previous *DMAPF* implementations to solve MAPF sub-problem instances, by eliminating unnecessary parameters. The results show that the new solver scales better and is more efficient than the previous versions.

1 Introduction

As the warehouse automation market worldwide is projected to double in market size in 2026[1] (from the time of this writing), the need for scalable systems that

---

[1] https://www.statista.com/statistics/1094202/global-warehouse-automation-market-size.

T.C. Son—Was partially supported by NSF grants 1812628, 1914635, and 1757207.

enable autonomous agents (e.g., robots) to collaborate efficiently is greater than ever [11]. One important function for warehouse robots to perform is to navigate without colliding with obstacles, be it static (c.g., walls, columns, packing stations) or dynamic (e.g., other robots, humans). This function is focused in the field called *Multi-Agent Path Finding* (MAPF), where the objective is to find a movement plan (i .e., a sequence of actions) for agents to reach their goals without a conflict [14].

There are various MAPF solvers. According to [13], they may be categorized into 3 groups: (*i*) fast solvers; (*ii*) optimal solvers; and (*iii*) approximately-optimal solvers. The 'fast' solvers are defined as those that have polynomial time complexity in the size of the graph and the number of agents in the worst-case scenario; the optimal solvers always return optimal solutions; and the approximately-optimal solvers relax the optimality to some definable degree and trade it for efficiency. *Distributed Multi-Agent Path Finder* (DMAPF) [9,10] is a distributed system that solves MAPF problems in a divide-and-conquer manner. It decomposes a given MAPF problem spatially into sub-problems with manageable sizes, assigns each sub-problem to a different distributed sub-solver to manage, then combines partial solutions from every sub-solver into the solution of the original problem. Motivated by the performance of compilation-based techniques in solving MAPF problems in dense, albeit small, maps [1,5], it employs *Answer Set Programming* (ASP) in solving MAPF sub-problem instances. The ASP encoding solves sub-problems optimally, but with exponential time complexity, therefore *DMAPF* also has exponential time complexity and cannot be grouped in the 'fast' solvers category. The aggregation of optimal, partial solutions, may result in a suboptimal solution to the original problem, therefore *DMAPF* may be categorized in the approximately-optimal solvers group. Even though *DMAPF* has exponential time complexity and is suboptimal, it has been shown in [9,10] that it can scale better than a solver such as *WHCA** [12] which employs the most popular method in the fast solvers category called *prioritized planning*, and *ECBS* [2] which is a well-known approximately-optimal solver.

The scalability of *DMAPF* comes from its design for parallel computing. After a given MAPF problem is decomposed and assigned to each sub-solver, the sub-solvers can then work on their given sub-problems in parallel (with some communication in between). Most other MAPF solvers solve the problem in a centralized manner. This usually allows them to perform well in problems with small to moderate sizes, but it would still be a challenge to apply them to the world of expanding autonomous infrastructure. The only idea that comes close to *DMAPF* is *Spatially Distributed Multiagent Planner* (SDP) [15]. In *SDP*, a given MAPF problem is first divided into *high-contention* areas using a number of patterns that are moved around in the map like a sliding window. Every remaining maximum contiguous area is considered a *low-contention* area. To speed up the solving time, the high-contention areas impose direction restrictions on certain highly congested nodes to eliminate potential conflicts between agents. There is a sub-solver (called a *controller*) responsible for each area, both in the high- and the low-contention areas. Each controller takes turn routing the agents in its area. At the end of its turn, it may communicate with its neighboring controller to accept some units that need to move across the areas, or it will return the solution if the global goal has been accomplished. In contrast, *DMAPF* does not impose a restriction on how the map is to be partitioned and the sub-solvers work together in parallel.

The previous publications [9,10] of *DMAPF* focus on how sub-solvers work together, but pay little attention to how the problem is decomposed. In the previous works, a given MAPF problem of the size $x \times y$ would be divided into $\lceil x/dx \rceil \cdot \lceil y/dy \rceil$ rectangular-shaped sub-problems of the sizes at most $dx \times dy$ where $0 < dx \leq x$ and $0 < dy \leq y$. In this paper, we name it the *naive* technique. While this *naive* technique works well for problems with a rectangular map and a uniform distribution of obstacles, it is not suitable for many problems where the opposite is true (e.g., problems with rooms or corridors). Using the *naive* technique on such problems could result in sub-problems that (*i*) vary greatly in the number of *nodes* (i.e., locations that agents can reside); or (*ii*) contain *disconnected areas* (i.e., groups of nodes within a sub-problem without a path connecting them). The two scenarios increase the chance of some sub-solvers having more workload than the others (i.e., unbalanced workload), and as a result can make *DMAPF*, which is a parallel system, less efficient.

Our contribution in this paper is threefold. **First**, we develop better problem decomposition techniques than the *naive* method, utilizing *k-means* [7] and *balanced k-means* [8]. Instead of dividing a map into smaller rectangular maps (as in the *naive* method), both techniques group nodes into clusters based on their distances. They result in sub-problems having less chance to contain disconnected areas. In addition, using *balanced k-means* produces sub-problems with roughly the same number of nodes. They are more suitable than the *naive* method to be applied to MAPF problems in general. **Second**, we introduce a mechanism to regulate the number of agents in sub-problems during the negotiation between sub-solvers. This ensures that agents will not overrun available nodes when sub-solvers make their movement plans, which was the main cause that made *DMAPF* fail in crowded problems (problems with relatively large number of agents compared to the number of nodes). **Third**, we improve the performance of the ASP encoding used for making agent movement plans by limiting the information encoded to bare minimum. The experiment shows significant improvement in the efficiency compared to the encoding used in [9].

The layout of this paper is as follows. Section 2 introduces MAPF, ASP, and *DMAPF* to serve as a background. Section 3 explains the introduced problem decomposition techniques in detail. Subsections 4.1 and 4.2 explain the introduced problem regulation and the improved ASP encoding, respectively. Section 5 evaluates the introduced improvements and discusses the results. Section 6 concludes by discussing future directions of the work.

2   Background

2.1   Multi-agent Path Finding

A *Multi-Agent Path Finding* (MAPF) problem can be defined as a quadruple $P = (G, A, S, T)$, where $G = (V, E)$ is a graph such that V is a set of vertices corresponding to locations (i.e., *nodes*) in the graph, and $E \subseteq V \times V$ denotes edges between two vertices; A is a set of agents; and $S, T \subseteq A \times V$ denote start and goal nodes of the agents, respectively. Each agent has a distinct start node.

Agents can move from v_1 to v_2 where $v_1, v_2 \in V$ in one time step if $(v_1, v_2) \in E$, under the restrictions [14]: (*a*) *vertex conflict* – each node can be occupied by at most one agent at a time; and (*b*) *swapping conflict* – two agents cannot swap nodes in a single time step. A *path* for an agent a is a sequence of vertices $\alpha_a = \langle v_1, \ldots, v_n \rangle$ such that (*i*) agent a starts at a vertex v_1 (i.e., $(a, v_1) \in S$); and (*ii*) for every positive integer i, there is an edge between any two subsequent vertices v_i and v_{i+1} (i.e., $(v_i, v_{i+1}) \in E$), or they are the same vertex (i.e., $v_{i+1} = v_i$). An agent a completes its order $T_a = \{v \mid (a, v) \in T\}$ via a path $\alpha_a = \langle v_1, \ldots, v_n \rangle_a$ if $T_a \subseteq \{v_1, \ldots, v_n\}$. A *solution* of a MAPF problem P is a collection of paths $Sol = \{\alpha_a \mid a \in A\}$ such that all orders in T are completed. The *makespan* and the *sum of cost* (SoC) are typically used to evaluate the solution quality. They are defined as the difference between the start time step of the first agent the completion time step of the last agent; and sum of the plan length of each agent, respectively.

In our work, we assume that (*i*) each agent either has no goal or has a distinct goal node; and (*ii*) every agent stays at its goal node (if there exists) in the last time step. These assumptions are common among various classical MAPF problems [14].

2.2   Answer Set Programming

In *Answer Set Programming* (ASP) [4], a problem is solved by first encoding it as an ASP program, whose answer sets correspond one-to-one to the solutions of the problem. The encoded ASP program is then given to an ASP solver (e.g., *Clingo* [3]) to compute answer sets. An ASP encoding consists of rules of the form:

$$a_0 \leftarrow a_1, \ldots, a_m, \; not \; a_{m+1}, \ldots, \; not \; a_n \tag{1}$$

where $0 \leq m \leq n$. Each a_i is an atom of a propositional language and *not* represents default negation. Intuitively, a rule states that if every positive literals a_i is believed to be true and no negative literal *not* a_i is believed to be false, then a_0 must be true. The '$\leftarrow$' symbol is written as :- in the encoding. For a rule of the form in 1, the *head* denotes a_0 and the *body* denotes the conjunction of literals $a_1, \ldots, a_m, \; not \; a_{m+1}, \ldots$, and *not* a_n. If the head is omitted, the rule is called a *constraint*, and its body must be false in any answer set. If $n = 0$, the rule is called a *fact*, and its head is considered to be true.

The ASP language also includes language-level extensions to facilitate the encoding. In *Clingo*, examples of such extensions[2] are

- A *conditional literal* of the form $L_0 : L_1, \ldots, L_n$ where $L_0, \ldots, L_n$ are literals. Intuitively, it says that L_0 matters only when the conjunction of $L_1, \ldots,$ and L_n is true. For example, the atom a in the encoded rule a :- b : c is true only when either c is false or both b and c are true. If $n = 0$, then we get a regular literal L_0.
- A *weight constraint literal* of the form $l \prec_1 \{\mathbf{L}\} \prec_2 u$ where $\mathbf{L} = L_0 : L_1, \ldots, L_n$ is a conditional literal and '$\prec$' denotes a comparison predicate. Intuitively, it says that the number of literal L_0 must be within a lower bound l and an upper bound u based on the comparison predicates used. The comparison predicates $\prec_1$ and $\prec_2$ can be dropped, which implies that '$\leq$' is used for the comparison. If l is not specified, then the lower bound is 0 by default. For example, an encoded rule m(D) : d(D) 1 says that there must be at most one $m/1$ atom in the answer sets.
- An *external* statement of the form #external $A : L_1, \ldots, L_n$ declares an external atom A if the conjunction of literals $L_1, \ldots,$ and L_n is true. An external atom is not subject to certain simplification, therefore its truth value can be modified at run time and may affect the answer sets.
- A *show* statement of the form #show p/n means that only atom p with n-arity will be shown in the answer sets.

2.3   Distributed Multi-agent Path Finder

Distributed Multi-Agent Path Finder (DMAPF) is a MAPF solver that focuses on scalability. It was first introduced in [10], and later extended to handle obstacles in [9]. It differs from other MAPF solvers by its use of distributed parallel computation to find a solution. In a high-level view, *DMAPF* consists of two steps: (*i*) *problem decomposition*; and (*ii*) *problem solving*.

The *problem decomposition* step divides a given MAPF problem into smaller and non-overlapping sub-problems. Its purpose is to partition a map into smaller sub-problems that the underlying sub-solvers can solve efficiently. This step is designed to be performed at any time before the problem solving step. There is no restriction on how the sub-problems should look like, but the rule of thumb is to partition the map in such a way that the workload is evenly distributed for every sub-solver, for the efficiency in parallel computation. As mentioned in the introduction, the previous works [9,10] on *DMAPF* simply divide the map of the size $x \times y$ into multiple smaller maps of the size $dx \times dy$ where $0 < dx \leq x$ and $0 < dy \leq y$.

The *problem solving* step takes the sub-problems as inputs to the distributed sub-solvers (that are run as processes). After receiving the inputs, each sub-solver first finds an *abstract plan* – a sequence of sub-problems that an agent needs to cross until it reaches the sub-problem that contains its goal node, for

---

[2] https://github.com/potassco/guide/releases/download/v2.2.0/guide.pdf.

each agent in its sub-problem. Then, the sub-solvers proceed to work together to solve the problem. This process involves interleaving of communication between the sub-solvers and movement planning. The way the sub-solvers communicate repeats between each *round*. A *round* is defined as the smallest number of time steps it takes for all the sub-solvers to finish their internal routing of agents. For example, let there be two sub-solvers: s_1 and s_2; and they contain agents a_1 and a_2, respectively. Supposed that s_1 (resp. s_2) moves a_1 (resp. a_2) to its assigned node in 5 (resp. 7) time steps; then, the current *round* amounts to 7 time steps. The communication between the sub-solvers is divided into 3 phases: (i) *negotiation*, (ii) *rejection*, and (iii) *confirmation*. In every phase, every sub-solver only communicate with its neighbors, one-to-one at a time, in the style of remote procedure call (RPC). Each sub-solver has a unique integer ID. Sub-solvers with lower IDs (i.e., *lower-ranked*) need to issue a *request* message to sub-solvers with higher IDs (i.e., *higher-ranked*); and the higher-ranked sub-solvers will return a *reply* message to the lower-ranked sub-solvers within the same RPC call.

In the *negotiation* phase, each sub-solver negotiates with its neighbors for agents that need to migrate, either in or out. The number of *borders* – nodes that connect to another sub-problem, can be different from the number of agents that need to migrate. Let n_a and n_b be the number of agents and available borders, respectively. The current heuristic is to first choose a set of 'at least' $min(n_a, n_b)$ agents that have the longest *abstract steps* – steps left in their abstract plans. If $n_a \leq n_b$, then a set of n_a agents is selected. If $n_a > n_b$, then a set of 'at least' n_b agents is selected. For example, supposed that agents a_1, a_2, a_3, and a_4 have 1, 2, 2, and 3 abstract steps; and there are two available borders; then, only agents a_2, a_3, and a_4 are going to be included in the set. After the set of agents has been selected, the *border assignment* – assigning borders to the (migrating) agents, is determined by guaranteeing border assignment to agents that do not have the shortest abstract steps, while agents with the shortest abstract steps will be selected using the smallest distance of the whole group to the borders. Continuing from the previous example, supposed that b_1 and b_2 denote the two available borders; and $d(a,b)$ – a Manhattan distance from the location of agent a to border b, are as follows: $d(a_2, b_1) = 2$, $d(a_2, b_2) = 3$, $d(a_3, b_1) = 3$, $d(a_3, b_2) = 4$, $d(a_4, b_1) = 4$, and $d(a_4, b_2) = 5$; then, as a result, there are two possible border assignments with the total distance to the borders equal to 7: $\{a_2 \rightarrow b_1, a_4 \rightarrow b_2\}$ and $\{a_2 \rightarrow b_2, a_4 \rightarrow b_1\}$. This seemingly complicated heuristic helps to improve the *makespan* – the shortest amount of time it takes for every agent to reach its goal.

In the *rejection* phase, each sub-solver checks for conflicted incoming (migrating) agents from its neighbors. The incoming agents are conflicted if they try to migrate into the same node. Only one of the conflicted agents is allowed to move in. The one to be kept is selected based on the shortest abstract steps. The (shortest) distance to border is next applied if there is a tie. The sub-solvers report to their neighbors a list of agents that they (the sub-solvers) do not allow to move in, so the neighbors will have to keep the rejected agents themselves at least for this round.

Between the *rejection* phase and the next phase, *confirmation*, each sub-solver proceeds to solve for *movement plans* – a sequence of movements for agents to reach their goal without a conflict, in parallel. This can be done because every sub-solver has agreed (from the previous two steps) on the assigned location of each agent it is responsible for. In solving for movement plans, one of the agent-goal assignments is removed at a time if a movement plan cannot be found. The algorithm returns no solution if the agent-goal assignments cannot be relaxed further and there is still no movement plan.

In the *confimation* phase, each sub-solver confirms with its neighbors a set of (migrating) agents that can actually move to their assigned borders (as a result of movement planning in the previous step). Those agents will be considered as disappeared from the sub-solver and will be in the care of the neighboring sub-solvers they move to in the next round.

3 A Novel Problem Decomposition

There are two steps in our proposed problem decomposition technique: (i) clustering; and (ii) merging small areas. Clustering groups close nodes together to form clusters – to be used as sub-problems. We prefer every cluster to have roughly the same number of nodes and a single connected area for efficiency in parallel computation; however, Fig. 1 shows that results after clustering sometimes have nodes disconnected from their groups. This is especially true when *balanced k-means* is used for a reason that will be explained in Subsect. 3.1. The purpose of merging small areas is to eliminate those disconnected areas. The resulting clusters after merging may have more discrepancy in their numbers of nodes, but it would typically be small since the sizes of disconnected areas are usually small.

Fig. 1. An example of disconnected areas after clustering. The map consists of 17 nodes, denoted by numbers from 1 to 17. It has been divided into two clusters denoted by either a letter 'A' or 'B' on the upper-right corner of each node. The yellow background for nodes in cluster 'A' is only for visual clarity. The area containing a single node, number 16, should be part of cluster 'A' instead of cluster 'B' since the area is small and is disconnected from other nodes in its assigned cluster. (Color figure online)

Algorithm 1. *k-means*

Input: N – a set of nodes; k – the number of desired clusters
Parameter: *max_iteration*
Output: $M: N \rightarrow \{1, \ldots, k\}$

1: $M[n] = 0$ for every node $n \in N$
2: Add k random nodes to C {a list of centroids}
3: **for** $i = 1$ to *max_iteration* **do**
4:      *changed* = **false**
5:      **for** each $n \in N$ **do**
6:          *min_dist* = $+\infty$
7:          **for** $j = 1$ to k **do**
8:              $d = Dist(n, C[j])$ {distance function}
9:              **if** $d < min\_dist$ **then**
10:                 *min_dist* = d, $j_0 = j$
11:         **if** $M[n] \neq j_0$ **then**
12:             $M[n] = j_0$, *changed* = **true**
13:     **if** *changed* = **true then**
14:         **for** $j = 1$ to k **do**
15:             $C[j] =$ (center of all nodes n where $M[n] = j$)
16:     **else**
17:         **break**
18: **return** M

3.1 Clustering

To improve the *naive* method mentioned in Sect. 1, we introduce the use of (i) *k-means* [7] and (ii) *balanced k-means* [8] for problem decomposition – each comes with advantages and disadvantages that will be discussed in Sect. 5.

Algorithm 1 shows how *k-means* is used to cluster nodes in our problem. It takes two inputs: (i) a set of nodes (i.e., N); and (ii) the number of desirable clusters (i.e., k). The integer k should be set to a value that makes the number of nodes per cluster appropriate to be solved efficiently by its underlying sub-solver. Having too many nodes in a sub-problem makes finding a movement plan more difficult, but having too few nodes also incur more communication overhead as more sub-solver processes have to be created and may also negatively affect the solution quality. The algorithm returns a mapping M of nodes to their assigned clusters. Initially, Line 1 assigns no cluster (denoted by the number '0') to every node. Line 2 initializes centroids of the k clusters. The centroids can actually be anywhere, preferably within the map boundary, but to keep it simple we pick k random nodes to be the centroids. The loop between lines 3-17 keeps assigning the nodes to their nearest cluster (line 12) using some function (line 8) to determine the distance between the nodes and the centroids. The distance function we currently use is either: (i) Manhattan distance: $Dist(a, b) = |a.x - b.x| + |a.y - b.y|$; ($ii$) Euclidean distance: $Dist(a, b) = (a.x - b.x)^2 + (a.y - b.y)^2$; or ($iii$) Real distance. The real distance from any node to a centroid is calculated by using *breadth-first search* starting from the centroid until every reachable node is traversed, while marking the distance it took to reach each of them along the way. The results of the searches are saved so that we can avoid future searches from the same centroids. After every node has been assigned to its nearest cluster, the centroids are updated to be at the center of all nodes assigned to them (line 15). The algorithm terminates at line 18 when there is either no change in centroid assigned to any node, or it has looped over a certain threshold defined in the integer *max_iteration*.

k-means is fast and not susceptible to outliers (that it is infamous for) because our problem has no outlier as every node needs to have a cluster assigned, but it could result in some discrepancy in the sizes of clusters. Clusters with congested nodes tend to contain a higher number of nodes compared to ones with sparse nodes. To mitigate this problem, *balanced k-means* [8] is investigated. *balanced k-means* works by instead of assigning each node to its nearest cluster (lines 5-12 in Algorithm 1), it considers distances from every node to every cluster at once, making it become the *assignment problem*. The assignment problem can be considered as a minimum-cost bipartite matching problem. Supposed there are two sets: A and B, with the same n number of elements, a cost matrix representing the assignment problem between the two sets can be constructed as a square matrix of the size $n \times n$ where its elements denote the costs between members in the two sets. The *Hungarian algorithm* [6] is a famous algorithm to solve the assignment problem represented as the cost matrix. We adapt the idea of the Hungarian algorithm to partition our map with n nodes into k clusters, where it is safe to assume that $k \leq n$, by constructing a square matrix with $k * (n/k)$ rows and n columns. Because the assumption that $k \leq n$, some rows may need to be duplicated to create a square matrix.

Cluster \ Node	1	2	3	4	5
1	0	2	4	8	10
1	0	2	4	8	10
2	9	7	5	3	1
2	9	7	5	3	1
3	5	4	3	4	5

Fig. 2. An example of a cost matrix constructed for a map with 5 nodes that is to be partitioned into 3 clusters. The columns denote nodes 1-5. The rows denote clusters 1-3. The elements in the matrix denote the cost (i.e., distance) between node and cluster in the corresponding column and row. Some rows are duplicated to create a square matrix which is required by the Hungarian algorithm.

To create a square cost matrix, each cluster occupies at least $\lfloor n/k \rfloor$ rows. The rows are duplicated if $\lfloor n/k \rfloor > 1$. One more row is added to a cluster c where $c \leq (n \mod k)$. Figure 2 shows an example of a cost matrix of a map with 5 nodes and 3 desired clusters. The columns denote the nodes from 1 to 5. The rows denote the clusters from 1 to 3. The rows for clusters 1 and 2 are duplicated to create a square matrix. The elements of the matrix denote the costs (i.e., distance) between nodes (in the column) and clusters (in the row). For example, the distances between node 4 and clusters 1-3 are 8, 3, and 4, respectively. In this cost matrix, the optimal matching (from nodes to clusters) – which is an answer to the assignment problem – would be $\{1{\to}1, 2{\to}1, 3{\to}3, 4{\to}2, 5{\to}2\}$, for the total cost of $0 + 2 + 3 + 3 + 1 = 9$. After the assignment problem is solved, the *balanced k-means* algorithm works in the same way as *k-means*. It will check whether there is any node that has changed its cluster. If so, the centroids are updated (line 15), then it loops back to construct another cost matrix, and so on. Otherwise, the algorithm terminates in the same way (line 18).

Using the Hungarian algorithm, however, has a big drawback in that it is not practical for many MAPF problems. If a map contains 1000 nodes, the cost matrix would need to hold one million elements. This number is still conservative since many of the problems in the benchmark[3] [14] contain more than 10000 nodes! We mitigate this problem by instead of having to solve a square cost matrix, we use a modified Hungarian algorithm[4] that can solve the rectangular assignment problem, thus reducing the size of the cost matrix from $n \times n$ to $n \times k$ ($k \ll n$ in practice). With this, instead of solving the assignment problem once per loop, it has to be solved $\lceil n/k \rceil$ times because only k elements will be matched at a time. Nodes that have clusters assigned are removed from the cost matrix between each time. Solving the rectangle assignment problem multiple times is much faster than solving a single big square matrix at once. The drawback is that the total cost assignment may not be optimal in the end, so there might be some disconnected areas within a cluster. This problem can be mitigated by merging small, disconnected areas, which will be explained in the next subsection.

3.2   Merging

As pointed out in the last part of Subsect. 3.1, the results of map partitioning may contain small, disconnected areas. While we prefer sub-problems to have roughly the same number of nodes, we also do not want them to have disconnected areas because it may create disproportionate workload among sub-solvers, which reduce the efficiency of parallel computing. To eliminate small, disconnected areas, the idea is to merge them with one of their nearby clusters. The merging process works by repeatedly initialize a breadth-first search on any 'unchecked' node and traverse through every connected node within the same cluster while marking them as 'checked', until there is no unchecked node. During the traversal, the numbers of border nodes (i.e., nodes that connect to another cluster) and which cluster they connect to are counted. At the end of the search, if the number of traversed nodes is less than a threshold, then the searched area is considered to be 'too small' and should be *merged* – become a

---

[3] https://movingai.com/benchmarks/mapf/index.html.
[4] https://github.com/mcximing/hungarian-algorithm-cpp.

part of another cluster, with the cluster that it shares most of its borders with. If there is no cluster to merge with or the cluster it is going to merge with has been checked, then all the traversed nodes remain checked after merging. Otherwise, the status of the traversed nodes will be reset (to 'unchecked') after merging. The process repeats, by initializing a breadth-first search on another unchecked node, until every node is checked. The current threshold is set to 25% of the number of nodes a cluster is expected to contain, viz., $\lfloor 0.25 \cdot n/k \rfloor$ where n and k denote the total number of nodes and the total number of clusters, respectively.

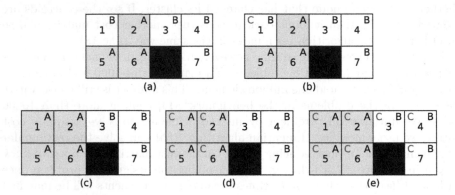

Fig. 3. An example showing how area merging works. The map consists of 7 nodes, denoted by numbers from 1 to 7. It has been divided into two clusters denoted by either a letter 'A' or 'B' on the upper-right corner of each node. The red letter 'C' on the upper-left corner of the nodes denotes that they have been 'checked', otherwise 'unchecked'. The yellow background for nodes in cluster 'A' is only for visual clarity. (a) The map after partitioning into two clusters. (b) The area containing node 1 is traversed. (c) Because the area containing node 1 is 'too small', it is merged with cluster 'A' which it shares most of its border nodes with. (d) The area containing nodes 1, 2, 5, and 6 is traversed. (e) The area containing nodes 3, 4, and 7 is traversed, and the merging algorithm terminates because every node has been checked. (Color figure online)

Figures 3 illustrates how the merging algorithm works with an example. In the example, the map contains $n = 7$ nodes denoted by numbers from 1 to 7; and has been partitioned into $k = 2$ clusters denoted by either a letter 'A' or 'B' on the upper-right corner of each node. The red 'C' letter on the upper-left corner of the nodes denote that they have been 'checked', otherwise 'unchecked'. Cluster 'B' contains two disconnected areas: one with 3 nodes on the right-hand side of the map and the other with 1 node on the top-left corner of the map. Assume that the threshold is set to 50%. It means that we expect every cluster to contain at least $\lfloor 0.5 \cdot n/k \rfloor = \lfloor 0.5 \cdot 7/2 \rfloor = 3$ nodes. Figure 3a depicts a map after partitioning, prior to merging. Figure 3b assumes node 1 is first checked. Because the area (of the same cluster) traversed from node 1 only contains one node (i.e., node 1), which is less than the minimum of 3 nodes that we expect, it is merged with cluster 'A' which it shares most of its border nodes with, resulted in Fig. 3c. Figures 3d and 3e assume that a node in cluster 'A' and a node in cluster 'B' are picked to be checked, respectively. Clusters 'A' and 'B' contain 4 and 3 nodes, respectively, not less than the 3 nodes threshold, so there is no need to merge them with any nearby cluster. The merging algorithm ends when every node is checked. The map after merging contains two clusters, each containing only one disconnected area. With this merging algorithm, it is possible for a map after merging to contain less clusters than what is specified in k.

4   Other Improvements

This section explains two other contributions in addition to the better problem decomposition techniques explained in Sect. 3: (i) improved problem regulation; and (ii) improved ASP encoding.

4.1   Improved Problem Regulation

The previous works on *DMAPF* [9,10] do not have a mechanism to control how many agents to migrate at a time, as long as they do not exceed the number of available borders. Such mechanism was not implemented to keep the communication overhead low, but this comes with a drawback that sub-solvers will fail to find a movement plan if they received more migrating agents than there are nodes available. Deciding which agents to reject is done in the *rejection* phase (see Subsect. 2.3). The design of the rejection phase in the previous work is simple. Each *lower-ranked* sub-solver simply sends a list of migrating agents it refuses to accept to their corresponding *higher-ranked* sub-solvers without having to synchronize in advance (recall that each sub-solver has a unique integer ID called *rank*). This design greatly reduces communication overhead in the *rejection* phase, but it imposes a restriction that higher-ranked sub-solvers can never have information to reply to lower-ranked sub-solvers during the *rejection* phase.

In this paper, we change the design as follows. First, a synchronization point is added before sub-solvers start to communicate in the *rejection* phase. Second, instead of accepting migrating agents from lower-ranked sub-solvers in a first-come-first-serve manner, higher-ranked sub-solvers select agents with the smallest *abstract steps* (followed by the shortest distance to their assigned borders if there is a tie) when there is a conflict (i.e., multiple agents want to move into the same node) between migrating agents. Third, every sub-solver restricts the number of agents in its map by maintaining the constraint $n - r - i \geq M$ where n, r, and i denote the number of nodes in the map, the number of agents in the map, and the number of incoming (migrating) agents, respectively; and $M \leq n$ denotes the required minimum number of *free* nodes – nodes without agents, in the map. The constraint states that at least M nodes must remain without agents in the map with n nodes and $r + i$ agents. If the constraint is unsatisfied, then $M - (n - r - i)$ incoming agents will be rejected. Selecting which incoming agents to reject is also based on the same heuristic previously mentioned in the second change. M is currently set to 2.

This new design comes with an overhead in synchronization, but allows *DMAPF* to solve more problems successfully, as shown in the experiment in Subsect. 5.2. The increased overhead is also greatly offset by the performance gain using the improved ASP encoding, explained in the next subsection.

4.2   Improved ASP Encoding

The ASP encoding currently employed by our sub-solvers to solve MAPF sub-problem instances is shown below:

```
#program p(t).                                      % Line 1
#external q(t).                                     % Line 2
{ m(R,D,t) : d(D) } 1 :- r(R), t>0.               % Line 3
:- a(R,C,0), o(C), not m(R,_,1), q(t).            % Line 4
a(R,C',t) :- a(R,C,t-1), m(R,D,t), x(C,C',D).     % Line 5
:- m(R,D,t), a(R,C,t-1), not x(C,_,D).            % Line 6
a(R,C,t) :- a(R,C,t-1), not m(R,_,t).             % Line 7
w(C,C',t) :- a(R,C,t-1), m(R,D,t), x(C,C',D).     % Line 8
:- w(C,C',t), w(C',C,t).                          % Line 9
:- {a(_,C,t)} > 1, i(C).                          % Line 10
g(t) :- a(R,C,t) : g(r(R),C).                     % Line 11
:- not g(t), q(t).                                 % Line 12
:- g(t), r(R,C,t), c(C), not g(r(R),C), q(t).     % Line 13
#show m/3.                                          % Line 14
```

where the meaning of each atom is as follows: $r(R)$ – agent R is a robot; $d(D)$ – D is a direction (e.g., $(1,0)$ means east); $i(C)$ – coordinate C is inside this map; $o(C)$ – coordinate C is outside this map (i.e., C is a border of a neighboring map); $c(C)$ – coordinate C is a corner node (i.e., a node that connects to more than one neighboring map); $q(t)$ – t is a time step used in multi-shot query; $m(R,D,t)$ – robot R moves in D direction at time step t; $a(R,C,t)$ – robot R is at coordinate C at time step t; $x(C,C',D)$ – coordinate C and C' are next to each other, where C' is in D direction of C; $w(C,C',t)$ – there is a robot going from coordinate C' to C' at time step t; $g(r(R),C)$ – the goal of robot R is at coordinate C. Line 3 generates an action for each robot R to either move in one of the directions D or stay. Line 4 forces every incoming (migrating) robot R to move in at the first time step. Line 5-6 imply results of the movement. Line 7 is the inertia rule. Lines 8-9 prevent the *swapping conflict*. Line 10 prevents the *vertex conflict*. Lines 11-12 enforce that every robot must reach its goal. Line 13 enforces that robots must not stay at a corner node unless it is their goal, viz., corners tend to be congested.

The encoding used in the previous work [9] contain unnecessary information that negatively impacts its performance. For example, the rule used to generate an action for each agent (i.e., our Line 3) was encoded as:

```
{ m(R,D,N2,t) : x(N1,N2,D) } :- r(R,N1,t-1).
```

Notice the extra parameters in atoms m and r. By streamlining the encoding, we noticed a great increase in the performance of *DMAPF*. It is the main contributing factor that allows our improved *DMAPF* to be more efficient than its previous work. Interested readers can refer to the previous work [9] for side-by-side comparison.

5   Experiments

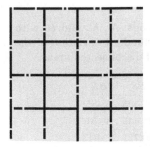

Fig. 4. Name: room-64-64-16 Dimension: 64×64 #Nodes: 3,646

Fig. 5. Name: maze-128-128-2 Dimension: 128×128 #Nodes: 10,858

Fig. 6. Name: lak303d Dimension: 194×194 #Nodes: 14,784

In the following subsections, we evaluate our improved *DMAPF* on maps shown in Figs. 4–6. The maps are taken from the MAPF benchmark [14]. They have different names, dimensions, sizes (i.e., #nodes), and how obstacles are distributed. In the figures, only the grayish-white cells are nodes. The other colors: green and black, are obstacles. We shorten the names of the maps in Tables 1 and 2, from room-64-64-16, maze-128-128-2, and lak303d, to Room, Maze, and Lak, respectively. We use $\mathcal{N}$, $\mathcal{K}$, and $\mathcal{B}$ to denote the *naive, k-means,* and *balanced k-means* methods, respectively; and $\mathcal{M}$, $\mathcal{E}$, and $\mathcal{R}$ to denote the distance functions: Manhattan, Euclidean, and real distances, respectively. Using *k-means* with real distance is denoted as $\mathcal{KR}$, for instance. The tests were performed on a Dell XPS 15 9510 laptop with Intel Core i7-11800H and 16 GB RAM; on Ubuntu 20.04 and *Clingo* [3] version 5.5.1.

5.1   Comparing Problem Decomposition Methods

Table 1 compares the quality of resulting partitioned maps and elapsed times for the different problem decomposition methods: *naive* (See Sect. 1), *k-means,* and *balanced k-means*, on different maps. The quality is objectively measured using (*i*) the standard deviation of the number of nodes in each area (denoted as *SD*); and (*ii*) the number of disconnected areas (denoted as #*Areas*). *SD* and #*Areas* are the primary factors in the comparison – the lower their values are, the better. A low *SD* means that areas in the partitioned map contain roughly the same number of nodes. The elapsed time is less important since problem decomposition can be performed at any time before the problem solving process. The parameter $dx \times dy$ of the *naive* method for sub-problem size is set to 12×12. The parameter k of the *k-means* and the *balanced k-means* methods for the number of clusters is set to $\lfloor n/100 \rfloor$, where n is the number of nodes in a map. For example, lak303d is to be partitioned into $k = \lfloor 14784/100 \rfloor = 147$ clusters. The *merging* technique (see Sect. 3.2) is only applied to $\mathcal{K}$ and $\mathcal{B}$, but not $\mathcal{N}$ since the technique was not implemented in the previous work [9].

Table 1. Comparison between problem decomposition methods: $\mathcal{N}$, $\mathcal{K}$, and $\mathcal{B}$, with different distance functions: $\mathcal{M}$, $\mathcal{E}$, and $\mathcal{R}$. *SD* denotes the standard deviation of the number of nodes in each area. *#Areas* denotes the number of disconnected areas.

	Map	$\mathcal{N}$	$\mathcal{KM}$	$\mathcal{KE}$	$\mathcal{KR}$	$\mathcal{BM}$	$\mathcal{BE}$	$\mathcal{BR}$
SD	Room	45.657	28.719	31.677	35.038	23.950	27.495	5.485
	Maze	18.501	27.615	29.657	106.33	27.207	26.445	40.51
	Lak	46.637	34.575	34.179	39.200	11.666	10.727	12.947

	Map	$\mathcal{N}$	$\mathcal{KM}$	$\mathcal{KE}$	$\mathcal{KR}$	$\mathcal{BM}$	$\mathcal{BE}$	$\mathcal{BR}$
#Areas	Room	51	38	42	36	40	42	36
	Maze	453	180	175	92	180	180	132
	Lak	219	123	120	138	150	149	147

	Map	$\mathcal{N}$	$\mathcal{KM}$	$\mathcal{KE}$	$\mathcal{KR}$	$\mathcal{BM}$	$\mathcal{BE}$	$\mathcal{BR}$
Elapsed time (in seconds)	Room	0.032	0.003	0.004	0.119	0.779	0.804	0.963
	Maze	0.242	0.033	0.033	5.233	8.8587	9.777	25.824
	Lak	0.683	0.056	0.056	7.080	23.165	28.977	29.177

5.2   Comparing Problem Solving Performances

Table 2 compares the performances of our improved *DMAPF* on the maps in Figs. 4–6, partitioned by different methods: $\mathcal{BR}$, $\mathcal{KR}$, and $\mathcal{N}$. The performance of the previous work [9] (denoted as $\mathcal{O}$) on the same maps partitioned by $\mathcal{BR}$ is also shown. From Table 1, $\mathcal{BR}$ is chosen to be used in the comparison because it gives partitioned map with the highest quality; $\mathcal{KR}$ is chosen to compare with $\mathcal{BR}$ to show the effect of problem decomposition on problem solving performances because it gives poor partitioned map quality from its high SD values, albeit the low numbers of areas; and $\mathcal{N}$ is chosen to show that better decomposition methods allow more problems to be solved successfully.

The results show that problem decomposition does impact the solving performance. Comparing between $\mathcal{BR}$ and $\mathcal{KR}$ shows that the same solver can scale better on the same maps if they were partitioned with better methods. Comparing between $\mathcal{BR}$ and $\mathcal{N}$ shows that the same solver fails to find a solution on crowded maps that were partitioned with the *naive* method. Using the *naive* method results in a partitioned map with multiple small areas due to the lack of the *merging* technique. No other agent can pass those areas if they are filled with agents that have reached their goals. Having multiple small areas increases the performance of *DMAPF*, but decreases the success rate and the solution quality [10]. Comparing between $\mathcal{BR}$ and $\mathcal{O}$ shows that our improved *DMAPF* performs better than the previous work [9] in every case. This is due to the introduced problem regulation and the more-efficient ASP encoding. The previous work also fails in the maze map, which is filled with small corridors, because it does not have the problem regulation implemented. There is no significant deviation in the solution qualities overall.

Table 2. Comparison of the performances of our improved *DMAPF* on maps partitioned by different methods: $\mathcal{BR}$, $\mathcal{KR}$, and $\mathcal{N}$. The performance of the previous work [9] on maps partitioned by $\mathcal{BR}$ is denoted as $\mathcal{O}$, and is highlighted with a gray background to distinguish it from the improved *DMAPF*. #A denotes the number of agents in the map. (T) denotes the elapsed time in seconds. (M) denotes the *makespan*. (S) denotes the *sum of costs* ×1000. '-' denotes that the solver still works on the problem after the timeout. 'F' denotes that the solver terminates without a solution before the timeout. The timeout is set to 10 mins. The agents are randomly assigned their start and goal nodes using the random scenario in the MAPF benchmark [14].

Map (#A)	$\mathcal{BR}$ (T)	$\mathcal{KR}$ (T)	$\mathcal{N}$ (T)	$\mathcal{O}$ (T)	$\mathcal{BR}$ (M)	$\mathcal{KR}$ (M)	$\mathcal{N}$ (M)	$\mathcal{O}$ (M)	$\mathcal{BR}$ (S)	$\mathcal{KR}$ (S)	$\mathcal{N}$(S)	$\mathcal{O}$ (S)
Room (100)	23.81	21.42	19.91	29.92	595	492	408	590	7.62	7.40	7.64	7.57
Room (200)	46.52	68.17	43.46	71.25	835	1196	672	853	16.4	16.3	16.7	15.9
Room (400)	283.80	586.49	–	–	2609	2825	–	–	52.2	44.0	–	–
Maze (100)	196.30	191.82	101.14	F	3583	3989	3499	F	59.0	58.7	58.0	F
Maze (200)	527.51	–	–	F	5897	–	–	F	135.8	–	–	F
Maze (400)	–	–	–	F	–	–	–	F	–	–	–	F
Lak (100)	42.62	38.45	–	46.67	913	757	–	917	21.7	21.1	–	21.8
Lak (200)	70.88	152.32	–	103.84	1373	2159	–	1369	44.5	42.2	–	44.7
Lak (400)	181.82	314.13	–	335.74	2103	3275	–	2113	101.0	90.9	–	97.8

6 Future Work

With the improved *DMAPF* that (*i*) has a mature way to decompose MAPF problems; and (*ii*) solves the problem of prematurely failure because of the lack of problem regulation in the previous works, we feel that it is time do extensive evaluation on the system. The evaluation should include the use of other MAPF solvers, that may be more efficient, as sub-solvers for *DMAPF*. It should also be done on hardware that allows more parallel computation, such as a cluster, to better study the performance of the system.

References

1. Achá, R.A., López, R., Hagedorn, S., Baier, J.A.: A new boolean encoding for mapf and its performance with asp and maxsat solvers. In: Proceedings of the International Symposium on Combinatorial Search, vol. 12, pp. 11–19 (2021). https://ojs.aaai.org/index.php/SOCS/article/view/18546

2. Barer, M., Sharon, G., Stern, R., Felner, A.: Suboptimal variants of the conflict-based search algorithm for the multi-agent pathfinding problem. In: Seventh Annual Symposium on Combinatorial Search (2014). https://doi.org/10.3233/978-1-61499-419-0-961

3. Gebser, M., Kaminski, R., Kaufmann, B., Schaub, T.: Clingo = ASP + control: Preliminary report. In: Technical Communications of the 13th International Conference on Logic Programming, vol. 14(4–5) (2014). https://arxiv.org/abs/1405.3694

4. Gelfond, M., Lifschitz, V.: Logic programs with classical negation. In: Logic Programming, Proceedings of the Seventh International Conference, pp. 579–597. MIT Press, Jerusalem, Israel (June 1990). https://dl.acm.org/doi/10.5555/87961.88030

5. Gómez, R.N., Hernández, C., Baier, J.A.: A compact answer set programming encoding of multi-agent pathfinding. IEEE Access **9**, 26886–26901 (2021). https://doi.org/10.1109/ACCESS.2021.3053547

6. Kuhn, H.W.: The hungarian method for the assignment problem. Naval Res. Logist. Quart. **2**(1–2), 83–97 (1955). https://doi.org/10.1002/nav.3800020109

7. MacQueen, J.: Classification and analysis of multivariate observations. In: Proceedings of the fifth Berkeley symposium on mathematical statistics and probability, Oakland, CA, USA, pp. 281–297 (1967)

8. Malinen, M.I., Fränti, P.: Balanced K-means for clustering. In: Fränti, P., Brown, G., Loog, M., Escolano, F., Pelillo, M. (eds.) S+SSPR 2014. LNCS, vol. 8621, pp. 32–41. Springer, Heidelberg (2014). https://doi.org/10.1007/978-3-662-44415-3_4

9. Pianpak, P., Son, T.C.: DMAPF: A decentralized and distributed solver for multi-agent path finding problem with obstacles. Electron. Proc. Theor. Comput. Sci. (EPTCS) **345**, 99–112 (2021). https://doi.org/10.4204/eptcs.345.24. Sep

10. Pianpak, P., Son, T.C., Toups, Z.O., Yeoh, W.: A distributed solver for multi-agent path finding problems. In: Proceedings of the First International Conference on Distributed Artificial Intelligence (DAI), pp. 1–7 (2019). https://doi.org/10.1145/3356464.3357702

11. Salzman, O., Stern, R.Z.: Research challenges and opportunities in multi-agent path finding and multi-agent pickup and delivery problems blue sky ideas track. In: 19th International Conference on Autonomous Agents and Multiagent Systems, AAMAS 2020, pp. 1711–1715. International Foundation for Autonomous Agents and Multiagent Systems (IFAAMAS) (2020). http://www.orensalzman.com/docs/AAMAS20.pdf

12. Silver, D.: Cooperative pathfinding. In: Proceedings of the AAAI Conference on Artificial Intelligence and Interactive Digital Entertainment, pp. 117–122 (2005). https://ojs.aaai.org/index.php/AIIDE/article/view/18726

13. Stern, R.: Multi-agent path finding - an overview. In: Osipov, G.S., Panov, A.I., Yakovlev, K.S. (eds.) Artificial Intelligence. LNCS (LNAI), vol. 11866, pp. 96–115. Springer, Cham (2019). https://doi.org/10.1007/978-3-030-33274-7_6

14. Stern, R., et al.: Multi-agent pathfinding: Definitions, variants, and benchmarks. Symposium on Combinatorial Search (SoCS), pp. 151–158 (2019). https://www.aaai.org/ocs/index.php/SOCS/SOCS19/paper/view/18341

15. Wilt, C.M., Botea, A.: Spatially distributed multiagent path planning. In: Twenty-Fourth International Conference on Automated Planning and Scheduling, pp. 332–340 (2014). https://www.aaai.org/ocs/index.php/ICAPS/ICAPS14/paper/view/7858/8043

Assume-Guarantee Verification
of Strategic Ability

Łukasz Mikulski[1,2]([✉]), Wojciech Jamroga[2,3], and Damian Kurpiewski[1,2]

[1] Faculty of Mathematics and Computer Science, Nicolaus Copernicus University,
Toruń, Poland
lukasz.mikulski@mat.umk.pl
[2] Institute of Computer Science, Polish Academy of Sciences, Warsaw, Poland
d.kurpiewski@ipipan.waw.pl
[3] Interdisciplinary Centre for Security, Reliability and Trust, SnT,
University of Luxembourg, Esch-sur-Alzette, Luxembourg
wojciech.jamroga@uni.lu

Abstract. Model checking of strategic abilities is a notoriously hard problem, even more so in the realistic case of agents with imperfect information. Assume-guarantee reasoning can be of great help here, providing a way to decompose the complex problem into a small set of exponentially easier subproblems. In this paper, we propose two schemes for assume-guarantee verification of alternating-time temporal logic with imperfect information. We prove the soundness of both schemes, and discuss their completeness. We illustrate the method by examples based on known benchmarks, and show experimental results that demonstrate the practical benefits of the approach.

Keywords: Model checking · Assume-guarantee reasoning · Strategic ability

1 Introduction

Multi-agent systems involve a complex network of social and technological components. Such components often exhibit self-interested, goal-directed behavior, which makes it harder to predict and analyze the dynamics of the system. In consequence, formal specification and automated verification can be of significant help.

Verification of Strategic Ability. Many important properties of multi-agent systems refer to *strategic abilities* of agents and their groups. *Alternating-time temporal logic* **ATL*** [2,37] and *Strategy Logic* **SL** [34] provide powerful tools to reason about such aspects of MAS. For example, the **ATL*** formula $\langle\langle taxi \rangle\rangle G \neg fatality$ expresses that the autonomous cab can drive in such a way that no one gets ever killed. Similarly, $\langle\langle taxi, passg \rangle\rangle F$ destination says that the cab and the passenger have a joint strategy to arrive at the destination, no matter what the other agents do. Specifications in agent logics can be used as input to algorithms and tools for *model checking*, that have been in constant development for over 20 years [3,6,7,20,27,30].

Model checking of strategic abilities is hard, both theoretically and in practice. First, it suffers from the well-known state/transition-space explosion. Moreover, the space of possible strategies is at least exponential *on top of the state-space explosion*, and incremental synthesis of strategies is not possible in general – especially in the realistic case of agents with partial observability. Even for the more restricted (and computation-friendly) logic **ATL**, model checking of its imperfect information variants is Δ_2^P- to **PSPACE**-complete for agents playing memoryless strategies [5,37] and **EXPTIME**-complete to undecidable for agents with perfect recall [12,16]. The theoretical results concur with outcomes of empirical studies on benchmarks [6,22,30], as well as recent attempts at verification of real-life multi-agent scenarios [21,26].

Contribution. In this paper, we make the first step towards compositional model checking of strategic properties in asynchronous multi-agent systems with imperfect information. The idea of *assume-guarantee reasoning* [10,36] is to "factorize" the verification task into subtasks where components are verified against a suitable abstraction of the rest of the system. Thus, instead of searching through the states (and, in our case, strategies) of the huge product of all components, most of the search is performed locally.

To achieve this, we adapt and extend the assume-guarantee framework of [31,32]. We redefine the concepts of modules and their composition, follow the idea of expressing assumptions as Büchi automata, and accordingly redefine their interaction with the computations of the coalition. Then, we propose two alternative assume-guarantee schemes for **ATL*** with imperfect information. The first, simpler one is shown to be sound but incomplete. The more complex one turns out to be both sound and complete. We illustrate the properties of the schemes on a variant of the Trains, Gate and Controller scenario [4], and evaluate the practical gains through verification experiments on models of logistic robots, inspired by [26].

Note that our formal treatment of temporal properties, together with strategic properties of curtailment,[1] substantially extends the applicability of schemes in [31,32] from temporal liveness properties to strategic properties with arbitrary **LTL** objectives. We also emphasize that our schemes are sound for the model checking of agents with *imperfect* as well as *perfect recall*. In consequence, they can be used to facilitate verification problems with a high degree of hardness, including the undecidable variant for coalitions of agents with memory. In that case, the undecidable problem reduces to multiple instances of the **EXPTIME**-complete verification of individual abilities.

Structure of the Paper. In Sect. 2, we present the model of concurrent MAS that we consider in this paper. In Sect. 3, we define the syntax and semantics

---

[1] Provided in the supplementary material, available at https://github.com/agrprim a22/sup.

of the logic used in the formulation of agents' strategic properties. In Sects. 4 and 5 we introduce the notions of assumption and guarantee, and utilize them to propose two schemes of assume-guarantee reasoning for strategic abilities. Finally, we present preliminary results of experimental verification in Sect. 6 and conclude the paper in Sect. 7.

Related Work. Compositional verification (known as *rely-guarantee* in the program verification community) dates back to the early 1970s s and the works of Hoare, Owicki, Gries and Jones [19,24,35]. Assume-guarantee reasoning for temporal specifications was introduced a decade later [10,36], and has been in development since that time [11,13,18,29,31,32]. Moreover, automated synthesis of assumptions for temporal reasoning has been studied in [9,15,17,25].

The works that come closest to our proposal are [11,14,31,32]. In [31,32], models and a reasoning scheme are defined for assume-guarantee verification of liveness properties in distributed systems. We build directly on that approach and extend it to the verification of strategic abilities. [11] studies assume-guarantee reasoning for an early version of **ATL**. However, their assume-guarantee rules are designed for perfect information strategies (whereas we tackle the more complex case of imperfect information), and targeted specifically the verification of aspect-oriented programs. Finally, [14] investigates the compositional synthesis of strategies for **LTL** objectives. The difference to our work is that they focus on finite-memory strategies while we consider the semantics of ability based on memoryless and perfect recall strategies. Another difference lies in our use of repertoire functions that define agents' choices in a flexible way, and make it closer to real applications. The advantage of the solution presented in [14] is the use of contracts, thanks to which it is possible to synthesize individual strategies using the knowledge of the coalition partners' strategies. We also mention [8] that studies the synthesis of Nash equilibrium strategies for 2-player coalitions pursuing ω-regular objectives. The authors call their approach *assume-guarantee strategy synthesis*, but the connection to assume-guarantee verification is rather loose.

A preliminary version of the ideas, presented here, was published in the extended abstract [33]. Our extension of the STV tool [27], used in the experiments, is described in the companion paper [28].

2 Models of Concurrent MAS

Asynchronous MAS have been modeled by variants of reactive modules [1,32] and automata networks [23]. Here, we adapt the variant of reactive modules that was used to define assume-guarantee verification for temporal properties in [32].

2.1 Modules

Let D be the shared domain of values for all the variables in the system. D^X is the set of all valuations for a set of variables X. The *system* consists of a number of *agents*, each represented by its *module* and a *repertoire* of available choices.

Every agent uses *state variables* and *input variables*. It can read and modify its state variables at any moment, and their valuation is determined by the current state of the agent. The input variables are not a part of the state, but their values influence transitions that can be executed.

Definition 1 (Module [32]). *A module is a tuple* $M = (X, I, Q, T, \lambda, q_0)$, *where:* X *is a finite set of state variables;* I *is a finite set of input variables with* $X \cap I = \varnothing$; $Q = \{q_0, q_1, \ldots, q_n\}$ *is a finite set of states;* $q_0 \in Q$ *is an initial state;* $\lambda : Q \to D^X$ *labels each state with a valuation of the state variables; finally,* $T \subseteq Q \times D^I \times Q$ *is a transition relation such that (a) for each pair* $(q, \alpha) \in Q \times D^I$ *there exists* $q' \in Q$ *with* $(q, \alpha, q') \in T$, *and (b)* $(q, \alpha, q') \in T, q \neq q'$ *implies* $(q, \alpha, q) \notin T$. *In what follows, we omit the self-loops from the presentation.*

Modules M, M' are *asynchronous* if $X \cap X' = \varnothing$. We extend modules by adding *repertoire functions* that define the agents' available choices in a way similar to [23].

Definition 2 (Repertoire). *Let* $M = (X, I, Q, T, \lambda, q_0)$ *be a module of agent* i. *The repertoire of* i *is defined as* $R : Q \to \mathcal{P}(\mathcal{P}(T))$, *i.e., a mapping from local states to sets of sets of transitions. Each* $R(q) = \{T_1, \ldots, T_m\}$ *must be nonempty and consist of nonempty sets* T_i *of transitions starting in* q. *If the agent chooses* $T_i \in R(q)$, *then only a transition in* T_i *can be occur at* q *within the module.*

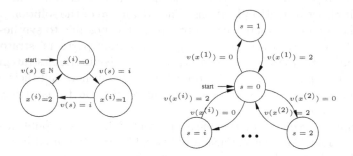

Fig. 1. A variant of TCG: Train synchronizing with a semaphore (left) and the controller (right).

We adapt the Train-Gate-Controller (TGC) benchmark [3] as our running example.

Example 1. The module $M^{(i)}$ of a train is presented in Fig. 1 (left). Its local states $Q^{(i)} = \{w^{(i)}, t^{(i)}, a^{(i)}\}$ refer, respectively, to the train waiting at the entrance, riding in the tunnel, and cruising away from the tunnel. The sole state variable $x^{(i)}$ labels the state with values 0, 1, and 2, respectively. $I^{(i)} = \{s\}$ consists of a single input variable that takes values from an external multi-valued semaphore. The train can enter and exit the tunnel only

if the semaphore allows for that, i.e., if $v(s) = i$. To this end, we define
$$T^{(i)} = \{(w^{(i)}, i, t^{(i)}), (t^{(i)}, i, a^{(i)}), (a^{(i)}, 0, w^{(i)}), (a^{(i)}, 1, w^{(i)}) \ldots, (a^{(i)}, n, w^{(i)})\} \cup$$
$$\{(w^{(i)}, j, w^{(i)}), (t^{(i)}, j, t^{(i)}) \mid j \neq i\} .^2$$

The module $M^{(C(n))}$ of a controller that coordinates up to n trains is depicted in Fig. 1 (right). Formally, it is defined by:

- $X = \{s\}$ (the semaphore),
- $I = \{x_1, \ldots, x_n\}$ (the positions of trains),
- $Q = \{r, g_1, \ldots, g_n\}$ (red or directed green light),

where a state with subscript 1 represents a tunnel shared with the other trains, $\lambda(g_i)(s) = i$, $\lambda(r)(s) = 0$, and r is the initial state.

The controller can change the light to green when a train is waiting for the permission to enter the tunnel, and back to red after it passed through the tunnel: $T = \{(r, v, g_i) \mid v(x_i) = 0\} \cup \{(g_i, v, r) \mid v(x_i) = 2\}$.

Each agent can freely choose the local transition intended to execute next. Thus, $R^{(i)}(q) = \{\{(q, \alpha, q')\} \mid (q, \alpha, q') \in T^{(i)}\}$, and similarly for $R^{(C(n))}$.

Note that all the modules in TCG are asynchronous.

2.2 Composition of Agents

On the level of the temporal structure, the model of a multi-agent system is given by the asynchronous composition $M = M^{(1)} | \ldots | M^{(n)}$ that combines modules $M^{(i)}$ into a single module. The definition is almost the same as in [32]; we only extend it to handle the repertoire functions that are needed to characterize strategies and strategic abilities.

We begin with the notion of compatible valuations to adjust local states of one agent with the labels of the actions performed by the other agent. Note that the local states of different asynchronous agents rely on disjoint sets of variables.

Let $Y, Z \subseteq X$ and $\rho_1 \in D^Y$ while $\rho_2 \in D^Z$. We say that ρ_1 is compatible with ρ_2 (denoted by $\rho_1 \sim \rho_2$) if for any $x \in Y \cap Z$ we have $\rho_1(x) = \rho_2(x)$. We can compute the union of ρ_1 with ρ_2 which is compatible with ρ_1 by setting $(\rho_1 \cup \rho_2)(x) = \rho_1(x)$ for $x \in Y$ and $(\rho_1 \cup \rho_2)(x) = \rho_2(x)$ for $x \in Z$.

Definition 3 (Composition of modules [32]). *The composition of asynchronous modules* $M^{(1)} = (X^{(1)}, I^{(1)}, Q^{(1)}, T^{(1)}, \lambda^{(1)}, q_0^{(1)})$ *and* $M^{(2)} = (X^{(2)}, I^{(2)}, Q^{(2)}, T^{(2)}, \lambda^{(2)}, q_0^{(2)})$ *(with* $X^{(1)} \cap X^{(2)} = \varnothing$*) is a composite module* $M = (X = X^{(1)} \uplus X^{(2)}, I = (I^{(1)} \cup I^{(2)}) \setminus X, Q^{(1)} \times Q^{(2)}, T, \lambda, q_0 = (q_0^{(1)}, q_0^{(2)}))$, *where*

- $\lambda : Q^{(1)} \times Q^{(2)} \to D^X$, $\lambda(q^{(1)}, q^{(2)}) = \lambda^{(1)}(q^{(1)}) \cup \lambda^{(2)}(q^{(2)})$,

---

^{2} By a slight abuse of notation, the valuation of a single variable is identified with its value.

– T is the minimal transition relation derived by the set of rules presented below:

$$\textbf{ASYN}_\textbf{L} \quad \frac{q^{(1)} \xrightarrow{\alpha^{(1)}}_{T^{(1)}} q'^{(1)} \quad q^{(2)} \xrightarrow{\alpha^{(2)}}_{T^{(2)}} q'^{(2)}}{(q^{(1)}, q^{(2)}) \xrightarrow{(\alpha^{(1)} \cup \alpha^{(2)}) \setminus X}_T (q'^{(1)}, q^{(2)})} \quad \alpha^{(1)} \sim \alpha^{(2)} \quad \lambda^{(1)}(q^{(1)}) \sim \alpha^{(2)} \quad \lambda^{(2)}(q^{(2)}) \sim \alpha^{(1)}$$

$$\textbf{ASYN}_\textbf{R} \quad \frac{q^{(1)} \xrightarrow{\alpha^{(1)}}_{T^{(1)}} q'^{(1)} \quad q^{(2)} \xrightarrow{\alpha^{(2)}}_{T^{(2)}} q'^{(2)}}{(q^{(1)}, q^{(2)}) \xrightarrow{(\alpha^{(1)} \cup \alpha^{(2)}) \setminus X}_T (q^{(1)}, q'^{(2)})} \quad \alpha^{(1)} \sim \alpha^{(2)} \quad \lambda^{(1)}(q^{(1)}) \sim \alpha^{(2)} \quad \lambda^{(2)}(q^{(2)}) \sim \alpha^{(1)}$$

$$\textbf{SYN} \quad \frac{q^{(1)} \xrightarrow{\alpha^{(1)}}_{T^{(1)}} q'^{(1)} \quad q^{(2)} \xrightarrow{\alpha^{(2)}}_{T^{(2)}} q'^{(2)}}{(q^{(1)}, q^{(2)}) \xrightarrow{(\alpha^{(1)} \cup \alpha^{(2)}) \setminus X}_T (q'^{(1)}, q'^{(2)})} \quad \alpha^{(1)} \sim \alpha^{(2)} \quad \lambda^{(1)}(q^{(1)}) \sim \alpha^{(2)} \quad \lambda^{(2)}(q^{(2)}) \sim \alpha^{(1)}$$

pruned in order to avoid disallowed self-loops. We use the notation $M = M^{(1)} | M^{(2)}$.

Note that the operation is defined in [32] for a pair of modules only. It can be easily extended to a larger number of pairwise asynchronous modules. Moreover, the order of the composition does not matter.

Consider agents $(M^{(1)}, R^{(1)}), \ldots, (M^{(n)}, R^{(n)})$. The *multi-agent system* is defined by $\mathcal{S} = (M^{(1)} | M^{(2)} | \ldots | M^{(n)}, R^{(1)}, \ldots, R^{(n)})$, i.e., the composition of the underlying modules, together with the agents' repertoires of choices.

Example 2. The composition $M^{(1)} | M^{(2)} | M^{(C(2))}$ of two train modules $M^{(1)}, M^{(2)}$ and controller $M^{(C(2))}$ is presented in Fig. 2. The asynchronous transitions are labelled by the agent performing the transitions. All the synchronous transitions performed by both trains are in red, while the synchronous transitions performed by a controller with one of the trains are in blue. There are two synchronous transition performed by all the agents, both in green.

Traces and Words. A trace of a module M is an infinite sequence of alternating states and transitions $\sigma = q_0 \alpha_0 q_1 \alpha_1 \ldots$, where $(q_i, \alpha_i, q_{i+1}) \in T$ for every $i \in \mathbb{N}$ (note that q_0 is the initial state). An infinite word $w = v_0 v_1, \ldots \in (D^X)^\omega$ is *derived* by M with trace $\sigma = q_0 \alpha_0 q_1 \alpha_1 \ldots$ if $v_i = \lambda(q_i)$ for all $i \in \mathbb{N}$. An infinite word $u = \alpha_0 \alpha_1, \ldots \in (D^I)^\omega$ is *admitted* by M with σ if $\sigma = q_0 \alpha_0 q_1 \alpha_1 \ldots$. Finally, w (resp. u) is derived (resp. admitted) by M if there exists a trace of M that derives (resp. admits) it.

3   What Agents Can Achieve

Alternating-time temporal logic **ATL*** [2,37] introduces *strategic modalities* $\langle\langle C \rangle\rangle \gamma$, expressing that coalition C can enforce the temporal property γ. We use the semantics based on *imperfect information strategies* with *imperfect recall* (ir) or *perfect recall* (iR) [37]. Moreover, we only consider formulas without the next step operator X due to its questionable interpretation for asynchronous systems, which are based on the notion of local clocks.

Syntax. Formally, the syntax of $\mathbf{ATL}^*_{-\mathbf{X}}$ is as follows:

$$\phi::= p(Y) \mid \neg\phi \mid \phi \wedge \phi \mid \langle\!\langle C \rangle\!\rangle \gamma\,, \qquad\qquad \gamma::= \phi \mid \neg\gamma \mid \gamma \wedge \gamma \mid \gamma\, \mathsf{U}\, \gamma$$

where $p : Y \to D$ for some subset of domain variables $Y \subseteq X$. That is, each atomic statement refers to the valuation of variables used in the system. U is the "strong until" operator of $\mathbf{LTL}_{-\mathbf{X}}$. The "sometime" and "always" operators can be defined as usual by $\mathsf{F}\,\gamma \equiv \top\, \mathsf{U}\, \gamma$ and $\mathsf{G}\,\gamma \equiv \neg\mathsf{F}\,\neg\gamma$. The set of variables used by the formula γ is denoted by $var(\gamma)$.

In most of the paper, we focus on formulas that consist of a single strategic modality followed by an $\mathbf{LTL}_{-\mathbf{X}}$ formula (i.e., $\langle\!\langle C \rangle\!\rangle \gamma$, where $\gamma \in \mathbf{LTL}_{-\mathbf{X}}$). The corresponding fragment of $\mathbf{ATL}^*_{-\mathbf{X}}$, called $\mathbf{1ATL}^*_{-\mathbf{X}}$, suffices to express many interesting specifications, namely the ones that refer to agents' ability of enforcing trace properties (such as safety or reachability of a winning state). Note that $\mathbf{1ATL}^*_{-\mathbf{X}}$ has strictly higher expressive and distinguishing power than $\mathbf{LTL}_{-\mathbf{X}}$. In fact, model checking $\mathbf{1ATL}^*_{-\mathbf{X}}$ is equivalent to $\mathbf{LTL}_{-\mathbf{X}}$ controller synthesis, i.e., a variant of $\mathbf{LTL}$ realizability.

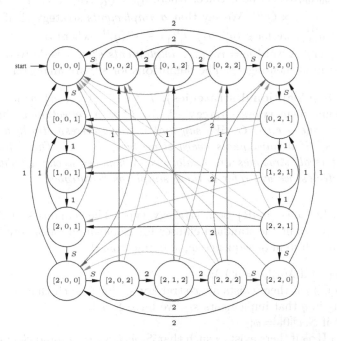

Fig. 2. Composition of modules: two trains $M^{(1)}, M^{(2)}$ and controller $M^{(C(2))}$. (Color figure online)

Nested strategic modalities might be sometimes needed to refer to an agent's ability to endow or deprive another agent with/of ability. We discuss assume-guarantee verification for such specifications in Sect. 5.4.

Strategies and Their Outcomes. Let S be a system composed of n agents with asynchronous modules $M^{(i)} = (X^{(i)}, I^{(i)}, Q^{(i)}, T^{(i)}, \lambda^{(i)}, q_0^{(i)})$ and repertoires $R^{(i)}$.

Definition 4 (Strategies). *A* memoryless strategy *for agent* i *(ir-strategy in short) is a function* $s_i^{\mathrm{ir}} : Q^{(i)} \to \mathcal{P}(\mathcal{P}(T^{(i)}))$ *such that* $s_i^{\mathrm{ir}}(q^{(i)}) \in R^{(i)}(q^{(i)})$ *for every* $q^{(i)} \in Q^{(i)}$. *That is, a memoryless strategy assigns a legitimate choice to each local state of* i.
   A perfect recall strategy *for* i *(iR-strategy in short) is a function* $s_i^{\mathrm{iR}} : (Q^{(i)})^+ \to T^{(i)}$ *such that* $s_i^{\mathrm{iR}}(q_1^{(i)}, \ldots, q_k^{(i)}) \in R^{(i)}(q_k^{(i)})$, *i.e., it assigns choices to finite sequences of local states. We assume that* s_i^{iR} *is stuttering-invariant, i.e.,*

$$s_i^{\mathrm{iR}}(q_1^{(i)}, \ldots, q_j^{(i)}, q_j^{(i)}, \ldots, q_k^{(i)}) = s_i^{\mathrm{iR}}(q_1^{(i)}, \ldots, q_j^{(i)}, \ldots, q_k^{(i)}).$$

Note that the agent's choices in a strategy depend only on its local states, thus being uniform by construction.

Let $\sigma = q_0 \alpha_0 q_1 \alpha_1 \ldots$ be a trace, where $q_j = (q_j^{(1)}, q_j^{(2)}, \ldots, q_j^{(n)})$ are global states in $Q^{(1)} \times \ldots \times Q^{(n)}$. We say that σ *implements* strategy s_i^{ir} if, for any j where $q_j^{(i)} \neq q_{j+1}^{(i)}$, we have $(q_j^{(i)}, \alpha_j, q_{j+1}^{(i)}) \in s_i^{\mathrm{ir}}(q_j^{(i)})$ where $\alpha_j : I^{(i)} \to D$ and $\alpha_j(x) = \lambda(q_j)(x)$. A word $w = v_0 v_1 \ldots$ *implements* s_i^{ir} if it is derived by S with some trace σ implementing s_i^{ir}. The definitions for s_i^{iR} are analogous.

Definition 5 (Coalitional strategies). *Let* $C \subseteq \{1, \ldots, n\}$ *be a coalition of agents. A* joint memoryless strategy s_C^{ir} *for* C *is a collection of memoryless strategies* s_i^{ir}, *one per* $i \in C$. *We say that a trace* σ *(respectively a word* w_σ*)* implements s_C^{ir} *if it implements every strategy* $s_i^{\mathrm{ir}}, i \in C$. *The definitions for joint perfect recall strategies are analogous. Whenever a claim holds for both types of strategies, we will refer to them simply as "strategies."*

Semantics. Let $x \in \{\mathrm{ir}, \mathrm{iR}\}$ be a strategy type. The semantics of $\mathbf{ATL}^*_{-\mathbf{X}}$ is given below (we omit the standard clauses for Boolean operators etc.). By $w[i]$, we denote the ith item of sequence w, starting from 0.

$S, q \models_x p(Y)$ if $\lambda(q)|_Y = p(Y)$;
$S, q \models_x \langle\langle C \rangle\rangle \gamma$ if there exists an x-strategy s_C for C such that, for any word w starting in q that implements s_C, we have $S, w \models \gamma$;
$S, w \models \phi$ if $S, w[0] \models \phi$;
$S, w \models \gamma_1 \, \mathrm{U} \, \gamma_2$ if there exists j such that $S, w[j, \infty] \models \gamma_2$, and $S, w[i, \infty] \models \gamma_1$ for each $0 \leq i < j$.

Finally, we say that $S \models_x \phi$ if $S, q_0 \models_x \phi$, where q_0 is the initial state of S.

Example 3. Let us consider the system $\mathcal{S}$ of Example 2 and the **1ATL*** formula $\phi \equiv \langle\langle 1, 2 \rangle\rangle (GFp^{(1)} \wedge GFp^{(2)})$, where $p^{(i)}(x^{(i)}) = 1$. That is, ϕ says that trains $1, 2$ have a strategy so that each visits the tunnel infinitely many times. Consider the joint strategy (σ_1, σ_2) with $\sigma_i(w^{(i)}) = \{(w^{(i)}, i, T^{(i)})\}$, $\sigma_i(T^{(i)}) = \{(T^{(i)}, i, A^{(i)})\}$, and $\sigma_i(A^{(i)}) = \{(A^{(i)}, 3-i, w^{(i)})\}$. All the traces implementing (σ_1, σ_2) alternate the visits of the trains in the tunnel, making the **LTL** formula $GFp^{(1)} \wedge GFp^{(2)}$ satisfied. Thus, $\mathcal{S} \models_x \phi$ for $x \in \{\text{ir}, \text{iR}\}$.

By the same strategy, we get $\mathcal{S} \models_x \langle\langle 1, 2 \rangle\rangle (GFq^{(1)} \wedge GFq^{(2)})$, where $q^{(i)}(s) = i$.

4   Assumptions and Guarantees

Our assume-guarantee scheme reduces the complexity of model checking by "factorizing" the task into verification of strategies of single agents with respect to abstractions of the rest of the system. In this section, we formalize the notions of *assumption* and *guarantee*, which provide the abstractions in a way that allows for simulating the global behavior of the system.

4.1   Assumptions

Definition 6 (Assumption [32]). *An* assumption *or an* extended module $(M, F) = (X, I, Q, T, \lambda, q_0, F)$ *is a module augmented with a set of accepting states* $F \subseteq Q$.

For assumptions, we use Büchi accepting conditions. More precisely, the infinite word $w = q_0 q_1, \ldots$ is *accepted* by extended module (M, F) with computation $u = \alpha_0 \alpha_1 \ldots$ if it is derived by M with a trace $\sigma = q_0 \alpha_0 q_1 \alpha_1 \ldots$ and $inf(\sigma) \cap F \neq \varnothing$. Thus, the assumptions have the expressive power of ω-regular languages. In practical applications, it might be convenient to formulate actual assumptions in **LTL** (which covers a proper subclass of ω-regular properties).

The definitions of Sects. 2 and 3 generalize to assumptions in a straightforward way. In particular, we can compose a module M with an assumption $A' = (M', F')$, and obtain an extended composite module $A = (M|M', F)$, where $F = \{(q, q') \in Q \times Q' \mid q' \in F'\}$. We use the notation $A = M|A'$. Moreover, let $\mathcal{A} = (A, R^{(1)}, \ldots, R^{(m)})$ be a MAS based on the extended module A with repertoires related to all components of M. The semantics of **1ATL**$^*_{-\mathbf{X}}$ extends naturally:

$\mathcal{A}, q \models_x \langle\langle C \rangle\rangle \phi$ iff there exists an x-strategy s_C for C such that, for any word $w = w[1]w[2] \ldots$ that implements s_C and is accepted by A, we have $\mathcal{A}, w \models_x \phi$.

Example 4. Recall module $M^{(C(2))} = (X, I, Q, T, \lambda, q_0)$ of the controller for 2 trains, with $Q = \{r, g^{(1)}, g^{(2)}\}$. We define four different assumptions about the behavior of the rest of the system, depicted graphically in Fig. 3:

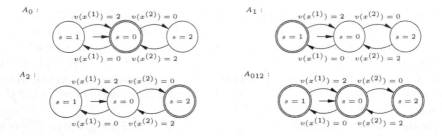

Fig. 3. Assumptions for the railway scenario

- $A_0 = (X, I, Q, T, \lambda, q_0, \{r\})$
- $A_1 = (X, I, Q, T, \lambda, q_0, \{g^{(1)}\})$
- $A_2 = (X, I, Q, T, \lambda, q_0, \{g^{(2)}\})$
- $A_{012} = (X, I, Q, T, \lambda, q_0, \{r, g^{(1)}, g^{(2)}\})$.

Note that we can identify each valuation with an element of the set $\{0, 1, 2\}$, i.e., the value of the only variable s. This way A_0 as well as A_{012} accept all infinite words of the ω-regular language $L = (0(1|2))^\omega$, while A_1 and A_2 accept only proper subsets of this language, namely $L \setminus (0(1|2))^*(02)^\omega$ and $L \setminus (0(1|2))^*(01)^\omega$.

4.2   Guarantees

We say that a sequence $v = v_1 v_2 \ldots$ over D^Y is a *curtailment* of a sequence $u = u_1 u_2 \ldots$ over D^X (where $Y \subseteq X$) if there exists an infinite sequence c of indices $c_0 < c_1 < \ldots$ with $c_0 = 0$ such that $\forall_i \forall_{c_i \le k < c_{i+1}} v_i = u_k|_Y$. We will denote a curtailment of u to D^Y by $u|_Y$ or $u|_Y^c$, and use it to abstract away from irrelevant variables and the stuttering of states.

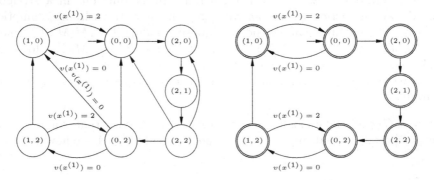

Fig. 4. Module $M^{(C(2))}|M^{(2)}$ (left). The edges are labeled only if the value of $x^{(1)}$ is relevant. Subsystem $M^{(2)}|A_{012}$ implementing strategy σ (right).

Definition 7 (Guarantee). *Let* $M^{(1)}, \ldots, M^{(k)}$ *be pairwise asynchronous modules, and* $A = (X^{(A)}, I^{(A)}, Q^{(A)}, T^{(A)}, \lambda^{(A)}, q_0^{(A)}, F^{(A)})$ *be an assumption with* $X^{(A)} \subseteq X = \bigcup_{i=1}^{k} X^{(i)}$ *and* $I^{(A)} \subseteq I = \bigcup_{i=1}^{k} I^{(i)}$.

We say that $M = M^{(1)} | \ldots | M^{(k)}$ *guarantees the assumption* A *(denoted* $M \models A$*) if, for every infinite trace* σ *of* M *with* $w \in (D^X)^\omega$ *derived by* M *with* σ *and* $u \in (D^I)^\omega$ *admitted by* M *with* σ*, there exists a curtailment* $w|_{X^{(A)}}^c$ *(*$c = c_1, c_2, \ldots$*) accepted by* A *with the computation* $u_{c_1-1}|_{I^{(A)}} \, u_{c_2-1}|_{I^{(A)}} \cdots$.

That is, every trace of M must agree on the values of $X^{(A)}$ with some trace in A, modulo stuttering.

Example 5. Consider the system $M^{(C(2))} | M^{(1)} | M^{(2)}$ presented in Example 2, its subsystem $M^{(C(2))} | M^{(2)}$ from Fig. 4, and the assumption A_{012} of Example 4.

If we focus on the changes s, the following words can be derived: $(0(1|2))^\omega$ for the trains taking turns in the tunnel forever, $(0(1|2))^* 01^\omega$ for the traces where the semaphore is stuck in state $(1, 0)$ because it never receives that $v(x^{(1)}) = 2$, and $(0(1|2))^* 02^\omega$ for ones that cycle forever in the right-hand part of $M^{(C(2))} | M^{(2)}$. In consequence, we have that $M^{(C(2))} | M^{(2)} \models A_{012}$, but not $M^{(C(2))} | M^{(2)} \models A_1$.

It is possible to relate the traces of a subsystem with the traces of the entire system in such a way that it is possible to verify locally defined formulas.

5 Assume-Guarantee Reasoning for 1ATL*

Now we propose our assume-guarantee schemes that decompose abilities of coalition C into abilities of its subcoalitions, verified in suitable abstractions of their neighbor modules.

5.1 Assume-Guarantee Rule for Strategies

Let $\mathcal{S}$ be a system composed of asynchronous agents $(M^{(1)}, R^{(1)}), \ldots, (M^{(n)}, R^{(n)})$. By $N_1^{(i)}$, we denote the direct "neighborhood" of agent i, i.e., the set of agent indices j such that $I_{M^{(j)}} \cap X_{M^{(i)}} \neq \varnothing$ or $I_{M^{(i)}} \cap X_{M^{(j)}} \neq \varnothing$. By $N_k^{(i)}$, we denote the agents connected to i in at most k steps, i.e., $(N_{k-1}^{(i)} \cup \bigcup_{j \in N_{k-1}^{(i)}} N_1^{(j)}) \setminus \{i\}$. Finally $Comp_k^{(i)}$ denotes the composition of all modules of $N_k^{(i)}$. That is, if $N_k^{(i)} = \{a_1, \ldots, a_m\}$ then $Comp_k^{(i)} = M^{(a_1)} | \ldots | M^{(a_m)}$.

Let ψ_i be an **LTL** formula (without "next"), where atomic propositions are local valuations of variables in $M^{(i)}$. Also, let $x \in \{\text{ir}, \text{iR}\}$. The scheme is formalized through a sequence of rules $\mathbf{R_k}$ which rely on the behaviour of the neighbourhoods of coalition C, limited by "distance" k:

$$\mathbf{R_k} \quad \frac{\forall_{i \in C} \, (M^{(i)} | A_i, R^{(i)}) \models_x \langle\!\langle i \rangle\!\rangle \psi_i \qquad \forall_{i \in C} \, Comp_k^{(i)} \models A_i}{(M^{(1)} | \ldots | M^{(n)}, R^{(1)}, \ldots, R^{(n)}) \models_x \langle\!\langle C \rangle\!\rangle \bigwedge_{i \in C} \psi_i}$$

The main challenge in applying the scheme is to define the right assumptions and to decompose the verified formula.

Example 6. Recall the multi-agent system $\mathcal{S}$ presented in Example 2, based on module $M^{(C(2))}|M^{(1)}|M^{(2)}$. We already argued that it satisfies $\phi \equiv \langle\langle 1,2\rangle\rangle(GFp^{(1)}) \wedge (GFp^{(2)})$ as well as $\phi' \equiv \langle\langle 1,2\rangle\rangle(GFq^{(1)}) \wedge (GFq^{(2)})$, for $p^{(i)}(x^{(i)}) = 1$ and $q^{(i)}(s) = i$, cf. Example 3. We will now see if the verification of the formulas can be decomposed using $\mathbf{R_k}$.

By Example 5 we know that $M^{(C(2))}|M^{(i)} \models A_{012}$, where A_{012} was an assumption defined in Example 4. It is easy to see that $M^{(C(2))} \models A_{012}$.

Consider the extended module $M^{(2)}|A_{012}$, which is nothing but $M^{(2)}|M^{(C(2))}$ with all the states marked as accepting. Assume further that agent 2 executes strategy σ_2 of Example 3. The resulting subsystem is presented in Fig. 4. Note that, if we focus on the values of variable s, the ω-regular language accepted by this automaton is $((01)|(0222(01)^*011))^{\omega}$, hence it periodically satisfies $p(\{s\}) = 1$. In consequence, σ_2 can be used to demonstrate that $(M^{(2)}|A_{012}, R^{(2)}) \models_{ir} \langle\langle 2\rangle\rangle GFq^{(1)}$, where $q^{(1)}(s) = 1$. Similarly, $(M^{(1)}|A_{012}, R^{(1)}) \models_{ir} \langle\langle 1\rangle\rangle GFq^{(2)}$, where $q^{(2)}(s) = 2$.

As a result, we have decomposed formula ϕ' and constructed independent strategies for agents 1 and 2. By the use of rule $\mathbf{R_1}$, we conclude that

$$(M, R^{(C(2))}, R^{(1)}, R^{(2)}) \models_{ir} \langle\langle 1,2\rangle\rangle(GFq^{(1)}) \wedge (GFq^{(2)}).$$

The situation for $\phi \equiv \langle\langle 1,2\rangle\rangle(GFp^{(1)}) \wedge (GFp^{(2)})$ is drastically different. We cannot use the analogous reasoning, because $\langle\langle i\rangle\rangle GFp^{(3-i)}$ is not a local constraint for $M^{(i)}$. There is a unique decomposition of ϕ into local constraints, but proving that $(M^{(1)}|A_{012}, R^{(1)}) \models_{ir} \langle\langle 1\rangle\rangle GFp^{(1)}$ fails, as the system can get stuck in the state where s equals 2 or infinitely loop between the states where $s = 2$ and $s = 0$. Changing the assumption would not help, since we cannot avoid the infinite exclusion of the considered train. Thus, while the scheme can be used to derive that $\mathcal{S} \models_{ir} \phi'$, it cannot produce the (equally true) statement $\mathcal{S} \models_{ir} \phi$.

5.2   Soundness and Incompleteness

The following theorem says that, if each coalition member together with its assumption satisfies the decomposition of the formula, and its neighborhood satisfies the assumption, then the original verification task must return "true."

Theorem 1. *The rule $\mathbf{R_k}$ is sound.*

Proof. Let $\forall_{i \in C} (M^{(i)}|A_i, R^{(i)}) \models_x \langle\langle i\rangle\rangle\psi_i$ with (memoryless or perfect recall) imperfect information strategy σ_i and $\forall_{i \in C} Comp_k^{(i)} \models A_i$. Here and in the rest of the proof, $x \in \{ir, iR\}$.

Let us consider $M = M^{(1)}|...|M^{(n)}$ such that $(M, R^{(1)}, \ldots, R^{(n)}) \models_x \langle\langle C\rangle\rangle\psi_i$ and fix its joint strategy σ for coalition C, where $\sigma(i) = \sigma_i$ for every $i \in C$.

We will prove the soundness by contradiction. Suppose that for every (memoryless or perfect recall) imperfect information joint strategy there exists an infinite word which implements this joint strategy, but do not satisfy $\bigwedge_{i \in C} \psi_i$, i.e. there exists $j \in C$ such that w does not satisfy ψ_j. Let $w = q_0 q_1 \ldots$ be such a word for the strategy σ and fix j.

Let us consider $M^{(j)}|A_j$, where $X_{M^{(j)}}$ and X_{A_j} are internal variables of $M^{(j)}$ and A_j, appropriately. By the construction and the presumption that $(M^{(j)}|A_j, \mathrm{R}^{(j)}) \models_x \langle\!\langle j \rangle\!\rangle \psi_j$ we get that every infinite word over $X_{M^{(j)}} \cup X_{A_j}$ which implement (memoryless or perfect recall) imperfect information strategy σ_j satisfy ψ_j.

However, the assumption A_j is guaranteed by $Comp_k^{(j)}$, hence for a word derived by $Comp_k^{(j)}$ we have its curtailment accepted by A_j. Moreover, every word accepted by $M^{(j)}|A_j$ is a curtailment of a word derived by M, and, in particular, w is such a word. However, there exists a curtailment $w|_{X_{M^{(j)}} \cup X_{A_j}}$ which satisfy strategy σ_j but is not accepted by $M^{(j)}|A_j$, which gives an obvious contradiction with $(M^{(j)}|A_j, R^{(j)}) \models_x \langle\!\langle i \rangle\!\rangle \psi_j$.

The obtained contradiction shows that there exists a joint strategy σ for the entire model and $(M^{(1)}|...|M^{(n)}, R^{(1)}, \ldots, R^{(n)}) \models_x \langle\!\langle C \rangle\!\rangle \bigwedge_{i \in C} \psi_i$, which concludes the proof.

Unfortunately, there does not always exist $k < n$ for which the rule $\mathbf{R_k}$ is complete, even in a very weak sense, where we only postulate the *existence* of appropriate assumptions.

Theorem 2. *The scheme consisting of rules $\{\mathbf{R_k} \mid \mathbf{k} \in \mathbb{N}\}$ is in general not complete.*

Proof. Follows directly from Example 6.

5.3   Coalitional Assume-Guarantee Verification

In Sect. 5.2, we showed that achievable coalitional goals may not decompose into achievable individual subgoals. As a result, the scheme proposed in Sect. 5.1 is incomplete. A possible way out is to allow for assume-guarantee reasoning about joint strategies of subcoalitions of C. We implement the idea by partitioning the system into smaller subsystems and allowing to explicitly consider the cooperation between coalition members.

Again, let $\mathcal{S} = (M^{(1)}, R^{(1)}), \ldots, (M^{(n)}, R^{(n)})$ be a system composed of asynchronous agents . Moreover, let $\{P_1, \ldots, P_k : P_i \subseteq \{1, 2, \ldots, n\}\}$, be a partitioning of coalition C, and let $\overline{C} = \{i : i \notin C\} = Ag \backslash C$ be the set of opponents of C. By $\mathcal{S}^{(P_i)}$ we denote the system composed of all the agents in $P_i = \{i_1, \ldots, i_s\}$, i.e., $(M^{(P_i)} = M^{(i_1)}|\ldots|M^{(i_s)}, R^{(i_1)}, \ldots, R^{(i_s)})$. $\mathcal{S}^{(\overline{C})}$ is defined analogously.

We extend the notion of neighbourhood to sets of agents as follows:

– $N_1^{P_i} = (\bigcup_{i \in P_i} N_1^{(i)}) \setminus P_i$, $N_k^{P_i} = (N_{k-1}^{P_i} \cup \bigcup_{j \in N_{k-1}^{P_i}} N_1^{(j)}) \setminus P_i$ for $k > 1$,
– $Comp_k^{P_i} = M^{(x_1)}|\ldots|M^{(x_s)}$ for $N_k^{P_i} = \{x_1, \ldots, x_s\}$.

Let $x \in \{\mathrm{ir}, \mathrm{iR}\}$. The generalized assume-guarantee rule is defined below:

$$\mathbf{Part_k^P} \quad \frac{\forall_{P_i \in P} (M^{(P_i)}|A_i, R^{(i_1)}, \ldots, R^{(i_s)}) \models_x \langle\!\langle P_i \rangle\!\rangle \bigwedge_{j \in P_i} \psi_j \qquad \forall_{P_i \in P} Comp_k^{P_i} \models A_i}{(M^{(1)}|\ldots|M^{(n)}, R^{(1)}, \ldots, R^{(n)}) \models_x \langle\!\langle C \rangle\!\rangle \bigwedge_{i \in C} \psi_i}$$

As it turns out, the new scheme is sound, conservative with respect to enlarging the neighborhood, and complete.

Theorem 3. *The rule* $\mathbf{Part_k^P}$ *is sound.*

Proof. Intuitively, we can proceed similarly to the proof of Theorem 1. Note that each component P_i can be seen as single composed module with a imperfect information strategy (memoryless or with perfect recall) being a joint strategy for the subset of coalition C which is the component P_i. Moreover, we can take instead of $Comp_k^{P_i}$ the union U of all the components P_j (and possibly $\overline{C}$) which intersection with $Comp_k^{P_i}$ is non-empty. It is easy to see, that if $Comp_k^{P_i} \models A_i$ then also $U \models A_i$.

This way we could fix the strategy for coalition C, deduce that every infinite word as a composition of strategies σ_{P_i} for its parts $(C \cap P_i)_{P_i \in P}$, and deduce that for every word w which do not satisfy $\bigwedge_{i \in C} \psi_i$ there exists a single component P_j containing M_i such that ψ_j would not be satisfied for any curtailment of w, while one of them implements strategy σ_{P_i} being at the same time accepted by $M^{(P_i)}|A_i$.

Proposition 1. *If* $Comp_k^{P_i} \models A_i$ *then* $Comp_{k+1}^{P_i} \models A_i$.

Proof. Let $N_{k+1}^{P_i} = \{i_1, \ldots, i_t\}$, $M = M^{(i_1)}|\ldots M^{(i_t)}$, $N_k^{P_i} = \{j_1, \ldots, j_{t'}\}$ and $M' = M^{(j_1)}|\ldots M^{(j_{t'})}$. Let us consider an infinite trace σ of M, with $w \in (D^X)^\omega$ and $u \in (D^I)^\omega$ and $\sigma' = w_1|_{X'} (u_1|_{I' \cap I} \cup w_1|_{I' \cap X}) w_2|_{X'} \ldots$. Note that one of the curtailments of a word $w_1|_{X'} w_2|_{X'} \ldots$ is derived by M', and thus its curtailment is accepted by A_i.

Theorem 4. *There exist a partition set P and $k \le n$ such that the rule* $\mathbf{Part_k^P}$ *is complete.*

Proof. Straightforward, as we can take $k = n$ and singleton partition $P = \{P_1\}$, where A_1 is an automaton constructed on the base of the system $M^{(\overline{C})}$, where all the states are accepting ones (hence $Comp_{P_1}^k \models A_1$ as every word accepted by A_1 is derived with a trace of $M_{\overline{C}}$).

Hence $(M^{(P_1)}|A_1, R^{(i_1)}, \ldots, R^{(i_s)}) \models_x \langle\!\langle P_1 \rangle\!\rangle \bigwedge_{j \in P_1} \psi_j$ is just an equivalent formulation of $(M^{(1)}|\ldots|M^{(n)}, R^{(1)}, \ldots, R^{(n)}) \models_x \langle\!\langle C \rangle\!\rangle \bigwedge_{i \in C} \psi_i$, for $x \in \{ir, iR\}$.

Remark 1 (Complexity). The assume-guarantee schemes provide (one-to-many) reductions of the model checking problem. The resulting verification algorithm for $\mathbf{ATL_{ir}^*}$ is **PSPACE**-complete with respect to the size of the coalition modules, the size of the assumptions, and the length of the formula. In the very worst case (i.e., as the assumptions grow), this becomes **PSPACE**-complete w.r.t. the size of the global model, i.e., no better than ordinary model checking for **ATL*** with memoryless strategies. On the other hand, our method often allows to decompose the verification of the huge global model of the system to several smaller cases. For many systems one can propose assumptions that are exponentially smaller than the size of the full model, thus providing an exponential gain in complexity.

Note also that the first scheme provides a model checking algorithm for $\mathbf{ATL}^*_{iR}$ that is **EXPTIME**-complete with respect to the size of the coalition modules, the size of the assumptions, and the length of the formula, i.e., an incomplete but decidable algorithm for the generally undecidable problem.

5.4   Verification of Nested Strategic Operators

So far, we have concentrated on assume-guarantee specification of formulas without nested strategic modalities. Here, we briefly point out that the schemes $\mathbf{R_k}$ and $\mathbf{Part}_k^P$ extend to the whole language of $\mathbf{ATL}^*_{-X}$ through the standard recursive model checking algorithm that verifies subformulas bottom-up. Such recursive application of the method to the verification of $S \models \phi$ proceeds as follows:

- For each strategic subformula ϕ_j of ϕ, do assume-guarantee verification of ϕ_j in S, and label the states where ϕ_j holds by a fresh atomic proposition p_j;
- Replace all occurrences of ϕ_j in ϕ by p_j, and do assume-guarantee verification of the resulting formula in S.

The resulting algorithm is sound, though there is the usual price to pay in terms of computational complexity. The main challenge lies in providing decompositions of **LTL** objectives for multiple strategic formulas, as well as multiple Büchi assumptions (one for each subformula). A refinement of the schemes for nested strategic abilities is planned for future work.

6   Case Study and Experiments

In this section, we present an experimental evaluation of the assume-guarantee verification schemes of Sect. 5. As the benchmark, we use a variant of the factory scenario from [26], where a coalition of logistic robots cooperate to deliver packages from the production line to the storage area.

6.1   Experiments: Monolithic Vs. Assume-Guarantee Verification

Decomposition to Individual Strategies. In the first set of experiments, we verified the formula

$$\psi \equiv \langle\!\langle R \rangle\!\rangle (\bigwedge_{r \in R} \text{energy}_r > 0)\, \text{U delivered}$$

expressing that the coalition of robots R can maintain their energy level above zero until at least one package is delivered to the storage area. Guessing that the first robot has enough energy to deliver a package on his own, we can decompose the formula as the conjunction of the following components:

$$\psi_d \equiv \langle\!\langle r_1 \rangle\!\rangle \text{F delivered}, \qquad \psi_e^{(i)} \equiv \langle\!\langle r_i \rangle\!\rangle \text{G energy}_{r_i} > 0, \quad i \in R.$$

188   Ł. Mikulski et al.

Note that, if $\psi_d \wedge \bigwedge_{i>1} \psi_e^{(i)}$ is true, then ψ must be true, too.

The experiments used the first (incomplete) scheme of assume-guarantee verification. The results are presented in Table 1. The first column describes the configuration of the model, i.e., the number of robots, locations in the factory, and the initial energy level. Then, we report the performance of model checking algorithms that operate on the explicit model of the whole system. The running times are given in seconds. *DFS* is a straightforward implementation of depth-first strategy synthesis. *Apprx* refers to the (sound but incomplete) method of fixpoint-approximation in [22]; besides the time, we also report if the approximation was conclusive.

Table 1. Results of assume-guarantee verification, scheme $\mathbf{R_k}$ (left), scheme $\mathbf{Part_k^P}$ (right).

Conf	Monolithic verif.			Ass.-guar. verif.		
	#st	DFS	Apprx	#st	DFS	Apprx
2,2,2	8170	<0.01	0.6/No	1356	<0.01	<0.01/Yes
2,3,3	1.1e5	0.02	13/No	9116	<0.01	0.5/Yes
3,2,2	5.5e5	timeout		2.7e4	<0.01	3/Yes
3,3,3	memout			4.4e5	<0.01	58/Yes
4,2,2	memout			5.2e5	timeout	

Conf	Monolithic verif.			Ass.-guar. verif.		
	#st	DFS	Apprx	#st	DFS	Apprx
2,3,1	522	<0.01	<0.01/No	522	<0.01	<0.01/No
2,4,2	3409	<0.01	<0.01/No	3409	<0.01	<0.01/No
4,3,1	memout			4.8e4	<0.01	4/No
6,3,1	memout			5.8e5	0.36	42/No
8,3,1	memout			timeout		

Coalitional Assume-Guarantee Verification. For the second set of experiments, the robots were divided in two halves, initially located in different parts of the factory. We verified the following formula:

$$\psi \equiv \langle\langle R \rangle\rangle F\,G\,(\bigwedge_{i \in \{1,2,...,n/2\}} (\mathsf{delivered}_i \vee \mathsf{delivered}_{i+n/2})),$$

expressing that the coalition of robots can delivered at least one package per pair to the storage area. Depending on the initial energy level of robots, the storage may not be reachable from the production line. That means that the robots must work in pairs to deliver the packages. We use this insight to decompose the verification into the following formulas:

$$\psi^{(i)} \equiv \langle\langle r_i, r_{i+n/2} \rangle\rangle F\,G\,(\mathsf{delivered}_i \vee \mathsf{delivered}_{i+n/2}).$$

The results are presented in Table 1.

Discussion of Results. The experimental results show that assume-guarantee schemes presented here enables to verify systems of distinctly higher complexity than model checking of the full model. We have also conducted analogous experiments on the Simple Voting scenario of [22], with very similar results; we do not report them here due to lack of space.

Interestingly, Table 1 shows that the application of incomplete assume-guarantee scheme to fixpoint approximation (in itself an incomplete method of model checking) often turns inconclusive verification into conclusive one. This is because fixpoint approximation works rather well for individual abilities, but poorly for proper coalitions [22]. Rule $\mathbf{R_k}$ decomposes verification of coalitional abilities (very likely to resist successful approximation) to model checking individual abilities (likely to submit to approximation). It is not true in the case of the second experiment, as this time we did not reduce the tested coalitions to singleton ones.

7   Conclusions

In this paper we propose two schemes for assume-guarantee verification of strategic abilities. Importantly, they are both sound for the memoryless as well as perfect recall semantics of abilities under imperfect information. Moreover, the second scheme is complete (albeit in a rather weak sense). The experiments show that both schemes can provide noticeable improvement in verification of large systems consisting of asynchronous agents with independent goals. Note also that the scheme $\mathbf{R_k}$ provides an (incomplete) reduction of the undecidable model checking problem for coalitions with perfect recall to decidable verification of individual abilities.

Clearly, the main challenge is to formulate the right assumptions and to decompose the verified formula. In the future, we would like to work on the automated generation of assumptions. The first idea is to obtain a larger granularity of the global model by decomposing agents into even smaller subsystems (and recomposing some of them as assumptions). This can be combined with abstraction refinement of the assumptions in case they are still too complex. We also plan to extend the notion of assumptions to capture the agents' knowledge about the strategic abilities of their coalition partners. Positive results in that direction would significantly increase the applicability of assume-guarantee schemes for model checking of asynchronous MAS.

Acknowledgement. The work was supported by NCBR Poland and FNR Luxembourg under the PolLux/FNR-CORE project STV (POLLUX-VII/1/2019), and the CHIST-ERA grant CHIST-ERA-19-XAI-010 by NCN Poland (2020/02/Y/ST6/00064). The work of Damian Kurpiewski was also supported by the CNRS IEA project MoSART.

References

1. Alur, R., Henzinger, T.: Reactive modules. Form. Meth. Syst. Des. **15**(1), 7–48 (1999)
2. Alur, R., Henzinger, T., Kupferman, O.: Alternating-time temporal logic. J. ACM **49**, 672–713 (2002)
3. Alur, R., Henzinger, T.A., Mang, F.Y.C., Qadeer, S., Rajamani, S.K., Tasiran, S.: MOCHA: modularity in model checking. In: Hu, A.J., Vardi, M.Y. (eds.) CAV 1998. LNCS, vol. 1427, pp. 521–525. Springer, Heidelberg (1998). https://doi.org/10.1007/BFb0028774

4. Alur, R., Henzinger, T., Vardi, M.: Parametric real-time reasoning. In: Proceedings of STOC, pp. 592–601. ACM (1993)
5. Bulling, N., Dix, J., Jamroga, W.: Model checking logics of strategic ability: complexity. In: Dastani, M., Hindriks, K., Meyer, J.J. (eds.) Specification and Verification of Multi-agent Systems, pp. 125–159. Springer, Boston (2010). https://doi.org/10.1007/978-1-4419-6984-2_5
6. Busard, S., Pecheur, C., Qu, H., Raimondi, F.: Reasoning about memoryless strategies under partial observability and unconditional fairness constraints. Inf. Comp. **242**, 128–156 (2015)
7. Cermák, P., Lomuscio, A., Murano, A.: Verifying and synthesising multi-agent systems against one-goal strategy logic specifications. In: Proceedings of AAAI, pp. 2038–2044 (2015)
8. Chatterjee, K., Henzinger, T.A.: Assume-guarantee synthesis. In: Grumberg, O., Huth, M. (eds.) TACAS 2007. LNCS, vol. 4424, pp. 261–275. Springer, Heidelberg (2007). https://doi.org/10.1007/978-3-540-71209-1_21
9. Chen, Y.-F., et al.: Comparing learning algorithms in automated assume-guarantee reasoning. In: Margaria, T., Steffen, B. (eds.) ISoLA 2010. LNCS, vol. 6415, pp. 643–657. Springer, Heidelberg (2010). https://doi.org/10.1007/978-3-642-16558-0_52
10. Clarke, E., Long, D., McMillan, K.: Compositional model checking. In: Proceeding of LICS, pp. 353–362. IEEE Computer Society Press (1989)
11. Devereux, B.: Compositional reasoning about aspects using alternating-time logic. In: Proceedings of FOAL, pp. 45–50 (2003)
12. Dima, C., Tiplea, F.: Model-checking ATL under imperfect information and perfect recall semantics is undecidable. CoRR abs/1102.4225 (2011)
13. Fijalkow, N., Maubert, B., Murano, A., Vardi, M.: Assume-guarantee synthesis for prompt linear temporal logic. In: Proceedings of IJCAI, pp. 117–123. ijcai.org (2020)
14. Finkbeiner, B., Passing, N.: Compositional synthesis of modular systems. Innov. Syst. Softw. Eng. **18**, 1–15 (2022)
15. Giannakopoulou, D., Pasareanu, C., Barringer, H.: Component verification with automatically generated assumptions. Autom. Softw. Eng. **12**(3), 297–320 (2005)
16. Guelev, D., Dima, C., Enea, C.: An alternating-time temporal logic with knowledge, perfect recall and past: axiomatisation and model-checking. J. Appl. Non-Classical Log. **21**(1), 93–131 (2011)
17. He, F., Mao, S., Wang, B.-Y.: Learning-based assume-guarantee regression verification. In: Chaudhuri, S., Farzan, A. (eds.) CAV 2016. LNCS, vol. 9779, pp. 310–328. Springer, Cham (2016). https://doi.org/10.1007/978-3-319-41528-4_17
18. Henzinger, T.A., Qadeer, S., Rajamani, S.K.: You assume, we guarantee: methodology and case studies. In: Hu, A.J., Vardi, M.Y. (eds.) CAV 1998. LNCS, vol. 1427, pp. 440–451. Springer, Heidelberg (1998). https://doi.org/10.1007/BFb0028765
19. Hoare, C.: An axiomatic basis for computer programming. Commun. ACM **12**(10), 576–580 (1969)
20. Huang, X., van der Meyden, R.: Symbolic model checking epistemic strategy logic. In: Proceedings of AAAI, pp. 1426–1432 (2014)
21. Jamroga, W., Kim, Y., Kurpiewski, D., Ryan, P.Y.A.: Towards model checking of voting protocols in UPPAAL. In: Krimmer, R., et al. (eds.) E-Vote-ID 2020. LNCS, vol. 12455, pp. 129–146. Springer, Cham (2020). https://doi.org/10.1007/978-3-030-60347-2_9
22. Jamroga, W., Knapik, M., Kurpiewski, D., Mikulski, Ł.: Approximate verification of strategic abilities under imperfect information. Artif. Int. **277**, 103172 (2019)

23. Jamroga, W., Penczek, W., Sidoruk, T.: Strategic abilities of asynchronous agents: Semantic side effects and how to tame them. In: Proceedings of KR, pp. 368–378 (2021)

24. Jones, C.: Specification and design of (parallel) programs. In: Proceedings of IFIP, pp. 321–332. North-Holland/IFIP (1983)

25. Kong, S., Jung, Y., David, C., Wang, B.-Y., Yi, K.: Automatically inferring quantified loop invariants by algorithmic learning from simple templates. In: Ueda, K. (ed.) APLAS 2010. LNCS, vol. 6461, pp. 328–343. Springer, Heidelberg (2010). https://doi.org/10.1007/978-3-642-17164-2_23

26. Kurpiewski, D., Marmsoler, D.: Strategic logics for collaborative embedded systems. SICS Soft. Int. Cyber-Phys. Syst. **34**(4), 201–212 (2019)

27. Kurpiewski, D., Pazderski, W., Jamroga, W., Kim, Y.: STV+reductions: towards practical verification of strategic ability using model reductions. In: Proceedings of AAMAS, pp. 1770–1772. ACM (2021)

28. Kurpiewski, D., Mikulski, Ł., Jamroga, W.: STV+AGR: towards verification of strategic ability using assume-guarantee reasoning. In: Proceedings of PRIMA (2022)

29. Kwiatkowska, M., Norman, G., Parker, D., Qu, H.: Assume-guarantee verification for probabilistic systems. In: Esparza, J., Majumdar, R. (eds.) TACAS 2010. LNCS, vol. 6015, pp. 23–37. Springer, Heidelberg (2010). https://doi.org/10.1007/978-3-642-12002-2_3

30. Lomuscio, A., Qu, H., Raimondi, F.: MCMAS: an open-source model checker for the verification of multi-agent systems. Int. J. Soft. Tools Tech. Trans. **19**(1), 9–30 (2017)

31. Lomuscio, A., Strulo, B., Walker, N., Wu, P.: Assume-guarantee reasoning with local specifications. In: Dong, J.S., Zhu, H. (eds.) ICFEM 2010. LNCS, vol. 6447, pp. 204–219. Springer, Heidelberg (2010). https://doi.org/10.1007/978-3-642-16901-4_15

32. Lomuscio, A., Strulo, B., Walker, N., Wu, P.: Assume-guarantee reasoning with local specifications. Int. J. Found. Comput. Sci. **24**(4), 419–444 (2013)

33. Mikulski, Ł., Jamroga, W., Kurpiewski, D.: Towards assume-guarantee verification of strategic ability. In: Proceedings of of AAMAS 2022, pp. 1702–1704. IFAAMAS (2022)

34. Mogavero, F., Murano, A., Perelli, G., Vardi, M.: Reasoning about strategies: on the model-checking problem. ACM Trans. Comp. Log. **15**(4), 1–42 (2014)

35. Owicki, S., Gries, D.: Verifying properties of parallel programs: an axiomatic approach. Commun. ACM **19**(5), 279–285 (1976)

36. Pnueli, A.: In transition from global to modular temporal reasoning about programs. In: Apt, K.R. (ed.) Logics and Models of Concurrent Systems. NATO ASI Series, vol. 13, pp. 123–144. Springer, Heidelberg (1984). https://doi.org/10.1007/978-3-642-82453-1_5

37. Schobbens, P.: Alternating-time logic with imperfect recall. Electr. Not. Theor. Comput. Sci. **85**(2), 82–93 (2004)

Sample Complexity of Learning Multi-value Opinions in Social Networks

Masato Shinoda[1], Yuko Sakurai[2(✉)], and Satoshi Oyama[3]

[1] Nara Women's University, Nara, Japan
shinoda@cc.nara-wu.ac.jp
[2] Nagoya Institute of Technology, Nagoya, Japan
sakurai@nitech.ac.jp
[3] Hokkaido University, Sapporo, Japan
oyama@ist.hokudai.ac.jp

Abstract. We consider how many users we need to query in order to estimate the extent to which multi-value opinions (information) have propagated in a social network. For example, if the launch date of a new product has changed many times, the company might want to know to which people the most current information has reached. In the propagation model we consider, the social network is represented as a directed graph, and an agent (node) updates its state if it receives a stronger opinion (updated information) and then forwards the opinion in accordance with the direction of its edges. Previous work evaluated opinion propagation in a social network by using the probably approximately correct (PAC) learning framework and considered only binary opinions. In general, PAC learnability, i.e., the finiteness of the number of samples needed, is not guaranteed when generalizing from a binary-value model to a multi-value model. We show that the PAC learnability of multi-value opinions propagating in a social network. We first prove that the number of samples needed in a multi-opinion model is sufficient for $(k-1)\log(k-1)$ times the number of samples needed in a binary-opinion model, when k (≥ 3) is the number of opinions. We next prove that the upper and lower bounds on the number of samples needed to learn a multi-opinion model can be determined from the Natarajan dimension, which is a generalization of the Vapnik-Chervonenkis dimension.

Keywords: PAC learning · Opinion estimation · Social network

1 Introduction

Today, many people exchange various opinions and information via social network services (SNSs). Therefore, SNSs have become an important means for individuals, companies, and other information sources to disseminate and propagate information such as opinions and product advertisements. To measure the

© The Author(s), under exclusive license to Springer Nature Switzerland AG 2023
R. Aydoğan et al. (Eds.): PRIMA 2022, LNAI 13753, pp. 192–207, 2023.
https://doi.org/10.1007/978-3-031-21203-1_12

effectiveness of an advertising campaign, it is necessary to know to whom the information has reached. However, for a large network, it is impractical to check whether everyone has received the information, so we have to rely on estimation based on sampling.

A recently proposed method [4] for estimating the extent of propagation of binary opinions in a social network uses the probably approximately correct (PAC) learning framework [10] to obtain the number of samples needed for estimation. The PAC learning framework is typically used for estimating the number of samples needed to learn an accurate classification model with high probability. PAC learning is a classical theory in the field of machine learning that has in recent years been applied to various multi-agent system (MAS) problems. For example, PAC learning has been applied to cooperative games [1,7,9,11] and has been combined with incentive design [12].

Conitzer et al. represented a social network as a directed graph with nodes as agents and edges as relations among agents and assumed that opinions propagated in accordance with the direction of edges [4]. The state of each agent is binary: either it has received an opinion (1) or it has not (0). Once an opinion enters an agent node through an incoming edge, the agent propagates the opinion through its outgoing edges. PAC learning is used to calculate the order of the number of samples (agents) that need to be asked whether they have an opinion needed to estimate, within a predefined error margin, the opinions of other agents in the network once opinion propagation has completed.

In their study, Conitzer et al. considered only binary opinions, but opinions are not always expressed in binary form. For example, a company may announce the scheduled release date of a new product and then change the date or product specifications. In this case, the company would probably want to know the extent to which the old information and the updated information have propagated. As another example, knowledge about a new infectious disease is constantly being updated, and knowing who has each stage of the information would be helpful in implementing effective countermeasures. Thus, the degree to which opinions and information have spread in social networks can have multiple uses. It is also practically necessary to determine the sample size needed to estimate the extent to which opinions have been reached in a social network.

Here, we generalize the problem setting used by Conitzer et al. [4]. More specifically, when $k(\geq 3)$ types of opinions (labels) propagate in a social network represented by a directed graph, we use PAC learning to determine the number of samples required to estimate labels other agents have when opinion propagation is completed. In general, when a binary model is extended to a multi-valued model, PAC learnability, i.e., the finiteness of the required number of samples, is not guaranteed. However, in our model of opinion propagation on a directed graph, generalization is possible because the hypothesis class $\mathcal{H}$ (the set of candidate labelings to be estimated) representing possible labeling patterns is determined from the propagation conditions of labels on the graph. We first show, as a relative comparison, that for a k (≥ 3)-valued model, $(k-1)\log(k-1)$ times the number of samples required for PAC learning of a binary model is sufficient. Next, we determine specific upper and lower bounds on the number of samples required for PAC training of a k (≥ 3)-valued model.

The rest of this paper is organized as follows. We first introduce previous related work in Sect. 2. In Sect. 3, we describe PAC learning for binary and multi-valued models. In Sect. 4, we present the problem setting considered in this paper. We compare binary and multi-valued models in Sect. 5. In Sect. 6, we define the Natarajan dimension in our problem setting and determine the upper and lower bounds on the number of samples needed for estimating the overall propagation of multiple opinions in a social network.

2   Previous Work

As mentioned in Sect. 1, PAC learning has been applied to various MAS problems.

Procaccia and Rosenschein investigated PAC learning for simple cooperative games in which the coalitions are partitioned into winning and losing coalitions. They analyzed the complexity of learning a suitable concept class via the Vapnik-Chervonenkis (VC) dimension and developed an algorithm that learns its class [9]. Balcan et al. concentrated on the core stability in cooperative games when agents' preferences are fully unknown [1]. They established a connection between PAC learnability and core stability: for games that are efficiently learnable, payoff divisions that are likely to be stable can be found by using a polynomial number of samples. Their defining of PAC stability led to studies of PAC stability. Sliwinski and Zick studied PAC stability in hedonic games (which are a variant of cooperative games) when agents' preferences are fully unknown [11].

Berenbrink et al. investigated an agent-based model for opinion formation in a social network in which the opinion of an agent depends both on its own intrinsic opinion and on those of its network neighbors [3]. They analyzed the convergence time of asynchronous Hegselmann-Krause opinion dynamics in arbitrary social networks. Irfan et al. addressed the problem of how to maximize the spread of information while minimizing the spread to unintended recipients under budget constraints [8].

Zhang and Conitzer considered PAC learning in the presence of strategic manipulation [12]. They addressed an incentive problem in which a point being classified may strategically modify its features in order to receive a more desirable outcome. Incentive design is an important MAS research area, and Zhang and Conitzer presented a new direction for combining machine learning and MAS techniques.

3   PAC Learning

In this section, we present several fundamental concepts of PAC learning.

3.1   PAC Learning for Binary Labels

PAC learning provides an estimate of the number of samples required to learn a hypothesis that guarantees a confidence level δ and generalization error ε for a learning problem with a hypothesis class $\mathcal{H}$. Suppose there exists a data set X ($|X| = n$) and a label set $W = \{0, 1, 2, \ldots, k - 1\}$ ($k \geq 2$). Suppose that each data item $x \in X$ is given a label $f(x) \in W$, and let W^X be the set of all possible labelings on X. The learner independently selects m points on the basis of probability distribution $\mathcal{D}$ on X and knows the value of f at each point. As an estimation of the label value $f = \{f(x)\}_{x \in X}$ from the sample data, one h is selected from the predefined hypothesis set $\mathcal{H} \subseteq W^X$.

The error between the true labeling f and its hypothesis h is defined as the probability that $f(x)$ and $h(x)$ differ when x is chosen on the basis of $\mathcal{D}$ and is denoted as

$$L_{\mathcal{D}, f}(h) = P_{\mathcal{D}}(f(x) \neq h(x)), \tag{1}$$

where $P_{\mathcal{D}}$ denotes the probability of choosing the point $x \in X$ in accordance with $\mathcal{D}$. That is, $L_{\mathcal{D}, f}(h)$ represents the error rate (measured in $\mathcal{D}$) of h when f is the correct answer.

For a given $\varepsilon, \delta > 0$, the goal of PAC learning is to determine the hypothesis $h \in \mathcal{H}$ satisfying $L_{\mathcal{D}, f}(h) \leq \varepsilon$ with probability greater than $1 - \delta$. The procedure to achieve this goal is outlined below.

1. The learner is given a hypothesis class $\mathcal{H}$, which is a subset of all possible labelings W^X. The learner knows nothing about the true labeling f to be guessed except that it is an element of W^X.
2. The m points $(x_1, x_2, \ldots, x_m) \in X^m$ chosen from X and the values of f at those points $(f(x_1), f(x_2), \ldots, f(x_m))$ are called a training set. The learner determines an algorithm to find a hypothesis $h \in \mathcal{H}$ as a guess of f from the given training set. We call the algorithm A henceforth.
3. True labeling $f \in W^X$ and probability distribution $\mathcal{D}$ on X are determined.
4. The m points $(x_1, x_2, \ldots, x_m)$ chosen independently from X in accordance with probability distribution $\mathcal{D}$ and labels $(f(x_1), f(x_2), \ldots, f(x_m))$ at those points are given to the learner as a training set. The learner determines hypothesis $h \in \mathcal{H}$ using algorithm A.
5. The obtained hypothesis h is evaluated using $L_{\mathcal{D}, f}(h)$, and if the value obtained is less than ε, the learning is considered successful.

The m points $x_1, x_2, \ldots, x_m$ chosen in step 2 must be considered in the case of overlap. The learner must decide algorithm A before step 3, i.e., without any information about $f, \mathcal{D}$. That is, A is a mapping from $(X \times W)^m$ to $\mathcal{H}$. Let $m_L(\varepsilon, \delta)$ be the smallest integer m for which algorithm A can be defined such that the probability of success in guessing is uniformly greater than $1 - \delta$ regardless of $\mathcal{D}$ and f. The condition corresponding to the assumption that f given in step 3 is in particular an element of $\mathcal{H}$; i.e.

$$\min_{h \in \mathcal{H}} L_{\mathcal{D},f}(h) = 0 \qquad (2)$$

is called the realizability condition. Here, PAC learning is performed under the assumption of this condition.

3.2 Vapnik-Chervonenkis Dimension

The VC dimension is used to characterize the sample complexity of learning a given hypothesis class $\mathcal{H}$ for a binary label set $W = \{0, 1\}$.

Definition 1 (VC dimension). *Let X be a non-empty set, and let $\mathcal{H}$ be a hypothesis class of functions from X to $\{0,1\}$; i.e., $\mathcal{H} \subseteq \{0,1\}^X$. We say that a subset $S \subseteq X$ is **shattered** by $\mathcal{H}$ if the restriction $\mathcal{H}|_S$ of $\mathcal{H}$ to S is identical to $\{0,1\}^S$. The VC dimension of a hypothesis class $\mathcal{H}$, denoted $d_{VC}(\mathcal{H})$, is the maximum size of a set $S \subseteq X$ that can be shattered by $\mathcal{H}$. If $\mathcal{H}$ can shatter sets of arbitrarily large size, we say that $\mathcal{H}$ has an infinite VC dimension.*

In other words, the VC dimension is the maximum size of a set of agents in which all combinations for any labels are feasible.

Example 1. We set $W = \{0, 1\}$ and $X = \{a, b, c\}$. If we denote the elements of $\mathcal{H}$ in the form $(h(a), h(b), h(c))$, the hypothesis class is $\mathcal{H} = \{(1, 0, 0), (0, 1, 0), (0, 0, 1), (1, 1, 0), (1, 0, 1), (0, 1, 1)\}$.

If we set $S_{abc} = \{a, b, c\}$, we have $\mathcal{H}|_{S_{abc}} = \mathcal{H}$. $\mathcal{H}|_{S_{abc}}$ does not include $(0, 0, 0)$ and $(1, 1, 1)$, so S_{abc} is not shattered by $\mathcal{H}$. If we set $S_{ab} = \{a, b\}$, we have $\mathcal{H}|_{S_{ab}} = \{(0, 0), (0, 1), (1, 1), (1, 0)\}$. $\mathcal{H}|_{S_{12}}$ consists of all feasible combinations for W. As a result, S_{ab} is shattered by $\mathcal{H}$, and $d_{VC}(\mathcal{H}) = 2$. Furthermore, if we set $S_{ac} = \{a, c\}$ and $S_{bc} = \{b, c\}$, both S_{ac} and S_{bc} are shattered by $\mathcal{H}$.

We estimate $m_L(\varepsilon, \delta)$ by applying the VC dimension under realizability assumption (2).

Theorem 1. [10]. *Let $\mathcal{H}$ be a hypothesis class of functions from a domain X to $\{0, 1\}$; that is, $\mathcal{H} \subseteq \{0, 1\}^X$. Assume that $d_{VC}(\mathcal{H}) < \infty$. Then, there are absolute constants $C_1, C_2 > 0$ such that*

$$C_1 \frac{d_{VC}(\mathcal{H}) + \log(1/\delta)}{\varepsilon} \leq m_L(\varepsilon, \delta) \leq C_2 \frac{d_{VC}(\mathcal{H}) \log(1/\varepsilon) + \log(1/\delta)}{\varepsilon}. \qquad (3)$$

This fundamental theorem states that, even if X is an infinite set, $\mathcal{H}$ is PAC learnable if its VC dimension is finite.

3.3 PAC Learning for Multiple Labels

We introduce PAC learning for $k(\geq 2)$ labels $W = \{0, 1, 2, \ldots, k - 1\}$ under realizability assumption (2) in which there exists a true label f in hypothesis class $\mathcal{H}$.

(a) Hypothesis H				
a	0	0	1	1
b	0	2	0	2
c	0	2	0	2

(b) Function g		
	a	b	c
0	0	2	2
1	1,2	0,1	0,1

(c) Labels g				
a	0	0	1	1
b	1	0	1	0
c	1	0	1	0

Fig. 1. Example of calculating graph dimension

To estimate the accuracy of hypothesis h, we define $l_{\mathcal{D},f}(h)$ in addition to error rate $L_{\mathcal{D},f}(h)$:

$$l_{\mathcal{D},f}(h) = E_{\mathcal{D}}(|f(x) - h(x)|). \tag{4}$$

$l_{\mathcal{D},f}(h)$ represents the expected value of the error rate, taking into account the difference in size between f and h, measured with respect to probability distribution $\mathcal{D}$. From this definition, we get

$$L_{\mathcal{D},f}(h) \leq l_{\mathcal{D},f}(h) \leq (k-1)L_{\mathcal{D},f}(h). \tag{5}$$

If $k = 2$, we have $L_{\mathcal{D},f}(h) = l_{\mathcal{D},f}(h)$ because the only possible values of f and h are 0 and 1. In PAC learning for multiple labels, when hypothesis h is estimated using $l_{\mathcal{D},f}(h)$ or $L_{\mathcal{D},f}(h)$, we say that the learner has succeeded in its prediction if the estimation does not exceed ε. Furthermore, the amount of training data needed so that the probability of successful prediction is equal to or more than $1 - \delta$ is denoted by $m_L(\varepsilon, \delta)$ or $m_l(\varepsilon, \delta)$ in accordance with the evaluation criterion.

To extend the VC dimension so that we can measure the complexity of hypothesis class $\mathcal{H}$ in the multi-valued case, consider $\mathcal{H}|_S$, which restricts $\mathcal{H}$ to S. As in Definition 1, one might think that one should look for the largest S such that $\mathcal{H}|_S$ coincides with $\{0, 1, \ldots, k-1\}^S$ and define $d_{VC}^{(k)}(\mathcal{H})$ as the number of its elements. However, it is known that, for $k > 2$, the case $m_L(\varepsilon, \delta), m_l(\varepsilon, \delta) = \infty$ occurs even if $d_{VC}^{(k)}(\mathcal{H}) < \infty$. Therefore, $d_{VC}^{(k)}(\mathcal{H})$ defined above is not useful for determining PAC learnability in the multi-valued case.

3.4 Graph and Natarajan Dimensions

We give the definitions of the Graph and Natarajan dimensions for PAC learning for multiple labels [5].

Definition 2 (Graph dimension). *Let X be a non-empty set, and let $\mathcal{H}$ be a hypothesis class of functions from X to $\{0, 1, \ldots, k-1\}$; i.e., $\mathcal{H} \subseteq \{0, 1, \ldots, k-1\}^X$. We say that a subset $S \subseteq X$ is **G-shattered** by $\mathcal{H}$ if there exists a $\{0, 1, 2, \ldots, k-1\}$-value function g over S such that, for any subset $T \subseteq S$, there exists an $h \in \mathcal{H}$ such that*

$$\forall x \in T, \ h(x) = g(x), \text{ and } \forall x \in S \backslash T, \ h(x) \neq g(x). \tag{6}$$

The Graph dimension of hypothesis class $\mathcal{H}$, denoted $d_G(\mathcal{H})$, is the maximum size of a set $S \subseteq X$ that can be G-shattered by $\mathcal{H}$.

(a) Hypothesis H				
a	0	0	1	1
b	0	2	0	2
c	0	2	0	2

(b) Functions g_1, g_2	a	b	c
g_1	0	2	0
g_2	1	0	2

(c) Labels g_1, g_2				
a	g_1	g_1	g_2	g_2
b	g_2	g_1	g_2	g_1
c	g_1	g_2	g_1	g_2

Fig. 2. Example of calculating Natarajan dimension

Function g converts multiple labels into binary labels by separating k labels into a single label and a set containing the remaining labels. It may differ by agent. The Graph dimension is the maximum size of a set of agents in which certain combinations of labels determined in accordance with g are feasible. We show an example of determining the Graph dimension.

Example 2. Let W be $\{0, 1, 2\}$ and X be $\{a, b, c\}$. If we denote the elements of H in the form $(h(a), h(b), h(c))$, the hypothesis class is $H = \{(0, 0, 0), (0, 2, 2), (1, 0, 0), (1, 2, 2)\}$, as shown in table (a) in Fig. 1.

Let us set function g as shown in table (b) in Fig. 1. Function g relabels 0 as 0 and 1 and 2 as 1 for agent a and relabels 2 as 0 and 0 and 1 as 1 for agents b and c. There exist all combinations of labels determined in accordance with g in $S = \{a, b\}$ shown in table (c) in Fig. 1. Furthermore, setting $S = \{a, c\}$ creates a set of agents in which all combinations for labels determined in accordance with function g are feasible. If $S = \{a, b, c\}$, certain combinations for labels determined in accordance with functions g are infeasible. As a result, the Graph dimension is 2.

Definition 3 (Natarajan dimension). *Let X be a non-empty set, and let H be a hypothesis class of functions from X to $\{0, 1, \ldots, k-1\}$; i.e., $H \subseteq \{0, 1, \ldots, k-1\}^X$. We say that a subset $S \subseteq X$ is **N-shattered** by H if there exists $\{0, 1, 2, \ldots,$*
$k-1\}$-value functions g_1 and g_2 over S such that for any subset $T \subseteq S$, there exists an $h \in H$ such that

$$\forall x \in T, \ h(x) = g_1(x), \text{ and } \forall x \in S \backslash T, \ h(x) = g_2(x). \tag{7}$$

The Natarajan dimension of hypothesis class H, denoted $d_N(H)$, is the maximum size of a set $S \subseteq X$ that can be N-shattered by H.

Intuitively, we first select binary labels from multiple labels. Then we consider the selected binary labels as g_1 and g_2; g_1 and g_2 may differ by agent. The Natarajan dimension is the maximum size of a set of agents in which all combinations for labels determined in accordance with functions g_1 and g_2 are feasible.

Example 3. Let W be $\{0, 1, 2\}$ and X be $\{a, b, c\}$. If we denote the elements of H in the form $(h(a), h(b), h(c))$, the hypothesis class is $H = \{(0, 0, 0), (0, 2, 2), (1, 0, 0), (1, 2, 2)\}$, as shown in table (a) in Fig. 2.

Let us set functions g_1 and g_2 as shown in table (b) in Fig. 2. For agent a, 0 and 1 indicate g_1 and g_2, respectively. There exist all combinations of labels determined in accordance with g_1 and g_2 in $S = \{a, b\}$, as shown in table (c) in Fig. 2. Furthermore, setting $S = \{a, c\}$ creates a set of agents in which all combinations for labels determined in accordance with functions g_1 and g_2 are feasible. If $S = \{a, b, c\}$, all combinations for labels determined in accordance with functions g_1 and g_2 are infeasible. As a result, the Natarajan dimension is 2.

The Natarajan and Graph dimensions are identical to the VC dimension when $W = \{0, 1\}$. From the definitions, if $d_{VC}^{(k)}(\mathcal{H}) \leq d_N(\mathcal{H}) \leq d_G(\mathcal{H})$ for any $k(\geq 2)$, we can estimate $m_L(\varepsilon, \delta)$ by using the Natarajan and Graph dimensions as follows.

Theorem 2 ([5]). *Let us assume that $d_G(\mathcal{H}) < \infty$. For the constants C_1, C_2, from Theorem 1, for every $\mathcal{H}$, we have*

$$C_1 \frac{d_N(\mathcal{H}) + \log(1/\delta)}{\varepsilon} \leq m_L(\varepsilon, \delta) \leq C_2 \frac{d_G(\mathcal{H}) \log(1/\varepsilon) + \log(1/\delta)}{\varepsilon}. \qquad (8)$$

The Natarajan and Graph dimensions can be used to estimate the amount of training data required for a general multi-valued model. Furthermore, Ben-David et al. proved the following relationships between $d_N(\mathcal{H})$ and $d_G(\mathcal{H})$ [2].

$$d_N(\mathcal{H}) \leq d_G(\mathcal{H}) \leq 4.67 \log_2 k \; d_N(\mathcal{H}). \qquad (9)$$

Thus, there is an equivalence between $d_N(\mathcal{H})$ being finite and $d_G(\mathcal{H})$ being finite.

4   Problem Setting

Let $G = (V, E)$ be a directed graph. The node set V corresponds to the set X in the general theory described in the previous section. When V is a finite set, the number of nodes is $|V| = n$. Let $(u, v) \in E$ denote the directed edge from node u to node v.

If there exists a sequence of nodes $u, u_1, u_2, \ldots, u_{l-1}, v$ connecting two nodes $u, v \in V$ by directed edges ($u_0 = u, u_l = v$, then, for $1 \leq i \leq l$ $(u_{i-1}, u_i) \in E$), the relationship is denoted as $u \to v$. Then, let $\rho(u, v)$ be the number of edges (l in the above notation) when the two nodes are connected by the shortest directed edge sequence. If $u \to v$ does not hold, then $\rho(u, v) = \infty$. Note that we write $\rho_U(u, v)$ when we restrict the sequence of nodes connecting two nodes to those contained in the subset U of V. For $u, v \in U$, $\rho(u, v) \leq \rho_U(u, v)$.

The set of labels given to each node is $W = \{0, 1, 2, \ldots, k-1\}$. The case $k = 2$ corresponds to binary labels. Each node u is given one of these k kinds of values, which we denote by $f(u)$. A greater or lesser value of this label represents greater or lesser information about a certain matter, and this information spreads through the directed edges of the graph; i.e.,

$$u \to v \quad \Longrightarrow \quad f(u) \leq f(v) \qquad (10)$$

is assumed to be satisfied.

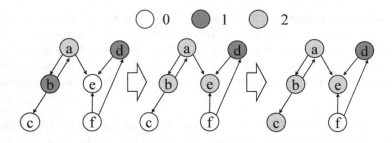

Fig. 3. Example of opinion flow

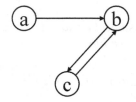

Fig. 4. Example of social network

In Conitzer et al.'s model [4], the state of each node is binary ($k = 2$) (it has or does not have the target information), and the set of nodes $S_0 \subseteq V$ that initially have that information is given as the initial state. The final state is represented by S_∞, and the objective is to estimate it. Once the information is acquired, it is not forgotten; i.e., if $u \in S_0$, then $u \in S_\infty$ is assumed. It is also assumed that the information is transmitted through directed edges; i.e., if $u \in S_0$ and $u \to v$, then $v \in S_\infty$ is also assumed. In our model, the above condition (10) is given by specifying the conditions that the final state must satisfy. We assume that each node u obtains information from nodes other than those connected by directed edges, and we allow the states $u \to v$ and $f(u) < f(v)$.

Example 4. Figure 3 shows how multiple opinions propagate in a social network. In this example, three opinions propagate. Initially, agent a has 2, agents b and d have 1, and the other agents have 0 as an opinion. Then, they share their opinions in accordance with the directions of their outgoing edges. Next, agents a, b, and e have 2 and d has 1. The opinion of agent b changes from 1 to 2 because 2 is stronger than 1. Although agent e receives both 1 and 2, opinion 2 is kept for the same reason. Finally, agents $a, b, c,$ and e have 2, agent d has 1, and agent f still has 0.

Of all possible labeling sets W^V on V, the subset that satisfies condition (10) is the hypothesis class and is denoted by $\mathcal{H}$. Hypothesis class $\mathcal{H}$, which is restricted to a subset V' of the node set V, is denoted by $\mathcal{H}|_{V'}$.

Example 5. Let $V = \{a, b, c\}$ denote the node set $E = \{(a, b), (b, c), (c, b)\}$, the edge set, as shown in Fig. 4. Let $k = 3$ be the number of labels. If we denote the elements of $\mathcal{H}$ in the form $(h(a), h(b), h(c))$, the hypothesis class is

$$\mathcal{H} = \{(0,0,0), (0,1,1), (0,2,2), (1,1,1), (1,2,2), (2,2,2)\};$$

and if we restrict the node set to $V' = \{a, c\}$, the restricted hypothesis class is

$$\mathcal{H}|_{V'} = \{(0,0), (0,1), (0,2), (1,1), (1,2), (2,2)\}.$$

In Conitzer et al.'s model [4] and the model used in this study, the learner is given information on the directed graph $G = (V, E)$ in step 1 of the learning procedure, as described in Sect. 3.1. At this point, the learner can define a subset of W^V that satisfies condition (10) as the hypothesis class $\mathcal{H}$. In the case of binary labels treated in Conitzer et al.'s study, the VC dimension of the hypothesis class $\mathcal{H}$ satisfying condition (10) is determined to be the maximum number of nodes in the graph that do not affect each other. Since the value of this dimension is determined from G, it is written as $d_{VC}(G)$. That is, the following holds for binary labels.

$$d_{VC}(G) = \max_{U \subseteq V}\{ |U| \mid {}^\forall u, v \in U, \rho_U(u, v) = \infty\} \tag{11}$$

Note that, if there exists a cycle in a directed graph G, i.e., a sequence of directed edges starting from $u \in V$ and returning to u, the label values of the nodes in the cycle must all be identical by condition (10). Therefore, it is sufficient to consider a directed acyclic graph in which all the nodes in a cycle in G are reduced to a single node, thereby removing all cycles. A directed acyclic graph can also be regarded as a partially ordered set. A subset of a partially ordered set for which none of its elements can be ordered is called an antichain. The number of elements in the largest antichain is called the width of the partially ordered set, which is in fact the right-hand side of Equation (11). It is known that the width of a partially ordered set can be determined by the polynomial order of the number of elements, which is the number of nodes in the corresponding directed acyclic graph [6]. Thus, variable d in inequality (3) of Theorem 1, which represents the estimated amount of training data needed, can be replaced by the width of the partially ordered set, which is a directed acyclic graph with cycles removed from the directed graph G.

In the following, we consider the case in which there are k kinds of labels $W = \{0, 1, 2, \ldots, k-1\}$, and hypothesis class $\mathcal{H}$, which is a set of candidate labelings of the entire V, is defined as the set of all f satisfying condition (10). In other words, realizability condition (2) is necessarily satisfied here. The learning problem is therefore to find f among the elements of the set $\mathcal{H}$ of W-valued functions on V. If parameters ε and δ are given, the amounts of training data required for PAC learning on $l_{\mathcal{D},f}(h)$ and $L_{\mathcal{D},f}(h)$ are defined as $m_l^{(k)}(\varepsilon, \delta)$ and $m_L^{(k)}(\varepsilon, \delta)$, respectively.

5   Comparison Between Binary and Multi-valued Models

In this section, we evaluate $m_l^{(k)}(\varepsilon, \delta)$ for a k-valued model compared with the binary model by using the following theorem.

Theorem 3. *Let the number of labels be* $k \geq 2$. *The following holds for* $m_l^{(k)}(\varepsilon, \delta)$, *i.e., the amount of training data required for PAC labeling.*

$$m_l^{(2)}\left(\frac{\varepsilon}{k-1}, \delta\right) \leq m_l^{(k)}(\varepsilon, \delta) \leq m_l^{(2)}\left(\frac{\varepsilon}{k-1}, \frac{\delta}{k-1}\right) \tag{12}$$

This theorem says that approximately $(k-1)\log(k-1)$ times the number of samples is sufficient for PAC learning for the k-valued model compared with the binary model. As for $m_l^{(k)}(\varepsilon, \delta)$ regarding the error rate, a similar evaluation formula can be obtained from the theorem and inequality (5).

Proof. The inequality on the left-hand side in Theorem 3 is shown because the error rate is exactly $k - 1$ times the error rate when the case in which the label of each node takes the value $\{0, 1\}$ in the binary model matches the case in which the label takes the value $\{0, k - 1\}$ in the k-valued model. The right-hand side inequality is shown below. Since the label of each node $v \in V$ can take k different values of $W = \{0, 1, 2, \ldots, k-1\}$, we divide these values into the following $k-1$ binary models: (i) $f(v) = 0$ or $f(v) > 0$, (ii) $f(v) \leq 1$ or $f(v) > 1$, and (iii) $f(v) \leq 2$ or $f(v) > 2 \cdots$. Then, each instance of $\left(\frac{\varepsilon}{k-1}, \frac{\delta}{k-1}\right)$-PAC learning is performed. That is, PAC learning of binary models (i), (ii), (iii), $\cdots$ is simultaneously performed using $m_L^{(2)}\left(\frac{\varepsilon}{k-1}, \frac{\delta}{k-1}\right)$ training data. This enables the following relationships to be satisfied.

(i) The probability of $P_D(f(u) = 0, h(u) \geq 1) + P_D(f(u) \geq 1, h(u) = 0) \leq \frac{\varepsilon}{k-1}$ is $1 - \frac{\delta}{k-1}$ or more.

(ii) The probability of $P_D(f(u) \leq 1, h(u) \geq 2) + P_D(f(u) \geq 2, h(u) \leq 1) \leq \frac{\varepsilon}{k-1}$ is $1 - \frac{\delta}{k-1}$ or more.

(iii) $\cdots$

The probability that all PAC learning of these $k - 1$ binary models will succeed, i.e., that the respective error rates will all be less than or equal to $\frac{\varepsilon}{k-1}$, is greater than or equal to $1 - \delta$. From this, it can be shown that

$$E_D(|f(u) - h(u)|)$$
$$= \sum_{i<j}(j-i)P_D(f(u) = i, h(u) = j) + \sum_{i>j}(i-j)P_D(f(u) = i, h(u) = j)$$
$$= \sum_{i \leq l < j} P_D(f(u) = i, h(u) = j) + \sum_{i > l \geq j} P_D(f(u) = i, h(u) = j)$$
$$\leq \sum_{l=0}^{k-2} \frac{\varepsilon}{k-1} = \varepsilon.$$

We obtain inequality (12) since $m_L^{(2)}\left(\frac{\varepsilon}{k-1}, \frac{\delta}{k-1}\right) = m_l^{(2)}\left(\frac{\varepsilon}{k-1}, \frac{\delta}{k-1}\right)$ when $k = 2$. $\qquad\square$

Next, we consider PAC learning when the possible label values are extended to real values. Let $W = [a, b]$, i.e., the label $f(u)$ of each node is a real value in the closed interval of a and b, and let $\mathcal{H}$ be the set of functions from V to W that satisfy condition (10). In this setting, as shown below, PAC learning is possible even though $|\mathcal{H}| = \infty$. The minimum number of samples for which the probability of selecting $h \in \mathcal{H}$ satisfying $E_{\mathcal{D}}(|f(u) - h(u)|) \leq \varepsilon$ is more than $1 - \delta$ is $m_l^{[a,b]}(\varepsilon, \delta)$. In this case, the following theorem can be obtained compared with that for the binary model.

Theorem 4.

$$m_l^{(2)}\left(\frac{\varepsilon}{b-a}, \frac{\delta}{b-a}\right) \leq m_l^{[a,b]}(\varepsilon, \delta) \leq m_l^{(2)}\left(\frac{\varepsilon^2}{2(b-a)}, \frac{\varepsilon\delta}{b-a}\right) \qquad (13)$$

Proof. Divide the interval $W = [a, b]$ into $K = \lceil \frac{b-a}{\varepsilon} \rceil$ intervals of width ε or less: $[a, a_1], (a_1, a_2], (a_2, a_3], \dots, (a_{K-1}, b]$. If $a_0 = a, a_K = b$, then, for $1 \leq i \leq K$, $a_i - a_{i-1} \leq \varepsilon$. We shall guess which interval the value of $f(u)$ at each node u is in and determine that, if $f(u) \in (a_{i-1}, a_i]$, then $h(u) = \frac{1}{2}(a_{i-1} + a_i)$. Similar to the proof of Theorem 3, we define the following $K - 1$ binary models: $[a_0, a_1]$ or $(a_1, a_K]$, $[a_0, a_2]$ or $(a_2, a_K]$, $\cdots$, $[a_0, a_{K-1}]$ or $(a_{K-1}, a_K]$. For these $K - 1$ binary models, $\left(\frac{\varepsilon}{2(K-1)}, \frac{\delta}{K-1}\right)$-PAC learnings are performed simultaneously. The probability that all the PAC learnings successfully estimate $f(u)$ within the range of error $\frac{\varepsilon}{2(K-1)}$ is $1 - \delta$ or better. The error rate in this case is within $\frac{\varepsilon}{2}$. In addition, the difference between a point within each interval and the midpoint of that interval is within a maximum of $\frac{\varepsilon}{2}$, which means that the error rate is kept within ε, the sum of these values. $\square$

6   Dimensions in Directed Graphs

The VC, Natarajan, and Graph dimensions are introduced as measures of the complexity of the set $\mathcal{H}$ of all possible labelings on V. The values of these dimensions are important when considering PAC learning, and in particular, whether these values are finite is a criterion for PAC learnability. According to Theorem 2, the Natarajan and Graph dimensions are used to estimate the upper and lower bounds on the amount of training data required for a multi-level model. As a comparison between these dimensions, inequality (9) holds as described in Sect. 3.4. Therefore, the evaluation of (8) can be expressed in terms of the Natarajan dimension only. It is known that the VC dimension of $\mathcal{H}$ satisfying condition (10) in the case of binary labels is determined from graph G as (11). Here, we show that the Natarajan and Graph dimensions of $\mathcal{H}$, which are defined as the set satisfying condition (10) in the case of multi-valued labels, can be specifically determined from G. This enables the upper and lower bounds on the amount of training data required for PAC learning to be expressed in terms of the properties of graph G.

Proposition 1. *The following holds for* $\mathcal{H}$, *which is defined as the set satisfying condition (10) on directed graph* $G = (V, E)$.

$$d_N^{(k)}(\mathcal{H}) = d_G^{(k)}(\mathcal{H}) = \max_{U \subseteq V}\{ |U| \mid {}^\forall u, v \in U, \rho_U(u, v) \neq k - 1\} \qquad (14)$$

Since the dimensions that can be determined as above are the values known from directed graph G, we will write them as $d_N^{(k)}(G)$ and $d_G^{(k)}(G)$. Note that condition $\rho_v(u, v) \neq k - 1$ on the right-hand side of Equation (14) means that no directed edge sequence of length $k - 1$ or more is contained within a subset U of V. Note that this coincides with (11) when $k = 2$. Also note that, in the k-valued model on directed graph G, the value of $d_{VC}^{(k)}(\mathcal{H})$ described in Sect. 3.2 coincides with $d_{VC}(G)$ defined by (11). Putting these together, we obtain

$$d_{VC}(G) = d_N^{(2)}(G) = d_G^{(2)}(G) \leq d_N^{(k)}(G) = d_G^{(k)}(G). \qquad (15)$$

Proof. It suffices to show the following. (i) If U is a subset V and contains no directed edge sequence of length $k - 1$ or more, then U is N-shattered by $\mathcal{H}$, which is determined from G. (ii) When U is a directed edge sequence of length $k - 1$ or more in G, U is not G-shattered by $\mathcal{H}$ determined from G.

(i) Let U be a subset of V that contains no directed edge sequence of length $k - 1$ or more. For each point u in this U, define $\beta(u)$ as

$$\beta(u) = \text{Maximum length of directed edge sequence ending at } u \text{ in } U,$$

where $0 \leq \beta(u) \leq k - 2$. Using this β, we define $g_1(u) = \beta(u), g_2(u) = \beta(u) + 1$. Then $0 \leq g_1(u) < g_2(u) \leq k - 1$, and $g_2(u) = g_1(u) + 1 \leq g_1(v)$ for any $u, v \in U$ satisfying $u \to v$. Let h be defined as follows. For any subset T of U, $h(u) = g_1(u)$ if $u \in T$ and $h(u) = g_2(u)$ if $u \notin T$. Such an h is contained in $\mathcal{H}$ determined from G because it satisfies $h(u) \leq h(v)$ if $u, v \in U$ and $u \to v$.

(ii) Suppose $U = \{u_0, u_1, u_2, \ldots, u_{k-1}\}$ and $(u_{i-1}, u_i) \in E$ for $1 \leq i \leq k - 1$. Also suppose that function g from U to $\{0, 1, \ldots, k - 1\}$ is contained in $\mathcal{H}$; that is, if $i \leq j$, then $g(u_i) \leq g(u_j)$ is satisfied. If we define a subset T of U from this g, as explained below, there does not exist an $h \in \mathcal{H}$ satisfying $h(u) = g(u)$ if $u \in T$ and $h(u) \neq g(u)$ if $u \notin T$.

(I) Let $u_0 \in T$ if $g(u_0) > 0$. Let $u_0 \notin T$ if $g(u_0) = 0$.
(II) For $1 \leq i \leq k - 1$
(a) Let $u_i \in T$ if $u_{i-1} \in T$ and $g(u_{i-1}) < g(u_i)$.
(b) Let $u_i \notin T$ if $u_{i-1} \in T$ and $g(u_{i-1}) = g(u_i)$.
(c) Let $u_i \in T$ if $u_{i-1} \notin T$ and $g(u_{i-1}) + 1 < g(u_i)$.
(d) Let $u_i \notin T$ if $u_{i-1} \notin T$ and $g(u_{i-1}) + 1 = g(u_i)$.
(e) Let $u_i \in T$ if $u_{i-1} \notin T$ and $g(u_{i-1}) = g(u_i)$.

For T defined in this way, let $\mathcal{H}_0$ be the set of functions h from U to $\{0, 1, \ldots, k - 1\}$ that satisfy the following conditions: $h(u_i) \leq h(u_j)$ if $i \leq j$, $h(u) = g(u)$ if $u \in T$, and $h(u) \neq g(u)$ if $u \notin T$. We show that $\mathcal{H}_0$ is an empty set.

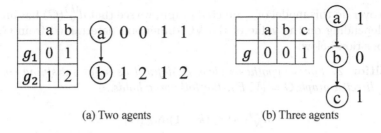

(a) Two agents   (b) Three agents

Fig. 5. Example of calculating Natarajan dimension on basis of Proposition 1

If $\mathcal{H}_0$ is not an empty set, we define $\tilde{h}(u_i) = \min_{h \in \mathcal{H}_0} h(u_i)$. If $i \leq j$, then $\tilde{h}(u_i) \leq \tilde{h}(u_j)$, so $\tilde{h}$ is also included in $\mathcal{H}_0$. From (I), $\tilde{h}(u_0) \geq 1$; furthermore, $\tilde{h}(u_0) = 1$ if $u_0 \notin T$. From the way (b) and (d) are determined, we know by induction with respect to i that $\tilde{h}(u_i) = g(u_i) + 1$ if $u_i \notin T$. Therefore, if $u_i \in T$ is determined by (e), then $\tilde{h}(u_{i-1}) > g(u_{i-1}) = g(u_i) = \tilde{h}(u_i)$, which is a contradiction. When $u_i \in T$ or $u_i \notin T$ is determined by (a), (b), (c), and (d), $\tilde{h}(u_{i-1}) < \tilde{h}(u_i)$ for $1 \leq i \leq k-1$. Therefore, $\tilde{h}(u_{k-1}) > \tilde{h}(u_0) + (k-1) > k-1$, which violates the assumption.   □

We show how we calculate the Natarajan dimension in the following example.

Example 6. Let X be $\{a, b, c\}$ and W be $\{0, 1, 2\}$. The structure of the social network is a line in which the edge from agent a goes to agent b and the edge from agent b goes to agent c. Here, since $k = 3$, we determine the maximum number of agents who do not have an edge sequence of length $2(= k - 1)$ or more.

For agents a and b, when we determine g_1 and g_2 as shown in (a) in Fig. 5, any assignment of g_1 and g_2 to agents a and b is monotonically non-decreasing on the path. Thus, $S = \{a, b\}$ is N-shattered by hypothesis $\mathcal{H}$. For agents $S = \{a, b, c\}$, we define g as shown in (b) in Fig. 5 for example. If we set $T = \{b, c\}$, then there is no h that satisfies $h(x) = g(x)$ for $x \in T$, $h(x) \neq g(x)$ for $x \in S \backslash T$ and is monotonically non-decreasing on the path. Thus, the Natarajan dimension is 2.

As a result, Theorem 2 can be rewritten in terms of the structure of directed graph G as follows.

Theorem 5. *When function f from V to $W = \{0, 1, \ldots, k-1\}$ on directed graph $G = (V, E)$ satisfies condition (10), we assume that the value $d_N^{(k)}(G)$ defined by Equation (14) is finite in PAC learning to guess this f. In this case, there exist positive constants C_1 and C_2 independent of $d_N^{(k)}(G), \varepsilon, \delta$, and the following holds.*

$$C_1 \frac{d_N^{(k)}(G) + \log(1/\delta)}{\varepsilon} \leq m_L(\varepsilon, \delta) \leq C_2 \frac{d_N^{(k)}(G) \log(1/\varepsilon) + \log(1/\delta)}{\varepsilon} \tag{16}$$

Moreover, in this model of a directed graph, we see that $d_N^{(k)}(G)$ has an upper bound depending on the value of the VC dimension determined from G, as in the proposition below.

Proposition 2. *For a hypothesis class $\mathcal{H}$ defined as a set satisfying condition (10) on directed graph $G = (V, E)$, the following holds.*

$$d_N^{(k)}(G) \leq (k-1)d_{VC}(G) \qquad (17)$$

From this proposition, it follows that models on directed graphs cannot have $d_N^{(k)}(G) < \infty$ and $d_{VC}(G) = \infty$. Therefore, it can be seen that a finite width of the partially ordered set corresponding to a directed acyclic graph is a necessary and sufficient condition for PAC learnability.

Proof. Let U be a subset of V that contains no directed edge sequence of length $k-1$ or more. If we define $\beta(u)$ for each node u in U as in the proof of Proposition 1, then $0 \leq \beta(u) \leq k-2$. From this definition, if $\beta(u) = \beta(v)$ for $u, v \in U$, then $u \not\to v$ and $v \not\to u$ in U. Let $U_l = \{u \in U | \beta(u) = l\}$ for $0 \leq l \leq k-2$. Each U_l is an antichain, and at least one U_l satisfies $|U_l| \geq \dfrac{1}{k-1}|U|$. Therefore,

$$d_{VC}(G) \geq \max_l |U_l| \geq \frac{1}{k-1}|U| \text{ holds.} \qquad \Box$$

7   Conclusion

We used the PAC learning framework to determine the number of samples needed to estimate the degree of propagation of multiple opinions in a social network. First, we compared the binary and multi-valued opinion cases. Next, we showed that the Natarajan dimension in this problem setup is determined by the size of the largest subset that does not contain directed edge sequences of length $k-1$ or more. We showed that the required number of samples can be estimated from above and below by using the Natarajan dimension. Furthermore, when the number of nodes in the graph is infinite, PAC learnability is determined by the structure of the graph, and the condition is the same for the binary and multi-valued cases.

Future work includes estimating the required sample size when the social network structure known to the learner is incorrect, when there is an agent that propagates a false opinion, and when agents follow the majority opinion upon receiving multiple opinions.

Acknowledgments. This work was partially supported by JSPS KAKENHI Grant Numbers JP18H03299, JP18H03337, JP21K12191, and JP21K19833 and by JST CREST Grant Number JPMJCR21D1.

References

1. Balcan, M-F., Procaccia, A.D., Zick, Y.: Learning cooperative games. In: Proceedings of the 24th International Joint Conference on Artificial Intelligence (IJCAI-2015), pp. 475–481 (2015)
2. Ben-David, S., Cesa-Bianchi, N., Haussler, D., Long, P.M.: Characterizations of learnability for classes of $\{0, \cdots, n\}$-valued functions. J. Comput. Syst. Sci. **50**, 74–86 (1995)
3. Berenbrink, P., Hoefer, M., Kaaser, D., Lenzner, P., Rau, M., Schmand, D.: Asynchronous opinion dynamics in social networks. In: Proceedings of the 21st International Conference on Autonomous Agents and Multiagent Systems (AAMAS-2022), pp. 109–117 (2022)
4. Conitzer, V., Panigrahi, D., Zhang, H.: Learning opinions in social networks. In: Proceedings of the 37th International Conference on Machine Learning (ICML-2020), vol. 119, pp. 2122–2132 (2020)
5. Daniely, A., Sabato, S., Ben-David, S., Shalev-Shwartz, S.: Multiclass learnability and the ERM principle. J. Mach. Learn. Res. **16**, 2377–2404 (2015)
6. Felsner, S., Raghavan, V., Spinrad, J.: Recognition algorithms for orders of small width and graphs of small Dilworth number. Order **20**, 351–364 (2003)
7. Igarashi, A., Sliwinski, J., Zick, Y.: Forming probably stable communities with limited interactions. In: Proceedings of the 33rd AAAI Conference on Artificial Intelligence (AAAI-2019), pp. 2053–2060 (2019)
8. Irfan, M.T., Hancock, K., Friel, L.M.: Cascades and overexposure in social networks: the budgeted case. In: Proceedings of the 21st International Conference on Autonomous Agents and Multiagent Systems (AAMAS-2022), pp. 642–650 (2022)
9. Procaccia, A.D., Rosenschein, J.S.: Learning to identify winning coalitions in the PAC model. In: Proceedings of the 5th International Joint Conference on Autonomous Agents and Multiagent Systems (AAMAS-2006), pp. 673–675 (2006)
10. Shalev-Shwartz, S., Ben-David, S.: Understanding Machine Learning - From Theory to Algorithms. Cambridge University Press, Cambridge (2014)
11. Sliwinski, J., Zick, Y.: Learning hedonic games. In: Proceedings of the 26th International Joint Conference on Artificial Intelligence (IJCAI-2017), pp. 2730–2736 (2017)
12. Zhang, H., Conitzer, V.: Incentive-aware PAC learning. In: Proceedings of the 35th AAAI Conference on Artificial Intelligence (AAAI-2021), pp. 5797–5804 (2021)

A Hybrid Model of Traffic Assignment and Control for Autonomous Vehicles

Jianglin Qiao[1,2]([✉]), Dave de Jonge[1], Dongmo Zhang[2], Carles Sierra[1],
and Simeon Simoff[2]

[1] IIIA-CSIC, Bellaterra, Catalonia, Spain
{davedejonge,sierra}@iiia.csic.es
[2] Western Sydney University, Penrith, NSW, Australia
{J.Qiao,D.Zhang,S.Simoff}@westernsydney.edu.au

Abstract. This paper proposes a multi-agent based method to describe traffic control optimization for autonomous vehicle assignment problems on road networks. We first present a formal model for abstract road networks. We then extend the road network model into a game-theoretical model based on population games to describe the behavior of autonomous vehicles under intelligent traffic control. Based on this model, we investigate a traffic control optimization problem that aims to improve the efficiency of road networks and provides an algorithm to find an approximate solution. Lastly, our algorithm significantly reduces the total delay of the road network, as demonstrated by the results of our experiments with the Aimsun (https://www.aimsun.com) simulation software.

Keywords: Multi-agent system · Transport and logistics · Intelligent traffic control

1 Introduction

Intelligent road infrastructures and traffic control technologies are crucial for future transport systems. Over the last decades, research on autonomous vehicles (AVs) has made revolutionary progress, giving us hope for safer, more convenient, and more efficient means of transportation. Most significantly, the advancement of artificial intelligence, especially machine learning, allows self-driving cars to learn and adapt to complex road situations with millions of accumulated driving hours, which is much more than any experienced human driver could ever reach [15,17]. However, autonomous vehicles on roads also introduce new challenges in traffic assignment and control due to the high sophistication and unpredictability of autonomous vehicles [1].

Traditional traffic control systems continue to suffer from several well-known flaws [7]. Current traffic control systems show ineffective time management at intersections, requiring vehicles to wait unnecessarily, resulting in congestion, pollution, and additional delays, among other things.

R. Aydoğan et al. (Eds.): PRIMA 2022, LNAI 13753, pp. 208–226, 2023.
https://doi.org/10.1007/978-3-031-21203-1_13

The most common traffic control protocols on major roads are based on traffic lights. The earliest versions of these traffic signal systems assigned a fixed amount of time for each traffic light to turn green, regardless of the number of vehicles or the density of traffic in the corresponding lane. However, as technology advanced, these traffic signal systems started to take into account different parameters, such as a distinction between day and night or between peak and off-peak periods, to determine the ratio between time in green and time in red. Some vision-based traffic management systems [11,18,29] use vision sensors to capture the flow of cars coming from different directions. To the best of our knowledge, these advanced management approaches target individual intersections and do not synergize with other intersections. Some roads may be busier than others at different times, which requires additional time to clear congestion on the road. An in-depth study of autonomous vehicle traffic management is in high demand. Almost all current road infrastructures and traffic control technologies depend on human driving [35]. Even self-driving cars are being trained to recognize human-oriented traffic signs and mimic human driving behaviors, which is by no means necessary for an efficient or reliable traffic management system.

Optimizing traffic control for autonomous vehicles has been studied for many years. Some of these studies range from optimizing vehicle routing to matching traffic control [21,39,40]. Others have proposed new traffic control methods to make autonomous vehicles more efficient [4,8,12]. Furthermore, some articles optimize existing traffic management protocols to adapt to changes in traffic flow [34,38]. Traditional vision-based traffic control facilities, such as traffic lights, roundabouts, and stop signs, are likely to be replaced by less visible but more efficient and effective algorithm-controlled road facilities as new technologies emerge for vehicle-based communication and intelligent traffic control [16]. A virtual roundabout traffic management protocol [26] is an example of an algorithmic traffic control protocol for autonomous vehicles or vehicles with vehicle-to-vehicle (V2V) or vehicle-to-infrastructure (V2I) communication. With the arrival of autonomous vehicles, better solutions have become necessary for intelligent traffic management systems that use the most advanced technologies [3]. Optimizing traffic control based on vehicle decisions has been an ongoing challenging problem.

The traffic assignment problem [5] is an important research topic in the field of transportation. In a road network, different numbers of vehicles pass between different origins and destinations. However, the different choice of vehicle routes can cause different congestion on different roads. Therefore, rational planning of vehicle choice is another important direction to improve traffic efficiency [14]. Traditionally, the traffic assignment problem has been formalized as a game theory problem. First, [30] proposed the task allocation problem, which, like the original traffic assignment problem, later becomes a congestion game. [31] uses non-cooperative games to explore the game theoretical properties of traffic assignment problems by considering vehicles as autonomous self-interested agents. [32] further simplifies this idea by focusing on population games and using potential functions to find equilibrium solutions. In addition, some studies focus on how to solve the traffic assignment problem in road networks using the existing model. The method of successive averages (MSA) is the algorithm most widely used to find the solution to traffic assignment [23]. [22] proposed a method of successive weighted averages (MSWA) to obtain results faster than the original MSA. There are also some common algorithms, such as origin-based algorithms [2], path-based algorithms [19] and the Frank-Wolfe algorithm [13]. Autonomous vehicles in our model are assumed to make self-interested decisions, like human drivers, who only consider their own interests, like how to reach their destination in the shortest possible time. The purpose of the road network model is to allow autonomous vehicles to reason about the network structure and traffic management protocols, which helps them to make decisions. The main motivation for our emphasis on autonomous driving is on the basis that vehicles have more powerful means of communication than humans to access more information about the road, which helps them make more informed decisions.

This paper presents a formal method to optimize traffic control with fully autonomous vehicles by combining a nonlinear optimization problem and a game-theoretical approach. We give a graph representation model of road networks based on graph theory to express the topological relationships between road lanes and intersections. We then introduce two additional relations to describe the connections and conflicts of each intersection. Based on the road network model, we can define traffic management protocols for each intersection, and these protocols provide the ability to optimize traffic control in different traffic scenarios. Due to autonomous vehicles' ability to make autonomous decisions, we build a game-theoretical model based on population games and congestion games, to describe the behavior of the vehicles. We then assume that an intersection manager controls all intersections, minimizes the total delay caused by changing traffic management protocols in a road network, and proposes a traffic control optimization problem. With the optimization problem, we have created a simple simulation environment by *Aimsun* and provided an algorithm to approximate the optimization solutions. Our proposed algorithm can successfully reduce the delay in the road network caused by static traffic assignment and traffic setting based on the traffic flow distribution generated by static traffic assignment, as demonstrated by the test results.

The structure of this paper is as follows. Section 2 introduces the graph representation of road networks, intersection relations, and traffic management protocols; in Sect. 3, we propose a formal definition of traffic network games based on the graph representation method in Section. Section 4 describes the traffic control optimization problem and the simulation-based algorithm to solve it. Section 5 concludes the paper and discusses future work.

2   Traffic Network Modeling

In this section, we present a formal model for describing road networks for autonomous vehicles capable of reasoning about the roads. This model is based on the model described in [28]. At first, we present a graph representation model for abstract road networks. Then, we introduce internal relations for each intersection that are used to specify internal connections and conflicts. Lastly, the formal definition of traffic management protocols for each intersection in a road network proposes the allocation proportion of all connections.

2.1 Road Network Model

Graph theory can provide a formal representation of intersections and has found a significant application in the analysis of road networks where there is an intuitive and obvious relationship between the links and nodes in a road network [20,24]. Furthermore, graph representations can also be used to represent traffic management protocols. For example, [27] manages autonomous vehicles using a time-based protocol or a priority-based protocol depending on the representation. Here, we will use labeled graphs to formalize road networks.

Definition 1. A road network $G = (N, A, L)$ is a labeled directed graph, where

- N is a set of nodes that represent intersections.
- $A \subseteq N \times N$ are the set of arcs, representing the roads that connect intersections.
- $L \subseteq A \times \mathbb{N}$ are the set of labeled lanes. $\mathbb{N}$ is the set of natural numbers. We use a natural number to label a lane on a road.

Intuitively, an intersection links roads and a road can be divided into several lanes. For example, an arc $(n, n') \in A$ represents a road on which vehicles can travel from n to n'. $(n, n', 1)$ and $(n, n', 2)$ are two lanes of the road[1]. The graph in Fig. 1 is an example of a road network. There are twelve intersections, and the arcs indicate the travel directions between the intersections. Figure 2

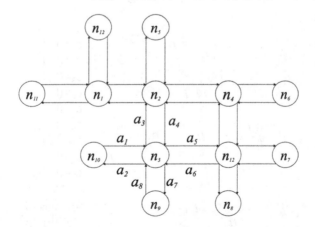

Fig. 1. Example of road graph

---

[1] Instead of denoting a lane as $((n, n'), 1)$, we simply write $(n, n', 1)$.

illustrates the labeled lanes. For example, road a_1 only has one lane l_1, however, road a_3 has two lanes $l_2 = (n_3, n_2, 1)$ and $l_3 = (n_3, n_2, 2)$. More specifically, the labels guarantee the uniqueness of each lane. For each intersection $n \in N$, let $L_n^{in} = \{(n', n, i) \in L : n' \in N \ \& \ i \in \mathbb{N}\}$ denote the set of all the incoming lanes, and let $L_n^{out} = \{(n, n', i) \in L : n' \in N \ \& \ i \in \mathbb{N}\}$ be the set of all the outgoing lanes.

2.2   Intersection Relations

This road network model describes the relationship between intersections, roads, and lanes. However, it does not represent the connection and conflict relationships between the road lanes at an intersection. For example, a vehicle approaching an intersection may wish to proceed straight, turn left, turn right, or make a U-turn, but the vehicle may not be allowed to travel in each of these directions. Therefore, we need to specify the connections between the road lanes at each intersection.

Furthermore, since these road connections at the same intersection can cross, vehicles crossing the intersection can collide if there is no traffic management protocol to avoid the collision. For example, if a vehicle travels from south to north while another is going from east to west, they may collide at that intersection. To specify such potential collisions between connections, we introduce a 'conflict relation' on top of the connection relation for each intersection. Formally, we define these two relationships as follows:

Definition 2. Given a road network $G = (N, A, L)$, we call $(C_n, Z_n)_{n \in N}$ an intersection relationship, where for each intersection $n \in N$,

- A connection relation $C_n \subseteq L_n^{in} \times L_n^{out}$ of the intersection is a binary relation between the sets of incoming and outgoing lanes.

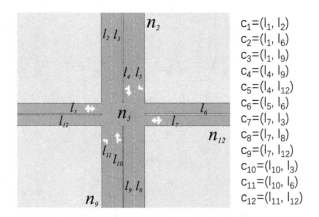

Fig. 2. Example of labeled lanes and connections

– A conflict relation $Z_n \subseteq C_n \times C_n$ is a symmetric binary relation over the connection relation C_n, which specifies potential collisions between connections. Symmetry means $(c, c') \in Z_n$ if and only if $(c', c) \in Z_n$ for all $c, c' \in C_n$.

The connection relation of an intersection specifies which outgoing lane can be reached from which incoming lane. Each $(l, l') \in C_n$ is called a *connection* between the incoming lane l and the outgoing lane l'. Intuitively, the connection c_1 means that the vehicles in l_1 are able to turn left at node n_3 toward l_2 in Fig. 2. We suppose that an U-turn is not allowed at intersection n_3, so (l_1, l_{12}) is not a connection in this case. It is worth mentioning that each incoming lane or each outgoing lane of an intersection should be contained in at least one connection. Figure 3 shows an example of a conflict relation Z_{n_3} of intersection n_3 in Fig. 1. The fact that the connection c_2 is linked to the connection c_4 in the conflict relation Z_{n_3} means that vehicles on l_1 that go straight could collide with vehicles on l_4 that go straight. Note that an intersection's collision relation only declares potential collisions between vehicles traveling in different connections, not actual collisions.

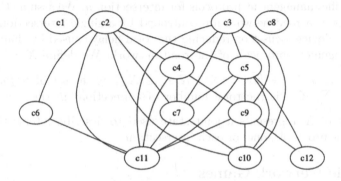

Fig. 3. Example of conflict relation

2.3 Traffic Management Protocols

Traffic must be controlled at intersections by traffic management protocols. Otherwise, there are potential vehicle collisions that can cause traffic accidents. Intuitively, the traffic management protocols of an intersection on a road network can be interpreted as the proportion of allocation of all connections per time unit from a macro-perspective in our road network model. For example, at an intersection under the management of traffic lights, the difference in the allocation proportion leads to changes in the green light time of that connection per unit time for each intersection connection. Obviously, the longer the traffic light is green, the more traffic can pass through that connection. Therefore, we can define the traffic management protocol for an intersection as the proportion of allocation to each connection at that intersection. Let $\overline{Z}_n$ denote the reflexive and transitive closure of Z_n. That is, $\overline{Z}_n := Z_n \bigcup \{(c, c) : c \in C_n\} \bigcup \{(c, c'') : (c, c'), (c', c'') \in Z_n\}$, so it forms an equivalence relation on C_n. For each $c \in C_n$, let $[c] = \{c' \in C_n : (c, c') \in \overline{Z}_n\}$ denote the equivalence class of c under C_n [33]. Formally, the traffic management protocol for an intersection is defined as follows:

Definition 3. Given a road network $G = (N, A, L)$ and its intersection relations $(C_n, Z_n)_{n \in N}$. For each intersection $n \in N$, a traffic management protocol x_n for the intersection is a function $x_n : C_n \rightarrow [0, 1]$ such that $\sum_{c' \in [c]} x_n(c') \leq 1$, which allocates a percentage of resources, such as time, flow, or capacity, to each connection at the intersection.

The condition shows that the sum of allocation proportion for all connections in the same equivalence class must be less than or equal to the unit of time. If we consider the traffic light as an example of the traffic management protocol at the intersection n, then the value $x_n(c)$ represents the percentage of time the traffic light for connection c is green. Furthermore, let X_n denote the set of all possible traffic management protocols for intersection n. We assume that all the intersections of a road network are controlled by a single intersection manager device. This device focuses on reducing the total delay caused by changes in the traffic management protocols of the road network. We define $X = \prod_{n \in N} X_n = \{x = (x_{n_1}, \ldots, x_{n_{|N|}}) \in [0, 1]^\sigma : n \in N, x_n \in X_n\}$ as the set of *traffic settings*, where $\sigma = \sum_{n \in N} |C_n|$ is the total number of connections in the road network. An element of X represents a joint state used to describe intersection traffic management protocols, one for each intersection.

3   Traffic Network Games

In this section, we present the formal definition of a traffic network game. A traffic network game is a model that describes the behavior of autonomous vehicles on a road network with intelligent traffic control. Each vehicle has a fixed origin and a fixed destination, but can choose which road it will take to reach its destination.

For a road network $G = (N, A, L)$, let $P \subseteq N \times N$ define a set of origin-destination pairs. For each such origin-destination pair, there is a population of vehicles that must travel from that origin to that destination. To simplify matters, we will not regard vehicles as discrete, countable objects, but rather as a continuous quantity (like a liquid). That is, for any origin-destination pair $p = (n, n') \in P$ the value $v_p > 0$ represents the vehicle 'density'. That is, the number of vehicles that travel from n to n' per unit of time. Furthermore, for each pair of origin-destination $p = (n, n') \in P$ we define $\Gamma_p = \{\gamma_1, \ldots, \gamma_{m^p}\}$ as the set of paths from n to n', in G where m^p is the total number of such paths. From now on, we will refer to such paths as *routes*. Formally, we define a route as follows:

Definition 4. Given a road network $G = (N, A, L)$ and its intersection relations $(C_n, Z_n)_{n \in N}$. For each origin-destination $(n, n') \in P$ and $n'', n''' \in N$, a route γ is a sequence $(l, l'') \to c_1 \to \cdots c_{m-1} \to (l''', l')$, where $l, l', l'', l''' \in L$, $l = (n, n'', i)$ and $l' = (n''', n', j)$, and satisfies for any u with $0 \leq u \leq m - 1$, such that $tail(c_u) = head(c_{u+1})$, where $head(c) = l$ and $tail(c) = l'$ for any connection $c = (l, l') \in C_n$.

Let $\Gamma = \bigcup\limits_{p \in P} \Gamma_p$ represent all possible routes for the road network, and the total number of routes for all origin-destination pairs is denoted by $m = \sum\limits_{p \in P} m^p$. Since every vehicle with the same origin-destination pair p has the same strategy space Γ_p, we can consider each origin-destination pair as a single player in the traffic network game to reduce the complexity of the model, which aims to assign individual vehicles to different routes. Therefore, the set of strategies of an origin-destination pair $p \in P$ is $S^p = \{s^p \in \mathbb{R}^{m^p} : \sum\limits_{\gamma \in \Gamma_p} s^p_\gamma = v^p\}$. The element $s^p_\gamma \in \mathbb{R}^+$ represents the mass of vehicles in the origin-destination pair p choosing strategy $\gamma \in \Gamma_p$. Specifically, a strategy for a given player assigns a certain percentage of all vehicles to each possible route. For example, it may assign 60% of the cars to route γ_1 and 40% of the cars to route γ_2. $S = \prod\limits_{p \in P} S^p = \{s = (s^{p_1}, \dots, s^{p_{|P|}}) \in \mathbb{R}^m : s^p \in S^p\}$ is a set of strategy profiles that describe the behavior of all players at once, and each strategy profile s is a vector of vehicle mass distributions, one for each origin-destination.

In a congestion game, the cost of each player is influenced by the facilities they select and the number of other players who also select those facilities. Next, we consider connections as facilities for a congestion game. For each node $n \in N$, each connection $c \in C_n$, $f_c(s)$ is the total mass of vehicles using the connection c. That is, $f_c(s)$ is determined from the strategy profile in the following way:

$$f_c(s) = \sum_{p \in P} \sum_{\gamma \in \Gamma_p} s^p_\gamma \delta_{c,\gamma} \tag{1}$$

where $\delta_{c,\gamma}$ is an indicator function that indicates whether a connection c is contained in a route γ. That is, $\delta_{c,\gamma} = 1$ if $c \in \gamma$; otherwise, $\delta_{c,\gamma} = 0$. Each connection has a cost function $d_c^x : \mathbb{R}^+ \to \mathbb{R}$ with connection traffic flow $f_c(s)$, which is total mass of vehicles using the connection under strategy profile s, as argument by given traffic setting x. Intuitively, the traffic setting affects the value of the cost function. We assume that vehicles in this paper are homogeneous vehicles, which means that the route cost is the cost of vehicles on that route. The cost of the vehicle is the travel time on the route it takes, which is the sum of the delays on its constituent connections and the free-flow travel time of the route. The delay on a connection is the number of vehicles that use that connection and the traffic management protocol applied to the connection. Subsequently, the free-flow travel time of a route is a constant number that depends on that route's length and speed limit. It is worth mentioning that the route's travel time does not represent the actual travel time for each vehicle; however, it shows the average travel time for all vehicles that choose that route. Formally, the cost for each route is calculated as follows:

$$F_\gamma^x(s) = \sum_{c \in \gamma} d_c^x(f_c(s)) + T_c \tag{2}$$

where x is a traffic setting and T_c is the free-flow travel time between the exit head intersection and the exit tail intersection. $F^x : S \to \mathbb{R}^m$ is a continuous map that assigns each strategy profile $s \in S$ to a vector of costs for a given traffic setting x, one for each route in each origin-destination. In summary, the traffic network game is defined as follows:

Definition 5. Given a road network $G = (N, A, L)$ and its intersection relations $(C_n, Z_n)_{n \in N}$. A tuple is called a traffic network game $(P, \Gamma, X, S, (F^x)_{x \in X})$, where

- P is the set of origin-destination pairs.
- Γ is the set of all routes.
- X is the set of traffic settings.
- S is the set of strategy profiles.
- $F^x : S \to \mathbb{R}^m$ is the cost function given the traffic setting $x \in X$.

Next, we need to define the equilibrium strategy profile of the traffic network games. In the field of transportation, Wardrop's first principle, known as "User Equilibrium", has been accepted as a simple and sound principle of conduct to explain the distribution of travel to alternative routes due to congestion [37]. Traffic flows adhering to this principle are referred to as user equilibrium flows, as each user chooses the best route. Formally, we have the following.

Definition 6. Given a traffic network game $(P, \Gamma, X, S, (F^x)_{x \in X})$ and a traffic setting $x \in X$, a strategy profile $s \in S$ is a user equilibrium (UE) if and only if for any origin-destination pair $p \in P$, any $\gamma \in \Gamma_p$ with $s_\gamma^p > 0$, and any $\gamma' \in \Gamma_p$, we have $F_\gamma^x(s) \le F_{\gamma'}^x(s)$ [37].

Specifically, a user equilibrium strategy profile is obtained if no vehicle could reduce travel time with one-sided measures. Furthermore, we use the following lemmas to show the properties of traffic network games based on the definition of population games, congestion games, and potential games.

Lemma 1. *Given a traffic setting x, any traffic network game $(P, \Gamma, \{x\}, S, F^x)$ is a congestion game.*

Lemma 1 is trivial. Based on the definition of congestion game [30], the cost of each player depends on the facility it chooses and the number of players who choose the same facility. In the traffic network game, we consider each origin-destination $p \in P$ to be a player and each connection c to be a facility. From the definition of the cost function (2), the cost of a player depends only on the traffic flow of the connections when the traffic setting x is given, which satisfies the definition of the congestion game.

Assumption 1. For each intersection $n \in N$ and each connection $c \in C_n$, suppose $g(s) = d_c^x(f_c(s))$, then $g(s)$ is a continuously differentiable function, and it satisfies the following properties:

- For any $n \in N$, $c \in C_n$ and $x \in X$, if $f_c(s) \le f_c(s')$, then $d_c^x(f_c(s)) \le d_c^x(f_c(s'))$ for any $s, s' \in S$;
- For any $n \in N$, $c \in C_n$ and $x^1, x^2 \in X$, if $x_n^1(c) \le x_n^2(c)$, then $d_c^{x^1}(f_c(s)) \ge d_c^{x^2}(f_c(s))$ for any $s \in S$;

That is, $d_c^x(f_c(s))$ does not decrease with increasing $f_c(s)$ when x is fixed, while it does not increase with increasing $x_n(c)$ when s is fixed.

Lemma 2. *Given a traffic setting x, the traffic network game $(P, \Gamma, \{x\}, S, F^x)$ is a potential game.*

Proof. From observation 3.1.1 in [32], it is easy to see that a game is a full potential game if and only if it satisfies full external symmetry. In a congestion game, a vehicle taking route $\gamma \in \Gamma_q$ affects the cost of vehicles choosing route $\gamma \in \Gamma_p$ through the marginal increases in congestion in the connections $c \in \gamma \bigcap \gamma'$ that the two routes have in common. Formally, we have

$$\frac{\partial F_\gamma^x(s)}{\partial s_{\gamma'}^q} = \sum_{c \in \gamma \bigcap \gamma'} d_c^x(f_c(s))' = \frac{\partial F_{\gamma'}^x(s)}{\partial s_\gamma^p} \tag{3}$$

for all $p, q \in P, \gamma \in \Gamma_p, \gamma' \in \Gamma_q$ and $s \in S$. Equation (3) satisfies full external symmetry, which means that the traffic network game is a potential game in a given traffic setting x.

Lemma 2 states that the traffic network game is a full potential game, which means that we can use the properties of the potential game to prove the existence of user equilibrium.

Theorem 1. *Given a traffic setting $x \in X$, the traffic network game $(P, \Gamma, \{x\}, S, F^x)$ has at least one user equilibrium strategy profile.*

Proof. Based on Lemma 1 and Lemma 2, it is possible to find a potential function [32] for the congestion game $(P, \Gamma, \{x\}, S, F^x)$ as follows:

$$\mathcal{F}^x(s) = \sum_{\gamma \in \Gamma} \int_0^{f_c(s)} F_\gamma^x(z) dz \tag{4}$$

So the task of finding the user equilibrium can be considered as the following non-linear optimization problem:

$$\min_{s \in S} \mathcal{F}^x(s) \tag{5}$$

subject to:

$$\sum_{\gamma \in \Gamma_p} s_\gamma^p = v^p, \quad \forall p \in P \tag{6}$$

$$s_\gamma^p \in [0, v^p], \quad \forall \gamma \in \Gamma_p \; \forall p \in P \tag{7}$$

According to Theorem 3.1.3 in [32] the solution of this non-linear problem is a user equilibrium.

Theorem 1 shows the existence of user equilibrium when the traffic setting x is fixed. For some given traffic network game, let $UE(x) = \{s \in S : p \in P, \gamma, \gamma' \in \Gamma_p, s_\gamma^p > 0 \to F_\gamma^x(s) \leq F_{\gamma'}^x(s)\}$ denote all user equilibrium strategy profiles for a given traffic setting x. It is easy to see that $UE(x) \neq \emptyset$ for all traffic settings $x \in X$. Next, we investigate an optimization problem to optimize traffic control for fully autonomous vehicles based on the model proposed in this section.

4   Traffic Control Optimization

In this section, we first introduce an optimization problem that aims to reduce the total delay of vehicles, based on the traffic network game model. Then, we present algorithms to find an approximate solution to this optimization problem. Lastly, we create a simple test environment to verify our algorithms and show some preliminary results.

4.1   Optimization Problem

The intersection manager aims to minimize the total delay caused by changing traffic settings. To find the minimum total delay for the intersection manager, we can formalize the problem as the following traffic control optimization problem:

$$\min_{x \in X, s \in UE(x)} \sum_{n \in N} \sum_{c \in C_n} f_c(s) d_c^x(f_c(s)) \tag{8}$$

subject to:

$$0 \leq x_n(c) \leq 1 \quad \forall c \in C_n \; \forall n \in N \tag{9}$$

$$\sum_{c' \in C_n, s.t. c' \in [c]} x_n(c') \leq 1 \quad \forall c' \in C_n \; \forall n \in N \tag{10}$$

$$f_c(s) \geq 0 \quad \forall c \in C_n \; \forall n \in N \tag{11}$$

$$\sum_{\gamma \in \Gamma_p} s_\gamma^p = v^p \quad \forall p \in P \tag{12}$$

$$s_\gamma^p \in [0, v^p] \quad \forall \gamma \in \Gamma_p \; \forall p \in P \tag{13}$$

The objective function (8) calculates the total delay of the road network. The $s \in UE(x)$ corresponds to the user equilibrium, which guarantees that no vehicle can experience a shorter travel time by unilateral deviation in an optimized traffic setting. The constraints (9)–(10) ensure the feasibility of traffic setting x. The constraint (11) specifies the positive traffic flow for all connections. Furthermore, the constraints (12)–(13) identify the feasibility of the strategy profile. The objective function cannot be solved by linear optimization when user equilibrium is used as a constraint. Additionally, when the road network is complex enough and the number of vehicles is large enough, finding a solution to the goal is also a complicated problem that requires further study. Therefore, we create a simple road network at *Aimsun* and provide an algorithm to provide an approximate solution to the objective function, which is proposed in the next section.

4.2 Simulation-Based Solution

The *Aimsun* simulation software provides an approximate user equilibrium strategy profile based on the method of successive averages (MSA) [6], which has been shown to converge to the equilibrium solution in static traffic assignment (STA) problems with well-behaved link cost functions [25]. Due to its simplicity and efficiency in computation, static traffic assignment has been widely used not only for estimating traffic demands on specific networks, but also for transportation planning and demand management policies concerning infrastructure investment [10,36]; it is the preferred tool for strategic transport planning [9]. Here, we have implemented a commonly used method in which, in each iteration, the traffic flow between routes is redistributed using MSA, and the demand percentages assigned to each route are updated. Let the predetermined sequence of steps size in the MSA algorithm be $\theta_i = \frac{1}{i}$, where i is the iteration number. Conventional MSA is calculated as

$$s_\gamma^{p,i+1} = s_\gamma^{p,i} + \theta_i(y_\gamma^{p,i} - s_\gamma^{p,i}) \tag{14}$$

where $y_\gamma^{p,i}$ is the auxiliary flow of connection c at iteration i. Also we can simplify the equation (14) as

$$s_\gamma^{p,i+1} = \frac{1}{i}(y_\gamma^{p,1} + \cdots + y_\gamma^{p,i}) \tag{15}$$

The proposed algorithm is considered to be converged if the average value of the user equilibrium relative gap becomes stable, where the related gap can be calculated as:

$$R_{gap}(i) = \frac{\sum_{\gamma \in \Gamma} s_\gamma^{p,i}(tt_\gamma^i - \pi_p^i)}{\sum_{\gamma \in \Gamma} s_\gamma^{p,i}\pi_p^i} \tag{16}$$

where i is the iteration number, $s_\gamma^{p,i}$ is the traffic flow on the route γ, $tt_\gamma^{p,i}$ is the travel experience time of the route γ collected by *Aimsun*, and π_p^i is the minimum travel time route from origin to destination p. The Algorithm 1 describes MSA based on our definition of notation, and we use $s = MSA(x)$ as user equilibrium strategies for a given traffic setting x in the remainder of the paper.

Algorithm 1. MSA Algorithm

Input: Traffic network game $(P, \Gamma, X, S, (F^x)_{x \in X})$, traffic setting x, gap tolerances θ, and the maximum iterations Λ.

Output: Approximate user equilibrium strategy profile s^*.

1: For each $p \in P$, $\gamma_p^* = \min_{\gamma \in \Gamma_p} \sum_{c \in \gamma} T_c$;

2: Initial strategy profile $s^0 = (s^{p,0}, \ldots, s^{p|P|,0})$, where $s_{\gamma_p^*}^{p,0} = v^p$ and $s_\gamma^{p,0} = 0$ for all $p \in P$;

3: $y_\gamma^{p,0} = v^p$, if $\gamma = \gamma_p^*$ for all $\gamma \in \Gamma_p \& p \in P$;

4: $y_\gamma^{p,0} = 0$, if $\gamma \neq \gamma_p^*$ for all $\gamma \in \Gamma_p \& p \in P$;

5: Run simulation in $Aimsun(s^0)$;

6: $i = 0$;

7: $R_{gap}(0) = \frac{\sum_{\gamma \in \Gamma} s_\gamma^{p,0}(tt_\gamma^{p,0} - \pi_p^0)}{\sum_{\gamma \in \Gamma} s_\gamma^{p,0} \pi_p^0}$;

8: **while** $R_{gap}(i) > \theta$ and $i < \Lambda$ **do**

9:    $y_\gamma^{p,i} = v^p$, if $\gamma = \pi_p^{i-1}$ for all $\gamma \in \Gamma_p \ \& \ p \in P$;

10:    $y_\gamma^{p,i} = 0$, if $\gamma \neq \pi_p^{i-1}$ for all $\gamma \in \Gamma_p \ \& \ p \in P$;

11:    $s_\gamma^{p,i+1} = \frac{1}{i}(y_\gamma^{p,1} + \cdots + y_\gamma^{p,i})$, for all $\gamma \in \Gamma_p \ \& \ p \in P$;

12:    $s^i = (s^{p,i}, \ldots, s^{p|P|,i})$;

13:    Run simulation in $Aimsun(s^*)$;

14:    $R_{gap}(i) = \frac{\sum_{\gamma \in \Gamma} s_\gamma^{p,i}(tt_\gamma^{p,i} - \pi_p^i)}{\sum_{\gamma \in \Gamma} s_\gamma^{p,i} \pi_p^i}$;

15:    $i = i + 1$;

16:    $s^* = s^i$

17: **end while**

Algorithm 2 is used to find the approximate solution of the traffic control optimization problem. The basic idea is to compare the conflict connection costs from the end-iteration. The proportion of allocations for each iteration increases or decreases proportionally to the difference between the total delays of two connections. In the next iteration, the higher total delay connection gets more allocation proportion than the ratio in the final iteration, and the lower total delay connection gets less allocation proportion than the ratio in the final iteration. If the new traffic setting reduces the total delay by more than a given threshold, then this traffic setting will be used as input for the next iteration by the MSA algorithm to find a user equilibrium. When the maximum number of iterations is reached, the algorithm is terminated. It is worth mentioning that the Algorithm 2 can only guarantee convergence to the local optimization solution, but cannot guarantee that the algorithm solution is the global optimization solution. Therefore, an accurate algorithm to find the global optimal solution is a critical task in the future.

Algorithm 2. Traffic Control Optimization

Input: Traffic network game $(P, \Gamma, X, S, (F^x)_{x \in X})$, objective function Ψ, gap tolerances ϵ, step size $\tau \subset [0, 1]$, and the maximum iterations Λ.

Output: Optimized traffic setting x^*.

1: Initial state $x^0 \in X$ and $s^0 = MSA(x^0)$;
2: $\Psi_c^0 = f_c(s^0) d_c^{x^0}(f_c(s^0))$, for all $c \in C_n$ and $n \in N$;
3: $\Psi^0 = \sum\limits_{n \in N} \sum\limits_{c \in C_n} \Psi_c^0$;
4: $i = 0$;
5: **while** $i < \Lambda$ **do**
6:    $j = 0$;
7:    $x_c^i = 1$, for all $n \in N$ such that $c, c' \in C_n$ and $(c, c') \notin Z_n$;
8:    $\eta_{(c,c')}^i = |\frac{\Psi_c^{i-1} - \Psi_{c'}^{i-1}}{\Psi_c^{i-1} + \Psi_{c'}^{i-1}}|$, for all $n \in N$, $c, c' \in C_n$ and $(c, c') \in Z_n$;
9:    **while** $j \in [0, 1]$ **do**
10:      $x_c^i = x_c^{i-1} + j\eta_{(c,c')}^i$, for all $n \in N$, $c, c' \in C_n$, $(c, c') \in Z_n$ such that $\Psi_c - \Psi_{c'} > 0$;
11:      $x_{c'}^i = x_c^{i-1} - j\eta_{(c,c')}^i$, for all $n \in N$, $c, c' \in C_n$, $(c, c') \in Z_n$ such that $\Psi_c - \Psi_{c'} < 0$;
12:      $s^i = MSA(x^i)$;
13:      $\Psi_c^i = f_c(s^i) d_c^{x^i}(f_c(s^i))$, for all $c \in C_n$ and $n \in N$;
14:      $\Psi^i = \sum\limits_{n \in N} \sum\limits_{c \in C_n} \Psi_c^i$;
15:      **if** $\frac{\Psi^{i-1} - \Psi^i}{\Psi^{i-1}} > \epsilon$ **then**
16:         *Break*;
17:      **else**
18:         $j = j + \tau$;
19:      **end if**
20:    **end while**
21:    $i = i + 1$;
22:    $x^* = x^i$
23: **end while**

4.3 Aimsun Setting and Results

We built a simple testing environment to test the algorithms in *Aimsun*, as shown in Fig. 4. It includes three different intersections, five origins, five destinations, and 20 origin-destination pairs. Each origin-destination pair has independent traffic demand. The total number of vehicles in the simulation is 5400. The simulation was performed using an Intel(R) Core(TM) $i9 - 10900$ K CPU @ 3.70 GHz and 64 GB of RAM. Since the algorithm only seeks to optimize the solution of the problem, it is not considered from the perspective of fast solutions. Therefore, iteration efficiency is not a research direction of the algorithm in this paper, and this issue is part of future work.

In the experimental set-up, each OD has a different traffic flow generated as a constant flow. In the initial traffic management setup, the ratio assigned to each connection is the same as the ratio of the total traffic passing through the

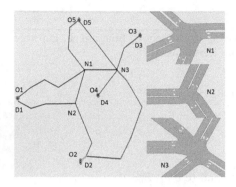

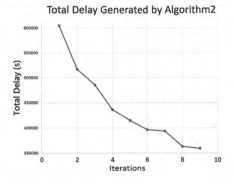

Fig. 4. Simulation setting   **Fig. 5.** Total delay on road network

intersection and the traffic of that connection by static user equilibrium, and each segment uses the BPR function, which is expressed as:

$$t_0 \cdot (1 + \alpha \cdot (\frac{volume}{capacity})^{\beta}) \tag{17}$$

where t_0 is the free flow travel time of the road lane, $\alpha = 0.15$, $\beta = 4$, *volume* is the assigned traffic in the road lane and *capacity* = 1800 for all the road lanes. The initial traffic setting is x^0, under the proportion of the traffic flow distribution by the static traffic assignment state s^0. It is worth mentioning that the system environment is the same during different iterations.

Figure 5 shows the preliminary result of *Aimsun* using Algorithm 2, and it is evident that each iteration reduces the total delay of the simulated road network. Further analysis shows that when changes in traffic settings are used as environmental variables, traditional static traffic assignment still has much room for optimization to reduce the overall delay in a road network. Although we used a simple road network model, the algorithm can still reduce the total delay in static traffic assignment by 40% without changing vehicle behavior based on the individual decision-making assumption.

The upper left of Fig. 6 shows the total number of vehicles that pass at each intersection during each iteration. The colored lines represent the number of cars at different intersections, one for each intersection in *Aimsun*. It can be seen from the graph that the change in traffic flow is almost constant at each intersection throughout the iteration. The rest of the subfigures in Fig. 6 show the total delay at each intersection for each iteration, one figure for one intersection. The overall delay in the road network decreases monotonically with increasing iterations. However, the total delay of vehicles at each intersection does not decrease monotonically. To put it simply, the autonomous decision of a car causes congestion at some intersections to make others more accessible, thus reducing the total delay on the road network.

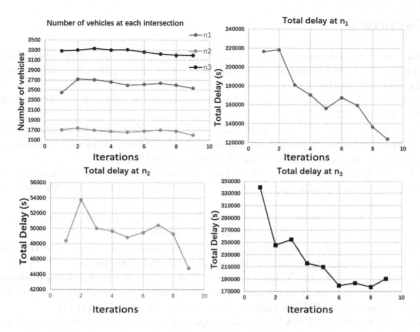

Fig. 6. Total number of vehicles and total delay at each intersection

5   Conclusion and Future Work

We consider problems in the future transport system: optimizing traffic control when fully autonomous vehicles can make individual decisions. This paper proposed a novel model to combine optimization and user equilibrium methods to increase the efficiency of road networks from a macroscopic point of view. Due to the complexity of the theoretical solution for traffic control optimization, we used a simulation-based approach to reach an approximate solution by implementing an iteration algorithm based on *Aimsun*. It can be seen from the experimental results that our proposed algorithm can effectively reduce the delay in the road network from static traffic assignment and traffic setting, which is based on the proportion of the traffic flow distribution generated by static traffic assignment.

Our work leaves some interesting unsolved problems in this paper. The essential work that needs to be done is to find meaning in the real world using some existing cost functions to give theoretical solutions to optimization problems that make sense. More efficient algorithms must be implemented so that global optimization is guaranteed. From a game theory point of view, future research should consider intersections as intelligent agents, giving them utility, such as toll policies, making the traffic network a different model. Another suggestion for the future is that we can extend our model to handle mixed autonomous traffic flows.

References

1. Bagloee, S.A., Tavana, M., Asadi, M., Oliver, T.: Autonomous vehicles: challenges, opportunities, and future implications for transportation policies. J. Mod. Transp. **24**, 284–303 (2016)
2. Bar-Gera, H.: Origin-based algorithm for the traffic assignment problem. Transp. Sci. **36**, 398–417 (2002)
3. Campisi, T., Severino, A., Al-Rashid, M.A., Pau, G.: The development of the smart cities in the connected and autonomous vehicles (CAVs) era: from mobility patterns to scaling in cities. Infrastructures **6**, 100 (2021)
4. Chen, S., Wang, H., Meng, Q.: An optimal dynamic lane reversal and traffic control strategy for autonomous vehicles. IEEE Trans. Intell. Transp. Syst. **23**, 3804–3815 (2021)
5. Dafermos, S.C., Sparrow, F.T.: The traffic assignment problem for a general network. J. Res. Natl. Bur. Stand. B. **73**, 91–118 (1969)
6. Daskin, M.S.: Urban transportation networks: equilibrium analysis with mathematical programming methods. Transp. Sci. **19**, 463–466 (1985)
7. Djahel, S., Doolan, R., Muntean, G.M., Murphy, J.: A communications-oriented perspective on traffic management systems for smart cities: challenges and innovative approaches. IEEE Commun. Surv. Tutor. **17**, 125–151 (2014)
8. Dresner, K., Stone, P.: A multiagent approach to autonomous intersection management. J. Artif. Intell. Res. **31**, 591–656 (2008)
9. Du, B., Wang, D.Z.W.: Solving continuous network design problem with generalized geometric programming approach. Transp. Res. Rec. **2567**, 38–46 (2016)
10. Du, B., Wang, D.Z.: Continuum modeling of park-and-ride services considering travel time reliability and heterogeneous commuters - a linear complementarity system approach. Transp. Res. Part E. Logist. Transp. Rev. **71**, 58–81 (2014)
11. Esteve, M., Palau, C.E., Martínez-Nohales, J., Molina, B.: A video streaming application for urban traffic management. J. Netw. Comput. App. **30**, 479–498 (2007)
12. Fernandes, P., Nunes, U.: Platooning of autonomous vehicles with intervehicle communications in sumo traffic simulator. In: 13th International IEEE Conference on Intelligent Transportation Systems, pp. 1313–1318 (2010)
13. Fukushima, M.: A modified frank-Wolfe algorithm for solving the traffic assignment problem. Transp. Res. Part B. Methodol. **18**, 169–177 (1984)
14. Golden, B.L., Raghavan, S., Wasil, E.A.: The Vehicle Routing Problem: Latest Advances and New Challenges. ORCS, vol. 43. Springer, New York (2008). https://doi.org/10.1007/978-0-387-77778-8
15. Grigorescu, S., Trasnea, B., Cocias, T., Macesanu, G.: A survey of deep learning techniques for autonomous driving. J. Field Robot. **37**, 362–386 (2020)
16. Gruel, W., Stanford, J.M.: Assessing the long-term effects of autonomous vehicles: a speculative approach. Transp. Res. Proc. **13**, 18–29 (2016)
17. Gupta, A., Anpalagan, A., Guan, L., Khwaja, A.S.: Deep learning for object detection and scene perception in self-driving cars: survey, challenges, and open issues. Array. **10**, 100057 (2021)
18. Javaid, S., Sufian, A., Pervaiz, S., Tanveer, M.: Smart traffic management system using internet of things. In: 2018 20th International Conference on Advanced Communication Technology (ICACT), pp. 393–398 (2018)
19. Jayakrishnan, R., Tsai, W.T., Prashker, J.N., Rajadhyaksha, S.: A faster path-based algorithm for traffic assignment (1994)

20. Karimi, K.: A configurational approach to analytical urban design:'space syntax' methodology. Urban Des. Int. **17**(4), 297–318 (2012)
21. Liard, T., Stern, R., Delle Monache, M.L.: Optimal driving strategies for traffic control with autonomous vehicles. IFAC-PapersOnLine. **53**, 5322–5329 (2020)
22. Liu, H.X., He, X., He, B.: Method of successive weighted averages (MSWA) and self-regulated averaging schemes for solving stochastic user equilibrium problem. Netw. Spatial Econ. **9**, 485–503 (2009)
23. Mounce, R., Carey, M.: On the convergence of the method of successive averages for calculating equilibrium in traffic networks. Transp. Sci. **49**, 535–542 (2015)
24. Porta, S., Crucitti, P., Latora, V.: The network analysis of urban streets: a dual approach. Phys. A Statist. Mech. App. **369**, 853–866 (2006)
25. Powell, W.B., Sheffi, Y.: The convergence of equilibrium algorithms with predetermined step sizes. Transp. Sci. **16**, 45–55 (1982)
26. Qiao, J., Zhang, D., de Jonge, D.: Virtual roundabout protocol for autonomous vehicles. In: Mitrovic, T., Xue, B., Li, X. (eds.) AI 2018: Advances in Artificial Intelligence, pp. 773–782 (2018)
27. Qiao, J., Zhang, D., de Jonge, D.: Graph representation of road and traffic for autonomous driving. In: Nayak, A.C., Sharma, A. (eds.) PRICAI 2019: Trends in Artificial Intelligence, pp. 377–384 (2019)
28. Qiao, J., Zhang, D., de Jonge, D.: Priority-based traffic management protocols for autonomous vehicles on road networks. In: Long, G., Yu, X., Wang, S. (eds.) AI 2021: Advances in Artificial Intelligence, pp. 240–253 (2022)
29. Reza, S., Oliveira, H.S., Machado, J.J., Tavares, J.M.R.: Urban safety: an image-processing and deep-learning-based intelligent traffic management and control system. Sensors. **21**, 7705 (2021)
30. Rosenthal, R.W.: A class of games possessing pure-strategy Nash equilibria. Int. J. Game Theory. **2**, 65–67 (1973)
31. Roughgarden, T., Tardos, E.: How bad is selfish routing? J. ACM. **49**, 236–259 (2002)
32. Sandholm, W.H.: Population Games and Evolutionary Dynamics. MIT Press, Cambridge (2010)
33. Schechter, E.: Handbook of Analysis and its Foundations. Academic Press, Cambridge (1996)
34. Sun, C., Guanetti, J., Borrelli, F., Moura, S.J.: Optimal eco-driving control of connected and autonomous vehicles through signalized intersections. IEEE Internet Things J. **7**, 3759–3773 (2020)
35. Wagner, P.: Traffic control and traffic management in a transportation system with autonomous vehicles. In: Maurer, M., Gerdes, J.C., Lenz, B., Winner, H. (eds.) Autonomous Driving, pp. 301–316. Springer, Heidelberg (2016). https://doi.org/10.1007/978-3-662-48847-8_15
36. Wang, D.Z., Du, B.: Continuum modelling of spatial and dynamic equilibrium in a travel corridor with heterogeneous commuters-a partial differential complementarity system approach. Transp. Res. Part. B. Methodolog. **85**, 1–18 (2016)
37. Wardrop, J.G.: Road paper some theoretical aspects of road traffic research. Proc. Inst. Civil Eng. **1**, 325–362 (1952)
38. Wu, Q., et al.: Distributed agent-based deep reinforcement learning for large scale traffic signal control. Knowl. Based. Syst. **241**, 108304 (2022)

39. Xu, W., Wei, J., Dolan, J.M., Zhao, H., Zha, H.: A real-time motion planner with trajectory optimization for autonomous vehicles. In: 2012 IEEE International Conference on Robotics and Automation, pp. 2061–2067 (2012)
40. You, C., Lu, J., Filev, D., Tsiotras, P.: Advanced planning for autonomous vehicles using reinforcement learning and deep inverse reinforcement learning. Robot. Auton. Syst. **114**, 1–18 (2019)

MTIRL: Multi-trainer Interactive Reinforcement Learning System

Zhaori Guo[✉], Timothy J. Norman, and Enrico H. Gerding

University of Southampton, Southampton, UK
{zg2n19,t.j.norman,}@soton.ac.uk, eg@ecs.soton.ac.uk

Abstract. Interactive reinforcement learning can effectively facilitate the agent training via human feedback. However, such methods often require the human teacher to know what is the correct action that the agent should take. In other words, if the human teacher is not always reliable, then it will not be consistently able to guide the agent through its training. In this paper, we propose a more effective interactive reinforcement learning system by introducing multiple trainers, namely Multi-Trainer Interactive Reinforcement Learning (MTIRL), which could aggregate the binary feedback from multiple non-perfect trainers into a more reliable reward for an agent training in a reward-sparse environment. In particular, our trainer feedback aggregation experiments show that our aggregation method has the best accuracy when compared with the majority voting, the weighted voting, and the Bayesian method. Finally, we conduct a grid-world experiment to show that the policy trained by the MTIRL with the review model is closer to the optimal policy than that without a review model.

Keywords: Interactive reinforcement learning · Human-in-the-loop reinforcement learning · Multiple people decision

1 Introduction

Reinforcement Learning (RL) is a machine learning method to train an agent to select actions in an environment to maximize a cumulative reward. In RL, the agent can usually be rewarded only at the end or at a particular state. This makes it difficult for the reward designer to quickly influence the knowledge of the agent in the key states. Therefore, the reward sparsity has limited the application scenarios of reinforcement learning [11,17]. One approach to solve this problem is the *interactive RL* (IRL), which allows humans to participate in the training process. Indeed, it has been shown that, through human feedback, the agent's learning is facilitated and, therefore, it is able to complete the training faster. In previous IRL research, people often focus on the interaction between a single human trainer and an agent [11,12,17]. However, this kind of methods require

R. Aydoğan et al. (Eds.): PRIMA 2022, LNAI 13753, pp. 227–242, 2023.
https://doi.org/10.1007/978-3-031-21203-1_14

a perfect trainer, that is a trainer whose feedback is always correct. Indeed, it has been shown that if the quality of the trainer's feedback is not perfect, it cannot effectively help an agent finish training [14]. For example, if the trainer gives wrong feedback on a critical state, the task will not be able to continue. Therefore, when a single trainer's trust is not enough, multiple trainers can make feedback more stable and reliable.

There are many scenarios in which MTIRL can be used fruitfully. Consider, for example, the asset portfolio management task, in which the agent has to decide on the best investment at every instant. Assuming that the trainer has a perfect knowledge of the market fluctuation is unfeasible. Another example is the patient's treatment. In this case, the experience of more doctors in training a medical agent is more reliable than a singular individual. To summarize, there are several contests in which one point of view is not enough to guarantee the level of knowledge that the agent needs to learn. Due to the novelty of the approach, the IRL community has not been studying multi-trainers methods in full. In this paper, we design the multi-trainer interactive reinforcement learning system (MTIRL), which can aggregate the binary feedback of multiple trainers into a reward that guides the agent training. The logical structure of MTIRL is composed of four parts. The first part is the feedback setting. Since it is important to reduce the cognitive load on trainers as much as possible, we use binary feedback, that is, every trainer can express opinions through a good-or-bad question.

The second part is the trust model, which takes care of understanding which of the trainers is more reliable than the others. We express the trustfulness of trainer x through a parameter $P(x)$, which roughly estimates the probability that the report made by trainer x is correct. The third part is the decision model, which, given the feedback and trustworthiness of the trainers, allows the system to decide whether the agent should receive a positive or negative reward. To decide what reward we should give to the agent, we combine a Bayesian model with a weighted voting model. The last part is the reviewing one, which allows the system to remember all the agent's answers in a specific state-action pair. Thanks to the reviewing part, the model is able to correct previously unreliable feedback by updating the trust levels and by asking more and different trainers.

The main contributions of the paper are the following: we propose and study a new aggregating method, and we compare it with the already known ones through several experiments. The results show that MTIRL has better accuracy. Moreover, the review model used in MTIRL has a smaller overall training cost and improves the accuracy. It is worthy of notice that the MTIRL method can be used as an alternative to all the single trainer IRL models.

The remainder of the paper is structured as follows. In Sect. 2, we provide an overview of related work. In Sect. 3, we formalize the problem. In Sect. 4, we introduce the details of the MTIRL system. The experimental setting is described in Sect. 5. Finally, in Sect. 6 we summarize the results of the paper and conclude.

2   Related Work

To begin with, several IRL works focus on how to improve the RL performance by human feedback [11,17], or how to use implicit feedback to give reward [1,5]. These two methods only allow one trainer to participate in the RL training loop and cannot aggregate feedback from multiple trainers.

In contrast, [15,21] enables multiple trainers to take part in IRL. However, they only select one trainer each time. If the quality of feedback from a single trainer is inaccurate, this will produce poor training accuracy. [14] filters trainer's bad advice by comparing Q-values. However, this approach relies on environmental rewards as ground truth. It will not work well when the rewards are highly sparse. In addition, the feedback of multiple people cannot be effectively used, which will cause more costs. Our approach does not rely on ground truth, and it can effectively utilize all feedback.

In addition, there is also a lot of research about how to aggregate the feedback from multiple participants. One approach is to complete the aggregation by using the similarity between users [7,22]. This is usually implemented by similarity matrix and distance function. The purpose of them is to obtain a consensus that is in line with the majority's preferences. Therefore, the consensus does not have correct or wrong, but the reward in RL has. In contrast, our work allows the agent to judge the correct probability of the reward and how much trust should it give to the reward.

Another approach to aggregate feedback is using weighted voting. This approach assigns weights to participants in different ways and accumulates them as the result of the final aggregation [6,20]. For example, [20] assigns fixed weights to different participants and aggregates them, whereas [6] uses the self-trust of participants to be the weights. The problem with the weighted voting method is that, if there is no ground truth, it cannot accurately represent the credibility of their aggregated results.

A third method is the distributed method, such as distributed RL and federated learning [3,16]. These methods usually do not aggregate the information for training, but pass the training results from the local to the center. They are efficient, but only if the rewards obtained from the environment are reliable, this also needs the ground truth to judge the noise from local thread. Also, these methods require higher computing power.

3   Problem Formalization

In this paper, we solve a multiple trainers decision problem without any ground truth in IRL. In more detail, the RL model is represented by a Markov Decision Process (MDP). It consists of 5 elements $\langle S, A, T, R, \gamma \rangle$, where: S is the set of states, also called the state space; A is the action space; T is the state transition function; and R is the reward function. Furthermore, $\gamma \in [0, 1]$ is the discount coefficient, which indicates the degree of influence of future rewards on the current state value. At each time t, the agent observes a state $s_t \in S$.

Then, it selects an action $a_t \in \mathcal{A}$ by policy $\pi(s_t|a_t)$; After this, it receives a reward r_t. The purpose of the RL task is to maximize the accumulated reward $R_t = \sum_{t=0}^{T} \gamma_t r_t$. In IRL, if human feedback is used as a reward, then it can be expressed as human reward r'_t.

In multi-trainers IRL, let $x \in X$ denote a set of trainers. We assume that more than half participants have a trust greater than the basic accuracy. After the agent performs action a_t, a set of trainers $Y_t \subseteq X$ gives feedback according to the state action pair (s_t, a_t). The feedback set can be denoted as F_t. In IRL, if human feedback is used as a reward, it can be expressed as human reward r'_t. Trainers' rewards are different from environmental rewards, and they may not be correct. Therefore, the system needs to use F_t to determine the final reward $r'_t = f(F_t)$ to improve the accuracy of the reward. Let r^*_t denote the correct rewards. Our goal is to maximize the number n of $r'_t = r^*_t$ under the feedback set F_t by the function $f(F_t)$. It can express as:

$$f^*(F_t) = \underset{f(F_t)}{\arg\max}\, n(r'_t = r^*_t | f(F_t)). \tag{1}$$

4   Multi-trainer Interactive Reinforcement Learning

MTIRL can aggregate the binary feedback of multiple trainers into an effective reward to help the agent training, which greatly improves the learning efficiency of the agent. The design of MTIRL considers four parts. The first part is the feedback setting. The second part is the trust model. The third part is the decision model. The last part is the review part. Figure 1 shows its structure.

4.1   Binary Feedback

In order to reduce the feedback pressure on trainers, MTIRL uses binary reward feedback $f \in \{r_{pos}, r_{neg}\}$. If the human believes the action taken by the agent is the best, then a positive reward r_{pos} is given. Otherwise, it is given a negative reward r_{neg}. There are two reasons for choosing it. Firstly, in the design of the feedback method, we plan to reduce the cognitive burden of human trainers as much as possible. Compared to the scoring reward, the binary reward can give humans less feedback pressure because humans only need to judge whether the current agent is performing the best action. Secondly, the binary reward is more robust to noise in feedback because it requires less cost than other methods to correct the noise.

4.2   Trainer Trust Model

Modeling the trustworthiness of trainers is essential because everyone's knowledge level is different, so the quality of their feedback is also different. Therefore, if the system aggregates their feedback, it is necessary to understand their trustworthiness.

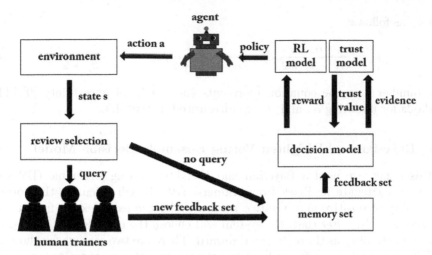

Fig. 1. The feedback selection model decides whether to query trainers according to the state-action pair. The decision model combines the trust value and the feedback set to determine the final reward given to the agent. The RL model updates the policy by the reward. The decision model sends the evidence to the trust model for updating trainers' trust after the decision.

Subjective logic is a method for modeling trust that is widely used [2,4,8]. There are three reasons to use it. Firstly, it can quantify the trustworthiness of the participants and the uncertainty of the trust. It provides each trainer with a trust score between 0 and 1 to measure the reliability of the trainer. Secondly, it can identify malicious users to defend against attacks. Thirdly, it can be combined with Bayesian methods for decision-making.

Evidence and Uncertainty. Given a set of trainers $x \in X$, let $b_x \in [0, 1]$ be the agent belief to trainer x, and $d_x \in [0, 1]$ denote the agent disbelief to trainer x. $u_x \in [0, 1]$ is the uncertainty assessment. It decreases from 1 as evidence increases. For example, 300 trials have less uncertainty in a coin toss experiment than three trials. a_x is a base rate , representing a prior degree of the trust before the model gets the evidence. If a_x is set to 0.5, it means that the trainers randomly select positive or negative with equal probability. The relationship between b_x, d_x and u_x satisfies:

$$b_x + d_x + u_x = 1 \tag{2}$$

The trainer's trustworthiness $P(x)$ can be expressed as:

$$P(x) = b_x + a_x u_x \tag{3}$$

After each feedback, the results provide the trainer with positive evidence α_x or negative evidence β_x observed by the agent, and then the system updates b_x, d_x

and u_x as follows:

$$b_x = \frac{\alpha_x}{\alpha_x + \beta_x + 2}, d_x = \frac{\beta_x}{\alpha_x + \beta_x + 2}, u_x = \frac{2}{\alpha_x + \beta_x + 2} \qquad (4)$$

The number 2 in the equation represents the weight of uncertainty [9]. The methods for updating α_x and β_x are introduced in Sect. 4.3.

4.3   Bayesian and Weighted Voting Ensemble Decision Model

In this paper, we used a Bayesian and Weighted Voting Ensemble (BWVE) model to aggregate feedback from trainers. BWVE will calculate the correct probability of positive and negative reward under the feedback set from trainers, respectively. After that, the system will choose the one who has the bigger correct probability as the aggregated reward. There are two reasons for choosing BWVE. Firstly, it can effectively utilize the trustworthiness of trainers to make the aggregation results more accurate. Secondly, its results are probability, which can measure the reliability of the aggregated reward.

Bayesian Probability. In RL, in each time t, the agent selects an action a_t under state s_t. A set of trainers $P_t \subseteq X$ gives positive feedback, whereas set of trainers $N_t \subseteq X$ gives negative feedback, and $P_t \cap N_t = \emptyset$. Under the condition P_t and N_t, the probability of the positive or negative feedback is right can be denoted as $P_t(f_{pos}|P_t, N_t)$ and $P_t(f_{neg}|P_t, N_t)$, respectively. Through the Bayesian method, they can be expressed as:

$$P_t(f_{pos}|P_t, N_t) = \frac{P(f_{pos})P_t(P_t, N_t|f_{pos})}{P(f_{pos})P_t(P_t, N_t|f_{pos}) + P(f_{neg})P_t(P_t, N_t|f_{neg})} \qquad (5)$$

$$P_t(f_{neg}|P_t, N_t) = \frac{P(f_{neg})P_t(P_t, N_t|f_{neg})}{P(f_{pos})P_t(P_t, N_t|f_{pos}) + P(f_{neg})P_t(P_t, N_t|f_{neg})} \qquad (6)$$

The $P(f_{pos})$ and $P(f_{neg})$ are the basic probability. For example, in the absence of prior information, if the trainer can randomly give the agent a r_{neg} or r_{pos} reward with the same probability, $P(f_{pos})$ and $P(f_{neg})$ are 0.5. $P_t(P_t, N_t|f_{pos})$ or $P_t(P_t, N_t|f_{neg})$ means given the condition that positive or negative feedback is correct, the probability that decision is correct under the condition P_t and N_t. They can be computed using the trustworthiness $P(x)$ mentioned in Sect. 4.2. So it can be expressed as:

$$P_t(P_t, N_t|f_{pos}) = \prod_{i \in P_t} \prod_{j \in N_t} P(i)(1 - P(j)) \qquad (7)$$

$$P_t(P_t, N_t|f_{neg}) = \prod_{i \in P_t} \prod_{j \in N_t} (1 - P(i))P(j) \qquad (8)$$

Weighted Voting Trust Initialization. In the initialization phase of the trust model, since the trust probability $P(x)$ of each trainer is not reliable, the performance of the Bayesian decision-making method is not reliable, which means that the Bayesian method are vulnerable to bad feedback. We use the weighted voting method to solve this problem because it is more stable in the initialization phase. The trainer's trustworthiness $P(x)$ is considered weights in the weighted voting method. The difference from the Bayesian method is that it only adds up each trainer's trust weight. The correct probability of positive and negative through weighted voting can be expressed as:

$$P_t^{wv}(f_{pos}|P_t, N_t) = \frac{\sum_{i \in P_t} P(i)}{\sum_{j \in P_t \cup N_t} P(j)} \tag{9}$$

$$P_t^{wv}(f_{neg}|P_t, N_t) = \frac{\sum_{i \in P_t} P(i)}{\sum_{j \in P_t \cup N_t} P(j)} \tag{10}$$

Bayesian and Weighted Voting Ensemble Decision Method. After getting the Bayesian (Eq. 5 and 6) and weighted voting probability (Eq. 9 and 10), the system uses the average uncertainty $\bar{u}_t$ of the trainers to combine and balance the Bayesian and the voting method. It represents the confidence or initialization level of the trust model. It can be expressed as:

$$\bar{u}_t = \frac{\sum_{i \in P_t \cup N_t} u_i}{n(P_t \cup N_t)} \tag{11}$$

The average uncertainty $\bar{u}_t$ decreases as time t increases, which means that the trust model becomes more and more believable. The correct probability of positive and negative through ensemble method can be expressed as:

$$P_t^{ag}(f_{pos}|P_t, N_t) = (1 - \bar{u}_t)P_t(f_{pos}|P_t, N_t) + \bar{u}_t P_t^{wv}(f_{pos}|P_t, N_t) \tag{12}$$

$$P_t^{ag}(f_{neg}|P_t, N_t) = (1 - \bar{u}_t)P_t(f_{neg}|P_t, N_t) + \bar{u}_t P_t^{wv}(f_{neg}|P_t, N_t) \tag{13}$$

As $\bar{u}_t$ decreases, the weights of the weighted voting methods are decreasing and the weights of the Bayesian methods are increasing. $P_t^{ag}(f_{pos}|P_t, N_t) + P_t^{ag}(f_{neg}|P_t, N_t) = 1$.

Decision Making and Update Trust Evidence. After aggregating the feedback, the system needs to compare $P_t^{ag}(f_{pos}|P_t, N_t)$ and $P_t^{ag}(f_{neg}|P_t, N_t)$. If $P_t^{ag}(f_{pos}|P_t, N_t)$ is bigger than $P_t^{ag}(f_{neg}|P_t, N_t)$, action a_t is considered to be the best action, the aggregating reward $r_t' = r_{pos}$. Otherwise, action a is not the best action, the aggregating reward $r_t' = r_{neg}$.

In Sect. 4.2, the computation of trainers' trust probability is closely related to evidence α and β. But the problem is that there is no ground truth to allow the agent to judge whether the reward r_t' is reliable in reward sparsity tasks. The difference of $P_t^{ag}(f_{pos}|P_t, N_t)$ and $P_t^{ag}(f_{neg}|P_t, N_t)$ can be the feedback confidence value i_t:

$$i_t = |P_t^{ag}(f_{pos}|P_t, N_t) - P_t^{ag}(f_{neg}|P_t, N_t)| \tag{14}$$

Here, i_t is a measure of the confidence of the aggregated reward. The greater i_t, the higher the credibility of r_t'. Evidence α_x and β_x updates should also be affected by i_t. Therefore, we use i_t as the step size for the evidence update. If $P_t^{ag}(f_{pos}|P_t, N_t) > P_t^{ag}(f_{neg}|P_t, N_t)$, it means the positive answer is more likely to be correct, so the evidence α_x and β_x is updated for each trainer using the following equation:

$$\forall x \in P_t, \quad \alpha_x \leftarrow \alpha_x + i_t$$
$$\forall x \in N_t, \quad \beta_x \leftarrow \beta_x + i_t \tag{15}$$

Similarly, if $P_t^{ag}(f_{neg}|P_t, N_t) > P_t^{ag}(f_{pos}|P_t, N_t)$, the negative answer is correct, and so we update α_x and β_x using:

$$\forall x \in P_t, \quad \beta_x \leftarrow \beta_x + i_t$$
$$\forall x \in N_t, \quad \alpha_x \leftarrow \alpha_x + i_t \tag{16}$$

4.4 Feedback Review Model

Human feedback is often expensive and time-consuming. In an IRL system, the designer needs to reduce the pressure of human feedback as much as possible. One way to reduce feedback is to avoid giving rewards to the state-action pair that has been feedback before. So in the MTIRL system, the system records feedback from trainers in each state-action pair. If the agent reencounters the same state, it uses the reward in the memory, greatly reducing the number of human feedback. However, the problem with doing this is that the future rewards are wrong if the previous reward is wrong. A review mechanism is applied in the MTIRL system to correct the wrong reward. The system re-asks those state-action pairs which have unreliable rewards.

$P_{s,a}$ and $N_{s,a}$ denote the positive and negative historical feedback sets of the state-action pair (s, a). At the time t, if the agent encounters a state-action pair that has already been asked, it needs to decide whether to ask the trainers again. The system needs to calculate $P_t^{ag}(f_{pos}|P_{s,a}, N_{s,a})$ (Eq. 12) and $P_t^{ag}(f_{neg}|P_{s,a}, N_{s,a})$ (Eq. 13) again with the latest trust model and $P_{s,a}$ and $N_{s,a}$. Then, the system can get the new reward $r_{s,a}'$ and the confidence value $i_{s,a}'$. The probability of review $P_{re}(s_t, a_t) \in [0, 1]$ can define as:

$$P_{re}(s_t, a_t) = 1 - i_{s,a}' \tag{17}$$

If $i_{s,a}'$ is larger, it means that the information of historical feedback is more reliable, and the probability of review is lower. On the contrary, if $i_{s,a}'$ is smaller, it means that the information of historical feedback is unreliable, and the probability of review is higher. If it is decided not to review, then the system can use the new reward $r_{s,a}'$ as reward r_t'. If it decides to query again, then the system firstly needs to combine the historical feedback with the new feedback to form a new feedback set $P_t' \leftarrow P_{s,a} \cup P_t$, $N_t' \leftarrow N_{s,a} \cup N_t$, and secondly calculate $P_t^{ag}(f_{pos}|P_t', N_t'), P_t^{ag}(f_{neg}|P_t', N_t')$ again to make the decision.

5 Experiments

In this paper, we designed two experiments. The first is a trainer feedback aggregation experiment, which is used to verify the performance of the trust model and the decision model. The second is grid-world experiment, which is used to test the performance of the review model and MTIRL. Our hypotheses are as follows:

H1. The BWVE is more accurate in estimating the correct reward in aggregating feedback from multiple trainers with varying trustworthiness than the Bayesian estimation, weighted voting and simple majority voting.

H2. The use of confidence measures calculated by BWVE enables MTIRL to construct policies from trainers that are close to the optimal policy.

In order to verify the reliability of the experimental results, we used Mann-Whitney U test combined with Bonferroni Correction to test the difference between the results of every two methods.

5.1 Trainer Feedback Aggregation

In this experiment, we test Hypotheses 5 to evaluate our BWVE model (Sect. 4.3). We do this through an agent questioning multiple trainers and using their feedback to estimate the feedback that would be received from a truthful advisor. (i.e. the correct reward) They are the Bayesian method (Eqs. 5 and 6), weighted voting method (Eqs. 9 and 10), majority voting method (weighted voting method without trust model,every trainer's trust is 1), BWVE (Eq. 12 and 13).

Trainer Feedback Aggregation Experimental Setting. There are 1000 independent questions with binary answers. Fifty simulated trainers participated in the experiment. An agent needs to answer 1000 questions in sequence, and it will query trainers for help before answering each question. Trainers do not always answer questions after query, whereas each trainer has a 10% probability to give feedback to each question.

Moreover, different trainers have different real trustworthiness. For example, if a trainer's real trustworthiness is 80%, he has 80% probability to give a correct answer. The trainers' real trustworthiness is generated by extended rectified Gaussian distribution with different mean and standard deviation [18]. To simulate the different trust distributions, we designed 6 groups of experiments with different standard deviations of trainers' trustworthiness (0, 0.1, 0.2, 0.3, 0.4, 0.5). The different standard deviations influence the difference between trainers' trust. Each group of experiments generated trainers' trust from a mean of 0.51 to 1 (increase 0.01 each set, a total of 50 sets), respectively.

After the agent has answered 1000 questions, we will count the number of correctly answered questions and calculate the accuracy under different aggregating methods as results. Each set of experiments was run 100 times. Table 1 shows the trainer feedback aggregation experimental setting.

Table 1. In every different method, there are 1000 questions and 50 trainers. 10% trainers give their answer in every question. Every set of experiment runs 100 times. There are 6 groups of experiments with different standard deviations (0, 0.1, 0.2, 0.3, 0.4, 0.5). Each group of experiments generated trainers' trust from a mean of 0.51 to 1.

Description	Value
Total number of questions	1000
Total number of trainers	50
Trustworthiness mean of trainers	From 0.51 to 1
Trustworthiness standard deviations of trainers	0, 0.1, 0.2, 0.3, 0.4, 0.5
Feedback probablity	10%
Experimental times	100

Trainer Feedback Aggregation Experimental Results. Figure 2 shows the six group of results of trainer feedback aggregation experiments.

Firstly, in varying standard deviation and mean of trainers' trustworthiness, BWVE almost has the best accuracy against Bayesian, weighted voting, and majority voting. Only if the trustworthiness of trainers is smaller than 0.75 and all trainers have identical trustworthiness (i.e. Figure 2a, the standard deviation of trainers' trustworthiness is 0), the voting methods is a little better than BWVE. We would argue that 0 standard deviation of trainers' trustworthiness in an MTIRL scenario is unlikely. In 900 pairs of the Mann-Whitney Test about BWVE, there are 487 (more than 50%) pairs $p < 0.0083(0.05/6)$. This supports hypotheses 5.

Secondly, compared to the Bayesian method in 6 sets of results, the error bar of BWVE is smaller than that of the Bayesian method in all the results, so BWVE is more stable than the Bayesian method.

Thirdly, the higher the standard deviation of trainers' trust, the more advantages Bayesian and BWVE methods over voting methods. When the standard deviation is greater than 0.2 (Fig. 2c, d, e, f), The average accuracy of BWVE and Bayesian method is better than the voting method.

Fourthly, the higher the standard deviation of the trainers' trust, the more efficient the trust model. Except for the result of 0 standard deviations (Fig. 2a) where the weighted voting and voting methods perform similarly, the rest show that the weighted voting consistently outperforms the voting method. In most results, the three other methods involving trust models are also preferred over voting methods.

Overall, BWVE considers the voting methods' stability and the Bayesian method's high accuracy to achieve better performance. In the initialization phase, the trust model is not reliable, so the Bayesian method doesn't work. Whereas BWVE can rely on the voting part to initialize trainers' trust, and then it gradually biases the decision weights towards the Bayesian part as the trust uncertainty decreases. So it almost always performs better than voting methods and has more stability than Bayesian methods.

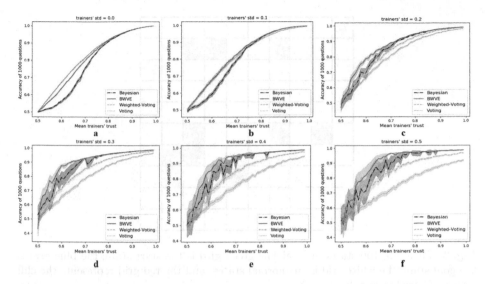

Fig. 2. This results are the answer accuracy as the trust mean increases (under 0 and 0.5 standard deviations of trainers' trust). The X-axis represents the mean of trainers' trust from 0.51 to 1. The Y-axis represents the average answer accuracy of 100 experiments. There are 50 points in every curve. Each point is the mean of 100 experimental results. The part with transparent color is the 95% confidence interval error bar.

5.2 MTIRL

In this experiment, we test Hypotheses 5 to evaluate our review model (Sect. 4.4) by grid-world task. We set up two additional multi-trainer IRL methods to compare with our MTIRL system. The first is MTIRL-no review. It does not use the review model and only provides feedback once for each state-action pair. The previous reward is used for the same state-action pair. The second is MTIRL-unlimited, which is that the agent gets feedback after every taking action.

Gird-World Experimental Setting. The experiment uses 10*10 grid-world as the experimental environment. It is a classic environment for testing the performance of RL algorithms and has been used in many studies [10,13]. Its module consists of 6 kinds of parts: agent, start state, goal state, normal state, and cliff state (Fig. 3). The start state (randomly selected in each episode) is where the agent is at the beginning of each game episode. If the agent reaches the goal state, it passes the game successfully. Normal states can walk freely, and the start state is also a normal state. If the agent reaches the cliff state, it will die.

Table 2 shows the experimental setting. There are five trainers and the trustworthiness of trainers is set the same as that in the trainer feedback aggregation experiment, but their standard deviation of trustworthiness is 0.2. Each set of experiments also needs to be repeated 100 times. The maximum episodes of the

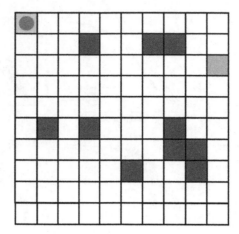

Fig. 3. There are 100 states in total.The green gird is the start state; the blue grid is the goal state; the white grid is the normal states. and the red grid represents the cliff states. (Color figure online)

10*10 cliff grid-world are set to 500. This is because the IRL method completes training in around 150 episodes without noise interference. Taking into account the effect of noise, we scaled up the maximum episodes. Moreover, the agent is easily going into a loop because of the noise, so the agent can perform at most 200 actions in each episode for saving computational power costs. If the agent finds the best solutions, it also stops training and records the results.

In the experiments, we use the state-action-reward-state-action (SARSA) algorithm as the basic algorithm for the experiment [19]. In interactive SARSA, its environmental rewards are replaced by human rewards. A convergent Q-table trained by the SARSA algorithm was used to simulate humans to give reward in the experiments.

Table 2. The max episodes are 500. Max number of actions in every episode is 200. Every experiment runs 100 times. There are 5 trainers.

Description	Value
Max episodes	500
Max action	200
Number of trainers	5
Trustworthiness means of trainers	From 0.51 to 1
Trustworthiness standard deviations of trainers	0.2
Feedback probablity	100%
Experimental times	100

MTIRL Girdworld Performance Results. Firstly, the policy trained by the MTIRL with the review model is closer to the optimal policy than that without a review model. At a mean of trainers' trustworthiness from 0.55 to 0.9, MTIRL with the review model has better performance than MTIRL-unlimit and MTIRL-no review methods. Three MTIRL methods have similar performance when the mean is less than 0.55 and greater than 0.9. In 100 Mann-Whitney hypotheses test results between MTIRL and the others without review model, 38 has $p < 0.0166(0.05/3)$, so it supports Hypotheses 5. Although the MTIRL-unlimit method can provide infinite feedback, indiscriminate feedback may revise the correct feedback into a wrong one. So that its feedback maintains a fixed accuracy rate, its performance is not prominent. This also shows that the review feedback without some evidence is not working to improve the efficiency of agent learning.

Secondly, the review model uses a small amount of feedback to improve the learning ability of the agent. In Fig. 5a, MTIRL-unlimit has the most feedback times and is around ten times more than the other two methods. MTIRL and MTIRL-no review have relatively low feedback costs, and MTIRL is slightly higher than MTIRL - no review. As can be seen from the figure, the amount of feedback from MTIRL decreases as the mean trainers' trust increases. When the trainers' trust is relatively low, the confidence value is very low, making the probability of review very large.

Thirdly, the review model reduces the risk of trapping the agent in a loop. Figure 5b shows the average number of training steps of three different MTIRL

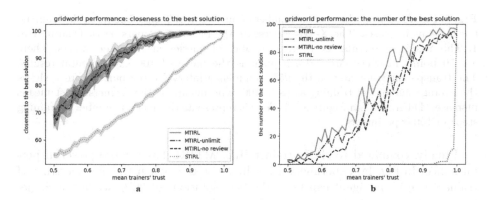

Fig. 4. The figure a shows the closeness to the best solution as the trainers' trust means increases. The X-axis represents the mean of trainers' trust from 0.51 to 1. The Y-axis represents the average closeness to the best solution at the end of training in 100 experiments. There are 50 points in every curve. Each point is the mean of 100 experimental results. The part with transparent color is the 95% confidence interval error bar. Figure b shows the number of the best solution in 100 experiments, as the trainers' trust means increases. The X-axis represents the mean of trainers' trust from 0.51 to 1. The Y-axis represents the number of the best solution in 100 experiments. There are 50 points in every curve.

methods in 100 experiments under different trust means. MTIRL-no review uses the most steps. When the mean is less than 0.8, the average training steps of MTIRL-no review are almost twice that of MTIRL. This means that if we only trust the first feedback result of each state-action pair, then the agent easily falls into a loop because of the wrong feedback. The MTIRL-unlimit method uses the fewest steps but requires a huge human cost. This is because, if the previous answer puts the agent in the loop, then the infinite queries have a big chance to change their answer, which can make the agent break out of the loop. Moreover, for MTIRL, because of the review model, there is also a chance that it will ask the trainers again, thus changing the wrong answer and getting the agent out of the loop.

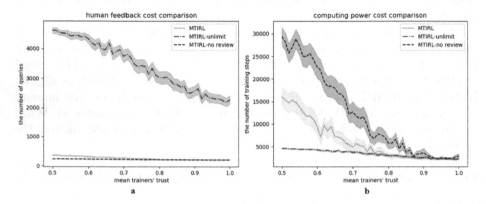

Fig. 5. Figure a shows the average number of queries in 100 experiments as the trainers' trust means increases. The X-axis represents the mean of trainers' trust from 0.51 to 1. The Y-axis represents the average number of queries in 100 experiments. There are 50 points in every curve. Each point is the mean of 100 experimental results. The transparent color area is the 95% confidence interval error bar. Figure b shows the average number of training steps in 100 experiments as the trainers' trust means increases. Different from Figure a, The Y-axis represents the average number of training steps in 100 experiments.

Finally, compared to single trainer IRL, MTIRL has a more powerful performance. In Fig. 4a, experimental results show that when the average trust of trainers is 0.7, the agent can learn the best solutions of 90%, while the single-trainer IRL can only learn around 70%. Before the mean trainer's trust was 95%, it was almost difficult for the single-trainer IRL method to learn all the best solutions, but MTIRL can learn the best solutions many times.

6 Conclusion

In this paper, we proposed MTIRL, which is the first IRL system that can combine advice from multiple trainers. It can aggregate a set of feedback from non-perfect trainers into a more reliable reward for RL agent training in a reward-sparse environment. We use a question-answer experiment to support the Hypotheses 5, that is, the BWVE is more accurate in estimating the correct reward in aggregating feedback from multiple trainers with varying trustworthiness than the Bayesian estimation, weighted voting, and simple majority voting. We also use the grid-world experiment to test Hypotheses 5. The results show that the policy trained by the MTIRL with the review model is closer to the optimal policy than that without a review model.

In future work, we will work on the optimization of two parts. First, we will consider the limit on the number of feedback trainers can give, that is, the system needs to maximize the value of each feedback, leveraging human feedback on more critical states. Second, the cost of each query needs to be considered, which means that the system should balance the cost and value to maximize the utility.

References

1. Bignold, A., Cruz, F., Dazeley, R., Vamplew, P., Foale, C.: Persistent rule-based interactive reinforcement learning. Neural Comput. Appl. 1–18 (2021)
2. Burnett, C., Norman, T.J., Sycara, K.: Bootstrapping trust evaluations through stereotypes. In: Proceedings of the 9th International Conference on Autonomous Agents and Multiagent Systems (AAMAS 2010), pp. 241–248. International Foundation for Autonomous Agents and Multiagent Systems (2010)
3. Cao, X., Fang, M., Liu, J., Gong, N.Z.: Fltrust: byzantine-robust federated learning via trust bootstrapping. In: ISOC Network and Distributed System Security Symposium (NDSS), (2021)
4. Cheng, M., Yin, C., Zhang, J., Nazarian, S., Deshmukh, J., Bogdan, P.: A general trust framework for multi-agent systems. In: Proceedings of the 20th International Conference on Autonomous Agents and MultiAgent Systems, pp. 332–340 (2021)
5. Cui, Y., Zhang, Q., Allievi, A., Stone, P., Niekum, S., Knox, W.: The empathic framework for task learning from implicit human feedback. In: Conference on Robot Learning (2020)
6. Fan, X., Liu, L., Zhang, R., Jing, Q., Bi, J.: Decentralized trust management: risk analysis and trust aggregation. ACM Comput. Surv. (CSUR) **53**(1), 1–33 (2020)
7. Goel, N., Faltings, B.: Personalized peer truth serum for eliciting multi-attribute personal data. In: Uncertainty in Artificial Intelligence, pp. 18–27. PMLR (2020)
8. Güneş, T.D., Norman, T.J., Tran-Thanh, L.: Budget limited trust-aware decision making. In: International Conference on Autonomous Agents and Multiagent Systems, pp. 101–110. Springer (2017). https://doi.org/10.1007/978-3-319-71679-4_7
9. Jøsang, A.: Subjective logic, vol. 3. Springer (2016). https://doi.org/10.1007/978-3-319-42337-1
10. Kazantzidis, I., Norman, T., Du, Y., Freeman, C.: How to train your agent: active learning from human preferences and justifications in safety-critical environments. In: International Conference on Autonomous Agents and Multiagent Systems (2022)
11. Knox, W.B., Stone, P.: Tamer: training an agent manually via evaluative reinforcement. In: 2008 7th IEEE international conference on development and learning, pp. 292–297. IEEE (2008)

12. Knox, W.B., Stone, P.: Combining manual feedback with subsequent mdp reward signals for reinforcement learning. In: Proceedings of the 9th International Conference on Autonomous Agents and Multiagent Systems, vol. 1, pp. 5–12. Citeseer (2010)
13. Knox, W.B., Stone, P.: Framing reinforcement learning from human reward: reward positivity, temporal discounting, episodicity, and performance. Artif. Intell. **225**, 24–50 (2015)
14. Kurenkov, A., Mandlekar, A., Martin-Martin, R., Savarese, S., Garg, A.: Ac-teach: a bayesian actor-critic method for policy learning with an ensemble of suboptimal teachers. In: Conference on Robot Learning, pp. 717–734. PMLR (2020)
15. Li, S., Zhang, C.: An optimal online method of selecting source policies for reinforcement learning. In: Proceedings of the AAAI Conference on Artificial Intelligence, vol. 32 (2018)
16. Ma, C., Li, J., Ding, M., Wei, K., Chen, W., Poor, H.V.: Federated learning with unreliable clients: performance analysis and mechanism design. IEEE Internet Things J. **8**(24), 17308–17319 (2021)
17. MacGlashan, J., et al.: Interactive learning from policy-dependent human feedback. In: International Conference on Machine Learning, pp. 2285–2294. PMLR (2017)
18. Palmer, A.W., Hill, A.J., Scheding, S.J.: Methods for stochastic collection and replenishment (scar) optimisation for persistent autonomy. Robot. Auton. Syst. **87**, 51–65 (2017)
19. Rummery, G.A., Niranjan, M.: On-line Q-learning using connectionist systems, vol. 37. University of Cambridge, Department of Engineering Cambridge, UK (1994)
20. Tittaferrante, A., Yassine, A.: Multi-advisor reinforcement learning for multi-agent multi-objective smart home energy control. IEEE Trans. Artif. Intell. **3**(4), 581–594 (2021)
21. Zhan, Y., Ammar, H.B., Taylor, M.E.: Theoretically-grounded policy advice from multiple teachers in reinforcement learning settings with applications to negative transfer. In: Proceedings of the Twenty Fifth International Joint Conference on Artificial Intelligence (2016)
22. Zhong, X., Xu, X., Pan, B.: A non-threshold consensus model based on the minimum cost and maximum consensus-increasing for multi-attribute large group decision-making. Inf. Fusion **77**, 90–106 (2022)

Action Languages Based Actual Causality in Decision Making Contexts

Camilo Sarmiento[1]([⊠]) [iD], Gauvain Bourgne[1] [iD], Katsumi Inoue[2] [iD], and Jean-Gabriel Ganascia[1] [iD]

[1] Sorbonne Université, CNRS, LIP6, 75005 Paris, France
{camilo.sarmiento,gauvain.bourgne,jean-gabriel.ganascia}@lip6.fr
[2] National Institute of Informatics, Tokyo, Japan
inoue@nii.ac.jp

Abstract. Rationally understanding the evolution of the physical world is inherently linked with the idea of causality. It follows that agents based on automated planning have inevitably to deal with causality, especially when considering imputability. However, the many debates around causation in the last decades have shown how complex this notion is and thus, how difficult it is to integrate it with planning. This paper's contribution is to link up two research topics—automated planning and causality—by proposing an actual causation definition suitable for action languages. This definition is a formalisation of Wright's NESS test of causation.

Keywords: Causality · Actual causality · Regularity theories of causation · Action languages

1 Introduction

Because of its essential role in human reasoning—both in trivial and in complex situations—numerous works in a variety of disciplines have tried—unsuccessfully—to propose a widely agreed upon theory of causation. The purpose of this article is not to enter into the debates that animate the community, but to propose a definition of causality that can be used by agents to enrich their knowledge of the world evolution and thus make better decisions. Since we are in an operational framework given that our focus is on decision making, we can make a couple of assumptions while remaining relevant. Therefore, we place ourselves in a classical planning framework which assumes problems are discrete and deterministic. Unlike *type causality* which seeks to determine general causal relationships, *actual causality* fits our purpose because it is concerned with particular events [18]. Limiting ourselves to a simplified framework and to actual causality does not make causality trivial, many issues remain.

Recent works [4,8,21,24] have attempted to link action languages and causation. However, each work has its own limitations. Thus, our work is a logical continuation of those mentioned above and our aim is to address the main remaining limitations: (i) a definition of actual causality conflating causality and responsibility, and (ii) a framework leaving aside the cases of overdetermination—subject of many crucial debates in the field of causality—by their inability to deal with concurrency of events. Overdetermined causation was defined by Wright [36] as:

> cases in which a factor other than the specified act would have been sufficient to produce the injury in the absence of the specified act, but its effects either (1) were preempted by the more immediately operative effects of the specified act or (2) combined with or duplicated those of the specified act to jointly produce the injury.

We deal with the first problem by imposing ourselves the constraints of factuality and independence of policy choices defended by Wright [36]. Regarding the second issue, the solution lies in the essential choice of the formalism encoding causal knowledge. The advanced state of maturity of PDDL [15,20], its vocation to facilitate interchangeability, and its use by a large community, are all meaningful arguments in favour of this formalism. However, the semantics of its ADL [33] fragment does not allow concurrency of events. To have a semantics that takes into account the concurrency it is necessary to jump directly to PDDL+ [12] whose semantics is adapted to durative actions, thus inconsistent with our discrete time assumption. We therefore base our approach on an action language whose semantics is an intermediate point between the ADL fragment of PDDL and PDDL+.

This paper is structured as follows. Section 2 discusses what is the appropriate approach to causation for our causal inquiry. In this section we explore two main highly influential theories of causation: *regularity* and *counterfactual*. Section 3 introduces the action language semantics—in which we encode causal knowledge—allowing concurrency of events. Section 4 offers a description of our actual causality definition proposal that we compare to Batusov and Soutchanski's approach [4]—the one we consider to be the most convincing so far. Finally, we conclude and give some perspectives in Sect. 5.

2   Adapted Causal Inquiry

Of the many fields studying causality, our approach is especially close to *tort law* whose interest is about causation in specific situations. Hence, works in this field are a good source of inspiration. In a series of influential papers [36,37], Wright demonstrates how essential a causal inquiry is in the process of determining *tort liability*. He emphasises the fundamental difference between causation and responsibility—or in the words of Vincent's taxonomy [35], between 'causal responsibility' and 'outcome responsibility'.

Wright argues that a satisfying tort liability analysis—which goal is to determine if a defendant is the 'responsible cause' of an injury—requires a factual and independent of policy choices causal inquiry. In his papers Wright criticises the processes to determine responsibility for an injury in which the causal inquiry is flawed and polluted with subjective aspects—a process where causality and responsibility are conflated. Wright's initial observation is that those two notions are too often conflated. The fact that 'the phrase *"the cause"* is simply an elliptical way of saying *"the responsible cause"'* [36] shows how thin the boundary between those notions is. To clarify this conflation, he describes the process to determine if an individual is legally responsible for an injury. This process has three stages: (i) *tortious-conduct inquiry*, where are identified the defendant's conducts that could potentially imply legal responsibility (intentional, negligent, hazardous, ...); (ii) *causal inquiry*, where is evaluated if the identified tortious conducts really contributed to cause the harm, i.e. if they can be considered as causes of the injury; (iii) *proximate-cause inquiry*, where other causes of the injury are considered, so as to evaluate if they mitigate or eliminate the defendant's legal responsibility for the injury. Of those three stages, only the second is entirely factual and independent of policy choices. It determines if a conduct was a cause of the injury. The two others are subject to policy considerations that 'determine which causes and consequences will give rise to liability' [36]. Not to yield into the easy confusion between responsibility and causality, our goal is to propose a definition of actual causality suitable for a causal inquiry as presented by Wright, i.e. factual and independent of policy choices.

The actual causation definitions based solely on strong necessity—also known as counterfactual dependence—fail to capture the commonly accepted intuition on overdetermination cases (early preemption, late preemption, and symmetric overdetermination) [17,28]. The commonly used in law *But-for test* is one of those unsuccessful definitions. This test states that 'an act was a cause of an injury if and only if, but for the act, the injury would not have occurred' [36]. 'In the context of structural equations, this flawed account can be described as equating causation with counterfactual dependence' [6]. Given that overdetermination cases are not just hypothetical and rare cases (cases of pollution, suicide, economic loss, ...), those strong necessity based approaches are not suitable for our purposes.

The dominant approach of actual causality—HP definition [18]—deals with those cases, but at the cost of the factualness of the causal inquiry. This definition has the same roots than the But-for test, Hume's definition of causation second formulation [22]:

> we may define a cause to be an object followed by another, and where all objects, similar to the first, are followed by objects similar to the second. Or, in other words, where if the first object had not been, the second had never existed.

It is the result of an iterative process that originates in Pearl's formalisation of Lewis' vision [25] in structural equations framework (SEF) [32]. HP approach is more complete than the But-for test in the sense that other elements in addition to counterfactual dependence where included in order to deal with some complex cases. One of those elements is interventionism. This assumption states that an event C causes a second event E if and only if, both events occur, and that, given an intervention allowing to fix the occurrence of a certain set of other events in the context—without being constrained to respect the physical coherence of the world—there is a context where if the first event had not occurred, the second would not have occurred either. This assumption is described by Beckers [6] using SEF notation as:

Interventionism They all share the assumption [HP-style definitions] that the relation between counterfactual dependence and causation takes on the following form: $C = c$ causes $E = e$ iff $E = e$ is counterfactually dependent on $C = c$ given an intervention $X \leftarrow x$ that satisfies some conditions P. The divergence between these definitions is to be found in the condition P that should be satisfied.

Interventionism—that Beckers' CNESS [6] and Beckers and Vennekens' BV [7] definitions reject—introduces non factual elements to the causal inquiry which appear problematic even for the author [19]:

if I fix BH [Billy hits] to zero here, I am sort of violating the way the world works. [...] I am contemplating counterfactuals are inconsistent with the equations but I seem to need to do that in order to get things to work out right. Believe me, we tried many other definitions.

In addition to non factual elements, the divergence on which 'conditions P' to apply can be equated with policy choices. These elements make HP-style definitions non adequate for our context.

STIT approaches are also part of this family where strong necessity is central. Usual STIT approaches focus on the relationship between the agent and the states of the world. In order to be closer to the philosophical tradition according to which the actual causal relationship is defined between two events, we find action languages ideal because the events are central elements. Because of their modal approach, STIT works such as [1,26] easily involve epistemic aspects—outside of the scope of this paper—fundamental when one wishes to go beyond causality by looking at responsibility.

The NESS test which subordinates necessity to sufficiency is an approach that deals with overdetermination cases [5,36–38] and that satisfies our inquiry needs. Introduced by Wright in response to But-for test flaws, this test states that [36,37]:

A particular condition was a cause of a specific consequence if and only if it was a necessary element of a set of antecedent actual conditions that was sufficient for the occurrence of the consequence.

Unlike approaches mentioned above, it belongs to a second high impact approach family, regularity theories of causation [2]. Those theories are also based on Hume's definition of causation, but on the first formulation. Specifically, the NESS test is closer to Mill's interpretation of this formulation which introduced that there are potentially a multiplicity of distinct, but equally sufficient sets of conditions [30]. The NESS test is even closer to Mackie's proposal. Indeed, unlike Mill's vision whereby the cause is the sufficient set, Mackie considers that each element of the set is a cause [27].

The actual causation definition we propose is an action languages suitable formalisation of Wright's NESS test. Even if accepted by influential counterfactual theories of causation authors as embodying our basic intuition of causation—such as Pearl [6]—criticism of the use of logic as formalism has prevented the popularisation of this test. What is argued is the inadequacy of logical sufficiency and logical necessity to formalise these intuitions. Recent works have shown that rejecting the formalism is not a reason to reject the idea behind it by successfully formalising the NESS test in causal calculus [9] and in the structural equations framework [6]. It is conceivable to work on a way of compiling existing action languages problems and translating them into SEF. However, works have shown SEF flaws [10] and that in complex evolving contexts [4,21] like ours, this translating approach is not necessarily desirable [21]:

> Structural causal models are excellent tools for many types of causality-related questions. Nevertheless, their limited expressivity render them less than ideal for some of the more delicate causal queries, like actual causation. These queries require a language that is suited for dealing with complex, dynamically changing situations.

Our contribution is to link automated planning and causality by continuing this momentum proposing an action languages suitable formalisation of Wright's NESS test.

3   Action Language Semantics

The whole purpose of an action language is to determine the evolution of the world given a set of actions corresponding to deliberate choices of the agent. Those actions might trigger some chain reaction through external events. As a result, we need to keep track of both: the state of the world and the occurrence of events—the term 'event' connoting 'the possibility of agentless actions' [34, chap 12]. This task is the simplest kind of temporal reasoning—temporal projection. Different action languages allowing temporal projection have been proposed such as PDDL [15,20] and action description languages $\mathcal{A}$, $\mathcal{B}$, and $\mathcal{C}$ [14]. However, the semantics of $\mathcal{A}$ [13], $\mathcal{B}$, and PDDL deterministic fragment—corresponding to ADL [33]—do not allow concurrency of events. To have a semantics that takes into account concurrency it is necessary to jump directly to $\mathcal{C}$ [16] or PDDL+ [12] which semantics is adapted respectively to non deterministic actions or durative actions, thus inconsistent with either our deterministic actions assumption or our discrete time assumption. The advanced state of maturity of PDDL [15,20], its vocation to facilitate interchangeability, and its use by a large community, are all meaningful arguments in favour of this formalism—gradually extended by different fragments. We therefore base our approach on an action language whose semantics is an intermediate point between the deterministic fragment of PDDL and PDDL+. This formalism works on a decomposition of the world into two sets: $\mathbb{F}$ corresponding to variables describing the state of the world, more precisely ground fluents representing time-varying properties; $\mathbb{E}$ representing variables describing transitions, more precisely ground events that modify fluents.

A fluent literal is either a fluent $f \in \mathbb{F}$, or its negation $\neg f$. We denote by $Lit_{\mathbb{F}}$ the set of fluent literals in $\mathbb{F}$, where $Lit_{\mathbb{F}} = \mathbb{F} \cup \{\neg f | f \in \mathbb{F}\}$. The complement of a fluent literal l is defined as $\bar{l} = \neg f$ if $l = f$ or $\bar{l} = f$ if $l = \neg f$. By extension, for a set $L \subseteq Lit_{\mathbb{F}}$, we have $\bar{L} = \{\bar{l}, l \in L\}$.

Definition 1 (state S). The set $L \subseteq Lit_{\mathbb{F}}$ is a state iff it is:

- Coherent: $\forall l \in L, \bar{l} \notin L$.
- Complete: $|L| = |\mathbb{F}|$, i.e. $\forall f \in \mathbb{F}, f \in L$ or $\neg f \in L$.

A complete and coherent set of fluent literals thus determines the value of each of the fluents. An incoherent set cannot describe a reality. However, in the absence of information or for the sake of simplification, we can describe a problem through a coherent but incomplete set. We will call such a set a partial state. We model time linearly and in a discretised way to associate a state S_t to each time point t of a set $\mathbb{T} = \{-1, 0, \ldots, N\}$. Having a bounded past formalisation of a real problem, we gather all states before $t = 0$—time point to which corresponds the state S_0 that we call initial state—in an empty state $S_{-1} = \varnothing$.

We place ourselves in a framework of concurrency where E_t is the set of all events which occur at a time point t. Therefore, E_t is what generates the transition between the states S_t and S_{t+1}. Thus, the states follow one another as events occur, simulating the evolution of the world. E_{-1} is the set that gathers all events which took place before $t = 0$, such that $E_{-1} = \{ini_l, l \in S_0\}$. Events are characterised by two elements: preconditions give the conditions that must be satisfied by the state in order for them to take place; effects indicate the changes to the fluents that are expected to happen if they occur. The preconditions and effects are respectively represented as formulas of the language $\mathcal{P}$ and $\mathcal{E}$ defined as follows:

$$\mathcal{P} ::= l | \psi_1 \wedge \psi_2 | \psi_1 \vee \psi_2 \qquad \mathcal{E} ::= [\psi]l | \varphi_1 \wedge \varphi_2$$

where $l \in Lit_{\mathbb{F}}$, $[\psi]l$ is the notation for the conditional effect indicating that l is an effect if the condition ψ is satisfied—$[\top]l$ is just written l—and the logical connectives $\wedge, \vee$ have standard first-order semantics. We can then deduce that if $\varphi \in \mathcal{E}$, $\varphi = \bigwedge_{i \in 1, \ldots, m} [\psi_i]l_i$. For the sake of brevity, we adopt a set notation for $\varphi \in \mathcal{E}$ which we will use where relevant, such that $\varphi = \{[\psi_i]l_i, i \in 1, \ldots, m\}$. We denote pre and eff the functions which respectively associate preconditions and effects with each event: $pre : \mathbb{E} \mapsto \mathcal{P}$, $eff : \mathbb{E} \mapsto \mathcal{E}$. Given the expression of E_{-1}, the application of eff to each element of the set is $eff(ini_l) = l$ with $l \in S_0$, thus $eff(E_{-1}) = S_0$. Moreover, given a formula $\psi \in \mathcal{P}$ and a partial state L, $L \vDash \psi$ is defined classically: $L \vDash l$ if $l \in L$, $L \vDash \psi_1 \wedge \psi_2$ if $L \vDash \psi_1$ and $L \vDash \psi_2$, and $L \vDash \psi_1 \vee \psi_2$ if $L \vDash \psi_1$ or $L \vDash \psi_2$.

Our work is a logical continuation of works such as [4,8,21,24], who attempted to link action languages and causation. To the best of our knowledge, [4,8] are the first to give a definition of actual cause in action languages.

However, each work has its own limitations that we try to address. In Batusov and Soutchanski's paper, many working perspectives are mentioned [4]:

> It is clear that a broader definition of actual cause requires more expressive action theories that can model not only sequences of actions, but can also include explicit time and concurrent actions. Only after that one can try to analyze some of the popular examples of actual causation formulated in philosophical literature. Some of those examples sound deceptively simple, but faithful modelling of them requires time, concurrency and natural actions.

At the moment, the proposed action language tackles both concurrency and time—at least discrete time. We will now introduce 'natural actions' that we denote exogenous events. These events are what distinguish our proposal from $\mathcal{A}_c$ [3]—the allowing concurrency version of $\mathcal{A}$. The set $\mathbb{E}$ is divided into two subsets: $\mathbb{A}$, which contains the actions carried out by an agent and thus subjected to a volition; $\mathbb{U}$, which contains the exogenous events—equivalent to :event in PDDL+ [12] and triggered axioms in Event Calculus [31]—which are triggered as soon as all the *pre* are fulfilled, therefore without the need for an agent to perform them. Thus, for exogenous events triggering conditions and preconditions are the same. In contrast, the triggering conditions for actions necessarily include preconditions but those are not sufficient. The triggering conditions of an action also include the volition of the agent or some kind of manipulation by another agent. To keep track of these subtleties that could be relevant in the causal inquiry we introduce triggering conditions represented as formulas of the language $\mathcal{P}$. We denote *tri* the function which associates triggering conditions with each event: $tri : \mathbb{E} \mapsto \mathcal{P}$.

The occurrence of events $(e, t) \in \mathbb{E} \times \mathbb{T}$ and $(e', t) \in \mathbb{E} \times \mathbb{T}$ in the state S_t is said to be interfering if the set $\{l, \exists \psi \in \mathcal{P}, S_t \models \psi, [\psi]l \in eff(e) \cup eff(e')\}$ is not coherent according to Definition 1.

Definition 2 (context κ). Given an initial state S_0, the context denoted as κ is the octuple $(\mathbb{E}, \mathbb{F}, pre, tri, eff, S_0, >, \mathbb{T})$, where $>$ is a partial order which represents priorities that ensure the primacy of one event over another when both are interfering.

As mentioned earlier, effects indicate the changes to the fluents that are expected to happen if an event occurs. Because of the complexity of reality, it may turn out that causally the action has more or less effects than those attributed by $\mathcal{E}$. Let's take the example of an agent who wants to turn on a light by pressing a switch. In a first scenario, it is possible that the agent's action causes an overheating in the electrical circuit and triggers a fire. When formalising the action of switching on the light, besides that it is not intuitive to take into account the overheating and then the fire as intrinsic effects, it affects the generality of the formalisation. In these cases, we will prefer to break down the process by introducing exogenous events. In the above fire example, we will therefore have an exogenous event corresponding to a fire outbreak—an agentless event—which will be triggered when a defective circuit is present and the switch is pressed. We are therefore in the presence of a causal chain. These cases where the action has more effects than those with which it has been formalised are typical cases where causality is necessary. In a second scenario, it may happen that the agent performs the action but the expected effects are not produced simply because the light was already on. This does not prevent the action from having been performed, and we want to keep a trace of the event without having to consider that its effect has taken place. This is especially the case if the action has several effects and only one of them does not actually occur. This second case can be resumed as cases where some of the fluents of the state have already the value attributed by an effect. Since the effects that an event had at the time it occurred is a basic causal information on which we will rely—inextricably linked to imputability—it is important to keep track of them.

Definition 3 (actual effects $actualEff(E, L)$). Given a context κ, the predicate $actualEff(E, L)$ which associates a set of events $E \in \mathbb{E}$ given a partial state L, to a partial state representing the actual effects of E when L is true, is defined as:

$$actualEff(E, L) = \bigcup_{e \in E} actualEff(\{e\}, L)$$
$$= \{l_i, \exists e \in E, [\psi_i]l_i \in eff(e), \ L \models \psi_i, \text{ and } l_i \notin L\}$$

For the sake of conciseness we adopt an update operator giving the resulting state when performing an event at a given state.

Definition 4 (update operator $\triangleright$). Given a context κ and set of events $E \in \mathbb{E}$, the update operator which we use as follows $S_t \triangleright E$ expresses $S_t \setminus \overline{actualEff(E, S_t)} \cup actualEff(E, S_t)$.

The information given by $actualEff(E, L)$ and $\triangleright$ can be equated to basic causal information given by the evolution of the world. Besides being causal, this information is directional since it is inconceivable in our semantics to say that the actual effect of the event is the cause of it. Therefore, we can rely on the events that occur and their actual effects to simulate the evolution of the world from the initial state S_0.

Definition 5 (induced state sequence $\mathcal{S}_\kappa$). Given a context κ and a sequence of events $\epsilon = E_{-1}, E_0, \ldots, E_n$, such that $n \leq |\mathbb{T}|$, the induced state sequence of ϵ is a sequence of complete states: $\mathcal{S}_\kappa(\epsilon) = S_0, S_1, \ldots, S_{n+1}$ such that $\forall t \in \{-1, \ldots, n\}$, $S_{t+1} = S_t \triangleright E_t$.

Though this can be defined for every ϵ, not all ϵ are possible given (i) the need to satisfy preconditions, (ii) the concurrency of events that must respect priorities, and (iii) the triggering of events that must respect priorities too.

Definition 6. Let ϵ be a sequence of events $\epsilon = E_{-1}, E_0, \ldots, E_n$, such that $n \leq |\mathbb{T}|$, and let's denote by $\mathcal{S}_\kappa(\epsilon) = S_0, S_1, \ldots, S_{n+1}$ its induced state sequence. We shall say that ϵ is:

- Executable in κ: if $\forall t \in \{0, \dots, n\}$, $S_t \models pre(E_t)$.
- Concurrent correct with respect to κ: $\neg \exists (e, e') \in E_t^2$, $e > e'$.
- Trigger correct with respect to κ: if $\forall t \in \{0, \dots, n\}$, $\forall e' \in \mathbb{E}$ such that $S_t \models tri(e')$, then $e' \in E_t$ or $\exists e \in E_t$, $e > e'$.
- Valid in κ: if and only if, executable in κ, concurrent correct with respect to κ, and trigger correct with respect to κ.

Finally, if we consider only a set of timed actions as an input which we call scenario, we have:

Definition 7 (traces $\tau_{\sigma,\kappa}^e$ and $\tau_{\sigma,\kappa}^s$). Given a scenario $\sigma \subseteq \mathbb{A} \times \mathbb{T}$ and a context κ, the event trace $\tau_{\sigma,\kappa}^e$ of σ, κ is the sequence of events $\epsilon = E_{-1}, E_0, \dots, E_n$ valid in κ, such that: $\forall t \in \{0, \dots, n\}, \forall e \in E_t$, $e \in \mathbb{A} \Leftrightarrow (e, t) \in \sigma$. Its induced state sequence is the state trace $\tau_{\sigma,\kappa}^s$.

We now have a tool for temporal projection. Since in future work we plan to evaluate the ethical permissibility of actions in a given scenario, this is sufficient. However, given the flexibility of answer set programming in which we have translated our action language, we could move at low cost to a planning tool managing concurrency of events and exogenous events—the latter allowing to handle dynamic environments. For more complex contexts involving multiple agents, this action language only gives a partial solution. Indeed, the actions of other agents can be represented as exogenous events. However, this solution does not capture the full complexity of multiagent contexts. In future work we plan to study this issue, in particular by formalising a causal relationship specific to these contexts, 'enables' [8,11].

4 Actual Causality

In the context of action languages, we consider that a first event is an actual cause of a second event if and only if the occurrence of the first is a NESS-cause of the triggering of the second. As commonly accepted by philosophers, the relation of causality we aim to define links two events. However, 'events are not the only things that can cause or be caused' [25]. Action languages represent the evolution of the world as a succession of states produced by the occurrence of events, thus introducing states between events. Therefore, we need to define causal relations where causes are occurrence of events and effects are formulas of the language $\mathcal{P}$ truthfulness. This section will introduce definitions which establish such a relation based on Wright's NESS test of causation.

Definition 8 (causal setting χ). The action language causal setting denoted χ is the couple (σ, κ) with σ a scenario and κ a context.

From now on, when reference is made to events and states, they will be those from $\tau_{\sigma,\kappa}^e$ and $\tau_{\sigma,\kappa}^s$ respectively. Thus, the set of all events which actually occurred at time point t is $E^\chi(t) = \tau_{\sigma,\kappa}^e(t)$. Following the same reasoning, the actual state at time point t is $S^\chi(t) = \tau_{\sigma,\kappa}^s(t)$. For the sake of brevity, when a set of occurrences of events $C = \{(e,t),\ e \in E^\chi(t),\ t \in \mathbb{T}\}$ will be used in the context of the update operator $\triangleright$ or the predicate $actualEff(E,L)$, it will actually only refer to the events of the couples in this set.

Definition 9 (Direct NESS-causes). Given a causal setting χ, the occurrence of events set $C = \{(e,t),\ e \in E^\chi(t),\ t \in \mathbb{T}\}$ is a sufficient set of direct NESS-causes of the truthfulness of the formula ψ at t_ψ, denoted $C \underset{W}{\rightsquigarrow} (\psi, t_\psi)$, iff there exists a partial state $W \subseteq Lit_\mathbb{F}$ that we call backing such that:

- Causal sufficiency and minimality of W: $W \vDash \psi$ and $\forall W' \subset W,\ W' \nvDash \psi$.
  There is a decreasing sequence $t_1, \ldots, t_k$ and a partition $W_1, \ldots, W_k$ of W such that $\forall i \in \{1, \ldots, k\}$, given $C(t_i) = C \cap E^\chi(t_i)$:
    - Weak necessity and minimality of C at t_i: $S^\chi(t_i) \triangleright C(t_i) \vDash W_i$ and $\forall C' \subset C(t_i),\ S^\chi(t_i) \triangleright C' \nvDash W_i$.
    - Persistency of necessity: $\forall t,\ t_i < t \leq t_\psi,\ S^\chi(t) \vDash W_i$.
- Minimality of C: $C = \bigcup_{i \in \{1, \ldots, k\}} C(t_i)$.

(e,t) is a direct NESS-cause of (ψ, t_ψ) iff $\exists C \subseteq \mathbb{E} \times \mathbb{T}$ such that $(e,t) \in C$, and $C \underset{W}{\rightsquigarrow} (\psi, t_\psi)$.

Wright's NESS test is based on three main principles which are formalised in Definition 9: (i) sufficiency of a set, (ii) weak necessity of the conditions in that set, and (iii) actuality of the conditions. (i) In this definition, the sufficient set is the partial state W. More precisely, given the directionality embedded in Sect. 3 semantics, we have causal sufficiency that Wright differentiates from logical sufficiency [38]: 'The successional nature of causation is incorporated in the concept of causal sufficiency, which is defined as the complete instantiation of all the conditions in the antecedent of the relevant causal law'. Moreover, Definition 9 introduces the constraint of necessity and sufficiency minimality which has been proven to be essential for regularity theories of causation [2,5,38]. The minimality of C condition ensures that weak necessity and minimality of C at t_i is applied to all elements in the set. In other words, it excludes the possibility to have in C an occurrence of event that has not occurred in one of the time points of the decreasing sequence $t_1, \ldots, t_k$. (ii) Definition 9 formalises weak necessity by subordinating necessity to sufficiency achieving that [38]: 'a causally relevant factor need merely be necessary for the sufficiency of a set of conditions sufficient for the occurrence of the consequence, rather than being necessary for the consequence itself'. It is worth mentioning that the condition $S^\chi(t_i) \nvDash W_i$—intuitively expected when referring to necessity—is included in the minimality condition by the case where $C' = \varnothing$, thus $S^\chi(t_i) = S^\chi(t_i) \triangleright \varnothing \nvDash W_i$. (iii) The actuality of the conditions is assured by the use of actual occurrence of events, which is implied by the presence of $E^\chi(t_i)$ in $C(t_i) = C \cap E^\chi(t_i)$.

Once causal sufficiency and minimality of the partial state W is defined, the causal inquiry is conducted by a recursive reasoning on a partition of W. The goal of this recursive reasoning is to identify the events which occurrence was necessary to the sufficiency of W. This reasoning is done by going back in time and analysing the information given by $\tau^s_{\sigma,\kappa}(t)$ and $\tau^e_{\sigma,\kappa}(t)$. Two limit cases can be identified. The first is when the partition set W_k is empty before its corresponding time t_k is equivalent to $t = 0$, meaning that all occurrences of events necessary for the sufficiency of W have been identified. When this is not the case, it means that there are fluent literals in W that were true in the initial state $S^\chi(0)$ and which value has not changed until $S^\chi(t_\psi)$. In this second case, the set C will contain the events $ini_l \in E^\chi(-1)$ whose l remains in W_k—events which symbolise events in the past beyond the framework of formalisation.

In practice, it is possible to study what will be considered as the direct NESS-causes of the truthfulness of ψ at t_ψ for each form that ψ may take. In the case where ψ is a fluent literal l, the direct NESS-causes will be the last occurrences of events to have made l true before or at t_ψ. In this basic case W is the singleton which unique element is that literal. This basic causal information is the one embedded in Sect. 3 action language semantics. In the case where ψ is a conjunction $\psi = l_1 \wedge \cdots \wedge l_m$ of fluent literals, the direct NESS-causes will be all the occurrence of events that are direct NESS-causes of the truthfulness of one of the literals l_i in the conjunction at t_ψ. Finally, the case where ψ is a disjunction of fluent literals, and more generally a disjunctive normal form, is by far the more interesting and challenging. Indeed, it is in this case that we can be confronted to situations of overdetermination. Whenever ψ is a disjunctive normal form, this means that there is a minimal causal sufficient backing W for each disjunct. Each of these backings is a possible way to cause the truthfulness of the formula ψ at t_ψ—in the same spirit as Beckers' paths [6]. Example 1 illustrates how Definition 9 handles one of those challenging situations.

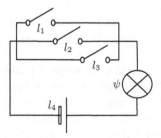

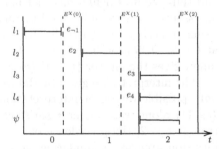

Fig. 1. Electrical circuit consisting of a voltage source, three switches, and an individual connected to electrodes.

Fig. 2. Evolution of fluents given κ in Example 1.

Example 1 (parallel switches and Milgram). Consider Fig. 1 simple electric circuit inspired by Milgram's experiment [29]. This circuit is made up of a voltage source, an individual strapped and connected to electrodes, and three switches connected in parallel. The positive literals $l_1, l_2, l_3, l_4 \in Lit_\mathbb{F}$ represent the closed state of each switch and the voltage source respectively—their respective complement thus represents the opened state. $\psi = (l_1 \wedge l_4) \vee (l_2 \wedge l_4) \vee (l_3 \wedge l_4)$ where $\psi \in \mathcal{P}$ represents the triggering conditions for the strapped individual being electrocuted. Thus, three backings are possible to cause ψ: $W = \{l_1, l_4\}$, $W' = \{l_2, l_4\}$, and $W'' = \{l_3, l_4\}$. $e_1, e_2, e_3 \in \mathbb{E}$ are the events which intrinsic effect is to close each switch respectively, $e_4 \in \mathbb{E}$ is an event which intrinsic effect is to close the voltage source, and $e_{\neg 1} \in \mathbb{E}$ is the event which intrinsic effect is to open the first switch. We assume that the situation involves five agents: the one strapped and four others—each controlling one of the four components of the circuit. The studied sequences illustrated by Fig. 2 and given by $\tau^e_{\sigma,\kappa}$ and $\tau^s_{\sigma,\kappa}$ are:

$$E^\chi(-1) = \{ini_{l_1}, ini_{\overline{l_2}}, ini_{\overline{l_3}}, ini_{\overline{l_4}}\}$$
$$S^\chi(0) = \{l_1, \overline{l_2}, \overline{l_3}, \overline{l_4}\}, E^\chi(0) = \{e_{\neg 1}, e_2\}$$
$$S^\chi(1) = \{\overline{l_1}, l_2, \overline{l_3}, \overline{l_4}\}, E^\chi(1) = \{e_3, e_4\}$$
$$S^\chi(2) = \{\overline{l_1}, l_2, l_3, l_4\}$$

Given the above traces, ψ is true at $t = 2$ by both W' and W''.

The question that arises in Example 1 is: what are the causes of ψ being true at $t = 2$? Said in another way, what are the causes of the strapped individual being electrocuted at $t = 2$? Batusov and Soutchanski's proposal will consider $(ini_{l_1}, -1)$ and $(e_4, 1)$ as 'achievement causes', and $(e_2, 0)$ as a 'maintenance cause'—'causes responsible for protecting a previously achieved effect, despite potential threats that could destroy the effect' [4]—this given that we omit to consider $(e_3, 1)$ in the comparison because it occurs at the same time as $(e_4, 1)$ and thus requires definitions that handle concurrency. Considering factuality as an essential feature of a causal inquiry, the presence of $(ini_{l_1}, -1)$ in the causes seems unacceptable. Factually, $(ini_{l_1}, -1)$ plays no role in the truthfulness of ψ at $t = 2$. Definition 9 gives the sets $\{(e_2, 0), (e_4, 1)\}$ and $\{(e_3, 1), (e_4, 1)\}$ which union gives the answer $\{(e_2, 0), (e_3, 1), (e_4, 1)\}$.

The interpretation given by Batusov and Soutchanski of Example 1 is not the only possible divergent interpretation. We wondered whether answer $\{(e_2, 0), (e_4, 1)\}$ alone was not more satisfactory given that, even if both l_2 and l_3 are true at $t = 2$, the precedence of l_2 could be taken into account. However, this intuition appears as conflating causality and responsibility. If we strictly limit ourselves to a factual causal inquiry as prescribed by Wright [36], both $(e_2, 0)$ and $(e_3, 1)$ are causes of the truthfulness of ψ at $t = 2$. The intuition that would induce us to take into account the precedence of $(e_2, 0)$ belongs to Wright's *proximate-cause inquiry* and not to the causal inquiry. Indeed, once $(e_2, 0)$ and $(e_3, 1)$ are identified as causes, there is a policy choice for which the precedence of $(e_2, 0)$ mitigates or eliminates the responsibility of $(e_3, 1)$ for the final effect. We suspect that Batusov and Soutchanski's choices—which led them to consider $(ini_{l_1}, -1)$ as a cause—were influenced by this same intuition, but taken even further.

Definition 9 gives us essential information about causal relations by looking to the actual effects of events. However, the set of direct NESS-causes of an effect may include exogenous events that are not necessarily relevant. This is especially true in a framework such as ours, where we are interested in agent's decisions thus actions. It is therefore essential to establish a causal chain by going back in time in order to find the set of actions that led to the effect. To this end, we must broaden our vision to look not only at the actual effects of events which are direct NESS-causes, but also (i) at the events that caused those events to be triggered and (ii) at the events that caused those events to have their actual effects.

Example 2 (causing events to have their actual effects). Consider the literals $l_1, l_2, l_3, l_{c_1}, l_{c_3} \in Lit_\mathbb{F}$, the formula $\psi = l_1 \wedge l_2 \wedge l_3$, events $e, e' \in \mathbb{E}$ where there respective effects are $eff(e) = \{[l_{c_1}]\overline{l_1}, [\top]l_2, [l_{c_3}]l_3\}$ and $eff(e') = \{[\top]\overline{l_{c_1}}, [\top]l_{c_3}\}$. The studied sequences illustrated by Fig. 3 and given by $\tau^e_{\sigma,\kappa}$ and $\tau^s_{\sigma,\kappa}$ are:

$$E^X(-1) = \left\{ ini_{l_1}, ini_{\overline{l_2}}, ini_{\overline{l_3}}, ini_{\overline{l_4}}, ini_{l_{c_1}}, ini_{\overline{l_{c_3}}}, \right\}$$
$$S^X(0) = \left\{ l_1, \overline{l_2}, \overline{l_3}, l_{c_1}, \overline{l_{c_3}} \right\}, E^X(0) = \{e'\}$$
$$S^X(1) = \left\{ l_1, \overline{l_2}, \overline{l_3}, \overline{l_{c_1}}, l_{c_3} \right\}, E^X(1) = \{e\}$$
$$S^X(2) = \left\{ l_1, l_2, l_3, \overline{l_{c_1}}, l_{c_3} \right\}$$

Given the above sequence, Definition 9 gives us the direct NESS-cause relation $C \underset{W}{\leadsto} (\psi, t_\psi)$ where C is the set $\{(e, 1), (ini_{l_1}, -1)\}$.

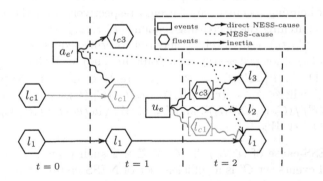

Fig. 3. Causal relations in Example 2.

In Example 2, the actual effects of the occurrence $(e, 1)$ were $actualEff(\{e\}, S^X(1)) = \{l_2, l_3\}$. In order to determine the desired causal chain, one of the steps requires to ask ourselves what occurrence of events caused $(e, 1)$ to have those effects—inquiry concerning exclusively conditional effects which condition is not $[\top]$. We distinguish two cases both illustrated by Fig 3. The two effects concerned are, $[l_{c_1}]\overline{l_1}$ and $[l_{c_3}]l_3$, each one representing a case. The effect $[l_{c_1}]\overline{l_1}$ corresponds to the case where the complement of the condition $[l_{c_1}]$ has been direct NESS-caused, thus causing $(e, 1)$ to 'maintain' l_1. The effect $[l_{c_3}]l_3$ corresponds to the case where the condition $[l_{c_3}]$ has been direct NESS-caused, thus causing $(e, 1)$ to 'produce' l_3 as an actual effect. The predicate $after(E, L_p, L_m)$—inspired by Khan and Lespérance's work [23]—gives the formula to direct NESS-cause in order to be considered a cause of an event having its actual effects. In the discussed example this formula is $\psi' = \overline{l_{c_1}} \wedge l_{c_3}$.

Definition 10 $(after(E, L_p, L_m))$. Given a causal setting χ, a set of events $E \in E^\chi(t)$, and partial states $L_m, L_p, W_{\psi'} \subseteq Lit_\mathbb{F}$ such that $S^\chi(t) \vDash L_m$ and $S^\chi(t) \nvDash L_p$, the predicate $after(E, L_p, L_m) = \psi'$ with $\psi' = \bigwedge_{l \in W_{\psi'}} l$ such that:

- Necessity and minimality of E: $W_{\psi'} \triangleright E \vDash L_p \cup L_m$ and $\forall E' \subset E, W_{\psi'} \triangleright E' \nvDash L_p \cup L_m$.
- Monotonicity: $\forall W', W_{\psi'} \subseteq W', W' \triangleright E \vDash L_p \cup L_m$.

Having introduced the predicate $after(E, L_p, L_m)$, we can now introduce NESS-causes that are found relying on the establishment of the causal chain.

Definition 11 (NESS-causes). Given a causal setting χ, the direct NESS-cause relation $C \underset{W}{\rightsquigarrow} (\psi, t_\psi)$, and the decreasing sequence $t_1, \ldots, t_k$ induced by the existing partition $W_1, \ldots, W_k$ of the backing W, the occurrence of events set $C' = \{(e, t), \ e \in E^\chi(t), \ t \in \mathbb{T}\}$ is a sufficient set of NESS-causes of the truthfulness of the formula ψ at t_ψ iff one of the following cases is satisfied:

- Base case: $C' = C$.
- Recursive case: Given the sets $C_R = C \setminus C'$ and $C_O = C' \setminus C$ of 'removable' and 'overwhelming' occurrence of events respectively, and the partitions of C and C_R matching the decreasing sequence $t_1, \ldots, t_k$—$C(t_1), \ldots, C(t_k)$ and $C_R(t_1), \ldots, C_R(t_k)$ respectively—there is a covering sequence of subsets $C_O = \bigcup_{i \in \{0, \ldots, k\}} C_{O_i}$ (not necessarily monotonic in time) such that:
$$\forall i \in \{1, \ldots, k\}, C_R(t_i) \neq \varnothing \implies (e, t) \in C_{O_i} \text{ are NESS-causes of}$$
(ψ', t_i), where $\psi' = tri(C_R(t_i)) \wedge after(C_R(t_i), L_p, L_m)$, $L_p = W_i \cap actualEff(C_R(t_i), S^\chi(t_i))$, and $L_m = [W_i \setminus actualEff(C_R(t_i), S^\chi(t_i))] \cup W_{i+1} \cup \cdots \cup W_k$.

(e, t) is a NESS-cause of (ψ, t_ψ) iff $\exists C' \subseteq \mathbb{E} \times \mathbb{T}$ such that $(e, t) \in C'$ and the occurrence of events set C' is a sufficient set of NESS-causes of (ψ, t_ψ). The set of NESS-causes $D = C \setminus C_R \cup C'$ is called a set of decisional causes if $D \subseteq \mathbb{A} \times \mathbb{T}$.

Definition 11 captures the two ways in which the occurrence of an event can have a causal relation with the truthfulness of ψ at t_ψ. First, by being a NESS-cause of the triggering conditions of an occurrence of event that is a NESS-cause of (ψ, t_ψ)—captured by the conjunct $tri(C_R(t_i))$. Second, by being a NESS-cause that the occurrence of an event that is a NESS-cause of (ψ, t_ψ) had its actual effects—captured by the conjunct $after(C_R(t_i), L_p, L_m)$.

Having determined the causal relations linking events and formulas of the language, we can now give a suitable for action languages definition of actual causality.

Definition 12 (actual cause). Given a causal setting χ and an event $e \in E^\chi(t_\psi)$, the actual causes of (e, t_ψ) are the NESS-causes of $(tri(e), t_\psi)$, i.e. the truthfulness of the triggering conditions of e at t_ψ.

5   Conclusion

The contribution of this paper is to link automated planning and causality by continuing the momentum established by recent papers [4,8,21,24] of proposing an action languages suitable definition of actual causality. By this proposal we address two of what we consider the main remaining limitations of this venture. First, not to yield into the easy confusion between responsibility and causality, our proposal is suitable for a factual and independent of policy choices causal inquiry. Second, not to disregard the much debated cases of overdetermination, our proposal is based on an action language semantics allowing concurrency of events. By taking as a base Wright's NESS test—as done recently in causal calculus [9] and in structural equation framework [6]—we are able to manage these cases satisfactorily. To the best of our knowledge, no other action languages suitable definition of actual causality has been able to handle those complex cases, yet essential. Our approach thus allows agents to handle complex cases of actual causality.

In future work we intend to propose a complete and sound translation into logic programming of this actual causation definition suitable for action languages. Then, we intend to extend the definition of causality by including the relation 'prevent' [8]. In Wright's conception of causality, causality can only be sufficient if we take into account—in addition to the positive causes—the conditions that were not true and whose absence was a necessary condition for the occurrence of the result. Then, the events being causes of their absence are also causes of the result. By working on fluent literals, our definition of causation already takes this notion into account. If we extend this reasoning, we could also take the case where the result did not occur because one of these negative conditions was made true. In such a case, the events being causes of the negative condition are causes of the non-occurrence of the result. We intend to define this causal relation given our more complex framework with events concurrency and disjunction.

References

1. Abarca, A.I.R., Broersen, J.M.: A stit logic of responsibility. In: 21st International Conference on Autonomous Agents and Multiagent Systems, pp. 1717–1719. International Foundation for Autonomous Agents and Multiagent Systems, Auckland, New Zealand (2022)
2. Andreas, H., Guenther, M.: Regularity and inferential theories of causation. In: Zalta, E.N. (ed.) The Stanford Encyclopedia of Philosophy. Metaphysics Research Lab, Stanford University, fall 2021 edn. (2021)
3. Baral, C., Gelfond, M.: Reasoning about effects of concurrent actions. J. Log. Program. **31**(1–3), 85–117 (1997)

4. Batusov, V., Soutchanski, M.: Situation calculus semantics for actual causality. In: McIlraith, S.A., Weinberger, K.Q. (eds.) Proceedings of the Thirty-Second AAAI Conference on Artificial Intelligence (AAAI-18), pp. 1744–1752. AAAI Press, New Orleans, Louisiana, USA (2018)

5. Baumgartner, M.: A regularity theoretic approach to actual causation. Erkenntnis **78**(1), 85–109 (2013). Dec

6. Beckers, S.: The counterfactual NESS definition of causation. Proc. AAAI Conf. Artif. Intell. **35**(7), 6210–6217 (2021). May

7. Beckers, S., Vennekens, J.: A principled approach to defining actual causation. Synth. **195**(2), 835–862 (2018)

8. Berreby, F., Bourgne, G., Ganascia, J.G.: Event-based and scenario-based causality for computational ethics. In: 17th International Conference on Autonomous Agents and Multiagent Systems, pp. 147–155. International Foundation for Autonomous Agents and Multiagent Systems, Stockholm, Sweden (2018)

9. Bochman, A.: Actual causality in a logical setting. In: Lang, J. (ed.) Proceedings of the Twenty-Seventh International Joint Conference on Artificial Intelligence, IJCAI 2018, July 13–19, 2018, pp. 1730–1736. Stockholm, Sweden (2018)

10. Bochman, A.: On laws and counterfactuals in causal reasoning. In: Thielscher, M., Toni, F., Wolter, F. (eds.) Principles of Knowledge Representation and Reasoning: Proceedings of the Sixteenth International Conference, pp. 494–503. AAAI Press, Tempe, Arizona (2018)

11. Bourgne, G., Sarmiento, C., Ganascia, J.G.: ACE modular framework for computational ethics: dealing with multiple actions, concurrency and omission. In: 1st International Workshop on Computational Machine Ethics. CEUR-WS.org (2021)

12. Fox, M., Long, D.: Modelling mixed discrete-continuous domains for planning. J. Artif. Intell. Res. **27**, 235–297 (2006). Oct

13. Gelfond, M., Lifschitz, V.: Representing action and change by logic programs. J. Log. Program. **17**(2-4), 301–321 (1993)

14. Gelfond, M., Lifschitz, V.: Action languages. Electron. Trans. Artif. Intell. **2**, 193–210 (1998)

15. Ghallab, M., et al.: PDDL - The planning domain definition language. Tech. Rep. CVC TR-98-003/DCS TR-1165, Yale Center for Computational Vision and Control (1998)

16. Giunchiglia, E., Lifschitz, V.: An action language based on causal explanation: preliminary report. In: Mostow, J., Rich, C. (eds.) Proceedings of the Fifteenth National Conference on Artificial Intelligence and Tenth Innovative Applications of Artificial Intelligence Conference, AAAI 98, IAAI 98, July 26–30, 1998, Madison, Wisconsin, USA, pp. 623–630. AAAI Press / The MIT Press (1998)

17. Hall, N., Paul, L.A.: Causation and Pre-emption. In: Clark, P., Hawley, K. (eds.) Philosophy of Science Today. Oxford University Press, Oxford, New York, May 2003

18. Halpern, J.Y.: Actual Causality. The MIT Press (2016)

19. Halpern, J.Y.: Actual causality: a survey: Joseph Halpern, 26:38–27:21 (2018). https://www.youtube.com/watch?v=hXnCX2pJ0sg

20. Haslum, P., Lipovetzky, N., Magazzeni, D., Muise, C.: An introduction to the planning domain definition language. No. 42 in Synthesis Lectures on Artificial Intelligence and Machine Learning, Morgan & Claypool Publishers. **13**(2), 1–187 (Apr 2019)

21. Hopkins, M., Pearl, J.: Causality and counterfactuals in the situation calculus. J. Log. Comput. **17**(5), 939–953 (2007). Oct

22. Hume, D.: Enquête sur l'entendement humain. No. 1305 in GF, Flammarion, Paris, 2006 edn. (1748)
23. Khan, S.M., Lespérance, Y.: Knowing why: on the dynamics of knowledge about actual causes in the situation calculus. In: Proceedings of the 20th International Conference on Autonomous Agents and MultiAgent Systems, pp. 701–709. International Foundation for Autonomous Agents and Multiagent Systems, Richland, SC (2021)
24. LeBlanc, E.C., Balduccini, M., Vennekens, J.: Explaining actual causation via reasoning about actions and change. In: Calimeri, F., Leone, N., Manna, M. (eds.) Logics in Artificial Intelligence - 16th European Conference, JELIA 2019, Rende, Italy, May 7–11, 2019, Proceedings. Lecture Notes in Computer Science, vol. 11468, pp. 231–246. Springer (2019). https://doi.org/10.1007/978-3-030-19570-0_15
25. Lewis, D.: Causation. J. Philos. **70**(17), 556–567 (1973), publisher: Oxford Up
26. Lorini, E., Longin, D., Mayor, E.: A logical analysis of responsibility attribution: emotions, individuals and collectives. J. Log. Comput. **24**(6), 1313–1339 (2014)
27. Mackie, J.L.: The Cement of the Universe: A Study of Causation. Oxford University Press, Oxford, Clarendon Library of Logic and Philosophy (1980)
28. Menzies, P., Beebee, H.: Counterfactual theories of causation. In: Zalta, E.N. (ed.) The Stanford Encyclopedia of Philosophy. Metaphysics Research Lab, Stanford University, winter 2020 edn. (2020)
29. Milgram, S.: Behavioral Study of obedience. J. Abnorm. Soc. Psychol. **67**(4), 371–378. publisher: American Psychological Association (1963)
30. Mill, J.S.: A system of logic, ratiocinative and inductive: being a connected view of the principles of evidence, and the methods of scientific investigation, cambridge library collection - philosophy, vol. 1. Cambridge University Press, Cambridge, 2011 edn. (1843)
31. Mueller, E.T.: Commonsense Reasoning: An Event Calculus Based Approach, 2nd edn. Morgan Kaufmann Publishers Inc., San Francisco, CA, USA (2014)
32. Pearl, J.: Causality: models, reasoning, and inference. Cambridge University Press, Cambridge, U.K.; New York (2000)
33. Pednault, E.P.D.: ADL: exploring the middle ground between STRIPS and the situation calculus. In: Proceedings of the First International Conference on Principles of Knowledge Representation and Reasoning, pp. 324–332. Morgan Kaufmann Publishers Inc., San Francisco, CA, USA (1989)
34. Russell, S., Norvig, P.: Artificial Intelligence - A Modern Approach. Pearson Education, third edn, Prentice Hall Series (2010)
35. Vincent, N.A.: A Structured Taxonomy of Responsibility Concepts. In: Vincent, N.A., van de Poel, I., van den Hoven, J. (eds.) Moral Responsibility, Library of Ethics and Applied Philosophy, vol. 27. Springer, Netherlands, Dordrecht (2011). https://doi.org/10.1007/978-94-007-1878-4_2
36. Wright, R.W.: Causation in tort law. Calif. L. Rev. **73**(6), 1735–1828 (1985), publisher: California Law Review Inc
37. Wright, R.W.: Causation, responsibility, risk, probability, naked statistics, and proof: pruning the bramble bush by clarifying the concepts. Iowa Law Review **73**, 1001 (1988). Dec
38. Wright, R.W.: The NESS account of natural causation: a response to criticisms. In: Goldberg, R. (ed.) Perspectives on Causation. Social Science Research Network, Rochester, NY, hart publishing edn. (2011)

Goal-Oriented Coordination
with Cumulative Goals

Aditya Ghose[1(✉)], Hoa Dam[1], Shunichiro Tomura[1], Dean Philp[2],
and Angela Consoli[2]

[1] Decision Systems Lab, University of Wollongong, Wollongong, NSW 2500, Australia
{aditya,hoa}@uow.edu.au,
st655@uowmail.edu.au
[2] Defence Science and Technology Group, Edinburgh, SA 5111, Australia
{dean.philp,angela.consoli}@dst.defence.gov.au

Abstract. Multi-actor coordination is in general a complex problem, with inefficient and brittle solutions. This paper addresses the problem of abstract coordination of multiple actors at the goal-level, which often enables us to avoid these problems. Goals in multi-actor settings often rely on the cumulative efforts of a group of distinct actors whose individual, measurable contributions accumulate to lead to the fulfillment of the goal. We formalize these as *cumulative goals* in a mathematical framework that permits us to measure individual actor contributions on a variety of scales (including qualitative ones). We view these as *softgoals*, a conception general enough to incorporate the more traditional *hardgoals*. Within this mathematical setting, we address the coordination problem as one of deciding which actor is allocated to fulfilling each goal of interest (and the associated problem of goal model maintenance). We also report some empirical evaluation results.

1 Introduction

Coordination is often a complex problem, with inefficient and brittle solutions. Goals afford a convenient means for managing complex underlying systems by enabling the use of high-level abstractions specifying the intent underpinning the behaviour being described. While the importance of multi-actor goal modelling is well-recognized in the literature [1], little attention has been paid to the problem of multi-actor *coordination* at the goal level ([2–4] address a version of the problem indirectly). This paper aims to address this gap. Our work views all goals as *softgoals*, which include *hard goals* as a special case. In our conception, goals may be relaxed (although we define specific conditions under which goal decompositions are valid) and provide directions for improvement (in a similar sense to non-functional requirements, such as the one for *usability*, which requires us to improve usability as much as possible within the applicable constraints).

Goals are organized in the form of (informally defined) AND-OR goal trees where goals higher up in the tree are decomposed (via AND-decomposition or

R. Aydoğan et al. (Eds.): PRIMA 2022, LNAI 13753, pp. 260–280, 2023.
https://doi.org/10.1007/978-3-031-21203-1_16

OR-decomposition) to lower level sub-goals. AND-decomposition involves situations where the parent goal is deemed to be fulfilled only if all of the sub-goals have been fulfilled. The correctness of an AND-decomposition is checked via three tests (originally articulated by Dardenne et al. [5]): (1) the conjunction of the goal conditions of the sub-goals must entail the parent goal condition (the *entailment* requirement; (2) the conjunction of the sub-goal conditions together with the parent goal condition must be consistent (the *consistency* requirement); (3) no subset of the sub-goals should satisfy the above two requirements (the *minimality* requirement). OR-decomposition involves situations where the parent goal is fulfilled if any one of the sub-goals are fulfilled. The correctness of an OR-decomposition is ensured by checking that each that the goal condition of each sub-goal entails the goal condition of the parent goal.

We introduce the notion of a *cumulative goal*. Informally, a cumulative goal is one where the goal state specification includes a measurable parameter whose target value is achieved by the *cumulative fulfillment* of its sub-goals. Thus a goal to make a cup of tea, AND-decomposed into three sub-goals (boil water, pour it into a cup and dunk a teabag in the cup) is not a cumulative goal since there is no measurable parameter with a target value. On the other hand, a goal to deliver 30 tons of produce, AND-decomposed into 3 sub-goals (each involving the delivery of 10 tons of produce, by a different trucking service provider in each case) is an example of a cumulative goal (the measurable parameter with a target value is the amount of produce delivered). We use the abstract algebraic framework of *c-semirings* [6] to formalize cumulative goals. This provides a general framework where the parameters of interest can be measured not just in terms of numeric weights as in the example of above (the *weighted* instance of a c-semiring) but also using fuzzy, probabilistic and even qualitative scales. Bistarelli et al. [6] also show that new c-semirings can be obtained from composing existing c-semirings.

We show that cumulative goals are *preferential* in the sense that they lead to *preference orderings* on states of affairs. This feature is particularly useful is viewing cumulative goals as softgoals (as an informal example, we prefer to achieve states s_1, failing which we prefer to achieve state s_2 and so on). We then outline the use of cumulative goals in multi-actor coordination. In the same way that goal-oriented modeling of behaviour is sequence-agnostic (it abstracts away detailed action sequencing), our approach also abstracts away action sequencing, task scheduling and so on. We define an algorithm for goal model maintenance in settings where new actors become available (leading to new goals becoming feasible) or existing actors retire (rendering existing goals infeasible). We finally provide an algorithm that addresses the fundamental coordination problem: which actor is allocated to fulfilling each goal. We provide experimental results which suggest that the approach can be computationally realized and discuss related work.

The approach to goal-oriented coordination can find application in a wide variety of settings. In addition to the logistics and bushfire-fighting applications that the examples in this paper briefly touch upon, this approach can be used in any setting where UXV (Unmanned Aerial/Maritime/land Vehicle) coordination is necessary. It can also be used in managing teams of humans (hence in organizational management in general), or managing mixed teams of human and machine actors, amongst many others.

2   Cumulative Goals

We leverage an approach to modelling *degrees of preference* using a subclass of semirings, formally defined below. A c-semiring is a tuple $\mathcal{V} = \langle V, \oplus, \otimes, \bot, \top \rangle$ satisfying (for all $\alpha \in V$) [6]:

- V is a set of abstract values with $\bot, \top \in V$.
- $\oplus$ is a commutative, associative, idempotent and closed binary operator on V with $\bot$ as unit element ($\alpha \oplus \bot = \alpha$) and $\top$ as absorbing element ($\alpha \oplus \top = \top$).
- $\otimes$ is a commutative, associative and closed binary operator on V with $\top$ as unit element ($\alpha \otimes \top = \alpha$) and $\bot$ as absorbing element ($\alpha \otimes \bot = \bot$).
- $\otimes$ distributes over $\oplus$ (i.e., $\alpha \otimes (\beta \oplus \gamma) = (\alpha \otimes \beta) \oplus (\alpha \otimes \gamma)$).

Informally, $\oplus$ helps us compare degrees of preference. For $a, b \in V$, $a \oplus b = b$ suggests that b is at least as preferred as a. Similarly, $\otimes$ helps us combine degrees of preference, as is illustrated in the examples below. Informally, $\bot$ is the least preferred value and $\top$ is the most preferred value.

The c-semiring instance that we have implicitly made reference to in the preceding examples is the *weighted* instance. Formally:

$$S_{weighted} = <\mathcal{R}^+, max, +, 0, +\infty> \tag{1}$$

In other words, we use the set of positive reals to measure the degree of preference (of a state, or a solution, depending on the application). The $\oplus$ operator is max, which means that we prefer higher weights. The $\otimes$ operator is arithmetic addition, which means that we combine weights by adding them. We can also define a fuzzy instance:

$$S_{fuzzy} = <\{x|x \in [0,1]\}, max, min, 0, 1> \tag{2}$$

In other words, we use reals between 0 and 1 to measure the degree of preference, max to compare fuzzy values (higher values are preferred) and min to combine. A probabilistic instance can be similarly defined:

$$S_{prob} = <\{x|x \in [0,1]\}, max, \times, 0, 1> \tag{3}$$

Consider a qualitative instance: $\langle \{High, Medium, Low\}, \oplus, \otimes, Low, High \rangle$. Here we may choose to define $\oplus$ by explicit enumeration as follows: $High \oplus Medium = High, High \oplus Low = High, Medium \oplus Low = Medium$. *otimes* is also defined by explicit enumeration: $High \otimes Medium = Medium, High \otimes Low = Low, Medium \otimes Low = Low$.

We assume that each goal is written in the following format:

$$\langle \phi, \{\langle \pi_0, v_0 \rangle, \ldots, \langle \pi_i, v_i \rangle, \ldots \langle \pi_n, v_n \rangle\}, C \rangle$$

Here:

- ϕ is a formal assertion which the goal seeks to *achieve* or *maintain*
- Each of $\pi_0, \ldots, \pi_n$ is a parameter with a specified *target value*
- $v_0, \ldots, v_n$ are the target values for the parameters (v_0 for π_0 and so on)
- C is a collection of constraints, on a signature that is possibly a superset of the set of parameters referred to above, that specify permitted combinations of values of the parameters.

Another instance of c-semirings makes it amenable to supporting reasoning in propositional logic. We have however not used that approach to encoding ϕ in a goal because the resulting representation would be much harder to understand. We shall refer to $\langle v_0, \ldots, v_n \rangle$ as the *level of satisfaction* of the goal. Most goals and sub-goals in a goal model are *normative* in nature - they do not describe current reality but specify how reality ought to be. However, leaf goals assigned to specific actors (which are responsible for their fulfillment) are *descriptive* in nature - they describe the current state of reality. In such situations, the satisfaction level of a leaf goal is contingent on the actor it is assigned to (since different actors can fulfill the same goal to different levels of satisfaction).

We are now in a position to define an extended version of the rules governing the AND-reduction of goals [5].

A set of subgoals $\{G_0, \ldots, G_m\}$ is a valid AND-reduction of a goal G if and only if each of the following conditions are satisfied:

- $\phi_0 \wedge \ldots \wedge \phi_i \wedge \ldots \phi_n \models \phi$ (here ϕ is the formal assertion associated with goal G, ϕ_i the formal assertion associated with G_i and so on)
- $\phi_0 \wedge \ldots \wedge \phi_i \wedge \ldots \phi_n \wedge \phi \not\models \bot$
- There exists no subset of $\{\phi_0, \ldots, \phi_i, \ldots \phi_n\}$ which also satisfies the two conditions above
- For each i, $v_{i1} \otimes \ldots \otimes v_{in} \oplus v_i = v_{i1} \otimes \ldots \otimes v_{in}$, where v_i is the target value for parameter π_i in parent goal G, v_{ij} is the target value for parameter π_i is subgoal G_j and so on.

Figure 1 is an example of a valid AND-decomposition. The setting involves water-bombing a bushfire (of the kind common in Australia) using water-carrying drones. In general, an area affected by bushfire would require water-bombing by a large number of drones, but we consider only two drones here to simplify the example and save space. We also assume the existence of a background knowledge base which specifies the following:

$$payload\text{-}deliv\text{-}drone1 \wedge payload\text{-}deliv\text{-}drone2 \models water - bombed$$

Figure 2 is an example of an invalid AND-decomposition according to the definition above. In addition to the water-quantity parameter, we introduce an additional parameter for precision, which assesses how precise a drone is in delivering its payload to the specified target area. The decomposition is invalid because while the first drone exhibits a high degree of precision, the second drone exhibits only a medium degree of precision and $High \otimes Medium = Medium$ (and the parent goal requires a high degree of precision.

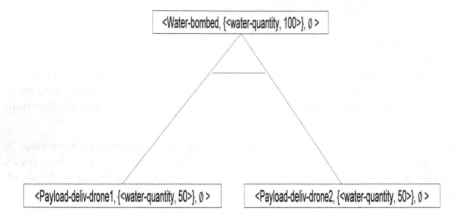

Fig. 1. Example of valid AND-decomposition

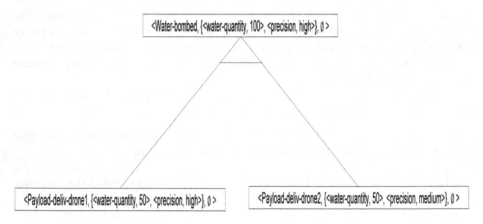

Fig. 2. Example of invalid AND-decomposition

3 Cumulative (Preferential) Goals

The notion of a *softgoal* has long been recognized in the literature. Softgoals are goals that do not mandatorily have to be satisfied (as opposed to *hard goals*) and admit some modicum of relaxation. They are typically used to model non-functional requirements, although they can also be useful in a range of other settings.

The conception of cumulative goal presented earlier in the paper allows us to view each such goal providing a preference ordering on a set of states.

A goal G of the form:

$$\langle \phi, \{\langle \pi_0, v_0 \rangle, \ldots, \langle \pi_n, v_n \rangle\}, C \rangle$$

leads to a preference ordering (most generally a partial order) $\prec_G$ on the set of states (this is based on a result in [6] that establishes that a c-semiring in general leads to a partially ordered set of preference values). Let state s_1 be of the form:

$$\langle \phi_1, \{\langle \pi_j, v_j \rangle, \ldots, \langle \pi_s, v_s \rangle\}, C_1 \rangle$$

Let state s_2 be of the form:

$$\langle \phi_2, \{\langle \pi_k, v_k \rangle, \ldots, \langle \pi_t, v_t \rangle\}, C_2 \rangle$$

$s_1 \prec_G s_2$ if and only if:

- $\phi_1 \models \phi$ and $\phi_2 \models \phi$
- Each of C, C_1 and C_2 are individually satisfiable
- $\{\pi_0, \ldots, \pi_n\} \cap \{\pi_j, \ldots, \pi_s\} \cap \{\pi_k, \ldots, \pi_t\} = \{\pi_u, \ldots, \pi_r\}$
- $v_{u1} \oplus v_{u2} = v_{u2}.v_{r1} \oplus v_{r2} = v_{r2}$ and so on, where v_{u1} is the value associated with parameter π_u in state s_1, v_{u2} is the value associated with parameter π_u in state s_2 etc.

4   Coordination with Cumulative Goals

We work from the premise that dynamic nature of the operating context triggers the need for goal-oriented coordination. New actorss with new capabilities may become available while existing actors might retire or otherwise become unavailable. The overall coordination model we work with assumes that there is a central coordinator agent that maintains the system-wide goal model while agents at the edge assume responsibility for the fulfillment of specific goals and opportunistically handover, or swap goals with other agents.

We outline a procedure (Algorithm 1 below) for maintaining goal models as new sub-goals become feasible to fulfill, or when existing goals or sub-goals become infeasible to fulfill. We use the notion of a *k-replacement goal model maintenance strategy*. In the case of new sub-goals becoming available, this involves taking any subset of size k of the set of new sub-goals and replacing a set of *sibling goals* (i.e., goals that share the same parent) with this set of size k. If the input set of newly feasible goals is of size n, we need to consider $\binom{n}{k}$ possibilities. In the case of existing sub-goals becoming infeasible, this involves picking any subset of length k from the set of available sub-goals (in Algorithm 1, this is SUBGOAL-LIBRARY, which is the set of sub-goals that the actor knows how to fulfill) and seeking to replace the infeasible sub-goal(s) with this set. If the size of the set of available sub-goals is of size m, we need to work through $\binom{m}{k}$ possibilities. Note that m is often much larger than n, but a variety of relevance reasoning techniques could be used to reduce the size of the set of available sub-goals at the pre-processing stages. In the following, we use a function SLEVEL() which returns the *satisfaction level* (as defined earlier) for the goal provided as input.

When a new sub-goal is introduced or an existing sub-goal is removed, the entire sub-tree rooted at the corresponding sub-goal is also removed. Algorithm 1 can be repeatedly called (in the REMOVAL mode) to re-populate these sub-trees. Including pseudo-code for this in Algorithm 1 would make it complex and difficult to explain (and understand); hence we have chosen to summarize it in this text fragment above.

Algorithm 1. Agent coordination with central coordinator

Input: model: goal model, indicator: represented as ADDITION or REMOVAL, NEW: a set of new subgoals in case of ADDITION, REMOVE: the specific subgoal to be removed in case of REMOVAL, SUBGOAL-LIBRARY: for available subgoals used in case of REMOVAL

Output: A new goal model

1: **if** indicator=ADDITION **then**
2:   **for each** non-root goal GOAL **do**
3:     SAT-LEVEL := satisfaction level of GOAL
4:   **end for**
5:   **for** i= 1 To |NEW| **do**
6:     **for each** subgoal G of GOAL **do**
7:       **for each** REPLACE = subset of size i of NEW **do**
8:         set GOAL-TMP := GOAL with G replaced with REPLACE, provided the replacement satisfies the rules for valid AND-decompositions
9:         **if** SLEVEL(GOAL-TMP) $\oplus$ SLEVEL(GOAL) = SLEVEL(GOAL-TMP) **then**
10:           set SAT-LEVEL := SLEVEL(GOAL-TMP) and GOAL := GOAL-TMP
11:         **end if**
12:       **end for**
13:     **end for**
14:   **end for**
15: **else if** indicator=REMOVAL **then**
16:   set GOAL to be the parent goal of the goal being removed
17:   set SAT-LEVEL := satisfaction level of GOAL
18:   **for each** REPLACE= subset of size i of SUBGOAL-LIBRARY **do**
19:     set GOAL-TMP := GOAL with REPLACE added as one or more additional subgoals, provided the result satisfies the rules for valid AND-decompositions
20:     **if** SLEVEL(GOAL-TMP) $\oplus$ SLEVEL(GOAL) = SLEVEL(GOAL-TMP) **then**
21:       set SAT-LEVEL := SLEVEL(GOAL-TMP) and GOAL := GOAL-TMP
22:     **end if**
23:   **end for**
24: **end if**

We next outline a procedure (Algorithm 2) to be used by agents to decide if a goal swap or handover is necessary. Recall that leaf-level goals are assigned to individual actors. These actorss thus assume responsibility for fulfillment of these leaf-level goals. In Algorithm 2, we only deal with leaf-level nodes, since these are only ones that can be assigned to different actors. $SLEVEL_A(G)$ refers to the satisfaction level of goal G when assigned to actor A.

Algorithm 2. Goal swap/handover

Input: model: goal model, A: an agent with specified capabilities
Output: A possibly modified goal model. The possible modification would involve the assignment of the input agent to a leaf-level goal.

1: set CANDIDATES := ∅
2: **for each** leaf-level goal G currently assigned to agent A' **do**
3:    **if** $SLEVEL_A(G) \oplus SLEVEL_{A'}(G) = SLEVEL_A(G)$ **then**
4:       set CANDIDATES := CANDIDATES ∪ {G}
5:    **end if**
6: **end for**
7: **for each** distinct GOAL∈CANDIDATES **do**
8:    **for any** DGOAL∈CANDIDATES **do**
9:       **if** $SLEVEL_A(GOAL) \oplus SLEVEL_A(DGOAL) = SLEVEL_A(GOAL)$ **then**
10:          set CANDIDATES := CANDIDATES − DGOAL
11:          non-deterministically select any goal from CANDIDATES and assign A to it
12:       **end if**
13:    **end for**
14: **end for**

---

5 Empirical Evaluation

In the following, we assume that the set of constraints is empty (i.e., the parameters are independent of each other). Including constraint satisfaction will lead to the well-known complexity of satisfiability checking.

5.1 Goal Satisfaction Check

We implemented the cumulative goal satisfaction check to show the achievability of our concept in reality. The aim of cumulative goal check is to investigate the efficiency of the c-semiring approach for measuring the cumulative goal satisfiability in various scenarios. We implement six respective checkers under respective scenarios; boolean, fuzzy, weight, quality, probability and integration scenarios. Through this experiment, we expect to assure the feasibility of the cumulative goal satisfiability check for all the respective checkers in a timely manner. The experimental result answers the question which expresses doubt in the realization of our ideas. This experiment consists of several steps.

1. Checker Design: Each case is designed based on the definitions discussed in the previous sections. There are three main components in each checker. The additive (⊕) and multiplicative (⊗) are the operators which compute the satisfiability level of each individual and cumulative goals. Each operator is structured differently by following the definitions.

2. Goal Generation: 10,000 goals are prepared for all the checkers except the integration checker (the total number of goals is 40,000). Each goal possesses five target variables. To simplify the experiment, target variable's desirable value as

Algorithm 3. Team activity initial setting

Input: model: goal model, C: a central system, T: a set of teams, A: a set of actors
Output: a model with team activities
```
 1: for each a ∈ A do
 2:     set team(a) := t ∈ T
 3:     an adequate team is assigned based on its capability
 4: end for
 5: for each t ∈ T do
 6:     for each a_t ∈ t do
 7:         set leader_rank(a_t) := rank(a_t)
 8:         rank(a_t) is determined by considering its capability as a leader
 9:     end for
10: end for
11: for each t ∈ T do
12:     set status_t = ∅
13:     for each a_t ∈ A_t do
14:         if status(a_t) ⊕ ⊥ = status(a_t) then
15:             status_t := status_t ∪ COMMIT
16:         else if status(a_t) ⊕ ⊥ = ⊥ or elapsed time > time limit then
17:             status_t := status_t ∪ CANCEL
18:         end if
19:         status is kept in the leader(t) (leader_rank(a_t) = 1) in each team
20:     end for
21:     send status_t to C
22: end for
23: C receives status_T
24: for each status_t ∈ status_T do
25:     if CANCEL in status_t then
26:         conduct Algorithm 1 with indicator = REMOVAL
27:         send START signal to leader(t) with updated team information
28:     else
29:         send START signal to leader(t)
30:     end if
31: end for
32: for each leader(t) ∈ leader(T) do
33:     if leader(t) receives START then
34:         for each a_t ∈ a_T do
35:             send START signal
36:         end for
37:     end if
38: end for
```

1 for the boolean, fuzzy, weight and probability checkers. The value is set as 3 for the quality checker. In the integration checker, 1 is the desirable value for the boolean, fuzzy, weight and probability checker parts while 3 is used for the quality checker as well. The satisfiability level of these individual goals determine the cumulative goal satisfiability level.

Algorithm 4. Leader replacement

Input: model: goal model, C: a central system, T: a set of teams, A^*: a set of leaders
Output: a model with possibly new leaders
 1: **for each** $a_t^* \in A^*$ **do**
 2:    **if** status$(a_t^*) \oplus \bot = \bot$ **then**
 3:       set $status_t :=$ FAILED
 4:       **for each** $a_t \in A_t$ **do**
 5:          **if** leader_rank$(a_t) =$ leader_rank$(a_t^*) -1$ **then**
 6:             set $a_t^* = a_t$
 7:             inform the leader replacement to the other actors in the same team
 8:             send $status_t$ to C
 9:             C receives $status_t$
10:             conduct Algorithm 1 with indicator = REMOVAL
11:             send UPDATED signal to leader(t) with updated team information
12:          **end if**
13:       **end for**
14:       a_t^* receives UPDATED
15:       set leader_rank$(a_{new}) :=$ rank(a_{new})
16:       **if** leader_rank$(a_{new}) >$ leader_rank(a_t^*) **then**
17:          set $a_t^* := a_{new}$
18:          inform the leader replacement to the other actors in the same team
19:       **end if**
20:    **end if**
21: **end for**

Algorithm 5. Actor assignment

Input: model: goal model, C: a central system, T: a set of teams
Output: a model with each actor being assigned to a goal
 1: **for each** t in T **do**
 2:    set $best\_comb := -1$
 3:    set $best\_result := -1$
 4:    **for each** $comb \in combination_t$ **do**
 5:       set result$:= sat_{comb\ goal\ 1} \otimes sat_{comb\ goal\ 2} \dots \otimes sat_{comb\ goal\ k}$
 6:       **if** result $> best\_result$ **then**
 7:          set $best\_comb := comb$
 8:          set $best\_result := result$
 9:       **end if**
10:    **end for**
11:    assign each actor in the team to a goal based on $best\_comb$
12: **end for**

---

3. Data Generation: Data is generated in order to simulate a real situation. For the boolean, fuzzy and weight, we generate random numbers for each actual observed value from the range of 0 to 2. Each observed value in the generated data for the quality checker is chosen from the integer number between 1 to 5. The probability checker uses the data with variables assigned either 'A', 'B', 'C', 'D' or 'E'. One character among them is selected under uniform probability.

The integration checker uses these three dataset types since it combines all the different checkers. All the datasets consist of 10,000 records (goals) with eight attributes for the first dataset and five attributes for the second and third dataset. For the first dataset, the labels for each checker are added as respective attributes beside the variables. The other datasets entail one label for the quality or probability checker. The last row in all the datasets show the labels for the cumulative goal satisfiability level of each checker. We create three datasets for each dataset type and hence nine different datasets are generated. In total, we execute the same experiment with different datasets to increase the result reliability.

4. Individual Goal Satisfiability Check: Each goal's target variable is compared with the corresponding actual observed value. A returned result from the individual goal satisfiability check function differs from checkers.

Boolean: If a variable is equal to 1, then 1 is returned to the variable. Otherwise, 0 would be output. If all the observed variable values in a goal are the same with the target variable value (if all the variables receive 1), then 1 is returned to the goal. If one of the observed variables obtains 0 for the return, then 0 is returned to the goal as well.

Fuzzy: A membership function is applied in the fuzzy checker, which allows the checker to represent the return value between 0 and 1 by providing a fuzzy level. The experiment sets all the fuzzy levels as 0.5. Any observed values larger than or equal to 0.5 and smaller than or equal to 1.5 return non zero values. If an observed variable value lies on the range, then the return can be expressed as a value larger than or equal to 0 and smaller than or equal to 1. The returned value depends on the satisfiability level of the value. If the observed variable is close to 1, it obtains a value close to 1. The fuzzy expression enables the checker to determine goal satisfiability at a fuzzy level as well. Among the returned results from each target variable, the minimum value is selected as the representation of the goal's satisfiability level.

Weight: Each variable possesses a weight. Five variables for each goal are set as 2, 4, 6, 8 and 10. Each goal obtains the total cost by summing all the possessing variables' weight. The multiplication of weight with corresponding variable's returned value reveals the cost. The returned value is decided based on the variables' values in a fuzzy way.

Quality: Based on the variable numbers, the quality level of each variable is determined. Since the target value is 3 (moderate) and hence the value evaluation is based on the number 3. If the values are lower than 3, either low or cool is assigned depending on the value. In contrast, warm or hot is given to the number higher than 3. The values 1, 2, 3, 4, 5 correspond with cold, cool, moderate, warm and hot.

Probability: Each variable receives either Prob(check) or 1 - Prob(check) as return. Prob(check) is probability that indicates the correctness of the check. We set 'A', 'B', 'C' and 'D' as correct values. Thus, if a variable contains either of the characters, then the checker considers that the variable matches with its target values and Prob(check) is returned. However, if the variable possesses 'E', then the value 1 - Prob(check) is returned. In our experiment, we set the P(check) as 0.7. In reality, the probability depends on the information or criteria from a certain domain. The arithmetic multiplication of all the returned values from each variable leads to the satisfiability level of the goal.

Integration: In this experiment, the integration consists of one boolean, fuzzy, weight, quality and probability checkers. For the boolean, fuzzy and weight parts, the same dataset is given. However, each checker examines the individual goal satisfiability level based on its own method. The quality and probability checkers use its own dataset and compute the satisfiability level based on their operators. Hence, the total number of goals is 40,000. All the parameter settings are the same with the ones discussed in the other subsections.

5. Cumulative Goal Satisfiability Computation: From individual goal satisfiability level, the cumulative goal satisfiability level is calculated by the multiplicative operator in each checker. For the integration checker, the cumulative result is shown as a collection of cumulative goal satisfiability levels from each checker.

The result from each checker is measured by two metrics. Accuracy measures the matching rate of the actual computed results with the labels. Since the experiment is conducted three times with different datasets, we average the observed accuracy. If all the actual components from a checker are identical with those from the expected result, the accuracy becomes 100%. For instance, the total labels for the boolean checker is 10,001 (10,000 goals plus 1 cumulative goal), and we check whether the returned values from the checker are identical with the labels. If all the components' values are the same with those from the expectation, then the accuracy is 100%. When the checker incorrectly computes the goal satisfiability level, then the returned result can differ from the expected result. This gap reduces the accuracy level. Large separation from the expected result leads to lower accuracy and indicates that it is infeasible to demonstrate our concept into actual implementation.

Another metric is time, which measures the computing time of each checker. The calculation includes the individual and cumulative goal satisfiability check. It is vital to achieve the small time value because it allows the checkers to be used in real-time goal satisfiability checking. If the checkers spend a large amount of time, then it is unrealistic to be exploited in reality. Time is averaged by the result from each round. We use a 4 GB memory, Intel(R) Core(TM) i5-7200U CPU, Surface Laptop. If the returned time is small although the device spec is not high, then we can demonstrate that the checkers are applicable to real issues.

The result of the experiment is shown in Table 1. As can be seen, the accuracy recorded as 100% for both individual and cumulative in all checkers, which validates the realization of our goal satisfiability level concept through the implementation. However, the accuracy is not supportive enough to conclude the achievability of our concept. The observation of recorded time is also required to check the ability of the checkers to check the goal satisfiability in real-time. From the Table 1, as the checkers become more complex (from the boolean to

Table 1. Accuracy and time from each checker

	Accuracy		Time (sec)
	Individual	Cumulative	
Boolean	1	1	0.035
Fuzzy	1	1	0.079
Weight	1	1	0.098
Quality	1	1	0.052
Probability	1	1	0.102
Integration	1	1	0.363

integration), the total amount of time increases. However, all the observed time is below one second and remains in small values with 10,000 goals checking for the first four checkers and 40,000 for the integration checker. This result demonstrates that our checkers can accurately check the goal satisfiability levels in a fast manner and can be used in real-time goal analysis if a single checker is given.

5.2 Time Increase Analysis for Integration Checker

In the previous experiment, the accuracy of each checker is validated. In this experiment, we investigate the time increase rate for the integration checker when the total number of checkers in the integration checker increases. The aim of this experiment is to observe the possibility of the integration checker being able to check the goal satisfiability level in a reasonable time manner when the total checker numbers and goals rise. We analyze the effect of checker number increase by different checker types. We expect the time to increase with a linear pace in all the checker types because other increase patterns such as polynomial and exponential growth can lead to prohibitive computational time.

We measure the time change by increasing each checker up to five. Each added checker examines the satisfiability level of additional 10,000 goals. Therefore, when five new checkers are added, the total goals number becomes 50,000. While increasing the total numbers of one checker type, the others checker types are not included. For example, in order to observe the time change by increasing the boolean checkers, we gradually augment the total number of the boolean checkers in the integration checker from one to five. When measuring the time difference, the other checker types are excluded in the integration checker. We use three different datasets to average the observed time. All the details of parameters in each checker type are the same with the ones in the previous experiment. The result is illustrated in Fig. 3.

The boolean checker achieves the lowest time rise at 0.55 s when the number is five, followed by quality and fuzzy at around 0.3 and 0.7 s respectively. The weight and probability checkers recorded longer time at approximately 0.6 for the former and 0.7 for the latter. One noticeable tendency is that though the slope of each line varies, their increase rates are in a linear form. We expect

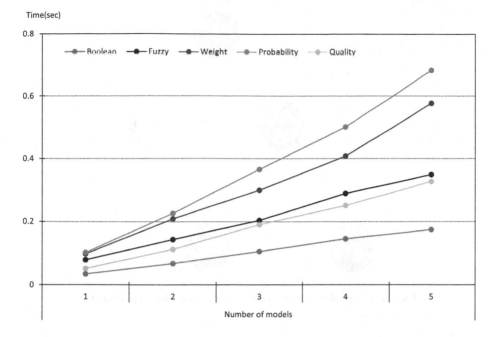

Fig. 3. Time change in integration checker by increasing checker numbers

to observe a linear increase as discussed previously. The checker computational time increase can be suppressed in a controllable level even though the number of any checker types and goals increases. By combining both accuracy and time observed in both experiments, we can demonstrate that our concept is achievable to be utilized in reality under reasonable computational time. Additional experimental results can be found at: https://github.com/ShunichiroTomura/G2I/blob/main/G2I.pdf.

5.3   Algorithm 1 Implementation

This experiment is designed to evaluate the achievability of the Algorithm 1. In our experiment, we assume that the indicator is set as addition. By showing that the addition operation can be implemented, then we can say that removal is also feasible because the only differences between the two indications are the motivation and a set of referred goals. In the addition indication, a set of new subgoals is given, and they may be replaced with the existing subgoals depending on the satisfiability level. In the removal indication, a removed subgoal is replaced with one of the achievable subgoals in the subgoal library. The core algorithm behind the scene is the same.

We consider one goal decomposition structure which is displayed in Fig. 4. The goal 0 is the root goal for the entire goals in this context, which is decomposed into the goal 1 and 2. The goal 1 is further decomposed into the goal 3 and 4. We assume that all the subgoals are AND-decomposed. Hence, the satisfaction

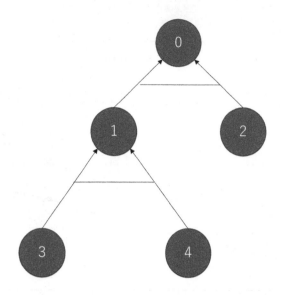

Fig. 4. The goal decomposition structure for this experiment

of all subgoals is required to measure the satisfiability of the parent goal, which is one requirement for the algorithm. We test the algorithm in three different scenarios; boolean, fuzzy and weight check. In each scenario. We assume that only one type of checker is required and each goal contains only one variable for simplicity. The initial parameter setting for each goal is shown in Table 2. We assume that all the target variable's value in every goal is 1 and hence if the observed variable value in one variable is 1, then it demonstrates the complete satisfaction of the goal. As can be seen, goal 3 has an issue in the satisfiability level in each case. Goals 0 and 1 are left blank because their results depend on their subgoals. Fuzziness shows the range of the membership function for the fuzzy and weight checks. The value is set as 0.5 for both checks. Cost indicates the weight for each goal used in the weight check. All the weights are set as 2.

Table 2. Initial setting

| | Observed variable value | | | | | Fuzziness | Cost | | | | |
	Goal 0	Goal 1	Goal 2	Goal 3	Goal 4		Goal 0	Goal 1	Goal 2	Goal 3	Goal 4
Boolean	–	–	1	0	1	–	–	–	–	–	–
Fuzzy	–	–	1	0.9	1	0.5	–	–	–	–	–
Weight	–	–	1	0.9	1	0.5	2	2	2	2	2

By implementing the three different scenarios with different checkers, the initial result of the goal satisfiability is shown as Fig. 5. The final goal satisfiability level for each scenario is 0, 0.8 and 5.6 respectively. As mentioned, due to the low

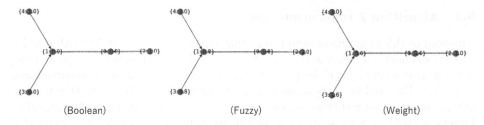

Fig. 5. Initial result from each scenario

goal satisfiability of the goal 3, the final goal from each scenario cannot achieve the highest satisfiability level.

Now we assume that we obtain several new subgoals which can be replaceable with goal 3. The details are illustrated in Table 3. The three goals are 6, 7 and 8. As can be seen, goal 8 seems to be able to achieve the highest satisfiability level among the new goals in all the scenarios. Based on the Algorithm 1, we compare the satisfiability of goal 3 with the new goals. We expect that the goal 3 is replaced with the goal 8 due to higher satisfiability level. By implementing the algorithm, we receive the result as Fig. 6. Through the addition operation, goal 3 is replaced with goal 8 because it can achieve higher goal satisfiability level. Consequently, the final goal satisfiability level increases to 1, 1 and 6 in each scenario. This result accords with our expectation and hence the Algorithm 1 is demonstrated as an executable mechanism in reality.

Table 3. New goals

	Observed variable values in new goals		
	6	7	8
Boolean	0	0	1
Fuzzy	0	0.6	1
Weight	0	0.6	1

Fig. 6. Addition result in each scenario

5.4   Algorithm 2 Implementation

The goal of this experiment is to investigate the achievability of Algorithm 2. In this experiment, we assume the structure of goal decomposition as Fig. 7. One noticeable difference from the previous experiment is the further decomposition in goal 2. The goal is AND-decomposed into two subgoals 5 and 6. Due to this extension, the goal structure is now represented in a binary form. Another difference is the existence of an actor. In this experiment, we explicitly denote the actor in order to check the correctness of the implementation. Actor A' is responsible for all the goal satisfiability activities. We also test the implementation of boolean, fuzzy and weight checkers by setting the three scenarios identical to the previous experiment. The initial parameter setting is summarized in Table 4. The Goal5 is the least satisfied goal in all the scenarios at 0. For the fuzzy and weight cases, the second lowest satisfiability level is observed in the goal 6. Two different low satisfiability level are set in both the cases to demonstrate the realization of our algorithm through the implementation. The fuzziness and cost for each goal is set as 0.5 and 2 in the specific cases.

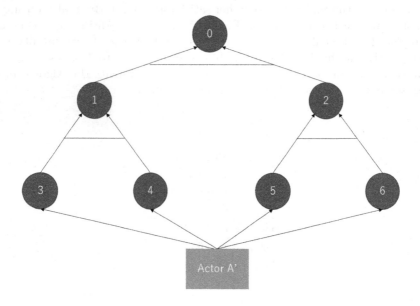

Fig. 7. The goal decomposition structure for this experiment

Based on this setting, we implement the boolean, fuzzy and weight cases. The result is shown in Fig. 8. Neither of the cases achieves the maximum satisfiability level at the goal 0. This is because at least one of the subgoal's satisfiability is not represented in the highest value that it can achieve (in this context, the value is 1). In particular, the fuzzy and weight cases possess two subgoals which are not fully satisfied. The actor A' seems to have a weakness at accomplishing

Table 4. Initial setting

| | Variable | | | | | | | Fuzziness | Cost | | | | | | |
	Goal 0	Goal 1	Goal 2	Goal 3	Goal 4	Goal 5	Goal 6		Goal 0	Goal 1	Goal 2	Goal 3	Goal 4	Goal 5	Goal 6
Boolean	–	–	–	1	1	0	1	–	–	–	–	–	–	–	–
Fuzzy	–	–	–	1	1	0	0.8	0.5	–	–	–	–	–	–	–
Weight	–	–	–	1	1	0	0.8	0.5	2	2	2	2	2	2	2

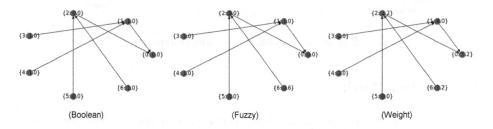

(Boolean)   (Fuzzy)   (Weight)

Fig. 8. Initial result from each scenario

the goal 5 for the boolean and goal 5 and 6 for the fuzzy and weight cases. We assume that there is another actor called A. The observed variable values of each subgoals by the actor A is shown in Table 5. In contrast, the actor A can achieve the goal 5 and 6 with higher satisfiability than the actor A' while the goal 3 and 4 cannot be accomplished. From this characteristic, if we assume that only goal can be swapped, then we expect the executor of goal 5 is handed over to the actor A' in all the cases. For the fuzzy and weight, the actor A' does not also fully satisfy the goal 6, but the degree of satisfiability is much closer to the highest than the goal5's and thus the goal5 is selected. By applying the Algorithm 2, the result changes as Fig. 9. The goal 5 is now under the actor A's responsibility and this swapping raised the final satisfiability level of the root goal. The satisfiability level for each case becomes 1, 0.6 and 7.2 respectively, which matches with our expectation. From this experiment, the achievability of the Algorithm, 2 is validated.

Table 5. Observed variable values in each subgoal by actor A

| | Observed variables | | | |
	3	4	5	6
Boolean	0	0	1	1
Fuzzy	0	0	1	1
Weight	0	0	1	1

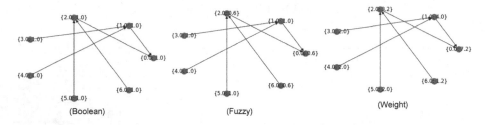

Fig. 9. Goal satisfiability after swapping

6 Related Work

The versatility of the c-semiring allows the fusion of the concept with other fields. One example is argumentation formulation. [7] applies c-semiring based constraint check on Dung argumentation. The output of the constraint is treated as weights, which can be represented as either boolean, fuzzy or other expressions depending on the requirements. These values are used as the attributes of edges between nodes as weights. The weights are served as attack levels to the directed nodes. This idea is materialized by the development of Conarg [8,9]. This Java-based software enables checking conflict levels in argumentation formulation. The ability of the proposed method is deepened by defending from attacks by comparing two attacks from the opposite directions [10].

Another application is security. [11] applies the essence of c-semiring to maintain desirable security degrees in multi-levels. One significant issue relating to security is the cascade elimination problems. The solution was considered an NP-hard problem. However, the generalization of this issue by using the c-semiring approach reduces the difficulty into polynomial time level. The c-semiring approach also can be applied to the security protocol proposed by [12]. One substantial difference from the other approaches is that the c-semiring based approach allows to represent the protocol compliance level in a non-boolean form by allowing constraint check result to express into non-crisp values such as fuzzy theory.

The goal oriented concept has been used in various realms as well. For instance, [13] extends the concept of i* as a text form, which is required to guarantee the scalability of the concept in a large project. Equipping i* with the ability of expression in a text form enables applying the concept into a complex problem. These instances assure the extensibility of the i* concept.

i* can even be utilized into the field of law constraint checking systems. [14] develops a model called Nomos, which allows the i* modeling to assure that any tasks entailing law constraints comply with the rules. For instance, tasks relating to clinical treatments are often restricted with a number of rules and requirements. These rules need to be represented together with the goals as well. Nomos is connected with VLPM [15] to be able to display the law constraints in UML diagrams.

7   Conclusions

The coordination problem is complex, admitting inefficient and brittle solutions, in a variety of important application domains, including logistics, natural disaster management and UXV coordination. This paper addresses the problem of lifting the coordination to the goal-level, thus avoiding some of the drawbacks mentioned above. We offer a novel conception of cumulative goals, which are implicitly softgoals that permit explicitly accounting for the cumulative contributions of a number of individual actors. Cumulative goals are defined in an innovative mathematical framework (previously used for solving over-constrained problems) that is general enough to admit a variety of useful instances. We define algorithms for goal model maintenance and the optimal allocation of actors to goals. We present experimental results that suggest that the approach can be computationally realized. In future work, we expect to be able to report on broader array of coordination algorithms and on more practical implementations.

References

1. Yu, E.S.: Towards modelling and reasoning support for early-phase requirements engineering. In: 1997 Proceedings of the IEEE International Symposium on Requirements Engineering, pp. 226–235. IEEE (1997)
2. Fuxman, A., Kazhamiakin, R., Pistore, M., Roveri, M.: Formal tropos: language and semantics. Univ. Trento IRST **55**, 123 (2003)
3. Giorgini, P., Kolp, M., Mylopoulos, J., Castro, J.: Tropos: a requirements-driven methodology for agent-oriented software. In: Agent-oriented methodologies, pp. 20–45. IGI Global (2005)
4. Bresciani, P., Perini, A., Giorgini, P., Giunchiglia, F., Mylopoulos, J.: Tropos: an agent-oriented software development methodology. Auton. Agent. Multi-Agent Syst. **8**(3), 203–236 (2004). https://doi.org/10.1023/B:AGNT.0000018806.20944
5. Dardenne, A.A., van Lamsweerde, A., Fickas, S.: Goal-directed requirements acquisition. Sci. Comput. Program. **20**(1–2), 3–50 (1993)
6. Bistarelli, S., Montanari, U., Rossi, F.: Semiring-based constraint satisfaction and optimization. J. ACM **44**(2), 201–236 (1997)
7. Bistarelli, S., Santini, F.: A common computational framework for semiring-based argumentation systems. In: ECAI 2010: 19th European Conference on Artificial Intelligence, vol. 215 (2010)
8. Bistarelli, S., Santini, F.: ConARG: a constraint-based computational framework for argumentation systems. In: 2011 IEEE 23rd International Conference on Tools with Artificial Intelligence, pp. 605–612 (2011)
9. Bistarelli, S., Santini, F.: Modeling and solving AFs with a constraint-based tool: ConArg. In: Modgil, S., Oren, N., Toni, F. (eds.) TAFA 2011. LNCS (LNAI), vol. 7132, pp. 99–116. Springer, Heidelberg (2012). https://doi.org/10.1007/978-3-642-29184-5_7
10. Bistarelli, S., Rossi, F., Santini, F.: A novel weighted defence and its relaxation in abstract argumentation. Int. J. Approx. Reasoning **92**, 66–86 (2018)

11. Foley, S.N., Bistarelli, S., O'Sullivan, B., Herbert, J., Swart, G.: Multilevel security and quality of protection. In: Gollmann, D., Massacci, F., Yautsiukhin, A. (eds.) Quality of Protection. Advances in Information Security, vol. 23, pp. 93–105. Springer, Boston (2006). https://doi.org/10.1007/978-0-387-36584-8_8
12. Bella, G., Bistarelli, S.: Soft constraint programming to analysing security protocols. Theory Pract. Logic Program. 4(5–6), 545–572 (2004)
13. Penha, F., Lucena, M., Lucena, L., Angra, C., Alencar, F.: A proposed textual model for i-star. In: iStar (2016)
14. Siena, A., Perini, A., Susi, A., Mylopoulos, J.: A meta-model for modelling law-compliant requirements. In: 2009 Second International Workshop on Requirements Engineering and Law (2009)
15. Villafiorita, A., Weldemariam, K., Susi, A., Siena, A.: Modeling and analysis of laws using BPR and goal-oriented framework. In: 2010 Fourth International Conference on Digital Society (2010)

Optimal Parameter Selection Using Explainable AI for Time-Series Anomaly Detection

Shimon Sumita$^{(\boxtimes)}$, Hiroyuki Nakagawa, and Tatsuhiro Tsuchiya

Osaka University, Osaka, Japan
{s-sumita,nakagawa,t-tutiya}@ist.osaka-u.ac.jp

Abstract. Time-series anomaly detection is a technique for detecting unusual values, changes, or movements in a large amount of data arranged in time-series. It is primarily used in the fields of intrusion detection, medical diagnosis, and industrial defect damage detection and necessary to realize agents that operate intelligently and autonomously, such as changing system behavior based on detected anomalies. SALAD is a real-time time-series anomaly detection method based on deep learning. It is lightweight and determines anomaly detection threshold flexibly; however, experts need to determine an appropriate value for a parameter so that it suits any given recurrent time series, and this inhibits the realization of the agent. In this study, we propose a method to determine automatically the optimal parameter value in SALAD's prediction model by utilizing XAI. We use SHAP, which provides interpretability to the prediction by the deep learning model. Through evaluation experiment, we demonstrate that our method is effective and provide an example of the use of XAI for time-series anomaly detection.

Keywords: Time-series anomaly detection · Self-adaptive anomaly detection · Explainable AI (XAI)

1 Introduction

With the recent rapid increase of data generation, anomaly detection, the process of detecting data that behaves differently from the majority of other data, has gained in importance. It is used in various fields, such as intrusion detection, fraud detection, medical diagnosis, image processing, and industrial defect damage detection. In terms of the realization of agent, anomaly detection is also very important. Agent is software that operates intelligently and autonomously. In order for agents to change their own behavior in response to changes in the environment, it is important to detect anomalies in real time. SALAD [5] is a real-time time-series anomaly detection method based on deep learning. It use simple LSTM and self-adaptive anomaly detection threshold to detect anomalies in recurrent time-series flexibly; however, experts need to determine hyperparameters to build optimal predictive models for anomaly detection. This precludes

© The Author(s), under exclusive license to Springer Nature Switzerland AG 2023
R. Aydoğan et al. (Eds.): PRIMA 2022, LNAI 13753, pp. 281–296, 2023.
https://doi.org/10.1007/978-3-031-21203-1_17

the realization of agents that behave autonomously. In this study, we propose a method to determine the optimal hyperparameters of SALAD automatically and efficiently by utilizing explainable AI. Explainable AI (XAI) is a technology that gives explanatory power to the black box predictions of AI. It provides humans with a visually clear explanation of the basis for the decisions made by AI models. We use SHAP (SHapley Additive exPlanation) [24] which is based on the game theoretically optimal Shapley values to build the proposed method. In the evaluation experiment, we used the NYC taxi dataset to show that our method is able to determine the optimal hyperparameter for SALAD. Our research addresses the following research questions.

RQ1: Is XAI useful in determining the optimal parameters for time series anomaly detection methods?
RQ2: Is the proposed method beneficial for agent implementation?

The remainder of the paper is organized as follows. Section 2 overviews anomaly detection and XAI and describes the time-series anomaly detection method, SALAD and XAI method, SHAP. In Sect. 3, we propose a method utilizing SHAP in SALAD. Section 4 describes the experiments conducted to verify the effectiveness of the proposed method. In Sect. 5, we discuss the results of the experiments, and finally, we summarize this study in Sect. 6.

2   Background

This section overviews anomaly detection method and XAI used in the proposed method.

2.1   Anomaly Detection

When analyzing real-world datasets, it is often required to determine the data that is different from the majority of other data. Such data is called anomalous. In particular, an anomaly is defined as "an observed value that deviates significantly from other observed values and is suspected to be generated by a different mechanism" [2]. Anomaly detection is a technique that detects such anomalies. A simple example of an anomaly is provided in Fig. 1. Given a such dataset, by considering the overall distribution, anomaly detection techniques identify the majority of the dataset clustered on the left as normal and the few data deviating from it as abnormal. Anomaly detection can handle tabular data, image data, and time series data.

Anomalies are broadly classified into three types: point, collective or group, and contextual. Point anomalies often represent randomly occurring irregularities or deviations that cannot be interpreted in any particular way. Collective or group anomalies appear to behave normally when viewed individually but exhibit

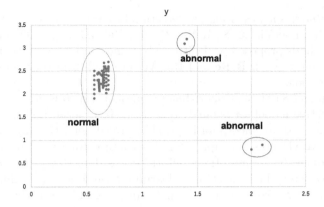

Fig. 1. Example of abnormal data.

abnormal characteristics when observed collectively. A contextual anomaly refers to data that may be considered anomalous in a particular context. Contextual anomalies are identified by considering both contextual and behavioral features. Contextual features typically use time and space, whereas behavioral features use arbitrary features to describe normal behavior, such as patterns in money usage or the occurrence of system log events.

In the past 10 years, various methods based on statistics (Hotelling's T-squared method) and machine learning (k-means method and one-class SVM [1]) have been studied as anomaly detection methods. These state-of-the-art studies include luminol [9] proposed by LinkedIn, Yahoo's EGADS [10], Lavin and Ahmad's hierarchical temporal memory (HTM) [11]. In addition, anomaly detection methods based on deep learning, particularly using CNNs and LSTMs, have attracted considerable attention in recent years. Zhang [12] and Mudassar [13] have achieved excellent results using these methods for IoT and big data; Erfurth [14] and Xu [15] applied them to the field of medicine, and Le [16] and HaddadPajouh [17] to the field of malware detection. Kanarachos et al. [18] and Shipmon et al. [19] have studied anomaly detection using deep learning on one-dimensional time-series.

SALAD (Self-adaptive lightweight anomaly detection) proposed by Ming-Chang Lee et al. [5] is an effective anomaly detection method for real-time time-series with periodic patterns. Real-world time-series, such as transit ridership, network traffic, energy usage, and human gait, have periodic patterns and are often generated in real time. Recently, anomaly detection methods based on statistics and machine learning have been proposed and actively studied in various fields. However, methods based on machine learning require labeled dataset, offline training, and extensive computation, and statistical methods require the time-series of the target in advance to build statistical models. Therefore, neither method suits real-time anomaly detection. By contrast, SALAD is a real-time time-series anomaly detection method that overcomes these issues and demonstrates a superior performance compared to five state-of-the-art anomaly detection methods such as AnomalyDetectionTs (ADT), AnomalyDetectionVec (ADV) [6], GrammerViz3.0 [8], ReRe [21] and RePAD [20]. ADT and ADV are statistical methods proposed by Twitter. GrammerViz3.0 is a statistical method proposed by Senin et al. ReRe and RePAD are real-time time series anomaly detection methods.

SALAD uses LSTM (long short-term memory), which is a type of RNN , to build a predictive model for anomaly detection. In general, LSTM has complex structures, and systems incorporating LSTM are computationally expensive. In particular, SALAD uses a simple LSTM structure (one hidden layer and 10 nodes) to reduce the computational effort as possible. However, such a simple LSTM structure may be ineffective for learning time-series that exhibit complex behavior. Therefore, instead of training a simple LSTM directly on the time-series to predict future data point and detect anomalies, the time-series data are converted in real time to a series of average absolute relative error (AARE) values [22], which is a well-known measure used to determine the prediction accuracy of prediction methods. SALAD uses past data to train a simple LSTM in a sliding window method. The AARE series data is much smoother than the original time series, making it useful for both learning and prediction. The AARE value is calculated by Eq. 1, where v_y the measured value, $\hat{v}_y$ is the predicted value, and b the number of past data used in training. The lower the AARE value, the closer the prediction is to the measured value.

$$AARE_t = \frac{1}{b} \cdot \sum_{y=t-b-1}^{t} \frac{|v_y - \hat{v}_y|}{v_y}, t \geq 2b - 1 \tag{1}$$

Once SALAD has derived a sufficient number of AARE values, it trains a simple LSTM using short-term past AARE values to predict future AARE values and begins detecting anomalies. Concurrently, SALAD continues to update the detection threshold based on all previously derived AARE values and the 3-sigma rule [7]. The detection threshold is calculated by Eqs. 2, 3, and 4.

$$thd_{AARE} = \mu_{AARE} + 3 \cdot \sigma \tag{2}$$

$$\mu_{AARE} = \frac{1}{t - b - 1} \cdot \sum_{x=2b-1}^{t} AARE_x \tag{3}$$

$$\sigma = \sqrt{\frac{\sum_{x=2b-1}^{t} (AARE_x - \mu_{AARE})^2}{t - b - 1}} \tag{4}$$

If the difference between the predicted and actual AARE values is greater than the detection threshold, which is continually updated as the environment changes, the corresponding data point is considered abnormal; otherwise, the data point is considered normal. The features of SALAD are summarized as follows.

- SALAD is an unsupervised anomaly detection method that does not require off-line learning. Experts are not required to build training or statistical models in advance or define detection thresholds.
- SALAD is a flexible anomaly detection method that automatically retrains the LSTM model and updates the detection threshold in response to changes in the pattern of the time-series data.
- SALAD is a lightweight and cost-effective anomaly detection method. By converting the complex original time-series data into a simpler series of AARE values, the use of LSTMs with complex structures is avoided, reducing computational complexity.

2.2   XAI

Machine learning and Deep Learning technologies have wide ranges of applications and have achieved good results in such areas as image recognition and natural language processing. However, their complex internal structure is a black box, and humans struggle to understand the basis on which AI make predictions. In recent years, XAI has been attracting attention, particularly in medical and financial industries, for providing explanatory power to AI predictions. XAI is not a term for a specific technology but a generic term for technologies being researched with the aim of understanding various types of AI from all perspectives.

Specific techniques include LIME [23], SHAP [24], permutation importance [29], partial dependence plot/individual conditional expectation [25,26], CAM/Grad-CAM [27,28], integrated gradients [30]. LIME uses linear approximation to explain the predictions of arbitrary AI models on various types of data such as images and text. SHAP uses a game-theoretic approach to indicate the contribution of features. Permutation importance shows the relationship between features and results based on the prediction errors of models produced by rearranging features. Partial dependance plot/individual conditional expectation show the effect of changing feature values on the prediction results of a machine learning model as a graph. CAM/Grad-CAM use the gradients of the convolution layer of a CNN-based model to generate a map highlighting important regions in the image. Integrated gradients approximates the integral of the input–output gradients of DNN-based models to assign importance scores to input features. We have applied the integrated gradients technique to reduce the adaptation space in the self-adaptation domain in the previous work [31]. In this study, we use SHAP as an XAI technique to improve the anomaly detection technique, because SHAP computes the contribution of each feature to the model's predictions and can be used for deep learning.

SHAP (SHapley Additive exPlanations) [24] is a game-theoretic approach for explaining the output of any machine learning model. It is based on the Shapley value, which represents the contribution of each player in game theory. SHAP allows us to calculate the contribution of each feature to the prediction made by the predictive model, i.e., SHAP value. By plotting the SHAP values, the contribution of each feature to a given forecast is displayed in an easy-to-see manner, as shown in Fig. 2.

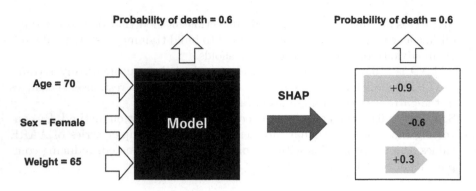

Fig. 2. Example of SHAP.

3   Optimal Window Size Determination

This section describes the proposed method which determine optimal SALAD parameter automatically and efficiently. First, we provide an overview of the proposed method. Next, we describe the algorithm.

SALAD uses historical time-series data to train LSTM-based prediction models using a sliding window method. If the window size is small, only the most recent data are provided as input values to make a prediction, which may result in localized predictions that do not consider the entire flow of data. Conversely, if the window size is large, the input data can include considerable data from the past to make a certain prediction such as a global prediction, which considers the entire flow of data, possible. However, the number of input values given to the LSTM increases, and the time required for training increases. The ideal prediction model for anomaly detection should be able to make global predictions that consider the entire data flow at high speed. Determining the optimal window size is necessary to achieve these goals. However, the optimal window size differs for each time-series dataset, and the appropriate value must be determined manually based on the final results.

In this study, SHAP, as a XAI technique, is used to automatically determine the appropriate window size. When SHAP is applied to a forecasting model built with simple LSTM, it calculates a SHAP value that indicates the contribution of historical data provided as input values to the forecast. Figure 3 presents an example.

This figure plots the SHAP values, which represent the contribution of each input value to the prediction, when the prediction model trained with a window size of 6 is given historical data at t = 571–576 and predicts the value one point ahead (t = 577). If the absolute value of the SHAP value is large, it makes a large contribution. Conversely, if the absolute value of the SHAP value which is near zero, it makes a small contribution. In this example, the contribution to the forecast decreases slightly with historical data, but all input values contribute to some degree.

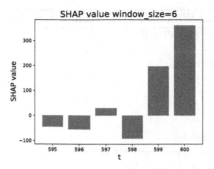

Fig. 3. Example of SHAP value.

We plotted the SHAP values at various window sizes and data points. From the results we found that as the window size is increased, the contribution of past data tends toward zero after a certain window size. As a concrete example, Figs. 4 and 5 show the SHAP values for window sizes of 36 and 96 respectively.

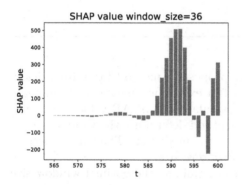

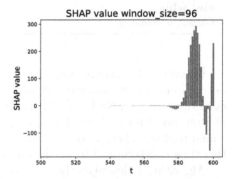

Fig. 4. Window_size = 36.   **Fig. 5.** Window_size = 96.

Figure 4 shows that when the window size is 36, the data before t = 570 contributes minimally to the prediction of t = 601. In addition, Fig. 5 shows that when the window size is 96, the previous data around t = 570 does not contribute to the prediction of t=601, unlike when the window size is 36. Increasing the window size increases the input values given to the LSTM prediction model and increases the time required for learning and prediction. Thus, omitting data that does not contribute as much as possible is intuitively better. However, the SHAP value alone cannot be used to determine that areas of past data that do not contribute to prediction actually do not affect anomaly detection accuracy. Therefore, the assumption is that if the window size exceeds a certain value and a section of the historical data does not contribute to the forecast, the subsequent anomaly detection accuracy does not change significantly.

Algorithm 1. Optimal Window Size Determination Algorithm

$window\_size \Leftarrow FIRST\_WINDOW\_SIZE$
$isUnbreak \Leftarrow True$
$time \Leftarrow START\_TIME$
$cycle \Leftarrow CYCLE$
$x \Leftarrow NUM$
$div \Leftarrow DIV$
while $isUnbreak$ **do**
   Build a forecasting model
   Build an explanatory model with SHAP
   while $time \leq t \leq time + cycle$ **do**
      Calculate SHAP value for the forecast at $t + 1$ point.
      Build a forecasting model
      if All of the previous x SHAP values are less than max(absolute SHAP values)/div **then**
         $isUnbreak \Leftarrow False$
         break
      end if
   end while
   $window\_size \Leftarrow window\_size + 1$
end while
output $window\_size$

Based on this assumption, this study proposes a method for automatically determining the optimal window size with fast execution time and high anomaly detection accuracy. In brief, the method calculates the SHAP value of the prediction model for each window size. The method determines the window size at which past data begins to not contribute to the prediction. The window size at this time is determined to be the optimal window size.

Algorithm 1 describes the process for determining the optimal window size for SALAD.

The algorithm begins with a window size of $FIRST\_WINDOW\_SIZE$ and searches for the optimal window size by gradually increasing the window size. For each window size, a prediction model is built, and an explanatory model is built to calculate the SHAP value for the prediction of the model. The constructed model is then used to calculate the SHAP value for one forecast ahead (at $t + 1$) in a certain interval ($time \leq t \leq time + cycle$). If all previous x SHAP values are smaller than max(absolute SHAP values)/div, then there is a portion of the past data after the window size that does not contribute, and the window size at that time is determined as the optimal window size.

Table 1. Dates defined as anomalies and their contents.

Month	Day	Content
2014/9	1	Labor Day
	21	Climate March
	28	Sunday event
10	5	Sunday event
	12	New York Comic Con
	19, 26	Sunday event
11	2	NYC Marathon
	9, 16	Sunday event
	23	Football match
	27	Thanksgiving
	30	Sunday event

Month	Day	Content
12	7	Sunday event
	13–14	Millions March NYC
	21	Sunday event
	25	Christmas
2015/1	1	New Year's Day
	11, 18	Sunday event
	19	MLK day
	26–27	Blizzard

4 Evaluation

4.1 Overview

We use the open-source time-series dataset New York City Taxi demand (NYC) published by the Numenta Anomaly Benchmark (NAB) [32]. This dataset is based on the total number of cab passengers in New York City from July 2014 to January 2015, aggregated every 30 min. It consists of 10,320 data items. The dataset has also been used in several studies for the purpose of evaluating anomaly detection accuracy [33,34].

This dataset includes 22 anomalies to be detected. These anomalies are defined by [33] and [5]. Most of the days defined as anomalies are holidays, anniversaries, and Sundays with special events. Table 1 lists the dates and contents defined as anomalies.

This study used data from 9840 cases from July 1, 2014 to January 21, 2015. The anomalies to be detected are the 21 abnormal days, omitting the blizzard January 26–27, 2015.

Figure 6 plots the entire NYC dataset. The y-axis represents the number of cab passengers in New York City every 30 min. The x-axis represents the time of day. Data for dates defined as anomalies are in red. Data for other normal days are in blue.

4.2 Evaluation Criteria

In this experiment, the F-measure, precision, recall, and execution time are used as evaluation criteria to compare SALAD's performance with different window sizes. The F-measure, precision, and recall are defined by Eqs. 5, 6 and 7, respectively.

$$F - measure = \frac{2 * Precision * Recall}{Precision + Recall} \tag{5}$$

$$Precision = \frac{TP}{TP + FP} \tag{6}$$

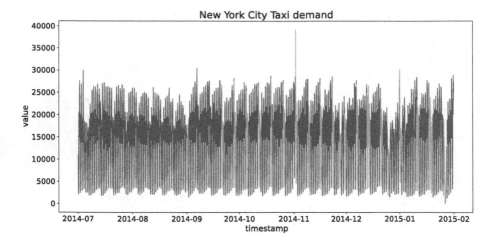

Fig. 6. New York City Taxi demand. (Color figure online)

$$Recall = \frac{TP}{TP + FN} \tag{7}$$

TP (true positive) is the number of days that SALAD detects as anomalies and are actually abnormal. FP (false positive) is the number of days that SALAD detects as anomalies but are not actually abnormal. FN (false negative) is the number of days that SALAD determines are not abnormal but are actually abnormal. The F-measure is the weighted harmonic mean of precision and recall. The execution time is the time required to run SALAD.

4.3 Experiment Details

In this experiment, the proposed method, called optimal window size determination, was executed and the correctness of the results was verified. First, the proposed method was executed and the optimal window size was output. SALAD was then run with that window size, and the recall, precision, F-measure, and execution time were measured. Subsequently SALAD was run with various values of window size (6, 24, 36, 48, 72, and 96) to evaluate whether the results are optimal. Anomaly detection accuracy and execution time were measured and compared to the results for the window sizes calculated by the proposed method. In this experiment, the algorithm constants were set to the values listed in Table 2.

The experiment environment was as follows:

- OS: macOS High Sierra 10.13.6
- CPU: Intel Core i5 1.8 GHz
- Memory: 8 GB.

Table 2. Constant values of the proposed method

Fixed number name	Value
FIRST_WINDOW_SIZE	3
START_TIME	576
CYCLE	48
NUM	3
DIV	200

Table 3. Results

Window size	Recall	Precision	F-measure	Run time (s)
6	0.381	0.800	0.515	417.4
24	0.809	0.654	0.723	999.1
30	0.857	0.667	0.750	1037.4
36	0.952	0.606	0.740	1238.2
48	0.857	0.667	0.750	1709.7
72	0.905	0.678	0.775	2223.7
96	0.952	0.625	0.755	2446.8

4.4   Results

The proposed method outputs that the optimal window size was 30. Therefore, we run SALAD with this window size, and measure the four metrics. Next, we run SALAD with various window sizes to examine whether the window size calculated by the proposed method was actually optimal. In this experiment, we run SALAD with window sizes of 6, 24, 36, 48, 72, and 96. Figure 7 and Table 3 present the SHAP value, anomaly detection accuracy, and execution time for each window size.

Figure 7 shows the SHAP values for a prediction of the model trained with various window sizes. This SHAP value shows the contribution of each input value to the prediction at $t = 601$ using data from $t = (600 - windowsize + 1)$ to $t = 600$ as input values. When the window size was 6, the data from the most recent point ($t = 595$) and data from the point closest to the forecast point ($t = 600$) have approximately the same contribution. However, as the window size increases, the historical data stop contributing to the forecast at window size 30. Table 3 summarizes the anomaly detection accuracy and execution time for various window sizes. The results show that the execution time increased as the window size increased, and that the accuracy of the F-measure improved until window size 30, but after that, the F-measure remained unchanged at approximately 0.75.

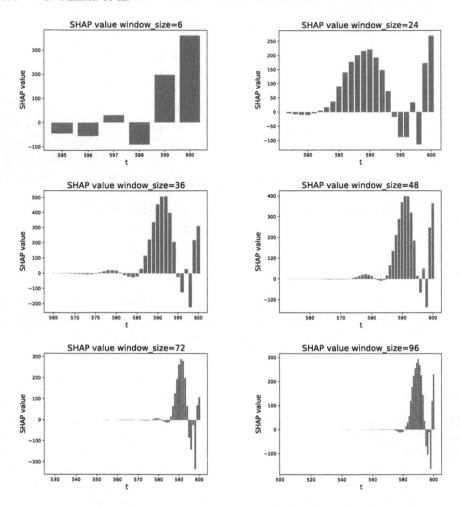

Fig. 7. SHAP value (window_size = 6, 24, 36, 48, 72, 96).

5 Discussion

In this section, we discuss results and revisit our research questions (RQs).

5.1 Results

From the results described in Sect. 4.4, our method can determine the optimal window size with high anomaly detection accuracy in the least amount of time for a real-time time-series anomaly detection method. We discuss the effectiveness of this method based on the results obtained. First, we found the following facts:

1. The execution time increases as the window size increases.

2. As the window size is increased, the anomaly detection accuracy improves until a certain window size and does not change thereafter.

For the first fact, a larger window size means more inputs for the LSTM-based forecasting model, which increases the time required for training and forecasting. Consequently, the overall execution time is also expected to increase. For the second fact, as can be seen from the SHAP values in Fig. 7, from a certain window size, the past data hardly contribute to the model prediction, and therefore, the prediction model does not change even if the window size is increased. This may produce the results where accuracy remains the same for various window sizes. Because the SHAP value can determine the nature of the prediction model to an extent and the prediction model is related to the anomaly detection accuracy, we consider that a relationship exists between the anomaly detection accuracy and the SHAP value. Therefore, we conclude that this method is effective in determining the optimal window size that achieves high anomaly detection accuracy and requires a relatively small execution time, and that XAI, which can quantify the learning status of predictive models, is useful for the practical application of a time-series anomaly detection method.

5.2   Answers to Research Questions (RQs)

In summary, the research questions (RQs) that were posed in Sect. 1 are answered as follows.

RQ1: Is XAI Useful in Determining the Optimal Parameters for Time Series Anomaly Detection Methods? The challenge with SALAD, which is the time-series anomaly detection method used in this study, is that the optimal parameters differ for each dataset and must be determined manually. Specifically, the optimal window size for training a prediction model is determined based on the results of running SALAD (the anomaly detection accuracy and execution time). In this study, we determined that the XAI method SHAP can determine the optimal parameter in advance for the contribution of input values to certain predictions of a forecasting model. XAI has the potential to solve the problem of automatically determining optimal parameters for time-series anomaly detection methods.

RQ2: Is the Proposed Method Beneficial for Agent Implementation? Information obtained from anomaly detection is useful for realizing agents that behave intelligently and autonomously. However, conventional anomaly detection methods require experts to set optimal parameters, and introducing such anomaly detection methods directly into agents would inhibit their autonomous and intelligent behavior. On the other hand, our proposed method is capable of determining the optimal parameters for anomaly detection automatically, which vary with dataset. Therefore, we conclude that our method is useful for agents to operate anomaly detection methods and determine their own behavior autonomously.

6   Conclusion

In this study, to apply anomaly detection to agents, we considered determining the optimal parameters for anomaly detection automatically and proposed the method using XAI for time-series anomaly detection. Our method utilizes the contribution of input values to the model's prediction calculated by SHAP to select the optimal parameter. To verify whether the parameter calculated by the proposed method is the actual optimal value, we ran SALAD with various parameter values and compared the results. Consequently, we concluded that this method can automatically select the optimal parameter value that allows SALAD to run quickly and accurately, and that it is useful for agents to operate anomaly detection and intelligently and autonomously change their own behavior. Few studies have been conducted on the use of XAI for time-series anomaly detection, and we believe that this study provides an example of its application.

Future works are as follows: This study only shows that the optimal parameters for anomaly detection could be determined automatically by using XAI, and thus evaluation experiments should be conducted in terms of time required for parameter determination and efficiency. In addition, the effectiveness of this method should be verified using various datasets, various XAI methods, and various hyperprameter tuning methods. We should investigate the linkages between anomaly detection and XAI and refine the theory of determining the threshold.

Acknowledgment. This work was supported by JSPS Grants-in-Aid for Scientific Research (Grant Numbers 17KT0043, 20H04167, and 18H03229).

References

1. Schölkopf, B., Platt, J.C., Shawe-Taylor, J.C., Smola, A.J., Williamson, R.C.: Estimating the support of a high-dimensional distribution. Neural Comput. **13**(7), 1443–1471 (2001)
2. Hawkins, D.: Identification of outliers. Chapman and hall, London (1980)
3. Chalapathy, R., Chawla, S.: Deep learning for anomaly detection: a survey. arXiv preprint arXiv:1901.03407 (2019)
4. Hayes, M.A., Capretz, M.A.M.: Contextual anomaly detection framework for big sensor data. J. Big Data **2**(1), 1–22 (2015). https://doi.org/10.1186/s40537-014-0011-y
5. Lee, M.-C., Lin, J.-C., Gran, E.G.: SALAD: self-adaptive lightweight anomaly detection for real-time recurrent time series. In: Proceedings of the 45th IEEE Computer Society Signature Conference on Computers, Software, and Applications (COMPSAC 2021), pp. 344–349 (2021). arXiv preprint arXiv:2104.09968
6. Hochenbaum, J., Vallis, O.S., Kejariwal, A.: Automatic anomaly detection in the cloud via statistical learning. arXiv preprint arXiv:1704.07706 (2017)
7. Pukelsheim, F.: The three sigma rule. Am. Stat. **48**(2), 88–91 (1994)
8. Senin, P., et al.: GrammarViz 3.0: interactive discovery of variable-length time series patterns. ACM Trans. Knowl. Discov. Data (TKDD) **12**(1), 1–28 (2018)
9. linkedin/luminol. https://github.com/linkedin/luminol

10. Laptev, N., Amizadeh, S., Flint, I.: Generic and scalable framework for automated time-series anomaly detection. In: Proceedings of the 21th ACM International Conference on Knowledge Discovery and Data Mining (SIGKDD), pp. 1939–1947 (2015)
11. lavin, A., Ahmad, S.: Evaluating real-time anomaly detection algorithms-the numenta anomaly benchmark. In: 2015 IEEE 14th International Conference on Machine Learning and Applications (ICMLA 2015), pp. 38–44 (2015)
12. Zhang, W., et al.: LSTM-based analysis of industrial IoT equipment. IEEE Access **6**, 23551–23560 (2018)
13. Mudassar, B.A., Ko, J.H., Mukhopadhyay, S.: An unsupervised anomalous event detection frame-work with class aware source separation. In: 2018 IEEE International Conference on Acoustics, Speech and Signal Processing (ICASSP), pp. 2671–2675 (2018)
14. Schmidt-Erfurth, U., Sadeghipour, A., Gerendas, B.S., Waldstein, M., Bogunovic, H.: Artificial intelligence in retina. Prog. Retinal Eye Res. **67**, 1–29 (2018)
15. Xu, H., et al.: Unsupervised anomaly detection via variational auto-encoder for seasonal KPIs in web applications. In: Proceedings of the 2018 World Wide Web Conference on World Wide Web, pp. 187–196 (2018)
16. Le, Q., Namee, B.M., Scanlon, M.: Deep learning at the shallow end: malware classification for non-domain experts. Digit. Investig. **26**, S118–S126 (2018)
17. HaddadPajouh, H., Dehghantanha, A., Khayami, R., Choo, K.-K.R.: A deep recurrent neural network based approach for internet of things malware threat hunting. Future Gener. Comput. Syst. **85**, 88–96 (2018)
18. Kanarachos, S., Christopoulos, S.-R.G., Chroneos, A., Fitzpatrick, M.E.: Detecting anomalies in time series data via a deep learning algorithm combining wavelets, neural networks and Hilbert transform. Expert Syst. Appl. **85**, 292–304 (2017)
19. Shipmon, D., Gurevitch, J., Piselli, P.M., Edwards, S.: Time series anomaly detection: detection of anomalous drops with limited features and sparse examples in noisy periodic data. Technical report, Google Inc. (2017). https://arxiv.org/abs/1708.03665
20. Lee, M.-C., Lin, J.-C., Gran, E.G.: RePAD: real-time proactive anomaly detection for time series. In: Barolli, L., Amato, F., Moscato, F., Enokido, T., Takizawa, M. (eds.) AINA 2020. AISC, vol. 1151, pp. 1291–1302. Springer, Cham (2020). https://doi.org/10.1007/978-3-030-44041-1_110
21. Lee, M-C., Lin, J-C., Gran, E.G.: ReRe: a lightweight real- time ready-to-go anomaly detection approach for time series.: In: Proceedings of the 44th IEEE Computer Society Signature Conference on Computers, Software, and Applications (COMPSAC 2020), pp. 322–327 (2020)
22. Lee, M.-C., Lin, J.-C., Gran, E.G.: Distributed fine-grained traffic speed prediction for large-scale transportation networks based on automatic LSTM customization and sharing. In: Malawski, M., Rzadca, K. (eds.) Euro-Par 2020. LNCS, vol. 12247, pp. 234–247. Springer, Cham (2020). https://doi.org/10.1007/978-3-030-57675-2_15
23. Ribeiro, M.T., Singh, S., Guestrin, C.: Why should I trust you?: explaining the predictions of any classifier. In: Proceedings of the 22nd ACM International Conference on Knowledge Discovery and Data Mining (SIGKDD), pp. 1135–1144 (2016)
24. Lundberg S., Lee, S.-I.: A unified approach to interpreting model predictions. In: NIPS 2017: Proceedings of the 31st International Conference on Neural Information Processing Systems, pp. 4768–4777 (2017)
25. Friedman, J.H.: Greedy function approximation: a gradient boosting machine. Ann. Stat. **29**, 1189–1232 (2001)

26. Goldstein, A., Kapelner, A., Bleich, J., Pitkin, E.: Peeking inside the black box: visualizing statistical learning with plots of individual conditional expectation. J. Comput. Graph. Stat. **24**(1), 44–65 (2015)
27. Zhou, B., Khosla, A., Lapedriza, A., Oliva, A., Torralba, A.: Learning deep features for discriminative localization (2016)
28. Selvaraju, R.R., Cogswell, M., Das, A., Vedantam, R., Parikh, D., Batra, D.: Grad-CAM: visual explanations from deep networks via gradient-based localization: Proceedings of the IEEE International Conference on Computer Vision (ICCV), pp. 618–626 (2017)
29. Fisher, A., Rudin, C., Dominici, F.: All models are wrong, but many are useful: learning a variable's importance by studying an entire class of prediction models simultaneously. arXiv:1801.01489 (2018)
30. Sundararajan, M., Taly, A., Yan, Q.: Axiomatic attribution for deep networks. In: ICML 2017: Proceedings of the 34th International Conference on Machine Learning, Vol. 70, pp, 3319–3328 (2017)
31. Diallo, A.B., Nakagawa, H., Tsuchiya, T.: Adaptation space reduction using an explainable framework. In: Proceedings of the IEEE 45th Annual Computers, Software, and Applications Conference (COMPSAC), pp. 1653–1660 (2021)
32. numenta/NAB. https://github.com/numenta/NAB
33. A tour of AI technologies in time series prediction. https://www.soa.org/resources/research-reports/2019/tourai-technologies/
34. Farahani, I.V., Chien, A., King, R.E., Kay, M.G., Klenz, B.: Time series anomaly detection from a Markov chain perspective. In: 2019 IEEE 18th International Conference on Machine Learning and Applications (ICMLA), pp. 1000–1007 (2019)

Does Order Simultaneity Affect the Data Mining Task in Financial Markets? – Effect Analysis of Order Simultaneity Using Artificial Market

Masanori Hirano$^{(\boxtimes)}$ (iD) and Kiyoshi Izumi (iD)

The University of Tokyo, Tokyo, Japan
research@mhirano.jp, izumi@sys.t.u-tokyo.ac.jp

Abstract. This study analyzed the effect of order simultaneity in financial markets on data mining tasks, using multi-agent simulations. In financial markets, multiple orders are submitted almost simultaneously or within very quick succession; such orders are thought of as independent of one another. We call this phenomenon order simultaneity. If order simultaneity increases, tick-time-level data mining methods are assumed to worsen because the randomness of the order sequences increases. The present study analyzed this effect using artificial market simulations, which enable experimentation in a fully-controlled environment. As a data mining task, we employed a Generative Adversarial Network (GAN) for the financial market to perform next order generation (prediction). We analyzed the impact of order simultaneity by applying the GAN to simulated data in artificial market simulations with various environmental parameters. We found that the effect of order simultaneity is limited for the next order generation task, which can be said to be the ultimate prediction task in financial markets. This analysis also supports the validity of the current approach of utilizing GANs to model order time series in financial markets. Moreover, our study demonstrates the utility of combining artificial market simulations and data mining.

Keywords: Financial markets · Data mining · Order simultaneity · Artificial market simulation · Generative Adversarial Network (GAN)

1 Introduction

In financial markets, trade is gradually accelerating. Although high-frequency trading (HFT) shares might be shrinking [22], the time priority principle, which is important for HFT, is still employed all over the world. Order speed is expected to continue to increase with technological advancement, as is mechanized order processing speed.

Given emerging HFTs, the advantages and disadvantages of HFT are also being discussed. For example, the risk of flash crashes is said to have increased

R. Aydoğan et al. (Eds.): PRIMA 2022, LNAI 13753, pp. 297–313, 2023.
https://doi.org/10.1007/978-3-031-21203-1_18

because of HFT. However, HFT is considered to offer the advantage of enhancing markets' price discovery function, especially in the short term.

To address the downside of HFT, speed bumps have been proposed. In the context of financial markets, speed bumps function as market architecture for delaying order processing. Speed bumps were introduced at New York Stock Exchange (NYSE) American in 2017. Speed bumps have also been discussed in European countries, such as in the MiFID II and the HFT Act. Also, batch auction is among the alternative actions to address the downside of HFT.

Related to the aforementioned speeding up and speed bumps, the idea of simultaneity is an important concept. When you attempt to place an order, the referenced information does not always reflect all previous orders ahead of yours in the queue because it is likely that other orders will be placed while yours is being submitted and processed. If speed bumps are introduced, simultaneity will increase. On the other hand, if market acceleration intensifies, simultaneity will decrease because speeding up lowers the probability that other orders will be placed during the submission and processing of your order. Simultaneity can thus be considered an enemy of HFT because it increases market uncertainty during trading operations, and the information time lag becomes relatively more significant. Hence, HFT regulation addresses the level of simultaneity. Ultimately, batch auction, where all orders are processed at the same time, has the highest degree of simultaneity.

Moreover, simultaneity nullifies the meaning of order sequences in short periods. It is possible that continuous orders issued at very short intervals could come in different random order sequences. Furthermore, it is hard to imagine that when orders are issued in quick succession, consideration is given to previous orders within that short period.

Order simultaneity also affects financial data mining. Recently, data augmentation with a Generative Adversarial Network (GAN) has been proposed, and its benefits for prediction tasks on financial markets have been espoused [33]. Using augmented tick (order) data improves prediction task performance. GANs usually only generate the next order, and the process is repeated to generate a longer augmented order series.

Does such order generation make sense under the assumption of simultaneity? If we assume that order simultaneity renders the sequence of orders within a short period meaningless, then only attempting to predict the next order seems nonsensical. The reason for this is because the randomness of the arrival of multiple orders dominates the prediction of the next order so intensely that it may be utterly unpredictable.

Therefore, in this study, we use multi-agent simulation to answer the following research question: If we assume randomness in the order sequence, does it make sense to generate the next order in GANs? In other words, we test the hypothesis that the simultaneity of orders significantly affects the accuracy of the next order generation (prediction) task. Regarding experiments, we use an artificial market data mining platform [17] that utilizes multi-agent simulation for the evaluation of data mining methods. Artificial market simulation makes it easy to verify the effect of order simultaneity because orders' origin trader, which would normally be unobservable, can be identified. We also employ the policy gradient stock GAN (PGSGAN) [18], given that it is a state-of-the-art GAN for financial markets. Consequently, we find that simultaneity exerts a limited effect on prediction; hence, the hypothesis is partially rejected.

2 Related Work

Edmonds *et al.* [11] argued that agent-based simulation is useful in the social sciences. Its importance, especially for financial markets, is discussed in [4,12]. For example, Lux *et al.* [27] showed that interaction between agents in financial market simulations is necessary to replicate stylized facts. Cui *et al.* [8] showed that the trader model used in artificial financial market simulations requires intelligence to replicate stylized facts. Mizuta [31] demonstrated that a multi-agent simulation of the financial market can contribute to the implementation of rules and regulations in actual financial markets. Torii *et al.* [41] used this approach to reveal how the flow of a price shock is transferred to other stocks. Indeed, based on data from an artificial market simulation, Mizuta *et al.* [32] tested the effect of price tick size, that is, the price unit for orders, which led to a discussion of tick size devaluation in the Tokyo Stock Exchange market. Hirano *et al.* [16] assessed the effect of regulation of the Capital Adequacy Ratio (CAR) and observed the resultant risk of market price shock and depression, based on generated data in the hypothetical situation realized in their artificial market simulation. Some studies have focused on flush crashes using artificial financial market simulations [24,35]. As an example of one such platform, Torii *et al.* [42] proposed the Plham [39]. In this study, we use PlhamJ platform [40], the updated version of Plham. Other artificial financial market simulators exist, such as the U-MART [37], the Santa Fe artificial stock market [3], and agent-based interactive discrete event simulation (ABIDES) [5].

In terms of order generation for financial markets, stock GAN [26], a GAN for stock markets, was designed to generate realistic order time series and best prices without real order book data via a continuous double auction (CDA) network. Naritomi *et al.* [33] presented a basic GAN model for stock markets and showed that its generated data are beneficial for predicting future price movement. In this study, we employ the PGSGAN [18], which can consider actual orders' discreteness to generate realistic fake orders. Moreover, there exist studies that have attempted to directly utilize GAN architecture for future price predictions [45,46].

GANs-related technology has improved in the following respects. Goodfellow *et al.* [13] proposed the original GAN. Mirza *et al.* [29] then proposed the conditional GAN. Radford *et al.* [36] subsequently proposed a deep convolutional GAN (DCGAN). Other learning architectures such as the least-squares GAN [28], the generalized f-GAN [34], the Laplacian pyramid GAN [9], the variational autoencoder GAN [23], the image-to-image translation GAN (known as pix2pix) [19], the self-attention GAN [45], the cycle GAN [7] for image translations, the style GAN [21] for style conversions, and the progressive growing GAN

[20] for high-resolution images were also proposed. Additionally, as an extension of GANs, adversarial feature learning [10] for embedding images into vectors and anomaly detections based on GAN [25,38,44] were proposed. The Wasserstein GAN (WGAN) [2] was suggested based on discussion about GANs' learning stability [1]. Gradient penalty [14] and spectral normalization [30] are the tools proposed for stabilizing the WGAN. The PGSGAN [18], which is employed in this study, is based on the WGAN and uses spectral normalization.

3   Model

In our model, we employed the concept of the artificial market data mining platform [17], which combines multi-agent simulation and data mining methods for financial markets, with the aim of revealing important factors of financial markets in terms of data mining performance. Hirano *et al.* [17] originally proposed this concept, along with a practical example.

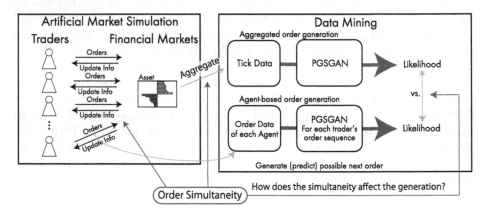

Fig. 1. Study outline.

We employed this concept and designed a different model for validating our hypothesis. The outline of our application of the concept is shown in Fig. 1. To create an artificial market simulation, we adopted a simulation model drawn from a previous work [41]; it comprises a continuous double auction market and traders who trade (submit orders) using order book information from the market. The advantage of using an artificial market simulation is that orders' origin trader, which would normally be unobservable, can be identified, which makes it easy to verify the effect of order simultaneity. Moreover, artificial market simulation renders the market environment fully controllable, enabling testing under various situations.

Orders are aggregated as tick data, and the PGSGAN [18] is applied as a data mining model for data training. The PGSGAN is primarily used to model the next order distribution via the GAN framework and generate the next order.

The reason we employed next order generation is that it is the ultimate prediction task among financial data mining tasks because we can generate the entire order sequence by repeating next order generation if we assume that actual next order generation is possible. Other than aggregated tick data, we also applied the PGSGAN to each individual trader's order sequence to reveal the effect of order simultaneity. Finally, we compared the likelihood of the aggregated and individual simulated next orders in the trained next order distribution in the PGSGAN. In the following section, we provide more details.

3.1   Artificial Market Simulation Model

Individual Agents' Decision Process. We used the stylized trader model that Torii *et al.* [41] proposed, based on [6].

At time t, a stylized trader agent i decides on their trading actions using the following criteria. This type of agent's actions are determined by three factors: fundamentalist, chartist (trends), and noise. Initially, agents calculate these three factors.

– Fundamentalist factor:

$$F_t^i = \frac{1}{\tau^{*i}} \ln \left\{ \frac{p_t^*}{p_t} \right\}, \tag{1}$$

where τ^{*i} is agent i's mean-reversion-time constant, p_t^* is the fundamental price at time t, and p_t is the price at time t.
– Chartist factor:

$$C_t^i = \frac{1}{\tau^i} \sum_{j=1}^{\tau^i} r_{(t-j)} = \frac{1}{\tau^i} \sum_{j=1}^{\tau^i} \ln \frac{p_{(t-j)}}{p_{(t-j-1)}}, \tag{2}$$

where τ^i is the time window size of agent i, and r_t is the logarithm return at time t.
– Noise factor:

$$N_t^i \sim \mathcal{N}(0, \sigma_N), \tag{3}$$

denoting that N_t^i obeys a normal distribution with a zero mean and variance $(\sigma_N)^2$.

Agents then calculate these three factors' weighted average.

$$\widehat{r_t^i} = \frac{1}{w_F^i + w_C^i + w_N^i} \left(w_F^i F_t^i + w_C^i C_t^i + w_N^i N_t^i \right), \tag{4}$$

where w_F^i, w_C^i, and w_N^i are the weights agent i assigns to each factor.

In the next step, agent i's expected price is calculated using the following equation:

$$\widehat{p_t^i} = p_t \exp\left(\widehat{r_t^i} \tau^i \right). \tag{5}$$

Then, using a fixed margin of $k^i \in [0, 0.1]$, the actual order prices are determined according to the following rules:

– If $\widehat{p_t^i} > p_t$, agent i places a bid (buy order) at the price

$$\left\lfloor \min\left\{ \widehat{p_t^i}(1 - k^i), p_t^{\text{bid}} \right\} \right\rfloor . \tag{6}$$

– If $\widehat{p_t^i} < p_t$, agent i places an ask (sell order) at the price

$$\left\lceil \max\left\{ \widehat{p_t^i}(1 + k^i), p_t^{\text{ask}} \right\} \right\rceil . \tag{7}$$

Here, p_t^{bid} and p_t^{ask} indicate the best bid and ask prices, respectively. $\lfloor \cdot \rfloor$ and $\lceil \cdot \rceil$ are the floor and ceiling functions, respectively. The floor and ceiling functions are applied because we set the price tick size (minimum price unit) to one in this simulation.

The parameters that we employed for this type of trader are $w_F^i \sim Ex(w_F)$, $w_C^i \sim Ex(w_C)$, $w_N^i \sim Ex(w_N)$, $w_N = 1.0$, $\tau^* \in [50, 100]$, and $\tau \in [100, 200]$, which were determined largely based on [41]. Here, $Ex(\lambda)$ indicates an exponential distribution with an expected value of λ. The values of w_F, w_C, and σ_N varied during our experiment.

Aggregation of Agents' Orders. At each step, agents submit an order. Before orders are registered in the order processing system, we assume all orders submitted at the same step will be randomized in the sequence.

3.2   Data Mining Model: PGSGAN

As a data mining model, we employed the PGSGAN [18]. As we mentioned in the Introduction, this study focuses on GANs for financial markets. Specifically, the PGSGAN generates the probabilistic distribution of fake orders, which is beneficial for our study because it allows us to calculate the likelihood. Here, we briefly introduce the PGSGAN and its application in this study.

The PGSGAN is designed to address some of the issues associated with other GANs for the financial market. For example, the authors pointed out that typical GANs for the financial market ignore order discreteness, such as tick price or minimum volume size. On the contrary, the PGSGAN breaks the GAN generator and critic gradient chains and instead employs a policy gradient algorithm for generator learning.

Figure 2 visually outlines the PGSGAN. The PGSGAN is based on the WGAN [2]. The PGSGAN is formulated as a min-max game, in a manner similar to typical GANs, as follows:

$$\min_{G} \max_{||C||_{L \leq 1}} \left\{ \mathbb{E}_{x \sim \mathbb{P}_r} \left[C(x) \right] - \mathbb{E}_{z \sim \mathbb{P}_z} \left[\mathbb{E}_{\tilde{x} \sim G(z)} \left[C(\tilde{x}) \right] \right] \right\} , \tag{8}$$

where z represents random variables (seed for the generator; in our experiment, $z \in \mathbb{R}^{10}$), $\mathbb{P}_z$ represent the distribution of random variables, $\mathbb{P}_r$ is the distribution of real data (simulation data), G represents the generator, C represents the

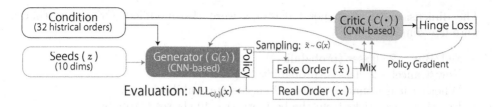

Fig. 2. Outline of the PGSGAN

critic, and $||f||_{L \leq 1}$ represents the 1-Lipschitz constraint for any function f. Given that $G(z)$ generates the probabilistic distribution of fake orders as a policy, it can be sampled. Moreover, in those formulations, in the interest of simplified notation, we skip conditional notation for both the generator and the critic, but the conditional inputs (32 historical orders) are actually input simultaneously. To address the disconnection between the generator and the critic, REINFORCE [43] with baseline is used for generator learning. Thus, the critic's and generator's loss functions are defined as:

$$L_C := \mathbb{E}_{\tilde{x} \sim G(z)}[C(\tilde{x})] - \mathbb{E}_{x \sim \mathbb{P}_r}[C(x)], \tag{9}$$

$$L_G := -(C(\tilde{x}) - B) \ln p_{G(z)}(\tilde{x}) = (C(\tilde{x}) - B) \cdot \mathrm{NLL}_{G(z)}(\tilde{x}), \tag{10}$$

respectively, where $p_{G(z)}(\tilde{x})$ is the probability for the sampled fake order $\tilde{x}$ according to the generated policy $G(z)$, $\mathrm{NLL}_{G(z)}(\tilde{x})$ is the negative log-likelihood (NLL) for the sampled fake order $\tilde{x}$ according to the generated policy $G(z)$ ($\mathrm{NLL}_{G(z)}(\tilde{x}) = -\ln\{p_{G(z)}(\tilde{x})\}$), and B is the baseline of REINFORCE, which is set to mean of G in one batch (See [18] for more details).

Our application also includes some minor environmental modifications. Firstly, we modified the order representation dimensions. Originally, there were seven dimensions:

- Sell/Buy
- New/Cancel
- Whether it is a market order
- Relative price (ticks from the best price)
- Volume (scaled by dividing by the minimum volume unit)
- Current relative best ask price
- Current relative best bid price

On the other hand, because the simulation we employed in this study does not publish cancel and market orders, and the volume is fixed due to simplification, there are only four dimensions:

- Sell/Buy
- Relative price (ticks from the best price)
- Current relative best ask price
- Current relative best bid price

The dimensions of the generated orders were also modified. Originally, there were five dimensions:

- Sell/Buy – 2 classes (probability)
- New/Cancel – 2 classes (probability)
- Whether it is a market order – 2 classes (probability)
- Relative price (ticks from the best price) – 40 classes (probability)
- Volume (scaled by dividing by the minimum volume unit) – 40 classes (probability)

However, in this study, there were two dimensions because of the same reasons as the order representation dimensions:

- Sell/Buy – 2 classes (probability)
- Relative price – 20 classes (probability)

Moreover, we employed 32 historical orders as a condition of the PGSGAN, instead of the original 20 historical orders. Corresponding to those modifications, we also changed the number of convolutional neural network (CNN) layers for both the generator and the critic. Other details were kept the same as the original PGSGAN. We also employed hinge loss in a manner identical to the original.

3.3 Hypothesis Testing

As we mentioned in the Introduction, we hypothesized that the simultaneity of orders significantly affects the accuracy of the next order generation (prediction) task. Here, to simplify the explanation, we assumed ten concurrencies of simultaneity (In our experiments, we employed ten concurrent agents). Simply phrased, ten orders can be considered published almost simultaneously. Thus, let x_i be ith order, and if x_i to x_{i+9} are generated simultaneously, we can assume the following equation:

$$P(x_i|x_{i-1}, x_{i-2}, \ldots, x_0) = P(x_{i+1}|x_{i-1}, x_{i-2}, \ldots, x_0) = \cdots \qquad (11)$$
$$= P(x_{i+9}|x_{i-1}, x_{i-2}, \ldots, x_0). \qquad (12)$$

This means that the generation task $P(x_i|x_{i-1}, x_{i-2}, \ldots, x_0)$ becomes harder if simultaneity exists because $x_{i+9}, x_{i+8}, \cdots, x_i$ possiblly become the next coming order, and x_i is just a realized next order.

In our model, the PGSGAN can be said to model $P(x_i|x_{i-1}, x_{i-2}, \ldots, x_{i-32})$ indirectly. Thus, if the PGSGAN models correctly, $P_{G(z)}(x)$, the probability of the actual order under the generated probability distribution (policy), will be higher (1.0 is the maximum value because it is a probability). Moreover, it can be the index for generation accuracy.

To test our hypothesis, we conducted comparison experiments as illustrated in Fig. 1:

1. Aggregated order generation (AggOG): Just modeling the next order.

2. Agent-based order generation (ABOG): Modeling each agent's next order generation.

In the latter experiments, we can exclude the randomized effect from order simultaneity. Moreover, in the case of the latter experiment, we will obtain ten PGS-GAN models for each agent and ten different likelihoods. Thus, by comparing the average likelihood, we evaluate the effect of order simultaneity for next order generation (prediction).

More practically, we employ the mean NLL, i.e., $\text{NLL}_{G(z)}(x)$ where x is the simulated next order, for AggOG or ABOG. Thus, if the NLL for AggOB exceeds the NLL for ABOG (a lower NLL means a better prediction, so zero is the smallest and the best NLL), it means that our hypothesis cannot be rejected, and there is a strong possibility that order simultaneity affects the next order generation (prediction) task. For a statistical test, we perform t-test and calculate p-value to evaluate the significance of the difference between the two NLLs.

4   Experiments

We conducted experiments to validate our hypothesis; this entailed changing some of the artificial market environment's parameters. The parameters modified in our simulation are:

- The weight of the fundamentalist factor: $w_F = 3.0, 10.0$.
- The weight of the chart factor: $w_C = 3.0, 10.0$.
- The noise scale: $\sigma_N = 10^{-2}, 10^{-3}, 10^{-4}$.

There are also fixed parameters, as follows:

- Simulation:
  - The weight of the noise factor: $w_N = 1.0$.
  - The number of agents: 10 (Assume simultaneity)
  - The opening price: 500
  - The fundamental price: $p_t^* = 500$ (const.)
  - The price tick size: 1
  - The steps of pre-opening session: 100 steps
  - The steps of one session: 10500 steps
- PGSGAN:
  - Learning epochs: 1000
  - Learning rate: 0.001
  - Two time-scale update rule [15]: G:C=1:5
  - Price classes: 20 (prices 20 and more price ticks away from the best price comprise the 20th class)
  - Historical input: 32 orders
  - The dimension of the random seed for the generator: 10
  - Training data: Data from 10000 steps of the session
  - Test data: Data from the last 500 steps of the session

For each parameter set, we ran 100 simulations with the different simulation random seeds and evaluated the NLL of both AggOG and ABOG. To calculate the NLLs, we performed 100 calculations with the different PGSGAN input seeds for each evaluation to reduce the randomness of the generated policy.

5 Result

Table 1. NLL results for AggOG and ABOG

w_F	w_C	σ_N	NLL (AggOG)	NLL (ABOG)	diff	t-value	p
10.0	10.0	10^{-4}	2.2415 ± 0.0465	1.0064 ± 0.0283	1.2352	229.2650	$\ll 0.01$
10.0	3.0	10^{-4}	2.3222 ± 0.0424	1.1098 ± 0.0211	1.2123	258.5539	$\ll 0.01$
3.0	10.0	10^{-4}	2.2354 ± 0.0491	1.1030 ± 0.0287	1.1324	200.9167	$\ll 0.01$
3.0	3.0	10^{-4}	2.3832 ± 0.0474	1.2646 ± 0.0242	1.1186	212.2086	$\ll 0.01$
10.0	10.0	10^{-3}	2.5712 ± 0.0407	1.7460 ± 0.0309	0.8251	163.0315	$\ll 0.01$
10.0	3.0	10^{-3}	2.6721 ± 0.0354	1.9832 ± 0.0315	0.6889	146.8755	$\ll 0.01$
3.0	10.0	10^{-3}	2.6388 ± 0.0415	1.9369 ± 0.0344	0.7019	131.6461	$\ll 0.01$
3.0	3.0	10^{-3}	2.7304 ± 0.0239	2.2019 ± 0.0269	0.5285	148.6249	$\ll 0.01$
10.0	10.0	10^{-2}	1.7224 ± 0.0411	1.7036 ± 0.0337	0.0188	3.5676	$\ll 0.01$
10.0	3.0	10^{-2}	1.4544 ± 0.0332	1.4768 ± 0.0305	-0.0225	-5.0303	$\ll 0.01$
3.0	10.0	10^{-2}	1.1071 ± 0.0323	1.1713 ± 0.0321	-0.0641	-14.2390	$\ll 0.01$
3.0	3.0	10^{-2}	1.0898 ± 0.0070	1.1432 ± 0.0092	-0.0535	-46.6007	$\ll 0.01$

Table 1 and Fig. 3 show the results of all the parameter sets we tested. NLL (AggOG) and NLL (ABOG) are the results of averaging the NLLs for AggOG and ABOG, respectively; smaller values mean a better fit of the PGSGAN next order generation to the simulated (actual) order. Moreover, "diff" in Table 1 indicates the difference between NLL (AggOG) and NLL (ABOG), which is technically defined as NLL(AggOG) − NLL(ABOG). Thus, a negative value for "diff" indicates that AggOG produced a better estimate of the next order than ABOG, which challenges our hypothesis. As statistical tests, the t- and p-value were calculated between NLL (AggOG) and NLL (ABOG).

The results show that GANs both in AggOG and in ABOG somehow successfully generated fake orders. The by-chance NLL is $\ln\{2 \times 20\} \approx 3.6889$ because the generated fake orders have two dimensions: two classes of sell/buy and 20 classes of relative price. Thus, an NLL below 3.6689 indicates superiority to random generation.

According to the results listed in Table 1, the effect of the noise scale σ_N is more dominant than the effects of either w_F or w_C. If the noise scale is small, the difference between AggOG and ABOG is great. On the other hand, if the noise scale is big, the difference vanishes. More interestingly, if the noise scale is set to $\sigma_N = 10^{-2}$, in some parameter sets, the NLL of ABOG exceeds the NLL of AggOG, indicating that next order generation is easier in the aggregated order sequence than in the sequence of each individual agent's orders. This result is in complete opposition to the hypothesis.

In terms of the effects of w_F and w_C, w_F is more effective than w_C. However, the effects are still smaller than those of the noise scale, as mentioned above.

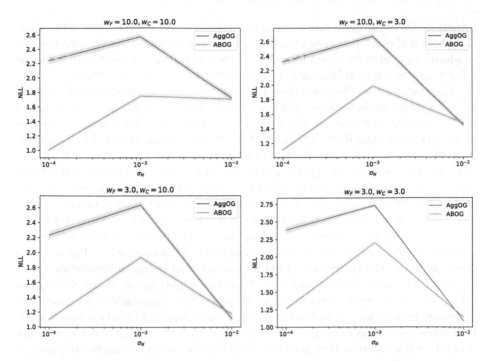

Fig. 3. Results of all parameter sets. The blue lines represent the NLL of AggOG, and the orange lines represent the NLL of ABOG for each parameter set. The filled area represents the standard deviations. (Color figure online)

6 Discussion

First, the results reveal the relationship between prediction (generation) difficulty and the noise scale. Interestingly, the moderate noise scale (in our experiment, $\sigma_N = 10^{-3}$) shows the highest NLL, indicating the lowest prediction accuracy and the highest degree of difficulty. We theorize the reasons for this phenomenon as follows. The first reason is the direct effect of the noise scale: the bigger noise makes prediction difficult, which is the very usual effect of the noise scale. The other reason is the indirect effect of the noise scale via agents' behavior: the bigger noise disables agents' ability to detect market direction, leading many agents to consistently publish similar or typical orders, which makes next order prediction easy. We assume that moderate noise makes next order generation (prediction) difficult due to a combination of those reasons. In terms of actualness, the parameter $\sigma_N = 10^{-3}$ was employed in [41] as the result of the hyperparameter fitting to the actual market. Thus, prediction on actual markets may be similarly difficult due to the two abovementioned reasons.

The simultaneity effect was larger when the noise scale was smaller. This can be observed in the difference between NLL (AggOG) and NLL (ABOG), as shown in the "diff" column in Table 1. With smaller noise, the direction of agents' behavior becomes evident because agents can clearly decide their order intention. Owing to this clarity regarding individual agents' behavior, the order-distributional overlap between each agent decreases, enhancing the effect of the randomness arising from simultaneity (If the distributional overlap is high, the identity of the agent submitting the next order becomes unimportant).

Thus far, we have discussed the noise analysis; the noise modeled in this study includes many kinds of noise. Noise is initially defined in Eq. 3 and included as a part of agent behavior via Eq. 4. In the modeling of stylized traders, noise is modeled on a normal distribution, but the actual meaning is broader. This noise includes a variety of types, such as observation noise regarding each agent's fundamentals, individual agents' prediction error, observation noise regarding external information, the noise associated with each agent's behavior decisions, market uncertainty, and others. Additionally, in actual financial markets, noise arises through the accumulation of events and the actions of individual stockholders. It is therefore acceptable to explain those types of noise using one random variable for each agent to maintain the simplicity of the simulation. The modeled noise facilitates the realization of actual market fluctuation in simulations.

Next, we discuss our hypothesis that the simultaneity of financial market orders significantly affects next order prediction (generation) accuracy. We employed next order generation because it is the ultimate prediction task since it facilitates generation of entire order sequences through repetition of next order generation if we assume that actual next order generation is completely possible. Although GANs usually have randomness in their generation, it can be seen as a prediction task if we eliminate the randomness over many generations. Additionally, thanks to the invention of the PGSGAN, we can generate next orders using the order distribution. We can therefore more accurately calculate the likelihood of the generation.

Based on the results, we can partially confirm the effect of order simultaneity and statistically reject that the difference between the NLL of AggOG and the NLL of ABOG is zero. This means that, because of order simultaneity, the generation task will be difficult.

However, even when the order simultaneity effect is confirmed, it is limited. In our experiments, the maximum NLL differences are less than 1.24. It is equivalent to the choices of $\exp(1.24) \approx 3.46$ patterns. In our experiments, we employed ten agents, which means that we assumed ten instances of order simultaneity. However, 3.46 is considerably lower than ten. This means that order simultaneity does not fully affect generation.

Moreover, compared with the chance rate, order simultaneity does not seem to prevent next order generation. As our calculations in the previous section showed, the by-chance NLL was 3.6889. However, even when we set order simultaneity (AggOG), the NLL is still far below the by-chance value. This also supports a limited order simultaneity effect.

Interestingly, in some cases of $\sigma_N = 10^{-2}$, a higher prediction likelihood was confirmed when aggregated data were used (AggOG). This challenges our hypothesis, given the inverse order simultaneity effect. Possible reasons are as follows. We assumed that it is because of the prediction difficulty, given the significant noise and the higher data volume due to order aggregation. As we mentioned earlier, the bigger noise can make prediction difficult. Under that condition, having more data is beneficial for constructing a prediction (generation) model. Thus, comparing data size between AggOG and ABOG, AggOG can utilize a larger amount of data for training a GAN model. In financial markets in particular, there exists inductive bias, which means that the realized market movement path is only a very small part of the possible paths. Thus, more data that are not divided by individual agents could be greatly beneficial.

Moreover, the lack of an order simultaneity effect also indicates the reasonability of aggregated order generation. According to rational expectation in financial markets, overall market movement is the expected value of people's price expectations. Thus, aggregated generation can be said to generate rational expectations. This also suggests that order prediction at the individual trader level is meaningless in some cases, such as predicting market movement.

Based on our results and discussion, a GANs approach using aggregated data is somehow reasonable and promising for modeling financial markets, even when the financial market has significant order simultaneity. Moreover, in terms of data augmentation methods for financial markets, the GANs approach, which comprehensively models the market, is also reasonable because the opposite approach that attempts to model each individual trader, such as financial market simulation, still has practical limitations outside of application to a hypothesis-testing study like the present study.

Finally, we will discuss the concept of an artificial market data mining platform. This study has confirmed that we can analyze and explain complex phenomena using this concept. This is the advantage of an artificial market data mining platform, as Hirano et al. [17] have also pointed out. This approach is still very new, but it seems promising. Future research should address other hypotheses using this concept. The concept may be useful not only in financial markets but also concerning other emergent multi-actor phenomena. Further, additional GANs development for financial markets using this concept is another possible future research direction.

7   Conclusion

This study focused on order simultaneity in financial markets. In financial markets, it is typical for orders to register in the market system almost simultaneously or in quick succession, such that traders cannot detect them before order submission. This study refers to that phenomenon as order simultaneity. With the development of GANs technologies, some studies have addressed next order generation for financial markets as data augmentation tools. However, order simultaneity and GANs-based next order generation seem to be conflicting ideas because the randomness of the next order would increase in a high simultaneity market. Thus, this study used the concept of artificial market data mining, which is a technology that combines artificial markets and data mining, to analyze the effect of order simultaneity in a fully controlled environment. For the analysis, we compared order generation performance using aggregated tick data, which includes order simultaneity, with that using individual traders' order data, where simultaneity is irrelevant. We could not confirm a significant order simultaneity effect, but we found that GANs can generate next orders with substantial accuracy. We also analyzed the effect in situations characterized by different market environment parameters, which revealed that the effect of order simultaneity nearly disappears in the presence of significant market noise. These analyses were only possible using the artificial market data mining platform, and through our study confirmed its usefulness. Future work should analyze the unknowns in financial markets using the artificial market data mining platform.

Acknowledgements. This work was supported by JSPS KAKENHI Grant Number JP 21J20074 (Grant-in-Aid for JSPS Fellows).

References

1. Arjovsky, M., Bottou, L.: Towards principled methods for training generative adversarial networks (2017). https://doi.org/10.48550/arXiv.1701.04862
2. Arjovsky, M., Chintala, S., Bottou, L.: Wasserstein GAN (2017). https://doi.org/10.48550/arXiv.1701.07875
3. Arthur, W.B., Holland, J.H., LeBaron, B., Palmer, R., Tayler, P.: Asset pricing under endogenous expectations in an artificial stock market. In: The Economy as an Evolving Complex System II, pp. 15–44 (1997). https://doi.org/10.1201/9780429496639-2
4. Battiston, S., et al.: Complexity theory and financial regulation: economic policy needs interdisciplinary network analysis and behavioral modeling. Science **351**(6275), 818–819 (2016). https://doi.org/10.1126/science.aad0299
5. Byrd, D., Hybinette, M., Hybinette Balch, T., Morgan, J.: ABIDES: towards high-fidelity multi-agent market simulation. In: Proceedings of the 2020 ACM SIGSIM Conference on Principles of Advanced Discrete Simulation, vol. 12 (2020). https://doi.org/10.1145/3384441.3395986
6. Chiarella, C., Iori, G.: A simulation analysis of the microstructure of double auction markets. Quant. Finance **2**(5), 346–353 (2002). https://doi.org/10.1088/1469-7688/2/5/303
7. Chu, C., Zhmoginov, A., Sandler, M.: CycleGAN, a Master of Steganography (2017). https://doi.org/10.48550/arXiv.1712.02950
8. Cui, W., Brabazon, A.: An agent-based modeling approach to study price impact. In: Proceedings of 2012 IEEE Conference on Computational Intelligence for Financial Engineering and Economics, CIFEr 2012, pp. 241–248 (2012). https://doi.org/10.1109/CIFEr.2012.6327798
9. Denton, E., Chintala, S., Szlam, A., Fergus, R.: Deep generative image models using a Laplacian pyramid of adversarial networks. Adv. Neural. Inf. Process. Syst. **28**, 1486–1494 (2015). https://doi.org/10.5555/2969239.2969405
10. Donahue, J., Krähenbühl, P., Darrell, T.: Adversarial Feature Learning (2016). https://doi.org/10.48550/arXiv.1605.09782
11. Edmonds, S.M., Bruce: towards good social science. J. Artif. Soc. Soc. Simul. **8**(4) (2005). https://www.jasss.org/8/4/13.html
12. Farmer, J.D., Foley, D.: The economy needs agent-based modelling. Nature **460**(7256), 685–686 (2009). https://doi.org/10.1038/460685a

13. Goodfellow, I., et al.: Generative adversarial nets. In: Advances in Neural Information Processing Systems, pp. 2672–2680 (2014). https://doi.org/10.1145/3422622
14. Gulrajani, I., Ahmed, F., Arjovsky, M., Dumoulin, V., Courville, A.: Improved training of Wasserstein GANs montreal institute for learning algorithms. Adv. Neural. Inf. Process. Syst. **30**, 5767–5777 (2017). https://doi.org/10.5555/3295222. 3295327
15. Heusel, M., Ramsauer, H., Unterthiner, T., Nessler, B., Hochreiter, S.: GANs trained by a two time-scale update rule converge to a local NASH equilibrium. In: Advances in Neural Information Processing Systems, vol. 30 (2017). https:// doi.org/10.5555/3295222.3295408
16. Hirano, M., Izumi, K., Shimada, T., Matsushima, H., Sakaji, H.: Impact Analysis of Financial Regulation on Multi-Asset Markets Using Artificial Market Simulations. J. Risk Fin. Manage. **13**(4), 75 (2020). https://doi.org/10.3390/jrfm13040075
17. Hirano, M., Sakaji, H., Izumi, K.: Concept and practice of artificial market data mining platform. In: 2022 IEEE Conference on Computational Intelligence for Financial Engineering Economics (CIFEr), pp. 1–10 (2022). https://doi.org/10. 1109/CIFEr52523.2022.9776095
18. Hirano, M., Sakaji, H., Izumi, K.: Policy gradient stock GAN for realistic discrete order data generation in financial markets (2022). https://doi.org/10.48550/arXiv. 2204.13338
19. Isola, P., Zhu, J.Y., Zhou, T., Efros, A.A.: Image-to-image translation with conditional adversarial networks. In: IEEE Conference on Computer Vision and Pattern Recognition, pp. 1125–1134 (2017). https://doi.org/10.1109/CVPR.2017.632
20. Karras, T., Aila, T., Laine, S., Lehtinen, J.: Progressive growing of GANs for improved quality, stability, and variation. In: 6th International Conference on Learning Representations (2018)
21. Karras, T., Laine, S., Aila, T.: A style-based generator architecture for generative adversarial networks. In: IEEE/CVF Conference on Computer Vision and Pattern Recognition, pp. 4401–4410 (2019). https://doi.org/10.1109/TPAMI.2020.2970919
22. Kohda, S., Yoshida, K.: Analysis of high-frequency trading from the viewpoint of tick distance and Execution [in Japanese]. In: Proceedings of the 22nd Meeting of Special Interest Group on Financial Informatics of Japanese Society for Artificial Intelligence (2019). https://sigfin.org/?022-02
23. Larsen, A.B.L., Sønderby, S.K., Larochelle, H., Winther, O.: Autoencoding beyond pixels using a learned similarity metric. In: International Conference on Machine Learning, pp. 1558–1566 (2016). https://doi.org/10.5555/3045390.3045555
24. Leal, S.J., Napoletano, M.: Market stability vs. market resilience: regulatory policies experiments in an agent-based model with low- and high-frequency trading. J. Econ. Behav. Organ. **157**, 15–41 (2019). https://doi.org/10.1016/j.jebo.2017.04. 013
25. Li, D., Chen, D., Goh, J., Ng, S.K.: Anomaly detection with generative adversarial networks for multivariate time series (2018). https://doi.org/10.48550/arXiv.1809. 04758
26. Li, J., Wang, X., Lin, Y., Sinha, A., Wellman, M.: Generating realistic stock market order streams. AAAI Conf. Artif. Intell. **34**(01), 727–734 (2020). https://doi.org/ 10.1609/aaai.v34i01.5415
27. Lux, T., Marchesi, M.: Scaling and criticality in a stochastic multi-agent model of a financial market. Nature **397**(6719), 498–500 (1999). https://doi.org/10.1038/ 17290

28. Mao, X., Li, Q., Xie, H., Lau, R.Y., Wang, Z., Paul Smolley, S.: Least squares generative adversarial networks. In: IEEE International Conference on Computer Vision, pp. 2794–2802 (2017). https://doi.org/10.1109/ICCV.2017.304

29. Mirza, M., Osindero, S.: Conditional Generative Adversarial Nets (1784), 1–7 (2014). https://doi.org/10.48550/arXiv.1411.1784

30. Miyato, T., Kataoka, T., Koyama, M., Yoshida, Y.: Spectral normalization for generative adversarial networks. In: 6th International Conference on Learning Representations (2018). https://doi.org/10.48550/arXiv.1802.05957

31. Mizuta, T.: An agent-based model for designing a financial market that works well (2019). https://doi.org/10.1109/SSCI47803.2020.9308376

32. Mizuta, T., et al.: Effects of price regulations and dark pools on financial market stability: an investigation by multiagent simulations. Intell. Syst. Account. Finance Manage. **23**(1–2), 97–120 (2016). https://doi.org/10.1002/isaf.1374

33. Naritomi, Y., Adachi, T.: Data augmentation of high frequency financial data using generative adversarial network. In: 2020 IEEE/WIC/ACM International Joint Conference on Web Intelligence and Intelligent Agent Technology (WI-IAT), pp. 641–648. IEEE (2020). https://doi.org/10.1109/WIIAT50758.2020.00097

34. Nowozin, S., Cseke, B., Tomioka, R.: f-GAN: training generative neural samplers using variational divergence minimization. In: 30th International Conference on Neural Information Processing Systems, pp. 271–279 (2016). https://doi.org/10.5555/3157096.3157127

35. Paddrik, M., Hayes, R., Todd, A., Yang, S., Beling, P., Scherer, W.: An agent based model of the E-Mini S&P 500 applied to flash crash analysis. In: Proceedings of 2012 IEEE Conference on Computational Intelligence for Financial Engineering and Economics, CIFEr 2012, pp. 257–264 (2012). https://doi.org/10.1109/CIFEr.2012.6327800

36. Radford, A., Metz, L., Chintala, S.: Unsupervised representation learning with deep convolutional generative adversarial networks (2015). https://doi.org/10.48550/arXiv.1511.06434

37. Sato, H., Koyama, Y., Kurumatani, K., Shiozawa, Y., Deguchi, H.: U-mart: a test bed for interdisciplinary research into agent-based artificial markets. In: Aruka, Y. (eds) Evolutionary Controversies in Economics, pp. 179–190. Springer, Tokyo (2001). https://doi.org/10.1007/978-4-431-67903-5_13

38. Schlegl, T., Seeböck, P., Waldstein, S.M., Schmidt-Erfurth, U., Langs, G.: Unsupervised anomaly detection with generative adversarial networks to guide marker discovery. In: Niethammer, M., et al. (eds.) IPMI 2017. LNCS, vol. 10265, pp. 146–157. Springer, Cham (2017). https://doi.org/10.1007/978-3-319-59050-9_12

39. Torii, T., et al.: Plham: platform for large-scale and high-frequency artificial market (2016). https://github.com/plham/plham

40. Torii, T., et al.: PlhamJ (2019). https://github.com/plham/plhamJ

41. Torii, T., Izumi, K., Yamada, K.: Shock transfer by arbitrage trading: analysis using multi-asset artificial market. Evol. Inst. Econ. Rev. **12**(2), 395–412 (2016). https://doi.org/10.1007/s40844-015-0024-z

42. Torii, T., Kamada, T., Izumi, K., Yamada, K.: Platform design for large-scale artificial market simulation and preliminary evaluation on the K computer. Artif. Life Robot. **22**(3), 301–307 (2017). https://doi.org/10.1007/s10015-017-0368-z

43. Williams, R.J.: Simple statistical gradient-following algorithms for connectionist reinforcement learning. Mach. Learn. **8**(3), 229–256 (1992). https://doi.org/10.1007/BF00992696

44. Zenati, H., Foo, C.S., Lecouat, B., Manek, G., Chandrasekhar, V.R.: Efficient GAN-Based Anomaly Detection (2018). https://doi.org/10.48550/arXiv.1802.06222
45. Zhang, K., Zhong, G., Dong, J., Wang, S., Wang, Y.: Stock market prediction based on generative adversarial. Network **147**, 400–406 (2019). https://doi.org/10.1016/j.procs.2019.01.256
46. Zhou, X., Pan, Z., Hu, G., Tang, S., Zhao, C.: Stock market prediction on high-frequency data using generative adversarial nets. Math. Prob. Eng. **2018** (2018). https://doi.org/10.1155/2018/4907423

Fine-Grained Prediction and Control of Covid-19 Pandemic in a City: Application to Post-Initial Stages

Souvik Barat[1(✉)], Vinay Kulkarni[1], Aditya Paranjape[1], Ritu Parchure[2], Srinivas Darak[2], and Vinay Kulkarni[2]

[1] Tata Consultancy Service Research, Pune 411013, India
{souvik.barat,vinay.vkulkarni,aditya.paranjape}@tcs.com
[2] Prayas Health Group, Pune 411004, India
{ritu,shirish,vinay}@prayaspune.org

Abstract. Predicting the evolution of the Covid-19 pandemic during its early phases was relatively easy as its dynamics were governed by few influencing factors that included a single dominant virus variant and the demographic characteristics of a given area. Several models based on a wide variety of techniques were developed for this purpose. Their prediction accuracy started deteriorating as the number of influencing factors and their interrelationships grew over time. With the pandemic evolving in a highly heterogeneous way across individual countries, states, and even individual cities, there emerged a need for a contextual and fine-grained understanding of the pandemic to come up with effective means of pandemic control. This paper presents a fine-grained model for predicting and controlling Covid-19 in a large city. Our approach borrows ideas from complex adaptive system-of-systems paradigm and adopts a concept of agent as the core modeling abstraction.

Keywords: Covid-19 modeling · Agent model · Complex system · Digital twin · Simulatable model

1 Introduction

The Covid-19 pandemic has impacted public health safety, economy and social well-being for more than two years. As we write this paper, globally more than 500 million people have been affected, 6 million have died, and brakes have been put on the global economy since the beginning of the Covid-19 pandemic [24]. This prolonged yet evolving situation has put forth a perpetual challenge to the policy makers and stakeholders for understanding the dynamics of the Covid-19 pandemic, as well as the factors influencing it, in order to enable a safer return to a new normal without compromising public health safety.

Stakeholders and decision-makers often attempt to gauge the dynamics and predict possible future outcomes by observing and interpreting Covid-19 dashboards [8,19] that show the trends on various aspects of interest *e.g.*, number

© The Author(s), under exclusive license to Springer Nature Switzerland AG 2023
R. Aydoğan et al. (Eds.): PRIMA 2022, LNAI 13753, pp. 314–330, 2023.
https://doi.org/10.1007/978-3-031-21203-1_19

of active infections, hospitalizations, critical cases and deaths. However, such an intuition-driven approach is often vulnerable to personal bias and inadequate exploration, putting public health and socio-economic matters at risk. To reduce such a risk, decision makers tend to enforce lockdowns, a proven and easy-to-implement intervention, when the situation appears to worsen beyond a limit.

The modeling and simulation (M&S) community has been active since the beginning of the Covid-19 pandemic, providing the necessary insights to understand and effectively control the situation. A wide range of modeling techniques have been repurposed and proposed, which include different form of traditional compartmental epidemic models (e.g., SEIR model [14] and SEIRD model [17]), historical data-centric statistical/AI models [1,11] and agent-based models [16,23]. Many of these models have demonstrated efficacy, albeit over a wide spectrum of accuracy across various levels of granularity. For example, a data-centric ARIMA-based statistical model can forecast Covid-19 infections over a 7–14 day horizon [10] and claims to predict the situation for ten countries, including US, UK, India and several European countries, with a 95% confidence interval. The SUTRA model [1], which leverages similar statistical rigor, has been able to predict infection surges in India. Covasim [16], an agent-based model, has been used to predict the situation for a dozen countries in Africa, Asia Pacific, Europe, and North America. Another agent-based model, INFEKTA [12], is used to understand the transmission dynamics of the Covid-19 under different social distancing policies for Bogota, Columbia. Our earlier work was effectively used to explore the efficacy of a wide range of non-pharmaceutical interventions for Pune, located in western India, using an agent based digital twin [3].

While these modeling techniques could predict the trajectory of the pandemic with a high degree of accuracy during its early phases, (i.e., waves due to *Alpha* variant [24]), most of them started faltering considerably as the number of influencing factors increased over time. The key reasons for such deviations are: a) increasing uncertainty about influencing factors such as the emergence of new variants, vaccines and their efficacy, and waning immunity, b) wide heterogeneity in the demographic characteristics of a given area, especially cities, in the pandemic control interventions and adherence to these interventions by the people, and c) poor quality and corpus of relevant data due to low testing uptake and under-reporting.

We believe that the dynamics of an airborne disease can be well understood for a the specific localized context (e.g., a city or country) by visualizing it from the lens of *complex adaptive system* (CAS) [5] and *system of systems* [4] paradigms. Here, we consider a city as key focus area and visualize it as multiple connected localities (i.e., system of systems) with varying socio-economic strata and a heterogeneous population. The evolution of a pandemic in such a city emerges from the stochastic interactions of its population, their visiting patterns, dominant pathogen variants and their characteristics, and other factors, such as the adoption of masks and social distancing, vaccines and non-pharmaceutical interventions. To predict the dynamics of Covid-19, we capture these aspects of interest of a city population via a purposeful, fine-grained, hi-fidelity simulatable

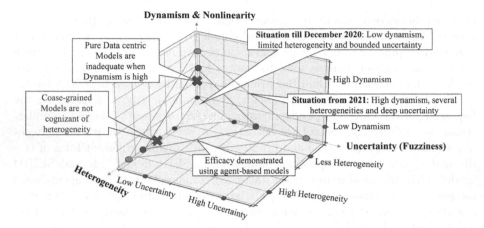

Fig. 1. Modeling complexities and state-of-the-art modeling and analysis techniques.

model; *i.e.*, a city digital twin. In a bottom-up modeling approach, we capture the demographic details of a heterogeneous population (*i.e.*, age, gender, comorbidities, adherence to Covid-appropriate behavior(CAB)), their business-as-usual behavior (*i.e.*, *who* does *what*, *where*, and *when*), the place characteristics (*i.e.*, *who* all congregate *where* and for *how* long), and the virus characteristics (*i.e.*, infectivity, severity, affinity for a specific comorbidity, vaccine escape) in the form of fine-grained *agents* [15]. We rely on probabilistic modeling to capture known uncertainties, *e.g.*, vaccine efficacy, loss of immunity over time, and compliance with CAB, as parameterized non-deterministic behaviors. These parameterized agents, and their stochastic behavior, help in hypothesis building and validation by designing suitable experiments with various potential and hypothetical influencing factors, such as the emergence of a new variant or the possibility of a new relaxation. We rely on simulation-led experiments involving a sufficiently large set of hypotheses to predict possible Covid-19 pandemic evolution.

In particular this paper discusses dynamics-induced complexities in predicting the evolution of Covid-19 pandemic in the face of deep uncertainty, highlights limitations of the existing modeling and analysis techniques, and presents an pragmatic agent-based modeling approach with a set of methodological considerations that are borrowed from modeling and simulation of complex adaptive systems to overcomes some of the limitations.

The rest of the paper is organized as follows: Sect. 2 evaluates current state of art and practice of Covid-19 pandemic models with respect to evolving modeling and analysis needs. Section 3 presents our approach as an advance over the state of art and practice. Section 4 illustrates our approach for Pune city[1] (an Indian city with 4 million population). Section 5 concludes with lesson learnt and future direction.

---

[1] https://en.wikipedia.org/wiki/Pune.

2   Review of the State-of-the-Art

The early phase of the Covid-19 pandemic was dominated by the *Alpha* variant across the world. Enforcement of strict lockdowns restricted people's movements within and across countries. Further, widespread compliance with *Covid-appropriate behavior* (CAB) slowed the progression of the pandemic across the globe. Differences in trends in infection count, number of critical cases, and death count in different parts of the world were primarily due to the heterogeneity of demographic characteristics (*e.g.*, age, gender and comorbidity), ease of access to healthcare systems, and variations in the non-pharmaceutical and pharmaceutical interventions. The dynamics were largely predictable and relatively devoid of uncertainty; thus, most Covid models predicted the peak of imminent waves and the time to reach the peak with high accuracy. However, the situation started evolving rapidly after the first wave faded away. The *Alpha* variant diminished significantly, and multiple factors and uncertainties started interfering with the pandemic dynamics. Here, we discuss how the evolving situation introduced a complexity that most of Covid-19 models could not cope with.

2.1   Contextual Complexities

From early 2021, it was observed that people started violating administrative interventions and social norms, such as the use of face mask and social distancing. Different forms of nonpharmaceutical interventions (*e.g.*, weekend lockdowns, night curfews and air travel bubbles) were introduced in place of strict lockdowns. Vaccines with different efficacy and emergent variants with varying characteristics started playing a critical role in the evolution of the pandemic. From a modeling perspective, all these factors contributed to increased complexity along three dimensions: a) heterogeneity, b) uncertainty, and c) dynamism and nonlinearity as shown in Fig. 1.

Heterogeneity: The heterogeneity that was limited to demographic factor (*e.g.*, age, gender and comorbidity), archetypes of people's profile (*e.g.*, office worker, student, banker, health worker) and place archetype (*e.g.*, office, school, market, and clinics) got extended to several other aspects that include different form of interventions and vaccine types. In particular, vaccination of the population was heterogeneous (*i.e.*, not same for different cities and different parts of the same city) and evolving. As a result, determining the susceptibility (and subsequent progression of infection) to these variants got complex. Moreover, the testing uptake varied significantly with time and place across cities. Strict norms of home and institutional quarantine faded away at varying levels.

Uncertainty: Compared to the *Alpha* [24] variant, there was significant uncertainty about the *Delta* and *Omicron* variants at the onset of the corresponding waves. Moreover, the existence of different variants and their lineages in a city, their distributions, and how these lineages are impacting city population became uncertain from the emergence of *Delta* variant. The lack of precise understanding of vaccine efficacy and effectiveness on individuals is another area, where certain assumptions can be made with a degree of uncertainty by interpreting established research findings [6,18,20]. Waning of vaccine- and infection-induced immunity over time are other uncertain area that make modeling task complex.

Dynamism and Non-linearity: Pandemic started evolving at faster rate as compared to the first wave as the infectivity of *Delta*, *Omicron* and their lineages are higher than *Alpha* [13]. More interestingly, these emerging factors exhibited overlapping and nonlinear effects on each other that varied over time thus making pandemic dynamics far more complex than before. For example, an effective vaccine and a less severe variant (*e.g.*, as for the case of *Omicron* variant) lead to less critical cases – an experience of such a trend makes people reluctant to comply with administrative and social norms. In the long run, such noncompliances and low testing uptake influence the number of infections as well as the number of detected and critical cases. Capturing the relevant details in a structured and machine processable form presents a challenge for the modeling community.

2.2   State of the Art Modeling and Analysis Techniques

Predictive models for pandemics are broadly classified into two categories: coarse-grained and fine-grained with former as the majority. Coarse-grained models adopt one of the two techniques to predict the future: (a) statistical modeling supported by historical data [1,10], including those based on AI [11]; or (b) compartmental models (*e.g.*, SEIR [2,14,17], and their variations).

Since data-centric statistical models rely exclusively on historical data to predict the future, they are often vulnerable to internal and external *threats to validity* [25]. External validity becomes prominent during the early phase of a new variant as one needs to rely on data collected from an altogether different geographical region. For example, the data collected from South Africa during the *Omicron* wave was used for predicting possible infection trends in other counties where the situations were vastly different due to the use of different vaccines, percent of population vaccinated, demographic details of the population and so on.

Internal validity is a concern for infection prediction as the observed cases in an area are not an accurate representation of the reality as detected cases in an area depends not only on actual infection but also on the ratio of asymptomatic cases and testing uptake. For example, analysis of infection spread of *Omicron* based on the observed data is more susceptible to ascertainment bias compared to earlier phases [9]. Primarily, increasing dynamics and unavailability of relevant data made the historical data-centric approaches inadequate as shown in Fig. 1. For instance, the trends predicted by SUTRA model[2] were grossly inaccurate during the early phase of the second wave (termed as *drift period*) due to rapid evolution of the pandemic and inappropriate correlation with historical data. As

---

[2] https://www.sutra-india.in/.

a result, the SUTRA model had to adjusted every week in March to May 2021 and November to December 2021 to keep it abreast of the emerging data.

Compartmental models describe the spread of infection in the form of differential equations [2]. While these models are usually computationally efficient, explainable (being based on well-understood mathematical techniques) and traditionally used over several decades, their shortcomings are particularly relevant in the context of Covid-19. They usually ignore the heterogeneity of the population [16], and fail to account for the micro-causality and emergent behavior in a cohort, *e.g.*, super-spreader events from social gatherings.

To overcome the limitations of coarse-grained models, fine-grained agent-based models have been employed as a competing approach. The key objective of these models is to capture the behavior of micro-elements such as people, households and places (*e.g.*, workplace, school, shops) to predict macroscopic indicators, such as the number of infected cases, critical cases and deaths. While agent models in general are capable of addressing high heterogeneity and dynamism, their utilization for Covid-19 prediction are limited to moderate heterogeneity and dynamism with less support for uncertainty as shown using yellow-colored hyper triangle in Fig. 1. Some of the agent models, such as INFEKTA [12], capture only the key entities (*e.g.*, people and places) as agents where behavior of each agent is specified in terms of aggregated equations. Therefore, they exhibit similar limitations as coarse-grained models for capturing emergent behavior and micro-causalities of pandemic dynamics. To the best of our knowledge, only a few agent models, such as Covasim [16], capture the individualistic behaviors of a wide range of micro-elements and their interactions. From a richness perspective, they capture demographic variations in the population, a wide range of places, and interventions. However, they simplify the dynamics to a large extent. Primarily, they aggregate the overlapping effect of demographic characteristics of the individual, variant characteristics and vaccine effects as predefined rules inside the person agent. This limits an ability to understand the emergent effect of a vaccine and the characteristics of a variant on an individual. Moreover, they address scalability by linearly scaling down the population (to the order of 10^3) to make the simulation manageable. Essentially, these models tend to establish a balance between richness and scale by compromising all three desired fronts, *i.e.*, heterogeneity, uncertainty and dynamism, as shown using yellow hyper triangle vs desired purple hyper triangle in Fig. 1.

3 Our Approach

We consider a city as a coherent unit connected with the rest of the world in terms of in and out flow of people. For modeling and comprehending the dynamics of Covid-19 within a city, we adopt a reductionist standpoint to visualize a city as a *system of systems* (SoS) [4] with inherent characteristics of a *complex adaptable system* (CAS) as opposed to an equilibrium-seeking system [5].

Conceptually, a city (*i.e.*, a context) is a collection of administrative wards (*i.e.*, constituent systems of SoS) with in and out flow of people, where each ward is a bottom-up composition of different types of places (*i.e.*, school, college, marker offices, *etc.*), household structures (household archetypes *e.g.*, small congested house with many household members, large house with less members), and people with unique set of socio-economic strata (citizen archetypes, *e.g.*, office worker, shop keepers, students, driver, *etc.*). Thus a ward, and consequently a city, is a *system of systems* with composite (*e.g.*, household, office, school are composed of people), dynamic (*e.g.*, an office/school/restaurant changes over time based on visitor footfall at that time), and emergent (*e.g.*, contact propensity emerges based on gathering of the people leading to a super-spreader event) elements.

People's behaviors are nondeterministic and evolve over time. We conceptualize people as complex composite elements with their own characteristics (*e.g.*, age, gender, comorbidity) and a set of spatiotemporal rules augmented by nondeterministic behaviors. The rules are bounded by who they are (*i.e.*, a student or an office worker), where they are (*i.e.*, at home, in office/school/clinic or in a restaurant) and the time of the day. Behavioral nondeterminism is primarily due to movements. Movements within a place (*i.e.*, inside household, office or in school) are inherently random with certain predefined pattern and bounded uncertainty. For example, a doctor stays in a specific location during clinic hours while patients have to wait in a waiting area for a specific time before consultation in the doctor's room. Movements across the places are also random but are guided by people archetype (*e.g.*, office worker goes to office if it is open, uses commuting means, occasionally goes to markets or restaurants, *etc.*).

The infection transmission and infection progression for an individual emerge from the composition of virus variant (when they get exposed), vaccines (if administered) and mask (if used). Important to note that infection transmission from one individual to another is nonlinear (*i.e.*, similar type of contact may result in different outcomes), and infection progression (*i.e.*, exposed to infectious, infectious to asymptomatic, mildly symptomatic or severe, respective state to recovered or dead) of an individual is path dependent (*i.e.*, based on infection history, vaccination details and infecting variant).

3.1   Agent-Based Realization

We use an extended agent based model to faithfully represent a city as complex adaptive system of systems incorporating inherent dynamism, path dependency, nondeterminism, nonlinearity, emergentism and composition of large number of heterogeneous elements as discussed. Agent topology of our digital twin is shown in Fig. 2. The *City, Ward, Place* and *Household* agents are configurable container agents – they do not have specific behavior; instead, they have finite areas where citizens can move. The behaviors of these agents emerge from their constituent elements. A city agent comprises tens of representative wards agents and a ward agent comprises significantly large numbers of heterogeneous citizen, place and household agents. The combination of citizens with different profile archetypes, place archetypes and household archetypes form representative ward archetype, such as slums, well-to-do localities, and market area. We consider 13 household

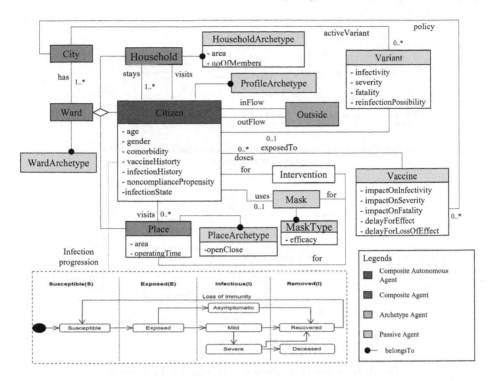

Fig. 2. Schematic representation of agent topology and relationships.

archetypes and 20 place archetypes that include representative commuting means (*i.e.*, own car, bus or shared cab). The household archetypes range from two-member family (1 Male and 1 Female) to twelve-member family (*i.e.*, 3 Male, 3 Female, 4 Children and 2 Senior Citizens). Place archetypes represent relevant places of a city where people frequently visit, spend time and make contacts, such as office, school, restaurants & pub, clinics, mall, market-place, worship place and so on. A typical ward of an Indian city contains tens of offices, tens of schools, tens of hundreds of other places and tens of thousands of households with varying number of family members. Citizens from well-to-do localities may stay in relatively bigger houses with few family members. On the other hand, slum areas are densely populated and have smaller houses with bigger families.

Citizen is a composite autonomous agent. It captures individualistic characteristics and behavior patterns including age, gender, comorbidity, profession, house-hold structure, vaccination status, and infection status. We consider 25 profile archetypes, including Kid, College Student, Senior Citizen, and Office Goers, to represent professions with different behavioral patterns. Each archetype has unique movements and contact patterns. For example, an office goer in a back-end role interacts only with colleagues, while a customer-facing bank employee interacts with colleagues as well as customers; a cab driver interacts with a large number of passengers, each belonging to a different archetype,

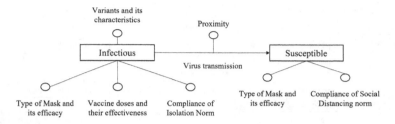

(a) Factors that influence virus transmission from source (infectious person) to target (susceptible person)

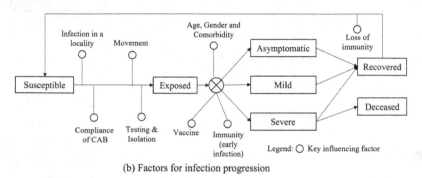

(b) Factors for infection progression

Fig. 3. Infection transmission and infection progression.

throughout the day; a small shop keeper interacts with customers for short intervals but in a congested place. We also capture the propensity of compliance with CAB and administrative interventions as behavioral patterns of the individuals.

In addition to their own behavior, a citizen may contain vaccine, variant and/or mask agents and can be influenced by them. Virus, vaccine and mask agents are configurable passive agents, which have their own (stochastic) characteristics but cannot act independently without a citizen. They contribute to the citizen behavior when a citizen is vaccinated with a vaccine, exposed to a variant and/or wearing mask. A vaccine agent captures the probability of reducing infection, severity and fatality as parameters; a variant agent defines (actual/hypothetical) virus characteristics including infectivity, severity, mortality, and probability of immune escape as parameters, and mask agent captures the propensity of reducing virus transmission. A citizen can get exposed to a variant if she comes into a proximal contact with another infectious citizen – this is an interplay between two citizen agents, place agent (characteristics of the place, *i.e.*, open vs close), infectivity of variant agent and mask characteristics of the source and target citizens (if they are wearing mask). Further, the progression of the infection in an exposed citizen (*i.e.*, exposed to infectious; infectious to asymptomatic, mildly symptomatic or severe; respective state to recovered or dead) and the possible degree of criticality of the citizen depends on the characteristics of the citizen, infection history, vaccine agent, and variant

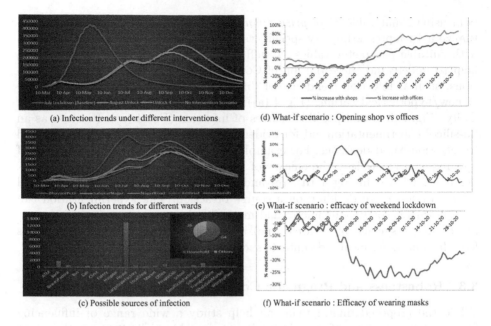

(a) Infection trends under different interventions

(d) What-if scenario : Opening shop vs offices

(b) Infection trends for different wards

(e) What-if scenario : efficacy of weekend lockdown

(c) Possible sources of infection

(f) What-if scenario : Efficacy of wearing masks

Fig. 4. Illustration of simulation led experimentation.

agent. Infection transmission and progression dynamics are highlighted in Fig. 3 (a) and (b) respectively.

A city may have a set of approved vaccines and an adoption policy. For example, a vaccine can be introduced from a specific day of a month to the population with a set of criteria on age (*e.g.*, 60+), comorbidity (*e.g.*, diabetes and hypertension) and profession (*e.g.*, medical professionals) with a specific rate and interval between doses. A new variant can be originated from the city or import from outside. We capture the import dynamics using an agent Outside and in/out flow to and from to *Outside* as shown in Fig. 2. Outside is a composite agent that a specific number of infected citizens with existing/new variant.

We consider three types of interventions, namely administrative, healthcare-related, and social, as spatiotemporal stochastic agents. Administrative interventions are related to citizens' movements, partial or full closure of places, and to capacity constraints on public transport. Interventions from health care standpoint include testing of mildly infected (in addition to severely infected) citizens, contact tracing and isolation of detected mildly infected citizens. Social interventions include mask usage. The intervention agents can be active for specific locality or citizen archetype in a time-bound manner, and influence the behavior of the place and citizen agents accordingly.

3.2 Simulation

To comprehend the evolution of Covid-19 pandemic in presence of different types of vaccines, variants and interventions in a city, we capture our digital twin using simulatable *Enterprise Simulation Language* (ESL) [7] and contextualize it by representing city specific wards, places, households and population with suitable parameter values. A sufficiently contextualized digital twin can help to understand the evolution of Covid-19 pandemic under different situations, such as infection trends under different interventions or in the presence of new/hypothetical variant (Fig. 4 (a)), infection trends for different wards of a city (Fig. 4 (b)), and possible sources of infection (Fig. 4 (c)). It serves as an 'in-silico' experimentation aid for evidence-backed decision-making as opposed to intuition-based decisions. For example, one can evaluate the consequence of opening shops vs offices, the efficacy of higher testing uptake, efficacy of wearing mask (shown in Fig. 4 (d), (e) and (f) respectively) and other potential interventions before deciding on a course of action. The experimentation can be constructed for various micro- and macro-level interventions (*e.g.*, for opening/closing a specific place archetype) and anticipated/hypothetical scenarios for a for analyzing localized contexts such as a ward or a city.

3.3   Robustness and Pragmatic Considerations

While the proposed digital twin can help study a wide range of influencing factors at various level of granularity, it is vulnerable to limitations. We adopt methodological rigor and pragmatic approaches to address them as discussed below.

Ensuring Faithfulness: Our model, like others, relies on a set of assumptions, where an inaccurate assumption may reduce the accuracy of model prediction. We adopt the established technique of *operational validity* [22] to ensure faithfulness of the digital twin, where historical situations are simulated using the digital twin and simulation results are compared with real observations to ensure faithfulness. Additionally, agent-based modeling abstraction with finer level of granularity helps to capture the relevant aspects of interest such as vaccines, variants and mask, as a modular and individual entity – this *separation of concern* ensures *conceptual validity* [22] to the extent possible. For example, an epidemiologist can capture virus characteristics from established research, vaccine efficacy can be specified independently, a demographic expert can solely focus on city and ward specific demographic distributions to define places of interest, a public health specialist can provide micro-level <age, gender, comorbidity> to severity correlation for specific variant, *etc.* This is a significant improvement over other models, including existing agent-based models [16,23]. However, such a model construction process requires a multidisciplinary team, including epidemiologists, demographic experts, public health specialists and computer modeling and simulation experts.

Managing Heterogeneity: Heterogeneity is addressed in existing agent-based models using archetypes as discussed here. However, they aggregate the behavior of the elements belonging to an archetype – it is a tradeoff between scalability and richness. We address the heterogeneity of wards, places, households, and citizens by adopting a pure form of bottom-up modeling technique. We define archetype-specific characteristics as parameters with a range of possible values leading to a fine-grained model.

Addressing Scale: Scalability is an inherent concern for any agent-based technique. Existing agent-based techniques, such as [16], proportionately reduce the population size to a range of 10^3 (from typical population of city of a range 10^6) using sampling technique to address scalability issue. It is important to note here that the typical number of active infection at peak is below 10% of the population and infection fatality rate is much lower than 1% – therefore significant reduction in population size breaks the probability distribution law to a large extent.

Though ESL can efficiently simulate millions of agents, the simulation of a city with a population of tens of million and a proportionate number of places of interest, households, multiple vaccines and variants using standard computing machine is a challenge. We adopt a reductionist view to divide a city-specific simulation into multiple ward-specific simulations by approximating the rest of the wards and other cities as 'Outside' agents and adjusting the flow of individuals between them. We simulate them in a distributed environment and combine simulation results for city level prediction.

Managing Uncertainty: Stochastic characteristics (*e.g.*, propensity of waning immunity, vaccine efficacies and variant characteristics) and behaviors (*e.g.*, movements within and across places) of the constituent elements make digital twin close to real. However, it poses a unique concern – each situation of same configuration may emerge differently. The dissimilarity is greater for those indicators which are rarely executed in a simulation, such as, the trend of deaths, active critical cases, and infection trend for citizens with age 70+. We overcome such limitation by repeating simulation multiple times to allow simulation trends to converge as suggested in [21]. We use a convergence rule to improve the confidence level of predicted trends:

Simulate N times and compute avg. of all indicators (I_{Avg}),
we set $N = 5$
While all Indicators haven't converged
Simulate and compute new average (I_{New}) from all simulation runs
For all Indiactors
If (($|I_{Avg} - I_{New}|$) < δ), where deviation (δ) is within a tolerable range
Converged = $True$
Else
$I_{Avg} = I_{New}$

4   Case Study

We contextualized our city digital twin for Pune city by configuring the demographic details and comorbidity distribution among citizens, household structures and prototypical areas that reflect socio-economic strata of the city, various professions and their movements, and prototypical places, such as offices, factories, schools, markets, worship places. We further introduced relevant Covid-19 interventions, vaccination policies as reported by Indian Government[3], and city specific vaccination rates. The trend predicted by our digital twin for Pune city, with *Alpha* variant, no vaccine, high compliance of Covid-19 interventions and moderate Covid-appropriate behavior (CAB), closely resembles the recorded data from March 2020 to February 2021 as shown using a grey line in Fig. 5 (a). However, our predicted trends started deviating significantly from March 2021 and the situation became unexplainable in April. None of the Covid-19 models were able to predict/explain the situation.

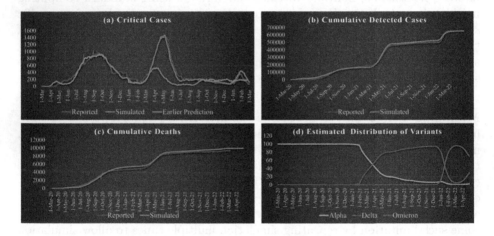

Fig. 5. Simulated vs reported cases in Pune.

Post facto experiments using our digital twin showed that situation in Pune from March 2021 to November 2021 represents a collective impact of the following factors: *Delta* variant starting to appear around February 2021; around 5−7% loss of immunity after 5−7 months of infection; two approved vaccines (*i.e.*, *Covishield* and *Covaxin*) with their reported efficacy and adoption rate in Pune; 10−15 days delay in implementing administrative interventions in March-April 2021, and 80−90% compliance during that period; 75−80% noncompliance with CAB and significant violation of public gatherings thereafter. The estimated trends of critical cases, detected cases and cumulative deaths, along with reported values, are shown in Fig. 5. In early December 2021, we introduced

---

[3] https://www.mohfw.gov.in/.

the *Omicron* variant into our digital twin, accompanied by further relaxation of administrative intervention, 10−15% greater noncompliance and significantly low testing uptake to predict the emerging situation. Our prediction (shown using orange line) closely matches the reported cases (shown using blue line in Fig. 5) until the end of the third wave. We also estimated the spread and distribution of different variants as shown in Fig. 5(d): this is difficult to validate in the absence of authentic data, but our results were considered highly plausible by public health experts during informal discussions.

4.1   Synthesis of Simulation-Led Experimentation

Hypotheses building and systematic simulation-led experimentation on city digital twin helped to justify the possible causes for perplexing situations observed during second and third waves. Our study indicates that the characteristics of dominant variants is not the only contributing factor for infection spread. People's movements along with the characteristics of variant play a critical role to determine the pace at which a wave will unfold in a city. For an instance, the first wave took around 160 days to peak in Pune city. In comparison, the second wave took 91 days, and the third wave took only 31 days to peak as shown Fig. 5(a). The key reasons for such differences are twofold: a) increased infectivity of the dominant variant *i.e.*, Omicron is more infective than Delta which is more infective than Alpha variant, and b) relaxation of movement-related restrictions and gradual reduction in adherence to Covid-appropriate behavior.

Detailed analysis of simulation results indicates that movement restrictions impacting open spaces (*i.e.*, strict lockdown) can at best delay the onset of a wave. Instead, controlling the mixing of people in closed places (such as, within schools, offices and business places) and limiting household infections lead to better results. Therefore, isolation in the form of strict home/institutional quarantine backed by effective strategies to reopen offices and schools can contribute the most towards reduced infection spread. Wearing face masks indoors also helps to curb the spread of infection to a large extent, as is already well-known. The infectivity and severity of a variant have a complex relationship with other factors that influence how quickly a variant can be the dominant one in a city. A variant with low infectivity and low severity (*e.g.*, Alpha) has a high chance to exponentially disappear from the community as we observed for Alpha vs Delta. Variants with low infectivity and high severity disappear much faster compared to a variant with low infectivity and low severity as severely infected people are likely to go for testing and subsequent isolation. Variants having high infectivity and low severity (*e.g.*, Omicron variant) quickly become dominant as shown for Omicron and Delta in Fig. 5(d). Variants with high infectivity and high severity can potentially be the most dangerous; however, high severity leads to early detection, thus limiting the impact significantly. This situation can be controlled through early testing, contract tracing and strict isolation. Therefore, a variant with high infectivity and high severity is unlikely to survive for long. A variant's ability to bypass immunity is another characteristic that needs to be considered carefully as it significantly contributes towards the magnitude of the peak of a wave.

Vaccination is the most critical factor controlling the severity of infection and the subsequent fatalities. This impact was evident during the later stages of the second (Delta-driven) wave and throughout the third (Omicron-driven) wave. However, reduced severity typically leads to reduced testing and lax compliance with isolation norms, as witnessed during the third wave. These factors might lead to greater infection spread, increasing the amount of risk in individuals with comorbidities.

Based on simulation results, we further argue that a major surge in infections is possible in the future only if: a) a new variant characterized by moderate to high infectivity, moderate severity, and immunity bypassing capability emerges, and/or b) significant chunk of population becomes susceptible due to immunity waning over time. The latter factor can cause a wave even in absence of the former factor, as most of the variants are likely to be around for a while and can cause a serge if waning immunity is significantly high.

5   Conclusion

During the last two years, we made several attempts to precisely understand the evolving dynamics of Covid-19 pandemic in the context of a moderately large city with significant heterogeneity and deep uncertainty. The notable takeaway from our experiments is as follows: the use of any of the modeling and analysis technique in its canonical form to address an exceedingly complex problem is not a pragmatic proposition. One needs to explore the problem space from the right lens to devise appropriate solutions. We adopted a reductionist view and critically reflected on core system modeling concepts namely, *system of systems* and *complex adaptive system*, and the modeling principle of *separation of concerns* to manage the inherent complexity of predicting the evolution of Covid-19 pandemic at various levels of granularity. We advocated a pure form of *bottom-up* modeling paradigm and *agent* model as a core modeling abstraction to achieve the desired modeling richness; leveraged a combined validation method that promotes domain-expert led *conceptual validity* along with traditional *operational validity* to address faithfulness; and adopted pragmatic considerations supported by suitable technology (*i.e.*, ESL) to establish a balance between precision and scalability. While we addressed all core concerns of modeling and predicting the evolution of the Covid-19 pandemic, there is significant scope to improve our digital twin from two perspectives: usability and greater rigor in validation. Pre-populated model parameters for prototypical cities and an automated data feed from authentic sources or Covid-19 dashboards will address the former. The latter is a key point for future investigation and research.

References

1. Agrawal, M., Kanitkar, M., Vidyasagar, M.: SUTRA: a novel approach to modelling pandemics with applications to Covid-19. arXiv preprint arXiv:2101.09158 (2021)
2. Anderson, R.M., Anderson, B., May, R.M.: Infectious Diseases of Humans: Dynamics and Control. Oxford University Press, Oxford (1992)
3. Barat, S., et al.: An agent-based digital twin for exploring localized non-pharmaceutical interventions to control COVID-19 pandemic. Trans. Indian Natl. Acad. Eng. **6**(2), 323–353 (2021). https://doi.org/10.1007/s41403-020-00197-5
4. Boardman, J., Sauser, B.: System of systems-the meaning of of. In: 2006 International Conference on System of Systems Engineering, p. 6. IEEE (2006)
5. Buckley, W.: Society as a complex adaptive system. In: Systems Research for Behavioral Sciencesystems Research, pp. 490–513. Routledge (2017)
6. Burki, T.K.: Omicron variant and booster COVID-19 vaccines. Lancet Respir. Med. **10**(2), e17 (2022)
7. Clark, T., Kulkarni, V., Barat, S., Barn, B.: ESL: an actor-based platform for developing emergent behaviour organisation simulations. In: Demazeau, Y., Davidsson, P., Bajo, J., Vale, Z. (eds.) PAAMS 2017. LNCS (LNAI), vol. 10349, pp. 311–315. Springer, Cham (2017). https://doi.org/10.1007/978-3-319-59930-4_27
8. Dong, E., Du, H., Gardner, L.: An interactive web-based dashboard to track COVID-19 in real time. Lancet. Infect. Dis. **20**(5), 533–534 (2020)
9. Elbanna, A.: Estimation of the ascertainment bias in Covid case detection during the Omicron wave. MedRxiv (2022). https://doi.org/10.1101/2022.04.22.22274198
10. Fatimah, B., Aggarwal, P., Singh, P., Gupta, A.: A comparative study for predictive monitoring of COVID-19 pandemic. Appl. Soft Comput. **122**, 108806 (2022)
11. Fayyoumi, E., Idwan, S., AboShindi, H.: Machine learning and statistical modelling for prediction of novel COVID-19 patients case study: Jordan. Mach. Learn. **11**(5), 3–11 (2020)
12. Gomez, J., Prieto, J., Leon, E., Rodriguez, A.: INFEKTA: a general agent-based model for transmission of infectious diseases: studying the COVID-19 propagation in Bogotá-Colombia. MedRxiv (2020)
13. Hansen, P.R.: Relative contagiousness of emerging virus variants: an analysis of the Alpha, Delta, and Omicron SARS-CoV-2 variants. Econom. J. **25**(3), 739–761 (2022)
14. He, S., Peng, Y., Sun, K.: SEIR modeling of the COVID-19 and its dynamics. Nonlinear Dyn. **101**(3), 1667–1680 (2020). https://doi.org/10.1007/s11071-020-05743-y
15. Hewitt, C.: Actor model of computation: scalable robust information systems. arXiv preprint arXiv:1008.1459 (2010)
16. Kerr, C.C., et al.: Covasim: an agent-based model of COVID-19 dynamics and interventions. PLoS Comput. Biol. **17**(7), e1009149 (2021)
17. Korolev, I.: Identification and estimation of the SEIRD epidemic model for COVID-19. J. Econom. **220**(1), 63–85 (2021)
18. Lipsitch, M., Dean, N.E.: Understanding COVID-19 vaccine efficacy. Science **370**(6518), 763–765 (2020)
19. Muhareb, R., Giacaman, R.: Tracking COVID-19 responsibly. Lancet (2020)
20. Olliaro, P., Torreele, E., Vaillant, M.: COVID-19 vaccine efficacy and effectiveness—the elephant (not) in the room. Lancet Microbe **2**(7), e279–e280 (2021)

21. Robinson, S.: Simulation verification, validation and confidence: a tutorial. Trans. Soc. Comput. Simul. **16**(2), 63–69 (1999)
22. Sargent, R.G.: Verification and validation of simulation models. In: Proceedings of the 2010 Winter Simulation Conference, pp. 166–183. IEEE (2010)
23. Silva, P.C., Batista, P.V., et al.: COVID-ABS: an agent-based model of COVID-19 epidemic to simulate health and economic effects of social distancing interventions. Chaos Solit. Fractals **139**, 110088 (2020)
24. WHO: Tracking SARS-CoV-2 variants. World Health Organization (2022). https://www.who.int/en/activities/tracking-SARS-CoV-2-variants
25. Winter, G.: A comparative discussion of the notion of validity in qualitative and quantitative research. Qual. Rep. **4**(3), 1–14 (2000)

Preference Aggregation Mechanisms for a Tourism-Oriented Bayesian Recommender

Errikos Streviniotis$^{(\boxtimes)}$ and Georgios Chalkiadakis

Technical University of Crete, Chania, Greece
{estreviniotis,gehalk}@intelligence.tuc.gr

Abstract. In this work, we employ various preference aggregation mechanisms from the social choice literature alongside with a multiwinner voting rule, namely the *Reweighted Approval Voting (RAV)*, to the group recommendations problem. In more detail, we equip with such mechanisms a Bayesian recommender system for the tourism domain, allowing for the effective aggregation of elicited group members' preferences while promoting *fairness* in the group recommendations. We conduct a systematic experimental evaluation of our approach by applying it on a real-world dataset. Our results clearly demonstrate that the use of multiwinner mechanisms allows for *fair* group recommendations with respect to the well-known m-*proportionality* and m-*envy-freeness* metrics.

Keywords: Group recommendations · Preference aggregation · Bayesian recommender system · Personalized recommendations

1 Introduction

Social choice theory (SCT) [5] is a theoretical framework that is widely deployed in various domains such as economics, political science, computer science etc. In recent years, there is an increasing interest in the SCT subdomain relating to *multiwinner elections*. Specifically, multiwinner elections employ mechanisms or voting rules that elect a subset of candidates instead of a single winner [10]. Such mechanisms can find application in a variety of domains, from picking parliaments to choosing contest winners to recommending products or services [11]. However, to the best of our knowledge multiwinner election mechanisms have not yet been used in real-world recommender systems, since such mechanisms have mostly been studied at a theoretical level.

In general, *Recommender Systems (RS)* are tools that help users browse and retrieve relevant information or items of interest (e.g., products or services) from large collections [28]; RS is an inherently multiagent domain, in which both users and the RS system itself can be viewed as (perhaps bounded) rational agents. Many RS provide personalized recommendations by analyzing the users' previous interactions with the system, or by exploiting available data (e.g., ratings from similar users). Recommender systems increase users' satisfaction, since they do not waste their time with items not matching their interests and preferences. Thus, popular travel platforms incorporate RS to enhance customer experience.

© The Author(s), under exclusive license to Springer Nature Switzerland AG 2023
R. Aydoğan et al. (Eds.): PRIMA 2022, LNAI 13753, pp. 331–346, 2023.
https://doi.org/10.1007/978-3-031-21203-1_20

Now, most of RS research focuses on recommendations for a single user, while in real life there is a plethora of scenarios where users form groups in order to experience some product or service, e.g., music in a car ride or a movie in the theater. However, group recommendations come in naturally in many domains—such as tourism, since usually users travel with company, e.g., friends or family. Thus, an RS in such a domain should take this aspect into account [9]; and, importantly, needs to ensure that recommendations are *fair* [32] with respect to the preferences of the individual group members. In general, the generation of group recommendations by a system is achieved by employing an *aggregation mechanism* that considers individuals' preferences [20]. However, there is a multitude of alternative ways to produce recommendations for groups of users [15], e.g., find the recommendations for each member of the group separately and produce the group recommendations by selecting items based on a preference aggregation technique; or build a group recommender model by merging group members into one [18].

In the tourism industry, RS serve as digital guides for the many activities a group of visitors may partake in according on their individual interests. On top of the preferences aggregation problem, RS in tourism have to deal with very sparse items ratings originating from the user(s) of interest, and thus the employment of classic RS approaches (e.g., collaborative filtering [28]) can be a complicated task [9]. Additionally, there are many kinds of short-term visitors, e.g., cruise tourists. This category of tourists have limited time when visiting a travel destination. As such, the cost of recommending wrong or irrelevant items is high. Thus, an RS should be able to provide effective recommendations in order to maximize user satisfaction via a lightweight user-system interaction process.

Against this background, we employ, for the first time in the literature, a multiwinner election mechanism, Reweighted Approval Voting (RAV) to the group recommendation problem; and show via a systematic experimental evaluation process that it outperforms several other well-known aggregation mechanisms with respect to standard fairness metrics. We used a real-world dataset for our evaluation, specifically one created for the needs of a real-world short-term visits planning recommender system built for the municipality of Agios Nikolaos, a popular travel destination in Crete. Real world data on *points of interests (POIs)* and users' preferences were collected by: *(i)* local knowledge, *(ii)* online sources, and *(iii)* questionnaires that were filled by tourists. Our mechanisms can be applied on top of *any* standard single-user recommender system. In this work, this was a personalized Bayesian recommender we put forward, along with a novel picture-based preference elicitation process.

2   Background and Related Work

In this section, we provide the necessary background for this work.

2.1   Social Choice Theory

In general, social choice theory studies aggregation mechanisms of individual preferences in order to reach a collective choice or decision [5]. Over the years, particular emphasis has been given to the scenario of electing a single "winner" over a set of items or alternatives. In more detail, given a set of voters or agents and their corresponding preferences, social choice theory studies efficient mechanisms and rules in order to elect the best alternative with respect to voters' preferences. Many single-winner voting rules have been proposed in the literature with most known *plurality, Borda count, Copeland, etc.* [5].

However, there is another type of elections that has recently gained the interest of researchers. Specifically, in this type of elections, the purpose is to select a k-sized group of alternatives, i.e., a *committee* of size k, rather than just a single winner, i.e., a single alternative. This type of elections are also known as *Multiwinner elections* [11]; and can be categorized as: *(i)* Shortlisting, *(ii)* Diverse Committee, and *(iii)* Proportional Representation mechanisms [10], based on their type and their properties. Intuitively, a Shortlisting mechanism elects a committee consisting of the alternatives that have the best quality with respect to some feature(s), e.g., on a job interview scenario the application of a shortlisting mechanism would result to a committee consisting of candidates that have similar skills and characteristics [11]. By contrast, a Diverse Committee mechanism elects a committee consisting of alternatives that are diverse based on some feature(s). For instance, consider a travel agency that recommends travel destinations to a customer. The employment of such mechanisms in this case could produce a set of k travel destination that differ with each other based on their location (or any other feature). As such, a capital city in South America, an exotic island in the Pacific ocean and a traditional village in Asia could be elected as the recommendations of the agency. Finally, a Proportional Representation mechanism selects a committee that captures all the different preferences of the voters proportionally.

An important class of voting rules are the so-called *approval-based* rules, in which voters indicate the alternatives they "approve". Perhaps the most well-known such mechanism is the Approval Voting (AV). Given a list of candidates, Approval Voting allows each voter to express her approval, i.e., her support, for many candidates. Then the mechanism elects the candidate who earned the greatest number of approval votes. In general, AV satisfies several desirable properties in the situation of a single winner, but it fails to attain proportionate representation in the case of multiwinner elections [1]. On the other hand, the PAV multiwinner election method is an approval-based rule that meets strong theoretical guarantees for election proportionality. In more detail, according to the PAV rule, the weight of each voter to the committee's final score is based on how many candidates from the voter's approval set were elected [1]. However, Skowron et al. [33] showed that winners determination under PAV is an NP-hard problem. To tackle this, a "sequential" PAV variant, namely the *Reweighted Approval Voting (RAV)*, which is essentially a "greedy" approximation of the PAV rule, has been introduced in the literature [11]:

Definition 1. (Reweighet Approval Voting - RAV [11]) Consider an election with n voters where the i-th voter approves candidates in the set A_i. RAV starts with an empty committee S and executes k rounds. In each round it adds to S a candidate c with the maximal value of $\sum_{i:c\in A_i} \frac{1}{|S\cap A_i|+1}$.

That is, according to this definition, at each iteration RAV re-adjusts the weights of each voter's ballot in order to achieve a proportional representation in the final committee.

To the best of our knowledge, such mechanisms have mostly been researched as theoretical tools, as they have not been implemented in real-world recommender systems—with the notable exception of Gawron and Faliszewski [13]: in that paper, the authors introduced a system that exploits multiwinner election mechanisms in order to produce a set of resources (or items) that are similar to a given query. In more detail, by employing different mechanisms the system is able to control the degree of relation between the recommended resources and the given query. However, their proposed system operates more like a search engine rather than a classic recommender system, since it elects items that are somewhat related to the given query, instead of recommending items that can increase the satisfaction of a specific user (i.e., they do not take into account user-specific features in order to provide personalized recommendations).

2.2   Personalized Recommendations

Tourism is a natural application domain for personalized RS, since users with variant preferences need to select items of different types (e.g., leisure or cultural POIs). Our work in this paper is related to the development of a real-world tour planning application. As such, we now discuss a few tourism related personalized recommender systems relating to this specific sub-problem.

Ziogas et al. [36] proposed a content-based tourism RS which provides personalized recommendations for touristic attractions. Specifically, the authors constructed hierarchies of items-to-be-recommended, and employed various hierarchical and non-hierarchical similarity measures in order to provide the final set of recommended POIs. In [31] the authors proposed a Crow Search Optimization-based Hybrid Recommendation model in order to produce recommendations to tourists by combining collaborative filtering and content-based filtering techniques. The accuracy of their approach was evaluated experimentally via a dataset provided by TripAdvisor, the well-known tourism platform. Kashevnik et al. [16] proposed a context-driven tour planning service by exploiting user's past interactions with the system. In this approach, authors employed the SCoR algorithm [26] in order to predict the ratings of a specific user for any given item and subsequently produce the final recommendations. In [19] personalized recommendation are provided to the users by a Hybrid recommender which employs three different types of filtering, namely collaborative filtering, along with content-based and demographic filtering. Gavalas et al. [12] introduced another personalized tour planner, that generates *personalized tours*. In more detail, a context-aware web/mobile application produces tailored multimodal tours based on a selection of urban attractions. On top of that each individual is able to define the starting and the ending point of her daily tours. The system was evaluated by actual users in city of Berlin. Finally, an extensive overview of recommender systems in tourism can be found in [4].

2.3 Group Recommendations

Traditionally, most RS research focuses on individuals by recommending items that maximise users' satisfaction. However, users often interact with one another, forming groups. This social aspect gives rise to the development of *group recommender systems*. In the literature, several RS have been proposed for groups in various domains, such as movies, music, TV programs, travel, etc. [8]. Briefly, in the movies domain such systems may operate by exploiting users' social and behavioral data [30], or by calculating the probability that a user likes a movie or not [14,35]. Additionally, some Collaborative Filtering approaches have been introduced [3,17]. MusicFX [22] is a group recommender system for music in shared environments, e.g., in gyms, which is also extended to other domains, i.e., restaurants [21].

In terms of work in our domain of interest, there is a number of tourism- or travel-oriented group RS. McCarthy et al. [23] introduced the CATS travel RS for groups of users. Specifically, CATS is a collaborative advisory travel system that recommends travel destinations to groups of at most 4 individuals. An extension of CATS, was proposed in [29], where an extra module of negotiation was added. Moreover, *Bayesian methods*, which maintain and exploit probabilistic beliefs regarding user preferences, are able to provide high quality recommendations for both individual tourists and groups; and, most importantly, such techniques can be applied for real-time mobile recommendation services [6]. The travel RS in [6] exploits data from the "community-contributed" photos by giving tags to the groups. Moreover, users can be categorized based on some user specific features (i.e., age, gender, etc.); whereas groups are categorized based on the type of the formed group (i.e., group of friends, family, etc). Finally, [27] employs Bayesian networks to recommend restaurants to groups of people in mobile environments.

3 Our Approach

The main aim of this work is to tackle the group recommendation problem in the tourism domain. To this end, we use "tools" from the social choice theory to effectively aggregate tourist group members' preferences in a fair manner. Specifically, in this section we proceed to show how to tackle the group recommendation problem via employing various preference aggregation mechanisms— and, importantly, for the first time in tourism-oriented RS, a multiwinner voting rule. We also describe the main workings of a Bayesian recommender system that we use in order to generate single-user preferences and feed these into the aggregation mechanisms tackling the group recommendation problem.

Figure 1 provides an overview of our approach. We see there that *any* single-user recommender method of choice can be employed in order to generate lists of single user preferences. These can be used either for recommending items to individual users; or, importantly, as input to a *group recommendation stage* that employs *preference aggregation mechanims* in order to come up with (hopefully effective and fair) recommendations for groups of users.

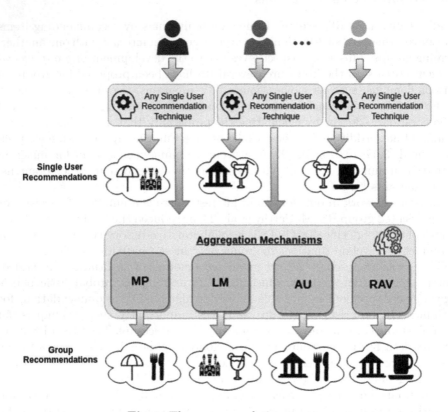

Fig. 1. The recommendation process.

3.1   Recommendation Process for Groups

We first describe how to apply our preference aggregation methods and mechanisms on top of any single user recommendation technique. In more detail, we consider a set of items (or alternatives) and a set of users (or agents), denoted as $\mathcal{I}$ and $\mathcal{U}$ correspondingly. We can employ *any* recommender system technique of choice (e.g., collaborative filtering, content-based, Bayesian, or any other), in order to generate a predicted score, $r_{u,i}$, for any possible combination of i and u, where $i \in \mathcal{I}$ and $u \in \mathcal{U}$—i.e., the (single-user) recommender system predicts that user u will rate item i with a score of $r_{u,i}$. Moreover, for each individual u, we can make the natural assumption that u prefers item i over j if the predicted score of i is larger than the one of j, i.e., $i \succ_u j$ if and only if $r_{u,i} > r_{u,j}$. Thus, our system is able to create the preference list for any individual u.

Now, assume that a group, denoted as g, consists of $|g|$ members corresponding to tourists, i.e., individual users. Our system is able to exploit the aforementioned preference list of every member of the group, derived after the employment of the single-user recommendation technique of choice during the (independent) interaction of each user with the system. Then, our group recommender system is able to produce group recommendations to any group g, by exploiting the preference lists of the group members and by applying *any* aggregation mechanism of choice.

In the experimental evaluation of our system, we explore several well-known aggregation strategies, such as the *Least Misery (LM)* strategy, *Most Pleasure (MP)* strategy and the *Additive Utilitarian (AU)* strategy. Formally, the LM mechanism provides recommendations (or items) that maximize the minimum individual rating among the members of the group, i.e., for each item $i \in \mathcal{I}$, LM mechanism assigns a score equal to $min_{u \in g,i}\{r_{u,i}\}$ and recommends the item(s) with the highest score(s). Similarly, the MP strategy elects the items that maximize the maximum individual rating among the members of the group, i.e., for each item $i \in \mathcal{I}$, MP assigns a score equal to $max_{u \in g,i}\{r_{u,i}\}$ and recommends the item(s) with the highest score(s); while the AU mechanism recommends the items that maximize the average individuals ratings among the members, , i.e., for each item $i \in \mathcal{I}$, AU assigns a score equal to $avg_{u \in g,i}\{r_{u,i}\}$ and recommends the item(s) with the highest score(s). Note that the LM, MP and AU aggregation strategies have been in the past employed for tackling the problem of group recommendations in the tourism domain [8].

In addition, we use the RAV multiwinner election mechanism (see Sect. 2.1)—for the first time in the recommender systems' literature. We remind the reader that RAV is a greedy multiwinner voting rule that elects a committee (i.e., a set of items), that represent proportionally the preferences of the voters, i.e., the members of the group. Generally, in the problem of group recommendations, such mechanisms can be very useful due to their properties, since the proportionality that is achieved by the elected committee provides a notion of fairness among the members of the group with respect to their preferences[1]. Furthermore, the RAV mechanism was selected since our purpose is to find a computationally efficient mechanism that is able to satisfy fairness in a real world application, where the group size can be large and the recommended items have to be displayed quickly in order to ensure that visitors would not waste their time waiting for the results, i.e., the final group recommendations. Note that all aforementioned aggregation mechanisms can be employed for any possible group size.

---

[1] Of course, proportionality is only one notion of fairness provided by some multiwinner election mechanims. In other cases, one may want to define a notion of fairness based on the properties of shortlisting or diversity that other multiwinner election mechanisms satisfy.

3.2   Deriving the Preferences of Individuals

In this section, we describe a recommendation process for individuals, which can be used to derive the preference lists to be fed into our aggregation mechanisms for the group recommendation stage (see Fig. 1). To this end, inspired by the work of [2], we designed a Bayesian RS that performs updating of beliefs in order to *learn* the users' preferences. The main idea of this approach is to model the users and the items (the tourist POIs) by a common representation; evolve user models via a Bayesian updating procedure; and provide as recommendations the items whose representation best-matches the evolved user models. The common representation used for users and POIs is *multivariate normal distributions*[2] of dimension D over ranges of values, describing the degree that each feature describes a specific user or item.

On top of that, our single-user recommendation module employs a lightweight, picture-based elicitation process in order to determine user's preferences. Such picture-based elicitation approaches have been shown to be efficient for tourism recommender systems [24,25], effectively tackling the inherent complexity of the domain [9], but have never been used for *Bayesian* recommenders, such as the one we use in this work.

To describe this process in some detail, in each iteration of the elicitation process our system presents n alternative *generic, travel-related pictures* to the user. As mentioned, each picture is represented as a multivariate Gaussian, and corresponds to a specific POI *type*, i.e., a restaurant, a monument, a beach and so on.

Note that our agent uses the well-known Boltzmann exploration technique [2] to select which generic pictures to present to the user, based on the available preference-related information in the user model (i.e., the multivariate distribution representing the user). However, the well-known "cold start" problem plaguing recommender systems is an issue to deal with in our case also: there is no information about new users entering the system. In such cases, our recommender *randomly* picks some generic pictures to show to the user during their very first interaction with the system—barring the possibility that some prior information regarding a user "category", "type", "class" already exists. In our work, we were able to exploit prior knowledge regarding the preferences of actual tourists of specific age categories visiting Agios Nikolaos (as we later explain), in order to show to new users pictures relating to tourists of the same age.

Now, once the user is presented with a set of generic pictures, she clicks the one image that she "likes" more, that is most "attractive" to her, *wrt* her interests, and subsequently rates it by giving it 1–5 stars. (Note that all this functionality is actually included in a real-world mobile app developed for the needs of Agios Nikolaos' visitors.) A "5-star" rating is interpreted by the system as a "perfect match" between the generic picture's representation model, and the actual user model; while lower ratings correspond to lower levels of matching among the models. The Bayesian updating process effectively aggregates all such information via a sampling based approach, as we now describe.

---

[2] Henceforth referred to as "multivariate Gaussians" or "Gaussians" for short.

Similarly to the work of [2], we compute the similarity of any item (POI or generic picture) and any user model via exploiting the well-known *Kullback-Leibler (KL) Divergence* criterion to assess the "distance" between their corresponding multivariate Gaussian distributions. As mentioned, we make the natural assumption that the more similar the Gaussians of a user u and an item i are, the higher the rating (of user u for item i) would be; while the smaller the KL-divergence between a Gaussian x and a Gaussian y is, the more similar these distributions are. As such, the (predicted) rating of a (represented as a Gaussian) user u for (a represented as a Gaussian) item i can be defined as:

$$r_{u,i} = M - \frac{KL(u\|i)}{M} \qquad (1)$$

with M being the maximum possible rating (i.e., 5). Given this predicted rating, the Bayesian recommender uses the *logistic function* [7] in order to draw an appropriate number of samples from the selected generic picture's distribution. Then, *Bayesian inference* [2,34] is employed so as to combine the prior user model and the new samples collected in order to produce an updated user model (that is, a posterior Gaussian distribution describing the user). This process then repeats for a pre-specified number of iterations, with the posterior becoming the new user prior, exploited to pick new generic pictures to present to the user in her next interaction with the system[3]. Following this elicitation process, the single-user recommendation module exploits the built user model in order to output a list of the most preferred POIs by this user (i.e., those POIs having the lower KL-divergence when compared with the user model); and provides it as input to the aggregation mechanisms used for group recommendations.

4   Experimental Evaluation

In this section we present a series of experiments, mainly to evaluate the fairness that is achieved by several well-known aggregation mechanisms for group recommendations. We use a real-world dataset including 430 POIs located in or around the city of Agios Nikolaos, Crete, Greece.

Evaluating Aggregation Mechanisms for Group Recommendations. In our experiments we evaluate the performance of different aggregation mechanisms for group recommendations, in terms of the standard *m-PROPORTIONALITY* and *m-ENVY-FREENESS* fairness metrics [32]. These respectively signify the percentages of users that consider m items in a recommended set to be either in their top $\Delta_p\%$ of preferred items, or for which the user belongs in some top $\Delta_e\%$ of users that are favored by the recommendation of these items (these will be clarified more below). We created synthetic groups g of users of various sizes—specifically, $|g| = \{5, 10, 15, 20\}$—and applied the following aggregation

---

[3] Obviously the user model can and will also be updated following an actual visit to and rating of a particular POI, via the exact same process.

strategies: *(i)* Least Misery (LM), *(ii)* Most Pleasure (MP), *(iii)* Additive Utilitarian (AU), and *(iv)* Reweighted Approval Voting (RAV).

In more detail, for the RAV mechanism, we assume that a user *approves* an item, i.e., a POI, if and only if her expected score (computed from Eq. 1) for this item is larger than 3. We note that in order to compute the expected user's rating for an item we use her inferred model (i.e. the model that our approach constructed via our preference elicitation process) and not her real one (since we want to assess our system's ability to provide fair recommendations, and the real user model is not known to the system). For the *m-PROPORTIONALITY* fairness metric we assume that Δ_p for all users is set to 0.1—i.e., a user *likes* a POI, if this POI is ranked in the top-10% of the user's preferences over all available POIs in the dataset. Additionally, for the *m-ENVY-FREENESS* fairness metric we assume that $\Delta_e = 0.4$—i.e., a user is *envy-free* for a POI, if for this POI the user is in the favored top-40% of the group (i.e., in the 40% of the group members that prefer the POI more than the rest 60%). Finally, for both *m-PROPORTIONALITY* and *m-ENVY-FREENESS* metrics we consider that the m items for which the corresponding property is required is set to:

$$m = \frac{\#\ of\ recommended\ POIs}{|g|} \tag{2}$$

where *# of recommended POIs* = 20.

Table 1. Fairness results (averages over 500 simulations per $|g|$).

Group size	Metrics	RAV	MP	LM	AU
$|g| = 5$	m-PROPORTIONALITY	0.93	0.79	0.72	0.83
	m-ENVY-FREENESS	0.79	0.62	0.65	0.62
$|g| = 10$	m-PROPORTIONALITY	0.96	0.89	0.87	0.88
	m-ENVY-FREENESS	0.92	0.79	0.75	0.78
$|g| = 15$	m-PROPORTIONALITY	0.98	0.97	0.95	0.94
	m-ENVY-FREENESS	0.97	0.92	0.86	0.92
$|g| = 20$	m-PROPORTIONALITY	0.98	0.97	0.95	0.94
	m-ENVY-FREENESS	0.97	0.92	0.85	0.92

Table 1 illustrates the results of our approach on this set of experiments. Note that the presented results are the average values over 500 simulations of experiments on settings with the same properties—i.e., we randomly generated 500 groups for each group size $|g|$ value, and ran one such simulation per generated group (i.e., we ran 2000 simulations in total). We can see that the RAV mechanism is able to provide very efficient group recommendations for every setting with respect to our fairness metrics, achieving consistently better performance compared to the other aggregation mechanisms. In fact, the RAV mechanism usually achieves a score over 92%, i.e., the proportionality and envy-freeness properties are achieved for almost all members of the group, irrespective of group size (with only one exception, for $|g| = 5$ when a 4-*ENVY-FREENESS* of 79% is achieved). Notice also that RAV's performance is significantly better than that of the other mechanisms for the smaller group sizes. In the case of larger groups, however, every aggregation mechanism achieves very high scores (signifying fair group recommendations), which are also comparable to each other. Such a result is expected, since for larger groups the m parameter for both metrics decreases (see Eq. 2). Thus, we need fewer items (i.e., m items) in the final set of recommendations, in order to consider this set of POIs fair for a member of the group with respect to our metrics. Additionally, for larger groups it is easier to find members that share similar interests—e.g., it is easier to recommend POIs that satisfy more than one members belonging to the group.

Validating the Underlying Single-User Bayesian RS. As noted earlier in the paper, any type of single-user recommender can be used to provide input to the aggregation mechanisms used for group recommendations. The experiments conducted above used as input the preference lists associated with user models created by the single-user Bayesian recommender presented in Sect. 3.2. An extensive evaluation of this single-user recommendations algorithm is provided in a RecTour-2022 workshop paper that is freely available online [34]. Since this single-user recommender approach is not the main focus of our work in this paper, and for the interest of conciseness, here we only present briefly the main findings of that evaluation.

Specifically, our results showed that given a specific user, the more she interacts with the system (by providing information regarding her interests via clicking on pictures she likes presented to her by the system), the Bayesian RS is able to produce a model that represents her preferences quite closely. Additionally, when more options are provided to the user by the system (i.e., when more pictures are included in the set of pictures presented to her by the system), then the quality of the recommendations increases. Indicatively, in the case where the user interacts with the system three times, i.e., each she selects an image from a tuple of three different pictures and then provides a rating for the selected picture during the elicitation process, our approach achieves a similarity score of 3.67 out of 5 with respect to the Kullback-Leibler metric, while in the case that the user interacts with the system five times the corresponding score stands at 3.92 out of 5. However, there is a trade-off between the satisfaction of user and the effectiveness of a recommender, i.e., as the number of user-system interaction increases the system is able to provide more efficient recommendations since it can exploit further information regarding the interests of the user, but it is also creates an emotion of dissatisfaction since the user has to provide more answers to the system. As such, our results indicate that our algorithm can produce a good model even with limited interaction, i.e., three, since the difference in terms of efficiency does not exceed a $5\% = (0.25/5)$ "penalty" compared to the case of five iterations. Finally, the employment of prior information regarding tourists' average preferences (in our experiments, this prior was constructed given information relating to the preferences of real tourists grouped by age), results to better performance (i.e., higher quality single-user recommendations), especially when the user-system interaction is limited.

5   Discussion

In this work, we employed the RAV multiwinner election mechanism for the challenging problem of group recommendations. Our choice for the particular mechanism was motivated by the following factors. First of all, RAV can be considered as a good greedy approximation algorithm for the PAV rule [11]. Noticeably, PAV is the only w-AV rule which satisfies the property of *Extended Justified Representation (EJR)* [1,11]. However, we highlight the fact that the purpose of this work is to produce recommendations of POIs for a real-world mobile application. Thus, we have to employ a computationally efficient mechanism, since mobile phones have limited processing power.

To the best of our knowledge, this work applies for the first time multiwinner elections in a real-world recommender system. As such, we chose to focus on the metrics of m-*PROPORTIONALITY* and m-*ENVY-FREENESS*, which are derived from the recommender systems literature; and exploit them for the first time for the evaluation of multiwinner rules. Our results clearly demonstrate that such techniques outperform other well-known mechanisms that have been employed for the group recommendation problem, especially when the size of the group is small, i.e., $|g| = 5$.

Now, note that many researchers have focused on fairness notions in the recommender systems literature. Note also that a recommender can use only the inferred model for generating recommendations. As such, as is natural and common in the literature, we exploit the *inferred* user model instead of the real one for producing recommendations.

Of course, the real user model can be exploited, for the evaluation of the *elicitation* procedure—i.e., for answering the question "How well our system has learned the (real) preferences of the user, via the selected elicitation process?". (We tackle this question when evaluating single-user recommendations, using the real model of the user and the corresponding metrics [34].) However, we believe that it is *not* appropriate to exploit the real user model to evaluate the mechanisms for group recommendations in real-world systems.

To explain this, assume that we employ any multiwinner mechanism that is able to perform *perfectly* with respect to our metrics. If our elicitation process cannot learn the users' preferences efficiently (e.g., due to a small number of interactions), then when evaluating our multiwinner mechanism with respect to m-*PROPORTIONALITY* and m-*ENVY-FREENESS*, the results would show that the mechanism does not perform well, when evaluated with respect to the real users' models. This effect however would be due to the fact that our inferred model does not describe efficiently the real users' preferences, and not because our mechanism is unable to provide a committee that satisfies to a large extent our selected metrics. Hence, we do not consider it appropriate to use the real user models for evaluating the multiwinner election mechanisms, as by doing so we would not be able to draw clear conclusions as to which component is responsible for potential poor performance of the real-world system, as our example indicates.

On the other hand, one could add to the pipeline a step in which the real users evaluate the final group recommendations (indeed, our real-world application includes such a step). This would result in an update of the inferred users' models (using any technique of choice), leading to improved recommendations in future interactions with the system.

Finally, we note that in [34] we introduced a novel social choice theory framework that is able to provide diverse personalized recommendations to a single user. In more detail, our system is able to exploit the mean vector that our system has constructed via the elicitation process, in order to create a *personalized election* that consists of *auxiliary* voters that represent proportionally each feature based on the corresponding scores of a specific user. Our results show that such an approach can improve the performance of our system especially when the user-system interaction is limited; while due to the nature of such a framework, one can employ any multiwinner election mechanism that results to a committee, i.e., final recommendations, that satisfy any desired property.

6   Conclusions and Future Work

In this work we put forward a recommender system to tackle the group recommendation problem in the tourism domain. Our approach utilizes a number of well-known preference aggregation mechanisms alongside a multiwinner voting rule, the *Reweighted Approval Voting (RAV)* mechanism. We also outlined the principal operations of a Bayesian recommender system that we employed in order to build the single-user preferences and feed them into aggregation techniques that address the group recommendation problem. Finally, we evaluated our methodology using a real-world dataset of a tourist destination. Our results confirm that the employment of the RAV multiwinner election mechanism results to *fair* group recommendations with respect to the fairness metrics of *m-PROPORTIONALITY* and *m-ENVY-FREENESS* derived from the recommender system literature. We note that RAV clearly outperforms its competitors for small tourist group sizes (which are in fact quite common in real life).

As future work, we intend to further evaluate our approach in scenarios in which different types of prior knowledge is available—i.e., when we have and can exploit information regarding the general preferences of a type of visitors not only based on the age group that they belong to, but also their nation, their gender etc. We also plan to employ other multi-winner election mechanisms, as well as equip our system with an additional *negotiations module* that helps the members of the group to decide fairly among the recommended POIs. Another interesting line of work would be the employment of other multiwinner election mechanisms that provide more theoretical guarantees derived from the social choice literature, e.g., *Justified Representation (JR)* and *Extended Justified Representation (EJR)*, in order to (i) evaluate them with respect to fairness metrics from other domains; (ii) find a brake-down point in terms of computational complexity. Finally, we plan to extensively test our group recommendations approach with actual tourists, via employing our real-world mobile application for short-term visits planning to this purpose; and try these ideas in other related domains of practical interest, such as road-trips planning.

Acknowledgments. This research has been co-financed by the European Union and Greek national funds through the Operational Program Competitiveness, Entrepreneurship and Innovation, under the call RESEARCH-CREATE-INNOVATE B cycle (project code: T2EDK-03135). E. Streviniotis was also supported by the Onassis Foundation - Scholarship ID: G ZR 012-1/2021-2022.

References

1. Aziz, H., Brill, M., Conitzer, V., Elkind, E., Freeman, R., Walsh, T.: Justified representation in approval-based committee voting. Soc. Choice Welfare **48**(2), 461–485 (2017). https://doi.org/10.1007/s00355-016-1019-3
2. Babas, K., Chalkiadakis, G., Tripolitakis, E.: You are what you consume: a Bayesian method for personalized recommendations. In: Proceedings of the 7th ACM Conference on Recommender Systems, pp. 221–228. RecSys 2013, ACM, NY, USA (2013)
3. Baltrunas, L., Makcinskas, T., Ricci, F.: Group recommendations with rank aggregation and collaborative filtering. In: RecSys 2010 (2010)
4. Borrás, J., Moreno, A., Valls, A.: Intelligent tourism recommender systems: A survey. Expert Syst. Appl. **41**(16), 7370–7389 (2014)
5. Brandt, F., Conitzer, V., Endriss, U., Lang, J., Procaccia, A.D.: Handbook of Computational Social Choice, 1st edn. Cambridge University Press, USA (2016)
6. Chen, Y.Y., Cheng, A.J., Hsu, W.H.: Travel recommendation by mining people attributes and travel group types from community-contributed photos. IEEE Trans. Multimedia **15**(6), 1283–1295 (2013)
7. Cox, D.R.: The regression analysis of binary sequences. J. Roy. Stat. Soc.: Ser. B (Methodol.) **20**(2), 215–232 (1958)
8. Dara, S., Chowdary, C.R., Kumar, C.N.: A survey on group recommender systems. J. Intell. Inf. Syst. **54**, 271–295 (2019)
9. Delic, A., Neidhardt, J.: A comprehensive approach to group recommendations in the travel and tourism domain. In: Proceedings of the 25th Conference on User Modeling, Adaptation and Personalization, pp. 11–16. UMAP 2017, ACM, NY, USA (2017)
10. Elkind, E., Faliszewski, P., Skowron, P., Slinko, A.: Properties of multiwinner voting rules. Soc. Choice Welfare **48**(3), 599–632 (2017)
11. Faliszewski, P., Slinko, A.M., Talmon, N.: Multiwinner Voting: A New Challenge for Social Choice Theory (2017)
12. Gavalas, D., Kasapakis, V., Konstantopoulos, C., Pantziou, G., Vathis, N., Zaroliagis, C.: The ecompass multimodal tourist tour planner. Expert Syst. Appl. **42**(21), 7303–7316 (2015)
13. Gawron, G., Faliszewski, P.: Using multiwinner voting to search for movies. In: EUMAS (2022)
14. Gorla, J., Lathia, N., Robertson, S., Wang, J.: Probabilistic group recommendation via information matching. In: Proceedings of the 22nd International Conference on World Wide Web, pp. 495–504. WWW 2013, Association for Computing Machinery, New York, NY, USA (2013)

15. Jameson, A., Smyth, B.: Recommendation to groups. In: Brusilovsky, P., Kobsa, A., Nejdl, W. (eds.) The Adaptive Web. LNCS, vol. 4321, pp. 596–627. Springer, Heidelberg (2007). https://doi.org/10.1007/978-3-540-72079-9_20

16. Kashevnik, A., Mikhailov, S., Papadakis, H., Fragopoulou, P.: Context-driven tour planning service: an approach based on synthetic coordinates recommendation. In: 2019 24th Conference of Open Innovations Association (FRUCT), pp. 140–147 (2019). https://doi.org/10.23919/FRUCT.2019.8711949

17. Kaššák, O., Kompan, M., Bieliková, M.: Personalized hybrid recommendation for group of users: top-N multimedia recommender. Inf. Process. Manag. **52**(3), 459–477 (2016)

18. Kaya, M., Bridge, D., Tintarev, N.: Ensuring fairness in group recommendations by rank-sensitive balancing of relevance, pp. 101–110. ACM, NY, USA (2020)

19. Kbaier, M.E.B.H., Masri, H., Krichen, S.: A personalized hybrid tourism recommender system. In: 2017 IEEE/ACS 14th International Conference on Computer Systems and Applications (AICCSA), pp. 244–250 (2017)

20. Masthoff, J.: Group recommender systems: combining individual models. In: Ricci, F., Rokach, L., Shapira, B., Kantor, P.B. (eds.) Recommender Systems Handbook, pp. 677–702. Springer, Boston, MA (2011). https://doi.org/10.1007/978-0-387-85820-3_21

21. McCarthy, J.F.: Pocket restaurantfinder: a situated recommender system for groups. In: Proceedings of the Workshop on Mobile Ad-Hoc Communication at the 2002 ACM Conference on Human Factors in Computer Systems. ACM, Minneapolis (2002)

22. McCarthy, J.F., Anagnost, T.D.: MusicFX: an arbiter of group preferences for computer supported collaborative workouts (1998)

23. McCarthy, K., Salamó, M., Coyle, L., McGinty, L., Smyth, B., Nixon, P.: Group recommender systems: a critiquing based approach. In: Proceedings of the 11th International Conference on Intelligent User Interfaces, pp. 267–269. IUI 2006, ACM, NY, USA (2006)

24. Neidhardt, J., Schuster, R., Seyfang, L., Werthner, H.: Eliciting the users' unknown preferences. In: Proceedings of the 8th ACM Conference on Recommender Systems, pp. 309–312. RecSys 2014, ACM, NY, USA (2014)

25. Neidhardt, J., Seyfang, L., Schuster, R., Werthner, H.: A picture-based approach to recommender systems. Inf. Technol. Tourism **15**, 49–69 (2015)

26. Papadakis, H., Panagiotakis, C., Fragopoulou, P.: SCoR: a synthetic coordinate based recommender system. Expert Syst. Appl. **79**, 8–19 (2017). https://doi.org/10.1016/j.eswa.2017.02.025, https://www.sciencedirect.com/science/article/pii/S0957417417301070

27. Park, M.-H., Park, H.-S., Cho, S.-B.: Restaurant recommendation for group of people in mobile environments using probabilistic multi-criteria decision making. In: Lee, S., Choo, H., Ha, S., Shin, I.C. (eds.) APCHI 2008. LNCS, vol. 5068, pp. 114–122. Springer, Heidelberg (2008). https://doi.org/10.1007/978-3-540-70585-7_13

28. Ricci, F., Rokach, L., Shapira, B.: Recommender Systems Handbook, vol. 1–35, pp. 1–35 (2010)

29. Salamó, M., McCarthy, K., Smyth, B.: Generating recommendations for consensus negotiation in group personalization services. Pers. Ubiquit. Comput. **16**, 597–610 (2011). https://doi.org/10.1007/s00779-011-0413-1

30. Sánchez, L.Q., Recio-García, J.A., Díaz-Agudo, B., Jiménez-Díaz, G.: Happy movie: a group recommender application in Facebook. In: FLAIRS Conference (2011)

31. Sarkar, M., Roy, A., Agrebi, M., AlQaheri, H.: Exploring new vista of intelligent recommendation framework for tourism industries: an itinerary through big data paradigm. Information **13**(2), 70 (2022)
32. Serbos, D., Qi, S., Mamoulis, N., Pitoura, E., Tsaparas, P.: Fairness in package-to-group recommendations, pp. 371–379. WWW 2017 (2017)
33. Skowron, P., Faliszewski, P., Lang, J.: Finding a collective set of items: from proportional multirepresentation to group recommendation. Artif. Intell. **241**, 191–216 (2016)
34. Streviniotis, E., Chalkiadakis, G.: Multiwinner election mechanisms for diverse personalized Bayesian recommendations for the tourism domain. In: 2022 Workshop on Recommenders in Tourism, RecTour 2022 (2022)
35. Yuan, Q., Cong, G., Lin, C.Y.: Com: a generative model for group recommendation. In: Proceedings of the 20th ACM SIGKDD International Conference on Knowledge Discovery and Data Mining, pp. 163–172. KDD 2014, Association for Computing Machinery, New York, NY, USA (2014)
36. Ziogas, I.P., Streviniotis, E., Papadakis, H., Chalkiadakis, G.: Content-based recommendations using similarity distance measures with application in the tourism domain. In: Proceedings of the 12th Hellenic Conference on Artificial Intelligence (2022)

Weaponizing Actions in Multi-Agent Reinforcement Learning: Theoretical and Empirical Study on Security and Robustness

Tongtong Liu[1], Joe McCalmon[1], Md Asifur Rahman[1], Cameron Lischke[2], Talal Halabi[3], and Sarra Alqahtani[1(✉)]

[1] Computer Science Department, Wake Forest University, Winston-Salem, NC, USA
{liut18,mccalmonjoe,rahmm21,alqahtas}@wfu.edu
[2] Computer Science Department, John Hopkins University, Baltimore, MD, USA
[3] Department of Computer Science and Software Engineering, Laval University, Quebec City, QC, Canada
talal.halabi@ift.ulaval.ca

Abstract. Cooperative Multi-Agent Reinforcement Learning (c-MARL) enables a team of agents to determine the global optimal policy that maximizes the sum of their accumulated rewards. This paper investigates the robustness of c-MARL to a novel adversarial threat, where we target and weaponize one agent, termed the *compromised agent*, to create natural observations that are adversarial for its team. The goal is to lure the compromised agent to follow an adversarial policy that pushes activations of its cooperative agents' policy networks off distribution. This paper shows mathematically the exploitation steps of such an adversarial policy in the centralized-learning and decentralized-execution paradigm of c-MARL. We also empirically demonstrate the susceptibility of the state-of-the-art c-MARL algorithms, namely MADDPG and QMIX, to the compromised agent threat by deploying four attack strategies in three environments in white and black box settings. By targeting a single agent, our attacks yield highly negative impact on the overall team reward in all environments, reducing it by at least 33% and at most 89.6%. Finally, we provide recommendations on improving the robustness of c-MARL.

Keywords: Multi-Agent Reinforcement Learning · Adversarial policies · Robustness · Security threats · Compromised agent

1 Introduction

The advances in single-agent Reinforcement Learning (RL) algorithms have sparked a new interest in cooperative Multi-Agent Reinforcement Learning (c-MARL). Several c-MARL training algorithms have been recently developed for deployment in several application domains such as cyber-physical systems [3], sensor networks, and social sciences. Nonetheless, these algorithms present new security vulnerabilities. For instance, it may not be surprising that adversarial attacks exist in RL to decrease the agent performance [8,14]. However, the

R. Aydoğan et al. (Eds.): PRIMA 2022, LNAI 13753, pp. 347–363, 2023.
https://doi.org/10.1007/978-3-031-21203-1_21

vulnerability of the compromised agent in c-MARL systems has been only investigated once in a white-box setting against the QMIX algorithm [13] using a modified version of the adversarial example attack JSMA [24] in one environment. Therefore, it is important and necessary to develop a systematic methodology for designing non-trivial adversarial attacks which can efficiently and effectively exploit the vulnerabilities of c-MARL in order to design more robust algorithms.

Adversarial attacks on c-MARL are different from those carried out against individual RL agents [8,11,25]. First, each agent in c-MARL interacts with and modifies the state of the environment not only for itself but also for its cooperative agents. For an episode of L timesteps, an adversary has $2^L \times N$ choices of attacking or not attacking at least one agent at each timestep in a system having N agents, which significantly amplifies the attack surface for c-MARL compared to RL. Second, an adversary to c-MARL may have different goals such as reducing the final rewards of the whole team or maliciously using some agents' actions to lure other agents to dangerous states. We call this vulnerability the *compromised agent vulnerability*, which is different from adversarial attacks against an individual RL agent that aim to directly minimize the agent's reward.

The compromised agent vulnerability is relevant to the robustness of multi-agent domains such as autonomous driving platoons [17], negotiation [21], and automated scalping trading [10]. In those settings, agents work in environments populated by other agents, including humans, which increases the number of potential adversaries against the system. In such domains, it is not usually feasible for the adversary to directly change the victim policy's input via adversarial examples; it can only modify the victim agent's observations via its own actions. For example, in autonomous vehicle platoons, pedestrians and other drivers cannot add noise to arbitrary pixels, or make a building disappear. Nonetheless, they can take adversarial actions that negatively affect the camera image, but only in a physically realistic fashion. Similarly, in financial trading, an adversary can send orders to an exchange which will appear in the victim's market data feed, but the attacker cannot modify the observations of a third party's orders.

In this paper, we present an algorithmic framework to study the robustness of c-MARL algorithms. First, we reverse engineer the c-MARL algorithms in the centralized-learning and decentralized-execution paradigm to exploit the compromised agent vulnerability. In this paradigm, the c-MARL algorithms use a centralised learning and make use of decentralised policies with only local observations during execution. Then, we empirically analyze the impact of this vulnerability on the robustness of two of the state-of-the-art algorithms in three different environments. We develop four attack strategies to exploit the compromised agent vulnerability in c-MARL in white-box and black-box settings, where the adversary has access to the reward function, state transition function, and the policies of all agents in the former settings and has no knowledge of these in the latter. Our contributions are threefold:

1. We show the feasibility of the compromised agent vulnerability by reverse-engineering the algorithms in the centralized-learning decentralized-execution paradigm of c-MARL.

2. We design four attack strategies to demonstrate the impact of the compromised agent vulnerability on the robustness of c-MARL algorithms.
3. We thoroughly analyze the robustness of the c-MARL algorithms MADDPG [16] and QMIX [18] under our attacks in three different environments involving cooperative and competitive tasks[1]. The designed attacks bring down the team reward in all environments by at least 33% and at most 89.6%.

The remainder of this paper is organized as follows. We discuss the background and related work on c-MARL robustness in Sect. 2. Section 3 formulates the threat model and introduces the proposed approach. Section 4 presents our experiments and discusses the results. We provide our recommendations in Sect. 5. Final remarks and conclusions are outlined in Sect. 6.

2   Background and Related Work

This section presents the background information necessary to fully understand our proposed attack strategies on c-MARL and discusses the related work.

2.1   C-MARL

In this paper, we model the c-MARL system using stochastic games [19]. For an n-agent stochastic game, we define a tuple:

$$G = \left(S, A^1, ..., A^n, r^1, ..., r^n, T, \gamma\right) \tag{1}$$

where S denotes the state space, A^i and r^i are the action space and the reward function for agent $i \in 1, ..., n$, respectively. γ is the discount factor for future rewards, and T is a joint state transition function $T : S \times A_1 \times A_2.. \times A_n \rightarrow \triangle(S)$ where $\triangle(S)$ is a probability distribution on S. Agent i chooses its action $a^i \in A^i$ according to its policy $\pi_{\theta^i}^i(a^i|s)$ parameterized by θ^i conditioning on some given state $s \in S$. The collection of all agents' policies π_θ is called the joint policy where θ represents the joint parameter. For convenience, we interpret the joint policy from the perspective of agent i as:

$$\pi_\theta = (\pi_{\theta^i}^i(a^i|s)\pi_{\theta^{-i}}^{-i}(a^{-i}|s)) \tag{2}$$

where $a^{-i} = (a^j)_{j \neq i}, \theta^{-i} = (\theta^j)_{j \neq i}$, and $\pi_{\theta^{-i}}^{-i}(a^{-i}|s)$ is a compact representation of the joint policy of all complementary agents of i [15]. At each stage of the game, actions are taken simultaneously. Each agent is assumed to pursue the maximal cumulative reward [20] expressed by:

$$\max \eta^i(\pi_{\theta^i}) = \mathbb{E}\left[\sum_{t=1}^{\infty} \gamma^t r^i(s_t, a_t^i, a_t^{-i})\right] \tag{3}$$

---

[1] https://github.com/SarraAlqahtani22/MARL-Robustness.

with (a_t^i, a_t^{-i}) sample from $(\pi_{\theta^i}^i, \pi_{\theta^{-i}}^{-i})$. Correspondingly, for a game with an infinite time horizon, the state-action Q-function can be defined by

$$Q_{\pi_\theta^i}^i(s_t, a_t^i, a_t^{-i}) = \mathbb{E}\left[\sum_{l=0}^{\infty} \gamma^l r^i(s_{t+1}, a_{t+1}^i, a_{t+1}^{-i})\right].$$

The centralized-learning and decentralized-execution paradigm of MARL has been followed by the major c-MARL algorithms including MADDPG [16], COMA [5], MF-AC [27], and Q-Mix [18]. Although those algorithms simplify the learning in multi-agent environments by using the non-correlated factorization of the joint policy, they are vulnerable to the compromised agent attack shown in this paper. This vulnerability arises when the implicit connections among the agents' actions are ignored. Agents trained with such algorithms cannot efficiently identify the normal and abnormal behaviors of other agents working together to accomplish certain tasks. This paper focuses on attacking MAD-DPG [16] and QMIX [18], the lead algorithms in the centralized-learning and decentralized-execution paradigm.

2.2 Related Work on Adversarial Attacks in MARL

Previous work has shown the vulnerability of individual RL agents to adversarial attacks, in which the adversary perturbs the agent's observation to degrade its performance [8]. Other attacks reduce the number of adversarial examples needed to decrease the agent's reward [14] or trigger its misbehavior [28]. However, the literature did not study the security of c-MARL and the effects of cooperation on the success of attacks. The closest work to our proposed threat model and attack strategies proposes a two-step attack against QMIX with the objective of reducing the total team reward by perturbing the observation of a single agent [13]. The authors extend an existing adversarial example method, namely JSMA [24], to create d-JSMA which is more suitable for attacking an RL model with a low-dimensional feature space. They focus on white-box settings to launch their attack by assuming the knowledge of the team reward function.

The approach proposed in this paper is fundamentally different since it involves a physically realistic attack model that does not depend on directly modifying the agents' observations with adversarial examples. Instead, we weaponize one agent to follow an adversarial policy that pushes activations of its cooperative agents' policy networks off distribution. We also conduct our attacks in both white and black box settings against QMIX and MADDPG in three different environments. Also, compared to the work of Lin et al. [13] which focuses on attacks in the competitive multi-agent setting, our threat model considers cooperative teams of agents in both fully-cooperative and competitive environments.

3   Proposed Adversarial Approach

We first describe our threat model then mathematically explain how an adversary can exploit the compromised agent vulnerability and carry out various attacks.

3.1   Threat Model

We assume that the attacker can take over at least one benign agent (the compromised agent m) and use it to create naturally adversarial observations via its actions to attack the other agents $-m$ in the system. Recall that the joint transition probability in c-MARL is $p(s_{t+1}|s_t, a^1, ..., a^n)$, indicating that the attack surface for c-MARL includes any perturbations to the state s_t through adversarial examples and any perturbations to the other agents' actions $a^1, ..., a^n$ through the compromised agent attacks. This threat targets the agents' actions instead of the states' features usually targeted by adversarial examples [8,14,28]. The attacker can only intercept the compromised agent's actions via network attacks such as hijacking, impersonation, and Man in The Middle (MiTM). Studies have shown that multi-agent systems are vulnerable to such attacks [1,4,7]. The attacker's goal is to weaponize actions taken by the compromised agent to distract team members from accomplishing their task either by preventing them from converging to the optimal policy or misleading them to a dangerous state.

In the white-box setting, the adversary may have access to the environment's reward function, the policies of every agent in the system, and the ground truth state transition probability $p(s_{t+1}|s_t, a_0, \ldots, a_n)$, where s_t is the concatenation of each agents' observations $(o_1, \ldots, o_n)$. Conversely, a black box adversary has no access to the internal configuration, rewards, or policies of benign agents including the compromised one.   We also assume that all agents, including the compromised one, follow fixed policies corresponding to the common case of a pretrained model deployed with static weights. This model holds particularly well for safety-critical systems, where it is a standard practice to validate a model, then freeze it, to ensure that it does not develop any new problems due to training [25]. Since the agents' policies are held fixed, the Markov game G in Eq. (1) reduces to a single-player MDP, denoted by $G_m = (S, A_m, T_m, R_m)$, that the adversary must solve to generate a new policy by which the compromised agent m will achieve the adversary's goal of attacking the other agents $-m$.

The compromised agent problem in c-MARL is defined by:

$$\max \sum_{t=0}^{t=T} \mathbf{KL}\ (p(a_t^{-m}|a_t^m, s_t)\|p(a_t^{-m}|a_t^{*m}, s_t)) \tag{4}$$

where a^{*m} represents the adversarial actions generated by the adversarial policies for the compromised agent m. This equation maximizes the KL-divergence between the conditional policy of $-m$ on the action a^m at time t and the same conditional policy if agent m deviates from its policy and takes an adversarial action a^{*m}. The adversary can then intervene on a_t^m by replacing it with the action a_t^{*m} which will be used to compute the next action of agents $-m$, $p(a_{t+1}^{-m}|a_t^{*m}, s_t^m)$, pushing the activations of their policy networks off distribution. Practically, we solve the problem in Eq. (4) by finding the adversarial actions a^{*m} for the compromised agent following one of the proposed attack strategies in Sect. 3.3 to maximize the KL-divergence.

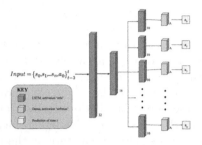

Fig. 1. The architecture of the deep learning-based behavioral cloning.

3.2 Exploiting the Compromised Agent Vulnerability

We now show the steps of exploiting the compromised agent vulnerability in the centralized-learning and decentralized-execution c-MARL algorithms. The goal is to reverse engineer the learning algorithm by correlating the learning process of agent m's policy with the learning of the conditional policies of agents $-m$. First, we collect state-action pairs by observing the agents during reconnaissance as a trajectory $\tau = [(s_1, a_1^m, a_1^{-m}), ..., (s_t, a_t^m, a_t^{-m})]$. We use τ for training an Adversarial Inverse RL (AIRL) algorithm [6] to discover the hidden reward function behind agent m's behavior, $r^m(s_t, a_t^m, a_t^{-m}, s_{t+1})$, while considering the actions taken by the other agents a_t^{-m} as part of the environment state.

The second step is to reverse engineer the joint policy in Eq. (2) to approximate the agents' policies. The joint policy can be reformulated as [23,26]:

$$
\pi_\theta(a^m, a^{-m}|s) = \underbrace{\pi_{\theta^m}^m(a^m|s)\pi_{\theta^{-m}}^{-m}(a^{-m}|s, a^m)}_{\text{Compromised agent's perspective}}
$$
$$
= \underbrace{\pi_{\theta^{-m}}^{-m}(a^{-m}|s)\pi_{\theta^m}^m(a^m|s, a^{-m})}_{\text{other agents' perspective}}
\tag{5}
$$

From the perspective of the compromised agent m, the first equality in Eq. (5) indicates that the joint policy can be essentially decomposed into two parts: agent m's policy and the conditional policies of agents $-m$. The conditional part of the first equality $\pi_{\theta^{-m}}^{-m}(a^{-m}|s, a^m)$ represents what actions would be taken by victim agents $-m$ given the fact that they know the current environment state and agent m's action, i.e., what the compromised agent believes the other agents might think based on their original policy.

In the white-box setting, the adversary has direct access to the agents' policies and the ground truth of the state transition function. In the black-box setting, the adversary needs to develop an approximation of the transition function and the conditional policies of the victims $\pi_{\theta^{-m}}^{-m}(a^{-m}|s, a^m)$ via the behavioral cloning model depicted in Fig. 1, which is trained by minimizing the loss function $L(a, \pi_\theta)$ to approximate each agent's policy $\rho_{\phi^{-m}}^{-m}(a^{-m}|s, a^m)$. The supervised learning model for the state transition function is similar to the behavioral cloning model with multiple heads but with different learnable parameters Φ:

$$T_\Phi = p(s_{t+1}|s_t, a^1, ..., a^n) \tag{6}$$

By approximating the actual policies of the victims $-m$, the learning task for the compromised agent m can be formulated by:

$$\underset{\theta^m, \phi^{-m}}{\arg\max} \left(\pi_{\theta^m}^m(a^m|s) \rho_{\phi^{-m}}^{-m}(a^{-m}|s, a^m) \right) \tag{7}$$

With the learning protocol in Eq. (7), the adversary can learn the compromised agent m's policy and approximate the conditional policy of the victim agents $-m$ given m's actions using probabilistic RL [12]. We first derive the probability of τ being observed during the reconnaissance phase as follows:

$$p(\tau) = \left[p(s_1) \prod_{t=1}^{T} p(s_{t+1}|s_t, a_t^m, a_t^{-m}) \right] \exp \left(\sum_{t=1}^{T} r^m(s_t, a_t^m, a_t^{-m}) \right) \tag{8}$$

Since we used AIRL to discover r^m using τ, the goal becomes to find the best approximation of $\pi_{\theta^m}^m(a_t^m|s_t) \rho_{\phi^{-m}}^{-m}(a_t^{-m}|s_t, a_t^m)$ to maximize Eq. (7) such that the induced trajectory distribution $\hat{p}(\tau)$ can match the ground-truth of trajectory probability $p(\tau)$:

$$\hat{p}(\tau) = p(s_1) \prod_{t=1}^{T} p(s_{t+1}|s_t, a_t^m, a_t^{-m}) \pi_{\theta^m}^m(a_t^m|s_t) \rho_{\phi^{-m}}^{-m}(a_t^{-m}|s_t, a_t^m) \tag{9}$$

We can now optimize the approximated policies of the victim agents by minimizing the KL-divergence between Eq. (8) and Eq. (9):

$$KL(\hat{p}(\tau)||p(\tau)) =$$

$$-\mathbb{E}_{\tau\ \hat{p}(\tau)}[\log p(\tau) - \log \hat{p}(\tau)] = - \sum_{t=1}^{t=T} \mathbb{E}_{\tau\ \hat{p}(\tau)} \left[r^m(s_t, a_t^m, a_t^{-m}) + \right. \tag{10}$$

$$\left. H\left(\pi_{\theta^m}^m(a_t^m|s_t) \rho_{\phi^{-m}}^{-m}(a_t^{-m}|s_t, a_t^m) \right) \right]$$

where H is the conditional entropy on the joint policy that potentially promotes the exploration for both the malicious agent m's best action and the victims' conditional policies. Minimizing Eq. (10) yields the optimal Q-function for agent m (Theorem 1 in [23]):

$$Q_{\pi_\theta}^m = \log \int_{a^{-m}} \mathbb{E}(Q_{\pi_\theta}^m(s, a^m, a^{-m})) da^{-m} \tag{11}$$

The corresponding $-m$ conditional policy becomes:

$$\rho_{\phi^{-m}}^{-m}(a_t^{-m}|s_t, a_t^m) = \frac{1}{Z} \mathbb{E}(Q_{\pi_\theta}^m(s, a^m, a^{-m}) - Q_{\pi_\theta}^m(s, a^m)) \tag{12}$$

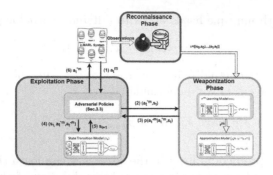

Fig. 2. The steps of exploiting the compromised agent vulnerability.

To solve Eq. (12), we maintain two Q-functions and iteratively update them using the learned reward function for agent m and the observations in τ as the ground-truth. Equation (11) approximates the original policy of m while considering the approximated conditional policies of agents $-m$ in Eq. (12). The overall steps of exploiting the compromised agent vulnerability are shown in Fig. 2. For the proof of Eq. (11) and Eq. (12), please check [23].

3.3   Attack Strategies

According to Fig. 2 and Eq. (10), we still need to generate the adversarial policies for the compromised agent to choose a_t^{*m}. In this section, we introduce our attack strategies to generate those policies under two different categories: attacks based on the compromised agent's self-destruction strategies, and attacks based on destructive strategies of other agents' objectives.

Self-Destruction Adversarial Policies. This category focuses on minimizing the compromised agent's individual reward which indirectly reduces the reward of the c-MARL team.

Randomly-Timed Attack: We attack the victims' policies by developing a set of randomized off-distribution adversarial policies for the compromised agent to sabotage the c-MARL system through its own actions. At a certain percentage of timesteps, the adversary changes the compromised agent's action into a_t^{*m} based on a random off-distribution policy.

Strategically-Timed Attack: This attack strategically selects a subset of timesteps to change the compromised agent's actions. We first calculate the c-function [14]:

$$\max_{a_t}(\pi_m(s_t, a_t)) - \min_{a_t}(\pi_m(s_t, a_t)) > \beta \tag{13}$$

and launch the attack if $c > b$, where b is a chosen threshold that indicates the desired attacking rate. The idea behind this attack is that the adversary chooses to alter the compromised agent's action only when it strongly prefers a specific action (the action has a relative high probability), which means that it is critical to perform that action; otherwise, its accumulated reward will be reduced.

Adversarial Policies for Destructing Other Agents. The other method to attack c-MARL algorithms is to sabotage the objectives of the other agents in the system using the compromised agent's actions, which directly pushes activations of c-MARL agents' policy networks off-distribution.

Counterfactual Reasoning-Based Attack: This attack predicts the compromised agent's counterfactual reasoning process about how its actions will affect the other agents and then postulates actions that would enable it to achieve maximal destruction of the system. We design a reward function for an RL agent to generate a long-term policy that replaces the original actions $a_t^m, ..., a_{t+l}^m$ to the best set of adversarial actions $a_t^{*m}, .., a_{t+l}^{*m}$. The RL agent would choose certain timesteps to attack instead of attacking each timestep based on how much divergence the attack is expected to produce. To do so, the reward function is crafted as follows:

$$r_{att} = \sum_t^l \gamma^t \, \mathbf{KL} \left(p(a_t^{-m}|a_t^m, s_t) \, || \, p(a_t^{-m}|a_t^{*m}, s_t) \right) \tag{14}$$

where a^{*m} represents the set of counterfactual actions to the action a^m generated by the original policy of agent m, $\pi_{\theta^m}^m$, and γ is a discount factor. The attack starts at timestep t, and l is the number of steps into the future when the attacker wants the event to take place. Equation (14) generates a combination of actions $a_t^{*m}, ..., a_{t+l}^{*m}$ for which the success rate is the highest possible. We train this adversarial policy using DDPG.

Zero-Sum Attack: We train another RL agent to learn an adversarial policy minimizing the global reward of the c-MARL system. We formulate this attack as a single agent RL problem to minimize the cumulative reward for the whole team as:

$$\theta^m \sum_{t=1}^{\infty} \gamma^t r_t(s_t, a_t^{*m}, a_t^{-m}, s_{t+1}), \tag{15}$$

where a_t^{*m} is the compromised agent's action at timestep t, θ^m parameterizes the compromised agent's policy, and r_t is the global reward recovered by [6]. (a_t^{*m}, a_t^{-m}) is sampled from $(\pi_{\theta^m}^m, \pi_{\theta^{-m}}^{-m})$ in the white box setting. In the black box setting, we sample from the approximated policies derived in Eq. (11) and (12). With Eq. (15), we train an adversarial policy that selects actions for the compromised agent that will minimize the reward r for the c-MARL team. In our implementation, we use DDPG to train this adversarial policy.

4   Experiments and Results

This section describes the implementation of our attacks and discusses the obtained results.[2]

---

[2] Our code and demos are available here:https://github.com/SarraAlqahtani22/MARL-Robustness.

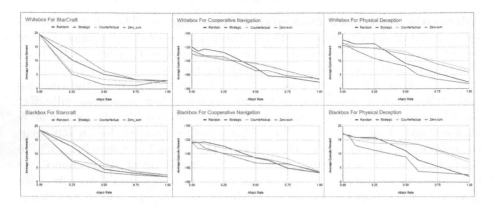

Fig. 3. The average episode rewards in 2 particle multi-agent environments (MAD-DPG) and StarCraft2 (QMIX) under our attacks as a function of attack rate.

4.1 Experimental Setup

We evaluate the robustness of the MADDPG algorithm under our attacks in both the white and black box settings in two particle environments [16]: cooperative navigation and physical deception with variant attacking rates. In the cooperative navigation environment, N cooperative agents must cover L landmarks, and the agents must learn to reach separate landmarks without communicating their observations to each other. In our experiments, we use $N = L = 3$. In the physical deception environment, N cooperative agents try to fool one adversarial agent. There are L total landmarks, with one being the 'target' landmark and only the cooperative agents know which landmark is the target one. The adversary must try to infer and reach the target landmark from the cooperative agents' positioning, and the cooperative agents must try to deceive the adversary by spacing out. The cooperative agents are rewarded as long a single member of their team reaches the target landmark. We use $N = L = 2$.

We evaluate the robustness of QMIX using StarCraft II, a real-time strategy game where two teams of agents can fight against each other. We use the "3m" SMAC map, which employs three "Marine" units on each team. A team wins by shooting the enemy team enough to drain their health. Our team consists of three cooperative agents working together to defeat the three enemy marines, which use fixed policies. For our attacks, we control one of the cooperative marines, and alter its actions using the aforementioned attack strategies.

4.2 Results and Discussion

We discuss the obtained results from two perspectives: the adversarial policies and c-MARL team reward, and the qualitative performance and behavioral analysis of the agents.

Adversarial Policies and Team Reward. To learn an adversarial policy for the compromised agent, we used the attack strategies explained in Sect. 3.3.

Table 1. The average number of occupied landmarks in the cooperative navigation, average distance between the cooperative agents and target landmark in physical deception [16], and win rate for the cooperative team in StarCraft II [18] for 25%, 50%, 75%, and 100% attack rates across all attack types in white and black box settings.

MADDPG: Cooperative navigation (occupied landmarks)								
	White box				Black box			
Attack rate	Random	Timed	Counterfactual	Zero-sum	Random	Timed	Counterfactual	Zero-sum
0%	1.611	1.611	1.611	1.611	1.611	1.611	1.611	1.611
25%	1.311	1.308	1.007	1.102	1.325	1.333	1.150	1.09
50%	0.958	0.955	0.786	0.868	1.058	1.048	1.002	0.847
75%	0.695	0.711	0.601	0.722	0.860	0.815	0.811	0.730
100%	0.502	0.562	0.489	0.573	0.502	0.688	0.547	0.519
MADDPG: Physical deception (average distance)								
	White box				Black box			
Attack rate	Random	Timed	Counterfactual	Zero-sum	Random	Timed	Counterfactual	Zero-sum
0%	0.163	0.163	0.163	0.163	0.163	0.163	0.163	0.163
25%	0.225	0.418	0.196	0.188	0.200	0.343	0.182	0.175
50%	0.326	0.470	0.211	0.277	0.324	0.499	0.201	0.2
75%	0.515	0.607	0.264	0.297	0.530	0.614	0.235	0.243
100%	0.540	0.688	0.427	0.423	0.654	0.680	0.412	0.356
QMIX: StarCraft II (win rate)								
	White box				Black box			
Attack rate	Random	Timed	Counterfactual	Zero-sum	Random	Timed	Counterfactual	Zero-sum
0%	0.955	0.955	0.955	0.955	0.955	0.955	0.955	0.955
25%	0.32	0.18	0.190	0.210	0.475	0.135	0.135	0.528
50%	0.065	0.0	0.060	0.050	0.015	0.0	0.080	0.144
75%	0.01	0.0	0.0	0.000	0.0	0.0	0.030	0.04
100%	0.0	0.0	0.0	0.000	0.0	0.0	0.0	0.0

To evaluate the performance of each policy, we directly change the actions of the compromised agent based on the output of the adversarial policy. We ran each attack with different attack episode lengths starting at 0% and moving to 100% by increments of 25%. We present the team average reward for the victim agents in Fig. 3. As the attack rate increases, the team reward decreases, indicating that each attack was successful at degrading the robustness of c-MARL algorithms. The strategically-timed attack has the highest negative impact on the team reward when the attack rate is higher. However, the zero-sum and counterfactual reasoning-based attacks perform better with less attack rates in the cooperative navigation environments.

In the physical deception environment, the strategically-timed attack achieved 86.6% and 85% reward drop for 100% attack rate in white-box and black-box settings, respectively. In the cooperative navigation environment, the strategically-timed attack achieved a reward drop of 33.1% and 33.0% for white-box and black-box settings, respectively. In the StarCraft II environment, the strategically-timed attack achieved a reward drop of 84% and 89.6% in the white-box and the black-box settings, respectively. The strategically-timed attack is the strongest because it attacks only at impactful timesteps as opposed to the randomly-timed attack which attacks at random timesteps during the episode.

The counterfactual reasoning-based attack is able to achieve similar levels of performance with respect to the strategically-timed attack in StarCraft. In Cooperative Navigation, both the counterfactual and zero-sum achieve similar

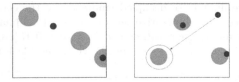

Fig. 4. Screenshots from replayed episodes of the cooperative navigation environment from MADDPG under the strategically-timed attack.

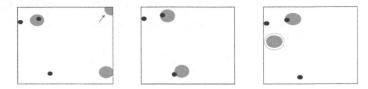

Fig. 5. Screenshots from replayed episodes of the cooperative navigation environment from MADDPG under the counterfactual reasoning-based attack.

performance as the strategically-timed attack, especially with low attack rates. We believe since those environments are purely cooperative, the adversarial policies trained to directly sabotage other agents' policies can better diminish the robustness of the algorithms in cooperative settings. However, in the physical deception environment that naturally involves an enemy, the counterfactual and zero-sum attacks have the least impact on the team reward.

Although the results in Fig. 3 and Table 1 show that the counterfactual reasoning-based attack succeeds, we observe an effect similar in nature to the canonical imitation learning problem. As we start attacking the system using the compromised agent's counterfactual actions, the impact of the attack was not as strong as the other attacks. We hypothesize that this is due to the inability of the behavioral cloning model to accurately capture the other agents' states that were not part of their optimal policies during reconnaissance. In general, the canonical problem of imitation learning accumulates the learning errors, resulting in the learner encountering unknown states [2]. Moreover, this attack builds its adversarial policy based on predicting each agent's action for a sequence of timesteps then finds the counterfactual actions with maximum KL divergence using those predictions. Hence, the prediction errors accumulate over the timesteps and hinder the attack.

Qualitative Performance and Behavioral Analysis. We evaluate the qualitative performance of c-MARL algorithms under our attacks using environment-specific metrics. In the cooperative navigation environment, we measure the average number of the occupied landmarks by the cooperative agents. In the physical deception environment, we measure the average distance between the cooperative agents and the target landmark. In StartCraft II, we use the team win rate to evaluate the attack impact. Table 1 shows the performance of each attack.

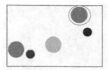 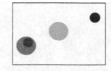

Fig. 6. Screenshots from replayed episodes of the physical deception environment from MADDPG under the strategically-timed attack. To the left, we see the beginning of the episode where the cooperative agents are splitting over the target and non-target landmarks. To the right, the compromised agent is moving away from the non-target landmark, leaking the information to the adversary.

 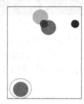

Fig. 7. Screenshots from replayed episodes of the physical deception environment from MADDPG under the counterfactual reasoning-based attack. To the left, we see the beginning of the episode. To the right, the compromised agent is moving away from the non-target landmark at a perfect timing to leak the information to the adversary which got the clue and moved towards the target.

In cooperative navigation, the number of occupied landmarks per timestep decreases as the compromised agent deviates more from its optimal policy. Similarly, in physical deception, the distance from the closest cooperative agent to the target landmark increases as we attack at more timesteps.

In StarCraft II, under the optimal QMIX policy, the c-MARL team of agents wins the battle around 95% of the time. As shown in the last part of Table 1, attacking during just 25% of timesteps can reduce the win rate by at least 18% for the strategically-timed attack in a white-box setting, and 13% in the black-box setting. In all attack strategies, a 100% attack rate decreases the win rate to 0%, and in most attacks, a 75% attack rate also does that. Overall, under the compromised agent attacks, the win rate decreases as the attack rate increases, and even a small attack rate has significant impact on the QMIX robustness.

We show here the qualitative analysis of the cooperative navigation environment under the strategically-timed and counterfactual reasoning-based attacks, chosen to represent the attacks in each category. During the strategically-timed attack, the compromised agent immediately moves away from the landmarks to prevent its teammates from covering all landmarks. In this environment, there is not much room for the agents to recover from the compromised agent's adversarial actions. The left figure in Fig. 4 shows the beginning of the episode where the agents attempt to cover the 3 landmarks (black circles). Then, in the right figure, the compromised agent (within the red circle) is moving away from its supposedly assigned landmark.

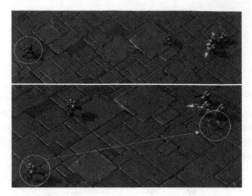

Fig. 8. Screenshots from replayed episodes of StarCraft II. The compromised agent is controlled by an adversarial policy trained with the strategically-timed attack (top) and counterfactual reasoning-based attack (bottom).

In the counterfactual reasoning-based attack, the compromised agent displays interesting behaviors. The first behavior is shown in Fig. 5. The compromised agent (pointed to with a red arrow) is moving away from the landmark just before its teammate(s) get to a landmark, which makes the affected agent (within a green circle) confused about which landmark to cover (stands in between the 2 empty landmarks for the remaining of the episode). This behavior suggests that the compromised agent succeeds by manipulating its teammate's observations through its actions. We notice another behavior under this attack strategy where the compromised agent moves to the same landmark that has been already covered by one of its teammate causing the team reward to decrease.

In the physical deception environment, during the strategically-timed attack, we notice that when the compromised agent moves away from the non-target landmark (Fig. 6), the other cooperative agent does not alter its behavior to move away from the target. This is a robustness issue in the MADDPG algorithm. Ideally, the agents should be robust enough to not have to rely on a teammate who is not doing its job. Similarly, when the compromised agent leaves the non-target landmark uncovered and moves towards the target landmark, the adversary does not always take advantage of this clue (Fig. 7). The optimal behavior of the adversary would be to move towards the only landmark which is being covered by a cooperative agent, instead it stands still. This behavior once again shows a lack of robustness in the agents under our attack.

In the StarCraftII, during all attacks except the counterfactual reasoning-based attack, we notice that the compromised agent moves away from its team until its teammates get defeated. Then, it moves towards the enemies to get killed. In the strategically-timed attack, the compromised agent runs away only when its team is getting closer to the enemy (top of Fig. 8). In the counterfactual reasoning-based attack, we notice that sometimes the compromised agent is luring one of its teammates to start attacking the enemy team then it itself runs away (bottom of Fig. 8) causing its team to get defeated.

5   Recommendations

The idea that slightly perturbing one compromised agent's observations can reduce performance at such a large scale is alarming. With the seemingly heavy dependence on small fractions of the global observations, attackers can implement similar attacks to go virtually unnoticed by detection models. By only compromising one agent, the entire system will be affected. And without reliable detection, it is clear that these attacks can be devastating.

The naive remedy once a compromised agent has been detected is to exclude it from the team and mark it as an adversary. However, the deviation in one agent's behavior could occur due to a security threat or its lack of knowledge about the environment which is reasonable considering the limited vision range and communication bandwidth in MARL systems. Thus, we think it is critical to extend the assured RL (ARL) techniques into c-MARL by embedding real-time formal verification methods in c-MARL algorithms, which would shield the agents from reaching the dangerous states by training them to trade off between performance and security/safety in the environments containing either malicious (adversarial) or faulty (dysfunctional) agents. Those methods should be developed for run-time verification focusing only on the agent's time-bounded, short-term behavior for scalability. This will increase the robustness of MARL systems functioning in uncertain and unpredictable environments.

To solve the non-correlated factorization problem of the MARL centralized learning-decentralized execution paradigm, the other agents' actions were taken into consideration by decoupling the joint policy as a correlated policy conditioned on the environment state and other agents' actions [9,22,23]. Those algorithms assume that agents participating in a joint activity act rationally and cooperate to achieve shared goals. However, relying only on this assumption to achieve joint goals without the establishment and reinforcement of trust opens a vulnerability similar to the one discussed here. Hence, studying the compromised agent vulnerability in this paradigm of c-MARL algorithms becomes essential.

6   Conclusion

We investigate the maleficence of c-MARL by targeting and weaponizing one agent, termed *compromised*, to follow an adversarial policy that pushes the activation of the cooperating agents' policy networks off distribution. We proposed four attack strategies to control the compromised agent: 1) randomly-timed attack, 2) strategically timed attack, 3) counterfactual reasoning-based attack, and 4) zero-sum attack. Our attacks reduce the overall team reward in all environments by at least 33% and at most 89.6%. In future work, we intend to develop more robust c-MARL algorithms by accounting for the compromised agent vulnerability during training. This will increase the robustness of c-MARL systems functioning in uncertain environments. Moreover, our attacks can be utilized to evaluate the robustness of c-MARL algorithms. We will make our code and demos available in the final submission.

Acknowledgment. This material is based upon work supported by the National Science Foundation (NSF) under grant no. 2105007.

References

1. Amoozadeh, M., et al.: Security vulnerabilities of connected vehicle streams and their impact on cooperative driving. IEEE Commun. Mag. **53**(6), 126–132 (2015). https://doi.org/10.1109/MCOM.2015.7120028
2. Bagnell, J.A.D.: An invitation to imitation. Technical report. CMU-RI-TR-15-08, Carnegie Mellon University, Pittsburgh, PA (2015)
3. Bakakeu, J., Kisskalt, D., Franke, J., Baer, S., Klos, H.H., Peschke, J.: Multi-agent reinforcement learning for the energy optimization of cyber-physical production systems. In: 2020 IEEE Canadian Conference on Electrical and Computer Engineering (CCECE), pp. 1–8 (2020). https://doi.org/10.1109/CCECE47787.2020.9255795
4. Dadras, S., Dadras, S., Winstead, C.: Collaborative attacks on autonomous vehicle platooning. In: 2018 IEEE 61st International Midwest Symposium on Circuits and Systems (MWSCAS), pp. 464–467 (2018). https://doi.org/10.1109/MWSCAS.2018.8624026
5. Foerster, J.N., Farquhar, G., Afouras, T., Nardelli, N., Whiteson, S.: Counterfactual multi-agent policy gradients. In: AAAI (2018)
6. Fu, J., Luo, K., Levine, S.: Learning robust rewards with adversarial inverse reinforcement learning (2018)
7. Higgins, F., Tomlinson, A., Martin, K.M.: Survey on security challenges for swarm robotics. In: 2009 Fifth International Conference on Autonomic and Autonomous Systems, pp. 307–312 (2009). DOI: https://doi.org/10.1109/ICAS.2009.62
8. Huang, S., Papernot, N., Goodfellow, I., Duan, Y., Abbeel, P.: Adversarial attacks on neural network policies (2017)
9. Jaques, N., et al.: Social influence as intrinsic motivation for multi-agent deep reinforcement learning (2019)
10. Jo, U., Jo, T., Kim, W., Yoon, I., Lee, D., Lee, S.: Cooperative multi-agent reinforcement learning framework for scalping trading (2019)
11. Kos, J., Song, D.: Delving into adversarial attacks on deep policies (2017)
12. Levine, S.: Reinforcement learning and control as probabilistic inference: tutorial and review (2018)
13. Lin, J., Dzeparoska, K., Zhang, S.Q., Leon-Garcia, A., Papernot, N.: On the robustness of cooperative multi-agent reinforcement learning (2020)
14. Lin, Y.C., Hong, Z.W., Liao, Y.H., Shih, M.L., Liu, M.Y., Sun, M.: Tactics of adversarial attack on deep reinforcement learning agents (2019)
15. Liu, M., et al.: Multi-agent interactions modeling with correlated policies (2020)
16. Lowe, R., Wu, Y., Tamar, A., Harb, J., Abbeel, P., Mordatch, I.: Multi-agent actor-critic for mixed cooperative-competitive environments. In: Proceedings of the 31st International Conference on Neural Information Processing Systems, pp. 6382–6393. NIPS 2017, Curran Associates Inc., Red Hook, NY, USA (2017)
17. Peake, A., McCalmon, J., Raiford, B., Liu, T., Alqahtani, S.: Multi-agent reinforcement learning for cooperative adaptive cruise control. In: 2020 IEEE 32nd International Conference on Tools with Artificial Intelligence (ICTAI), pp. 15–22 (2020). https://doi.org/10.1109/ICTAI50040.2020.00013

18. Rashid, T., Samvelyan, M., de Witt, C.S., Farquhar, G., Foerster, J., Whiteson, S.: Qmix: monotonic value function factorisation for deep multi-agent reinforcement learning (2018)
19. Shapley, L.S.: Stochastic games. Proc. National Acad. Sci. **39**(10), 1095–1100 (1953). https://doi.org/10.1073/pnas.39.10.1095, https://www.pnas.org/content/39/10/1095
20. Sutton, R.S., Barto, A.G.: Reinforcement Learning: An Introduction. A Bradford Book, Cambridge, MA, USA (2018)
21. Tang, Y.C.: Towards learning multi-agent negotiations via self-play (2020)
22. Tian, Z., et al.: Learning to communicate implicitly by actions (2019)
23. Wen, Y., Yang, Y., Luo, R., Wang, J., Pan, W.: Probabilistic recursive reasoning for multi-agent reinforcement learning (2019)
24. Wiyatno, R., Xu, A.: Maximal Jacobian-based saliency map attack (2018)
25. Wu, X., Guo, W., Wei, H., Xing, X.: Adversarial policy training against deep reinforcement learning. In: 30th USENIX Security Symposium (USENIX Security 21), pp. 1883–1900. USENIX Association (2021). https://www.usenix.org/conference/usenixsecurity21/presentation/wu-xian
26. Xia, Y., Qin, T., Chen, W., Bian, J., Yu, N., Liu, T.Y.: Dual supervised learning (2017)
27. Yang, Y., Luo, R., Li, M., Zhou, M., Zhang, W., Wang, J.: Mean field multi-agent reinforcement learning (2018)
28. Zhao, Y., Shumailov, I., Cui, H., Gao, X., Mullins, R., Anderson, R.: Blackbox attacks on reinforcement learning agents using approximated temporal information (2019)

Learning to Classify Logical Formulas Based on Their Semantic Similarity

Ali Ballout[1], Célia da Costa Pereira[2], and Andrea G. B. Tettamanzi[1(✉)]

[1] Université Côte d'Azur, CNRS, Inria, I3S, Villeurbanne, France
`ali.ballout@inria.fr`, `andrea.tettamanzi@univ-cotedazur.fr`
[2] Université Côte d'Azur, CNRS, I3S, Villeurbanne, France
`Celia.DA-COSTA-PEREIRA@univ-cotedazur.fr`

Abstract. An important task in logic, given a formula and a knowledge base which represents what an agent knows of the current state of the world, is to be able to guess the truth value of the formula. Logic reasoners are designed to perform inferences, that is, to decide whether a formula is a logical consequence of the knowledge base, which is stronger than that and can be intractable in some cases. In addition, under the open-world assumption, it may turn out impossible to infer a formula or its negation. In many practical situations, however, when an agent has to make a decision, it is acceptable to resort to heuristic methods to determine the probable veracity or falsehood of a formula, even in the absence of a guarantee of correctness, to avoid blocking the decision-making process and move forward. This is why we propose a method to train a classification model based on available knowledge in order to be able of accurately guessing whether an arbitrary, unseen formula is true or false. Our method exploits a kernel representation of logical formulas based on a model-theoretic measure of semantic similarity. The results of experiments show that the proposed method is highly effective and accurate.

1 Introduction and Related Work

A defining feature for intelligent agents is their ability to reason, that is to draw logical conclusions from the available premises, which constitute their knowledge [3,5]. While this capability is very important, an equally important and useful, but weaker, capability for an agent would be to be able to recognize if a given formula is likely to be true or false, given the current knowledge, *in the current state of the world*, even though not necessarily in general.

As a matter of fact, we often experience situations where our incomplete knowledge would not allow us to make exact inferences, yet this does not prevent us to make decisions, because even when we don't know a fact that we need in order to move forward, we are able to make an educated guess (i.e., a prediction based on what we already know) about the veracity of that fact and proceed with our decision making.

© The Author(s), under exclusive license to Springer Nature Switzerland AG 2023
R. Aydoğan et al. (Eds.): PRIMA 2022, LNAI 13753, pp. 364–380, 2023.
https://doi.org/10.1007/978-3-031-21203-1_22

It is this weaker task that we are interested in studying here. We propose a simple but effective idea, which is to train a classifier against the knowledge base of the agent, which may be viewed as a set of formulas labeled with their truth value. The formulas are represented as vectors of similarities to the labeled formulas; to this end, we propose a model-theoretic semantic similarity measure which can be computed efficiently. This kernel-representation and its associated similarity measure are the key ingredients of our proposal.

Recently, a rise of interest in developing connectionist methods for reasoning can be observed, with proposals such the so-called Logic Tensor Networks [4], or the Logic-Integrated Neural Network [14] to integrate the power of deep learning and logic reasoning, or approaches that employ state-of-the-art methods for training deep neural networks to learn to perform some basic ontology reasoning tasks [11]. As a further witness of the attention this research field is attracting, some conferences are beginning to feature tutorials on it, like KDD'21 [15] and there is even an upcoming Dagstuhl seminar on "Machine Learning and Logical Reasoning: The New Frontier"[1].

Unlike these approaches, what we propose does not require sophisticated neural architectures or resource-intensive deep learning; in addition, we do not attack the more ambitious challenge of logical deduction, but just that of heuristically guessing (as human beings do), the truth value of a formula, independently of its being logically entailed by the available knowledge.

Actually, what people do in case of incomplete knowledge is to somehow measure the similarity between known/familiar situations and unknown/unfamiliar situations [16]. Several cognitive tasks, such as *learning* and *interpolation* require the concept of similarity to be performed [9]. There exists a vast literature on similarity measures, with many proposal arising in the field of machine learning [7]. However, it appears that the problem of measuring the similarity of logical formulas has been less investigated and, when it has, that's often in relation with specific contexts.

While not directly addressing the problem of defining similarity among logical formulas, Bowles [6] studies the nature of relevance and irrelevance of a proposition with respect to another. His work shares with the definition of semantic similarity that we propose here, a basic intuition, which is that the probability that one proposition is true given that another one is true should play a central role. The definition of relevance proposed by Makinson in [13], instead, is not in line with what we are proposing here because it is defined in terms of letter-sharing. A way of measuring the similarity of a Boolean vector to a given set of Boolean vectors, motivated in part by certain data mining or machine learning problems, was proposed by Anthony and Hammer [2]. A similarity measure for Boolean function was proposed by Fišer *et al.* [10] in a quite different context, that of circuit synthesis, which explains the differences with our proposal. One measure of similarity between functions is the existence of a Lipschitz mapping (with small constant) between them [12]. A problem somehow related to the one

---

[1] Dagstuhl Seminar 22291, July 17–22, 2022.

we are dealing with is the problem of measuring the similarity between logical arguments, which has been studied by Amgoud and David [1].

Through an empirical validation we show that the framework we propose allows a number of quite standard and unsophisticated classification techniques, like support-vector machines, to learn very accurate models that are capable of "guessing" whether a given, unseen formula is true or false in the current state of affairs, without the need to perform any logical deduction.

The rest of the paper is structured as follows: Sect. 2 states the problem of formula classification; Sect. 3 defines a semantic similarity measure for formulas that is the cornerstone of the proposed approach. Section 4 provides an empirical validation of the approach and Sect. 5 draws some conclusions and suggestions for future work.

2 Problem Statement

Let Φ be a set of formulas in a logical language $\mathcal{L}$ and let $\mathcal{I}$ be an interpretation, which represents a particular state of affairs or the current state of the world. Under interpretation $\mathcal{I}$, the formulas in Φ may be labeled as being true or false. One could thus construct a table

$$\begin{bmatrix} \phi_1, \phi_1^{\mathcal{I}} \\ \phi_2, \phi_2^{\mathcal{I}} \\ \vdots \quad \vdots \end{bmatrix},$$

where $\phi_i \in \Phi \subset \mathcal{L}$, for $i = 1, 2, \ldots$, and $\phi_i^{\mathcal{I}}$ is the truth value of ϕ_i according to interpretation $\mathcal{I}$. This table can be viewed as a representation of a knowledge base K consisting of all the formulas $\phi_i \in \Phi$ such that $\phi_i^{\mathcal{I}} = T$ and all the formulas $\neg\phi_i \in \Phi$ such that $\phi_i^{\mathcal{I}} = F$. K represents what an agent knows (or believes) about the current state of affairs but, of course, $\mathcal{I}$, the actual state of affairs, is not known in full, which is like saying that the open world hypothesis holds.

Consider now the problem of guessing or predicting whether a new formula $\psi \notin \Phi$ is true or false in $\mathcal{I}$, given K. To be sure, one could use a reasoner to check whether $K \vdash \psi$ or $K \vdash \neg\psi$. If the reasoner is sound and complete, this can even allow one to decide whether $K \models \psi$ or $K \models \neg\psi$. However, even in cases where $K \not\models \psi$ and $K \not\models \neg\psi$, which are entirely possible in an open world, it would be useful for an agent to be able to make educated guesses at the truth value of ψ. By an *educated guess* we mean a prediction, based on the truth values of the formulas the agent already knows. If a model to make that type of predictions existed and were fast and accurate enough, the agent might even used it *instead* of the reasoner, for time-critical tasks where having a quick answer is more important than having an answer that is guaranteed to be always correct.

What we have just described is a classification problem, where given a set of labeled examples (here, formulas with their truth value), a model is sought for that is able to accurately predict the label of an unseen case (i.e., a new formula).

To solve this problem, we propose to use a kernel representation, i.e., to represent formulas **as vectors of similarities to a restricted set of formulas whose label is already known** (Φ) and to train a classification model on these labeled examples, later to be used to classify new, unseen formulas. To this aim, we will stick to very standard and unsophisticated classification methods.

3 Semantic Similarity

We need to define similarity among logical formulas. It is quite obvious that such a similarity should not be based on syntax, due to the fact that formulas with widely different syntactical forms may be equivalent. Now, the semantics of logical formulas is defined in model-theoretic terms. What we are looking for is, therefore, a model-theoretic notion of formula similarity.

To keep technical complications at a minimum and without loss of generality, let us consider propositional logic. As a matter of fact, more expressive logical languages can be mapped to the propositional case (e.g., description logics and first-order logic under the Herbrand semantics).

Definition 1 (Language). *Let $\mathcal{A}$ be a* finite *set of atomic propositions and let $\mathcal{L}$ be the propositional language such that $\mathcal{A} \cup \{\top, \bot\} \subseteq \mathcal{L}$, and, $\forall \phi, \psi \in \mathcal{L}$, $\neg \phi \in \mathcal{L}$, $\phi \wedge \psi \in \mathcal{L}$, $\phi \vee \psi \in \mathcal{L}$.*

Additional connectives can be defined as useful shorthands for combination of connectives of $\mathcal{L}$, e.g., $\phi \supset \psi \equiv \neg \phi \vee \psi$.

We will denote by $\Omega = \{0,1\}^{\mathcal{A}}$ the set of all interpretations on $\mathcal{A}$, which we may also call the "universe". An interpretation $\mathcal{I} \in \Omega$ is a function $\mathcal{I} : \mathcal{A} \to \{0,1\}$ assigning a truth value $p^{\mathcal{I}}$ to every atomic proposition $p \in \mathcal{A}$ and, by extension, a truth value $\phi^{\mathcal{I}}$ to all formulas $\phi \in \mathcal{L}$; $\mathcal{I} \models \phi$ means that $\phi^{\mathcal{I}} = 1$ ($\mathcal{I}$ is a model of ϕ); if $S \subseteq \mathcal{L}$ is a set of formulas, $\mathcal{I} \models S$ means $\mathcal{I} \models \phi$ for all $\phi \in S$; $S \models \phi$ means that $\forall \mathcal{I} \models S$, $\mathcal{I} \models \phi$. The notation $[\phi]$ denotes the set of all models of formula $\phi \in \mathcal{L}$: $[\phi] = \{\mathcal{I} \in \Omega : \mathcal{I} \models \phi\}$. The semantics of a formula $\phi \in \mathcal{L}$ is the set of its models, $[\phi]$.

We might begin by defining the semantic distance between two formulas ϕ and ψ as the Hamming distance between the two binary string that represent their respective sets of models:

$$d(\phi, \psi) = \sum_{\mathcal{I} \in \Omega} [\phi^{\mathcal{I}} \neq \psi^{\mathcal{I}}], \tag{1}$$

where [expr] denotes the indicator function, which equals 1 if expr is true and 0 otherwise.

According to this definition, $d(\phi, \neg \phi) = \|\Omega\|$ and $d(\phi, \phi) = 0$, which is in good agreement with our intuition. Also, two formulas that are totally unrelated[2], like,

---

[2] Two formulas may be said to be totally unrelated if knowing the truth value of one does not give any information about the truth value of the other.

say, p and q, where $p, q \in \mathcal{A}$, will have a distance which is half-way in between these two extreme cases, $d(p, q) = \frac{1}{2}\|\Omega\|$.

One problem with this notion of distance is that the distance between two given formulas depends on the number of propositional constants in the language, which is a little counter-intuitive. For instance, $d(p, q) = 2$ if $\mathcal{A} = \{p, q\}$, but $d(p, q) = 4$ if $\mathcal{A} = \{p, q, r\}$, and so on. In addition, to compute it, we have to consider all interpretations in Ω, even though many of them might be indifferent when it comes to two given formulas: for example, pqr and $pq\bar{r}$ are indifferent when comparing p to q.

The former problem disappears if, instead of a distance, we define a similarity, ranging between 0 and 1 based on the same idea, as follows:

$$\mathrm{sim}(\phi, \psi) = \frac{1}{\|\Omega\|} \sum_{\mathcal{I} \in \Omega} [\phi^{\mathcal{I}} = \psi^{\mathcal{I}}]. \tag{2}$$

The latter problem is also solved by defining $\mathcal{A}_\phi \subseteq \mathcal{A}$ as the set of atoms that occur in formula ϕ and by letting $\Omega_{\phi, \psi} = 2^{\mathcal{A}_\phi \cup \mathcal{A}_\psi}$; Eq. 2 can now be rewritten as

$$\mathrm{sim}(\phi, \psi) = \frac{1}{\|\Omega\|} \sum_{\mathcal{I} \in \Omega} [\phi^{\mathcal{I}} = \psi^{\mathcal{I}}] = \frac{1}{\|\Omega_{\phi, \psi}\|} \sum_{\mathcal{I} \in \Omega_{\phi, \psi}} [\phi^{\mathcal{I}} = \psi^{\mathcal{I}}]. \tag{3}$$

According to this definition, for all formula $\phi \in \mathcal{L}$, $\mathrm{sim}(\phi, \phi) = 1$, $\mathrm{sim}(\phi, \neg\phi) = 0$ and, no matter how many atoms are involved, if $\mathcal{A}_\phi \cap \mathcal{A}_\psi = \emptyset$, $\mathrm{sim}(\phi, \psi) = \frac{1}{2}$.

Another interesting property of this semantic similarity is the following, which ensures that the proposed similarity is consistent with logical negation.

Theorem 1. *Let ϕ ψ be any two formulas of $\mathcal{L}$. Then*

$$\mathrm{sim}(\phi, \psi) = 1 - \mathrm{sim}(\neg\phi, \psi).$$

Proof. For all interpretation $\mathcal{I}$, $\phi^{\mathcal{I}} = \psi^{\mathcal{I}} \Leftrightarrow \neg\phi^{\mathcal{I}} \neq \psi^{\mathcal{I}}$ and $\phi^{\mathcal{I}} \neq \psi^{\mathcal{I}} \Leftrightarrow \neg\phi^{\mathcal{I}} = \psi^{\mathcal{I}}$. Therefore, $\{\mathcal{I} : \phi^{\mathcal{I}} = \psi^{\mathcal{I}}\} = \{\mathcal{I} : \neg\phi^{\mathcal{I}} \neq \psi^{\mathcal{I}}\} = \Omega \setminus \{\mathcal{I} : \neg\phi^{\mathcal{I}} = \psi^{\mathcal{I}}\}$ and we can thus write

$$\mathrm{sim}(\phi, \psi) = \frac{1}{\|\Omega\|} \sum_{\mathcal{I} \in \Omega} [\phi^{\mathcal{I}} = \psi^{\mathcal{I}}] = \frac{1}{\|\Omega\|} \|\{\mathcal{I} : \phi^{\mathcal{I}} = \psi^{\mathcal{I}}\}\|$$

$$= \frac{1}{\|\Omega\|} \|\Omega \setminus \{\mathcal{I} : \neg\phi^{\mathcal{I}} = \psi^{\mathcal{I}}\}\| = \frac{\|\Omega\|}{\|\Omega\|} - \frac{1}{\|\Omega\|} \|\{\mathcal{I} : \neg\phi^{\mathcal{I}} = \psi^{\mathcal{I}}\}\|$$

$$= 1 - \frac{1}{\|\Omega\|} \sum_{\mathcal{I} \in \Omega} [\neg\phi^{\mathcal{I}} = \psi^{\mathcal{I}}] = 1 - \mathrm{sim}(\neg\phi, \psi).$$

$\square$

Another interesting property of the semantic similarity, as we have defined it, is that, if $\Omega_{\phi, \psi}$ is too large, we are not obliged to perform an exact computation of $\mathrm{sim}(\phi, \psi)$, but we can approximate it with acceptable accuracy by randomly sampling n interpretations from $\Omega_{\phi, \psi}$ and counting for how many of them $\phi^{\mathcal{I}} = \psi^{\mathcal{I}}$. Indeed, $\text{sim}(\phi, \psi)$ may be construed as a probability, namely the probability that, in a random interpretation, ϕ and ψ are both true or both false. What we get is an unbiased estimator of $\text{sim}(\phi, \psi)$, which behaves like a binomial parameter $\hat{s}_{\phi,\psi}$, whose confidence interval is given by the Wald confidence interval, based on the asymptotic normality of $\hat{s}_{\phi,\psi}$ and estimating the standard error. This $(1 - \alpha)$ confidence interval for $\text{sim}(\phi, \psi)$ would be

$$\hat{s}_{\phi,\psi} \pm z_{\alpha/2} \sqrt{\hat{s}_{\phi,\psi}(1 - \hat{s}_{\phi,\psi})/n}, \tag{4}$$

where z_c denotes the $1 - c$ quantile of the standard normal distribution.

For example, if we set $n = 30$, with a 99% confidence, the actual similarity will be within a deviation of $2.576\sqrt{1/120} = 0.2351$ from $\hat{s}_{\phi,\psi}$, in the worst case, which corresponds to $\hat{s}_{\phi,\psi} = 0.5$; for $n = 100$, the approximation error will be less than 0.1288 and for $n = 1000$ it will be less than 0.0407. As a matter of fact, a precise computation of the similarity between formulas is not really required for the proposed approach to work.

This also suggests a way to deal with non-finite interpretations, which might arise in expressive languages involving variables and functions.

4   Experiments and Results

4.1   An Example from the Block World

As a first test and example of our proposal, we define a language with four individual constants, A, B, C, $Table$, one unary predicate, $\text{covered}(\cdot)$, and one binary predicate $\text{on}(\cdot, \cdot)$. The Herbrand base of this language is finite and consists of twenty ground atoms, but we can only consider a subset of it, after dropping atoms like $\text{on}(A, A)$, $\text{covered}(Table)$, and $\text{on}(Table, A)$, which would always be false in every state of the block world:

$$\mathcal{A}_{12} = \{\, \text{covered}(A), \text{on}(A, B), \text{on}(A, C), \text{on}(A, Table),$$
$$\text{covered}(B), \text{on}(B, A), \text{on}(B, C), \text{on}(B, Table),$$
$$\text{covered}(C), \text{on}(C, A), \text{on}(C, B), \text{on}(C, Table) \,\}.$$

Notice that, given this $\mathcal{A}_{12}$, $\|\Omega_{12}\| = 2^{12} = 4,096$. By adding another block D to this world we can obtain a larger set of atoms

$$\mathcal{A}_{20} = \{\, \text{covered}(A), \text{on}(A, B), \text{on}(A, C), \text{on}(A, D), \text{on}(A, Table),$$
$$\text{covered}(B), \text{on}(B, A), \text{on}(B, C), \text{on}(B, D), \text{on}(B, Table),$$
$$\text{covered}(C), \text{on}(C, A), \text{on}(C, B), \text{on}(C, D), \text{on}(C, Table),$$
$$\text{covered}(D), \text{on}(D, A), \text{on}(D, B), \text{on}(D, C), \text{on}(D, Table) \,\},$$

of size 20, with $\|\Omega_{20}\| = 2^{20} = 1,048,576$, and, similarly, by adding a further block E, a set $\mathcal{A}_{30}$ of 30 atoms, with $\|\Omega_{30}\| = 2^{30} = 1,073,741,824$.

The language may then be completed by a minimal set of logical operators, $\neg$, $\wedge$, $\vee$. Then we select a reference interpretation, for example

$$\mathcal{I}_{12}^{*} = \{\text{on}(A, Table), \text{on}(C, Table), \text{on}(B, A), \text{covered}(A)\},$$

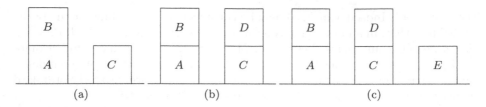

Fig. 1. The three block worlds corresponding to the reference interpretations, respectively, (a) to $\mathcal{I}_{12}^*$, (b) to $\mathcal{I}_{20}^*$, and (c) to $\mathcal{I}_{30}^*$.

corresponding to a given state of a very simple block world containing one table and three blocks, arranged as in Fig. 1a.

We then generate a set Φ of random logical formulas and we assign them a truth label based on $\mathcal{I}^*$ and train various models on it.

4.2 Experimental Protocol

The experiment was divided into two parts. In the first part, we created 3 datasets, each of which is based on a different universe generated using the language explained in Sect. 4.1. The universes are depicted in Fig. 1. We used these sets to test the performance of models learned using our proposed similarity measure. We considered different universe complexities and used very small training sets to simulate a realistic scenario. For this part, no sampling was done, all interpretations in $\Omega_{\phi,\psi}$ were considered as per Eq. 3. This can be very time-consuming when the two formulas involve many atoms. For the second part, we created 3 additional sets for each of the universes used in the first part. These additional sets contain the exact same formulas as those in the first part, the only difference being the way the similarity was calculated. To investigate what we mentioned in Sect. 3 regarding the ability to approximate the similarity with acceptable accuracy by randomly sampling n interpretations, we approximated the similarities for each of the 3 additional sets using $n = 30$, $n = 100$, and $n = 1000$ respectively. We then compared the performance of each of these sets with the base one created in the first part[3].

Part One: Baseline Experiment. To see how the proposed method performs, we created the 3 universes depicted in Fig. 1, and denoted by Ω_{12}, Ω_{20}, and Ω_{30}. The universes consist of 12, 20, and 30 atoms respectively (sets $\mathcal{A}_{12}$, $\mathcal{A}_{20}$, and $\mathcal{A}_{30}$ as defined above). The following are the reference interpretations:

- $\mathcal{I}_{12}^* = \{\mathsf{on}(A, \textit{Table}), \mathsf{on}(C, \textit{Table}), \mathsf{on}(B, A), \mathsf{covered}(A)\}$, cf. Fig. 1a;
- $\mathcal{I}_{20}^* = \{\mathsf{on}(A, \textit{Table}), \mathsf{on}(C, \textit{Table}), \mathsf{on}(B, A), \mathsf{on}(D, C), \mathsf{covered}(A), \mathsf{covered}(C)\}$, cf. Fig. 1b;

---

[3] All the code and data used for the experiments described in this paper can be found in the following repository: https://github.com/ali-ballout/Learning-to-Classify-Logical-Formulas-based-on-their-Semantic-Similarity.

- $\mathcal{I}_{30}^*$ = {on(A, *Table*), on(C, *Table*), on(E, *Table*), on(B, A), on(D, C), covered(A), covered(C)}, cf. Fig. 1c;

Following that, we generated 500 random formulas for each of the universes using Algorithm 1. Algorithm 1 generates a given number N of random formulas, taking as input a list of ground atoms $\mathcal{A}$. It is recursive and chooses its next step and which symbols to add at random. It uses a variable that reduces the probability of adding a nested subformula the more complex a formula becomes.

We then labeled each of the formulas with its truth, based on the reference interpretation of its universe. The next step was to create the similarity matrix for each set of formulas. For this part, no sampling was done, in other words all interpretations were taken into account and no noise was added. The similarity between each formula and all other formulas in the set is calculated using Eq. 3. To simplify, we compare formula ϕ to all other formulas in the set of 500 formulas. At each comparison we check all the unique atoms included in the compared formulas ϕ and ψ, for an example of what atoms are refer to $\mathcal{A}_{12}$ in Sect. 4.1. We then generate all interpretations for this set of unique atoms extracted from both formulas. Then we record the truth for each of the formulas based on each of the generated interpretations. After that, we count the instances where the truth of formulas ϕ and ψ are the same. We divide that number by the total number of generated interpretations and the result obtained is the similarity between ϕ and ψ. We do this, once, for all pairs of formulas to obtain a symmetric similarity matrix of the shape 500 × 500. Figure 2 depicts the similarity matrix between formulas of a set of formulas of size m with S being the similarity between each pair. The diagonal is all 1 since it is the similarity between a formula ϕ and itself. The truth labels of all the formulas are attached as column *Truth* to the similarity matrix to obtain the final product of the process, which is the input to be used for training and testing a machine learning model.

$Truth$	$Formula$	ϕ_0	ϕ_1	$\cdots$	ϕ_m
$Truth_0$	ϕ_0	1	$S_{0,1}$	$\cdots$	$S_{0,m}$
$Truth_1$	ϕ_1	$S_{1,0}$	1	$\cdots$	$S_{1,m}$
$\vdots$	$\vdots$	$\vdots$	$\vdots$	$\ddots$	$\vdots$
$Truth_{m-1}$	ϕ_{m-1}	$S_{m-1,0}$	$S_{m-1,1}$	$\cdots$	$S_{m-1,m}$
$Truth_m$	ϕ_m	$S_{m,0}$	$S_{m,1}$	$\cdots$	1

Fig. 2. Formula similarity matrix with truth labels.

Now that we have created our labeled datasets, we need to choose a machine learning method that is suitable for the task. Through a process of model selection we decided to use a support vector classifier, it performed the best with the small training sets that we provided. After performing a grid search we determined the best hyper parameters, we set the regularization parameter C to 0.1 and the kernel type to *polynomial*, of degree 3. We ran, for each of the 3 datasets, a 20-fold cross validation processes to establish the baseline performance of our proposed method. All results presented in Table 1 are averages of the scores obtained from all the runs for each dataset. Similarly, confusion matrices displayed in Fig. 3 are the result of summing up all confusion matrices of the 20 runs and then normalizing them. We set the number of formulas included in the training sets of each universe to less than or equal to $\|\mathcal{A}\|$ of said universe, the training set sizes were as follows: 10 for Ω_{12}, 20 for Ω_{20}, and 30 for Ω_{30}. Table 2 presents the labeled formulas used in the training set of one of the runs for Ω_{12}.

No agent, human or artificial, has in its knowledge the exhaustive list of all possible formulas. The rationale for using small training sets in our experiments is that the knowledge base of an agent is unlikely to contain many formulas; some of them might be handcrafted and be part of the "background knowledge" of the agent, and the others acquired through sensors or messages received from other agents. In any case, it is a principle of economy that the knowledge of an agent be encoded using as few and as simple formulas as required. We want to test our proposal against a realistic scenario in which the available knowledge (the formulas whose truth value is known) is very small compared to the number of semantically distinct formulas that can be stated in the language. This also has the advantage of demonstrating the generalization capability of our models.

Notice that, for a language whose set of interpretations is Ω, there are $2^{\|\Omega\|}$ semantically distinct formulas, which is a really huge number, although most of them would be very complicated formulas that one would not expect to find in a real knowledge base. However, even factoring out very complicated formulas, the number of possible formulas would be exceedingly large.

To be sure, there exists a choice of formulas that would make the problem we are studying absolutely trivial. That is when the training set contains at least $\|\mathcal{A}\|$ formulas, each consisting of a single literal (i.e., a positive or negated atom), such that the atoms of these formulas are all distinct. It is easy to see that those formulas, with their truth labeling, would directly give the reference interpretation, from which the truth value of any other formula can be mechanically computed in linear time with respect to the length of the formula, *without performing any logical deduction or reasoning.*

This is the reason why the formulas of each dataset are extracted from a distribution that is skewed in favor of simpler (i.e., realistic), but not too simple formulas. Indeed, we ensure that the training set does not contain literals for all the atoms, by counting the number of literals that are randomly generated and rejecting additional literals once the maximum number of literals has been reached. That maximum is set to $\|\mathcal{A}\|/2$, well below $\|\mathcal{A}\|$.

Since the dataset consists of randomly generated formulas, it is unbalanced[4], so in addition to the accuracy score, which we report because it gives an intuitive idea of the probability that the prediction is correct, we will provide the

---

[4] The dataset for universe Ω_{12} has 272 false formulas and 227 true ones (1 missing because it was a duplicate), for universe Ω_{20} 278 false and 222 true, and for universe Ω_{30} 300 false and 200 true; of course, these figures vary (between training and test set) for every fold obtained from these datasets.

Matthews correlation coefficient (MCC) which is a statistical rate between -1 and 1 that produces a high score only if the prediction obtained good results in all of the four confusion matrix categories (true positives, false negatives, true negatives, and false positives), proportionally both to the size of positive elements and the size of negative elements in the dataset. So its a very good metric when we don't have a perfectly balanced dataset [8]. Results of this part of the experiment are presented in Table 1.

Algorithm 1. Generating random formulas

Require: A set of atoms $\mathcal{A}$
Ensure: $formulas$, a list of generated formulas
  $N \leftarrow Number\ of\ random\ formulas\ to\ generate$
  $f \leftarrow one\ randomly\ generated\ formula$
  $literals \leftarrow 0$ ▷ A counter used to limit the number of literals as sentences
  for $i = 1 \rightarrow N$ **do**
    $i \leftarrow i + 1$
    $f \leftarrow$ RANDOM_FORMULA$(\mathcal{A}, 0)$
    if $f\ in\ formulas$ **then**
      $i = i - 1$
      $continue$
    else if $length(f.symbols) == 1$ **then**
      if $literals < length(\mathcal{A})/2$ **then**
        $literals = literals + 1$
      else
        $i = i - 1$
        $continue$
      end if
    else
      $formulas.append(f)$
    end if
  end for

  function RANDOM_FORMULA$(\mathcal{A}, level)$
    ▷ Recursive; the nesting $level$, initially $= 0$, is used to progressively reduce the probability of adding nested subformulas
    if RANDRANGE$(level + 4)$ **then**   ▷ $\frac{level+3}{level+4}$ probability of stopping
      return CHOICE$(\mathcal{A})$
    end if
    if RANDRANGE$(3) = 0$ **then**   ▷ with probability $\frac{1}{3}$
      return $\neg$RANDOM_FORMULA$(\mathcal{A}, level + 1)$
    end if
    return RANDOM_FORMULA$(\mathcal{A}, level + 1) \cdot$ CHOICE$(\wedge, \vee)\cdot$
      RANDOM_FORMULA$(\mathcal{A}, level + 1)$
  end function
Note: The generation process is slightly biased towards sentences that are neither too simple, nor too complex.

Part Two: Sampling Experiment. In this part of our experiment we investigate a property of our proposed similarity, which is the ability to approximate $sim(\phi, \psi)$ with acceptable accuracy by randomly sampling n interpretations from $\Omega_{\phi,\psi}$. We will name this approximation $\hat{s}_{\phi,\psi}$.

To this end, we created 3 new matrices for each set of formulas used in Sect. 4.2. We ended up with 9 new datasets, 3 for each of the universes depicted in Fig. 1 and describe in Sect. 4.2. The similarity in the 9 new matrices was calculated differently than in Sect. 4.2. For this part, we approximated the similarity

---

Algorithm 2. Approximating the similarity by sampling interpretations

---

Require: 2 formulas ϕ *and* ψ to be compared
Require: a sample size n
Ensure: ϕ *and* ψ, in the same universe Ω
Ensure: $n > 0$
$\quad \mathcal{A} \leftarrow \phi.atoms \cup \psi.atoms$
$\quad interpretations \leftarrow$ SAMPLE_INTERPRETATIONS($\mathcal{A}$, n)
$\quad counter \leftarrow 0$
$\quad$**for** w in $interpretations$ **do**
$\quad\quad$**if** $\phi.truth(w) == \psi.truth(w)$ **then**
$\quad\quad\quad counter \leftarrow counter + 1$
$\quad\quad$**end if**
$\quad$**end for**
$\quad \hat{s}_{\phi,\psi} \leftarrow \frac{counter}{n}$

$\quad$**function** SAMPLE_INTERPRETATIONS($\mathcal{A}$, n)
$\quad\quad interpretations \leftarrow array(size = n)$ ▷ Array to store n interpretations
$\quad\quad$**for** $i = 0 \rightarrow n - 1$ **do**
$\quad\quad\quad b \leftarrow array(size = \mathcal{A}.length)$ ▷ Array the size of the list of atoms
$\quad\quad\quad$**for** $j = 0 \rightarrow \mathcal{A}.length - 1$ **do**
$\quad\quad\quad\quad b[j] \leftarrow$ RANDRANGE(2)
$\quad\quad\quad$**end for**
$\quad\quad\quad interpretations[i] \leftarrow b$
$\quad\quad$**end for**
$\quad\quad$**return** $interpretations$
$\quad$**end function**

---

between formulas by randomly sampling a set number n of all interpretations, instead of taking all of them into account as we did in Sect. 4.2. The number of random samples n considered for creating the matrices is $n = 30$, $n = 100$, and $n = 1000$. This allows us to simulate the scenario of having a machine with low computational capacity trying to process a set of interpretations that is too large, and utilizing sampling as a solution. It also allows us to see how the method performs when noise is introduced.

The way the similarity is approximated using sampling is not much different from how it is calculated: we still count the instances where formulas ϕ and ψ have the same truth, but for n randomly sampled interpretations instead of *all* interpretations. Algorithm 2 is used to approximate the similarity between two formulas. In simple terms, when Algorithm 2 compares two formulas ϕ and ψ, instead of generating all interpretations corresponding to the set of unique atoms $\mathcal{A}$ composing those formulas, it generates a number n of these interpretations randomly. This sampling is done with replacement, which means that it is possible that a given interpretation gets sampled multiple times, especially in case n is larger than the number of all interpretations. We then proceed to count the instances where formulas ϕ and ψ have the same truth out of these sampled interpretations. After that, we divide the obtained number by n, the size of the sample, since we are now dealing with n interpretations and not all of them. The result from that division is the approximation $\hat{s}_{\phi,\psi}$ of the similarity $sim(\phi, \psi)$ between ϕ and ψ. We do this for the sets of formulas we randomly generated in Sect. 4.2 for each of our universes 3 times, once for each number n of samples we mentioned.

With these 9 new matrices we are able to study how the sample size n might affect the performance of the method when dealing with different universe complexities. It will also show us how well an approximation of the similarity performs. We used the same model to test the performance and the same scoring metrics as the baseline. We used the same training set sizes for each universe as in the baseline. The results of this part of the experiment are available in Table 1.

Table 1. Accuracy and MCC for experiments done on each universe.

Universe	Training set Size	sample size	Accuracy score	MCC
Ω_{12}	10	no sampling	0.77	0.56
		30	0.76	0.54
		100	0.77	0.56
		1000	0.77	0.55
Ω_{20}	20	no sampling	0.81	0.63
		30	0.81	0.62
		100	0.82	0.63
		1000	0.82	0.65
Ω_{30}	30	no sampling	0.83	0.66
		30	0.79	0.56
		100	0.82	0.62
		1000	0.83	0.64

4.3   Results and Analysis

Baseline Results. We start our analysis with the first part of our experiment, detailed in Sect. 4.2. The results can be found in Table 1 and the corresponding confusion matrices to offer support in Fig. 3. A small sample of formulas from the test set for the smallest universe, with the labels predicted by the model, is provided in Table 3. From this experiment we can determine:

1. The overall performance of our proposed method without sampling while dealing with universes of different complexities, using very small training sets.
2. The effect the training set size has on performance with respect to the complexity of the universe addressed.

Regarding the first, Table 1 shows that the overall performance of our proposed method is good. The highest accuracy achieved was 83% for a training set size of 30 formulas and a universe of complexity 30, MCC being 0.66 which is a very good result when training using an unbalanced set. As a worst case, the method achieved 77% accuracy with a minimal training set size of 10 formulas and universe complexity of 12, MCC of 0.56 is acceptable considering the small training set relative to the complexity of the universe. Indeed, 30 formulas for a language with 30 propositional symbols is a really sparse training set, when one thinks that this language has $\sim 10^9$ interpretations and there exist $\sim 10^{300,000,000}$ semantically distinct formulas one can construct!

Table 2. A sample training set made of 10 formulas from universe Ω_{12}.

Formula	Label
$(\text{on}(C, B) \wedge \text{on}(B, C)) \vee (\neg\neg\neg\neg\text{on}(A, B) \vee \text{on}(B, A))$	True
$\neg(\neg(\text{on}(A, B) \wedge ((\text{on}(C, Tbl) \vee \neg\neg\text{on}(C, B)) \wedge \text{covered}(A))) \vee (\text{on}(C, A) \vee \text{on}(B, C)))$	False
$\neg(((\text{covered}(B) \vee \neg\text{on}(B, A)) \vee (\text{on}(B, Tbl) \wedge (\text{on}(B, A) \wedge \text{on}(C, A)))) \wedge \text{covered}(B))$	True
$\neg\neg\neg\text{on}(A, C)$	True
$(\text{on}(B, C) \vee \text{covered}(A)) \vee \text{covered}(A)$	True
$\neg(\neg\text{on}(A, C) \wedge \neg\text{covered}(C))$	False
$(\text{on}(A, C) \vee \text{on}(C, A)) \wedge \neg(\text{covered}(C) \wedge \text{on}(A, Tbl))$	False
$\text{on}(C, Tbl) \wedge \text{on}(C, B)$	False
$\text{on}(C, B) \vee \text{on}(B, C)$	False
$\neg\text{on}(C, B) \wedge (\neg\neg\neg\text{on}(C, B) \wedge \text{covered}(B))$	False

After demonstrating that our proposed method is capable of achieving good results with very small training sets, we move on to the second point. We can see that the proposed method can achieve an average accuracy of 80% throughout the runs that use a very small training set of 10 formulas for Ω_{12}, 20 formulas for Ω_{20}, and 30 formulas for Ω_{30}. It would be natural to think that as the universe complexity increases, a model would require a larger training set to maintain performance, which is what the results shown in Table 1 and Fig. 3 confirm. From the results see in Table 1 where no sampling was considered, we can see that increasing the number of formulas included in the training set had a very significant effect on performance. This effect was not limited to maintaining performance, but it resulted in an improvement of up to 8% in accuracy and 0.14 in terms of MCC.

To put things into perspective, for Ω_{12} we used for training 10 formulas out of a possible $\sim 10^{1233}$ compared to 30 out of a possible $\sim 10^{300,000,000}$ for Ω_{30}. In other words, the transition from Ω_{12} with 4096 interpretations to Ω_{30} with $\sim 10^9$, resulted in a gain of 8% accuracy by just adding 20 formulas to the training set. The increase in the size of the training set is modest relative to the size of Ω_{30} or the number of semantically distinct formulas that can be constructed, while the gain of accuracy and balance in predictions in terms of MCC is significant.

We observed that the truth value of "simple" formulas turns out to be harder to predict for the trained models than that of "complicated" formulas (see, e.g.,

Table 3. A small sample of the test set with formulas varying in complexity from universe Ω_{12}.

Formula	Actual	Predicted
$\neg(\neg(\neg(\text{on}(B, A) \wedge \text{covered}(B)) \vee ((\text{covered}(C) \vee \text{on}(A,)B) \wedge \text{on}(C, Tbl))) \vee \neg((\text{on}(B, A) \wedge \text{on}(A, Tbl)) \wedge \neg\text{covered}(A)))$	False	False
$(\text{on}(A, Tbl) \wedge \text{on}(B, A)) \vee \neg\neg((\text{on}(A, C) \wedge ((\text{on}(A, Tbl) \vee \text{covered}(A)) \wedge \text{covered}(A))) \vee \text{on}(C, B))$	True	True
$\text{covered}(B) \wedge \text{on}(A, Tbl)$	False	True
$((\text{covered}(B) \vee (\neg\text{on}(A, B) \wedge \text{on}(C, Tbl))) \wedge (((\text{on}(B, A) \wedge (\text{on}(A, C) \wedge \text{on}(C, Tbl))) \vee (\text{on}(C, A) \vee \text{on}(A, Tbl))) \wedge \text{on}(A, Tbl))) \vee \text{on}(C, A)$	True	True
$((\text{covered}(A) \wedge \text{covered}(B)) \vee (\text{covered}(A) \vee \neg(((\text{covered}(A) \vee \text{on}(B, C)) \vee (\text{on}(B, C) \wedge \text{on}(B, Tbl))) \vee \text{on}(C, A)))) \vee ((\text{on}(B, A) \vee \text{on}(A, C)) \wedge (((\text{on}(C, Tbl) \wedge \text{on}(B, C)) \wedge \text{on}(A, C)) \wedge \text{covered}(A)))$	True	True
$\text{covered}(B) \wedge (((\text{on}(C, B) \vee ((\text{on}(C, B) \wedge \text{on}(B, Tbl)) \wedge ((\neg\text{covered}(B) \vee (\text{on}(A, B) \wedge \neg\text{on}(A, C))) \vee (\neg\neg\text{on}(B, C) \wedge (\text{covered}(C) \vee \text{on}(A, B))))))) \vee \text{covered}(C)) \wedge (\neg(\text{on}(A, C) \vee \text{on}(B, C)) \wedge ((\text{covered}(A) \vee \text{on}(C, B)) \vee (\text{on}(A, Tbl) \wedge (\text{on}(A, Tbl) \vee \text{on}(C, B))))))$	False	False

Table 3). While this must have to do with the geometry of the space of the kernel representation of formulas induced by the semantic similarity, this phenomenon will have to be the object of further investigation.

Sampling Results. We now shift our attention to part two of the experiment detailed in Sect. 4.2. The results of this experiment are also shown in Table 1 and the corresponding confusion matrices to offer support are found in Fig. 3.

At first glance at Table 1, we can tell that the overall performance of the model does not degrade much when the similarity is approximated using the lowest number of samples $n = 30$. Indeed, we have a loss of accuracy of almost 4% for 2 of our universes. But this is an acceptable result when considering that in this case we would no longer have to calculate the exact similarity especially when we are limited by computational power. In fact, in this case, we would be looking at 30 random interpretations instead of $\sim 10^9$ for a universe the size of Ω_{30}.

The degradation in accuracy and MCC decreases as we increase the number of samples from 30 to 100 and then to 1000, it even approaches baseline performance. This proves what we mentioned in Sect. 3, we are able to approximate the similarity with very high accuracy even with a low number of sampled interpretations when compared to the number of *all* interpretations.

On the other hand, another increase in the number of samples from 100 to 1000 has no significant effect on performance, which is interesting considering that this introduces noise (since we allow for repetitions) yet it does not degrade performance. It also means that for a universe of complexity $\|\mathcal{A}\|$ there exists an optimal number of samples n that achieves baseline-similar performance.

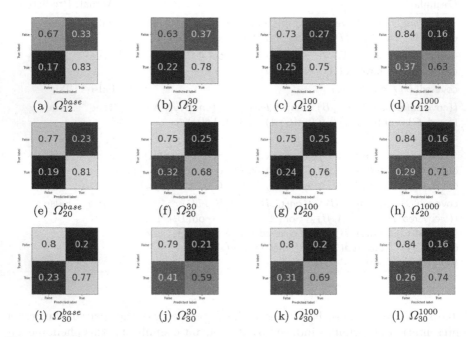

Fig. 3. Confusion matrices of the similarity approximation using sampling experiment for each universe. Each row represents 4 cases for each universe, starting with the baseline (no sampling) and then $n = 30$, $n = 100$, and $n = 1000$ respectively. Each sub-figure is captioned by the universe notation $\Omega_{12,20,30}$ and in superscript the sample size n used to approximate similarity.

5   Conclusion

We have proposed a framework that allows an agent to train, based on a set of formulas whose truth values are known, a classification model that predicts the truth-value of a new, arbitrary formula. This framework uses a semantic similarity between formulas, which is a key ingredient of our proposal, to perform a kernel encoding of the formulas, which is then exploited by the classification model. We have tested an implementation of this framework using SVM, showing that the classification model is highly accurate (with accuracy around 80%) even when the similarity is approximated by severely undersampling the interpretations. The practical implications of these results are that the proposed approach is tractable even for languages with a large (or infinite but enumerable) number of atoms; indeed, computing a good approximation of the similarity of two formulas can be done in linear time, as it depends only on the size of the (random) interpretations sampled.

There is no guarantee that all the predictions made by a model be altogether consistent. There is no built-in mechanism to ensure that and the mutual consistency of all the prediction is not part of the measure of the quality of a classifier: every prediction is made by the model and assessed independently of the others. Of course, if the predictions were all correct, they would also be consistent and that's what we observe empirically, that the predictions tend to be mostly consistent.

Since the knowledge of an agent may not be complete, some formulas, which are not entailed by it and whose negation is not entailed either, both predictions would be acceptable, and one might be tempted to count them as correct. However, this is not what we did: for the purpose of testing our method, what we did was to arbitrarily fix one interpretation and say it corresponded to the actual state of affairs; use it to label the training set and evaluate the predictions of the classifiers against the label that would be thus assigned, even for those formulas whose truth value is not constrained by the available knowledge. In a sense, we were as strict as one can be when judging a classifier.

Future work might involve testing other more sophisticated classification methods and applying the proposed framework to real-world scenarios.

Acknowledgments. This work has been partially supported by the French government, through the 3IA Côte d'Azur "Investments in the Future" project managed by the National Research Agency (ANR) with the reference number ANR-19-P3IA-0002, as well as through the ANR CROQUIS (Collecte, représentation, complétion, fusion et interrogation de données de réseaux d'eau urbains hétérogènes et incertaines) project, grant ANR-21-CE23-0004 of the French National Research Agency (ANR).

References

1. Amgoud, L., David, V.: Measuring similarity between logical arguments. In: Thielscher, M., Toni, F., Wolter, F. (eds.) Principles of Knowledge Representation and Reasoning: Proceedings of the Sixteenth International Conference, KR 2018, Tempe, Arizona, 30 October–2 November 2018, pp. 98–107. AAAI Press (2018)
2. Anthony, M., Hammer, P.L.: A Boolean measure of similarity. Discrete Appl. Math. **154**(16), 2242–2246 (2006)
3. Antoniou, G., Ghose, A.: What is default reasoning good for? applications revisited. In: 32nd Annual Hawaii International Conference on System Sciences (HICSS-32), 5–8 January 1999, Maui, Hawaii, USA. IEEE Computer Society (1999)
4. Badreddine, S., d'Avila Garcez, A., Serafini, L., Spranger, M.: Logic tensor networks. Artif. Intell. **303**, 103649 (2022). https://doi.org/10.1016/j.artint.2021.103649
5. Blee, J., Billington, D., Sattar, A.: Reasoning with levels of modalities in BDI logic. In: Ghose, A., Governatori, G., Sadananda, R. (eds.) PRIMA 2007. LNCS (LNAI), vol. 5044, pp. 410–415. Springer, Heidelberg (2009). https://doi.org/10.1007/978-3-642-01639-4_39
6. Bowles, G.: Propositional relevance. Informal Logic **2**(12), 65–77 (1990)
7. Cheruvu, A., Radhakrishna, V.: A survey of similarity measures for time stamped temporal datasets. In: DATA, pp. 193–197. ACM (2021)

8. Chicco, D., Jurman, G.: The advantages of the Matthews correlation coefficient (MCC) over F1 score and accuracy in binary classification evaluation. BMC Genomics **21**(1), 1–13 (2020). https://doi.org/10.1186/s12864-019-6413-7

9. Esteva, F., Godo, L., Rodriguez, R.O., Vetterlein, T.: On Ruspini's models of similarity-based approximate reasoning. In: Lesot, M.-J., et al. (eds.) IPMU 2020. CCIS, vol. 1237, pp. 3–13. Springer, Cham (2020). https://doi.org/10.1007/978-3-030-50146-4_1

10. Fišer, P., Kubalík, P., Kubátová, H.: Output grouping method based on a similarity of Boolean functions. In: Proceedings of 7th International Workshop on Boolean Problems (IWSBP), Freiberg (Germany), 21–22 September, pp. 107–113 (2006)

11. Hohenecker, P., Lukasiewicz, T.: Ontology reasoning with deep neural networks. J. Artif. Intell. Res. **68**, 503–540 (2020)

12. Johnston, T., Scott, A.: Lipschitz bijections between boolean functions. Comb. Probab. Comput. **30**, 513–525 (2021)

13. Makinson, D.: Propositional relevance through letter-sharing. J. Appl. Log. **7**(4), 377–387 (2009)

14. Shi, S., Chen, H., Ma, W., Mao, J., Zhang, M., Zhang, Y.: Neural logic reasoning. In: d'Aquin, M., Dietze, S., Hauff, C., Curry, E., Cudré-Mauroux, P. (eds.) CIKM 2020: The 29th ACM International Conference on Information and Knowledge Management, Virtual Event, Ireland, 19–23, 2020 October, pp. 1365–1374. ACM (2020). https://doi.org/10.1145/3340531.3411949

15. Tran, T., Le, V., Le, H., Le, T.M.: From deep learning to deep reasoning. In: KDD 2021: Proceedings of the 27th ACM SIGKDD Conference on Knowledge Discovery & Data Mining, pp. 4076–4077 (2021)

16. Wendler, J., Bach, J.: Recognizing and predicting agent behavior with case based reasoning. In: Polani, D., Browning, B., Bonarini, A., Yoshida, K. (eds.) RoboCup 2003. LNCS (LNAI), vol. 3020, pp. 729–738. Springer, Heidelberg (2004). https://doi.org/10.1007/978-3-540-25940-4_72

Time Series Predictive Models
for Opponent Behavior Modeling
in Bilateral Negotiations

Gevher Yesevi[1]([⊠])(iD), Mehmet Onur Keskin[1](iD), Anıl Doğru[1](iD),
and Reyhan Aydoğan[1,2](iD)

[1] Computer Science, Özyeğin University, Istanbul, Turkey
{gevher.yesevi,onur.keskin,anil.dogru}@ozu.edu.tr,
reyhan.aydogan@ozyegin.edu.tr
[2] Interactive Intelligence, TU Delft, Delft, The Netherlands

Abstract. In agent-based negotiations, it is crucial to understand the opponent's behavior and predict its bidding pattern to act strategically. Foreseeing the utility of the opponent's coming offer provides valuable insight to the agent so that it can decide its next move wisely. Accordingly, this paper addresses predicting the opponent's coming offers by employing two deep learning-based approaches: Long Short-Term Memory Networks and Transformers. The learning process has three different targets: estimating the agent's utility of the opponent's coming offer, estimating the agent's utility of that without using opponent-related variables, and estimating the opponent's utility of that by using opponent-related variables. This work reports the performances of these models that are evaluated in various negotiation scenarios. Our evaluation showed promising results regarding the prediction performance of the proposed methods.

Keywords: Automated negotiation · Multi-agent systems ·
Time-series prediction · Utility prediction

1 Introduction

Autonomous negotiating agents decide on their behaviors by considering various factors such as time pressure, the competitiveness of the underlying negotiation domain, the opponent's collaborative level, and so on [8,14]. Sophisticated strategies aim to detect the opponent's behaviors and make reciprocating moves. Thus, understanding the fundamental causes of behavior is one of the essential research questions in agent-based negotiation systems. Once the underlying causes of their opponent's behaviors are observed, negotiating agents can act strategically to get better negotiation outcomes sooner. Consequently, agents can target to maximize their utility or increase social welfare depending on the context.

In autonomous negotiations, decisions on when to accept the opponent's counter-offer or what offer to make (i.e., acceptance and bidding) are made according to the employed strategies. These strategies are often defined based on the target utility calculations [2,7,11]. Therefore, predicting opponents' target utility for future rounds would be an excellent approach to grasp their behaviors. In the literature, some attempts aim to detect the opponent's moves/target utilities and act accordingly [4,7]. For instance, Williams *et al.* present a Gaussian process to foresee the concession rate of the opponent [19]. Furthermore, researchers apply reinforcement learning to determine their target utility based on the exchanged offers and remaining negotiation time during the negotiation [1,16]. Those studies implicitly take the opponent's behavior into account. Moreover, Chen *et al.* suggest applying transfer learning in negotiation to benefit from previous negotiation experiences [5].

With the growing need for decision-making processes in complex domains, there is an increasing interest in understanding the behavior of other agents such as logistics and transportation [6,8,16]. Some of them focus on learning the patterns and trends in an agent's behavior. For this type of prediction, time series analysis is a promising approach to build such predictors. In automated negotiation, Li *et al.* recently adopt such a time series analysis to recognize the opponent's strategy during the negotiation [12]. In their work, the agent aims to classify what strategy its opponent employs by analyzing the history of the offers made by the opponent. Inspired by that study and considering the importance of the target utility estimation in negotiation, we propose adopting time series predictors to guess the utility of the opponent's coming offers so that the agent can strategically make its decisions.

Accordingly, the goal of this study can be summarized twofold: (i) introducing two deep learning-based models, namely Long short-term memory (LSTM) [10] and Transformer models [18], to guess the utility of the opponent's following offers, and (ii) studying the effect of opponent's strategy and the size of the negotiation domain on the performance of the implemented predictors. This work could lead to a promising research direction toward recognizing the opponent's strategy. We believe that predicting the utility of the opponent's following offers (i.e., next-step utility prediction) helps the agent developers design resilient and robust negotiation strategies.

The following sections in this paper are as follows: Sects. 2 and 3 provide the information on the reviewed literature and the necessary background about automated negotiations. The proposed approach and the details of the prediction models are explained in Sect. 4 while its evaluation is elaborately reported in Sect. 5. Finally, Sect. 6 concludes this paper with future work.

2   Related Work

Various negotiation strategies have been proposed in the literature. Existing strategies usually calculate a target utility at each round and generate a bid with that utility. Time-based strategies such as Conceder and Boulware agents determine the target utility through a function of remaining negotiation time [7]. Opponent agents can straightforwardly exploit such strategies since they do not consider opponent's behaviors. Thus, strategies like Tit-for-Tat consider opponent's consecutive offers to determine their coming offers by mimicking their opponent to some extent. For a more robust strategy, Faratin *et al.* suggest adopting a hybrid strategy, which combines both time and behavior-dependent tactics similar to the strategy presented in [11]. Moreover, another strategy determines several negotiation states and proposes adopting a specific bidding tactic for each state while considering the opponent's consecutive offers [15].

The aforementioned strategies consider their opponent's behavior based on their previous offers during the negotiation. Besides, guessing an opponent's future moves may enable a negotiating agent to act strategically. Regarding predicting the opponent's future behavior, there is some literature work. For instance, Williams *et al.* present a Gaussian process to predict the utility of the opponent's next offer [19] by assuming that the opponent concedes over time. Consequently, the agent can estimate its opponent's future concession.

Another direction is to build a prediction model for the opponent's strategy. Accordingly, Li *et al.* introduce the idea of applying a time series prediction model to classify an opponent's strategy among a predefined set of strategies [12]. It is claimed that the proposed idea can be adopted independently from the domain. For this purpose, the authors use the agents of the negotiation platform called Genius [13]. Notably, they use the LSTM model for recognizing the opponent's strategy. In some cases, such classifiers may not perform well, especially when facing an opponent employing a sophisticated unknown strategy. Therefore, unlike that study, we propose adopting time series models such as LSTM [10] and Transformers [18] to predict the utility of the opponent's following offers. To our knowledge, Transformers have not been used yet in this context.

3   Automated Negotiation

In automated negotiation, agents negotiate over a finite set of n issues $\mathcal{I} = \{1, 2, \ldots, n\}$. Each issue $i \in \mathcal{I}$ has a range $\mathcal{D}_i$ of possible instantiations. An outcome, $o \in \Omega$, is a complete assignment to the set of issues where Ω is the Cartesian Product of the ranges of instantiations per issue. Formally, the set of all possible outcomes is defined as $\Omega = \mathcal{D}_1 \times \mathcal{D}_2 \times \ldots \times \mathcal{D}_n$. The assessment of each offer/outcome is done using a utility function mapping each negotiation outcome to a real number $[0, 1]$, the desirability of that outcome. The utility function is a mathematical representation of the agent's preferences. As usual, additive utility functions are used for this purpose [8]. Eq. 1 shows the function where w_i represents the importance of the negotiation issue I_i (i.e., issue weight), o_i represents the value for issue i in offer o, and V_i is the valuation function for issue i, which returns the desirability of the issue value. Without losing generality, it is assumed that $\sum_{i \in n} w_i = 1$ and the domain of V_i is $(0, 1)$ for any i. An issue value is preferred when its valuation value V_i is higher. A negotiating agent utilizes its utility function to determine what to offer and when to accept.

$$\mathcal{U}(o) = \sum_{i=1}^{n} w_i \times V_i(o_i) \tag{1}$$

Stacked Alternating Offers Protocol (SAOP) governs the interaction among agents (i.e., what actions can be taken under which condition and when to stop the negotiation) [3]. As there is a deadline to reach an agreement, the interaction ends when agents find a consensus or reach the deadline. The interaction starts with an offer made by one of the agents. In each turn, the agent receiving an offer can (i) *accept* the current offer, (ii) make a *counteroffer*, or (iii) *end* the negotiation without an agreement. The interaction continues in a turn-taking fashion and ends until reaching an agreement or deadline. Agents generally do not know their opponent's preferences or negotiation strategies. However, they can try to learn those preferences/strategies over time by analyzing offer exchanges as we aim in this study.

To analyze the behavioral changes of negotiating agents during the negotiation, Hindriks *et al.* define six negotiation moves. A move is determined based on the utility difference of the negotiator's subsequent offers for both sides. These moves are defined as follows: *fortunate, nice, concession, selfish, unfortunate,* and *silent* [9]. Table 1 demonstrates the calculation of move types of a player where ΔU_A and ΔU_{Op} represent the utility difference for the negotiator itself and that for the opponent, respectively.

Table 1. Move specification of a negotiator [9]

	Self difference	Opponent difference
Silent	$\Delta U_A = 0$	$\Delta U_{Op} = 0$
Nice	$\Delta U_A = 0$	$\Delta U_{Op} > 0$
Concession	$\Delta U_A < 0$	$\Delta U_{Op} > 0$
Unfortunate	$\Delta U_A < 0$	$\Delta U_{Op} < 0$
Fortunate	$\Delta U_A > 0$	$\Delta U_{Op} > 0$
Selfish	$\Delta U_A > 0$	$\Delta U_{Op} < 0$

4   Proposed Prediction Approach

The main focus of this study is to build a prediction module that generates next-step utility value predictions during bilateral negotiations to improve the decision-making process of the agents. Consequently, agents may avoid making an offer whose utility is lower than the utility of its opponent's next offer (i.e., leaving money on the table). In particular, when the agent negotiates with the same opponent several times, it can foresee its behavior and act wisely to find a consensus sooner. Those predictions may play an essential role in capturing the trends of opponent behavior and help to recognize the opponent's strategies.

Accordingly, this study aims to predict the utility of the opponent's following offers to design sophisticated and robust negotiation strategies by adopting the three objectives listed below:

- **Objective 1:** Predicting the utility of its opponent's coming offer for itself, $U_A(o_{t+1})$, based on remaining time and bid exchanges so far.
- **Objective 2:** Improving the performance of the prediction gained in Objective 1 by considering additional features such as estimated opponent utility, Nash Distance, and opponent's moves.
- **Objective 3:** Predicting its opponent's estimated utility of its opponent's next offer, $\widehat{U}_{Op}(o_{t+1})$, based on remaining time, bid exchanges so far and additional features used in *Objective 2*.

Accordingly, Fig. 1 illustrates the inputs used within our next-step utility prediction for achieving each objective mentioned above. For any kind of analysis, a negotiating agent can keep track of all offers made during the negotiation and calculate their utilities for itself by using its utility function ($< U_A(o_0), ..., U_A(o_t) >$) at time t. To achieve the first objective, we suggest adopting a time series predictor that can be fed by the remaining time (t_{remain}) and the agent's utility of a chunk (we will refer to it as 'window' for the rest of the paper) of previous consecutive offer exchanges ($< U_A(o_{t-k}), ..., U_A(o_t) >$). The designer can choose the size of the window k to be used for each training set[1].

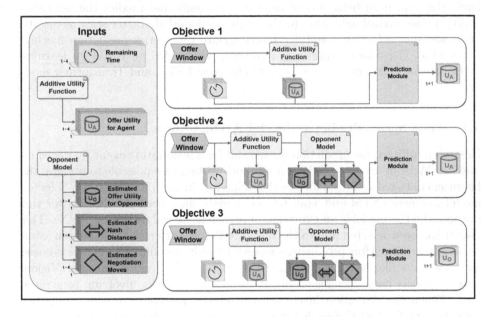

Fig. 1. Inputs and outputs for next-step utility prediction

For *Objective 2*, we suggest including the opponent's utilities of the offer exchanges, negotiation move analysis, and the Nash distances. Although the agent has no access to the opponent's preferences, it could employ an opponent

---

[1] In our work, we consider five previous consecutive offer exchanges.

modeling for learning the opponent's preferences over time in terms of utilities. Any opponent modeling study from the literature [4] could be utilized for this purpose. For our work, a frequency-based opponent modeling mechanism is chosen [17]. Consequently, the agent can exploit additional estimated information such as the opponent's utility of a given offer, negotiation move types, and the Nash distances of the given offers. It is worth noting that the accuracy of the selected opponent model may affect the predictor's performance for the next-step utility value. To sum up, the following inputs feed the second predictor:

- Agent's utilities for the offer window, $< U_A(o_{t-k}), ..., U_A(o_t) >$,
- Estimated opponent utilities for the offer window, $< \widehat{U}_{Op}(o_{t-k}), ..., \widehat{U}_{Op}(o_t) >$,
- Nash distances for the offer window, $< \Delta N_{(o_{t-k})}, \Delta N_{(o_t)} >$,
- Estimated moves for the offer window, $< m(o_{t-k}, o_{t-k+1}), ..., m(o_{t-1}, o_t) >$,
- Remaining negotiation time, t_{remain}.

To accomplish the third object, we utilize the same inputs used for *Objective 2*, but the output of the model is the estimated opponent's utility of the opponent's coming offer, $\widehat{U}_{Op}(o_{t+1})$. All offer-related inputs can be kept as a time series during negotiation. This allows us to use supervised learning models to learn the sequential behaviors of negotiating agents and predict the next-step utility values accordingly. Due to the sequence-based characteristics of negotiation sessions, selecting a suitable multi-variate time series prediction method is essential. Considering these requirements, we decided on two deep learning architectures with sequence processing behaviors: LSTM and Transformer models.

4.1   Time Series Predictive Model Architectures

Next-step utility value prediction is essential for a negotiating agent for decision-making. With time series prediction methods, it becomes possible to observe the historical data patterns and foresee the behaviors in the following steps. Selected models, namely LSTM and Transformer models, have been used widely for this purpose. LSTM model is an extension of recurrent neural networks (RNN). This model has been selected due to the high predictive performance in similar competitive markets. After producing successful results on different sequence-based learning tasks like Natural Language Processing (NLP) and Computer Vision, LSTM models have become prevalent in regression tasks involving sequential data. When the Attention layers are introduced to replace RNNs, many use cases that prefer LSTM models have considered Transformer models in different learning tasks like NLP and Computer Vision. Therefore, we included Transformer models in our prediction module to test this assumption for next-step utility predictions.

Sequential information is fed to the aforementioned models with a sliding window approach. This approach first requires a number of time steps to decide the window size of data it will carry. Then, each iteration utilizes this window in the computations by sliding the window by one step. The inputs of each iteration not only depend on the current step but are also fed by the previous inputs received by the window, as can be seen in Fig. 2.

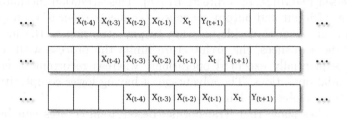

Fig. 2. Sliding window approach of model input and output

Long Short-Term Memory (LSTM) Model Architecture: Recurrent Neural Network (RNN) deep learning architectures are designed for processing sequential inputs. It is a widely used neural network since its ability to model the time dependency in its architecture. There are many variations of RNN to improve its efficiency. One of these variations is LSTM [10]. Mainly, deep neural networks suffer from the vanishing gradient problem, which occurs when the calculated gradient gets close to zero value during back-propagation operation. This situation causes the information to be lost during the model training. To resolve this problem, LSTM architecture introduces memory gates to control the input flow. This way, the information of long sequences can be preserved during the training and processed in a unidirectional way.

The LSTM architecture we employed contains one LSTM layer with 45 units and a fully connected layer to produce the predictions, as shown in Fig. 3. The model takes last five inputs; $X_{(t-4)}$, $X_{(t-3)}$, $X_{(t-2)}$, $X_{(t-1)}$, $X_{(t)}$ as a sequence and predicts next value $Y_{(t+1)}$. The data is processed in the model with a batch size of 32. 'Mean Squared Error' is used as the loss function, whereas 'RMSProp' is selected as the optimizer since it is widely preferred for regression problems. The model is trained for 50 epochs with a 0.001 learning rate.

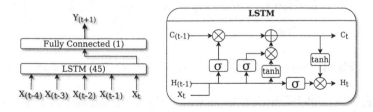

Fig. 3. The left-hand side demonstrates the proposed LSTM model, while the right-hand side demonstrates the LSTM architecture

Transformer Architecture: Transformer models stand out with the self-attention mechanism they employ to draw dependencies between inputs and outputs instead of focusing on recurrence in neural networks (i.e., allowing data to be processed regardless of a direction) [18]. This attention mechanism takes the positions of input and output sequences, connects them to each other, and traverses among them to decide on what to pay attention to the most. While connecting the sequences, the architecture limits the process with a constant number of sequentially executed operations, whereas recurrent layers require $O(n)$ sequential operations. The advantage of having lower complexity pays off when the tasks involve very long sequences.

Recent studies show that Transformer-based architectures can be used to predict time series [21]. Wu *et al.* use an encoder-decoder based approach for time series prediction in their study [20]. Their model takes the time series inputs with a window size of five, and the output as a sequence with the shifted input indices. After experimenting with various Transformer-based architectures for our task, we propose an encoder-decoder model with shifted inputs. Figure 4 shows the Transformer block and input-output design of this architecture that is used in our study.

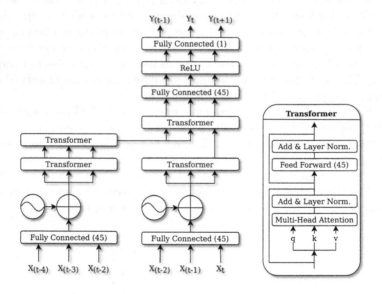

Fig. 4. Proposed Transformer based encoder-decoder model

Encoder: The model's encoder is shown on the left-hand side of Fig. 4. It takes the first 3 inputs of sequence $(X_{(t-4)}, X_{(t-3)}, X_{(t-2)})$. In the study introducing attention layers, Vaswani et al. use input embedding for the 'token2vector' operation [18]. However, we prefer to use a fully connected layer instead of input embedding to adapt the original structure of Transformer models to time series prediction tasks, similar to the work of Wu et al. [20]. Note that the other components of the original Transformer structure remained the same. The encoder of the model has two Transformer blocks.

Decoder: The model's decoder is shown on the right-hand side of Fig. 4. It takes the last 3 inputs of sequence $(X_{(t-2)}, X_{(t-1)}, X_t)$, and predicts the corresponding shifted outputs $(Y_{(t-1)}, Y_t, Y_{(t+1)})$. Similar to the encoder, the decoder uses a fully connected layer instead of input embedding and contains two Transformer blocks. The inputs used in both Transformer blocks are the same, except the inputs obtained from the encoder and fed into the decoder. The decoder part of the architecture contains two fully connected layers right after the second Transformer block.

Similar to the LSTM architecture, we build the Transformer model with a window size of five and batch size of 32, then train it for 50 epochs. 'Mean Squared Error' is selected as the loss function while 'RMSProp' optimizer is used with a 0.001 learning rate.

5   Evaluation

The objectives of this study have been evaluated elaborately in varying negotiation settings (i.e., different negotiation scenarios and opponent strategies). We pre-trained the selected model architectures with historical negotiation sessions to feed the prediction models with the defined input and target variables. This section reports the actions taken for model training and evaluations of three different objectives. Accordingly, Sect. 5.1 describes our experimental setting where the results are analyzed and discussed in Sect. 5.2.

5.1   Experimental Setup

Defined model architectures must be fed with historical negotiation sessions to capture the opponent agent's behaviors during the negotiation. For this reason, multiple negotiations with different settings have been conducted using the GeniusWeb negotiation framework [13] whose collected sessions are used for model training purposes. Note that GeniusWeb is the Web version of Genius, which allows agent developers to design their agents in Python. It supports machine learning libraries that are available in Python for time series predictions. Unfortunately, we cannot directly use agents available in Genius on this platform. There are a few agent strategies available at this moment. For the baseline agent that performs the learning process, we implemented an additional strategy – a hybrid bidding strategy [11] with a frequency-based opponent model [17]. The negotiations have been conducted between this baseline agent and five available agents, which employ Boulware, Conceder, behavior-based, hybrid, and another hybrid strategy with opponent modeling. The brief information about those agents is given below:

- **Time-based strategies**: These strategies calculate a target utility considering the remaining time and generate an offer with that utility [7]. The agents adopt a function of normalized negotiation time to determine the utility of their coming offer. They tend to concede on their target utility over time. The main difference between the Conceder and Boulware agents is their concession curve. While the Conceder agent concedes quickly over time, the Boulware agent tends to concede only when the deadline is approaching.
- **Behaviour-based strategy**: The opponents that employ this strategy are expected to be opponent-aware and behave accordingly. The agents that adopt a behavior-based strategy mimic the behavior of the opponent. To do so, the agent calculates the utility difference between the opponent's two consecutive offers and applies the concession amount proportionally [7].
- **Hybrid strategy**: The agents employing the hybrid strategy make their decisions by considering both remaining time and the behaviors of the agent they negotiate with. The target utility is a linear combination of the target utilities calculated by time-based and behavior-based strategies as shown in Eq. 2 [11]. The principal intuition is that when time is not crucial (e.g., at the beginning of the negotiation), the agent pays more attention to its opponent's behavior while deciding on its next bid's target utility. As the deadline approaches, it tends to find an agreement urgently; therefore, it cares more about the remaining time. We use two versions of this agent with and without opponent modeling in our work.

$$TU_{Hybrid} = (t^2) \times TU_{Times} + (1 - t^2) \times TU_{Behavior} \qquad (2)$$

To assess the performance of the proposed approaches, we run negotiation tournaments with varying negotiation scenarios (i.e., domain with two preference profiles for bilateral negotiation). For this purpose, we selected nine negotiation domains available in the GeniusWeb negotiation platform. Table 2 shows the selected domain information of negotiation sessions that are used for training and testing purposes. In order to evaluate the effect of domain sizes, two large, two medium, and two small-sized domains have been selected for training sessions, whereas one domain for each size group has been selected for testing purposes. The baseline agent negotiates with all opponents for each domain and preference profile. The negotiations are repeated ten times for each negotiation configuration with a session deadline of three minutes. After completing the negotiation sessions with five opponents, two preference profiles, and six domains ten times, we obtained 600 different negotiation sessions for training purposes. Other than that, 60 negotiation sessions are collected for testing purposes after negotiating with five opponents, two profiles, and three different domains twice.

In addition to feeding all collected data into the models, the filtered sessions of the small, medium, and large domains have been trained separately. Therefore, collected negotiation sessions have been grouped by domain sizes before training models. When the training data becomes ready, training sessions for each objective have been conducted with prepared data sets.

Table 2. Domain details for both training and test data

	DomainID	Category	Issue & Value List	Bid Space	Opposition
Train	1	Small	[2, 3, 2, 2, 2, 3, 3]	432	0.189
	2	Small	[8, 2, 2, 8, 2]	512	0.096
	3	Medium	[5, 11, 8, 9]	3,960	0.260
	4	Medium	[17, 4, 5, 3, 2]	2,040	0.056
	5	Large	[26, 20, 8, 4]	16,640	0.281
	6	Large	[26, 22, 10, 8]	45,760	0.255
Test	7	Small	[2, 3, 2, 2, 11, 2]	528	0.080
	8	Medium	[4, 3, 2, 2, 5, 5, 3]	3,600	0.191
	9	Large	[26, 8, 26, 2]	10,816	0.280

5.2   Results

After training the neural networks (LSTM and Transformer) with 600 negotiation sessions with given configurations, we generate the predictions of the opponent's next-step utility values on the test data for all rounds after the fifth round. Predicted values are compared with the actual values by using two evaluation metrics; the root-mean-square error (RMSE) and the mean absolute percentage error (MAPE). Recall that we make predictions for 60 negotiation sessions in total. For the final results, we take the average of calculated RMSE and MAPE metrics. Additionally, we analyze the effect of the domain size per each objective. Remind that *Objective* 1 and *Objective* 2 have a shared target variable which is the agent's utility value of the opponent's next offer, whereas *Objective* 3 makes use of the same opponent-related input variables as *Objective* 2 during training. However, its target is to guess the opponent's utility. Therefore, the evaluations are formed with the consideration of these differences.

We first evaluate the performance of the predictions regarding to *Objective* 1 and *Objective* 2. Figure 5 shows the MAPE scores of each model on each domain size for both objectives. The blue bars show their prediction performance on all test scenarios. It can be said that the *Objective* 1 achieved prediction with 17% and 18% MAPE by Transformer and LSTM, respectively. Here, the performance of the Transformer is slightly better than the LSTM. Moreover, it is obvious that the prediction error decreases when the models consider the opponent-related features (i.e., estimated opponent's utility of its previous offers, their Nash distances, and estimated opponent moves described in Table 1). Therefore, we can say that *Objective* 2 is achieved.

To investigate the effect of the domain size on Transformer and LSTM models, we train separate predictors for different sized scenarios (i.e., small, medium, and large), which are shown by orange, grey, and yellow bars, respectively. We observed that predicting agents' utilities on large domains have the highest error rates regardless of the chosen model. This situation may mainly stem from the

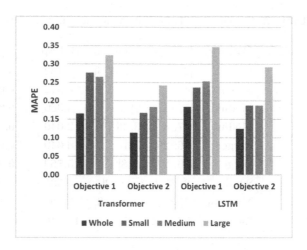

Fig. 5. Model comparison among different domain sizes for Objectives 1 & 2

high complexity of possible offer distributions in large negotiation domains. Compared to other domain sizes, a regular negotiation session in large domains covers a small portion of the bid space, which might decrease the model's generalization ability. On the other hand, the models trained with whole data show the best performances among others since they are introduced to more diverse examples in the training data. For more detailed analysis, Fig. 6 elaborately summarizes both MAPE and RMSE scores per each setting for *Objective* 1 and *Objective* 2. According to the RMSE and MAPE scores of *Objective* 1 and *Objective* 2, it can be observed that both metric scores of *Objective* 2 are lower than of *Objective* 1. This observation shows that both models are improved as they are enriched with additional opponent-related variables, as expected.

Domain	Model	MAPE		RMSE	
		OBJ 1	OBJ 2	OBJ 1	OBJ 2
Whole	Transformer	0.17	0.11	0.10	0.08
	LSTM	0.18	0.12	0.12	0.08
Small	Transformer	0.28	0.17	0.17	0.11
	LSTM	0.24	0.19	0.16	0.13
Medium	Transformer	0.26	0.18	0.13	0.11
	LSTM	0.25	0.19	0.13	0.11
Large	Transformer	0.32	0.24	0.16	0.13
	LSTM	0.35	0.29	0.22	0.18

Fig. 6. Model comparison among different domain sizes for Objectives 1 & 2

The evaluation of *Objectives* 1 and 2 is important to understand the opponent's attitude from the agent's utility change perspective. Besides, it is crucial to predict the opponent's utilities of their coming offers since most of the opponents generate their offers by considering their utility. Accordingly, *Objective* 3 aims to learn opponent's utility. Note that the agent does not know the opponent's utility function. Therefore, we first assess the predictor's performance by comparing the predictions with the estimated utilities by relying on the current opponent model. Then, we compare these predictions with actual utilities calculated by the opponent's utility function in the system. It is worth noting that these actual utilities are not accessible by the agent during the training process and the adopted opponent modeling approach may affect the performance of this comparison between predicted opponent utilities and the actual opponent utilities since the models are trained with the estimations. Implicitly, this comparison can give some insights about the performance of the opponent modeling technique employed by the agent.

Figure 7 compares the predictions with estimated and actual opponent utilities. For both models, the predictions have higher error rates when compared to the actual opponent utilities as expected. However, the performance of predicting the estimated values shows the positive impact of utilizing opponent-related inputs to predict opponent utility. Inherently, this shows that improving the employed opponent model's accuracy might help obtaining lower error rates while predicting actual opponent utilities, which can lead to an interesting research direction. In general, the performance of the LSTM models seems to be slightly better than Transformer in all domain categories except small domains.

Domain	Model	MAPE		RMSE	
		EST	REAL	EST	REAL
Whole	Transformer	0.12	0.22	0.14	0.19
	LSTM	0.11	0.19	0.12	0.17
Small	Transformer	0.08	0.20	0.08	0.15
	LSTM	0.11	0.27	0.11	0.17
Medium	Transformer	0.16	0.30	0.18	0.22
	LSTM	0.14	0.29	0.15	0.20
Large	Transformer	0.12	0.39	0.12	0.19
	LSTM	0.09	0.27	0.09	0.17

Fig. 7. Model comparison among different domain sizes for Objective 3 according to estimated & real values

We also analyze how well the general models work against different opponents as far as the different characteristics of the opponents are concerned. Figure 8 shows the error distribution of the general models among different opponent strategies regarding the *Objectives* 1 and 2. We might think that learning the utilities of the opponent's next offers would be easier when they employ a time-based concession strategy since they are generated through a function of normalized negotiation. However, the *Objectives* 1 and 2 aim to learn the agent's utility, not the opponent's utility. Therefore, there may not be a regular pattern as far as the agent's utility is concerned due to varying opposition of the domains as shown in Table 2. In other words, the received utilities by the agent may have some fluctuations. On the other hand, we expect behavior-based strategies to show a more regular pattern since they consider the other side's utilities. Therefore, the predictors' performance against such agents is lower than the behavior-based agents. The performance of the predictors is better for the *Objective* 2 because of considering opponent-related features. While the models perform best against behavior-based opponents, their performance drastically drops due to the stochastic behavior shown by the hybrid agents.

Opponent	Model	MAPE		RMSE	
		OBJ 1	OBJ 2	OBJ 1	OBJ 2
Whole	Transformer	0.22	0.15	0.14	0.10
	LSTM	0.21	0.15	0.13	0.10
Behavior Based	Transformer	0.21	0.17	0.14	0.12
	LSTM	0.19	0.16	0.13	0.11
Boulware	Transformer	0.29	0.18	0.15	0.10
	LSTM	0.29	0.19	0.15	0.10
Conceder	Transformer	0.29	0.21	0.15	0.12
	LSTM	0.28	0.21	0.15	0.12
HybridW	Transformer	0.27	0.25	0.18	0.17
	LSTM	0.25	0.23	0.17	0.16
HybridWO	Transformer	0.31	0.20	0.19	0.13
	LSTM	0.30	0.20	0.19	0.13

Fig. 8. Model comparison among different opponents for Objectives 1 & 2

Figure 9 shows the model comparison against each opponent strategy for *Objective* 3 and demonstrates the metrics for estimated and actual opponent utilities. In general, next-step utility predictions against Hybrid strategies demonstrate lower performance than time-based and behavior-based strategies, as expected, since they have higher complexity for involving time-based and behavior-based strategies. However, predictions against Hybrid strategies only perform better while comparing Objective 3 predictions with the real opponent utilities in terms of MAPE. This can stem from estimating the opponent's offers by the employed opponent model.

To sum up, it is observed that there is no significant difference between LSTM and Transformer results. RMSE and MAPE values were observed similarly for each objective, as shown in Fig. 10. The similarity of the model performances can also be interpreted by the prediction examples shown in Fig. 11. Although the models can be refined by adding more complexity and potentially achieving higher success, this study used basic architectures to focus on the prediction generalization capability on different domain sizes and employed opponent strategies.

		MAPE		RMSE	
Opponent	Model	EST	REAL	EST	REAL
Whole	Transformer	0.11	0.23	0.12	0.18
	LSTM	0.11	0.21	0.12	0.18
Behavior Based	Transformer	0.09	0.15	0.10	0.15
	LSTM	0.09	0.16	0.10	0.16
Boulware	Transformer	0.11	0.25	0.12	0.17
	LSTM	0.11	0.22	0.12	0.16
Conceder	Transformer	0.10	0.28	0.10	0.16
	LSTM	0.10	0.25	0.10	0.16
HybridW	Transformer	0.12	0.23	0.14	0.21
	LSTM	0.14	0.21	0.15	0.20
HybridWO	Transformer	0.12	0.19	0.13	0.17
	LSTM	0.12	0.19	0.14	0.18

Fig. 9. Model comparison among different opponents for Objective 3 according to estimated & real values

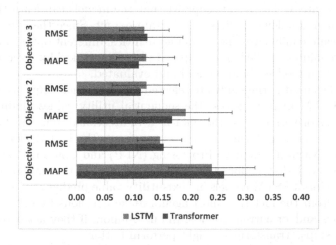

Fig. 10. Averaged RMSE and MAPE results models for different objectives

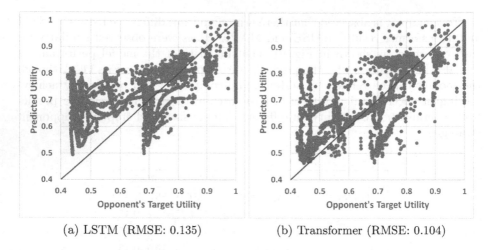

(a) LSTM (RMSE: 0.135)   (b) Transformer (RMSE: 0.104)

Fig. 11. Comparing predicted utilities in Objective 3 for a large domain

6 Conclusion

This study proposes time series predictive models, namely LSTM and Transformers, to guess the utility values of the opponent's coming offers during the bilateral negotiation. Three different objectives have been introduced with the motivation to foresee the utility of the opponent's next offer from the agent's and opponent's perspectives and investigate the effect of the opponent-related features. To assess the performance of the proposed approaches, we trained LSTM and Transformer models with data obtained from 600 negotiation sessions. The results are analyzed elaborately by considering the effect of domain size and the opponent's strategy. The results support that the models can learn the utilities of the opponent's following offers to a certain extent. Since the opponent modeling significantly influences the estimated utilities, different opponent modeling approaches could be applied and compared in future work. Moreover, other time series prediction models could be used and evaluated.

The models used in the study are selected based on their sequence processing behaviors. LSTM models process the sequential utility values unidirectionally, whereas Transformers process the data in a bidirectional manner. The bidirectional behavior of Transformer models outperforms the LSTM models in some tasks such as Natural Language Processing (NLP) and Computer Vision. However, we observed that it does not significantly exceed the unidirectional processing behavior of LSTM models in next-utility value predictions. The situation might stem from the fact that most agents make decisions by only considering their previous and/or current rounds. In our opinion, if they act by considering their future steps, Transformers might perform better.

References

1. Arslan, F., Aydogan, R.: An actor-critic reinforcement learning approach for bilateral negotiation. Turk. J. Electr. Eng. Comput. Sci. 1–20 (2022)
2. Aydoğan, R., et al.: Challenges and main results of the automated negotiating agents competition (ANAC) 2019. In: Bassiliades, N., Chalkiadakis, G., de Jonge, D. (eds.) EUMAS/AT -2020. LNCS (LNAI), vol. 12520, pp. 366–381. Springer, Cham (2020). https://doi.org/10.1007/978-3-030-66412-1_23
3. Aydoğan, R., Festen, D., Hindriks, K.V., Jonker, C.M.: Alternating offers protocols for multilateral negotiation. In: Fujita, K., et al. (eds.) Modern Approaches to Agent-based Complex Automated Negotiation. SCI, vol. 674, pp. 153–167. Springer, Cham (2017). https://doi.org/10.1007/978-3-319-51563-2_10
4. Baarslag, T., Hendrikx, M.J.C., Hindriks, K.V., Jonker, C.M.: Learning about the opponent in automated bilateral negotiation: a comprehensive survey of opponent modeling techniques. Auton. Agent. Multi-Agent Syst. 30(5), 849–898 (2015). https://doi.org/10.1007/s10458-015-9309-1
5. Chen, S., Ammar, H., Tuyls, K., Weiss, G.: Transfer learning for bilateral multi-issue negotiation. In: Proceedings of the BNAIC 2012, pp. 59–66 (2012)
6. Eran, C., Keskin, M.O., Cantürk, F., Aydoğan, R.: A decentralized token-based negotiation approach for multi-agent path finding. In: Rosenfeld, A., Talmon, N. (eds.) EUMAS 2021. LNCS (LNAI), vol. 12802, pp. 264–280. Springer, Cham (2021). https://doi.org/10.1007/978-3-030-82254-5_16
7. Faratin, P., Sierra, C., Jennings, N.R.: Negotiation decision functions for autonomous agents. Robot. Auton. Syst. 24(3), 159–182 (1998)
8. Fatima, S., Kraus, S., Wooldridge, M.: Principles of Automated Negotiation. Cambridge University Press, Cambridge (2014)
9. Hindriks, K., Jonker, C., Tykhonov, D.: Let's dans! an analytic framework of negotiation dynamics and strategies. Web Intell. Agent Syst. 9, 319–335 (2011)
10. Hochreiter, S., Schmidhuber, J.: Long short-term memory. Neural Computation (1997)
11. Keskin, M.O., Çakan, U., Aydoğan, R.: Solver agent: towards emotional and opponent-aware agent for human-robot negotiation. In: Proceedings of the AAMAS 2021, pp. 1557–1559. AAMAS 2021, International Foundation for Autonomous Agents and Multiagent Systems, Richland, SC (2021)
12. Li, M., Murukannaiah, P.K., Jonker, C.M.: A data-driven method for recognizing automated negotiation strategies. ArXiv abs/2107.01496 (2021)
13. Lin, R., Kraus, S., Baarslag, T., Tykhonov, D., Hindriks, K.V., Jonker, C.M.: Genius: an integrated environment for supporting the design of generic automated negotiators. Comput. Intell. 30(1), 48–70 (2014)
14. Marsa-Maestre, I., Klein, M., Jonker, C.M., Aydoğan, R.: From problems to protocols: towards a negotiation handbook. Decis. Support Syst. 60, 39–54 (2014)
15. Sanchez-Anguix, V., Tunali, O., Aydoğan, R., Julián, V.: Can social agents efficiently perform in automated negotiation. Appl. Sci. 11(13), 6022 (2021)
16. Sengupta, A., Mohammad, Y., Nakadai, S.: An autonomous negotiating agent framework with reinforcement learning based strategies and adaptive strategy switching mechanism. CoRR abs/2102.03588 (2021)
17. Tunalı, O., Aydoğan, R., Sanchez-Anguix, V.: Rethinking frequency opponent modeling in automated negotiation. In: An, B., Bazzan, A., Leite, J., Villata, S., van der Torre, L. (eds.) PRIMA 2017. LNCS (LNAI), vol. 10621, pp. 263–279. Springer, Cham (2017). https://doi.org/10.1007/978-3-319-69131-2_16

18. Vaswani, A., et al.: Attention is all you need. CoRR abs/1706.03762 (2017)
19. Williams, C.R., Robu, V., Gerding, E.H., Jennings, N.R.: Using gaussian processes to optimise concession in complex negotiations against unknown opponents. In: Proceedings of the 22nd International Joint Conference on Artificial Intelligence, 15–21 July 2011, pp. 432–438 (2011)
20. Wu, N., Green, B., Ben, X., O'Banion, S.: Deep transformer models for time series forecasting: the influenza prevalence case. CoRR (2020)
21. Zeng, A., Chen, M., Zhang, L., Xu, Q.: Are transformers effective for time series forecasting? (2022)

An MCTS-Based Algorithm to Solve Sequential CFGs on Valuation Structures

Tabajara Krausburg[1]([⊠])[iD], Jürgen Dix[1][iD], and Rafael H. Bordini[2][iD]

[1] Department of Informatics, TUC, Clausthal-Zellerfeld, Germany
{tkr19,dix}@tu-clausthal.de
[2] School of Technology, PUCRS, Porto Alegre, Brazil
rafael.bordini@pucrs.br

Abstract. In recent work, a generalised form of characteristic function games has been introduced, where certain sequences of coalition structures (and not a single one) are considered as solutions. Such games have later been extended to allow valuation structures to be used to restrict the allowed solutions for each game in the sequence; the resulting game is called SEQVS. This paper introduces an algorithm to solve instances of SEQVS based on Monte Carlo Tree Search. We experimentally evaluate the algorithm by comparing its performance against a heuristic algorithm appearing in the literature. We show that in settings containing many constraints, our algorithm outperforms the existing heuristic approach.

Keywords: Sequential CFGs · Valuation Str. · Monte Carlo Tree Search

1 Introduction

There is a lot of work on cooperative game theory [16,18], in particular on the Coalition-Structure Generation (CSG) problem [7,12,14]. However, most of the research is theoretical. Inspired by a practical disaster-rescue scenario, a new problem in Characteristic-Function Games (CFG) was introduced in [9]. It was noted that, in some scenarios, there are repeated episodes of coalition formation, and the choice of coalition structure in one episode affects the subsequent ones. The notion of a Sequential Characteristic-Function Game (SCFG) was defined, a game where there are h different CFGs that need to be solved in accordance with a binary relation that determines whether a particular coalition structure can follow another in the sequence.

Solving an instance of the SCFG game requires finding an optimal Feasible Coalition-Structure Sequence (FCSS), which typically does not equate to finding the individually optimal coalition structure for each CFG because of the relation constraining the allowed solution sequences. SCFG was then extended to SEQVS [10], where Valuation Structures (VS) [7] are used to further constrain the coalition structures that can be generated at each level of a sequence (see Sect. 2 for the motivation of this extension).

In this paper, we introduce a new algorithm for SEQVS called UCT-Seq. The algorithm is based on a Monte Carlo Tree Search (MCTS) technique and explores the generation of pairs of coalition structures. We propose a general procedure to generate coalition structures by exploiting the available valuation structures. In doing so, we assume that the binary relation is given as a procedure that checks whether a pair is in the relation or not. We have run many experiments to evaluate the performance of our algorithm with MC-Link [10] for both small instances (to compare them with optimal solutions) and large instances (up to 50 agents in the experiments reported here). Our main finding is that our algorithm performs better than the existing heuristic algorithm when there is a high number of constraints that the sequence of CFGs needs to satisfy.

The remainder of the paper is structured as follows. In Sect. 2, we introduce a running example to motivate our approach. We also state the background for the games we use throughout this work and discuss related work. Section 3 introduces our main contribution, our MCTS-based approach. In Sect. 4, we extensively experiment with UCT-Seq and two existing algorithms that solve SEQVS problems. We discuss the results of our algorithm in Sect. 4.4. Finally, we conclude and point out future work in Sect. 5.

2 Motivation and Background

Example 1 (Disaster response operation). We consider a disaster response operation in which 28 personnel (i.e., responders) participate and form a hierarchy as depicted in Fig. 1. This forms a chain of command which is a key part of the ICS framework [6] and makes sure each personnel has a single person to report to. A *superior*, responsible for supervising a set of personnel, is shown at the uppermost position within a circle, which stands for a coalition. The hierarchy is represented as a sequence of coalition structures. Even though each personnel has a single superior, one may interpret a coalition of upper levels as the set of agents affected by the decisions made by that coalition superior. A superior at an upper level remains in a singleton coalition in the remaining levels to show it does not directly contribute to any coalition at it. Here, only 28 agents are required. Depending on the magnitude of a disaster incident, that number could easily pass hundreds of personnel.

To avoid overwhelming superiors, a **span of control** [6, Section III.A] is defined: It establishes the maximum number of subordinate units a superior can manage (it is three in Fig. 1). The resulting hierarchy must not violate that constraint.

How to model a span of control? In the last hierarchical level, the answer is trivial: a coalition must have at most the span of control plus one (the superior) agents. In the remaining levels, we need to consider how we organize those coalitions. Addressing a single level at a time might lead to suboptimal solutions.

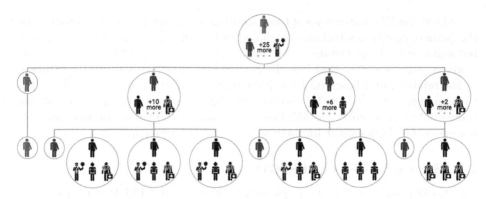

Fig. 1. Three-level hierarchy for a disaster response operation represented as a *sequence* of coalition structures (one per level). The uppermost responder in each circle represents a superior of the corresponding coalition.

Even worse, depending on how we model the problem, the resulting hierarchy might not follow the defined span of control at all. By modelling each hierarchical level as a coalition structure, one can see that individually feasible coalition structures might be incompatible when observing a span of control.

A SCFG allows us to model the span of control by determining which coalition structures may follow the preceding one in the sequence. It was later used as the basis for SEQVS [10], an extension of SCFG where Valuation Structures (VS) [7] are used to further constrain the coalition structures that can be generated at each level of a sequence. According to that definition, each of the h CFGs of a sequence has its own valuation structure establishing constraints on the coalitions allowed to form: This greatly facilitates the modelling of SCFGs for real-world problems.

Example 2 (Disaster response operation: Adding valuation structures). We extend our disaster example above. A superior usually commands at a single given hierarchical level. For instance, a superior at the last hierarchical level is not superior at the top level. At the top level stays the command centre which needs to manage the entire disaster response operation. Then, we need a way to model different superiors at different levels. Moreover, superiors of the same level must stay in different coalitions. A valuation structure introduces the concept of *pivotal agents*, which are supposed to stay in different coalitions.

To avoid exhaustively enumerating all possible combinations of pairs of coalition structures compatible with one another in a binary relation, it is a common practice to assume it is given in an algorithmic form that either generates those pairs or checks the compatibility of any two coalition structures. To the best of our knowledge, there exist only two algorithms that solve SCFG-based problems: (i) an exact dynamic-programming algorithm for SEQVS [10], and (ii) a heuristic approach based on hierarchical clustering (called MC-Link) [9].

Algorithm (i) computes an optimal solution assuming a procedure to generate the pairs of coalition structures contained in the binary relation and therefore is not suitable for large instances. Algorithm (ii) assumes that the binary relation is given as a procedure that can check whether a pair of coalition structures is in the relation, and based on that, it computes a solution for the problem. It is then further extended in [10] to deal with SEQVS problems, however, it was shown in the same work that MC-Link is not complete. That is, for some solvable instances, MC-Link cannot find any solution for the problem.

2.1 Sequential CFGs and SEQVS

An SCFG is built on top of a sequence of CFGs [9]. A CFG Γ is a tuple $\langle A, v \rangle$ where A is a set of agents and v is a valuation function assigning to each coalition a value, $2^A \to \mathbb{R}$. The solution concept is a Coalition Structure (CS) which is a partition of A and we use $\mathbf{CS}^A$ to denote the set of all CSs. Then, an SCFG is a tuple $\langle A, \mathcal{H}, \mathcal{R} \rangle$, where $A = \{a_1, \ldots, a_n\}$ is a set of agents, $\mathcal{H} = \langle \Gamma_1, \ldots, \Gamma_h \rangle$ is an ordered set of CFGs, and $\mathcal{R} \subset \mathbf{CS}^A \times \mathbf{CS}^A$. The main point is that all games in $\mathcal{H}$ are played by the same set of agents A and we aim to form a *feasible coalition-structure sequence* $\mathbf{CS} = \langle CS_1, \ldots, CS_h \rangle$ such that $CS_i \, \mathcal{R} \, CS_{i+1} : 1 \leq i < h$. In doing so, $\mathcal{R}$ determines the constraints to be observed to compute a solution for the interdependent games in $\mathcal{H}$. Note that each CS CS_i is a solution for the corresponding CFG $\Gamma_i \in \mathcal{H}$.

Given the fact that all contiguous pairs of CSs in an FCSS must be in $\mathcal{R}$, the authors in [10] proposed the integration of SCFG and Valuation Structures (VS) [7] to model constraints that are specific to each particular CFG. As introduced in [10], a VS σ induced over a CFG Γ, denoted Γ^σ, is a tuple $\sigma = \langle G, S \rangle$, where G is an interaction graph $(A, E) : E \subseteq A \times A$ and S is a set of pivotal agents $S \subseteq A$.

A VS has specific semantics: coalition C is allowed to form if (i) the induced sub-graph of C over G is connected, and (ii) $|C \cap S| \leq 1$. We use $\mathcal{C}^\sigma$ to refer to the set of all coalitions allowed by VS σ. We now define a SEQVS.

Definition 1 (Sequential CFGs induced by VSs [10]). *A sequential CFG induced by a sequence of VSs is a tuple $\mathcal{G} = \langle A, \mathcal{H}, \Pi, \mathcal{R} \rangle$, where:*

- *A is a set of agents;*
- *$\mathcal{H}$ is a totally ordered set $\Gamma_1 = \langle A, v_1 \rangle, \ldots, \Gamma_h = \langle A, v_h \rangle$ of CFGs;*
- *Π is a totally ordered set $\sigma_1 = \langle G_1, S_1 \rangle, \ldots, \sigma_h = \langle G_h, S_h \rangle$ of VSs;*
- *$\mathcal{R} \subset (\mathbf{CS}^A \cup \{\varnothing\}) \times \mathbf{CS}^A$: $\varnothing$ is a dummy to specify via "$\varnothing \, \mathcal{R} \, CS_1$" the first entry.*

This tuple determines the sequence $\boldsymbol{\Gamma} = \langle \Gamma_1^{\sigma_1}, \ldots, \Gamma_h^{\sigma_h} \rangle$ of CFGs induced by VSs, with $\Gamma_i = \langle A, v_i \rangle$ and $\sigma_i = \langle G_i, S_i \rangle$, where v_i are characteristic functions and $\sigma_i \in \Pi$, for $i = 1, \ldots, h$.

In Example 2, as mentioned above, the valuation structures are used to formulate constraints (the pivotal agents in Fig 1: red agents and superiors at the top of each coalition), and the coalition structures correspond to the levels in the hierarchy. The solution concept for such a game is defined as follows.

Definition 2 (SEQVS optimisation problem, solution FCSS). *Given a sequence* $\boldsymbol{CS} = \langle CS_1, \ldots, CS_h \rangle$ *of coalition structures from* $\boldsymbol{CS}^A$, $\boldsymbol{CS}$ *is a potential solution for* $\langle \Gamma_1^{\sigma_1}, \ldots, \Gamma_h^{\sigma_h} \rangle$ *if:*

(i) each CS_i is a solution of $\Gamma_i^{\sigma_i}$;
(ii) $\varnothing \, \mathcal{R} \, CS_1$; and
(iii) it follows the relation $\mathcal{R}$: $CS_i \, \mathcal{R} \, CS_{i+1}$, $1 \leq i < h$.

Such a sequence is called a Feasible Coalition-Structure Sequence (FCSS). A solution for a SEQVS game instance is an optimal FCSS $\boldsymbol{CS}^*$ with

$$\boldsymbol{CS}^* = \arg\max_{\boldsymbol{CS}} \mathcal{V}(\boldsymbol{CS}),$$

where the function $\mathcal{V}$ is defined by $\mathcal{V}(\boldsymbol{CS}) = \sum_{i=1}^{h} V_i(CS_i)$ with $V_i(CS_i) = \sum_{C \in CS_i} v_i(C)$ (for a given FCSS $\boldsymbol{CS}$).

In Example 2, the relation $\mathcal{R}$ makes sure that only those sequences of coalition structures are considered that are compatible with it.

2.2 Monte Carlo Tree Search (MCTS) Method

In the MCTS method [3], one iteratively builds a tree in which each node in the tree is one of the possible states of the problem. A transition from the current node to one of its child nodes is given by an action being carried out at that state. Given this method, an MCTS-based algorithm implements four main steps: (i) recursively *select* child nodes until a terminal or not fully expanded node is reached; (ii) *expand* the tree with a child node of the selected node; (iii) *simulate* (aka play-out or roll-out) how promising a subtree rooting at the added node is by reaching a terminal state; and (iv) *backpropagate* statistical results throughout the path that led to the simulated node.

The select and expand steps constitute the *tree policy* whilst the simulation step is called *default policy*. A standard algorithm for MCTS is called UTC [8] and applies the UCB1 heuristics to select a node among the child nodes addressing the problem of exploring and exploiting paths in the tree. As in MCTS one deals with intractable search spaces, the four steps above are repeated until a halting criterion is met; usually a time budget or a number of iterations. To return a solution for the problem, different strategies might be employed, for instance, one may choose the most visited child node of the root (see [3]).

2.3 Related Work

To the best of our knowledge, our work on the SCFG problem is original. Only two algorithms are available in the literature. MC-Link [9] is a clustering-based algorithm inspired by C-Link [5] to solve SCFG instances. It starts off with a sequence of coalition structures of singletons and merges two coalitions based on the numeric gain of the merger. No merger can be undone. Moreover, the resulting coalition must be feasible according to $\mathcal{R}$ and given the current preceding

CS in the sequence. The algorithm stops either when there is no gain in merging coalitions, or all mergers are constrained. Another algorithm is called SDP and is based on dynamic programming to compute an optimal solution for SEQVS instances [10]. In their experiments, the authors further extended MC-Link to cope with SEQVS problems as well.

MCTS has recently been investigated to solve the coalition structure generation problem (i.e., a single CFG). In [19], the authors proposed the CSG-UCT algorithm, which is based on UCT [8]: each node in the tree corresponds to a CS $CS \in \mathcal{CS}^A$. The root node is the CS containing only singleton coalitions. The set of actions available at each node contains all pairwise union operations that can be performed on the corresponding CS. For instance, the CS $\{\{a_1\}, \{a_2\}, \{a_3\}\}$ has the child nodes $\{\{a_1, a_2\}, \{a_3\}\}$, $\{\{a_1, a_3\}, \{a_2\}\}$, and $\{\{a_1\}, \{a_2, a_3\}\}$. To select a node, the authors apply the UCB1 heuristics, where the exploitation component is the maximum value found for a node in the corresponding subtree. A roll-out consists in merging two coalitions that result in the greatest gain until the CS of the grand coalition is found. Once the iteration budget is out, one performs a best-first search to retrieve the best solution.

MCTS is also applied to a similar problem in which each coalition is allocated to a task in an *ordered coalition structure* [13]. Given a vector of m tasks, one aims to form an ordered partition of A of size m, so that each task is assigned to at most one coalition. An MCTS search is conducted over one agent at a time, choosing a position in the CS where to place it. Therefore, a node is a composition of agents already allocated to coalitions and a permutation of the remaining agents to the m positions. To define a priority among child nodes, the authors add a third component to UCB1 representing a possible derivation of the child node.

3   A Monte-Carlo Approach to SEQVS

We introduce a general MCTS approach to solve the problem of finding a sequence of coalition structures based on UTC [8]. In this formulation, it is not a single node that is seen as a solution to the SCFG problem, instead, each node represents a single CS. Thus, we are interested in finding a path in the tree that reaches level h. This path corresponds to an FCSS. A node x in the tree looks as follows: $x = \langle parent, CS, l, children, N, val, expanded, terminal, i \rangle$, where:

- x.*parent* is a pointer to the parent node;
- x.*CS* is from $\mathcal{CS}^A \cup \{\varnothing\}$;
- x.*l* is the level where x is placed in the tree;
- x.*children* is a finite list of child nodes;
- x.*N* $\in \mathbb{Z}^+$ is a counter of visits to the node;
- x.*val* $\in \mathbb{R}$ is the cumulative reward of the node;
- x.*expanded* is a Boolean variable to denote if x has been fully expanded;
- x.*terminal* is a Boolean variable stating whether the node is terminal; and
- x.*i* is an index with the specific purpose explained below.

Alternatively, we use y and z to refer to nodes as well. Moreover, we use $X^{CS} = \{CS' \in \boldsymbol{CS}^A \mid CS\,\mathcal{R}\,CS'\}$ and $X_l^{CS} = \{CS' \in X^{CS} \mid CS' \subseteq \boldsymbol{C}^{\sigma_l}\}$.

The Boolean variable x.*expanded* is true when the whole set $X_{x.l}^{x.CS}$ has been added to the x.*children*. The Boolean variable x.*terminal* is set to true either if: (i) x.$l = h$; or (ii) x.*expanded* $\wedge$ |x.*children*| $= 0$. The last attribute x.i is used to retrieve a CS from a list that corresponds to $X^{x.CS}$: during the search we construct the set X^{CS} based only on $\mathcal{R}$. Each node at a different level filters out incompatible CSs given the VS constraints of the subsequent level.

3.1   Constructing the Tree

At the beginning of the execution, the tree contains only node root where root.$CS = \varnothing$. To select a node, we apply a tree policy that returns a node. To select an action (i.e., a transition from one CS to another) that can be applied at that particular state, we assume a generative algorithm $gen(CS)$ to generate compatible CSs. If it is efficient, then $\{CS' : CS'$ generated by $gen(x.CS)\} = X^{x.CS}$. But we also investigate procedures that can deal with any $\mathcal{R}$ by generating many more CSs than needed, thus $\{CS' : CS'$ generated by $gen(x.CS)\} \supseteq X^{x.CS}$. Such a procedure, for instance, can generate the set $\boldsymbol{CS}^A$. We discuss the generation of CSs in Sect. 3.2. Doing so, we construct $X^{x.CS}$ on the fly and use a list $Act[x.CS]$ to store the compatible CSs.

As the set $X^{x.CS}$ may be very large, we apply a progressive widening mechanism. In particular, we follow [11] and use the heuristics in Eq. 1 in order to expand the list of child nodes of a non-terminal node x:

$$\lfloor x.N^\alpha \rfloor \geq |x.children| \tag{1}$$

where $\alpha \in [0, 1]$ is an expansion factor. If the above condition holds, then we retrieve a CS from $Act[x.CS][x.i]$. In case a node x has already added all CSs from that list as its child nodes, we call the generative algorithm. To select a node from the current node x, we execute Eq. 2 on its list of child nodes.

$$y = \arg \max_{z \in x.children} \mathrm{UCB1}(z) \tag{2}$$

We use heuristics UCB1 [1] to establish a priority among the current child nodes. This heuristics is given in Eq. 3,

$$\mathrm{UCB1}(z) = \frac{z.val}{z.N} + c\sqrt{\frac{\log z.parent.N}{z.N}} \tag{3}$$

where c is an *exploration factor* set to the standard value $\sqrt{2}$ [4]. If Eq. 2 does not have a unique solution, we randomly select a node among the options.

Once a node has been selected to be simulated, we estimate how good its subtree can be by carrying out the *default policy*. This is another challenging part of the problem as we do not know which actions can be carried out at the selected node. We perform a depth-first search to try to reach an end of a sequence (that is, a coalition structure at level h). Our approach generates a baseline coalition structure by performing *split* operations on the simulated CS. A split operation divides a coalition into two or more subsets. From this baseline CS, we start carrying out *merger* operations. A single merger operation merges two coalitions. We discuss how we apply those operations in Sect. 3.3. However, the above heuristics is neither guaranteed to find a subsequent CS nor to reach the end of a sequence. Therefore, we assume as input: (i) a maximum number of attempts $\bar{b}$ to generate CSs at each level; and (ii) a maximum relative depth $\bar{d}$ to simulate in the subtree.

The last step is to update the tree statistics according to the new simulated node (and its subtree). Usually, x.val is a cumulative value of all rewards collected up to that point, averaged by the number of visits on the given node [3]. We update the cumulative rewards of the nodes throughout the path with the value generated by the roll-out. In case a selected node has already been simulated (e.g., no action available in the selected path), we return a reward of 0. In doing so, nodes in which it is difficult to find actions (i.e., compatible coalition structures) gradually decrease their priority in Eq. 3. All that is left to do at this stage is to update the visited nodes' counters.

In case the selected node is a terminal node at level h, we are in a position to evaluate an FCSS. Recall that each path *path* reaching level h in the tree corresponds to an FCSS. At this point, if it leads to the best solution found so far, then we store it, otherwise, we continue the search. Otherwise, we remove it from the tree so as not to bias the search toward it.

3.2 The Generation of Coalition Structures

We remind the reader that our problem of finding a sequence of coalition structures is to find a path in the tree introduced in the previous section, where each node represents a single CS.

An important part of the general MCTS method is to select an *action* to be applied to a state and expand the tree. If the set of actions is small, one can select an action based on some distribution. For instance, in Go, one has approximately 250 actions available at each state [17]. In a continuous-action space, for instance, in [11], an action is sampled from a computed policy network (the same policy is used during a roll-out). *How are we using* MCTS *and which actions are appropriate for our purpose?* Note that each node corresponds to a CS, and this CS might be represented as a graph over its coalitions: we make sure (in the following two definitions) that an edge connecting any two coalitions is coloured either green or red.

To generate a new node, one green edge in the parent node is chosen to be contracted, i.e. *two coalitions are merged*. After merging the coalitions, a new graph (i.e., a tree node) is generated, and the contracted edge is coloured red at the parent graph. This algorithm is inspired by CFSS [2] (see Fig. 2 and the discussion after Definition 4). CFSS continues merging green edges until only reds are available in the entire tree. That means all feasible coalition structures have been evaluated.

Selecting an action in the general MCTS is thus *choosing a green edge*. Although our set of actions is finite, it is intractably large, namely of size $\Omega(n^{\frac{n}{2}})$.

Definition 3 (2-coloured graph G^cinduced by Γ^σ). *Given a CFG $\Gamma = \langle A, v \rangle$ induced by an VS $\sigma = \langle G, S \rangle$, where $G = \langle A, E' \rangle$, we define a 2-coloured graph G^{Γ^σ}induced by Γ^σ as a tuple $\langle V, E, c, gain \rangle$ with:*

- $V \subseteq 2^A$, $\{a\} \in V$ *for all* $a \in A$;
- $E \subseteq 2^A \times 2^A$, $(\{u\}, \{r\}) \in E$ *for all* $(u, r) \in E'$;
- c *is a function* $E \to \{green, red\}$; *and*
- $gain : 2^A \times 2^A \to \mathbb{R}$; $(C_i, C_j) \mapsto v(C_i \cup C_j) - v(C_i) - v(C_j)$.

During the process just described (more formally in the next definition), V, E, and c are constructed incrementally (with the minimal requirements for V and E as stated). Function *gain* is used to govern this construction.

To colour an edge, we first check the VS constraints. Given an edge $e = (u, r)$, if $u \cup r \notin \mathcal{C}^\sigma$, then $c(e) = red$. The remaining edges are initially coloured green. We follow a similar procedure introduced in [2, Definition 3] to contract a green edge. Their definition is adapted to our context and introduced below.

Definition 4 (Green edge contraction). *Given a 2-coloured graph $G^{\Gamma^\sigma} = \langle V, E, c, gain \rangle$ and a green edge $e = (u, r)$, where $e \in E$, the result of the contraction of edge e is a graph $G^{\Gamma^{\sigma'}}$ obtained by performing the contraction of the edge e in graph G^{Γ^σ}. Whenever two parallel edges are merged into a single one, the resulting edge is coloured red either if at least one of them is red-coloured or the resulting coalition $u \cup r \notin \mathcal{C}^\sigma$. It is coloured green otherwise.*

Let CS^e be the coalition structure represented by graph $G^{\Gamma^{\sigma'}}$ after the contraction of edge e in G^{Γ^σ}. Then, given the previous CS CS in the sequence, we construct $\bar{E} = \{e \in E \mid c(e) = green, CS^e \in \mathcal{CS}^\sigma, (CS, CS^e) \in \mathcal{R}\}$, the set of all edges that result in a CS compatible with CS. We select first an edge with $\arg\max_{e \in \bar{E}} w(e)$ for contraction. Then, the generator is suspended and UCT-Seq continues the search having CS^e as a child node. In case $\bar{E} = \emptyset$, the generator selects an edge $\arg\max_{e \in E} w(e)$. It then attempts to find an edge $e \in \bar{E}$ up to 5 times. After that, it hands over the algorithm execution back to MCTS, which will decide the next step of the execution.

Consider again Example 2. We depict a possible modelling of the VS of the second game in Fig. 2. Moreover, the procedure explained above is generating coalition structures for the preceding CS containing only the grand coalition. To improve readability, we omit the values computed for the edges. The dashed lines coloured green mean a feasible merger between two coalitions, which does not lead to a feasible coalition structure according to $\mathcal{R}$ yet. On the other hand, the solid green lines indicate a compatible coalition structure will be generated.

To speed up the search, we keep in memory a list of CSs compatible with x.CS (i.e., the CS represented by node x) regardless of the level in which x is in the tree. Let $Act[CS]$ be a such list. Once $gen(CS)$ terminates, then $Act[CS] \supseteq X_l^{CS}$.

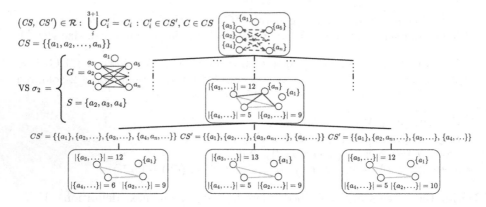

Fig. 2. The generation of coalition structures in Example 2.

3.3 Simulation of a Sequence of CSs

The generator discussed above addresses a single level of the sequence. In a simulation, one is interested in quickly reaching a terminal state, which, for an SCFG problem, is a CS at level h. A standard approach for this is to select actions randomly at each level of the simulated subtree [3]. One can also perform an informed search to reach a terminal node [19]. In our case, we do not know beforehand which actions are applicable at the node of interest. By employing an informed search, it is not guaranteed that the procedure will reach a terminal state. In fact, the values assigned to coalitions might not be related to the constraints posed by $\mathcal{R}$ and the VSs. That means well-evaluated coalitions might lead to dead ends in a sequence of CSs.

In a simulation, we conduct a series of split and merger operations on the CS CS of the newly expanded node. The split operations are first based on: (i) the VS constraints of the subsequent level $l+1$; then on (ii) random operations. Given a coalition C, if $|C \cap S_{l+1}| > 1$, then we split the pivotal agents into singleton coalitions. Let $\widehat{CS}$ be a set of coalitions containing initially only singletons of pivotal agents. For each remaining agent $a \in C \setminus S_{l+1}$, we decide whether to include it in a coalition $C \in \widehat{CS}$ (iff $C \cup \{a\} \in \mathcal{C}^{\sigma_{l+1}}$) or keep it in a singleton $\{a\} \in \widehat{CS}$ with a probability of 50%. In case $|C \cap S_{l+1}| \leq 1$, the disconnected components of C induced over G_{l+1} become new coalitions and we let any agent $a \in C$ form a singleton coalition with a probability of 50%.

The procedure described above produces a single coalition structure. We now merge two coalitions $C, C' \in CS'$ iff $C \cup C' \in \mathcal{CS}^{\sigma_{l+1}}$ with a probability of 50%. In case a merger is feasible, i.e., allowed by $\mathcal{R}$, $(CS_l, CS') \in \mathcal{R}$, then we return CS' and repeat the procedure until we reach the maximum depth in a simulation; otherwise, we try other mergers until no further mergers are possible. Additionally, as CS' is compatible with CS_l, we add it to the list $Act[CS_l]$. In doing so, two distinct local searches contribute to constructing the set X^{CS}, namely the generator and the simulation.

4   Experiments

We compare UCT-Seq with MC-Link using also SDP [10] as a reference. For small instances, we compare the quality of the solutions with an optimal FCSS computed by SDP. We then increase the size of the set of agents and compare the performance of UCT-Seq with MC-Link in more challenging instances.

4.1   Metrics AOR and QIR

To compare the algorithms, we pick valuation functions available in the CSG literature [12]: Modified Uniform, Modified Normal, and NDCS. We shall use two metrics to evaluate the quality of an outcome. The first one (Definition 5) computes the distance of a sub-optimal solution to the one computed by SDP. When computing an optimal solution is not possible, we compute the distance between the solutions outputted by the heuristic algorithms (Definition 6).

Definition 5 (Averaged Optimal Ratio (AOR)). *Given an FCSS CS computed by either MC-Link or UCT-Seq, and an optimal solution CS^* computed by SDP, the AOR metric is calculated as follows:* $\frac{\mathcal{V}(CS)}{\mathcal{V}(CS^*)}$.

Definition 6 (Quality Improvement Ratio (QIR)). *Given an FCSS CS computed by MC-Link and an FCSS CS' computed by UCT-Seq, the QIR is computed as follows:* $\frac{\mathcal{V}(CS')}{\mathcal{V}(CS)} - 1$.

Regarding the VS constraints, an edge in an interaction graph connects any two agents if $p \leq 60$ where $p \sim U(0, 100)$. We randomly pick q agents and insert them into the corresponding set of pivotal agents, where $q \sim U(0, \lceil n \times 0.2 \rceil)$. We use $n \times 0.2$ to avoid picking up all agents from A. Out of the four binary relations used in the experiments with SDP [10], we chose to evaluate the worst-case relation and the one that enforces a hierarchy of agents:

$\mathcal{R}_1$: $(CS, CS') \in \mathcal{R}_1$ iff $CS \neq CS'$; and
$\mathcal{R}_3$: $(CS, CS') \in \mathcal{R}_3$ iff $\forall\, C' \in CS' \,\exists\, C \in CS$ st $C' \subseteq C$ and $|CS| < |CS'|$.

The heuristic algorithms, i.e., MC-Link and UCT-Seq, make use of algorithms to check if a pair of CSs are compatible. On the other hand, SDP uses a generative algorithm for each $\mathcal{R}$ of interest. All algorithms are implemented in Python 3.8.10. We conduct all experiments in a machine with 32 GB of RAM and a CPU with four single cores of 3400 MHz MHz each.

4.2   Approximation of the Optimal Value

We compare how close the solutions computed by MC-Link and UCT-Seq are to the optimal one found by SDP. For $\mathcal{R}_1$, we experiment with $n = 3, \ldots, 7$ and 10 CFGs. For $\mathcal{R}_3$, we use $n = 5, \ldots, 10$ and 4 CFGs. Note that we need at least five agents to form a four-level hierarchy. Before each experiment, we

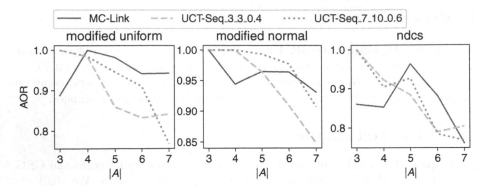

Fig. 3. Comparison of MC-Link and UCT-Seq solution quality ($h = 10$, $\mathcal{R} = \mathcal{R}_1$).

draw, for each game $\Gamma \in \mathcal{H}$, a value for each coalition $C \in 2^A$ and store it in a table. We always generate a new set of VS constraints in each experiment. For UCT-Seq, we experiment with the simulation depth and degree, as well as the exploration factor. To improve readability, we select only two configurations that obtained dissimilar results in the corresponding set of experiments to depict in the charts; they have the form UCT-Seq_DEGREE_DEPTH_FACTOR. Moreover, we let UCT-Seq run for 60 s in each instance.

We report in Fig. 3 the results when $h = 10$ and $\mathcal{R} = \mathcal{R}_1$. In general, UCT-Seq achieves results that are slightly inferior to the ones produced by MC-Link. Both algorithms in all distributions tend to have a negative steepness as we increase the number of agents, which indicates they will have poor performance in larger instances. Moreover, small values of UCT-Seq parameters seem to lead to better quality solutions. This is particularly the case for the exploration factor, as in $\mathcal{R}_1$ there exist many FCSSs.

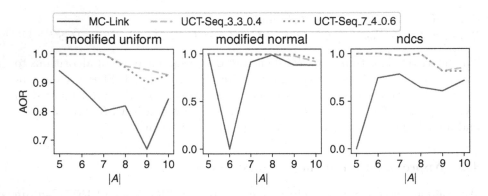

Fig. 4. Comparison of MC-Link and UCT-Seq solution quality ($h = 4$, $\mathcal{R} = \mathcal{R}_3$).

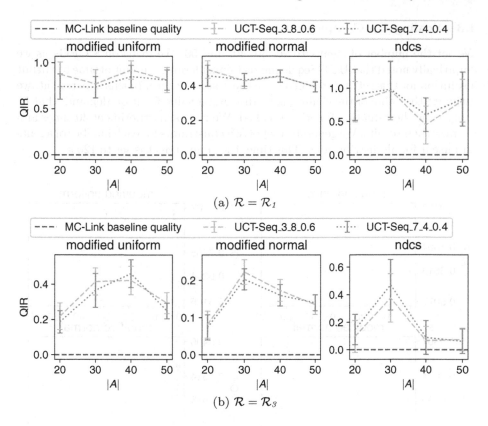

Fig. 5. Comparison of MC-Link and UCT-Seq performance (8 CFGs).

What about running times? For UCT-Seq, we look at each instance individually and depict the amount of time required by MC-Link to output a solution (solid circle in the charts), then we compare it with UCT-Seq. In Fig. 6a we depict the results when $n = 7$. We see that, in general, MC-Link is faster to compute a solution of better quality than the ones produced by UCT-Seq in that same amount of time. Similar running times for an approximate solution quality occur only for instances in which the coalition values were drawn from the NDCS distribution, which is known for producing an unbiased search space.

We now consider relation $\mathcal{R}_3$, which significantly reduces the search space. We depict in Fig. 4 the results when $h = 4$. One can see that the performance of UCT-Seq improves in the experiments conducted with $\mathcal{R}_1$. In fact, UCT-Seq, in general, outperforms MC-Link in the long term and also in the solution reached after a similar amount of time (see Fig. 6b). Moreover, in some cases ($n = 6$ and $n = 5$) MC-Link cannot find a solution for the problem at all.

4.3   Scaling Up Comparison

We set the number of agents to 20, 30, 40, and 50. We focus on 8 CFGs as we empirically noted that UCT-Seq demands a considerable amount of time to output a solution for this setting (we introduce the results below). In this experiment, we estimate the value of the coalitions by drawing a value for it on demand, that is, every time the valuation function is called. We run each experiment 30 times and average their results. We generate a set of VS constraints for each number of agents and use it for all distributions. This time, the time budget is set to 120 s.

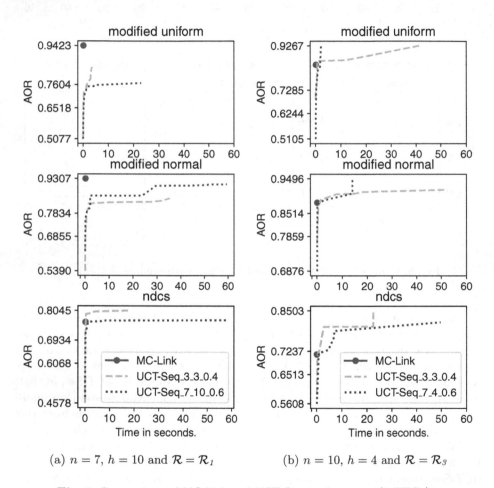

(a) $n = 7$, $h = 10$ and $\mathcal{R} = \mathcal{R}_1$ (b) $n = 10$, $h = 4$ and $\mathcal{R} = \mathcal{R}_3$

Fig. 6. Comparison of MC-Link and UCT-Seq performance (4 CFGs).

We depict the results in Fig. 5. The error bars in the charts stand for a confidence interval of 95% on the 30 solutions calculated based on the t distribution. UCT-Seq computes solutions of better quality for $\mathcal{R}_1$ in all distributions (Fig. 5a). However, when it comes to $\mathcal{R}_3$ (Fig. 5b), one can clearly see that the

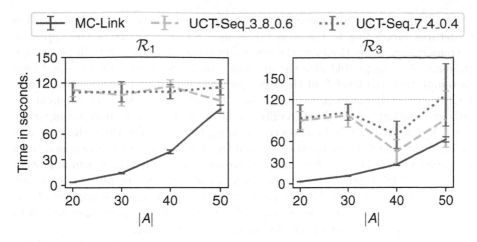

Fig. 7. Comparison of MC-Link and UCT-Seq running time.

performance of UCT-Seq decreases. In fact, for the NDCS distribution, the confidence interval dropped below the MC-Link baseline quality. Also, one can see no clear best combination of UCT-Seq parameters.

What about the running time of both algorithms as we scale up the number of agents? We record the precise moment (in seconds) that the last FCSS was found by UCT-Seq. Moreover, we keep UCT-Seq running until it finds at least one solution for the problem; even if the time budget is finished. We consider only the NDCS distribution as it provides unbiased search spaces [15].

We depict the running time results in Fig. 7. UCT-Seq requires more time than MC-Link to find a good solution. In fact, UCT-Seq keeps finding better solutions even when the time budget is almost out (red dotted line). This is particularly the case for $\mathcal{R}_1$ as it is easier to find an FCSS for that relation. On the other hand, for $\mathcal{R}_3$, we notice that the time budget of 120 s is not enough for computing FCSSs, as the confidence interval indicates the expected running time above the time threshold.

4.4   Discussion

The experiments above show that the MCTS method provides an interesting approach to the SEQVS problem. Due to the large search space, the heuristics explained in Sect. 3 for the tree expansion selects promising nodes to investigate. This allows the algorithm to explore distinct paths in the tree, which minimises the impact of the initial decisions that lead to an unfeasible sequence of coalition structures. Such a behaviour is observed in MC-Link leading to no computed solution (Fig. 4).

Applying the method above to any domain by generating compatible coalition structures (according to the constraints in VSs and $\mathcal{R}$) makes the approach extremely appealing. However, the generality comes at a price. If both generation (finding CSs compatible with the previous one in the sequence) and simulation (attempt to reach level h of the tree) procedures fail to produce child nodes, UCB1 can easily converge to a value for all child nodes. From that moment on, only exploration is carried out (a different node at every visit) until a compatible CS is found. This might increase the running time in cases where the only way forward is through the generation procedure: One needs to run the generator a few times until it finds a CS of interest. So one can (1) investigate running other instances of UCT-Seq for the same problem at different points in the search space, or (2) adjust the MCTS parameters based on the convergence of the tree policy at any given node. Further efforts in those directions may pay off to increase the performance of the aforementioned algorithm.

In particular, a simulation (i.e., play-out) is a key component to solving SEQVS instances. To reach level h, the algorithm has to find compatible CSs through subsequent games. Not only does it require clever procedures to generate compatible CSs, but it should quickly assess whether it is worth exploring that branch of the tree. It seems interesting to consider an informed search. This strategy is adopted in CSG-UCT [19], in which the authors, in simulation steps, continuously merge the two coalitions that lead to the greatest gain until the grand coalition is formed. However, one must ensure that the valuation functions are aligned with the VSs and $\mathcal{R}$ constraints.

The overall approach seems promising for the SEQVS problem. The generation of compatible CSs and the simulation of a path in the tree remain the main challenges to be addressed.

5   Conclusions and Future Work

In previous work we have introduced the idea of certain sequences of coalition structures as solutions for newly introduced games SCFG and SEQVS. We have also investigated how to use these games to model interesting real-world applications and gave a heuristic algorithm, MC-Link, to compute solutions. In this paper, we concentrated on a class of Monte-Carlo algorithms for solving our optimisation problem. We proposed a new algorithm based on Monte Carlo Tree Search, UCT-Seq, and compared it with MC-Link.

We experimented extensively and concluded the following: While often MC-Link is faster than UCT-Seq to find and compute a solution, UCT-Seq eventually outperforms MC-Link in terms of the quality of the outcome. This is because UCT-Seq can explore different parts of the search space, given enough time.

In future work, we intend to address two main challenges in our UCT-Seq approach: the simulation of a path in the tree and the generation of compatible pairs of coalition structures. We also believe that for particular instances of $\mathcal{R}$, improvements are possible by investigating patterns in the search space.

References

1. Auer, P., Cesa-Bianchi, N., Fischer, P.: Finite-time analysis of the multiarmed bandit problem. Mach. Learn. **47**, 235–256 (2002). https://doi.org/10.1023/A: 1013689704352
2. Bistaffa, F., Farinelli, A., Cerquides, J., Rodríguez-Aguilar, J., Ramchurn, S.D.: Anytime coalition structure generation on synergy graphs. In: Proceedings of the 13th International Conference on Autonomous Agents and Multi-agent Systems, pp. 13–20. IFAAMS (2014)
3. Browne, C.B., et al.: A survey of monte Carlo tree search methods. IEEE Trans. Comput. Intell. AI Games **4**, 1–43 (2012)
4. Dann, M., Thangarajah, J., Yao, Y., Logan, B.: Intention-aware multiagent scheduling. In: Proceedings of the 19th International Conference on Autonomous Agents and Multiagent Systems, pp. 285–293. IFAAMS (2020)
5. Farinelli, A., Bicego, M., Bistaffa, F., Ramchurn, S.D.: A hierarchical clustering approach to large-scale near-optimal coalition formation with quality guarantees. Eng. Appl. Artif. Intell. **59**, 170–185 (2016)
6. FEMA: National Incident Management System. Independently Published (2017)
7. Greco, G., Guzzo, A.: Constrained coalition formation on valuation structures. Artif. Intell. **249**, 19–46 (2017)
8. Kocsis, L., Szepesvári, C.: Bandit based monte-Carlo planning. In: Fürnkranz, J., Scheffer, T., Spiliopoulou, M. (eds.) ECML 2006. LNCS (LNAI), vol. 4212, pp. 282–293. Springer, Heidelberg (2006). https://doi.org/10.1007/11871842_29
9. Krausburg, T., Dix, J., Bordini, R.H.: Feasible coalition sequences. In: Proceedings of the 20th International Conference on Autonomous Agents and MultiAgent Systems, pp. 719–727. IFAAMAS (2021)
10. Krausburg, T., Dix, J., Bordini, R.H.: Computing sequences of coalition structures. In: Proceedings of the 2nd Symposium Series on Computational Intelligence, pp. 01–07. IEEE (2021)
11. Lee, J., Jeon, W., Kim, G., Kim, K.: Monte-Carlo tree search in continuous action spaces with value gradients. In: Proceedings of the 34th Conference on Artificial Intelligence, pp. 4561–4568. AAAI Press (2020)
12. Michalak, T., Rahwan, T., Elkind, E., Wooldridge, M., Jennings, N.R.: A hybrid exact algorithm for complete set partitioning. Artif. Intell. **230**, 14–50 (2015)
13. Präntare, F., Appelgren, H., Heintz, F.: Anytime heuristic and monte Carlo methods for large-scale simultaneous coalition structure generation and assignment. In: Proceedings of the 35th Conference on Artificial Intelligence, pp. 11317–11324. AAAI Press (2021)
14. Rahwan, T., Michalak, T.P., Wooldridge, M., Jennings, N.R.: Coalition structure generation: a survey. Artif. Intell. **229**, 139–174 (2015)
15. Rahwan, T., Ramchurn, S.D., Jennings, N.R., Giovannucci, A.: An anytime algorithm for optimal coalition structure generation. J. Artif. Intell. Res. **34**, 521–567 (2009)
16. Shapley, L.S.: Cores of convex games. Int. J. Game Theory **1**(1), 11–26 (1971)
17. Silver, D., et al.: Mastering the game of go with deep neural networks and tree search. Nature **529**, 484–489 (2016)

18. Skibski, O., Michalak, T.P., Sakurai, Y., Wooldridge, M.J., Yokoo, M.: Partition decision trees: representation for efficient computation of the Shapley value extended to games with externalities. Auton. Agent. Multi-Agent Syst. **34**, 1–39 (2020)
19. Wu, F., Ramchurn, S.D.: Monte-Carlo tree search for scalable coalition formation. In: Proceedings of the 29th International Joint Conference on Artificial Intelligence, pp. 407–413. IJCAI Organization (2020)

The FastMap Pipeline for Facility Location Problems

Omkar Thakoor[1]([✉]), Ang Li[1], Sven Koenig[1], Srivatsan Ravi[2], Erik Kline[2], and T. K. Satish Kumar[2]

[1] Department of Computer Science, University of Southern California, Los Angeles, USA
{othakoor,ali355,skoenig}@usc.edu
[2] Information Sciences Institute, University of Southern California, Los Angeles, USA
{sravi,kline}@isi.edu

Abstract. Facility Location Problems (FLPs) involve the placement of facilities in a shared environment for serving multiple customers while minimizing transportation and other costs. FLPs defined on graphs are very general and broadly applicable. Two such fundamental FLPs are the Vertex K-Center (VKC) and the Vertex K-Median (VKM) problems. Although both these problems are NP-hard, many heuristic and approximation algorithms have been developed for solving them in practice. However, state-of-the-art heuristic algorithms require the input graph G to be complete, in which the edge joining two vertices is also the shortest path between them. When G doesn't satisfy this property, these heuristic algorithms have to be invoked only after computing the metric closure of G, which in turn requires the computation of all-pairs shortest-path (APSP) distances. Existing APSP algorithms, such as the Floyd-Warshall algorithm, have a poor time complexity, making APSP computations a bottleneck for deploying the heuristic algorithms on large VKC and VKM instances. To remedy this, we propose the use of a novel algorithmic pipeline based on a graph embedding algorithm called FastMap. FastMap is a near-linear-time algorithm that embeds the vertices of G in a Euclidean space while approximately preserving the shortest-path distances as Euclidean distances for all pairs of vertices. The FastMap embedding can be used to circumvent the barrier of APSP computations, creating a very efficient pipeline for solving FLPs. On the empirical front, we provide test results that demonstrate the efficiency and effectiveness of our novel approach.

1 Introduction

Facility Location Problems (FLPs) are constrained optimization problems that seek the optimal placement of facilities for providing resources and services to multiple customers in a shared environment. They are used to model decision problems related to transportation, warehousing, polling, and healthcare, among many other tasks, for maximizing efficiency, impact, and/or profit. From an agent-centric perspective, FLPs serve the purpose of orchestrating shared

R. Aydoğan et al. (Eds.): PRIMA 2022, LNAI 13753, pp. 417–434, 2023.
https://doi.org/10.1007/978-3-031-21203-1_25

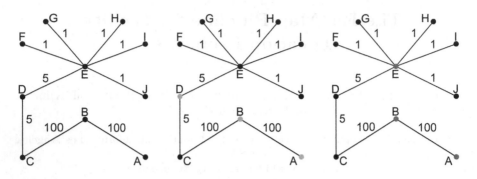

Fig. 1. Examples of the VKC and the VKM problems on the same input graph: The two problems have different optimal solutions for the same value of K. The left panel shows the input graph. The middle panel shows the optimal solution in red for the VKC problem with $K = 3$. The right panel shows the optimal solution in blue for the VKM problem with $K = 3$. (Color figure online)

resources between multiple agents. FLPs can be defined on geometric spaces or on graphs, on continuous or discrete spaces, and with a variety of distance metrics and objectives. A compendium of FLPs along with various algorithms and case studies can be found in [24].

FLPs defined on graphs are very general and broadly applicable. The Vertex K-Center (VKC) problem and the Vertex K-Median (VKM) problem are two such fundamental FLPs defined on graphs. The VKC (VKM) problem seeks K vertices on the input graph for the placement of facilities so as to minimize the farthest (aggregate) distance of all vertices to their nearest facility. Both the VKC and the VKM problems have many real-world applications—often in the same domain but with slightly different objective functions. For example, in urban development, they can be used to optimally place various public service centers within a city. In communication networks, they can be used to determine the optimal placement of computation sites for critical multiplexing and the optimal placement of traffic merging sites while deploying network coding.

Formally, in both the VKC and the VKM problems, we are given an undirected edge-weighted graph $G = (V, E)$ and seek a subset of vertices $S \subseteq V$ of cardinality K. In the VKC problem, we are required to minimize $\max_{v \in V} \min_{u \in S} d(v, u)$ while, in the VKM problem, we are required to minimize $\sum_{v \in V} \min_{u \in S} d(v, u)$. Here, $d(u, v) = d(v, u)$ is the shortest-path distance between u and v in G. Figure 1 shows examples of both these problems posed on the same graph for $K = 3$.

Both the VKC and the VKM problems are computationally NP-hard to solve optimally [33]. However, many heuristic and approximation algorithms have been developed for solving them in practice. For example, the Gonzalez (GON) algorithm [21,31] is among the fastest algorithms proposed to solve the VKC problem in $O(K|V|)$ time, achieving a factor-2 approximation. Similarly, Partition Around Medoids (PAM) [55], a local search procedure proposed for the

VKM problem [5] arrives at a near-optimal solution by repeatedly swapping a vertex from its current solution S with a vertex in $V \setminus S$. It converges very quickly; and by restricting the number of swaps to a large enough constant, it terminates in $O(K^2|V|^2)$ time. We discuss more algorithms for these two problems in the Related Work section.

Despite the existence of many previous works, one of the drawbacks of the existing heuristic algorithms for the VKC and the VKM problems is that they require the input graph G to be complete, in which the edge joining two vertices is also the shortest path between them. This assumption is primarily made so that the heuristic algorithms can focus on the combinatorially hard part of the problem. If G doesn't satisfy this property, these heuristic algorithms can still be effective but should be invoked only after computing the metric closure of G.

Technically, the metric closure of G can be computed in polynomial time by calculating the all-pairs shortest-path (APSP) distances. However, APSP algorithms, such as the Floyd-Warshall algorithm [25], are computationally expensive with their running time complexity typically being cubic in $|V|$. Because of these limitations, APSP algorithms quickly become a computational bottleneck for deploying heuristic algorithms on large VKC and VKM instances.

Some APSP algorithms are based on fast matrix multiplication and achieve sub-cubic running time complexities, but these are better than the Floyd-Warshall algorithm only for very large values of $|V|$. There also exist several other algorithms with better running time complexities [3, 35], but these are much more complicated than the Floyd-Warshall algorithm and rely on complicated data structures. Hence, in most cases, the Floyd-Warshall algorithm is still the APSP algorithm of choice, notwithstanding the issue of being the bottleneck for solving large VKC and VKM instances.

In this paper, we address this issue by using a novel algorithmic pipeline based on a graph embedding algorithm called FastMap. In general, graph embeddings have been used in many different contexts such as for shortest-path computations [15], multi-agent meeting problems [46], community detection and block modeling [45], and social network analysis [51]. They are useful as they facilitate geometric interpretations and algebraic manipulations in vector spaces. FastMap [15, 46] is a recently developed graph embedding algorithm that runs in near-linear time[1]. It embeds the vertices of a given undirected graph into a Euclidean space such that the pairwise Euclidean distances between vertices approximate the shortest-path distances between them in the graph.

We use the FastMap embedding as an alternative to APSP algorithms, creating a very efficient pipeline for solving FLPs on graphs. We provide empirical results demonstrating the efficiency and effectiveness of our proposed FastMap pipeline for the VKC and the VKM problems. We show that, for the same or similar qualities of solutions, the FastMap pipeline is significantly faster than the Floyd-Warshall pipeline.

---

[1] Linear time after ignoring logarithmic factors.

2 FastMap

FastMap [23] was introduced in the Data Mining community for automatically generating Euclidean embeddings of abstract objects. For many real-world objects such as DNA strings, multi-media datasets like voice excerpts or images, medical datasets like ECGs or MRIs, there is no geometric space in which they can be naturally visualized. However, there is often a well-defined distance function for every pair of objects in the problem domain. For example, the edit distance[2] between two DNA strings is well defined although an individual DNA string cannot be conceptualized in geometric space.

FastMap embeds a collection of abstract objects in an artificially created Euclidean space to enable geometric interpretations, algebraic manipulations, and downstream Machine Learning algorithms. It gets as input a collection of abstract objects $\mathcal{O}$, where $D(O_i, O_j)$ represents the domain-specific distance between objects $O_i, O_j \in \mathcal{O}$. A Euclidean embedding assigns a κ-dimensional point $p_i \in \mathbb{R}^\kappa$ to each object O_i. A good Euclidean embedding is one in which the Euclidean distance χ_{ij} between any two points p_i and p_j closely approximates $D(O_i, O_j)$. For $p_i = ([p_i]_1, [p_i]_2 \ldots [p_i]_\kappa)$ and $p_j = ([p_j]_1, [p_j]_2 \ldots [p_j]_\kappa)$, $\chi_{ij} = \sqrt{\sum_{r=1}^{\kappa}([p_j]_r - [p_i]_r)^2}$.

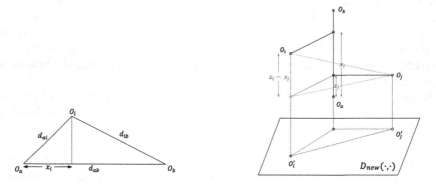

Fig. 2. Illustration of how coordinates are computed in FastMap, borrowed from [15]: The left panel illustrates the "cosine law" projection in a triangle. The right panel illustrates the process of projecting onto a hyperplane that is perpendicular to $\overline{O_a O_b}$.

FastMap creates a κ-dimensional Euclidean embedding of the abstract objects in $\mathcal{O}$, for a user-specified value κ. In the very first iteration, it heuristically identifies the farthest pair of objects O_a and O_b in linear time. Once O_a and O_b are determined, every other object O_i defines a triangle with sides of lengths $d_{ai} = D(O_a, O_i)$, $d_{ab} = D(O_a, O_b)$, and $d_{ib} = D(O_i, O_b)$, as shown in Fig. 2 (left panel). The sides of the triangle define its entire geometry, and the projection of O_i onto the line $\overline{O_a O_b}$ is given by

---

[2] The edit distance between two strings is the minimum number of insertions, deletions, or substitutions that are needed to transform one to the other.

$$x_i = (d_{ai}^2 + d_{ab}^2 - d_{ib}^2)/(2d_{ab}).$$ (1)

FastMap sets the first coordinate of p_i, the embedding of O_i, to x_i. In the subsequent $\kappa - 1$ iterations, the same procedure is followed for computing the remaining $\kappa - 1$ coordinates of each object. However, the distance function is adapted for different iterations. For example, for the first iteration, the coordinates of O_a and O_b are 0 and d_{ab}, respectively. Because these coordinates fully explain the true domain-specific distance between these two objects, from the second iteration onward, the rest of p_a and p_b's coordinates should be identical. Intuitively, this means that the second iteration should mimic the first one on a hyperplane that is perpendicular to the line $\overline{O_a O_b}$, as shown in Fig. 2 (right panel). Although the hyperplane is never constructed explicitly, its conceptualization implies that the distance function for the second iteration should be changed for all i and j in the following way:

$$D_{new}(O_i', O_j')^2 = D(O_i, O_j)^2 - (x_i - x_j)^2.$$ (2)

Here, O_i' and O_j' are the projections of O_i and O_j, respectively, onto this hyperplane, and $D_{new}(\cdot, \cdot)$ is the new distance function.

Algorithm 1: FastMap: A near-linear-time graph embedding algorithm.

Input: $G = (V, E)$, κ, and ϵ.

Output: $p_i \in \mathbb{R}^r$ for all $v_i \in V$.

1 **for** $r = 1, 2 \ldots \kappa$ **do**
2 $\quad$ Choose $v_a \in V$ randomly and let $v_b = v_a$;
3 $\quad$ **for** $t = 1, 2 \ldots C$ **do**   // C is a constant.
4 $\quad\quad$ $\{d_{ai} : v_i \in V\} \leftarrow$ ShortestPathTree(G, v_a);
5 $\quad\quad$ $v_c \leftarrow \text{argmax}_{v_i} \{d_{ai}^2 - \sum_{j=1}^{r-1}([p_a]_j - [p_i]_j)^2\}$;
6 $\quad\quad$ **if** $v_c == v_b$ **then**
7 $\quad\quad\quad$ Break;
8 $\quad\quad$ **else**
9 $\quad\quad\quad$ $v_b \leftarrow v_a$; $v_a \leftarrow v_c$;
10 $\quad$ $\{d_{ai} : v_i \in V\} \leftarrow$ ShortestPathTree(G, v_a);
11 $\quad$ $\{d_{ib} : v_i \in V\} \leftarrow$ ShortestPathTree(G, v_b);
12 $\quad$ $d_{ab}' \leftarrow d_{ab}^2 - \sum_{j=1}^{r-1}([p_a]_j - [p_b]_j)^2$;
13 $\quad$ **if** $d_{ab}' < \epsilon$ **then**
14 $\quad\quad$ Break;
15 $\quad$ **for** each $v_i \in V$ **do**
16 $\quad\quad$ $d_{ai}' \leftarrow d_{ai}^2 - \sum_{j=1}^{r-1}([p_a]_j - [p_i]_j)^2$;
17 $\quad\quad$ $d_{ib}' \leftarrow d_{ib}^2 - \sum_{j=1}^{r-1}([p_i]_j - [p_b]_j)^2$;
18 $\quad\quad$ $[p_i]_r \leftarrow (d_{ai}' + d_{ab}' - d_{ib}')/(2\sqrt{d_{ab}'})$;

19 **return** p_i for all $v_i \in V$.

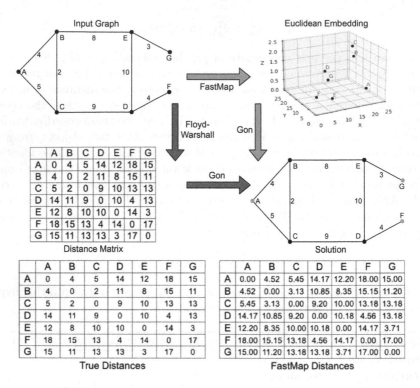

Fig. 3. The FastMap pipeline and its comparison with the Floyd-Warshall pipeline: The FastMap pipeline uses a Euclidean embedding instead of an APSP distance matrix (left). The distortion in the APSP distances implicitly produced by FastMap (right) rarely affects the quality of the final solution.

FastMap can also be used to embed the vertices of a graph in a Euclidean space to preserve the pairwise shortest-path distances between them. The idea is to view the vertices of a given graph $G = (V, E)$ as the objects to be embedded. As such, the Data Mining FastMap algorithm cannot be directly used for generating an embedding in linear time. This is because it assumes that the distance d_{ij} between any two objects O_i and O_j can be computed in constant time, independent of the number of objects in the problem domain. However, computing the shortest-path distance between two vertices depends on the size of the graph.

The issue of having to retain (near-)linear time complexity can be addressed as follows: In each iteration, after we heuristically identify the farthest pair of vertices O_a and O_b, the distances d_{ai} and d_{ib} need to be computed for *all* other vertices O_i. Computing d_{ai} and d_{ib} for any single vertex O_i can no longer be done in constant time but requires $O(|E|+|V| \log |V|)$ time instead [27]. However, since we need to compute these distances for all vertices, computing two shortest-path trees rooted at each of the vertices O_a and O_b yields all necessary distances in one shot. The complexity of doing so is also $O(|E| + |V| \log |V|)$, which is only linear in the size of the graph[3]. The amortized complexity for computing d_{ai} and d_{ib} for any single vertex O_i is therefore near-constant time.

The foregoing observations are used in [46] to build a graph-based version of FastMap that embeds the vertices of a given undirected graph in a Euclidean space in near-linear time. The Euclidean distances approximate the pairwise shortest-path distances between vertices. Algorithm 1 presents the pseudocode for this algorithm.

A slight modification of this FastMap algorithm, presented in [15], can also be used to preserve *consistency* and *admissibility* of the Euclidean distance approximation used as a heuristic in A* search for shortest-path computations. In both [15] and [46], κ is user-specified, but a threshold parameter ϵ is introduced to detect large values of κ that have diminishing returns on the accuracy of approximating pairwise shortest-path distances.

3   The FastMap Pipeline

We will now exploit the efficiency of the FastMap algorithm towards APSP computations. After FastMap computes the Euclidean embedding of the given graph in near-linear time, the Euclidean distance between any pair of its vertices serves to approximate the shortest-path distance between them. Since Euclidean distances can be computed in $O(\kappa)$ time, independent of the size of the graph, FastMap efficiently sets up the groundwork for solving the VKC and VKM problems.

Figures 3 and 4 show the FastMap pipeline in comparison with the Floyd-Warshall pipeline for solving the VKC and VKM problems. While both pipelines can invoke the same heuristic algorithm of choice for solving the VKC or VKM problem, the FastMap pipeline is much faster because of its efficiency in the APSP computations.

For the VKC problem, we can use the GON algorithm [21,31]. It is simple to implement, has a low running time complexity, and yields a factor-2 approximation. In the first iteration, it picks a random vertex and nominates it as a center. In each subsequent iteration, it picks a vertex that is farthest away from any of the existing centers and nominates it as an additional new center. Thus, a solution is obtained after K iterations. GON runs in $O(K|V|)$ time and produces a factor-2 approximation.

For the VKM problem, we can use the PAM algorithm [55]. Although PAM has several variants, a simple version of it with a naive implementation suffices for demonstrating the effectiveness of our FastMap pipeline. In fact, improved versions of PAM increase the benefits of the FastMap pipeline since the bottleneck of APSP computations becomes more pronounced. PAM constructs an initial solution greedily. It then invokes local search to improve the quality of the solution by repeatedly swapping a vertex from its current solution S with a vertex in $V \setminus S$. While a non-trivial bound on the number of iterations required for

---

[3] Unless $|E| = O(|V|)$, in which case the complexity is near-linear in the size of the input because of the $\log |V|$ factor.

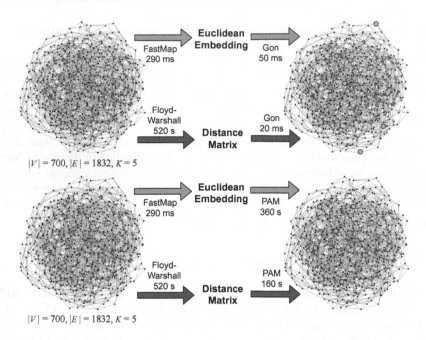

Fig. 4. Efficiency of the FastMap pipeline for solving the VKC (top) and VKM (bottom) problems: For the same quality of the final VKC solution, FastMap+GON takes 0.34 s, while Floyd-Warshall+GON takes 520 s. Here, the FastMap pipeline yields a 1529× speedup. For the same quality of the final VKM solution, FastMap+PAM takes 360 s, while Floyd-Warshall+PAM takes 680 s. Here, the FastMap pipeline yields a 1.887× speedup. The final solutions are marked by the green vertices. (Color figure online)

convergence is not known, fewer than K iterations are usually observed in practice [57,63]. In addition, with slightly modified swapping conditions, convergence within a polynomial number of iterations can be guaranteed [5].

Of course, the FastMap pipeline introduces some intermediate distortion in the APSP distances. But this distortion is usually not much and is a very small price to pay for huge benefits in running times, both complexity-wise and in actual wall-clock times. In fact, for the examples chosen in Figs. 3 and 4, the FastMap pipeline does not change the qualities of the final solutions. But it runs several orders of magnitude faster than the Floyd-Warshall pipeline. The running time of the GON or PAM algorithm is slightly higher in the FastMap pipeline compared to that in the Floyd-Warshall pipeline. This is because, in the FastMap pipeline, the pairwise distances cannot be looked up in a distance matrix but should now be computed using the Euclidean coordinates, requiring $O(\kappa)$ time. However, since κ is a small number, usually less than 5, the enormous savings in the APSP computations continue to be the dominant factor benefiting the FastMap pipeline.

Table 1. Results for VKC on DIMACS.   **Table 2.** Results for VKC on Small World.

K	Instance	Vertices	Edges	Quality factor	Speedup	K	Instance	Vertices	Edges	Quality factor	Speedup
5	queen7_7	49	476	0.800	3.483	5	n0100k6p0.6	100	483	1	22.704
	myciel7	191	2360	0.889	50.328		n0300k4p0.3	300	776	1	290.837
	queen16_16	256	6320	1.167	60.620		n0600k6p0.6	600	2865	1	810.219
	le450_25b	450	8263	1.333	254.702		n0600k4p0.3	600	1564	1	1197.670
10	queen8_8	64	728	1.000	3.585	10	n0100k4p0.6	100	315	1	12.446
	games120	120	638	0.750	16.598		n0400k4p0.6	400	1277	1.333	267.190
	myciel7	191	2360	1.500	24.973		n0700k6p0.6	700	3355	1	537.126
	le450_5c	450	9803	1.333	98.959		n0700k4p0.3	700	1832	1	771.443
20	myciel6	95	755	1.000	5.887	20	n0100k4p0.3	100	262	1	9.831
	miles1000	128	3216	1.333	4.728		n0200k4p0.6	200	651	1.5	40.005
	queen14_14	196	4186	1.500	13.760		n0600k6p0.6	600	2865	1	278.556
	le450_5d	450	9757	1.250	59.687		n0700k6p0.3	700	2705	1.333	472.860
40	queen10_10	100	1470	1.500	3.348	40	n0100k4p0.6	100	315	2	6.049
	games120	120	638	1.167	7.991		n0400k6p0.6	400	1951	1	88.304
	queen12_12	144	2596	1.333	6.263		n0600k4p0.3	600	1564	1.333	268.690
	queen16_16	256	6320	1.000	13.227		n0700k4p0.6	700	2244	1.333	209.628

The same patterns in the benefits of the FastMap pipeline are also observed on several kinds of benchmark problem instances, as reported in the next section.

4 Experimental Results

In this section, we present experimental results comparing the FastMap pipeline and the Floyd-Warshall pipeline for solving VKC and VKM problem instances. For solving the VKC problem instances, the FastMap pipeline uses FastMap+GON and the Floyd-Warshall pipeline uses Floyd-Warshall+GON. For solving the VKM problem instances, the FastMap pipeline uses FastMap+PAM and the Floyd-Warshall pipeline uses Floyd-Warshall+PAM. We implemented all algorithms and experimentation procedures using Python3 with the NetworkX library. For the Floyd-Warshall algorithm, several state-of-the-art implementations with code-level optimizations are available. They work particularly well for certain classes of graphs. However, due to the inherent difference in the asymptotic complexities of the two pipelines, on large enough instances with no special properties, the Floyd-Warshall pipeline can be shown to be significantly slower than the FastMap pipeline. Hence, for a fair comparison of the two pipelines on benchmark problem instances, while focusing on the quality of the solutions produced, we used a vanilla implementation of the Floyd-Warshall algorithm meant for general graphs. For the FastMap algorithm in Algorithm 1, we used $\kappa = 4$ and $\epsilon = 10^{-4}$. All experiments were conducted on a laptop with a 1.6 GHz Intel Core i5 processor and 8 GB 1600 MHz DDR3 memory.

Table 3. Results for VKC on ORLib.

K	Instance	Vertices	Edges	Quality factor	Speedup
5	pmed2	100	193	0.859	5.550
	pmed9	200	785	1.018	11.435
	pmed29	600	7042	0.943	33.606
	pmed39	900	15896	–	–
10	pmed5	100	196	0.865	3.189
	pmed13	300	1760	1.174	10.573
	pmed21	500	4909	0.962	14.950
	pmed38	900	15898	–	–
20	pmed10	200	786	0.971	3.633
	pmed17	400	3142	1.020	7.908
	pmed29	600	7042	1.105	11.721
	pmed39	900	15896	–	–
40	pmed6	200	786	1.460	2.813
	pmed14	300	1771	1.204	4.100
	pmed28	600	7054	1.129	6.985
	pmed40	900	15879	–	–

Table 4. Results for VKC on Tree.

K	Instance	Vertices	Edges	Quality factor	Speedup
5	n0100	100	99	0.981	36.152
	n0300	300	299	1.168	346.328
	n0600	600	599	1.036	1437.121
	n1000	1000	999	–	–
10	n0200	200	199	0.841	83.738
	n0500	500	499	1.027	495.447
	n0700	700	699	0.974	1008.908
	n1000	1000	999	–	–
20	n0300	300	299	1.020	110.636
	n0400	400	399	1.217	200.612
	n0600	600	599	0.888	301.079
	n1000	1000	999	–	–
40	n0300	300	299	1.452	76.859
	n0500	500	499	1.549	220.077
	n0700	700	699	1.051	446.138
	n1000	1000	999	–	–

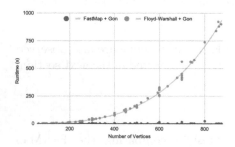

Fig. 5. Runtime scaling for VKC.   **Fig. 6.** Runtime scaling for VKM.

We used both VKC and VKM problem instances derived from different benchmark datasets. These include the DIMACS[4], Small World, ORLib[5], Tree, and MovingAI[6] datasets. For the DIMACS instances, each edge was assigned an integer weight chosen uniformly at random from the interval $[1, 10]$. The Small World instances were generated using the Newman-Watts-Strogatz graph generator in NetworkX. All edges were assigned a unit weight. The names of these instances indicate the parameter values for n (the number of vertices), k (the number of neighbors in a ring), and p (the probability of adding a new edge). The original ORLib graphs already have weights on the edges, although different

---

[4] The DIMACS instances were generated using the DIMACS graphs from http://networkrepository.com/dimacs.php and https://mat.tepper.cmu.edu/COLOR/instances.html.

[5] The ORLib instances were generated using the ORLib graphs from http://people.brunel.ac.uk/~mastjjb/jeb/orlib/pmedinfo.html.

[6] The MovingAI instances were generated using the MovingAI graphs from https://movingai.com/benchmarks.

Table 5. Results for VKC on Moving-gAI.

K	Instance	Vertices	Edges	Quality factor	Speedup
5	orz106d	335	602	0.846	316.146
	lak102d	519	920	1.000	839.839
	hrt002d	754	1300	1.192	2093.917
	lak526d	954	1715	–	–
10	orz203d	244	442	1.000	106.603
	den404d	358	632	0.889	219.150
	orz105d	679	1245	1.000	733.192
	lak526d	954	1715	–	–
20	ost102d	249	447	1.000	65.042
	lak105d	443	766	1.167	222.258
	lak104d	851	1570	1.125	822.030
	den009d	1003	1863	–	–
40	den404d	358	632	1.333	97.559
	den408d	548	991	1.250	226.418
	lak104d	851	1570	1.200	582.540
	den009d	1003	1863	–	–

Table 6. Results for VKM on DIMACS.

K	Instance	Vertices	Edges	Quality factor	Speedup
5	queen7_7	49	476	1.244	0.647
	queen10_10	100	1470	1.064	1.625
	queen14_14	196	4186	1.153	2.116
	queen16_16	256	6320	1.194	2.302
	le450_15c	450	16680	1.178	3.947
	p-hat700-1	700	60999	1.213	5.905
10	queen5_5	25	160	1.136	0.686
	miles500	128	1170	1.208	0.805
	queen14_14	196	4186	1.193	1.199
	le450_5d	450	9757	1.159	1.036
	le450_5a	450	5714	1.183	1.776
	p-hat700-1	700	60999	–	–

Table 7. Results for VKM on Small World.

K	Instance	Vertices	Edges	Quality factor	Speedup
5	n0300k6p0.3	300	1168	1.133	1.691
	n0400k6p0.3	400	1562	1.120	2.244
	n0500k4p0.3	500	1281	1.241	2.107
	n0600k4p0.3	600	1564	1.253	2.912
	n0700k6p0.3	700	2705	1.173	3.157
	n0800k4p0.6	800	2561	–	–
10	n0200k6p0.3	200	787	1.187	0.971
	n0300k6p0.6	300	1440	1.124	1.008
	n0400k6p0.3	400	1951	1.211	1.492
	n0700k6p0.3	700	2705	1.157	2.200
	n0800k4p0.3	800	2062	1.214	1.781
	n0800k4p0.6	800	2561	–	–

Table 8. Results for VKM on ORLib.

K	Instance	Vertices	Edges	Quality factor	Speedup
5	pmed8	200	792	1.242	0.853
	pmed14	300	1771	1.236	1.139
	pmed20	400	3144	1.410	1.200
	pmed22	500	4896	1.153	1.350
	pmed28	600	7054	1.411	3.035
	pmed39	900	15896	–	–
10	pmed2	100	193	1.162	1.020
	pmed14	300	1771	1.195	1.206
	pmed15	300	1754	1.197	1.152
	pmed17	400	3142	1.261	1.204
	pmed28	600	7054	1.279	1.894
	pmed39	900	15896	–	–

values of K were chosen for the experiments. The Tree instances were generated using NetworkX. Each edge was assigned an integer weight chosen uniformly at random from the interval $[1, 10]$. For the MovingAI instances, all edges were assigned a unit weight.

Because various components of the two pipelines use randomization, we used 5 trials for each pipeline on each problem instance and compared the best solutions found by them. This comparison is reported as a "Quality Factor". In essence, the Quality Factor is the cost of the solution found by the FastMap pipeline divided by the cost of the solution found by the Floyd-Warshall pipeline. If the Quality Factor $= 1$, the FastMap pipeline retains the same quality of the final solution as the Floyd-Warshall pipeline. If it is > 1, the FastMap distor-

Table 9. Results for VKM on Tree.

K	Instance	Vertices	Edges	Quality factor	Speedup
5	n0100	100	99	1.287	1.140
	n0200	200	199	1.398	2.469
	n0300	300	299	1.393	1.624
	n0500	500	499	1.447	3.398
	n0700	700	699	1.361	4.695
	n0900	900	899	–	–
10	n0100	100	99	1.435	1.160
	n0200	200	199	1.484	0.971
	n0300	300	299	1.593	1.354
	n0400	400	399	1.511	1.301
	n0500	500	499	1.405	1.515
	n0800	800	799	–	–

Table 10. Results for VKM on MovingAI.

K	Instance	Vertices	Edges	Quality factor	Speedup
5	lak110d	168	290	1.070	1.452
	orz203d	244	442	1.037	2.013
	den404d	358	632	0.988	1.239
	ht_store	490	910	1.030	4.428
	orz105d	679	1245	1.027	4.059
	den405d	925		–	–
10	lak110d	168	290	1.018	1.342
	orz203d	244	442	1.041	1.688
	den404d	358	632	1.004	1.716
	lak107d	393	710	1.038	2.272
	den408d	548	991	1.025	1.476
	orz102d	738	1359	–	–

tion in the APSP distances produces a costlier solution compared to the Floyd-Warshall pipeline. Sometimes, the Quality Factor can even be < 1, indicating that the FastMap pipeline produces a better solution compared to the Floyd-Warshall pipeline. This can happen because of randomization and other heuristic components in the two pipelines. We also report a "Speedup" factor, which is the time taken by the Floyd-Warshall pipeline in the 5 trials divided by the time taken by the FastMap pipeline in the 5 trials.

Tables 1, 2, 3, 4, and 5 show the results on some representative VKC problem instances derived from the DIMACS, Small World, ORLib, Tree, and MovingAI datasets, respectively. In these tables, a "–" indicates that the Floyd-Warshall pipeline timed out after 1000 s on each of the 5 trials. In such cases, the FastMap pipeline still generated a solution. The FastMap pipeline yields significant speedup on all the datasets for only marginal compromises on the solution qualities. In fact, the FastMap pipeline is orders of magnitude faster than the Floyd-Warshall pipeline for larger problem instances. Figure 5 visualizes and compares the running times of the two pipelines on all the problems instances, barring the ones on which the Floyd-Warshall pipeline timed out.

Tables 6, 7, 8, 9, and 10 show the results on some representative VKM problem instances derived from the DIMACS, Small World, ORLib, Tree, and MovingAI datasets, respectively. In these tables, a "–" indicates that the Floyd-Warshall pipeline timed out after 1000 s on each of the 5 trials. In such cases, the FastMap pipeline still generated a solution. The FastMap pipeline yields significant speedup on all the datasets for only marginal compromises on the solution qualities. Figure 6 visualizes and compares the running times of the two pipelines on all the problems instances, barring the ones on which the Floyd-Warshall pipeline timed out. The speedup for VKM problem instances is less than that for VKC problem instances since the PAM algorithm is not as efficient as the GON algorithm.

5   Related Work

The VKC problem we considered in this paper is the *uncapacitated unweighted* version. Several other variants have been studied. These include the *capacitated* VKC problem [43], where each center can serve only a fixed number of vertices, the *heterogeneous capacitated* VKC problem [8], which is similar to the capacitated VKC problem, except that the capacities of different centers may be different, the *aligned K-center* problem in Euclidean space [6], where the centers must be selected from a line or a polygon, the *edge-dilation* VKC problem [44], where the goal is to minimize the maximum ratio of the distance between two vertices via their respective centers to their shortest-path distance, the *fault-tolerant* VKC problem [42], where each selected center must have a set of $\alpha \leq K$ centers close to it, the *p-neighbor* VKC problem [12], where, given an integer p, the goal is to minimize the maximum distance of any non-center vertex to its pth closest center, among many other variants.

Several exact algorithms have been proposed for the VKC problem considered in this paper. They are primarily based on Integer Programming or Mixed Integer Programming formulations [1,7,13,16,18,22,49]. None of them run in polynomial time since the VKC problem is NP-hard to solve optimally. Several meta-heuristic algorithms have also been proposed, such as Tabu Search [48], Variable Neighborhood Search [37,48], Scatter Search [50], GRASP [50], Memetic Genetic Algorithms [53], Harmony Search [41], and Bee Colony Optimization [19]. While these algorithms may provide better performance in practice, they are not guaranteed to converge quickly or to find optimal solutions. The VKC problem is factor-2 approximable in polynomial time. The polynomial-time algorithms that guarantee this approximation include the SH algorithm [52,59], and its refinements—the GON algorithm [21,31], and the HS algorithm [36,52]. The greedy GR algorithm [54,56], the SCR algorithm [56], and the CDSH algorithm [30] are among the polynomial-time heuristic algorithms that yield the best empirical performance. However, these algorithms are significantly slower than the GON algorithm. In this paper, we used the GON algorithm because of its lower runtime.

The VKM problem is closely related to the general uncapacitated facility location problem [17], with a restriction on the number of facilities (centers) that can be opened, but with no costs for opening them. One of the early proposals for solving the VKM problem was a reverse greedy algorithm [14]. It starts by opening all vertices as centers and, in each iteration, closes a center that increases the total cost by the least amount, until K of them remain. It achieves an $O(\log |V|)$ approximation factor. A frequently used local search algorithm is the PAM algorithm [55]. It iteratively finds cost-lowering swaps of vertices into and out of the current candidate solution, until convergence to a local optimum is achieved. While we used a simple version of PAM in this paper, a more generalized version with p swaps allowed in each iteration, along with a slight modification in the swapping condition, is presented in [5]. This generalized version of PAM expends $O(|V|^{O(p)})$ time in each iteration but is guaranteed to converge after a polynomial number of iterations, achieving an approximation factor of $3 + 2/p$. Another polynomial-time algorithm that yields a factor-$6\frac{2}{3}$ approximation is based on a Linear Programming relaxation and rounding scheme [10]. Similar techniques have also been proposed by others. A factor-4 polynomial-time approximation algorithm is presented in [38,39]. An algorithm that achieves an approximation factor of $3.25(1+\delta)$ with running time $O(K^3|V|^2/\delta^2)$ is presented in [11]. This algorithm outperforms PAM empirically [20]. However, PAM is still very competitive and is used in this paper for its simplicity. Another algorithm that achieves an approximation factor of $1 + \sqrt{3} + \epsilon$ with running time $|V|^{O(1/\epsilon^2)}$ is presented in [47].

A classical algorithm for APSP computations is the Floyd-Warshall algorithm [25]. It uses dynamic programming and runs in $O(|V|^3)$ time. Johnson's algorithm [40] runs in $O(|V||E|+|V|^2 \log |V|)$ time, but it assumes the absence of negative-cost cycles in the graph. For directed graphs with non-negative weights on the edges, APSP computations are closely related to the *distance product* of two matrices. A popular algorithm that exploits this connection has running time $O(|V|^3(\log \log |V|/ \log |V|)^{1/2})$ [26,60]. For graphs with integer weights on the edges, [34] presents an algorithm that runs in $O(|V||E| + |V|^2 \log \log |V|)$ time. For undirected graphs with integer weights on the edges, the running time can be improved to $O(|V||E|)$ [61,62]. For general graphs, several algorithms have improved logarithmic factors in their running times. For example, [35] achieves a running time of $O(|V|^3 \log \log |V|/ \log^2 |V|)$. Algorithms for fast matrix multiplication can also be invoked to obtain sub-cubic-time APSP algorithms for a large class of "geometrically weighted" graphs [9]. For graphs embedded in a 2D Euclidean space, such an algorithm has running time $O(|V|^{2.922})$. Several other works, such as [3,4,28,29,58] have shown that APSP computations can be done in $\tilde{O}(M(|V|))$ time for unweighted graphs and in $\tilde{O}(\sqrt{|V|^3M(|V|)})$ time for weighted graphs, where $M(n)$ is the time complexity of $n \times n$ matrix multiplication, currently known to be $O(n^{2.37286})$ [2].

6   Conclusions and Future Work

FastMap is a near-linear-time algorithm that embeds the vertices of a graph in a Euclidean space while approximately preserving the shortest-path distances as Euclidean distances for all pairs of its vertices. In this paper, we presented a FastMap-based approach for solving FLPs, adding to the list of FastMap's previous applications in multi-agent domains. We demonstrated the efficiency and effectiveness of our novel FastMap pipeline on two fundamental and vital FLPs defined on graphs: the VKC and the VKM problems. Both these problems are NP-hard to solve optimally; but enabling efficient heuristics and approximation algorithms is the key to solving them well in practice. Existing state-of-the-art heuristic algorithms rely on the input being a complete graph with edges representing shortest paths. Consequently, an input graph that doesn't satisfy this property has to be first rendered amenable by computing its metric closure via APSP algorithms like the Floyd-Warshall algorithm, which becomes a critical bottleneck when deploying fast heuristics on large VKC and VKM instances.

Our proposed FastMap pipeline circumvents this barrier of APSP computations. Through empirical results on a wide variety of VKC and VKM instances, we showed that the distortion of pairwise distances in the FastMap embedding does not affect the quality of the final output by much: For the same or similar qualities of solutions, the FastMap pipeline is significantly faster than the Floyd-Warshall pipeline.

In future work, we will consider reducing the distortion of APSP distances caused by the FastMap embedding using Machine Learning techniques to learn the correction factors. In fact, the FastMap coordinates can themselves be used as features for the learning, as illustrated in [32]. The key challenge for such a self-supervised approach is to minimize the number of training samples and retain the end-to-end efficiency of the pipeline. Another direction of future work is to apply our efficient FastMap pipeline to other kinds of FLPs.

References

1. Al-Khedhairi, A., Salhi, S.: Enhancements to two exact algorithms for solving the vertex p-center problem. J. Math. Model. Algorithms **4**(2), 129–147 (2005). https://doi.org/10.1007/s10852-004-4072-3
2. Alman, J., Williams, V.V.: A refined laser method and faster matrix multiplication. In: Proceedings of the 2021 ACM-SIAM Symposium on Discrete Algorithms (SODA), pp. 522–539. SIAM (2021)
3. Alon, N., Galil, Z., Margalit, O.: On the exponent of the all pairs shortest path problem. J. Comput. Syst. Sci. **54**(2), 255–262 (1997)
4. Alon, N., Naor, M.: Derandomization, witnesses for boolean matrix multiplication and construction of perfect hash functions. Algorithmica **16**(4), 434–449 (1996). https://doi.org/10.1007/BF01940874
5. Arya, V., et al.: Local search heuristics for k-median and facility location problems. SIAM J. Comput. **33**(3), 544–562 (2004)
6. Brass, P., Knauer, C., Na, H.S., Shin, C.S., Vigneron, A.: The aligned k-center problem. Int. J. Comput. Geom. Appl. **21**(02), 157–178 (2011)
7. Calik, H., Tansel, B.C.: Double bound method for solving the p-center location problem. Comput. Oper. Res. **40**(12), 2991–2999 (2013)
8. Chakrabarty, D., Krishnaswamy, R., Kumar, A.: The heterogeneous capacitated k-center problem. In: Eisenbrand, F., Koenemann, J. (eds.) IPCO 2017. LNCS, vol. 10328, pp. 123–135. Springer, Cham (2017). https://doi.org/10.1007/978-3-319-59250-3_11
9. Chan, T.M.: More algorithms for all-pairs shortest paths in weighted graphs. In: Proceedings of the Thirty-Ninth Annual ACM Symposium on Theory of Computing, pp. 590–598. Association for Computing Machinery (2007)
10. Charikar, M., Guha, S., Tardos, É., Shmoys, D.B.: A constant-factor approximation algorithm for the k-median problem. J. Comput. Syst. Sci. **65**(1), 129–149 (2002)
11. Charikar, M., Li, S.: A dependent lp-rounding approach for the k-median problem. In: Czumaj, A., Mehlhorn, K., Pitts, A., Wattenhofer, R. (eds.) ICALP 2012. LNCS, vol. 7391, pp. 194–205. Springer, Heidelberg (2012). https://doi.org/10.1007/978-3-642-31594-7_17
12. Chaudhuri, S., Garg, N., Ravi, R.: The p-neighbor k-center problem. Inf. Process. Lett. **65**(3), 131–134 (1998)

13. Chen, D., Chen, R.: New relaxation-based algorithms for the optimal solution of the continuous and discrete p-center problems. Comput. Oper. Res. **36**(5), 1646–1655 (2009)
14. Chrobak, M., Kenyon, C., Young, N.: The reverse greedy algorithm for the metric k-median problem. Inf. Process. Lett. **97**(2), 68–72 (2006)
15. Cohen, L., Uras, T., Jahangiri, S., Arunasalam, A., Koenig, S., Kumar, T.K.S.: The FastMap algorithm for shortest path computations. In: Proceedings of the 27th International Joint Conference on Artificial Intelligence (2018)
16. Contardo, C., Iori, M., Kramer, R.: A scalable exact algorithm for the vertex p-center problem. Comput. Oper. Res. **103**, 211–220 (2019)
17. Cornuéjols, G., Nemhauser, G., Wolsey, L.: The Uncapacitated Facility Location Problem. Cornell University Operations Research and Industrial Engineering, Technical report (1983)
18. Daskin, M.S.: A new approach to solving the vertex p-center problem to optimality: algorithm and computational results. Commun. Oper. Res. Soc. Japan **45**(9), 428–436 (2000)
19. Davidović, T., Ramljak, D., Šelmić, M., Teodorović, D.: Bee colony optimization for the p-center problem. Comput. Oper. Res. **38**(10), 1367–1376 (2011)
20. Dohan, D., Karp, S., Matejek, B.: K-median Algorithms: Theory in practice. Princeton University Computer Science, Technical report (2015)
21. Dyer, M.E., Frieze, A.M.: A simple heuristic for the p-centre problem. Oper. Res. Lett. **3**(6), 285–288 (1985)
22. Elloumi, S., Labbé, M., Pochet, Y.: A new formulation and resolution method for the p-center problem. INFORMS J. Comput. **16**(1), 84–94 (2004)
23. Faloutsos, C., Lin, K.I.: FastMap: a fast algorithm for indexing, data-mining and visualization of traditional and multimedia datasets. In: Proceedings of the 1995 ACM SIGMOD International Conference on Management of Data (1995)
24. Farahani, R.Z., Hekmatfar, M.: Facility Location: Concepts. Algorithms and Case Studies. Springer Science & Business Media, Models (2009). https://doi.org/10.1007/978-3-7908-2151-2
25. Floyd, R.W.: Algorithm 97: shortest path. Commun. ACM **5**(6), 345 (1962)
26. Fredman, M.: New bounds on the complexity of the shortest path problem. SIAM J. Comput. **5**, 83–89 (1976)
27. Fredman, M.L., Tarjan, R.E.: Fibonacci heaps and their uses in improved network optimization algorithms. J. ACM **34**(3), 596–615 (1987)
28. Galil, Z., Margalit, O.: All pairs shortest paths for graphs with small integer length edges. J. Comput. Syst. Sci. **54**(2), 243–254 (1997)
29. Galil, Z., Margalit, O.: Witnesses for boolean matrix multiplication and for transitive closure. J. Complex. **9**(2), 201–221 (1993)
30. Garcia-Diaz, J., Sanchez-Hernandez, J., Menchaca-Mendez, R., Menchaca-Mendez, R.: When a worse approximation factor gives better performance: a 3-approximation algorithm for the vertex k-center problem. J. Heuristics **23**(5), 349–366 (2017). https://doi.org/10.1007/s10732-017-9345-x
31. Gonzalez, T.F.: Clustering to minimize the maximum intercluster distance. Theoret. Comput. Sci. **38**, 293–306 (1985)
32. Gopalakrishnan, S., Cohen, L., Koenig, S., Kumar, T.K.S.: Embedding directed graphs in potential fields using FastMap-D. In: Proceedings of the 13th International Symposium on Combinatorial Search (2020)
33. Guo-Hui, L., Xue, G.: k-center and k-median problems in graded distances. Theoret. Comput. Sci. **207**(1), 181–192 (1998)

34. Hagerup, T.: Improved shortest paths on the word RAM. In: Montanari, U., Rolim, J.D.P., Welzl, E. (eds.) ICALP 2000. LNCS, vol. 1853, pp. 61–72. Springer, Heidelberg (2000). https://doi.org/10.1007/3-540-45022-X_7

35. Han, Y., Takaoka, T.: An $o(n^3 \log \log n / \log^2 n)$ time algorithm for all pairs shortest paths. J. Discrete Algorithms **38–41**, 9–19 (2016). https://doi.org/10.1007/978-3-642-31155-0_12

36. Hochbaum, D.S., Shmoys, D.B.: A best possible heuristic for the k-center problem. Math. Oper. Res. **10**(2), 180–184 (1985)

37. Irawan, C.A., Salhi, S., Drezner, Z.: Hybrid meta-heuristics with vns and exact methods: application to large unconditional and conditional vertex p-centre problems. J. Heuristics **22**(4), 507–537 (2016). https://doi.org/10.1007/s10732-014-9277-7

38. Jain, K., Mahdian, M., Markakis, E., Saberi, A., Vazirani, V.V.: Greedy facility location algorithms analyzed using dual fitting with factor-revealing lp. J. ACM (JACM) **50**(6), 795–824 (2003)

39. Jain, K., Vazirani, V.V.: Approximation algorithms for metric facility location and k-median problems using the primal-dual schema and lagrangian relaxation. J. ACM (JACM) **48**(2), 274–296 (2001)

40. Johnson, D.B.: Efficient algorithms for shortest paths in sparse networks. J. ACM (JACM) **24**(1), 1–13 (1977)

41. Kaveh, A., Nasr, H.: Solving the conditional and unconditional p-center problem with modified harmony search: a real case study. Sci. Iranica **18**(4), 867–877 (2011)

42. Khuller, S., Pless, R., Sussmann, Y.J.: Fault tolerant k-center problems. Theoret. Comput. Sci. **242**(1–2), 237–245 (2000)

43. Khuller, S., Sussmann, Y.J.: The capacitated k-center problem. SIAM J. Discret. Math. **13**(3), 403–418 (2000)

44. Könemann, J., Li, Y., Parekh, O., Sinha, A.: An approximation algorithm for the edge-dilation k-center problem. Oper. Res. Lett. **32**(5), 491–495 (2004)

45. Li, A., Stuckey, P., Koenig, S., Kumar, T.K.S.: A FastMap-based algorithm for block modeling. In: Proceedings of the International Conference on the Integration of Constraint Programming, Artificial Intelligence, and Operations Research (2022). https://doi.org/10.1007/978-3-031-08011-1_16

46. Li, J., Felner, A., Koenig, S., Kumar, T.K.S.: Using FastMap to solve graph problems in a Euclidean space. In: Proceedings of the International Conference on Automated Planning and Scheduling (2019)

47. Li, S., Svensson, O.: Approximating k-median via pseudo-approximation. SIAM J. Comput. **45**(2), 530–547 (2016)

48. Mladenović, N., Labbé, M., Hansen, P.: Solving the p-center problem with tabu search and variable neighborhood search. Netw. Int. J. **42**(1), 48–64 (2003)

49. Özsoy, F.A., Pınar, M.Ç.: An exact algorithm for the capacitated vertex p-center problem. Comput. Oper. Res. **33**(5), 1420–1436 (2006)

50. Pacheco, J.A., Casado, S.: Solving two location models with few facilities by using a hybrid heuristic: a real health resources case. Comput. Oper. Res. **32**(12), 3075–3091 (2005)

51. Perozzi, B., Al-Rfou, R., Skiena, S.: Deepwalk: online learning of social representations. In: Proceedings of the 20th ACM SIGKDD International Conference on Knowledge Discovery and Data Mining (2014)

52. Plesník, J.: A heuristic for the p-center problems in graphs. Discret. Appl. Math. **17**(3), 263–268 (1987)

53. Pullan, W.: A memetic genetic algorithm for the vertex p-center problem. Evol. Comput. **16**(3), 417–436 (2008)

54. Rana, R., Garg, D.: The analytical study of k-center problem solving techniques. Int. J. Inf. Technol. Knowl. Manag. **1**(2), 527–535 (2008)

55. Rdusseeun, L., Kaufman, P.: Clustering by means of medoids. In: Proceedings of the Statistical Data Analysis Based on the L1 Norm Conference, Neuchatel, Switzerland, pp. 405–416 (1987)

56. Robič, B., Mihelič, J.: Solving the k-center problem efficiently with a dominating set algorithm. J. Comput. Inf. Technol. **13**(3), 225–234 (2005)

57. Schubert, E., Rousseeuw, P.J.: Fast and eager k-medoids clustering: O(k) runtime improvement of the pam, clara, and clarans algorithms. Inf. Syst. **101**, 101804 (2021)

58. Seidel, R.: On the all-pairs-shortest-path problem in unweighted undirected graphs. J. Comput. Syst. Sci. **51**(3), 400–403 (1995)

59. Shmoys, D.B.: Computing near-optimal solutions to combinatorial optimization problems. Comb. Optim. **20**, 355–397 (1995)

60. Takaoka, T.: A new upper bound on the complexity of the all pairs shortest path problem. Inf. Process. Lett. **43**(4), 195–199 (1992)

61. Thorup, M.: Undirected single-source shortest paths with positive integer weights in linear time. J. ACM (JACM) **46**(3), 362–394 (1999)

62. Thorup, M.: Floats, integers, and single source shortest paths. J. Algorithms **35**(2), 189–201 (2000)

63. Whitaker, R.: A fast algorithm for the greedy interchange for large-scale clustering and median location problems. INFOR Inf. Syst. Oper. Res. **21**(2), 95–108 (1983)

An Axiomatic Approach to Formalized Responsibility Ascription

Sarah Hiller[1,3]($\boxtimes$) ⓘ, Jonas Israel[2] ⓘ, and Jobst Heitzig[3] ⓘ

[1] Free University Berlin, Institute for Mathematics, Berlin, Germany
sarah.hiller@fu-berlin.de
[2] Technische Universität Berlin, Research Group Efficient Algorithms,
Berlin, Germany
[3] Potsdam Institute for Climate Impact Research, Potsdam, Germany

Abstract. A formalized and quantifiable responsibility score is a crucial component in many aspects of the development and application of
multi-agent systems and autonomous agents. We can employ it to inform
decision making processes based on ethical considerations, as a measure
to ensure redundancy that helps us in avoiding system failure, as well as
for verifying that autonomous systems remain trustworthy by testing for
unwanted responsibility voids in advance. We follow recent proposals to
use probabilities as the basis for responsibility ascription in uncertain environments rather than the deterministic causal views employed in much
of the previous formal philosophical literature. Using an axiomatic approach we formally evaluate the qualities of (classes of) proposed responsibility functions. To this end, we decompose the computation of the responsibility a group carries for an outcome into the computation of values
that we assign to its members for individual decisions leading to that outcome, paired with an appropriate aggregation function. Next, we discuss
a number of intuitively desirable properties for each of these contributing
functions. We find an incompatibility between axioms determining upper
and lower bounds for the values assigned at the member level. Regarding
the aggregation from member-level values to group-level responsibility we
are able to axiomatically characterise one promising aggregation function.
Finally, we present two maximally axiom compliant group-level responsibility measures – one respecting the lower bound axioms at the member
level and one respecting the corresponding upper bound axioms.

Keywords: Responsibility under uncertainty · Agency · Formal
ethics · Trustworthy autonomous systems · Axiomatic evaluation

1 Background and Introduction

One important challenge in the development and deployment of trustworthy
autonomous and multi-agent systems is a formalized and quantifiable responsibility measure. Internally to a system we can use responsibility as a value which
informs decision making processes, while from an external point of view we can

R. Aydoğan et al. (Eds.): PRIMA 2022, LNAI 13753, pp. 435–457, 2023.
https://doi.org/10.1007/978-3-031-21203-1_26

use shared responsibility as a measure to ensure redundancy and avoid system failures in the case of an agent failure. Finally, in the evaluation of autonomous agents interacting with humans it is important to verify the requirement of meaningful human control [28]. The study of responsibility in multi-agent systems lies at the intersection of game theory, formal ethics, logic, and computer science. For a recent overview of open questions regarding responsibility formalisation in autonomous systems applications see [35]. In the current paper we focus on backward looking responsibility for groups of agents in complex scenarios including uncertainty.

In order to arrive at a formalized responsibility representation we need to take two steps: First, we need to represent the situation in which responsibility is to be ascribed. The way this is implemented varies considerably between approaches from a philosophical tradition versus ones from a computer science background. Second, we need to look at the criteria for responsibility ascription and how these can be modelled in the given situation.

Braham and van Hees [4] model the decision situations in which responsibility is assigned using normal-form games. That is, several players may interact, but decisions are all made at one single point in time, after which the outcome is clear. Contrastingly, in the field of *stit* logics, decisions take place at a moment in an infinitely branching history. Every choice is represented by a new branching off of possible futures [3,14]. Other approaches employ a dynamic epistemic logic for the representation of decision situations, where agents' actions correspond to transitions between a possibly infinite set of possible worlds [19,27]. Similarly, Yazdanpanah et al. [34] use concurrent game structures where agents' actions initiate a change between finitely many possible states of a system, with the possibility of revisiting a state more than once. Beyond these, there are many other ways to model the relevant decision situations for the study of responsibility ascription (e.g., see [1,9]) which are, however, less relevant to our approach. Our representation is somewhere in between the previously mentioned approaches of using normal-form games, infinite Kripke frames, and concurrent games. Namely, we use extensions of extensive-form game trees. These extend normal-form games with a temporal component, or, viewed from a different angle they represent finite fragments of infinite stit frames [7]. They are perhaps most similar to the concurrent epistemic game structures used by [34] or the Coalition Dynamic Logic in [19,27], with several interacting agents having the choice to influence the system. Like the latter, we acknowledge that agents may not always know about the consequences of their choices in interactive settings. Therefore, we include the option of consequences being uncertain, both probabilistic and non-quantifiable[1].

---

[1] Note that while our approach is able to represent situations in which an agent carries responsibility due to the fact that they influenced another agent's actions, this responsibility is still of a direct or *primary* nature when considering distinction between direct/primary and indirect/secondary responsibility as e.g. described in [21].

The criteria for responsibility ascription are mostly consistent throughout the philosophical literature. Free choice and the capability for moral reasoning [26,31] are generally assumed to hold for all agents and actions (possibly after an appropriate restriction). Most attention tends to be focused on the analysis of a causal relation between the action or event in question and an undesirable outcome. Implementations of causality include NESS causation [4,33], or modelling causality as *seeing to it that* a certain outcome obtains in stit logics [3,14]. Very similar to this strict view, several approaches represent responsibility as the possibility to avoid a certain outcome, that is, seeing to it or allowing that it's opposite holds [19,22,27,34]. Lorini et al. [20], who use an epistemic extension of STIT logic to model decision situations, integrate both views by differentiating actively seeing to it that an outcome holds from passively allowing it to happen by not acting. The logical representations in [19,20,27] are additionally able to include notions of (missing) knowledge as an excuse. Further elements such as intention [10] or other excuses [8] may be added or left out, depending on the desired complexity of the representation.

In contrast to the often unquestioned assumption of actual causation as a precondition for responsibility there are scenarios in which there is no actual causality but we would still want to speak of responsibility. For example, in legal contexts 'attempts' are well-known cases of non-actualized causal relations [24]. Baltag et al. [2] try to solve this by retroactively equipping stit logics with a notion of *action failure* or *attempt*. More comprehensively, in some of the occasions in which we want to assign responsibility but cannot fall back on actual causation it has been observed that the action in question *increased the probability* of the outcome [6]. Note, however, that we can have both causation without probability increase – due to an initial lowering of the probability of unlikely causes – and probability increase without causation – due to fizzling or probabilistic preemption[2]. Thus, attempts to reduce causation to probability raising, as described by [13,16,31], do not seem very promising.

We argue that causation is not probability increase, but that both are separate grounds for responsibility, as was already suggested by Moore [25]: "These metaphysical conclusions are enough to make possible the moral thesis I now want to advance: that chance-raising is an independent desert basis [for responsibility], along with causation and counterfactual dependence[3]" We assume here

---

[2] Fizzling here describes an event in which the probability of the outcome was increased but stays below 1 and the unwanted outcome does not occur due to chance. Probabilistic preemption is simply preemption in a probabilistic context, that is, the event which increased the probability of the outcome does not turn out to be a cause as a different event interrupts the causal chain by causing the outcome first.

[3] The well worked out reduction by Halpern and Pearl [11] of causation to counterfactual dependence *in an appropriately modified context* may serve as an argument to disregard the third disjunct. Specifically, treating probability raising independently from causation thus also implies an independence from counterfactual dependence (such as the popular account by Lewis [17,18]). This fact – that conditional probabilities fail to capture counterfactual relations – has been well-known since early works on counterfactual analyses of causation [13].

that both responsibility due to causation and responsibility due to probability increase each form a lower bound on overall responsibility.

As responsibility due to actual causation has been the focus in the literature so far, we now analyse the aspect of responsibility due to probability increase. In a previous work (that is currently under review) a subset of the authors suggested some functions for computing responsibility based on probability increase and evaluated these according to a number of paradigmatic example scenarios. The current work provides a more formalised and in-depth examination of the properties of responsibility functions. We decompose the responsibility computation for a group of agents into two parts: First we compute values for individual decisions by group members leading to the outcome, before aggregating these values into the final group responsibility.

In order to evaluate proposed responsibility functions we employ an axiomatic method [30]. That is, we formulate desirable properties which our responsibility functions are to have in the form of axioms, and assess the quality of (sets of) proposed functions according to these axioms. Additionally, we will present certain incompatibility and implication results between the axioms and a characterisation of one specific subset of functions. Two responsibility functions will be singled out to be maximally axiom-compliant with respect to our impossibility result, one respecting the lower-bound axioms and one respecting the upper-bound ones. Proofs omitted in the paper can be found in the long submitted manuscript [12].

2   Framework and Responsibility Functions

We are interested in modelling decision situations of several agents interacting over time. Additionally, we want to allow for the presence of various forms of uncertainty, resulting from the interactive nature of the scenario or from an inherent uncertainty (both probabilistic or not) regarding the outcomes of actions. As noted earlier, the framework presented here also occurs in a different work currently under review which is authored by a subset of the authors.

2.1   Framework

In order to represent decision scenarios we use extensive-form game trees equipped with specific additions for the features mentioned above. Formally, the framework is the following.

Definition 1 (Decision tree). *A morally evaluated multi-agent **decision tree** with uncertainty (without possible confusion in the remainder abbreviated as* tree*) is a tuple*

$$\mathcal{T} = \langle I, V, E, \sim, (A_v), (c_v), (p_v), \epsilon \rangle$$

where:

- I *is a nonempty finite set of* agents *(or players).*
- $\langle V, E \rangle$ *is a directed rooted tree with nodes V and edges E. $V - \bigcup_{i \in I} V_i \cup V_a \cup V_p \cup V_o$ is partitioned into a set of* decision nodes V_i *for each agent $i \in I$, a set of* ambiguity nodes V_a, *a set of* probabilistic uncertainty nodes V_p, *and a set of* outcome nodes V_o, *that are exactly the leaves of the tree. We denote the set of all decision nodes by $V_d := \bigcup_{i \in I} V_i$.*
- $\sim$ *is an equivalence relation on V_d so that $v \sim w$ implies $v, w \in V_i$ for the same agent $i \in I$. We call $\sim$* information equivalence *and the equivalence classes of $\sim$ in V_i the* information sets *of i.*
- A_v *is a nonempty, finite set of i's possible* actions *in v, for each agent $i \in I$ and decision node $v \in V_i$. Whenever $v \sim w$, $A_v = A_w$. Let $\bigcup_{v \in V_d} A_v =: \mathcal{A}$.*
- $c_v : A_v \to S_v$, *where $S_v := \{w \in V : (v, w) \in E\}$, is a bijective* consequence function *mapping actions to successor nodes for each node $v \in V \setminus V_o$.*
- $p_v \in \Delta(S_v)$ *for $v \in V_p$, with $\Delta(A)$ being the set of all probability distributions on a given set A, is a probability distribution on the set of possible successor nodes for each probability node.*
- $\epsilon \subseteq V_o$ *is a set of ethically undesirable outcomes.*

The set of *agents* and the *directed tree* encode a multi-agent decision situation with the direction of the tree showing the temporal progression. *Decision, ambiguity* and *probability nodes* receive their intuitive interpretation. We use the term ambiguity specifically to denote unquantifiable uncertainty, in contrast to quantifiable probabilistic uncertainty. We argue that both quantifiable and unquantifiable uncertainty do arise in decision situations and it is necessary to represent both in order to adequately capture responsibility, rather than aiming to reduce one to the other. Information equivalence $\sim$ encodes which nodes are indistinguishable to an agent at a given time. Note that only decision nodes of one agent may be related – that is, i) agents always know whether or not it is their turn, and ii) we do not need to index the equivalence relation with the agent under consideration. We use the term *uncertainty* as an umbrella term for information uncertainty, ambiguity and probabilistic uncertainty[4].

Graphical Representation. We represent these features graphically as follows. An example of two simple scenarios is depicted in Fig. 1.

Directed edges are shown as arrows labelled with actions, descriptions of the situation, or probabilities, depending on the preceding node. Decision nodes are depicted as diamonds labelled with the respective agent and ambiguity nodes are empty diamonds, in line with the intuition that these can be regarded as a decision node of a special agent that represents the decision scenario's environment.

---

[4] Note that according to this representation we do not assign probabilities to any player's actions. While it can very well be argued that people do indeed reason using subjective probability distributions over other players' actions, we do not include this here for several reasons. The first one is that it is extremely difficult, if not impossible, to assess these probabilities objectively. The other reason is that including reasoning via other agents' expected actions leads to possible excuses in responsibility ascription that we do not want to permit.

Probabilistic uncertainty nodes are depicted as empty squares. Outcome nodes are represented as circles, with undesirable ones shaded in gray. Information sets are connected via a dotted line.

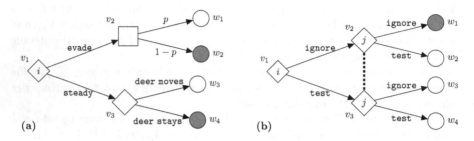

Fig. 1. Graphical representation of interactive decision scenarios with uncertainty in the described framework. (a) An autonomous vehicle (agent i) approaches a deer on a street. It can either try to evade the deer with a computed success rate of p or keep steady, resulting in a crash if the deer does not move. (b) Agents i and j are two instances in a distributed system which may perform a costly test for the failure of a component, with i coming before j. Both may either perform the test or ignore it, but j has no way of knowing whether i performed the test. If they both ignore the test a failure is overlooked.

Further Notions. Additionally, we will need formal representations of the following notions defined on this framework: that of *past* and *future* of a certain node, that of *strategies*, which tell us for a given set of agents G all future decisions of G, and that of *scenarios*, which tell us about others' future decisions and resolve all non-probabilistic uncertainty. Formally, these are defined as follows.

Definition 2 (History, Branch, Information Branch). *Let a tree $\mathcal{T}$ and a node $v \in V$ be given. Then the **history** of v is*

$$H(v) := \{v' \in V \mid \exists v_1, \ldots, v_n \in V \ s.t. \ (v', v_1), (v_1, v_2), \ldots, (v_n, v) \in E\},$$

*and the **branch** of v is*

$$B(v) := \{v' \in V \mid v \in H(v')\},$$

*that is, all possible futures after v. The **information branch** of v is $B^{\sim}(v) := \bigcup_{v' \sim v} B(v')$, that is, all futures considered possible in the information set of v.*

Given a group G, we call their decision nodes $V_G := \bigcup_{i \in G} V_i$, and the decision nodes of all agents not in the group $I \setminus G$ together with all ambiguity nodes $V_{-G} := \bigcup_{i \in I \setminus G} V_i \cup V_a$. With these two notations we can define the terms *strategy* and *scenario*.

Definition 3 (Strategy). *Let a tree $\mathcal{T}$, a group $G \subseteq I$, and a node $v \in V$ be given. Then a **strategy** for G at v is a function*

$$\sigma \colon V_G \cap B^{\sim}(v) \to \bigcup_{v_d \in V_G \cap B^{\sim}(v)} A_{v_d}$$

that chooses an action for every one of G's future decision nodes considered possible according to the information set in v, i.e., $\sigma(v) \in A_v$. Additionally, we require that the actions selected are not just logically but also practically possible, that is, a strategy must select the same action for all nodes in one information set: $\sigma(v_d) = \sigma(v_d')$ for all $v_d, v_d' \in V_G \cap B^\sim(v)$ s.t. $v_d \sim v_d'$[5]. We denote the set of all these functions by $\Sigma(\mathcal{T}, G, v)$.

Definition 4 (Scenario). *Again, let a tree $\mathcal{T}$, a group $G \subseteq I$, and a node $v \in V_G$ be given. Then a **scenario** for G at v is a node $v_\zeta \sim v$ together with a function*

$$\zeta \colon V_{-G} \cap B(v_\zeta) \to \bigcup_{v' \in V_{-G} \cap B(v_\zeta)} S_{v'}$$

that chooses successor nodes $\zeta(v')$ for all future decision nodes by non-members of G or ambiguity nodes, i.e., $\zeta(v) \in S_v$. The node v_ζ is considered the actual node in scenario ζ, thus resolving information uncertainty. The function ζ resolves non-probabilistic uncertainty regarding what will happen in the future (disregarding G's own actions).

We denote the set of all these functions by $Z^\sim(\mathcal{T}, G, v)$. Note that the specification of v_ζ is implicit in the definition of ζ.

Given a node $v \in V_G$, a strategy $\sigma \in \Sigma(\mathcal{T}, G, v)$, and a scenario $\zeta \in Z^\sim(\mathcal{T}, G, v)$, one can easily compute in a recursive way the conditional probability to end in an outcome node w given that the current node is actually v_ζ and the choices in non-probabilistic nodes are made according to what σ and ζ specify. Let's call this conditional probability the *likelihood* $\ell(w|v, \sigma, \zeta)$. We are often interested in the likelihood of ending in any undesirable outcome node $w \in \epsilon$ for which we slightly abuse notation and write $\ell(\epsilon|v, \sigma, \zeta) := \sum_{w \in \epsilon} \ell(w|v, \sigma, \zeta)$.

In the remainder of the paper, unless specified otherwise, we will use $v, v_1, v_2, \ldots$ to indicate decision nodes and $w, w_1, w_2, \ldots$ to indicate outcome nodes.

2.2 Responsibility Functions

We are interested in assigning backward looking moral responsibility to a (possibly singleton) group for a certain outcome. In order to compute this, we utilize the path from the root node of the decision tree to the given outcome node. We will assign an intermediate value, which we call "member contribution", for single decisions by individual group members in a given node. Consequently, we use an aggregation function to combine these values into the final "outcome responsibility"[6].

---

[5] This is sometimes called a *uniform strategy* [34], however, as this is the only kind of strategy we use here we leave out the qualification. Also, our restriction is only concerned with individual knowledge at the agent level and does not concern any kind of group knowledge or coordination. Therefore, we can employ this restriction without going into the debate about what actions a group can collectively select.

[6] By outcome responsibility we mean moral responsibility assigned at an outcome node as opposed to at an intermediate node, and not non-moral causal responsibility (as it is sometimes understood in the literature, e.g. [32]).

Member contribution is not computed irrespective of an agent's group membership but precisely with this information in mind. Thus, the point of view we take here does not stand in contrast to non-reducibility results known from the literature [5,7,29].

It is important to note that we place no restrictions on which agents can form a group. This is a decision the modeler takes at the time of the computation of responsibility. Therefore, we also do not place any *a priori* restrictions on the level of coordination within an arbitrary group. Finally, we always assume common knowledge of the full decision situation.

Member contribution is a function of the individual agent and the group that they are a member of, the node in which the current decision is taken as well as the action which the agent selects. All of this is considered within a given decision situation. We measure contribution as an increase in probability. Therefore the range of this function will be the interval $[0,1]$.[7]

Definition 5 (Member Contribution). *Let a tree $\mathcal{T}$ be given. **Member contribution** is a function mapping a set ('group') of agents $G \subseteq I$, an agent $i \in G$, a node $v \in V_i$ and an action $\mathbf{a} \in A_v$ to values in the interval $[0,1]$:*

$$\mathbf{r} \colon \mathcal{P}(I) \times I \times V_d \times \mathcal{A} \to [0,1].$$

Whenever $i \notin G$, $v \notin V_i$, or $\mathbf{a} \notin A_v$ the function is not defined.

Next we define the general form of the functions we use to aggregate member contribution into outcome responsibility (see [23] for a general introduction to aggregation functions).

Definition 6 (Aggregation function). *For $n \geq 1$ an **n-ary aggregation function** is a function $\mathbf{agg}^{(n)} \colon [0,1]^n \to [0,1]$ that is non decreasing in each entry and fulfills the following boundary conditions*

$$\inf_{\mathbf{x} \in [0,1]^n} \mathbf{agg}^{(n)}(\mathbf{x}) = \inf[0,1] = 0 \quad and \quad \sup_{\mathbf{x} \in [0,1]^n} \mathbf{agg}^{(n)}(\mathbf{x}) = \sup[0,1] = 1.$$

*An **extended aggregation function** is a function $\mathbf{agg} \colon \bigcup_{n \in \mathbb{N}_{\geq 1}} [0,1]^n \to [0,1]$ such that for all $n > 1$, $\mathbf{agg}^{(n)} = \mathbf{agg} \restriction_{[0,1]^n}$ is an n-ary aggregation function and $\mathbf{agg}^{(1)}$ is the identity on $[0,1]$.*

Finally, outcome responsibility will be a function of a group of agents and an outcome node, again in a specified decision situation.

Definition 7 (Outcome responsibility). *Let a tree $\mathcal{T}$ be given. **Outcome responsibility** is a function of a group of agents $G \subseteq I$, and an outcome node $w \in V_o$ to the reals:*

$$\mathcal{R} \colon \mathcal{P}(I) \times V_o \to \mathbb{R}.$$

---

[7] Note that a member contribution function $\mathbf{r}$ only receives information internal to the scenario modeled in the decision tree. The ascribed contribution is thus invariant under any outside information. This includes invariance with respect to the specific name an agent is given as well as any form of duty or other historic information.

We consider outcome responsibility for group $G \subseteq I$ at node w to be a function of the member contribution values of the individual decisions of agents $i \in G$ which lead to the outcome w:

$$\mathcal{R}(G, w) := \mathbf{agg}\left((\mathbf{r}(G, i, v, \mathbf{a}_{v \to w}))_{i \in G, v \in V_i \cap H(w)}\right),$$

for an appropriate aggregation function $\mathbf{agg}$. $\mathbf{a}_{v \to w}$ is that action available in v for which the successor node lies on the path to w.

In the following three sections we provide an axiomatic study of member contribution, aggregation functions and outcome responsibility.

3   Member Contribution Functions

We start our analysis by considering member contribution functions in more detail. After establishing a list of interesting axioms that reflect certain moral desiderata we present three functions capturing different notions of contribution. We conclude by qualitatively evaluating the presented functions with respect to the axioms.

3.1   Axioms for Member Contribution Functions

The axioms described here demand certain contribution values in clearly defined situations. This reflects some moral desiderata that might (or might not) be important in different situations. The first axiom reflects the idea that in situations the agent can not discern between they should not be treated differently.

(KSym) *Knowledge Symmetry.* The same action taken in the same information set produces the same contribution value. Let $v \sim v'$ and $\mathbf{a} \in A_v = A_{v'}$. Then $\mathbf{r}(G, i, v, \mathbf{a}) = \mathbf{r}(G, i, v', \mathbf{a})$.

The following axioms bound the assigned contribution value either to 0 or to 1 for taking specific actions. For both pairs of axioms it is easy to see that the version of the axiom considering all information branches (marked by the $\sim$) is logically implied by the original one.

(AMC) *Avoidance of member contribution.* Consider a tree $\mathcal{T}$, a group $G \subseteq I$ and a node $v \in V_i$ for some $i \in G$ with $A_v = \{\mathbf{a}, \mathbf{b}_1, \ldots, \mathbf{b}_m\}$, where $m \geq 0$, such that choosing $\mathbf{a}$ certainly leads to a desirable outcome and choosing any other option certainly leads to an undesirable outcome. Then $\mathbf{r}(G, i, v, \mathbf{a}) = 0$.

(AMC$\sim$) *Avoidance of member contribution in information branches.* Consider a tree $\mathcal{T}$, a group $G \subseteq I$ and a node $v \in V_i$ for some $i \in G$ with $A_v = \{\mathbf{a}, \mathbf{b}_1, \ldots, \mathbf{b}_m\}$, where $m \geq 0$, such that choosing $\mathbf{a}$ in any $v' \sim v$ certainly leads to a desirable outcome and choosing any other option certainly leads to an undesirable outcome. Then $\mathbf{r}(G, i, v, \mathbf{a}) = 0$.

(FMC) *Full member contribution.* Consider a tree $\mathcal{T}$, a group $G \subseteq I$ and a node $v \in V_i$ for some $i \in G$ with $A_v = \{\mathsf{a}, \mathsf{b}_1, \ldots, \mathsf{b}_m\}$, where $m > 0$[8], such that choosing a certainly leads to an undesirable outcome and choosing any other option certainly leads to a desirable outcome. Then $\mathbf{r}(G, i, v, \mathsf{a}) = 1$.

(FMC~) *Full member contribution in information branches.* Consider a tree $\mathcal{T}$, a group $G \subseteq I$ and a node $v \in V_i$ for some $i \in G$ with $A_v = \{\mathsf{a}, \mathsf{b}_1, \ldots, \mathsf{b}_m\}$, where $m > 0$, such that choosing a in any $v' \sim v$ certainly leads to an undesirable outcome and choosing any other option certainly leads to a desirable outcome. Then $\mathbf{r}(G, i, v, \mathsf{a}) = 1$.

The axioms (AMC) and (FMC) represent notions of *seeing to it that* [3]. They request that if an agent ensures a desirable or undesirable outcome through a single action in one decision node, i.e. she *sees to it that* this outcome holds, she is to be assigned no or full contribution value, respectively.

3.2   Proposed Functions

We consider three different member contribution functions. The first follows an ad-hoc way of measuring responsibility through increased likelihood of an undesirable outcome. The other two use more elaborate notions of responsibility through risk taking and through negligence. Let a tree $\mathcal{T}$, group $G \subseteq I$, agent $i \in G$ and node $v \in V_i$ be given.

Contribution Through Increase in Guaranteed Likelihood. Here, agent i is assigned contribution value for the undesirable outcome if, and to the degree that, their action increased the *guaranteed likelihood* of ϵ. This is often the first intuition when adopting a probabilistic view of causation in responsibility ascription, see e.g. [15], or [31]: "I shall assume that the relevant causal connection is that the choice increases the objective chance that the outcome will occur". We define the *known guaranteed likelihood* of ϵ at node $v \in V$ as

$$\gamma(v) := \min_{\sigma \in \Sigma(\mathcal{T}, G, v)} \min_{\zeta \in Z^\sim(\mathcal{T}, G, v)} \ell(\epsilon | v, \sigma, \zeta).$$

The member contribution we assign to agent $i \in G$ for performing action $\mathsf{a} \in A_v$ in node $v \in V_i$ is measured as the increase in guaranteed likelihood as follows

$$\mathbf{r}^{\text{like}}(G, i, v, \mathsf{a}) := \Delta\gamma(v, \mathsf{a}) := \gamma(c_v(\mathsf{a})) - \gamma(v).$$

Contribution Through Risk Taking. This variant assigns a contribution value to an agent if their action can be seen as some kind of risk taking. We define taking a risk here as not avoiding a possible bad outcome. We define the *optimal avoidance* of ϵ by group G given a scenario $\zeta \in Z^\sim(v)$ as

$$\omega(v, \zeta) := \min_{\sigma \in \Sigma(\mathcal{T}, G, v)} \ell(\epsilon | v, \sigma, \zeta).$$

---

[8] Note that it is important here to enforce that there is actually a choice for the agent, i.e., that $m \neq 0$.

We now measure member contribution as the shortfall in avoiding ϵ due to action **a** at v

$$\mathbf{r}^{\mathrm{risk}}(G, i, v, \mathbf{a}) := \max_{\zeta \in Z^{\sim}(\mathcal{T}, G, v)} \Delta\omega(v, \zeta, \mathbf{a}) := \max_{\zeta \in Z^{\sim}(\mathcal{T}, G, v)} [\omega(c_v(\mathbf{a}), \zeta) - \omega(v, \zeta)].$$

That is, rather than assuming a single scenario we compare G's strategies over all scenarios.

Contribution Through Negligence. The third and final variant we study in this paper assigns the contribution value in a similar way to the previous variant but deducts a baseline of unavoidable risk. This ensures that in situations where all available actions produce some risk of leading to an undesirable outcome the agent is only assigned a contribution value when choosing negligently. We define the minimal risk formally through

$$\underline{\rho}(G, i, v) := \min_{\mathbf{a} \in A_v} \rho(G, i, v, \mathbf{a}) = \min_{\mathbf{a} \in A_v} \max_{\zeta \in Z^{\sim}(\mathcal{T}, G, v)} \Delta\omega(v, \zeta, \mathbf{a}) = \min_{\mathbf{a} \in A_v} \mathbf{r}^{\mathrm{risk}}(G, i, v, \mathbf{a}).$$

With that we define this variant of member contribution as

$$\mathbf{r}^{\mathrm{negl}}(G, i, v, \mathbf{a}) := \Delta\rho(G, i, v, \mathbf{a}) := \max_{\zeta \in Z^{\sim}(\mathcal{T}, G, v)} \Delta\omega(v, \zeta, \mathbf{a}) - \underline{\rho}(G, i, v).$$

3.3   Application to Example Scenarios

The suggested functions give the following results for the examples from Fig. 1 and Fig. 2. We can see that in many situations $\mathbf{r}^{\mathrm{like}}$ is not very fine-grained. Contribution values for members of the group $\{i, j\}$ are often zero as we can assume that the other group members will follow a strategy that avoids the undesirable outcome. Also, we see that in accordance with our intentions $\mathbf{r}^{\mathrm{risk}}$ may assign contribution values where $\mathbf{r}^{\mathrm{negl}}$ fails to do so (Table 1).

Table 1. Evaluation of member contribution values with $\mathcal{T}$ as in the examples from Fig. 1 and Fig. 2. G and **a** are as specified, v is clear from the context. In cases where $G = \{i, j\}$ the values for agents i and j are the same. We assume $p < 1 - p$.

| | Figure 1(a) | | Figure 1(b) | | | | Figure 2 | | | |
| | $G = \{i\}$ | | $G = \{i\}$ or $G = \{j\}$ | | $G = \{i, j\}$ | | $G = \{i\}$ or $G = \{j\}$ | | $G = \{i, j\}$ | |
	evade	steady	ignore	test	ignore	test	left	right	left	right
$\mathbf{r}^{\mathrm{like}}$	1-p	0	0	0	0	0	0	0	0	0
$\mathbf{r}^{\mathrm{risk}}$	1-p	p	1	0	0	0	1	1	0	0
$\mathbf{r}^{\mathrm{negl}}$	1-2p	0	1	0	0	0	0	0	0	0

Table 2. Summary of the compliance by the three proposed functions with the considered axioms. "✓" denotes that the function satisfies the axiom whereas "×" denotes that there are instances where the axiom is not satisfied.

	(KSym)	(AMC)	(AMC~)	(FMC)	(FMC~)
r^{like}	×	✓	✓	✓	✓
r^{risk}	✓	×	✓	✓	✓
r^{negl}	✓	✓	✓	×	✓

3.4   Evaluation of Proposed Functions

In this section we check compliance of the member contribution functions described earlier with our axioms. Note that the coordination game as depicted in Fig. 2 works as a counterexample for all negative results.

Proposition 1. *The three functions* r^{like}, r^{risk} *and* r^{negl} *satisfy the given axioms as specified in Table 2.*

We now show that one has to choose between assigning unavoidable contribution values in some situations – and thus violating an axiom like (AMC) – or having situations where we cannot assign full contribution values – and in turn violating an axiom like (FMC). We will come back to this point later for similar axioms regarding aggregated outcome responsibility.

Proposition 2. *No function can simultaneously satisfy (KSym), (AMC), and (FMC).*

Proof. Consider the coordination game depicted in Fig. 2 and assume that the member contribution function r satisfies (KSym), (AMC) and (FMC). By (AMC), $r(j, v_1, \texttt{cinema}) = r(j, v_2, \texttt{theater}) = 0$ and by (FMC) we have $r(j, v_1, \texttt{theater}) = r(j, v_2, \texttt{cinema}) = 1$. But this contradicts (KSym) as $r(j, v_1, \texttt{cinema}) \neq r(j, v_2, \texttt{cinema})$. □

On the other hand, we can see in Table 2 that each combination of two out of the three axioms (AMC), (FMC), and (KSym) is possible. We would argue that sacrificing (KSym) might not be satisfactory in most instances, as responsibility assignment should not depend on factors outside the agents' knowledge. Instead, one could require (KSym) together with the corresponding weakened variants (AMC~) and (FMC~).

4   Aggregation Functions

After studying member contribution functions and their axiomatic compliance, we will now turn to aggregation functions. Again, we start by defining a number of axioms applicable to these, before presenting a set of possible functions that could be used as aggregation functions and qualitatively compare them using the axioms.

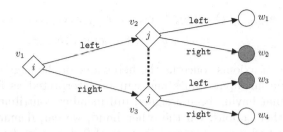

Fig. 2. A coordination game where two autonomous vehicles (agents i and j) approach each other on a street with two lanes, destined to crash into each other if they don't evade. The crash is avoided if and only if both vehicles move to their respective right or both move to their respective left.

4.1   Axioms for Aggregation Functions

As a first axiom we consider monotonicity. If we input more entries of non-zero member contribution into the computation, we will want the outcome responsibility to increase as well. Similarly, if we input the same number of member contributions but some of them have larger values, we also expect the outcome responsibility to be larger (instead of just larger or equal, as is demanded in the definition of aggregation functions).

(BSM$^+$) *Bounded strict monotonicity under adding non-zero entries.* For $[x_1, \ldots, x_n] \in [0,1]^n$ and $x_{n+1} \in (0,1]$ it holds that

$$\text{either} \quad \mathbf{agg}([x_1, \ldots, x_n]) = 1 \quad \text{or} \quad \mathbf{agg}([x_1, \ldots, x_n]) < \mathbf{agg}([x_1, \ldots, x_n, x_{n+1}]).$$

(BSM$^>$) *Bounded strict monotonicity under increasing entries.* For $[x_1, \ldots, x_n], [y_1, \ldots, y_n] \in [0,1]^n$ where there is a $j \in \{1, \ldots, n\}$ s.t. $x_j < y_j$ and $x_i = y_i$ for all $i \neq j$ it holds that

$$\text{either} \quad \mathbf{agg}([x_1, \ldots, x_n]) = 1 \quad \text{or} \quad \mathbf{agg}([x_1, \ldots, x_n]) < \mathbf{agg}([y_1, \ldots, y_n]).$$

(BSM) *Bounded strict monotonicity.* Both of the above hold.

Strengthening this idea, we can ask for the aggregation function to not only be monotone, but linear in each component. That is, if we keep the other input values fixed, the influence of one member contribution on the outcome should be linear. In order to define this we use the following notational convention. For an n-ary aggregation function $\mathbf{agg}^{(n)}$, an n-dimensional vector $\bar{\mathbf{r}} = (\mathbf{r}_1, \ldots, \mathbf{r}_n)$, and an index $i \leq n$, let $\mathbf{agg}^{(n)}_{\bar{\mathbf{r}}, -i}(x) := \mathbf{agg}^{(n)}(\mathbf{r}_1, \ldots, \mathbf{r}_{i-1}, x, \mathbf{r}_{i+1}, \ldots, \mathbf{r}_n)$ be the function obtained from $\mathbf{agg}^{(n)}$ by keeping all input values fixed as given by $\bar{\mathbf{r}}$, except for the i-th entry.

(LIN) *Linearity in each component.* For each $n \in \mathbb{N}_{\geq 1}$, for each input vector of length n, $\bar{\mathbf{r}} \in [0,1]^n$ and for each index $i \leq n$, $\mathbf{agg}^{(n)}_{\bar{\mathbf{r}}, -i}$ is a linear function. That is,

$$\mathbf{agg}_{\bar{\mathbf{r}},-i}^{(n)}(x) = \mathbf{agg}^{(n)}(\mathbf{r}_1, \ldots, \mathbf{r}_{i-1}, x, \mathbf{r}_{i+1}, \ldots, \mathbf{r}_n)$$
$$= ax + b \qquad \text{for some } a, b \in \mathbb{R}.$$

The third set of axioms concerns the behaviour of the aggregation function under certain special input values and can be interpreted as follows. Firstly, we can require that having been assigned full member contribution can not be relativized by other actions. On the other hand, we can demand that adding a decision which had a member contribution of 0 does not change an agents', or their groups', assigned outcome responsibility. Lastly, one could require that doing something "equally bad" multiple times does not change the ascribed outcome responsibility.

(AN1) *Annihilator 1.* For each $n \in \mathbb{N}_{\geq 1}$ and all $[x_1, \ldots, x_n] \in [0, 1]^n$ it holds that if $x_k = 1$ for some $k \in \{1, \ldots, n\}$ then

$$\mathbf{agg}([x_1, \ldots, x_n]) = 1.$$

(NE0) *Neutral element 0.* For each $n \in \mathbb{N}_{\geq 1}$, all $[x_1, \ldots, x_n] \in [0, 1]^n$ such that $x_i = 0$ for some $i \in \{1, \ldots, n\}$ it holds that

$$\mathbf{agg}([x_1, \ldots, x_n]) = \mathbf{agg}([x_1, \ldots, x_{i-1}, x_{i+1}, \ldots, x_n]).$$

(SIP) *Strong idempotency.* For all $k \in \mathbb{N}$ and $\mathbf{x} \in \bigcup_{n \in \mathbb{N}_{\geq 1}} [0, 1]^n$ it holds that

$$\mathbf{agg}(\underbrace{\mathbf{x} \oplus \ldots \oplus \mathbf{x}}_{k \text{ times}}) = \mathbf{agg}(\mathbf{x}),$$

where $\mathbf{x} \oplus \ldots \oplus \mathbf{x} \in [0, 1]^{kn}$ is the vector obtained by concatenating $\mathbf{x}$ with itself k times.

The next axiom, *anonymity*, requires that it does not matter who exactly makes a certain decision, only the 'value' of their decision matters for the final evaluation. Additionally, one can require that the time of the decision making has no effect.

(AAT) *Anonymity (with respect to agents and time).* For any $\mathbf{x} \in [0, 1]^n$ and any permutation π of the entries in $\mathbf{x}$ it holds that $\mathbf{agg}(\mathbf{x}) = \mathbf{agg}(\pi(\mathbf{x}))$.

Finally, we consider an axiom which seems very natural if we hold that outcome responsibility and member contribution are intended to capture aspects of the same concept: that outcome responsibility is to be zero exactly in those cases where all member contributions which we provide as an input are also zero.

(RED) *Reducibility.* For any $\mathbf{x} \in [0, 1]^n$ it holds that $\mathbf{agg}(\mathbf{x}) = 0$ iff $\mathbf{x} = (0, \ldots, 0)$.

4.2   Proposed Aggregation Functions

Having developed a set of possibly desirable properties for aggregation functions we now continue by suggesting specific functions. We will discuss the full matrix of axiom compliance in Sect. 4.3. Let a tree $\mathcal{T}$, group of agents $G \subseteq I$ and outcome node $w \in V_o$ be given. We drop $\mathcal{T}$ and G from the notation. Note that the first proposed aggregator, the sum, is technically not an aggregation function in the sense of our definition in Sect. 2, as it might exceed the interval $[0, 1]$. We still include it here as it is a natural way to aggregate member contributions.

Variant 1, sum.

$$\mathbf{sum}[(\mathbf{r}(i, v, \mathbf{a}_{v \rightarrow w}))_{i \in G, v \in V_i \cap H(w)}] := \sum_{i \in G, v \in V_i \cap H(w)} \mathbf{r}(i, v, \mathbf{a}_{v \rightarrow w})$$

Variant 2, average.

$$\mathbf{avg}[(\mathbf{r}(i, v, \mathbf{a}_{v \rightarrow w}))_{i \in G, v \in V_i \cap H(w)}] := \frac{1}{|\{ v \in V_i \cap H(w) \mid i \in G \}|} \sum_{i \in G, v \in V_i \cap H(w)} \mathbf{r}(i, v, \mathbf{a}_{v \rightarrow w})$$

Variant 3, maximum.

$$\mathbf{max}[(\mathbf{r}(i, v, \mathbf{a}_{v \rightarrow w}))_{i \in G, v \in V_i \cap H(w)}] := \max_{i \in G, v \in V_i \cap H(w)} \mathbf{r}(i, v, \mathbf{a}_{v \rightarrow w})$$

Variant 4, modified product.

$$\mathbf{mprod}[(\mathbf{r}(i, v, \mathbf{a}_{v \rightarrow w}))_{i \in G, v \in V_i \cap H(w)}] := 1 - \prod_{i \in G, v \in V_i \cap H(w)} (1 - \mathbf{r}(i, v, \mathbf{a}_{v \rightarrow w})).$$

4.3   Evaluation of Proposed Aggregation Functions

In addition to the axioms introduced in Sect. 4, we include one more property in our axiomatic analysis. As we noted above, the sum technically is not an aggregation function. To make this explicit we add the following property that is satisfied by all aggregation functions in the sense of the definition in Sect. 2 but is violated by the sum.

(01B) *0,1-boundedness.* $\mathbf{agg}(\bigcup_{n \in \mathbb{N}_{\geq 1}} [0, 1]) \subseteq [0, 1].$

Proposition 3. *Compliance of the candidate aggregation functions with the axioms from Sect. 4.1 and (01B) is as depicted in Table 3.*

Validating the compliance as noted in the above proposition is mostly straight-forward. We refer the proof to the full version of the paper.

Table 3. Summary of axiom compliance by the proposed aggregation functions.

	(01B)	(BSM$^+$)	(BSM$^>$)	(LIN)	(AN1)	(NE0)	(SIP)	(AAT)	(RED)
sum	✓	✓	✓	✓	×	✓	×	✓	✓
avg	✓	×	✓	✓	×	×	✓	✓	✓
max	✓	×	×	×	✓	×	✓	✓	✓
mprod	✓	✓	✓	✓	✓	✓	×	✓	✓

The sum fulfills monotonicity, anonymity and reducibility. However, it fails 0,1-boundedness and thus is not an aggregation function. Averaging the sum remains 0,1-bounded but fails monotonicity under adding entries. As the same reasoning applies to other normalisation methods we move away from considering normalisations of the sum. We mention the maximum for reasons of completeness, despite it clearly not fulfilling any monotonicity requirements. The same would hold for the product, which is why it is not not mentioned in detail and does not appear in the table. However, a modification of the product seems promising: The issue with the first three proposed functions seems to be that they do not correctly include additional contributions when considering several actions, thus either failing 0,1-boundedness or monotonicity. The rationale behind the modified product becomes clearer when we look at an example of a repeated action. Consider the scenario depicted in Fig. 3, and consider the path where agent i selects continue twice and then repair. If we assume that continuing once with a 90% chance of disaster produces a member contribution of 0.9, then in the given example continuing the first time adds 0.9 to the outcome responsibility, continuing the second times adds 0.9 of the remaining interval (i.e. 0.09), and the final decision to repair does not reduce any of the previously gained contributions. This example also shows that the modified product does not fulfill (SIP) and hints at non-compliance with (SIP) being in fact desirable in certain cases.

From the proposed aggregation functions, **mprod** is the only one that is a proper aggregation function for any input member contribution values and which fulfills all the described axioms except for (SIP).

Moreover, we can even show the stronger statement that **mprod** is characterised by a combination of the discussed axioms and properties[9].

Theorem 1. *The axioms (LIN), (AAT), (NE0) and (AN1) together uniquely characterise* **mprod** *among all aggregation functions.*

We only present the main idea of the proof here. For the full details we refer to the full version of the paper.

---

[9] We require (LIN) for this characterisation. As one might argue against this axiom due to it being very strong and rather technical it is important to point out that even without the characterisation result, **mprod** is the most highly axiom compliant function out of the ones we suggested.

Proof (Sketch). Linearity in each component together with a subset of the other axioms constrains the function to

$$\mathbf{agg}([\mathbf{r}_1, \ldots, \mathbf{r}_n]) =$$
$$b + \sum_{i=1}^{n} a_i \mathbf{r}_i + \sum_{\substack{i,i'=1 \\ i<i'}}^{n} a_{i,i'} \mathbf{r}_i \mathbf{r}_{i'} + \cdots + \sum_{\substack{i^{(1)}, \ldots, i^{(n-1)}=1 \\ i^{(1)}<\ldots<i^{(n-1)}}} a_{i^{(1)}, \ldots, i^{(n)}} \mathbf{r}_{i^{(1)}} \cdots \mathbf{r}_{i^{(n-1)}} + a_{1,\ldots,n} \mathbf{r}_1 \cdots \mathbf{r}_n.$$

Further axioms restrict the values of the coefficients as follows. (AAT) implies that $a_1 = \ldots = a_n =: a^{(1)}$, $a_{1,2} = \ldots = a_{n-1,n} =: a^{(2)}$ etc. Since an aggregation function is the identity on $[0,1]$, we know that $a^{(1)} = 1$, (NE0) additionally implies that $b = 0$ and with $(AN1)$ we can inductively prove that $a^{(k)} = (-1)^{k-1} \quad \forall k \geq 1$, which results precisely in the function **mprod**.

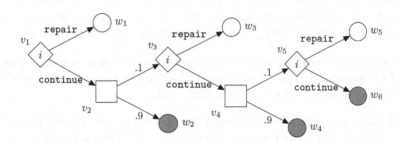

Fig. 3. Representation of an example scenario of a repeated action. The operator of a large machine can either ignore a warning of the machine and continue using it, knowing that this has a high chance of irreversible damage or perform a repair. At some point in time the last chance to repair the machine is reached.

5   Outcome Responsibility Functions

After exploring member contribution functions and aggregation functions on their own we will now turn our attention to outcome responsibility as a combination of the two previously mentioned classes of functions. Again, we first propose a set of axioms that capture interesting properties before checking axiom compliance for a set of proposed functions.

5.1   Axioms for Outcome Responsibility Functions

The following four axioms give upper and lower bounds on the assigned responsibility and in that sense follow a similar rationale as (AMC) and (FMC) for member contribution functions. The first two axioms present upper bounds by determining that there are cases in which no responsibility is to be ascribed. The first one captures the idea that if an agent has complete control over the situation and steers it towards a desired outcome, that agent should not be assigned responsibility. The second axiom requires that agents have initial strategies which avoid responsibility. The fact that there is a qualitatively different action available is seen by some authors as one of the fundamental criteria for assigning responsibility. For example Braham and van Hees [5] introduce an *avoidance opportunity condition*, which requires that a person has an opportunity to avoid contributing to an outcome in order for responsibility ascription to be appropriate. A similar – but not equivalent – idea is captured by the second axiom.

(CC) *Complete control.* Given a tree $\mathcal{T}$, a singleton group $G = \{i\}$ and a desirable outcome node $w \in V_o \setminus \epsilon$ such that the path to w involves only decisions of agent i and no decision nodes of other agents nor ambiguity or probability nodes, $H(w) \subseteq V_i$. Then $\mathcal{R}(w, i) = 0$.

(NUR) *No unavoidable responsibility.* Given a tree $\mathcal{T}$, each group $G \subseteq I$ must have an original strategy that is guaranteed to avoid any outcome responsibility. That is, denoting the root node of $\mathcal{T}$ by v_r, for every group of agents $G \subseteq I$ there must be a strategy $\sigma \in \Sigma(\mathcal{T}, G, v_r)$, such that $\mathcal{R}(G, w) = 0$ for all outcomes $w \in V_o \cap \sigma(V_G \cap B^\sim(v_r))$ reachable with that strategy.

The next two axioms are lower bounds in the sense that they require a certain amount of responsibility to be attributed. Specifically, they request the absence of (individual or group-wise) responsibility voids.

(NRV) *No responsibility voids.* Given a tree $\mathcal{T}$ with no uncertainty nodes, $V_a = V_p = \emptyset$, and a set of undesirable outcomes $\epsilon \neq V_o$. Then for each undesirable outcome $w \in \epsilon$, some group is at least partially responsible, i.e., there exists a $G \subseteq I$ with $\mathcal{R}(G, w) > 0$.

(NIRV) *No individual responsibility voids.* Given a tree $\mathcal{T}$ with no uncertainty nodes, $V_a = V_p = \emptyset$, and a set of undesirable outcomes $\epsilon \neq V_o$. Then for each undesirable outcome $w \in \epsilon$, there is an individual agent $i \in I$ with $\mathcal{R}(\{i\}, w) > 0$.

Note that as we allow group composition to inform member contribution functions it is not necessarily the case that (NRV) together with (RED) implies (NIRV).

The absence of individual responsibility in the presence of group responsibility is discussed repeatedly in the literature. That is, cases where (NRV) holds, but (NIRV) for members of the same group does not. For example, in the presentation by Duijf [7] the premises we provide in our axioms place us in a cooperative decision context with no external uncertainty but with coordination uncertainty. This combination is shown to allow for the absence of individual responsibility in the presence of group responsibility. Similarly, Braham and van Hees [5] show that this combination is possible if a mechanism does not allow for the attribution of different aspects of an outcome to varying individuals but only for an overall attribution of responsibility at large, which is the case in our representation.

In addition to the above axioms that are specifically designed for outcome responsibility functions, we also say that an outcome responsibility function satisfies (KSym), (AMC) or (FMC) – as well as their weaker versions (AMC$^\sim$) and

(FMC~) – if the underlying member contribution function satisfies the respective axiom. Using this we prove the following impossibilities.

Proposition 4. *For any outcome responsibility function $\mathcal{R}$ the following impossibilities hold.*

(i) $\mathcal{R}$ can not simultaneously satisfy (KSym), (FMC), and (NUR).
(ii) $\mathcal{R}$ can not simultaneously satisfy (KSym), (NRV), and (NUR).

5.2   Evaluation

In the following we show the compliance of certain classes of responsibility functions with these new axioms, with the full overview being visible in Table 4.

Proposition 5. *Let* **agg** *be an aggregation function fulfilling (BSM) and (RED) and let $\mathbf{r}^{\triangle}$ for $\triangle \in \{$ like, risk, negl $\}$ be as defined earlier. Then the compliance of the responsibility function $\mathcal{R}^{\triangle} := \mathbf{agg} \circ \mathbf{r}^{\triangle}$ with the axioms (NRV), (NIRV), (NUR) and (CC) is as presented in Table 4.*

This result immediately leads us to the following conclusion.

Table 4. Summary of axiom compliance by the three variants of member contribution from Sect. 3.1 combined with an aggregation functions **agg** that satisfies (BSM) and (RED). For the axioms initially defined for member contribution functions on the right hand side of the table we say that the combined function satisfies the axiom if its member contribution function satisfies it.

	(NRV)	(NIRV)	(NUR)	(CC)	(KSym)	(AMC)	(FMC)
agg $\circ$ **r**^{like}	✓	✓	✓	✓	×	✓	✓
agg $\circ$ **r**^{risk}	✓	✓	×	✓	✓	×	✓
agg $\circ$ **r**^{negl}	×	×	✓	✓	✓	✓	×

Corollary 1. *Given a tree $\mathcal{T}$, a group of agents $G \subseteq I$ and an outcome node $w \in V_o$. Then the following two statements hold.*

*(i) **mprod**$\circ$**r**^{risk} fulfills all the axioms we discussed in Sect. 4 (except for (SIP)) as well as (KSym), (FMC), (NRV), (NIRV), and (CC).*
*(ii) **mprod**$\circ$**r**^{negl} fulfills all the axioms we discussed in Sect. 4 (except for (SIP)) as well as (KSym), (AMC), (NUR), and (CC).*

The results presented here show that if we constrain ourselves to functions that satisfy (KSym), we have to choose between fulfilling (NUR) and thus ensure some upper bound on the ascribed responsibility or fulfilling (NIRV) and (FMC) and ensure some lower bound. The two combinations discussed in the above lemma provide solutions to both choices, while being maximally compliant with the other presented axioms.

5.3   Application to Example Scenario

In the example presented in Fig. 3 we obtain the following outcome responsibility values using the two functions determined above: **mprod** $\circ$ $\mathbf{r}^{\mathrm{risk}}$ and **mprod** $\circ$ $\mathbf{r}^{\mathrm{negl}}$. The results are summarised in Table 5. Note that as selecting `repair` always results in a member contribution of zero, $\mathbf{r}^{\mathrm{risk}}$ and $\mathbf{r}^{\mathrm{negl}}$ actually return the same results.

Table 5. Summary of the outcome responsibility values for all outcomes in the example in Fig. 3.

	w_1	w_2	w_3	w_4	w_5	w_6
mprod $\circ$ $\mathbf{r}^{\mathrm{like}}$	0	0.9	0.9	0.99	0.99	1
mprod $\circ$ $\mathbf{r}^{\mathrm{risk}}$	0	0.9	0.9	0.99	0.99	1

6   Conclusion

We employed an axiomatic analysis of responsibility quantification in complex decision situations containing interactions and uncertainty. The model is based on representing appropriate decision scenarios via an extension of extensive form game trees and assigning (moral) responsibility for a certain outcome to a group of agents as a value between 0 and 1, based on the change in the probability of an undesirable outcome.

We split responsibility functions for outcomes into member contribution functions and aggregation functions. The former can be viewed as functions for member contribution assigned to individuals as part of a group, while the latter determine the aggregation of these individual values into a group evaluation. This separation enables a more fine-grained analysis of the functions' properties. We translated different kinds of desiderata from the literature on (moral) responsibility into this setting and formulated respective axioms for the contributing functions.

We presented an impossibility result for three axioms regarding member contribution. This elucidates the intuition that a principled and sensible assignment of responsibility in coordination games is impossible. We were then able to single out two promising candidates that satisfy the two opposing points of view in situations such as the coordination game, and that satisfy all of the other considered axioms for member contribution functions.

We were able to derive a characterisation of an appealing aggregation function, the modified product, using five intuitive axioms. For outcome responsibility functions we prove compliance with respective axioms for classes of combinations of member contribution functions and aggregation functions. The previously mentioned impossibility result transfers to the case of outcome responsibility. When we require that agents are assigned the same member contribution in all situations they cannot discern between, then a responsibility function has to either allow for voids or for unavoidable responsibility. The same pair of member contribution functions which we determined earlier, paired with the selected aggregation function, is able to capture each side of this division.

The work presented in this paper can be continued in various directions. First of all, we can use the functions which we determined here as fulfilling most of the desired properties in real-world application scenarios. Next, a characterisation of the space of all three functions using appropriate axioms would be ideal. Another promising direction for future research is a differentiation of the proposed responsibility functions, including for example the distinction between primary and secondary responsibility or the introduction of weighted aggregation functions that are not indifferent to the time at which a decision was taken. The latter enables the study of responsibility in settings where more recent actions or decisions should carry more weight than more distant ones. Finally, it would be very interesting to integrate our approach within a full epistemic logic such as those mentioned in the introduction, in order to capture notions of knowledge on a group level like distributed or common knowledge, as well as beliefs etc. and the dynamics and interrelations of these notions within the system.

Acknowledgements. We would like to thank the three anonymous reviewers for their valuable comments regarding an earlier version of the paper. Additionally, we want to thank Alexandru Baltag, Markus Brill, Rupert Klein, the rest of the Efficient Algorithm research group at Technical University Berlin, as well as the copan collaboration at the Potsdam Institute for Climate Impact Research for fruitful discussions and comments.

The research leading to these results received funding from the Deutsche Forschungsgemeinschaft (DFG, German Research Foundation) under Germany's Excellence Strategy – The Berlin Mathematics Research Center MATH+ (EXC-2046/1, project ID: 390685689) and under grant BR 4744/2-1.

References

1. Baldoni, M., Baroglio, C., Boissier, O., May, K.M., Micalizio, R., Tedeschi, S.: Accountability and responsibility in agent organizations. In: Miller, T., Oren, N., Sakurai, Y., Noda, I., Savarimuthu, B.T.R., Cao Son, T. (eds.) PRIMA 2018. LNCS (LNAI), vol. 11224, pp. 261–278. Springer, Cham (2018). https://doi.org/10.1007/978-3-030-03098-8_16
2. Baltag, A., Canavotto, I., Smets, S.: Causal agency and responsibility: a refinement of STIT logic. In: Giordani, A., Malinowski, J. (eds.) Logic in High Definition. TL, vol. 56, pp. 149–176. Springer, Cham (2021). https://doi.org/10.1007/978-3-030-53487-5_8
3. Belnap, N., Perloff, M., Xu, M.: Facing the Future. Agents and Choices in our Indeterminist World. Oxford University Press (2001)
4. Braham, M., van Hees, M.: An anatomy of moral responsibility. Mind **121**(483), 601–634 (2012)
5. Braham, M., van Hees, M.: Voids or fragmentation: moral responsibility for collective outcomes. Econ. J. **128**(612), F95–F113 (2018)

6. Broersen, J.: Modeling attempt and action failure in probabilistic STIT logic. In: Proceedings of the 22nd International Joint Conference on Artificial Intelligence (IJCAI), pp. 792–797. IJCAI (2011)
7. Duijf, H.: Responsibility voids and cooperation. Philos. Soc. Sci. **48**(4), 434–460 (2018)
8. Fischer, J.M., Tognazzini, N.A.: The Physiognomy of responsibility. Philosophy Phenomenological Res. **LXXXII**(2) (2011)
9. Glavaničová, D., Pascucci, M.: Formal analysis of responsibility attribution in a multimodal framework. In: Baldoni, M., Dastani, M., Liao, B., Sakurai, Y., Zalila Wenkstern, R. (eds.) PRIMA 2019. LNCS (LNAI), vol. 11873, pp. 36–51. Springer, Cham (2019). https://doi.org/10.1007/978-3-030-33792-6_3
10. Halpern, J.Y., Kleiman-Weiner, M.: Towards formal definitions of blameworthiness, intention, and moral responsibility. In: Proceedings of the AAAI Conference on Artificial Intelligence, vol. 32, no. 1, pp. 1853–1860 (2018)
11. Halpern, J.Y., Pearl, J.: Causes and explanations: a structural-model approach. Part I causes. Br. J. Philos. Sci. **56**(4), 843–887 (2005)
12. Hiller, S., Israel, J., Heitzig, J.: An Axiomatic Approach to Formalized Responsibility Ascription. arXiv preprint (2022). https://arxiv.org/abs/2111.06711
13. Hitchcock, C.: Probabilistic Causation. The Stanford Encyclopedia of Philosophy (2021). https://plato.stanford.edu/archives/spr2021/entries/causation-probabilistic/
14. Horty, J.F.: Agency and Deontic Logic. Oxford University Press (2001)
15. Kaiserman, A.: 'More of a cause': recent work on degrees of causation and responsibility. Philosophy Compass (2018)
16. Kvart, I.: Probabilistic cause and the thirsty traveller. J. Philos. Log. **31**, 139–179 (2002). https://doi.org/10.1023/A:1015507124004
17. Lewis, D.: Counterfactuals. Blackwell Publishing (1973)
18. Lewis, D.: Causation as Influence. J. Philos. **97**(4), 182–197 (2000)
19. de Lima, T., Royakkers, L., Dignum, F.: A logic for reasoning about responsibility. Logic J. IGPL **18**(1), 99–117 (2010)
20. Lorini, E., Longin, D., Mayor, E.: A logical analysis of responsibility attribution: emotions, individuals and collectives. J. Log. Comput. **24**(6), 1313–1339 (2014). https://doi.org/10.1093/logcom/ext072
21. Lorini, E., Sartor, G.: Influence and responsibility: a logical analysis. In: Proceedings of the 28th International Conference on Legal Knowledge and Information Systems (JURIX 2015), pp. 51–60. IOS press (2015)
22. Lorini, E., Schwarzentruber, F.: A logic for reasoning about counterfactual emotions. In: Proceedings of the 21st International Joint Conference on Artificial Intelligence (IJCAI), pp. 867–872. Pasadena, California, USA (2009). https://doi.org/10.1016/j.artint.2010.11.022
23. Mesiar, R., Kolesárová, A., Calvo, T., Komorníková, M.: A review of aggregation functions. In: Bustince, H., Herrera, F., Montero, J. (eds.) Fuzzy Sets and Their Extensions: Representation, Aggregation and Models, pp. 121–144. Springer, Berlin Heidelberg, Berlin, Heidelberg (2008). https://doi.org/10.1007/978-3-540-73723-0_7
24. Moore, M.: Causation in the law. In: Zalta, E.N. (ed.) The Stanford Encyclopedia of Philosophy. Metaphysics Research Lab, Stanford University, winter 2019 edn. (2019). https://plato.stanford.edu/archives/win2019/entries/causation-law/
25. Moore, M.S.: Causing, aiding, and the superfluity of accomplice liability. Univ. Pa. Law Rev. **156**(2), 395–452 (2007)

26. van de Poel, I.: The relation between forward-looking and backward-looking responsibility. In: Vincent, N.A., van de Poel, I., van den Hoven, J. (eds.) Moral Responsibility. Beyond Free Will and Determinism. Springer (2011). https://doi.org/10.1007/978-94-007-1878-4_3

27. Royakkers, L., Hughes, J.: Blame it on me. J. Philos. Log. **49**, 315–349 (2020). https://doi.org/10.1007/s10992-019-09519-7

28. Santoni de Sio, F., van den Hoven, J.: Meaningful human control over autonomous systems: a philosophical account. Front. Robot. AI **5**(15) (2018)

29. Tamminga, A., Hindriks, F.: The irreducibility of collectivce obligations. Philos. Stud. **177**, 1085–1109 (2020). https://doi.org/10.1007/s11098-018-01236-2

30. Thomson, W.: On the axiomatic method and its recent applications to game theory and resource allocation. Soc. Choice Welf. **18**(2), 327–386 (2001). https://doi.org/10.1007/s003550100106

31. Vallentyne, P.: Brute luck and responsibility. Politics Philos. Econ. **7**(1), 57–80 (2008)

32. Vincent, N.A.: A structured taxonomy of responsibility concepts. In: Vincent, N.A., Poel, I.v.d., Hoven, J.v.d. (eds.) Moral Responsibility. Beyond Free Will and Determinism. Springer (2011). https://doi.org/10.1007/978-94-007-1878-4_2

33. Wright, R.W.: Causation, responsibility, risk, probability, naked statistics, and proof: pruning the bramble bush by clarifying the concepts. Iowa Law Rev. **73**, 1001–1077 (1988)

34. Yazdanpanah, V., Dastani, M., Jamroga, W., Alechina, N., Logan, B.: Strategic responsibility under imperfect information. In: Proceedings of the 18th International Conference on Autonomous Agents and Multiagent Systems (AAMAS 2019). Montreal, Canada (2019)

35. Yazdanpanah, V., Gerding, E.H., Stein, S., Dastani, M., Jonker, C.M., Norman, T.J.: Responsibility research for trustworthy autonomous systems. In: Proceedings of the 20th International Conference on Autonomous Agents and Multi-Agent Systems (AAMAS 2021). Online (2021)

Task Selection Algorithm for Multi-Agent Pickup and Delivery with Time Synchronization

Tomoki Yamauchi(✉) ⓘ, Yuki Miyashita ⓘ, and Toshiharu Sugawara ⓘ

Computer Science and Communications Engineering, Waseda University,
Tokyo, Japan
{t.yamauchi,y.miyashita,sugawara}@isl.cs.waseda.ac.jp

Abstract. In this paper, we formulate the material transportation problem as a *multi-agent pickup and delivery with time synchronization* (MAPD-TS) problem, which is an extension of the well-known multi-agent pickup and delivery (MAPD) problem. In MAPD-TS, we consider the synchronization of the movement of transportation agents with that of external agents, such as trucks arriving and departing from time to time in a warehouse and elevators that transfer materials to and from different floors in a construction site. We then propose methods via which agents autonomously select the tasks for improving overall efficiency by reducing unnecessary waiting times. MAPD is an abstract formation of material transportation tasks, and a number of methods have been proposed only for efficiency and collision-free movement in closed systems. However, as warehouses and construction sites are not isolated closed systems, transportation agents must sometimes synchronize with external agents to achieve real efficiency, and our MAPD-TS is the abstract form of this situation. In our proposed methods for MAPD-TS, agents approximately estimate their arrival time at the carry-in/out port connected with external agents and autonomously select the task to perform next for improved synchronization. Thereafter, we evaluate the performance of our methods by comparing them with the baseline algorithms. We demonstrate that our proposed algorithms reduce the waiting times of both agents and external agents and thus could improve overall efficiency.

Keywords: Multi-agent pickup and delivery tasks · Multi-agent path finding · Multi-agent task selection · Decentralized robot path planning

1 Introduction

Technology for *multi-agent systems* used in enormous and complex real-world delivery/transportation applications, such as autonomous multi-vehicle systems in automated warehouses [15], delivery systems with multiple drones [4], and ride-sharing services [18] has been attracting considerable attention in recent years. However, increasing the number of agents often causes inefficiency owing

R. Aydoğan et al. (Eds.): PRIMA 2022, LNAI 13753, pp. 458–474, 2023.
https://doi.org/10.1007/978-3-031-21203-1_27

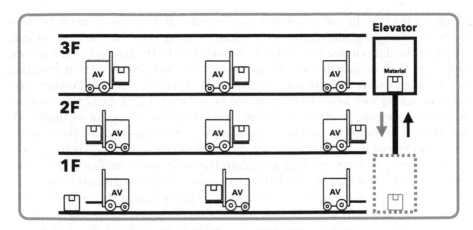

Fig. 1. Three-dimensional material transportation systems.

to redundant movement, collisions, and other resource conflicts. Thus, coordinated actions among agents are essential to avoid adverse effects and improve overall performance. Particularly, in pickup and delivery systems in a restricted environment wherein large heavy-duty *autonomous vehicle* (AV) agents carry heavy and large-sized materials, avoidance of collisions and deadlocks among agents is a crucial issue.

The problems involved in these applications are often formulated as the *multi-agent pickup and delivery* (MAPD) problem [7], in which pickup and delivery tasks are assigned to agents simultaneously. The agent with a task moves to the material storage area, load the specified material, deliver it to the specified location, and then unload it; thereafter, it will be assigned another task. Therefore, an MAPD problem instance with numerous tasks can be seen as the iteration of *multi-agent path-finding* (MAPF) problems, in which multiple agents generate collision-free paths to their current destinations. However, obtaining the optimal solution to the MAPF problem is generally NP-hard [8], which suggests that an MAPD problem is even more complex and time-consuming to solve.

Although many studies [6,7,10] have focused on the MAPD problem, most conventional studies assume closed systems with no interference with external systems. However, real-world MAPD application is generally not an isolated closed system, and thus, we have to consider some interference with an external system. Therefore, tasks may need to meet time requirements for synchronization. For example, let us consider a three-dimensional material transportation system in a building construction site where there are a few cargo elevators for vertical transportation of building materials and several AV agents in each maze-like floor for horizontal transportation as our target application (see Fig. 1). If AV agents and materials are considerably heavy such that they cannot board the elevators, AV agents in a floor must arrive and standby near the elevator to carry in and out the materials in coordination with other *external agents* (simply called ext-agents), such as *elevator control agents*. Although the time requirements may be soft constraints, AV agents are required to perform these tasks in a timely manner to prevent a long waiting time for the elevator cars owing to the limited number of elevators compared to the number of AV agents; moreover, their delay will result in the delay in vertical transportation, resulting in cascading delays to horizontal transportation on other floors. Furthermore, the time agents wait near elevators should be reduced. This type of time requirements also appears in other situations; in a retail warehouse, for example, AV agents need to complete carrying in packages of purchased goods by the time the outbound trucks leave, although they do not load and unload goods together.

For these problems, we first formulate the *multi-agent pickup and delivery with time synchronization* (MAPD-TS) problem, which is an extension of an MAPD problem by assuming coordination between agents to meet the time requirements. In MAPD-TS, a task set consists of different types of tasks: (1) *normal tasks* that require completion as quickly as possible, similar to the conventional MAPD problem, and (2) *synchronizing tasks* (we call them *sync-tasks*) that has the time requirement to effectively synchronize the movement of agents with that of other ext-agents, such as elevators and transport trucks.

Considering the aforementioned task characteristics, sync-tasks arrive dynamically according to requests from other ext-agents. Although several MAPD algorithms have been proposed, we focus on *standby-based deadlock avoidance* (SBDA) method [17] because it efficiently works in the maze-like environments that we envision. Furthermore, it seems well-suited for our targeted issue because several agents can stand by near the elevator for carrying-in/out the materials and make effective use of the limited access paths to it in a maze-like environment by increasing the degree of parallelism of task executions.

Therefore, we integrate the proposed task selection methods into SBDA to apply it to our MAPD-TS problems. We propose two task selection algorithms, *earliest loadable/unloadable time first* (ELUF) and *synchronization of arrival time with loadable/unloadable time first* (SALUF), in which agents autonomously select the task considering the time requirements of ext-agents to reduce unnecessary waiting time for both agents and ext-agents for improving overall transportation efficiency. We evaluate the performance of our proposed algorithms by comparing them to baseline methods under various experimental settings. Thereafter, we demonstrate that our proposed algorithms, especially SALUF, reduce the waiting time of agents and ext-agents and improve the overall efficiency in the MAPD-TS problem. Finally, we analyze the features of SALUF through experiments with various parameter settings.

2   Related Work

There have been studies on various perspectives on the MAPF/MAPD problem [11]. A major perspective is the coordination structure between agents, which can be broadly classified into centralized and decentralized coordination. Centralized planning and scheduling [1,6,12] includes the well-known *conflict-based search* algorithm proposed by Sharon et al. [12]. However, although we can expect completeness and optimality for MAPF/MAPD instances, centralized methods have scalability and robustness issues because the computational cost increases rapidly for an increasing number of agents [7].

In contrast, many decentralized methods with high scalability and robustness have also been proposed [7,10,16,17]. However, the solution quality of decentralized methods for the MAPD problem is not ensured because agents generate plans individually. Furthermore, they require specific constraints on, for example, environmental structure and task selection to detect and resolve conflicts and deadlocks among plans and guarantee completeness. For example, Ma et al. [7] proposed *token passing* (TP) using the *holding task endpoints* (HTE) [5,6], in which agents select tasks whose destinations do not overlap with currently executed tasks by other agents and generate plans that avoid collisions and deadlocks. However, although TP is effective in grid-like environments with an abundance of *endpoints*, where agents can stay for any finite period of time without blocking the movement of other agents, our maze-like environments usually have few endpoints, and task execution parallelism is reduced by HTE. Thus, the application of TP may reduce the transportation efficiency. In contrast, the SBDA proposed by Yamauchi et al. [17] achieves high transportation efficiency even in a maze-like environment with few endpoints; therefore, we believe that SBDA is suitable for integrating our methods for our target applications.

From the task assignment aspect of the MAPD problem, TP [7] and other studies [5,10,16,17] employ a simple method that assigns the task with the smallest travel time from the current location to the pickup location. In contrast, some studies [2,3,6,14] proposed task assignment methods similar to our approach. For example, Liu et al. [6] proposed a method to construct a directed complete graph with agents and tasks as vertices for an MAPD instance, plan a Hamiltonian cycle on the constructed graph by solving the associated traveling salesman problem, and convert a cycle to the task sequences to be assigned to each agent. This method improves the transportation efficiency but assumes the offline version of MAPD, where information on all tasks is known a priori. Therefore, we cannot apply it to an MAPD-TS problem, because any task, especially sync-tasks, can be dynamically generated upon requests from ext-agents. Wu et al. [14] formulated an extension of the MAPD considering task deadline requirements and proposed a priority-based framework that integrates task assignment and path planning. This method defines a metric, called flexibility, which is the task deadline minus the earliest possible completion time among all agents executing the target task and assigns tasks based on this metric. The main purpose of this method is to complete the task earlier than the deadline. However, in MAPD-TS, the agent cannot complete the sync-task even if the agent arrives at the carry-in/out port connected with ext-agents much earlier than the arrival time of the ext-agent, and the agent would be forced to wait a long time owing to the ext-agent. Thus, this method is not suitable for our purposes and cannot apply to MAPD-TS because it also assumes offline MAPD. Our target application is not a closed system; hence, transportation agents must sometimes synchronize with the ext-agents to some degree to achieve real efficiencies. However, to the best of our knowledge, there have been no studies that consider the synchronization of the movement of transportation agents with that of external agents in the conventional MAPD problem.

3 Preliminaries

3.1 MAPD Problem Formulation

An MAPD problem is described by the agent set $A = \{1, \ldots, M\}$, a finite set of (unexecuted) tasks $\mathcal{T} = \{\tau_1, \ldots\}$, and an environment represented by an undirected connected planar graph $G = (V, E)$ that can be embedded in a two-dimensional Euclidean space. Node $v \in V$ and edge $(u, v) \in E$ $(u, v \in V)$ denote a location and a path with length $l(u, v)$ in the environment, respectively, and an agent can move between u and v along (u, v). Let $V_{ep} (\subset V)$ be the set of *endpoints* that are *task endpoints*, which are nodes where materials can be picked up and delivered, and *non-task endpoints*, at which agents can stay indefinitely. We represent the set of task endpoints v_{tsk} by $V_{tsk} (\subset V_{ep})$, and the parking node [6] of agent $i \in A$ by $park_i$, which is unique to each agent. We assume that $park_i \in V_{ep} \setminus V_{tsk}$ is included in the non-task endpoints. Because we consider a maze-like environment, endpoints are set to the dead-ends in G, wherein a dead-end is a node with only one associated edge in G.

Our agent is, for example, a forklift-type AV with a picker or an arm in front that can load/unload a material using it in a specified direction at a specified node. This means that agents' orientations cannot be neglected; rather, agents can move back and forth without changing orientation. We introduce a discrete-time $t \in \mathbb{Z}^+$, where $\mathbb{Z}^+$ is the set of positive integers. The state of agent i at time t can be expressed by the pair of its *orientation* $o_i^t \in \mathbb{Z}^+$ and the moving *direction* $d_i^t \in \mathbb{Z}^+$, where $0 \leq o_i^t, d_i^t < 360$ in D $(\in \mathbb{Z}^+)$ increments. We define $o_i^t = 0$ and $d_i^t = 0$ as the north orientation/direction in G. Although D can have any number depending on the environmental structure (i.e., agents can move around in more than just a grid structure), we assume $D = 90$ for simplicity. Thus, the set of possible orientations is $\mathcal{D} = \{0, 90, 180, 270\} \ni o_i^t, d_i^t$.

Agents can execute actions *move*, *rotate*, *wait*, *load*, and *unload* on any node. We denote the durations of these actions by $T_{mo}(l)$, $T_{ro}(\theta)$, $T_{wa}(t)$, T_{ld}, and T_{ul}, respectively, where $l = l(u, v)$ is the length of the edge to move along, $\theta \in \mathbb{Z}^+$ is the rotation angle, and t is the waiting time. Suppose that agent i is on node v at t. The *move* action of agent i makes it move forward or backward along edge (u, v) to node u, after i has oriented appropriately at v. With *rotate* action, i can rotate D degrees clockwise (D) or counter-clockwise $(-D)$ from o_i^t, i.e., $o_i^{t+T_{ro}(D)} = o_i^t \pm D$, staying at v. Agent i starts from its own parking node $park_i \in V_{ep} \setminus V_{tsk}$ at $t = 0$ and stays back there if i has no task to fulfill.

An MAPD task $\tau_j \in \mathcal{T}$ is expressed by a tuple $\tau_j = (\sigma_{\tau_j}^{ld}, \sigma_{\tau_j}^{ul}, \phi_{\tau_j})$, where $\sigma_{\tau_j}^{ld} = (v_{\tau_j}^{ld}, o_{\tau_j}^{ld})$ $(\in V \times \mathcal{D})$ are the location and orientation for loading a material ϕ_{τ_j}, and $\sigma_{\tau_j}^{ul} = (v_{\tau_j}^{ul}, o_{\tau_j}^{ul})$ $(\in V \times \mathcal{D})$ are the location and orientation for unloading ϕ_{τ_j}. The agent needs to orient itself in the direction of $o_{\tau_j}^{ld}/o_{\tau_j}^{ul}$ when loading/unloading the material. Agents can carry only one material at a time. Agents have exclusive access to $\mathcal{T}$ and must complete $\forall \tau_j \in \mathcal{T}$ without deadlocks regarding the movement of agents and collisions (conflicts), then plan a path to their $park_i$ and return there. A conflict is defined as a situation where multiple agents occupy the same node or cross the same edge simultaneously.

3.2   Standby-Based Deadlock Avoidance

We briefly describe the SBDA [17], focusing on the relevant part of the task selection process because it is also key to our proposed methods. *Standby nodes* are nodes that are guaranteed for agents to stay for a finite period of time and are identified in real-time. In the graph $G = (V, E)$, a node is an *articulation point* (AP) if and only if removing it with the associated edges splits the connected area of G and increases the number of connected components. A node that is neither endpoint, dead-end, nor AP in G is a *potential standby node* used as a standby node when necessary. The set of all potential standby nodes in G is denoted by $\mathcal{S}_{psn}(G)$ ($\subset V$). If G is a connected graph and $\mathcal{S}_{psn}(G) \neq \varnothing$, then the subgraph obtained by removing any node in $\mathcal{S}_{psn}(G)$ from G is also a connected graph. Therefore, even if an agent stays at a potential standby node for a finite period of time, SBDA enables other agents to generate paths to reach their destinations without passing through that node. $\mathcal{S}_{psn}(G)$ can be efficiently identified using *articulation-point-finding* (APF) algorithms, such as Tarjan's algorithm [13] with a computational complexity of $O(|V| + |E|)$ [9].

When a standby node is reserved by an agent, other agents cannot pass through it. This means that removing standby nodes and associated edges temporarily modifies the structure of the graph G. Denoting the modified graph at time t as $G_t = (V_t, E_t)$, the set of potential standby nodes in G_t is denoted by $\mathcal{S}_{psn}(G_t)$. $\mathcal{S}_{psn}(G_t)$ can be also efficiently identified using the APF algorithm. Note that $G = G_0$. A potential standby node $v \in \mathcal{S}_{psn}(G_t)$ becomes a standby node when agent $i \in A$ reserves a stay. Conversely, when i leaves standby node v, then v is no longer a standby node. The set of all standby nodes reserved by agents is denoted by $\mathcal{S}_t = \{(v, i) \mid i \in A$ reserves v as standby node$\}$.

Before agents begin the MAPD tasks, SBDA generates the set of associated potential standby nodes $s(v_{tsk}) = \{v_{psn} \in \mathcal{S}_{psn}(G) \mid dist(v_{psn}, v_{tsk}) \leq \alpha\}$ for $\forall v_{tsk}$ ($\in V_{tsk}$), where $dist(v_1, v_2)$ is the shortest path length between v_1 and v_2 and parameter α (≥ 0) is the threshold for the shortest path length between the endpoint and the standby node. Note that it is possible that $s(v_{tsk}) \cap s(v'_{tsk}) \neq \varnothing$ and $s(v_{tsk}) = \varnothing$ for $v_{tsk}, v'_{tsk} \in V_{tsk}$. Let $s_t(v_{tsk}) = s(v_{tsk}) \cap \mathcal{S}_{psn}(G_t)$ denote the set of potential standby nodes for v_{tsk} at t. Thus, $s(v_{tsk}) = s_0(v_{tsk})$ is the set of initial potential standby nodes for G ($= G_0$). The set of *free potential standby nodes* at t that are not included in the associated potential standby nodes is defined as $\mathcal{S}^c_{psn}(G_t) = \mathcal{S}_{psn}(G_t) \setminus \bigcup_{v_{tsk} \in V_{tsk}} s_t(v_{tsk})$.

SBDA uses a sharable memory area, the *status management token* (SMT), which can be accessed exclusively by one agent at a time for managing the status of planning, agents, and standby nodes, as well as for detecting conflicts with other agents. SMT comprises the *task execution status table* (TEST), the *reservation table* (RT), and the *standby-node status table* (SST). TEST is a set of tuples (τ, v, i), where τ is the currently executing task by agent i and v is the load or unload node specified by τ. Thus, i adds two tuples (τ, v^{ld}_τ, i) and (τ, v^{ul}_τ, i) to the TEST when i selects τ, and removes the corresponding entry when i arrives at v^{ld}_τ or v^{ul}_τ. RT is a set of *valid tuples* $(v, [s^i_v, e^i_v], i)$ when $e^i_v \geq t$ (t is the current time), where $[s^i_v, e^i_v]$ is the time interval while i occupies node

Fig. 2. Loadable time and unloadable time.

v. Agents use the reservation data in RT to generate collision-free plans. Note that a tuple is deleted from RT when it expires and becomes invalid.

Finally, SST is used to manage the state of all standby nodes that are dynamically referenced and modified by SBDA. The SST at t consists of (1) the initial set of potential standby nodes, $\mathcal{S}_{psn}(G)$, (2) the initial set of all pairs of endpoints and associated potential standby nodes, $\{(v_{tsk}, s(v_{tsk})) \mid v_{tsk} \in V_{tsk}\}$, (3) the set of pairs of standby nodes and the agent i that reserves the nodes, $(v_{sn}, i) \in \mathcal{S}_t$, and (4) *crowded list*, C_L ($\subset A$), which is the set of agents that temporarily stay at a free potential standby node in $\mathcal{S}_{psn}^c(G_t)$.

4   Proposed Method

4.1   MAPD-TS Problem Formulation

We formulate the MAPD-TS problem, which is an extension of the conventional MAPD problem by introducing the special task endpoints, *carrying-in/out ports* (simply called ports) $v_{prt} \in V_{prt}$ ($\subset V_{tsk}$), at which agents can load and unload the material into/from ext-agents such as elevators/truck agents. A task in MAPD-TS is described by $\tau_j = (\sigma_{\tau_j}^{ld}, \sigma_{\tau_j}^{ul}, \phi_{\tau_j})$, where $\sigma_{\tau_j}^{ld} = (v_{\tau_j}^{ld}, o_{\tau_j}^{ld}, t_{\tau_j}^{ld})$ ($\in V \times \mathcal{D} \times \mathbb{Z}^+$) and $t_{\tau_j}^{ld}$ is *loadable time* for a material ϕ_{τ_j}, and $\sigma_{\tau_j}^{ul} = (v_{\tau_j}^{ul}, o_{\tau_j}^{ul}, t_{\tau_j}^{ul})$ ($\in V \times \mathcal{D} \times \mathbb{Z}^+$) and $t_{\tau_j}^{ul}$ is *unloadable time* for ϕ_{τ_j}. For the sake of simplicity, we assume that there is no τ_j which is $v_{\tau_j}^{ld} \in V_{prt}$ and $v_{\tau_j}^{ul} \in V_{prt}$.

As a port is a node for access to an ext-agent, then $t_{\tau_j}^{ld}$ (or $t_{\tau_j}^{ul}$) > 0 only if $v_{\tau_j}^{ld}$ (or $v_{\tau_j}^{ul}$) $\in V_{prt}$; otherwise, $t_{\tau_j}^{ld}$ and/or $t_{\tau_j}^{ul} = 0$, meaning that an agent can load and/or unload it anytime. If $v_{\tau_j}^{ld}, v_{\tau_j}^{ul} \notin V_{prt}$, τ_j is a normal task that has nothing to do with ext-agents, so $t_{\tau_j}^{ld}, t_{\tau_j}^{ul} = 0$; otherwise, τ_j is a sync-task. We denote the set of the sync-tasks as $\mathcal{T}^{syn}$ ($\subset \mathcal{T}$); thus, $\mathcal{T} \setminus \mathcal{T}^{syn}$ is the set of normal tasks. The set of sync-tasks whose load or unload node is $v_{prt} \in V_{prt}$ is denoted by $R^{ld}(v_{prt}) = \{\tau \in \mathcal{T}^{syn} \mid v_{prt} = v_{\tau}^{ld}\}$ or $R^{ul}(v_{prt}) = \{\tau \in \mathcal{T}^{syn} \mid v_{prt} = v_{\tau}^{ul}\}$, respectively.

Upon a request at t from an ext-agent whose port is $v_{prt} \in V_{prt}$, at most C_{prt} ($\in \mathbb{Z}^+$) sync-tasks whose loading or unloading nodes are v_{prt} (thus, a total of at most $2C_{prt}$ sync-tasks) are generated and added to $\mathcal{T}$ (thus, they are also added to $R^{ld}(v_{prt})$ or $R^{ul}(v_{prt})$). Parameter C_{prt} is the *maximum capacity* of an ext-agent at v_{prt}. For a generated sync-task $\tau_j^{syn} \in \mathcal{T}^{syn}$, its loadable and unloadable time are set to $t_{\tau_j^{syn}}^{ld}$ (or $t_{\tau_j^{syn}}^{ul}$) $\leftarrow t + \gamma$ if $v_{\tau_j^{syn}}^{ld}$ (or $v_{\tau_j^{syn}}^{ul}$) $\in V_{prt}$; otherwise, it is set to $t_{\tau_j^{syn}}^{ld}$ (or $t_{\tau_j^{syn}}^{ul}$) $\leftarrow 0$, where $\gamma \in \mathbb{Z}^+$ is the time required for the ext-agent to

---

Algorithm 1. Task selection by agent i at time t for MAPD-TS in SBDA

1: **function** SELECTTASK(i)
2:    $\mathcal{T}^C =$ Set of tasks $\tau \in \mathcal{T}$ satisfying Conditions (C1), (C2) and (C3).
3:    // $\tau = (\sigma_\tau^{ld}, \sigma_\tau^{ul}, \phi_\tau)$, $\sigma_\tau^{ld} = (v_\tau^{ld}, o_\tau^{ld}, t_\tau^{ld})$, and $\sigma_\tau^{ul} = (v_\tau^{ul}, o_\tau^{ul}, t_\tau^{ul})$
4:    // v_c^i is current node, and o_c^i is current orientation.
5:    **if** $\mathcal{T}^C \neq \varnothing$ **then**
6:       $\tau^* \leftarrow \arg\min_{\tau \in \mathcal{T}^C} h(v_c^i, v_\tau^{ld}, o_c^i, o_\tau^{ld})$ // Greedy Method
7:       // The above greedy method can be replaced by our ELUF and SALUF.
8:       $\mathcal{T} \leftarrow \mathcal{T} \setminus \{\tau^*\}$; **return** τ^*
9:    **else return** false // i returns to $park_i$.
10:   **end if**
11: **end function**

---

arrive at v_{prt} and thus indirectly related to the frequency of arrival of a request from the ext-agent.

The ext-agent whose port is v_{prt} requests the generation of sync-tasks only when all of the following conditions are met to avoid redundant requests: (1) $R^{ld}(v_{prt}) \cup R^{ul}(v_{prt}) = \varnothing$, and (2) no agent has started to execute a sync-task toward v_{prt} to load/unload. Furthermore, under these conditions, we do not consider for simplicity the situation where, while the first ext-agent requests the generation of sync-tasks and moves to v_{prt}, the subsequent ext-agent requests the generation of sync-tasks for the same v_{prt}, simultaneously. We also assume that agents can preemptively start working on the tasks before the ext-agent arrives. We do not consider the order of loading and unloading at v_{prt}.

The conceptual examples of loadable/unloadable time of sync-tasks with the involved elevator ext-agent are shown in Fig. 2. Loadable/unloadable time implies the arrival time of an ext-agent at its carrying-in/out port $v_{prt} \in V_{prt}$, and the sync-task is generated before the arrival of an ext-agent. It is possible that agent i with τ_j reaches v_{prt} before $t_{\tau_j}^{ld}$ (or $t_{\tau_j}^{ul}$) but cannot load (or unload) the material and, as such, must wait until $t_{\tau_j}^{ld}$ (or $t_{\tau_j}^{ul}$); thus, it is inefficient to wait too long. Conversely, if i arrives late, the involved elevator agent are forced to wait longer, which may result in further delays in the MAPD-TS planning in other floors. Therefore, we have to reduce these waiting times of both agents, especially ext-agents, for the overall efficiency.

4.2 Task Selection for MAPD-TS

In SBDA, agent i has exclusive access to the SMT and selects a task to execute according to the function SELECTTASK(i), which uses the potential standby nodes for temporary waiting; however, we slightly modified it from the original SELECTTASK(i) in SBDA [17] (see the pseudo-code in Algorithm 1). Agent i selects a task in this function only when $\mathcal{T} \neq \varnothing$, otherwise it returns to parking node $park_i$. For $v_{psn} \in \mathcal{S}_{psn}(G_t)$, let $e_{v_{psn},t}^*$ be the last time that all agents would have passed through v_{psn} according to all current plans; this can be calculated by element $(v_{psn}, [s^j_{v_{psn}}, e^j_{v_{psn}}], j)$ in the RT of the SMT, or set to $e^*_{v_{psn},t} = t'$ (t' is the time when $e^*_{v_{psn},t}$ is calculated) if no such an element exists in the RT.

Agent i first generates a set $\mathcal{T}^C$ of tasks $\tau = (\sigma^{ld}_\tau, \sigma^{ul}_\tau, \phi_\tau) \in \mathcal{T}$ that satisfy the following conditions (C1), (C2) and (C3) at t, where v^i_c is the current node of i, $\sigma^{ld}_\tau = (v^{ld}_\tau, o^{ld}_\tau, t^{ld}_\tau)$, $\sigma^{ul}_\tau = (v^{ul}_\tau, o^{ul}_\tau, t^{ul}_\tau)$, and δ (≥ 0) is a threshold parameter of the time margin for standby node reservation, owing to i's inability to begin a stay at v_{psn} before $e^*_{v_{psn}}$ [Line 2].

(C1) If i is staying at its parking node at t (i.e., $v^i_c = park_i$), the C_L is empty.

(C2) Its load node v^{ld}_τ is *open* (i.e., the *RT* does not include it as an endpoint), or $s_t(v^{ld}_\tau) \neq \varnothing$ and $\exists v_{psn} \in s_t(v^{ld}_\tau)$ such that $e^*_{v_{psn}} - t \leq \delta$.

(C3) $|s_t(v^{ul}_\tau)| + 1$ is greater than the number of tuples with destination v^{ul}_τ included in the *TEST*.

Then, i selects task τ^* from $\mathcal{T}^C$ minimizing the heuristic function h of travel time from v_{src} to v_{dst} [Lines 5–8], where

$$h(v_{src}, v_{dst}, o_{src}, o_{dst}) = T_{mo}(dist(v_{src}, v_{dst})) + T_{ro}(diff(o_{src}, o_{dst})), \quad (1)$$

o_{src} is the orientation at v_{src}, o_{dst} is the orientation at v_{dst}, and $diff(o_1, o_2)$ is the difference between the orientation o_1 and o_2. We call this selection strategy the *greedy* method, which is a straightforward extension of the original SBDA. Note that this task selection strategy in Line 6 of Algorithm 1 is replaceable; thus, we will use the proposed methods in Sect. 4.3 in this line, instead of the greedy method. Therefore, although the loadable/unloadable time in Algorithm 1 is not used, the proposed methods will use them. i adds two TEST tuples of τ^* to the TEST of the SMT when i selects τ^*, and removes the corresponding entry when i arrives at $v^{ld}_{\tau^*}$ or $v^{ul}_{\tau^*}$ and completes loading/unloading after $t^{ld}_{\tau^*}$ or $t^{ul}_{\tau^*}$. If $\mathcal{T}^C = \varnothing$, i returns to $park_i$ [Line 9]. However, while staying at or en route to $park_i$, i can occasionally check whether some endpoints or standby nodes become open owing to the completions of other agents' tasks. Note that when $\mathcal{T}^C = \varnothing$, i can move to a standby node instead of $park_i$ and stay there for any finite period of time. However, staying at a standby node unnecessarily may force other agents to take long detours, because reserving a standby node by an agent temporarily modifies the structure of the graph G. Therefore, i returns to the agent-specific $park_i$, which does not affect other agents from the viewpoint of transportation efficiency. Furthermore, this action and conditions (C1), (C2) and (C3) might be able to reduce the number of agents to avoid an overcrowded environment.

4.3   Proposed Algorithms for MAPD-TS

We propose two novel task selection algorithms, ELUF and SALUF, for the MAPD-TS problem to reduce the waiting time of both agents and ext-agents for the overall transportation efficiency. Intuitively, in ELUF, agents preferentially select the sync-tasks with the earliest loadable/unloadable time. Therefore,

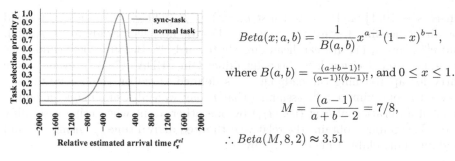

$$Beta(x; a, b) = \frac{1}{B(a, b)} x^{a-1}(1 - x)^{b-1},$$

where $B(a, b) = \frac{(a+b-1)!}{(a-1)!(b-1)!}$, and $0 \leq x \leq 1$.

$$M = \frac{(a - 1)}{a + b - 2} = 7/8,$$

$$\therefore Beta(M, 8, 2) \approx 3.51$$

Fig. 3. Task selection priority p_τ of SALUF ($a = 8, b = 2, \xi = 2000$, and $\omega = 0.2$).

although ELUF can reduce the waiting time of ext-agents, it does not consider the arrival time of the agents at the port, which may cause them to arrive later than the loadable/unloadable time, or conversely, arrive much earlier and wait too long.

In SALUF, agents individually decide the priority for task selection by considering the estimated arrival time at the specified port, the specified loadable/unloadable time, and the *probability density function* (PDF) derived from a *beta distribution* shown in Fig. 3, where M is the *mode* of the beta distribution. SALUF attempts to synchronize the arrival time of the agent with the loadable/unloadable time, which is also the arrival time of the ext-agent and, thus, can eliminate the unnecessary waiting time for both agents and the ext-agents. To set the priority asymmetrically between early and late estimated arrival times of agents for loadable/unloadable time, we use the beta distribution $Beta(x; a, b)$ whose the *skewness* of PDF can be easily controlled by parameters a and b. Furthermore, by setting the priority of the normal task as a constant, we can control the starts of normal tasks and sync-tasks.

ELUF. Agent i calculates the remaining time $rem(\tau, t)$ at t until the loadable/unloadable time of task $\tau \in \mathcal{T}^C$ by

$$rem(\tau, t) = \begin{cases} \max(t_\tau^{ld}, t_\tau^{ul}) - t & (\tau \in \mathcal{T}^{syn}) \\ \eta & (\tau \in \mathcal{T} \setminus \mathcal{T}^{syn}), \end{cases}$$

where η (≥ 0) is a threshold to prevent the agent from waiting too long for the arrival of the ext-agent. Thereafter, i generates a set $\mathcal{T}^F = \{\tau \in \mathcal{T}^C | rem(\tau, t) \leq \eta\}$. Finally, i selects task $\tau^* = \arg\min_{\tau \in \mathcal{T}^F} rem(\tau, t)$ (i uses the greedy method for tie-breaking) if $\mathcal{T}^F \neq \varnothing$, otherwise it returns to $park_i$. Thus, if both normal tasks and sync-tasks are included in $\mathcal{T}^F$, a sync-task will be selected.

SALUF. Agent i calculates the estimated arrival time t_τ^{est} for the sync-task $\tau \in \mathcal{T}^C \cap \mathcal{T}^{syn}$ using the heuristic function h from Formula (1) at time t by

$$t_\tau^{est} = \begin{cases} t + h(v_c^i, v_\tau^{ld}, o_c^i, o_\tau^{ld}) & (v_\tau^{ld} \in V_{prt}) \\ t + h(v_c^i, v_\tau^{ld}, o_c^i, o_\tau^{ld}) + (1 + s) \cdot T_{ld} + h(v_\tau^{ld}, v_\tau^{ul}, o_\tau^{ld}, o_\tau^{ul}) & (v_\tau^{ul} \in V_{prt}), \end{cases}$$

where $s \in \{0,1\}$ and $s = 0$ if $dist(v_c^i, v_\tau^{ld}) \leq \beta$ (where $\beta > \alpha$ is a threshold for direct heading toward the endpoint [17]) or no agent heads to an $s_t(v_\tau^{ld})$, and v_τ^{ld} is open, i.e., if i can head directly toward v_τ^{ld}. Because some conditions of destination decision have been introduced in SBDA [17] to prevent a side entry for approaching the endpoint, s is defined based on those conditions. i uses s to approximate t_τ^{est}, assuming that i may wait at a minimum the equivalent of a duration of *load* (i.e., T_{ld}) by one other agent when using a standby node. Thereafter, i obtains the relative estimated arrival time t_τ^{rel} using t_τ^{est} and loadable/unloadable time t_τ^{ld} or t_τ^{ul} by

$$t_\tau^{rel} = \begin{cases} t_\tau^{est} - t_\tau^{ld} & (v_\tau^{ld} \in V_{prt}) \\ t_\tau^{est} - t_\tau^{ul} & (v_\tau^{ul} \in V_{prt}). \end{cases}$$

Using beta distribution $Beta(x; a, b)$ with $a, b > 1$ ($\in \mathbb{Z}^+$), agent i then determines the synchronization degree $syn(t_\tau^{rel})$ ($0 \leq syn(t_\tau^{rel}) \leq Beta(M; a, b)$) of the estimated arrival time to the loadable/unloadable time using t_τ^{rel} by

$$syn(t_\tau^{rel}) = \begin{cases} Beta\left(\frac{t_\tau^{rel}}{\xi} + M\right) & (-\xi M \leq t_\tau^{rel} \leq \xi - \xi M) \\ 0 & (\text{otherwise}), \end{cases}$$

where ξ (> 0) is the parameter that magnifies $Beta(x; a, b)$ in the x-axis direction. Thereafter, i calculates the priority p_τ ($0 \leq p_\tau \leq 1$) of task $\tau \in \mathcal{T}^C$ at t using

$$p_\tau = \begin{cases} \dfrac{syn(t_\tau^{rel})}{Beta(M)} & (\tau \in \mathcal{T}^{syn}, t_\tau^{ld} > t \text{ or } t_\tau^{ul} > t) & (2) \\ 1 & (\tau \in \mathcal{T}^{syn} \text{ and } t_\tau^{ld}, t_\tau^{ul} \leq t) & (3) \\ \omega & (\tau \in \mathcal{T} \setminus \mathcal{T}^{syn}), & (4) \end{cases}$$

where constant ω ($0 \leq \omega \leq 1$) is the uniform priority parameter for all normal tasks. An example of p_τ (Formulae (2) and (4)) when $a = 8, b = 2, \xi = 2000$, and $\omega = 0.2$ is shown in Fig. 3. Agent i attempts to not exceed the loadable/unloadable time significantly. Thus, $t_\tau^{rel} > 0$ means that i's estimated arrival time will be past t_τ^{ld} (or t_τ^{ul}) of sync-task τ; however, because another agent may be able to arrive before t_τ^{ld} (or t_τ^{ul}) if it is located near the loading node, i decreases p_τ by Formula (2) to let another agent perform τ. However, if the current time t has already passed t_τ^{ld} (or t_τ^{ul}), p_τ continues to decrease over time by Formula (2), and thus τ may not be selected by any agent. Therefore, i immediately select τ (Formula (3)). Finally, i selects the highest priority task $\tau^* = \arg\max_{\tau \in \mathcal{T}^C} p_\tau$ (i uses the greedy method for tie-breaking).

5   Experiments and Discussion

5.1   Experimental Setting

We experimentally evaluated the performance of our proposed methods for MAPD-TS, by comparing it to that of SBDA with greedy (SBDA-greedy) and

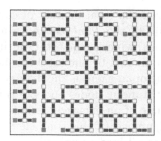

Fig. 4. Environment.

Table 1. Parameter values.

Description	Param. value
No. of agents	$M = 2$ to 20
Orientation/direction increments	$D = 90$
Duration of *move* per length 1	$T_{mo}(1) = 10$
Duration of *rotate*	$T_{ro}(D) = 20$
Durations of *load* and *unload*	$T_{ld}, T_{ul} = 20$
Duration of *wait*	$T_{wa}(t) = t$
Threshold for $dist(v_{psn}, v_{tsk})$	$\alpha = 8$
Threshold for direct heading endpoint	$\beta = 20$
Margin time for reserving v_{sn}	$\delta = 100$

the well-known deadlock avoidance method HTE [5,6] with greedy as the baseline methods. In HTE, the agent i first generates $\mathcal{T}^C$ from $\mathcal{T}$, which is a set of tasks whose load/unload node does not overlap with the endpoints of tasks currently executed by other agents. Thereafter, i selects a task from $\mathcal{T}^C$ with a task selection algorithm such as the greedy method (HTE-greedy) or ELUF (HTE-ELUF). i plans a path to the load node of the selected task and proceeds, followed by planning a path to the unload node. In HTE, i heads directly to the task endpoint because it cannot standby. If $\mathcal{T}^C = \varnothing$, i returns to $park_i$. Both SBDA and HTE used space-time A^* for the path-finding algorithm.

Assuming one floor of a three-dimensional material transportation system in a construction site, we conducted the experiments in a maze-like environment with few task endpoints ($|V_{tsk}| = 6$), as shown in Fig. 4, where red squares are parking nodes, blue squares are task endpoints except the ports, orange squares are ports connected with ext-agents, hollow-green squares are normal nodes, and black squares are edges. Note that this environment meets the well-formed conditions of SBDA [17] and HTE, so completeness (i.e., well-formed MAPD instances are solvable) is guaranteed. Agents can rotate, wait, and load/unload materials only at these nodes, including endpoints. The edge breaks in the figure represent blocks of length 1. The initial location of an agent is randomly assigned to a parking node.

Fifty normal tasks are generated at $t = 0$ and added to $\mathcal{T}$. For $t > 0$, one normal task is generated and added to $\mathcal{T}$ if one normal task is completed. The maximum capacities of all ext-agents arriving at $\forall v_{prt}$ are identically set to $C_{prt} = 2$. Upon a request from the ext-agent whose port is v_{prt}, C_{prt} sync-tasks with v_{prt} as the load or unload node are generated, respectively. Therefore, a total $2C_{prt}$ ($= 4$) sync-tasks are added to $\mathcal{T}$ per request. The parameter γ to set the loadable/unloadable time is a random number following a normal distribution with mean 2000 and standard deviation 500. Although the ext-agent can request the sync-tasks at arbitrary times, for example, considering its movement status, we assume that the ext-agent requests them approximately 2000 timesteps before the loadable/unloadable time (i.e., arrival time) for the sake of simplicity.

To evaluate the proposed methods, we measured the total number of completed sync-tasks and normal tasks until $t = 50000$, the *total waiting times* (TWTs) of all agents and all ext-agents per sync-task, which is the total waiting time for sync-tasks of all agents (or all ext-agents) divided by the total number of completed sync-tasks. Note that the waiting time of an agent is the difference between the time on arrival at the port or nearby standby nodes and the time when its load/unload is completed. The waiting time of an ext-agent is defined by the difference from the time it is ready to load/unload (if this is an elevator agent, time when it arrives at the floor) to the time all load or unload tasks at the port in the requested sync-tasks are completed. Note that the agent cannot stand by near the port in HTE, thus waiting times of the agent are measured from the arrival time at the port. We used $a = 8$, $b = 2$, $\xi = 2000$, and $\omega = 0.2$ as the parameter values of SALUF. Other parameter values used in the experiments are presented in Table 1. Our experiments were performed on a 3.20-GHz Intel 16-Core Xeon W with 112 GB of RAM. The following experimental results are the average of 100 trials with different random seeds.

5.2 Performance Comparison

In the first experiment, we compared the performances of the HTE-greedy, HTE-ELUF, SBDA-greedy, SBDA with ELUF (SBDA-ELUF), and SBDA with SALUF (SBDA-SALUF). Note that SALUF does not apply to HTE because it uses standby node information to estimate the arrival time of the agent at the port. We set $\eta = 1000$, i.e., in ELUF, agents start sync-tasks when the time until the involved ext-agent arrives is less than 1000 timesteps, as it is obvious that if agents start tasks very early, the TWTs of the agents will unnecessarily be large; thus, this time was set so that the TWTs would be sufficiently small. The results are plotted in Fig. 5.

Figures 5a and 5b show the TWTs of ext-agents and agents per sync-task, respectively. First, Fig. 5a indicates that SBDA-SALUF reduced the TWTs of ext-agents the most. This is because, in addition to SALUF considering the estimated arrival time of the agent at the port and the arrival time of the ext-agent, SBDA-SALUF effectively used standby nodes, where agents could stand by on approach to the port before the arrival of the ext-agent, to increase the parallelism of task executions. Thus, these agents could reach the port one after another. However, HTE-greedy/ELUF allowed only one agent to approach the port because of the limitation of HTE. Moreover, we confirmed the effectiveness of ELUF because HTE-ELUF could reduce TWTs of ext-agents compared to HTE-greedy, even under the limitation of HTE. SBDA-greedy could also use standby nodes effectively but, unlike SBDA-ELUF/SALUF, did not consider the arrival time of the ext-agent. Therefore, the TWTs of ext-agents for SBDA-greedy were large. Although the plot is omitted, when the number of agents $|A| = 2$, the TWTs of ext-agents for SBDA-greedy increased to nearly 3000 timesteps.

In contrast, Fig. 5b indicates that the TWTs of agents in HTE-ELUF is the smallest; however, this is obvious as almost all sync-tasks were executed after

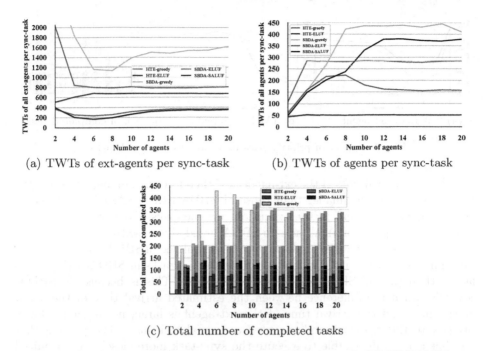

(a) TWTs of ext-agents per sync-task   (b) TWTs of agents per sync-task

(c) Total number of completed tasks

Fig. 5. Comparison of HTE-greedy/ELUF and SBDA-greedy/ELUF/SALUF.

the ext-agent arrived because of the insufficient parallelism, so the ext-agent always waits longer. HTE/SBDA-greedy did not consider the arrival time of the ext-agent, thus some agents arrived at the port earlier than necessary and had to wait a long time. Meanwhile, agents in SBDA-ELUF/SALUF could start executing a number of sync-tasks and stand by the port or nearby standby nodes. Thus, multiple agents waited simultaneously and these waiting times added to the multiplicity, causing the TWTs of agents to increase rapidly according with the increase of $|A|$. This suggests that the long waits of agents in SBDA-ELUF/SALUF did not reduce the entire performance.

This suggestion also supported by the stacked bar graph in Fig. 5c, which shows the total number of tasks completed until $t = 50000$ for the sync-tasks in darker colors and the normal tasks in lighter colors. Therefore, it indicates the real efficiency of all methods. First, we can see that HTE-greedy/ELUF exhibits a slightly better performance than SBDA-greedy/ELUF/SALUF only when $|A|$ is low because parallelism is limited owing to the small number of agents; thus, agents with SBDA-greedy/ELUF/SALUF rarely used the standby nodes. However, when $|A| \geq 4$, the number of completed tasks in HTE-greedy/ELUF was almost identical regardless of the number of agents owing to the limited capability of HTE. In SBDA-greedy/ELUF/SALUF, the standby nodes were effectively used and, thus, the number of completed tasks increased until $|A| = 8$. Thereafter, it slightly decreased according to the increase in $|A| \geq 10$. This may be because standby nodes are also finite and limited, and agents may have to take long routes to the task endpoint and nearby standby nodes. SBDA-greedy did not

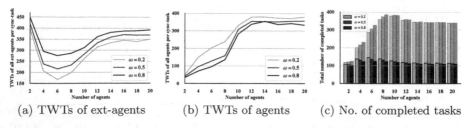

(a) TWTs of ext-agents   (b) TWTs of agents   (c) No. of completed tasks

Fig. 6. Impact of priority parameter ω for all normal tasks.

consider the arrival time of the ext-agent and therefore the number of completed sync-tasks was much smaller than those of SBDA-ELUF/SALUF. Meanwhile, because of the trade-off in the execution of sync-tasks and normal tasks, the number of completed normal tasks in SBDA-greedy increased when $|A|$ was low.

We can observe that the numbers of tasks completed in SBDA-ELUF/SALUF were almost identical but the number of completed tasks in SBDA-SALUF was larger than that in SBDA-ELUF when $|A| \geq 10$. This is because in SBDA-SALUF, when the difference between the estimated arrival time of the agent at the port and the arrival time of the ext-agent is large, it assigned a lower priority to the sync-task and executed a normal task instead, expecting that another agent will be able to execute the sync-task more closely synchronized with the arrival of the ext-agent. As the number of agents increases, more agents will meet that expectation, resulting in the improved overall efficiency. Thus, in MAPD-TS, whose task set consists of different types of tasks (normal tasks and sync-tasks), SBDA-SALUF allows the agent to select a more appropriate task.

Finally, notably, it is more critical to reduce the TWTs of ext-agents because increases in the TWTs of ext-agents will affect the delay in the external systems. For example, if the ext-agents are elevators, it will cause delays on other floors, and if the ext-agents are trucks, the work at their delivery points or tasks for the next trucks may be delayed. In this sense, SBDA-SALUF appears better than other methods (see Fig. 5a).

5.3   Ablation Study: Features of SBDA-SALUF

We also investigated the impact of ω, the priority parameter for all normal tasks on the entire performance of SBDA-SALUF. The results of SBDA-SALUF when $\omega = 0.2, 0.5$, and 0.8 are plotted in Fig. 6. We can see from Figs. 6a and 6b that for larger values of ω, the TWTs of ext-agents increase and those of agents decrease, because the agents preferentially selects the normal tasks (Fig. 3). However, when the number of agents are larger ($|A| \geq 10$), the entire performance does not change significantly, as shown in Fig. 6c. Thus, if we consider the negative effect on the external systems, we believe that ω should be small but we also have to consider the executions of normal tasks.

Conversely, in SBDA-SALUF, an environment has its upper limit on the number of the standby nodes near the task endpoint owing to the threshold parameter α. When ω is larger, the agents were likely to select the normal task, resulting in the congestion near the task endpoints except the ports. Therefore, when $|A| \leq 8$, the larger ω facilitate the execution of normal task, but when the agents further increased, the difference in efficiency due to ω was small.

6 Conclusion

We have formulated MAPD-TS, which is an extension of MAPD by considering synchronization of the movement of the agents with that of external agents such as trucks transporting from/to other warehouses and elevators transporting from/to other floors. We then proposed methods to reduce unnecessary waiting time for synchronization on both sides for better overall efficiency through autonomous task selection. Thereafter, we integrated the proposed methods with the SBDA to effectively use the standby nodes to approach the ports to reduce the waiting time. We evaluated the performance of the proposed methods, SBDA-ELUF/SALUF, by comparing them with baseline methods in an environment based on our target application, where the external agents were elevators to transport construction materials to different floors of a construction site. Experimental results demonstrate that the proposed methods can reduce the waiting time for both agents for MAPD and the external agents, thereby obtaining a better overall transportation efficiency.

We believe that practical MAPD systems are not isolated; in contrast, they face interference with external systems. Therefore, for wider applicability, we plan to study learning methods for coordinated behavior with an external system by dynamically adjusting parameter values, such as the priority parameter ω. Furthermore, we will consider coordination among agents, such as negotiating swaps of their selected tasks to further improve overall transportation efficiency.

Acknowledgements. This work was partly supported by JSPS KAKENHI Grant Number 20H04245.

References

1. Andreychuk, A., Yakovlev, K., Surynek, P., Atzmon, D., Stern, R.: Multi-agent pathfinding with continuous time. Artif. Intell. **305**, 103662 (2022). https://doi.org/10.1016/j.artint.2022.103662
2. Farinelli, A., Contini, A., Zorzi, D.: Decentralized task assignment for multi-item pickup and delivery in logistic scenarios. In: Proceedings of the 19th International Conference on Autonomous Agents and MultiAgent Systems, pp. 1843–1845. IFAAMAS (2020)
3. Gong, X., Wang, T., Huang, T., Cui, Y.: Toward safe and efficient humanswarm collaboration: a hierarchical multi-agent pickup and delivery framework. IEEE Trans. Intell. Veh. 1–13 (2022). https://doi.org/10.1109/TIV.2022.3172342
4. Krakowczyk, D., Wolff, J., Ciobanu, A., Meyer, D.J., Hrabia, C.E.: Developing a distributed drone delivery system with a hybrid behavior planning system. In: German/Austrian Conference on Artificial Intelligence, pp. 107–114. Springer (2018). https://doi.org/10.1007/978-3-030-00111-7_10

5. Li, J., Tinka, A., Kiesel, S., Durham, J.W., Kumar, T.S., Koenig, S.: Lifelong multi-agent path finding in large-scale warehouses. In: Proceedings of the AAAI Conference on Artificial Intelligence, vol. 35, pp. 11272–11281 (2021)
6. Liu, M., Ma, H., Li, J., Koenig, S.: Task and path planning for multi-agent pickup and delivery. In: Proceedings of the International Joint Conference on Autonomous Agents and Multiagent Systems (AAMAS), pp. 1152–1160. IFAAMAS (2019)
7. Ma, H., Li, J., Kumar, T., Koenig, S.: Lifelong multi-agent path finding for online pickup and delivery tasks. In: Proceedings of the 16th Conference on Autonomous Agents and MultiAgent Systems, pp. 837–845. IFAAMAS (2017)
8. Ma, H., Tovey, C., Sharon, G., Kumar, T.S., Koenig, S.: Multi-agent path finding with payload transfers and the package-exchange robot-routing problem. In: The 30th AAAI Conference on Artificial Intelligence (2016). https://doi.org/10.1609/aaai.v30i1.10409
9. Nuutila, E., Soisalon-Soininen, E.: On finding the strongly connected components in a directed graph. Inf. Process. Lett. **49**(1), 9–14 (1994). https://doi.org/10.1016/0020-0190(94)90047-7
10. Okumura, K., Machida, M., Défago, X., Tamura, Y.: Priority inheritance with backtracking for iterative multi-agent path finding. In: Proceedings of the 28th International Joint Conference on Artificial Intelligence, IJCAI-19, pp. 535–542 (2019). https://doi.org/10.24963/ijcai.2019/76
11. Salzman, O., Stern, R.: Research challenges and opportunities in multi-agent path finding and multi-agent pickup and delivery problems. In: Proceedings of the 19th International Conference on Autonomous Agents and MultiAgent Systems, pp. 1711–1715 (2020)
12. Sharon, G., Stern, R., Felner, A., Sturtevant, N.R.: Conflict-based search for optimal multi-agent pathfinding. Artif. Intell. **219**, 40–66 (2015). https://doi.org/10.1016/j.artint.2014.11.006
13. Tarjan, R.: Depth-first search and linear graph algorithms. SIAM J. Comput. **1**(2), 146–160 (1972). https://doi.org/10.1137/0201010
14. Wu, X., et al.: Multi-agent pickup and delivery with task deadlines. In: IEEE/WIC/ACM International Conference on Web Intelligence and Intelligent Agent Technology, pp. 360–367. Association for Computing Machinery (2021). https://doi.org/10.1145/3486622.3493915
15. Wurman, P.R., D'Andrea, R., Mountz, M.: Coordinating hundreds of cooperative, autonomous vehicles in warehouses. AI Mag. **29**(1), 9–20 (2008). https://doi.org/10.1609/aimag.v29i1.2082
16. Yamauchi, T., Miyashita, Y., Sugawara, T.: Path and action planning in non-uniform environments for multi-agent pickup and delivery tasks. In: European Conference on Multi-Agent Systems, pp. 37–54. Springer (2021). https://doi.org/10.1007/978-3-030-82254-5_3
17. Yamauchi, T., Miyashita, Y., Sugawara, T.: Standby-based deadlock avoidance method for multi-agent pickup and delivery tasks. In: Proceedings of the 21st International Conference on Autonomous Agents and Multiagent Systems, pp. 1427–1435. IFAAMAS (2022)
18. Yoshida, N., Noda, I., Sugawara, T.: Distributed service area control for ride sharing by using multi-agent deep reinforcement learning. In: Proceedings of the 13th International Conference on Agents and Artificial Intelligence - Volume 1: ICAART, pp. 101–112. INSTICC, SciTePress (2021). https://doi.org/10.5220/0010310901010112

Dynamic Continuous Distributed Constraint Optimization Problems

Khoi D. Hoang$^{(\boxtimes)}$ and William Yeoh

Washington University in St. Louis, St. Louis, USA
{khoi.hoang,wyeoh}@wustl.edu

Abstract. The Distributed Constraint Optimization Problem (DCOP) formulation is a powerful tool to model multi-agent coordination problems that are distributed by nature. While DCOPs assume that variables are discrete and the environment does not change over time, agents often interact in a more dynamic and complex environment. To address these limiting assumptions, researchers have proposed Dynamic DCOPs (D-DCOPs) to model how DCOPs dynamically change over time and Continuous DCOPs (C-DCOPs) to model DCOPs with continuous variables and constraints in functional form. However, these models address each limiting assumption of DCOPs in isolation, and it remains a challenge to model problems that *both* have continuous variables and are in dynamic environment. Therefore, in this paper, we propose *Dynamic Continuous DCOPs (DC-DCOPs)*, a novel formulation that models both dynamic nature of the environment and continuous nature of the variables, which are inherent in many multi-agent problems. In addition, we introduce several greedy algorithms to solve DC-DCOPs and discuss their theoretical properties. Finally, we empirically evaluate the algorithms in random networks and in distributed sensor network application.

Keywords: Multiagent systems · Distributed constraint optimization problems · Continuous DCOPs · Dynamic DCOPs

1 Introduction

Distributed Constraint Optimization Problems (DCOPs) [7,22,24,37] are problems where agents coordinate their value assignments to maximize the sum of the utility functions. The model has been applied to solve a wide range of multi-agent coordination problems including distributed meeting scheduling [20,35], sensor and wireless network coordination [6,37], multi-robot coordination [40], smart grid optimization [10,18,21], smart home automation [9,27], and cloud computing applications [15,23].

Typically, DCOPs assume that the domains of variables are discrete and the environment does not change over time. However, in many distributed multi-agent problems, agents often interact in a more dynamic and complex environment. For example, in distributed sensor networks, targets usually move from

© The Author(s), under exclusive license to Springer Nature Switzerland AG 2023
R. Aydoğan et al. (Eds.): PRIMA 2022, LNAI 13753, pp. 475–491, 2023.
https://doi.org/10.1007/978-3-031-21203-1_28

one location to another location over time, and to adapt to such a dynamic environment, the sensors should be augmented with the capability to change their sensing directions accordingly. To address this concern, researchers have proposed *Dynamic DCOPs (D-DCOPs)* [19,25,26], which model how the problem evolves during the solving process. Additionally, to better sense the targets of interest, whose locations correspond to a wide range of possibilities (i.e., the set of all possible locations in a two-dimensional plane or three-dimensional space of the network), the sensors should be equipped with a continuous range of sensing directions. Therefore, researchers have introduced *Continuous DCOPs* (C-DCOPs) [29,32], which model continuous variables with a bounded domain and represent the constraints in functional form.

While D-DCOPs and C-DCOPs have been proposed to address the two limiting assumptions of DCOPs, the two models only address these assumptions in isolation. Thus, it remains a challenge to model and solve the problems that are both dynamically changing over time and have continuous variables. Therefore, in this paper, we propose *Dynamic Continuous DCOPs (DC-DCOPs)*, a novel formulation that models both the dynamic environment and continuous variables, which are present in many multi-agent problems. In addition, we introduce several greedy algorithms to solve DC-DCOPs and discuss their theoretical properties. Finally, we empirically evaluate the algorithms in random networks and in a distributed sensor network application.

2   Background

In this section, we provide a brief overview of DCOPs, Dynamic DCOPs, and Continuous DCOPs.

2.1   Distributed Constraint Optimization Problems (DCOPs)

A *Distributed Constraint Optimization Problem (DCOP)* [7,22,24] is a tuple $\langle \mathbf{A}, \mathbf{X}, \mathbf{D}, \mathbf{F}, \alpha \rangle$, where:

- $\mathbf{A} = \{a_i\}_{i=1}^{p}$ is a set of *agents*.
- $\mathbf{X} = \{x_i\}_{i=1}^{n}$ is a set of *decision variables*.
- $\mathbf{D} = \{D_x\}_{x \in \mathbf{X}}$ is a set of finite *domains*, where each variable $x \in \mathbf{X}$ takes values from the set $D_x \in \mathbf{D}$.
- $\mathbf{F} = \{f_i\}_{i=1}^{m}$ is a set of *utility functions*, each defined over a set of decision variables: $f_i : \prod_{x \in \mathbf{x}^{f_i}} D_x \rightarrow \mathbb{R}_0^+ \cup \{-\infty\}$, where infeasible configurations have $-\infty$ utilities and $\mathbf{x}^{f_i} \subseteq \mathbf{X}$ is the *scope* of f_i.[1]
- $\alpha : \mathbf{X} \rightarrow \mathbf{A}$ is a function that associates each decision variable to one agent.

A *solution* σ is a value assignment to a set $\mathbf{x}_\sigma \subseteq \mathbf{X}$ of decision variables that is consistent with their respective domains. The utility $\mathbf{F}(\sigma) = \sum_{f \in \mathbf{F}, \mathbf{x}^f \subseteq \mathbf{x}_\sigma} f(\sigma)$ is the sum of the utilities across all applicable utility functions in σ. A solution σ is *complete* if $\mathbf{x}_\sigma = \mathbf{X}$. The goal of a DCOP is to find an optimal complete solution $\mathbf{x}^* = \mathrm{argmax}_{\mathbf{x}} \mathbf{F}(\mathbf{x})$.

---

[1] The scope of a function is the set of variables that are associated with the function.

2.2   Dynamic DCOPs

A *Dynamic DCOP (D-DCOP)* [19,25,26,36] is defined as a sequence of DCOPs with changes between them. Changes between DCOPs occur over time due to addition or removal of variables, addition or removal of values in the variable's domain, addition or removal of utility functions, and increase or decrease in the utility values. Solving a D-DCOP optimally means finding a utility-maximal solution for each DCOP in the sequence. Therefore, this approach is *reactive* since solving each DCOP in the sequence does not consider future changes. Its advantage is that solving a D-DCOP is no harder than solving h DCOPs, where h is the horizon of the problem. Researchers have used this approach to solve D-DCOPs, where they introduce search- and inference-based approaches that are able to reuse information from previous DCOPs to speed up the search for the solution for the current DCOP [25,36]. Alternatively, a *proactive* approach predicts future changes in the D-DCOP and finds robust solutions that require little or no changes in the sequence of DCOP solutions despite future changes to the DCOP [12–14].

2.3   Continuous DCOPs

A *Continuous DCOP (C-DCOP)* [15,29,32] is defined as a DCOP where the variables take values from a continuous domain. In a typical (discrete) DCOP, constraints are represented in tabular form, which enumerates all possible values of the discrete variables involved in the constraint. Since variables in C-DCOPs are continuous, the model represents the constraints in functional forms such as linear piecewise function, quadratic function, or a more general differentiable function. Recently, researchers have proposed several algorithms to solve C-DCOPs including approximate approaches [3,15,28] and exact approach that solves C-DCOP under a specific setting [15].

3   Motivating Application: Distributed Radar Coordination and Scheduling Problem

We motivate our work using the *Distributed Radar Coordination and Scheduling Problem (DRCSP)* [12], which is based on NetRad, a real-time weather radar sensor system [4,17,39]. The NetRad system is consisted meteorological command and controls (MCCs), each controls a set of radars with a limited sensing range. The radars in NetRad are tasked by the MCCs to scan a specific area of interest in a coordinated fashion, where each radar takes 360° volume scan. For example, in Fig. 1, the NetRad system has five radars scanning the area with two weather phenomena, represented as a yellow star and a red star. The goal of a DRCSP is to find a coordination strategy that maximizes the aggregated utility by scanning the highest-utility phenomena in the area. Since each sensor is able to take a continuous 360° scan, we model the sensing direction of the sensors with the continuous variables. In addition, since the weather phenomena may move continuously over time, we model this dynamism by incorporating random variables representing the weather phenomena.

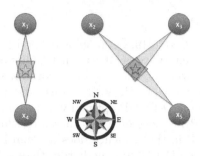

Fig. 1. Distributed radar coordination and scheduling problem

4   Dynamic Continuous DCOP Model

A *Dynamic Continuous DCOP (DC-DCOP)* is a tuple $\langle \mathbf{A}, \mathbf{X}, \mathbf{Y}, \mathbf{D_x}, \mathbf{D_y}, \mathbf{F}, p_{\mathbf{Y}}^0, \mathbf{T}, \gamma, h, \mathbf{C}, \alpha \rangle$, where:

- $\mathbf{A} = \{a_i\}_{i=1}^p$ is a set of *agents*.
- $\mathbf{X} = \{x_i\}_{i=1}^n$ is a set of *decision variables*, which are variables controlled by the agents.
- $\mathbf{Y} = \{y_i\}_{i=1}^m$ is a set of *random variables*, which are variables that are uncontrollable and model stochastic events (e.g., weather phenomena location or intensity)
- $\mathbf{D_x} = \{D_x\}_{x \in \mathbf{X}}$ is a set of continuous *domains* of the decision variables. Each variable $x \in \mathbf{X}$ takes values from the interval $D_x = [LB_x, UB_x]$.
- $\mathbf{D_y} = \{D_y\}_{y \in \mathbf{Y}}$ is a set of continuous state space of the random variables. Each variable $y \in \mathbf{Y}$ has state space $D_y \in \mathbf{D_y}$.
- $\mathbf{F} = \{f_i\}_{i=1}^k$ is a set of *utility functions*, each defined over a mixed set of decision and random variables: $f_i : \prod_{x \in \mathbf{X} \cap \mathbf{x}^{f_i}} D_x \times \prod_{y \in \mathbf{Y} \cap \mathbf{x}^{f_i}} D_y \to \mathbb{R}_0^+ \cup \{-\infty\}$, where infeasible configurations have $-\infty$ rewards and $\mathbf{x}^{f_i} \subseteq \mathbf{X} \cup \mathbf{Y}$ is the scope of f_i. We divide the set of utility functions into two sets: $\mathbf{F_X} = \{f_x\}$, where $\mathbf{x}^{f_x} \cap \mathbf{Y} = \emptyset$, and $\mathbf{F_Y} = \{f_y\}$, where $\mathbf{x}^{f_y} \cap \mathbf{Y} \neq \emptyset$. Note that $\mathbf{F_X} \cup \mathbf{F_Y} = \mathbf{F}$ and $\mathbf{F_X} \cap \mathbf{F_Y} = \emptyset$.
- $p_{\mathbf{Y}}^0 = \{p_y^0\}_{y \in \mathbf{Y}}$ is a set of initial *probability density functions* of the random variable $y \in \mathbf{Y}$.
- $\mathbf{T} = \{T_y\}_{y \in \mathbf{Y}}$ is a set of *transition functions*, where each transition function is a conditional density function $T_y : D_y \times \mathcal{P}(D_y) \to [0, 1]$ that specifies the transition from a value $d_y \in D_y$ to a subset of D_y.
- $\gamma \in [0, 1]$ is a *discount factor*, which represents the decrease in the importance of future rewards.
- $h \in \mathbb{N}$ is a finite *horizon*.
- $\mathbf{C} = \{c_x\}_{x \in \mathbf{X}}$ is a set of *switching cost functions*, each defined over a set of decision variables: $c_x : D_x \times D_x \to \mathbb{R}_0^+$. Each switching cost function c_x models the cost associated with the change in the value of the decision variable x from one time step to the next.
- $\alpha : \mathbf{X} \to \mathbf{A}$ is a function that associates each decision variable to one agent.

Throughout this article, we assume that each agent controls exactly one decision variable and that each utility function is associated with at most one random variable.[2] In the case where one agent controls more than one variable, one can use standard DCOP reformulation techniques [2,38], such as *compilation*, where each agent creates a new *pseudo-variable*, whose domain is the Cartesian product of the domains of all variables of the agent; and *decomposition*, where each agent creates a *pseudo-agent* for each of its variables. More recently, researchers have also proposed a multi-variable decomposition method that exploits the co-locality of variables to more efficiently solve the problem [8].

The goal of a DC-DCOP is to find a sequence of $h+1$ assignments $\mathbf{x}^*$ for all the decision variables in $\mathbf{X}$:

$$\mathbf{x}^* = \text{argmax}_{\mathbf{x} = \langle \mathbf{x}^0, \ldots, \mathbf{x}^h \rangle \in \Sigma^{h+1}} \mathcal{F}^h(\mathbf{x})$$

$$\mathcal{F}^h(\mathbf{x}) = \underbrace{\sum_{t=0}^{h} \gamma^t \left[\mathcal{F}_x^t(\mathbf{x}^t) + \mathcal{F}_y^t(\mathbf{x}^t) \right]}_{\mathbf{P}} - \underbrace{\sum_{t=0}^{h-1} \gamma^t \left[C_{\mathbf{x}}(\mathbf{x}^t, \mathbf{x}^{t+1}) \right]}_{\mathbf{Q}}$$

where Σ is the assignment space for the decision variables of the DC-DCOP. The first term $\mathbf{P}$ refers to the optimization over $h+1$ time steps, with:

$$\mathcal{F}_x^t(\mathbf{x}) = \sum_{f_i \in \mathbf{F}_{\mathbf{X}}} f_i(\mathbf{x}_i)$$

$$\mathcal{F}_y^t(\mathbf{x}) = \sum_{f_i \in \mathbf{F}_{\mathbf{Y}}} \int_{D_{y_i}} f_i(\mathbf{x}_i, y_i) \cdot p_{y_i}^t(y_i) dy_i$$

where $\mathbf{x}_i$ is an assignment for all the variables in the scope $\mathbf{x}^{f_i}$ of the function f_i; $p_{y_i}^t$ is the probability density function of the random variable y_i at time step t, and defined as:

$$p_{y_i}^t(y_i) = \int_{D_{y_i}} p_{y_i}^{t-1}(y_i) \cdot T(y_i, D_{y_i}) dy_i$$

The second term $\mathbf{Q}$ considers the penalty due to changes in decision variables' values during the optimization process:

$$C_{\mathbf{x}}(\mathbf{x}^t, \mathbf{x}^{t+1}) = \sum_{x \in \mathbf{X}} c_x(x^t, x^{t+1})$$

is a penalty function that takes into account the difference in the decision variable assignments between two time steps.

---

[2] If multiple random variables are associated with a utility function, w.l.o.g., they can be merged into a single variable.

5   DC-DCOP Algorithms

We now introduce our DC-DCOP algorithms, which are built upon two sequential greedy Dynamic DCOP algorithms: FORWARD and BACKWARD [14]. The two algorithms have been applied to solve the Dynamic DCOPs where each subproblem is a *discrete* DCOP. However, in DC-DCOPs, the subproblem at every time step is a *Continuous* DCOP. Thus the original version of FORWARD and BACKWARD cannot be applied to solve DC-DCOPs. In this section, we propose a new version of the two algorithms that can address and solve the C-DCOP at every time step.

5.1   FORWARD

In general, FORWARD greedily solves each subproblem in DC-DCOPs one time step at a time starting from the first time step. In other words, it successively solves the C-DCOP at each time step starting from $t = 0$ to $t = h$. When solving each C-DCOP, it takes into account the switching cost incurred by changing the solution from time step $t - 1$ to the optimal solution at time step t. Specifically, before solving the C-DCOP at each time step, the agents run a pre-processing step, where they (1) reformulate the constraint between decision and random variables, and (2) capture the cost of switching values between time steps in new unary constraints of decision variables. For each constraint $f_i \in \mathbf{F}_Y$ between decision variables $\mathbf{x}_i$ and a random variable y_i, the following new constraint is created for each time step $0 \le t \le h$:

$$F_i^t(\mathbf{x}_i) = \int_{D_{y_i}} f_i(\mathbf{x}_i, y_i) \cdot p_{y_i}^t(y_i) dy_i \tag{1}$$

where $p_{y_i}^t(\cdot)$ is the probability density function of random variable y_i at time step t.

After reformulating the constraints between decision variables and random variable, the agents create a new constraint to capture the cost of switching values across time steps. Specifically, for each decision variable $x \in \mathbf{X}$, the following new unary constraint is created for each time step $0 < t \le h$:

$$C_x^t(x^t) = -c_x(x^{t-1}, x^t) \tag{2}$$

After adding the switching cost constraints, the agents successively solve each C-DCOP from time step $t = 0$ onwards using any off-the-shelf C-DCOP algorithm.

In this paper, we use the following off-the-shelf C-DCOP algorithms to solve the problem at each time step: *AC-DPOP, CAC-DPOP, HCMS*, and *C-DSA* [15]. AC-DPOP, CAC-DPOP, and HCMS are *inference*-based algorithms, while C-DSA is a *local search* algorithm. AC-DPOP solves C-DCOPs by first discretizing the domains of the variables into initial discrete values and then using gradient methods to move the values of the parent and psedo-parent variables in order to better approximate the constraint utilities. CAC-DPOP is a variant of AC-DPOP that reduces the memory and time consumption of AC-DPOP by clustering the values of the agents before sending them up the pseudo-tree. Instead of using pseudo-tree, HCMS uses a factor graph to represent C-DCOPs and gradually adjusts agents' values over a number of iterations. Finally, C-DSA is a continuous *stochastic* algorithm, where each agent communicates their assignment with neighboring agents and stochastically determines to keep the current assignment or change to a better one.

5.2 BACKWARD

Instead of solving the DC-DCOP one time step at a time forward starting from $t = 0$ towards h, one can also greedily solve the problem backwards from $t = h$ towards the first time step. Similar to FORWARD, before solving the C-DCOP at each time step, agents in BACKWARD run a pre-processing step to reformulate the constraint between decision and random variables, and to capture the switching cost between two time steps. To reformulate the constraints between decision variables and a random variable, the agents calls Eq. (1) and create a new constraints for each time steps $0 \leq t \leq h$. However, the key difference between BACKWARD and FORWARD is how the agents compute the new switching cost constraint at each time step t. Specifically, when solving the C-DCOP at time step t, instead of taking into account the switching cost between time step t and time step $t - 1$, agents in BACKWARD takes into account the switching cost between time step t and time step $t + 1$.

Specifically, before solving each subproblem, BACKWARD creates a unary constraint for each time step $0 \leq t < h$:

$$C_x^t(x^t) = -c_x(x^t, x^{t+1}) \tag{3}$$

After adding the switching cost constraints and the reformulated constraints between decision variables and a random variable, the agents successively solve each C-DCOP from time step $t = h$ backward using any off-the-shelf C-DCOP algorithm. Similar to FORWARD, we use AC-DPOP, CAC-DPOP, HCMS, and C-DSA to solve the C-DCOP at each time step. We will empirically evaluate both greedy versions of these C-DCOP algorithms in the experimental result section and will also discuss their theoretical properties in Sect. 6.

6 Theoretical Properties

We now describe below some theoretical properties on the error bounds and communication complexities for some of our algorithms.

We denote U^∞ as the optimal solution quality of a DC-DCOP with an infinite horizon and U^h as the optimal solution quality when the horizon h is finite. Let $F_\mathbf{y}(\mathbf{x})$ be the utility of a regular C-DCOP where the decision variables are assigned $\mathbf{x}$ given values $\mathbf{y}$ of the random variables. We define $F_\mathbf{y}^\Delta = \max_{\mathbf{x} \in \Sigma} F_\mathbf{y}(\mathbf{x}) - \min_{\mathbf{x} \in \Sigma} F_\mathbf{y}(\mathbf{x})$ as the maximum loss in solution quality of a regular DCOP for a given random variable assignment $\mathbf{y}$ and $F^\Delta = \max_{\mathbf{y} \in \Sigma_\mathbf{Y}} F_\mathbf{y}^\Delta$ where $\Sigma_\mathbf{Y} = \prod_{y \in \mathbf{Y}} \Omega_y$ is the assignment space for all random variables.

Theorem 1. *When $\gamma < 1$, the error $U^\infty - U^h$ of the optimal solution from solving DC-DCOPs with a finite horizon h instead of an infinite horizon is bounded from above by $\frac{\gamma^h}{1-\gamma} F^\Delta$.*

PROOF. Let $\hat{\mathbf{x}}^* = \langle \hat{\mathbf{x}}_0^*, \ldots, \hat{\mathbf{x}}_h^*, \hat{\mathbf{x}}_{h+1}^*, \ldots \rangle$ be the optimal solution of DC-DCOPs with infinite horizon ∞:

$$U^\infty = \sum_{t=0}^\infty \gamma^t \left[\mathcal{F}_x^t(\hat{\mathbf{x}}_t^*) + \mathcal{F}_y^t(\hat{\mathbf{x}}_t^*) - C_{\mathbf{x}}(\hat{\mathbf{x}}_t^*, \hat{\mathbf{x}}_{t+1}^*) \right]$$

Ignoring switching costs after time step h, an upper bound U_+^∞ of U^∞ is defined as:

$$U_+^\infty = \sum_{t=0}^{h-1} \gamma^t \left[\mathcal{F}_x^t(\hat{\mathbf{x}}_t^*) + \mathcal{F}_y^t(\hat{\mathbf{x}}_t^*) - C_{\mathbf{x}}(\hat{\mathbf{x}}_t^*, \hat{\mathbf{x}}_{t+1}^*) \right]$$
$$+ \sum_{t=h}^\infty \gamma^t \left[\mathcal{F}_x^t(\hat{\mathbf{x}}_t^*) + \mathcal{F}_y^t(\hat{\mathbf{x}}_t^*) \right]$$

Let $\mathbf{x}^* = \langle \mathbf{x}_0^*, \ldots, \mathbf{x}_h^* \rangle$ be the optimal solution of the DC-DCOPs with a finite horizon h:

$$U^h = \sum_{t=0}^{h-1} \gamma^t \left[\mathcal{F}_x^t(\mathbf{x}_t^*) + \mathcal{F}_y^t(\mathbf{x}_t^*) - C_{\mathbf{x}}(\mathbf{x}_t^*, \mathbf{x}_{t+1}^*) \right]$$
$$+ \sum_{t=h}^\infty \gamma^t \left[\mathcal{F}_x^t(\mathbf{x}_h^*) + \mathcal{F}_y^t(\mathbf{x}_h^*) \right]$$

For $\hat{\mathbf{x}}^*$, if we change the solution for every C-DCOP after time step h to $\hat{\mathbf{x}}_h^*$, as $\langle \hat{\mathbf{x}}_0^*, \ldots, \hat{\mathbf{x}}_h^*, \hat{\mathbf{x}}_h^*, \ldots \rangle$, we get a lower bound U_-^∞ of U^h:

$$U_-^\infty = \sum_{t=0}^{h-1} \gamma^t \left[\mathcal{F}_x^t(\hat{\mathbf{x}}_t^*) + \mathcal{F}_y^t(\hat{\mathbf{x}}_t^*) - C_{\mathbf{x}}(\hat{\mathbf{x}}_t^*, \hat{\mathbf{x}}_{t+1}^*) \right]$$
$$+ \sum_{t=h}^\infty \gamma^t \left[\mathcal{F}_x^t(\hat{\mathbf{x}}_h^*) + \mathcal{F}_y^t(\hat{\mathbf{x}}_h^*) \right]$$

Therefore, we get $U_-^\infty \leq U^h \leq U^\infty \leq U_+^\infty$.

Next, we compute the difference between the two bounds:

$$U^\infty - U^h \leq U_+^\infty - U_-^\infty$$
$$= \sum_{t=h}^\infty \gamma^t \left[(\mathcal{F}_x^t(\hat{\mathbf{x}}_t^*) + \mathcal{F}_y^t(\hat{\mathbf{x}}_t^*)) - (\mathcal{F}_x^t(\hat{\mathbf{x}}_h^*) + \mathcal{F}_y^t(\hat{\mathbf{x}}_h^*)) \right]$$

Notice that the quantity $(\mathcal{F}_x^t(\hat{\mathbf{x}}_t^*) + \mathcal{F}_y^t(\hat{\mathbf{x}}_t^*)) - (\mathcal{F}_x^t(\hat{\mathbf{x}}_h^*) + \mathcal{F}_y^t(\hat{\mathbf{x}}_h^*))$ is the utility difference between the value assignment $\hat{\mathbf{x}}_t^*$ and $\hat{\mathbf{x}}_h^*$ for a subproblem in time step t, and thus is bounded by the maximum loss of a regular C-DCOP:

$$(\mathcal{F}_x^t(\hat{\mathbf{x}}_t^*) + \mathcal{F}_y^t(\hat{\mathbf{x}}_t^*)) - (\mathcal{F}_x^t(\hat{\mathbf{x}}_h^*) + \mathcal{F}_y^t(\hat{\mathbf{x}}_h^*)) \leq F^\Delta$$

Thus,

$$U^\infty - U^h \leq U_+^\infty - U_-^\infty$$

$$\leq \sum_{t=h}^{\infty} \gamma^t \left[\mathcal{F}_x^t(\hat{\mathbf{x}}_t^*) + \mathcal{F}_y^t(\hat{\mathbf{x}}_t^*) - \mathcal{F}_x^t(\hat{\mathbf{x}}_h^*) - \mathcal{F}_y^t(\hat{\mathbf{x}}_h^*) \right]$$

$$\leq \sum_{t=h}^{\infty} \gamma^t F^\Delta$$

$$\leq \frac{\gamma^h}{1-\gamma} F^\Delta$$

which concludes the proof.   □

Error Bounds from C-DCOP Algorithms: For each reward function $f(x_i, x_{i_1}, \ldots, x_{i_k})$ of an agent x_i and its separator agents $x_{i_1}, \ldots, x_{i_k}$, assume that agent x_i discretizes the domains of the reward function into hypercubes of size m (i.e., the distance between two neighboring discrete points for the same agent x_{i_j} is m). Let $\nabla f(v)$ denote the gradient of the function $f(x_i, x_{i_1}, \ldots, x_{i_k})$ at $v = (v_i, v_{i_1}, \ldots, v_{i_k})$:

$$\nabla f(v) = (\frac{\partial f}{\partial x_i}(v_i), \frac{\partial f}{\partial x_{i_1}}(v_{i_1}), \ldots, \frac{\partial f}{\partial x_{i_k}}(v_{i_k}))$$

Furthermore, let $|\nabla f(v)|$ denote the sum of magnitude:

$$|\nabla f(v)| = |\frac{\partial f}{\partial x_i}(v_i)| + |\frac{\partial f}{\partial x_{i_1}}(v_{i_1})| + \ldots + |\frac{\partial f}{\partial x_{i_k}}(v_{i_k})|$$

Assume that $|\nabla f(v)| \leq \delta$ holds for all utility functions in the DCOP and for all v.

Theorem 2. *The error of* AC-DPOP-*based algorithms is bounded above by* $h \cdot |\mathbf{F}|(m + |\mathbf{A}|k\alpha\delta)\delta + (h-1) \cdot \Theta|\mathbf{A}|$, *where* k *is the number of times each agent "moves" values of its separator, and* $\Theta = \max_{x \in \mathbf{X}} c_x(v, v')$ *is the maximum of the bounded switching cost functions.*

PROOF. According to Theorem 5.2 by Hoang *et al.* [15], the error bound of solving a C-DCOP using AC-DPOP algorithm is $|\mathbf{F}|(m + |\mathbf{A}|k\alpha\delta)\delta$. In DC-DCOPs, there are h C-DCOPs, each is a subproblem at every time step. Without taking into account the switching cost, the error bound of AC-DPOP-based algorithms (e.g., Forward-AC-DPOP and Backward-AC-DPOP) is $h \cdot |\mathbf{F}|(m + |\mathbf{A}|k\alpha\delta)\delta$. Given $\Theta = \max_{x,x'} c(x, x')$ as the maximum value of switching cost between two time steps, and considering there are at most $h-1$ switching times between h time steps from $|\mathbf{A}|$ agents, the upper bound is thus $h \cdot |\mathbf{F}|(m + |\mathbf{A}|k\alpha\delta)\delta + (h-1) \cdot \Theta|\mathbf{A}|$.   □

Theorem 3. *In a binary constraint graph* $G = (\mathbf{X}, E)$, *the number of messages of* HCMS-*based algorithms and* C-DSA-*based algorithms with* k *iterations is* $h \cdot 4k|E|$ *and* $h \cdot 2k|E|$, *respectively. The number of messages of* AC-DPOP-, *and* CAC-DPOP-*based algorithms is* $h \cdot 2|\mathbf{X}|$.

PROOF. According to Theorem 5.3 by Hoang *et al.* [15], the number of messages of *HCMS*-based algorithms and *C-DSA*-based algorithms with k iterations is $4k|E|$ and $2k|E|$, respectively. The number of messages of *AC-DPOP*-, and *CAC-DPOP*-based algorithms is $2|\mathbf{X}|$. Since solving a DC-DCOP is equivalent to solving h C-DCOPs, each at a time step, the number of messages is thus h times the number of messages needed to solve a single C-DCOP.   □

7   Related Work

Aside from the D-DCOP model described in the introduction and background, several approaches have been proposed to solve related constraint models with discrete variables including *Dynamic CSPs*, where value assignments of variables or utilities of constraints may change according to some probabilistic model [16, 33]. The goal is typically to find a solution that is robust to possible changes. Other related models include *Mixed CSPs* [5], which model decision problems under uncertainty by introducing state variables, which are not under control of the solver, and seek assignments that are consistent to any state of the world; and *Stochastic CSPs* [31,34], which introduce probability distributions that are associated to outcomes of state variables, and seek solutions that maximize the probability of constraint consistencies. While these approaches have been used to solve CSP variants, they have not been used to solve D-DCOPs with continuous variables to the best of our knowledge.

Researchers have proposed several algorithms to solve C-DCOPs. One of such algorithms is Continuous Max-Sum (CMS) [29], which is based on Max-Sum [6], a belief propagation algorithm. To represent the constraints, CMS uses multivariate continuous piecewise linear functions (CPLFs) and later encodes the n-ary CPLFs as n-simplexes. To add two CPLFs, CMS partitions the domains of the two functions and then finds the simplexes that make up the resulting summation function. To project a CPLF, the function is projected onto the corresponding plane and the result is the upper envelope of the simplexes. However, CMS is not suitable for the problems where constraint functions are smooth, and it does not provide quality guarantee for the solution. Later, Voice *et al.* [32] proposed Hybrid Continuous Max-Sum (HCMS) to solve C-DCOPs with differentiable functions. Instead of working directly on continuous domains, HCMS first discretizes the domain into a number of initial discrete points and then uses continuous non-linear optimization techniques such as gradient method and Newton method to optimize the marginal function at each variable. However, similar to CMS, HCMS does not provide solution quality guarantee. Recently, Choudhury *et al.* [3] proposed *Particle Swarm Optimization Based Functional DCOP (PFD)* which is based on the *Particle Swarm Optimization (PSO)* technique. While being an iterative and a heuristic algorithm, PFD shares the same limitation with CMS and HCMS that they do not provide guarantee for their solutions. Finally, Fransman *et al.* [11] proposed *Bayesian DPOP (B-DPOP)*, a Bayesian optimization based algorithm, to solve C-DCOPs. While B-DPOP guarantees that it will eventually converge to the global optimum for Lipschitz-

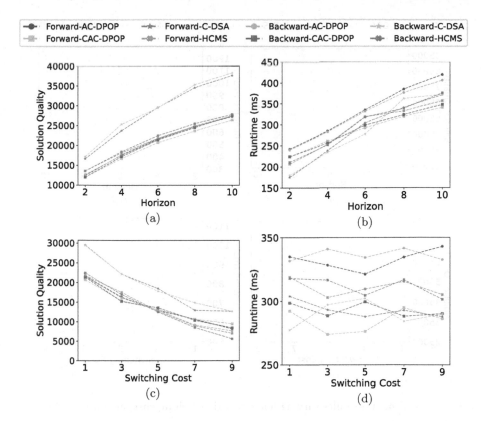

Fig. 2. Experimental results varying horizon and switching cost on sparse random networks

continuous objective functions, it does not provide guarantees on intermediate solutions prior to convergence.

8   Experimental Evaluations

We empirically evaluate the following DC-DCOP algorithms: FORWARD-(labeled 'F-' in the tables) and BACKWARD- (labeled 'B-' in the tables) versions of AC-DPOP, CAC-DPOP, C-DSA, and HCMS [15] on random networks and distributed sensor network problems. Our experiments are performed on a 2.1 GHz machine with 16 GB of RAM using JADE framework [1]. We report solution quality and simulated runtime [30] averaged over 30 independent runs, each with a timeout of 30 min.

8.1   Random Networks

We use the following default configuration: Number of agents and random variables $|\mathbf{A}| = |\mathbf{X}| = |\mathbf{Y}| = 12$; domains of decision and random variables

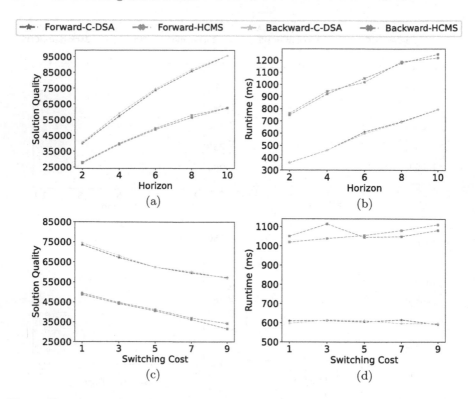

Fig. 3. Experimental results varying horizon and switching cost on dense random networks

$D_x = D_y = [-10, 10]$; discount factor $\gamma = 0.9$; horizon $h = 6$; switching cost function $c(x, x') = c \cdot (x - x')^2$ with the default cost $c = 1$. We set the number of discrete points to 3 for AC-DPOP-, CAC-DPOP-, and HCMS-based algorithms. For all algorithms, we set the number of iterations as 20.[3]

We first vary the horizon h to evaluate the performance of the algorithms with different horizon length. Figures 2(a) and 2(b) show the solution quality and runtime with horizon varying from 2 to 10 on sparse networks with $p_1 = 0.2$. When the horizon increases, both FORWARD-C-DSA and BACKWARD-C-DSA produce the highest solution quality and outperform all other algorithms. The reason is that C-DSA-based algorithms do not depend on a number of initial discrete points and thus they are free to explore the search space. Interestingly, when the horizon becomes longer, their runtime is as small as other algorithms. This result shows that while C-DSA-based algorithms have the best solution quality, they do not come with the cost of higher runtime. Since AC-DPOP takes the longest time to solve each single C-DCOP [15], FORWARD-AC-DPOP

---

[3] For AC-DPOP- and CAC-DPOP-based algorithms, that is the number of iterations to move the values of parent and pseudo-parent variables. For HCMS- and C-DSA-based algorithms, it is the number of iterations to perform the local search.

Table 1. Varying the Number of Agents on Sparse Random Networks with $p_1 = 0.2$

|A|	F-AC-DPOP		B-AC-DPOP		F-CAC-DPOP		B-CAC-DPOP		F-C-DSA		B-C-DSA		F-HCMS		B-HCMS	
	q	t	q	t	q	t	q	t	q	t	q	t	q	t	q	t
8	20789	285	20467	280	20778	284	20656	281	25824	280	26354	272	18668	285	18792	285
12	27269	420	27356	406	26378	341	27445	348	37653	371	38306	372	27423	357	27780	376
16	42473	111276	43327	119863	37708	874	39005	870	59390	542	59296	545	43511	611	44373	591
20	–	–	–	–	65345	3697	65075	3690	100725	690	102904	709	73269	751	74140	760
24	–	–	–	–	70058	49275	68965	43269	134213	774	134964	782	93427	958	94610	956
28	–	–	–	–	88135	493444	88156	524903	176429	884	175571	887	120822	1247	120917	1259
32	–	–	–	–	–	–	–	–	224743	1014	227258	1015	162918	1498	163627	1623

Table 2. Varying the number of agents on dense random networks with $p_1 = 0.7$

|A|	F-CAC-DPOP		B-CAC-DPOP		F-C-DSA		B-C-DSA		F-HCMS		B-HCMS	
	q	t	q	t	q	t	q	t	q	t	q	t
8	30359	6604	31158	6229	47747	436	47594	418	33166	684	32958	674
12	–	–	–	–	95133	782	96722	791	62861	1289	62767	1273
16	–	–	–	–	160255	1273	160713	1289	109128	2222	110232	2227
20	–	–	–	–	217548	1603	215767	1601	148709	3243	149640	3284
24	–	–	–	–	281505	1842	283987	1836	196808	4508	196467	4453
28	–	–	–	–	375106	1972	374697	1986	255482	5565	252306	5643
32	–	–	–	–	466945	2138	463594	2121	313125	6891	318854	6860

Table 3. Varying the number of agents on sensor networks

|A|	F-AC-DPOP		B-AC-DPOP		F-CAC-DPOP		B-CAC-DPOP		F-C-DSA		B-C-DSA		F-HCMS		B-HCMS	
	q	t	q	t	q	t	q	t	q	t	q	t	q	t	q	t
4	4750	108	5053	104	4750	171	5052	168	7302	131	7432	136	4344	127	4406	125
8	19166	275	21155	263	19287	296	19208	298	24958	252	25045	253	17415	282	17969	282
12	31809	387	31916	387	31116	411	30773	418	40014	392	40912	404	28357	373	28892	358
16	37842	507	38427	493	36007	450	36615	469	50069	459	51274	458	36454	412	36265	411
20	58987	696	60088	695	51418	570	51265	567	70953	513	71888	514	52402	444	52201	465

and BACKWARD-AC-DPOP are the slowest algorithms across different horizon length. Similarly, on dense networks with $p_1 = 0.7$, Figs. 3(a) and 3(b) show that both versions of C-DSA again outperform the HCMS-based algorithms in terms of solution quality with smaller runtime. We do not include AC-DPOP- and CAC-DPOP-based algorithms in Fig. 3 since they time out on the dense networks.

Figures 2(c) and 2(d) show the result of varying the switching cost c in the switching cost function $c \cdot (x - x')^2$. The result shows that the solution quality of all algorithms decreases when the switching cost increases. If there is no switching cost (i.e., $c = 0$), the optimal solution of DC-DCOP consists of the optimal solution of the C-DCOP at each time step. However, with higher switching cost, the solution quality found by algorithms is likely to decreases due to the higher penalty incurred by different solutions across time steps. We also observe that C-DSA-based algorithms have the best solution quality, which is consistent with the result on dense graph reported in Figs. 3(c) and 3(d).

Finally, we vary the number of agents $|\mathbf{A}|$ (and thus the number of decision $|\mathbf{X}|$ and random variables $|\mathbf{Y}|$) of the problems from 8 to 32 with horizon $h = 10$. Table 1 tabulates the solution quality (denoted by q) and simulated runtime (denoted by t in ms) of the algorithms on sparse networks with $p_1 = 0.2$. Since AC-DPOP takes the longest time to solve the C-DCOP at each time step, both FORWARD-AC-DPOP and BACKWARD-AC-DPOP can only solve small instances with 8, 12 and 16 agents and time out with larger instances. CAC-DPOP, which is the clustering version of AC-DPOP, reduces the memory used in the UTIL phrase and is more scalable to solve C-DCOPs with more number of agents [15]. Thus both FORWARD- and BACKWARD-CAC-DPOP are able to solve instances with more number of agents than AC-DPOP-based algorithms and only time out with 32 agents. On the other hand, since C-DSA and HCMS are more scalable, it takes less time for them to solve each individual C-DCOP, and their DC-DCOP algorithms are able to solve all instances with much smaller runtime than AC-DPOP and CAC-DPOP. Interestingly, HCMS-based algorithms report a slightly larger runtime than C-DSA-based algorithms. Similar to the results from Fig. 2, C-DSA-based algorithms report the highest solution quality than those from AC-DPOP-, CAC-DPOP-, and HCMS-based algorithms on different numbers of agents.

Table 2 shows the result varying agents on a dense random networks with $p_1 = 0.7$. Since both FORWARD- and BACKWARD-AC-DPOP time out with 8 agents, we do not include these algorithms in the table. While CAC-DPOP-based algorithms are able to solve the instances with 8 agents, they time out on larger instances. Both C-DSA- and HCMS- based algorithms are able to scale to solve larger instances with incremental runtime. While C-DSA-based algorithms outperform HCMS-based algorithms on all instances, it also takes them less time than the counterpart algorithms.

8.2   Distributed Sensor Network Problems

We evaluate our DC-DCOP algorithms on distributed sensor network problems, which is our motivating application described in Sect. 3. We use grid networks to represent the sensor networks where sensors are arranged in a rectangular grid. Each sensor is connected to its four neighboring sensors in the cardinal direction. Those sensors on the edges are connected to three neighboring sensors, and corner sensors are connected to two neighbors. The random variables, which represent the possible location of the targets, are randomly placed on the network.

Table 3 shows the quality solution and runtime (in ms) of DC-DCOP algorithms on sensor network problems with agents varying from 4 to 20. Both AC-DPOP- and CAC-DPOP-based algorithms run from smaller (4 sensors) to larger instances (20 sensors) without timeout and have slightly higher solution quality than HCMS-based algorithms. However, both versions of C-DSA outperform all other algorithms by providing the best solution quality from small to large instances. In addition, C-DSA-based algorithms have smaller runtime than AC-DPOP- and CAC-DPOP-based since C-DSA is a local search algorithm on

C-DCOP. However, on grid network problems, HCMS-based algorithms execute faster than C-DSA-based algorithms.

9   Conclusions

In many real-world applications, agents often act in a complex and dynamic environment. While DCOPs have been widely used to solve several multi-agent problems, the formulation lacks the capability to model the dynamic and continuous nature in complex environments. Consequently, researchers have proposed D-DCOPs to model how the environment changes over time and C-DCOPs to model the continuous domain of decision variables. However, they can only address the DCOP limitations in isolation. In this paper, we introduced Dynamic Continuous DCOPs (DC-DCOPs), which model *both* the dynamic environment *and* decision variables with continuous domain. To solve DC-DCOPs, we proposed several sequential greedy algorithms that can use any off-the-shelf C-DCOP algorithms to solve DC-DCOPs and we discussed their theoretical properties. Finally, we evaluated our algorithms on random networks and on distributed sensor network problems, which are our motivating application for this line of work.

Acknowledgments. This work is partially supported by NSF grants 1812619 and 1838364. The views and conclusions contained in this document are those of the authors and should not be interpreted as representing the official policies, either expressed or implied, of the sponsoring organizations, agencies, or the U.S. government.

References

1. Bellifemine, F., Bergenti, F., Caire, G., Poggi, A.: Jade — a java agent development framework. In: Bordini, R.H., Dastani, M., Dix, J., El Fallah Seghrouchni, A. (eds.) Multi-Agent Programming. MSASSO, vol. 15, pp. 125–147. Springer, Boston, MA (2005). https://doi.org/10.1007/0-387-26350-0_5
2. Burke, D., Brown, K.: Efficiently handling complex local problems in distributed constraint optimisation. In: Proceedings of ECAI, pp. 701–702 (2006)
3. Choudhury, M., Mahmud, S., Khan, M.M.: A particle swarm based algorithm for functional distributed constraint optimization problems. In: Proceedings of AAAI (2020)
4. Deng, Y., An, B.: Speeding up incomplete GDL-based algorithms for multi-agent optimization with dense local utilities. In: Proceedings of IJCAI, pp. 31–38 (2020)
5. Fargier, H., Lang, J., Schiex, T.: Mixed constraint satisfaction: a framework for decision problems under incomplete knowledge. In: Proceedings of AAAI, pp. 175–180 (1996)
6. Farinelli, A., Rogers, A., Petcu, A., Jennings, N.: Decentralised coordination of low-power embedded devices using the max-sum algorithm. In: Proceedings of AAMAS, pp. 639–646 (2008)
7. Fioretto, F., Pontelli, E., Yeoh, W.: Distributed constraint optimization problems and applications: a survey. J. Artif. Intell. Res. **61**, 623–698 (2018)

8. Fioretto, F., Yeoh, W., Pontelli, E.: Multi-variable agents decomposition for DCOPs. In: Proceedings of AAAI, pp. 2480–2486 (2016)
9. Fioretto, F., Yeoh, W., Pontelli, E.: A multiagent system approach to scheduling devices in smart homes. In: Proceedings of AAMAS, pp. 981–989 (2017)
10. Fioretto, F., Yeoh, W., Pontelli, E., Ma, Y., Ranade, S.: A DCOP approach to the economic dispatch with demand response. In: Proceedings of AAMAS, pp. 999–1007 (2017)
11. Fransman, J., Sijs, J., Dol, H., Theunissen, E., Schutter, B.D.: Bayesian-DPOP for continuous distributed constraint optimization problems. In: Proceedings of AAMAS, pp. 1961–1963 (2019)
12. Hoang, K.D., Fioretto, F., Hou, P., Yeoh, W., Yokoo, M., Zivan, R.: Proactive dynamic distributed constraint optimization problems. J. Artif. Intell. Res. **74**, 179–225 (2022)
13. Hoang, K.D., Fioretto, F., Hou, P., Yokoo, M., Yeoh, W., Zivan, R.: Proactive dynamic distributed constraint optimization. In: Proceedings of AAMAS, pp. 597–605 (2016)
14. Hoang, K.D., Hou, P., Fioretto, F., Yeoh, W., Zivan, R., Yokoo, M.: Infinite-horizon proactive dynamic DCOPs. In: Proceedings of AAMAS, pp. 212–220 (2017)
15. Hoang, K.D., Yeoh, W., Yokoo, M., Rabinovich, Z.: New algorithms for continuous distributed constraint optimization problems. In: Proceedings of AAMAS, pp. 502–510 (2020)
16. Holland, A., O'Sullivan, B.: Weighted super solutions for constraint programs. In: Proceedings of AAAI, pp. 378–383 (2005)
17. Kim, Y., Krainin, M., Lesser, V.: Effective variants of the max-sum algorithm for radar coordination and scheduling. In: Proceedings of WI-IAT, pp. 357–364 (2011)
18. Kumar, A., Faltings, B., Petcu, A.: Distributed constraint optimization with structured resource constraints. In: Proceedings of AAMAS, pp. 923–930 (2009)
19. Lass, R., Sultanik, E., Regli, W.: Dynamic distributed constraint reasoning. In: Proceedings of AAAI, pp. 1466–1469 (2008)
20. Maheswaran, R., Tambe, M., Bowring, E., Pearce, J., Varakantham, P.: Taking DCOP to the real world: efficient complete solutions for distributed event scheduling. In: Proceedings of AAMAS, pp. 310–317 (2004)
21. Miller, S., Ramchurn, S., Rogers, A.: Optimal decentralised dispatch of embedded generation in the smart grid. In: Proceedings of AAMAS, pp. 281–288 (2012)
22. Modi, P., Shen, W.M., Tambe, M., Yokoo, M.: ADOPT: asynchronous distributed constraint optimization with quality guarantees. Artif. Intell. **161**(1–2), 149–180 (2005)
23. Paulos, A., et al.: A framework for self-adaptive dispersal of computing services. In: IEEE Self-Adaptive and Self-Organizing Systems Workshops (2019)
24. Petcu, A., Faltings, B.: A scalable method for multiagent constraint optimization. In: Proceedings of IJCAI, pp. 1413–1420 (2005)
25. Petcu, A., Faltings, B.: Superstabilizing, fault-containing multiagent combinatorial optimization. In: Proceedings of AAAI, pp. 449–454 (2005)
26. Petcu, A., Faltings, B.: Optimal solution stability in dynamic, distributed constraint optimization. In: Proceedings of IAT, pp. 321–327 (2007)
27. Rust, P., Picard, G., Ramparany, F.: Using message-passing DCOP algorithms to solve energy-efficient smart environment configuration problems. In: Proceedings of IJCAI, pp. 468–474 (2016)
28. Sarker, A., Choudhury, M., Khan, M.M.: A local search based approach to solve Continuous DCOPs. In: Proceedings of AAMAS, pp. 1127–1135 (2021)

29. Stranders, R., Farinelli, A., Rogers, A., Jennings, N.: Decentralised coordination of continuously valued control parameters using the Max-Sum algorithm. In: Proceedings of AAMAS, pp. 601–608 (2009)
30. Sultanik, E., Lass, R., Regli, W.: DCOPolis: a framework for simulating and deploying distributed constraint reasoning algorithms. In: Proceedings of AAMAS, pp. 1667–1668 (2008)
31. Tarim, S.A., Manandhar, S., Walsh, T.: Stochastic constraint programming: a scenario-based approach. Constraints $11(1)$, 53–80 (2006)
32. Voice, T., Stranders, R., Rogers, A., Jennings, N.: A hybrid continuous max-sum algorithm for decentralised coordination. In: Proceedings of ECAI, pp. 61–66 (2010)
33. Wallace, R., Freuder, E.: Stable solutions for dynamic constraint satisfaction problems. In: Proceedings of CP, pp. 447–461 (1998)
34. Walsh, T.: Stochastic constraint programming. In: Proceedings of ECAI, pp. 111–115 (2002)
35. Yeoh, W., Felner, A., Koenig, S.: BnB-ADOPT: an asynchronous branch-and-bound DCOP algorithm. J. Artif. Intell. Res. 38, 85–133 (2010)
36. Yeoh, W., Varakantham, P., Sun, X., Koenig, S.: Incremental DCOP search algorithms for solving dynamic DCOPs. In: Proceedings of IAT, pp. 257–264 (2015)
37. Yeoh, W., Yokoo, M.: Distributed problem solving. AI Mag. $33(3)$, 53–65 (2012)
38. Yokoo, M. (ed.): Distributed Constraint Satisfaction: Foundation of Cooperation in Multi-agent Systems. Springer, Cham (2001). https://doi.org/10.1007/978-3-642-59546-2
39. Zink, M., et al.: Meteorological command and control: an end-to-end architecture for a hazardous weather detection sensor network. In: Workshop on End-to-End, Sense-and-Respond Systems, Applications, and Services. USENIX Association (2005)
40. Zivan, R., Yedidsion, H., Okamoto, S., Glinton, R., Sycara, K.: Distributed constraint optimization for teams of mobile sensing agents. J. Auton. Agents Multi-Agent Syst. $29(3)$, 495–536 (2015)

DITURIA: A Framework for Decision Coordination Among Multiple Agents

Helena Ibro[1](✉)[ID], Geeta Mahala[1], Simon Pulawski[1], Steven Harvey[2], Alexis Andrew Miller[3], Aditya Ghose[1], and Hoa Khanh Dam[1]

[1] University of Wollongong, Wollongong, NSW 2522, Australia
{hi852,gm168,spp701,aditya,hoa}@uow.edu.au
[2] Illawarra Shoalhaven Medical Imaging, Wollongong Hospital,
Wollongong, NSW 2500, Australia
steven.harvey@health.nsw.gov.au
[3] Illawarra Cancer Care Centre, Wollongong Hospital,
Wollongong, NSW 2500, Australia

Abstract. Decision making in multi-agent settings is a complex exercise where agents have to handle incomplete knowledge of the complete problem. Agents are interdependent in multi-agent decision making, being subject to the decisions of other agents who bring to bear other qualitative and quantitative criteria. Some aspects of this problem have been addressed in the Distributed Constraint Optimisation Problems (DCOP) and Markov Decision Processes literature. Taking inspiration from a medical example, our objective in this paper is to provide a framework to support multi-agent decision coordination. This method can be applied in scenarios where we seek to combine qualitative preferences on projected final states with assessment made using utility/objective functions, while accounting for partial agent knowledge.

Keywords: Decision coordination · Decision optimisation · Adversarial search

1 Introduction

Supporting multi-agent decision making is a complex problem. A multitude of techniques have been developed, with widely varying antecedents. The closest starting point is the literature on Distributed Constraint Optimisation Problems (DCOPs) [5]. A variety of other problem formulations, with antecedents as varied as game theory, probabilistic reasoning and formal argumentation theory have been explored in the literature. The resulting smorgasbord of techniques have not come together into a unified, coherent framework. In many practical application domains, the available techniques leave much to be desired.

A hospital for example, is required to treat a large number of patients every day, while seeking to optimise on multiple dimensions. The overarching objective

© The Author(s), under exclusive license to Springer Nature Switzerland AG 2023
R. Aydoğan et al. (Eds.): PRIMA 2022, LNAI 13753, pp. 492–508, 2023.
https://doi.org/10.1007/978-3-031-21203-1_29

is to maximise the quality of the clinical outcome for each patient. Subsidiary objectives relate to the improvement of the efficiency of clinical processes, such as reducing the average duration of hospital stay per patient, maximising the utilisation of medical resources, cost reduction and so on.

A patient arriving at a hospital is associated with a potentially complex sequence of decisions. These include decisions on a preliminary diagnosis, the types of medical imaging required, the battery of other tests to be performed, and decisions on surgical procedures to be executed, amongst many others. There are multiple agents taking these decisions, including paramedics, nurses, junior doctors, specialists, lab technicians, physiotherapists and radiology equipment operators. There are constraints governing these decisions (a pregnant patient should not be subjected to high doses of radiation in imaging procedures such as CT scans, for instance). There are also sequencing constraints governing these decisions (a decision on medical imaging modality can only be taken after a decision on preliminary diagnosis has been arrived at). Some of these decision combinations have efficiency implications that can be assessed using utility/objective functions. Others can only be assessed by considering the final state of affairs achieved, parts of which cannot be assessed using purely numeric measures (but instead by using preferences over states). Individual agents are usually faced with decisions based on incomplete knowledge, and might have to resort to minimax or maximin reasoning of the kind used in adversarial search that will handle said gaps in its knowledge.

In this paper, we present the DITURIA (Albanian for "knowledge") framework, which builds upon early work on decision interdependency networks [23], to address such problems. We begin with a multi-agent formulation that resembles a distributed constraint network like those found in Distributed Constraint Optimisation Problems (DCOPs) [5]. There are, nevertheless, significant distinctions. In general, DCOP formulations do not allow for precedence constraints between decisions, whereas DITURIA does. It is feasible to gain a representation of the state of affairs (often a partial state) that arises after any allowed series of decisions using a multi-agent decision problem (MADP) represented in DITURIA. With DCOP formulations (which do not support the relatively sophisticated machinery required to map a set of value assignments to a set of decision variables to a perhaps non-deterministic group of states), this is not achievable. The value gained for each agent-specific objective function, as well as a preference relation on the states that arise following a given sequence of choices (the values assigned to decision variables), determine the optimal combinations of choices. For a DCOP formulation, the whole *schema* or *signature* of the problem must be specified *a priori*, although in the case of the DITURIA framework, they can be revealed sequentially. A first-cut version of a MADP in DITURIA can be retrieved from widely available process models, unlike a DCOP formulation.

Look-ahead search plays a role in 2 different ways in DITURIA. First, we use look-ahead search in a manner akin to standard constraint-solving by (possibly temporarily) reducing the domains of the variables that are yet to be assigned values in response to a potentially tentative assignment of value to a decision variable. Second, we leverage value from viewing adversarial game tree search as look-ahead search by having each agent compute the worst possible outcome that might accrue by performing look-ahead search on decisions taken by other agents in its *neighbourhood* (i.e., agents that it shares constraints with and knows about). It does this for each available decision option (possible value to assign to a decision variable), computes how desirable the resulting state would be and then picks the best of the worst-case scenarios (the least desirable state that would accrue) for each decision option. The best of the worst-case scenarios thus determines the decision to be taken at any point in time.

The rest of the paper is organised into Sect. 2 which presents the formal foundations and outlines the DITURIA problem solving procedure, Sect. 3 which provides theoretical proofs of the framework's correctness and optimality, Sect. 4 which presents an illustration and evaluation of the algorithm, Sect. 5 which positions these results relative to existing work, and finally Sect. 6 which presents conclusions and directions for future work.

2   The DITURIA Framework in Detail

Definition 1. The DITURIA framework is our approach to solving a multi-agent decision problem (MADP), which is formally defined as a tuple $\langle A, X, D, KB, \Psi, C, F, E, G \rangle$, comprised of:

- A set of *agents* $A = \{a_1, \ldots, a_m\}$, where m denotes the quantity of agents.
- A set of *decision variables* $X = \{x_1, \ldots, x_n\}$, where n is the number of variables[1] each with a distinct *domain*.
- A collection of *domains* $D = \{D_1, \ldots, D_n\}$, where each domain D_i is the set of possible values $\{d_j \mid d_j \in D_i\}$ for a decision variable x_i.
- A *knowledge base* KB consisting of rules that every valid system state must satisfy.
- The universe of possible *partial states* Ψ. Subsets of Ψ are denoted as θ.
- A set of *constraints* C, each constraint $c \in C$ being a tuple with the value $\langle scope, type, rel \rangle$.
- The *agent assignment function* $F : A \longrightarrow 2^X$ that takes as input an agent ID and returns the set of variables that is associated with that agent.
- The *decision-to-state mapping function* $E : D_1 \times \ldots \times D_m \longrightarrow 2^\Psi$ that maps variable assignments to a set of partial states, where m is the number of decision variables being considered, n is the total number of decision variables in the system (and $m \leq n$).
- A set of agent-specific *assessment functions* G where each $g_i \in G$ represents the machinery that agent a_i uses to assess the desirability of a set of decisions (assignments of values to decision variables). The assessment function involves the application of the following two sub-functions[2]:

---

[1] In this paper we refer to decisions, decision variables and variables interchangeably.
[2] We do not prescribe the details of exactly how these functions are applied - these can be configured to meet the needs of the application domain.

- A *qualitative comparison function* $q : 2^{\Psi} \times 2^{\Psi} \longrightarrow 2^{\Psi} \times 2^{\Psi}$ that takes two sets of states and returns a tuple of two elements.
- A utility function $u : 2^{\Psi} \longrightarrow \mathbb{R}$ that receives a state and returns a number.

In the proposed constraint tuple, *scope* is a tuple of decision variables that are part of a constraint, e.g., $\langle x_1, x_2 \rangle$. Note that in this study, we only consider binary constraints for the sake of simplicity, therefore *scope* is a tuple with two variables. *type* is the sort of constraint between the variables in a *scope*. We will look at two sorts of constraints in this paper: *prec* and *value* constraints. *value* constraints place certain restrictions on the possible combinations of *values* that can be assigned between the variables, whereas *precedence* constraints, or *prec*, stipulate that one decision variable must be assigned before another. *rel* is the constraint-imposed relationship between the variables. In the case of *prec* constraints, *rel* is a tuple that specifies the order in which the variables must be assigned. For value constraints, *rel* is a logical rule that expresses an n-ary relation (where n is the number of variables in *scope*). The same tuple of variables can be constrained in multiple ways. However, only one *prec* constraint can exist between a pair of variables, whereas there may be numerous *value* constraints between a tuple of variables.

A partial state $\psi \in \Psi$ is an assignment of truth values to a set of literals which might not include all the literals required to specify a complete system state, i.e., there can potentially be multiple complete system states and the latter may sometimes not require all the variables that are included in the framework to be assigned a value for that partial assignment to be considered complete. In the rest of this paper, we simplify matters by assuming that each agent is associated with exactly one variable, hence function F will return only one variable per agent. Various methods already exist in the literature that deal with using similar frameworks in more complex settings where multiple variables are assigned per agent. For example, one of the methods suggested in [32] is creating multiple virtual agents within a single real agent where each of the former gets assigned one local variable. The E function views each decision as leading to an action. It thus applies a *state update operator* (such as PWA [8] or PMA [28]) which updates the prior state with the post-conditions of the corresponding action. In general, each application of a state update operator can lead to multiple non-deterministic outcomes. Hence a sequence of decisions could lead to a potentially large number of possible partial states that may accrue consequently.

The agent specific g functions are "projections" of the global G function to the signatures of individual agents. Each assessment function is defined as $g_i : 2^{D_1 \times \ldots \times D_m} \longrightarrow D_1 \times \ldots \times D_m$. In other words, given a set of decisions taken by a set of agents (given by assignments of values to the corresponding variables), the assessment function selects the most preferred combination of decisions by using a lexicographic strategy. A lexicographic strategy in this context is selecting the assignment that leads to the minimisation of the utility function while also yielding the most desirable set of partial states, or vice versa, the assignment that leads to the most desirable set of partial states that also minimise the utility function. The tuple returned by the function q contains both the input sets if they are equally desirable or, if one set is conclusively more desirable than the other, a tuple where the least desirable set of states is given as $\varnothing$. The utility function can be used to describe *soft* constraints such as temporal or fiscal cost.

Definition 2. A *local assignment* ρ_{a_i} for agent a_i is a value assignment for the subset of variables in X that is assigned to agent a_i and its *direct neighbours*.

A local assignment ρ_{a_i} is an input to function E when an agent computes its set of partial states using the partial state mapping function, e.g., $\theta_{a_i} = E(\rho_{a_i})$.

Definition 3. The optimal solution to an MADP in DITURIA when following a lexicographic strategy of maximising the desirability of the state and then minimising the utility function is a local assignment $\rho_{a_{i_{sol}}}$ to each agent $a_i \in A$ which satisfies the set of conditions listed below:

$$\text{for each } \rho_{a_{i_{sol}}}, \ \rho_{a_{i_{sol}}} \cup C \not\models \bot \tag{1}$$

$$\theta_{a_{i_{sol}}} = E(\rho_{a_{i_{sol}}}) \tag{2}$$

$$\neg \exists \theta_{other} \subset \Psi, \ q(\theta_{a_{i_{sol}}} \theta_{other}) = \langle \varnothing, \ \theta_{other} \rangle \tag{3}$$

$$\rho_{a_{i_{sol}}} = \operatorname*{argmin}_{\rho_{a_i} \in P} \sum_{a_i \in A} u(\rho_{a_i}) \tag{4}$$

where P is the set of all partial assignments ρ_{a_i} an agent can take that satisfy Eq. 2 and Eq. 3.

The DITURIA Algorithm: Acquiring the optimal solution by utilising the approach introduced in our framework consists of two phases: *Extraction* and *Solution*. During the former, the agents order themselves into a network that forms the first cut of the multi-agent system. In this phase we utilise a similar approach to the one presented in [23] to acquire all the necessary inputs for a DITURIA framework. In [23] a new approach is implemented, where decisions are extracted from semantic effect annotations. Accordingly, the process model is annotated with the *immediate effects* (or post-conditions) of each task. Immediate effects are a way of describing what becomes true in the world after the execution of the task. The process model is also accompanied by a KB, extra knowledge in the form of rules on how the process functions and knowledge about the domain in which the process executes. The above establishes all the necessary inputs to also extract a DITURIA framework which we assume is a completed step prior to our algorithm. During the latter solution phase, the agents explore different assignments for their decision variables by engaging in interaction with their neighbours. The agent interaction protocol (to be explained below) will incrementally reveal to agents a (potentially partial) view of the system state, which in turn plays a role in the reasoning that agents perform to decide values for their associated variables. Agents update their assignments using a protocol that considers: (1) constraints governing the inter-relationships between decisions; (2) utility/objective functions defined on (possibly a subset of) the decision variables; (3) partial system states arrived at as a consequence of taking a sequence of decisions. The solution computation strategy involves a combination of distributed constraint satisfaction, distributed optimisation and maximin reasoning of the kind used in look-ahead search, including viewing adversarial game tree search as such (Algorithm 1 provides the details). We acknowledge that some application domains of DITURIA may involve malicious agents and that communications may be unreliable, but this has been excluded from the scope of this paper where said domains have all neighbour agents always positively cooperative (no one is malicious) and communications are consistently effective and reliable.

We define below some notations that will be used in the remainder of this section. In general, an agent may be associated with more than one decision variable. To simplify matters, we assumed that each agent corresponds to a single decision variable. Thus, we will refer to agent's value and variable's value interchangeably. Each agent contains:

- The *current value:* The value currently assigned to the variable associated with the agent.
- *Neighbours:* The set of agents with whom the current agent shares constraints.
- The *current domain:* This is the subset of the domain (i.e., the set of values that a variable can take) that is consistent (in terms of satisfying the applicable constraints) with the current domains of all the agent's neighbours.
- *Constraints:* The set of rules that specify the allowed combinations of values that an agent and each of its neighbours can take.
- *View:* This is the (potentially incomplete) specification of the complete system state that an agent is able to construct based on its knowledge of itself and its neighbours and the messages it receives from its neighbours.

The messages that an agent sends or receives can be of two types: *VIOLATION* and *VALUE*. An agent sends a *VIOLATION* to its neighbours when it has no value in its domain that is consistent (i.e., constraint-satisfying) given the current values of its neighbours. An agent sends a *VALUE* message to its neighbours every time it updates its value. The message contains both the new value and the partial state that accrues from the current values of the agent and its neighbours (this is computed using the E function). When selecting a value, an agent's goal is to maximise the desirability of the partial state that accrues from this value. Recall that the choice of a value for a single agent/variable does not, in general, determine the complete system state, but a *set* of system states (all of which are consistent with the agent's value). Recall also that an agent does not always have access to complete system states but only potentially incomplete states that it is able to construct from the *VALUE* messages from its neighbours (who are in turn able to construct their views of the system state from the *VALUE* messages they receive from their neighbours, and so on). When selecting its first value, the agent must consider the fact that the partial state is the result of not just its value assignment, but also that of its neighbours, over which it has no control. To account for this, the agent assumes the worst case and performs an adversarial game tree search [27]. The agent assumes its neighbours are rational agents who will select variable assignments that min-imise the desirability of its partial state. As such, the agent searches the space of partial states using an adversarial game tree search algorithm such as MAXMIN, where the agent is the MAX player and its neighbours are the MIN player. The actions available to the agent are the values it can assign to its variable, while the actions available to the MIN player are the combinations of variable assignments that its neighbours can select. The agent selects the value that maximises the desirability of the final outcome while assuming that its neighbours will select values that minimise that outcome, the max-min partial state.

The Solution Phase of our framework (as shown in Algorithm 1) consists of two main processes, namely *Value selection* and *Message checking*. Initially, an agent a_i will begin its decision process in regard to their variable x_i only if they do not have a *prec* constraint where they are the dependent agent (i.e., they will only be included in the system if another agent has assigned to their variable a certain value as specified in the *prec* constraint). This differs from previous algorithms that always establish a hierarchy among the agents (i.e., children and parents). In those algorithms, the agent may have to wait for communication from one of its children, or the agent may be unable to interact directly with another agent with whom it shares a constraint. At this instant, due to their lack of view regarding the system state, the agent's G function (Function 1: Line 8) will select that value from the domain that does not violate the variable's internal constraints, minimises/maximises its utility function and yields the preferred state. Once the value is selected, the agent sends a *VALUE* message to all its neighbours and then waits to receive messages from them.

When messages are received, the agent classifies them into their correspond-ing types and begins processing them starting from the *VIOLATION* ones (this ordering is not necessary for the algorithm's accuracy, but it does help with performance). For every *VIOLATION* message, the agent updates its internal constraints for the variable that the message is directed to, noting that the value currently assigned to that variable is no longer satisfactory. Subsequently, for each *VALUE* message, the agent first checks that the received value does not cause an arc-inconsistency for its variable. According to the result, the agent will send back a *VIOLATION* message to that neighbour if the arc-inconsistency did occur or update its partial view of the system state correspondingly to the partial state received from the message (Algorithm 1: Line 7–15).

Once the first round of messages is processed, the agent proceeds to choose a new value for its variable by consulting its internal G function[3]. The function takes a variable's current domain and partial view of the system state from the agent and initially uses look-ahead search as a reaction to a possible tentative assignment of value to a decision variable to temporarily reduce the domain. Following that, for each $d_i \in D$ adversarial game tree search reasoning is used to compute the worst partial states that can occur based on what its neighbours have decided so far and choose the value assignment that will lead to the most

---

[3] We note that there might be instances where despite the new information an agent has gained for its variables, their G function may still choose the same value.

preferred partial state out of them all (Function 1: Line 2–6). The reason behind this approach comes as an attempt to avoid the instances where some agents may have values that they prefer in relation to the ones that do not cause arc-inconsistency with their neighbours, but require them to change the value of their variables (i.e., no *VIOLATION* message is received when such values are sent). Hence, the agent may try to "convince" its neighbours to change their value so it can choose/keep the value it prefers. This could be followed up the same way by its neighbours, leading to an infinite exchange of *VALUE* messages between agents.

Following the return value from the G function, if that differs from the one previously assigned for the variable, the agent will notify its neighbours about the change, otherwise it will just wait for any further communication (Algorithm 1: Line 17–19). We note that when an agent selects a value for its variable, before sending any *VALUE* messages to its neighbours, it will first assess if that value satisfies any of the *prec* constraints that the variable might be involved with. Assuming that the latter is true, the other agent involved in this constraint will be added to the network by also receiving a *VALUE* message. This process is repeated by each agent until all of them are in a waiting state.

Definition 4. An agent $a_i \in A$ of the DITURIA framework is in a waiting state when:

$$x_i \leftarrow d_j \mid d_j \in D_i \text{ where } d_j \rightarrow C \not\models \bot \qquad (5)$$

$$\left\{ \begin{array}{c} \text{VIOLATION messages} \\ \text{VALUE messages} \end{array} \right\} \not\models \bot \qquad (6)$$

Thenceforth the algorithm terminates and the optimal solution is acquired by taking the value from each variable in the system.

Function 1: G()

Input : a variable's current domain and/or the agent's current view on the partial system state from his neighbours

Output: a value assignment for the agent's decision variable

1 **begin**
2   **if** $\top(\rho_{a_i})$ **then**
3   **foreach** $d_i \in D_i$ **do**
4        $\lfloor$ Compute worst $\psi_{a_i} = E(\rho_{a_i})$ that satisfies all constraints c_i
5      $\psi_{a_i}* \leftarrow$ most preferred partial state from the ones computed above using maxmin reasoning (i.e. is the most preferred ψ_{a_i} based on the functions q and u)
6   **return** $d_i \rightarrow \psi_{a_i}*$
7   **else**
8      $\lfloor$ **return** most preferred $d_i \in D_i$ based on the functions q and u

---

Algorithm 1: DITURIA's solving algorithm

    Input : *a DITURIA specification in the form of a multi-agent system*
    Output: *some assignments of variables:* $D_1 \times ... \times D_n$

1 **while** *Not terminated* **do**
2   **foreach** $a_i \in A$ **do**
3   **if** $\nexists prec \in agent's\ C_i \lor \forall\ prec : C_i(prec)$ *is true* **then**
4   **if** x_i *has no value* **then**
5                 $x_i \leftarrow G(D_i)$
6   Send *VALUE* message to neighbours
7   **if** a_i *has received messages* **then**
8   Classify messages into their corresponding types:
                    VIOLATIONS $\land$ *VALUES*
9   **foreach** $m_i \in VIOLATIONS$ **do**
10   Add content into agent's C_i
11   **foreach** $m_i \in VALUES$ **do**
12   **if** *value* $\implies D_i \equiv \bot$ **then**
13   Send VIOLATION message to sender
14   **else**
15   Update ρ_{a_i}
16                 $x_i \leftarrow G(D_i, \rho_{a_i})$
17   **if** *new value* $\neq$ *previous value* **then**
18   Send *VALUE* message to neighbours
19   Wait for new messages
20   Accumulate all variable assignments

---

3 Theoretical Analysis

In this section, we first demonstrate that the DITURIA framework will always choose an optimal solution at termination, implying that the quality of DITURIA's solutions improves monotonically. Then we look at DITURIA's guarantee to terminate with said solution, followed by an evaluation of the algorithm's complexity.

Optimality: Based on Definition 3 we proceed to demonstrate the framework's optimality by contradiction. We approach this event by assuming that the DITURIA algorithm gives a sub-optimal solution $\rho_{sol} = D_1 \times ... \times D_m$. This indicates that there exists another solution $\rho'_{sol} = D'_1 \times ... \times D'_m$ that is more optimal than the selected ρ_{sol}. The proposed framework uses agent-specific assessment functions $g_i \in G$ that access the desirability of a set of decisions through a lexicographic approach. As stated in Definition 1, G is composed of a qualitative comparison function q and a utility function u that determine the most desirable set of decisions. There are two ways the algorithm determines the most desirable solution: (1) $q \to \langle 2^{\Psi_{sol}}, \varnothing \rangle$ which indicates that the states differ in desirability by returning the most desirable state[4] or (2) $q \to \langle 2^{\Psi_{sol}}, 2^{\Psi'_{sol}} \rangle$ which implies that the states are equally desirable and therefore the solution with the smaller value retrieved from the utility function u is selected. In saying that, there will be an instance i where the algorithm will be situated such that:

$$E(\rho_{sol}) \longrightarrow 2^{\Psi_{sol}} \text{ and } E(\rho'_{sol}) \longrightarrow 2^{\Psi'_{sol}} \text{ where } \rho_{sol}, \; \rho'_{sol} \cup C \not\models \bot$$

$$g_i \left(2^{\Psi_{sol}}, 2^{\Psi'_{sol}} \right) \to q \left(2^{\Psi_{sol}}, 2^{\Psi'_{sol}} \right) \cup \underset{2^{\Psi_i} \, \in \, (2^{\Psi_{sol}}, 2^{\Psi'_{sol}})}{\operatorname{argmin}} \sum u(2^{\Psi_i})$$

Case I. If the states differ in desirability :

$$g_i \left(2^{\Psi_{sol}}, 2^{\Psi'_{sol}} \right) \to \langle \varnothing, 2^{\Psi'_{sol}} \rangle$$

Case II. If the states are equal but have different utility values:

$$g_i \left(2^{\Psi_{sol}}, 2^{\Psi'_{sol}} \right) \to \langle 2^{\Psi_{sol}}, 2^{\Psi'_{sol}} \rangle \cup \mathbb{R}'$$

where $u(2^{\Psi_{sol}}) \to \mathbb{R}$ and $u(2^{\Psi'_{sol}}) \to \mathbb{R}'$

The above shows that the algorithm will indeed choose ρ'_{sol} if that is an existent, more optimal solution, which contradicts the initial assumption of the choice of the sub-optimal solution ρ_{sol}.

Termination: The proposed algorithm will terminate when all the agents in the system are in a waiting state. An agent goes into a waiting state after they have chosen a value for their decision variable(s) from the corresponding domain(s) and have received no messages from their neighbours regarding their value changes or possible violations as presented in Definition 4. Similarly, we suppose that the algorithm does not terminate. For that to be the case, there will exist at least one agent that is not in a waiting state due to either Eq. 5 or Eq. 6 not being true. If the former holds, in the first timestamp (T_1) the algorithm will indicate for a_i to assign a value $d_j \in D_i$ for x_i and send a VALUE message to its neighbours and go into a waiting state. If in the next timestamp (T_2) the agent has received no further messages and its neighbours also remain in a waiting state, we will have all agents in a waiting state and hence the algorithm will terminate. Likewise, if the agent has received messages (i.e., Eq. 6 is not true), it will process those messages, reevaluate its value assignment and following a similar approach as described above will eventually go into a waiting state which contradicts our initial presumption of the algorithm not terminating.

---

[4] Note that when the g function selects between two states, it gives priority to the q function and refers to the states' utility values when there is equal desirability between the said states.

Complexity: Due to DITURIA's nature of dealing with MADPs and constraint optimisation, we face a worst-case scenario of time complexity being exponential regarding the number of variables X (on the grounds of our simplification that $m = n$). This aligns with the known NP-hard nature of constraint optimisation algorithms [29]. The worst-case space complexity that each agent faces is solely related to the size of the domain D_i for their corresponding variable x_i, since the agents are equipped with a view of the system state based on the knowledge acquired from its neighbours. This reduces a potentially polynomial worst-case space complexity to a linear $n \times |D_i|$. Further insight on the complexity of the algorithm has been demonstrated via some experimental results when testing the scalability of our implementation in Sect. 4.

4   Illustration and Evaluation

In this section, we first provide a detailed illustration of the algorithm in action. We then evaluate the scalability of the algorithm empirically by examining the impact of the following on the performance of the algorithm (with a random scenario generator): (1) domain sizes of the variables and (2) the number of agents/variables. All the experiments are executed using Python as a programming language in Google Colab, which had the following specs at the time of execution: 2.30 GHZ CPU Freq.; 2 CPU Cores and 12 GB RAM.

Illustration of the Algorithm: Consider a simple multi-agent system problem for which we generate both a manual solution and a solution using the implementation of the algorithm. There are five agents/variables which are connected as shown in Fig. 1.

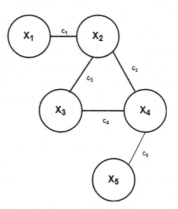

Fig. 1. Example multi-agent system

The aim of the problem is to find the optimal solution while satisfying the following constraints:

- A variable cannot be assigned its numeric value (i.e. x_1 cannot be 1).
- All neighbouring variables must have different values (i.e., $x_1 \neq x_2$ as represented by c_1).
- The preferred partial state ψ_{a_i} has the most positive literals. For our example, a variable assignment creates a partial state with positive literals if it is assigned an even number, while an odd number of assignments leads to a state with negative literals.
- The utility function of an agent depends on their numerical name. If an agent's variable is an odd named variable (e.g., x_1), the utility function prefers the larger variable assignment that gives the most preferred state. The opposite holds for even numbered variables.

Initially, all the agents have a domain $D_i = \{1, 2, 3, 4\}$ for their corresponding variables, which is later modified by their variable specific constraints, so each domain does not contain the variables number as an option (i.e., $D_1 = \{2, 3, 4\}$). When the problem was run through our DITURIA algorithm, we acquired a final solution of $v_{sol} = \{x_1 = 4, x_2 = 3, x_3 = 4, x_4 = 1, x_5 = 4\}$.

If we were to solve the same problem manually following the steps in Algorithm 1, it would take us three iterations to reach the optimal solution. In the first timestamp (T_1), a_1 would pick the value 4 for its variable since it is the largest assignment that would guarantee some positive literals in the final state even if its neighbour chooses a variable that gives negative ones. Similarly based on their numerical naming and look-ahead results, a_3 and a_5 would also choose 4 while a_2 and a_4 would pick the value 1. After the messages from their corresponding neighbours are received, in T_2 the agents reevaluate their choices and a_2 changes to 3 (thinking its neighbours might not change their value), while the other 4 agents do not change their values. In T_3, a_1 is notified about a_2's value change but does not change its value. Since no other messages are transmitted, the solution is the one remaining under each agent for their corresponding variables, which is the same as the one obtained from the algorithm.

Scalability of the DITURIA Algorithm: In this section, we run two sets of experiments to test our implementation's performance. There are two factors that we anticipate will impact the algorithm's efficiency: the domain size per variable and the number of agents in the system.

We have created a random multi-agent system generator that will take the number of agents and the domain size as input and produce similar scenarios to the one presented in Fig. 1. We start by testing the impact of the domain size by keeping a constant number of variables to 100 and increasing the domain size from 10 to 90 by 10 each time. The results are plotted in Fig. 2.

The line graph has a positive slope, indicating that the more we increase the domain size per variable, the more time it will take for the optimal solution to be calculated. With each increase, we observe a constant increase of $\approx 1.4\times$ the previous amount per change. This can be seen as a result of the adversarial maxmin reasoning that each agent utilises when deciding on the best assignment

#Variables/Agents=100 & Varying Domain Values

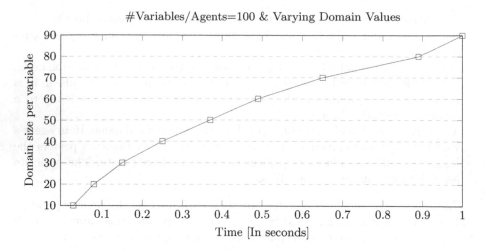

Fig. 2. Scalability: #variables/agents = 100 & varying domain sizes

Domain Value = 25 & Varying No. of Variables/Agents

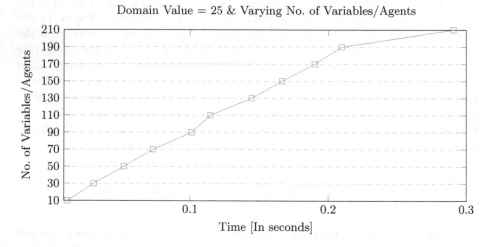

Fig. 3. Scalability: domain size = 30 & varying no. of variables/agents

for their variable. The bigger the domain size, the more possible partial states need to be computed.

The graph in Fig. 3 plots the results from the experiments where the domain size per variable is kept constant at 30, while the number of agents is increased by 20 each time, starting at 10. This line graph has an even deeper upright slope compared to the one in Fig. 2, indicating that despite the increase on the number of agents, the algorithm manages to obtain the optimal solution fairly quickly.

Based on the experimental results presented above, we establish that the domain size has a greater impact on the performance of our algorithm as opposed to the number of the decision variables/agents in the system.

5   Background and Related Work

A multi-agent system (MAS) is a system where multiple agents communicate with each other to achieve goals. The interaction among agents in a shared environment can use direct or indirect communication messages. Within a MAS, agents may cooperate to achieve a common goal or compete to achieve their own goals. MAS has a major role in distributed artificial intelligence which allows the modeling of real-world problems where information and control are decentralised and distributed among a set of agents.

A very important part in MAS is obtaining the optimal sequence of decisions that will yield the desired outcome. The emphasis is on selecting the *optimal* solution among these options, that is, the solution that best achieves a specified goal. Constraint optimisation methods employ mathematical techniques to select the best solution from among all possible solutions to a problem while taking into account all relevant constraints. Similar techniques have been used in business re-engineering to model problems and aid decision making for processes [3,26].

The issue in distributed artificial intelligence is how to model multi-agent systems where autonomous intelligent agents coordinate with each other while each having its own goals and preferences in order to achieve a mutual goal. The Recursive Modeling Method (RMM) has been proposed to model such situations where agents can make rational and coordinated decisions [9]. In the approach presented in [9] agents can explicitly reason on how collective actions can affect the utilities of individual actions. Hence, agents can maximise their individual utility by knowing the actions of other agents. In MAS, multiple agents achieve their own goals in parallel while communicating with other agents forming a single shared environment [13]. Accordingly, an outcome achieved by a single agent depends on the set of actions taken by other agents. To address such scenarios, adversarial search is often used to analyse an adversarial setting and determine what moves an agent should make to successfully reach its goal. Given a current state, the minmax values for all states are computed to determine the best next move [27]. In our approach, we also utilise a minmax application to figure out the best next state among all possible sets of worst states.

Decision model and notation (DMN) is used to model the decision logic by determining which decisions are made, what information is used to make the decisions and where the information can be found and how this is processed to generate the decision result [2,21]. The DMN is used to define different levels of The *decision requirements* and *decision logic* to model decision logic [2]. The *decision requirements* depicts how decisions are interdependent and what data is accessible for decision-making, linking these nodes together by information requirement edges. The textitdecision logic determines the output by an undirected connection.

DCOPs have been used to model autonomous behaviour. Distributed Constraint Optimisation algorithms and communication models are driven by the structure of the specific problem. Agents have to decentralise their value assignments in DCOPs in order to optimise their objective functions [6,14,19,22,31]. This method seeks the global optimum given a collective agent interaction graph.

Since its inception, this model has undergone continuous evolution to represent a wide range of agent behaviours and the environments in which they operate. Researchers proposed a variety of DCOP frameworks that differ in expressiveness and issue classes that can be addressed, enabling the DCOP model to now handle both dynamic and uncertain situations [5]. We need to assume that utilities are known and deterministic in DCOPs, which means that DCOP algorithms cannot handle the situation where we have stochastic utilities. Later work was developed by [12,30] that considered such conditions by using an extra random variable for each constraint or by relaxing certain assumptions respectively for them to handle the stochastic utilities. All current DCOP approaches differ greatly from DITURIA due to the latter's inclusion of state preferences and look-ahead search techniques such as adversarial reasoning in constraint optimisation.

Bayesian Networks (BNs) [11], Influence Diagrams (IDs) [1], and Decision Trees (DTs) [18] are other decision-making approaches that have been employed in the literature. In many ways, BNs diverge from our suggested DITURIA architecture. For instance, a conditional probability table with directed edges illustrating the cause-and-effect linkages for the variables in BNs does not make them decision variables [10] (in situations where there is far less knowledge available, our methodology can still be useful). Later, BNs were expanded into IDs, which increased the network's functionality by adding utility and decision nodes [15]. While in our approach we have a utility function which DITURIA seeks to minimise or maximise accordingly, these utility nodes are employed to assign a value to particular outcomes indicated by a node's current state. Additionally, the study of the business process' decision points have been done using the well-known DTs approach [24]. The primary idea is to turn the decision points into a classification problem [18], with the various decisions as classes. The authors in [24] have established the DT, which consists of nodes representing the decision point in the business process (like XOR) and edges representing the branches that emanate from the decision point, using historical execution data. DITURIA differs from DTs in three ways: it is not produced as a classification issue, it has a set of agents, and it takes into account a collection of all potential states.

6   Conclusions and Future Work

In this paper, we took inspiration from the complex decision processes found in medical settings, where professionals are often faced with complex combinations of decisions made by independent decision makers which must satisfy inter-decision constraints, which are often based on incomplete knowledge and where the optimality of a set of decisions can only be assessed via some modicum of look-ahead search. These decisions require minimax or maximin reasoning of the kind used in adversarial search in order to handle such gaps in their knowledge. We introduced a novel approach called the DITURIA framework that effectively uses look-ahead searches to support multi-agent decisions. We evaluate our work's correctness both theoretically and experimentally. The former demonstrates the algorithm's optimality, termination and complexity, while the latter solves a simple MAS and further showcases its performance through testing its scalability. These results yielded positive outcomes that demonstrate the worth of further evaluating such an approach. In the future, we intend to investigate whether this approach can be applied to solve more complex, real-life based medical scenarios in the Radiology environment. Future work will also address the formation of agent coalitions [25], belief merging [16,17], the mining of decision sequences [7], decision sequence merging [20] as well as risk prediction [4].

References

1. Agogino, A.M., Rege, A.: IDES: influence diagram based expert system. Math. Model. **8**, 227–233 (1987)
2. Batoulis, K., Meyer, A., Bazhenova, E., Decker, G., Weske, M.: Extracting decision logic from process models. In: Zdravkovic, J., Kirikova, M., Johannesson, P. (eds.) CAiSE 2015. LNCS, vol. 9097, pp. 349–366. Springer, Cham (2015). https://doi.org/10.1007/978-3-319-19069-3_22
3. Bel, G., Rota, K., Thierry, C.: Constraint optimization as a tool for business process re-engineering. In: Modelling Techniques for Business Process Re-engineering and Benchmarking. IAICT, pp. 164–173. Springer, Boston, MA (1997). https://doi.org/10.1007/978-0-387-35067-7_15
4. Choetkiertikul, M., Dam, H.K., Tran, T., Ghose, A.: Characterization and prediction of issue-related risks in software projects. In: 2015 IEEE/ACM 12th Working Conference on Mining Software Repositories, pp. 280–291. IEEE (2015)
5. Fioretto, F., Pontelli, E., Yeoh, W.: Distributed constraint optimization problems and applications: a survey. J. Artif. Intell. Res. **61**, 623–698 (2018)
6. Gershman, A., Meisels, A., Zivan, R.: Asynchronous forward bounding for distributed cops. J. Artif. Intell. Res. **34**, 61–88 (2009)
7. Ghose, A., Koliadis, G., Chueng, A.: Rapid business process discovery (R-BPD). In: Parent, C., Schewe, K.-D., Storey, V.C., Thalheim, B. (eds.) ER 2007. LNCS, vol. 4801, pp. 391–406. Springer, Heidelberg (2007). https://doi.org/10.1007/978-3-540-75563-0_27
8. Ginsberg, M.L., Smith, D.E.: Reasoning about action I: a possible world approach. Artif. Intell. **35**(2), 165–195 (1988). https://doi.org/10.1016/0004-3702(88)90011-2
9. Gmytrasiewicz, P.J., Durfee, E.H., Wehe, D.K.: A decision-theoretic approach to coordinating multi-agent interactions. In: IJCAI, vol. 91, pp. 63–68 (1991)
10. Heckerman, D.: A tutorial on learning with Bayesian networks. In: Holmes, D.E., Jain, L.C. (eds) Innovations in Bayesian Networks. Studies in Computational Intelligence, vol. 156, pp. 33–82. Springer, Heidelberg (2008). https://doi.org/10.1007/978-3-540-85066-3_3
11. Jensen, F.V.: Decision graphs. In: Bayesian Networks and Decision Graphs. Statistics for Engineering and Information Science, pp. 109–155, Springer, NY (2001). https://doi.org/10.1007/978-1-4757-3502-4_4
12. Le, T., Fioretto, F., Yeoh, W., Son, T.C., Pontelli, E.: ER-DCOPs: a framework for distributed constraint optimization with uncertainty in constraint utilities. In: Proceedings of the 2016 International Conference on Autonomous Agents & Multiagent Systems, pp. 606–614 (2016)

13. Lisỳ, V., Bošanskỳ, B., Vaculín, R., Pěchouček, M.: Agent subset adversarial search for complex non-cooperative domains. In: Proceedings of the 2010 IEEE Conference on Computational Intelligence and Games, pp. 211–218. IEEE (2010)
14. Mailler, R., Lesser, V.: Solving distributed constraint optimization problems using cooperative mediation. In: Proceedings of the Third International Joint Conference on Autonomous Agents and Multiagent Systems, 2004. AAMAS 2004, pp. 438–445. IEEE (2004)
15. Mead, R., Paxton, J., Sojda, R., et al.: Applications of Bayesian networks in ecological modeling. In: IASTED International Conference on Environmental Modelling and Simulation. St. Thomas, US Virgin Islands. Citeseer (2006)
16. Meyer, T., Ghose, A., Chopra, S.: Social choice, merging, and elections. In: Benferhat, S., Besnard, P. (eds.) ECSQARU 2001. LNCS (LNAI), vol. 2143, pp. 466–477. Springer, Heidelberg (2001). https://doi.org/10.1007/3-540-44652-4_41
17. Ishizuka, M., Sattar, A. (eds.): PRICAI 2002. LNCS (LNAI), vol. 2417. Springer, Heidelberg (2002). https://doi.org/10.1007/3-540-45683-X
18. Mitchell, T.M.: Does machine learning really work? AI Mag. **18**(3), 11 (1997)
19. Modi, P.J., Shen, W.M., Tambe, M., Yokoo, M.: ADOPT: asynchronous distributed constraint optimization with quality guarantees. Artif. Intell. **161**(1–2), 149–180 (2005)
20. Morrison, E.D., Menzies, A., Koliadis, G., Ghose, A.K.: Business process integration: method and analysis. In: Proceedings of the Sixth Asia-Pacific Conference on Conceptual Modelling (2009)
21. OMG: Decision model and notation (2021). https://www.omg.org/spec/DMN/
22. Petcu, A., Faltings, B.: DPOP: a scalable method for multiagent constraint optimization. In: IJCAI 2005, pp. 266–271. No. CONF in 19 (2005)
23. Pulawski, S., Ibro, H., Mahala, G., Ghose, A., Dam, H.K.: Extracting and leveraging value from a decision interdependency network (DIN) in a policing/law enforcement setting. In: International Workshop on AI-Enabled Policing and Law Enforcement. The Enterprise Computing conference, Gold Coast, Australia (2021)
24. Rozinat, A., van der Aalst, W.M.P.: Decision mining in ProM. In: Dustdar, S., Fiadeiro, J.L., Sheth, A.P. (eds.) BPM 2006. LNCS, vol. 4102, pp. 420–425. Springer, Heidelberg (2006). https://doi.org/10.1007/11841760_33
25. Sombattheera, C., Ghose, A.K., Hyland, P.: A framework to support coalition formation in supply chain collaboration. In: ICEB 2004 Proceedings (2004)
26. Tsang, E.P.: Constraint satisfaction in business process modelling. Tech. rep., Technical Report CSM-359, University of Essex, Colchester, UK (2002)
27. Wilson, B., Zuckerman, I., Parker, A., Nau, D.S.: Improving local decisions in adversarial search. In: ECAI 2012, pp. 840–845. IOS Press (2012)
28. Winslett, M.: Reasoning about action using a possible models approach. In: AAAI (1988)
29. Woeginger, G.J.: Exact algorithms for NP-hard problems: a survey. In: Jünger, M., Reinelt, G., Rinaldi, G. (eds.) Combinatorial Optimization — Eureka, You Shrink! LNCS, vol. 2570, pp. 185–207. Springer, Heidelberg (2003). https://doi.org/10.1007/3-540-36478-1_17
30. Wu, F., Jennings, N.: Regret-based multi-agent coordination with uncertain task rewards. In: Proceedings of the AAAI Conference on Artificial Intelligence, vol. 28 (2014)
31. Yeoh, W., Yokoo, M.: Distributed problem solving. AI Mag. **33**(3), 53 (2012)
32. Yokoo, M.: Distributed constraint satisfaction: foundations of cooperation in multiagent systems. Springer, Heidelberg (2012). https://doi.org/10.1007/978-3-642-59546-2

Evaluating Adaptive and Non-adaptive Strategies for Selecting and Orienting Influencer Agents for Effective Flock Control

James Hale(✉), Adam Dees, Jayson Garrison, and Sandip Sen

The University of Tulsa, Tulsa, OK 74104, USA
{jah6484,apd615,jcg5493,sandip}@utulsa.edu

Abstract. Flocks navigate for large distances, moving in a coherent path through space, under mutual influence of flock members. Such influences may include repulsion, orientation, and attraction. Certain applications give rise to the need to control the movements of flocks, e.g., circumventing critical zones. Researchers have investigated the problem of seeding flocks with a percentage of externally controlled agents to achieve effective flock control. Recent studies of flock control include orthogonal directions of (a) selecting influencing or leader agents and (b) orienting the leader agents. We build on these studies and evaluate combinations of selecting and orienting choices for fast convergence of the flock to follow desired travel directions with both adaptive and non-adaptive selection and orientation algorithms. We evaluate the effectiveness of combined flock control strategies under different physical world models. We explore the case of non-looping (non-toroidal) environments and attempt to overcome their challenges. (This is a continuation of work presented here [3]).

Keywords: Biologically-inspired approaches · Flock control · Adaptation

1 Introduction

Multiagent system researchers are interested in designing and analyzing ad hoc and emergent coordination among agents. Of particular interest to us is the topic of synthesizing coordinated behavior in groups without any explicit communication or prior agreements such as abiding by coordination protocols. Coordination in such scenarios emerges from interaction or behavioral rules followed by agents in a group. Individual agents in such groups, often referred to as flocks, swarms, or herds, use innate behaviors to respond to sensory stimuli from neighboring agents. Sensory stimuli can include positions, orientations, velocities, etc. of neighboring agents. Behavioral influences from other agents include repulsion, attraction, orientation, etc. that shape the movement of each agent in addition

© The Author(s), under exclusive license to Springer Nature Switzerland AG 2023
R. Aydoğan et al. (Eds.): PRIMA 2022, LNAI 13753, pp. 509–522, 2023.
https://doi.org/10.1007/978-3-031-21203-1_30

to any other existing environmental influences. In this paper, we use the term flocks and flocking to refer to a range of coordination scenarios and behaviors that include situations which have been traditionally referred to as flocking, swarm control, herding behaviors, etc. in the literature [19].

We, like other multiagent system researchers [4–9,11,17,18,21–24], however, are interested in studying flocks of artificial agents, either robotic or virtual. The generic task that we investigate is the control of a large group of artificial agents whose behavioral characteristics are well-documented, i.e., we know how these agents respond to sensory stimuli. The research goal is to strategically place a few carefully designed influencer or leader agents in the flock to control flock movement to follow the desired trajectory.

Most of the existing literature on flock control, with few exceptions [7], primarily focus on investigating options for only one aspect of flock control while fixing the other attributes of the agent or the domain. We investigate combinations of the most promising influence selection and orientation strategies and identify some novel approaches that perform well in various environments. We also experiment with multiple influence models, environments or physical realities governing how agents influence one another.

In particular, we are interested in studying the relative advantages of adaptive versus non-adaptive algorithms. In the current context, *non-adaptive strategy* choices by influencer agents ignore the positions and the likely decisions of other influencer agents, while *adaptive* strategy choices do take those factors into consideration. While the former can be computationally cheaper and requires less sensory and processing capabilities, the latter might be more robust and effective. Our results indicate that different influencer selection and orientation behaviors are best suited for different environments (influence models).

2   Related Work

Prior work on agent-based flock control have investigated various key aspects including the following:

Leader Selection: Various strategies have been investigated to either select leaders from the available agents [5,23] or place new leaders in locations that will maximize their ability to control the flock [4,7,10].

Leader Orientation: Various behaviors have been investigated to determine the direction and timing of orientation and velocities to be chosen by the leaders to most effectively control the flock [4,7].

Leader Roles: Some research has investigated a democratic process of electing leaders periodically and hence leadership can change over time [24] and leaders can be user-controlled mediators, who perform diverse roles in the flock [12].

Other Leader Behaviors: In certain situations, such as under sparse and distributed agent scenarios, leaders may first strategically position themselves in the group, which might include waiting in a holding pattern, before triggering their influencing orientation behaviors [4].

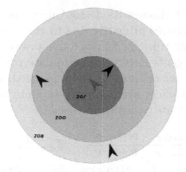

Fig. 1. The zonal influence model showing zones of repulsion (ZOR), orientation (ZOO), and attraction (ZOA). Slightly modified figure from Tiwari *et al.* [23].

Human Control: Human controllers can exert either indirect control through changing environmental features [13,25] or direct control by changing agent parameters [2,19], providing intermittent or continuous inputs [1,15].

Influence Models: An influence model determines how agents are influenced by other agents in their neighborhood. Influence models vary in terms of the effect of distance of the neighbor and a subset of attractive, repulsive and orientation effects exerted on an agent by its neighbors [12,23] (see Fig. 1). The influencer agents exert influence on others but are not influenced by others. However, follower agents cannot distinguish between influencer and other follower agents. Further, some research has been done with deep reinforcement learning in this area [16,20,26].

3 Model

A flock is composed of a set of influencer agents $\mathcal{I}$ and follower agents $\mathcal{F}$. Each agent a has a two-dimensional position vector $\mathbf{p}_a$ and a two-dimensional velocity vector $\hat{\mathbf{v}}_a$, the latter vector always has a magnitude equal to 1 to maintain constant and equal speed for all agents. Every agent has three concentric circular zones, defined in order of increasing size, one of which is a circle called the "zone of repulsion", $\mathcal{Z}_{R,a}$, and the other two are annuli with inner radii set such that they do not overlap with the zones smaller than them called the "zone of orientation", $\mathcal{Z}_{O,a}$, and the "zone of attraction", $\mathcal{Z}_{A,a}$ (see Fig. 1).

We initialize flocks by setting agent positions $\mathbf{p}$ uniformly within a circle of radius 0.2 centered around the position (0.5, 0.5). We consider two initial flocking configurations: aligned and unaligned corresponding to a coordinated or uncoordinated flock respectively. In the aligned case, all agents have the same starting direction, with a target direction 90° away. Whereas, in the unaligned case, all agents start ±90° from their target direction.

The simulation progresses in discrete time-steps which are divided into a phase of velocity update and a phase of position update. During the velocity update phase, each agent chooses its desired next orientation. All agents ultimately update their velocities primarily due to the conditions of their zones of repulsion. Velocity update rules for follower agents vary depending on the influence model. Influencer agents have velocity update rules which vary depending on the particular influencer orientation strategy used. However, only in one of the four cases of the influencer agent velocity update function (given below) is the specific orientation strategy algorithm used.

$$\hat{\mathbf{v}}_a(t + \Delta t) = \begin{cases} -\frac{\sum_{b \in \mathcal{Z}_{R,a}} \mathbf{P}(a,b) - \mathbf{P}_a}{\|\sum_{b \in \mathcal{Z}_{R,a}} \mathbf{P}(a,b) - \mathbf{P}_a\|} & \mathcal{Z}_{R,a} \neq \emptyset \\ OrientationStrategy & \mathcal{Z}_{R,a} = \emptyset \wedge \mathcal{Z}_{O,a} \neq \emptyset \\ \frac{\sum_{b \in \mathcal{Z}_{A,a}} \mathbf{P}(a,b) - \mathbf{P}_a}{\|\sum_{b \in \mathcal{Z}_{A,a}} \mathbf{P}(a,b) - \mathbf{P}_a\|} & \mathcal{Z}_{R,a} = \mathcal{Z}_{O,a} = \emptyset \wedge \mathcal{Z}_{A,a} \neq \emptyset \\ \hat{\mathbf{v}}_a(t) & Otherwise \end{cases}$$

All velocities changes are bounded by a maximum turn of ω (5° for influencers and 2° for followers) per time-step toward their desired velocity. Once velocities are processed, we update the positions of agents accordingly:

$$\mathbf{p}_a(t + \Delta t) = \mathbf{p}_a(t) + \Delta t * \hat{\mathbf{v}}_a(t + \Delta t)$$

We next test for convergence of the flock following Tiwari *et al.* [23]. If the average direction of follower agents, $\theta \in \theta_f \pm 0.1\,radians$ for three time-steps in a row, the flock has converged.

3.1   Influence Models

Distinct Zonal (3Z): Follower agents in this model are either repelling from, orienting with, or attracting to other agents. These are discrete cases where repelling has ultimate priority, then orientation, and lastly attraction. The follower velocity update function is defined as such:

$$\hat{\mathbf{v}}_a(t + \Delta t) = \begin{cases} -\frac{\sum_{b \in \mathcal{Z}_{R,a}} \mathbf{P}(a,b) - \mathbf{P}_a}{\|\sum_{b \in \mathcal{Z}_{R,a}} \mathbf{P}(a,b) - \mathbf{P}_a\|} & \mathcal{Z}_{R,a} \neq \emptyset \\ \frac{\sum_{b \in \mathcal{Z}_{O,a}} \hat{\mathbf{v}}_b}{\|\sum_{b \in \mathcal{Z}_{O,a}} \hat{\mathbf{v}}_b\|} & \mathcal{Z}_{R,a} = \emptyset \wedge \mathcal{Z}_{O,a} \neq \emptyset \\ \frac{\sum_{b \in \mathcal{Z}_{A,a}} \mathbf{P}(a,b) - \mathbf{P}_a}{\|\sum_{b \in \mathcal{Z}_{A,a}} \mathbf{P}(a,b) - \mathbf{P}_a\|} & \mathcal{Z}_{R,a} = \mathcal{Z}_{O,a} = \emptyset \wedge \mathcal{Z}_{A,a} \neq \emptyset \\ \hat{\mathbf{v}}_a(t) & Otherwise \end{cases}$$

Inverse Zonal (IZ): All zones are active but the influence of other agents is inversely proportional with distance from the agent by an inverse cubed law. This model is equivalent to Couzin *et al.* zonal with all three zone equations summed and normalized. This is a novel model.

Couzin *et al.* Zonal (PZ): The orientation and attraction zones work in tandem when the follower agent is not forced to repulse itself from other agents.

It is designed such that each agent is equally weighted, as opposed to equally weighting each zone. The follower velocity update function is defined as such:

$$
\hat{\mathbf{v}}_a(t + \Delta t) =
\begin{cases}
-\dfrac{\sum_{b \in \mathcal{Z}_{R,a}} \mathbf{p}(a,b) - \mathbf{p}_a}{\|\sum_{b \in \mathcal{Z}_{R,a}} \mathbf{p}(a,b) - \mathbf{p}_a\|} & \mathcal{Z}_{R,a} \neq \emptyset \\[3mm]
\hat{\mathbf{v}}_a(t) & \mathcal{Z}_{R,a} = \mathcal{Z}_{O,a} = \mathcal{Z}_{A,a} = \emptyset \\[3mm]
\dfrac{\sum_{b \in \mathcal{Z}_{O,a}} \hat{\mathbf{v}}_b + \sum_{b \in \mathcal{Z}_{A,a}} \frac{\mathbf{p}(a,b) - \mathbf{p}_a}{\|\mathbf{p}(a,b) - \mathbf{p}_a\|}}{\|\sum_{b \in \mathcal{Z}_{O,a}} \hat{\mathbf{v}}_b + \sum_{b \in \mathcal{Z}_{A,a}} \frac{\mathbf{p}(a,b) - \mathbf{p}_a}{\|\mathbf{p}(a,b) - \mathbf{p}_a\|}\|} & Otherwise
\end{cases}
$$

3.2 Influencer Selection Strategies

Center (C): Center placement attempts to make the most connected and central agents influencer agents by first discarding the convex hull of the agents from consideration. Afterward it selects the most central $|\mathcal{I}|$ agents according to $|\mathcal{Z}_{O,a} \cup \mathcal{Z}_{R,a}|$ to be influencer agents. This selection algorithm is considered non-adaptive as it assigns leadership to agents near the center, without considering the proximity of other leaders.

Periphery (P): The objective of this placement is to border the flock of agents with the influencer agents. The method achieves this by repeated taking the convex hull of the agent positions and setting those positions to be influencer agents so long as we still have influencer agents to place. If the convex hull size happens to be greater than the number of influencer agents still to place, we randomly select an equal number of positions from this hull to be influencer agents. This algorithm is considered non-adaptive as it randomly assigns leadership to agents on the convex-hull.

k-Means (K): The k-Means clustering algorithm [14] is used to select k leaders located near the center of different clusters of agents on the plane. This selection algorithm is adaptive as leader selections affect each other.

Attraction-Repulsion (AB): The motivation for this approach is to select leaders that are close to clusters of agents while still being somewhat evenly dispersed in the population so that almost all follower agents are being influenced. To achieve this, k target positions for influencers are identified that balance attractive forces from all follower agents, weighted by an attraction parameter, A, and repulsive forces from all other target positions, weighted by a repulsion parameter, R. Subsequently the nearest agent to each of the identified points is chosen as the influencer agents. This algorithm is adaptive as it considers the locations of other selected leaders when assigning leadership roles. The algorithm, developed for this paper, is presented in detail within Algorithm 1.

3.3 Influencer Orientation Strategies

Face Target Direction (FT): The simplest of all the orientation algorithms, with complexity O(1) is when all influencers orient towards the target direction.

```
Input   :  α ← .3: Attraction value
           β ← .7: Repulsion value
           I: Set of influencer agents (initially randomly assigned)
           F: Set of following agents
1  I' ← I
2  for c ∈ I' do
3      vectorSumInfluencers ← (0,0)
4      vectorSumFollowers ← (0,0)
5      for a ∈ F ∪ I do
6          if a ∈ F then
7              vectorSumInfluencers ← vectorSumInfluencers − pₐ + p_c
8          else
9              vectorSumFollowers ← vectorSumFollowers + pₐ − p_c
10     point ←
       p_c + (vectorSumInfluencers * β/|I|) + (vectorSumFollowers * α/|F|)
11     newLeader ← arg min_{a∈F} d(a, point)
12     I ← I − {c} ∪ {newLeader}
13     F ← F ∪ {c} − {newLeader}
```

Algorithm 1: Attraction-Repulsion influencer selection algorithm.

This is the only non-adaptive orientation algorithm we use. The agent's actions are not influenced by other members of the flock.

One-Step Lookahead (OSL, 1): From Genter *et al.* [5], each influencer agent performs a one-step lookahead to check, for each of its possible orientations, the resultant orientation of its followers after one step. The influencer then chooses the orientation that results in the closest alignment of the followers one step into the future. This algorithm is adaptive as an agent's decisions are determined by the movements of surrounding agents. It has a complexity of $O(nZ^2)$, where Z is the total number of agents and n is the number of directions the agent considers.

Augmented OSL (AOSL, R1): A novel variation of OSL which will not consider influencer agents in its own orientation zone. AOSl considers agents $b \in \mathcal{Z}_{O,a} \cap \mathcal{F}$ instead. This is because OSL calculates the orientations of those in the $\mathcal{Z}_{O,b}$ as if $\hat{\mathbf{v}}_b$ will tend toward *choice* should a adopt it, which does not necessarily follow for another influencer agent b. This algorithm is adaptive, for similar reasons to OSL. the same reasoning as OSL and has the same complexity.

Minimizing Lost Influencers: An influencer that focuses only on orientation may get detached from the flock. To mitigate this, we use an augmentation: at the start of simulation, each influencer counts the number of agents in its ZOO. If an influencer loses all follower agents from its ZOO, it tries to move back towards its ZOA (if its ZOA lacks follower agents, it keeps its current velocity) until it regains a fraction (half in our experiments) of its initial ZOO size.

Table 1. Symbols and corresponding parameters

Symbol	Parameter	Default value
$\mathcal{F}$	Follower agents	$|\mathcal{F}| = 180$
$\mathcal{I}$	Influencer agents	$|\mathcal{I}| = 20$
$\mathcal{A}$	Agents (the flock)	$\mathcal{F} \cup \mathcal{I}$
a	Agent a	
$\mathbf{p}_a$	a's position vector	$\forall i, \mathbf{p}_{a,i} \in [0,1]$
$\hat{\mathbf{v}}_a$	a's velocity vector	$||\hat{\mathbf{v}}_a|| = 1$
$d(a,b)$	Distance between a and b	
$\mathcal{Z}_{R,a}$	a's Zone of repulsion	$\{b \in \mathcal{A}|d(a,b) \in [0,0.01]\} - \{a\}$
$\mathcal{Z}_{O,a}$	a's Zone of orientation	$\{b \in \mathcal{A}|d(a,b) \in (0.01,0.1]\}$
$\mathcal{Z}_{A,a}$	a's Zone of attraction	$\{b \in \mathcal{A}|d(a,b) \in (0.1,0.13]\}$
θ_f	Target angle	$\theta_f \sim \mathcal{U}(0,2\pi)$
Δt	Time-step	.001
ω_f	Follower max turn per time-step	$2°$
ω_i	Influencer max turn per time-step	$5°$
n	Influencer angle options	16

3.4 Adaptive vs. Non-adaptive Approaches

We were interested in the effectiveness of adaptive selection and orientation algorithms when compared to non-adaptive models for flock control. In our experiments, an adaptive behavior is one which alters its behavior based on the state of other agents. A non-adaptive behavioral model dictates an agent ignore the actions of other agents in its vicinity. The OSL and AOSL orientation algorithms are adaptive while the FT algorithm is non-adaptive. For the influencer selection strategies, the k-Means and the Attraction-Repulsion algorithms are adaptive, while the Center and Periphery algorithms are non-adaptive.

4 Experiments

All experiments used parameters as listed in Table 1; like Genter & Stone [5], we use 200 agents, with 10% leaders. Further, we use widths for $\mathcal{Z}_{R,a}$, $\mathcal{Z}_{O,a}$ and $\mathcal{Z}_{A,a}$ proportional to those from Tiwari *et al.* [23]. Every combination of influence model, influencer selection, and influencer orientation strategy was tested for both initially aligned and unaligned conditions. Data presented in Tables 2, 3, and 4 present flock convergence time means and standard deviations averaged over 200 simulations for each of these cases, along with the average performance of particular strategies across combinations. A graphical representation of mean convergence times for the aligned and unaligned cases are shown in Figs. 3 and 4 respectively. We run each simulation for a maximum of $\lfloor (.5 - .2)/\Delta t \rfloor = 300$

Lost agents

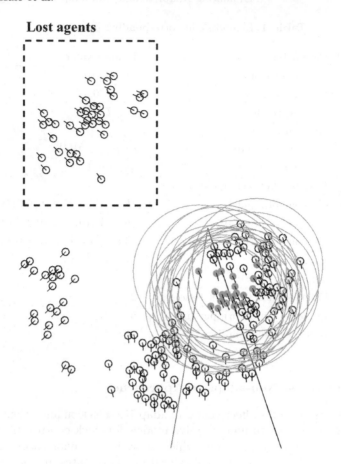

Fig. 2. A fragmented flock in the Inverse Zonal world where follower agents are black, influencer agents are green (surrounded by their ZOA, also in green), the target angle is black, and the current mean heading is red. (Color figure online)

time-steps; i.e. we ran for just enough time-steps such that an agent placed on the periphery of the placement radius could not escape the boundary.

We also measure the number of lost agents in each simulation, and the number of simulations for a configuration in which at least one agent becomes lost. We define a lost agent as an agent that cannot be reached by starting at an influencer agent and traversing ZOOs. Let $G = (V, E)$ be a graph in which $V = \mathcal{I} \cup \mathcal{F}$, and $v_i \in ZOO(v_j) \wedge v_j \in ZOO(v_i) \Rightarrow (v_i, v_j) \in E$. Now, let G_a be a connected sub-graph such that agent a is a vertex in G_a. If a is a follower agent and G_a has no vertexes in $\mathcal{I}$, then a is lost. Figure 2 shows an example of a flock fragmenting, which causes lost follower agents.

Table 2. Distinct zonal influence model convergence times

	Selection Orientation	Mean/Standard deviation	
		Aligned	Unaligned
Selection-Orientation Combinations	A-AOSL	138.6/37.3	65.6/11.7
	A-FT	181.9/42.3	94.3/27.6
	A-OSL	138.6/37.4	65.7/11.7
	Center-AOSL	170.3/47.1	83.7/22.6
	Center-FT	179.2/43.7	97.6/26.3
	Center-OSL	171.9/47.9	85.2/23.3
	K-Means-AOSL	**132.9/35.1**	**65.1/10.5**
	K-Means-FT	176.0/42.9	94.4/25.0
	K-Means-OSL	133.2/36.2	65.3/11.0
	Periphery-AOSL	147.7/40.8	68.0/12.8
	Periphery-FT	199.4/48.2	102.7/29.7
	Periphery-OSL	147.2/40.2	68.3/13.1
Average Selection	A	152.8/44.0	75.2/23.0
	Center	173.9/46.4	88.8/24.9
	K-Means	**147.3/43.1**	**75.0/21.8**
	Periphery	164.3/49.5	79.7/25.9
Average Orientation	AOSL	**147.0/42.6**	**70.6/17.0**
	FT	184.0/45.1	97.2/27.4
	OSL	147.3/43.0	71.1/17.6

Table 3. Inverse zonal influence model convergence times

	Selection-Orientation	Mean/Standard deviation	
		Aligned	Unaligned
Selection-Orientation Combinations	A-AOSL	148.9/49.8	104.1/24.8
	A-FT	162.8/50.3	117.8/31.7
	A-OSL	149.7/51.4	104.5/25.0
	Center-AOSL	198.2/50.8	136.2/46.1
	Center-FT	194.3/47.8	185.2/70.1
	Center-OSL	201.6/50.5	138.1/47.3
	K-Means-AOSL	146.0/50.3	**95.5/21.3**
	K-Means-FT	150.1/53.1	105.8/26.9
	K-Means-OSL	**145.7 50.1**	96.7/23.0
	Periphery-AOSL	185.1/39.5	113.2/32.2
	Periphery-FT	247.9/27.8	128.0/39.0
	Periphery-OSL	187.0/39.1	111.9/32.0
Average Selection	A	153.8/50.8	108.8/28.1
	Center	198.1/49.8	150.6/58.3
	K-Means	**147.3/51.1**	**99.3/24.3**
	Periphery	202.9/45.8	117.5/35.2
Average Orientation	AOSL	**168.0/52.5**	**112.1/35.8**
	FT	184.3/59.4	130.9/51.7
	OSL	169.4/53.2	112.5/36.5

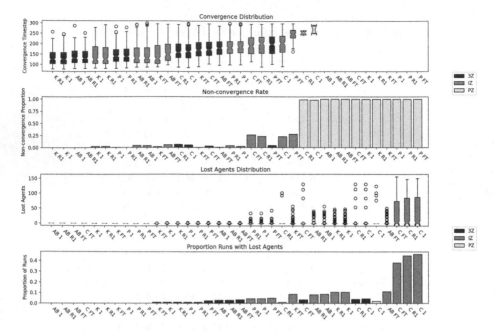

Fig. 3. Aligned case

5   Discussion

Influence Model Hierarchy: Likely the most obvious trend in the results is the overwhelming determinant of performance that is the influence model. Essentially, productive alignment work is only done by the effects of orientation; attraction and repulsion generally disorient a flock member. Thus models are essentially easier whenever the effects of attraction and repulsion are minimized. This is mostly the case in the distinct zonal model, where agents will always try to enter the orientation zone of another agent if they are not already in one, and when they are able to orient, they exclusively devote themselves to this task. In the case of inverse zonal, repulsion and attraction are always present on some level, making it more difficult to form cohesive flocks. Lastly, the Couzin *et al.* model always forces an agent to devote itself largely to attraction or repulsion, and orientation is rarely given full control. The flock tends to collapse upon itself in this model and is very difficult to steer. Although these effects largely negate the occurrences of isolation, it makes a turn very difficult to accomplish.

Adaptive Orientation Algorithms Suffer with Center Selection: Adaptive orientation algorithms AOSL and OSL use predictive models to guide their choices. These predictive models rely on assumptions which are not necessarily correct, and which have a greater magnitude of error especially when center selection is used. Pertinent assumption 1 is shared by both algorithms: other

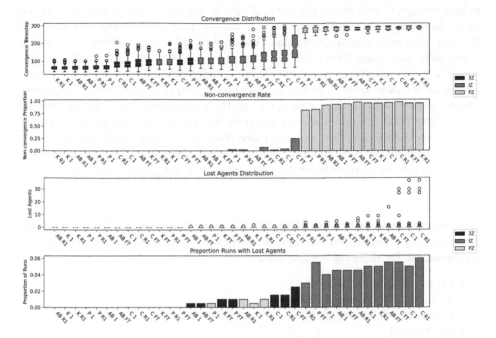

Fig. 4. Unligned case

Table 4. Couzin *et al.* influence model convergence times.

	Selection-Orientation	Mean/Standard Deviation	
		Aligned	Unaligned
Selection-Orientation Combinations	A-AOSL	N/A/N/A	278.4/14.5
	A-FT	N/A/N/A	282.8/7.1
	A-OSL	N/A/N/A	279.2/14.2
	Center-AOSL	**256.0/15.6**	286.7/7.5
	Center-FT	N/A/N/A	284.1/12.3
	Center-OSL	271.3/21.2	285.6/10.1
	K-Means-AOSL	N/A/N/A	289.2/7.2
	K-Means-FT	N/A/N/A	288.1/9.5
	K-Means-OSL	N/A/N/A	284.6/11.0
	Periphery-AOSL	N/A/N/A	275.4/16.9
	Periphery-FT	N/A/N/A	281.5/13.7
	Periphery-OSL	N/A/N/A	**273.8/16.4**
Average Selection	A	N/A/N/A	279.4/13.3
	Center	**266.2/19.5**	285.2/10.2
	K-Means	N/A/N/A	287.3/9.2
	Periphery	N/A/N/A	**275.5/16.3**
Average Orientation	AOSL	**256.0/15.6**	278.9/15.4
	FT	N/A/N/A	284.1/11.3
	OSL	271.3/21.2	**277.7/15.3**

influencer agents will adopt the same choice as the one being considered in the algorithm. There is a reason to believe this so long as the neighborhoods of the two influencer agents are similar. Assumption 2 belongs to OSL only, which is precisely the assumption eliminated by AOSL: influencer agents will be influenced in a similar manner as follower agents, and it is equally useful to influencer agents as follower agents. AOSL solves this by skipping over other influencer agents when trying to minimize error, as their alignment does not determine convergence, and they do not obey the influence model like the follower agents. Both these assumptions are violated more often when there is a high amount of influencer agents in an influencer agent's zone of orientation. This is, of course, the case in the center placement strategy, which initially places leaders in a dense circle.

Orientation and Selection Best Performers Vary by Influence Model: The following summarizes the best performing (lowest mean convergence time) combinations for different environments:

- Distinct zonal
  - Aligned: K-Means-AOSL
  - Unaligned: K-Means-AOSL
- Inverse zonal
  - Aligned: K-Means-OSL
  - Unaligned: K-Means-AOSL
- Couzin *et al.* zonal
  - Aligned: Center-AOSL
  - Unaligned: Periphery-OSL

Notably, no one combination of methods works best in each setting. The adaptive orientation update rules (AOSL in all but two cases), perform best in each influence model. Additionally, Distinct Zonal and Inverse zonal favor a more spread-out initial influencer placement, while Couzin *et al.* prefers center or peripheral placement. This may be explained by an influencer's propensity, in 3Z, to become detached from the flock as it initially settles, as in center placement the influencers more so struggle to make their way to the periphery of the flock.

6 Conclusions and Future Work

We experimented with different approaches for effective flock control. We tried all possible combinations of two previously used and one novel influencer selection schemes and two existing and two novel orientation schemes in two existing and one new world (influence models) for both initially aligned and unaligned flocks. Performance is measured in terms of the time steps taken for the flock to converge to the desired orientation.

Many interesting and subtle takeaways resulted from the complexity of the interactions between these three aspects, alongside other generalizations that can be made across individual combinations. These are important and complex implications for the efficacy of flock control that we have not seen investigated within the existing literature, which often assume a single and simple physical world, and only a single orientation or placement strategy. Physical worlds played a dominant role in determining the effectiveness of approaches, leading us to the conclusion that the study of flock control relies on the accuracy of the physical model which simulates the flock. It is therefore more urgent that more study is put forth into the physical models often used in flock control, as its inaccuracy risks the efficacy of the field of study. In harmony with this conclusion, it was observed that adaptive orientation algorithms thrived to the degree that their predictive models reflected the reality of the model.

The next step of this research would be to characterize abstract features that would be predictive of successful leader placement and orientation strategies. We also plan to more thoroughly analyze the reasons why the Couzin *et al.* is particularly challenging for all approaches tested and even more so for the aligned case. Other characterizations of convergence, starting configurations, maneuvers, etc. can also be investigated. In particular, it would be particularly useful to identify flock control mechanisms that are more robust to different initial flock orientations and target maneuvers.

References

1. Alboul, L., Saez-Pons, J., Penders, J.: Mixed human-robot team navigation in the guardians project. In: IEEE International Workshop on. Safety, Security and Rescue Robotics, SSRR 2008, pp. 95–101. IEEE (2008)
2. Couzin, I.D., Krause, J., James, R., Ruxton, G.D., Franks, N.R.: Collective memory and spatial sorting in animal groups. J. Theor. Biol. **218**(1), 1–11 (2002)
3. Dees, A., Hale, J., Sen, S.: Evaluating adaptive and non-adaptive strategies for selecting and orienting influencer agents for effective flock control
4. Fu, D.Y., Wang, E.S., Kraft, P.M., Grosz, B.J.: Influencing flock formation in low-density settings. In: Proceedings of the 17th International Conference on Autonomous Agents and Multiagent Systems (AAMAS-1), pp. 1604–1612 (2018)
5. Genter, K., Stone, P.: Ad hoc teamwork behaviors for influencing a flock. Acta Polytech. J. **56**(1) (2016)
6. Genter, K., Stone, P.: Adding influencing agents to a flock. In: Proceedings of the 15th International Conference on Autonomous Agents and Multiagent Systems (AAMAS-16), pp. 615–623 (2016)
7. Genter, K., Zhang, S., Stone, P.: Determining placements of influencing agents in a flock. In: Proceedings of the 2015 International Conference on Autonomous Agents and Multiagent Systems (AAMAS-15), pp. 247–255 (2015)
8. Han, J., Li, M., Guo, L.: Soft control on collective behavior of a group of autonomous agents by a shill agent. J. Syst. Sci. Complex. **19**(1), 54–62 (2006)
9. Han, X., Rossi, L.F., Shen, C.C.: Autonomous navigation of wireless robot swarms with covert leaders. In: Proceedings of the 1st international Conference on Robot Communication and Coordination, p. 27. IEEE Press (2007)
10. Hussein, A., Petraki, E., Elsawah, S., Abbass, H.A.: Autonomous swarm shepherding using curriculum-based reinforcement learning. In: AAMAS, pp. 633–641 (2022)

11. Jadbabaie, A., Lin, J., Morse, A.S.: Coordination of groups of mobile autonomous agents using nearest neighbor rules. IEEE Trans. Autom. Control **48**(6), 988–1001 (2003)
12. Jung, S.Y., Brown, D.S., Goodrich, M.A.: Shaping couzin-like torus swarms through coordinated mediation. In: IEEE International Conference on Systems, Man, and Cybernetics (SMC), 2013, pp. 1834–1839. IEEE (2013)
13. Kolling, A., Nunnally, S., Lewis, M.: Towards human control of robot swarms. In: Proceedings of the Seventh Annual ACM/IEEE International Conference on Human-robot Interaction, pp. 89–96. ACM (2012)
14. MacKay, D.: An example inference task: clustering. In: Information Theory, Inference and Learning Algorithms, pp. 284–292. Cambridge University Press (2003)
15. Olfati-Saber, R.: Flocking for multi-agent dynamic systems: algorithms and theory. IEEE Trans. Autom. Control **51**(3), 401–420 (2006)
16. Qiu, Y., Zhan, Y., Jin, Y., Wang, J., Zhang, X.: Sample-efficient multi-agent reinforcement learning with demonstrations for flocking control. arXiv preprint arXiv:2209.08351 (2022)
17. Qu, S., Abouheaf, M., Gueaieb, W., Spinello, D.: A policy iteration approach for flock motion control. In: 2021 IEEE International Symposium on Robotic and Sensors Environments (ROSE), pp. 1–7. IEEE (2021)
18. Raj, J., Raghuwaiya, K., Sharma, B., Vanualailai, J.: Motion control of a flock of 1-trailer robots with swarm avoidance. Robotica **39**(11), 1926–1951 (2021)
19. Reynolds, C.W.: Flocks, herds and schools: a distributed behavioral model. In: ACM SIGGRAPH Computer Graphics, vol. 21, pp. 25–34. ACM (1987)
20. Salimi, M., Pasquier, P.: Deep reinforcement learning for flocking control of UAVs in complex environments. In: 2021 6th International Conference on Robotics and Automation Engineering (ICRAE), pp. 344–352. IEEE (2021)
21. Shrit, O., Filliat, D., Sebag, M.: Iterative learning for model reactive control: Application to autonomous multi-agent control. In: 2021 7th International Conference on Automation, Robotics and Applications (ICARA), pp. 140–146. IEEE (2021)
22. Su, H., Wang, X., Lin, Z.: Flocking of multi-agents with a virtual leader. IEEE Trans. Autom. Control **54**(2), 293–307 (2009)
23. Tiwari, R., Jain, P., Butail, S., Baliyarasimhuni, S.P., Goodrich, M.A.: Effect of leader placement on robotic swarm control. In: Proceedings of the 16th Conference on Autonomous Agents and MultiAgent Systems, pp. 1387–1394. AAMAS 2017 (2017)
24. Walker, P., Amraii, S.A., Lewis, M., Chakraborty, N., Sycara, K.: Control of swarms with multiple leader agents. In: IEEE International Conference on Systems, Man and Cybernetics (SMC), 2014, pp. 3567–3572. IEEE (2014)
25. Werfel, J., Nagpal, R.: Extended stigmergy in collective construction. IEEE Intell. Syst. **21**(2), 20–28 (2006)
26. Zhang, H., Cheng, J.: Deep reinforcement learning approach for flocking control of multi-agents. In: 2021 40th Chinese Control Conference (CCC), pp. 5002–5007. IEEE (2021)

A Proportional Pricing Mechanism
for Ridesharing Services with Meeting Points

Lucia Cipolina-Kun[1]([⊠]) [iD], Vahid Yazdanpanah[2] [iD], Sebastian Stein[2] [iD],
and Enrico H. Gerding[2] [iD]

[1] Electrical and Electronic Engineering, University of Bristol, Bristol, UK
lucia.kun@bristol.ac.uk
[2] Electronics and Computer Science, University of Southampton, Southampton, UK
v.yazdanpanah@soton.ac.uk, {ss2,eg}@ecs.soton.ac.uk

Abstract. Ridesharing is a promising approach for reducing congestion and pollution, and many variants have been studied in the literature over the past decades. In this paper, we consider a novel setting where individuals walk to a common pick-up point and ride together to a single drop-off point from where they walk to their final destination. This setting requires finding the optimal composition of riders and pick-up and drop-off meeting points, as well as an equitable distribution of the costs whereby riders are incentivised to participate. Based on game-theoretic principles, we propose a methodology to determine the optimal pick-up and drop-off points, together with a cost allocation method that is equitable in the sense that it ensures proportionality for sharing the costs, i.e., those who walk more should pay less. We present a formal evaluation of our cost allocation method and empirical evaluation against the Shapley value using real-world and simulated data. Our results show that our approach is computationally more tractable than the Shapley value, as it is linear in time while guaranteeing individual rationality under certain conditions.

Keywords: Ridesharing · Cost sharing · Smart mobility · Multi-agent systems for transportation

1 Introduction

Ridesharing services allow individuals with similar itineraries to share a car and split the cost of the trip. As a mobility option, ridesharing presents advantages on several fronts. From a social point of view, it contributes to lower congestion, bringing a positive externality to traffic [21,25]. From the user's standpoint, ridesharing is usually more affordable than travelling alone [14]. For these reasons, ridesharing services have become a popular mobility option across big cities. In recent years, several commercial platforms have started to offer ridesharing services, such as Uber[1], Lyft[2] and DiDi[3], as a sign of the changing landscape in mobility patterns. According to the *US Census*

---

[1] https://www.uber.com.
[2] https://www.lyft.com.
[3] http://www.didiglobal.com.

© The Author(s), under exclusive license to Springer Nature Switzerland AG 2023
R. Aydoğan et al. (Eds.): PRIMA 2022, LNAI 13753, pp. 523–539, 2023.
https://doi.org/10.1007/978-3-031-21203-1_31

Bureau [27], by 2019, ridesharing represented approximately 8–11% of the transportation modality in Canada and the USA.

Our approach considers a ridesharing setting where users walk to a common pick-up point and take a car to a single drop-off point, from where they walk to their own destinations. The walking requirement is a common practice in ridesharing services, as it provides efficiency to the system by optimizing the car route and avoiding detours [25]. Example scenarios include the case of friends arranging a private trip and meeting at the car rental place; commuters using private cars (a similar case is considered in [30]); or companies providing ridesharing services to their facilities (as considered by [12]). In all these cases, there are pre-specified pick-up and drop-off points for the car and a walking effort required from passengers to walk to/from those points. Our proposed methodology starts by determining these pick-up and drop off points in a way such that the total walking time of individuals is minimized. Additionally, we consider the walking time as a non-transferable cost for individuals. As such, we propose a method where we factor the walking time into the total trip cost using the concept of value-of-time [22] to account for the monetary value of walking. In this way, the total cost of a trip is composed of the car cost and the walking-time cost. With the travel cost defined in this manner, we find the socially optimal car allocation of passengers such that the travel cost is minimized. A central aspect we consider is the distribution of the trip cost among ridesharing passengers. For this, we propose an *equitable* cost allocation method that explicitly recognizes the walking time as a cost and we propose a cost allocation method that compensates users for their walking time when splitting the car cost.

Our research problem is two-fold: given the origin and destination coordinates for each rider (from the set of riders), we first determine the pick up and drop-off points such that the walking time is minimized and we obtain the socially optimal way to allocate riders to different cars such that the total travel cost is minimized (including the walking and car cost).[4]. Secondly, we focus on the final cost-allocation method for the trip cost. In this part, the goal is to provide an equitable cost allocation mechanism for the socially optimal coalition structure while being computationally tractable.

1.1   Introductory Example

Consider a group of friends who want to share a ride after a night out, or colleagues who live close-by and want to share a ride. In both cases, riders meet at a pick-up point and ride together to a drop-off point. Given a set of riders, and assuming an infinite number of cars, there are many possible ways to allocate riders into cars. Our premise is that individuals choose with whom to share a ride based on the cost of the trip, including riding and walking costs. We illustrate the interplay between walking and riding costs below.

As an example, consider Fig. 1 below. There are 3 individuals $\{A, B, C\}$ who choose to share a car. In the left panel, each individual walks from their individual origins to a common departure point **O** and then drive to a single drop-off point **D**, from where they walk to their individual destinations. This is just one example of a possible arrangement of riders, but there can be many others. For example, on the right

---

[4] This problem will be formally presented in Sect. 3, Definition 5.

panel $\{A, B\}$ ride-share together while $\{C\}$ travels alone (and therefore has no need for walking). Indeed, there are five possible combinations in which three individuals can be arranged. The formation of these possible travel arrangements, their cost optimality, and the fair cost distribution is the subject of this paper.

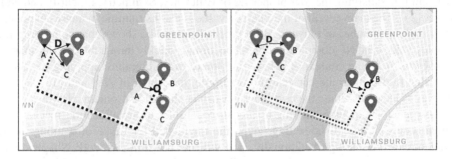

Fig. 1. Example of a ridesharing formation for three individuals. The arrows show their walking distance to the common O-D points and the dotted line the distance travelled by the car. On the left panel, the three riders share a car, while on the right panel A,B share a car.

1.2 Related Literature

Ridesharing has motivated the production of academic studies on its different aspects. Several authors have approached the rider-matching problem using game-theoretic solutions by modelling ridesharing as a cooperative game. Under this framework, a set of trip requests is partitioned as a coalition structure, where each subset is a coalition whose members will share a car based on some cost-optimization rule [10, 11, 15]. Another traditional area of study has been the matching problem between trip requests and available cars. For example, the work by [2] uses cooperative game theory to find the optimal combination of riders that minimises the system-wide travel cost. These approaches, like many others, assume that cars make multiple stops and riders are not required to walk, which is unrealistic in a ridesharing setting. Recently, there has been an increasing body of literature recognizing the importance of the walking requirement for the efficiency of the ridesharing system. For example, authors like [25] highlight the benefits of introducing meeting points in a ridesharing system. They show that allowing for meeting and drop-off points introduces flexibility in the system and increases the feasible matches between riders and drivers (i.e., demand and supply). More recently, the work of [9] shows that the introduction of a small walking requirement of about one minute increases the system's efficiency (as considered by the matches of trip demand and supply) by 80%. While these works highlight the importance of walking options in the efficiency of ridesharing, they focus on the matching problem between riders and drivers. Our approach deviates from these approaches, which are rooted in matching theory, and is the first one to capture walking in a game-theoretical model for ridesharing by integrating walking time as a non-transferable cost in the so-called *ridesharing games*.

Another related question is how to distribute the trip cost among riders sharing a car. It is a common approach to use game-theoretic solutions to guarantee desirable theoretical properties of the proposed cost allocation method. A traditional method is the Shapley value [18], which compensates each player by the weighted average of his/her marginal contributions. It is a widely accepted solution concept, as it is the only payment rule satisfying the four properties of Efficiency, Symmetry, Linearity and Null player [24]. The main caveat of the Shapley value is that its runtime increases exponentially with the number of players. More precisely, it can be shown that computing the Shapley value is an NP-complete problem, becoming quickly intractable for ridesharing settings [6,8]. In the context of ridesharing, there exists literature applying the Shapley value to distribute the car cost. For example, the works of [29] and [13] use the Shapley value to distribute the cost in a rider-driver allocation problem. However, none of these methods include walking as a cost to consider in the allocation mechanism, which seems an unrealistic setting, given the mentioned relevance of walking in the efficiency of ridesharing. Additionally, as it will be shown in this work, Shapley does not guarantee proportionality of the cost allocation with respect to the walking effort.

1.3 Contributions

Our contributions are as follows:

1. Existing work on ride sharing assume the meeting points for pick-up and drop-off are fixed. To address this, we are the first to propose a method to determine the pick-up and drop-off points based on the geometric median of coordinates, which minimizes the walking distance of riders[5].
2. For the first time in the ridesharing literature, our methodology models the walking cost as a non-transferable cost to determine the optimal allocation of riders.
3. We are the first to propose a cost allocation methodology that is equitable in the sense that it compensates riders for the walking effort to join the coalition.
4. The proposed cost allocation method is individually rational (under certain conditions) and has linear time complexity.

The next sections describe our proposed methodology for walking cost and the payment vector. Lastly, we evaluate the payment-allocation method theoretically and empirically and compare it with a Shapley-based cost allocation method.

2 Formal Preliminaries

This section introduces the notation for cooperative games and successive sections expand on the definitions used within the context of ridesharing. Following [19] and [16], in cooperative games, a set of agents $A = \{a_1, ..., a_n\}$ work together by forming coalitions and taking joint actions to maximize their utility. The goal is to find what is the best coalition structure to form. A coalitional cost game can be described in terms of its *characteristic function*, which expresses the cost of each coalition. Intuitively, this is the cost that a subset of agents face and need to pay collectively.

---

[5] The idea behind this approach was presented in an early pre-print [3].

Definition 1. *A coalitional cost game with transferable utilities (TU) is the tuple* (A, C) *where* A *is the set of agents and* C *is a characteristic function* $C : 2^A \to \mathbb{R}$ *that returns the cost that a subset* $S \subseteq A$ *of agents face on their own regardless of what the remaining agents do (i.e., without any externality present).*

Given a coalitional cost game (A, C), the Coalition Structure Generation (CSG) problem focuses on generating a coalition structure (as a partition of the set of agents A) with desirable properties, e.g., those that yield a minimum cost.

Definition 2. *Given a coalitional cost game* (A, C), *a coalition structure* $\mathbb{C} = \{S_1, \ldots, S_m\}$, *is a partition of* A, *with* $m \leq n$. *That is, for arbitrary distinct* $1 \leq k, l \leq m$ *with* $k \neq l$, *we have that* $S_k \subseteq A$, $S_l \subseteq A$, $S_k \cap S_l = \varnothing$, *and* $\bigcup_{k=1}^{m} S_k = A$. *The set of all possible coalition structures is denoted by* $\mathscr{C}$.

2.1 Ridesharing as a Coalitional Cost Game

A ridesharing game is a tuple (A, C, M), where $A = \{a_1, .., a_n\}$ is the set of riders, $C : 2^A \to \mathbb{R}$ is the characteristic function, and $M : A \to \mathbb{R}^2 \times \mathbb{R}^2$ is the coordinate function that yields the origin and destination coordinates for each rider, i.e., $M(a_i) = (o_i, d_i)$, where $o_i \in \mathbb{R}^2$ and $d_i \in \mathbb{R}^2$ are the origin and destination coordinates of a rider, respectively. The objective in a ridesharing game is to find the socially-optimal coalition structure with the minimum travel cost. For simplicity, we consider an unbounded supply of cars with up to four seats each. The following sections cover how to calculate the coalition cost and how the optimal coalition structure is obtained.

2.2 Cost Calculation

In contrast to the most common coalition structure generation literature, where a cost table is given, our model provides a contextual function to calculate ridesharing costs. In particular, the main contribution of our cost calculation methodology is the explicit modelling of walking costs on top of the car cost. In a sense, the walking cost can be viewed as the *cost of entry* into a coalition, as it represents the time investment required to join a ridesharing car. The walking *distance* of each individual depends on the central origin and destination points, while the walking *cost* depends on the monetary value of time, as explained below.

Determination of the Central O-D Points. The first step is to calculate the pick-up and drop-off points for all riders sharing a car. Our approach determines these points using the geometric median of the individuals' coordinates (as given by the function M).[6] We choose this approach since it minimizes the distance walked by all individuals, while being computationally tractable.[7] Once the walking points are set, the next step is to assign a (monetary) cost to the walking time.

---

[6] The geometric median of a set of points is defined as the point minimizing the sum of Euclidean distances to all points [5]. For its implementation we used the Weiszfeld algorithm [28].

[7] Note that for simplicity, we assume that the O-D points can lie anywhere on the Cartesian plane. In a real system, one could use the nearest feasible points on the actual road network.

Cost of Walking. In order to assign a monetary value to the walking effort, we use the concept of value of time (VoT), which accounts for the opportunity cost of the walking time. Following [9], we assume that there is a walking threshold for reasonable walking distance, beyond which individuals prefer to take a car (typically, 800 m is accepted as the walking threshold [23]). We model this trade off between walking and riding using a function similar to a Cobb-Douglas utility function [4] as in Eq. 1 to express the fact that the cost of walking increases more than proportional to the distance walked. Lastly, the VoT is re-scaled by a constant representing the taxi cost per distance, to account for the fact that after a certain tolerance threshold, walking is more expensive (in terms of VoT) than taking a car. The VoT of walking from point o to d is modeled as:

$$VoT(o, d) = dist(o, d)^{\alpha}.K \tag{1}$$

where K is a constant representing the taxi fare, $dist(\cdot)$ is a distance function in the Cartesian plane, and $\alpha > 1$ is an arbitrary parameter related to the function's convexity and the walking threshold. The higher the α value, the higher the opportunity cost of walking compared to taking a car.

Cost of Riding. The cost of riding a car from coordinates o to d is simply the distance travelled times a constant K accounting for the taxi fare, i.e.:

$$P_{car}(o, d) = dist(o, d).K \tag{2}$$

Coalition Cost. The first step to obtain the travel cost for a set of riders (i.e., a coalition) $S \subseteq A$ is to calculate the central pick-up and drop-off coordinates as explained in Sect. 2.2. From there, one can obtain the walking and car costs using Eqs. 1 and 2 above. The total cost of the trip for this coalition (i.e., the characteristic function of the ridesharing game) is defined as the sum of walking and riding costs, as expressed in Eq. 3. For individuals traveling alone, the cost of travel is the minimum between the taxi and walking, while for riders in a coalition, we assume that they choose to share a car instead of walking to their destination.

$$C(S) = \begin{cases} min\{VoT(o_i, d_i), P_{car}(o_i, d_i)\}, & \text{if } |S| = 1 \\ P_{car}(\bar{o}, \bar{d}) + \Sigma_{i \in S}[VoT(o_i, \bar{o}) + VoT(d_i, \bar{d})], & \text{otherwise} \end{cases} \tag{3}$$

where $(\bar{o}, \bar{d})$ are the pick-up and drop-off coordinates of the shared car, calculated as the geometric median of the riders' origin and destination coordinates respectively and (o_i, d_i) are the origin and destination coordinates of individual i. Lastly, from Definition 2, the total cost of a coalition structure $\mathbb{C}$ is simply the sum of the costs of its component coalitions:

$$\mathbb{C}_{cost}(\mathbb{C}) = \Sigma_{S \in \mathbb{C}} C(S) \tag{4}$$

3   Optimal Coalition Structure

Next, we explain how to find the optimal coalition structure that minimises the total travel cost given by Eq. 4.

3.1 Dimensionality Reduction

The problem of searching for optimal structures is generally computationally intractable because the number of different possible coalitions is exponential in the number of coalition members (since there are 2^n possible coalitions for a set of n riders)[8]. Additionally, ridesharing presents the complexity of a high volume of trip requests in a short period of time, especially when considering the trips demand in densely populated areas. To reduce the dimensionality of the problem, it is common within the ridesharing literature to introduce a series of constraints and heuristics, composed of certain spatio-temporal rules that make the coalition generation problem tractable [15]. Following those approaches, we define a number of constraints that help reduce the search space. The first constraint is a spatial constraint guaranteeing that only riders within a certain radius are considered for riding together (i.e., for forming a coalition), which leads to the spatial clustering of trips.

Definition 3 (ϵ-**Feasible Coalition**). *In a ridesharing game* (A, C, M), *we say a coalition* $S \subseteq A$ *is ϵ-feasible if all of its members are interior points of a closed ball* $N_\epsilon(p) = \{q \in \mathbb{R}^4 \mid dist(p, q) \leq \epsilon\}$, *where the $dist(\cdot)$ function is the Euclidean distance between points in a four-dimensional space,* $q = \{[o_i^\top, d_i^\top]^\top : o_i \in M(a_i), d_i \in M(a_i)\}$ *where o_i, d_i are the individual's origin and destination vectors respectively, ϵ is an arbitrary radius in 4D, and p is an arbitrary point in this space.*

Definition 4 (ϵ-**Feasible Coalition Structures**). *By $\mathscr{C}^\epsilon$, we denote the set of coalition structures that only contain ϵ-feasible coalitions.*

To exemplify Definitions 3 and 4, consider Fig. 1 where riders $\{A, B, C\}$ have close origin and destination points, up to a walking radius of 800m. Then they will be allocated into the same ϵ-feasible coalition structure. Any other rider farther apart, will be placed on a different coalition structure.

Constraint 1 (**Car capacity**). *We assume the maximum capacity of a car is four passengers.*

The next definition formalizes the idea that the optimal arrangement of riders in cars is the one that minimizes the travel cost across riders.

Definition 5 (**Optimal Coalition Structure of a Ridesharing Game**). *Within the set of ϵ-feasible coalitions structures $\mathscr{C}^\epsilon$, satisfying the car capacity constraint, the optimal coalition structure is* $\mathbb{C}^* = \arg\min_{\mathbb{C} \in \mathscr{C}^\epsilon}\{\mathbb{C}_{cost}(\mathbb{C})\}$.

The next section describes the steps to calculate the optimal coalition structure of a ridesharing game.

---

[8] The number of coalition structures is given by the Bell number [1], while the number of possible coalitions is 2^n.

3.2 Optimal Coalition Structures in a Ridesharing Game

The objective is to find the $\mathscr{C}^\epsilon$ coalition structure that minimizes the total traveling cost. Below we outline the procedure to find such structure and provide a concrete example of the steps.

- The first step is to group riders by proximity on their origin and destination coordinates and obtain the ϵ-feasible coalitions as in Definition 3. This can be achieved with clustering algorithms such as DBSCAN [7].
- The next step is to calculate all the possible coalition structures among the riders of a cluster. One can use exhaustive search or other coalition formation algorithms (see for example [17]). Regardless of the partition algorithm, the idea is to input the list of individuals in a cluster and return a set of coalition structures alongside their total riding cost, as in Eq. 4.
- The last step is to follow Definition 5 and select the coalition structure with the minimum travel cost per cluster. If there is more than one coalition structure with the minimum cost, we (randomly) select one with the lowest number of coalitions, as this means more members per coalition.

Example 1. Consider for example riders A, B, and C on Fig. 1 and note that they are within 800m of each other's origin-destination, falling into the same cluster. The first step is to calculate the travel cost of all possible coalition structures in the cluster. Following Definition 2, there are five possible coalition structures for three riders $\{A, B, C\}$, $\{\{A, B\}, \{C\}\}$, $\{\{A, C\}, \{B\}\}$, $\{\{B, C\}, \{A\}\}$, $\{\{A\}, \{B\}, \{C\}\}$. On the left-side panel of Fig. 1 we present one example of such structures for the grand coalition $\{A, B, C\}$ together with its pick-up and drop-off points, calculated using the geometric median. The right-side panel of the same figure presents the coalition structure $\{\{A, B\}, \{C\}\}$ with its respective pick up-and drop-off points. We then calculate the total travel cost of each coalition structure following Eqs. 3 and 4. For example, let the total travel cost of each of the five coalition structure be: 50, 55, 60, 65, 70, then following Definition 5, the optimal coalition structure is $\{A, B, C\}$ with a travel cost of 50.

4 Cost Allocation Problem

After obtaining the socially optimal coalition structure C^*, the next question is how to split the cost of the car across the coalition members. This aspect is important, as it determines whether individuals would prefer ridesharing over traveling alone and, thus, whether a coalition can be formed. The goal is to calculate a payoff vector $\vec{c}$, representing the share of the car cost allocated to riders of S, $\forall S \in C^*$. Following [16], we define a cost allocation as follows:

Definition 6. *A cost allocation is a vector* $\vec{c} = (c_1, ..., c_n)$, *such that* $c_i \geq 0$. *Moreover, if* $\sum_{i=1}^{n} c_i = P_{car}$, *then* $\vec{c}$ *is efficient.*

In the context of ridesharing, an allocation method is individually rational if the travel cost of joining a coalition, as given by Eq. 3 (with its corresponding walking cost plus the share of the car fare) is less or equal than traveling alone (which does not involve walking).

Definition 7. *A cost allocation $\vec{c}$ is individually rational if $c_{total_i} \leq C(\{i\})$.*

Here, C is the coalition cost from Eq. 3 and c_{total_i} is the total travel cost composed by the share of the car cost (Eq. 2) plus the walking cost (Eq. 1). The challenge in distributing the cost of the car in ridesharing games is that the walking part of the cost is a non-transferable utility (NTU) component and the only part of the cost that has transferable utilities is the cost of the car. Our method resolves this by linking the individual share of the car with the walking effort, as explained in the next section.

4.1   Inversely-Proportional Cost Allocation

Once the optimal coalition has been determined and the central O-D points have been established, the only difference on the cost contribution across riders is their walking effort. As such, our method seeks to compensate riders for this cost in an equitable way.

To allocate P_{car}, we start by splitting the total amount in two, as: $\gamma P_{car} + (1-\gamma)P_{car}$, with $0 < \gamma < 1$. The first quantity, γP_{car}, can be seen as the flag-fall price and will be equally allocated across all drivers[9]. The remaining amount, $(1 - \gamma)P_{car}$, will be distributed proportionally to the walking effort done by each rider, in what we call the inversely-proportional cost allocation method. The idea of the inversely-proportional cost allocation method is to translate the walking effort into a payment reduction, so those who walked relatively more in the coalition will pay relatively less of the car share. Let $w_i = \frac{VoT_i}{\sum_{i \in S} VoT_i}$ be the proportion of walking done by rider a_i after joining coalition S. Let w_i' be the proportion of the car price paid by rider a_i. The goal is to find a proportional split such that the usual condition holds:

$$\sum_{a_i \in S} w_i' = 1 \qquad (5)$$

As an additional condition, we want the proportion of the car price paid by rider a_i to be inversely proportional to the walking effort, i.e.,[10]:

$$w_i' = \frac{1}{w_i} \cdot \kappa \qquad (6)$$

where the κ term is a re-scaling term needed for Eq. 5 to hold. To determine κ we plug Eq. 6 into Eq. 5, obtaining $\kappa = \frac{1}{\sum \frac{1}{w_i}}$. Finally, the payment allocation of the car price by each member a_i of coalition S is:

$$c_i = (1 - \gamma) \cdot P_{car}(\bar{o}, \bar{d}) \cdot w_i' \qquad (7)$$

---

[9] A 'flag fall' is a fixed initial charge incurred at the start of a taxi journey, as part of the overall fare.

[10] Although a zero walking cost is unlikely, in our implementation we have added a small constant of 0.01% in the denominator to avoid the division by zero.

The total cost of ridesharing for an individual a_i in coalition S is the summation of the car cost and the walking cost as follows:

$$c_{total_i} = \frac{1}{|S|} \cdot \gamma \cdot P_{car}(\bar{o}, \bar{d}) + (1 - \gamma) \cdot P_{car}(\bar{o}, \bar{d}) \cdot w'_i + VoT_i(o_i, d_i) \quad (8)$$

5   Formal Evaluation and Properties

This section analyses the properties of the inversely-proportional cost allocation algorithm. Equation 5 guarantees that the inverse-walking payment allocation is efficient. We say that this cost allocation method is equitable in the sense that it compensates individuals for their walking effort, which is seen as the cost of entry into a coalition. We outline two properties of our method. (a) *Equal treatment*: if two individuals have walked in the same proportion, their cost allocation will be equal (i.e. if $w_i = w_j$ then $w'_i = w'_j$) and also (b) *Proportionality to walking effort*: if the VoT of individual i is p times more than individual j, then $w'_i = \frac{1}{p} w'_j$. The formal results for the desired properties of our approach are further described in Sect. 5.1.

5.1   Conditions for the Individual Rationality of the Inversely-Proportional Method

This section analyzes the conditions that have to be met for the socially-optimal coalition to be individually rational. In particular, the method presents stronger guarantees when individuals are closer in origin and destination and the distance travelled by car justifies the walking effort. Below we formalize this idea.

Theorem 1. *In a ridesharing game, the inversely-proportional cost allocation method guarantees individual rationality if $dist(\bar{o}, \bar{d}) \geq \frac{2}{\gamma} (\epsilon + \epsilon^\alpha)$.*

Proof. We derive the conditions under which the proposed allocation method is individually rational. From Definition 7, a payment allocation c_{total_i} is individually rational if: $c_{total_i} \leq C(\{i\})$. Using Eq. 8, and assuming the car price is 1, the cost equations are:

$$\frac{1}{|S|} \cdot \gamma \cdot dist(\bar{o}, \bar{d}) + (1 - \gamma) \cdot dist(\bar{o}, \bar{d}) \cdot w'_i + \left[VoT(o_i, \bar{o}) + VoT(d_i, \bar{d}) \right] \leq dist(o_i, d_i)$$

Expanding the VoT by its expression in Eq. 1, we obtain:

$$\frac{1}{|S|} \cdot \gamma . dist(\bar{o}, \bar{d}) + (1 - \gamma) . dist(\bar{o}, \bar{d}) \cdot w'_i + \left[dist^\alpha(o_i, \bar{o}) + dist^\alpha(d_i, \bar{d}) \right] \leq dist(o_i, d_i).$$

The strategy is to write the LHS as a function of the geometric median and find an upper bound depending on the choice of ϵ (which acts a universal constant arbitrarily chosen). By the spatial constraint 3, the *total* walking distance of the riders in S is bounded by ϵ (for example, individuals are required to walk no more than 800 m in total, considering the sum of the walking at origin and destination). Then, the VoT is upper-bounded by ϵ^α, therefore:

$$\frac{1}{|S|} \cdot \gamma.dist(\bar{o}, \bar{d}) + (1 - \gamma).dist(\bar{o}, \bar{d}) \cdot w_i' + \left[dist^\alpha(o_i, \bar{o}) + dist^\alpha(d_i, \bar{d}) \right] \le$$

$$\frac{1}{|S|} \cdot \gamma.dist(\bar{o}, \bar{d}) + (1 - \gamma).dist(\bar{o}, \bar{d}) \cdot w_i' + c^\alpha$$

Rearranging terms and noting that $|S| \ge 2$ and $w_i' \le 1$, the upper bound on the LHS is: $dist(\bar{o}, \bar{d}) \cdot \left(\frac{1}{|S|} \cdot \gamma \cdot + (1 - \gamma) \cdot w_i' \right) + \epsilon^\alpha \le dist(\bar{o}, \bar{d}) \cdot \left(1 - \frac{1}{2} \cdot \gamma \right) + \epsilon^\alpha$.

The RHS is lower-bounded by using the triangle inequality: $dist(\bar{o}, \bar{d}) \le d(\bar{o}, o_i) + d(d_i, \bar{d}) + d(o_i, d_i)$. The lower bound for the RHS is: $dist(\bar{o}, \bar{d}) - \epsilon \le dist(o_i, d_i)$.

Rearranging the LHS and RHS, and noting that $|S| \ge 2$ we obtain $dist(\bar{o}, \bar{d}) \cdot \left(1 - \frac{1}{2} \cdot \gamma \right) + \epsilon^\alpha \le dist(\bar{o}, \bar{d}) - \epsilon$. Equivalently, $dist(\bar{o}, \bar{d}) \ge \frac{2}{\gamma} \left(\epsilon + \epsilon^\alpha \right)$.   □

The theorem shows that the inversely-proportional cost allocation scheme achieves individual rationality in settings with maximum utilisation of car capacity, relatively small epsilon and relatively small walking distance (as compared with the trip's length) and overall, the distance of the shared car compensates for the walking cost. The next section provides an evaluation analysis of the inversely-proportional allocation method.

6   Evaluation of the Cost Allocation Method

The aim of this section is to study the performance of the proposed cost allocation method under different configuration settings and compare it against established methods such as an even split and the Shapley value. Section 6.1 uses simulated trip data to ablate the performance of the proposed cost allocation method under different value of time settings. Section 6.2 studies the performance of the method under different trip lengths using real New York City taxi data, [26] as used by [9]. We compared the inversely-proportional cost allocation method to the Shapley value. The Shapley value ϕ_i of rider i in a ridesharing game (S, C, M), which takes place among riders in S who are sharing a ride, is i's average marginal contribution to the game. Formally, it is specified as $\phi_i(C)$ which is equal to $\sum_{T \subseteq S \setminus \{i\}} \frac{t!(s-t-1)!}{s!} (C(T \cup \{i\}) - C(T))$ where t and s represent the cardinality of T and S, respectively [16]. Due to the non transferable part of ridesharing games (i.e., the walking costs), there are several alternative ways to obtain the share of the car from the Shapley value. The first variant takes the total cost $C(S)$ of the coalition as input of the ϕ function and subtracts the individual cost of walking to arrive to the car cost allocation.

Shapley-total-input: $c_{car_i} = \phi_i(C) - \left[VoT(o_i, \bar{o}) + VoT(d_i, \bar{d}) \right]$ (9)

An alternative way of using the Shapley value to split the car cost is to use the coalition's car price as input (i.e., $C(S)$ without considering the walking cost). This variation is calculated as:

Shapley-car-input: $c_{car_i} = \phi_i(P_{car})$ (10)

Lastly, following the rationale from the inversely-proportional method, the Shapley value (calculated with walking and car costs as inputs) can be used to weight the car cost as below:

$$\textbf{Shapley-weighted: } c_{car_i} = P_{car} \cdot \frac{\phi_i(C)}{C(S)} \tag{11}$$

The next sections provides further detail on the numerical experiments and their results.

6.1 Simulated Network

The first experiment analyzes the equitability of different cost allocation methods. For a given optimal coalition structure, and given car trip, we study how each method compensates riders for their walking effort. Table 1 shows the car split for the trips depicted in Fig. 1, on its left panel, panels (a) and (b) shows the optimal coalition structure where $\{A, B\}$ rideshare together and $\{C\}$ travels alone (thus, no walking). In the case of a two-person coalition, the central O-D coordinates (pick-up and drop-off points) are half-way between both members $\{A, B\}$; therefore, the walking cost is the same for both. Since each coalition member walks the same amount of time and they travel the same car distance (as there is a single stop), it is expected that both pay an equal share of the car price. We see that the inversely-proportional allocation method yields an equal payment for $\{A, B\}$ given equal travel costs (i.e., each pays 50% of the trip) which is not the case with any of the Shapley variants. The reason for this difference is that Shapley responds to different desiderata, as it determines the cost allocation based on the individual trip distance, which is more applicable in a multiple-stop taxi problem with no walking cost (see for example, the taxi problem in [20]).

On Table 1(b), the optimal coalition structure is for $\{A, B, C\}$ to rideshare together. Our desideratum of equitability seeks to compensate B for its walking cost, since it has to bear the most walking effort (48.47%), then C has walked the less (12.44%) so we expect this will be reflected in a higher percentage of the car share, In other words, the walking effort is ordered as: $VoT_B > VoT_A > VoT_C$ and the car cost allocation given by the inversely proportional method is ordered as: $c_C > c_A > c_B$, as expected. None of the Shapley methods have such ordering in the car cost allocation, and thus, they are not equitable.

Next we compare the performance of the different allocation methods with respect to the individual rationality property 7 (i.e., the individual cost of riding alone versus the cost of ridesharing) for a three-rider coalitions. On this particular case, we have increased the convexity of the VoT from *Weak* $\alpha = 1.008$ to *Medium* $\alpha = 1.21$, to *Strong* $\alpha = 1.45$ convexity, to increment the monetary value of the walking effort. Our results show that as the cost of walking increases, the inversely-proportional method compensates individuals for the walking cost, holding the individual rationality property for the three riders until the *Medium* VoT convexity, whereas when the cost of walking is too onerous, Shapley methods become less applicable to ridesharing games, as they are unable to compensate for the NTU cost of those who walk more in the car share. For all the Shapley methods, one out of three riders had car costs that were not individually rational when the cost of walking is beyond weakly convex.

Table 1. Car cost split under different methodologies. The share of car cost is expressed as percentage of the total fare.

<table>
<tr><td colspan="4">(a) A, B share a car, C travels alone</td><td colspan="4">(b) Riders A, B, C share a car</td></tr>
<tr><td></td><td>A</td><td>B</td><td>C</td><td></td><td>A</td><td>B</td><td>C</td></tr>
<tr><td>Walking cost</td><td>50%</td><td>50%</td><td>0%</td><td>Walking cost</td><td>39.09%</td><td>48.47%</td><td>12.44 %</td></tr>
<tr><td>Inv-proportional</td><td>50%</td><td>50%</td><td>100%</td><td>Inv-proportional</td><td>20.87%</td><td>17.15%</td><td>61.98%</td></tr>
<tr><td>Even split</td><td>50%</td><td>50%</td><td>100%</td><td>Even split</td><td>33%</td><td>33%</td><td>33%</td></tr>
<tr><td>Shapley-tot-input</td><td>52.07%</td><td>47.93%</td><td>100%</td><td>Shapley-tot-input</td><td>31.63%</td><td>33.89%</td><td>34.48%</td></tr>
<tr><td>Shapley-car</td><td>52.07%</td><td>47.93%</td><td>100%</td><td>Shapley-car</td><td>31.82%</td><td>34.36%</td><td>33.82%</td></tr>
<tr><td>Shapley-weighted</td><td>51.31%</td><td>48.69%</td><td>100%</td><td>Shapley-weighted</td><td>32.06%</td><td>34.72%</td><td>33.23%</td></tr>
</table>

On the next experiment, we simulated $10K$ random coordinates uniformly in the square $[0, 300] \times [0, 300]$, as shown on Table 2. We run the different cost allocation methods under varied VoT settings to show the sensitivity of the individual rationality property to the convexity of the walking function. The configuration for the experiment is: car price K = 1, $\gamma = 0.05$ and the DBSCAN's $\epsilon = 25$.[11] The Euclidean distance was used across all experiments. For each run, we calculated the percentage of riders who satisfied the individual rationality condition under each method. The results of our simulations are as expected, the higher the cost of walking, the more costly it is to join a coalition, and thus, the individual rationality decreases across all methods. The said table shows that all methods perform similarly; however, the individual rationality decreases on the Shapley-car and Shapley-weighted at much faster pace than the inversely-proportional method. Notwithstanding the Shapley's onerous computational time, which will be analyzed on Sect. 6.3.

6.2 NYC Network

The NYC dataset allows us to test the performance of the cost allocation methods under different trip lengths. The length of a trip plays a relevant role in the determination of the individual rationality of the inversely-proportional method, as shown in the proof in Sect. 5.1 which links the individual rationality condition to the length of the trip with the ϵ and γ parameters of the walking cost. Given a fixed ϵ of 800 m, when the trip length increases, the proportion of car cost over the walking cost increases as well, making the cost allocation individually rational. As shown on Table 3 the scenario 'NYC' includes a random selection of 15,000 taxi trips across all boroughs. This scenario contains a mix of trips leaning towards shorter trips. The 'Manhattan' scenario contains medium distance trips from lower downtown to the Central Park area, which are the common trips expected during rush hours. As shown in the said table, for the given ϵ an average trip of 7 mi is enough to guarantee all methods to be individually rational. The last scenario 'Airport trips' includes long-distance trip requests from Manhattan's Midtown to Newark and LaGuardia airports. As the average trip length increases, all methods are individually rational. The configuration for the experiment for all the three scenarios is

---

[11] The choice of ϵ in the case of random points is proportional to the point's standard deviation.

Table 2. Percentage of individually rational riders for different walking costs. Mean over 10K random coordinates.

Allocation method	Convexity of the VoT function		
	Weak	Medium	Strong
Inv-proportional	$99.59 \pm 0.1\%$	$99.09 \pm 0.19\%$	$98.2 \pm 0.26\%$
Even split	$99.53 \pm 0.1\%$	$98.36 \pm 0.23\%$	$96.31 \pm 0.35\%$
Shapley-tot-input	$100 \pm 0\%$	$99.87 \pm 0.08\%$	$99.84 \pm 0.08\%$
Shapley-car-input	$99.87 \pm 0.1\%$	$98.94 \pm 0.20\%$	$97.67 \pm 0.28\%$
Shapley-weighted	$99.72 \pm 0.1\%$	$98.16 \pm 0.27\%$	$96.12 \pm 0.37\%$

$\alpha = 1.0085$, which corresponds to peak of the VoT at the 800 m mark. The price of car $= 1$ and $\gamma = 0.05$ for the portion of the price related to the flag-fall.

Table 3. Average of individual rationality per rider across different methodologies for 15K NYC trips. In parentheses is the 95% confidence interval.

Allocation method	Average trip length		
	Entire NYC (4 mi avg trip)	Manhattan only (7mi avg trip)	Airport trips (12 mi avg trip)
Inv-proportional	$99.07 \pm 0.04\%$	$100 \pm 0\%$	$100 \pm 0\%$
Even split	$99.0 \pm 0.05\%$	$100 \pm 0\%$	$100 \pm 0\%$
Shapley-tot-input	$99.89 \pm 0.02\%$	$100 \pm 0\%$	$100 \pm 0\%$
Shapley-car-input	$99.71 \pm 0.02\%$	$100 \pm 0\%$	$100 \pm 0\%$
Shapley-weighted	$99.32 \pm 0.03\%$	$100 \pm 0\%$	$100 \pm 0\%$

6.3   Time Complexity Comparison of the Cost Allocation Method

The inversely-proportional cost allocation method is linear ($O(n)$) in the number of agents, since their inputs are the individuals' value of time (which is $O(n)$ as per Eq. 1), the rescaling term κ and the inversely proportional payment terms which are also linear in the number of riders as can be seen from Eqs. 5–8. This is a more tractable computational time as compared with Shapley's time complexity, which is exponential, as it requires the calculation of the characteristic function of all sub sets within a coalition.

Table 4 shows the result of an example study on the running time comparison for different number of riders between the inversely proportional cost allocation method and the Shapley-total-input. As it can be seen, for a three-person coalition our algorithm takes 20% less time to run, and as the number of riders increases, the time difference between both methods increases as well[12]. Building on these preliminary results, we aim for further investigations to establish time-savings in different settings and against other forms of Shapley-based cost allocation.

---

[12] Results calculated on a 2.3 GHz Quad-Core Intel Core $i7$.

Table 4. Average *time saving* between the inversely proportional cost allocation method and Shapley *total input* method for different number of riders.

Number of riders	n = 3	n = 10	n = 20
Inv-proportional (in secs)	0.0010	0.00081	0.0014
Shapley-total-input (in secs)	0.0014	0.0028	0.026
Inv-prop vs Shapley-total-input	20%	71%	94%

Table 5. Comparison of properties across different allocation methods.

Allocation method	Efficiency	Indiv. rationality	Equitability	Time complexity
Inv-proportional	YES	Conditional	YES	Linear
Even allocation	YES	NO	YES	Linear
Shapley-total-input	YES	Conditional	NO	Exponential
Shapley-car-input	YES	Conditional	NO	Exponential
Shapley-weighted	YES	Conditional	NO	Exponential

7 Conclusions and Future Work

In this work we show that the socially-optimal ridesharing problem can be modelled as a coalition formation problem and solved within the framework of game theory. We propose a method to determine the optimal pick-up and drop-off points so that the distance walked by all coalition members is minimal. We describe a methodology to include the cost of walking as part of the coalition's cost together with a methodology to allocate the car cost among coalition members, called the inversely-proportional method. This method is computationally tractable, yet effective on its intended application. We provide conditions under which individual rationality is guaranteed and tested it using randomly generated data as well as the NYC taxi dataset. We show that this method is equitable, as it allocates costs proportionally to the walking effort. The equitability, individual rationality (under conditions) and computational tractability make this method a valuable alternative to the traditional Shapley value, which does not hold the said conditions. Table 5 summarizes the performance of different methods across the experiments performed. The individual rationality condition on the second column is guaranteed under certain conditions for the presented methods, for Shapley it is the non-empty core condition [16] and for the inversely-proportional method it is the condition from Sect. 5.1.

In this work we compared the inversely-proportional cost allocation method against Shapley, as an established method. However, we have not investigated the stability of the coalitions formed, since the focus was put on the equitability of the method. For future work, we would like to compare against additional cost allocation methods, and test stability concepts like the core or kernel. One extension could also be to include multiple stops in the car route.

Data Access Statement. This study was a re-analysis of data that are publicly available from the *TLC Trip Record Data* dataset [26].

Acknowledgements. We thank the anonymous reviewers for their incisive comments that were most useful in revising this paper. This work was supported by the UK Engineering and Physical Sciences Research Council (EPSRC) through a Turing AI Fellowship (EP/V022067/1) on Citizen-Centric AI Systems (https://ccais.ac.uk/) and the platform grant entitled "AutoTrust: Designing a Human-Centred Trusted, Secure, Intelligent and Usable Internet of Vehicles" (EP/R029563/1). Lucia Cipolina-Kun is funded by British Telecom (R122171-101). For the purpose of open access, the author has applied a creative commons attribution (CC BY) licence to any author accepted manuscript version arising.

References

1. Bell, E.T.: Exponential polynomials. Ann. Math. **35**(2), 258–277 (1934)
2. Bistaffa, F., Farinelli, A., Ramchurn, S.D.: Sharing rides with friends: a coalition formation algorithm for ridesharing. Proc. AAAI **1**, 608–614 (2015)
3. Cipolina-Kun, L., Yazdanpanah, V., Gerding, E., Stein, S.: Coalition formation in ridesharing with walking options. In: ICLR 2022 Workshop on Gamification and Multiagent Solutions (2022)
4. Cobb, C., Douglas, P.: A theory of production. Am. Econ. Rev. **18**, 139–165 (1928)
5. Cohen, M., Lee, Y., Yin, T., Miller, G., Pachocki, J., Sidford, S.: Geometric median in nearly linear time. In: ACM Symposium on Theory of Computing (2016)
6. Deng, X., Papadimitriou, C.H.: On the complexity of cooperative solution concepts. Math. Oper. Res. **19**(2), 257–266 (1994)
7. Ester, M., Kriegel, H., Sander, J., Xu, X.: A density-based algorithm for discovering clusters in large spatial databases with noise. In: Proceedings of the Second International Conference on Knowledge Discovery and Data Mining (1996)
8. Faigle, U., Kern, W.: The shapley value for cooperative games under precedence constraints. Int. J. Game Theory **21**(3), 249–266 (1992). https://doi.org/10.1007/BF01258278
9. Fielbaum, A., Bai, X., Alonso-Mora, J.: On-demand ridesharing with optimized pick-up and drop-off walking locations. Transp. Res. Part C Emerg. Technol. **126**, 103061 (2021)
10. Fielbaum, A., Kucharski, R., Cats, O., Alonso-Mora, J.: How to split the costs and charge the travellers sharing a ride? aligning system's optimum with users' equilibrium. Eur. J. Oper. Res. **301**, 956–973 (2021)
11. Foti, L., Lin, J., Wolfson, O.: Optimum versus Nash-equilibrium in taxi ridesharing. GeoInformatica **25**(3), 423–451 (2021). https://doi.org/10.1007/s10707-019-00379-6
12. Kaan, L., Olinick, E.V.: The vanpool assignment problem: optimization models and solution algorithms. Comput. Ind. Eng. **66**(1), 24–40 (2013)
13. Li, S., Fei, F., Ruihan, D., Yu, S., Dou, W.: A dynamic pricing method for carpooling service based on coalitional game analysis. In: 2016 IEEE 18th International Conference on High Performance Computing and Communications, pp. 78–85 (2016)
14. Li, Y., et al.: Top-k vehicle matching in social ridesharing: a price-aware approach. IEEE Trans. Knowl. Data Eng. **33**(3), 1251–1263 (2021)
15. Lu, W., Quadrifoglio, L.: Fair cost allocation for ridesharing services - modeling, mathematical programming and an algorithm to find the nucleolus. Transp. Res. Part B Methodol. **121**, 41–55 (2019)
16. Nisan, N., Roughgarden, T., Tardos, É., Vazirani, V. (eds.): Algorithmic Game Theory. Cambridge University Press, Cambridge (2007)

17. Rahwan, T., Tomasz, P., Michalak, M., Wooldridge, N., Jennings, R.: Coalition structure generation: a survey. Artif. Intell. **229**(2), 139–174 (2015)
18. Roth, A.E. (ed.): The Shapley Value: Essays in Honor of Lloyd S. Shapley. Cambridge University Press, Cambridge (1988)
19. Rothe, J. (ed.): Economics and Computation. STBE, Springer, Heidelberg (2016). https://doi.org/10.1007/978-3-662-47904-9
20. Ruibin, B., Jiawei, L., Jason, A., Graham, K.: A novel approach to independent taxi scheduling problem based on stable matching. J. Oper. Res. Soc. **65**(10), 1501–1510 (2014)
21. Santos, D.O., Xavier, E.C.: Taxi and ride sharing: a dynamic dial-a-ride problem with money as an incentive. Expert Syst. Appl. **42**(19), 6728–6737 (2015)
22. Santos, G.: Road pricing theory and evidence. Res. Transp. Econ. **9**(3), 2–308 (2004)
23. Shrestha, R.M., Zolnik, E.J.: Eliminating bus stops: evaluating changes in operations, emissions and coverage. J. Publ. Transp. **16**(2), 153–175 (2013)
24. European Mathematical Society: Encyclopedia of Mathematics. Springer Verlag GmbH
25. Stiglic, M., Agatz, N., Savelsbergh, M., Gradisar, M.: The benefits of meeting points in ridesharing systems. Transp. Res. Part B Methodol. **82**, 36–53 (2015)
26. Taxi, N., record data, L.C.: American community survey, 2019 (2017). https://www1.nyc.gov/site/tlc/about/tlc-trip-record-data.page Accessed 30 May 2022
27. US census bureau: American community survey, 2019 (2020). https://www.census.gov/programs-surveys/acs/data.html Accessed 25 Feb 2022
28. Weiszfeld, E.: Sur le point pour lequel la somme des distances de n points donnés est minimum. Tohoku Math. J. **43**, 355–386 (1937)
29. Yan, P., Lee, C., Chu, C., Chen, C., Luo, Z.: Matching and pricing in ride-sharing: optimality, stability, and financial sustainability. Omega **102**, 102351 (2021)
30. Ye, Y., Zheng, L., Chen, Y., Liao, L.: Discovering stable ride-sharing groups for commuting private car using spatio-temporal semantic similarity. In: Qiu, H., Zhang, C., Fei, Z., Qiu, M., Kung, S.-Y. (eds.) KSEM 2021. LNCS (LNAI), vol. 12816, pp. 636–646. Springer, Cham (2021). https://doi.org/10.1007/978-3-030-82147-0_52

Short Papers

Privacy-Aware Explanations for Team Formation

Athina Georgara[1,2(✉)], Juan Antonio Rodríguez-Aguilar[1], and Carles Sierra[1]

[1] Artificial Intelligence Research Institute, CSIC, Barcelona, Spain
{ageorg,jar,sierra}@iiia.csic.es
[2] Enzyme Advising Group, Barcelona, Spain

Abstract. Over the recent years there is a growing move towards explainable AI (XAI). The widespread use of AI systems in a large variety of applications that support human's decisions leads to the imperative need for providing explanations regarding the AI system's functionality. That is, explanations are necessary for earning the user's trust regarding the AI systems. At the same time, recent legislation such as GDPR regarding data privacy require that any attempt towards explainability shall not disclose private data and information to third-parties. In this work we focus on providing privacy-aware explanations in the realm of team formation scenarios. We propose the means to analyse whether an explanation leads an explainability algorithm to incur in privacy breaches when computing explanation for a user.

Keywords: Privacy awareness · Explainable AI (XAI) · Team formation · Explainable multi-agents environments (xMASE)

1 Introduction

Over the past decades there is wide interest in using artificial intelligence (AI) to aid humans to carry out complex, hard, and time-consuming tasks. As AI systems pervade our lifes, people are becoming curious regarding the rationale and the methodology of these systems; thus we observe a new surge of interest towards *explainable AI (XAI)* [10,22]. XAI provides "inside information" regarding the inner functionality of an AI system in an attempt to be transparent, and earn in this way the users' trust. More and more applications turn to AI in order to ease and automate complex procedures, and demand understanding the solutions recommended by such systems. Besides the growing need for explanations, Goodman and Flaxman [15] point out that legislation such as the GDPR recently put forward by the EU leads to the *right to explanation*. That is, a user providing personal information as input data to some AI algorithm,

Research supported by projects AI4EU (H2020-825619), TAILOR (H2020-952215), 2019DI17, Humane-AI-Net (H2020-952026), Crowd4SDG (H2020-872944), and grant PID2019-104156GB-I00 funded by MCIN/AEI/10.13039/501100011033.

has the right to know why the algorithm makes a decision with their input data instead of another one.

Došilović et al. in [10] thoroughly discuss the intererpretability and the explainability of supervised machine learning models. The main focus of recent literature in explainability lies on machine learning (ML) models [1, 8, 10, 16, 23, 28, 29] and recommender systems [4, 17, 20, 21, 24, 33], which are usually considered as 'black-boxes', and transparency is a necessity. Beyond ML, Borg and Bex [6] recently introduced a general framework to provide contrastive explanations for (abstract) argumentation-based conclusions; Nardi et al. in [25] and Boixel and Endriss in [5] developed algorithms to justify outcomes (i.e., winners) in voting settings; and Georgara et al. in [13] propose a general algorithm to deliver explanations in team formation scenarios.

Recently, Kraus et al. [19] have raised awareness on the need for explanations in multiagent environments (xMASE), and they have identified the key challenges towards xMASE. Among other challenges—such as the development of appropriate algorithms for generating explanations and the user modelling to appropriately tailor explanations and increase user satisfaction—Kraus et al. refer to the issue of non-disclosing private data and information. Note that in any AI system that assists people in making a decision or solve a problem, individuals need to feed the system with information (possibly private), which is therefore utilised by the system to reach a solution. As such, within environments where explanations need to justify solutions involving many individuals, it is of utmost importance to ensure that private information remain private.

Need for privacy-awareness has risen as more and more data become available to AI systems. Considering the online social networks, we find privacy issues as people may expose data not only about themselves bat also about others (e.g., via pictures, check-ins, etc.). Such and Criado in [32] discuss the multi-party privacy problem on online social networks, and highlight the need for mechanism that preven privacy violations in such environments. [18] works towards privacy in social networks, and develops a tool for detecting privacy violations in such settings using an agent-based representation for social networks. In a different to social media domain, Sörries et al. in [30] study privacy preserving technologies by design within the domain of healthcare. Now in XAI, Puiu et al. in [26] present recent developments on explainability and interpretability along with the limitation of data accessibility due to ethical constraints in cardiovascular diagnosis; while Sorvano et al. in [31] make a separation between *explainable* (X-) and *explanatory* (Y-) AI, and propose a model for YAI under GPDR guidelines.

In this paper we address the challenge of preserving privacy upon providing explanation within multi-agent environments, and specifically in team formation scenarios. Specifically, we argue that an AI system should only offer explanations that are guaranteed not to breach privacy. To the best of our knowledge this is the first work tackling this challenge in team formation. As such here we propose a *privacy breach detector* capable of finding whether a given explanation is bound to lead to privacy breaches. That is, we describe how our privacy breach detector interacts with a team formation algorithm (AI system) and an explanatory algorithm (XAI system) to approve or disapprove explanations within a general framework for privacy-aware explanations in team formation.

2   Background: Team Formation and Explanations

A team formation problem [2,3,7,9,12,14] deals with situations where individuals must be grouped in teams to work on some task(s). In general, in such a problem there is a set of tasks that need to be tackled; while each task is assigend to a team of agents (denoted as $\mathcal{A}$) who collectively work towards the task. There is a plethora of team formation algorithms, referred to as TFA, that solve the team formation problem. A TFA takes as input data regarding agents' characteristics along with data regarding tasks' descriptions, and outputs a team-to-task allocation (denoted as g), i.e., a mapping from tasks to teams of agents. The team-maker is the one who invokes the TFA to generate an allocation. Throughout the paper we will be using as a running example the "classroom scenario": a teacher needs to split their students into teams that work on different projects each. As such, we will be considering algorithms as the one proposed in [12,14], since it applies best in our classroom scenario.

In the context of team formation, Georgara et al. [13] propose a general scheme that demonstrates explanations using a many teams to many tasks TFA. Specifically, [13] proposes a general explanatory algorithm that *wraps* existing team formation algorithms in order to build *contrastive explanations* regarding a team-to-tasks allocation. As highlighted in [22], contrastive explanations are based on findings in the philosophical and cognitive sciences literature indicating that people are not interested in the causes leading to a particular outcome (in our case an allocation) per se, but, on the contrary, they are interested in the causes that explain a non-occurring outcome. In other words, people are interested in (and also tend to give) explanations regarding questions of the type "Why X instead of Y?". As such, a contrastive explanation provides the reasons why outcome X is preferred to another outcome Y.

A contrastive explanation within team-to-tasks allocation problems corresponds to information coming from the comparison between two allocations that justify why one is preferred to the other. In [13], the authors build explanations of the form: "If team A was assigned to task τ instead of B, it would result in task τ being assigned to a team (A) that is worse than its current team (B) with respect to property f". According to [13] the TFA at hand forms teams based on some *desired properties*, while there is a way to measure the matching quality of a team being assigned to a task toward some desired property. Therefore, they exploit these desired properties in order to justify why one task assignment $\langle team_1, task_1 \rangle$ in an allocation is better than a task assignment $\langle team_2, task_2 \rangle$ in an alternative allocation. Now, in our classroom example, we consider the following four desired properties: *(1)* a team shall be *skilled* for its assigned task, *(2)* a team shall be diverse in terms of individuals' personalities, *(3)* a team shall be satisfied with their assigned task, and *(4)* a team shall be socially coherent. As such, here we use *individuals' features* (skills, personality) and *individuals' preferences* (over projects, over potential team-mates) in order to measure the matching quality of a team with a task *wrt.* each one of the desired properties.

With this desired properties in mind, the teacher uses the TFA which forms a teams-to-tasks allocation. Then a student, namely Beth, challenges the

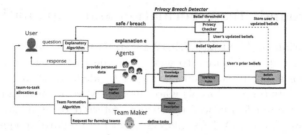

Fig. 1. General framework for privacy-aware explanations for team formation

explanatory algorithm (e.g., the one in [13]) with the following query: "Why is Jack in my team instead of Alex?". Given the query, the EA (according to [13]) computes an alternative allocation that *enforces* Beth and Alex to work together. Then the EA computes the differences between the teams in both allocations for Beth. That is, let according to the current allocation Beth be working with Jack on project Maths Game, while according to the alternative allocation Beth is working with Alex on project Creative Writing. The EA would compare ⟨Beth and Jack, Maths Game⟩ against ⟨Beth and Alex, Creative Writing⟩ with respect to the properties: each team being *(a)* skilled for their assigned project; *(b)* diverse in terms of personality; *(c)* satisfied with their assigned project in terms of individuals' preferences over projects; and *(d)* socially coherent in terms of individuals' preferences over team-mates. Then the explanation that the EA builds would be: "If Alex was on your team instead of Jack, then you would be in a less diverse team in terms of personality than the the team you are currently in". Notably, according to the EA, the desired property that justifies best why Beth should be working with Jack and not with Alex, is that of personality.

3   A General Framework for Privacy-Aware Explainable Team Formation

In this section we describe a general framework that combines team formation solutions, explanations over these solutions, and a mechanism for checking whether some explanation may cause a privacy breach. Assume we have a team formation scenario and a set of agents along with a set of task in our disposal. Moreover, let o be the 'orchestrator' or team-maker, i.e., the person who requests the forming of a team-to-tasks allocation using some team formation algorithm. A user is someone that challenges the teams-to-tasks allocation, and is either the team-maker or an agent. In this work we assume that each agent holds a view of the world which consists of: *(i) known facts* such as their own private information, the description of the tasks, and the teams-to-tasks allocation; and *(ii) beliefs* over other agents' private information. Similarly, the team-maker also holds their own view of the world, consisting of some known facts and their beliefs over the agents' private information. Figure 1 illustrates our proposed framework, which in a nutshell consists of the following components:

1. A team formation algorithm (TFA) that forms a teams-to-tasks allocation.
2. An explanatory algorithm (EA)—interacting with the TFA—that generates explanations regarding a teams-to-tasks allocation.
3. A privacy breach detector (PBD) that assesses whether an explanation may incur in privacy breaches. The PBD is composed of:
   (a) a belief updater (BU) that computes posterior beliefs that the user is expected to form upon receiving an explanation; and
   (b) a privacy checker (PC) that assesses whether the user's expected posterior beliefs exceed a belief threshold.

In more details, the team-maker uses the TFA to solve a team formation problem and form an allocation; while the TFA notifies the team-maker and the agents with the allocation formed. As we mentioned in Sect. 2, there is a plethora of TFAs solving different team formation problems, as such depending on the problem at hand, one shall use the corresponding TFA. For example, a teacher in a classroom acts as the team-maker and uses a TFA to group their students (who correspond to agents) into teams in order to work on their mid-term projects (which correspond to tasks). The TFA computes the teams along with their allocation to projects. Thereafter, the TFA communicates the resulting teams and allocations to both the teacher and the students.

Then, say that some user challenges the TFA's result. That is, a user may argue that there is a better allocation than the one yielded by the TFA. Hence, the user poses a question to the explanatory algorithm. For example, student Beth asks why Jack is in her team instead of her friend Alex. The EA processes the user's question and, by interacting with the TFA, builds an appropriate explanation. For example, the EA builds the following explanation: "If Alex was on your team instead of Jack, then you would be in a less diverse team in terms of personality than the the team you are currently in".

Next, the EA passes the generated explanation to the privacy breach detector, and in particular to the belief updater. As mentioned before, each agent holds knowledge regarding the world, and beliefs over other agents' private information. The BU is responsible for exploiting the information conveyed by an explanation, combining it with the user's knowledge and current beliefs in order to extract valuable conclusions. Specifically, the BU follows a theory of mind [11] on the user to simulate the reasoning that the user is expected to follow (based on the user's knowledge and beliefs). As a result, the BU forms an updated version of beliefs which the user is expected to reach after receiving the explanation. For example, Beth is expected to update her beliefs on Alex's and Jack's personalities based on the explanation from the EA.

After that, the BU passes the expected posterior beliefs to the privacy checker. The PC is responsible for assessing whether the user's expected posterior beliefs exceeds the belief threshold ε. The belief threshold corresponds to a maximum probability with which a user may believe that some agent's information is true, without violating this agent's privacy. For example, with a belief threshold $\varepsilon = 0.5$, if Beth is expected to update her beliefs that Alex is of personality role 'leader' to 0.3, then this causes no violation of Alex's privacy. On the other hand, if Beth is expected to update her beliefs that Jack is of personality 'implementer' to 0.7, then this *causes* a violation of Jack's privacy.

Finally, the privacy checker outputs an answer for the explanatory algorithm. Specifically, the PC responds with an appropriate message indicating whether the explanation is *safe* if our PBD detected no privacy breaches on private information, or otherwie. Depending on the PC's response, the explanatory algorithm either provides the explanation to the user, or *handles* this situation by e.g. computing a different explanation or denying to answer due to a privacy breach.

4   Representing Knowledge and Beliefs

In this section we discuss how to represent *knowledge* and *beliefs* used within our framework (see Fig. 1). Recall that, as mentioned in Sect. 3, both the agents and the team-maker hold a view of the team formation problem which consists of known facts and beliefs. *Knowledge* corresponds to known facts that an agent has over the team formation scenario. Such known facts include the tasks' description and the team-to-tasks allocation published by the TFA. Moreover, for an agent, known facts also include their own personal characteristics, i.e., this agent's features and preferences. Besides knowledge, an individual can form over others. Specifically, an individual forms beliefs regarding knowledge they do not own, i.e., beliefs over another agent's personal characteristics.

Agent's Knowledge. An agent holds *knowledge* that can be either *private* or *public*. Given an agent $a \in \mathcal{A}$, their *private knowledge* refers to characteristics that comprise agent's a own profile i..e, their features and preferences. Each agent holds their own private knowledge, withheld from anyone else. For example, "John is capable in Maths" corresponds to agent John's private knowledge. *Public knowledge* refers to the tasks made public by the team-maker and the team-to-tasks allocations received from the TFA. All agents at the outset share the same public knowledge, i.e. public knowledge is common to all agents. For example, "John has been allocated to work on the Maths-Game task" is an example of public knowledge.

We represent knowledge using *first-order predicates* with *ground terms*. For an agent $a \in \mathcal{A}$ we denote the private knowledge of a as Γ_a corresponding to a set of first-order predicates with ground terms referring to a. For instance, predicate $acquire(John, maths) \in \Gamma_{John}$ corresponds to some of John's private knowledge. In our running example, the predicates that exist in agent's a private knowledge are: $acquires(a, skill)$, $personality(a, role)$, $wants\_to\_work\_on(a, \tau)$, and $wants\_to\_work\_together(a, b)$, where $skill$ is some skill that agent a acquires, $role$ is agent's a personality role, τ is some task that a wants to work on, and $b \in \mathcal{A}$ is some agent that a wants to work with. We denote with Γ_τ the public knowledge that each agent initially holds regarding task τ—for example, $size(Maths - Game, 3) \in \Gamma_{Maths-Game}$; and with Γ_g the public knowledge that each agent initially holds regarding the team-to-tasks allocation—for example, $worksOn(g, John, \tau) \in \Gamma_g$, which is read as "According to allocation g, John is assigned to work on the Maths-Game task".

Team-Maker's Knowledge. The team maker only holds public knowledge regarding the tasks' description and team-to-tasks allocations. Thus, the team-maker's knowledge is $\Gamma_o \equiv \Gamma_\tau \cup \Gamma_g$.

Agents' Beliefs. Each agent holds beliefs over other agents' private knowledge. That is, an agent sets a probability with which they believe that some private knowledge of another agent is true. For example, let Beth believe that John is knowledgeable in maths with probability 0.7, this comprises Beth's belief over some of John's private knowledge. This belief is in fact a probability over a predicate in Γ_{John}, i.e., $P[acquires(John, maths)] = 0.7$. Thus, an agent's a beliefs correspond to a probability function over predicates in $\bigcup_{b \in \mathcal{A}} \Gamma_b$.

Team-Maker's Beliefs. The team-maker holds beliefs over the agents' private information as well. Similarly, the team-maker's beliefs correspond to a probability function over predicates in $\bigcup_{a \in \mathcal{A}} \Gamma_a$.

5 Inference Rules

Here we discuss about the *inference rules* used by our model within the privacy breach detector (see Fig. 1). We use 'IF-THEN' rules that guide the BU component to reason over new information deriving from an explanation. Specifically, we discern rules that *(i)* determine when a team satisfies a desired property, and *(ii)* interpret a comparison described in an explanation.

Considering our classroom example, we have one rule per desired property to determine when a team satisfies this property. For example, such a rule is: "IF the team members are of different personality roles THEN the team is diverse", which using first order predicates is written as: $\forall\, x, y\ \forall p\ inTeam(x, A) \wedge inTeam(y, A) \wedge personality(x, p) \wedge \neg personality(y, p) \Rightarrow isDiverse(A)$. We also have rules for interpreting a comparison described in explanations. The comparison of an explanation is in the form of "team A assigned to τ satisfies property f, while team B assigned to σ does not" or "both team A assigned to τ and team B assigned to σ (do not) satisfy property f"; which using first-order predicates is written as: $isAssigned(A, \tau) \wedge isAssigned(B, \sigma) \wedge isBetter(A, B, f) \Rightarrow satisfies(A, \tau, f) \wedge \neg satisfies(B, \sigma, f)$ and $isAssigned(A, \tau) \wedge isAssigned(B, \sigma) \wedge isEqual(A, B, f) \Rightarrow (satisfies(A, \tau, f) \wedge satisfies(B, \sigma, f)) \vee (\neg satisfies(A, \tau, f) \wedge \neg satisfies(B, \sigma, f))$.

Given these rules, we can handle the process of inference with a rule-based forward reasoner [27]; while the inference is used to update the beliefs that the explainee holds over private information of the agents appearing in the explanation, following a theory of mind approach [11].

6   Conclusions

In this paper we tackled the challenge of preserving privacy when providing explanations within the multi-agent setting of team formation. We argue that providing explanations should guarantee that agents' private information is not disclosed. Towards this, we propose a general framework that combines team formation solutions and explanations over these solutions, while it detects potential privacy breaches upon offering explanations. In particular, we put forward a privacy breach detector that complements an explanatory algorithm as the one proposed in [13], and assesses the explanations built *wrt.* privacy breaches.

References

1. Adadi, A., Berrada, M.: Peeking inside the black-box: a survey on explainable artificial intelligence (xai). IEEE Access **6**, 52138–52160 (2018)
2. Anagnostopoulos, A., Becchetti, L., Castillo, C., Gionis, A., Leonardi, S.: Power in unity: forming teams in large-scale community systems, pp. 599–608 (01 2010)
3. Andrejczuk, E., Berger, R., Rodríguez-Aguilar, J.A., Sierra, C., Marín-Puchades, V.: The composition and formation of effective teams: computer science meets organizational psychology. Knowl. Eng. Rev. **33**, e17 (2018)
4. Antognini, D., Musat, C., Faltings, B.: Interacting with explanations through critiquing. In: Zhou, Z.H. (ed.) Proceedings of the Thirtieth International Joint Conference on Artificial Intelligence, IJCAI-21, pp. 515–521 (8 2021), main Track
5. Boixel, A., Endriss, U.: Automated justification of collective decisions via constraint solving. In: Proceedings of the 19th International Conference on Autonomous Agents and MultiAgent Systems, pp. 168–176. AAMAS '20 (2020)
6. Borg, A., Bex, F.: Contrastive explanations for argumentation-Based conclusions. In: Proceedings of the 21st International Conference on Autonomous Agents and Multiagent Systems (2022)
7. Capezzuto, L., Tarapore, D., Ramchurn, S.D.: Anytime and efficient coalition formation with spatial and temporal constraints (2020)
8. Carvalho, D.V., Pereira, E.M., Cardoso, J.S.: Machine learning interpretability: a survey on methods and metrics. Electronics **8**(8), 832 (2019)
9. Crawford, C., Rahaman, Z., Sen, S.: Evaluating the efficiency of robust team formation algorithms. In: Osman, N., Sierra, C. (eds.) Autonomous Agents and Multiagent Systems, pp. 14–29. Springer International Publishing, Cham (2016). https://doi.org/10.1007/978-3-319-46882-2_2
10. Došilović, F.K., Brčić, M., Hlupić, N.: Explainable artificial intelligence: a survey. In: 2018 41st International Convention on Information and Communication Technology, Electronics and Microelectronics (MIPRO), pp. 0210–0215 (2018)
11. Frith, C., Frith, U.: Theory mind. Curr. biol. **15**(17), R644–R645 (2005)
12. Georgara, A., Rodriguez-Aguilar, J.A., Sierra, C.: Allocating teams to tasks: an anytime heuristic competence-based approach. In: Baumeister, D., Rothe, J. (eds.) Multi-Agent Systems - 19th European Conference, EUMAS 2019, pp. 14–16. Germany, September, Düsseldorf (2022)
13. Georgara, A., Rodríguez-Aguilar, J.A., Sierra, C.: Building contrastive explanations for multi-agent team formation. In: Proceedings of the 21st International Conference on Autonomous Agents and MultiAgent Systems (AAMAS '22), pp. 516–524 (2022)

14. Georgara, A., et al.: An anytime heuristic algorithm for allocating many teams to many tasks. In: Proceedings of the 21st International Conference on Autonomous Agents and MultiAgent Systems, pp. 1598–1600 (2022)
15. Goodman, B., Flaxman, S.: European union regulations on algorithmic decision making and a "right to explanation". AI Magazine **38**(3), 50–57 (2017)
16. Holzinger, A.: From machine learning to explainable ai. In: 2018 World Symposium on Digital Intelligence for Systems and Machines (DISA), pp. 55–66 (2018)
17. Kleinerman, A., Rosenfeld, A., Kraus, S.: Providing explanations for recommendations in reciprocal environments. In: Proceedings of the 12th ACM Conference on Recommender Systems, pp. 22–30. RecSys '18, Association for Computing Machinery, New York, NY, USA (2018)
18. Kökciyan, N., Yolum, P.: PriGuard: a semantic approach to detect privacy violations in online social networks. IEEE Trans. Knowl. Data Eng. **28**(10), 2724–2737 (2016)
19. Kraus, S., et al.: Ai for explaining decisions in multi-agent environments. Proceedings of the AAAI Conference on Artificial Intelligence, pp. 13534–13538 (2020)
20. Kunkel, J., Donkers, T., Michael, L., Barbu, C.M., Ziegler, J.: Let me explain: impact of personal and impersonal explanations on trust in recommender systems. In: Proceedings of the 2019 CHI Conference on Human Factors in Computing Systems, pp. 1–12. Association for Computing Machinery, New York, NY, USA (2019)
21. Lipton, Z.C.: The mythos of model interpretability: in machine learning, the concept of interpretability is both important and slippery. Queue **16**(3), 31–57 (2018)
22. Miller, T.: Explanation in artificial intelligence: Insights from the social sciences. Artif. Intell. **267**, 1–38 (2019)
23. Mohseni, S., Zarei, N., Ragan, E.D.: A multidisciplinary survey and framework for design and evaluation of explainable ai systems (2020)
24. Mosca, F., Such, J.M.: ELVIRA: an Explainable Agent for Value and Utility-Driven Multiuser Privacy, pp. 916–924. International Foundation for Autonomous Agents and Multiagent Systems, Richland, SC (2021)
25. Nardi, O., Boixel, A., Endriss, U.: A graph-based algorithm for the automated justification of collective decisions. In: Proceedings of the 21st International Conference on Autonomous Agents and Multiagent Systems (AAMAS '22), pp. 935–943 (2022)
26. Puiu, A., Vizitiu, A., Nita, C., Itu, L., Sharma, P., Comaniciu, D.: Privacy-preserving and explainable AI for cardiovascular imaging. Stud. Inf. Control, ISSN 1220–1766 **30**(2), 21–32 (2021)
27. Rattanasawad, T., Saikaew, K.R., Buranarach, M., Supnithi, T.: A review and comparison of rule languages and rule-based inference engines for the semantic web. In: 2013 International Computer Science and Engineering Conference (ICSEC), pp. 1–6 (2013)
28. Rosenfeld, A., Richardson, A.: Explainability in human-agent systems. Autonom. Agent. Multi-Agent Syst. **33**(6), 673–705 (2019)
29. Samek, W., Müller, K.-R.: Towards explainable artificial intelligence. In: Samek, W., Montavon, G., Vedaldi, A., Hansen, L.K., Müller, K.-R. (eds.) Explainable AI: Interpreting, Explaining and Visualizing Deep Learning. LNCS (LNAI), vol. 11700, pp. 5–22. Springer, Cham (2019). https://doi.org/10.1007/978-3-030-28954-6_1
30. Sörries, P., et al.: Privacy needs reflection: conceptional design rationales for privacy-preserving explanation user interfaces. Mensch und Computer 2021-Workshopband

31. Sovrano, F., Vitali, F., Palmirani, M.: Making things explainable vs explaining: requirements and challenges under the GDPR. In: Rodríguez-Doncel, V., Palmirani, M., Araszkiewicz, M., Casanovas, P., Pagallo, U., Sartor, G. (eds.) AICOL/XAILA 2018/2020. LNCS (LNAI), vol. 13048, pp. 169–182. Springer, Cham (2021). https://doi.org/10.1007/978-3-030-89811-3_12
32. Such, J.M., Criado, N.: Multiparty privacy in social media. Commun. ACM **61**(8), 74–81 (2018)
33. Zhang, Y., Chen, X.: Explainable recommendation: a survey and new perspectives. Found. Trends Inf. Retrieval **14**(1), 1–101 (2020)

A New Semantics for Action Language mA*

Loc Pham$^{(\boxtimes)}$, Yusuf Izmirlioglu$^{(\boxtimes)}$, Tran Cao Son, and Enrico Pontelli

New Mexico State University, Las Cruces, NM, USA
{locpham,yizmir,epontell}@nmsu.edu, tson@cs.nmsu.edu

Abstract. The action language mA* employs the notion of update models in defining transitions between states. Given an action occurrence and a state, the update model of the action occurrence is automatically constructed from the given state and the observability of agents. A main criticism of this approach is that it cannot deal with situations when agents' have incorrect beliefs about the observability of other agents. The present paper addresses this shortcoming by defining a new semantics for mA*. The new semantics addresses the aforementioned problem of mA* while maintaining the simplicity of its semantics; the new definitions continue to employ simple update models, with at most three events for all types of actions, which can be constructed given the action specification and independently from the state in which the action occurs.

Keywords: Epistemic reasoning · Update models · Action language

1 Introduction

In multi-agent environments, agents not only need to reason about properties of the world, but also about agents' knowledge and beliefs. Among the various formalisms for reasoning about actions in Multi-Agent Systems (MAS), a commonly used one is the *action model*, introduced in [1,2] and later extended to the *update model* [5,9]. Update models have been employed in the study of epistemic planning problems in MAS [3,6,11]. The action language mA*, proposed in [4], and its earlier versions are among the first action languages that utilize update models in defining a transition function based semantics for multi-agent domains. Update models have also been adopted in [13]. Given an action occurrence, a corresponding update model is automatically derived from the action description and the pointed Kripke model encoding the current state of the world and the state of beliefs/knowledge of agents; such update model is used to compute the resulting state from the action occurrence. This simple construction only uses update models with at most three events. However, as discussed in [4,8], the simplicity of mA* presents some challenges for its application.

Example 1. Three agents, A, B and C, are in a room with a box containing a coin. It is common knowledge that: (1) no agent knows whether the coin lies

R. Aydoğan et al. (Eds.): PRIMA 2022, LNAI 13753, pp. 553–562, 2023.
https://doi.org/10.1007/978-3-031-21203-1_33

heads or tails up; (2) the box is locked and only A can open it; (3) an agent needs to peek into the open box to learn the position of the coin; and (4) if one agent is looking at the box and a second agent peeks into the box, then the first agent will learn that the second agent knows the status of the coin; nevertheless, the first agent's knowledge about which face of the coin is up will not change.

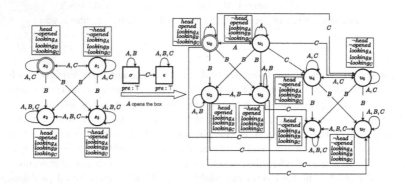

Fig. 1. A opens the box

Suppose that only A and B are looking at the box. However, B believes that all three agents have their eyes on the box. The situation is illustrated by the pointed Kripke structure on left of Fig. 1. Assume that A opens the box and anyone who is looking at the box will observe this action. Intuitively, after A opens the box, B should believe that C is also aware of the box being open. The design of m$\mathcal{A}^*$ produces the pointed Kripke structure on the right of Fig. 1, leading to the conclusion that B thinks that C considers the box still closed. This is because the current update models in m$\mathcal{A}^*$ assume that all full observers know about the observability of all other agents. While this assumption is reasonable in many situations, it implies that the use of m$\mathcal{A}^*$ requires very careful considerations by the domain designers, as pointed out in [4].

In this paper, we propose an extension of the language m$\mathcal{A}^*$ that can handle situations where agents' have incorrect beliefs about the observability of other agents, using *edge-conditioned event update models*, introduced by [7]. We begin with a short review of m$\mathcal{A}^*$, then show how to apply the edge-conditioned event update models to help m$\mathcal{A}^*$ solve the problems mentioned in the previous example. We prove relevant properties and provide final considerations.

2   Background

Belief Formulae. A *multi-agent* domain $\langle \mathcal{AG}, \mathcal{F} \rangle$ includes a finite and non-empty set of agents $\mathcal{AG}$ and a set of fluents (atomic propositions) $\mathcal{F}$ encoding properties of the world. *Belief formulae* over $\langle \mathcal{AG}, \mathcal{F} \rangle$ are defined by the BNF: "$\varphi ::= p \mid \neg\varphi \mid (\varphi \wedge \varphi) \mid (\varphi \vee \varphi) \mid \mathbf{B}_i\varphi$" where $p \in \mathcal{F}$ is a fluent and $i \in \mathcal{AG}$. We refer to a belief formula which does not contain any occurrence of $\mathbf{B}_i$ as *a fluent formula*. In addition, for a formula φ and a non-empty set $\alpha \subseteq \mathcal{AG}$, $\mathbf{B}_\alpha \varphi$ and $\mathbf{C}_\alpha \varphi$ denote $\bigwedge_{i \in \alpha} \mathbf{B}_i \varphi$ and $\bigwedge_{k=1}^{\infty} \mathbf{B}_\alpha^k \varphi$, where $\mathbf{B}_\alpha^1 \varphi = \mathbf{B}_\alpha \varphi$ and $\mathbf{B}_\alpha^k \varphi = \mathbf{B}_\alpha^{k-1} \mathbf{B}_\alpha \varphi$ for $k > 1$, respectively. $\mathcal{L}_{\mathcal{AG}}$ denotes the set of belief formulae over $\langle \mathcal{AG}, \mathcal{F} \rangle$.

Satisfaction of belief formulae is defined over *pointed Kripke structures* [10]. A Kripke structure M is a tuple $\langle S, \pi, \{\mathcal{B}_i\}_{i \in \mathcal{AG}} \rangle$, where S is a set of worlds (denoted by $M[S]$), $\pi : S \mapsto 2^{\mathcal{F}}$ is a function that associates an interpretation of $\mathcal{F}$ to each element of S (denoted by $M[\pi]$), and for $i \in \mathcal{AG}$, $\mathcal{B}_i \subseteq S \times S$ is a binary relation over S (denoted by $M[i]$). For convenience, we will often draw a Kripke structure M as a directed labeled graph, whose set of labeled nodes represents S and whose set of labeled edges contains $s \xrightarrow{i} t$ iff $(s, t) \in \mathcal{B}_i$; the label of each node is the name of the world and its interpretation is displayed as a text box next to it (see, e.g., Fig 1). For $u \in S$ and a fluent formula φ, $M[\pi](u)$ and $M[\pi](u)(\varphi)$ denote the interpretation associated to u via π and the truth value of φ with respect to $M[\pi](u)$. For a world $s \in M[S]$, (M, s) is a *pointed Kripke structure*, hereafter called a *state*.

The satisfaction relation $\models$ between belief formulae and a state (M, s) is defined as follows: (1) $(M, s) \models p$ if p is a fluent and $M[\pi](s)(p)$ is true; (2) $(M, s) \models \neg \varphi$ if $(M, s) \not\models \varphi$; (3) $(M, s) \models \varphi_1 \wedge \varphi_2$ if $(M, s) \models \varphi_1$ and $(M, s) \models \varphi_2$; (4) $(M, s) \models \varphi_1 \vee \varphi_2$ if $(M, s) \models \varphi_1$ or $(M, s) \models \varphi_2$; and (5) $(M, s) \models \mathbf{B}_i \varphi$ if $\forall t.[(s, t) \in M[i] \Rightarrow (M, t) \models \varphi]$.

Edge-Conditioned Update Models. The formalism of *update models* has been used to describe transformations of states according to a predetermined transformation pattern (see, e.g., [1,5]). This formalism makes use of the notion of $\mathcal{L}_{\mathcal{AG}}$-substitution, which is a set $\{p_1 \rightarrow \varphi_1, \ldots, p_k \rightarrow \varphi_k\}$, where each p_i is a distinct fluent in $\mathcal{F}$ and each $\varphi_i \in \mathcal{L}_{\mathcal{AG}}$. $SUB_{\mathcal{L}_{\mathcal{AG}}}$ denotes the set of all $\mathcal{L}_{\mathcal{AG}}$-substitutions. To handle the nested belief about agents' observability problem, in this extension of m$\mathcal{A}^*$, we will utilize the *edge-conditioned event update models* as proposed by [7]. An edge-conditioned event update model Σ is a tuple $\langle \Sigma, \{R_i\}_{i \in \mathcal{AG}}, pre, sub \rangle$ where Σ is a set of events, $R_i \subseteq \Sigma \times \mathcal{L}_{\mathcal{AG}} \times \Sigma$ is the accessibility relation of agent i between events, $pre : \Sigma \rightarrow \mathcal{L}_{\mathcal{AG}}$ is a function mapping each event $e \in \Sigma$ to a formula in $\mathcal{L}_{\mathcal{AG}}$, $sub : \Sigma \rightarrow SUB_{\mathcal{L}_{\mathcal{AG}}}$ is a function mapping each event $e \in \Sigma$ to a substitution in $SUB_{\mathcal{L}_{\mathcal{AG}}}$. Elements of R_i are of the form (e_1, γ, e_2) where γ is a belief formula. In the graph representation, such an accessibility relation is shown by a directed edge from e_1 to e_2 with the label $i : \gamma$. We will omit γ and write simply i as label of the edge when $\gamma = \top$.

Given an edge-conditioned update model Σ, an *update instance* ω is a pair (Σ, e) where e is an event in Σ, referred to as a *designated event* (or *true event*). For simplicity of presentation, we often draw an update instance as a graph whose events are rectangles, whose links represent the accessibility relations between events, and a double square represents the *designated event* (see, e.g., Fig. 2).

Given a Kripke structure M and an edge-conditioned update model $\Sigma = \langle \Sigma, \{R_i\}_{i \in \mathcal{AG}}, pre, sub \rangle$, the *update* of M induced by Σ results in a new Kripke structure M', denoted by $M' = M \otimes \Sigma$, defined by: **(i)** $M'[S] = \{(s, \tau) \mid \tau \in \Sigma, s \in M[S], (M, s) \models pre(\tau)\}$; **(ii)** $((s, \tau), (s', \tau')) \in M'[i]$ iff (s, τ),

$(s', \tau') \in M'[S]$, $(s, s') \in M[i]$, $(\tau, \gamma, \tau') \in R_i$ and $(M, s) \models \gamma$; and **(iii)** for all $(s, \tau) \in M'[S]$ and $f \in \mathcal{F}$, $M'[\pi]((s, \tau)) \models f$ if $f \rightarrow \varphi \in sub(\tau)$ and $(M, s) \models \varphi$.

An *update template* is a pair (Σ, Γ), where Σ is an update model with the set of events Σ and $\Gamma \subseteq \Sigma$. The update of a state (M, s) given an update template (Σ, Γ) is a set of states, denoted by $(M, s) \otimes (\Sigma, \Gamma)$, where $(M, s) \otimes (\Sigma, \Gamma) = \{(M \otimes \Sigma, (s, \tau)) \mid \tau \in \Gamma, (M, s) \models pre(\tau)\}$.

Syntax of $m\mathcal{A}^*$. An action theory in the language $m\mathcal{A}^*$ over $\langle \mathcal{AG}, \mathcal{F} \rangle$ consists of a set of action instances $\mathcal{AI}$ of the form $a\langle \alpha \rangle$, representing that a set of agents α performs action a, and a collection of statements of the following forms:

a	**executable_if**	ψ	(1)		a	**announces**	φ	(4)
a	**causes** ℓ **if**	φ	(2)		z	**observes** a **if**	δ_z	(5)
a	**determines**	φ	(3)		z	**aware_of** a **if**	θ_z	(6)

where ℓ is a fluent literal (a fluent $f \in \mathcal{F}$ or its negation $\neg f$), ψ is a belief formula, φ, δ_z and θ_z are fluent formulae, a $\in \mathcal{AI}$, and $z \in \mathcal{AG}$. (1) encodes the executability condition of a. (2) describes the effect of the ontic (i.e., world-changing) action a. (3) enables the agents who execute a to learn the value of the formula φ. (4) encodes an *announcement* action, whose owner announces that φ is true. (5) indicates that agent z is a full observer of a if δ_z holds. (6) states that agent z is a partial observer of a if θ_z holds. It is assumed that the sets of ontic actions, sensing actions, and announcement actions are pairwise disjoint. Furthermore, for every pair of a and z, if z and a occur in a statement of the form (5) then they do not occur in any statement of the form (6) and vice versa. An action domain is a collection of statements (1)–(6). An action theory is a pair of an action domain and a set of statements of the form "**initially** ψ", indicate that ψ is true in the initial state. By this definition, action domains are deterministic in that each ontic action, when executed in a world, results in a unique world.

3   Edge-Conditioned Event Update Models

In this section, we will show how to define the transition function $m\mathcal{A}^*$ using edge-conditioned event update models. We will use Example 1 as a running example to illustrate the application of edge-conditioned event update models. We follow the same notation and rules as in Sect. 2.

Let us denote the multi-agent domain described in Example 1 by D_{coin}. For this domain, we have that $\mathcal{AG} = \{A, B, C\}$. The set of fluents $\mathcal{F}$ for this domain consists of *head* (the coin is heads up), *looking$_x$* (agent x is looking at the box where $x \in \{A, B, C\}$), and *opened* (the box is open). D_{coin} has two actions: *open* and *peek*, that can be represented by the following $m\mathcal{A}^*$ statements:

$$open\langle x\rangle \textbf{ causes } opened \quad (7)$$

$$peek\langle x\rangle \textbf{ executable\_if } opened \quad (8)$$

$$peek\langle x\rangle \textbf{ determines } head \quad (9)$$

$$x \textbf{ observes } open\langle x\rangle \quad (10)$$

$$y \textbf{ observes } open\langle x\rangle \textbf{ if } looking_y \quad (11)$$

$$x \textbf{ observes } peek\langle x\rangle \quad (12)$$

$$y \textbf{ aware\_of } peek\langle x\rangle \textbf{ if } looking_y \quad (13)$$

where $x, y \in \{A, B, C\}$ and $x \neq y$.

Initially, the coin is heads up, the box is closed and A, B are looking at it; however, B thinks that all three agents are looking at the box. The initial state (M_0, s_0) of D_{coin} is on the left of Fig. 1. Suppose that agent A would like to know whether the coin lies heads or tails up. She would also like to let agent B know that she knows this fact. However, she would like to make B also thinks that agent C is aware of this fact. Intuitively, because B has already believed that C is looking at the box, agent A could achieve her goals by: (1) opening the box; and then (2) peeking into the box.

Observe that under the current semantics of m$\mathcal{A}^*$ [4], A could not achieve her goal by executing the above sequence of actions. This is because B believes that C does not know that the box is open (as showed in Fig. 1), therefor B would conclude that C is not observing the execution of the action of A opening the box. When A peeks into the box, B reasons that C is still thinking that A knows nothing because, according to B, C still believes that the box is closed. Therefore, B will think that C's belief about A's belief about the state of the coin does not change. This is not intuitive. A more intuitive outcome with respect to B's beliefs after the execution of the plan $[open\langle A\rangle; peek\langle A\rangle]$ is as follows: B should believe that C knows that the box is open and that A knows the value of the coin after the execution of the plan.

The main reason for the above inadequacy of m$\mathcal{A}^*$ lies in the fact that the construction of the update models in m$\mathcal{A}^*$ assumes that full observers have the correct observability of *all agents,* which is not the case for B, who is a full observer, and C: B believes that C is a full observer while C is not. One possible way to address the above issue is to create different update models, whose set of events depends on the effects of actions, as done in [13], or to define transition functions by directly manipulating the accessibility relations and the worlds in the resulting Kripke structure as in [8]. In this paper, we introduce a different approach to this problem, through the use of edge-conditioned update models.

3.1 Ontic Actions

We assume that an action domain D is given. As in m$\mathcal{A}^*$, we assume that an agent can either observe or not observe the execution of an ontic action, i.e., for an ontic action instance a, there exists no statement of the form (6) whose action is a.

Definition 1 (Ontic Actions). *Let* a *be an ontic action instance with the precondition* ψ. *The update model for* a, *denoted by* $\omega(\mathsf{a})$, *is defined by* $\langle \Sigma, \{R_i\}_{i \in \mathcal{AG}},$ *pre, sub*$\rangle$ *where: (1)* $\Sigma = \{\sigma, \epsilon\}$; *(2)* $R_i = \{(\sigma, \delta_i, \sigma), (\sigma, \neg\delta_i, \epsilon), (\epsilon, \top, \epsilon)\}$ *where*

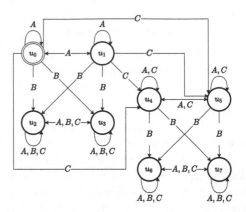

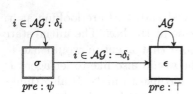

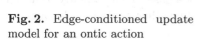

Fig. 2. Edge-conditioned update model for an ontic action

Fig. 3. (M_1, v_0) after A opened the box using edge-conditioned update model

"i **observes** a if δ_i" belongs to D; (3) $pre(\sigma)=\psi$ and $pre(\epsilon)=\top$; and (4) $sub(\epsilon)=\emptyset$ and $sub(\sigma) = \{p \to \Psi^+(p, \mathsf{a}) \vee (p \wedge \neg\Psi^-(p, \mathsf{a})) \mid p \in \mathcal{F}\}$, where $\Psi^+(p, \mathsf{a}) = \bigvee\{\varphi \mid$ [a **causes** p **if** $\varphi]\in D\}$ and $\Psi^-(p, \mathsf{a}) = \bigvee\{\varphi \mid$ [a **causes** $\neg p$ **if** $\varphi]\in D\}$.

When an ontic action occurs, an agent may or may not observe its occurrence. As such, $\omega(\mathsf{a})$ has two events. σ is the designated event representing the true occurrence of the action whereas ϵ denotes the null event representing that the action does not occur. σ is the event full observers believe occurring and ϵ is the event seen by oblivious agents. Figure 2 shows the edge-conditioned update model of an ontic action a. In the figure, we use $i \in X : \delta_i$ as a shorthand for the set of links with labels $\{i : \delta_i \mid i \in X\}$.

Observe that the presence of the condition attached to the link and the definition of the cross product between a Kripke structure and the update model enable a flexible update of the accessibility relations, allowing us to eliminate the problem of the definition in [4]. For example, given a state (M, s), the link $(\sigma, i : \delta_i, \sigma)$ in $\omega(\mathsf{a})$ indicates that $((\sigma, s), i, (\sigma, s))$ is an element in the accessibility relation of i in the state resulting from the execution of a in (M, s) iff $(M, s) \models \delta_i$.

The update induced by the edge-conditioned update model for $open\langle A\rangle$ on the pointed Kripke structure at the left of Fig. 1 is shown in Fig. 3. In this figure, the worlds and their interpretations are the same as in the pointed Kripke structure at the right of Fig. 1. The differences lie in the removal of the links labeled C from u_2/u_3 to u_6/u_7 and the addition of the loops labeled C at u_2/u_3. The loops labeled C at u_2 and u_3, denoting the worlds (s_2, σ) and (s_3, σ), respectively, are added because $(M_0, s_2) \models looking_C$ and $(M_0, s_3) \models looking_C$ hold. This is also the reason for the removal of the links labeled C from u_2 and u_3 to u_6 and u_7.

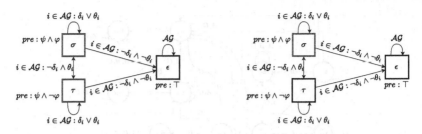

Fig. 4. Edge-conditioned update models for sensing action (left) and truthful announcement Action (right)

3.2 Sensing Actions and Announcement Actions

An agent can either observe, partially observe, or not observe the occurrence of a sensing or announcement action occurrence. Therefore, the update models for sensing or announcement actions are different from that of update models for ontic actions. They are defined as follows.

Definition 2 (Sensing and Announcement Actions). *Let* a *be a sensing action instance that senses* φ *or an announcement action instance that announces* φ *with the precondition* ψ. *The update model for* a, *denoted by* $\omega(\mathsf{a})$, *is defined by* $\langle \Sigma, \{R_i\}_{i \in \mathcal{AG}}, pre, sub \rangle$ *where: (1)* $\Sigma = \{\sigma, \tau, \epsilon\}$; *(2)* $R_i = \{(\sigma, \delta_i \vee \theta_i, \sigma), (\tau, \delta_i \vee \theta_i, \tau), (\sigma, \neg\delta_i \wedge \theta_i, \tau), (\tau, \neg\delta_i \wedge \theta_i, \sigma), (\sigma, \neg\delta_i \wedge \neg\theta_i, \epsilon), (\tau, \neg\delta_i \wedge \neg\theta_i, \epsilon), (\epsilon, \top, \epsilon)\}$ *where "i* **observes** *a if* δ_i" *and "i* **aware_of** *a if* θ_i" *belong to* D; *(3)* $pre(\sigma) = \psi \wedge \varphi$, $pre(\tau) = \psi \wedge \neg\varphi$ *and* $pre(\epsilon) = \top$; *and (4)* $sub(x) = \emptyset$ *for each* $x \in \Sigma$.

Observe that an update model of a sensing or announcement action instance has three events. However in sensing actions, the true event can be σ or τ whereas in announcement actions, the true event is σ. As for ontic actions, ϵ is the "null event" representing that the action does not occur. Sensing and announcement actions do not alter the state of the world and thus *sub* is empty for every event. Figure 4 illustrates the edge-conditioned update model for an announcement a that truthfully announces φ (right) and a sensing action a that determines φ (left).

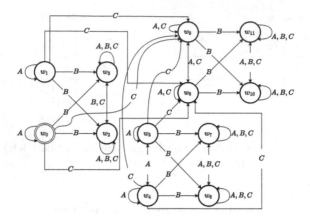

Fig. 5. (M_2, w_0) after A peeked into the box

The application of the edge-conditioned update model for $peek\langle A\rangle$ in the state (M_1, u_0) from Fig. 3 is given in Fig. 5. In this figure, w_0-w_3 have the same interpretation as u_0-u_3; and w_4-w_{11} have the same interpretation as u_0-u_7. Observe that A now achieves her goals: not only does A realize that the coin lies head up $((M_2, w_0) \models \mathbf{B}_A head)$ but B also believes that C knows the fact that A knows the value of the coin now $((M_2, w_0) \models \mathbf{B}_B\mathbf{B}_C(\mathbf{B}_A head \lor \mathbf{B}_A \neg head))$. This example shows that the use of edge-conditioned update models enables $\mathsf{m}\mathcal{A}^*$ to avoid the side problem discussed in [4].

Having defined the update models for actions in a multi-agent domain D, we can define the transition function Φ_D in D in the similar fashion as in [4]. We omit the details for brevity.

3.3   Properties of Edge-Conditioned Update Models

The use of edge-conditioned update models enables the modification of the semantics of $\mathsf{m}\mathcal{A}^*$ that takes into consideration the observability of the agents at the local level. A consequence of this treatment is that the belief of an agent i about the belief of another agent j with respect to the action occurrence will change in accordance to the belief of i about j before. The following proposition indicates these properties of edge-conditioned update models.

Proposition 1. *Let (M, s) be a state and a be an ontic action instance that is executable in (M, s) and $\omega(\mathsf{a})$ be given in Definition 1. It holds that:*

1. *For every agent $x \in \mathcal{AG}$, $[x$ **observes** a **if** $\delta_x]$ and $[\mathsf{a}$ **causes** ℓ **if** $\varphi]$ belong to D, if $(M, s) \models \delta_x$, $(M, s) \models \mathbf{B}_x\varphi$ and $(M', s') = (M, s) \otimes (\omega(\mathsf{a}), \sigma)$ then $(M', s') \models \mathbf{B}_x\ell$.*

2. *For every pair of agents $x, y \in \mathcal{AG}$, $[\mathsf{a}$ **causes** ℓ **if** $\varphi]$, $[x$ **observes** a **if** $\delta_x]$ and $[y$ **observes** a **if** $\delta_y]$ belong to D, if $(M, s) \models \delta_x$, $(M, s) \models \mathbf{B}_x\delta_y$, $(M, s) \models \mathbf{B}_x\mathbf{B}_y\varphi$ and $(M', s') = (M, s) \otimes (\omega(\mathsf{a}), \sigma)$ then $(M', s') \models \mathbf{B}_x\mathbf{B}_y\ell$.*

3. *For every pair of agents $x, y \in \mathcal{AG}$, a belief formula η, $[x$ **observes** a **if** $\delta_x]$ and $[y$ **observes** a **if** $\delta_y]$ belong to D, if $(M, s) \models \delta_x$, $(M, s) \models \mathbf{B}_x \neg \delta_y$, $(M, s) \models \mathbf{B}_x \mathbf{B}_y \eta$ and $(M', s') = (M, s) \otimes (\omega(\mathsf{a}), \sigma)$ then $(M', s') \models \mathbf{B}_x \mathbf{B}_y \eta$.*

Proof. All proofs are omitted for lack of space and detailed in [12].

The second and third item of Proposition 1 show that a full observer will update her beliefs about another agent's beliefs, if she thinks that the agent is also a full observer, or her own beliefs about the other agent will not change if she believes that such agent is unaware of the action occurrence. These two items do not hold w.r.t. the old semantics of m$\mathcal{A}^*$. Similar propositions can be established for sensing/announcement actions and can be found in [12].

4   Discussion and Related Work

Update models have been used in formalizing actions in multi-agent domains by several authors [1,2,5,6,9,11]. However, the automatic generation of update models from an action description has only been discussed with the introduction of actions languages for multi-agent domains in [3] and subsequent versions of languages like m$\mathcal{A}^*$. To the best of our knowledge, the present work is among the first that attempts to use edge-conditioned update models, introduced by [7], in an action language. As shown in Proposition 1, the use of edge-conditioned update models eliminates the problem encountered by earlier semantics of m$\mathcal{A}^*$. We note that [7] discussed only edge-conditioned update models for world-altering actions (ontic actions), while we use it in modeling other types of actions as well.

The use of event models for reasoning about effects of actions in multi-agent domains is also studied in [13] within the language DER. In this language, the observability of agents is encoded by an observations set $\mathcal{O}$ and no distinction between ontic, sensing, and announcement actions is made. Comparing with the update models used in [13], we can see that updated models used in the present paper have a fixed number of events, given the type of the action: two events for ontic actions and three events for sensing/announcement actions. On the other hand, the number of events in DER can vary given the number of statements specifying its effects and observations. We believe that this feature might bring some advantages if update models are used for planning, where efficient construction of update models is critical (in the new m$\mathcal{A}^*$, the model need to be constructed only once).

5   Conclusion

We define a new semantics for the high-level action language m$\mathcal{A}^*$ using edge-conditioned update models. In this method, edge-conditioned update models are constructed directly from the domain specification and are independent from the states in which the action occurs. We prove that the new semantics satisfies a desirable property that second order beliefs of agents about other agents' beliefs change consistently with its first-order beliefs about observability of action occurrence, i.e., it overcomes a problem of the earlier semantics of $m\mathcal{A}^*$. This overcomes a limitation of the earlier version of $m\mathcal{A}^*$, which requires a careful domain design for dealing with certain types of questions as described in [4].

Acknowledgments. The authors have been partially supported by NSF grants 2151254, 1914635 and 1757207. Tran Cao Son was also partially supported by NSF grant 1812628.

References

1. Baltag, A., Moss, L.: Logics for epistemic programs. Synthese **139**, 165–224 (2004)
2. Baltag, A., Moss, L., Solecki, S.: The logic of public announcements, common knowledge, and private suspicions. In: 7th TARK, pp. 43–56 (1998)
3. Baral, C., Gelfond, G., Pontelli, E., Son, T.C.: Reasoning about the beliefs of agents in multi-agent domains in the presence of state constraints: the action language mAL. In: Leite, J., Son, T.C., Torroni, P., van der Torre, L., Woltran, S. (eds.) CLIMA 2013. LNCS (LNAI), vol. 8143, pp. 290–306. Springer, Heidelberg (2013). https://doi.org/10.1007/978-3-642-40624-9_18
4. Baral, C., Gelfond, G., Pontelli, E., Son, T.C.: An action language for multi-agent domains. Artif. Intell. **302**, 103601 (2022)
5. van Benthem, J., van Eijck, J., Kooi, B.P.: Logics of communication and change. Inf. Comput. **204**(11), 1620–1662 (2006)
6. Bolander, T., Andersen, M.: Epistemic planning for single and multi-agent systems. J. Appl. Non-Classical Logics **21**(1), 9–34 (2011)
7. Bolander, T.: Seeing is believing: formalising false-belief tasks in dynamic epistemic logic. In: van Ditmarsch, H., Sandu, G. (eds.) Jaakko Hintikka on Knowledge and Game-Theoretical Semantics. OCL, vol. 12, pp. 207–236. Springer, Cham (2018). https://doi.org/10.1007/978-3-319-62864-6_8
8. Buckingham, D., Kasenberg, D., Scheutz, M.: Simultaneous representation of knowledge and belief for epistemic planning with belief revision, pp. 172–181 (2020)
9. van Ditmarsch, H., van der Hoek, W., Kooi, B.: Dynamic Epistemic Logic, 1st edn. Springer, Heidelberg (2007). https://doi.org/10.1007/978-1-4020-5839-4
10. Fagin, R., Halpern, J., Moses, Y., Vardi, M.: Reasoning About Knowledge. MIT press, Cambridge (1995)
11. Löwe, B., Pacuit, E., Witzel, A.: DEL planning and some tractable cases. In: van Ditmarsch, H., Lang, J., Ju, S. (eds.) LORI 2011. LNCS (LNAI), vol. 6953, pp. 179–192. Springer, Heidelberg (2011). https://doi.org/10.1007/978-3-642-24130-7_13
12. Pham, L., Izmirlioglu, Y., Son, T.C., Pontelli, E.: A new semantics for the action language ma*. Technical report, NMSU (2022). https://github.com/phhuuloc/New-semantic-mAstar
13. Rajaratnam, D., Thielscher, M.: Representing and reasoning with event models for epistemic planning. In: Proceedings of the 18th International Conference on Principles of Knowledge Representation and Reasoning, pp. 519–528 (11 2021)

Coalition Logic for Specification and Verification of Smart Contract Upgrades

Rustam Galimullin[1]([✉])(iD) and Thomas Ågotnes[1,2]

[1] University of Bergen, Bergen, Norway
[2] Southwest University, Chongqing, China
{rustam.galimullin,thomas.agotnes}@uib.no

Abstract. It has been argued in the literature that logics for reasoning about strategic abilities, and in particular coalition logic (CL), are well-suited for verification of properties of smart contracts on a blockchain. Smart contracts, however, can be upgraded by providing a new version of a contract on a new block. In this paper, we extend one of the recent formalisms for reasoning about updating CL models with a temporal modality connecting a newer version of a model to the previous one. In such a way, we make a step towards verification of properties of smart contracts with upgrades. We also discuss some properties of the resulting logic and the complexity of its model checking problem.

Keywords: Coalition logic · Smart contracts · Blockchain · Model checking

1 Introduction

Smart Contracts. Smart contracts (SCs) [3, Chapter 7] are programs, usually written in a high-level programming language like Solidity [1], that are stored on a blockchain [17] and executed by nodes of a given distributed ledger. Probably the most well-known blockchain that supports storing and execution of SCs is Ethereum [20]. Since SCs are stored on a blockchain, once deployed, they are immutable. This, however, does not necessarily mean that SCs cannot be amended, in the case of critical bugs, or upgraded. There are several ways to upgrade SCs, including using a separate contract as a proxy, and splitting one contract into several smaller ones. In this paper, we do not discriminate between different ways of upgrading SCs, and focus on upgrades themselves.

Verification and Specification of Smart Contracts. Logic-based verification of blockchain systems and SCs is a nascent field (see a recent survey [19]). For example, authors of [11] use a classic runs-and-system approach to analyse the notion of consensus on a blockchain from an epistemic perspective. A logic for reasoning about blockchain updates was presented in [4], where the authors

R. Aydoğan et al. (Eds.): PRIMA 2022, LNAI 13753, pp. 563–572, 2023.
https://doi.org/10.1007/978-3-031-21203-1_34

follow the lead of *dynamic epistemic logic* (DEL) [6]. In [14] a variant of temporal logic is used to focus on properties of a blockchain in a permissionless setting.

It is argued in [15,16] that logics for reasoning about abilities of agents, in particular *coalition logic* (CL) [18] and ATL [2], have great potential for verification of properties of SCs. However, none of the proposed logical approaches allows one to reason about upgrades of SCs.

One conceptual difficulty we have to overcome is that in the context of blockchains we can have several iterations of an SC recorded on several blocks. New iterations may come about as updates of a contract triggered by new financial policies or amendments to the existing features. This highlights the fact that SCs on a blockchain allow for *introspection* [12]: it is possible to reason about current properties of a contract based on its earlier versions.

To the best of our knowledge, the only extension of CL or ATL that allows for updating agents' abilities is a recently introduced *dictatorial dynamic coalition logic* (DDCL) [7]. DDCL follows the paradigm which is pretty much ubiquitous in DEL: *model + update = updated model*. As its name suggests, DDCL can express updating dictatorial powers of single agents either by granting such powers or revoking them.

Contribution of the Paper . In Sect. 2.1 we present an extension of DDCL with temporal 'yesterday' relations between a model and the corresponding updated model. Moreover, we consider chain models that are a natural extension of the 'model → updated model' approach. Introduced temporal relations refer to a previous version of a contract, thus adding introspection to the setting. After that, in Sect. 2.2, we tackle the model checking problem of the introduced logic by showing that it is P-complete. We conclude in Sect. 3.

2   Reasoning About Abilities of Agents on Chain Models

In this section we first introduce *temporal DDCL* (TDDCL), which is an extension of DDCL [7], and then study the complexity of its model checking problem.

2.1   Syntax and Semantics

Let P be a countable set of *propositional variables*, and A be a finite set of *agents*. Subsets C of A are called *coalitions*.

Definition 1. *The language* $\mathcal{TDDCL}$ *is given by the following BNF:*

$$\mathcal{TDDCL} \ni \varphi \ ::= p \mid \neg\varphi \mid (\varphi \wedge \varphi) \mid \Diamond\varphi \mid \langle\!\langle C \rangle\!\rangle\varphi \mid [+U]\varphi \mid [-U]\varphi$$
$$+U ::= (\varphi, a, \varphi)^+ \mid (\varphi, a, \varphi)^+, +U$$
$$-U ::= (\varphi, a, \varphi)^- \mid (\varphi, a, \varphi)^-, -U$$

where $p \in P$, $a \in A$, $C \subseteq A$. *The duals are defined as* $[C]\varphi := \neg\langle\!\langle C \rangle\!\rangle\neg\varphi$, $\langle+U\rangle\varphi := \neg[+U]\neg\varphi$, $\langle-U\rangle\varphi := \neg[-U]\neg\varphi$, *and* $\Box\varphi := \neg\Diamond\neg\varphi$.

Formulas of the form $\langle\langle C \rangle\rangle \varphi$ are read as 'coalition C can force φ', and expressions $\Diamond\varphi$ mean that 'φ is the case in the previous version of a contract'. Constructs $+U$ are called *positive updates*, and formulas $[+U]\varphi$ are read as 'after (positive) update $+U$, φ is true'. Constructs $-U$ are called *negative updates*, and formulas $[-U]\varphi$ are read as 'after (negative) update $-U$, φ is true'[1].

The fragment of $\mathcal{TDDCL}$ with only positive updates is $\mathcal{TDDCL}^+$; the fragment with only negative updates is $\mathcal{TDDCL}^-$. The *language of positive DDCL* $\mathcal{DDCL}^+$ is obtained from $\mathcal{TDDCL}$ by omitting $[-U]\varphi$ and $\Diamond\varphi$, and the *language of negative DDCL* $\mathcal{DDCL}^-$ is obtained from $\mathcal{TDDCL}$ by omitting $[+U]\varphi$ and $\Diamond\varphi$. Finally, the fragment of $\mathcal{TDDCL}$ that excludes updates and $\Diamond\varphi$ is called *coalition logic* $\mathcal{CL}$ [18].

Formulas of $\mathcal{TDDCL}$ are interpreted on *chain models* that, in turn, are sequences of *concurrent game models*.

Definition 2. *A concurrent game model (CGM), or a model, is a tuple $M = (S, Act, act, out, L)$ consisting of the following elements:*

- *S is a non-empty set of states, and Act is a non-empty set of actions.*
- *Function $act : A \times S \to 2^{Act} \setminus \emptyset$ assigns to each agent and each state a non-empty set of actions. A C-action at a state $s \in S$ is a tuple α_C such that $\alpha_C(i) \in act(i, s)$ for all $i \in C$. The set of all C-actions in s is denoted by $act(C, s)$. We will also write $\alpha_{C_1} \cup \alpha_{C_2}$ to denote a $C_1 \cup C_2$-action with $C_1 \cap C_2 = \emptyset$.*
  A tuple of actions $\alpha = \langle \alpha_1, \ldots, \alpha_k \rangle$ with $k =\mid A \mid$ is called an action profile. An action profile is executable in state s if for all $i \in A$, $\alpha_i \in act(i, s)$. The set of all action profiles executable in s is denoted by $act(s)$. An action profile α extends a C-action α_C, written $\alpha_C \sqsubseteq \alpha$, if for all $i \in C$, $\alpha(i) = \alpha_C(i)$.
- *Function out assigns to each state s and each $\alpha \in act(s)$ a unique output state.*
- *$L : S \to 2^P$ is the valuation function.*

We will denote a CGM M with a designated, or current, state s as (M, s). Also, we will use superscript M to refer to elements of the corresponding tuple.

Example 1. Consider model M_1 in Fig. 1 on page 5. In the vein of [15, 16] we can think of CGMs as abstract descriptions of contracts specifying what participating parties can and cannot achieve. For the sake of the example, let agents a, b, and c be directors of a company. State s then corresponds to agents discussing whether they should issue stock options. The only way for stock options to be issued is by a and b agreeing to do so (choosing actions a_1 and b_1). All other agents' decisions lead to them staying in the discussion phase. Also observe that agent c does not influence the decision. If a and b agree on issuing stock options (action profile $a_1b_1c_0$), the system transitions to state t meaning that the options has been issued. From this state, agents can either return to the discussion phase (action profile $a_1b_1c_0$) or continue issuing options (all other action profiles).

---

[1] We will sometime use U to denote both positive and negative updates.

In the model, we have that no agent can force p on their own, written as $(\mathcal{C}_1, M_1, s) \models [\![a]\!]\neg p \wedge [\![b]\!]\neg p \wedge [\![c]\!]\neg p$. At the same time, a coalition consisting of agents a and b can force a state satisfying p (by choosing actions a_1 and b_1) since agent c has no action to preclude such a transition: $(\mathcal{C}_1, M_1, s) \models \langle\!\langle\{a, b\}\rangle\!\rangle p$.

Updates allow us to modify a CGM by adding or removing action profiles. Given a positive update $+U$ and a CGM M, we denote *updated* CGM as M^{+U}. Similarly, we write M^{-U} in the case of a negative update $-U$.

Unfortunately, due to the lack of space, we cannot present formal definitions for updated CGMs, and instead resort to intuitive explanations and examples. Since the particularities of such updates are not the focus of this work, we believe that this omission does not hinder the readability of the paper. For definitions and details the interested reader is referred to [7,9].

To provide the intuition behind updates, we first define forcing actions, i.e. actions that allow a particular single agent to force a specific outcome no matter which actions other agents choose. Formally, the set of *forcing actions* for agent i and state s, denoted as $\mathfrak{f}(i, s)$, is $\{\alpha_i \in act(i, s) \mid \forall \alpha, \beta \in act(s) : (\alpha_i \sqsubseteq \alpha$ and $\alpha_i \sqsubseteq \beta)$ implies $out(\alpha, s) = out(\beta, s)\}$.

Now, the intuition behind $[+U]\varphi$ is as follows. Each $(\varphi, a, \psi)^+$ specifies between which states agent a will be granted a *new* forcing action. In case if multiple states satisfy φ or ψ, agent a will have a new action for each pair of states. Negative updates, on the other hand, specify between which states forcing actions should be *preserved*. In other words, if agent a has a forcing action from a state satisfying φ to a state satisfying ψ, then they will retain the action if triple $(\varphi, a, \psi)^-$ appears in $-U$, and lose it otherwise.

Example 2. Consider once again CGM M_1 depicted in Fig. 1. Assume that the initial version of the contract has led to a and b abusing their power and issuing stock options (staying in state t) without ever discussing it (not transitioning to state s). To mitigate this, a new policy has been issued: agent c should decide whether the company continues issuing stock options or enters a discussion state. Moreover, the new policy also requires that agent a's decision is enough to issue stock. Such a policy can be described by update $+U^1 = \{(\neg p, a, p)^+, (p, c, \neg p)^+\}$. The result of updating the existing contract with this new policy is model M_2. In M_2 we indeed have that in all $\neg p$-states (state s) agent a has a new forcing action a_2 to force p-states (state t). Similarly, agent c now has a new forcing action c_1 to force state s from state t. We thus have that $(\mathcal{C}_1, M_1, t) \models \langle\!\langle\{a, b\}\rangle\!\rangle p \wedge [+U^1][\![\{a, b\}]\!]\neg p$ meaning that in state t of CGM M_1 a coalition of agents a and b can force a p state, but after update $+U^1$ they lose such a power.

As a result of the update, model M_2 has the following non-empty sets of forcing actions: $\mathfrak{f}(a, s) = \{a_2\}$ and $\mathfrak{f}(c, t) = \{c_1\}$. Continuing with the company setting, assume that the next policy was to revoke the ability of agent c to force the discussion phase (state s) from the state of issuing stocks (state t). Such a policy can be represented by a negative update $-U^2 = \{(\neg p, a, p)^-\}$ where triple $(\neg p, a, p)^-$ prescribes to preserve a's power to force a p-state from a $\neg p$-state. Since there are no more triples in $-U^2$, we remove all other forcing actions and corresponding action profiles. The result of updating M_2 with $-U^2$ is M_3, where there is only forcing action left is $f(a, s) = \{a_2\}$. Observe that action profiles containing c_1 were removed from the model. Formally, it holds that $(\mathcal{C}_1, M_2, t) \models \langle\!\langle c \rangle\!\rangle \neg p \wedge [-U^2][\![c]\!]p$ meaning that in state t of CGM M_2, agent c can force $\neg p$, but after negative update $-U^2$ she loses such an ability.

Definition 3. *A* minimal chain model $\mathcal{C}$ *is a pair* $(\mathcal{M}, \leftsquigarrow)$, *where* $\mathcal{M}$ *is a non-empty set of CGMs, and* $\leftsquigarrow$ *is a possibly empty relation between* $S^M \times S^N$, *where M and N are CGMs such that* $M, N \in \mathcal{M}$. *A minimal chain model with a designated state s of CGM M is denoted by* $(\mathcal{C}, M, s)$.

Definition 4. *Let* $\mathcal{C} = (\mathcal{M}, \leftsquigarrow)$ *be a minimal chain model,* $M \in \mathcal{M}$ *be a CGM, and U be an update. The result of executing U in CGM M on* $\mathcal{C}$ *is* $\mathcal{C}^U = (\mathcal{M}^U, \leftsquigarrow^U)$, *which we call* updated minimal chain model, *where* $\mathcal{M}^U = \mathcal{M} \cup \{M^U\}$, *and* $\leftsquigarrow^U = \leftsquigarrow \cup \{(s, s) \mid \pi_1((s, s)) \in S^M \text{ and } \pi_2((s, s)) \in S^{M^U}\}^2$.

Updating a model M in a minimal chain model $\mathcal{C}$ adds updated CGM M^U to $\mathcal{C}$ and connects each state of M^U with a corresponding state of M with temporal relation $\leftsquigarrow$ (represented by dashed arrows in Fig. 1).

Example 3. The previously considered examples of positive and negative updates in Fig. 1 can be viewed now as a single chain structure. CGM M_1 can be considered as an initial version of an SC. After incorporating new policy $+U^1$, a new version of the contract, M_2, is added to the initial one. The two contracts

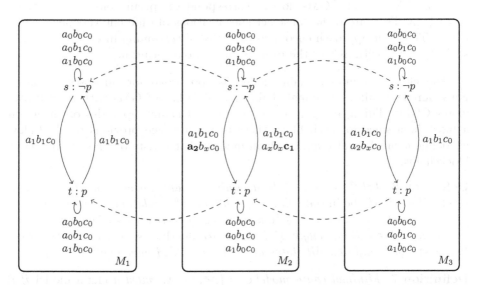

Fig. 1. Chain model $\mathcal{C}_1$ consisting of CGMs M_1, M_2, and M_3. Dashed arrows represent temporal relations, and bold actions depict new action profiles required by an update. Symbol x stands for elements of $\{0, 1\}$.

---

[2] π_1 and π_2 are left and right projections of an ordered pair.

are now also connected by a temporal relation such that M_1 is reachable from M_2. Adding a third version M_3 as a result of updating M_2 with $-U^2$ makes the chain longer So, having the latest version of a contract, M_3, we can express, for example, that now agent a can on her own force the company to issue stocks (transition to state t) while it was not possible two iterations of the contract ago. Formally, $(C_1, M_3, s) \models \langle\langle a \rangle\rangle p \wedge \Diamond\Diamond\neg\langle\langle a \rangle\rangle p$, where C_1 refers to the whole chain, and M_3 refers to the third version of the contract.

Upgrading smart contracts in the blockchain setting preserves history i.e. updating a chain model does not alter the already existing CGMs and their order. Thus, we can reason introspectively about the *evolution* of a smart contract.

Definition 5. *Let (C, M, s) be a pointed minimal chain model. The semantics of TDDCL are defined recursively as follows, where Boolean cases are omitted:*

$$(C, M, s) \models \Diamond\varphi \quad \text{iff } \exists N \in M, t \in S^N : t \rightsquigarrow s \text{ and } (C, N, t) \models \varphi$$
$$(C, M, s) \models \langle\langle C \rangle\rangle\varphi \text{ iff } \exists\alpha_C, \forall\alpha_{\overline{C}} : (C, M, t) \models \varphi, \text{ where } t = out(s, \alpha_C \cup \alpha_{\overline{C}})$$
$$(C, M, s) \models [+U]\varphi \text{ iff } +U \text{ is executable in } M \text{ implies } (C^{+U}, M^{+U}, s) \models \varphi$$
$$(C, M, s) \models [-U]\varphi \text{ iff } -U \text{ is executable in } M \text{ implies } (C^{-U}, M^{-U}, s) \models \varphi$$

We call a formula φ valid if for all (C, M, s) it holds that $(C, M, s) \models \varphi$.

The *executability* condition in the above definition stems from the fact that not all updates can be executed. More on this in [7].

Remark 1. Note that CGMs do *not* correspond to specific blocks on a given blockchain. They are rather abstract specifications of different versions of contracts. Thus, our approach encompasses *software versioning* in general. We will stick, however, with SCs as the prime source of our intuitions.

The class of minimal chain models is too broad for purposes at hand. For example, it allows minimal chain models to have CGMs with several previoius CGMs. This goes against the intuition of having upgrades of an SC on a blockchain since for each block there is at most one previous block. Below we define a subclass of minimal chain models that satisfy our intuitions about blockchains.

Definition 6. *Let $C = (M, \rightsquigarrow)$ be a minimal chain model, and $M \in \mathcal{M}$ be a CGM. We call M the initial CGM if for all $s \in S^M$, relation $\rightsquigarrow$ is empty.*

Let $\ldots \rightsquigarrow t_1 \rightsquigarrow \ldots \rightsquigarrow t_n \rightsquigarrow s$ be a sequence of $\rightsquigarrow$-relations of maximal length ending in s. We call the length of the sequence depth of s, and write $d(s)$. Note that $d(s)$ can be infinite. All states in the initial CGM have depth 0.

Definition 7. *Minimal chain model $C = (M, \rightsquigarrow)$ is called a chain model if it satisfies the following properties.*

1. The initial CGM: *there is a single $M \in \mathcal{M}$ such that M is the initial CGM.*
2. CGM-definedness: *for all states s, t, and u, if $t \rightsquigarrow s$ and $u \rightsquigarrow s$, then $t = u$. In other words, for each state in a CGM there is only one previous state.*

3. Depth-definedness: $d(s) \neq \infty$ for all s.
4. Valuation preservation: for all states s and t belonging to some M and N, if $s \leftrightsquigarrow t$, then $s \in L^M(p)$ if and only if $t \in L^N(p)$. The property reflects that updates do not change valuations of propositional variables.
5. Update-definedness: for all $s \in S^M$, $t \in S^N$, if $s \leftrightsquigarrow t$, then there is a U s.t. $M^U = N$. Each new CGM is a result of updating the previous one.

Depth-definedness implies *acyclicity* and *irreflexivity* of $\leftrightsquigarrow$. On the other hand, depth-definedness does not imply finiteness. Indeed, our chain models are, in fact, tree-like, and thus they allow a possibly infinite number of children at a given node. Moreover, *intransitivity* of $\leftrightsquigarrow$ follows from irreflexivity and CGM-definedness. Also note that both chain and minimal chain models do not allow agents to force transitions between different blocks (the *synchronicity* property).

Theorem 1. *Let $\mathcal{C} = (\mathcal{M}, \leftrightsquigarrow)$ be a chain model, and let U be an update. The result $\mathcal{C}^U$ of updating $\mathcal{C}$ with U is a chain model.*

Proposition 1. *The following formulas are valid on chain models.*

$$1. \Diamond(\varphi \wedge \psi) \leftrightarrow \Diamond\varphi \wedge \Diamond\psi \qquad 2. \neg\Diamond\varphi \leftrightarrow \Diamond\neg\varphi \qquad 3. \varphi \rightarrow [U]\Diamond\varphi$$

The first formula expresses the property that there is only one previous CGM. The second property states that $\Diamond$ is its own dual. Observe that the first two items are not valid on minimal chain models. Finally, the third validity shows that adding a new CGM does not change the existing CGMs.

2.2 Model Checking

The model checking problem for DDCL$^+$ and DDCL$^-$ is investigated in [9], where it is shown to be P-complete for both logics. The provided algorithms label each state of a given model by a subformula of a given formula. The labelling is inspired by the classic model checking algorithm for CTL [5]. There are two separate algorithms, one for DDCL$^+$ and one for DDCL$^-$, because it is not yet clear how we can combine positive and negative updates in such a way that the resulting complexity is still in P. Thus, we will present extentions of the algorithms from [9] so that they work with formulas of $\mathcal{TDDCL}^+$ and $\mathcal{TDDCL}^-$.

Given a formula φ we organise the list of its subformulas in such a way that formulas within updates are evaluated before formulas that are in the scope of these updates. It allows us to know the effect of an update before we have to evaluate formulas that are affected by the update. As an example, consider formula $\varphi := [(q, b, \neg q)^+]\Diamond p$ with $+U^1 := (q, b, \neg q)^+$. The ordered labelled list $sub(\varphi)$ looks as follows: q, $\neg q$, $(p)^{+U^1}$, $(\Diamond p)^{+U^1}$, $[(q, b, \neg q)^+]\Diamond p$.

Algorithm 1. An algorithm for global TDDCL$^+$ model checking

---

1: **procedure** GLOBALTDDCL$^+(\mathcal{C}, M, \varphi)$
2:     **for all** $\psi^\sigma \in sub(\varphi)$ **do**
3:         **for all** $M \in \mathcal{M}$ **do**
4:             **for all** $s \in S^M$ **do**
5:                 **case** $\psi^\sigma = (\Diamond\chi)^\sigma$
6:                     **if** there is a t such that $t \leftsquigarrow s$ and t is labelled with χ^σ **then**
7:                         label s with $(\Diamond\chi)^\sigma$
8: **end procedure**

Algorithm 1 is a modification of the corresponding algorithm for DDCL$^+$. The main idea behind it is that while checking $\psi^\sigma = (\langle\!\langle C \rangle\!\rangle\chi)^\sigma$, we need to 'model' the effects of positive updates $+U$. To do this we check for each update in σ, starting from the last one, whether it affected agents from C.

Compared to the algorithm for DDCL$^+$, GLOBALTDDCL$^+$ has an additional loop over CGMs in the given blockchain model $\mathcal{C}$ (line 3), and an additional case for $(\Diamond\chi)^\sigma$ (lines 5–7). All other case are the same as in [9] and we omit them. It is clear Algorithm 1 follows the semantics, and thus its correctness can be shown by the induction on φ. Moreover, the case for $(\Diamond\chi)^\sigma$ takes polynomial time.

Theorem 2. *Complexity of TDDCL$^+$ model checking problem is P-complete.*

Model checking TDDCL$^-$ is similar to model checking TDDCL$^+$. It also requires preparation of list $sub(\varphi)$ with the only difference that now after we are done with labelling subformulas within update $-U$, we include $-U$ in the list right after the subformulas. For example, having a formula $\varphi := [(q, b, \neg q)^-]\Diamond p$ with $-U^1 := (q, b, \neg q)^+$, the ordered labelled list $sub(\varphi)$ looks as follows: $q, \neg q,$ $-U^1, (p)^{+U^1}, (\Diamond p)^{+U^1}, [(q, b, \neg q)^+]\Diamond p$.

The model checking algorithm for TDDCL$^-$ is a modification of the one for DDCL$^-$ exactly in the same way as in Algorithm 1. To model negative updates, the DDCL$^-$ algorithm marks action profiles with a sequence of negative updates meaning that the corresponding action profile has been preserved after these updates. Similarly to GLOBALTDDCL$^+$, case $(\Diamond\chi)^\sigma$ takes polynomial time.

Theorem 3. *Complexity of TDDCL$^-$ model checking problem is P-complete.*

3 Conclusion

We presented TDDCL, a logic that allows us to reason about SC upgrades in the blockchain setting: we considered its properties and the model checking problem. Since this is a first step towards specification of SCs on a blockchain, there is a plethora of open problems.

First, our model checking algorithm works with fragments of $\mathcal{TDDCL}$, either with the positive or negative version. So far, it is not clear how one can combine both types of updates while maintaining polynomial time complexity. In the future, we would like to provide a general algorithm and implement it as an extension of one the tools for strategic logics (e.g. MCMAS [13], MCK [10]).

Updates of CGMs in our case are restricted to granting and revoking dictatorial powers of single agents. Finding other, more general, ways of updating SCs is an exciting avenue of further research. An approach we find most tempting is incorporating chain structures to a recent dynamic CL with action models [8]. Similar goals can be set out for base languages that are more expressive than CL, like ATL and ATL*.

References

1. Solidity programming language. https://soliditylang.org, Accessed 20 Jan 2022
2. Alur, R., Henzinger, T.A., Kupferman, O.: Alternating-time temporal logic. J. ACM **49**, 672–713 (2002). https://doi.org/10.1145/585265.585270
3. Antonopoulos, A.M., Wood, G.: Mastering Ethereum. O'Reilly, Newton (2018)
4. Brünnler, K., Flumini, D., Studer, T.: A logic of blockchain updates. J. Logic Comput. **30**(8), 1469–1485 (2020). https://doi.org/10.1093/logcom/exaa045
5. Clarke, E.M., Emerson, E.A.: Design and synthesis of synchronization skeletons using branching time temporal logic. In: Kozen, D. (ed.) Logic of Programs 1981. LNCS, vol. 131, pp. 52–71. Springer, Heidelberg (1982). https://doi.org/10.1007/BFb0025774
6. van Ditmarsch, H., van der Hoek, W., Kooi, B.: Dynamic Epistemic Logic, Synthese Library, vol. 337. Springer, Heidelberg (2008). https://doi.org/10.1007/978-1-4020-5839-4
7. Galimullin, R., Ågotnes, T.: Dynamic coalition logic: granting and revoking dictatorial powers. In: Ghosh, S., Icard, T. (eds.) LORI 2021. LNCS, vol. 13039, pp. 88–101. Springer, Cham (2021). https://doi.org/10.1007/978-3-030-88708-7_7
8. Galimullin, R., Ågotnes, T.: Action models for coalition logic. In: Proceedings of the 4th DaLí (2022). (to appear)
9. Galimullin, R., Ågotnes, T.: Dictatorial dynamic coalition logic. Manuscript. Submitted to a journal (2022). https://rgalimullin.gitlab.io/DDCL/ddcldraft.pdf
10. Gammie, P., van der Meyden, R.: MCK: model checking the logic of knowledge. In: Alur, R., Peled, D.A. (eds.) CAV 2004. LNCS, vol. 3114, pp. 479–483. Springer, Heidelberg (2004). https://doi.org/10.1007/978-3-540-27813-9_41
11. Halpern, J.Y., Pass, R.: A knowledge-based analysis of the blockchain protocol. In: Lang, J. (ed.) Proceedings of the 16th TARK. EPTCS, vol. 251, pp. 324–335 (2017). https://doi.org/10.4204/EPTCS.251.22
12. Herlihy, M., Moir, M.: Blockchains and the logic of accountability: keynote address. In: Grohe, M., Koskinen, E., Shankar, N. (eds.) Proceedings of the 31st LICS, pp. 27–30. ACM (2016). https://doi.org/10.1145/2933575.2934579
13. Lomuscio, A., Qu, H., Raimondi, F.: MCMAS: an open-source model checker for the verification of multi-agent systems. Int. J. Softw. Tools Technol. Transfer **19**(1), 9–30 (2015). https://doi.org/10.1007/s10009-015-0378-x
14. Marinkovic, B., Glavan, P., Ognjanovic, Z., Studer, T.: A temporal epistemic logic with a non-rigid set of agents for analyzing the blockchain protocol. J. Logic Comput. **29**(5), 803–830 (2019). https://doi.org/10.1093/logcom/exz007
15. van der Meyden, R.: On the specification and verification of atomic swap smart contracts. CoRR abs/1811.06099 (2018). http://arxiv.org/abs/1811.06099

16. van der Meyden, R.: On the specification and verification of atomic swap smart contracts (extended abstract). In: Proceedings of the 1st ICBC, pp. 176–179. IEEE (2019). https://doi.org/10.1109/BLOC.2019.8751250
17. Nakamoto, S.: Bitcoin: a peer-to-peer electronic cash system (2008). https://bitcoin.org/bitcoin.pdf
18. Pauly, M.: A modal logic for coalitional power in games. J. Logic Comput. **12**(1), 149–166 (2002). https://doi.org/10.1093/logcom/12.1.149
19. Tolmach, P., Li, Y., Lin, S., Liu, Y., Li, Z.: A survey of smart contract formal specification and verification. ACM Comput. Surv. **54**(7), 148:1–148:38 (2022). https://doi.org/10.1145/3464421
20. Wood, G.: Ethereum: a secure decentralised generalised transaction ledger. Ethereum Project (2014). https://ethereum.github.io/yellowpaper/paper.pdf

Collaborative Multi-agent System for Automatic Linear Text Segmentation

Filipo Studzinski Perotto[✉][ID]

ONERA/DTIS, University of Toulouse, 31055 Toulouse, France
`filipo.perotto@onera.fr`

Abstract. This paper proposes a collaborative multi-agent system for splitting documents into semantically coherent text chunks, labeling them according to a given segmentation structure. Diverse linear text segmentation methods can be incorporated into the system by introducing new agents, which allows to combine complementary approaches: domain-specific, supervised and unsupervised. The system must be supplied with a representative set of previously segmented documents from the target corpus, which are used both to train the supervised agents and to evaluate every agent within the system, similar to ensemble methods. The accuracy of each agent determines its weight in a subsequent aggregation phase, when a common solution is agreed on. The proposed approach presented promising results on segmenting documents from a juridical corpus.

1 Introduction

Linear Text Segmentation (LTS) is the task of breaking a document into semantically coherent or meaningful consistent parts, identifying distinct contiguous segments by mapping neighbor phrases or paragraphs that share common characteristics. The automation of this task constitutes a current and active research problem within the *Natural Language Processing* (NLP) community. LTS can also help to address other problems, such as *text mining*, *synthesis*, *labeling*, and *categorization*, as well as *document search* and *visualization*. In particular, LTS can be useful to non-expert readers for interpreting complex documents. This is the case of the legal language employed in court decisions and law related documents in general, for which the technicality and harshness of the employed vocabulary can be compensated by highlighting their implicit organization.

This paper focuses on the LTS scenarios into which a common segmentation structure is shared by all the documents within the considered corpus. That structure is supposed to be linear, constant, and well-defined, where non-overlapping labeled segments follow each other in a known order. Our contribution for approaching that particular kind of LTS problem is the proposition of a collaborative multi-agent architecture where a set of agents attempt to jointly solve the given segmentation task by combined their solutions. Each considered segmentation algorithm, implemented as an agent within the system, must be

R. Aydoğan et al. (Eds.): PRIMA 2022, LNAI 13753, pp. 573–581, 2023.
https://doi.org/10.1007/978-3-031-21203-1_35

able to break any new unseen document according to the given segmentation structure, associating a *confidence* to its own proposition. The final solution is obtained through a weighted majority rule, similar to ensemble methods. The weight of each agent corresponds to its *quality* on the segmentation task, measured by its accuracy on chunking a set of documents to which the correct segmentation is known. The intuition is that the system can increase the chances of proposing the right segmentation by joining the strengths of different methods. The architecture, illustrated in the Fig. 1, allows different approaches to collaborate: supervised and unsupervised methods, as well as heuristics conceived by domain experts.

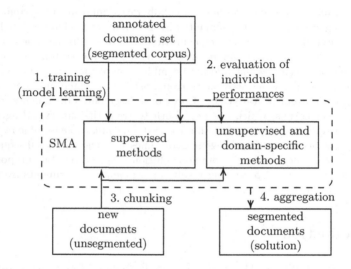

Fig. 1. Sketch of the proposed collaborative multi-agent system. A given set of segmented documents is used either for training the supervised models and for evaluating the performance of every method within the system. Those evaluations work like weights in a subsequent aggregation phase. When new unseen documents are presented to the system, each method declares its preferences on how to segment the given text. In the aggregation phase, such preferences are combined based on the weight of each method.

The system must be provided with a set of previously segmented documents used for both training and evaluating the different agents. In the case of unsupervised and domain-specific methods, there is no previous learning involved, then the entire document set can be used to evaluate the quality of the agent in terms of accuracy in the segmentation task. Supervised agents, however, need to use the given document set to learn their models, in a preliminary training phase. For this reason, their quality must be averaged through cross-validation. That estimated quality can be interpreted as how reliable or trustworthy each method is, providing its weight in a subsequent decision phase, when a common solution is obtained from the aggregation of the different propositions made by the agents. The quality of the final multi-agent solution depends, besides the complexity of the underlying segmentation criteria, on how representative the training corpus is for the target domain, and on how complementary and robust are the agents participating into the system.

The proposed approach has been tested on a corpus extracted from an online document base[1] specialized in the French common law (*jurisprudence*). A hundred justice decisions from second instance courts have been manually segmented by an expert, who also defined a set of heuristic segmentation rules implemented by one of the agents in the system. In that experimental scenario, the multi-agent solution presented improved performances when compared to any of the implemented methods taken separately.

2   Background and Related Work

Three distinct approaches for LTS can be identified in the literature: domain-specific, supervised, and unsupervised. *Domain-specific* methods are based on expert knowledge and can be expressed through a set of lexical rules aiming to find the segment boundaries. Those rules can describe a known normative model related to the domain, or can implement a heuristic strategy for identifying segment changing into the text, generally based on *cue-phrases*.

Unsupervised methods try to identify segments in the document by analyzing its inherent characteristics, such as the vocabulary variation throughout the text. Quantifying the *lexical cohesion* between different parts of a document helps to partitioning the text into a set of thematically coherent segments. That strategy is particularly adapted to identify topic shift within an open segmentation structure. That is the case of `TextTiling` [10], an early method which traverses the document using two fixed length and adjacent blocks of text to draw a function of the similarity given the boundary. Boundaries with lowest scores are selected as potential candidates for chunking the document. The notion of lexical similarity can be replaced by semantic relatedness, like in `OntoSeg` [2], which uses ontology-based similarity to assess the correlation between text blocks.

Recent LTS solutions have been moving away from bag-of-word representations toward word embeddings and latent representations [12,14], which encode each word into a dense vector that captures its relative meaning within the context. That is the case of `GraphSeg` [7], which exploits word embeddings to construct a semantic relatedness graph representation of the document in terms of connected sentences, then deriving semantically coherent segments from the graph. Another example is `TopicTiling` [18], which uses *Latent Dirichlet Allocation* (LDA) for representing segments as dense vectors of dominant topics of terms they contain.

Supervised methods can be used when a representative set of segmented documents is available and provides a *description by extension* of the segmentation criteria. The combination of text processing methods with supervised learning

---

[1] https://www.legifrance.gouv.fr/search/juri.

algorithms is then used to build a classifier system able to identify starting or ending paragraphs of the different segments, or to associate the content of paragraphs to the typical content of the segments [3]. The aim is to extract features that are correlated with the presence of boundaries in labeled training text.

PatSeg [9] implements a two-step approach, where a document is first segmented into text blocks in an unsupervised fashion followed by a supervised classification step for each identified segment, using semantic word embeddings in both phases, and applying a sequential learning algorithm for the second step. In [11], a hierarchical neural model is proposed, in which a lower-level network creates sentence representations from word tokens, and then a higher-level network classifies the belonging of each sentence to a specific segment.

Many algorithms have been proposed in the literature, and an exhaustive overview is not in the scope of this paper. The state of the art concerning automatic LTS can be found in recent surveys [15], comparative studies [8], and related work [1,5,6,9,11–13,17,21]. The idea of using ensemble methodologies for text segmentation also appears in [13], but in a clustering approach. The particular application of supervised learning techniques for legal text segmentation also appears in [20]. An overview of ensemble classifiers is presented in [19]. A survey about collaborative multi-agent systems can be read in [16].

3   Proposed Multi-agent Solution

This paper proposes a solution that consists in the collaborative use of a chosen collection of algorithms within a multi-agent system, allowing the constitution of hybrid strategies. The choice of an adequate function for merging or combining the different results expressed by the different agents within the system constitutes a *preference aggregation* problem [4]. In the case of text segmentation, a weighted majority rule can be applied, taking two factors in account: the *quality* of each method, and the *confidence* that a method declares on its own suggestions.

Having several segmentation methods at hand and a representative set of examples showing how documents in the corpus should be segmented, it is possible to estimate the accuracy of each method. The *quality* of a given agent corresponds to its previously measured segmentation accuracy against the validation dataset. Indeed, when proposing a solution, an agent declares its own *confidence* on the suggested answer. Both values, *quality* and *confidence*, are used to calculate the weight of each response during a later aggregation phase. In this way, the final solution can be seen as the result of an agreement to maximize the chance of proposing the right segmentation. In certain situations, an agent who is not necessarily very efficient in general can nevertheless provide a good answer with a high level of confidence for a specific case.

Formally, let $D = \{d_1, d_2, \cdots, d_i, \cdots, d_n\}$ be a set of annotated text documents, where $n = |D|$ is the number of documents into the dataset. Each document d_i is a sequence of paragraphs. Let the length $l(d_i)$ be the number of paragraphs within document d_i. Different documents can have different lengths.

Every document within the corpus is chunked into $k+1$ segments. The boundary position $b(d_i, j)$, indicated by the index of its first paragraph, is known for each boundary $j \in \{1, \cdots, k\}$ of each document $d_i \in D$. The objective is to build a model for automatically identifying the boundaries between those segments in unseen documents.

Let $A = \{a_1, a_2, \cdots, a_m\}$ be a set of segmenter agents, ready to chunk any document like the ones that compose D. When a new unseen document d' containing $l(d')$ paragraphs is presented, an agent a is expected to return a proposition of chunking in the form of k mass functions $v_{a,j}(d', x)$ representing its own *confidence* in the fact that paragraph x is a good candidate for boundary j in document d'. A mass function is, by definition, constraint to $\sum_{x=1}^{l(d')}[v_{a,j}(d', x)] = 1$. Each segment contains at least one paragraph and each paragraph is contained into exactly one segment. There is no intersections, overlaps or gaps between the segments.

Let $w_{a,j}(D)$ be the *quality* of the agent a in segmenting the dataset D concerning the boundary j. The quality of unsupervised methods corresponds to their accuracy in finding the correct position of each boundary j on the dataset D, so as, $\forall a \in A$, $\forall j \in \{1, \cdots, k\}$:

$$w_{a,j}(D) = \max\left\{0\,,\, \frac{1}{n}\sum_{i=1}^{n}\left[v_{a,j}\big(d_i, b(d_i, j)\big) - \frac{1}{l(d_i)}\right]\right\}. \tag{1}$$

The Eq. 1 is designed to return normalized values, i.e. $w_{a,j}(D) \in [0, 1]$. An hypothetical oracle method, which always returns $v_{a,j}(d_i, x) = 1$ when $x = b(d_i, j)$, i.e. the correct answer for the boundary with 100% of confidence, and 0 otherwise, presents a quality $w_{a,j}(D) = 1$. An uninformative method, which always returns $1/l(d_i)$ of confidence for all possible positions (a uniform guess), presents a quality $w_{a,j}(D) = 0$. Any method that, in average, performs worst than uniform is also evaluated to zero. Any method that can do better than uniform presents a quality between 0 and 1. The quality of supervised methods corresponds to their average accuracy in a z-fold cross-validation.

The overall quality w_a of a given agent a, which represents its general accuracy in segmenting dataset D concerning any boundary, is done by the average quality over the different boundaries:

$$w_a(D) = \frac{1}{k}\sum_{j=1}^{k} w_{a,j}(D). \tag{2}$$

When segmenting an unseen document d', all the agents are asked to present their solutions in the form of k mass functions $v_{a,j}$. Then, an aggregation method based on a weighted majority rule makes emerge a single answer for each boundary j. The final segmentation is chosen by selecting the combination of boundaries that maximizes the weighted average score and respects the constraint of order between the segments:

$$\underset{\{x_1,\cdots,x_j,\cdots x_k\}}{\arg\max} \left\{ \sum_{a\in A} \sum_{j=1}^{k} \left[\left(w_{a,j}(D)\right)^{\tau} v_{a,j}(d',x_j) \right] \right\} \qquad (3)$$

subject to $x_1 < \cdots < x_j < \cdots < x_k$, and where $\tau \in [0,\infty)$ is a parameter allowing to favor the answers given by the most trustworthy methods. When $\tau \to 0$, the quality of the method is ignored, and all the methods are taken with uniform weight. When $\tau \to \infty$, the method with higher quality tends to decide alone.

4   Corpus and Implemented Agents

In France, aiming to enhance transparency and clarity of justice, a significant number of court decisions is released online, digitized and anonymized, freely accessible at https://www.legifrance.gouv.fr/search/juri. Currently, almost 580,000 documents are available under the category *law-cases*. A corpus containing 96 decisions, written in French, produced at different times and locations, by different judges, in diverse *Courts of Appeal* (the second instance), was used as experimental scenario. The considered documents presented an average size of 164 paragraphs and 3843 words, the smallest with 38 paragraphs and 1083 words, and the longest with 758 paragraphs to 17106 words. After tokenization, the considered vocabulary retained 6504 terms.

Each of these documents has been manually partitioned into 4 segments: (1) **header**, where information such as the name of the court, the judge, the city, the date and the name of the parties in dispute is declared; (2) **facts**, where the judge recalls the context of the disagreement, as well as the claims of appellants and respondents, and the verdict proffered by the lower court; (3) **reasons**, where the judge sets out the arguments that justify the new decision; (4) and **conclusion**, where the judge declares and substantiates a new sentence, accepting or rejecting the plea, and stating a final verdict.

Five different agents have been implemented within the proposed multi-agent approach, in order to make a test of concept. The first agent is the classic unsupervised `TextTiling` algorithm [10], adapted to retain only the k stronger candidates. The second agent, `RegEx`, uses a domain-specific strategy by implementing a set of rules written as regular expressions by an expert. The rules are designed to find occurrences of certain expressions that frequently appear in the first paragraph of each searched segment. When the expression is found in the text, the agent returns a confidence of $1/s$ for the corresponding paragraphs, where s is the number of matches, and returns 0 for all the other paragraphs. If the expression does not match any paragraph, the agent returns a uniformly distributed confidence among all paragraphs (uninformative). The third agent, `RelativePosition`, simply predicts the boundaries based on the average relative size of each segment. The agent uses the training set D to calculate the mean and variance of the relative position of each one of the k boundaries. When segmenting a new document d', the method returns confidence values corresponding to the normal probability density function for the relative position of each paragraph. The last two agents, `ClassifierKeyStart` and `ClassifierParagraph`, are based on a multi-layer perceptron (MLP) trained, respectively, to predict if a paragraph is the starting paragraph of a given segment, and to associate a paragraph to a segment. `RegEx` and `TextTiling` do not need to be trained, then their evaluation can be made directly against the given document set. `RelativePosition`, `ClassifierKeyStart` and `ClassifierParagraph` use supervised learning strategies, then their accuracy is evaluated through cross-validation.

5   Empirical Results

For the experiments, the set of documents was divided into 8 folds, and the performance of each configuration evaluated trough cross-validation, using, at each iteration, 84 documents for learning and 12 for testing, then taking the average accuracy. In the case of the supervised agents, at each iteration, the given 84 documents were redivided into other 12 folds, then another cross-validation process is used to calculate their quality, with, at each iteration, 77 documents for training, and 7 for validation, defining the weight of the agent into the system by the average accuracy. In Table 1 we can compare the accuracy of each one of the agents separately, and then the accuracy of our multi-agent system, implementing a collaboration between them. We can see that our approach leads to a performance improvement, if compared to the other methods alone. `RegEx` agent was able to correctly find almost 90% of the boundaries between the segments in the set of documents in question. That high performance is due to the fact that in most of the documents there is an intention of clearly distinguishing the passage between the segments by the use of conventional formulas. The documents into the corpus, representing justice decisions made by the French Court of Appeal, are not forms but free texts. However, it is common to observe the use of *keyphrases* to indicate the beginning of each segment. In addition, the accuracy rate can be expected to drop as soon as the rules are applied to other documents, outside of the studied D. Finally, the weakness of the method comes from the 10% of incorrect segmentation. These are the cases for which no rule

Table 1. Comparison of the different tested LTS algorithms.

Method	Accuracy	per Boundary
`TextTilling`	.02	.05, .01, .00
`RegEx`	.89	.80, .99, .87
`RelativeSize`	.05	.03, .04, .08
`ClassifierKeyStart`	.49	.54, .50, .41
`ClassifierParagraph`	.60	.78, .43, .58
`MultiAgent`	.92	.89, .99, .88

can be applied, and therefore no suggestion can be returned, or cases where several matches are found.

The challenge posed by the presented scenario was, in fact, to be more precise than the heuristics provided by a human expert. Unsupervised methods, based on lexical cohesion were not very effective, presenting a fairly low precision. This is not surprising given that the corpus contains long documents segmented in a domain-specific manner, quite far from the principle which governs topic segmentation. This also suggests that there is a common vocabulary throughout the entire document.

Finally, the supervised learning approach represented by `ClassifierKey Start` and `ClassifierParagraph` presented a correct performance, but significantly worse than `RegEx`. A classifier of the type MLP with 100 nodes in the hidden-layer was trained to identify the initial paragraphs of the different segments, or to associate paragraphs to segment labels, using a tokenized and filtered *bag-of-words* representation. The important result is that the multi-agent solution was able to reach an improved performance, even compared to the best isolated method, which evidences the capacity of combining the solutions.

6   Conclusions and Furure Works

We proposed a multi-agent architecture for LTS into which multiple algorithms can be introduced, allowing to combine the power of diverse strategies (domain-specific, supervised and unsupervised). A set of annotated documents was used for training the supervised agents, and for evaluating all the agents. The aggregation of different solutions using an adapted weighted majority rule allowed to improve the accuracy of predictions when compared to the performance of any isolated agent. However, the interaction of the agents in the system is quite limited, the solution is not negotiated, but voted, and it makes the mechanism closer to ensemble methods than multi-agent systems. In the future, more complex agents can be imagined in order to increase interaction and negotiation possibilities.

Many performing strategies proposed in the literature were not implemented in our simple experimental setup. In further analysis, other state-of-the-art algorithms must be included into the system, and the multi-agent approach deserves to be tested against bigger benchmark datasets. Further discussions should be done about aggregation alternatives, represented features, and different possible classification methods.

References

1. Arnold, S., Schneider, R., Cudré-Mauroux, P., Gers, F.A., Löser, A.: SECTOR: a neural model for coherent topic segmentation and classification. Trans. ACL **7**, 169–184 (2019)
2. Bayomi, M., Levacher, K., Ghorab, M.R., Lawless, S.: OntoSeg: a novel approach to text segmentation using ontological similarity. In: ICDMW 2015, Proceedings, pp. 1274–1283. IEEE (2015)

3. Beeferman, D., Berger, A.L., Lafferty, J.D.: Statistical models for text segmentation. Mach. Learn. **34**(1–3), 177–210 (1999)
4. Conitzer, V.: Making decisions based on the preferences of multiple agents. Commun. ACM **53**(3), 84–94 (2010)
5. Dadachev, B., Balinsky, A., Balinsky, H.: On automatic text segmentation. In: Proceedings of the ACM Symposium on Document Engineering. DocEng 2014, pp. 73–80. ACM (2014)
6. Ghinassi, I.: Unsupervised text segmentation via deep sentence encoders: a first step towards a common framework for text-based segmentation, summarization and indexing of media content. In: 2nd DataTV, Proceedings. Zenodo (2021)
7. Glavaš, G., Nanni, F., Ponzetto, S.P.: Unsupervised text segmentation using semantic relatedness graphs. In: 5th SEM, Proceedings, pp. 125–130. ACL (2016)
8. Gupta, V., Zhu, G., Yu, A., Brown, D.E.: A comparative study of the performance of unsupervised text segmentation techniques on dialogue transcripts. In: SIEDS 2020, Proceedings, pp. 1–6 (2020)
9. Habibi, M., et al.: Patseg: a sequential patent segmentation approach. Big Data Res. **19–20**, 100133 (2020)
10. Hearst, M.A.: TextTiling: segmenting text into multi-paragraph subtopic passages. Comput. Linguist. **23**(1), 33–64 (1997)
11. Koshorek, O., Cohen, A., Mor, N., Rotman, M., Berant, J.: Text segmentation as a supervised learning task. In: NAACL, Proceedings, vol. 2, pp. 469–473. ACL (2018)
12. Li, W., Matsukawa, T., Saigo, H., Suzuki, E.: Context-aware latent Dirichlet allocation for topic segmentation. In: Lauw, H.W., Wong, R.C.-W., Ntoulas, A., Lim, E.-P., Ng, S.-K., Pan, S.J. (eds.) PAKDD 2020. LNCS (LNAI), vol. 12084, pp. 475–486. Springer, Cham (2020). https://doi.org/10.1007/978-3-030-47426-3_37
13. Memon, M.Q., Lu, Y., Chen, P., Memon, A., Pathan, M.S., Zardari, Z.A.: An ensemble clustering approach for topic discovery using implicit text segmentation. J. Inf. Sci. **47**(4), 431–457 (2021)
14. Misra, H., Yvon, F., Jose, J.M., Cappe, O.: Text segmentation via topic modeling: an analytical study. In: CIKM 2009, Proceedings, pp. 1553–1556. ACM (2009)
15. Pak, I., Teh, P.L.: Text segmentation techniques: a critical review. In: Zelinka, I., Vasant, P., Duy, V.H., Dao, T.T. (eds.) Innovative Computing, Optimization and Its Applications. SCI, vol. 741, pp. 167–181. Springer, Cham (2018). https://doi.org/10.1007/978-3-319-66984-7_10
16. Panait, L., Luke, S.: Cooperative multi-agent learning: the state of the art. Auton. Agent. Multi-agent Syst. **11**, 387–434 (2005)
17. Pethe, C., Kim, A., Skiena, S.: Chapter Captor: text segmentation in novels. In: EMNLP 2020, Proceedings, pp. 8373–8383. ACL (2020)
18. Riedl, M., Biemann, C.: Text segmentation with topic models. J. Lang. Technol. Comput. Linguist. **27**(47–69), 13–24 (2012)
19. Rokach, L.: Ensemble-based classifiers. Artif. Intell. Rev. **33**, 1–39 (2010)
20. Wagh, R.S., Anand, D.: A novel approach of augmenting training data for legal text segmentation by leveraging domain knowledge. In: Thampi, S.M., et al. (eds.) Intelligent Systems, Technologies and Applications. AISC, vol. 910, pp. 53–63. Springer, Singapore (2020). https://doi.org/10.1007/978-981-13-6095-4_4
21. Zeinab Shahbazi, Y.C.B.: Analysis of domain-independent unsupervised text segmentation using LDA topic modeling over social media contents. Int. J. Adv. Sci. Technol. **29**(06), 5993–6014 (2020)

Start Making Sense: Identifying Behavioural Indicators When Things Go Wrong During Interaction with Artificial Agents

Sara Dalzel-Job[1]([✉]) [iD], Robin Hill[1] [iD], and Ron Petrick[2] [iD]

[1] University of Edinburgh, Edinburgh, Scotland
sdalzel@ed.ac.uk
[2] Heriot-Watt University, Edinburgh, Scotland

Abstract. This project looks at how people approach collaborative interactions with humans and virtual humans, particularly when encountering ambiguous or unexpected situations. The aim is to create natural and accurate models of users' behaviours, incorporating social signals and indicators of psychological and physiological states (such as eye movements, galvanic skin response, facial expression and subjective perceptions of an interlocutor) under different conditions, with varying patterns of feedback. The findings from this study will allow artificial agents to be trained to understand characteristic human behaviour exhibited during communication, and how to respond to specific non-verbal cues and biometric feedback with appropriately human-like behaviour. Continuous monitoring of "success" during communication, rather than simply at the end, allows for a more fluid and agile interaction, ultimately reducing the likelihood of critical failure.

Keywords: Virtual humans · AIs · Eye tracking · Facial expression · Social interaction · Task-focused interaction · Biometrics · GSR · Trust

1 Introduction

Virtual humans – computer-controlled agents or human-controlled avatars – are widely used in online social interaction and task-oriented communication. Historically, virtual humans have been used in support and health [1–3], and areas such as teaching and training [4, 5]. Increasingly relying on physically distanced interaction, we need to understand more about how technologically mediated communication (i.e., not face-to-face) may lose essential social cues. Retaining non-verbal social information in such situations enables replication of an interaction as similar to face-to-face as possible, given the constraints of technology available. Furthermore, it should be possible to use real-time feedback from a user to tailor a virtual human's behaviour to a specific situation, resulting in increased trust, confidence, and task performance.

With a wealth of investigation into how to design virtual humans for maximum success during interaction with users [6–13], it has been found that the optimum behaviour of a virtual human can vary, depending on the interaction [14, 15]. This study aims to

© The Author(s), under exclusive license to Springer Nature Switzerland AG 2023
R. Aydoğan et al. (Eds.): PRIMA 2022, LNAI 13753, pp. 582–591, 2023.
https://doi.org/10.1007/978-3-031-21203-1_36

establish which combination of behavioural patterns maximise confidence in, and other positive perceptions of, a virtual human interlocutor. The results will be utilised in a proposed study, applying them in real-time during embodied virtual human design ensuring high levels of trust with and confidence in virtual humans.

2 Aims

The primary aim of this research is to understand more about how people respond in ambiguous or unexpected situations. If an instruction giver directs a follower to a target landmark, for example, but the follower's response is unexpected, how does the instruction giver respond? How do biometric responses alter in ambiguous or unexpected situations? Can certain behaviours predict increased or decreased user confidence? With this information, we can understand more about how non-verbal behaviours relate to perceived confidence during an interaction with a human or a virtual human. This study looks at objective measures (behavioural and biometric), and subjective responses during interactions with virtual humans, giving an insight into what the user believes and how they instinctively respond to specific situations. The data can subsequently be used to generate a model of objective and subjective measures, enabling development of an AI instruction giver. In the proposed experiment, the roles will be reversed, with the virtual human instruction giver guiding a human follower to locate targets. The AI's appearance and behaviours associated with high and low confidence levels (from the current study) will be systematically varied throughout the proposed interaction. The participant's biometric responses will be utilised in real-time by the AI to identify instances of low confidence by the participant, enabling it to alter its instructions accordingly for a successful interaction (see Fig. 13).

3 Current Study: Measuring Confidence

3.1 Design

The current study was based on a previous paradigm where a virtual human instruction giver guided a human follower through tasks in a virtual environment [7, 13, 15, 16]. Behavioural cues identified differences in social perceptions of an interlocutor, undetected by traditional questionnaires. This study aimed to extend the previous paradigm by measuring user's biometric responses and perception of and behaviour towards a virtual human while systematically varying the virtual human's behavioural cues. Participants' eye movements, galvanic skin response (GSR) and facial expressions were measured during an interaction with a virtual human (human-controlled avatar or computer-controlled agent). The participant also recorded confidence in the interaction, resulting in both objective and subjective responses to the interaction.

3.2 Method

Stimuli. A human instruction giver (IG) in a lab guided an instruction follower (IF) round a map to landmark. Figure 1 shows the view that the instruction giver had of a human instruction follower in the centre of the map, allowing the IG to be able to easily switch their view between the IF's behaviour and the surrounding landmarks. This also, crucially, allowed the IG to access shared gaze, or knowing where the IF was looking, to identify whether she had located the correct landmark. Each instruction giver guided both a human and a virtual human instruction follower (see Fig. 1 and Fig. 2, respectively). The virtual and human IF's response behaviours were actually pre-recorded The virtual human was created using *Facerig* software and behaved identically to the human IF, minimising unintended experimental artefacts and enabling maximum experimental control.

Fig. 1. "We're looking for the purple mountain" – the instruction giver can see that the human follower has located and is looking at the *correct* landmark.

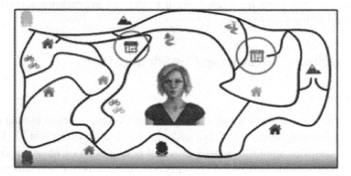

Fig. 2. The virtual IF: the *ambiguous* target is 'the café', but it could be either one.

Variables: *Feedback.* The IF may or may not correctly locate the target landmark, resulting in *correct* and *wrong* conditions. She did not communicate verbally, but instead looked at the target to inform the IG that the correct landmark had been located (see Fig. 1). By not looking at a different landmark, she indicated she had gone wrong. In the *ambiguous* condition, the IG may be told that the target landmark is 'the café', when there are two cafés on the map, as shown in Fig. 2. This feedback was designed to elicit a variety of IG responses, reflecting how people behave in ambiguous or unexpected situations, compared with when the response was predictable.

Follower type. The instruction giver did the experiment once with a human IF (Fig. 1) and once with a virtual human (Fig. 2). The human and virtual human behaved identically, and the order of presentation was alternated between participants.

Agency. In the virtual human condition (Fig. 1), half of the participants believed that they were interacting with a computer-controlled *agent*, and half that it was a human-controlled *avatar*. This was the only difference between conditions, ensuring that any differences in the IG's behaviour were due to the agency manipulation.

Measures: *Confidence.* After each interaction, the IG was asked how confident they were in their own instructions, and also in whether the IF found the correct target.

Eye movements. The IGs' eye movements were recorded using an Eyetribe remote eye tracker. The scene was divided into task-related areas of interest (AOIs). The proportion of fixations within, and number or unique visits to AOIs were recorded.

Galvanic skin response (GSR). The IGs attached two sensors to their fingers to record changes in sweat gland activity, or skin conductance, which can indicate changes in emotional arousal. It was hypothesised that GSR may identify decreases in confidence, an indication that things may be going wrong. The nature and valency of the arousal cannot be determined by these measures alone; peaks could indicate positive or negative affect – anger/joy; or frustration/excitement – requiring interpretation in conjunction with other measures, and within the context of the interaction.

Facial expression. Participants were video recorded during the interaction, and facial expressions were recorded and analysed using *Affectiva* and *iMotions* software.

Procedure. Thirty-two participants (mean age: 25.5; 10M) were recruited and ethical approval was granted by the university's ethics panel. These IGs were presented with the name of a target landmark, then the map with the IF in the centre (Fig. 1, Fig. 2). They were told to guide the IF to the target landmark, using verbal instructions, and that they would be able to tell if the follower had located the target by where she looked. Following each task, the IG answered the two confidence questions and was debriefed concerning the experimental deception techniques. Appropriate ethical approval was secured from Edinburgh University.

3.3 Results

Gaze. A main effect of response type on fixation duration was found $(F(2,58) = 5.703, p = .005, \eta p^2 = .164$, see Fig. 3), with more fixations in the correct than ambiguous condition $(t(37) = 2.89, p = .006; Means: 6.66, 5.72; sd: 4.13, 3.83, respectively)$. There were also significantly more fixations within AOIs when the wrong condition than in the ambiguous $(t(37) = 3.49, p = .001; Means: 7.08, 5.72; sd: 4.59, 3.83, respectively)$.

A significant interaction was found between response type and follower type $(F(2,58) = 3.806, p = .028, \eta p^2 = .116)$. Within the virtual condition only, ambiguous responses resulted in shorter fixation durations than wrong $(t(37) = 3.668, p = .001; Means: 7.68, 5.80; sd: 6.33, 4.10, respectively)$ or correct responses $(t(37) = 3.617, p = .001; Means: 7.43, 5.80; sd: 5.38, 4.10$, respectively, see Fig. 4).

There was a significant main effect of response type on number of revisits to AOIs ($F(2,58) = 10.729$, $p < .001$, $\eta p^2 = .270$). There were more revisits in the correct condition than in ambiguous *(t(37) = 5.317, p < .001; Means: 3.61, 2.95; sd: 1.77, 1.72, respectively),* and more revisits in correct than in the wrong condition *(t(37) = 2.416, p = .021; Means: 3.61, 3.25; sd: 1.77, 1.93, respectively,* see Fig. 5).

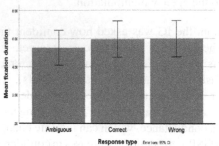

Fig. 3. Fixation duration by response type.

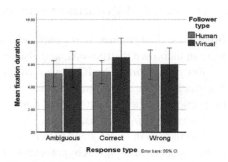

Fig. 4. Fixation duration by response type and follower type.

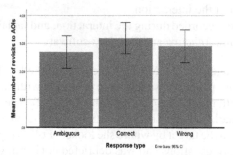

Fig. 5. Revisits to AOIs by response type.

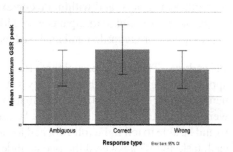

Fig. 6. Response type by maximum GSR peak.

Galvanic Skin Response (GSR). A main effect of response type was found on maximum peak (F(2,46) = 15.862, p < .001, ηp² = .408). The ambiguous condition elicited significantly lower peaks than the correct condition (t(33) = 2.553, p = .015; Means: .66, .56; sd: .54, .46, respectively). The wrong condition also elicited significantly lower peaks than the correct condition (t(33) = 2.544, p = .016; Means: .66, .55; sd: .54, .49, respectively, see Fig. 6).

Confidence. The data revealed a main effect of response type on IG confidence in themselves *(F(4, 144) = 6.285; p < .001, ηp² = .149).* IGs were significantly more confident in their own instructions in the correct condition than in the ambiguous condition *(t(37) = 5.60, p < .001; means: 3.12, 2.88; sd: .51, .50, respectively)* and were more confident in themselves when the response was correct than when the response was wrong *(t(37) = 3.15, p = .003; means: 3.12, 2.97; sd: .51, .57, respectively* see Fig. 7).

A main effect was found between the three response conditions for confidence in the IF having located the correct landmark *(F(2, 72) = 37.266, p > 0.001, ηp² = 0.509)*. IGs were more confident in the IF's success in the correct condition than when instructions were ambiguous *(t(37) = 5.64, p < .001; Means: 3.61, 3.14; sd:.70, .83, respectively)*. IGs were also more confident in the IF in the correct than wrong condition *(t(37) = 7.48, p < .001; Means: 3.61, 2.84; sd:.70, .79, respectively)*. They were also more confident in the IF in the ambiguous condition than in wrong *(t(37) = 3.79, p = .001; Means: 3.14, 2.84; sd: .83, .79, respectively see Fig. 8)*.

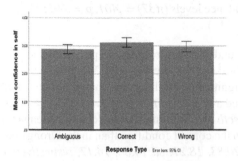

Fig. 7. IG self-confidence by response type   **Fig. 8.** IG confidence in IF by response type

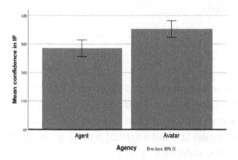

Fig. 9. IG confidence in IF by Agency   **Fig. 10.** IG confidence in the IF by IF type.

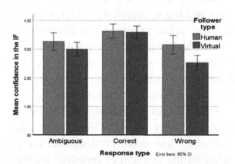

Fig. 11. IF confidence X response & IF type   **Fig. 12.** Engagement by agency & response

A main effect of agency was found on IF confidence $(F(1,36) = 11.01, p < .002, \eta p^2 = .234$, see Fig. 9), with more confidence in the IF having located the correct target in the avatar condition than the agent condition *(Means: 3.53, 2.86; sd: .52, .72, respectively)*. There was higher IF confidence in the human condition than the virtual $(F(1,36) = 8.014, p = .008, \eta p2 = .182;$ *means: 3.35, 3.04; sd: .86, .70,* see Fig. 10).

A significant interaction between IF type and response type was found $(F(2,72) = 11.380, p < .001, \eta p^2 = .240)$. When the instruction was ambiguous, the IG was more confident in the human IF than in the virtual IF $(t(37) = 3.99, p < .001;$ *Means: 3.15, 2.53; sd:1.00, .85, respectively)*. When the correct target was selected, however, there was no difference between the IF type confidence levels $(t(37) = .401, p = .691;$ *Means: 3.63, 3.58; sd:.81, .76, respectively,* see Fig. 11).

Facial Expression. An interaction was found between response type and agency for engagement $(F(2,70) = 3.479, p = .036, \eta p^2 = .090,$ see Fig. 12). When things were going wrong, engagement was found to be significantly higher in the computer-controlled agent condition than in the human-controlled avatar *condition* $(t(36) = 2.076, p = .045;$ *Means: 24.95, 18.21; sd:20.17, 14.17, respectively)*. Within the avatar condition, engagement was found to be significantly higher in the correct condition than in the wrong condition $(t(18) = 2.951, p = .009;$ *Means: 20.83, 18.21; sd:14.88, 14.17, respectively,)*. All other differences failed to reach significance following Bonferroni adjustments for multiple comparisons. Finally, a negative correlation was found between brow raise and confidence in follower $(r(36) = -.366 \ p = .028)$.

3.4 Discussion

IGs had more confidence in a human IF than a virtual one, and more confidence when they believed a virtual IF was controlled by a human than controlled by a computer. In unexpected and ambiguous situations, IGs were more confident in a human IF than in a virtual one. There was higher arousal with a human IF than a virtual human when things went wrong, but no difference in the other two conditions.

As predicted, unexpected events elicited variations in biometric and subjective responses. There were shorter fixations and more revisits to AOIs in ambiguous than in correct, perhaps reflecting less focused looking and more 'searching'. Ambiguous also elicited higher GSR peaks than correct (reflecting higher arousal when the pressure is on the IF to disambiguate the target), less self-confidence and less IF confidence. There were fewer revisits to AOIs in wrong than in correct, as well as lower GSR peaks and lower overall confidence. These could both be strong indicators that things are going wrong. Ambiguity produced higher self-confidence and longer fixations than the wrong condition. The human elicited higher arousal (more peaks per minute) and higher confidence ratings than the virtual human when things went wrong. This suggests that a virtual human may be more useful in situations where low arousal is desirable. The next step is to quantify the users' responses in terms of the confidence outcome measures. This information will be used in the proposed study.

4   Proposed Study: Predicting Confidence, Measuring Trust

The aim of the proposed follow-up study will be to utilise the behavioural and biometric data to enable an AI to predict levels of confidence in a human during a task-focused interaction (see Fig. 13). In this study, the AI IG will guide a human IF through a map to a target landmark. The AI will continuously monitor biometric feedback from the IF, enabling it to respond to cues of confusion, or low confidence (as previously defined). The emphasis will be on behavioural and biometric cues – eye movements, facial expression, GSR – as these can be processed and responded to in real-time. While the AI will respond to non-verbal cues from the participant, it will also display systematically varied levels of confidence, as defined by the pre-defined behaviours and biometric responses from the study. It is anticipated that different levels of 'confident' behaviour will result in varying levels of trust in the AI. This will be measured using a standard trust questionnaire after each task. Once the data from the proposed study has been collected, the answers to two research questions will become clearer:

1. What combination of behavioural patterns and appearance should a virtual human exhibit to maximise levels of confidence and trust during an interaction? Does it matter if the virtual human is controlled by a human or a computer?
2. Can 'confidence' behaviours in humans be detected in real-time and utilised by an AI to adjust its responsive behaviours?

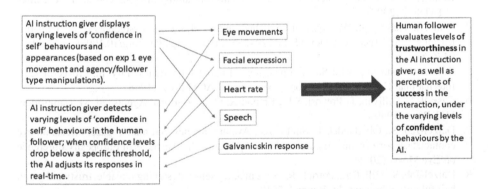

Fig. 13.   Utilise the identified behaviours to design a confident AI and measure trustworthiness.

This could improve human-computer interaction, with moment-to-moment feedback modulating responses from an AI, ensuring any instances of confusion or uncertainty, or more positive situations, such as where the human displays biometric responses associated with high confidence, are detected and responded to appropriately. This could, in turn, increase the effectiveness of human-AI interactions, in terms of task performance, as well as trust in a virtual interlocutor.

5 Conclusions

In situations where a virtual human may be beneficial in assisting a user to complete a task, manipulating its behaviour can lead to a more successful interaction (as found in [15]). When face-to-face communication is not possible (due to geographical, temporal, or financial considerations), a virtual human with task-appropriate behaviour can be used for successful remote mediated communication. In some situations, virtual humans could be potentially more effective than a real human (such as those where a lower level of arousal is desirable). It is anticipated that the paradigm from the proposed study will result in the potential to create an interactive and responsive virtual human, reacting in real-time to behavioural and biometric cues from its human interactant. These results could be applied to a diverse variety of applications – including education, training, health, wellness, commerce, mediation – each producing a customisable, interactive, responsive, truly trustworthy, effective virtual human.

References

1. Kang, S., et al.: Does the contingency of agents' nonverbal feedback affect users' social anxiety? In: Proceedings of the International Joint Conference on Autonomous Agents & Multiagent Systems-vol. 1 (2008)
2. Yuen, E.K., et al.: Treatment of social anxiety disorder using online virtual environments in second life. Behav. Ther. **44**(1), 51–61 (2013)
3. Kenny, P., et al.: Building interactive virtual humans for training environments. In: Proceedings of I/ITSEC (2007)
4. Kim, Y., Thayne, J., Wei, Q.: An embodied agent helps anxious students in mathematics learning. Educ. Tech. Res. Dev. **65**(1), 219–235 (2016). https://doi.org/10.1007/s11423-016-9476-z
5. Rickel, J., Johnson, W.L.: Steve: a pedagogical agent for virtual reality. In: Proceedings of International Conference on Autonomous Agents. ACM Press (1998)
6. Cassell, J., Sullivan, J., Prevost, S.E.: Embodied Conversational Agents, ed. M. Cambridge. MIT Press (1999)
7. Dalzel-Job, S., Oberlander, J., Smith, T.J.: Avatars, agency and mutual gaze: effects on eye contact, task performance & perceived social presence. In: Abstracts of European Conference on Eye Movts (2011)
8. Dalzel-Job, S., Hill, R.L., Petrick, R.: Start making sense: designing likeable, trustworthy and helpful virtual humans. In: Beyond (2019)
9. Dalzel-Job, S., Hill, R.L., Petrick, R.: Start making sense: predicting confidence in virtual human interactions using biometric signals. In: International Conference on Methods & Techniques in Behavioral Research (2020)
10. Andrist, S., et al.: Designing effective gaze mechanisms for virtual agents in CHI 2012, Austin, Texas, USA (2012)
11. Appel, J., et al.: Does humanity matter? Analyzing the importance of social cues and perceived agency of a computer system for the emergence of social reactions during human-computer interaction. In: Advances in HCI, p. 13 (2012)
12. Bailenson, J.N., et al.: The Independent and Interactive Effects of Embodied-Agent Appearance and Behavior on Self-Report, Cognitive, and Behavioral Markers of Copresence in Immersive Virtual Environments Presence (2005)

13. Dalzel-Job, S., Nicol, C., Oberlander, J.: Comparing behavioural and self-report measures of engagement with an embodied conversational agent: a first report on eye tracking in Second Life. In: Proceedings of ETRA. ACM.
14. Dalzel-Job, S., Oberlander, J., Smith, T.J.: Don't look now: the relationship between mutual gaze, task performance and staring in second life. In: Annual Conference on Cognitive Science (2011)
15. Dalzel-Job, S.: Social interaction in virtual environments: the relationship between mutual gaze, task performance and social presence. In: Informatics 2015, Edinburgh: Unpublished doctoral dissertation (2015)
16. Dalzel-Job, S., Oberlander, J., Smith, T.J.: Contested staring: issues & the use of mutual gaze as online measure of social presence. In: ISPR (2011)

Comparing Mediated and Unmediated Agent-Based Negotiation in Wi-Fi Channel Assignment

Marino Tejedor Romero[1](✉) [iD], Pradeep Kumar Murukannaiah[2] [iD],
Jose Manuel Gimenez-Guzman[3] [iD], Ivan Marsa-Maestre[1] [iD],
and Catholijn M. Jonker[2] [iD]

[1] University of Alcala, Alcala de Henares, Spain
{marino.tejedor,ivan.marsa}@uah.es
[2] Technical University of Delft, Delft, The Netherlands
{P.K.Murukannaiah,C.M.Jonker}@tudelft.nl
[3] Universitat Politècnica de València, València, Spain
jmgimenez@upv.es

Abstract. Channel allocation in dense Wi-Fi networks is a complex problem due to its nonlinear and exponentially sized solution space. Negotiating over this domain is a challenge, since it is difficult to estimate opponent's utility. Based on our previous work in mediated techniques, we propose the first two fully-distributed multi-agent negotiations for Wi-Fi channel assignment. Both of them use a simulated annealing sampling process and a noisy model graph estimation. One is designed for Alternating Offers protocols, while the other uses the novel Multiple Offers Protocol for Multilateral Negotiations with Partial Consensus (MOPaC), with experimental promising features for our particular domain. Our experiments compare both proposals against their mediated counterparts, showing similar results on social welfare, Nash product and fairness, but improving privacy and communication overhead.

Keywords: Wi-Fi · Simulated annealing · Automated negotiation

1 Introduction

Wi-Fi channel assignment is clearly a distributed problem, where each access point (AP) may autonomously choose the channel it operates in, and its performance depends both on its choice and the choices of the APs in interference range. In fact, Least Congested Channel search (LCCS) [1], the *de facto* standard for dense, uncoordinated Wi-Fi networks is distributed. But this uncoordinated search often yields suboptimal distributions. In order to solve this, most managed settings design channel distributions for their devices centrally.

In previous work, we proposed Wi-Fi channel assignment as a realistic and challenging benchmark for complex automated negotiations [2,6,11]. In this setting, different agents negotiate the distribution of the channels used by the access

© The Author(s), under exclusive license to Springer Nature Switzerland AG 2023
R. Aydoğan et al. (Eds.): PRIMA 2022, LNAI 13753, pp. 592–601, 2023.
https://doi.org/10.1007/978-3-031-21203-1_37

points (APs) of the network, where the objective is to maximize the network throughput. This technique is coordinated and distributed. We proposed a number of approaches, but the complexity of the negotiation domain, along with the difficulty to estimate utility, forced us to resort to mediated settings. The most successful approach was based on simulated annealing [11], which clearly outperformed LCCS, at the cost of a large number of bidding rounds.

In this work, we propose fully-distributed and unmediated alternatives for negotiation in Wi-Fi channel assignment based on our previous techniques. The experimental results (Sect. 5.3) show that mediated and unmediated negotiation approaches are similar in terms of social welfare, nash product and fairness. In addition, we observe an advantage in terms of network efficiency and privacy.

2   Wi-Fi Channel Assignment as a Negotiation Problem

In this section we briefly review the characteristics of the negotiation domain, the problems it presents, and the utility metric we use.

IEEE 802.11 based networks are commercially known as Wi-Fi networks. In the infrastructure mode operation there are two types of devices: access points (APs) and stations or clients(STAs). Each client will connect to an access point in order to communicate with the rest of the network, which will act like a bridge.

One of the reasons for the great popularity of Wi-Fi networks is that users can connect wirelessly over unlicensed frequency bands. The most frequent of these operating unlicensed frequency bands are the so-called 2.4 GHz and 5 GHz frequency bands. For the moment, we focus on the 2.4 GHz (IEEE 802.11n or Wi-Fi 4) one since it is the most congested, where our proposal can be more beneficial, but our work can be easily extrapolated to others. In this frequency band, there are 11 possible channels for each access points and its associated clients, which partially overlap, which makes the problem even more challenging.

To study the problem of Wi-Fi channel assignment, we have modeled Wi-Fi networks by means of geometric 3D graphs. This way, we can keep the model abstract and reusable. Formally, a graph can be defined as a set of vertices (V) and a set of edges (E) connecting those vertices, $E \subseteq \{(u,v) \mid u,v \in V\}$. The vertices represent APs and STAs. The set of edges contains useful signals (signal between a station and its access point) and interfering signals (any signal between two devices that are not communicating). With this graph, we can compute the Signal-to-Interference-plus-Noise Ratio (SINR) for every station as the quotient between the power of the received signal from its access point divided by the sum of the powers of all the interferences plus the thermal noise. SINR is a key performance parameter that will define the throughput. Depending on the SINR, a certain Modulation and Coding Scheme (MCS) can be used. In other words, as the SINR grows, we will be able to use more aggressive coding schemes with less redundancy and more bits per symbol, in exchange. These powers need to be calculated using a specific propagation model. We have used the indoor propagation model proposed by ITU-R in the Recommendation P-1230-10.

Given the above discussion, we formally define different elements of the problem.

- A solution or deal is expressed as a vector $S = (s_1, s_2, s_3, \ldots, s_{n_{AP}})$, where each $s_i \in \{1, \ldots, 11\}$, represents the assignment of a Wi-Fi channel to the i-th access point.
- The global utility for a solution S is $u(S)$ and can be calculated as the sum of all throughput values. The partial utility obtained by an agent A for a solution S is $u_A(S)$, and can be calculated as the sum of the throughput of all stations attached to the access points depending on the agent A. The opponent utility for an agent A for a solution S is $u_A^o(S)$, and can be calculated as the complementary measure of the previous utility, this is, the sum of the throughputs of all stations attached to access points not controlled by said agent A. These utilities are defined in absolute terms, but can also be expressed in a relative way, normalized.

3   Previous Work

In our previous work on this setting [2, 6, 11], we used several variations of the simple text mediation protocol [9]. Before we describe our new approach, it is helpful to review a common algorithm family: Simulated Annealing.

3.1   Simulated Annealing

Simulated annealing (SA) [8] is a family of heuristic algorithms. Its goal is to find a global optimal solution in a complex non-linear discrete space, and it is best used when the complete solution space is large and rough, this is, there are many local maxima that make it difficult to find the global optimal solution.

The principle behind SA is to roam across the solution space jumping from one neighbour to another, trying to maximize the utility while being able to escape local maxima. The steps are randomly chosen, and then evaluated. If the candidate yields better utility, it is always accepted. Otherwise, it is decided randomly depending on the current iteration count, and how much worse the new utility is. The exact implementation of simulated annealing depends on the particular problem.

3.2   Mediated Negotiation for Wi-Fi Channel Assignment

Based on simulated annealing, we developed a mediated multi-agent distributed algorithm. It needs a mediator and a number of agents. It works as follows:

1. The mediator starts with a randomly-generated solution, the vector (S_0) and it becomes the current channel vector.
2. In each iteration t, the current channel vector is S_t. The mediator proposes a new candidate S_t^c, changing a random access point to a new random channel.
3. Each agent A either accepts or rejects the candidate S_t^c. Their votes follow the same principle explained in the Simulated Annealing section. They evaluate their own partial utility difference between the new candidate and the current

state, this is $\Delta u_A = u_A(S_t^c) - u_A(S_t)$. With the utility difference and the current temperature (determined by the initial temperature and the cooling schedule), they calculate the probability of acceptance.
4. If all agents have accepted the new candidate S_t^c, it will become the new current state of the algorithm $S_{t+1} = S_t^c$. Otherwise, it will be discarded, maintaining the previous state $S_{t+1} = S_t$. The process moves to step 2.
5. After a fixed number of iterations, the mediator advertises the last mutually accepted contract as final.

Although the negotiation mechanism above yielded satisfactory results in terms of social welfare, it had a number of limitations. First, since it optimized the sum of utilities, it had a tendency to produce unfair assignments. Second, it needed the agents to vote over thousands of contracts during the negotiation, which involved a significant communication overhead and a potential privacy concern. Our hypothesis is that these limitations can be overcome by using unmediated negotiation approaches, which we propose next.

4   Unmediated Techniques for Wi-Fi Channel Negotiation

We propose the first unmediated negotiation approaches succeeding in this domain. The special characteristics of the Wi-Fi channel domain were preventing the application of state-of-the-art negotiation techniques for these reasons:

1. The high cardinality of the solution space, which makes an exhaustive search unfeasible. For instance, in the biggest scenario in our experiments, a residential building with 40 access points, the number of bids is 11^{40}. This is clearly an obstacle since many negotiation approaches, such as the ones implemented in GENIUS [5], rely on the agent having an ordered set of bids.
2. The lack of negotiation predictability. Being able to estimate the preference profile of the opponents makes it easier to make an effective offer, and it increases the chances of reaching a good outcome more quickly [12]. In our scenario, this problem is, at the same time, twofold. First, the utility space are highly rugged, so linearity, concavity or convexity assumptions are not possible. Second, the estimated utility for the agents depend on the accuracy of the positions of both access points and stations at a given time. Therefore, there is an uncertainty not only about the opponent's utility function, but also about the agent's own one.

In the following, we describe the techniques used to overcome these two challenges, and then the protocols used for the negotiation.

4.1   Estimating Utility Through the Graph Model

First, in order to address the difficulty of estimating the utility functions ($u_A(S)$ and $u_A^o(S)$), we rely on the graph model.

We assume that each agent can determine the accurate location of their access point and its connected clients, but this is not enough to obtain the estimated throughput. For the rest of positions, agents can use Wi-Fi state-of-the-art localization techniques such as [4,10]. These two sources present results with an average error below 1.7 m. Thus, it is realistic to assume a mixed positioning approach. Each agent will have a different version of the graph, where its access points and stations will have accurately positioned, and the rest of the devices will have an approximate position.

4.2   Simulated Annealing One-Sided Exploration

To allow agents to have a tractable and ordered set of bits to choose from during the negotiation, we leverage the success of the previous approach. The variant of this heuristic executed by each agent, prior to the negotiation, in order to sample the bid space in a directed way, works as follows:

1. Each agent A starts with a randomly-generated current state vector S_0.
2. In each iteration t, the current state is S_t. The agent generates a new candidate as a simple mutation of the current state S_t^c.
3. The agent stores this new candidate S_t^c, its utility for the agent $u_A(S_t^c)$, and the opponent utility $u_A^o(S_t^c)$.
4. The agent calculates the difference of utility $\Delta u_A = u_A(S_t^c) - u_A(S_t)$. With the utility loss and the current temperature, the agent obtains an acceptance probability. If the candidate is accepted, it will become the current state $S_{t+1} = S_t^c$. If it is discarded, the previous state is maintained, $S_{t+1} = S_t$.
5. After a fixed number of iterations, the agent stops exploring and obtains a set of bids with associated utilities for itself and for the opponents.

The most important part of this variation is to store all the steps, and associated estimated utilities. This allows to have an ordered subset of the bid space that covers a range of aspiration levels for the agent. This detail will enable conventional negotiation strategies to be deployed over this domain.

4.3   Bilateral Unmediated Negotiation

We are going to introduce briefly an example of how to negotiate in the Wi-Fi channel domain using standard techniques, covering the simplest case: a bilateral negotiation. For this part, we have chosen Simple Alternating Offering Protocol (SAOP) [3]. In this protocol, for each round of negotiation, one of the agent proposes a bid, and the other agent evaluates it, accepting it or not. In the next round, their roles will be reversed. The negotiation ends when a bid is accepted by any of the agents or when they reach a fixed number of rounds.

In order to test our annealing exploration and the utility estimation method, we have created a simple agent for SAOP that includes frequently used techniques. It is based on time-dependent agents, which start proposing the bid which yields maximum utility for themselves, but start conceding throughout the negotiation rounds, lowering their utility goals until they reach a common agreement. This simple agent proceeds as follows:

1. The agent runs one or several simulated-annealing-based explorations, according to the technique explained in Sect. 4.2. This is a preparation stage, prior to any communication between agents.
2. Every round, the agent calculates its utility goal. Without loss of generality, in this work we use a linear concession strategy to compute the utility goal at each round.
3. If it is the agent's turn to offer a contract, it extracts the subset of contracts that satisfy its own utility goal and sends the contract with the greater estimated opponent utility. On the contrary, if the agent evaluates an incoming offer, it simply checks if the received contract satisfies the goal.

4.4 Multi-party Unmediated Negotiation

The next objective is to extrapolate this simple approach towards an unmediated negotiation with multiple agents. In this step, we have chosen a new negotiation protocol. We choose the Multiple Offers Protocol for Multilateral Negotiations with Partial Consensus (MOPaC) [13]. In MOPaC, at the beginning of a round, every agent proposes a contract to a common pool. Then, every agent evaluates every contract in the pool and vote them, including a minimum and maximum consensus threshold. This protocol does not require a full consensus, and can be configured to search for multiple partial consensus.

It works in a similar fashion as in the SAOP-based protocol: the agent explores the bid space using SA. Then, for each round, the agents calculate their utility goal. Given an utility goal the agent extracts the subset of bids which satisfy the corresponding goal and propose the one that yields more estimated opponent utility. As a last step, in the voting phase, agents vote using their utility goal, looking for consensus.

5   Experimental Evaluation

5.1   Considered Scenario

We conduct our experiments in a realistic scenario that models a 5-floor residential building as a paradigmatic example where multiple Wi-Fi networks coexist. In this setting, each floor has a length, width and height of 40, 30 and 3 m, and there are eight flats in each floor in a 4×2 layout. Using this building model, we have generated three different buildings, configured with two, four, and six stations per access point, respectively. For each flat, the position of the AP and its STAs follows a uniform distribution in the x and y-axis, and a normal distribution in the z-axis ($\mu = 1.5$ m, $\sigma = 0.5$ m). In summary, our experimental scenarios contain 40 APs distributed along 5 floors and $40 \times 2 = 80 \; STAs$, $40 \times 4 = 160 \; STAs$, or $40 \times 6 = 240 \; STAs$.

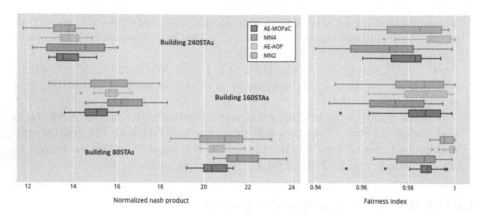

Fig. 1. Normalized nash product ($\frac{\text{Number of agents}}{\sqrt{\text{Nash product}}}$ /Number of stations per agent) and Jain's fairness index for mediated and unmediated negotiations in different buildings according to our experiments.

5.2   Experimental Settings

We summarize here again the techniques used for evaluation, for convenience.

- *Mediated negotiation with two and four agents (MN-2 and MN-4)*: The mediated approach we used in our previous works [2,6,11]. To allow for a better comparison, we run experiments with two and four agents.
- *Annealer exploration and alternating offers protocol (AE-AOP)*: Here, we perform the initial exploration of the agent utility spaces described in Sect. 4.2, and then we use a bilateral SAOP (Sect. 4.3) for the negotiation.
- *Annealer exploration and MOPaC (AE-MOPaC)*: Again, we perform the initial exploration of the agent utility spaces described in Sect. 4.2, but then we use MOPaC (Sect. 4.4) with four agents for the negotiation.

Agent utility functions were generated making noisy estimations of the real Wi-Fi graph as described in Sect. 4.1. The precision of the unknown devices is modeled adding a random distance determined by a gaussian distribution with $\sigma = 1.7$ in a random direction. These estimations were generated randomly for each agent and trial. Each technique was run for 20 times for the three scenarios described above. All the SA explorations use 3000 iterations and 1 as the initial temperature. We measured measure the following metrics:

- *Social Welfare*: Sum of all throughputs, and global utility of a solution.
- *Communication Overhead*: Number of messages sent during the negotiation.
- *Nash product*: Product of the utility obtained by each one of the agents.
- *Jain index* [7]: Fairness index calculated with all the partial utilities obtained by each one of the agents.

The last two metrics can only be compared with the same number of agents, and for the same distribution of access points between these agents.

5.3 Experimental Results

Table 1, summarize our results. At the same time, we present a graphical summary of these tables in the 1.

The tables show the overall performance of the unmediated proposals is generally similar to the mediated ones (clearly superior to LCCS in our previous work). Communication overhead depends on the protocol. Mediated negotiation requires as many messages as contracts proposed by SA. In our experiments, we have used 3000 iterations for all SA executions. In unmediated negotiations, agents run their annealing exploration processes independently, eliminating this overhead. In this case, the communication overhead depends on the negotiation rounds. We used 50 rounds for our experiments.

With these results, we can tell that unmediated negotiations generally show a similar performance to the mediated counterpart, with clear advantage over the current standard. Unmediated negotiations, however, offer a communication overhead and privacy advantage, at no performance cost.

Table 1. Results for the experiments.

	Social welfare		Nash product		Jain's fairness		Comm. overhead
	Avg	CI	Avg	CI	Avg	CI	Avg
2 stations per access point							
MN-2	1669.85	49.88	$6.97 \cdot 10^5$	$4.16 \cdot 10^4$	0.996	0.001	$3 \cdot 10^3$
AE-AOP	1655.22	23.78	$6.84 \cdot 10^5$	$2.00 \cdot 10^4$	0.998	0.001	$5 \cdot 10^1$
MN-4	1755.00	36.47	$3.63 \cdot 10^{10}$	$3.23 \cdot 10^9$	0.985	0.005	$3 \cdot 10^3$
AE-MOPaC	1646.45	23.94	$2.80 \cdot 10^{10}$	$1.66 \cdot 10^9$	0.986	0.005	$5 \cdot 10^1$
4 stations per access point							
MN-2	2526.87	94.28	$1.58 \cdot 10^6$	$1.12 \cdot 10^4$	0.984	0.007	$3 \cdot 10^3$
AE-AOP	2524.92	43.30	$1.57 \cdot 10^6$	$5.19 \cdot 10^4$	0.986	0.005	$5 \cdot 10^1$
MN-4	2655.90	82.69	$1.89 \cdot 10^{11}$	$2.40 \cdot 10^{10}$	0.975	0.007	$3 \cdot 10^3$
AE-MOPaC	2420.60	45.60	$1.31 \cdot 10^{11}$	$9.63 \cdot 10^9$	0.984	0.006	$5 \cdot 10^1$
6 stations per access point							
MN-2	2526.87	94.28	$1.58 \cdot 10^6$	$1.12 \cdot 10^4$	0.984	0.007	$3 \cdot 10^3$
AE-AOP	2524.92	43.30	$1.57 \cdot 10^6$	$5.19 \cdot 10^4$	0.986	0.005	$5 \cdot 10^1$
MN-4	2655.90	82.69	$1.89 \cdot 10^{11}$	$2.40 \cdot 10^{10}$	0.975	0.007	$3 \cdot 10^3$
AE-MOPaC	2420.60	45.60	$1.31 \cdot 10^{11}$	$9.63 \cdot 10^9$	0.984	0.006	$5 \cdot 10^1$

6 Conclusions and Future Work

Optimizing resource use in wireless networks is a challenging and increasingly critical real-world problem, which we had successfully addressed in the past using mediated negotiation. This paper studies and evaluates the use of distributed negotiation techniques for WiFi-channel assignment. We compare the negotiation-based approaches with our previous mediated approach. Experiments show that the distributed approach is similar to the mediated approach in terms of performance, but involves a privacy and communication overhead advantage.

Although our experiments yield satisfactory results, there are several of research directions. An open challenge of our approach is how to use opponent's bids to refine the utility model throughout the negotiation. We also want to explore different partial consensus formation approaches for MOPaC. Finally, we are interested in evaluating the strategic properties of the mechanisms, to see how they perform when agents may use different strategies to their advantage.

Acknowledgements. M. Tejedor Romero, J. M. Gimenez-Guzman and I. Marsa-Maestre are supported by Project SBPLY/19/180501/000171 of the Junta de Comunidades de Castilla-La Mancha and FEDER, by Projects UCeNet (CM/JIN/2019-031) and WiDAI (CM/JIN/2021-004) of the Comunidad de Madrid and University of Alcalá (UAH), and by Project PID2019-104855RB-I00/AEI/10.13039/501100011033 of the Spanish Ministry of Science and Innovation. M. Tejedor is funded by UAH PhD program.

References

1. Achanta, M.: Method and apparatus for least congested channel scan for wireless access points, 6 April 2006. US Patent App. 10/959,446
2. De La Hoz, E., Marsa-Maestre, et al.: Multi-agent nonlinear negotiation for Wi-Fi channel assignment. In: Proceedings of the 16th Conference on Autonomous Agents and MultiAgent Systems, pp. 1035–1043. IFAAMAS (2017)
3. Fatima, S., Kraus, S., Wooldridge, M.: Principles of Automated Negotiation: Cambridge University Press, Cambridge, October 2014
4. Han, K., Yu, S.M., Kim, S.L., Ko, S.W.: Exploiting user mobility for WIFI RTT positioning: a geometric approach. IEEE IoT J. **8**(19), 14589–14606 (2021)
5. Hindriks, K., Jonker, C.M., et al.: Genius: negotiation environment for heterogeneous agents. In: Proceedings of the 8th International Conference on Autonomous Agents and Multiagent Systems, vol. 2, pp. 1397–1398 (2009)
6. de la Hoz, E., Gimenez-Guzman, J.M., Marsa-Maestre, I., Orden, D.: Automated negotiation for resource assignment in wireless surveillance sensor networks. Sensors **15**(11), 29547–29568 (2015)
7. Jain, R.K., Chiu, D.M.W., Hawe, W.R., et al.: A quantitative measure of fairness and discrimination. Digital Equipment Corporation, Hudson, MA 21 (1984)
8. Kirkpatrick, S., Gelatt, C.D., Vecchi, M.P.: Optimization by simulated annealing. Science **220**(4598), 671 (1983). https://doi.org/10.1126/science.220.4598.671
9. Klein, M., Faratin, P., Sayama, H., Bar-Yam, Y.: Negotiating complex contracts. Group Dec. Negot. **12**(2), 111–125 (2003). https://doi.org/10.1023/A:1023068821218
10. Li, S., Hedley, M., Bengston, K., Humphrey, D., Johnson, M., Ni, W.: Passive localization of standard WiFi devices. IEEE Syst. J. **13**(4), 3929–3932 (2019)

11. Marsa-Maestre, I., Gimenez-Guzman, J.M., et al.: Nonlinear negotiation approaches for complex-network optimization: a study inspired by Wi-Fi channel assignment. Group Decis. Negot. **28**(1), 175–196 (2019)
12. Marsa-Maestre, I., Klein, M., Jonker, C.M., Aydoğan, R.: From problems to protocols: towards a negotiation handbook. Dec. Support Syst. **60**, 39–54 (2014)
13. Murukannaiah, P.K., Jonker, C.M.: MOPaC: the multiple offers protocol for multilateral negotiations with partial consensus (2022). https://doi.org/10.48550/ARXIV.2205.06678, arxiv:2205.06678

Design of Conversational Components to Facilitate Human-Agent Negotiation

Dale Peasley[✉], Bohan Xu, Sami Abuhaimed, and Sandip Sen

The University of Tulsa, Tulsa, OK 74104, USA
{dfp3395,bohan-xu,saa8061,sandip-sen}@utulsa.edu

Abstract. With burgeoning interest in the industry and among citizens about the potential of human-AI partnerships [10], academic researchers have been pushing the frontier of new modalities of peer-level and ad-hoc human-agent collaboration [5,11]. We are particularly interested in research on agents representing human users in negotiating deals with other human and autonomous agents [9]. We present the design motivation and critical components of the conversational aspect of our agents entry into the *Human-Agent League* of the Automated Negotiation Agent Competition. We explore how language can be used to promote human's likeability, even in the domain of a competitive negotiation.

Keywords: Human-agent negotiation · Conversational agent

1 Introduction

With breakthrough advances in AI science and technology in recent years, there has been significant interest in both industry and the general populace about the future potential of human-AI collaboration [4,6]. Our current research in this space is on autonomous agents representing user interest while negotiating with other automated agents and human users. Possible real-world applications of AI and intelligent agents include the legal, business, and industrial sectors where there is an increased demand for automated systems that can accurately represent a party in a negotiation to secure better deals for both parties [12].

In this paper, we discuss the effect of the use of effective language model to improve human engagement when they negotiate with an autonomous agent. We improved the language model of an agent designed for the Human-Agent League (HAL) of 2019 Automated Negotiation Agent Competition (ANAC). We developed, implemented and tested three agents with divergent language models:

Base: An agent that has concise and direct communication to engage the user. The language model, though not fully explanatory, was a significant improvement on the terse and abrupt language model of the 2019 agent, which users often found opaque and even overbearing.

© The Author(s), under exclusive license to Springer Nature Switzerland AG 2023
R. Aydoğan et al. (Eds.): PRIMA 2022, LNAI 13753, pp. 602–611, 2023.
https://doi.org/10.1007/978-3-031-21203-1_38

Fig. 1. The interface of IAGO platform (agent assists the user to navigate through the Draft protocol).

Chatty: An agent that uses colloquial phrasing and "small talk" banter, irrelevant to the task, to attract the user's attention.

Explaining: An agent, more articulate than the Base agent, focusing brief and pertinent explanations of its behavior.

We chose these agents to see if different language models have different effects on user satisfaction, engagement, and negotiation outcome. The experiments are implemented using the Interactive Arbitration Guide Online (IAGO) platform [7] and the data are collected through Amazon MTurk [3]. Our analysis shows that user engagement can be improved with short but informative messages.

2   ANAC Human Agent Negotiation League

The ANAC Human Agent Negotiation competition involves the allocation of a set of issues between autonomous agents and human participants with asymmetric preferences. The negotiation is performed using the IAGO platform, which is developed at the University of Southern California [7]. Human participants are recruited on Amazon MTurk [3] for the competition, and communicate with autonomous agents only via the predefined sets of actions, emojis, and sentences as shown in Fig. 1. The agent is represented by an avatar, can express basic emotions, and can send customized utterances.

One complete game between one agent and one participant contains three rounds, and the negotiation space for each round can be represented as follows. Let $\mathcal{I}$ be the set of negotiated items. $\forall i \in \mathcal{I}$, n_i is the number of units available for item i. An offer O is a set of triplets $O(i) = (i, n_{O,i}^h, n_{O,i}^{AI})$ where $\forall i \in \mathcal{I}$ and $n_{O,i}^h + n_{O,i}^{AI} \leq n_i$. $n_{O,i}^h$ and $n_{O,i}^{AI}$ are the units of item i allocated in offer O to the human and agent, respectively. An offer O is a *complete offer* iff $n_{O,i}^h + n_{O,i}^{AI} = n_i$ where $\forall i \in \mathcal{I}$. $U(O) = \sum_{i \in \mathcal{I}} w_i n_{O,i}^{AI}$ is the utility of offer O to the agent, where w_i is the per unit utility of item i to the agent.

3   Agent Design

We now present the core agent design shared by all of our agents. Our agents' strategy relies on the human player's cooperation, which creates a need to convince the human to cooperate with the agent through engagement. Our agent's goal is to build trust across the repeated rounds of negotiation. These skills are valuable for agents to have, especially as there is a widely perceived need for developing human-agent collaborative teams [10].

3.1   The Draft Protocol

A key challenge of negotiation is to understand and effectively utilize the utility preferences of one's opponent [1]. As the human opponent's utility is unknown at the outset of a negotiation round, it must be learned or approximated to allow for strategic negotiation. This core functionality of our agents is provided by adapting an existing negotiation protocol[1].

We present an interaction strategy based around the "Draft": both parties alternately select their preferred issue until all the issues are exhausted. This procedure may repeat more than once and be followed with some simple questions to obtain the complete human player's preference profile [13]. The "Draft" process aims at (1) obtaining the necessary information for the agent to generate a fair initial complete offer, (2) guiding the generation of counter offers, and (3) providing some knowledge about the agent's preference to the human player.

3.2   First Post-"Draft" Offer

After the agent has the human player's preference profile, it generates and sends out an offer based on this knowledge. We build a preference profile for the agent, which takes both the quantity and utility of an issue into account. In order to make the offer acceptable to the human, the agent attempts to give them the items with the higher utility regarding the human's preference. At the same time, the agent wants to maximize its own reward as well. For any items which share the same positions on both preference profiles, an even split of those issues will be made. The detailed implementation is presented in Algorithm 1. Our goal is to create an offer which is fair to both parties. The purpose of providing a fair

---

[1] This protocol is a variation of the *Strict alteration* protocol, in which agents take alternate turns and in each turn an agent selects one resource from the set of resources not yet allocated. Selected resource is removed from the negotiation set [2].

Algorithm 1. First Post-"Draft" Offer Generation

1: **procedure** INITIALOFFER(P_h, P_{AI})
2: **if** P_h is not empty **then**
3:    **if** $P_h(first) = P_{AI}(first)$ **then**
4:      allocate half of $P_h(first)$ items, subject to truncation, to each player
5:    **else**
6:      allocate all $P_h(first)$ items to human, and all $P_{AI}(first)$ items to agent
7:    $P_{alloc} = \{P_h(first)\} \cup \{P_{AI}(first)\}$
8:    Remove P_{alloc} from both P_h and P_{AI}
9:    InitialOffer(P_h, P_{AI})

P_h and P_{AI} refer to the human and agent preference profiles, respectively.

offer instead of attempting to trick the player is to promote cooperation across all three rounds of the negotiation in a complete game. Our strategy is more aggressive in the final round.

3.3   Counter-Offer Generation

Algorithm 2 describes the agent generating a counter-offer midway between an offer O_h made by the human and O_{AI}, the last offer from the agent itself.

Algorithm 2. Counter-Offer Generation

1: **procedure** COUNTEROFFER(O_{AI}, O_h, P_h, P_{AI})
2: $loss = U(O_{AI}) - U(O_h)$
3: **if** $loss < 0$ **then**
4:    Accept O_h
5: **else**
6:    $O = O_h$; $P = P_h$; increment $= -1$
7:    itemPreferenceOrder $= |P| - 1$
8:    **if** P_h is empty **then**
9:      $P = P_{AI}$; increment $= 1$; itemPreferenceOrder $= 1$
10:   **while** $loss > 0$ **do**
11:     $i = P(\text{itemPreferenceOrder})$; $n = n_{O_h,i}^h$
12:     **if** $n > 0$ **then**
13:       $itemsSwapped = \min(n, \lceil \frac{loss}{w(i)} \rceil)$
14:       $loss = loss - itemsSwapped * w(i)$
15:       $O = (O \setminus O(i)) \cup \{(i, n - itemsSwapped, n_i - (n - itemsSwapped))\}$
16:     itemPreferenceOrder $=$ itemPreferenceOrder $+$ increment
17:   Counter offer O

3.4   Anchoring

For the 2020 agents, an "anchor offer" is sent to human players at the beginning of each negotiation. If this anchor offer is rejected, the "Draft" protocol will start to determine the human's preference. The use of anchoring is motivated by the fact that many human negotiators prefer even splits, and humans will often begin by negotiating around splits that are close to 50–50. We use a basic form of anchoring [9]. The agent presents an initial deal in which it would receive roughly 70% of its max utility. Given most negotiations, 70% was experimentally shown to be about half of the total number of items being negotiated. This threshold is to be set for avoiding proposing worse than optimal offers and the negotiation is usually able to achieve a Pareto-optimal outcome.

4   Language and Intent

When designing the Base, Chatty, and Explaining agents, we focus on adding a more dynamic language model. We consider several aspects of the language models with each agent laying primary emphasis on one of these aspects.

Ease of Understanding: Large volumes of information can be exchanged within a short time in agent-to-agent interactions. However, human-agent negotiation scenarios involve imbalanced communication [8]. A human has the ability to articulate preference in a manner that the agent cannot interpret, whereas the agent can communicate copious information that can easily overwhelm humans. Concise, judicious communication facilitates human-agent interaction and makes the information accessible to the human, particularly so under time constraints. To apply this concept to our 2020 agents, we simplify the phrasing while still communicating required information. The Base agent's language model keeps messages brief and breaks a long message into several shorter messages.

Non-monotonic Nature: The 2019 agent only had a single response for any given situation. The 2020 agents change their languages to not only reflect the current state of the negotiation, but also choose randomly from several equivalent phrasings if a situation is repeated. Consider the following equivalent phrasings used by the Base agent to reject offers from the human: (1) *"That deal does not seem fair to me."* (2) *"I can't accept that."* (3) *"I have to decline this offer."*

Our goal of choosing between equivalent phrases is to present a more dynamic and intelligent agent. Equivalent phrasings are constructed for (i) proposing, accepting, and rejecting an offer, (ii) being rejected, (iii) timing language, etc.

The Chatty agent uses humor to engage with and entertain the player. Some examples of how the Chatty agent rejects an offer from the human:

(1) *Nah, I have to pass on that one!*
(2) *Wish I could, but I really, Really, REALLY can't*
(3) *You are going to kill me! But I have magic powers to survive; bring it on!* A more engaging agent is expected to be more successful in earning the trust of the human to continue negotiation.

Guiding the Human Negotiator: A source of frustration with the 2019 agent is the human player getting lost during the "Draft". To help with that, we modify the language model to guide the human player through the "Draft". We assume the human is new to this form of negotiation, and provide sequenced messages that facilitate the "Draft. The following is an example of how the Explaining agent introduces the "Draft" in the first round: *"To find a WIN-WIN outcome, first let's take turns choosing our favorite items! Then I can use that draft to make a good deal for both of us. You choose an item first.".* Also, the agent would persist in the "Draft" until it meets an exit condition, then a new negotiation through offer modification procedures would take over. This avoids scenarios with awkward interaction sequences.

Another change in the 2020 agents is our response to a non-cooperative opponent. In our 2019 agent, we respond with a hardline "take it or leave it" response. However, our 2020 agents are designed to be less combative. Where the human appears to be hostile such as threatening Best Alternative To Negotiated Agreement (BATNA), or presenting terrible deals, the 2020 agents opt to give the human the benefit of the doubt and act as if they are misunderstood, since it is often the case that human's negotiating is truthful, given their preferences [8].

5   Interactions During Negotiation

5.1   Initiating the Draft

The 2019 agent immediately launches into the "Draft" with a direct message attempting to explain the "Draft", while all of our 2020 agents start by offering an anchor deal. If the anchor offer is rejected, the 2020 agents will guide the human player through the "Draft". The proposal of the "Draft" is accompanied by an explanation of the player's role in the "Draft", such as this from the Chatty agent: *"So it's just like last time we'll take turns choosing issues. You can go first and send me an offer after taking all items of the issue you want. I will then pick the next issue and so on. Go ahead and make an offer.".* The agents would clear the negotiation space of the anchoring deal, in preparation for the human to select an issue to begin the "Draft". This assumption of cooperation is to corral the player into beginning the "Draft".

5.2   Dealing with Uncooperative Opponents

If the human either did not cooperate with the "Draft" or makes mistakes, the 2019 agent would respond critically. However, our 2020 agents gently corrects them with a message which assumes that the player has good intentions and has made a mistake. The goal of this simple strategy is not to offend a player who is merely having difficulty. Without sensitive and sensible feedback, achieving cooperation may become harder going forward. Second, if the player is deliberately not cooperating and is being confrontational, the direct rebuttal will likely exacerbate the situation. If the player does not cooperate more than five times, the agent sends a message acknowledging the failure of the "Draft" such as: *"I don't think this is working well; here's an offer that should work."*. From there, we begin to make friendly offers to continue the negotiation on a positive note.

6 Experimental Results

To investigate the effects of various language models on user likeability, the human participants are asked to complete questionnaires after each round of the negotiation as well as after the entire game. The questionnaire after each round only contains only one 7-point Likert scale question: "How much do you like your opponent?". The post-game questionnaire includes 6 questions. Each question measures, on a 7-point Likert scale, the likeability from a different perspective. We calculate an averaged likeability of the post-round questionnaire over all human players and only for the first two rounds, since the agents use a more aggressive strategy in the third round of negotiation. The post-game questionnaire is added for only the 2020 agents.

Table 1. Averaged likeability of post-round questionnaire

2019 agent	2020 agent		
	Base	Chatty	Explaining
3.93	5.13	5.42	5.42

Table 2. Averaged human utility for 2020 agents

Base	Chatty	Explainable
54.23	52.50	49.86

Number of human participants pitted against the 2019 agent is 24, and the number of human players negotiating with 2020 Base, Chatty, and Explaining agents are 24, 19, and 19 respectively.

6.1 Post-Round Questionnaire Results

The language of the 2019 agent is monotonic, while the 2020 agents respond with a randomly selected message from several equivalent phrasings. This major difference between the 2019 and three 2020 agents, is reflected in the average likeabilities for each agent (see Table 1). According to the p-value of 0.68 of the one-way analysis of variance (ANOVA) test using this likeability rating, there is no statistical difference among the 2020 agent variants on this measurement.

6.2 Post-Game Questionnaire Results

We developed a post-game questionnaire for evaluating user understanding of the negotiation process, satisfaction with the outcome, motivation to engage with the agent, informativeness of the communication, agent friendliness, trust in the agent, and likelihood of future engagement:

(1) *I trust my negotiation partner and would like to work with it on other tasks.*
(2) *I found the negotiation process or protocol easy to follow or use.*
(3) *I was satisfied with the negotiation results.*
(4) *I was encouraged/motivated to negotiate with the agent.*
(5) *I found the agent to be approachable and friendly.*
(6) *The agent negotiator responses were relevant and informative.*

We initially expected the Chatty and Explaining agents to obtain higher scores in Question 2, which is about guiding the human participants, since the Chatty agent is more humorous and the Explaining agent is more informative. However, the Base agent shows the best performance on this question as listed in Table 3. A possible explanation could be that the human participants may have difficulty reading longer messages sent by Chatty or Explaining agents given a limited time. In contrast, the short messages from the Base agent contain sufficient information to guide human players. For Questions 5 and 6, the polite messages from the Explaining agent either clearly conveys the agent's motivation/purpose or effectively communicates to the human players the following steps, which may result in the highest scores on these two questions among the 2020 agents. On the other hand, the Chatty agent's long messages may have too much irrelevant information, which some human player may even find to be distracting. The large p-values from the ANOVA test using these ratings, listed in Table 3, indicate these differences are not significant.

Table 3. Averaged likeability of post-game questionnaire for 2020 agents

	Q1	Q2	Q3	Q4	Q5	Q6
Base	5.04	**5.08**	**5.29**	5.75	5.29	5.21
Chatty	4.95	4.79	5.00	**5.89**	5.00	5.05
Explaining	**5.21**	4.58	4.68	5.58	**5.47**	**5.63**

We compare user engagement and likeability with the threee agent types:

Base Agent: The Base Agent receives the highest rating on Questions 2 and 3 from the users. One possible explanation for this is the higher utility received by the human user with the Base Agent (see Table 2). The bare bones communication content of the Base agent may be easier for the users to follow.

Chatty Agent: The Chatty Agent receives highest rating on Question 4. Its conversational component may be attractive to the user and hence promote engagement as was the motivation behind this agent.

Explaining Agent: The Explaining Agent receives the highest rating on Questions 1, 5, and 6 from the users. These are important issues as they represent both how the agent communication is perceived to be relevant to the task at hand, addresses trust in the agent, and influences the willingness of the user to continue interacting with the agent in the future.

Each agent outperforms the others in certain aspects of user interaction and engagement. This suggests future investigation in invoking different agent characteristics at different stages of negotiating with a human user. One such possible combination might be a chatty welcoming agent, a basic agent explaining the working of the protocol, and an explaining agent providing clarifications of why an offer was made or an offer from the user was not acceptable.

7   Conclusions and Future Work

Here are some guidelines for designing agent negotiators for improving human engagement that are supported by our experiments with the 2019 HAL entrant and the 2020 Base, Chatty, and Explaining agents.

- Use of conversational language helps human engagement.
- Multiple equivalent phrases reduces the appearance of a static or simple agent.
- Important information should be communicated succinctly.
- Explanations can help to break impasse and guide a human user.
- Direct, chatty, and explaining behaviors can be invoked strategically at different stages of negotiation to optimize outcomes and user satisfaction.

Continuously adapting facial expressions and emotions, as opposed to the discrete emotions available on this platform, may prove to be more effective in human-agent interactions. Possible improvement can also be made by keeping track if a certain line of negotiation is stalling or repeating, and then redirecting it to facilitate further productive negotiation. An adaptive conversational approach, strategically invoking direct, chatty, and explaining capabilities can be developed to leverage complementary strengths of these communication modes.

References

1. Baarslag, T., Gerding, E.H.: Optimal incremental preference elicitation during negotiation. In: Twenty-Fourth International Joint Conference on Artificial Intelligence, pp. 3–9 (2015)
2. Brams, S.J., Taylor, A.D.: The Win-Win Solution: Guaranteeing Fair Shares to Everybody. WW Norton & Company, Boston (2000)
3. Crowston, K.: Amazon mechanical turk: a research tool for organizations and information systems scholars. In: Bhattacherjee, A., Fitzgerald, B. (eds.) IS&O 2012. IAICT, vol. 389, pp. 210–221. Springer, Heidelberg (2012). https://doi.org/10.1007/978-3-642-35142-6_14
4. Dellermann, D., Calma, A., Lipusch, N., Weber, T., Weigel, S., Ebel, P.: The future of human-ai collaboration: a taxonomy of design knowledge for hybrid intelligence systems. arXiv preprint arXiv:2105.03354 (2021)

5. Hafızoğlu, F.M., Sen, S.: The effects of past experience on trust in repeated human-agent teamwork. In: Proceedings of the 17th International Conference on Autonomous Agents and MultiAgent Systems, pp. 514–522. International Foundation for Autonomous Agents and Multiagent Systems (2018)

6. Kamar, E.: Directions in hybrid intelligence: complementing AI systems with human intelligence. In: IJCAI, pp. 4070–4073 (2016)

7. Mell, J., Gratch, J.: Iago: interactive arbitration guide online. In: AAMAS, pp. 1510–1512 (2016)

8. Nazari, Z.: Automated Negotiation with Humans. Ph.D. thesis, University of Southern California (2017)

9. Rosenfeld, A., Zuckerman, I., Segal-Halevi, E., Drein, O., Kraus, S.: Negochat-a: a chat-based negotiation agent with bounded rationality. Auton. Agents Multi-Agent Syst. **30**(1), 60–81 (2016)

10. Seeber, I., et al.: Machines as teammates: a research agenda on AI in team collaboration. Inf. Manag. **57**(2), 103174 (2020)

11. Stone, P., Kaminka, G.A., Kraus, S., Rosenschein, J.S.: Ad hoc autonomous agent teams: collaboration without pre-coordination. In: AAAI (2010)

12. Verhagen, T., Van Nes, J., Feldberg, F., Van Dolen, W.: Virtual customer service agents: using social presence and personalization to shape online service encounters. J. Comput.-Mediat. Commun. **19**(3), 529–545 (2014)

13. Xu, B., Hale, J.A., Pritchard, S., Sen, S.: An application of the infinite framework in a human-agent negotiation competition. In: Proceedings of the 8th International Conference on Human-Agent Interaction, pp. 32–40 (2020)

AN Using Local Search in Multi-issue Bilateral and Repeated Negotiation

Galit Haim[✉], Jonathan Langer, and Raz Yaniv

The College of Management Academic Studies, Rishon Lezion, Israel
galita@colman.ac.il, {jona.lan03,rrttou}@cs.colman.ac.il

Abstract. Designing an automated agent for Human-Agent Negotiation is a challenging task. Especially in the domain that combines multi-issue bilateral negotiations and repeated negotiations. In this domain, the agents negotiate with humans over more than one item, and there are several rounds of negotiation in each game.

Designing this kind of agent can be very challenging. Our agent needs to estimate the preferences of the human opponent in real-time, proposing fair offers that will be excepted by the human opponent but taking into account, not proposing offers that don't increase the agent's score.

On the other hand, local search algorithms have proven to be effective in a variety of fields in artificial intelligence.

In this paper, we present a novel approach for an automated agent for this type of negotiation by using local search algorithms, in particular: Simulated Annealing and Hill Climbing.

As we analyze the results from our experiments and compare the local search algorithms, we show that local search algorithms can be more efficient in Human-Agent negotiation than traditional methods. Moreover, our agent is capable of negotiating efficiently and outperforming the human opponent.

Keywords: Human-agent negotiation · Multi-issue bargaining · Repeated negotiations · Local search · Simulated annealing · Hill climbing

1 Introduction

In this paper we combine two particular problems in Human-Agent Negotiations:

- Multi-Issue Bilateral Negotiations
- Repeated Negotiations

Multi-Issue Bilateral Negotiations - Bilateral negotiation is a process that involves two people meeting to resolve various issues. When two people are negotiating over more than one issue or item, it is commonly referred to as multi-issue negotiation.

© The Author(s), under exclusive license to Springer Nature Switzerland AG 2023
R. Aydoğan et al. (Eds.): PRIMA 2022, LNAI 13753, pp. 612–620, 2023.
https://doi.org/10.1007/978-3-031-21203-1_39

Repeated Negotiations - Series of negotiations the agent plays with the same human opponent. The agent has more time to learn and model the human behavior, and through it, he will be able to establish a cooperative relationship with the human participant.

In this paper, we propose a novel approach for an automated agent for this type of negotiation by using optimization techniques for local search, in particular: Simulated Annealing and Hill Climbing.

The results of our experiments have shown, that our agent is capable of negotiating efficiently, outperforming the human opponent, and reaching multi-attribute agreements in such an environment.

2   Related Work

Our agent design is based on the IAGO platform [6] and inspired by earlier work in the bilateral multi-issue Human-Agent negotiation field. A paper that was written by G. Koley and S. Rao - "Adaptive Human-Agent Multi-Issue Bilateral Negotiation Using the Thomas-Kilmann Conflict Mode Instrument" [4], uses an adaptive agent. Their agent's main objective is to identify human preferences in real-time and propose offers that the human will most likely accept, using heuristic functions.

In their work, they mainly refer to what the human has offered or agreed to accept over time. In real-time, the agent has to decide whether to be fair, assertive, competitive, uncooperative, or adopt such qualities.

For example, if the person accepts certain offers, or offers the same things for himself, the agent will assume that the items he proposed are the items he prefers. In their agent design, they use the Thomas-Kilmann Conflict Mode Instrument (TKI) to determine the opponent's strategy and adapt the agent's bidding strategy. The TKI is designed to assess a person's behavioral response to conflict situations. "Conflict situations" are those where the interests or concerns of two people are seemingly incompatible. In such a situation, an individual's behavior has two dimensions: (1) assertiveness, the extent to which the person attempts to fulfill their own interests, and (2) cooperativeness, the extent to which the person attempts to fulfill the opponent's interests.

Their methods provided the probability of the negotiated agreement resulting in an optimal distribution of points between the human and the agent as 97.7%.

Research by Johnathan Mell and Jonathan Gratch [7], presents the differences between agent-agent negotiation, human-human negotiation, and agent-human negotiation (Also through the IAGO platform). Their research highlighted the importance of emotional and language expression in influencing negotiation.

Another research that was written by Lichun Yuan, Siqi Chen, Zili Zhang - "A Novel Strategy for Complex Human-Agent Negotiation" [5], proposes a novel strategy in human-agent negotiation in multiple issues domain, unknown opponent preferences as well as real-time constraints. This novel strategy can model opponent behavior during negotiation sessions and make reasonable decisions to establish agreements with human players.

Designing our agent, we address in **real time** to the following: whether the human threatened the agent, whether he accepted the previous offers or rejected them, and whether he revealed his preferences. We do not count items that the person has agreed to, refused, or offered, but instead, we mainly refer to his behavior during the negotiation.

We use local search algorithms as the agent's bidding strategy. The purpose of these algorithms is to look for a local maximum according to the current state of the game. Moreover, these algorithms use states. States will be influenced by the human's actions in the game, and the decision whether to offer the human his favorite items or random items will be affected by his previous behavior (threat, rejection, etc').

3   Experimental Setting

Our agent is built on the Interactive Arbitration Guide Online (IAGO) negotiation framework [6]. IAGO is a framework for designing automated agents that can negotiate with humans.

The human and the agent had to negotiate over a set of 4 items when there are 5 of each item. The human and the agent were assigned predefined and not necessarily similar values over the set of the 4 items. The maximum score a participant could get is 50 points. Each game has 3 rounds of negotiation, and each round has a time limit of 3 min.

A negotiation will only end when all the items are assigned to either the agent or the human participant, or the 3-min time limit for the negotiation has expired. In the case that time expires with no full offer, which means that some items remain on the table and are considered "undecided", each player will take points equal to their respective Best Alternative To Negotiated Agreement (BATNA). BATNA is the most advantageous alternative that a participant in negotiation can take if negotiations fail and an agreement cannot be made.

Our game setting has several challenges with which our agent deals:

- Our game consists of up to 3 negotiation rounds. Human players have the chance to "opt out" of engaging in a third negotiation. Therefore, our agent has to take into consideration this and persuade the human to continue negotiating. Failing to "retain" the human player will result in fewer points overall.
- Incomplete Information - Preferences will be unknown to the opposing side at the beginning of the three negotiations.
- The human's point values and BATNA will not be revealed.

4   Agent Design

Our agent's main objective is to maximize his overall points after all 3 rounds of negotiation.

In order to do so, our agent has to persuade a person to continue negotiating, even if he will be given an opportunity to leave after the second round (failing to "retain" the player will result in fewer points overall).

Our agent's design relies on the agent architecture that was presented by Baarslag [1], and combines three distinct components of a negotiating agent strategy:

1. Bidding Strategy
2. Opponent Model
3. Acceptance strategy

As recalled, in this paper we present 2 approaches for bidding strategies using 2 well-defined techniques for the optimal local search: Simulated Annealing and Hill Climbing.

4.1   Defining State

One of the advantages of local search algorithms such as simulated annealing and hill-climbing is that there is no need to maintain and handle a search tree or graph as it only keeps a single current state. The following definition describes the state that is used in our algorithms. Our state consists of the following:

- The items that are currently assigned to the human opponent.
- The items that are currently undecided" by being in the middle of the table.
- The items that are currently assigned to the agent.
- *isThreatMe* - A boolean that indicates if the human opponent has threatened the agent until the current state.
- *lastOfferRejected* - A boolean that indicates if the last offer that was proposed by the agent has been rejected by the human opponent.
- *toGive* - A rational number from 0 to 1 that tells if the agent has to give more or fewer items to the opponent when he generates a new state and wants to split the issue between him and the opponent.

4.2   Reward Function

In addition, we define a heuristic function for evaluating states:

$$f(S) = BATNA + \frac{1}{totalPointsOfFree + totalPointsOfOpponent}$$

The aim of the reward function is to minimize the total points of the issues which do not belong to the agent. The points that don't belong to the agent are the sum of:

1. *totalPointsOfFree* - The total points of the issues that are left in the middle of the negotiation table in the current state ("undecided items").

2. *totalPointsOfOpponent* - The total points of the issues that are currently assigned to the opponent.

Notice that the minimum number of points that each of the participants can get in a round is equal to their BATNA for the current round (this can happen when the negotiation fails). This means that it's should be impossible to get a reward on a state which is lower than the BATNA value.

4.3 Generating Neighboring States

Most of the local search algorithms are short-sighted, they are unable to see far because they are generating in each iteration only neighboring states. Generating neighboring states means the discovery of possible offers from the current state of the game. When we discover neighbors we want to be able to address the fact that the human opponent may leave and pay attention to the opponent's actions and the current state of the game. Therefore, of all the possible states that can be reached from the current state, we would like to find out the states that will make the opponent stay in the game. To do this, we address the variables: *isThreatMe* and *doesLastOfferRejected* in the generation of neighboring states.

4.4 Hill Climbing

Hill Climbing is a local search algorithm (heuristic search) used for mathematical optimization problems in the field of Artificial Intelligence. Our Hill Climbing algorithm gets an initial state and searches for a local maximum between 5 neighboring states.

Where there is a given state, the algorithm discovers 5 more neighbors and selects the state with the maximum utility (We can't discover all the neighboring states, because there are many of them, so we decided to discover only 5 neighboring states). The Hill-Climbing is described in detail in Algorithm 1.

Algorithm 1. Hill Climbing

```
 1: function HILL-CLIMBING(state)
 2:     if state ≠ ∅ then
 3:         currentState ← updateState(state)
 4:     else
 5:         Hill-Climbing(generateState(state))
 6:     end if
 7:     if size(stateList) ≥ 5 then
 8:         S_max = findMaxState(stateList)
 9:         return S_max
10:     end if
11:     insert currentState into stateList
12:     return Hill-Climbing(generateOffer(currentState))
13: end function
```

4.5 Simulated Annealing

Simulated Annealing is a probabilistic/heuristic method proposed in Kirkpatrick, Gelett and Vecchi [3] and Cerny [2], and was inspired by the annealing procedure of liquid. The simulated Annealing algorithm adopts an iterative movement according to the variable temperature parameter which imitates the annealing transaction of the liquids. We did fine-tuning to the original Simulated Annealing so it will fit our domain and requirements.

It's worth noting that our fine-tuned Simulated Annealing runs until the size of the result is 5. This means that our algorithm generates a finite number of states, unlike the original algorithm, which makes it a local search algorithm.

Note that We chose a limit of 5 states in the result of the Simulated Annealing (as well as in Hill Climbing). This is because we want that the execution of the algorithm will last a short time. If we give a higher threshold (i.e. above 5 states in the result), it will take the agent more time to generate and calculate all the required states and as a result, it will work slower in the bidding stage (it will take him a long time to make an offer).

Algorithm 2 shows in detail our fine-tuned Simulated Annealing that the agent use as his bidding strategy.

Algorithm 2. Simulated Annealing

1: **function** SIMULATED-ANNEALING(state)
2:     currentStateUtil ← $getReward$(currentState)
3:     curTemp ← $startTemperature$
4:     **while** $curTemp > endTemperature$ **do**
5:         **for** $iteration = 1, 2, \ldots, numberOfSteps$ **do**
6:             nextState ← $generateState$(currentState)
7:             nextStateUtil ← $getReward$(nextState)
8:             **if** maxState $= \emptyset$ or nextStateUtil $\geq$ maxStateUtil **then**
9:                 maxState ← nextState
10:                maxStateUtil ← nextStateUtil
11:            **end if**
12:        **end for**
13:        $\Delta E \leftarrow$ maxStateUtil - currentStateUtil
14:        $P \leftarrow e^{\frac{\Delta E}{curTemp}}$
15:        **if** $\Delta E > 0$ or $P > random()$ **then**
16:            currentState ← maxState
17:            currentStateUtil ← maxStateUtil
18:        **end if**
19:        **if** $size$(stateList) < 5 **then**
20:            **insert** currentState **into** stateList
21:        **else**
22:            **return** stateList[$size$(stateList)]
23:        **end if**
24:        curTemp ← curTemp * $getCool$();
25:    **end while**
26: **end function**

4.6 Opponent Model

In our game setting, we deal with incomplete information in several ways.

Regarding the preferences, we ask the opponent in each round of negotiation after 60 s what his preferences. As soon as the opponent gives the agent an answer about his preferences, the agent will propose an offer in favor of the opponent, in which he will offer to bring more items to the opponent from the type he prefers.

It is important to note that we also analyze the opponent's behavior by addressing in the state definition to the rejection of offers by him, and his threats. These variables help us characterize the opponent's negotiation style and accordingly propose offers that will suit him and the current state of the game.

4.7 Acceptance Strategy

Accepting offers policy is derived from a few options depending on the game mode:

1. As long as time allows, and there were no threats or doubts from the human, we will examine whether the total bid value to the agent is greater than or equal to the total bid value to the human (as you recall, the participants has not necessarily similar values over the set of the items). If so, the agent will accept the offer. If not, the agent will reject and propose a counteroffer following the current policy.
2. If there are less than 45 s left to the round, and the agent has not reached his minimum goal, we will allow faster progress in receiving bids and even offer bids that will end the game to reach at least the minimum goal (BATNA).
3. The most naive way in which the agent chooses whether to accept an offer or not is to check if the offer it received is better than the current situation (which is always true), and this is done when it will have to accept more items in a short time.

5 Results and Analysis

Overall, we conducted a total of 40 games for both algorithms. Each human opponent played 2 games with the agent. First, with the Hill Climbing algorithm, and the second game, with the Simulated Annealing algorithm. For each game, we produced 3 graphs (one graph for each round which compares the 2 algorithms that we used for the bidding strategy). Each graph represents the total sum of points that the agent obtained as a function of time. During each round, we sampled every five seconds the total number of points the agent scored up to the current point in time.

In this section, we present results of one game. The flow of the other games is not described since their results were almost the same.

We show that it is possible to use local search algorithms for Human-Agent negotiation. We conclude from the results that the Simulated Annealing algorithm, outperformed the Hill-Climbing algorithm and reached a higher total sum of points. In addition, we showed that the Simulated Annealing algorithm is reaching the local maximum slower than the Hill Climbing, but is more stable. Therefore, the Simulated Annealing algorithm will yield a better result when it comes to repeated negotiations. The Simulated Annealing algorithm has outperformed the human opponent and can be used in Human-Agent negotiations (Fig. 1).

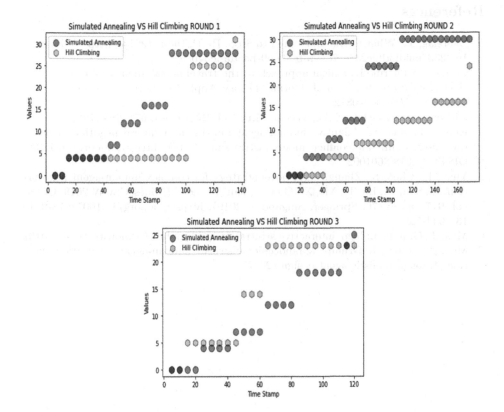

Fig. 1. Full game that includes three rounds when using the Hill Climbing algorithm

6 Conclusions

In this paper, we proposed a novel approach for designing an automated agent in multi-issue bilateral and repeated negotiations using local search algorithms for the agent's bidding strategy, in particular: Hill Climbing and Simulated Annealing.

We conducted 40 experiments overall for both algorithms against human opponents and compared their results. We have shown that the local search algorithms are more efficient and outperform rule-based agents and other traditional approaches.

From the results presented, we see that the Simulated Annealing algorithm outperforms the Hill-Climbing algorithm over time. In addition, we see that the Simulated Annealing algorithm outperforms the human opponent. Therefore, the Simulated Annealing algorithm is a good bidding strategy and can be used in multi-issue bilateral and repeated negotiations.

References

1. Baarslag, T.: What to Bid and When to Stop. Ph.D. thesis (2014). https://doi.org/10.4233/uuid:3df6e234-a7c1-4dbe-9eb9-baadabc04bca
2. Cerny, V.: Thermodynamical approach to the traveling salesman problem: an efficient simulation algorithm. J. Optim. Theory Appl. **45**(4151) (1985). https://doi.org/10.1007/BF00940812
3. Kirkpatrick, S., Gelatt, C.D., Vecchi, M.P.: Sci. **220**(4598), 671–680 (1983)
4. Koley, G., Rao, S.: Adaptive human-agent multi-issue bilateral negotiation using the thomas-kilmann conflict mode instrument (2018). https://doi.org/10.1109/DISTRA.2018.8601002
5. Yuan, L., Chen, S., Zhang, Z.: A novel strategy for complex human-agent negotiation. In: Sun, Y., Lu, T., Xie, X., Gao, L., Fan, H. (eds.) ChineseCSCW 2018. CCIS, vol. 917, pp. 66–76. Springer, Singapore (2019). https://doi.org/10.1007/978-981-13-3044-5_5
6. Mell, J., Gratch, J.: Iago: interactive arbitration guide online (demonstration) (2016)
7. Mell, J., Gratch, J.: Grumpy & pinocchio: answering human-agent negotiation questions through realistic agent design (2017)

Ontology-Based Reflective Communication for Shared Human-AI Recognition of Emergent Collaboration Patterns

Emma M. van Zoelen[1,2]($\boxtimes$), Karel van den Bosch[2], David Abbink[1], and Mark Neerincx[1,2]

[1] Delft University of Technology, Mekelweg 5, 2628 CD Delft, The Netherlands
e.m.vanzoelen@tudelft.nl
[2] TNO, Kampweg 55, 3769 DE Soesterberg, The Netherlands

Abstract. When humans and AI-agents collaborate, they need to continuously learn about each other and the task. We propose a Team Design Pattern that utilizes adaptivity in the behavior of human and agent team partners, causing new Collaboration Patterns to emerge. Human-AI Co-Learning takes place when partners can formalize recognized patterns of collaboration in a commonly shared language, and can communicate with each other about these patterns. For this, we developed an ontology of Collaboration Patterns. An accompanying Graphical User Interface (GUI) enables partners to formalize and refine Collaboration Patterns, which can then be communicated to the partner. The ontology was evaluated empirically with human participants who viewed video recordings of joint human-agent activities. Participants were requested to identify Collaboration Patterns in the footage, and to formalize patterns by using the ontology's GUI. Results show that the ontology supports humans to recognize and define Collaboration Patterns successfully. To improve the ontology, it is suggested to include pre- and post-conditions of tasks, as well as parallel actions of team members.

Keywords: Human-agent team · Ontology · Collaboration Patterns · Co-learning

1 Introduction

A growing body of research on human-agent teaming [1, 2] and human-robot collaboration [3] studies how to make optimal use of the qualities of both humans and AI agents by making them team partners. An important aspect of becoming successful team members is to continuously learn about each other and the task, to make sure the team becomes a fluently functioning unit; a process called co-learning [4].

To us humans, adapting to and learning with our fellow human team members often comes natural. In a hybrid human-agent team, successful adaptation and learning is not self-evident, as humans and AI agents differ in the way in which they learn and adapt. Still, implicit co-adaptation is bound to occur as the learning processes of human and agent will influence each other while they collaborate on a task. As a result, new team behaviors will emerge [5]; successful emergent team behaviors (coordination and

R. Aydoğan et al. (Eds.): PRIMA 2022, LNAI 13753, pp. 621–629, 2023.
https://doi.org/10.1007/978-3-031-21203-1_40

cooperation as defined by [6]) can be specified as 'Collaboration Patterns[1]'. To make sure that the team can successfully co-learn by achieving reflective communication (the highest quality collaboration [6]), it is necessary for team members to consolidate and organize their collaborative efforts by developing a shared model of the collaboration.

Based on exploratory work done in [5], this process can be expressed as a Team Design Pattern (Table 1) that describes how human and agent team members co-learn by communicating about emergent Collaboration Patterns. In this paper we address the following research question:

What kind of model and communication interface enables a human-agent team to establish shared recognitions of emergent Collaboration Patterns?

Existing frameworks of collaboration usually predefine Collaboration Patterns (e.g. as Plays [7] or Social Practices [8]), and do not study how Patterns can be created or updated through communication during human-agent collaboration. We propose a model in the form of an ontology, along with an accompanying communication interface that can be used for communication about and formalization of emergent Collaboration Patterns. An advantage of ontologies is that they provide shared univocal conceptualizations that can be used for communication and reasoning [9]. The concepts and structure of the ontology and its communication interface were evaluated empirically, with human participants. With this ontology-based reflective communication we aim to enable human-agent co-learning of successful coordination and collaboration behaviors.

Table 1. Team design pattern for co-learning in a human-agent team. The pattern supports definition of emergent Collaboration Patterns in a shared ontology, enabling partners to communicate about them. In this paper we focus on the dashed arrows on the human side.

Name	Human-AI Co-Learning
Description	When human and an adaptive AI agent collaborate as team partners, they both adapt their behavior constantly to dynamically changing requirements of the task. When doing so, Collaboration Patterns emerge. A team member recognizes a CP as valuable to the task, and communicates this to its team member. By jointly reflecting on the CP they can refine or adjust the CP until they agree on its value and use. The CP is defined and stored in the shared ontology; now both team partners are explicitly aware of this CP, and can use it when relevant.
Structure	

Communicate and store in model   Communicate and store in model

Choose fitting CP   Choose fitting CP

Recognize the CP   Recognize the CP

Emergent Collaboration Pattern

Interact and adapt

---

[1] Previously called 'Interaction Patterns' in [5].

2   Ontology: Requirements and Background

2.1   Requirements for Collaboration Pattern Ontology

To enable an agent to reason and communicate about patterns of collaboration, the agent needs a model representing the relevant concepts that underlie the collaboration. Relevant concepts are, for example, the entities (e.g. actors, objects) that take part in the collaboration, details about the actions that should be executed (e.g. which actions, when, and in what order) and the context in which the Collaboration Pattern takes place (e.g. when does it start and end). Using these concepts, an agent can connect a particular pattern of actions to a particular instance of a context. In addition, the model should allow the agent to define the success of a Collaboration Pattern, in terms of its contribution (or harm) to the team's task.

As the model will be used for storing and updating newly emergent CPs, and for communication during collaboration, it is necessary that it can be dynamically updated. Given that the ontology should function as a shared model between team members, the structure and concepts of the ontology should be fixed, while instances of specific Collaboration Patterns can be updated. This is analogous to a frame-based approach, in which an *Upper Ontology* describes concepts and relations in a generic manner, while a *Lower Ontology* describes unique instances of the concepts and relations [9].

To summarize, the requirements for the ontology are as follows: (1) it should store and specify the structure of patterns of collaboration; (2) it should contain a model of context at a level that is understandable by humans; (3) it should support the agent to reason about the appropriateness of patterns in specific contexts; (4) it should allow live updating; (5) there should be a distinction between high level concepts (Upper Ontology) that provide the structure of the model, and low level instances (Lower Ontology) that can be used directly in a task by the team members.

2.2   Ontologies in Human-Agent Teaming

There are several existing ontologies in the areas of human-agent teaming and human-robot collaboration. Some of these address team configuration [10, 11], but do not cover collaborative actions, hence are not directly useful for our purposes. Ontologies that do represent coordinated actions focus on high-level tasks and goals (e.g. [12]). Some more recent papers touch upon complex aspects of team behavior, such as the integration of intent (e.g. [2]), or a combination of tasks, goals and intent by introducing the concept of 'Plays' in their ontology (e.g. [1, 13]). 'Plays' were introduced and are used mostly in human-agent teaming applications in the military [7]. A play is a set of instructions that tells actors in a team how to act in a particular situation. This concept is similar to our notion of Collaboration Patterns, although a play is a predefined set of instructions, whereas CPs emerge and develop during collaboration. While the concept of plays is relevant for our work, the reported ontologies that represent plays do not provide information on the structure of a play and therefore do not meet requirement 1.

For human-robot collaboration, many ontologies exist that enable robots to behave autonomously in a certain practical task [14]. They contain concepts such as object, task, actor, etc., and have a large overlap with task models (such as [15]), but add aspects that are required for robots, such as hardware knowledge (e.g. about sensors and actuators that the robot is equipped with). Some of these ontologies support communication to humans, but with a focus on context-dependent information sharing. The task model related aspects of these ontologies are reusable for the description of context in our ontology (requirement 2).

In conclusion, existing ontologies that use task models as described in [14, 15] can provide a basis for formalizing context within an ontology. We used these as a starting point for designing the context part of our ontology (requirement 2).

2.3   Frameworks for Describing Patterns of Collaboration

We have also looked at frameworks that describe patterns of collaboration between partners, for example from sociology, that have not been formalized in an ontology. As we aim to represent CPs that are defined while collaborating, we are looking for a structure of the concepts and relations that build up a CP, to incorporate that in the ontology.

One such framework is Social Practices, which originates from sociology, although it has been formalized for agent reasoning [8]. Social Practices are described as ways of doing things that are shared between actors. They contain patterns of behavior that are strongly tied to the specific contexts in which they are executed. Social Practices emerge as humans interact with each other in a particular environment. Although Social practices are predefined (and not emergent) in the formalization in [8], the formalization is detailed and contains the elements that build up a Social Practice. The formalization in [8] uses concepts such as Actors, Roles, and Places to describe context, and also includes concepts such as Possible Actions and Strategies to describe expected sequences of behavior.

We used the Social Practice formalization as a starting point for designing the part of the ontology that represents Collaboration Patterns (requirement 1).

3   Collaboration Pattern Ontology

Using the aforementioned frameworks, we chose a minimal set of concepts and relations, that can be extended for use in specific domains. This minimal set of concepts and relations serves as the Upper Ontology. In choosing the concepts and relations, we have based ourselves on previous work; we wanted to ensure that our ontology could at least describe CPs found in [5]. An example of such a CP is 'Alternating actively working on the task and waiting for a team member'; in this CP, a human team member clears away some small rocks from a pile, then waits for their agent team member to clear away large rocks from that pile. This CP would take place when there is a rock pile that contains both large and small rocks. A definition of a CP based on this example needs tasks (clear away, wait), actors (human, robot) and objects (small and large rocks), as well as a way to describe the order in which tasks happen, and a condition to choose the CP. Figure 1 presents a graphical overview of the ontology.

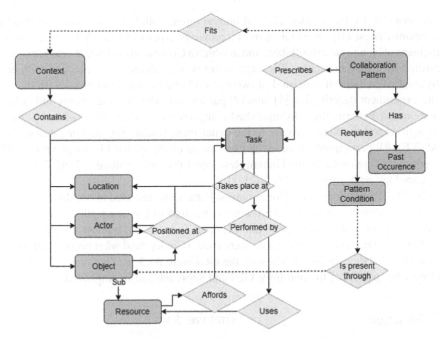

Fig. 1. An overview of the Collaboration Pattern ontology. The red items are the concepts, the yellow items are the relations. Dashed lines represent relations that enable an agent to reason about whether CPs fit a certain context. (Color figure online)

4   Ontology in Practice: Translation to Context

To evaluate whether the chosen approach supports humans in expressing Collaboration Patterns to agents, we chose to use a USAR task in which a human-agent team collaborated in saving an earthquake victim from underneath a pile of rocks (see [5]). We created a context-dependent set of specifications for several concepts, as well as a communication interface, based on use of the ontology within this task. The context-dependent set of specifications are translations of the concepts specified in Fig. 1.

To support a human team partner in defining and communicating a Collaboration Pattern and the contextual conditions for its application to their agent team partner, a drag-and-drop graphical user interface (GUI) was developed (see Fig. 2). The GUI consisted of predefined 'building blocks' based on the context-dependent concepts.

4.1   Evaluation Goals and Method

The evaluation addressed whether human participants were able to identify emergent Collaboration Patterns in video footage. We verified whether the detected patterns matched those previously identified by the researchers, as well as what the differences and similarities were. Moreover, we investigated whether participants were able to describe these CPs with the ontology and the designed GUI, as well as what combinations of the concepts they used to create their descriptions.

A series of 14 short video clips of human-agent collaboration were presented to participants. These clips were taken from a previous experiment [5]. All clips contained a fragment of human-agent collaboration in which a Collaboration Pattern was previously identified by the experimenter. The experiment was conducted by video call with each individual participant. It consisted of two parts: (1) participants practiced with the task of the experiment described in [5], and (2) participants watched the videos and defined Collaboration Patterns they distinguished using the GUI. They were asked to clarify their actions and thinking verbally to the experiment leader. Ten students participated (7 M, 3 F). All participants were in the final stages of AI-related Master programs. The procedure was approved by the Human Research Ethics Committee at Delft University of Technology on November 12th, 2021.

The GUI descriptions of the Collaboration Patterns were coded in two different ways: (1) correct, incorrect or semi-correct when compared to CP descriptions made by the researchers prior to the experiment, and (2) open coded based on how the descriptions were built up. The verbal clarifications were used to understand what participants meant in case their CP descriptions made with the GUI were unclear. They were also used to explore what aspects of the ontology, GUI and approach can be improved.

Fig. 2. An example Collaboration Pattern and accompanying Pattern Condition in the GUI. The user selects context-factors from colored blocks and drags them into the left grey area ("Situation") to define the contextual conditions of the CP, and into the right grey area ("What we do") to define the actions constituting the CP. The description portrayed is the example mentioned in Sect. 3, 'Alternating actively working on the task and waiting for a team member'.

4.2 Results: Correctness of Collaboration Patterns Recognized

One participant (participant 13) did not follow the syntax of the GUI as instructed, and described Collaboration Patterns in an extremely minimal manner. As no feedback was given on the descriptions during the experiment, there was limited opportunity for them to learn. All participants had difficulty understanding what was happening in video 5, which was understandable, as the course of actions was dependent on the implicit intentions of the human, and not very apparent in the behavior. We observed that participants became better at recognizing and describing that the human was directing the robot as the experiment progressed. Overall, they were able to create descriptions that made sense and at least partly fit with the descriptions made by the researchers.

Interestingly, anything that required the human to wait for the robot was ignored in the descriptions. On the other hand, waiting behavior by the robot was expressed often. Moreover, some participants decided to decouple the human and robot behavior completely, describing both separately and therefore ignoring any interaction or coordination between the two team members. Most participants did this for some descriptions.

4.3 Results: Patterns of Descriptions

Many participants noticed that the human team member directed the robot in several of the videos. However, they differed in the way they accounted for this in their CPs. They would for example describe the human standing still, or moving back and forth, they sometimes described 'Robot move to Human', and some by put the human actions in the situation description. Several participants also indicated that they had difficulty expressing this kind of behavior. Participants indicated that they felt the need to describe causality. They sometimes attempted to create a pre-condition or trigger for an action, but sometimes also a post-condition or consequence of an action.

Contextual information (such as locations, objects or agents) was often left out of action descriptions, possibly because participants deemed the information self-evident (e.g. the information is already in the situation description, or two consecutive actions that are done by the same agent). Sometimes, participants added extra information to make their descriptions more specific, for example by using double location specifications to describe a more specific location.

About half of the participants took a modular approach in describing the Collaboration Patterns. They used several small CPs to describe behavior observed in one video. Some participants created separate CPs for the human and the robot. These participants often attempted to create a complete set of CPs that would describe all possible behavior sequences observed; therefore, many of these small CPs were reused in several videos.

5   Discussion

Our work presents an approach for enabling a human-agent team to co-learn, and to identify and share emergent Collaboration Patterns. The ontology has been designed to be generic; it can be used in or easily adapted to other contexts. It should be seen as a first iteration for creating a model to formalize emergent CPs, that can be built upon.

To enable a human-agent team to use the ontology of CPs, we designed an interface. We chose to design a drag-and-drop GUI (rather than, e.g., a natural language interface), to restrict formalization of and communication about the CPs to concepts and relations present in the ontology. The GUI allowed us to perform an experiment with human participants. The results show that it supports people in formalizing CPs within the boundaries of the ontology. Research into what interfaces are suitable for communicating about CPs in different task contexts will be valuable.

Results of the evaluation can be used to improve the design of the ontology and the GUI. Participants tended to not explicitly formalize information that was described earlier in the same CP. To ensure that this does not hamper the process of developing shared representations of CPs, we might want to equip the agent with inferencing capabilities, or expand the interface to guide the human in checking whether assumptions are met. Several participants also formalized human and agent behavior separately. The GUI should support the user more extensively in formalizing the interactions as a CP, rather than a sequential series of actions. This requires elaboration of the ontology, by allowing parallel tasks, and/or the coupling of actions through pre- and post-conditions.

The evaluation was done offline, through video recordings, instead of on-task, based on experienced collaboration. Therefore, it does not address how descriptions might change over time due to behavior portrayed by the agent team partner. A next challenge is to implement the additional design requirements obtained in this study, and to investigate whether they support human-agent co-learning on the job. This will improve our understanding of how participants' perception of task, agent and CPs evolves over time.

6 Conclusion

The ontology in this paper enables a human-agent team to represent emergent Collaboration Patterns explicitly, thus making them available for use in future task situations. The formal representation in the ontology enables partners to correct and refine CPs, based upon new experiences or reflections. This way, the ontology system supports co-learning within the team. The drag-and-drop graphical user interface that we presented provides a common language for the team members by translating high-level concepts from the ontology to more contextualized concepts. Evaluation with human participants showed that people are able to identify relevant CPs from videos, and that they were able to formalize them using the GUI. CPs in which the human directs the agent proved difficult to describe. It is therefore considered necessary to expand the ontology system with a function to represent behaviors conducted in parallel by human and agent, as well as to explicitly provide ways of representing pre- and post-conditions.

Our work contributes to developing representations of emergent Collaboration Patterns that support co-learning by humans and agents. Further research is needed to evaluate, expand and refine the proposed ontology system.

References

1. van Diggelen, J., Barnhoorn, J., Post, R., Sijs, J., van der Stap, N., van der Waa, J.: Delegation in human-machine teaming: progress, challenges and prospects. In: Russo, D., Ahram, T., Karwowski, W., Di Bucchianico, G., Taiar, R. (eds.) IHSI 2021. AISC, vol. 1322, pp. 10–16. Springer, Cham (2021). https://doi.org/10.1007/978-3-030-68017-6_2
2. Schneider, M.F., Miller, M.E., Ford, T.C., Peterson, G., Jacques, D.: Intent integration for human-agent teaming. Syst. Eng. 1–13 (2022). https://doi.org/10.1002/sys.21616
3. Ajoudani, A., Zanchettin, A.M., Ivaldi, S., Albu-Schäffer, A., Kosuge, K., Khatib, O.: Progress and prospects of the human–robot collaboration. Auton. Robot. 42(5), 957–975 (2017). https://doi.org/10.1007/s10514-017-9677-2

4. Schoonderwoerd, T.A.J., van Zoelen, E.M., van den Bosch, K., Neerincx, M.A.: Design patterns for human-AI co-learning: a wizard-of-Oz evaluation in an urban-search-and-rescue task. Int. J. Hum.-Comput. Stud. **164**, 102831 (2022). https://doi.org/10.1016/j.ijhcs.2022.102831

5. van Zoelen, E.M., van den Bosch, K., Neerincx, M.: Becoming team members: identifying interaction patterns of mutual adaptation for human-robot co-learning. Front. Robot. AI. **8**, 200 (2021). https://doi.org/10.3389/frobt.2021.692811

6. Engeström, Y.: Interactive expertise: studies in distributed working intelligence. Research Bulletin 83. Department of Education, University of Helsinki, Bulevardi 18, SF-00120 Helsinki, Finland (1992)

7. Miller, C.A.: Delegation architectures: playbooks and policy for keeping operators in charge. Presented at the Workshop on Mixed-Initiative Planning and Scheduling, Monterey, California, USA (2005)

8. Dignum, F.: Interactions as social practices: towards a formalization. ArXiv180908751 Cs (2018)

9. Fensel, D.: Ontologies: a silver bullet for knowledge management and electronic commerce (2001)

10. van Diggelen, J., Neerincx, M., Peeters, M., Schraagen, J.M.: Developing effective and resilient human-agent teamwork using team design patterns. IEEE Intell. Syst. **34**, 15–24 (2019). https://doi.org/10.1109/MIS.2018.2886671

11. Pico-Valencia, P., Holgado-Terriza, J.A., Sierra Martínez, L.M.: A preliminary ontology for human-agent collectives. In: De La Prieta, F., et al. (eds.) PAAMS 2019. CCIS, vol. 1047, pp. 176–187. Springer, Cham (2019). https://doi.org/10.1007/978-3-030-24299-2_15

12. Madni, A.M., Madni, C.C.: Architectural framework for exploring adaptive human-machine teaming options in simulated dynamic environments. Systems **6**, 44 (2018). https://doi.org/10.3390/systems6040044

13. Kasmier, D., et al.: Ontology of plays for autonomous teaming and collaboration. In: Proceedings of the XIV Seminar on Ontology Research in Brazil, ONTOBRAS, pp. 9–22 (2021)

14. Olivares-Alarcos, A., et al.: A review and comparison of ontology-based approaches to robot autonomy. Knowl. Eng. Rev. **34**, 1–29 (2019). https://doi.org/10.1017/S0269888919000237

15. van Welie, M., van der Veer, G.C., Eliëns, A.: An Ontology for task world models. In: Markopoulos, P., Johnson, P. (eds.) Design, Specification and Verification of Interactive Systems 1998. Eurographics, pp. 57–70. Springer, Vienna (1998). https://doi.org/10.1007/978-3-7091-3693-5_5

Accounting for Strategic Response in Limit Order Book Dynamics

Ji Qi[(✉)] and Carmine Ventre

King's College London, Strand, London WC2R 2LS, UK
{k19076785,carmine.ventre}@kcl.ac.uk

Abstract. The orders of traders in financial markets are typically stored in so-called limit order books. It is well understood that the mechanisms used to rank buy and sell orders affect the behavior of traders and ultimately market fundamentals. Research has focused on different design paradigms, alternative to the commonly used price-time priority, in the attempt to reduce volatility, maintain traded volumes and reduce toxic order flows. We here examine spread/price-time priority, introduced in [8], where the spread of two-sided orders contributes to the determination of the ranking. In contrast to previous simulation and numerical results, we account for the strategic response of traders. We consider different order aggression levels as pure strategies, and adopt a sound empirical game-theoretic analysis to analyze the market at equilibrium. Our results indicate that volatility is reduced by spread/price-time priority whereas the total trading volume is highly related to its spread weight: there is a sharp drop of trading volume when spread dominates the ranking over price. Our analysis shows that a 70% ranking contribution of price and a 30% ranking contribution of spread is a suitable setting that can lower the market volatility without decreasing trading volume. Our study confirms that spread/price-time priority is beneficial to financial markets, even when trader incentives are considered, while clarifying that its parameters need to be appropriately set.

1 Introduction

Nowadays most financial transactions are electronic and at high frequency. Limit Order Books (LOBs) are chiefly used to facilitate electronic trading [9]. A LOB can be regarded as a file storing a list of all market participants' orders for a specific asset; it contains a time record for each order, with position (sell/buy) and corresponding quantity. LOBs rank orders at either side of the market and, depending on the market rules, periodically match and execute the top ranked buy and sell orders. Currently, the majority of financial markets adopt price-time priority rules, whereby price will be considered first and time will be the next indicator in a First-In-First-Out fashion [1]. The trade occurs immediately once the orders match in the market (buy price is at least as much the sell price); executed orders are deleted from the LOB. LOBs are a simple way to

© The Author(s), under exclusive license to Springer Nature Switzerland AG 2023
R. Aydoğan et al. (Eds.): PRIMA 2022, LNAI 13753, pp. 630–639, 2023.
https://doi.org/10.1007/978-3-031-21203-1_41

summarise the complex dynamics of financial markets, where micro interactions between traders result in complicated macro phenomena [21]. The study of the microstructure of LOBs is also attractive for researchers and regulators, since it can be used to understand price discovery and market efficiency. Several examples can be found in the literature [3,6,10,17]. In addition, the analysis of LOBs can contribute to trading mechanism design, whereby the rules are designed to keep the market stable [8] also when the incentives of the traders are taken into account [4,5,13]. From this perspective, price-time priority encourages high-frequency traders to submit orders with very low latency and near the half point between best bid and best ask (a.k.a., *mid-price*), since the order received first will be executed first. This aggressive behaviour should provide liquidity and maintain price movement within reasonable limits. However, their incentives may lead to different outcomes as demonstrated by the 2010 flash crash, when orders became very unbalanced very quickly [11]. To overcome these misaligned incentives, [8] proposed spread/price-time priority, which involves two dimensions (in addition to time used as a tie breaker) to determine an order priority: spread and price. This algorithm is designed to encourage traders to post orders near the mid-price price but also to submit two-sided orders (i.e., to be *market makers*) with a narrow spread so to offer both liquidity and market stability. The strength of these two pulls depends on their relative weight. The numerical results in [8], achieved through an agent-based model of LOB dynamics, allow to conclude that spread/price-time priority reduces market volatility, maintains trading volumes (a proxy for liquidity) and achieves its goals, irrespectively of the weight of spread and price. However, their conclusion is not robust to the incentives of traders who are guided by their profit. We here revisit the validity of spread/price-time priority by looking at the trading setup as a game, where the aggression levels are strategic choice, and the traders behave in the market with the aim to maximize their profits. Traders choose the strategy in response to the different matching mechanisms and the actions of the others. Our research employs empirical game-theoretic analysis (EGTA) to solve the game and analyze the market at equilibrium. In particular, we will adopt an evolutionary game-theoretic dynamic and study markets in the evolutionary stable states of price-time priority and spread/price-time priority, with different weights. Our results qualitatively change the conclusions of [8] in that they show that spread/price-time priority does not always perform better than price-time priority and suggest that a 30%–70% split for spread and price weights, respectively, can lower market volatility without affecting the total traded volume.

2   Background

We will build upon the multi-agent model to describe the high-frequency market presented in [2] and later updated by [8]. The initial model is rather simple but is able to reproduce the so-called stylized facts (i.e., several empirical features) of the high-frequency trading dynamics of the stock market. A discrete-time step is adopted, and participants are regarded as agents who aim to make a profit by trading. Public information is referring to perceived information such as mid-price, best ask, best bid and volatility. Private information is independent of each other and sampled from a Gaussian distribution with zero mean and standard deviation proportional to the market perceived volatility [2]. In the financial market, agents access public information from LOB and their private information to take corresponding decisions-active trading, cancel previous limit orders or wait until a good opportunity to enter the market arises. Trading activation will lead to the subsequent central part-order generation step where an order will be posted in the LOB including type (market or limit), size and price (when needed). Agents can also choose to close their position in the LOB due to the status of the market, and the LOB will be updated accordingly. Moreover, if a limit order has not been executed in a stipulated time, the order will also be removed due to timeout. Orders are matched following **price-time priority**, best ask/bid price will be executed first. If prices of different orders are the same, the ranking will be that the oldest is the first to be executed. LOB updates over time which determines a time series. One important limitation for our purposes is the absence of market making, which is later introduced by [8]. The authors adopt this model to evaluate the impact on market liquidity and volatility of spread/price-time (discussed in detail below) as opposed to price-time priority. They present the results, assuming that the probability for submitting two-sided orders, denoted p in the sequel, is related to the total turnover of volume.

Spread/Price-Time Priority. High-frequency traders need to risk their own capital and pay for the costly transaction costs to trade in the market and contribute to providing ample liquidity [8]. The transaction cost is classified as advanced technology, complex models, trading commission fees, etc. However, there are no more discussions on the incentives for high-frequency traders to submit limit orders in the market. As mentioned above, [8] develop a new matching system spread/price-time priority mechanism based on price-time priority. The spread is another indicator for ranking the orders for execution. The basic idea is to offer a new way to reward participants who submit two-sided limit orders rather than one-sided ones. Spread/price-time priority has two ranking attributes, price and spread. In this setup, the lowest ranking will execute first with the highest priority. The ranking is a weighted average ranking of price ranking and spread ranking based on a parameter $\alpha \in [0, 1]$:

$$rank(\alpha) = \alpha \cdot price + (1 - \alpha) \cdot spread, \tag{1}$$

where $price$ and $spread$ ranking are defined next. Price ranking $price$ is the distance from the best ask/bid:

$$price = \begin{cases} ask - ask^{best}, & \text{sell limit order} \\ bid^{best} - bid, & \text{buy limit order} \\ 0, & \text{new best buy/sell price} \end{cases} \tag{2}$$

The second attribute spread measures how narrow the order is, and considers its two "sides".

$$spread = \begin{cases} ask - bid, & \text{two-sided limited order} \\ spread^{max}, & \text{one-sided limit order} \end{cases} \quad (3)$$

where $spread^{max}$ is the worst spread of a two-sided limit order in the LOB. The orders with a smaller spread will lead to a more balanced market. On the contrary, if the spread is large, the market is volatile. Therefore, the smaller the spread the higher the priority, with two-sided order getting higher spread priority than one-sided limit orders. To sum up, spread/price-time is a smoothed version of price-time priority, where α is used to "tune" the significance of spread versus price for primary ranking. Moreover, it rewards participants to submit two-sided limit orders (to give more liquidity), and smaller spread with prices near the mid-price (to keep the market balanced).

(Evolutionary) Game Theory. A normal form game involves players, viable strategies and corresponding payoffs for a single round strategic interaction. When a game becomes complex with more players and strategies, the number of entries in the payoff matrix will exponentially increase. For simplicity, a meta-game model is proposed to analyze complex game with meta strategies [19]. Instead of exploring all the possible strategies, meta strategies are a kind of classification of all possible strategies based on atomic actions, and it can be defined as the strategy set. For instance, in the context of trading where the set of atomic strategies can be very rich, one could define a set of two simple meta-strategies $S = \{$"Low Aggressiveness, High Aggressiveness"$\}$.

We will adopt an evolutionary game theory (EGT) approach and compute evolutionary stable strategies (ESS). The logic of evolutionary game theory is similar to dynamics in classical game theory, in that they both focus on how the strategy choices evolve in time. Whereas dynamics in game theory focuses on best responses, in EGT we use a natural selection that focuses on population changes in terms of imitation of best strategy in the game. The basic logic is that if a strategy survives over time, then it must be optimal for otherwise more efficient strategies would eventually come to dominate the population. The optimal strategy computed by the so-called replicator dynamics [18] is an evolutionary stable strategy (ESS), and ESS is an equilibrium refinement of the Nash equilibrium. Under this ESS, the population frequencies will not change, and there is no incentive for players to imitate other agent's strategies. In the next section, we will talk about a 3-strategy symmetric meta-game in high-frequency market.

3   Experimental Set-Up

We will enrich the ABM in Sect. 2 and build a game where we treat the agents as players and each agent with different aggression levels as endogenous variables which will determine trading actions. Each strategy chosen by the player is directly linked to corresponding actions (setting limit prices and size of the order) that will result in market price changes and the player's payoffs. We let the strategy of each player be her aggression level according to the original setting in [2]. In particular, a strategy $\lambda \in (-25, 50)$ will measure how far away from the mid-price are the prices of the submitted order. For example, a player adopting a strategy $\lambda = 0$ will submit orders (when relevant) at the mid-price. The size of each order is instead not part of a player's strategy and is randomly generated as in the original ABM. To define the payoff of each player, we need to define some key quantities. The wealth $W_i(t)$ of a player i at time t is defined as $W_i(t) = E_i(t) \cdot p(t) + C_i(t)$ where $p(t)$ is the mid-price in LOB at time t, $E_i(t)$ is the amount of the asset that the player i holds at t and $C_i(t)$ is the cash position of the player. $E_i(t)$ may be positive, meaning the player holds an amount of the asset, or negative, indicating a short position. $C_i(t)$ changes in each period based on purchases or sales of the asset. A negative $C_i(t)$ indicates a debt position. The payoff of player i at time $t + 1$ adopting strategy λ is defined as $\pi_i^\lambda(t) = W_i^\lambda(t) - W_i(t - 1)$, where $W_i^\lambda(t)$ is the wealth of the player at time t after having played strategy λ.

A meta-game will be used to simplify the analysis of this game [19]. We will represent all the possible atomic strategies $\lambda \in (-25, 50)$ into three categories: $\lambda \in (-25, 0)$ means highly aggressive (HA), $\lambda \in (0, 25)$ means medium aggressive (MA) and $\lambda \in (25, 50)$ means lowly aggressive (LA). Hence, for each player i, the pure strategy set of the meta-game can be represented as $S = \{LA, MA, HA\}$. Each meta-strategy can be interpreted as a player choosing a class of trading strategies, akin to a species in biology. Payoffs in the meta-game will be computed as an average payoff for each group. More specifically, for $s \in S$, we let $N_s(t)$ denote the set of players choosing meta-strategy s at time t and $\lambda_j(s)$ denote the atomic strategy chosen by player $j \in N_s(t)$. We define the utility associated to s as $U_s(|N_s(t)|) = \frac{\sum_{j \in N_s(t)} \pi_j^{\lambda_j(s)}(t)}{|N_s(t)|}$ if $|N_s(t)| \geq 0$ and 0 oth.

Environment Parameters. We let n be a positive integer denoting the total number of players. In our experiments, n is set to be $1,000$ ($n = 10,000$ as in previous work [2,8] was computationally out of reach due to the EGTA part). We let G represent a matrix, whose rows represent a discrete distribution for the 1000 players over the strategy set S; G_s represents the number of players taking strategy s. Each row in G will be simulated with the ABM and we get a vector of corresponding expected average payoffs according to (??) by uniformly at random selecting an atomic strategy $\lambda_j(s)$ in the interval induced by s for each player j playing meta-strategy s. We let U denote this matrix and call $P = (G|U)$ the meta-game payoff matrix. We show below a simplified meta-game payoff table for the 1000-player meta-game and the three meta strategies in S with $(1001 + 1) * 1001/2 = 501,501$ entries; P is much more compact than the classical payoff table with 3^{1000} entries. In each row of G, the vector (G_{LA}, G_{MA}, G_{HA}) represents the combination of the 1000 players with three positive integers summing to 1000. Thus, a mixed evolutionary strategy is induced as vector $(G_{LA}/1000, G_{MA}/1000, G_{HA}/1000)$ corresponding to the probabilities that players over one entire simulation pick a meta-strategy. Each row in the payoff table P can be obtained by one simulation, and an entire meta payoff table will require $501, 501$ simulations.

$$P = \begin{pmatrix} 2 & 2 & 996 & U_{LA}(2) & U_{MA}(2) & U_{HA}(996) \\ 10 & 0 & 990 & U_{LA}(10) & U_{MA}(0) & U_{HA}(990) \\ \vdots & \vdots & \vdots & \vdots & \vdots & \vdots \\ 300 & 200 & 500 & U_{LA}(300) & U_{MA}(200) & U_{HA}(500) \end{pmatrix}$$

The $1,000$ agents include inactive and active traders simultaneously, meaning that the orders might not be enough to fill the LOB. To deal with this problem, we change two of the ABM parameters of [2,8]: we decrease by 10% the probability of order cancellation and increase by 10% the probability to enter the market for each agent, while we maintain all the other features of the model. Meanwhile, we add 50 noisy traders to our environment to make the simulated market more reliable. These noisy traders will select a $\lambda \in (50, 200)$ uniformly at random in each time step. We use 500-time steps for every single simulation and set the timeout T_{max} (i.e., orders are cancelled if not executed before T_{max}) to 100. (For completeness, the simulation in [8] had 1000-time steps and $T_{max} = 200$.)

In our experiments, we have two degrees of freedom: p (recall that p represents the probability of submitting two-sided orders) and α ($(1 - \alpha)$ setting the spread contribution to the rank). We will test the following combination of values: $\alpha \in \{0.1, 0.3, 0.5, 0.7, 0.9, 1\}$ and $p \in \{0.1, 0.3, 0.5, 0.7, 0.9\}$ for a total of 30 games to analyse: twenty-five for the spread/price-time priority mechanism and five games for price/time priority ($\alpha = 1$).

EGTA Process. We will adopt EGTA to analyze our meta-games. EGTA is proposed in [20], with many subsequent papers [4,7,12,14,15,19]. In a nutshell, EGTA uses simulations to estimate a game and solve the game. We will analyze the population dynamics of the corresponding three meta-strategies in the game based on evolutionary game theory and solve the game by the EGTA method.

4   Experimental Results and Evaluation

Since we have slightly modified some parameters of the original model, we replicate the original experiments to make sure that ours is a fair comparison. The experimental results show the same trend as [8]. (Details omitted).

To account for incentives, we obtain 30 evolutionary dynamics by solving 30 games for each of our (α, p) pairs. We conduct 30 simulations and use the solver of [16] to compute the evolutionary dynamics. We show two typical dynamics for different α's under two fixed values of p (0.3 and 0.7) to represent different levels of market making involved, cf. Figure 1. The 2-dimensional triangles represent the state of the 3-dimensional population frequencies during our simulations. The coordinate for each point refers to the mixed evolutionary strategy, which is the corresponding percentage of the different populations summing to 1. For instance, the coordinate of the left bottom corner is $(1, 0, 0)$ with 100% of the

more aggressive population. The circles in the triangles represent the evolutionary stable states where the population frequency is an equilibrium. (There are
many overlapping ESS and circles are not always visible, whereas it is clear that
the trajectories always end on a side of the triangle.) This diagram makes the
evolutionary dynamics visible among the 3-meta-strategy game.

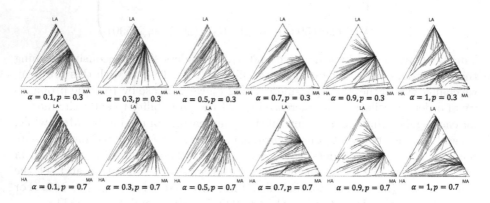

Fig. 1. Evolutionary dynamics of different α (for $p = 0.3$ and $p = 0.7$)

Figure 1 indicates similar population changes among each different α, for both
"small" and "large" probability to submit two-sided orders (that is, triangles in
each column show similar patterns). In our analysis, the basin changes can be
quantified and visible in response to the different tuning of spread/price-time
priority. Firstly, it can be seen that the pure strategy equilibrium of 100% population adopting the less aggressive strategy is attractive when spread becomes
dominant in the algorithm ($\alpha = 0.1$ and $\alpha = 0.3$). Secondly, we can see a discrete
mixed strategy equilibrium along the LA-MA edge when spread and price take
50% contribution each. Finally, for price contribution over 50%, we can see a
concentrated trend of the mixed strategy equilibrium moving from the middle
to the right bottom corner. Meanwhile, it can be found that some trajectories
terminate at the point near the top when $\alpha = 0.9$ and $\alpha = 1$. Two distinct
trajectories occur for price-time priority ($\alpha = 1$), with more ESS in the right
bottom corner and fewer at the top.

These results give us novel findings that spread contribution in the mechanism not only encourages players to submit two-sided orders but also leads to a
proportional increase of the less aggressive population. Moreover, the price of the
orders will become farther away from the mid-point price following the population changes, which means these orders will be executed with a lower probability
since we consider the real market involving a large number of market orders. It is
well known that one of the benefits offered by the high-frequency trader is providing ample liquidity. Our analysis reveals that when spread is dominant, there
will not be effective liquidity ($\alpha = 0.1$ and $\alpha = 0.3$). Furthermore, a suitable
setting of value α is essential for the health of the market.

To evaluate the performance of the two proposed matching mechanisms from a game theory perspective, we take the mixed evolutionary stable strategy with the highest frequency representing the stable market state of the corresponding game. We follow the same process to run experiments at these equilibria. Table 1 demonstrates that the conclusion that spread/time-priority can indeed reduce the volatility is confirmed, as price-time priority ($\alpha = 1$) always leads to the highest volatility. The volatility shows a downward trend while α decreases from 1 to 0.5 (price takes a dominant position for ranking). Moreover, Table 1 clearly shows that spread/price-time priority can increase total trading volume when spread give 10% of execution ranking ($\alpha = 0.9$). However, the volume will experience a decreasing movement as α declines from 0.9 to 0.1. Therefore, α is highly related to the trading volume.

Table 1. Average (over 100 runs) market data of ABM simulations with incentives

α		$Volume$						$Volatility$				
		$p = 0.1$	$p = 0.3$	$p = 0.5$	$p = 0.7$	$p = 0.9$		$p = 0.1$	$p = 0.3$	$p = 0.5$	$p = 0.7$	$p = 0.9$
								$Volatility\ increases$				
1	↑	60336	87514	85018	95037	98038	↑	317804	325779	632567	518078	525008
0.9		96383	92525	90852	102070	86260		184892	222225	368226	498034	455440
0.7		76955	78134	85244	96550	94091		184341	185597	351230	340534	444131
0.5		13924	17786	15498	10833	14549		830	629	707	580	706
		$Volume\ increases$										
0.3		10834	19997	21100	21379	24026		1248	2157	1746	1790	1810
0.1		6833	6700	10396	11181	12222		2289	2297	1343	1382	841

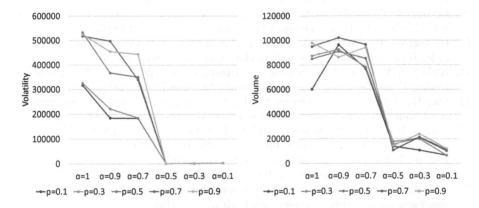

Fig. 2. Total volume and average volatility of different α and p at equilibrium.

Overall, the two graphs in Fig. 2 give us the market state when taking into account strategic responses, whereby players adjust their strategy to maximize the basic need to make a profit. They reveal that the novel algorithm proposed in [8] can lower market volatility as the volatility decreases with the spread involved, and the same finding is that $\alpha = 0.5$ will lead to the lowest volatility. However, $\alpha = 0.5$ is not proper for spread/price-time priority due to a relatively small transaction volume. From this game-theoretic perspective, with the combination of the market volatility and trading volume, the simulation results suggest that $\alpha = 0.7$ can lower market volatility without reducing the trading volume. To sum up, our analysis confirms the validity of spread/price-time priority as a matching mechanism even when incentives are taken into consideration while highlighting that tuning it right is essential.

References

1. Abergel, F., Anane, M., Chakraborti, A., Jedidi, A., Toke, I.M.: Limit Order Books. Cambridge University Press, Cambridge (2016)
2. Bartolozzi, M.: A multi agent model for the limit order book dynamics. Eur. Phys. J. B **78**(2), 265–273 (2010)
3. Bookstaber, R.M., Paddrik, M.E.: An agent-based model for crisis liquidity dynamics. Office of Financial Research Working Paper, pp. 15–18 (2015)
4. Brinkman, E., Wellman, M.P.: Empirical mechanism design for optimizing clearing interval in frequent call markets. In: EC, pp. 205–221 (2017)
5. Budish, E., Cramton, P., Shim, J.: The high-frequency trading arms race: frequent batch auctions as a market design response. Q. J. Econ. **130**, 1547–1621 (2015)
6. Chan, S.H., Kim, K.A., Rhee, S.G.: Price limit performance: evidence from transactions data and the limit order book. J. Emp. Financ. **12**(2), 269–290 (2005)
7. Cheng, F., Wellman, M.P.: Accounting for strategic response in an agent-based model of financial regulation. In: EC, pp. 187–203 (2017)
8. Golub, A., Dupuis, A., Olson, R.: High-frequency trading in FX markets. High-frequency Trading: New Realities for Traders, Markets and Regulators (2013)
9. Gould, M.D., Porter, M.A., Williams, S., McDonald, M., Fenn, D.J., Howison, S.D.: Limit order books. Quant. Financ. **13**(11), 1709–1742 (2013)
10. Huang, W., Rosenbaum, M., Saliba, P.: From Glosten-Milgrom to the whole limit order book and applications to financial regulation. SSRN (2019)
11. Kirilenko, A., Kyle, A.S., Samadi, M., Tuzun, T.: The flash crash: high-frequency trading in an electronic market. J. Financ. **72**(3), 967–998 (2017)
12. Liu, B., Polukarov, M., Ventre, C., Li, L., Kanthan, L.: Agent-based markets: equilibrium strategies and robustness. In: ICAIF, pp. 24:1–24:8. ACM (2021)
13. Liu, B., Polukarov, M., Ventre, C., Li, L., Kanthan, L.: Call markets with adaptive clearing intervals. In: AAMAS, pp. 1587–1589. ACM (2021)
14. Liu, B., Polukarov, M., Ventre, C., Li, L., Kanthan, L., Wu, F., Basios, M.: The spoofing resistance of frequent call markets. In: AAMAS, pp. 825–832 (2022)
15. Phelps, S.: An empirical game-theoretic analysis of the dynamics of cooperation in small groups. J. Artif. Soc. Soc. Simul. **19**(2), 4 (2016)
16. Phelps, S., McBurney, P., Parsons, S.: Evolutionary mechanism design: a review. Auton. Agent. Multi-Agent Syst. **21**(2), 237–264 (2010)
17. Riccó, R., Rindi, B., Seppi, D.J.: Information, liquidity, and dynamic limit order markets. Liquidity, and Dynamic Limit Order Markets (March 1, 2020) (2020)
18. Schuster, P., Sigmund, K.: Replicator dynamics. J. Theor. Biol. **100**(3), 533–538 (1983)

19. Tuyls, K., Perolat, J., Lanctot, M., Leibo, J.Z., Graepel, T.: A generalised method for empirical game theoretic analysis. arXiv preprint arXiv:1803.06376 (2018)
20. Wellman, M.P.: Methods for empirical game-theoretic analysis. In: AAAI, pp. 1552–1556 (2006)
21. Zare, M., Naghshineh Arjmand, O., Salavati, E., Mohammadpour, A.: An agent-based model for limit order book: Estimation and simulation. Int. J. Financ. Econ. **26**(1), 1112–1121 (2021)

Multi-Agent Modelling Notation (MAMN): A Multi-layered Graphical Modelling Notation for Agent-Based Simulations

Johannes Nguyen[1,2]([✉]), Simon T. Powers[2], Neil Urquhart[2], Thomas Farrenkopf[1], and Michael Guckert[1]

[1] KITE, Technische Hochschule Mittelhessen, Friedberg 61169, Germany
johannes.nguyen@mnd.thm.de
[2] School of Computing, Engineering and the Built Environment, Edinburgh Napier University, Edinburgh EH10 5DT, UK

Abstract. Cause-effect graphs have been applied in non agent-based simulations, where they are used to model chained causal relations between input parameters and system behaviour measured by appropriate indicators. This can be useful for the analysis and interpretation of simulations. However, multi-agent simulations shift the paradigm of chained causal relations to multiple levels of detail and abstraction. Thus, conventional cause-effect graphs need to be extended to capture the hierarchical structure of causal relations in multi-agent models. In this paper, we present a graphical modelling method that we call *Multi-Agent Modelling Notation (MAMN)*, with which global aspects of the simulation as well as detailed interior mechanisms of agent behaviour can be described. We give proof of concept by showing how the logic that connects individual agent behaviour to global outcomes in a previously published simulation model can be expressed in a concise diagrammatic form. This provides understanding into what drives the model behaviour without having to study source code. We go on to discuss benefits and limitations as well as new opportunities that arise from this type of model analysis.

Keywords: Cause-effect modelling · AOSE · Multi-agent simulations

1 Introduction and Motivation

The abstraction of a given real-world issue into a simulation model requires formalisation of causal relations and quantification of determining factors. Defining input variables and configuration parameters is an integral part of the modelling process. Multi-agent simulations try to recreate global system characteristics by

This research was supported by the Karl-Vossloh-Stiftung (S0047/10053/2019).

modelling individual agents. System behaviour, which is often mirrored into output variables (key performance indicators), depends on both the modelled input as well as the internal mechanisms and dynamics of agent decisions. Crucially, direct and indirect consequential effects are the outcome of calculations according to mathematical functions and formulas expressed in the model. Chaining these calculations and corresponding intermediate variables reveals causal relations between input and output variables. These relations are complicated, but visualisation in a computational graph can make the internal mechanism of the model more accessible. Cause-effect graphs have already been applied for visualising aspects of simulation models [10,12]. These approaches differ in the type of cause-effect relations modelled in the graphical representation, e.g. [12] focuses on modelling cause-effect relations between abstract events, rather than the computational aspects of key performance indicators. However, cause-effect relations between input parameters and performance indicators are of particular interest for policy-making. Current variations of cause-effect graphs typically model relations between variables on a common level of abstraction but the application of agent methods changes the paradigm from modelling chained causal relationships to multiple levels of detail and abstraction. This implies that the use of graphs working on a single level of abstraction is not appropriate and that a hierarchical approach separating individual and global perspectives would be more suitable. The semantics of a graphical notation needs to capture the internal aspects of individual agents, i.e. preferences and their decision-making behaviour, as well as their context in the computation of performance indicators at the global system level. In this paper, we propose a novel graphical modelling method that captures the hierarchical structure of causal relations between input and output variables in agent-based traffic simulations. This improves the transparency of agent-based models, by allowing the causal connections from input parameters and agent action selection functions to the result variables of the model to be clearly expressed in a manuscript. We establish a set of notation elements and define rules to represent the main logical constructs commonly used to simulate agents in route choice scenarios. Although code generation is typically a natural application for this type of graphical specification, our interest lies in finding an appropriate graph structure to improve the analysis and validation of agent-based simulations. In scope of this paper, we focus on collecting the necessary requirements for capturing the hierarchical structure of cause-effect relations in agent-based traffic simulations before further elaborating in subsequent work on how this graphical method can be leveraged for the analysis and validation of real applications. As we progress with tool implementation, we intend to assess which meta-model is best suited as a reference for this type of modelling.

The following section provides an overview of related work and discusses capabilities and scope of related modelling methods. Following this, in Sect. 3 we introduce a new set of notation elements and define rules for our proposed graph structure. In Sect. 4, we demonstrate usage of our graphical notation for representing a published simulation model from the traffic domain (see [8]). This allows us to represent the core logic that connects individual agent behaviours to global performance indicators in a diagrammatic form that fits in a manuscript. This avoids readers having to look at source code or pseudocode to try and uncover the connections. We then discuss how this can be used to improve analysis of multi-agent simulations. Finally, in Sect. 5 conclusions are drawn and possible options for future work are indicated.

2   Related Work

Cause-effect graphs have previously been used for a number of purposes, including software testing [15], system dynamics models [14], and for management tools [11]. They are an explicit and precise formalisation of logical systems and serve as a compact visualisation. Cause-effect graphs have been used in software testing to specify test cases for combinations of input and output variables [15]. Input variables define causes, while effects are represented as output variables. A specific variation of cause-effect graphs are causal loop diagrams which is used in system theory to model mutual effects between variable entities, e.g. mutual influence between predators and prey in an ecological system (see [10]). The system theoretical view of reducing complexity of information from reality to formal systems is an essential prerequisite for building computable simulation models. Building richer simulation models typically involves modelling of more system variables. Thus, observed effects are not a direct consequence of a single variable but of multiple causative variables (or chains of variables). *Bayesian networks* are an example of cause-effect graphs that allow output variables to be linked back to possible (chains of) input causes based on probabilities. However, applying cause-effect graphs to agent models has been difficult due to causal relations being emergent result of behavioural patterns of a large set of individuals which changes the paradigm from chained causal relations to several levels of detail and abstraction.

Visualisation of multi-agent systems has focused primarily on system design by extending traditional methods from software engineering (e.g. [6,16]). Some of these methods have been implemented as tools to guide the software developing process of multi-agent systems [5,9] and even dealt with system design from a more behavioural perspective [4,17]. However, these modelling methods have a primary focus on the technical design of software components, rather than the cause-effect relations of performance indicators in a simulation model. In this paper, we want to focus on exactly this type of causal relations between input parameters and performance indicators on the social-behavioural level as these are particularly relevant for policy-making. Another type of visualisation that has been applied to computer-based simulations are event graphs [12]. This type of graph focuses on modelling the relations between abstract events, which is a concept from *complex event processing*. [7] defines an event as a record of an activity in a system which is linked to other events by aggregation, time, or causal conditions. The aggregation of events into different levels of detail has led to the extension of event graphs with a hierarchical structure [13]. However, aggregation into different levels of abstraction in event processing is different from what is required for modelling causal relations of performance indicators in multi-agent systems. Global performance indicators are emergent results of the decisions of a large set of autonomous individuals, which in the graph leads to changing aggregation mechanisms depending on the context of decisions and the simulation scenario. Hence, there is a need for a new modelling method that is specifically designed for modelling the different levels of abstraction for causal relations of performance indicators in multi-agent systems.

3 Method

We have developed a new graphical notation to model the hierarchical structure of cause-effect relations between input and output variables in multi-agent simulations. We focus on modelling the main logical constructs commonly used to simulate agents in route choice scenarios. Balke and Gilbert [1] have given an overview of established agent architectures used in literature for modelling decision behaviour. For this work, we focus our method on modelling agent behaviour according to the commonly used *Belief-Desire-Intention (BDI)* model based on [3]. The BDI model allows internal agent aspects to be abstracted into separate mental-levels [3] providing a uniform basis for the comparison of agent behaviour [2] and thus facilitates the analysis of simulations. A distinctive property of multi-agent simulations is their focus on the modelling of individuals and their actions. Output variables in such simulations typically describe the system behaviour using performance indicators on the global level, whereas input variables model internal details of agents on the individual level. Based on this, we model the different levels of a simulation as separate graphs and establish a modelling method that allows for their conjunction through appropriate notation elements. Formally, let $G = (V, E)$ be a directed labeled graph with vertices V and edges E. $V = N \cup F$ is a heterogeneous set of vertices with N the set of **variable** nodes and F the set of **functional** nodes. Vertices $v \in V$ are

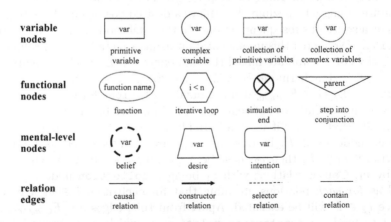

Fig. 1. Notation elements.

modelled using geometric shapes (see Fig. 1). In particular, vertices $n \in N$ serve as variables that contain either `primitive` (rectangles) or `complex` information (circles). This type of vertex is used to define input parameters and performance indicators of the simulation, as well as relevant intermediary variables that are produced during the computation of performance indicators. The outline of these variable nodes $n \in N$ indicates whether n is a `single` variable (solid) or a `collection` of variables (dotted). Vertices $f \in F$ are used to model aggregations of functional sequences as well as termination of the simulation. For example, route selection of traveller agents can be complex and is usually implemented using established, externally implemented algorithms, e.g. Dijkstra's algorithm or A*. As we are interested in modelling cause-effect relations of input and output variables, functional nodes $f \in F$ serve as an abstraction of the implemented logic used to compute output variables. This abstraction allows cause-effect relations between variables on the same level to be modelled as input/output chains while at the same time details of functions are shifted to a sub-level as a separate graph. Functional sequences that are moved to a sub-level are indicated using a `step-into conjunction` node (downward pointing triangle) on the upper level. Algorithms or mathematical formulas for computing intermediary or output variables are modelled as an ellipse using the `function` node. In addition to this, we have added one more notation element (hexagon) to model an `iterative loop` with a termination clause. A special type of nodes in N and F are *mental-level* nodes N_M and F_M which are based on the basic BDI model [3] and are used to represent internal aspects of agents. `Beliefs` are variables N_M that contain information about the current internal state of an agent as well as perceived information about its surrounding environment. This is modelled using a circle element with a bold dashed border. In addition to this, `desires` and `intentions` are functional nodes F_M that model agent behaviour. `Desires` define goals of an agent to maintain or achieve a certain state. In the context of mobility, this can also be referred to as *travel purpose*. Mobility of individuals typically is a necessary means for pursuing personal objectives, such as travelling to work or going to shop for groceries. In our notation, we model these desires using a trapezium. To achieve a desired goal agents have to perform actions or a series of subsequent actions. In the BDI model, this is referred to as `intentions`. We model this in our notation using a rectangle with rounded corners. Vertices of a graph are linked through edges $e \in E$ which are pairs (v_1, v_2) with $v_1, v_2 \in V$. Furthermore, $E = E_{Causal} \cup E_{Constructor} \cup E_{Selector} \cup E_{Contain}$ (see Fig. 1). Edges $e \in E_{Causal}$ define `causal relations` for which v_2 is causally dependent on v_1. This type of edge can only link variable nodes and functional nodes in alternation i.e. if v_1 is a variable node $v_1 \in N$, then v_2 must be a functional node $v_2 \in F$. In this case, v_1 can be interpreted as input to v_2. Otherwise, if $v_1 \in F$, then v_2 must be a variable node $v_2 \in N$ which is computed by v_1. Causal relations with v_1 being a `collection` node $v_1 \in N$, are defined as *for each* relations, meaning that for each item $i \in v_1$ a functional sequence $v_2 \in F$ will be executed. Apart from this, edges $e \in E_{Constructor}$ can be used to model a `constructor relation` in which v_2 is created from v_1.

In this case, v_1 must be a functional node $v_1 \in F$ that results in a variable node $v_2 \in N$. Edges $e \in E_{Selector}$ model a relation in which one item is being selected from a collection which serves as input to a function. Thus, v_1 must be a collection node $v_1 \in N$ and v_2 a functional node $v_2 \in F$. Finally, the last type of edges $e \in E_{Contain}$ defines a relation in which a complex variable node $v_1 \in N$ contains the information of $v_2 \in N$. In the case that v_1 is a collection of complex variables, e represents a *for each* relation, meaning that each item in v_1 holds its own information v_2. This concludes definitions for our proposed graph structure. In the next section, we give an example of how this can be applied to a simulation model from the traffic domain.

4   Use Case

As an example, we discuss the MAMN graph for the simulation model presented by the authors in [8]. This model is agent-based and was designed for measuring environmental impact of traffic caused by individuals and their travel behaviour. From a global perspective, input parameters of the simulation determine population size, potential home and supermarket locations as well as persona for agent characteristics on the individual level. The causal relations between these input parameters, agent behaviours, and key performance indicators such as average distance travelled are expressed in ca. 119.100 lines of source code. We now show how these can be expressed graphically in a succinct manner using MAMN. Based on notation elements presented in Fig. 1, population size is modelled as a primitive variable whereas relevant locations and agent persona are collections of complex variables (see Fig. 2). Relevant details of complex variables such as the attributes of agent persona (age, gender, etc.) are modelled as variable nodes and linked to the persona node using a contain relation. Information from input parameters is used to generate a population of shopping agents. This process is modelled using an iterative loop as a functional node with an outgoing creator relation. The resulting population of shopping agents can be represented as a collection of complex variables. Shopping agents in the simulation follow the BDI model and therefore details

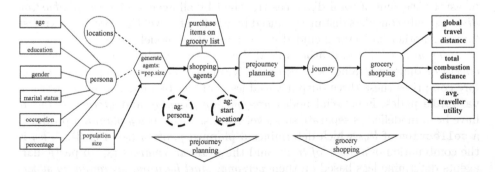

Fig. 2. MAMN graph from the global perspective.

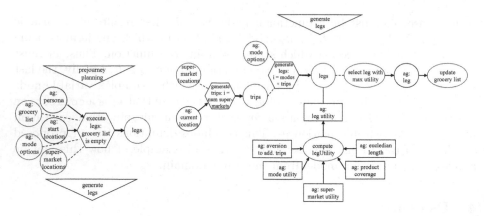

Fig. 3. MAMN graph for pre-journey planning.

Fig. 4. MAMN graph for processing the shopping list.

about their knowledge and behaviour are mapped to the corresponding mental-level nodes. Agents are assigned a persona and a start location as `beliefs` which is specified using the `contain relations`. Furthermore, agent behaviour is motivated by their purpose of travel to purchase groceries which is expressed using a `desire` node together with the associated `contain relation`. In order to satisfy their desire, agents perform a series of actions (`intentions`) initiated by `causal relations`. Agents determine modes of travel and supermarkets to be visited in *pre-journey planning*. This information is used to create a *journey* which is modelled using a `constructor relation` that results in a `complex variable`. Details about decision processes in *pre-journey planning* are moved to a separate graph (see Fig. 3). This is indicated on the top-level using a conjunction element positioned at the bottom of the graph (see Fig. 2). Agents can then use information from pre-journey planning to go grocery shopping. Again, details of this activity are moved to a separate graph (see Fig. 5). Performance indicators of the system are obtained based on movements of agents during their grocery shopping. For example, environmental impact is measured using performance indicators on aggregated travelled distances. *Global travel distance* measures the sum of total distances travelled by all agents whereas *combustion distance* only considers distances caused by modes of travel that produce exhaust fumes. Another indicator included in the simulation model refers to the *average traveller utility*. This indicator is used during the experimentation to measure effects of different traffic policies on individuals. The simulation model therefore comprises these three output variables that can be modelled as `primitive variable` nodes. Functional nodes *pre-journey planning* and *grocery shopping* have been modelled as separate sub-level graphs. *Pre-journey planning* produces a `collection` of *legs* which determines a planned *journey* (see Fig. 3). A *leg* is the combination of a *mode of travel* and the *next supermarket* [8]. In particular, agents determine legs based on their *persona, start location, surrounding supermarkets, mode options* and items on their *grocery list*. The process of generating

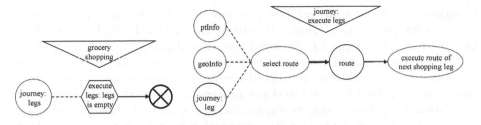

Fig. 5. MAMN graph for grocery shopping.

Fig. 6. MAMN graph for route selection.

the *collection of legs* requires a functional node with an outgoing `constructor` `relation`. Agents may need to process several legs until all items on their grocery list are purchased. Thus, we use an `iterative loop` with a termination clause depending on remaining items on their grocery list. Details of this loop are once more moved to a sub-level (see Fig. 4). In the sub-level, the agent first computes the set of all possible legs L for which applies $L = T \times M$ with M the set of available mode options and T the set of potential trips. L, M and T can therefore be modelled as `collections of variable nodes`. A trip $t \in T$ is a combination of a start location and a destination. Thus, T is the Cartesian product of the current location of the agent and the set of unvisited supermarkets. Furthermore, for each leg $l \in L$ a leg utility $u_a(l)$ is computed based on attributes of agent a and the leg. The agent then chooses a leg with maximum utility and updates its grocery list. Computation of the leg utility as well as the selection process are both modelled using `function nodes`. In this context, `function nodes` are the abstract representation of mathematical formula. This concludes the graph structure for *pre-journey planning*. Grocery shopping can be modelled as an `iterative loop` that processes all legs from the planned journey (see Fig. 5). The simulation is terminated upon completion of this loop. Analogous to the previous examples, details of this loop are modelled in a separate sub-level graph (see Fig. 6). The agent uses information on timetables for public transport as well as geographic map data to determine a route for the leg to be processed and then repeats the process for the next leg. Formalisation of cause-effect relations between input and output variables as an MAMN graph serves as a compact representation of the simulation model. This allows complex scenarios to be presented in a transparent and comprehensible manner that can be presented inside a manuscript. In particular, the representation as MAMN graphs offers insight into simulation models from a *social-behavioural* perspective, which is currently not supported by existing modelling notations and visualisations such as UML-based approaches as they focus on a more *technical* view of the simulation (e.g. system design). Event graphs may be positioned somewhere in between the *social-behavioural* and *technical* view, but are not specialised to model the hierarchical structure of cause-effect relations between input parameters and output indicators in multi-agent simulations. However, the social-behavioural perspective together with a focus on cause-effect relations is highly relevant for transportation planners using simulations based on individual traffic participants. Thus, with our MAMN method we address the lack of a modelling technique for the social-behavioural perspective of agent-based simulation models. Leveraging this, there are new opportunities to improve the development and evaluation process of agent-based simulations. Graph structures can be utilised in a bi-directional process to either transfer a theoretical simulation model into a concrete implementation as an executable piece of code (*forward engineering*) or to visualise information from a given implementation (backward engineering) which can be used to increase transparency and explainability of a system. As stated previously our interest lies in the second manner for which we establish MAMN as a basis for subsequent work on building tools for validation and analysis of agent-based simulations.

5   Conclusion and Future Work

Cause-effect graphs can provide insight into how simulation output is computed, but have previously lacked the concepts to capture the hierarchical structure of cause-effect relations in multi-agent simulations. In this paper, we have presented a new graphical method to model cause-effect relations from input parameters on the individual level to performance indicators at the global system level. This is achieved by shifting details of functional relations to a sub-level as a separate graph and through the use of appropriate conjunction elements. For future work, we will improve our graph by adjusting it to an appropriate meta-model and work on tools to improve analysis and validation of agent-based simulations.

References

1. Balke, T., Gilbert, N.: How do agents make decisions? a survey. J. Artif. Soc. Soc. Simul. **17**(4), 13 (2014)
2. Brafman, R., Tennenholtz, M.: Modeling agents as qualitative decision makers. Artif. Intell. **94**(1–2), 217–268 (1997)
3. Bratman, M., Israel, D., Pollack, M.: Plans and resource-bounded practical reasoning. Comput. Intell. **4**(3), 349–355 (1988)
4. Bresciani, P., Perini, A., Giorgini, P., Giunchiglia, F., Mylopoulos, J.: Tropos: an agent-oriented software development methodology. Auton. Agent. Multi-Agent Syst. **8**, 203–236 (2004)
5. Cossentino, M., Gaud, N., Hilaire, V., Galland, S., Koukam, A.: Aspecs: an agent-oriented software process for engineering complex systems. Auton. Agent. Multi-Agent Syst. **20**(2), 260–304 (2010)
6. Gonçalves, E., et al.: Mas-ml 2.0: supporting the modelling of multi-agent systems with different agent architectures. J. Syst. Softw. **108**, 77–109 (2015)
7. Luckham, D.: The Power of Events: An Introduction to Complex Event Processing in Distributed Enterprise Systems. Addison-Wesley (2002)
8. Nguyen, J., Powers, S., Urquhart, N., Farrenkopf, T., Guckert, M.: Modelling the impact of individual preferences on traffic policies. SN Comput. Sci. **3**, 1–13 (2022)

9. Padgham, L., Winikoff, M.: Prometheus. In: Proceedings of the First International Joint Conference on Autonomous Agents and Multiagent Systems Part 1 - AAMAS 2002, pp. 174–185. Springer, ACM Press (2002)

10. Schaub, H.: Simulation als entscheidungshilfe: Systemisches denken als werkzeug zur beherrschung von komplexität. Entscheiden in kritischen Situationen (2003)

11. Schoeneborn, F.: Linking balanced scorecard to system dynamics (2003)

12. Schruben, L.: Simulation modeling with event graphs. Commun. ACM **26**(11), 957–963 (1983)

13. Schruben, L.: Building reusable simulators using hierarchical event graphs. In: Winter Simulation Conference Proceedings, 1995, pp. 472–475. IEEE (1995)

14. Sterman, J.: Business Dynamics. McGraw-Hill, Inc. (2000)

15. Ufuktepe, D., Ayav, T., Belli, F.: Test input generation from cause-effect graphs. Softw. Quality J., 1–50 (2021)

16. Wagner, G.: The agent-object-relationship metamodel: towards a unified view of state and behavior. Inf. Syst. **28**(5), 475–504 (2003)

17. Wooldridge, M., Jennings, N.R., Kinny, D.: The gaia methodology for agent-oriented analysis and design. Autonomous Agents and multi-agent systems 3 (2000)

On Reachable Assignments Under Dichotomous Preferences

Takehiro Ito[1], Naonori Kakimura[2], Naoyuki Kamiyama[3](✉),
Yusuke Kobayashi[4], Yuta Nozaki[5], Yoshio Okamoto[6],
and Kenta Ozeki[7]

[1] Graduate School of Information Sciences, Tohoku University, Sendai, Japan
takehiro@tohoku.ac.jp
[2] Faculty of Science and Technology, Keio University, Yokohama, Japan
kakimura@math.keio.ac.jp
[3] Institute of Mathematics for Industry, Kyushu University, Fukuoka, Japan
kamiyama@imi.kyushu-u.ac.jp
[4] Research Institute for Mathematical Sciences, Kyoto University, Kyoto, Japan
yusuke@kurims.kyoto-u.ac.jp
[5] Graduate School of Advanced Science and Engineering, Hiroshima University,
Higashi-Hiroshima City, Japan
nozakiy@hiroshima-u.ac.jp
[6] Graduate School of Informatics and Engineering, The University of
Electro-Communications, Chofu, Japan
okamotoy@uec.ac.jp
[7] Faculty of Environment and Information Sciences, Yokohama National University,
Yokohama, Japan
ozeki-kenta-xr@ynu.ac.jp

Abstract. We consider the problem of determining whether a target
item assignment can be reached from an initial item assignment by a
sequence of pairwise exchanges of items between agents. In particular,
we consider the situation where each agent has a dichotomous preference
over the items, that is, each agent evaluates each item as acceptable
or unacceptable. Furthermore, we assume that communication between
agents is limited, and the relationship is represented by an undirected
graph. Then, a pair of agents can exchange their items only if they are
connected by an edge and the involved items are acceptable. We prove
that this problem is PSPACE-complete even when the communication
graph is complete (that is, every pair of agents can exchange their items),
and this problem can be solved in polynomial time if an input graph is
a tree.

Keywords: Item assignment · Dichotomous preference ·
Combinatorial reconfiguration

The full version is available at arXiv (arXiv:2209.10262). This work was sup-
ported by JSPS KAKENHI Grant Numbers JP18H04091, JP19K11814, JP20H05793,
JP20H05795, JP21H03397, JP19H05485, JP20K14317, JP20K11670, JP18K03391,
JP22H05001.

1   Introduction

1.1   Our Contributions

We consider the following problem. We are given a set of agents and a set of items. There are as many items as agents. Each agent has a *dichotomous preference* over the items, that is, each agent evaluates each item as acceptable or unacceptable. (See, e.g., [6] for situations where dichotomous preferences naturally arise.) Over the set of agents, we are given a communication graph. We are also given two assignments of items to agents, where each agent receives an acceptable item. Now, we want to determine whether one assignment can be reached from the other assignment by rational exchanges. Here, a rational exchange means that each of the two agents accepts the item assigned to the other, and they are joined by an edge in the communication graph.

We investigate algorithmic aspects of this problem. Our results are two-fold. We first prove that our problem can be solved in polynomial time if the communication graph is a tree. Second, we prove that our problem is PSPACE-complete even when the communication graph is complete (that is, every pair of agents can exchange their items). This PSPACE-completeness result shows an interesting contrast to the NP-completeness in the strict preference case [17].

The question studied in this paper is related to the generation of a random assignment. Bogomolnaia and Moulin [6] stated several good properties of random assignments in situations with dichotomous preferences. One of the typical methods for generating a random assignment is based on the Markov chain Monte Carlo method [14]. In this method, we consider a sequence of small changes for assignments and hope that the resulting assignment is sufficiently random. For this method to work, we require all possible assignments can be reached from an arbitrary initial assignment, i.e., the irreducibility of the Markov chain. This paper studies such an aspect of random assignments under dichotomous preferences from the perspective of combinatorial reconfiguration [19].

Due to space limitations, we omit the proofs except Lemma 1.

1.2   Backgrounds

The problem of assigning indivisible items to agents has been extensively studied in algorithmic game theory and computational social choice (see, e.g., [13,16]). Applications of this kind of problem include job allocation, college admission, school choice, kidney exchange, and junior doctor allocation to hospital posts. When we consider this kind of problem, we implicitly assume that agents can observe the situations of all the agents and freely communicate with others. Recently, assignment problems without these assumptions have been studied. For example, fairness concepts based on limited observations on others have been considered in [2,3,5,8,9]. In a typical setting in this direction, we are given a graph defined on the agents and fairness properties are defined on a pair of agents joined by an edge of the graph or the neighborhoods of vertices. This paper is concerned with the latter assumption, that is, we consider assignment problems in the situation where the communication between agents is limited.

Our problem is concerned with situations where each agent is initially endowed with a single item: Those situations commonly arise in the housing market problem [20]. In the housing market problem, the goal is to reach one of the desired item assignments by exchanging items among agents from the initial assignment. For example, the top-trading cycle algorithm proposed by Shapley and Scarf [20] is one of the most fundamental algorithms for this problem, and variants of the top-trading cycle algorithm have been proposed (see, e.g., [1, 4]). As said above, in the standard housing market problem, we assume that any pair of agents can exchange their items. However, in some situations, this assumption does not seem to be realistic. For example, when we consider trading among a large number of agents, it is natural to consider that agents can exchange their items only if they can communicate with each other. Recently, the setting with restricted exchanges has been considered [10,11,15,17]. More precisely, we are given an undirected graph defined on the agents representing possible exchanges, and a pair of agents can exchange their items only if they are joined by an edge.

Gourvès, Lesca, and Wilczynski [10] initiated the algorithmic research of exchanges over social networks in the housing market problem. They assumed that each agent has a strict preference over the items, and considered the question that asks which allocation of the items can emerge by rational exchanges between two agents. More concretely, they considered the problem of determining whether a target assignment can be reached from an initial assignment by rational exchanges between two agents. Here a rational exchange means that both agents prefer the item assigned to the other to her/his currently assigned item and they are joined by an edge. We can see that if the target assignment is reachable from the initial assignment, then the target assignment can emerge by decentralized rational trades between agents. Gourvès, Lesca, and Wilczynski [10] proved that this problem is NP-complete in general, and can be solved in polynomial time when the communication graph is a tree. Later, Müller and Benter [17] proved that this problem is NP-complete even when the communication graph is complete, and can be solved in polynomial time when the communication graph is a cycle.

In addition to reachability between assignments by rational exchanges, the problem of determining whether an assignment where a specified agent receives a target item can be reached from an initial assignment by rational exchanges has been studied. Gourvès, Lesca, and Wilczynski [10] proved that this problem is NP-complete even when the communication graph is a tree. Huang and Xiao [11] proved that this problem can be solved in polynomial time when the communication graph is a path. In addition, they proved the NP-completeness and the polynomial-time solvability in stars for preferences that may contain ties.

Li, Plaxton, and Sinha [15] considered the following variant of the model mentioned above [10,11,17]. In their model, we are given a graph defined on the items and an exchange between some agents is allowed if their current items are

Fig. 1. The graph representation. Graph G is shown in red, and graph H is shown in gray. (Color figure online)

joined by an edge. For this model, Li, Plaxton, and Sinha [15] proved similar results to the results for the former model [10,11,17].

Our problem can be regarded as one kind of problems where we are given an initial configuration and a target configuration of some combinatorial objects, and the goal is to check the reachability between these two configurations via some specified operations. In theoretical computer science, this kind of problem has been studied under the name of *combinatorial reconfiguration*. The algorithmic studies of combinatorial reconfiguration were initiated by Ito et al. [12]. See, e.g., [19] for a survey of combinatorial reconfiguration. In Sect. 4, we use a known result in combinatorial reconfiguration.

2 Preliminaries

Assume that we are given a finite set N of agents and a finite set M of items such that $|N| = |M|$. For each item $j \in M$, we are given a subset N_j of agents who can accept j. For each agent $i \in N$, define a subset $M_i \subseteq M$ as the set of acceptable items in M, i.e., $j \in M_i$ if and only if $i \in N_j$. For a subset $X \subseteq M$, we define $N_X = \bigcup_{j \in X} N_j$. We define the ordered families $\mathcal{M}$ and $\mathcal{N}$ as $\mathcal{M} = (M_i \mid i \in N)$ and $\mathcal{N} = (N_j \mid j \in M)$. Furthermore, we are given an undirected graph $G = (N, E)$.

The setup can be rephrased in terms of graphs. From the family $\mathcal{N} = (N_j \mid j \in M)$, we may define the following bipartite graph H. The vertex set of H is $N \cup M$, and two vertices $i \in N$ and $j \in M$ are joined by an edge if and only if $i \in N_j$ (or equivalently, $j \in M_i$). The graph G is defined over the set N. See Fig. 1.

A bijection $a \colon N \to M$ is called an *assignment* if $a(i) \in M_i$ for every agent $i \in N$, i.e., $a(i)$ is an item that is acceptable for i. By the assignment a, we say an item j is *assigned* to an agent i if $a(i) = j$. In terms of the graph H, an assignment corresponds to a *perfect matching* of H. Hall's marriage theorem states that a perfect matching of H exists if and only if $|S| \le |N_S|$ for all $S \subseteq M$. Hall's marriage theorem is used to prove our theorems.

For a pair of assignments $a, b \colon N \to M$, we write $a \to b$ if there exist distinct agents $i, i' \in N$ satisfying the following two conditions.

- For every agent $k \in N \setminus \{i, i'\}$, $a(k) = b(k)$.
- $a(i) = b(i')$, $a(i') = b(i)$, and $\{i, i'\} \in E$.

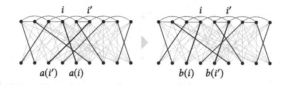

Fig. 2. An exchange operation. Assignments are drawn with thick black segments as perfect matchings.

See Fig. 2. As a handy notation, we use $a(Y) = \{a(i) \mid i \in Y\}$ for every $Y \subseteq N$.

Our problem is defined as follows. An instance is specified by a 6-tuple $\mathcal{I} = (N, M, \mathcal{N}, G, a, b)$, where a and b are assignments. The goal is to determine whether there exists a sequence $a_0, a_1, \ldots, a_\ell$ of assignments such that $a_{t-1} \rightarrow a_t$ for every integer $t \in \{1, 2, \ldots, \ell\}$, $a_0 = a$, and $a_\ell = b$. In this case, we say that a can be *reconfigured* to b, or b is *reachable* from a. Observe that $a_0^{-1}(j), a_1^{-1}(j), \ldots, a_\ell^{-1}(j)$ are in the same connected component of $G[N_j]$, where $G[N_j]$ is the subgraph of G induced by N_j. Thus, when we consider the reachability of the assignments, we may assume that $G[N_j]$ is connected for every $j \in M$ without loss of generality.

For the family $\mathcal{N}$, a non-empty subset $X \subseteq M$ of items is *stable* if $|X| = |N_X|$. We remind that $N_X = \bigcup_{j \in X} N_j$. A stable subset $X \subseteq M$ is *proper* if $\emptyset \neq X \subsetneq M$.

3   Trees

In this section, we consider the case when G is a tree. We give a sufficient condition for the reachability of the assignments, which is essential to design a polynomial-time algorithm. As described in the previous section, it suffices to deal with the case when $G[N_j]$ is connected for every $j \in M$.

Theorem 1. *Suppose that G is a tree and $G[N_j]$ is connected for every $j \in M$. If there exists no proper stable subset of items in M, then every assignment can be reconfigured to any other assignment.*

Theorem 1 leads to the following polynomial-time algorithm to determine whether two given assignments can be reconfigured to each other.

Theorem 2. *We can determine in polynomial time whether for a given instance $(N, M, \mathcal{N}, G, a, b)$, a can be reconfigured to b, when G is a tree.*

Recall that we may assume that $G[N_j]$ is connected for every $j \in M$. To prove Theorem 2, we first give a polynomial-time algorithm to find a proper stable subset of items, if it exists.

Lemma 1. *We can determine in polynomial time whether for a given instance $(N, M, \mathcal{N}, G, a, b)$, there exists a proper stable subset of items and find one with minimum size if it exists, when G is a tree.*

Below we present a proof for Lemma 1 using submodular functions. Before the proof, we summarize definitions and properties of submodular functions that we use in the proof.

For a finite set Ξ, the *power set* of Ξ is the family of all subsets of Ξ and denoted by 2^Ξ. A function $f \colon 2^\Xi \to \mathbb{R}$ is *submodular* if $f(X) + f(Y) \geq f(X \cup Y) + f(X \cap Y)$ for all $X, Y \subseteq \Xi$. The submodular function minimization is a problem to find a set $X^* \subseteq \Xi$ such that $f(X^*) \leq f(X)$ for all $X \subseteq \Xi$; such a set X^* is a *minimizer* of f. Here, the submodular function f is not given explicitly, but it is given as oracle access. Namely, we assume that we may retrieve the value $f(X)$ for each set $X \subseteq \Xi$ in polynomial time.

A minimizer of a submodular function f does not have to be unique. If X^* and Y^* are minimizers of f, then $X^* \cup Y^*$ and $X^* \cap Y^*$ are also minimizers of f, which can easily be seen from the submodularity of f. This implies that there exists a unique minimum-size minimizer of any submodular function. A minimum-size minimizer of a submodular function (given as oracle access) can be obtained in polynomial time [18].

Proof (Lemma 1). For each item $j \in M$, we define the function $f_j \colon 2^{M \setminus \{j\}} \to \mathbb{R}$ as

$$f_j(X) = |N_{X \cup \{j\}}| - |X \cup \{j\}|$$

for all $X \subseteq M \setminus \{j\}$. Since H has the assignment a, $f_j(X) \geq 0$ for all $X \subseteq M \setminus \{j\}$ by Hall's marriage theorem. Thus, since $f_j(M \setminus \{j\}) = 0$, the minimum value of f_j is zero. Notice that $f_j(X) = 0$ if and only if $X \cup \{j\}$ is stable.

It is easy to see that the function f_j is submodular, and for any submodular function, a unique minimum-size minimizer can be found in polynomial time as noted above. Let X_j be the unique minimum-size minimizer of f_j and let $X_j^* = X_j \cup \{j\}$. Then, X_j^* is the unique minimum-size stable subset containing j.

Let $j^* \in M$ be an item that minimizes $|X_j^*|$. Since X_j^* is the unique minimum-size stable subset containing j for each $j \in M$, $X_{j^*}^*$ is the minimum-size nonempty stable subset of items. Therefore, a proper stable subset exists if and only if $X_{j^*}^* \neq M$, which can be determined in polynomial time by computing $X_{j^*}^*$. Furthermore, if $X_{j^*}^* \neq M$, then $X_{j^*}^*$ is a proper stable subset with minimum size. $\square$

For our algorithm, we first decide whether, there exists a proper stable subset for a given instance $(N, M, \mathcal{N}, G, a, b)$. If none exists, then Theorem 1 implies that a can be reconfigured to b, and we are done. Assume that there exists a proper stable subset of items for the instance. Let X be one with minimum size.

We first observe that, by the minimality, $G[N_X]$ is connected. To see this, assume to the contrary that $G[N_X]$ is not connected. Let $(Y_1, \ldots, Y_p)$ be the partition of X such that $G[N_{Y_t}]$ forms a connected component of $G[N_X]$ for each $t \in \{1, \ldots, p\}$, where $p \geq 2$. Note that such a partition exists, because $G[N_{j'}]$ is connected for all $j' \in X$. Since X is a minimum-size proper stable set, it holds that $|N_{Y_t}| > |Y_t|$ for all $t \in \{1, \ldots, p\}$. This implies that $|N_X| - |X| = \sum_{t=1}^p (|N_{Y_t}| - |Y_t|) > 0$, which is a contradiction.

We then apply our algorithm recursively to the instances obtained by $G[N_X]$ and $G[N \setminus N_X]$, respectively. Here, $G[N \setminus N_X]$ consists of several connected components, whose vertex sets are denoted by $N^1, \ldots, N^\ell$, for some $\ell \geq 1$, and $G[N \setminus N_X]$ yields ℓ instances.

The following lemma is crucial. For $i = 1, \ldots, \ell$, define $M^i = a(N^i)$.

Lemma 2. *Let $(N, M, \mathcal{N}, G, a, b)$ be an instance such that G is a tree and let X be a proper stable subset of items. If there exists an item $j \in M^i$ such that $b^{-1}(j) \notin N^i$, then a cannot be reconfigured to b.*

Armed with Lemmas 1 and 2, we are ready for describing our algorithm.

Step 1. Decide whether a proper stable subset exists. If there is none, then we answer Yes. Otherwise, let X be a proper stable subset with minimum size, and proceed to Step 2.

Step 2. The subgraph $G[N \setminus N_X]$ consists of several connected components, whose vertex sets are denoted by $N^1, \ldots, N^\ell$, for some $\ell \geq 1$. For $i = 1, \ldots, \ell$, define $M^i = a(N^i)$. Check whether there exists an item $j \in M^i$ such that $b^{-1}(j) \notin N^i$. If there exists such an item, then we answer No. Otherwise, proceed to Step 3.

Step 3. We construct $\ell + 1$ smaller instances as follows. The first instance is $(N_X, X, \mathcal{N}_X, G[N_X], a_X, b_X)$, where $\mathcal{N}_X = (N_j \mid j \in X)$ and $a_X, b_X \colon N_X \to X$ are the restrictions of a, b to N_X, respectively. The other instances are $(N^i, M^i, \mathcal{N}^i, G[N^i], a_i, b_i)$ for $i = 1, \ldots, \ell$, where $\mathcal{N}^i = (N_j \cap N^i \mid j \in M^i)$ and $a_i, b_i \colon N^i \to M^i$ are the restrictions of a, b to N^i, respectively. By the assumption of Step 3, those instances are well-defined. Those $\ell + 1$ instances are solved recursively. If the answers to the smaller instances are all Yes, then the answer to the whole instance is also Yes. Otherwise, the answer to the whole instance is No.

The correctness is immediate from Theorem 1 and Lemma 2, and the running time is polynomial by Lemma 1. Thus, the proof of Theorem 2 is completed.

4   Complete Graphs

In this section, we prove that our problem is PSPACE-complete even when G is a complete graph.

Theorem 3. *The problem is PSPACE-complete even if G is a complete graph.*

This results can be proved by reduction from the bipartite perfect matching reconfiguration problem defined as follows. We are given a bipartite graph H' and two perfect matchings M_1, M_2 of H', and we are asked to decide whether M_1 can be transformed to M_2 by a sequence of exchanges of two matching edges with two non-matching edges such that those four edges form a cycle of H'. Note that the bipartite perfect matching reconfiguration problem is PSPACE-complete even when the input graph has a bounded bandwidth and maximum degree five [7].

For strict preferences, the problem in complete graphs is NP-complete [17]. Thus, we encounter a huge difference between the complexity status for dichotomous preferences (PSPACE-complete) and strict preferences (NP-complete). This is because with strict preferences each exchange strictly improves the utility of the two agents involved in the exchange, and thus the length of a reconfiguration sequence is always bounded by a polynomial of the number of agents. On the other hand, with dichotomous preferences, a reconfiguration sequence can be exponentially long.

5 Concluding Remarks

Further studies are required for the following research directions. The complexity status for other types of graphs G is not known. The shortest length of a reconfiguration sequence is not known even for trees. In particular, when there is a reconfiguration sequence, we do not know whether the shortest length is bounded by a polynomial in $|N|$. We may also study other types of preferences.

References

1. Abdulkadiroğlu, A., Sönmez, T.: House allocation with existing tenants. J. Econ. Theory **88**(2), 233–260 (1999). https://doi.org/10.1006/jeth.1999.2553
2. Abebe, R., Kleinberg, J., Parkes, D.: Fair division via social comparison. In: Larson, K., Winikoff, M., Das, S., Durfee, E.H. (eds.) Proceedings of the 16th Conference on Autonomous Agents and Multiagent Systems, pp. 281–289. International Foundation for Autonomous Agents and Multiagent Systems, Richland, SC (2017)
3. Aziz, H., Bouveret, S., Caragiannis, I., Giagkousi, I., Lang, J.: Knowledge, fairness, and social constraints. In: McIlraith, S.A., Weinberger, K.Q. (eds.) Proceedings of the 32nd AAAI Conference on Artificial Intelligence, pp. 4638–4645. AAAI Press, Palo Alto, CA (2018)
4. Aziz, H., De Keijzer, B.: Housing markets with indifferences: a tale of two mechanisms. In: Hoffmann, J., Selman, B. (eds.) Proceedings of the 26th AAAI Conference on Artificial Intelligence, pp. 1249–1255. AAAI Press, Palo Alto (2012)
5. Beynier, A., et al.: Local envy-freeness in house allocation problems. Auton. Agent. Multi-Agent Syst. **33**(5), 591–627 (2019). https://doi.org/10.1007/s10458-019-09417-x
6. Bogomolnaia, A., Moulin, H.: Random matching under dichotomous preferences. Econometrica **72**(1), 257–279 (2004). https://doi.org/10.1111/j.1468-0262.2004.00483.x
7. Bonamy, M., et al.: The perfect matching reconfiguration problem. In: Rossmanith, P., Heggernes, P., Katoen, J. (eds.) Proceedings of the 44th International Symposium on Mathematical Foundations of Computer Science. Leibniz International Proceedings in Informatics, vol. 138, pp. 80:1–80:14. Schloss Dagstuhl - Leibniz-Zentrum für Informatik, Wadern, Germany (2019). https://doi.org/10.4230/LIPIcs.MFCS.2019.80
8. Bredereck, R., Kaczmarczyk, A., Niedermeier, R.: Envy-free allocations respecting social networks. Artif. Intell. **305**, 103664 (2022). https://doi.org/10.1016/j.artint.2022.103664

9. Flammini, M., Mauro, M., Tonelli, M.: On social envy-freeness in multi-unit markets. Artif. Intell. **269**, 1–26 (2019). https://doi.org/10.1016/j.artint.2018.12.003
10. Gourvès, L., Lesca, J., Wilczynski, A.: Object allocation via swaps along a social network. In: Sierra, C. (ed.) Proceedings of the 26th International Joint Conference on Artificial Intelligence, pp. 213–219. AAAI Press, Palo Alto (2017). https://doi.org/10.24963/ijcai.2017/31
11. Huang, S., Xiao, M.: Object reachability via swaps under strict and weak preferences. Auton. Agent. Multi-Agent Syst. **34**(2), 1–33 (2020). https://doi.org/10.1007/s10458-020-09477-4
12. Ito, T., et al.: On the complexity of reconfiguration problems. Theoret. Comput. Sci. **412**(12–14), 1054–1065 (2011). https://doi.org/10.1016/j.tcs.2010.12.005
13. Klaus, B., Manlove, D.F., Rossi, F.: Matching under preferences. In: Brandt, F., Conitzer, V., Endriss, U., Lang, J., Procaccia, A.D. (eds.) Handbook of Computational Social Choice, pp. 333–355. Cambridge University Press, Cambridge (2016). https://doi.org/10.1017/CBO9781107446984.015
14. Levin, D.A., Peres, Y.: Markov Chain and Mixing Times: Second Edition. AMS, Providence, RI (2017). https://doi.org/10.1090/mbk/107
15. Li, F., Plaxton, C.G., Sinha, V.B.: Object allocation over a network of objects: Mobile agents with strict preferences. In: Dignum, F., Lomuscio, A., Endriss, U., Nowé, A. (eds.) Proceedings of the 20th International Conference on Autonomous Agents and Multiagent Systems, pp. 1578–1580. International Foundation for Autonomous Agents and Multiagent Systems, Richland, SC (2021)
16. Manlove, D.F.: Algorithmics of Matching Under Preferences. World Scientific, Singapore (2013). https://doi.org/10.1142/8591
17. Abramowitz, B., Shapiro, E., Talmon, N.: In the beginning there were n agents: founding and amending a constitution. In: Fotakis, D., Ríos Insua, D. (eds.) ADT 2021. LNCS (LNAI), vol. 13023, pp. 119–131. Springer, Cham (2021). https://doi.org/10.1007/978-3-030-87756-9_8
18. Murota, K.: Discrete Convex Analysis, SIAM Monographs on Discrete Mathematics and Applications, vol. 10. SIAM, Philadelphia (2003). https://doi.org/10.1137/1.9780898718508
19. Nishimura, N.: Introduction to reconfiguration. Algorithms **11**(4), 52 (2018). https://doi.org/10.3390/a11040052
20. Shapley, L., Scarf, H.: On cores and indivisibility. J. Math. Econ. **1**(1), 23–37 (1974). https://doi.org/10.1016/0304-4068(74)90033-0

Identifying Necessary and Sufficient Conditions for the Enforcement Problem of Argumentation Frameworks

Huan Zhang[1,2](✉) and Songmao Zhang[1]

[1] Key Laboratory of MADIS, Academy of Mathematics and Systems Science, Chinese Academy of Sciences, Beijing 100190, China
smzhang@math.ac.cn
[2] School of Mathematical Sciences, University of Chinese Academy of Sciences, Beijing 100049, China
zhanghuan@amss.ac.cn

Abstract. In the dynamics research of argumentation frameworks (AFs), the enforcement problem deals with changing an AF for the purpose of ensuring that a certain set of desired arguments becomes (part of) an extension. In this paper we focus on expansions of an AF where solely the addition of new arguments and attacks is allowed and the original framework remains unchanged. Existing results about the enforcement problem under strong and normal expansion are all sufficient conditions. We argue that necessary and sufficient conditions are essential concerning the solvability of the enforcement problem. Specifically, two necessary and sufficient conditions are identified for the non-strict enforcement in respectively the odd-length cycle free and the even-length cycle free AFs under strong expansion. This result can be used to determine that when new arguments satisfying the condition are unavailable, enforcing the desired set simply becomes unsolvable.

Keywords: Argumentation framework · Enforcement problem · Necessary and sufficient condition

1 Introduction

Argumentation stands as one of the core intellectual activities of mankind, and thus has been a research subject of Artificial Intelligence ever since its beginning. A landmark work is the abstract argumentation framework (AF) proposed by Dung in 1995 [1]. Since then, extensive research has flourished concerning diverse aspects of AF. Among them, the dynamics of AF studies the change in arguments and their relations and the resultant effect on the extensions, i.e., the justified

This work was supported in part by funding from the National Natural Science Foundation of China (61621003).

sets of arguments according to various kinds of semantics [2–5]. One of the most interesting dynamics problems is the so-called *enforcement problem* [6], which deals with changing an AF for the purpose of ensuring that a certain set of desired arguments becomes an extension or at least part of an extension [7]. Concretely, there are constraints on the allowed changes to the given AF: enforcing a set of arguments via the addition or deletion of arguments and attacks. Under the addition situation, the expansion is called *normal* when original arguments and attacks are kept intact [6], of which *weak* and *strong expansion* are two specific types.

For expansions, there already exist results about whether it is possible or how to find solutions of enforcement problem [6,8]. It has been shown that under weak expansion it is impossible to enforce a desired set that is not included in an extension for most semantics [8]. For normal and strong expansions, as we know, the existing results are all sufficient conditions, e.g., [6] shows that as long as the new argument attacks all the original arguments except the desired ones, the new and desired arguments constitute an extension under strong expansion. In this paper, we are concerned with the situation when arguments satisfying such sufficient conditions are not found. Take the medical group consulting for example. When evidence at hand cannot justify the desired treatment, one needs to perform more tests and gather more supportive knowledge so as to meet some sufficient condition. When such new arguments turn out unavailable in reality, should one keeps searching or simply abandons the desired treatment? The question arises here is when one can decide that the enforcement problem is unsolvable. This calls for the identification of necessary and sufficient conditions for the enforcement problem.

In this paper, we focus on the enforcement problem under strong expansion, and identify two necessary and sufficient conditions respectively for two classes of argumentation frameworks. To the best of our knowledge, this is the first time that such conditions are studied.

The paper is organized as follows. In Sect. 2, we briefly introduce the argumentation framework and the enforcement problem. The necessary and sufficient conditions are then presented in Sect. 3. Lastly in Sect. 4, we discuss related work and conclude the paper.

2   Background

The background knowledge in this section includes the basic notions of AF, extensions, allowed expansions, and the enforcement problem.

2.1   Argumentation Framework and Its Extension-Based Semantics

Firstly, we introduce Dung's definition of abstract argumentation frameworks.

Definition 1 [1]. *An argumentation framework is a tuple $F = (A, R)$, where A is a set of arguments and $R \subseteq A \times A$ a set of attacks. Moreover, from the perspective of graph theory, an argumentation framework can be represented as a directed graph, whose nodes represent arguments and edges attacks.*

We use $(a, b) \in R$ to denote that argument a attacks argument b, and call that a is an attacker of b. Moreover, for a set $S \subseteq A$, if an argument a attacks or is attacked by some argument in S, we say that a attacks or is attacked by S, respectively. We use S^+ and S^- to denote the sets of arguments that respectively are attacked by S and attack S. Besides, we use $F \downarrow_S$ to denote an argumentation framework whose set of arguments is S and set of attacks $R \cap (S \times S)$.

The following example illustrates an argumentation framework.

Example 1. Let $F_{exm} = (\{a_1, a_2, a_3, a_4, a_5, a_6, a_7, a_8\}, \{(a_1, a_2), (a_2, a_3), (a_3, a_4),$ $(a_4, a_1), (a_3, a_5), (a_5, a_6), (a_6, a_7), (a_7, a_8), (a_8, a_5)\})$ be an AF. Its corresponding directed graph is depicted in Fig. 1. In F_{exm}, for a set of arguments $S = \{a_1, a_2\}$, one can see that a_4 attacks S and a_3 is attacked by S. Moreover, $S^+ = \{a_2, a_3\}$, $S^- = \{a_1, a_4\}$, and $F_{exm} \downarrow_S = (\{a_1, a_2\}, \{(a_1, a_2)\})$.

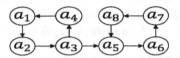

Fig. 1. The directed graph of F_{exm}.

As stated in [1], the fundamental problem is to determine the arguments that can be justified by AF, and accordingly the extension-based semantics is proposed where an extension represents a set of arguments that are considered jointly acceptable. The relevant notions are defined as follows.

Definition 2 [1]. *Let $F = (A, R)$ be an argumentation framework.*

- *A set $S \subseteq A$ of arguments is conflict-free iff $\nexists a, b \in S$, s.t. $(a, b) \in R$.*
- *An argument $a \in A$ is acceptable w.r.t. a set $S \subseteq A$ of arguments iff $\forall (b, a) \in R$, $\exists c \in S$, s.t. $(c, b) \in R$.*
- *A conflict-free set of arguments $S \subseteq A$ is admissible iff each argument in S is acceptable w.r.t. S.*
- *S is a preferred extension iff S is a $\subseteq$-maximal admissible set of arguments.*

The preferred extension constitutes only one of many existing semantics, for which a complete introduction can be found in [9], including the grounded extension, stable extension and complete extension originally defined in [1]. Among various semantics, the preferred extension-based semantics represents the main contribution in Dung's theory, as "it allows multiple extensions (differently from grounded semantics), the existence of extensions is always guaranteed (differently from stable semantics), and no extension is a proper subset of another extension (differently from complete semantics)" [10]. We focus on preferred extensions in this paper.

2.2   The Enforcement Problem of Argumentation Frameworks

The dynamics of argumentation frameworks can correspond to the multi-agent context: the framework evolves as the agents put forward new arguments. In such a context, new arguments and attack relations combined with the original ones form a new argumentation framework, often called an expansion. In this paper we focus on expansions of an AF where new arguments and attacks are added while attacks among the original arguments remain unchanged. The basic assumption behind such expansions is that the original attacks have been fully clarified and there is no dispute over these relations. Regarding expansions of argumentation frameworks, the following concepts are defined.

Definition 3 [6]. *An AF F' is an expansion of AF $F = (A, R)$ iff $F' = (A \cup A', R \cup R')$ for some nonempty A' disjoint from A. An expansion is*

1. *normal ($F \prec^N F'$) iff $\forall a, b((a, b) \in R' \rightarrow a \in A' \vee b \in A')$,*
2. *strong ($F \prec_S^N F'$) iff $F \prec^N F'$ and $\forall a, b((a, b) \in R' \rightarrow \neg(a \in A \wedge b \in A'))$,*
3. *weak ($F \prec_W^N F'$) iff $F \prec^N F'$ and $\forall a, b((a, b) \in R' \rightarrow \neg(a \in A' \wedge b \in A))$.*

Normal expansions contain new arguments and possibly new attack relations, and the latter are only allowed between new arguments or between new and original arguments. Strong and weak expansions are two kinds of particular normal expansions, which restrict the possible attacks between new and original arguments to a single direction. Figure 2 illustrates the three types of expansions, where g is a new argument and dashed arrows represent the added attacks.

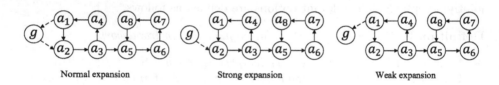

Normal expansion   Strong expansion   Weak expansion

Fig. 2. Three expansions of F_{exm}.

The enforcement problem, as the core problem in the dynamics of argumentation frameworks, aims to modify an AF such that a desired set of arguments becomes an extension (called *strict enforcement*) or included in an extension of the modified AF (called *non-strict enforcement*). One of the well-known results about the enforcement problem is that, as stated in [8], "under normal expansion, it's impossible to make a set of argument which is not an extension in original AF be an extension in modified AF in a strict way". Therefore we only take the non-strict enforcement problem into account in this paper.

3   Necessary and Sufficient Conditions for the Enforcement Problem Under Strong Expansion

In this section, we propose two necessary and sufficient conditions for the enforcement problem under strong expansion. Without loss of generality, we only consider adding one new argument, and all the results hold when the addition becomes a conflict-free set of new arguments. Moreover, we consider two classes of argumentation frameworks separately, those without odd-length cycles and those without even-length cycles, where the cycles are defined as follows.

Definition 4. *In a directed graph of argumentation framework, a directed cycle is a node sequence $(a_1, a_2, ..., a_n)(n \geq 2)$ such that the only repeated nodes are the first and the last. If the number of distinct nodes of a directed cycle is odd (even, respectively), we call this directed cycle an odd-length (even-length, respectively) cycle.*

Example 2 (Example 1 continued). In Fig. 1, the node sequence $(a_1, a_2, a_3, a_4, a_1)$ is an even-length cycle. There are none odd-length cycles in F_{exm}.

3.1   The First Necessary and Sufficient Condition

In this subsection, we focus on the enforcement problem of argumentation frameworks without odd-length cycles under strong expansion. The identified necessary and sufficient condition is presented in Theorem 1, which specifies that the desired set together with the new argument become a preferred extension if and only if the new argument attacks every original argument out of the scope of the desired set as well as those attacked by the desired set.

Theorem 1. *Given an AF $F = (A, R)$ without odd-length cycles, a conflict-free set of arguments $E \subseteq A$ and a new argument g. Let $R_g = \{(g, b)|b \in A\}$ denote the attacks from g. The following conclusion holds: $E \cup \{g\}$ is a preferred extension of $F' = (A \cup \{g\}, R \cup R_g)$ iff g attacks each argument in $A\backslash(E \cup E^+)$.*

Proof. ($\Leftarrow$) Since there are none attacks between E and g, $E \cup \{g\}$ is a conflict-free set. Moreover, according to the definition of E^+, we can infer that $\forall a \in A\backslash(E \cup \{g\}), \exists b \in E \cup \{g\}, (b, a) \in R_g$, which means that $E \cup \{g\}$ can attack each one of its attackers and $E \cup \{g\}$ is a $\subseteq$-maximal conflict-free set. Consequently, $E \cup \{g\}$ is a preferred extension of $F' = (A \cup \{g\}, R \cup R_g)$.

($\Rightarrow$) We prove that each admissible set of $F'\!\downarrow_{A\backslash(E\cup\{g\}\cup E^+\cup\{g\}^+)}$ together with $E \cup \{g\}$ is admissible. Let Γ be an admissible set of $F'\!\downarrow_{A\backslash(E\cup\{g\}\cup E^+\cup\{g\}^+)}$. Firstly, due to the definition of preferred extension, we know that there are none attacks between $E \cup \{g\}$ and Γ, which means that $E \cup \{g\} \cup \Gamma$ is conflict-free. Secondly, since $E \cup \{g\}$ and Γ are admissible, each attacker of $E \cup \{g\} \cup \Gamma$ can be attacked by $E \cup \{g\}$ or Γ, which means that $E \cup \{g\} \cup \Gamma$ is also admissible. Hence, each admissible set of $F'\!\downarrow_{A\backslash(E\cup\{g\}\cup E^+\cup\{g\}^+)}$ together with $E \cup \{g\}$ is still admissible.

Furthermore, according to the proof of Proposition 5.1 in [11], we know that any AF without odd-length cycles contains a non-empty admissible set. Hence, unless $F'{\downarrow}_{A\backslash(E\cup\{g\}\cup E^+\cup\{g\}^+)}$ contains no arguments, $E \cup \{g\}$ would not be a maximal admissible set. This means that $A\backslash(E \cup \{g\} \cup E^+ \cup \{g\}^+)$ is empty. Since g does not belong to A, $A\backslash(E\cup E^+)$ is a subset of $\{g\}^+$ consequently, i.e., g has to attack each argument in $A\backslash(E \cup E^+)$.

Example 3 (Example 1 continued). Argumentation framework F_{exm} in Example 1 is one without odd-length cycles. Suppose a desired set $E = \{a_1, a_3, a_7\}$ and a new argument g. Based on Theorem 1, we know that $E \cup \{g\}$ is a preferred extension of $F' = (A\cup\{g\}, R\cup R_g)$ iff g attacks a_6 which is the only argument in $A\backslash(E\cup E^+)$. The expansion F' of F is depicted in Fig. 3, where the dashed arrow represents the added attack. This result reveals that when the argument that attacks a_6 cannot be found, the non-strict enforcement of E becomes unsolvable.

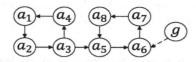

Fig. 3. An example illustrating Theorem 1.

3.2   The Second Necessary and Sufficient Condition

In this subsection, we focus on the enforcement problem of argumentation frameworks without even-length cycles under strong expansion. For such a class of AFs, [12] has presented a condition that suffices to guarantee a unique preferred extension, which is empty set.

Lemma 1 [11]. *For any argumentation frameworks $F = (A, R)$, if there are no even-length cycles in F and $\forall a \in A, \exists b \in A, (b, a) \in R$, then there are none non-empty preferred extensions of F.*

In order to enforce the desired set of arguments E in an AF without even-length cycles, certain arguments have to be attacked to make E admissible. Such arguments can be obtained in a constructive way as specified by Definition 5.

Definition 5 (Must-attack set). *Let $F = (A, R)$ be an argumentation framework without even-length cycles and $E \subseteq A$ a conflict-free set of arguments. We set:*

- $\Phi_0(F, E) = E^-\backslash E^+$
- $US_i(F, E) = \{a\in A\backslash(E\cup E^+\cup\Phi_i(F, E))\mid \nexists b\in A\backslash(E\cup E^+\cup\Phi_i(F, E)), (b, a)\in R\}$
- $\Phi_{i+1}(F, E) = \begin{cases} \Phi_i(F, E) & US_i(F, E) = \emptyset \\ \Phi_i(F, E)\cup US_i(F, E) & otherwise \end{cases}$

The must-attack set of arguments for E to become admissible is $\Phi(F, E) = \Phi_n(F, E)$ such that $\Phi_n(F, E) = \Phi_{n+1}(F, E)$.

Based on Lemma 1 and Definition 5, a necessary and sufficient condition for the enforcement problem of AF without even-length cycles can be identified, as in Theorem 2. It specifies that the desired set together with the new argument become a preferred extension if and only if the new argument attacks every original argument in the must-attack set for the desired set.

Theorem 2. *Given an AF $F = (A, R)$ without even-length cycles, a conflict-free set of arguments $E \subseteq A$ and a new argument g. Let $R_g = \{(g, b)|b \in A\}$ denote the attacks from g. The following conclusion holds: $E \cup \{g\}$ is a preferred extension of $F' = (A \cup \{g\}, R \cup R_g)$ iff g attacks each argument in $\Phi(F, E)$ obtained in Definition 5.*

Proof. ($\Leftarrow$) Firstly, we know that $E \cup \{g\}$ is conflict-free. Secondly, since g attacks each argument in $E^- \backslash E^+$, we can infer that $\forall a \in A$, if $\exists b \in E \cup \{g\}, (a, b) \in R \cup R_g$, then $\exists c \in E \cup \{g\}, (c, a) \in R \cup R_g$. Therefore, $E \cup \{g\}$ is admissible. Lastly, because each argument in $E^- \cup E^+ \cup \Phi(F, E)$ is attacked by an argument in $E \cup \{g\}$, it is impossible to add arguments of $E^- \cup E^+ \cup \Phi(F, E)$ to $E \cup \{g\}$ to get a larger admissible set. Besides, we know that there exists no even-length cycle and unattacked argument in $F'\downarrow_{A \backslash (E^- \cup E^+ \cup \Phi(F, E))}$. According to Lemma 1, we can infer that there are no non-empty preferred extensions of $F'\downarrow_{A \backslash (E \cup E^- \cup E^+ \cup \Phi(F, E))}$. Hence, $E \cup \{g\}$ is a $\subseteq$-maximal admissible set, i.e., a preferred extension of $F' = (A \cup \{g\}, R \cup R_g)$.

($\Rightarrow$) Let us compute step by step the set of arguments that g must attack, which is denoted by $\Psi_i, i \geq 0$. Firstly, by the admissibility of preferred extensions, g has to attack each argument in $E^- \backslash E^+$, so to start with $\Psi_0 = E^- \backslash E^+$. Secondly, if there are arguments in $A \backslash (E \cup E^+ \cup \Psi_0)$ which are not attacked by any other arguments in $A \backslash (E \cup E^+ \cup \Psi_0)$, then these arguments must be attacked by g; otherwise, these arguments together with $E \cup \{g\}$ can form a larger admissible set, which contradicts with that $E \cup \{g\}$ is a preferred extension. Therefore, $\Psi_1 = (E^- \backslash E^+) \cup \{a \in A \backslash (E \cup E^+ \cup \Psi_0)| \not\exists b \in A \backslash (E \cup E^+ \cup \Psi_0), (b, a) \in R\}$. Further, this goes by iteration, i.e., those not attacked by any other arguments in $A \backslash (E \cup E^+ \cup \Psi_i)$ must be attacked by g, and thus need to be added to Ψ_{i+1}. Lastly, the iteration stops when $\Psi_{n+1} = \Psi_n (n \geq 0)$, and Ψ_n is the set consisting of all arguments that g must attack. Based on Definition 5, we can infer that $\Phi(F, E) \subseteq \Psi_n$, which means that g attacks every argument in $\Phi(F, E)$.

Example 4. Given an argumentation framework $F = (\{a_1, a_2, a_3, a_4, a_5, a_6, a_7, a_8\}, \{(a_1, a_2), (a_2, a_3), (a_2, a_4), (a_4, a_1), (a_3, a_5), (a_5, a_6), (a_6, a_7), (a_7, a_8)\})$, a desired set $E = \{a_1, a_5\}$ and a new argument g. Based on Theorem 2, we know that $E \cup \{g\}$ is a preferred extension of $F' = (A \cup \{g\}, R \cup R_g)$ iff g attacks a_3, a_4, a_7 and a_8 simultaneously. This says that when no such new arguments can be found, the non-strict enforcement of E is simply unsolvable. The resultant expansion F' of F and intermediate results in constructing following Definition 5 are depicted in Fig. 4, where dashed arrows represent the added attacks.

Obtaining the must-attack set for enforcing E	AF being considered
$F = (A = \{a_1, a_2, a_3, a_4, a_5, a_6, a_7, a_8\}, R = (a_1, a_2), (a_2, a_3), (a_2, a_4),$ $(a_4, a_1), (a_3, a_5), (a_5, a_6), (a_6, a_7), (a_7, a_8)\}), E = \{a_1, a_5\}.$	
$E^+ = \{a_2, a_6\}$	
$E^- = \{a_3, a_4\}$	
$\Phi_0(F, E) = \{a_3, a_4\}$	
$US_0(F, E) = \{a_7\}$	
$\Phi_1(F, E) = \{a_3, a_4, a_7\}$	$F\downarrow_{A\setminus(E\cup E^+ \cup \Phi_0(F,E))}:$
$US_1(F, E) = \{a_8\}$	
$\Phi_2(F, E) = \{a_3, a_4, a_7, a_8\}$	$F\downarrow_{A\setminus(E\cup E^+ \cup \Phi_1(F,E))}:$
$US_2(F, E) = \{\}$	$F\downarrow_{A\setminus(E\cup E^+ \cup \Phi_2(F,E))}:$
Must-attack set: $\Phi(F, E) = \{a_3, a_4, a_7, a_8\}$	$F':$

Fig. 4. An example illustrating Definition 5 and Theorem 2.

Both Theorems 1 and 2 cover the argumentation frameworks without any cycles. For such an AF F, according to Definition 5 and Theorem 2, a new argument should attack each argument in $E^- \setminus E^+$, i.e., $(E^- \setminus E^+) \subseteq \Phi(F, E)$. Moreover, for $\forall i \geq 0$, since there are no cycles in $F\downarrow_{A\setminus(E\cup E^+ \cup \Phi_i(F,E))}$, we know that US_i is empty only when $A\setminus(E \cup E^+ \cup \Phi_i(F, E))$ is empty, which means that each argument in $A\setminus(E\cup E^+ \cup (E^- \setminus E^+))$ will be added into $\Phi(F, E)$ eventually. Therefore, the $\Phi(F, E)$ obtained in Definition 5 is $A\setminus(E \cup E^+)$, which coincides with the result by Theorem 1.

4   Related Work and Conclusions

Baumann et.al proposed the enforcement problem for the first time in [6], and extensive research has followed from the perspective of the type of enforcement [11,13,15], the algorithm [7,15], and the computational complexity [15]. This includes incorporating other formalisms into AF theories so as to take advantage of the both [16]. Generally speaking, there are two types of enforcements. The first type takes an argument-fixed way, i.e., solely changing the attack relations between arguments so as to enforce a set of desired arguments. For this direction, algorithms and solvers have been proposed [14,15]. Particularly, [8] shows a necessary and sufficient condition for enforcing the stable extension in argument-fixed way, and the condition requires that for a desired set E and $a \in E$, add an attack relation from a to every argument that is not attacked by E.

On the other hand, the second type focuses on an expansion way, which is what we follow in this paper. Compared with the first type, there are fewer algorithms and solvers for the expansion-based enforcement. The results about this direction can be found in [6,8], which contain the conclusion of impossibility of enforcement under weak expansion, and sufficient conditions for the enforcement problem under strong and normal expansion.

In this paper, we argue that necessary and sufficient conditions are essential concerning the solvability of the enforcement problem. Specifically, we have identified two necessary and sufficient conditions respectively for the odd-length cycle free and the even-length cycle free AFs under strong expansion. Previous studies show certain properties of these two classes of AFs that enable the conditions in this paper to be found.

Those not covered in our results are the argumentation frameworks with both odd-length and even-length cycles, for which exploring necessary and sufficient conditions for the enforcement problem shall be within our future work. Other types of semantics except preferred extensions are worth investigation as well. We also plan to develop corresponding tools and algorithms based on the conditions in this paper in order to deliver the utility for real-world scenarios such as medical decision making.

References

1. Dung, P.M.: On the acceptability of arguments and its fundamental role in non-monotonic reasoning, logic programming and n-person games. Artif. Intell. **77**(2), 321–357 (1995)
2. Boella, G., Kaci, S., van der Torre, L.: Dynamics in argumentation with single extensions: abstraction principles and the grounded extension. In: Sossai, C., Chemello, G. (eds.) ECSQARU 2009. LNCS (LNAI), vol. 5590, pp. 107–118. Springer, Heidelberg (2009). https://doi.org/10.1007/978-3-642-02906-6_11
3. Cayrol, C., de Saint-Cyr, F.D., Lagasquie-Schiex, M.: Change in abstract argumentation frameworks: adding an argument. J. Artif. Intell. Res. **38**, 49–84 (2010)
4. Bisquert, P., Cayrol, C., de Saint-Cyr, F.D., Lagasquie-Schiex, M.-C.: Change in argumentation systems: exploring the interest of removing an argument. In: Benferhat, S., Grant, J. (eds.) SUM 2011. LNCS (LNAI), vol. 6929, pp. 275–288. Springer, Heidelberg (2011). https://doi.org/10.1007/978-3-642-23963-2_22
5. Liao, B., Jin, L., Koons, R.C.: Dynamics of argumentation systems: a division-based method. Artif. Intell. **175**(11), 1790–1814 (2011)
6. Baumann, R., Brewka, G.: Expanding argumentation frameworks: enforcing and monotonicity results. COMMA **10**, 75–86 (2010)
7. Coste-Marquis, S., Konieczny, S., Mailly, J.G., Marquis, P.: Extension enforcement in abstract argumentation as an optimization problem. In: Twenty-Fourth International Joint Conference on Artificial Intelligence (2015)
8. Baumann, R., Doutre, S., Mailly, J.G., Wallner, J.P.: Enforcement in formal argumentation. J. Appl. Logic **2**, 1623–1677 (2021)
9. Baroni, P., Caminada, M., Giacomin, M.: An introduction to argumentation semantics. Knowl. Eng. Rev. **26**(4), 365–410 (2011)
10. Cerutti, F., Giacomin, M., Vallati, M., Zanella, M.: An SCC recursive meta-algorithm for computing preferred labellings in abstract argumentation. In: Fourteenth International Conference on the Principles of Knowledge Representation and Reasoning (2014)

11. Baumann, R., Ulbricht, M.: On cycles, attackers and supporters–a contribution to the investigation of dynamics in abstract argumentation. In: Twenty-Ninth International Joint Conference on Artificial Intelligence, vol. 2, pp. 1780–1786 (2021)
12. Dunne, P.E., Bench-Capon, T.J.: Complexity and combinatorial properties of argument systems. Technical report, Department of Computer Science (ULCS), University of Liverpool (2001)
13. Baumann, R.: What does it take to enforce an argument? Minimal change in abstract argumentation. In: ECAI, vol. 12, pp. 127–132 (2012)
14. Niskanen, A., Wallner, J.P., Järvisalo, M.: Optimal status enforcement in abstract argumentation. In: IJCAI, pp. 1216–1222 (2016)
15. Wallner, J.P., Niskanen, A., Järvisalo, M.: Complexity results and algorithms for extension enforcement in abstract argumentation. J. Artif. Intell. Res. **60**, 1–40 (2017)
16. Niskanen, A., Wallner, J.P., Järvisalo, M.: Extension enforcement under grounded semantics in abstract argumentation. In: Sixteenth International Conference on Principles of Knowledge Representation and Reasoning (2018)

Collaborative Filtering to Capture AI User's Preferences as Norms

Marc Serramia[1]($\boxtimes$), Natalia Criado[2], and Michael Luck[1]

[1] Department of Informatics, King's College London, London, UK
marc.serramia_amoros@kcl.ac.uk
[2] Escuela Técnica Superior de Ingeniería Informática,
Universitat Politècnica de València, Valencia, Spain

Abstract. Customising AI technologies to each user's preferences is fundamental to them functioning well. Unfortunately, current methods require too much user involvement and fail to capture their true preferences. In fact, to avoid the nuisance of manually setting preferences, users usually accept the default settings even if these do not conform to their true preferences. Norms can be useful to regulate behaviour and ensure it adheres to user preferences but, while the literature has thoroughly studied norms, most proposals take a formal perspective. Indeed, while there has been some research on constructing norms to capture a user's privacy preferences, these methods rely on domain knowledge which, in the case of AI technologies, is difficult to obtain and maintain. We argue that a new perspective is required when constructing norms, which is to exploit the large amount of preference information readily available from whole systems of users. Inspired by recommender systems, we believe that collaborative filtering can offer a suitable approach to identifying a user's norm preferences without excessive user involvement.

Keywords: Norms · Collaborative filtering · Preferences · Privacy

1 Introduction

Artificial Intelligence (AI) technologies are becoming commonplace in our lives. From smart watches to AI assistants they bring new functionalities to help us with daily tasks. However, each user of these technologies expects them to function in different ways. For example, in the case of AI assistants, different users have different privacy preferences and would expect the AI assistants to adhere to them. Some might prefer to share their data to enable a tailored experience, while others might prefer to keep their data private. While these AI devices and services usually allow users to customise their preferences, it is far too common that users disregard this option and accept the default settings. For example,

Research funded by the project SAIS: Secure AI AssistantS via Grant EP/T026723/1 from the UK Engineering and Physical Sciences Research Council.

© The Author(s), under exclusive license to Springer Nature Switzerland AG 2023
R. Aydoğan et al. (Eds.): PRIMA 2022, LNAI 13753, pp. 669–678, 2023.
https://doi.org/10.1007/978-3-031-21203-1_45

a large proportion of users in social networks do not change default privacy settings [18], demonstrating a wider problem, which is that while users expect AI devices and services to act as they desire, they don't want to invest time in customising them. A common approach to capturing user preferences is to question users when necessary. Unfortunately, the effects of this approach can be even worse, as receiving constant questioning both annoys users and triggers automatic acceptance of the default settings, as mentioned above. To address this problem we must take a smarter approach that does not rely on excessive user involvement.

In order to solve this problem of customising AI devices and services without excessive user input, we aim to exploit a common aspect of these technologies. In particular, we can see these technologies not as individual devices or services of an individual user, but as a multiagent system. Here, each user is represented by an agent (be it a smart watch, an AI assistant, an app, a service, etc.) and these agents interact with other agents (other devices, third party services or skills, etc.). This allows us not only to capture user preferences as norms regulating the behaviour of each agent, but it also allows us to exploit system-wide knowledge of all users' preferences in doing so.

Since this multiagent system has large numbers of users (just considering smart speakers, it is reported that 500 million units were installed as of Q4 2021 [34]), even if there is only partial knowledge of each user's preferences, we can use all available knowledge to make further inferences about their preferences. Inspired by recommender systems, we consider collaborative filtering to be a suitable approach to this end. In recommender systems, collaborative filtering is well-established for predicting items a user may like [15]. Given some known user preferences, these methods find similar items the user may like and suggest them to the user. Hence, in a sense, the user profile is completed from predictions with regard to similar items or to users with similar tastes. Following this idea, we can exploit user similarities with regard to their known preferences towards AI technologies to predict unknown preferences. This approach would allow us to construct a full profile of preferences while reducing interactions to a minimum and still capturing the user's real preferences with better success than current approaches.

To motivate this problem, in the following section we examine the particular problem of privacy in AI assistants.

2   Motivation: Privacy in AI Assistants

The advent of the internet has opened a door into a new world of opportunities and faster communication. Nonetheless, this same door has also allowed service providers, organisations, and enterprises to peek into our private lives. Studies show that users are deeply concerned about how their data is being collected online [20]. For example, 81% of surveyed users in [20] feel not very secure sharing private information with trusted persons or organisations through social networks. Yet even though users are concerned about their privacy online, they feel unable to control how their information is being transmitted. Paradoxically, this causes them not to protect their privacy, a behaviour known as privacy cynicism [14].

Legislators have tried to put regulations in place to protect user privacy, such as those proposed by the European Union [11], the United Kingdom [13], or California [33]. Among other things, these laws require users to be informed about how their data is being collected and used, as well as requiring their consent for doing so. However, while these regulations have, for example, increased the number of cookie banners on web pages, in most cases these banners inform or require consent but do not allow users to easily opt-out [8]. Furthermore, in the cases where users *can* opt-out, the banners are designed to guide users towards accepting the privacy policy (for example, by hiding the decline button while highlighting the accept one) [19]. A user navigating several web pages is thus overwhelmed with a large number and variety of such banners, and evidence shows that these are not effective in capturing the true preferences of the user. As found by Kretschmer et al. [17], banners are ignored by users 70% of the time, while only 10% of the time are they clicked for privacy reasons. This behaviour is not limited to cookie banners: Obar and Oeldorf-Hirsch [26] show that most users skip reading privacy policies when signing up to a social network, while those that start reading the policies become overloaded with information and stop reading shortly after. This behaviour can be explained as a result of privacy fatigue, which has been shown to have a stronger effect on users than privacy concerns, and leads them to cynicism [6].

A particular platform that has recently raised privacy concerns is that of AI assistants. Be it through smart speakers or our mobile phones, we use these assistants to check the weather, set reminders, or even buy things online. However, due to their only very recent adoption, these systems still have numerous security and privacy problems [10], which have already led to undesirable situations, such as recording private conversations and sending them to a random contact [37]. Apart from violating user privacy, these issues threaten user trust in AI assistants, causing users to disable functionalities or to implement coping mechanisms [1], thus threatening the adoption of the technology.

In consequence, it is paramount that we ensure AI assistants are secure and align with the privacy expectations of users. This requires a novel method to capture user preferences, one that does not rely on constant and overwhelming user interaction. As an example, imagine that a user asks their AI assistant about the weather, but before completing that task the weather app then asks the user to access their contacts to send them a message recommending that app. The user, who might be in a rush or tired, replies affirmatively, against their true preferences, just to quickly get the weather information. Instead, as an alternative approach, we can examine the pool of users of that app, find some with similar privacy preferences to the user and infer a predicted preference from them. This would at least help to tailor the interaction with the user to the predicted outcome, or even skip the interaction completely, assuming the user had provided the agent consent to decide on these interactions. In this way, we advocate for a technique to capture user preferences that does not require excessive user involvement, and that can be readily deployed in any AI device or service without the need for domain knowledge (i.e., contextual information). This technique should exploit system-wide information (like similarities between users) to build preference predictions.

3   Related Work

In our consideration of related work, we review three bodies of literature, namely privacy and AI assistants, normative multiagent systems, and AI ethics.

Firstly, some papers have addressed the problem we have outlined here in the particular domain of privacy and AI assistants. Abdi et al. [2] conducted a user survey and crowdsourced norms from the commonly agreed opinions of the users. While the approach in this paper would be useful for specifying default preferences, it is not able to tailor them to each individual user. Using that dataset, Zhan et al. [38] presented a model to predict privacy norms. Here, norms are predicted using a machine learning model with an accuracy of 70–80%. Both of these approaches are based on the idea of contextual integrity [25], which states that the privacy preferences of users depend largely on the context. For example, in a social network, a user may share a photo with their friends but not with the general public. Here, the receiver of the photo is the context that determines the preferences of the user. Therefore, while Zhan et al.'s work [38] seems promising, we argue that a more general approach is needed. Note that constructing predictions based on context requires knowledge of the possible contexts and their connections, and this knowledge is dependent on the domain. For example, the contexts to be considered in a social network will be different from those to be considered in an AI assistant. However, assuming this knowledge will be available is too strong. Instead, as discussed previously, we aim at a technique that can readily be used with any AI device or service without the need for specific knowledge.

Seeing that both of these works address the problem by resorting to norms, we also consider the normative multiagent system literature to see if any current approaches to constructing norms can be readily adopted for our purposes. Indeed, norms have been long studied in the multiagent systems literature as a means to coordinate agents [4]. In technical terms, there are two main methods for developing norm systems, known as top-down and bottom-up approaches. On the one hand, top-down approaches consider a system-wide perspective and norms are constructed and enacted by a central authority (for example, norm synthesis approaches [22,23]). The aim of these approaches is to exploit system-wide knowledge to build a system-wide norm system. While we also want to exploit system-wide knowledge, we differ in our goals, as we are concerned with developing individual norm systems for each agent. On the other hand, bottom-up approaches construct norms at an agent level based on the agent's experience and view of the environment (for example, norm emergence approaches [27,31,35]). Here, while norms are built at an agent level, they are only created considering agent level knowledge which, for our purposes, would require unwanted user interaction. Instead, the method we envision has elements of both top-down and bottom-up approaches, in that a norm system would be built individually and independently for each agent but considering system-wide knowledge of all agents' preferences to do so. Another aspect of differentiation between approaches is the time at which norm systems are constructed. On the one hand, off-line approaches like those in [3,30], build norm systems at a point in time, considering the information they have at that point. In contrast, given that user preferences may change over time and new situations will arise, our aim is for an online approach, like those in [22,23], which are able to construct norms during execution of the multiagent system or, in our case, during the life of the AI device or service in question.

Another focus of the literature is producing norm systems that satisfy desirable properties. There has been vast research on building norm systems satisfying properties such as: conflict-avoidance [16,36] (ensuring that the resulting norms do not conflict with each other); minimality [12,24] (avoiding over-regulation); compactness [22] (producing small norm systems); and many others. While these formal properties are important, our main focus is the alignment between user preferences and norms (regardless of the properties satisfied). In this sense, the approach to solving our problem should be closer to that of the field of AI Ethics. Recent work here has studied the engineering of moral value-aligned norm systems. For example, the work of Serramia et al. [28,29] composes sets of norms considering (and maximising) their alignment with moral values and known moral value preferences. Sierra et al. [32] propose a formal approach to finding value-aligned norms based on guiding the multiagent system to those states that promote the desirable moral values. Finally, Montes and Sierra [21] tweak parameters in norms to maximise their promotion of moral values (such as equality or fairness). Note that moral values are the criteria by which we distinguish between good and bad behaviour [5,9]. Therefore, ensuring AI works as expected by the user is in turn making AI aligned with the user's morality. For example, applying our approach to the AI devices of a user that highly values privacy will result in those devices respecting the user's privacy. Therefore, while work in the area of AI and ethics could be used to address the goals of this paper, they require knowing the moral value preferences beforehand, which is also too strong an assumption. Furthermore, all these approaches are off-line, which are unable to adapt to changing environments.

To conclude, while contextual integrity or morality are highly relevant to assert a user's preferences, we cannot assume explicit knowledge of either of these two aspects. Hence, our aim should be a new technique that does not require this knowledge.

4   Our Proposal: Capturing User Preferences as Norms

In this section we discuss several ideas to address the shortcomings we have identified in the literature. Firstly, we consider the possibility of exploiting user similarities in order to predict user preferences. Secondly, we discuss applying this idea to the task of specifying a collaborative filtering method for predicting a user's preference norms.

4.1 Exploiting User Similarities

A common trait of AI devices and services is their large pool of users, and the vast amount of available information about them. As a result, it might not be necessary to ask a user for all their preferences, and we might instead predict them. Note that we have partial knowledge over the preferences of each user. Individually, these preferences can be seen in bounded numerical form[1]. Thus, collectively these preferences are defined in a multi-dimensional real space (where the number of dimensions is the number of elements over which preferences are defined, i.e. the actions that AI devices can perform). This multi-dimensional space represents all possible preferences over all possible behaviours of the AI device in question. Then, the preferences of each individual user of the AI device are a point in this space (where each position of the point refers to a preference with regard to some action the AI device can perform). Since not all preferences are known, each user's point has many gaps (i.e. a gap in each position of the point representing an unknown preference). But even just considering the known positions in the point, we can establish distances between user preference profiles. For example, considering the real distance for known preferences and maximum distance for unknown ones. The overall distance between two users tells us how similar or dissimilar users are with regard to their preferences. Those with small distances will have very little divergence of preferences and therefore can be considered similar with regard to them.

Note that user preferences are not independent; for example, in the case of privacy preferences users might want to protect their privacy, leading to preferences against sharing data, or they might not care about their privacy, leading to preferences in favour of sharing data. Therefore, it is highly probable that, if users are similar with regard to their known preferences, they will also be similar with regard to unknown preferences. Therefore, even if we only have partial preferences for most users, we can still predict the missing preferences by inferring them from similar users. While this idea has been commonly used in areas like recommender systems, to the best of our knowledge it is a novel idea in the context of setting preferences about how an AI agent should behave. Importantly, this approach would not require knowledge of what the preferences mean, or information about contexts or the morality of the user which, as we have seen in Sect. 3, are common assumptions in the literature. Instead, this approach can readily be used in any application where we know partial preferences for each of the users, without the need for extra information. In fact, in this case, knowledge about the context and morality of decisions is considered implicitly, as similar users might have similar morality and views on contextual integrity.

---

[1] For numeral preferences, since the number of users and preferences is finite, there will always be an upper and lower bound. For ordinal preferences, we can define a transformation function that transforms an order into numerical preferences in a bounded interval.

4.2   Collaborative Filtering to Predict Norms

When it comes to specifying how AI agents should behave, we resort to norms. Firstly, norms serve as a concise way to define preferences in complex domains with a multitude of contexts, roles, etc. As new norms are created, we can combine them into more general norms. We are also able to detect inconsistencies (i.e. the newly created norm may contradict already established norms) and resolve them (for example, by abolishing the older norm). Secondly, agents may represent several humans with different preferences, in the particular case of AI assistants it is common for whole families to use a single smart speaker. Hence, norms can be a useful means to reason about multiple users' preferences and reach a consensus set of norms representing them all. Thirdly, considering the ecosystem of AI devices or services as a multiagent system, norms could help create an expectation or provide guidance for behaviour to other devices or services in this ecosystem. For example, in the case of AI assistants, if a user has several norms prohibiting the device from sharing information during night-time, other services requiring information might wait until daytime to request it. Finally, norms not only serve as a means to regulate agent behaviour but are also useful to *explain* agent behaviour as they are natural for humans. Thus, we can use the user's norms to construct explanations of agent behaviour that are easily understood by them, if need be. Importantly, since this process does not require explicit knowledge of context, roles, etc. it can adapt to different definitions of norms, as simple or as complex as required by the application domain.

Adopting the approach of the previous subsection, we are able to predict preferences of a user with regard to how their AI devices should behave. Note, however, that here user preferences strictly determine how the agent should act. If a user of an AI assistant sets their preferences to not share any data, it should imply that the AI assistant will not share any data. Therefore, depending on the predicted preferences, we can directly infer a norm regulating the behaviour of the AI agent. A strong negative predicted preference toward some action implies the agent should be prohibited from performing that action. Conversely, a strong preference in favour of the action, should imply the agent is obliged to perform it. Thus, in essence, when performing collaborative filtering we are not only predicting user preferences, we are also predicting norms.

Technically speaking, predicting norms is a two-strep process: first we predict the numerical preference, and then we feed it into a function that transforms the numerical preference into a norm. Note, however, that only clearly positioned preferences must lead to a norm. Neutral or close to neutral preferences are not strong enough to infer a norm, so in these cases the function should result in no norms being constructed. Furthermore, even in cases where we have clear predictions, we must consider prediction confidence to minimise the chance of constructing incorrect norms. Prediction confidence assesses the quality of the knowledge used to make the prediction. This can be calculated from both the similarity measured between the target user and its similar users, and from the amount of known preferences they have in common. Therefore, we can fix a threshold of necessary confidence to construct norms. Secondly, we may also consider context sensitivity (as has been considered previously when constructing privacy norms with regard to information transmissions in online social networks [7]). In our case, sensitivity can be inferred from the pool of users; for example, contexts that are usually part of norms forbidding interaction might be sensitive. In sensitive contexts, it might be better to interact directly with the user instead of constructing predicted norms.

Note that whenever interaction is needed (e.g., sensitive contexts), we can still tailor the interaction using our predictions. Hence, we argue that with this less invasive and more meaningful interaction, users will pay attention to consent requests and provide truthful answers. These truthful answers and norms, stemming from high confidence predictions, will ensure that the user's real preferences guide the behaviour of agents in the multiagent system.

Finally, it is worth mentioning that norm predictions are also useful to detect preference changes. As time progresses, we gather more knowledge on all users, so that when a preference norm has been in place for some time, we can test if it still holds by re-predicting it. If the predicted preferences remain the same we maintain the norm, whereas if they have changed we can update the norm directly or interact with the user if we lack prediction confidence or the context is sensitive.

5 Conclusions

Current methods to capture user preferences are ineffective and need to be improved. This is particularly crucial for AI technologies, which take decisions independently and therefore must understand user preferences to behave as users would expect. Methods relying on constant interaction and questioning annoy users and prevent them from achieving their goals when using these technologies. Furthermore, they fail at obtaining real answers, as usually users answer automatically just to swiftly deal with questions. Given the large amount of information already available from the large pool of users using the same devices and services, we advocate for minimising interaction, and for predicting preferences from knowledge of other users. This will decrease the amount of annoying interruptions, and therefore give more importance to questions. Users are therefore more likely to give truthful answers, as the smaller number of interactions might not be perceived as constant disturbance but as warnings. By completing the preferences with predictions, we should be able to obtain a complete set of preferences reasonably close to reality, or at least much better than those obtained with current methods. Note, too, that for critical preferences in which interactive questioning is required (e.g., when dealing with highly sensitive data), preference prediction could be used to rephrase the question to ask, for example for confirmation of the predicted preferences.

References

1. Abdi, N., Ramokapane, K.M., Such, J.M.: More than smart speakers: security and privacy perceptions of smart home personal assistants. In: Proceedings of the 15th SOUPS, pp. 451–466. USENIX Association, Santa Clara, August 2019
2. Abdi, N., Zhan, X., Ramokapane, K.M., Such, J.: Privacy norms for smart home personal assistants. In: Proceedings of CHI 2021. Association for Computing Machinery (2021)
3. Ågotnes, T., Van Der Hoek, W., Sierra, C., Wooldridge, M.: On the logic of normative systems. In: Proceedings of the 20th IJCAI, pp. 1175–1180 (2007)
4. Boella, G., van der Torre, L., Verhagen, H.: Introduction to normative multiagent systems. Comput. Math. Org. Theory **12**(2–3), 71–79 (2006)
5. Charisi, V., et al.: Towards moral autonomous systems (2017)
6. Choi, H., Park, J., Jung, Y.: The role of privacy fatigue in online privacy behavior. Comput. Hum. Behav. **81**, 42–51 (2018)
7. Criado, N., Such, J.M.: Implicit contextual integrity in online social networks. Inf. Sci. **325**(C), 48–69 (2015)
8. Degeling, M., Utz, C., Lentzsch, C., Hosseini, H., Schaub, F., Holz, T.: We value your privacy ... now take some cookies: measuring the GDPR's impact on web privacy. In: Proceedings of the Network and Distributed System Security Symposium, San Diego, USA, pp. 1–15 (2019)
9. Dignum, V.: Responsible autonomy. In: Proceedings of the Twenty-Sixth International Joint Conference on Artificial Intelligence (IJCAI-2017), pp. 4698–4704 (2017)
10. Edu, J.S., Such, J.M., Suarez-Tangil, G.: Smart home personal assistants: a security and privacy review. ACM Comput. Surv. **53**(6) (dec 2020)
11. European Union: General data protection regulation (2018)
12. Fitoussi, D., Tennenholtz, M.: Choosing social laws for multi-agent systems: minimality and simplicity. Artif. Intell. **119**(1–2), 61–101 (2000)
13. Government of the United Kingdom: Data protection act (2018). https://www.gov.uk/data-protection. Accessed April 2022
14. Hoffmann, C., Lutz, C., Ranzini, G.: Privacy cynicism: a new approach to the privacy paradox. Cyberpsychol. J. Psychosoc. Res. Cyberspace **10** (2016)
15. Hong, J., Su, X., Khoshgoftaar, T.M.: A survey of collaborative filtering techniques. Adv. Artif. Intell. **2009**, 421425 (2009)
16. Kollingbaum, M.J., Norman, T.J., Preece, A., Sleeman, D.: Norm conflicts and inconsistencies in virtual organisations. In: Noriega, P., et al. (eds.) COIN -2006. LNCS (LNAI), vol. 4386, pp. 245–258. Springer, Heidelberg (2007). https://doi.org/10.1007/978-3-540-74459-7_16
17. Kretschmer, M., Pennekamp, J., Wehrle, K.: Cookie banners and privacy policies: measuring the impact of the GDPR on the web. ACM Trans. Web **15**(4), 1–42 (2021)
18. Krishnamurthy, B., Wills, C.E.: On the leakage of personally identifiable information via online social networks. In: Proceedings of the 2nd WOSN, pp. 7–12. ACM, NY, USA (2009)
19. Laine, J.: There is no decision: design of cookie consent banner and its effect on user consent. Ph.D. thesis, Tampere University (2021)
20. Madden, M.: Public perceptions of privacy and security in the post-Snowden era (2014). Pew Research Center, Accessed April 2022

21. Montes, N., Sierra, C.: Value-guided synthesis of parametric normative systems. In: Proceedings of the 20th AAMAS, pp. 907–915 (2021)
22. Morales, J., Lopez-Sanchez, M., Rodriguez-Aguilar, J.A., Vasconcelos, W., Wooldridge, M.: On-line automated synthesis of compact normative systems. TAAS **10**(1), 2:1–2:33 (2015)
23. Morales, J., Lopez-Sanchez, M., Rodriguez-Aguilar, J.A., Wooldridge, M., Vasconcelos, W.: Automated synthesis of normative systems. In: AAMAS 2013, pp. 483–490 (2013)
24. Morales, J., Lopez-Sanchez, M., Rodriguez-Aguilar, J.A., Wooldridge, M., Vasconcelos, W.: Minimality and simplicity in the on-line automated synthesis of normative systems. In: AAMAS 2014, pp. 109–116. IFAAMAS, Richland, SC (2014)
25. Nissenbaum, H.: Privacy as contextual integrity. Washington Law Rev. **79**, 119 (2004)
26. Obar, J.A., Oeldorf-Hirsch, A.: The biggest lie on the internet: ignoring the privacy policies and terms of service policies of social networking services. In: Proceedings of the 44th TPRC, pp. 1–20. Information, Communication and Society, Arlington, VA, USA (2018)
27. Savarimuthu, B.T.R., Purvis, M., Cranefield, S., Purvis, M.: Mechanisms for norm emergence in multiagent societies. In: Proceedings of the 6th AAMAS, pp. 173:1–173:3 (2007)
28. Serramia, M., López-Sánchez, M., Moretti, S., Rodríguez-Aguilar, J.A.: On the dominant set selection problem and its application to value alignment. JAAMAS **35**(2) (2021)
29. Serramia, M., et al.: Moral values in norm decision making. In: Proceedings of the 17th AAMAS, pp. 1294–1302 (2018)
30. Shoham, Y., Tennenholtz, M.: On social laws for artificial agent societies: off-line design. Artif. Intell. **73**(1–2), 231–252 (1995)
31. Shoham, Y., Tennenholtz, M.: On the emergence of social conventions: modeling, analysis, and simulations. Artif. Intell. **94**(1–2), 139–166 (1997)
32. Sierra, C., Osman, N., Noriega, P., Sabater-Mir, J., Perello-Moragues, A.: Value alignment: a formal approach. In: RAIA Workshop in AAMAS. Montreal, Canada (2019)
33. State of California Department of Justice: California Consumer Privacy Act (2018). https://oag.ca.gov/privacy/ccpa. Accessed April 2022
34. Strategy analytics: Global smart speaker and screen vendor & os shipment and installed base market share by region: Q4 2021 (2021)
35. Sugawara, T.: Emergence and stability of social conventions in conflict situations. In: Proceedings of the 22nd IJCAI, pp. 371–378. AAAI Press (2011)
36. Vasconcelos, W.W., Kollingbaum, M.J., Norman, T.J.: Normative conflict resolution in multi-agent systems. Auton. Agent. Multi-Agent Syst. **19**(2), 124–152 (2009)
37. Wolfson, S.: Amazon's Alexa recorded private conversation and sent it to random contact. The Guardian (2018)
38. Zhan, X., Sarkadi, S., Criado, N., Such, J.: A model for governing information sharing in smart assistants. In: Proceedings of AIES 2022, pp. 845–855 (2022)

Influence of Expertise Complementarity on Ad Hoc Human-Agent Team Effectiveness

Sami Abuhaimed[(✉)] and Sandip Sen

The University of Tulsa, Tulsa, USA
saa8061@utulsa.edu

Abstract. As autonomous agents become more capable and widely deployed, teams of human and agent members will be seen more frequently. Ad hoc human-agent teams, formed with team members without prior experience with current teammates and deployed only for a limited number of interactions, will find diverse applications in dynamic environments. We focuses on ad-hoc team scenarios pairing human with agent where both need to assess and adapt to the capabilities and expertise of partner to maximize team performance. We investigate influence of different agent expertise distributions on effectiveness of such ad-hoc teams. We designed, implemented, and experimented with an environment in which human-agent teams repeatedly collaborate to complete heterogeneous task sets where agent and human expertise vary over different task types. Several hypotheses about effect of complementarity of team members on team performance and human satisfaction are evaluated.

Keywords: Human-agent collaboration · Team performance · Human satisfaction · Task allocation

1 Introduction

Teams of humans and agents are increasingly commonplace where human and agent team members play different team roles. As agent capabilities improve, they can assume roles of increasing importance in new environments and where they are peers, in their work responsibilities, with their human partners. We are interested in human-agent collaboration in *ad hoc teams* where team members have no prior knowledge of or interaction experience with their teammates: *An ad hoc team setting is one in which teammates must work together to obtain a common goal, but without any prior agreement regarding how to work together* [2].

We study ad hoc teams trying to accomplish a set of tasks chosen from diverse task types. We assume that different human users' expertise competence levels over various task types will vary. Agent expertise distribution is fixed, and simulated, over the task types. It is then necessary to use different task allocation

ⓒ The Author(s), under exclusive license to Springer Nature Switzerland AG 2023
R. Aydoğan et al. (Eds.): PRIMA 2022, LNAI 13753, pp. 679–688, 2023.
https://doi.org/10.1007/978-3-031-21203-1_46

distributions to the team members based on the expertise of the human team member to optimize the performance of a given human-agent team.

We believe team effectiveness and continued human engagement in human-agent teams and engagement with agent partners will depend on, among other factors, how satisfied the human is with how the team operates, the distribution of workload in the team, the behavior of their agent partner, and the performance of the team in early interactions.

Similar to humans, agents have different expertise over task types. The critical question on task allocation decisions and human-agent ad hoc team efficacy that we study in this paper is the following: *How does varying the agent's expertise distribution influence team's performance and the associated human user's satisfaction?* An effective team must judiciously leverage team member capabilities over task types. In this paper, we present results and analysis from experiments conducted to understand how the change of agent expertise distributions influence the effectiveness of human-agent teams.

2 Related Work

Human-agent teams have been studied in different domains such as space robotics [3], and examine human perceptions such as trust [6]. Much of the focus in existing research is on agents who play supportive roles to human teammates [7], and mostly in robotic and simulation settings.

However, our interest differs from previous studies in several aspects. We focus on ad hoc environments, whereas other studies [3] incorporate training or interaction sessions with agent and/or environment prior to experimentation. We are also interested in agents that are autonomous; DeChurch and Larson view an autonomous agent as a "team member fulfilling a distinct role in the team and making a unique contribution" [8].

Task allocation has been studied extensively in multi-agent teams [10]. The focus is on designing efficient mechanisms for agents to distribute items or tasks within their society. It is also studied in humans' team literature; the mechanism of task allocation, which includes capabilities identification, role specification, and task planning, is considered an important component of teamwork [9]. For any organization to achieve its goals, Puranam points that it needs to solve four universal problems, which includes task allocation [11].

In addition to performance, human's satisfaction is recognized as a major component of team effectiveness in team models [4]. Moreover, well-known human team frameworks, such as Input-Process-Output (IPO) model, examine teamwork through different dimensions, which include members, process in which they interact, and teamwork outcome [9]. It is worth mentioning that majority of human-agent team studies don't fully recognize these distinctions when measuring human perceptions. Furthermore, to the best of our knowledge, there is little investigation of satisfaction in human-agent team literature.

In summary, studies that investigate task allocation within teams composed of humans and autonomous agents in ad hoc environments over repeated interactions are limited. We study the effect of varying agent expertise distribution over task types on the effectiveness of ad hoc human-agent teams.

3   Research Hypotheses

As is often the case in real-world teams, members have diverse characteristics, capabilities, and qualities. An effective team needs to harness team members' complementary strengths for a productive and successful collaboration. To achieve that, team member capabilities need to accurately identified and task allocation mechanism used must match available tasks with members' capabilities.

Members of human-agent teams formed in ad hoc environments can have different levels of expertise over task types (we use expertise and confidence level of an agent in a task type interchangeably to represent the likelihood of the agent successfully completing a task of that type). For a given task type, the expertise of the human team member may be similar to or very different from the expertise level of the agent for that task type. An expertise profile represents the distribution of a team member's expertise over different task types. We conjecture that team effectiveness, including team performance and user satisfaction, will be critically dependent on the relation between the performance profiles of the human and agent teammates.

Hypothesis 1 (H1): *Team performance will vary with varying agent expertise profile over task types.*

We expect team performance and satisfaction to decrease when human and agent have low expertise on the same task type. Complementary team member expertise, on the contrary, is expected to produce better team performance as each task may be allocated to the team member with higher expertise.

Hypothesis 2 (H2): *Team performance is higher when the agent expertise profile is complementary, rather than being similar, to the human teammate.*

We also conjecture that humans will prefer to work with agents having complementary expertise profiles.

Hypothesis 3 (H3): *Humans are more satisfied with agents with complementary, rather than similar, expertise profiles.*

We further conjecture that the larger the difference between the expertise profiles of the human and agent teammates, the better off the team is in terms of success in completing tasks.

Hypothesis 4 (H4): *The larger the difference between the agent and human expertise vectors, the better is the overall team performance.*

4   Methodology

4.1   Collaborative Human-Agent Taskboard (CHATboard)

We developed CHATboard, an environment that facilitates human-agent, as well as human-human, team coordination, that may apply for different domains.

CHATboard contains a graphical interface that supports human-agent team coordination to complete a set of tasks. CHATboard allows for displaying the task sets to be completed, supports multiple task allocation protocols, communication between team members for expressing confidence levels, displaying task allocations and performance by team members on assigned tasks, etc. The framework utilizes the concept of tasks posted on blackboards, often used in coordination within human teams. Blackboards have been effectively used in agent teams as a common repository for information sharing between agents.

We incorporate three task boards in our task sharing framework: one shared board, which includes set of team tasks organized by type, and two other boards respectively for the tasks assigned to the human and the agent team member. These task boards facilitate coordination and are easily navigable repositories for team information allowing team members to share and view information.

4.2   Interaction Protocol

We design one interaction protocol to guide task allocation process in an ad hoc environment: Agent Allocator Protocol. It assigns the allocator role to Agent teammate. The human teammate provide preferences over task types to agent, and the agent is responsible of task allocation. The protocol does not dictate task allocation strategy used by the allocator. We use a perfect information scenario, where all team information, such as set of team tasks, task assignments to team members, and the task performance are fully observable to all team members.

4.3   Agent Characteristics

Expertise: A fixed agent expertise profile lists expertise for each task type, represented as a vector of probabilities for successful completion of task types.[1]

Agent Allocator Strategy: We assume each task is allocated to and performed by a single team member and does not require work from multiple individuals, i.e., $A_{i,e} \cap A_{j,e} = \phi$. We additionally required that the total number of tasks assigned to each team member be the same, i.e., $\forall x, y, |A_x| = |A_y|$. Different number of tasks can however be assigned to two team members for different task types. The primary allocation goal is to maximize utilization of the available expertise in the team subject to the constraint of equal task load for team members. The agent stores and uses estimates of task completion rates by task types for the human team member in the allocation procedure.

$$\max \sum_{y \in M} (x_y a(y) + (1 - x_y) h(y)); s.t. \forall y, x_y \in 0, 1, \text{where } \sum_{y \in M} x_y = \sum_{y \in M} (1 - x_y) = \frac{|M|}{2}.$$

In the above equations, x_y are binary variables indicating whether a task type, y, is assigned to human or agent, based on the current performance estimate of the human, $h(y)$, and agent, $a(y)$, on that task type. As per requirement, each team member is assigned exactly half of the task types. This is an

---

[1] Agent expertise is simulated by flipping a coin with success probability of P_t.

Algorithm 1. Agent Allocator Strategy

Input: $N = \{p_h, p_g\}, M = \{y_1, \ldots, y_m\}, E$

```
 1: for e = 1....E do
 2:    if e = 1 then
 3:        Q_{i,y_j} ← p_i(y_j), ∀p_i ∈ N, y_j ∈ M
 4:        each T_{y_j} is partitioned into n equal size subsets, which are randomly allo-
           cated to agent i to form A_{i,1}, for each p_i ∈ N
 5:    else
 6:        A_{i,e} ← getAllocations(Q_{i,e})
 7:    end if
 8:    if y_j is allocated to p_i then
 9:        Q_{i,y_j} ← (1 − α) · Q_{i,y_j} + α · μ_{i,y_j,e}
10:    end if
11: end for
```

---

unbalanced assignment problem, as number of task types is greater than number of team members $(m > n)$. It can be solved by transforming it into a *balanced* formulation, e.g., adding dummy variables, and using the Hungarian algorithm. We utilize the SCIP mixed integer programming solver, represented by `getAllocations()` procedure in Line 6 of Algorithm 1, to find the allocation that maximizes utilization of team's confidence levels.

In many task allocation formulations, e.g., matching markets, assignment problems, and others, participants' preferences or confidence levels are assumed to be accurately known [13]. In our formulation, however, learning is needed as we expect human participant's estimates of their capabilities to be inaccurate. Since this is an ad hoc environment, the second goal of our agent is to quickly learn about its partner's expertise levels and quickly adapt the allocations accordingly for improved team performance. After each interaction, e, the agent updates the expertise model, Q_{i,y_j}, of team member, p_i, for each task type, y_j, from the observed performances, $\mu_{i,y_j,e}$, as follows: $Q_{i,y_j} \leftarrow (1 - \alpha) \cdot Q_{i,y_j} + \alpha \cdot \mu_{i,y_j,e}$ (we used $\alpha = 0.4$ since ad hoc situations require agents to quickly learn about teammate's capabilities). In the first episode, however, the agent allocator explores team member's capabilities by partitioning task items within each task type, T_{y_j}, equally among team members, as shown in Line 4 in Algorithm 1.

4.4 Evaluation Metrics

Team Performance: A task allocated to a team member is either successfully completed or a failure is reported. Team overall performance is measured as the percentage of successful completion of assigned tasks over all episodes: Unweighted Team Performance is measured as the average team performance over episodes, $\frac{1}{E} \sum_{e=1}^{E} R_{team,e}$, where $R_{team,e}$ is the team performance in episode e, which is the average performance, μ, of all team members over all task types in that episode $R_{team,e} \leftarrow \frac{1}{mn} \sum_{i=1}^{n} \sum_{j=1}^{m} \mu_{i,y_j,e}$.

Human Satisfaction: We measure satisfaction with three team dimensions: interaction protocol, teamwork outcome, and agent teammate. We adapt the satisfaction survey proposed by [5] and [12] with four questions for each dimensions. The survey follows a 5-point Likert scale setting administered at the end of the study. Internal consistency estimates (α coefficients) for our sample were high: 0.91 (Team Outcome), 0.94 (Protocol), and 0.91 (Agent). We present sample questions for each survey dimension:

Task Allocation Protocol: *"I feel satisfied with the processes used in the team's task allocation protocol."*

Agent teammate: *"I am satisfied with my agent teammate."*

Team Outcome: *"I feel satisfied with the things we achieved in the team's task allocation protocol."*

Table 1. Expertise profiles, expected allocations & payoff.

	y_1	y_2	y_3	y_4	ProfDist	ExpPayoff
H	79.6	59.4	88.2	42.2		
p_A	5	95	5	95	246	89.5
Exp Alloc	h	a	h	a		
p_B	5	95	95	5	154	78
Exp Alloc	h	a	a	h		
p_C	85	10	90	15	83.8	69.2
Exp Alloc	a	h	a	h		

4.5   Experimental Configurations

We conduct experiments with teams of one human and one agent ($n = 2$), $N = \{p_a, p_h\}$. We use four task types ($m = 4$), M: $\{y_1, y_2, y_4, y_4\}$, which are *Identify Language, Solve WordGrid, Identify Landmark*, and *Identify Event*. The task types are selected so that, for each type, sufficient expertise variations in recruited human subjects are likely. For example, *Identify Language* is a task type in which team are asked to identify the language, e.g. Japanese, in a text message from a number of options, e.g., Japanese, German, Hebrew, Arabic.

We ran experiments with ad-hoc teams interacting over four episodes ($E = 4$). 32 ($r = 8$) task item instances are assigned to the team in each episode. Confidence levels for tasks are stated in a [1,100] range, which are scaled by agents into a [0,1] range and interpreted as task completion probabilities.

We used data from pilot experiments to form estimates of average human participant expertise profile, **H**=$\{y_1 : 76.6, y_2 : 59.4, y_3 : 88.2, y_4 : 42.2\}$. We found notable variations in expertise over different task types. While constructing agent profiles, we wanted to construct agent profiles that will lead to different allocations of task types to the human and agent team members. Based on the **H** expertise profile, we constructed three agent expertise profiles:

Complementary agent profile: $p_A=\{y_1 : 5, y_2 : 95, y_3 : 5, y_4 : 95\}$ is one where the agent does well on task types that humans tend to under-perform, and has lower performance in task types on which humans do well.
Intermediate agent profile: $p_B:\{y_1 : 5, y_2 : 95, y_3 : 95, y_4 : 5\}$, agent shares some of the human performance traits and have complementary expertise in others.
Similar agent profile: $p_C:\{y_1 : 85, y_2 : 10, y_3 : 90, y_4 : 15\}$, profile similar to **H**.
Table 1 presents these profiles together with the sum of the differences of the three agent profiles with **H** (246, 154, and 83.8 respectively). The table also presents the optimal allocation for each agent profile, where 'h' and 'a' refers to that task type to be allocated to humans and agents respectively, and the expected team payoff. Note that actual payoffs and even allocations may vary due to the expertise level of human participant and their task completion rates.

We recruited 195 participants from Amazon Turk with 65 subjects for each of three conditions (agent expertise profiles) as recommended for a medium-sized effect [1]. We use between-subject study and an agent with randomly selected expertise profile is assigned to each team. Participants start first episode after agreeing to Informed Consent Form, and read study description. Each episode contains three phases: task allocation, task completion, and task results. Both overall and per task type performance are shared with human and agent teammates after each episode. After four episodes are completed, participants are asked to complete a survey, including satisfaction on various aspects of teamwork. We incorporate random comprehension attention checks to ensure result fidelity. Participants receive a bonus payment based on team performance.

5   Experimental Results

Performance: We plot performance distribution for the three agent expertise profiles in Fig. 1 (the performance means and standard deviations are $M_{p_A} = 83$, $SD_{p_A} = 5.09$; $M_{p_B} = 72$, $SD_{p_B} = 6.7$; $M_{p_C} = 69.6$, $SD_{p_C} = 7.8$). One-way ANOVA finds that team performances for the three agent profiles are significantly different, $F=78.06$, $p < 0.001$. **Hypothesis 1 is supported.**

We ran post-hoc analysis using Tukey's HSD Test to understand how complementary profile, p_A, compares with the other profiles. We found significant difference between complementary profile and others, $p_A - p_C = 13.8$, $p < 0.001$; $p_A - p_B = 10.9$, $p < 0.001$. The comparison shows that teams with complementary profile significantly outperforms those with other profiles. **Hypothesis 2 is supported.**

We also analyze the differences between team members' expertise distribution to understand its relation to team performance. For each profile, we compute the average of the total differences between human and agent expertise over the four task types. We found the difference in p_A to be largest ($p_{A_{diff}} = 59.47$), followed by p_B ($p_{B_{Diff}} = 36.68$), and p_C ($p_{C_{Diff}} = 29.76$). This ranking is also reflected in corresponding team performances: the largest difference has the highest performance, the second largest has the second highest performance, and the lowest difference has the lowest performance. **Hypothesis 4 is supported.**

Satisfaction: For each profile, we analyze human satisfaction with following dimensions: Team Outcome, Protocol, and Agent. We found significant difference in human satisfaction with Protocol between agent profiles, $M_{p_A} = 4.28$, $M_{p_B} = 3.62$, $M_{p_C} = 3.54$, $F = 13.04$, and $p < 0.001$. We also found significant difference in satisfaction with Outcome, $M_{p_A} = 4.16$, $M_{p_B} = 3.67$, $M_{p_C} = 3.59$, $F = 11.7$, and $p < 0.001$. Lastly, we found significant difference in satisfaction with Agent, $M_{p_A} = 3.98$, $M_{p_B} = 3.48$, $M_{p_C} = 3.54$, $F = 8.9$, and $p < 0.001$.

Though we found that a significant difference exists between human satisfaction in three team dimensions, we wanted to further analyze how satisfaction differ when agent posses complementary expertise, p_A, with other profiles. We run post-hoc analysis using Tukey's HSD Test and found significant difference in human satisfaction in Protocol between complementary agent profile and others, $p_A - p_B = 0.65$, $p < 0.001$, and $p_A - p_C = 0.73$, $p < 0.001$. We also found significant difference in satisfaction in Team Outcome between complementary agent and other profiles, $p_A - p_B = 0.48$, $p < 0.001$, and $p_A - p_C = 0.56$, $p < 0.001$. Lastly, we found significant difference in satisfaction in Agent between complementary agent and other profiles, $p_A - p_B = 0.49$, $p < 0.001$, and $p_A - p_C = 0.52$, $p < 0.001$. The former comparisons show that humans are more satisfied with Team Outcome, Protocol, and Agent when the agent possess complementary expertise. **Hypothesis 3 is supported.**

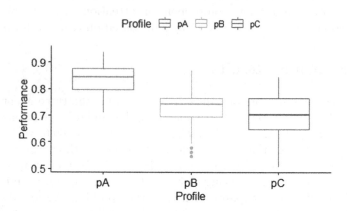

Fig. 1. Team Performance Distribution for three Agent Expertise Profiles.

6   Discussion and Future Work

We introduced CHATboard, task allocation framework between human and agent team members for ad hoc scenarios. We showed its efficacy in supporting collaboration between one human and one autonomous agent. CHATboard can be configured to support larger teams and more complex constraints between tasks. We also presented Agent Allocator Protocol, interaction protocol that guides team interactions, i.e., assigns allocator role to agent teammate.

We investigated effect of agent expertise distribution on team effectiveness, including performance and satisfaction. We deployed three agents with different expertise. Results show that human-agent teams with complementary agent expertise have higher performance and satisfaction with Outcome, Protocol, and Agent than with other expertise profiles. We also show that larger differences between team members' expertise distributions produce higher team performance.

The observations from this paper can inform the design of ad hoc human-agent teams. The observed high performance and user satisfaction in teams with complementary agent highlights the importance of finding task allocation mechanisms that emphasizes discovery of capabilities of not only agent but also human teammates. Finding the best task match for human and agent is critical for team success. These results also emphasizes the need for human-agent team designers to ensure complementary skill sets when matching humans and agents.

While our work provides interesting insights into task allocation mechanisms in human-agent teams, we identify limitations and future directions. The team only allocates intellective tasks, and it is unclear how the results would generalize if team is responsible for other classifications of task types. As future work, we plan to develop an understanding of how team dynamics changes when human assumes allocator role in the protocol. We also plan to study how dynamics of human-agent teams change when team consists of more than two members.

References

1. Brinkman, W.P.: Design of a questionnaire instrument. In: Handbook of Mobile Technology Research Methods, pp. 31–57. Nova Publishers (2009)
2. Genter, K., Agmon, N., Stone, P.: Role-based ad hoc teamwork. In: Proceedings of the Plan, Activity, and Intent Recognition Workshop at the Twenty-Fifth Conference on Artificial Intelligence (PAIR-11) , August 2011
3. Gervits, F., Thurston, D., Thielstrom, R., Fong, T., Pham, Q., Scheutz, M.: Toward genuine robot teammates: improving human-robot team performance using robot shared mental models. In: AAMAS, pp. 429–437 (2020)
4. Gladstein, D.L.: Groups in context: a model of task group effectiveness. Adm. Sci. Q. **29**, 499–517 (1984)
5. Green, S.G., Taber, T.D.: The effects of three social decision schemes on decision group process. Organ. Behav. Hum. Perform. **25**(1) (1980)
6. Hafızoğlu, F.M., Sen, S.: The effects of past experience on trust in repeated human-agent teamwork. In: Proceedings of the 17th International Conference on Autonomous Agents and MultiAgent Systems, pp. 514–522 (2018)
7. Lai, V., Tan, C.: On human predictions with explanations and predictions of machine learning models: a case study on deception detection. In: Proceedings of the Conference on Fairness, Accountability, and Transparency, pp. 29–38 (2019)
8. Larson, L., DeChurch, L.A.: Leading teams in the digital age: four perspectives on technology and what they mean for leading teams. Leadersh. Q. **31**(1), 101377 (2020)

9. Mathieu, J.E., Hollenbeck, J.R., van Knippenberg, D., Ilgen, D.R.: A century of work teams in the journal of applied psychology. J. Appl. Psychol. **102**(3), 452 (2017)
10. Mosteo, A.R., Montano, L.: A survey of multi-robot task allocation. Instituto de Investigacin en Ingenierła de Aragn (I3A), Tech. Rep (2010)
11. Puranam, P., Alexy, O., Reitzig, M.: What's "new" about new forms of organizing? Acad. Manag. Rev. **39**(2), 162–180 (2014)
12. Reinig, B.A.: Toward an understanding of satisfaction with the process and outcomes of teamwork. J. Manag. Inf. Syst. **19**(4), 65–83 (2003)
13. Shoham, Y., Leyton-Brown, K.: Multiagent Systems: Algorithmic, Game-Theoretic, and Logical Foundations. Cambridge University Press, Cambridge (2008)

Demo Papers

STV+AGR: Towards Verification of Strategic Ability Using Assume-Guarantee Reasoning

Damian Kurpiewski[1,2]($\boxtimes$), Łukasz Mikulski[1,2], and Wojciech Jamroga[1,3]

[1] Institute of Computer Science, Polish Academy of Sciences, Warsaw, Poland
d.kurpiewski@ipipan.waw.pl,lukasz.mikulski@mat.umk.pl
[2] Faculty of Mathematics and Computer Science, Nicolaus Copernicus University, Toruń, Poland
[3] Interdisciplinary Centre for Security, Reliability and Trust, SnT, University of Luxembourg, Esch-sur-Alzette, Luxembourg
wojciech.jamroga@uni.lu

Abstract. We present a substantially expanded version of the open source tool **STV** for strategy synthesis and verification of strategic abilities. The new version provides a web interface and support for assume-guarantee verification of multi-agent systems.

Keywords: Model checking · Assume-guarantee reasoning · Strategic ability

1 Introduction

Model checking of multi-agent systems (MAS) allows for formal (and, ideally, automated) verification of their relevant properties. Algorithms and tools for model checking of *strategic abilities* [1,17,19] have been in development for over 20 years [2–4,7,9,12,13]. Unfortunately, the problem is hard, especially in the realistic case of agents with imperfect information [6,19].

In this paper, we propose a new extension of our open source experimental tool **STV** [12] that facilitates compositional model checking of strategic properties in asynchronous MAS through assume-guarantee reasoning (AGR) [5,18]. The extension is based on the results in [16], itself an adaptation of the AGR framework for liveness specifications from [14,15].

Many important properties of MAS refer to *strategic abilities* of agents and teams. For example, the **ATL*** formula $\langle\langle taxi, passg \rangle\rangle$F destination expresses that the cab and the passenger have a joint strategy to arrive at the destination, no matter what the other agents do, while $\langle\langle taxi \rangle\rangle$G¬fatality says that the autonomous cab can drive in such a way that no one gets ever killed. Another intuitive set of strategic requirements is provided by properties of secure voting systems [20]. As shown by case studies [8,10] practical verification of such properties is still infeasible due to state-space and strategy-space explosion. **STV+AGR** addresses the specification and verification of such properties, as well as a user-friendly creation of models to be verified.

© The Author(s), under exclusive license to Springer Nature Switzerland AG 2023
R. Aydoğan et al. (Eds.): PRIMA 2022, LNAI 13753, pp. 691–696, 2023.
https://doi.org/10.1007/978-3-031-21203-1_47

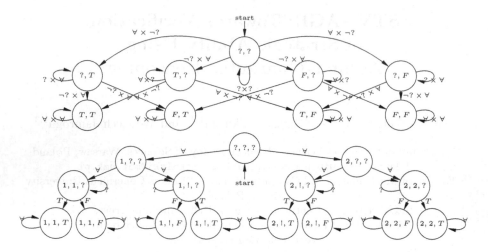

Fig. 1. Two modules: a coercer[2] (up) and a voter (down)

2 Simple Voting Scenario

To present the capabilities of **STV+AGR**, we designed an asynchronous version of the Simple Voting scenario [9]. The model consists of two types of agents, presented in Fig. 1, and described below.

Voter. Every voter agent has three local variables: $vote_i$, $reported_i$ and $pstatus_i$, where ? means no decision while ! means that the voter decided not to share her vote with the coercer. Each voter i can also see the value of the pun_i variable of the coercer. The voter first casts her vote, then decides whether to share its value with the coercer. Finally, she waits for the coercer's decision on punishment.

Coercer. The coercer[k] has one local variable for each of k voters: pun_i. Moreover, he can observe the value of $reported_i$ for each voter and has two available actions per voter: to punish the voter or to refrain from punishment.

3 Formal Background

Modules. The main part of the input is given by a set of asynchronous modules inspired by [15], where local states are labelled with valuations of state variables. The transitions are valuations of input variables controlled by the other modules. The multi-agent system is defined by a composition of its modules.

Strategies. A strategy is a conditional plan that specifies what the agent(s) are going to do in every possible situation. Here, we consider the case of *imperfect information memoryless strategies*, represented by functions from the agent's local states (or, equivalently, its epistemic indistinguishability classes) to its available actions. The *outcome* of a strategy from state q consists of all the infinite paths starting from q and consistent with the strategy.

Logic. Given a model M and a state q in the model, the **1ATL*$_{-X}$** [11] formula $\langle\langle a \rangle\rangle\varphi$ holds in the pointed model (M, q) iff there exists a strategy for agent a that makes φ true on all the outcome paths starting from any state indistinguishable from q. The semantics of coalitional abilities is analogous, for joint strategies of coalitions. Following this concept, the formula $\langle\langle C \rangle\rangle\varphi$ holds in (M, q) iff there exists a joint strategy (a set of strategies for every agent) of coalition C that makes φ true on all the outcome paths starting from any state indistinguishable from q.

Assume-Guarantee Reasoning. The theory behind the present extension of the **STV** tool is discussed in the companion paper [16]. The main idea is to cope with the state-space explosion by decomposing the goal φ of coalition C into local goals $\varphi_i, i \in C$, and verify them one by one against abstractions of each agent's environment. An abstraction for i is obtained by defining a single module, called the *assumption*, which *guarantees* that all the paths present in the original system have their counterparts in the composition of module i and its associated assumption. Those counterparts may reduce finite fragments of considered paths if nothing noticeable to the agents takes place. Moreover, we use a distance between modules, based on shared synchronization actions, so that only "close" agents are taken into account when preparing the assumption for i. This way, one can deduce the existence of a joint strategy to obtain φ from the existence of individual strategies that achieve local goals φ_i.

Automated Generation of Assumptions. The main difficulty in using assume-guarantee reasoning is how to define the right assumptions for the relevant modules. To this end, we propose an automated procedure that generates the assumptions, based on the subset of modules that are "close" to the given module M_i. The abstraction is obtained by composing all the "close" modules, abstracting away their state labels and variables except for the inputs of M_i, as well as removing all their input variables which are not state variables of M_i.

4   Technology

STV+AGR does *explicit-state model checking*. That is, the global states and transitions of the model are represented explicitly in the memory of the verification process. The tool includes the following new functionalities.

User-Defined Input. The user can load and parse the input specification from a text file that defines the groups of modules. The modules are local automata representing the agents. The groups define the partition for the assume-guarantee verification. Each group that describes the part of the coalition must also define the formula to be verified.

Web-Based Graphical Interface. The generated models and the verification results are visualized in the intuitive web-based graphical interface. The GUI is implemented in Typescript and uses the Angular framework.

Table 1. Results of assume-guarantee verification (times given in seconds)

V	Monolithic model checking				Assume-guarantee verification			
	#st	#tr	DFS	Apprx	#st	#tr	DFS	Apprx
2	529	2216	<0.1	<0.1/Yes	161	528	<0.1	<0.1/Yes
3	12167	127558	<0.1	0.8/Yes	1127	7830	<0.1	<0.1/Yes
4	2.79e5	6.73e6	memout		7889	1.08e5	<0.1	0.8/Yes
5	memout				5.52e4	1.45e6	<0.1	11/Yes

Evaluation. The assumption-guarantee scheme has been evaluated on the asynchronous variant of Simple Voting, using the formula $\varphi \equiv \langle\!\langle Voter_1 \rangle\!\rangle G(\neg pstatus_1 \vee voted_1 = 1)$. Note that the coalition consisted of only one agent, which made the decomposition of the formula trivial. The results are presented in Table 1. The first column describes the configuration of the benchmark, i.e., the number of voters. Then, we report the performance of model checking algorithms that operate on the explicit model of the whole system vs. assume-guarantee verification. *DFS* is a straightforward implementation of depth-first strategy synthesis. *Apprx* refers to the method of fixpoint-approximation [9]; besides the time, we also report if the approximation was conclusive.

Usage. The tool is available at stv.cs-htiew.com. The video demonstration of the tool is available at youtu.be/1DrmSRK1fBA. Example specifications can be found at stv-docs.cs-htiew.com. The presented tool **STV+AGR** allows to: Generate and display the composition of a set of modules into the model of a multi-agent system; Generate and display the automatic assumption, given a module and a distance bound; Provide local specifications for modules, and compute the global specification as their conjunction; Verify a **1ATL$^*_{-X}$** formula for a given system (using the verification methods available in the **STV** package); Verify a **1ATL$^*_{-X}$** formula for a composition of a module and its automatic assumption (using the methods in **STV**); Verify a **1ATL$^*_{-X}$** formula for a composition of a module and a user-defined assumption (using the methods in **STV**); Display the verification result, including the relevant truth values and the winning strategy.

5   Conclusions

Much complexity of model checking for strategic abilities is due to the size of the model of the system. **STV+AGR** addresses the challenge by implementing a compositional model checking scheme, called assume-guarantee verification. No less importantly, our tool supports user-friendly modelling of MAS, and automated generation of abstractions that are used as assumptions in the scheme.

Acknowledgement. The authors thank Witold Pazderski and Yan Kim for assistance with the web interface. The work was supported by NCBR Poland and FNR Luxembourg under the PolLux/FNR-CORE project STV (POLLUX-VII/1/2019), as well as the CHIST-ERA grant CHIST-ERA-19-XAI-010 by NCN

Poland (2020/02/Y/ST6/00064). The work of Damian Kurpiewski was also supported by the CNRS IEA project MoSART.

References

1. Alur, R., Henzinger, T., Kupferman, O.: Alternating-time temporal logic. J. ACM **49**, 672–713 (2002)
2. Alur, R., Henzinger, T.A., Mang, F.Y.C., Qadeer, S., Rajamani, S.K., Tasiran, S.: MOCHA: modularity in model checking. In: Hu, A.J., Vardi, M.Y. (eds.) CAV 1998. LNCS, vol. 1427, pp. 521–525. Springer, Heidelberg (1998). https://doi.org/10.1007/BFb0028774
3. Belardinelli, F., Lomuscio, A., Murano, A., Rubin, S.: Verification of multi-agent systems with imperfect information and public actions. In: Proceedings of AAMAS'17, pp. 1268–1276 (2017)
4. Čermák, P., Lomuscio, A., Mogavero, F., Murano, A.: MCMAS-SLK: a model checker for the verification of strategy logic specifications. In: Biere, A., Bloem, R. (eds.) CAV 2014. LNCS, vol. 8559, pp. 525–532. Springer, Cham (2014). https://doi.org/10.1007/978-3-319-08867-9_34
5. Clarke, E., Long, D., McMillan, K.: Compositional model checking. In: Proceedings of LICS'89, pp. 353–362. IEEE Computer Society Press (1989)
6. Dima, C., Tiplea, F.: Model-checking ATL under imperfect information and perfect recall semantics is undecidable. CoRR abs/1102.4225 (2011)
7. Huang, X., van der Meyden, R.: Symbolic model checking epistemic strategy logic. In: Proceedings of AAAI'14, pp. 1426–1432 (2014)
8. Jamroga, W., Kim, Y., Kurpiewski, D., Ryan, P.Y.A.: Towards model checking of voting protocols in UPPAAL. In: Krimmer, R., et al. (eds.) E-Vote-ID 2020. LNCS, vol. 12455, pp. 129–146. Springer, Cham (2020). https://doi.org/10.1007/978-3-030-60347-2_9
9. Jamroga, W., Knapik,, Kurpiewski, D., Mikulski, Ł.: Approximate verification of strategic abilities under imperfect information. Artif. Int.ell. **277** (2019)
10. Jamroga, W., Kurpiewski, D., Malvone, V.: Natural strategic abilities in voting protocols. In: Groß, T., Viganò, L. (eds.) STAST 2020. LNCS, vol. 12812, pp. 45–62. Springer, Cham (2021). https://doi.org/10.1007/978-3-030-79318-0_3
11. Jamroga, W., Penczek, W., Sidoruk, T., Dembinski, P., Mazurkiewicz, A.: Towards partial order reductions for strategic ability. J. Artif. Intell. Res. **68**, 817–850 (2020)
12. Kurpiewski, D., Pazderski, W., Jamroga, W., Kim, Y.: STV+Reductions: towards practical verification of strategic ability using model reductions. In: Proceedings of AAMAS'21, pp. 1770–1772. ACM (2021)
13. Lomuscio, A., Qu, H., Raimondi, F.: MCMAS: an open-source model checker for the verification of multi-agent systems. Int. J. Soft. Tools Tech. Trans. **19**(1), 9–30 (2017)
14. Lomuscio, A., Strulo, B., Walker, N., Wu, P.: Assume-guarantee reasoning with local specifications. In: Dong, J.S., Zhu, H. (eds.) ICFEM 2010. LNCS, vol. 6447, pp. 204–219. Springer, Heidelberg (2010). https://doi.org/10.1007/978-3-642-16901-4_15
15. Lomuscio, A., Strulo, B., Walker, N., Wu, P.: Assume-guarantee reasoning with local specifications. Int. J. Found. Comput. Sci. **24**(4), 419–444 (2013)
16. Mikulski, Ł., Jamroga, W., Kurpiewski, D.: Assume-guarantee verification of strategic ability. In: Proceedings of PRIMA (2022, to appear)

17. Mogavero, F., Murano, A., Perelli, G., Vardi, M.: Reasoning about strategies: on the model-checking problem. ACM Trans. Comp. Log. **15**(4), 1–42 (2014)
18. Pnueli, A.: In transition from global to modular temporal reasoning about programs. In: Logics and Models of Concurrent Systems. NATO ASI Series, vol. 13, pp. 123–144. Springer, Heidelberg (1984). https://doi.org/10.1007/978-3-642-82453-1
19. Schobbens, P.: Alternating-time logic with imperfect recall. Electr. Not. Theor. Comput. Sci. **85**(2), 82–93 (2004)
20. Tabatabaei, M., Jamroga, W., Ryan, P.Y.A.: expressing receipt-freeness and coercion-resistance in logics of strategic ability: Preliminary attempt. In: Proceedings of PrAISe@ECAI'16, pp. 1:1–1:8. ACM (2016)

Author Index

Printed in the United States
by Baker & Taylor Publisher Services